THE INDELIBLE RED STAIN

the destruction of a tropical paradise

a Cold War story

Book 2

Return to Conflict, Intrigue, Anguish
Fire, Killings, and Exodus

The Firebrand from Central Kitty

Mohan Ragbeer

THE INDELIBLE RED STAIN

Book 2

Copyright © 2011 by Dr Mohan Ragbeer

Dedication

To my late Parents, sister Mahadai and her husband Tulla, my mentors and role models, and to my extended and divided families who sacrificed so much in enduring the hardships of a cruel dictatorship and had the courage to start new lives in cold and often hostile lands.

To our Canadian, American, British and other children who ought to know something of their past history.

and

To My Wife Mary for her patient, meticulous and dedicated editing and critical appraisal of this voluminous and strange story.

Table of Contents-Book 2

Preface..1

Introduction to Book 1...3

Chapter 1 13

Chapter 2 43

Chapter 3 61

Chapter 4 83

Chapter 5 131

Chapter 6 281

Chapter 7 311

Chapter 8 335

Chapter 9 349

Chapter 10 367

Chapter 11 377

Chapter 12 405

Chapter 13 425

Chapter 14 487

Chapter 15 519

Chapter 16 545

Chapter 17 577

Chapter 18 599

Chapter 19 623

Chapter 20 655

Epilogue...677

Appendix..690

Acknowledgements

Many people--family and friends—contributed to the completion of this project. Foremost is Mary--my wife, confidante and critic--who shares in the dedication. David, our son, kept my computers functional, scanned the photos and helped with the cover. He had heard many of the anecdotes in childhood.

The five precious children of my first marriage--Phillip, Peter, Ranji, Devika and Cary—provided years of enormous pleasure as we grew up and cared for one another, in three different countries; they and their families continue to be a great joy; my niece Savitri has been more like a cherished and faithful daughter. My many nephews and other nieces, especially Kanhai, remain sources of inspiration. They all shared in the BG tragedy and today have forged enterprises, despite racial barriers, in the USA, Canada and UK, while few remain in Guyana.

My Wappai co-mates, colleagues at the Georgetown Hospital and my family willingly explored areas of darkness and reached for racial and religious harmony despite many obstacles. Unhappily Cpl. Doris died by drowning while on duty soon after independence and was thus mercifully spared the revelation that his hero Burnham was indeed a vicious tyrant denounced by his own sister, Jessie, also a previous comrade in politics.

The late Dr Stanley Luck encouraged and supported me through the long years of our close friendship. His notes provided some of the data used in the book; he, with Jinni, an Indo-Guianese poet, Elizabeth, a Franco-Anglo-American reformist and Winston, a Trinidadian émigré in London were insistent that I write this. Elizabeth's brief but powerful influence was clearly predestination or *karma*; she had an uncanny insight into events in BG, a place she did not know, and entered my life to give timely guidance and share her knowledge and vision.

Several Indian and British contacts gave data on Indian history and the British Raj, endorsing accounts by Dr Brahmam, Jaiṇ and my earlier teachers, notably Mr Latchman, the scholarly farmer.

Here in Canada friends encouraged me to complete the work seeing the distress of *hundreds of thousands* of Guianese including most of my large family, exploited and exiled by the very forces that had promised to emancipate them. Their losses and dashed hopes are the real tragic outcomes of a sad period of world history when the Cold War allowed the ambitions of greedy men to corrupt and despoil a population so completely that it should have been a warning to others. Instead, those errors are repeated today as powerful nations-- as divided as ever, and much more vitriolic--become more corrupt, and greedy egos trump morality and ethics to rule our world.

I especially thank my friend Ram Jagessar of Toronto—scholar, writer and an exile himself from Trinidad--for his persistence in pushing me to revive and conclude this work after many years of cynicism and indecision, and for arranging the publication. Kay Smart, late of St Kitts, painted the forest scene (Book 1 cover); Margit Bardos helped with the mob scene cartoon; Ram and David did the cover.

Ancaster, ON, Canada 1986-2011

Preface

Book 1 described a forensic expedition to a remote Carib village nestled in the dark virgin forests of British Guiana close to the Venezuelan border, and likened the difficulties of the journey to that of the political one to independence that the country had begun under Dr Jagan, a devoted Marxist.

We traced the progress in European colonial politics to the **inevitability** of decolonisation whose imminence by 1950 seemed to hinge on two main factors: the economic importance of the colony to the colonial power and its significance to Cold War combatants. By 1953 it was clear that the Soviets could exploit the Marxist ascendancy in British Guiana to secure a beachhead in the Americas akin to NATO bases littered in Germany, Turkey and elsewhere in Europe, quite close to Soviet republics. The expulsion in 1953 of the Peoples Progressive Party led by Dr Jagan and Mr Burnham ended that speculation and placed BG under direct UK control and covert scrutiny by an increasingly paranoid US State Department, the CIA and the US military that had left its WWII bases in BG not too long ago. (Many believed that if BG could have provided a resort-like environment, like Guantanamo Bay, Cuba, or full social and recreational amenities like West Germany or England, the US Armed Forces would have stayed indefinitely; it had an excuse!)

A hiatus thus followed during the mid-1950s in the constitutional development of the country in which Cold War issues and the anti-communist McCarthy machine revved up in the USA to the point that *"I am not now nor have ever been a member of the Communist Party"* became a mantra that reverberated across the nation, defined it and would become entrenched in the oath new citizens must swear in addition to renouncing a previous citizenship. Anyone who criticised the Government or country was quickly branded a communist and security risk.

This US itchiness allowed it to respond irrationally even to legitimate actions of sovereign states where these *might* eat into the profits or power of US or its subsidiary Canadian interests, especially business. Guzman's exile from Guatemala is a case in point where the stingy response by an extractive company trumped a nation's attempts to improve modestly the lot of its citizens. Thus the USA became the shining knight of the new imperialism dedicated to self-interest and expansion and to the destruction of the Soviet Union and its sympathisers and the eradication of Communism.

The Cold War had begun hardly had WWII ended, with the combatants – USA and communist states – fighting first ideologically then militarily in Korea and Southeast Asia, achieving mere stalemates in each zone, while McCarthyism raged in the USA and stained the entire Western Hemisphere. Meanwhile more thoughtful Americans formed the *Citizens for Global Solutions* aiming for a *"future in which nations work together to abolish war, protect our rights and freedoms and solve the problems facing humanity that no nation can solve alone"* and working to build *—the political will in the United States"* to realize this aim. And while they pondered noble ideals, their government and its CIA were doing the opposite in many lands.

By 1960 the CIA had already drawn blood in Latin America, Iran and the Congo and at home with subornation of major media. By sponsoring the World Bank and the International Monetary Fund at the 1944 Bretton Woods Conference in New Hampshire the USA gained virtual control of global finance, which it now dominates. Initially conservative the institutions changed focus under different directors and went through a period of profligate lending that created some of the world's largest personal fortunes and highest debts in Third World countries. To recoup payment World Bank developed the infamous *structural adjustment programs* in the late 1980s that are responsible for third world poverty today. Among the worst afflicted is the Republic of Guyana whose genesis forms the subject of this work.

We described in Book 1 the efforts of well-wishers to influence Dr Jagan's adoption of a moderate or centrist economic, political and social agenda. In this book we describe the return journey from Wappai, under increasingly difficult conditions and shortage of food. We explore the events and circumstances that were turning the small, quiet and simple nation, hardly born, into a cauldron of Cold War hostilities. We debate the role of race and the separation of Indians and Africans by long-standing British propaganda aimed to keep them from uniting in protest against servile working conditions. We used the long empty hours and slow progress on a treacherous river to present an account of India's long and rich history and the circumstances that brought it under a British *aristocracy* that raped India, subjugated its peoples and distorted its history and education, the while deceiving its more modest middle and lower class citizens at home with grand tales of might and heroism laced with 19th century notions of eugenics and race superiority that distracted them from their own oppression and assorted miseries.

We returned to a troubled city where racial polarisation, mob violence and CIA covert actions had already begun to increase fears and reveal signs of an imminent cataclysm.

Introduction to Book 1

A nation's history rightly includes accounts of its minorities – why they settled where they did, even among unfriendly and unwelcoming hosts, knowing that they will be underdogs. For Canada and the USA this includes a substantial minority of East Indians. Why did they leave their homelands to struggle in Canada knowing its history of bias and rejection where until 1967 Indians were not welcomed? Canada's *'whites only'* policy gelled with the Komagatu Maru incident of 1913 and the resulting federal decision to exclude Indians using some of the most hypocritical legislative ruses one can find anywhere.

I recall vividly in 1964, soon after completing specialisation I visited family in Kitchener, Ontario, briefly en route to New York. One day a physician friend informed me of a new position in a southern Ontario hospital in my specialty that had remained unfilled for over two years; he called the administrator who was delighted with my qualifications and invited me to apply. I already had an excellent offer at Columbia University, New York, but was persuaded to visit the Kitchener immigration office to inquire about migrant visas. I was rudely told by the officer answering my question--himself a migrant from somewhere in Eastern Europe, judging by his name and accent--that I should get out of Canada before he changed his mind and arrested me for breach of Canadian entry regulations. Shades of *Komagatu Maru*! It seemed that the mere act of inquiry from an Indian was then enough to trigger horrendous fears of a brown invasion. He even extended his threat to the hospital director, himself a physician, who had offered to speak to any officer who might wish to call for verification. Changes began slowly after 1967, just in time to provide a destination for the many persons--Indians especially, since they were previously specifically barred-- displaced by the rise of 'socialist' dictators in newly independent ex-colonies of the Caribbean, South America and Africa.

In the last forty years over 400,000 people have fled from Guyana--formerly British Guiana (BG) — mainly to the USA, Canada and the UK--to brave these uncertain, cold and hostile environments when a US-supported Marxist dictator, Forbes Burnham, methodically began to savage their businesses, farms, shops, professions and persons. Who are these exiles, and why did they leave? Was Burnham the only culprit? Their story goes back over 170 years but immediately to the two decades post-WWII which saw dramatic political changes in BG. In this book I trace conditions in the country--events, peoples and their leaders, their origins, culture, education, attitudes, needs, prospects, philosophies and relationships — and the leaders emerging as imperial powers declined and began to shed "unprofitable" colonies, and the actions that provoked the massive exodus.

Every major war has the cathartic potential to heal and re-direct humanity. WWII could have taught mankind a lesson in "live and let live" and steered it to what is good, just and right. Instead it yielded to intransigent corporate capitalists and their opposites, socialist iconoclasts who seized control of the USA and USSR, respectively, the giant powers that emerged from the wreckage of war. US leaders were less interested in "freeing" colonies--despite advocating the end of colonialism at the United Nations--than in nationalism and rampant capitalism, pushed by greed to grab assets and markets as Empires crumbled.

The USSR wished to seize new nations as tools in its campaign for global Communism. WWII thus failed when victors polarized into right and left, each consumed with the belief that it was right and best. So began the infamous and degrading Cold War which embroiled many, even obscure small states then emerging from the wreckage of empires. The Cold War coincided with the rise of anti-colonialism locally and at the UN, fuelled by the spirited socialism then sweeping the world, touching everyone, even the USA, corporatism's bastion. To its discredit the USA reacted rather childishly, if not stupidly, pushed by business paranoia, heedless of Dwight Eisenhower's parting caution: *"Beware the military-industrial complex!"*

Denied a voice or vote for generations few colonial peoples were educated enough to contribute wisely to the electoral process when adult franchise arrived, or to benefit from the change to full autonomy, and thus fell easy prey to young greenhorn socialist militants bursting on the scene, who exploited the UN resolution on Colonies, enticing the masses with impossible promises to capture their allegiance and votes. In the early 1960s the British government used this very deficiency and inexperience among colonials as a reason to delay independence.

To understand the gullibility of people one must recall that no European power, least of all Britain (and Portugal), had predicted the speed and inevitability of decolonisation. Churchill, as Prime Minister of the UK, had proclaimed the permanence of Empire. Thus both colonisers and the colonised were unprepared for independence, the latter discouraged from seeking it. For example, Indian leaders were snubbed by British authorities in the years before and during WWII, and India was denied Dominion status which had been given to white colonies. Netaji S.C. Bose was even refused audience by Conservative officers at that time, having advocated force to achieve self-rule when Britain absorbed itself in WWII. Post-war, at the nadir of her power, the Empire, to Churchill's dismay, unravelled.

Unfortunately for BG Britain also reneged on pre-war promises to modernise infrastructure and society generally, a small and deserved reward. Britain had methodically seized native lands and businesses globally, exploited their assets and squeezed every cent of revenue from the poorest up, from the widest imaginable range of taxes, fees, charges, licenses etc. (even the meanest transaction carried a stamp tax). She had exercised xenophobic power, sharing native lands to favourites, denying subjects fairness and rights and even plain good manners. Touting white power, they split the races in every colony — people they had imported as workers--and convincing each of exclusive British favour and goodwill: *divide and rule*!

Of all British derelictions, however the worst was to deny a good education and even a semblance of equal opportunity to the majority despite good intentions legislated from time to time, and despite the widely-known successes of students who had squeezed scholarships, benefits, titles, prizes, and other "favours" from British parsimony. Wealth generated in colonies was exported to Britain--except as needed for *colonial* businesses locally — to build mansions around the Squares of west central London, leaving no capital to build local capacity, whether in services or infrastructure. Thus colonies amassed a huge structural deficit in every sphere of social, cultural and economic need. Yet the British would criticise colonials for being naïve or inexperienced and undeveloped. Catch 22!

Consumed with the Cold War and one of its most vicious products, McCarthyism, the world paid little notice to colonies, yet their plight was emblematic of global fears of neo-imperialism as the US and USSR sparred for power. If anything, the Cold War increased the rapacity of the powerful and exposed the failure of the moral and rational world, as represented by its media, to denounce biases and oppression. Edmund Burke had observed *"All that is necessary for the triumph of evil is that good men do nothing."*

But while imperialists had created the economic monster called colonialism--with white superiors and coloured and poor inferiors, kept in place by tight policing and poor education, especially about one another--the militants who raged against them took their rhetoric to wild extremes and misrepresented the political position and economic and social realities.

In 1960, the population of BG--area 83,000 square miles – was just 560,000. It was, and remains a microcosm of the world, with six races and mixtures of them, 50% Indian (from India), 34% African, 10% Coloured and the remainder Native, Portuguese, Chinese, White and their hybrids, few of whom knew much about one another's basic culture.

Yet despite division into discrete racial enclaves the races did develop a law-abiding and congenial relationship, and interacted civilly in the workplace, in schools, in sports activities and to some extent socially. They were generally industrious, enterprising, craved education and advancement and took pride in civility. By the 1960s some had achieved a measure of wealth and higher education. But the rural majority remained neglected and the infrastructure primitive. Whites generally remained condescending and aloof, an attitude mimicked by the near-white and high-coloureds--octoroons and quadroons in the USA--who dominated middle and junior grades of the civil service.

Despite British parsimony and repressions through swift and often brutal Police responses to dissent, especially on sugar plantations, local men and women of intellect and vision had persevered in discreet groups since WWI to work for change, preferring the certainty of a peaceful, well-crafted and responsible strategy to achieve their goals i.e. subtlety and playing "their" game, over militancy, and to avoid the obstacles and distress that had dogged India's path to independence. The slow-down due to WWII blunted their credibility and reach among the masses making them prime targets for post-war militants who usurped the "freedom" movement and took sides as the Cold War escalated.

Not surprisingly Guianese masses heeded the militants' sweeping condemnation of everything and everyone British and flocked to their side; the broad brush tainted even those who had been kindly and done a lasting good--physicians, teachers and intellectuals, and people of high moral calibre. Their whiteness united them with the servant-bullies, uncouth estate managers, "security" thugs and police forces that British businesses and governments were wont to employ, and paid well to repress dissent..

Flush with the adulation of followers who had begun to expect a final release from bondage and the promised material gains thereafter, militants rejected the Fabian plans crafted by more experienced contemporaries and forerunners which were prudent, sound and likely to get UK support for the works needed and to produce an educated and informed electorate that would be less easily enticed with impractical and irrational promises.

Inevitably the populace fell to socialist demagoguery. The colony might have escaped US scrutiny were it not strategically located on the shoulder of South America, an ICBM's flight from the largest centres of industry and population in the USA and Latin America. It had been an important link in the chain of operational bases for Atlantic security during World War II, but became a source of tension in Washington when Cuba embraced the Soviets. The USA became paranoid that an independent Guiana might emulate Cuba, in view of the overt Marxism of Dr Cheddi Jagan, an Indian dentist and close family friend, and of Black lawyer Forbes Burnham, who had come together in the first political Party – the Peoples' Progressive Party – and had governed briefly in 1953 with Dr Jagan as head, under an internally self-governing constitution.

When the British Conservative Government "fired" Jagan's party for "threatening" Communism, Burnham, an occult Marxist, split off with his African support, but lost to Jagan in two subsequent elections, in 1957 and 1961. For the 1961 contest three parties had emerged: Jagan's PPP, Burnham's Peoples National Congress (PNC) and the United Force (UF) headed by liquor businessman Peter D'Aguiar, all supporting self-rule.

But BG was technically and financially unprepared for this or for the intense mob violence that followed Jagan's third victory in August 1961 incited by the fiery polemics of opposition leaders and their retinue who defied Police, Government and the law. Tensions rose and mob violence terrorised Indians. A few repercussions entrenched the conflict.

On a visit to Washington DC in October 1961 to meet with President Kennedy Jagan waffled on the issue of his ideology ignoring sage advice of several strong delegations to downplay communism and adjust his platform to support a mixed economy to permit growth of capital, infrastructural development, local enterprises and to create a sustaining tax base. He was reminded that as early as 1950--as the Cold War heated up--George Kennan, who had drafted America's anti-Soviet policies, had stated to US Chiefs of Mission in Rio de Janeiro that the purpose of US policy in Latin America was "*to protect the vital supplies of raw materials which Latin American countries export to the USA; to prevent the 'military exploitation of Latin America by the enemy' (the Soviet Union); and to avert 'the psychological mobilization of Latin America against us'.*"

Either he had forgotten this or he had put an unusual emphasis on a casual remark by JFK that he would have no problem with a democratically elected Communist. Jagan returned empty-handed, much to the disappointment of the Guianese people. The letdown deepened the divisions between the majority Indians and Blacks; the latter became convinced that Jagan would not give up on communism even to save the country, and that any advance to independence under him would be a ticket to poverty and enslavement, Soviet style.

At the dawn of December 1961, with gloom and inter-racial tensions heavy in the air, a forensic expedition of twelve persons journeyed deep into the BG forests to the tiny village of Wappai--buried in virgin tropical forest in the Amakura Mountains near the BG-Venezuela border, an area still largely unknown--to conclude the investigation of a murder. The journey, expected to take 5 to 6 days, lasted 17, resulting in insecurity, added dangers and food shortage among the men "imprisoned" in a small cramped boat on a treacherous river, and in open camps in a huge and trackless forest, with no means to communicate with the city.

The team was a microcosm of the country's major racial groups consisting of five policemen–four Black and one Arawak/Portuguese mix; three Indian laboratory workers; and four Carib natives. They had to work cooperatively and under duress, despite personal alliance, to complete the mission safely. They achieved their primary objective to assemble evidence for a murder trial. But the isolation and confinement, the shortage of food and the challenges of the river at low water presented a priceless reward: it gave the men and the people they met--native villagers and hunters and non-native miners--a unique opportunity to examine and unravel, without interruption, their dominant concern: Guianese social, economic and political realities, and the forces that exploited racial allegiances and the Cold War to disrupt society and change government by might, not ballots. The forces of law and order, most of whom were Black and supported the main opposition PNC were especially challenged. The turmoil brewing in the city when we left threatened to morph into outright armed rebellion. Poor planning for our trip put us at needless risk and revealed a troubling element of distraction and carelessness in high ranks of the Force.

The Chiefs, shamans and natives of two villages were exceptional sources of wisdom and new knowledge, including details of a secret Intelligence visit to BG-Venezuela borderlands at the dawn of WWII, and provided a different perspective on the emerging nation that few besides them appreciated. The discussions challenged individual beliefs which forced the men to recognize the growth of biases and conflicts that imperialists had used to entrench racial divisions, allowing a small well-armed ruling class of 3000 to dominate a population of 600,000, and a small island nation to command a huge global empire.

Fairly intense and frank discussion, at times threatening the most cherished views, suggested ways in which the races could learn from one another, develop mutual respect, cooperate and grow an exemplary multiracial society, and expunge the biases and schemes that the Opposition was fomenting to terrorise, ruin and murder citizens. The camaraderie that developed after two weeks of intense cultural examination and information-sharing suggested a model for all society, if only the scenario and motivation could be duplicated!

Three years of turmoil followed that trip. Jagan had naïvely enlisted with the USSR in the Cold War, following Castro's lead. This consolidated US fears of another Cuba in the Americas, especially after the CIA's *Bay of Pigs* debacle of April 1961 and the further failure of its *Operation Mongoose*--aimed to deride Castro and rattle Cuban society with disruptions and sabotage—ended Allen Dulles' headship of the CIA in November 1961. These failures finally convinced the Americans that they needed to learn facts not hearsay about the peoples of the world. They're still trying.

But Jagan did not take advantage of the lessons that emerged. In October 1962 Kennedy's successful confrontation with Khrushchev over missile bases being built in Cuba--the so-called Cuban missile crisis or prelude to World War III and John Dulles' *Mutually Assured Destruction* (MAD)-- did soften the Soviet approach to the West. But it did not change Jagan's policies as he firmly believed he could get the same extent of Soviet support as Castro had obtained--$100 million initially--after the US had severed ties. For this reason Kennedy deviated from his continental European tour in 1963 to visit London to "advise" the British to dismiss Jagan, as they had done in 1953. Thus, even if the UK had wished, it could not have surrendered the colony to Communist control. Premier Jagan stubbornly and foolishly ignored this reality, sacrificing Indians but incredibly retaining their unqualified allegiance.

The main alternative to him was Burnham, shunned by both US and UK agents as sly and deceitful. A second (minority) opposition came, as noted, from the *laissez faire* capitalist Peter D'Aguiar, whose inane policies and fanciful and strident claims fed the Marxist argument, when he should have followed sage advice to develop cogent alternatives to it. Each Party leader stood on a solid racial base that he manipulated at will.

Early in 1962 opposition mobs began disruptive activities, assisted by the CIA and other US agents and agencies to terrorise, kill, burn and bomb Indians, their homes and businesses. The destabilisation progressed apace in 1962-64 creating further fear, dissension and hate as Dr Jagan incredulously rejected renewed pleas to renounce Communism and follow a moderate mixed economic plan that had been first presented to him in 1950-53 by early financial backers.

The US actions seemed rather heavy-handed especially after Khrushchev had removed his missiles from Cuba and East-West relationships had warmed. It is said that the panoply of fears instilled in Americans in the previous decade by the chicanery, innuendos, accusations, lies and human wreckage caused by McCarthy and his fundamentalists had turned Americans to suspicions, hatreds, isolationism and terror, becoming a nation of self-righteous fools, even at the highest levels of government.

The prolonged general strike of 1963 and campaign of terror against Indians had damaged society and threatened to destroy it completely. This was a period of personal travail and distress which I wanted desperately to forget if only to put behind me images and expressions that at one time had kept me in disturbed wakefulness. It was during this strike that a citizens group examined and argued for separate development by peaceful planned partition but political leaders rejected the proposal without examination fearing loss of their monopoly iso-racial following. Jagan instead opted to induce opponents into a coalition, but failed.

Soon after, during the independence conference in London, Jagan also rejected a substantial financial offer from a group of exiles in London to salvage his government, again in favour of his Soviet contacts. In an act of infinite folly he also deferred to the Secretary of State for Colonies, Duncan Sandys, the final choice of constitutional instrument for independence, despite numerous exhortations and warnings to avoid that! Sandys shocked no one but Jagan by selecting Proportional Representation, which pleased the opposition parties.

Resulting political intrigues and social turmoil eventually led to repeated acts of racial savagery that culminated in the May 1964 massacre of Indians by Blacks in the town of Wismar-McKenzie (now Linden). Elections forced by the Colonial Office in December 1964 unseated Jagan's Party, despite his winning most seats, and paved the way for independence under Burnham and his establishment soon after of a savage dictatorship.

In the decolonisation process in Africa, Asia and the Caribbean militant socialists pursued power through demagoguery, agitation and in-fighting which in multiracial BG led to violent racial divisions, extreme hardship and a massive drain of brain and money to the USA, Canada, UK and Caribbean islands. Thus rich nations benefitted from the devastation of the poor! Extractive colonialism at its best. Those who fled were from the middle class--skilled and enterprising people with assets--not the unskilled who had put the dictator in place expecting hand-outs and fulfillment of promises of an easy life. The developed world in any case had no use for the unskilled. Guyana thus lost thrice: first the fruits of enterprise—buying power, taxes, investments etc.; second, moneys spent on training those that had left; and third, the loss of their skills which could not be easily or cheaply replaced.

I focus on the majority, the Indians, for reasons covered in the text, whom I know best and whom history will show as agents of their own distress. The exiles have settled mainly in the Greater Toronto Area of Canada and a somewhat larger number in the USA, chiefly in Queens, New York City. Few got the welcome or jobs their skills merited, simply because they were not white! Their hosts, though basically polite, did not see them as equals, not by race or religion--since the majority was Indian and non-Christian, and the remainder although Christian was Black or coloured, with a few Portuguese, Chinese or Whites, who were better received.

But they were proud, industrious and enterprising and despite biases soon created niches in their host countries' economies and enriched society with elements of their culture. Some have become millionaires, others professionals, academics, educators, technicians and civil servants. Many re-educated themselves to their host country norms, often a step-down from what they were. Few, if any, are on welfare despite stereotyping by host populations, which remain largely ignorant of things beyond their local horizons, and know little of the history and geography of fellow citizens. The same ignorance existed in colonial BG and persists today.

The second and third generations of these exiles are growing up with a native ethic—Canadian, American, British--and know little or nothing of their parents' homeland. Those who do, mourn the death of a promise that their ancestors had made less than a century ago to create a peaceful, prosperous and cultured haven for their offspring, something of a model for others to follow. They could afford to make this promise then, because they had little and saw much in the harsh but rewarding land which they had served with energy and faith. Most of them today knew little of history beyond the adulation of Jagan, so effective has been the campaign to discredit his predecessors, anoint him as a saviour and erase completely all memory of the good work done before him and the ideas which he had seized and failed to adapt to a communist template.

Why should any large power care about the fate of an insignificant and strange minority? Well, nearly half a million of them are now citizens of North America and Europe and doing quite well, while the nation they were forced to leave flounders in a morass of poverty, corruption, racism and drug-dealing, all sequels of a dictatorship that fattened on Cold War fears.

The economy has been drained of its best minds, who—mired in nostalgia and despite reduction to a second-class status—daily add value to their host nations while regretting the fall in value of their native dollar from 42 cents to 0.005 cents US within three decades, during which Cold War combatants poured capital into leaky purses of poor country dictators–to a level that no sane banker would have objectively approved--until debt payments equalled the borrowers'

GNP! Predictably at that stage the IMF, acting as agent for rapacious lenders, took over debtors' accounts and imposed on them its destructive *Structural Adjustment Program* (SAP) aimed to sap the lifeblood from those they had made anaemic and near dead.

I started this book in 1963 from a skeletal account of the forensic *trip to Wappai* that I had filed with the Ministries of Home Affairs and Health, Georgetown. The first chapters were completed and the outlines of the rest drafted by 1968; the book was concluded by 1984 but further progress gave way to other more pressing family and professional demands.

When I doubted whether any purpose would be served by continuing I was encouraged by several keen minds displaced by Guyana's decline and fall, who had once supported the architects of the decline on both sides. Many still carry the torch for these men especially those who had supported Dr Jagan, completely oblivious of this other side or more likely not wanting to know it existed. I am indebted to those who urged its telling and had hoped to complete a presentable account much earlier, during the lifetime of the prime political protagonists. The flaws can no doubt be corrected, but time flies and interest wanes.

The characters and events portrayed are real and few if any had in their time received any more than local publicity. The contributions and experiences of the individuals named illustrate what might have prevented the BG disaster. To preserve anonymity, some people have been given pseudonyms e.g. "Flora Pierce", "Indar" "Jinni", "Ram", "Rahim", "Sam", "Singh", Alvin "Chin Sang", "John Mohamed" and several others. Jain is a composite of a real person by that name plus two others with similar experience, background and views whose transit through the story was altogether too brief for individual preservation and little was lost in the amalgamation. The names of the men in the "secret" British expedition into the tepui are as Hari recalled them and almost certainly are code names.

Most of the dialogue is reconstructed from notes and may not always represent the exact words used at the time, but contains the germ of what was said, in the speakers' styles and includes original remarks.

I chose to render dialogue in Standard English for the most part or close enough, and omitted oaths--actual or minced, lively and colourful though they were in the Guianese idiom--to avoid misconstruction and to make reading easier for those unfamiliar with Guianese or Caribbean dialects and accents, as I feel that the story should be read by host populations and interest those touched or displaced by demagoguery, who in this generation might also be living the anguish of the multitudes forced to flee their homelands; to many of these English is a second language, and I hope to spare them the difficulties of reading an English dialect peppered with foreign words. Dialect was used in places-- where meaning was clear--to create atmosphere and emphasis, which translation might have missed. The meetings at my brother-in-law's place are faithfully reported, but abbreviated and edited.

The events covered affected Guyana but the lessons have a global reach. I expect this story to interest victims of the Cold War, displaced people everywhere, nationals of the countries involved--the USA, Canada, UK, India and Caribbean nations especially--the agencies mentioned, historians, academics and politicians and anyone interested in the problems of extremist behaviour as today exemplified in the clashes between militant Islam (Wahhabism) and its extremist foils among Christians, Jews and some of its own sects. I hope the view presented would counter some of the misinformation around the genesis of the decline of British Guiana from a promising new nation to today's hotbed of violence, crime, corruption, racial polarisation and involvement in the illicit drug industry.

I hope that this story would interest the young and enable them to see in these events how the lust for power can corrupt leaders and lead to the collapse of law and order, destroy nations, especially the weak and poor as we see in so many regions of Africa today. The success of demagogues is the root of many large migrations. The current economic collapse is a similar phenomenon for which the mighty barons and financiers of Wall Street, New York, and other global banking centres can take credit.

The rise of the Internet and its increasing use by the young will hopefully provide them with quick information which they can use after appropriate verification to avoid or mitigate future calamities, if we recover from the present widespread depression that has victimized the young especially. By a curious irony one of the great predators of today, the US Army, was the proprietor of this same Internet that can force them to greater accountability and a more responsible and humane behaviour.

The struggle between left and right rages on, despite the fall of the USSR, as rich countries outpace the poor, as sickness and global ecological damage threaten the integrity of nations and capitalist economies totter under the excesses of a few while the rest of the world becomes poorer and heads to the proverbial abyss. Sad to say the power of Corporations has increased and the gap between rich and poor, even in the wealthiest nations, has widened alarmingly, as events of recent decades reveal the stark and painful truth in Dwight Eisenhower's parting caution to the USA and the world: *"Beware the military-industrial complex!..."*

Just as a biopsy aids a physician to identify a cancer, the forces and events that made British Guiana a hot spot in the Cold War and impoverished it illustrate how the affairs of small, forgotten places can supply lessons to enlighten people and guide nations that today dominate world affairs purely by economic clout, not wisdom or justice.

Mohan Ragbeer 1997, rev. 2009

Chapter 1

We begin the slow and difficult journey downriver; we dig deeper into our dwindling supplies--conserved somewhat in the past four days--to share with the officers; this spontaneous act brings the group closer and the officers come to appreciate traditional Indian food choices, already known to the photographer whose wife is Indian. We reflect on current attitudes among colonial peoples seeking independence, identity and a harmonious *modus vivendi* in a multiracial environment. Colonial Indians stand out because they retained ancestral culture, wherever numbers permitted, despite a hostile environment. We review the causes and effects of cultural losses or retention, including devious and coercive methods of invaders to indoctrinate and subjugate peoples, to keep races separate for ease of control, and the social, economic and political consequences when colonies are abandoned. The impact of the Cold War and of antagonistic ideologies on an emerging nation could be ruinous by depleting it of skilled people when it needs them most. The rise of a rabid CIA-backed *laissez faire* capitalist in BG deepens tensions. Cpl Doris supports Burnham and incredibly thinks Indians should return to India. This is hotly debated.

Day 8, Mazawini landing to Aranka, on the river

"The Cultivators of Hindustan are known to be peaceable and industrious. An extensive introduction of that class of people to live on the produce of their own labour ... would probably be the best experiment for the population of this island... but without their priests, their chiefs, their families, their artisans, their plants and seeds, the success of such a plan could not be expected. "   19th century Governor of Trinidad

"The natives of India with their love of land and fondness for agriculture and pastoral pursuits will probably have a greater influence on the future of the colony than all the other races put together"
                                        R. Duff, Immigration Agent

"A new race is being born in this Colony free from the soul-killing rigours of caste and unreasoning social and religious practices and helping to enrich the life of the Colony and to gain the respect of the other races."
                            Diwan Bahadur Pillai, Madras, ca 1930

The urgent chatter of early morning life in the forest had already awakened the camp and the activities of camp break-up were well underway by the time I heaved out of my hammock. I had had strange dreams in one of which tall men dressed all in dirty green, their faces covered with broad brown leaves were tramping through the forest in phalanx formation, marching towards a frail almost invisible figure clothed in white *kurta* and *dhoti* who stood squarely in their path.

I was viewing this from behind the small figure, who became less and less significant as the enlarging phalanx advanced as if to crush him. Each man in the phalanx carried a huge axe, which he swung rhythmically with precision in an oblique circle around his head and neck, the blades inches away from the next man. As they swung, they got taller and taller until their eyes were level with the forest canopy, which they then swiftly beheaded in one sweeping blow. The limbs came crashing to the ground all around the little figure, almost smothering him. I wanted to run to his aid, but could not move. My feet were immobile, as if encased in concrete.

I called for help, but no voice came. I struggled to release myself. A pale figure appeared from the gloom off to one side floating sedately in mid-air, fully dressed in Government khakis, wearing a brown cork hat (sun helmet) and smoking a pipe; I recognised him as a District Commissioner, the Government's local representative. As I called to him for help, he removed the pipe from his mouth and began to laugh, at first noiselessly, then with a harsh and staccato sound, which became so loud that it boomed through the forest and shook the trees, those that were still standing. It was a terrifying sound, so close to the little man that it must have deafened him as he struggled to rise. Finally the little man stood up and turned to face his tormentors. It was then that I saw that he was

Hari, his clothing soiled in the fall. He stood his ground without flinching, his arms raised, even though the axes were now so close that their next swing would surely sever us in two.

They ignored his anguished plea, *"Spare the trees! Spare the trees! We need the oxygen! We need the Oxygen!"* I was so startled that I awoke, my left arm raised across my brow to fend off the dream-swing, my hammock shaking. It must have been about midnight. The lone camp light glowed dimly. There were snores everywhere. Rodriques was on watch duty, unaware of my adventure. The symbolism was obvious; it echoed Hari's clear concerns for the future of his forest. Was the Government's position with regards to the forest as callous as my dream portrayed? And would the advancing exploiters be as heinous as my dream depicted them?

We started downstream gingerly feeling our way into the channel. The sun had not yet topped the trees, which, silent, innocent and trusting, closed in around us. So far these majestic trees were being spared, as unrestricted logging by large companies had not yet reached the Barama. I imagined what this area would look like from the air: the monotony of an endless dark green canvass relieved only by the thin wavy brown ribbon of the river's mainstream. The tributaries would be too narrow to be seen from above, the canopy easily spanning the gaps they created, and closing over them.

The endless stretch of green would look so impressive, so strong, so overwhelming. But who looking from above would guess how frail, how vulnerable it all was, that human greed could lay it all to waste in less than a generation, with no hope of recall, no second chance to regenerate the work of millennia? Harry was right: society was all wrong; the rewards should go to the natives for preserving the forest not to those who profited from destroying trees.

We smelled of citronella or whatever particular personal insect repellent each was using. I had, from the first day, assiduously painted my exposed parts with the oily liquid every morning and after each wash. It was probably unnecessary since I was almost surely immune to the worst strains of the malarial parasite, having almost died of cerebral malaria due to the *falciparum* species when I was 15, and, like all in the party, had been inoculated against Yellow Fever and Poliomyelitis. But sporadic cases of jungle yellow fever did occur in BG[1], although rarely.

I disliked being stung and always got itchy red bumps when in mosquito-infested areas. The oiling was probably not necessary while we were on the water, under open sky and sun, although a few day-time biters were blown in on the cool wind that swept up from the water, or when awakened from their habitats in still leaf-covered pools filling little inlets along the bank, which the boat disturbed when it came too close, sending a spray of the little pests into the air. Somehow these were less ugly and less painful and even tolerable if you could accept the risk of some unknown disease, probably not malaria, since the

---

[1] In the months that followed I diagnosed two cases, one presenting classically with acute fulminant liver failure. The other was a perplexing case of a middle-aged man who had presented with a strange psychosis and after a week under observation at the Georgetown Hospital, he was being readied for transfer to the Mental Hospital, New Amsterdam, when he developed sudden vomiting, jaundice, liver failure and rapidly died of YF. Both men had been recently to the Mazaruni and Potaro regions of the hinterland. Cases of other liver, skin and heart infections transmitted by mosquitoes and sand flies had been reported in people returning from the deep forests, all presumed due to viruses. This new and rapidly expanding field of Virology was only at the research stage in BG and the Caribbean, although some diagnostics had begun at TRVRL, Trinidad and the UCHWI, Jamaica.

Anopheles were night feeders, although they did swarm and sting when disturbed in the daytime.

The natives of Wappai knew neither Malaria nor Yellow Fever. Presumably centuries of exposure had made them immune, an aspect of their biology not yet investigated. We knew that tribes downriver habitually drank infusions of the bark of the greenheart tree — which they called *bebeeru*--and other plant preparations regularly as preventatives or to treat illness. Thus their immune status to endemic illnesses would be of considerable value in planning for their health and improving ours.

Though we did not have all the needed technology or financial resources in BG, I knew that I could get serological and other complex analytical studies done at the Centres for Disease Control in Atlanta, Georgia, USA, or at one of the Institutes of Tropical Medicine in the UK, or through the World Health Organisation/Pan American Health Organisation. But my job allowed scant opportunity for a personal involvement in this, so I proposed to apply for a research grant to hire scientists for this work.

(When on returning to Georgetown I presented the idea to the Ministry of Health, officials shrugged it off in private, although they were overtly not totally opposed, merely invoking lack of resources and the more pressing needs of those on the heavily populated coastal strip.

This was almost certainly an expression of the low priority of natives and the hinterland in the Government's national plan regardless of any intrinsic scientific value. This, mind you, from the people who wished soon to take over as governors of an independent Guiana. No wonder Hari had been so pessimistic about my chances when I had broached the possibility of the study to him, "I will help you get to all the villages I know, but I doubt whether anyone will support you. They didn't listen to that white doctor years ago." This referred to the work of Dr CR Jones, previously cited.)

I sat next to the Inspector, burdened by my newly learned concern for the forest and the fragility of the natives' way of life, and ultimately their survival, as Dr Jones had noted eleven years earlier. I spoke instead of other things, other urgencies, particularly the increasing worry over the slow pace the numerous fallen trees had forced on us. Rodriques was at the bow keenly searching for any sign of the rock that could rip our boat apart. There was always that one, the one you took for granted, the bane of the bowman, such as had taken Zeke's life. "No, not on my turn at duty", Rodriques would say. In a sense the low water had made it easier for him to spot the signs, sometimes subtle, of flow obstruction. And so we crawled agonisingly downstream, perking up on the rare times when we got up to 3 knots.

"This thing bothers me; at this rate, we'll be three, four days getting to Cokerite." Inspector Bacchus interrupted my reverie, reading my mind. I was learning to read the signs on the river even as Rodriques played his pole, now left, now right, periodically pushing a floater away. And so we crawled all day until we reached the place where we had camped at the end of our third day, near *Parapimol,* west of the *Wiamu*. The markers we had left were firmly in place; in due course our camp was up and we ate frugally, sharing with the police.

"How are you for food?" Inspector Bacchus had asked me just before dinner.

Balgobin confirmed that we had rice, noodles, canned fish, salted cod, canned peas and fruit for a week for three of us at current rate of two spare meals per day. We still had half a can of crackers, and enough butter and cooking oil. The natives had supplies of cassava bread and some dried meat and fish. When asked, they said they were okay. The police team was almost out of everything; they had corned beef for just two more meals.

Listening to the inventory of our supplies emphasised the differences in the basic diet of Indians and others. Diet, politics, culture, religion, appearance, life style priorities: we differed in so many things. To dwell together in harmony we would have to have either total cultural synthesis or a tremendous understanding of, and respect for one another and be prepared to make many compromises on all sides. It was sad to note that attitudes had hardened by historical confrontations that had more to do with the interests of sugar bosses than with basic human foibles, and that misinformation had kept apart the two dominant populations of the colony.

The Indian had the advantage of knowing much more about the African than vice versa, which added to African resentment, and despite Jagan's claims the two were no closer than they were ten years ago.

"I think we eat too much meat, but that's all we have left," the Inspector said, "you Indians can do without the stuff."

"Most of us do," I said, "But we grew up on a mixed diet of milk, fish, shrimp, crab—these were plentiful in our area--and of course a wide range of vegetables, which every family grew; my mother was an ace at it and could get things to grow even in dry times. We also raised chickens, and had lamb from time to time. Beef and pork and exotic meats, no, we do not eat those. But my father once brought home a deer he had hunted, when I was a toddler."

"But your religion prevents you from eating meat, right?"

"Not really. It depends on the individual, and which religion. But you're right; vegetarianism is a Hindu thing. Especially among Buddhists and Jains. It's not basic to the religion and is more recent, speaking in historical terms; it has to do with respect for life and to some extent disease prevention. India's cuisine is very varied and has always included excellent meat dishes, and there are specialties from every region of the country. The *tandoori* style is well known in the Northwest and in Indian restaurants in Europe and America. Muslims eat meat, almost by preference; that has to do more with the fact that Islam originated in Arabia, a desert country with sheep, goats and camels as staples; agriculture is possible only in the oases; they grow dates and various crops, although in the distant past they had orchards and vineyards; those near the sea get seafood as well. In India, Pakistan and so on they have a wide variety of vegetables, grains and fruits, like us here."

"We only know Christianity, nothing really about Hindus or Muslims; we were always taught that those were false doctrines."

I heard Jain laugh.

"Inspector, false ones are people who preach theirs is only true doctrine. Hinduism is very old inclusive religion, based on mathematics and science, only one like that. Hindus do not try to convert anybody. Anyone from any religion can be Hindu at same time. You too can be Hindu, if you wish. Other religions say they're the only true one and therefore superior, and try to make converts." He paused and added cynically, "Mostly for the tithes, I think."

"But Mr Jain, I didn' know you was a Hindu. I thought you was Muslim." Balgobin said-- more a question than a statement.

"Right, I'm not strictly Hindu, my religion is Jainism; we believe in many same things. Just like different Christians."

"Jainism?" Brewster asked, "I never heard of that one. Sounds like you made it up out of your own name." Everyone laughed, Jain the heartiest; in his naturally exuberant way.

"Jainism is an Indian religion," I said, "derived from Hinduism, just as Calvinists, Lutherans, Catholics are variants of Christianity; the followers are called Jains. Mahatma Gandhi was a Jain."

"But hold on, Doc," Brewster continued, "Mr Jain telling us 'bout Hindus, and you 'bout Jainism, but each of you belong to the other. How so? Who is Calvinist? We have any here?"

"I believe there is a Calvinist church in Kingston," Bacchus offered.

"It's amazing; you people all live here together, and yet you are so separate; you know so little outside your own kind," Jain said, a bit unkindly.

"Come on, Naresh," I said, "you make it sound as if things are perfect where you come from, you know that's not so. Indians are even worse."

"Yes, true," he said, "India is huge, over 300 *millions* and people very clannish, and still stick to their silly castes. But here you have this tiny population, no bigger than one big Indian village; you have all this land, plenty for everyone, and some left over for me, but you separate yourselves into little racial groups, and fight over the same small piece of mudflat, when you have all this." He waved his arms dramatically in a wide circle. Hari's recitation of Indar's vehement condemnation of British "divide and rule" policy came to mind.

"It's not that bad; mos' people live well togedda; it's in town where things heat up. I have Indian friends; we all have Indian friends." Brewster said, wishing to steer away from any dissension, unsure of how too frank a discussion might evolve in this remote place.

Brewster had covered several sensational cases before this assignment, his first in the interior. He had dreaded the adventure and saw it only as a heavy demand on his physique relieved only by the slightly less objectionable boredom and confinement of a river trip in a cramped boat. But he had to follow orders. His racial outlook tended towards egalitarianism, and he dealt easily and smoothly with everyone in the party.

He shared however the prevailing prejudices against the natives and regarded them as lazy, inferior and unenterprising. Rodriques was the first native police officer he had met and he had some difficulty adjusting to the fact. To his credit, however, he had softened his views as he saw Rodriques in action, later the methodical and scientific way in which Joe, our chief guide, had verified our position and direction and their subtle ways of identifying features of the forest with personal marks to guide their way, and he confessed freely at the end that "we could be wrong about them."

"That's how Europeans enslaved Africans: by demeaning their value to the world, to justify slavery." I said.

He paused reflectively, then said, "I never thought of it that way."

Jain put in, "Don't forget though that slave trade was already part of African commerce when Europeans went there; I believe first ones were Portuguese. British brought slaves from African slavers, like they were buying cloth and spices in India!"

"Then how I read that they raided villages and captured the people?" Brewster asked.

"Well, I don't know if that happened, if it did, it was probably not too often. You know, Arabs came all the way from Middle East to buy West African slaves; and that's how they converted a lot of Africans to Islam."

"You confuse me, Mr Jain, what Islam got to do with Africa? Islam is Muslims, right?"

"Islam is religion of Muslims," Jain agreed, "and all North Africans and a lot of West, Central and East Africans are Muslims. In fact Islam is dominant religion of Africa."

"When you say West Africans, you mean like Nigeria, Ghana and so on; that can't be right; they don't have Muslims, eh Doc?"

"What can I say? Half of Nigeria and Chad are Muslim; there are Muslims in each country all the way round to Morocco and as Naresh said, all countries of North Africa are Muslim--Algeria, Libya, Tunisia — and in the east Egypt, Sudan, Somalia are mostly Muslim; Tanzania, Kenya and other east and south African states have Muslim populations. Yes, Islam is the main religion of Africa."

"You can't say that; many are Christian countries." Doris interjected.

"Christian by British propaganda; you go check for yourself! BG *is* Christian, but half the people are Hindus and Muslims!" Jain emphasised.

Cpl. Doris was perplexed; his notion of Africa was a lot of red stains on its map, each signifying an area of British domination, more than half the continent, he thought, and being British meant being Christian, since there was no organised native African religion. This was what he had learned in school, what all Africans had learned about Africa, from books and teachers, themselves mostly Africans, who by indoctrination to the British way had painted Africa as backward and homogeneous, the "Dark Continent", considering themselves fortunate to be out of it.

In the same way most ranks--as the constables were referred to within the Force--knew little about Indians, even though some had them as neighbours. Brewster had heard Police talk in their recreation room. He knew that many of their assertions and beliefs about Indians were incorrect, especially about religion; the comments and opinions seemed based on missionary propaganda. His Indian friends used to tease him that although he was African he had British names and thought like the British, but when Africans went to England white children would follow them and peek around their backsides to look for tails!

The European civilisation the Africans had adopted had shorn them of all traces of Africa, barring what remained in the few words that had entered the Caribbean lexicon, like *quashie, ackee, kokobeh, bakra, queh-queh*, or what had survived in their popular beliefs and cuisine, such as *obeah* and *fufu*. Doris himself had expressed some of these beliefs, for example when he had warned us in his briefing not to call the names of predators at night; he couldn't say why, except that it could bring bad luck. So if you must refer to them, he had told us, use euphemisms or false names. And if you innocently said the real name, you must immediately make a fist, put it in your mouth and bite down on it to cancel the call. Wasn't this a throwback to the West African myth that the night creatures could hear their names called and would interpret that as an invitation to come visiting? Wasn't this similar to Carib lore that long ago animals and plants did communicate? Owls and bats were said to be devilish creatures that stole the souls of the dead at night. West Africans hated them for this and so did Caribbean Africans. Similarly there was the belief I had heard as a child from our African neighbour that if you stepped over a mark or anything shaped like an X, bad luck would get you unless you closed your eyes and stepped backward over it, leading with your left foot.

"The English civilisation that your folks adopted is less than a thousand years old, while Hindus can trace ours back at least ten, twelve thousand years. The Jews go back 6000 years; in fact if you believe their story, their God created the world just about then, in 4004 BC."

"Incredible, that's why they live in their own world!" Jain said uncharitably, with a guffaw.

"Anyway, Christian memory is a short 2,000 years and Islam has been around for just under 1,350--1,339 to be exact. The history of both of these is full of wars and conquests, of grief and wrong and misrepresentation, all in the name of religion. Just read the history of the Popes and of the Vatican and of the Muslims in India for a real eye-opener. West African history--your ancestry-- includes civilisations as old as, or older than any European, which for some reason disintegrated, leaving only traces and many tribal divisions--for survival, I think.

"But while you've lost continuity with the past, we've carefully kept ours – it's the world's longest continuous record of a people and religion--and we pass that on to our children in all those lessons and ceremonies that you folks call backward and heathen. We don't correct you because there's never been a climate here of acceptance of non-Christian beliefs, especially of Hinduism, which the missions have specially targeted, blasting away in India. Even among Christian groups, denominations exist in a kind of hierarchy, each in its own cocoon. Do you know that Roman Catholics do not study the Bible the way the Presbyterians do?"

I could not resist the chance to say that. How many times at the UCWI I had had to correct the misinformation about Indians, especially to Afro-Jamaican students, among them aspiring politicians like Patterson[2], Lashley and Nettleford[3], who to a man nursed the belief that we Indians were some kind of an aberration, a blot on the scutcheon of black solidarity in the Caribbean, an inferior "heathen" people who must join them. They wanted us to divest ourselves of culture and other unique identifiers, integrate and be swallowed up, like most Jamaican Indians, by the anglicised Creole culture that had evolved and was presented as prototype "Caribbean," dressed in turgid academic prose.

None of these young intellectuals nor their counterparts from the other Caribbean islands had any knowledge of anything Indian, yet were quick to draw adverse conclusions. None had even studied Indian history, though a few might have dipped into the bastardised version given by British writers of textbooks for high schools, notably by Woodward, Williamson and their equivalents. These were full of distortions created by nineteenth century British revisionists who wished to paint a picture of Indians as an inferior people, to a Europe and America then consumed with white supremacy theories, and notions of a saviour mission for white Christians to reform the heathen non-Christian world, first by conquest, then by dogma. It's all there, in the words of Brian

---

[2] Later Prime Minister of Jamaica, 1992-2006
[3] Later Vice-Chancellor of the University of the West Indies 1996-2004

Edwards, Edward Long, Thomas Carlyle, Charles Kingsley, Thomas Macaulay, Rudyard Kipling, and in the work of Alfred Tennyson and a host of empire builders: Hastings, Clive, Wellesley, Chelmsford, Rhodes, Curzon, Kitchener and others, not to mention US counterparts like Thomas Jefferson, Senator Albert Beveridge and numerous others.

Benjamin Yesu Das, the Deputy Principal at Berbice High School in my time there, had refused to include Indian history in our curriculum choices, for the reason that the story in the prescribed texts was a distortion and misrepresentation, to put it mildly. The black students of the Antilles were spared both the distortion and the truth, since the issue never arose, as the few Indians who had settled in those islands had disappeared in the racial mélange within a few generations, or had become thoroughly Christianised. Their ignorance of history was profound. If Indian history was not taught among Indians, how much less likely was it to be taught among Africans? You cannot really teach culture in school, I would suggest; culture had to be experienced and lived, beginning from birth or early life.

I had excused Indo-Jamaicans their ignorance of the uniqueness of Indian culture because their island lacked a representative or vital Indian presence, the leadership and community institutions that could have informed them, and the critical mass required to preserve their culture and so withstand the social forces that had threatened it and scoffed at traditional practices, branding them as inferior, or worse, barbaric.

Within a few generations they had submitted and had been reduced to an ethnic anomaly that black intellectuals of Jamaica wished that all Caribbean Indians should become and "integrate" into the "Caribbean culture", that is, to give up, forego and sacrifice millennia of enduring values and a powerful philosophy, for an amalgam of divisive and militant European Christianity spiced with Caribbean mento, limbo and calypso on a backdrop of blue skies, sea, sand and waving palms!

Those few enclaves or households that retained their Indian identity had lost most of the elements of their true culture, and hung nostalgically to a few surviving symbols, which they would try to express and revive when they met Indians from Trinidad and BG, from whom they discovered that most Indians were actively Hindus and that separation from India was not, as they felt, a death sentence on cultural retention and preservation. "Who in hell would want just the last 100 years, when you can weave them into the variety, depth and wealth of 12 *thousand* years of Indian culture that flows in your veins?" I had asked my Indo-Jamaican fellow students. Most had scoffed and rejected my arguments.

I recall many "bull" sessions at the UCWI Students Union when, over a beer, I would be drawn into a critique of the obvious anti-Indian prejudices and ignorance of Africans and mulattoes, especially people who had political aspirations, like the acerbic Shirley Field-Ridley[4], herself a Guianese of mixed blood, Wm Cartey of Trinidad and Jamaican Cliff Lashley et al., who were equally dismissive of Indians. "Isn't that what we are here for?" I asked, "to learn objectivity, search for truth, and dispel untruth? The Nazis were not the first to

---

[4] She married PJ Patterson, the Jamaican PNP activist who would later become Prime Minister, as noted above; they divorced early and she returned to Guyana, became a Minister in Burnham's government in the early seventies, and married his deputy, Hamilton Green; she died under mysterious circumstances soon after.

distort history to their purpose!" Barbadian Blacks had had little or no contact with Indians, and were more cautious, being still, in the fifties, victims of the island's apartheid.

Many from Grenada and St Lucia -- including Derek Walcott, with whom I worked briefly on *Pelican,* the campus newspaper, and developed a friendship-- had been positively influenced by their Indian high school teachers from BG. Many from the islands were fair-minded and willing to accept critiques of what they had learned, like true intellectuals, and admit the valid claims of Indians and of others—Chinese, Portuguese, whites, and others—who had made major contributions to the region, and in fact controlled much of its assets. Some of my Indian friends thought I was "nuts" to argue and should leave well alone and take the path of least resistance. (Some of these would later come to gripe in private against the hegemony of Burnham or Eric Williams while publicly working on their agenda; others quietly joined the brain drain from the West Indies).

The white academic staff were surprisingly quite deferential and not overtly prejudiced towards us. What biases they had were more benign and subtler when shown at all and a sharp contrast to the wild, almost vituperative rage that the aspiring Africans of Trinidad and BG and to some extent Jamaica, were developing against us. The campus ferment of the fifties reflected the push of the major Caribbean territories – Jamaica, BG, Trinidad and Barbados -- for independence as unit states, while the British were concurrently promoting a West Indian Federation. Like their parents black students believed they were "natural heirs and leaders" of the nations in that Federation, in which Indians would play a supportive political role, if any, in Trinidad and Guiana, and little in a Federation comprised of a majority of "Africans".

Jagan's ascendancy stalled this argument. The likelihood by then of his becoming the first Indian premier of a self-governing state in the region belied the notion of an exclusive African succession. And the fact that Burnham was Jagan's second-in-command puzzled many as it belied the notion of Afro-Caribbean supremacy. The apparent successful union of Indians and Africans to a common purpose confused them, caused some to re-think their premises, but the die-hards remained sceptical. Later, in 1957-8 Jagan's refusal to join the ill-conceived West Indian Federation would justify this scepticism and consolidate anti-Indian feelings, as people wrongly leapt to the conclusion that Jagan's action was due to his "Indian-ness", and lack of sentiment for West Indian unity.

The approach they promoted might have been acceptable if there were such a thing as a West Indian (Caribbean) culture; the islands did have a few features in common, but they related only to the Creoles and educated Africans who felt that their absorption of Anglo-Christian values enabled them to replace the departing colonials. But *a* culture? Hardly yet.

The Creoles of the Caribbean have had little opposition, except latterly from Indians, to this claim of an African birthright, which they promoted aggressively and pretentiously in asserting their primacy as "first-come". Yet the cultural base was a blur and its ingredients a hodgepodge of hand-me-downs of various classes of British society, grafted on a multiplicity of African tribal customs and dominated by the values of planters and their lower class minions.

For two centuries the latter had been the cultural role models for workers, spiced with trace contributions from the white mandarins of the colonial bureaucracy, and dashes of African memorabilia. It was fairly plain sailing politically now for the Africans of Jamaica, Barbados and the Antilles where this belief went unchallenged. But Trinidad and BG presented a problem, an "Indian question", like a recrudescent ghost of British India come to haunt the emergent Afro-Caribbeans and disturb their smooth acquisition of ownership and power.

That power, once gained, Indians felt, could be used to re-create pre-slavery African tribal fiefdoms, modified by accretions from the more complex caste systems of Europe, to establish a local coloured elite. To achieve that in Trinidad and BG the Indians must be dealt with—assimilated, neutralised, sidelined or expelled. That task would fall to Eric Williams in Trinidad and Forbes Burnham in British Guiana.

The missionary view of Indians was that they were a lost heathen people to be rescued, and that Christianisation would "save" them! The British in India had gone further, and had started a campaign of propaganda to distort and degrade the history, literature and culture of India. In the19[th] century[5], agents like James Mill, H.H. Wilson, Max Müller and M. Monier-Williams, had promulgated the preposterous hypothesis that the civilisers of India were not native Indians, but a mythical "aryan" race from Central Asia that had invaded and conquered the indigenous people[6], who were assumed to have fled south. In 1856 Roman Catholic missionary Bishop Caldwell wrongly applied the term *"Dravidian"* to describe South Indians to distinguish them from *Aryans*; he thus ascribed an ethnic meaning to a regional geographic term, just as Müller had transformed the adjective *"aryan"* into a proper noun. The British—scholars and missionaries, following Macaulay's doctrine[7]--went on to disseminate authoritatively as "fact" the Aryan-Dravidian *hypothesis*. It took root and has flourished worldwide even today, so embedded has it become in Western and Indian thought.

To conform to Müller's hypothesis, *Vaidic* records were compressed to fit with Biblical accounts of creation and human civilisation, thus taking *a priori* reasoning to a ridiculous degree. A huge English literature grew to promote the myth, which was taught in the new Indian universities built for the express purpose of anglicising Indians to achieve imperial aims.

Despite coercion by British authorities Indian scholars--led by Shri Aurobindo, Bal Gangadhar Tilak, Swami Moolsankar Dayānanda Saraswati and many others--had rejected Muller's hypothesis of Indian origins, showing that it was based solely on flawed philology, denial of a vast and contradictory record of *Vaidic* chronology, dating back at least to 10,000 BC. Shri Aurobindo scoffed and dismissed it as *"a conjecture based on other conjectures"*!

In BG, as in India, Indians continued to practise, nurture and teach their own religions; indeed they revelled in their cultural expressions, promoted and embellished their rituals and festivals, which they celebrated with great pride. Even the Canadian Presbyterian Mission, the most successful missionary group

---

[5]In 1850 the first English version of the *Rig Veda* was published by H.H. Wilson, first holder of the University of Oxford's Boden Chair, which was created *"to promote the translation of the (Hindu) Scriptures into English, so as to enable his countrymen to proceed in the conversion of the natives of India to the Christian religion."* Max Muller in 1853 used the term Aryan to describe a fictional progenitor of Indian peoples. Sir M. Monier-Williams (1819-99) published an *English-Sanskrit Dictionary* in 1851; his *Sanskrit-English Dictionary* took 30 years to complete and was published in 1899, the year he died.

[6] See Book 1, Chapter 2, 12; Book 2, Ch. 4 and 5and footnotes.

[7] Ibid, p 12-13

among Indians in BG and Trinidad, would privately admit that they had learned more about morality and spirituality from Hindus than they dared admit in public. They did make converts, but the majority of those were converts of convenience, in that the conversion had brought an immediate material, as distinct from spiritual benefit to the converted.

Few non-Indians knew or had thought much of these things, and had simply accepted as fact the many pejorative anti-Indian assertions they had heard over the years. Brewster said that he believed, like most of his friends that all that was known or thought great were discovered or invented by the Europeans starting with the Greeks down to today.

The East beyond Egypt and Palestine was to most, if not all, a huge unknown, an area of darkness lightened here and there by *The Arabian Nights* or *Jungle Boy*. Even Africa was almost only a name to Afro-Guianese, even though they had roots there; more often than not Africa meant the sub-Saharan countries which were despised and viewed through British eyes as backward, primitive and disreputable, noted only for the exploits of ancient Egypt or modern white heroes like Rhodes, Livingstone, Schweitzer and *Tarzan of the Apes*.

If they had to represent the world on a pie diagram according to perceived importance, Britain would occupy the largest segment, the rest of Europe next, then USA, USSR, Canada, Japan, Brazil, the Caribbean and Australia. South Africa, the rest of Africa, China and India would trail behind and together occupy less than 10 percent of the globe. Pathetic, when you think of it, but that was reality of their indoctrination.

As to knowledge of history, the less said the better. Brewster, for example, admitted that he did not know that British agents, Rhodes especially, had "stolen" southern Africa to get at its large deposits of diamonds and gold. He had heard of Lumumba but knew little of the Congo and was astonished to hear that Belgian king Leopold had *purchased* the territory for a song and exploited its mineral wealth for his personal gain under conditions worse than slavery.

Other Europeans had staked similar claims to sub-Saharan Africa merely treating the continent as vacant and thus "up for grabs", a *terra nullius,* as Governor Bourke had proclaimed Australia in 1835, summarily seizing all native lands there. Brewster was stunned and unsure how to deal with this new information.

"If I put all this stuff in my head, won't it take up space needed for my real work?"

"I don't think the brain works that way; in fact the more you learn the better it gets."

"You sure 'bout that? People say too much study hurt you' head!"

"'Nancy story, I assure you."

The city-bred Indians who had managed to enter the Police Force were an ambivalent group. Many were Christians and tended to be more adversely critical of Hindus than even the Africans were, and often tougher on Indians, as if to prove their impartiality. They kept their politics to themselves. Those who had black friends tended to learn much about their ways, but the reverse was rarely true.

It was common knowledge that if you put Indians in the company of other races in Guyana, the Indian would come away knowing about the others but none would know anything about the Indian. Thus many Indians had come to know the ways of Africans and to gain insights into Christianity and into various aspects of "British" character; they would begin to doubt the fable learnt in school from books that showed the British as "civilisers" of the world. Africans were in general loyal to the crown, while Indians were ambivalent. Those Africans known as "high coloured" were singularly devoted.

I asked Brewster, "Constable, these Indians whom you know, are they friends, real friends, or just acquaintances?" Before he could answer Cpl Doris interjected, breaking his silence.

"The same goes for Indians; how many have black friends?"

"That's just the point." I said. "Here we have a country with six distinct races, supposedly living together in harmony, according to Government propaganda. But who is the Government fooling? That harmony is only superficial. The two major races are split in every conceivable way. Right now they face deep political divisions that could lead to bloodshed. And what are the leaders doing about it? Creating even deeper division and stirring up rabble emotions with race talk."

"The PPP started that, in the '57 elections. You remember *"apana jaat?"*

"That may be so, but don't forget that much of that was due to the Burnham split of the PPP and the withdrawal of most Africans from the PPP."

"We know that racial divisions have been around for centuries," Bacchus said. "It got worse here after the first migrant workers came after emancipation; that killed the hopes of the freed men to bargain with the estates for higher wages. It got worse when the first ones began to leave the sugar estates and compete with us for jobs, especially in the city. We have to learn to live better with this inter-racial competition. We have to live together."

"You must remember that Indians didn't come freely; they were forced by lousy conditions created by conquest including famine and wars and were not the first; the first were Negroes from the West Indies and USA, then Portuguese and others before Indians. Africans rioted against Portuguese in 1854 or '56 and in 1889. Chinese came later and escaped that; also their numbers were small. Today Indians are still not equally treated. You know how hard it is for an Indian to get an ordinary Government job? The biases are huge. Look, Indians are 52% of the population, they have barely 10% of Civil Service positions, less than 10% in the Police Force, Post Office or Transport and they're every bit as smart or educated or loyal as any other group. That restriction forced many to go into business; most started on a shoestring, like Palestinians or Lebanese, who too did not qualify for government jobs; they saved every penny of profit to reinvest in goods; they skimped and in time built up capital.

Indians went into agriculture, worked swampy lands and abandoned sugar estates in the three counties. Now everyone complains that Indians dominate those things, and both Jagan and Burnham are out to ruin them. Few have done really well. Most ordinary Indians are still buried in the sugar estates, trying to dig themselves out. They are Jagan's main support; they believe his claims that he's the only one fighting for them; they believe in his promises, but they don't know he can't deliver and in fact will harm their cause in the long run!

As for Burnham he will get Black support even though few who know him will trust him behind their backs, especially with money. Jagan at least has not so far dipped into the public till."

I was surprised how animated I had become. The conversation was taking an uncomfortable turn, but there were things that had to be aired and dispassionately to the point of debate, without rancour, if we were to avoid racial conflict and a permanent state of animosity among the peoples of the coast. Those Africans who had recently begun to call for Indians to return to India were unrealistic and chauvinistic. Reasonable and cooperative people would choose tolerance over bigotry and peaceful co-existence with equality over any attempt at racial dominance.

I believed strongly that the hope of political unity was already remote, if not lost altogether, that the intelligentsia was too weak numerically to influence either opinion or the polls, and that the real struggle would be for the attention of the working classes in the cities and farming communities. Once that was obtained it would take a major educational effort to convince them of the folly of voting on the basis of race alone, or of trusting the governance of the land to self-serving men and women who were seeking power for themselves and their obsessions only, who placed ambition above the popular issues that they had championed in the election campaign.

The educational adjustments should have begun ten years ago, with changes in the elementary curriculum to portray accurately the origins and values of the constituent peoples and not to stigmatise or belittle anyone. Each had to feel proud of his heritage, not apologise for it. And all in the community had to develop respect and tolerance for one another from this basis of knowledge.

An educated population, barring the Hitler syndrome, was less likely to be fooled by self-promoting national claimants or political posturing, and could then demand attention to issues more related to advancement of the *whole* society rather than specific sectors. Ignorance was no basis for development, and has been the major hindrance to dismantling the social and cultural barriers built by the British to facilitate control of the majority — the "divide and rule" approach so evident in Guianese society which had so far prevented the ordinary citizen from shedding biases and resentments that poisoned interactions with other races.

Once in power politicians had done as they wished. The PPP illustrated that. Despite massive support they had failed at the start, and more recently Dr Jagan had continued the neglect. Four years after regaining power, and after re-election in 1961, he had yet to devise an education plan or take other concrete steps to address racial justice and equality, and balance in Government recruitment. His current Minister of Home Affairs, Mr B. S. Rai wished to introduce measures and set quotas to begin the process, only to see Jagan veto its implementation. The PPP, one critic had concluded, had changed from *plucky, purposeful, and popular* to *petty political pricks*.

This unusual forum deep in the forest would probably have as good a chance as any, or better, perhaps, of achieving some understanding by dispelling widely held misconceptions. We had nothing to distract us, not even a radio, and no place of escape for anyone. We were prisoners whether on the boat or encamped. But we had become comfortable enough with one another to speak freely and not fear retribution or ridicule, both of which were common and powerful ways in which arguments often ended when the sides held fixed positions, especially when one of the sides held jurisdiction or authority, such as the police. Here, instead, we could keep an open mind. Besides we had to depend on one another to get us all safely back home. The wish to survive could be a strong determinant of reason and nobility, just as it could make us do the most unreasonable and inhuman things.

"Doc, tell me, how long you bin away?" Brewster asked. "You know what's bin going on with all these politicians fighting to reach the top?"

"Nearly ten years, but I did come home a few times, and kept informed. I've followed politics since I was 15, when I met Dr Jagan and the PAC set; JB Singh, JN, and a lot of the others are family friends; I know Burnham since 1950 and others in the PNC before the PNC formed: Kendall, Carter, Hart, Pilgrim, Barrow, Denbow, Wills, Green, Jackson and several others; the last three I knew at Queen's; I met Mann and Shirley Field-Ridley at University. My family was very close to the Jagans and my brother-in-law helped them a lot in the early years. Since coming back I met McKay and the Weithers brothers who are close to Odo, and the newer Ministers Rai, Ramsahoye and others."

"Okay, well you know that when Burnham and Jagan were together, the people did unite, and t'ings looked good. Since the break-up, this racial t'ing set in. And it getting' worse since Jagan win again, 'cos this time he's Premier with more real power than when he had to keep lookin' over 'e shoulder because the Brits were there, up close."

"Well, he has less power now than in '53. But in this term, it's not the British who will have the real say; it's the Americans. They've been busy for some time, as you know, collecting data on people and the politicians. They had some info on the politicians, but nothing much about the ordinary people; especially Indians, how they felt, what they thought, you know the sort of thing that social scientists talk about; people's beliefs, way of life, their ambitions, their education, economics and so on."

"Who doin' this for them?" he asked.

I reminded them about Steve (see Book 1 Ch. 7) and his various interests since coming to BG. "What do you think all this activity is about?"

"They spyin'; is de CIA they really workin' for!" Balgobin interjected. "The Americans don' know not'ing 'bout we. They think that we stupid because we not rich. All they do is scheme to put crooked dictators in power anywhere they want, control them with pay-off, and throw out the people's choice and honest people because that don't suit them. They plot against President Arbenz in Guatemala and now they trying to get rid of Castro because he show them some backbone. They did swear Jagan was going to lose the '57 election; remember how they back Latchmansingh and Jainarinesingh when it did look as if they would join up with Burnham 'gainst the PPP? But what happen surprise them. So they husslin' to find out 'bout we now. Whoever tell them things in the past must be from Georgetown; they don' know what really goin' on in the country or how people really feel. Or maybe they only listen to what they like to hear. None ah we can go in America and strong-arm them like how they do here. Everything must go their way. They just big bullies!" Balgobin was emphatic and sure of his ground.

In all this Inspector Bacchus hardly said anything, as if he was sitting on the sidelines watching a cricket game, and wondering who will play what stroke, when, and score what runs, or whether the bowlers would win the day.

"What I t'ink the Americans worry about most is Communism, like we were saying the other night at Tilbury's," he offered finally. "They don' want a second Communist Government at their back door now. Castro surprised them in Cuba. They feel betrayed, 'cos they did help him get rid of Battista. Then when they ask him 'bout elections, he hit them with a one party state. They don't want another one, not here, but they will get what they want here by squeezing the British. They're the power here now anyway; the British will be history soon."

He was careful not to reveal his loyalties. What he said was widely known and therefore did not threaten his neutrality as an officer of the crown. Then he addressed me and asked, "'Bout this fella Steve, where is he now?"

"I really don't know. I saw him a few weeks before we left town. We'd gone with my friend to a social at one of his relatives' on the West Coast. He was interested in anything and everything concerning Indians. I was amazed how little he knew and that "little" was wrong. He thought all Indians were the same--poor and uneducated–was surprised to see them driving cars and living in fancy houses. My friend took him to that office building in Croal St that's full of lawyers' offices across from the Law Courts, and watched him photograph the hundred names of lawyers there, 90% Indian. He was stunned. They don't have a clue about Indian culture, or religions, or that Hinduism and Islam are different. Couldn't tell the difference between church, temple and mosque; but they know all about synagogues!

"But then Americans are like that; they know almost nothing about other peoples. Not that they care to know, really. In fact, they know little about their own country, as I found out in New York last year! They know damn all about Africa too. They're learning about Jews though, because Jews control money flow and soon will own all of Wall St. Yet just twenty years ago US had turned them away." Heads nodded.

"True, true, Doctor; that's America!" Jain interjected. "The world's most powerful nation; in India we know they know nothing and we make fun of them when they try to say names; they're vairy vairy ignorant people; love themselves too much; vairy pushy. We laugh when we hear them talk about India! Some live in my building. You will not believe what they say when they chat. They're not aware enough to be ashamed of how little they know. And some of them come here as experts!" Noises of derision and condemnation greeted this.

"You mean they didn't brief the man on things like that before he left Washington?" The Inspector was incredulous. "So what else did he do, Doc?"

"Actually he seems a nice man; he mixes well with the folks, he's tall like you, good-looking and girls like him, and it seems he's taken a liking for one of them; he's been talking with young and old, told them he worked with the Consulate, was new to BG, and wanted to know the people and their customs so that he could do his job better.

He asked them many questions, about schools, work, fields and crops, taxes, hospitals, roads, water supply, and about Dr Jagan. And they were frank with him. You know how open and hospitable country people are. He didn't realise that they treated him like an insider because he had come with one of the family, until my friend told him. He thought it was because he had worked so hard to gain their confidence. That first time we spent the whole day there. And the family invited him back, as they would any friend of a family member, in true BG style."

"So you think he collecting data for the CIA?" the Inspector asked.

"The CIA, the Consulate, the same. I believe he doesn't know yet that the information is going to the CIA. Or maybe he's trained to put up a front."

"What's all this information they collectin', what for?" Balgobin was curious. I was sure he knew the answer.

It was Benn who spoke, and for the first time in the conversation, "It's obvious to me. They want to know which way the politics would go, left up to the people. If that don' suit them, they would have to put a plan in place to move things their way. That's how big governments work. It's just like wartime, man!"

"The US must have had spies on the major politicians for at least ten years." I said. "Before that the Brits had dossiers on everyone, and still collecting. The Russians too have agents here. BG is deep in the Cold War; its economy may be small but the location has value to both sides. Each wants to influence or control this country when it becomes independent."

"US is obsessed with keeping Commies out. That's the heart of the matter." Bacchus noted.

"If Russia try to get the upper hand here, the US would stop that fast!" Bal observed.

"That's why they need to know how the ordinary citizen thinks–are they Communists or what? As Bal said; in '57, the US got burned because they were told Indians would vote for Latchmansingh and Jainarine, and Jagan would lose. The opposite happened, because their ideas about the people were wrong. They had listened to the wrong Indians: a few Georgetown lawyers, civil servants and businessmen, Luckhoo, Gajraj, Hanoman, Kawall, Balwant Singh, Ramphal, Searwar those chaps–all Georgetown Indians, mostly wealthy, some Christians, who don't really know the rural people. And I'll tell you, because many of these businessmen employ people who follow orders at work, they think they will follow their orders on how to vote. Were they ever wrong! Now the US wants to get closer to real people, to get better information. That's what Steve does and whoever working among Africans."

"Jagan tell Luckhoo he's a Communist in '56. But Indians vote for him every time. You think the Indians are Communists, Doc?"

Cpl Doris could not rightly miss this opportunity to press his argument against Jagan, whom he might have opposed, Communist or not, simply because he was Indian. I've often wondered what would have happened in BG had Jagan listened to Tulla and other early supporters and followed a middle-of-the-road social and economic policy. Would the Africans have flocked to Burnham when so many were questioning everything about him: his motives, his honesty, his integrity, his colossal selfishness and penchant for self-aggrandisement, acquisitiveness, flamboyance and dictatorship?

"No, only a few are real Communists; most use the lingo, without knowing what' behind it. I know Jagan is Communist, but that's not why Indians vote for him. They vote for him because he's Indian," and before he could say anything, I quickly added, "in the same way most Africans vote for Burnham. It's emotion, not conviction. That's why the PPP missed the boat when they didn't start with educating the masses in '53. But maybe that was deliberate. Let's face it; the curriculum is more important than who runs the school. Jagan is more interested in *running* the schools. And remember Burnham was Minister of Education in the first PPP government. He was the pilot that ran us aground!"

The way was opened for a "reckoning"-- to use a popular Guianese word for a spirited debate, with potential for acrimony, but the Inspector would not have allowed that to develop. Yet I sensed that he could not let this unique opportunity pass to hear, in the seclusion and protection of the wilderness, opposing views of people who had obviously followed the events of the past fifteen years fairly closely.

Balgobin cited instances of Burnham's alleged "crookedness," two of which I knew first hand, as they had involved family acquaintances. Georgetown was, after all, a small place and few events affecting newsmakers were ever left untold, and quite often the real news would not be the one in the press or on radio, but the one told in whispers among the cognoscenti. Doris quoted examples of Jagan's intransigence and ignoring of important information.

Despite or perhaps because of arrogant treatment of individuals by both men each had no difficulty maintaining a fawning retinue that knew how favours and perquisites invariably flowed to the blindly loyal. To many the mere presence of the leader nearby was enough to increase their sense of importance. A handshake was an occasion for great celebration. A few personal words induced near ecstasy. Having a meal with the leader or getting him to attend a function at one's home was the high point of a lifetime. Sycophants referred to them as 'Cheddi' and 'Odo' in the hope that the vicarious intimacy would impress listeners and elevate them socially. Among supporters, the two men were welcomed, fêted extravagantly and venerated in the fashion of kings.

Criticism from any source, however justified, was treated as blasphemy and imperilled the critic. Thus supported, protected and exalted, they had come to dominate the country in every way save that of controlling the largest purse strings outside of Government's, that is, Bookers enterprises and the Bauxite companies. And both had cast covetous eyes on these businesses, as well as towards other moneyed enterprises like the large lumber and commercial companies, Jagan to collect them into a basket of state-controlled enterprises, Burnham to have them at his personal disposal.

"The way I see it," Doris was saying, incredulously, "India is independent now, so you people should all go back there, and leave this country to us. We bin here longer than you. We people slave to make it what it is today."

I was stunned into silence by the suddenness of this assertion, and the nerve it took for him to make it, even though I had heard it before, the last time just two months earlier from Leila's narration of her travail in the wards of the Georgetown Hospital. But it was Balgobin who spoke first.

"And if it wasn't for we people, you would be starving today, especially in Georgetown. Don't forget that if it wasn't for Indians sugar estates would be dead today; and BG would be dead, like Haiti. You want another Haiti?" Balgobin asked, sucking his teeth in derision.

He was most upset at the turn in the conversation. His voice had kept its normal low pitch, and hardly betrayed his feelings. He was a fair man, proud, generous and forgiving, whose relatively low station in the hierarchy of Government concealed a considerable talent, intellect and common sense that could have taken him to the highest ranks of a profession or Government had he the benefit of a higher education.

He was industrious, tolerant of constructive criticism and learned quickly, which was why I had chosen him for training as our first Pathology Assistant. He was recognised as such within the laboratory and hospital, and had already become almost indispensable to me. (But the Government had yet to approve such a radical innovation in its personnel structure, although recommended by the Chief Medical Officer.)

He was better informed on political issues than most and was in every way capable of sound debate. What he lacked in detailed knowledge was made up in willingness to seek information and to make sure he was misleading no one. He respected me in a way that was flattering, and often came to me with questions outside of medicine. What I did not know I would refer to an appropriate source. He was always deferential, though never obsequious, and polite in all his dealings with people. Though his boss, I never allowed myself to show anything but respect for him, his work, his attitudes and his industry. He was at his feisty best when confronted with what he thought to be unfairness. In this exchange of views and opinions, I did not feel any need to restrain him.

"Because of what we did, we can make the same claim, no matter whether you came first; you too can go back to Africa, if you know where to go, but I don' think they will tek you." he added, seething.

"My people was captured and brought here and turned into slaves; we had no contract like y'all."

"But it was you own people who sell dem matty; you own people did that. You trade one another like animals. Don't forget that. Wha' mek you think that Burnham wouldn' do the same to you? He already gat people, specials too and old police, running round like ants makin' mischief. You is a policeman; you mus' know!"

"Careful, Bal," Brewster said quickly, "don' let you' feelings run away with you' good sense."

"The police have information about all kinds of goings-on, and we don' take sides. If a policeman takes sides, he's acting alone, not for the Force." Inspector Bacchus intervened, more to set the record straight than to quell argument. He seemed interested to hear where this debate would go, since he had had no prior opportunity to hear two opposing partisans on this particular topic.

"Sorry, I di'n' mean to be personal, but you all know what I want to say. Things happenin'; PNP people saying they don' want we here; we must go 'way. I born hey, not India. You born hey. Why I must leave and not you? If I must leave all of us must leave and give the place back to the bucks."

Everyone laughed, somewhat nervously.

"*Haré, Rāma,*" Jain said.

(Aside, Brewster asked me, "Wha' that?", "I hear it befo' and always wonder what it mean."

("Literally, 'Hail to Lord Rāma'. He was an avatar, or messenger, of God to ancient India, like Jesus Christ; he came over six thousand ago."

("And I hear the same Haré Kishen?"

("Krishna, he was an avatar of God, about five thousand years ago."

("What, another one?"

("Yes Hindu history has ten major avatars, and many minor; nine have come. It's a long story; I'll tell you more later if you're interested." He nodded.)

Meanwhile Balgobin and Doris had continued, the former saying,

"Is true we Indians here for only 120 years or so, not as long as you. That does not mean I have less rights because I'm second generation and you fifth; neither o' we own this land; we only join with the people that steal it from the natives; but we can claim birth rights."

"Like I said befo', my parents spilled their blood here, their sweat and tears." Doris averred.

"And mine too, in the same fields as yours. And yours killed many of mine; we never spill your blood; we never shoot down any of you. That's a big difference."

"We were promised this land."

"Who by? The thieves who steal the land from the rightful owners! You would put me in jail if I did that. But it's the law of the thieves that rule us now. If we want to be fair and decent, we should give it all back to the bucks and let them decide. I'm willing to do that, how 'bout you?"

"I say that Indians can go back to India, because there's money fo' the passage, money in England, since Queen Victoria time," said Doris, pursuing his original point. "We don' have such money. Besides, is true that none o' we know whey we really come from, I mean, which village or town or country. And we cyaan speak African; alyuh know whey you come from, or can find out from the Immigration office. Every one of you register there. You know that. We know that." Doris remained adamant and sounded triumphant.

"So when you send we back after a hundred years, which village or town you goin' send us to, and when we get there, wha' language we goin' speak, you think o' that?" Balgobin asked, equally defiant.

"Indian, or English; all the Indians I see from India speak English. Look at Mr Jain; he speak English, better than me."

A great guffaw from Jain greeted this remark. I was amazed at Doris's ignorance, and more so at his willingness to display it. This was not the first time I had heard such obvious errors pronounced as fact, even among University students, a telling commentary on the lack of education on the history of migrant peoples, even though migration has always been a dominant issue among the world's peoples, ancient and modern, whether accomplished peacefully or through invasions and conquests.

"Isn't your main language called Hindustani?" asked the Inspector.

Jain was still venting his amusement as he spoke through his disbelief, and either didn't hear the Inspector or delayed his reply, preferring to address Doris.

"Mr Doris. How little you know, and yet your opinion is so strong. India is big as Europe; it has nearly half a billion people, billion, not million, Mr Doris, one thousand people for every one in BG. It has 15 or 16 major languages. Hindi is official language, but only one in three people speak it. English is used in Government as well, even though less than 3 per cent of Indians speak it. Sounds small but that's over 2 million people. That is because the British did everything in English, just like here; if you want to be government worker you must learn English. We still have all institutions Brits left behind that still use English; my university courses were all English; in time that might change. But I tell you Indians would not understand Guianese English."

"Well, what about Hindustani?" asked Inspector Bacchus, "I thought that was the main language in India, and that our local Indians speak it."

"No, and yes," Jain said, his voice reverberating in the darkness. "Hindustani is Delhi Hindi language named *Khari Boli* mixed with words from Muslim languages — Arabic, Persian, Turk — and is official language of Pakistan, also spoken in India. Guianese Hindi is mostly *Bhojpuri* and some *Brajbhasa* depending on where people came from. The Brits I think called everything *Hindustani.*

"You know, Guianese Indians would have tough time in India, except with lots of money. In past many who returned to India came back here after a while.

India changed for them. I think you too would not be heppy if you went to Africa. And Corporal, there is no language called African; there are hundreds of dialects in West Africa alone, where your people came from; and they speak English or French, depending."

In the silence that followed you could almost hear them mulling over Jain's simple statements of fact, which emphasised the misinformation that supported so much of political opinion in BG, on both sides of the racial spectrum. For example, not all Africans supported Burnham's ambition. Many among the intellectuals were vehemently opposed though most with political ambition had already joined up with him and the PNC.

The fact was that the Indians had been held in such low esteem by the ruling classes that no one outside the Indian community had bothered to learn anything about them, much less about developments, political or otherwise, taking place in their huge mother country. Nor, for that matter did anyone know much about Portugal (not even among the Portuguese in the colony) or China, about which only rudimentary information existed, and least among the local Chinese, especially now that Mao Tse Tung was holding such a tight rein on censorship and free speech in that vast land.

The dialogue was interesting and revelatory. So much needed to be set straight, on all sides. Indians were clear on their region of origin and identity. It was equally clear that few Africans knew their origins and could only guess at specifics from historical records of where their ancestors might have been enslaved or from physical characteristics, though cross breeding over the three hundred years of their relocation could have destroyed much of that evidence. There was no residue of distinctive language or cuisine, barring a few words and traces of culinary influences already noted.

There was a lot that could be said to clear the air, but I had the distinct feeling that it would do no good, sway no one. The year 1961 was ending. The erroneous propaganda had been circulating for over a hundred years. People had absorbed it, and their children had grown up accepting what their parents believed and expressed. Opinions had formed. Minds had been made up and polarised. The wheel that had started turning was unwieldy and heavy. It would be easier to turn around a battleship in the narrow Georgetown harbour than to put together the resources needed to combat the ingrained misinformation and distortions that so suited the political camps. Any change would have to start in early childhood education and honestly conceived.

"You ain't saying anything, Doc," Bacchus' voice broke through my reverie. "What d'you think of all this?"

"I wanted to keep out of this; it's futile to argue without facts. Politicians are making decisions based on ignorance. A lot of misinformation about people, about history, about what is possible has spread in BG to the point that even intelligent people believe and share it. The politicians have done it, the unions have done it, and those with knowledge have either kept silent or were brushed aside because what they had to say did not fit party propaganda. Right now all this racial talk of going back or sending back people wherever is a big red herring. It's not helpful. It creates bad blood. And it's based on a falsehood that the logical successor to this land is the African. The African might as well lay claim to the United States on that argument. And what does that claim do to native rights? Or for that matter the rights of the other races?"

"We sweat blood and tears to build this country; the bucks are just as backward as they were then; they ain't do nothin'!" Doris was emphatic.

"They'll disagree with you; they will tell you they've preserved this place for thousands of years, and you're destroying it. Surely their views should count for something? But none of us gives a fig for them really. We're like children in a family whose parents are dying and about to share out their business and property. Do they give it all to the first-born, or do they divide it among all their children? Most would opt for a fair division.

"Cpl Doris claims he is the first born. He thinks everything should go to him. Now that's not what he himself would do to his children. Nor indeed any one of us. So why expect the Brits to do that? If you compare BG to a business which won't survive division, wise parents would insist that it continue intact in the family, to preserve all that it has gained and so maintain its reputation. That way it will stay whole and keep its customers. If one of those children is more greedy and ambitious than the rest and also thinks he's the best steward of the business, what will he do but try to seize it all? I believe that Mr Burnham is that wanton child, and wants to seize the country for himself --for himself, Corporal, not for you--even though you and thousands others will willingly help him."

Doris objected, but I continued, "No wait, hear me out, you'll have equal opportunity to rebut. To seize this land Burnham will have to banish the other claimants; or dispose of them some other way. I believe he is ruthless enough to do that. I don't believe that any of us has seen the real man yet. Beware, Corporal, I hope I'm wrong. I don't want you to like Mr. Burnham less, nor anyone to change loyalties, but for heaven's sake know why you're giving your support, know the facts of every issue, know both sides, or all sides before you choose a path that could be divisive and destructive. That is, if you want peace. One last thing, Corporal. The money you mentioned had been set aside for repatriation of those who qualify, but will pay only half the fare for a man and two-thirds for a woman. That money was put in escrow as they call it, for that one purpose only; very few grants have been given in recent times, and the last people to return did so in 1949. Besides most of us do not qualify today; we lost any claim because our parents might have taken advantage of one of the schemes the planters tried in the last century to get out of paying those passages, for example land grant schemes like the ones at Whim, or at Helena, Mahaica, or Bush Lot."

"Also," Balgobin explained, "people who didn' go back to India before independence or didn' register citizenship when they had the chance, lost out because the BG government didn' inform them of their right, as it had promised to do. I believe all they did was put a notice in the *Official Gazette*; we don't get papers much *less Gazette*! My parents wanted to go back, but lost their passages because of this, and no appeal help them."

"That's a shame," Brewster sympathised; he had said little during this exchange, complaining that hunger did not encourage conversation, but he listened and made appropriate noises.

"In the late thirties the British Raj advised planters not to repatriate people because of problems they had adjusting, since many had found village life changed beyond recognition as Jain said. Now if I wish to settle in India, I'd have to apply as a migrant. The same goes for a Portuguese in Portugal or a Chinaman in China, but not to you if you wish to settle in British Africa. You can go without hindrance to any country in British Africa right now without a visa. But if you wish to go to what was a French West African colony you're out of luck, even if your ancestors had come from there; last year all became independent.

" So you cannot glibly talk of sending people born here to some other place. What will happen, as this kind of talk increases, is that the best people will leave before their British citizenship lapses, and they won't be going to Africa or India. *That will have the same effect as if your family business fired all your best workers. Your business will go belly up!* If things continue the way they're going, it won't be long before all of us here will wish we can turn the clock back to the bad colonial times!"

Both Brewster and the Inspector said complimentary things, and agreed on the need for prudence and fact finding. Doris on the other hand was unmoved, or so he sounded. It was a distinct disadvantage not seeing one another's faces in this eerie conversation, where you identified speakers by sound and direction, in the dim cocoons silhouetted by the two oil lamps that hung at our perimeter.

"So you say if you want to go back to India, you have to get a visa?" asked Doris.

"What do you mean '*back*'? I've never been there. You keep forgetting that I and others like me were born here. Just like you! My parents were born here. This is as much my home as it is yours, no matter what the propaganda machine says! And I stand ready to defend my rights here."

"And me too," Balgobin said, with emphasis.

"Hear, hear!" Jain trumpeted, like a schoolboy at a house rally.

Doris did not apologise nor concede, but then I did not expect him to. It was not in his nature to do either. Whether surliness was ingrained in his character was to me as yet uncertain, but I had rarely seen him otherwise since our meeting. The deep frown lines that I'd seen across his forehead seemed permanently etched there.

It was clear that his stance derived from staunch allegiance to the PNC, and had fed on some ancient hurt, as yet unknown even to him. Perhaps, as one born into a poor family, he might have felt dispossessed, and following Burnham's hypothesis, widely trumpeted at political rallies, he had come to blame Indians for his low estate.

In a sense I felt sorry for him, to have his political partisanship wage war against his policeman's pledge of neutrality and vows of service, and what I sensed as his basic decency. I noticed too that Bacchus, who had at first tried to restrain Doris' expressions of partisanship, had all but given up on that. Perhaps too, he had reasoned, our current locale was so surreal and the group all government workers that some latitude was permissible, as among those indulging in cathartic common room chat. Doris remained uninhibited and spoke his mind.

"What I mean is you cyaan jus' pack up and go to India?"

"No, I can't; but I'll tell you this again; you can go to any country in British Africa, anytime you want. But will you want to do that? I don't know any West Indian who has gone there and not come back, cursing the people and the lousy reception they got. For a start, you have lost almost everything except your colour; even your bloodlines have become mixed. Your African clothes, customs, language, religion, all are gone. All you have in common is roots, and those don't show. What you will find is that most Africans never heard of the slave trade that took their fellows to the Americas, and when you try to speak to them, they won't understand you, nor you them. You still have your British passport, and that's all you need to roam the Empire. But you can't go to India either, just like me.

"You and I have the same basic documents, however different we might look. When the British let go and we become independent both you and I will become Guianese, no more British passport, and we'll be lucky to travel to Trinidad. Of course, that won't affect the majority, so it's not a concern. But if you try to send a Guianese to India or wherever, Corporal, you'll have a problem. That's what I'm afraid of; if the demagogues and ignoramuses take hold of this country, heaven help us. I can see blood spilling. It's happened before. Is that what you want, Corporal?"

"Even America had to fight to get independence; blood spill when you have to fight," he said defiantly, without apology.

"God save us from political Corporals!" I replied, exasperated. "You know, the last one who felt he was the only one entitled to the world nearly destroyed it. Barely 16 years have passed and that lesson in hate is already forgotten. Why does each generation think it can justify and get away with such brutality? Look at how the Jews murdering and displacing the Palestinians over there; they already forgot that Hitler did the same to them. Is that what you want to do to us?"

"I don't think that will happen here," said Brewster reassuringly.

"I will tell you this, Constable Brewster and to anyone who wants to listen, and to sleep on it for a while, better to split the country into two, one part to each side, than to risk the conflict that will surely follow the PNC line. I will be prepared to take the smaller and poorer part in such a division. That way, if we do it right, we can remain on good terms. I know that the vast majority of ordinary people do not want to fight one another. Only the greedy, the hateful and belligerent want that. The real problem is almost too deeply rooted; your people can't put yourself in my shoes and our people can't imagine you; you don't want to know about us but most of us know something about you. More interest in each other and less ill-feeling will help a hell of a lot, but I don't think today's politicians want that."

A low drone from Benn's hammock followed by a quick snort gave testimony to his views on the matter. He was easy-going and tolerant; he felt that there was more room in the country than anyone needed and didn't see what the politicians and their sycophants were fussing about. He had dismissed them all as a bunch of arrogant Georgetown types with more ambition than substance and a persuasive way of speaking, appealing to the lowest levels of race and emotion. Not good, he felt.

The British had done a great job of dividing and ruling their colonies. That much was verified history. What was needed now was the opposite, unity. He rather hoped to hear more of that kind of talk, not of riot and of arson. So he generally bowed out of discussions like this, especially among policemen, who were nearly all pro-PNC. Besides he had more pressing things on his mind; the lives of a dozen men (counting his own) depended on his skills on the water. He needed rest to clear his mind. The next day's run would be taxing on him and his craft, he had said; both must be in tip-top shape. He had taken his nightcap of high wine, and had drifted quickly into sleep.

"I don' think we'll solve anything tonight. That's a big earful you all left us with, eh, Doc?" Inspector Bacchus brought closure to the debate. "We can talk about this further as we go, clear up some fuzzy areas that could do us all harm;

we have lots of time, a golden opportunity to really find out more about one another. Most of this debate is something I never expected to hear and I am so glad it's happening. When I think of it, I am amazed how much I learned from Hari and Tilbury, and from all of you. I wish I could understand the Caribs; I know they can teach us things about their way of life; I don't think we should dismiss them; we're all guilty of that. Anyway let's get a good night's sleep, and pray that we can cover more miles tomorrow than we did today."

The familiar night sounds enveloped the camp adding background to the snores and periodic snorts that would come from the various cocoons. It was too early to sleep and so I began to ponder the politics and personalities that would make or break the fledgling colony. The conversation echoed in my mind and I marvelled at the differences in perspectives that our small group displayed -- perhaps symbolic of the larger society -- and how frighteningly tenuous was the information base that fed thought and conclusion at this troubling time in the colony's history. Ignorance and prejudices were powerful political tools and our leaders were exploiting both.

It was no secret that the philosophy of the PPP was a radical socialism, and its leaders were already in bed with the USSR, but Burnham had been cagey and so far had not admitted that he held the same views; it was widely known, however, that he would do anything to seize the reins of government as an essential prelude to establishing his dictatorship. Most observers felt that while Jagan was absorbed in his Party's romance with the USSR and trying to distract the US suitor (by a curious display of antagonism one moment and imploring for help the next), Burnham was fine-tuning his plans to complete the subversion of Government during this current term.

He had for some time been openly using his wiles and the black Washington lobby to get the USA to back his bid to head an independent government, whenever that came, and by whatever means, fair or foul. Since he would lose in any legitimate ballot, revolutionary action could be justified on the grounds of anti-communism and he could justifiably claim that Jagan did not represent Georgetown—the capital city and heart of Guianese commerce— having treated the city contemptuously by failing to field a single candidate in the elections.

Destabilisation of government was a known undercover technique at such times and freely and brazenly practised by the US government which ruthlessly protected US business, regardless of the popularity, fairness or legitimacy of its actions, enabling US supra-national corporations aiming to dominate global trade to ravage Latin America for decades. Its use had extended elsewhere, as presently to the Congo and other African states "threatened" with Communism. The Cold War was, after all, quite hot, despite Khrushchev's declaration of "peaceful co-existence".

Already Burnham had started to boycott Parliament and had gone further than anyone had done before to obstruct its processes; Georgetown trade unions, his power base, were ready to strike against the Government at the first opportunity, legitimate or not, fully anticipating US support as its anti-Communist paranoia intensified. Burnham's emphasis on this would play well in Washington, and strengthen his lobby there to offset the negative opinion of US authorities in Georgetown who would rather not deal with him or his Party and still pursued all diplomatic means to bring Jagan to their side. Rumours of escalating anti-government action by the Opposition were troubling. Even the Police central command was unsure of how to react, although deep in probing secret partisan plots, torn by divided loyalties as many of its members were known to share the racial orientation of the PNC.

Jagan's response as Premier was weak and indecisive, as he usually was in confrontations with his friend Odo. His excuse in marking time was "to avoid racial strife at all costs". Yet each day's inaction increased racial tensions and US diplomatic frustration as Africans attacked, robbed and wounded Indians, often severely, all across the city, mostly unpublicised. This was the first phase of the much-rumoured and threatened campaign of terror advertised by PNC gangs.

The unrest and rumours of unrest had unsettled major sectors of society. Many professionals and small businessmen had elected to take the extreme step of closing down — with or without liquidation — and migrating to the cold north. Parents with means were increasingly sending their children to Britain, buying rental properties there to provide an income to support their education or entrepreneurial activities.

Foreign-born doctors at the Georgetown Hospital, including natives of India, had begun to leave, or talk of leaving their comfortable and lucrative practices and escaping to Britain at the end of current contracts. It was not easy for them, as they had to obtain migrant visas, unlike Guianese who as "citizens of the United Kingdom and Colonies" needed only the passage money to get there. If Guianese ran into financial trouble once there, the dole would tide them over temporarily until they could find their feet, as most quickly did.

Caribbean islanders, especially Jamaicans and Barbadians, had been making this UK trek for more than a century. The flow north had increased since the end of WWII, pushed by anglophile fears that independence would jeopardize their way of life, and pulled by the promise of jobs in the rebuilding of Britain. Many of the richer groups in BG, the white and almost white, the anglicised coloureds and Indians, had been moving back and forth, between BG and the UK, as early as the late forties, building an overseas financial base while maintaining their Guianese sources of income.

The net outflow, of people and capital, had spiked at the time of the first PPP government in 1953 and in its aftermath when the antics of the Interim Government merely served to convince sceptics that the future would be gloomy and painful, rife with cronyism and corruption, regardless of which "ism" triumphed. A minority, mostly Portuguese, had chosen Canada as their nesting place, helped by immigration practices that treated them as "Europeans" and thus preferred to other racial groups. Some, especially Africans, were heading for the USA, where many had connections, some dating from the time, more than a century ago, when Afro-Americans had come to the Caribbean and BG as slaves or as freed men, to fill labour demands after emancipation. Indians however faced huge obstacles to entry into North America and had to apply under India's meagre quota; thus the flow there was a trickle compared to the steady stream entering Britain.

The threat of violence was troubling, abetted by the prospect of communistic seizures and repressions under Jagan portrayed in a hideous Stalinesque moustache and garb waving the hammer and sickle under the direction of commissars all looking grimly like Jo Stalin and Lavrenty Beria. The alternative of a predatory Duvalier-type dictatorship under Burnham, policed by a private army (his own *ton ton m'acoute*) and riddled with marauding thieves and parasites, was equally distressing, even though it did not get the same publicity.

The latter frightened Indians pushing them into Jagan's arms despite his neglect of their main concerns. Both leaders were fully seized with the general public's anticipation of doom and gloom but they ignored it, or rather tacitly promoted it as a necessary price that they must pay as tribute to their leader. Each used it to censure the other and in so doing fashioned a climate of terror among the non-partisan populace and hastened their migration.

The third political party in the legislature, the United Force (UF) was militantly anti-communist, and favoured the status quo. Its strident and often irrational ranting against Socialism and its extravagant promises of plenty under an "unbridled" pro-American capitalism repelled middle class thinkers, the broad-minded and the uncommitted, who saw its stance and its actions as backward, simplistic inventions and as despotic as that of its opponents.

A UF victory was a clear impossibility in a free election since its support was so constricted, and yet the Party took such a polarised stance as relegated it, *ab initio*, to the status of a nuisance. Now the fear was that the US could use him to seize BG and turn into another Haiti. This was not what level-headed moderates like co-founder Patraj Singh, businessman—who had tried to persuade Tulla years earlier to abandon Jagan--had hoped for, at its formation; they had anticipated an inclusive and sensible platform, carefully and methodically constructed to attract all races, economic strata and religions.

Instead, under Peter D'Aguiar, a Roman Catholic businessman--some said *barbarian*--the UF adopted idiocy as its emblem and vituperation as its tool. Its good press derived largely from the Catholic community through the publication *The Catholic Standard* and from D'Aguiar's major shareholding in one of the three daily newspapers, *The Daily Chronicle*. The most respected of the dailies, *The Daily Argosy*, was philosophically and editorially conservative, pro-establishment, anti-PPP, but financially troubled and dominated by C.V. Wight, a creole white businessman and politician. *The Daily Chronicle* espoused urban middle class values but had become stridently and sometimes irrationally anti-PPP and increasingly militant in its support of the opposition. The *Guiana Graphic* was a popular paper, the least one-sided in its presentations, but did show a pro-PNC bias.

Recently a fourth had appeared, the *Evening Post* with a strong anti-communist stance and at times did present socialist views, but rarely rose to true impartiality. The *Post* had attracted a wide readership and often printed controversial matters and breaking news ahead of the others. It was particularly forthright in its treatment of legislative issues and claimed to be the only paper that investigated its leads before printing stories. Many felt that opposition politicians in the UF habitually fed its newsroom and its biases.

The papers uniformly presented government as shallow, blinkered and unmindful of public opinion and interests including those of its electoral base, and keener to erect totalitarian structures than address the declining economy. They presented evidence of mass disaffection as judged by falling real income, job losses, decline in job creation and rising migration to which Government's response seemed woolly and retrograde. The PPP matrix of theoretical ideas, the press argued, was rigid, while Premier Jagan walked a tightrope between two poles of crumbling infrastructure and an alienated government work force, both of which were rapidly approaching the breaking point.

Map of Guyana incorporating situations covered in text; *arrow* shows trip to Kamarang

Dr Jagan, victory salute, August 1961

PPP cabinet, Sept 1961, with Dr Jagan seated at head of table. See Appendix p. 690 for composition of the Legislature

British Empire in 1900

South to North (L to R): The tepuis Roraima, Kukenaam, Yuruani, Guadacapiapuey (God's finger), Karaurin and Ilu-tramen (courtesy, Supt McLeod)

Towakaima Falls, upper level

(L) SM Luck, an extraordinary general physician, patriot and political/social critic
(R) H.Annamunthodo, eminent surgeon, who exiled himself soon after specialising and had a distinguished career at the University of West Indies, Kingston, Jamaica, and was largely ignored, as were so many other professionals, by both Jagan and Burnham, who preferred to seek less critical ar relevant sources of "expert" guidance. Being Indian did not help as he once told me. His name is most likely a British corruption of Hanumantharao, a well-known South Asian appellation.

The western Cuyuni as it enters Venezuela and relationship to Wappai

Chapter 2

Our team is subdued, by argument as by hunger. I have heard nothing to change my mind about our prospects politically: The options are clear: Communism under Jagan with inevitable US intervention versus a dictatorship under Burnham which will force Indians into exile or servitude; the prospects are depressing and increase the brain drain, now beginning to involve established families. We fear that society is too fractured to accept a victory by either major leader. The hurdles include social divisions--class; rural/urban; racial (the LCP labels Indians a 'threat'); employment biases against Indians in the Civil Service and large businesses; religious, etc.—and the adjustments and understanding required, which seem to baffle those politically polarised. The PPP organisation is well-constructed and would withstand threats to its integrity. JFK will support Jagan if he renounces Communism, as other colonial politicians have done. This position is widely publicised. The dilemma of one entrepreneurial family supporting Jagan is presented. On the river a sudden change dumps Rod into the fast current but he surfaces just as help was reaching him and escapes with a bump on the head.

Day 9: Meandering through tacubas

"A man all wrapped up in himself makes a small package"   Marshall McLuhan

Admirer (proudly): "Cheddi and Odo resonate nicely in their speeches."   Overheard, 1950
Bystander (cynically): "Hollow objects resonate the most."

"Economics determines human action and institutions; change requires class struggle to overthrow imperialism and capitalism which the world over will fall to communism, and we will achieve the classless society…"
                                                                                            C Jagan, 1957

"I should hope that all of us on both sides of the table will so conduct our affairs, so plan our strategy, our tactics, that there can be no mistaken conception of the fact that we want not only a free country, but a country in which the people are free and enjoy human rights"   LFS Burnham, 1958

The way east remained depressingly slow. We weaved our way between the *tacubas* and several times rode over floating logs invisible in the chocolate water, each time breaking the propeller pin, which forced a stop. On occasion when the turbulence had eased and the flow moderated Benn would allow the boat to float downstream while he did the repair, usually in a minute or so. On these occasions we all acted as lookouts for floating debris, rocks or change in the current and helped to steer. That relieved the tedium, which threatened to create some raw nerves, making moods testy and conversation difficult, except for the most innocuous or urgent matters.

The prevailing hunger did not help; frequent drinks from the river helped to stem hunger and the thirst that came with rising temperature and sweating. For a time a heavy atmosphere prevailed, no doubt because of the baring of political loyalties within the group. Inspector Bacchus had tried during the discussion to maintain an even-handed stance. My position had been made quite clear, and even the militantly anti-PPP (and anti-Indian) Cpl Doris had acknowledged that what I had said was "fair", that it was "a pity more Indians di'n' think like you."

"But there are, believe me, more than you think. And tell me, corporal, what of your people, the Africans of this country, shouldn't they be fair too? Why is it that the people who agitate the most for something are the ones least likely to offer it in return?"

He had said nothing, but the point was made. Brewster's reaction was a little different; he claimed to have learned something about leaders that he had not known at all or only vaguely, and in any case had not allowed to occupy his time.

"I'll have to pay more attention to these things," he acknowledged.

Benn was dismissive "I don' go in for politics; that's for politicians; I don' trus' them, black, brown, yellow or white. I keep away from them. Most are crooks, anyway, looking for easy pickin's!"

Jain said, "Hear, hear!"

Balgobin maintained his respect and admiration for Dr Jagan. "He's a great man, and he don't steal, you can trust him with money anytime; you can't trust Burnham!" Privately to me he would express some misgivings. "Is he a Communist, doc?" I told him yes, and that Burnham too was Marxist.

"They close, but ah didn't t'ink Cheddi woulda make Burnham his son godfather. He insulted his mother's religion," he said regretfully.

Balgobin was glad that his eldest son was safely in Britain where he had joined the British navy and was an ensign, serving on a destroyer then based at Scapa Flow. He proudly displayed two wallet-sized photographs of a handsome youth, in navy blues with a thick high turtleneck, leaning against a gun turret "What kind of life would he 'ave here, if Burnham win?" This question, then asked in fear among Indians with young families in many communities throughout the country, would soon become the *raison d'être* for mass migration of young people and a continuous flight of skills. Even so, the adulation of the Indians for Jagan changed little despite his obvious failure to secure their welfare.

As the day wore on the desultory conversation of the morning was replaced by a brooding silence. No one wanted to refer to or recall the weighty issues that had been explored the previous night, perhaps superficially, certainly incompletely, and were perhaps preying on some minds, certainly mine, and, I felt sure, Corporal Doris's. I wondered whether he was concerned that he had not displayed in his arguments the sense of fairness, if not reason, expected of a policeman subjected to the power of logical analysis. Despite this, his stance was overtly and staunchly partisan extending even to blind acceptance of the misconceptions that characterised PNC propaganda--a behaviour that would make its Secretary most pleased.

How would Doris in his position as a police officer behave in an independent country, were his party to gain power? Would dissenting Indians and others begin to disappear, as they had done in totalitarian and police states elsewhere? Look around, in every Latin American dictatorship, in the Communist states, in some so-called democracies, people were "misplaced" or "lost" every day. Even Fidel Castro, so morally strong in his purpose against Dictator Fulgencio Battista, had stooped to arbitrary detention and sacrifice of life. And, of course, who would forget the myriad covert disappearances of anti-colonial activists all over the world while in Police custody, and the mass executions of tens of millions of Indians by Muslims over the 700 hundred years of their rule? The British had killed untold numbers of Indians by deprivation and famine and by savage armed repression of protesters, and similarly elsewhere during the period of their hegemony. Millions of Germans had been gassed by Hitler, Russians slaughtered by Stalin, Armenians and others by the Ottomans, Chinese by other Chinese, Palestinians by Jews--just a few of the countless atrocities of man against man.

Here many were fond of saying that BG was a melting pot! However comforting that sentiment might have been to those who voiced it, that certainly was not so, except for that tiny minority that had innocently or thoughtlessly intermarried. The pots were boiling alright, sometimes even on the same stove, but like dishes for a feast, each was to the eye homogeneous, and hardly touched in any real way with the substance of the others, save that their odours mingled in the air. Each would aim to tease the palate with its special savour, to be appreciated in its own right, to complement one another so as to please and satiate. That was the common purpose.

And so we too shared a common purpose, to improve and advance, to do what was possible and sensible to make our land a symbol of what was best in humankind. To do that we needed to show that our divided microcosm could become the laboratory where we could discover a way to strive together in unity, not to widen divisions nor create a master race. Hitler had tried that, and with all the might at his command, had failed, as had many demagogues before him. And yet despite all these failures each new tyrant would convince himself that he had the unique attribute to make him the model of success that had eluded his predecessors.

The history of man is a history of ambition and avarice, and of retaliatory struggles against the overly ambitious and greedy. Nothing has changed through time. Perhaps we were fooling ourselves, those of us who felt that we could dwell together in harmony, that the road there had only to cross the morass of ignorance and prejudice, which was achievable since the swamps were shallow and the dangers surmountable, as long as we pooled our strengths and pursued the task with fairness and resolution. But that attitude did not take sufficient account of political forces ranged in favour of division and disharmony, nor of the legitimate fears of people whose traditions and culture might be lost in the game of compromise, if the players were not sufficiently briefed, sensitive or enlightened.

I suspected that Inspector Bacchus, from his overly deferential attitude to my party all day, might be feeling embarrassed by the strong and disturbing exclusionary sentiments expressed by Cpl Doris, but I was not perturbed, believing sincerely that every person in a just and democratic society was entitled to speak freely. I expected though that they should do so from knowledge, and with fairness, sensitivity and regard for the truth. One recognised the varying perceptions of truth, and I have heard it argued that what was fair in one setting might not be so in another, a proposition I had to take "on advisement," as the lawyers were wont to say. Sensitivity was a more difficult issue. It was a matter of breeding and style, and not easy to achieve without indoctrination, though there were a few special souls gifted with this quality. I would thus allow Cpl Doris his right to his point of view but he must be prepared to allow me mine, deal with informed challenge and answer those with facts and argument, not with commotion, fists, bullets and bombs.

The Inspector shared my concerns, as did Brewster. Balgobin summarised our feelings "Everyone o' we want to better weself, to live good with other people whoever they be, feel free to do whatever work we can do, as long as it's legal, eh, Inspector, and feel safe whether we brown or black or white, or whether we agree or disagree with one anodda!"

This sentiment, or something like it, had been continually expressed by political activists in the country, as a kind of rallying call for many decades; small gains had been made and lost. In the infancy of popular politics--now just over a decade old in BG--the parties and individual activists had purported to speak for everyone regardless of race or colour.

Their platforms were clearly non-racial in concept, but in reality they reflected the conditions of the major groups, addressing poor working conditions, inequities, injustice and exploitation, none of which had changed for a century. Thus poverty, denial of basic rights such as freedom of speech or association, the right to vote, fair pay for work done, the right to withhold labour, release from servile contracts remained, *inter alia*, the rallying points. These applied equally to city and rural folk, of all shades. But by their very nature these things were not the prime concern of the privileged, of any stripe, in business or in the professions.

These latter groups had begun to segregate themselves into clubs and cliques of like-minded and mutually sustaining people, containing layers according to achievement, prestige, primacy, education, success and wealth, the last distinguishing the most influential in the group. They uniformly put personal ambition and goals first, became heroes to their families and friends, and as they rose, detached and distanced themselves from their group or place of origin and strove to rise, like a balloon filling with air, up, up and away from the masses.

Thus many high-echelon or upwardly moving Indians avoided popular political pressure groups, which they considered to be radical, disruptive and vulgar, and interfered with ambition's orderly and sure ascent up the social and economic ladder. They would have excluded themselves also from debates on the issues, though conceivably they might have argued with their less affluent or privileged relatives in the privacy of their homes, or at family socials and religious gatherings. The latter were often the only occasions when family members of all social classes might meet according to custom. On the specific issue of rights the more privileged would have conceded that rights should flow to members of the underclass when they showed the discipline and tenacity to better themselves enough to qualify for rights and for the privileges that followed. This was the fulcrum on which the seesawing would occur.

The determination and imposition of conditions had obstructed progress on the rights issue, especially the right to vote, which political activists from the turn of the century had seen as the prime instrument of political reform and popular power. A vote for every adult had become commonplace in democracies, and therefore, it was argued, states that imposed property and other qualifications were not "democratic".

The opponents of this view, however, noted that the cradles of democracy--Videha[8] in northern India and later Athens—had strict requirements for voters, to ensure that the voter was one who could exercise the right knowledgeably, freely and responsibly. The rabble was too impressionable and ill-informed, and clearly not ready for the responsibility of selecting their country's leaders. And even if they were misguidedly allowed to vote, the country itself might not be organised enough to deal with such an extension of the franchise. Premature enfranchisement on the basis of "any adult, one vote" would therefore be the final nail in the coffin of economic and social stability since any broadening of the suffrage would inevitably place the nascent society--with its 'unsophisticated majority' as one radio commentator put it–squarely at risk of takeover by

---

[8] I had learned in my Classics classes that democracy had emerged in pre-Christian Greece, only to fall under the axe of empire-builders. But a much earlier attempt to form a democratic republic had taken place in Bihar and Oudh, India, when the kingdoms of Videha and Vidarbha had sought to unite early in the first millennium BC.

'demagogue and dictator'.

Mr Jainarine Singh had argued feverishly in favour of rights. To this end he had led, with Jagan and others, the defiant march on the city, following the Enmore massacre of 1948 and at one point had dared to confront armed police, challenging them to shoot him, dramatically baring his chest at the head of the procession as it entered the intersection of the Sea Wall and Vlissengen Roads. However the subsequent glory would go to Jagan, who--helped by his plantation origin, rural connections and his opportunistic and much-publicised pledge to dedicate himself in the Legislature to the cause of sugar workers--quickly displaced the more volatile, urban middle-class Mr Singh from the BG political scene.

The incident had made a telling impression on me, then a teenager, and on countless others who had seen that day an army of unarmed workers--Indians mainly and some rural Africans, toting placards--come head to head with a phalanx of riflemen, all African, led by a white officer, and incredibly, defiantly stood their ground. Nothing Mr Singh did after that, not even his portentous 1958 motion in the House to seek independence from Britain, would equal this deed for valour.

Other leaders of the proletariat would later use the incident for propaganda, while others would reflect on the disturbing composition of the groups that day. The many previous imbroglios between Africans and Indians were amply chronicled. But to be close to the scene and *see* the stark difference in racial composition of the opposing groups which the photograph of Mr Singh and the riflemen reinforced so powerfully made an indelible stamp on the mind of thinking witnesses.

The Police were African, led by white men; the targets were mainly Indians–a reprise of many similar confrontations that had occurred in the previous 100 years on the sugar estates! The image clearly defined the allegiances and exposed them to tormenting reality, like a veiled woman suddenly relieved of her occlusive *burka,* her face bared for the first time. For months after that, in all manner of forums, one took care in debate or in simple conversation to avoid actions and language that would give the smallest hint of a racial bias.

In fact discrimination was rife throughout the land, and practiced at every level, surviving WWII. Much of it was subtle, much open. The non-Indian Christian population of BG had remained largely underprivileged after centuries of subjugation, inured to strict obedience of their superiors in business or the bureaucracy and fearful of authority. Acceptance into the Civil Service, especially the more prestigious Clerical Branch (the other was Technical) was a badge of honour bought with devotion and silence. Mulattos, Blacks, Chinese and Portuguese were absorbed readily, because they were Christians, but Indians were problematic even though they had begun to break barriers by WWII.

The labouring class also toed the line except for rare excursions into strikes and protests over jobs and conditions of work and living. Though steeped in this serf mentality Blacks would unhesitatingly lambaste Indians, particularly Hindus, for their customs, practices, dress, food, religion, music, the caste system, and so on whenever an occasion arose. Christianised Indians, alas, shared in the denunciation and some even rejected or sought to ablate Indian history. Why did they not see that this practice demeaned them and fellow Indians throughout BG society, and that the acceptance of the teachings of Christ did not mean that they should reject the pre-Christian millennia of *Vaidic* (Hindu) thought that Christ himself had imbibed and infused into his own doctrines? Did they not plainly see that rejection of their heritage would make the British feel and act even more superior and demean them more?

In the mid-1940s mulatto and African civil servants celebrated when Mr L.E. Kranenberg, became the first mulatto Colonial Secretary and took up residence in the stately Red House on High St, Kingston, the first non-white to do so. It was said of him that he was the first to see grey, not white paint on the rungs and sides near the top of the ladder he had climbed, a reference to the increasing lightness of shade that the new recruit would see as he stood on the bottom rung of the promotional ladder in the British Colonial Service. At that time few Indians were in that Service and Dr Jagan himself had failed in his efforts to join it on graduating from Queen's College during the mid-1930's despite possessing the basic qualification of a good School Certificate. Fifteen years later, even with a Higher School Certificate, it would be touch and go for me, with no contacts in the Service, while all around me--Africans, mulattoes, Chinese and Portuguese--were accepted more easily with only the lesser School Certificate qualification.

Indian high school graduates who failed to gain a Civil Service post would join a business or learn a trade. Others took to teaching, at one of the many emerging high schools set up by people often with no higher qualifications than theirs; many applied to work in rural Church schools, but found they had to convert to Christianity to get a job; and many did so. Others articled to lawyers or accountants; a few tried journalism.

The more intrepid and ambitious with enough money for a year of subsistence and tuition went off to the USA, or failing that Britain, to study and work, and hoped to save enough to complete higher education. The USA was the preferred destination for this group because of superior economic and job prospects and less rigorous educational curricula, which permitted students to work at a job or business while studying—an academic format not readily available in Britain except perhaps to those enrolled as part-time students.

Besides, there was an advantage in going to the USA where a London University Higher School Certificate could get you first year exemptions from many US Colleges and so lead to a degree in two years from sixth form, versus three in Britain. You could then pursue a profession, if you had the ambition, the academic ability and the resources. This was the route to a dental degree that Dr Jagan had taken after failing to get the Civil Service job that many of his white and coloured classmates had obtained.

By that time Guianese society had evolved as two distinct and in many ways irreconcilable groups, one urban (including the large villages), and predominantly non-Indian, the other rural and largely Indian. Urban society was organised in parallel vertical groupings by race, as I have already noted, each cloistered in its exclusive social and sports clubs, and openly identified as such, for example, the Chinese Sports Club, the Portuguese Club, and the BG East Indian Cricket Club. Those catering exclusively to the British were simply "The Georgetown this or that". (The British excluded most Portuguese, classifying them, not as Europeans, but as Madeirans, who as Roman Catholics, did not in any case belong among colonial Anglicans!) The Africans had followed the lead of their masters, and given their clubs more euphemistic names, such as the Malteenoes Sports Club and the Demerara Cricket Club. The YMCA and its

Sports Club were overwhelmingly African and served their interests primarily, though they did admit a few Indians and others from time to time, and I had joined their debating arm, the Y's Men's Club. The British Guiana Cricket Club catered almost exclusively to Civil Servants and was dominated by mulattoes and those not white enough for the Georgetown Cricket and Football Clubs.

Inter-racial socialising did, of course, occur, and followed an elaborate set of manners along quasi-Victorian lines, that was wondrous to observe and comedic in its form. Intermarriages produced coloured's, or mulatto (Afro-Caucasian), doglas (Afro-Indian), bovianders (Afro-Native) and so on. The races worked harmoniously enough, played "together" on the same national teams, especially cricket, competed at sports, but kept apart for cultural and religious purposes. Even in the national teams, the races kept to themselves, simply because they had not, with few exceptions, learned to socialise together. In making their way to the top in local sports, they had often played against one another, but representing the colony was often the first time they had played on the *same* team.

Religion dominated this separation. Christianity was, and has remained the official religion of British Guiana and the religion of the Africans. Hinduism, the majority religion of the Indians, and Islam, a minority, were tolerated, by necessity, but, being "heathen", did not count where it mattered. Many belonging to these two religions would claim to be Christian to get a job, a reference, a hearing or to claim civil rights.

So entrenched and respected had the colonial hierarchy become and so damned by Indian organisations and individuals that the League of Coloured Peoples (LCP), a branch of the multi-racial LCP of Britain--but in BG dominated by Africans--had come to declare Indians as "a threat to social order", and by 1948, had become openly anti-Indian, regarding the burgeoning militancy and aspirations of Indians as an assault on the positions the coloureds and Africans had expected to hold in perpetuity.

A broad sand bank jolted me out of my reverie. It rose suddenly in front of us on rounding a sharp bend in the river as it descended a rough patch creating an expanse of white water. Although the gradient was manageable the current had narrowed so much that it caused a sudden turbulence around the curve. This called for speedy course correction beyond the capability of the craft, even though Benn had entered the curve quite gingerly and with good control. Bbut with the bouncing flow the boat dipped down, rolled slightly at the wrong angle and was tossed abruptly onto the bank. Rodriques had tried to correct the movement with his pole but the change had taken place so fast it caught him off balance; the pole snagged on something, perhaps between rocks, held fast and, acting like a catapult as the boat swung sideways, lifted him off his feet and tossed him into the channel, barely clear of a huge menacing rock awash in spume; Rod was quickly carried away submerged in the hurrying stream.

There were shouts and I instinctively pulled my shirt off to go after him--a throwback to my emergency training in the QC swimming team's life-saving squad--when I saw him come up and paw the water with frenzied outstretched hands striking for the shallows. A few strokes carried him to his depth, about thirty yards away at the far end of the bank. He waded a little, then stood up in waist deep water, wiping his face, coughing and spluttering. He seemed unharmed as he slowly trudged through the water to rejoin us now standing beside the grounded boat, all eyes on him.

"Oh shit! Wha' happen to you?" Benn's concern was genuine and fraternal.

"You alright?" the Inspector inquired.

"I'm okay, Inspector," Rod replied, but we could clearly see a line of blood running from his forehead on to his left cheek. I walked over to meet him and saw a bump, a haematoma, an inch in diameter over his left eye, and at its centre a small laceration, skin deep, oozing blood. I was more concerned about the possibility of a skull injury beneath the haematoma. I led him to sit on a rock on the bank, while the others, assured he was all right, returned to free the boat.

Rodriques was as surprised as the rest of us at the sight of his blood.

"I ain't feel a thing," he declared, "must have been a rock; I went down a few feet; it happen so quick, but I feel alright," he repeated reassuringly.

I could feel no break but the clot interfered. He seemed indeed to have only this minor injury and had not fainted nor felt dizzy. I dug into my bag of supplies, found a roll of bandage and some Cetavlon antiseptic. I cleansed the area and closed the wound with the bandage. It would be easy to monitor his behaviour for the rest of the journey.

"I don' remember the water so low at this point," Benn said standing in ankle deep water helping to heave the boat back into the narrow deep. "This stretch of river is not shown as rapids on the map; that tells you how really low the water is. I hope the level is higher further down," he added, thinking of the inflow, however reduced, from the many small tributaries we would be passing. The air was hot and humid, and the exertion had raised a sweat, which lingered in the high humidity. The coolness of the water was such a striking and refreshing contrast I wanted to remain in it.

Benn scanned the boat for damage and found a few long surface streaks, but nothing significant; it did not leak when re-floated. We re-boarded and proceeded gingerly downstream. Doris and Joe relieved Rod at the prow. The water bobbed and swirled making swishing and gurgling sounds, and at times leapt and darted up as it negotiated the rocky course taking with it all the fallen leaves and twigs that had escaped the clutches of the many obstacles of rock and *tacuba*s along the way; some remained trapped in littoral eddies separated from the mainstream, and continued to swirl aimlessly getting nowhere. Like so many people.

Now that the sun was behind us, the confusing reflections were no longer a factor and identification of hazards became easier. We continued carefully, going at the pace of the current, which at times seemed too fast for the conditions, especially as we had to pick our way through a litter of rocks and shallows, and the ubiquitous fallen trees. At about four thirty we came to the largest obstruction so far that day, a massive fallen mora that spanned the river just beyond a bend that cradled a wide sandy beach. The men began chopping a path through the trunk. It was slow going. We decided to camp for the night on the beach.

Inspector Bacchus issued Doris and Benn a few rounds of ammunition for a hunting trip, accompanied by Joe and Mike. The rest of us pitched tent and prepared for the night. There was an hour of daylight left and the police were almost out of food, even with sharing ours. We had for several days gotten by on two meagre meals a day, with decreasing amounts each day, filling grumbling stomachs with copious amounts of the fresh river water. An hour later the two policemen returned, empty-handed. No shots had been fired, the failure deepening Doris's gloom, but the natives remained unmoved, Joe remarking that a successful hunting expedition was far from a casual evening stroll. The forest was generous only to those who knew how to get its riches; hunts had to be carefully planned and patiently carried out; they were rarely productive otherwise.

After a frugal meal and desultory conversation—perhaps because of the lingering tensions from the "frankness" of the previous day's--we focussed on our situation anticipating a difficult passage the next day, (not unlike the path Jagan had chosen for himself) and accepted the inevitability of eight or ten days total delay and to conserve supplies and personal energies for the challenges to come. In the hour before I dozed off I scribbled notes in my diary and listened to the world around me humming with the myriad noises of the woods that we had come to accept and ignore. Reflecting on Doris's remarks on repatriation of Indians and Balgobin's news of his son's adjustment to life in the British Navy brought to mind with some poignancy my recent meeting with an old acquaintance who had returned from England to BG for a family reunion.

The Migrant

The political situation was debated, increasingly and hotly, in many homes and often created divisions among otherwise closely-knit families. When I arrived that rather warm and humid September noon two months ago at the home of Karan's uncle, the party honouring him had already begun. Karan had migrated to England in 1953, qualified as an engineering technician a few years later, settled in Southampton with a construction company and had just earned a promotion. This was his first real holiday in eight years. He was regaling them with tales of his early days in England "on the dole".

"You din' feel cheap, takin' the dole money like that?" someone had asked him.

"Look, my dear chap," He had absorbed both the dialect and the accent of southern England, "my father and grandfather slaved for the bloody Brits on a stinking sugar estate. I have no compunctions whatever in taking back some of what they gave with their blood and tears."

With unabashed emotion he thumped the table so hard, the glass of rum and coke jumped off the surface, spilled the fluid, which ran in a broadening stream across the new laminate (Formica) surface then becoming fashionable, to stop at the slightly raised aluminium border.

"Sorry, *māmie*,[9]" he said contritely to his hostess, as he lowered his voice, and hastily mopped up the spill with tissue paper from the new box on the table. "I'm not drunk, but I had to deal with a lot of jokers who told me I was sponging on the country, that the Africans and Indians were lazy good-for-nothings looking for something and returning nothing. I am daily telling these ignorant English people how their people raped treasuries all over the world. Why, only a few years ago just before they left India, they were scooping out precious stones from the tiles of the Tāj Mahal. I've seen the photos. And whose diamond is the *Koh-i-Noor*?" he paused expectantly, studying each face, "Eh?"

"It's Indian," someone said.

"You damned right it's Indian," he said vehemently, "and most of the

---

[9] Maternal uncle's *(mamoo's)* wife

crown jewels, the rubies, the sapphires, all of it, Indian! You should see how they shine in the Tower." He paused dramatically, and took a swig of his drink. "Yes," he said more soberly, emphasising each word, "I had no qualms about living off the state. The state had lived off the backs of my people for centuries. What minuscule amount I took back is exactly that, almost nothing. I have a hell of a lot more to take back to get even! I won't live long enough to do that, but perhaps my children will, when I get children!"

The exchanges that followed emphasised the plight of the Guianese people, torn between attraction to their local "heroes" and an increasing impatience with the slow, painful attention to pressing problems which heroic words were promising but political actions clearly obstructing. More and more the young and not so young were concluding that BG was inexorably drifting towards totalitarianism, so far prevented only by the delay of full independence. Karan studied his *māmoo* seated in his favourite rocking chair and spoke reflectively.

"You know, *māmoo*, I'm glad you decided to send these two boys with me, to finish school in England. This place has no future. Not for education, anyway; Jagan and Burnham will ruin it and ruin all of you, mark my words! You should hear those two jokers when they go to London. Pompous, as bad as those bloody Africans. All those blokes want is bloody power, and when they get that, they will rape the lands, drain the treasuries and fatten themselves, just as the Brits did."

In that bright and spacious living room, with overhead fans whirring, where the ambience reflected prosperity and success the sentiment seemed inappropriate, if not unjustified.

"So what you think will happen here, baye?" his *māmoo* asked him, in a tone that suggested that he was humouring his favourite nephew.

There were eight to twenty people in the room at any one time, moving in and out between the kitchen and living room to replenish the bowls of *bhoonjal* mutton, *phulourie* and *channa*, all hotly spiced, that were *de rigueur* at a Sunday party like this one. Another wave of people would arrive in the evening for dinner and an hour or two of dancing. The air in the room was thick with the fragrances of the many spices used in the dishes already spread before them and assembled for the main meal that the ladies were busy preparing. A group of us stayed put and talked. Having just returned to BG I was content to listen and like others interject views as events dictated.

Māmoo was a man of about 40, his wife a few years younger and Karan had just turned 33. He was still unmarried, and had bought a house in Southampton that same year and felt properly poised to launch his family into Britain. Years ago he had sold life insurance briefly in Georgetown, but had given it up in 1953, concluding that the days of free enterprise were coming to an end. In a show of bravado still openly possible then, he had shredded his party card at the door of the PPP headquarters, and sailed off to Britain, having warned his friends that all their plans to start businesses would come to nothing as the Jagans were determined to take over all business activity.

He had felt betrayed by this trend in Dr Jagan's politics, and had said so repeatedly. He had joined the party in 1950 and served it unquestioningly and somewhat emotionally despite the elevation of Burnham to the chairmanship, which as a youth delegate he had vigorously opposed. I had met him that year when we played against each other in a Rajah Cup cricket match, and we had become friends; I had tried to get him to play on our team, the Stabroek Cricket Club, of which I was captain and co-founder with my friend Rudolph Ramdhar.

I was then Secretary of the Rajah Cup Committee, whose Chairman, Mohamed Rajah, the Cup donor--who owned a thriving sporting goods store on Regent Street or Indian Row, as some called it--he was looking for help part-time and I thought Karan might be interested. He was sensible and intense, including his attachment to Cheddi Jagan, a relationship we shared. He had joined the Pioneer Youth League, the youth arm of the PPP when it was formally inaugurated in August 1952. In my interview with him earlier that summer Jagan had asked me to join the PYL but I had excused myself as I would be leaving soon to rejoin the UCWI.

When I last saw Karan, in 1952, he was deeply involved in youth politics, organising and campaigning in the countryside, especially in the districts of West Coast Demerara where he had his family roots and connections. He had taken me on one of those weekend sallies with a team of similarly dedicated and single-minded admirers of Dr and Mrs Jagan ("I love the woman, maan!" he had confessed, "I would do any thing for she!") They had worked hard to set up discrete cells of adherents in every district, however small, and had given each a formal structure, with the most articulate or single-minded man at the head. Each group would liaise with others in adjacent districts and reported to and was serviced by the area leader, and so on up a hierarchical ladder to PPP headquarters at Freedom House, with Jagan at the pinnacle. There was no question of the thoroughness of their coverage and the extent and strength of the organisation's base. Each cell linked with its neighbour and allotted delegates to conventions. All members chose these by secret ballot; in the estates this was a novel, bold and uplifting endeavour for people more accustomed to orders and impositions. It bolstered self-esteem as everyone felt appreciated, empowered and honoured to be in the Party. The bond to Jagan, their messiah, thus became inviolable.

At previous years I had become involved with friends in long rambling nocturnal discussions of the policies of the party in relation to the needs of the country. I shared what I learned from sources in the Civil Service, but was dismayed to find that few of the youths had any insight into or interest in the workings of the party machine. Most did as they were told and were discouraged from asking questions, especially those relating to policy. Karan, for example, was unaware, despite his interest, of the support given the PPP by Indian businessmen, including his uncle and family, and was astonished when I told him that my brother-in-law was one of Jagan's chief advisers and backer.

He had absorbed and recited Jagan's blanket denunciation of "business" as exploitative and suppressive, which the PYL had indiscriminately and injudiciously applied to *all* business. Party literature made no distinctions to assist them in developing their opinions and attitudes objectively; instead it parroted the condemnations liberally spread through the pages of *Thunder* and regurgitated at each group meeting by the local leader or, in the early cementing days, by Jagan himself, Janet, Carter or Westmaas.

The more analytical conversations in our group—which included Ossie Belgrave and John Moses, two who could hold forth on any topic--had upset Karan and he had confessed that he had begun to assemble a dossier on the more aggressive entrepreneurs in his family, his uncle being a prime target. Later he would discover the truth and feel wretched for "betraying" his family, even though he had not done them any real harm. "But I came so close!" he had exclaimed ruefully at his 'going-away' party soon after the fall of the first PPP government.

In time he had tried to be more objective and to ask questions. The more he probed, the more he read about politics, the more disturbed he had become, despite the euphoria of the 1953 victory. He was aware of all the communist labels placed on the PPP and on the Jagans in particular, but like the majority of youth members, had dismissed them as cheap shots and low blows by a retreating and doomed opposition scraping the bottom of the barrel of dirt to smear that honourable and dedicated pair.

He had believed literally in Jagan's description of himself as a socialist and had never once heard him admit that he was a communist. He had been briefly perplexed however when in February 1953 the PYL became affiliated with the World Federation of Democratic Youth (WFDY), a known Communist organisation. But like so many others his trust in Jagan as academic authority and teacher had been absolute; he had linked him with Clement Attlee, the British prime minister, a model socialist, and therefore ignored the WFDY linkage. However, the events in the House in 1953 during the PPP's term and the revelations after the fall had stunned him. Feeling confused and betrayed, and seeing the 'red' he had vehemently rejected previously, he quit the party and left for England along with other similarly disillusioned young activists.

The 1955 split in the PPP had vindicated our position about Burnham. We were certainly not alone. He recalled his friend Lalta Pāl whom Jagan had censured for racial bias when he questioned Burnham's loyalties. Lalta's personal allegiance had not been questioned but his ideology was when he later joined an insurance company's sales force. Soon he too had begun to find holes in the PPP strategy when he joined a group of party youths helping Janet to research facts for use in campaigns, meetings and publications, especially anent historical references, facts on migration, education, colonial development plans for British Guiana, and other major policy areas.

His contributions to party meetings had become more moderate, more analytical and less strident. He had joined the camp advocating a cautious and unhurried approach to independence, to make sure that they had all the data on fiscal and security matters including development projects previously approved by the British but held in abeyance pending clarification of the ideological stance of the party likely to form the government. British plans had been revealed to the party brass, but had remained secret. Lalta's final regret was the rejection of known moderates as candidates for several constituencies in the 1957 elections.

Karan, reverting to dialect, reminisced, "Lalta was me good friend, we play cricket together, we work together for the party on the West Coast, he too din' like Burnham and when he say so the top boys criticise he, say he had to get rid of the prejudice in he veins; but he wasn't prejudiced, even de Negro boys on the team agree with he. He work real hard and they shoulda let he run but they say he din' have de right attitude, he sold insurance so that mek him a capitalist stooge. So he pack up and went to England in 1957, just after the PPP win; he said he didn' see hope for progress and that as soon as Cheddi get in he gon turn de country communist, and bring Burnham back. But Burnham din' come back; in fact he got he own party and want to rule now, and *dat* is big trouble."

Karan, like everyone else present, had confirmed that day that his *māmoo* and *māmee* were staunch Jaganites, contributing regularly to PPP funds, and attended meetings at Freedom House.

"I believe," he continued, taking care to choose words that would not offend his *māmoo*, with whom he had always had a fond relationship, more that of brother than uncle. "I believe the Commies fooling the people; they will try to take over this country, the same way they doing in Cuba, but the US will not allow Dr Jagan to do that."

He reached into the bowl for a piece of the fragrant *bhoonjal* duck and followed it with a *phulourie* and, after he had finished chewing, downed a mouthful of rum and coke. He swilled the drink gingerly and politely swallowed the liquid and the fragments of meat and starch dislodged in the process. He felt the fire rise in his gullet and the warmth spread through his stomach; he took a second gulp. His *māmoo* said, equally carefully, "I don' think so. Dr Jagan is not Communist. He tell everybody that. He will tell President Kennedy that. I ask he this very question jus' las' week." He paused for a bite and a drink.

"I believe that Cheddi is straight," one of the younger men said, "some people say he lyin' to us, that he sending lots of youth to Russia to train fo' guerrilla. I don' believe that. I know two boys my age from Corentyne who got PPP scholarships and they already lef', one name Vidya Persaud, he gone to East Germany to study Medicine, and de other one, a fullamaan, Farook -- I forget he last name--to Russia to do physics. Dem boys not Communists!"

"Who say they not Communist? To besides; some people will do anything, lie, cheat whatever to get scholarship; it's a big break! The real Commie ones go to Moscow to do Economics."

"Well, even if they is Communist and Cheddi too, is that so bad?" *Māmoo* asked, naively.

Karan was dumbfounded at this question.

"*Māmoo*, me dear *māmoo*," he said melodramatically, "if this was a communist state, you couldn't own this business that made you rich. You're a capitalist. *Nāna* started this business with a few dollars that the family scrape together, like so many country coolie; he buy and sell; he and you and my otha *māmoos* build it up, you reinvest all you' profits, you skimp and save and live in a small house, all t'ree of you with wife and pickney dem, all in one small house, how many ah you, nine, ten, till you all had enough to spare to buy a little more comfort, and get you' own house. And look whey you dey today! Twenty years! Think o' that! Long time! And all ah you still in the same yard, but separate houses, big and full of nice furniture, and inside toilets! Which bank help ah you?

"No bank help you. No government help you. You' own business sense and hard work built what you have today. Everybody say you rich. You tell me, What else beside free enterprise can turn a poor man with only fifth standard education into a wealthy man? In Communism the state employs everybody, directly or indirectly; what kind of job you think fift' or six standard will get you? Labouring! Not manager of a big business like you got! You can see the future right now, and tell me if me wrong."

Māmoo was out of his depth; he had simply not considered things like academic qualifications as relevant to business. To him and his brothers business came naturally; it was a passion that he felt required no schooling beyond the three R's. He was sure that Karan exaggerated, and said so, so gently that Karan almost missed it.

"If you think so, *māmoo*, explain this. The biggest business job Cheddi got he give to an ignorant and mouthy young University graduate, Lawrence Mann, not to a successful businessman like you, with experience. You'll see the controls and new business taxes that Mann will soon announce, and what that goin' do to *you*! And tell me, how can he put somebody like that in charge of Import Export? Parading him in Kissoon store; you watch! Kissoon and the wife goin' both regret that piece of ass-licking! Mann younger than me, he barely out of school, he family was labourers; what he know 'bout business? Is all ideology, *māmoo*. Besides, he black and he too ass-lick Jagan! Big plusses for him! Ah wish ah was wrong. It hurt me to see these young bayes running around like rabbits calling themselves Progressive Youths."

He looked at Rai, the young man who had risen to Jagan's defence. He shook his head and stressed, "All o' you running errands against yourselves. All o' you love Jagan, I know. I still like him, as a person. But Jagan, the palitishun, you can have him. I don' mean that with any disrespect."

Māmoo felt uneasy with such talk; he had heard it before from business colleagues, not close family, and had dismissed it as politics since most of Jagan's detractors were among the better-off classes; he had not looked in his personal mirror nor at the basic philosophy in the way of his nephew. He had preferred to be loyal, avoided argument in areas where he knew little, especially when it came to this or that "ism", and so chose to humour his nephew. Besides, the rum might be getting to Karan's head, loosening his tongue. He must watch that; after all, he mused, they didn't get good rum in England; one drink of the stuff you got there would make you sick!

"What d'you say to that, Rai?" he turned to his son.

"I know if we don' back Dr. Jagan Burnham will win, and that will be worse!" Rai replied.

"And dat is our real problem," said *māmoo*, given a way out of the predicament into which his nephew had placed him. "We can deal with Cheddi, but Burnham, that is a different story, that man will be a dictator. He nowhere yet, but you should see how he push people around a'ready. That man is going to do somet'ing real nasty before dis year is out. Everybaddy want Cheddi to make good with de States. And I believe the States would come round to he and help he."

"But you know what, *māmoo*, only if he's *not* a Communist. He will have to tell Kennedy that he's not a Communist. As simple as that! There's no other way. Look, America just not too long ago finish a bad war in Korea, a Communist war. What happen? You end up with a communist state, the same thing they wanted to prevent. Loss number 1. Then they help Castro in Cuba. Castro take over. And they wait for the elections that Castro promised. Instead of elections, he set up a Commie state; thousands run away to Miami. Today Miami filling up with Cubans, Battista Cubans, some of the worst people you'll find anywhere; Castro glad they left, his gain, America loss. Loss number 2. BG is the only English-speaking country in South America. We have a strategic location. Remember not so long ago, they had an air base at Atkinson Field, which did a big job in the last war. You think America will allow loss number 3? Especially when Kennedy touting the *Alianza*. T'ink 'bout that."

Rai offered, "You right, they won't. They have this Monroe doctrine which the papers say they follow and will use to interfere in this area if we do anything to t'reaten them."

"You jokin'! How can we t'reaten a big place like the States?" *Māmoo* asked in disbelief.

"With missiles, *māmoo*, atomic missiles. On top o' rockets, like they send to the moon. Already both sides have them. They can go two, three, four thousand miles. If we become Communist and we accept aid, trade and 'advisers' from Russia, their missiles will be shipped here soon after and we will become a launching base. You want that?"

"Come now, Karan, na mek you' dislike for Cheddi go so far. That will never happen."

He wanted to challenge that with "Want to bet the business?" but he repeated only, "No get me wrong, I still like Cheddi as a person, but as a politician I have me doubts."

Māmoo continued in a tone of concern "You say that so many Cubans leavin' Cuba. Whey yuh get that news? I don' see that here." He pointed to the *Mirror* lying folded on the coffee table.

"Yes, pa, the *Argosy* had something 'bout that. And *Voice of America* radio." Rai offered.

"I don' read that paper. Everything it write is against the PPP. I read the *Mirror* same way the Black people read *New Nation*. And wha' mek yuh t'ink *Voice of America* tell the trut'?"

Karan felt uncomfortable, and wished to avoid having to delve into and clear the morass of ignorance that clearly enveloped his uncle. To relieve that would be a trying and divisive process which could await a better opportunity. But he felt the matter too important for his family's welfare to drop it completely. He would avoid an argument over loyalties and beliefs and focus on the family's welfare and interests.

"Tell me, *māmoo*," he said hurrying his words a little, "we done arrange that these boys will come with me when I leave next month, right? They will study, four, five years, whatever education they can take. They will be safe with me. What will happen to the rest of you if things go bad, if Jagan don't do well with the US?"

"Na t'ink of that one; me sure Cheddi will do awright, we talk; he gun do w'at is right."

"Ah hope you right. But jus' tell me this, if he don' do well, t'ings will go bad for BG. If Jagan don' please Kennedy, all de African lobby in Washington will be at Kennedy door. You know these Denbow people them, they is one o' de links, they and they friends. And they are the PNC."

Māmoo was unsure, wary, worried even, as Karan's remark had struck a chord.

The fact of a strengthening and increasingly militant African lobby in Washington had been drawn to the PPP's attention by the Americans themselves who were prepared to work with Jagan provided he renounced Communism. They did not think much of Burnham. Why in the face of all this, *māmoo* had wondered, in moments of introspection, would Jagan pursue a Communist and pro-USSR line? It just did not make sense. No more sense than not to pursue development monies that Britain had withheld for nearly 12 years, ever since the PPP was formed. No, he had concluded, Jagan could not do such a stupid thing. And yet he recalled a conversation seven or so years ago with Tulla Hardeen, one of the first businessmen to support the PPP; Tulla had encouraged other Indian businessmen to do the same. But in that conversation he had scathingly criticised Jagan for his intransigence and had blamed him squarely for the debacle in 1953.

But Jagan had done his penance in jail and had seemed more aware of people's real needs and since then had been more encouraging on the role of business in the new Guiana. Indeed the past four years of governing seemed to have matured him enough to allay the fears of the business community. And so he and other businessmen, emotionally and somewhat wistfully attached to Jagan, and in fear of Burnham, had supported him in the 1961 campaign. They continued to overlook what was obvious to outsider analysts that the actions of the PPP were clearly consistent with a pro-Soviet agenda, and the strident clamour for immediate independence was a necessary item on that agenda.

"I don' know," he said, eventually, "I never think of that, I believe that Cheddi will do what's right and good for us. He is a great man."

"Anyway it wouldn't hurt to keep a sharp lookout," Karan cautioned. "I wouldn't trust anybody in politics today. I still say PPP foolin' you all. You watch what kind of man Jagan put in key places. That will tell you all you need to know. Chandisingh in Health, Moses Bhagwan at Freedom House, Janet in Labour and Housing, all three solid Communists; I know them well; none of them want private enterprise; all want central control; they ain't changing. And now Mann..."

Māmoo was shaking his head.

"Don' say no to that, *māmoo*; everybody who know them say they are true commies, and no PPP official deny that yet."

Lallo, a slow-witted man, a cousin of Karan's and the same age, had a few minutes earlier joined the group; they had been together in the PYL and Lallo had quickly accepted the militancy which Jagan had advocated from the start, and been unafraid to use his physical toughness to win arguments. He had risen to delegate status within the PPP, a low level considering his dedication and hours of service at Freedom House and in the field. Since entering the room he had been content to listen and deal first with hunger and thirst, quietly filling up with *dahlpuri* and *ghosht* and putting away two or three rums; now fed, he entered the fray, disagreeing, "That's a lot of balls; you don't know what you talking about; you just come back an' you think you know everything; you rass nah change at all; you only repeat what the white man say."

"Hey, don' get so hot, maan; is only my opinion. You think Mann should be in that job?"

"Mann is a qualified social scientist, he got talent, he's the future of the Party; look, even Kissoon had he in he store showing he off; Kissoon is a big businessman; he not stupid." As he spoke his voice had risen almost to a shout. He had missed Karan's previous reference to the Kissoons. I was about to comment on Mann, but held off sensing a rift deeper than this exchange.

"Tek it easy, maan, we gaffing, we not fighting. This is not one of you PPP meeting, Lallo." Karan said, perhaps with less tact than needed, but he too had had quite a few drinks, and tongues were getting loose. "So how you do? I didn't see when you come."

Karan tried to lighten the mood. But he had not recognised his cousin's ire. Lallo was a short burly man known to be bellicose, short on facts and therefore unable to deal with disagreement, settling differences with fisticuffs; he had been arrested a few times for fighting at parties. Within the PPP he had a reputation as an enforcer.

"Me dey awright, no thanks to you; you look out for you'self; this is not white maan country; this is me own. You bad-talk we! What you know about we policy, eh, what you know?"

Lallo's slurring of words was not surprising; he had started drinking well before lunch, and since arriving, had drunk freely from the array of drinks on the table.

Karan said, "Lallo, na fight me! I did want to have a drink with you, but I see you had enough a'ready; why you don't stretch out in that Berbice chair? The cool breeze will do you good."

Lallo did not need this tactless aggravation; he exploded, and with a lurch, was beside Karan, grabbing at his shirt, shouting, his right arm raised, his stance unsteady, "You fuckin' scunt! You want stretch out? Ah gon' stretch you rass out fo' good!"

Māmoo had felt jittery from the moment Lallo had walked in; he knew his volatility, his dim-wittedness and his hatred of his smart cousin since childhood. Fearing violence as the conversation heated up, he had risen, ostensibly to go to the bathroom and was close enough to the pair to grab Lallo's uplifted arm as he tried to hammer Karan. The moment's reprieve allowed Karan to duck and back his chair off with a screech that, with the shouting, had brought *māmee* into the living room, the steel ladle she had been using to stir *dahl* still clutched in her hand.

"Lallo!" she exclaimed, and lowering her voice, continued, "stop that, we not going to have no fight today. This is a happy time for we; this boy bin away nea'ly eight years; is you cousin, you first cousin, like you brother, and you bigger than he; you goin' hit 'e? Nah shame me here today; go sit down in you chair or come with me over here."

Lallo had lowered his fist and gazed at the floor as his *chacha* continued to hold his wrist and switching it to a handshake led him to a chair at the far side of the table.

Karan paused briefly, then said, "I sorry, maan, I only say what I feel; is still a free country; le' we shake on that." He walked over to Lallo and held his hand out. But the other did not accept it. Instead, he said gruffly, looking at his *chachee*, standing apprehensively a few feet off, "Is okay."

Dinner guests had begun to arrive, most unknown to me--young couples, older folk and a few children, all nicely dressed, prosperous-looking. After polite greetings, introductions and a welcoming drink, they were called to dinner. The room was rich with the fragrance of all the spices that had gone into the building of empires, and led to the European conquest of India, Malaya, Indonesia, Indo-China and the Pacific islands. The commingled smells so cannily put together in the array of chicken, duck, mutton, roti and vegetable dishes that crowded the tables, evoked the great desires that had led the Europeans so far afield, and were even today inspiring modern adventurers.

As they settled into the generous spread, *Māmoo* said, trying to lighten the mood, "Karan, hear this joke. This African man was saying that Guiana is an African country, and when the PNC take over, they will send everybaddy back to where they come fram. He say, 'We go sen' all the white man them back a England; we go sen' all de chinee man them back a China; we go sen' all the coolie them back a India, and the putaguee them … but befo' he finish, a coolie baye shout out and say 'yes, maan, send all the Putaguee them back to Canada!'"

orchid

Chapter 3

Water levels remain low and passage further obstructed; frustrations increase. We are three days overdue and families would begin to believe their worst fears. We ponder the poor communications, misinformation, our inadequate and layered education and its anglocentric curriculum that either ignored or denied much of what we have reviewed; I recall a spirited discussion at university of *"language as a colonising factor,"* and a former history teacher's views on European colonialism.

Day 10: Language as weapon

"Let me make this clear in case there should be any mistake about it. We mean to hold our own. I have not become the King's first Minister to preside over the liquidation of the British Empire."   W. Churchill, 1942

"When the British came to Africa, they had Bibles and we had land, today we have the Bibles and they own all the land!"
Anon. African lament

"…change comes slowly, and as a result of different pressures; … it is very important to devote ourselves to a continuous effort to promote that change through education and meaningful action…if we are too precipitous, there is danger of walking backward and delaying the desirable change." Samuel Bosch, Argentinian scholar

"… in my experience, if you put off independence because you fear you will get a left wing government, the most likely thing to happen is that you will get a government even further to the left."
Iain Mac Leod, former Colonial Secretary, House of Commons, UK, 1964

W e broke camp and were soon on our way, certain only of the delays ahead, and hoping they would be no worse than those of the day before. The stream ran quite briskly and varied in width and depth. Soon it took a wide sweeping turn to the right to run almost directly east, its surface glittering in the blinding morning sun, increasing caution and slowing us down.

The stretch of river immediately ahead contained no obvious major obstructions, according to the list we had made on the way in, but great care had to be taken to keep to the main channel and avoid the many minor hazards, floating and fixed. Several small tributaries would be flowing in from the north and one or two from the south, hopefully with enough water to raise the level at least to permit safe passage over the *tacubas* and rapids. We might then cover 25 miles or more before the day's end. But that was not to be. By late afternoon we had done barely 15 miles.

This was a disappointment and did little for morale, especially as we had no way of changing our situation. All day long the sun bore harshly down and the sky burned cloudless, as it had done every day. In the slothful progress, we felt the frustration, spoke desultorily and shallowly, too concerned with our different anxieties to concentrate on any meaningful conversation, other than the recurrent speculation on how Georgetown would explain the delay to our families, keep them from worrying, and what, if anything, they might be doing, or could usefully do to ascertain our situation and condition.

Sitting in our small boat struggling to find its way through the treacherous rocks and fallen trees that littered the river, we passed the time in reverie, which at times for me sank into brooding, puffing aimlessly on a cigarette, watching the lazy smoke curl upwards to float uncertainly to the rear; we played desultorily at cards or dozed in the shade of the overhanging forest when stopped to cut through obstructing *tacubas*, which had become exasperatingly more frequent. At one of these stops we had a light lunch--there *was* no other kind! We crunched Edger Boy biscuits in the midday shade and drank river water. While boldly assuring the team that the water was safe I kept wondering what the real likelihood of getting an infection was. So far we had intermittently drunk the water "raw", boiling a quantity each evening equal to the capacity of our water canteens. In the heat and sweat of the day water went fast. The natives drank the water straight from the river, as did Doris, Benn, Balgobin, Rodriques and I. I would watch the natives go to a point in the stream where it ran swift and deep and collect enough for the occasion. This is exactly how we were taught as children to identify safe water when minding cattle in the fields.

"Only drink the water if it's not running, the faster the better! And *never* where the cows shit!" was the universal injunction.

Inspector Bacchus, Brewster and Jain were a bit less trusting, a reflection of their urban upbringing, no doubt, but they too, by now, had drunk enough fresh from the river without any immediate discomfort or illness to remove at least their acute concerns. Brewster's remark concerning the natives, "They accustomed to this; that's all they got" summarized the difference of view between the city-raised man and the forester or rural dweller.

I thought of all the water-borne pathogens I had studied during my training in Microbiology and doubted that I would find any in infectious quantities in this river. In the interest of caution and science, however, I collected samples duly labelled from each drinking source, fixed one from each in formalin, and injected another in a liquid culture medium which I would keep as cool as possible to retard growth and examine each day for turbidity, and a third without treatment similarly kept and observed.

I hoped that what germs there might be in the sample would survive the journey and remain identifiable, or if any grew would not overwhelm the medium in the week before we could reach Mabaruma. The men were to report to me any symptoms, regardless of their nature. (I received none by the end of the trip, nor at any time thereafter). In my daily checks the untreated water had remained clear and nothing emerged for a week to suggest a growing parasite. Similarly the culture medium showed little significant change after five days. I kept them all for later study.

By mid-afternoon we had passed several small northern tributaries whose names have escaped me; then we came to the *Mamukani* and were again disappointed to note the low level of this southern stream. This observation did not help morale, as it presaged no smoother passage through the rough waters to come.

After a few tedious hours of bewildering sameness we reached a pleasant wide beach just beyond the place where the *Ianna* River joined the main stream from the south, and decided to pitch camp. Here we were just west of the point where the main stream began its fall of about 100 feet in a series of rapids over a distance of five miles.

Most of the traverse through that section, though rough and bumpy, should be manageable, save for that one drop that had provided some excitement and trepidation on the inbound trip a week earlier. The river from this beach veered slightly in an east-north-easterly direction, which would take us out of direct line with the sun. That would help with visibility and rate of progress in the early morning.

Each setback reminded us of the bungled planning for this trip, and criticism of high-ranking desk-bound officers who had over-ruled their field juniors and had opted for short-term parsimony instead of good sense. The resulting plan had exposed the party to grave dangers.

The severe restriction of ammunition for the two guns, for example, was difficult to understand, even allowing for an uneventful journey. It was perhaps symptomatic of changing Government ways and means, and how resources were being used, but Doris felt that it was systemic.

Thus the talk drifted inexorably to political agendas and direction, after some initial discussion on how our delay, now that we were two days overdue, would be affecting our principals and families in Georgetown. The length of that delay before a message could be sent to Georgetown was still unknown. Tilbury had expressed surprise that we had made the journey without a short-wave communicator. Already our delay had proven the need for one. We were sure that a needless and costly flight had been made to Barama Mouth by the plane returning on schedule, as any message from Tilbury would have been too late to stop it.

We had been in addition totally unaware of what was happening on the coast. My pocket battery-operated transistor radio had worked acceptably on the inward journey up to Cokerite. Further inland the static had become increasingly thick and the voices, faint at the best of times, had been swallowed up one by one in the harsh crackle that sprang to life each time I turned it on, and its squawking would ebb and flow as the dial searched the ether for a clear signal. Soon the radio was out of the range of all transmissions from Georgetown and Port of Spain. Either our location or the humidity or both must have interfered with radio reception, although we did hear the Voice of America faintly and briefly one night a week back.

We wondered how the authorities would explain our delay to worrying families. With no news from us and no way to contact us, what could they say? Tilbury's remark about radio was pure common sense. Why did trained officers not think of providing us with some means to communicate should an emergency occur? Did their planning not include dealing with contingencies? We were, after all, journeying into a little known area of the country at a difficult time. If they had not thought of this, why not? I worried lest this lapse symbolised a general weakness in police methodology — the last thing we needed in these troubled times.

In jest Jain said, "I have no one to miss me; only the girls." And everyone laughed, a little nervously.

"You shouldn't joke 'bout that, Mr J ain," Balgobin scolded, "this is serious. Inspector, if my wife goes to the Police in Brickdam will anybody tell her anything?"

"I don't know, Bal, they'll tell her not to worry," the Inspector said. Balgobin muttered something under his breath.

I had told my family, (and had advised Balgobin to do the same), that we might not be back for at least ten days, instead of the seven suggested by the Police. Since I was not involved in the planning nor in any discussion of alternative routes, I had had no prior knowledge of how thorough planning had been. In any case I did not know the area, except notionally, and had simply accepted the statements and estimates the Police had given. But I had been sceptical. My scepticism had been based on nothing more than plain intuition and past experience.

In the course of growing up a variety of incidents had taught me to allow more time for projects involving unknowns since tight schedules depended on everything going right and being done right, starting with the plan. I recalled several such incidents as I was growing up where an undesirable result was due mainly if not entirely to lack of a means to communicate a change of circumstances.

At that time few homes had telephones so even public ones were of limited usefulness for emergency contacts with home. So unforeseen delays brought anguish to the child who was kept back and to the parent awaiting him, and depending on the parent's mood and commitments, could get the child punishment without a hearing.

Once in New Amsterdam Sukhdeo and I had been sent to represent the family at an evening function and were five hours late getting home due to failure of our bicycle lamp and "arrest" by a Special Constable--a sort of policeman's assistant--for the infraction. My story revealed something of prevailing racial stereotyping and lightened the atmosphere considerably. Oddly it was Doris who found it quite hilarious as he told me later that the man sounded like someone he knew.

We had gone two miles outside of New Amsterdam and had left at midnight after a bicycle repairman who had attended the function had spent nearly two hours vainly trying to rewind a spent generator. We left with a rather weak flashlight riding slowly in the darkness and as we passed the Mental Hospital we narrowly escaped assault from an unseen voice that had risen out of the darkness at the side of the road and threw a cutlass at us when we ignored his order to halt! It hit the rear fender as we pedalled furiously away from him! We were rather relieved to enter the lit Main St after half a mile of cold sweat and fear. In the centre of town two blocks from home, at two o'clock in the morning we were stopped by a black Special Constable (nearly all of them then were black), demanding, "Whey you' light?"

He had an awfully sour and rummy smell, which struck me like a blow; I felt nauseous. He must have seen me grimace and withdraw in reaction. He pounced upon me, "Wha' happen to you, baye? You gat fits, or you t'ink you a' maan!"

He spoke with a slur and immediately accused us of being thieves, and that he would charge us for riding without a light. In the commotion that had overtaken us in the past half an hour, we had not noticed that our faint light, which had made an impact only in the blackest of gloom, had quit and gone unnoticed once the street lamps had appeared. Sukhdeo told him who we were, where we lived and recited our adventures that night. He could not, nor did he want to countenance any reference to a Hindu function, and thought our experience a fabrication, dismissing the fresh sharp dent in the rear carrier of the bike, which we were looking at for the first time. (Sukhdeo was right; it did look like a cutlass wound.) The man merely dismissed it all with derision.

"You coolies always full a' excuse!" he accused. "Wey you say you live? New Street? You daady name Latchmun? Ah don' know no Latchmun livin' in New Street." He said that in a manner suggesting that "Mr Latchmun" could be of no consequence or a fabrication, being unknown to him. For no reason except that he might pay heed to someone of stature I blurted, "I know Mr Tulloch and Mr Hanoman on Main Street, Mr Romalho in Cooper Street and Mrs Akai in Chapel Street, and my uncle Latchman teaches Mr Jairam's son at Hindi school."

I was sleepy and scared. Perhaps it was my fear alone or simply a defensive desire to impress him to let us go as I had heard it said that Specials were always deferential to people with money or power. As I finished I pointed to the business house cum residence looming tall and grand at the northeast corner of Main and Pitt Streets a few yards from where we stood. He read the sign pronouncing, in large bold letters, 'Jairam and Sons General Store, Wholesale and Retail'.

"How so you lil coolie know all these rich people?" He asked incredulously.

"They have children in my high school class, my friends."

"You lil' coolie rass, you lil pipsqueak! You go a high school? You lie; you look too small. Wha' you age?"

He leaned closer to me and his offensive odour made me wince once again. I felt the nausea rise and was sure I would vomit if he came any closer. I moved back.

"Ten," I said, trying to hold my breath. "And I also know Mr Chapman!"

"The Mayor, you know the Mayor? Whey you know he? Ah is a Special Constable and ah never meet he."

He was sufficiently distracted contemplating all these names of power in the small town, that he looked at us sternly and said, "Ah gun gi'e you all a break. Gwan home befo' ah change me mind. Hey bye, befo' you go, stan' me a drink." Sukhdeo fished in his pocket. He had exactly three cents, which he handed over. "Da' is all you gat? Nuh mek joke. You look old enough to tek one!" Sukhdeo was 17 and had never had alcohol; he emptied his pockets.

"Wha' you gat in you packet?" I turned my pockets inside out. Nothing but a 2-inch piece of pencil.

"Is wha in de bag?"

"Parsaad".

"Wha' de hell is dat?"

"Offering" Sukhdeo said. He sucked his teeth, a long suck.

"Offering? Alyou coolie strange no rass!" expressed his fury and perhaps his ignorance of anything relating to our customs, our religion or us. And even if he did know anything, he would probably think it alien, heathen and ridiculous.

We reached home to face the enormous and to me incomprehensible, although expected ire of Latchman chacha who accused us, even as the policeman had done, of doing wrong before he had heard us out. He actually punished Sukhdeo physically to ease his frustration, angered that Sukhdeo had not taken the proper spare flashlight intended for just such an emergency, and had put me, a child and a guest in the house, at risk. The youth could have retaliated but didn't, accepting his error and his responsibility philosophically.

I was hurt that he did not also punish me, for I was every bit as involved as Sukhdeo, even though I was in his care. But the error was so innocent, and he had asked me, not Sukhdeo to explain. He had taken my word, which corroborated his son's account, yet he was so unwilling to believe his own son, another form of punishment. I thought that was so grossly unfair, for Sukhdeo was a kind and generous person, smart and sensitive, learned in his religion, a fine singer, and lacking only the great assertiveness that his father had wanted in a son to match the boy's intelligence. It was doubtful whether that lack was ever verified or properly defined. But the point was not lost on me; knowing that so many misunderstandings stem from failures of communication and omission of a clear need. And I learned that even the learned and experienced can make mistakes.

Now here I was with a work party, twenty years later, unable to communicate with our principals two hundred miles away, in an age of wireless and new gadgets that technology had spawned to aid communication. Yet from the characteristics of our location, its isolation and lack of any means of speedy contact with the outside world, or any way out but the river, we might as well have been lost in the darkest corner of the world. Inspector Bacchus felt acutely embarrassed, as he had admitted to me much earlier in the trip, that he had not thought of the possibility that we might need to contact the city, having been so convinced by his superiors that the trip was "just a routine, take it like a short holiday". He was pleased that my group had planned for extra days.

Dinner was a quiet affair. It seemed as if no one wanted to expose more of their innermost fears, nor face so soon another examination of their private views. Everyone looked wary, and whatever conversation there was, was limited to essentials, much as it had been all day.

Out in communities, the lines had been drawn mainly on political passion and racial preference, not the sturdiest basis for critical assessment and not many seemed willing to retreat from them. Rational debate between opposing supporters was seldom possible, as Bal had noted, although desired. Questions or disagreement thus rapidly deteriorated to personal name-calling or physical exchanges.

If only these people could be induced to stop and think! And to seek evidence. However, the political leaders feared that enlightening their followers might have negative consequences: informed and thoughtful listeners might ask awkward questions, demand changes from their leaders, or worse withdraw support. The third party, the United Force, had a power base, which though wealthy, was so narrow that it was in danger of toppling on itself, and therefore not a serious contender.

I was mulling over these things and wondering what everyone else was thinking. Perhaps they were concerned less with political tensions, and more with the current difficulties on the river and our inadequate food supply. Almost as a distraction we began to talk about the case that we had come to investigate; this led to a consideration of the state of forensic sciences in BG, a field in which Insp. Bacchus was developing an interest. He described the initiatives of the new Minister of Home Affairs, Mr Balram Singh Rai who wished to place all forensic activities under a single "roof and direction," a task that would take all the energy and enthusiasm of the new unit director, Superintendent McLeod. Bacchus would be part of that unit.

McLeod was even at that moment taking steps to bring together representatives of all Government departments involved in forensic work to discuss the Home Affairs plan. Our Laboratory would be a key participant; it had long developed a reputation for forensic pathology in BG and throughout the Lesser Antilles, whose governments had used the services, since the days of its predecessor, the Clearkin Laboratory.

The sand flies were moderately active requiring a repellent, which I had begun to use, rather sparingly like everything else. Most of the party complained about the flies yet had less of a red reaction to insect bites than I had. Certainly the natives seemed oblivious to them and clearly had developed a tolerance or immunity to the bites.

Brewster, sitting beside me, sipped on his nightcap, tossed a pebble into the water flowing past his extended leg, ruminating, as the conversation sank into a lull. I smoked a cigarette, without really inhaling, not the dedicated way that Doris did, with deep drags and slow even exhalations, nor the measured approach that Benn and Bacchus used. Each man almost revealed his character in his handling of the cigarette; the swirling plumes of smoke seemed to keep off the insects.

Brewster said, "Doc, I remember reading in school that the British civilised America and before that everybody was backward, heathen and primitive, lived in tents, same in Africa, that we were cannibals, and in India people were dacoits, went about naked, worshipped Satan, and even drink dey urine."

"Wow; that sounds like pure hog doodoo! Hardly a trace of truth." I had of course heard this before. "We become victims of our education, when we stop too soon. You notice how carefully stratified our education is. First, there are few schools so few get schooling. In school the system controls what's taught and tailors it to what it wants each level to learn, what each level can access or relate to in open society. So if you complete 6th standard, as everyone here has done, you can move on to high school or get a job somewhere or start something on your own, a trade or similar; and you have enough basic knowledge to negotiate the fringes of the British social system. You can read well enough to decide which way to do things; you can farm, buy and sell, and even get rich; but that's it. For complicated stuff you need more; that means high school.

"But there are too few of those and none in rural areas, so few go on; they control high school content by recognising only UK examinations. So high schools don't take you where you might want to go; they take you where the Brits want to take you. So first you must qualify, by money or brains to squeeze into that system, and when you do, you begin four to five years of indoctrination that will take you up to the first rung of the British hierarchical ladder.

"Apart from Mathematics and General Science, all subjects--Languages, Literature, History, Geography, Religion--are part of a British menu, each ingredient carefully chosen to make the curriculum a tasty blend, like curry, that all, regardless of interest or background or where you are in the Empire, will eat and digest, getting more and more the same as you climb each step. At the end, if you do well, you'll get an embossed parchment Certificate that could lead to greater things, from better navigation of the "system" to jobs or a University career in Britain or one of her satellites, where the process of indoctrination continues.

"At this point you've had twelve years of brainwashing and you can now believe all of the fables the curriculum taught you, including all the half-truths you mentioned. It is only when you get to University level that you can meet teachers who could shake prior beliefs and throw out the half-truths you learned earlier, because this is the rung from which rulers are drawn.

"Less than 5% of high school graduates get this chance at correction, and even so the shock can make some lose their sanity as I've seen already, especially among those who had believed genuinely all that they'd been taught and already used that knowledge, for example to teach it to others, an especially dangerous thing here where very few high school teachers outside of Queens, Bishop's, St Stans, Ursuline and one or two others have a higher qualification, and knowing no better, teach only the half-truths they had learned.

"The teaching deficit is particularly bad with ideas on democracy. The British parliament is a real thing; you can see it in action, and believe that Government happens there; it doesn't; that's just the last step in debating and they make a convincing show of it. The real action is behind the scenes where power and wealth--same thing really--do their stuff.

"The casual learner even at University can come away thinking Parliament is democracy and worth copying, and reason that if the lessons about it were right, then the rest of the message, the half-truths taught earlier, becomes fully believable. So, perfectly rational people outside and inside the House of Commons believed that aboriginals everywhere had no culture, that Australia had no owners –they had given it a fancy label *terra nullius* or no man's land-- when in fact Natives might have something superior to what the Europeans have put in its place.

"You see, those natives have not had the same twelve years to tell you about their way of life. And twelve thousand years of Indian civilisation can be dismissed in a stupid sentence because there is no one to challenge it where it was taught. Sure India has its dacoits; but more so the Brits, who have legalised theirs, and every other nation has its bandits. That's why you chaps have a job!"

Brewster chuckled. "You're saying that we're all brain-washed to believe this propaganda; how do we tell what's right and what's wrong?"

"No one hustling a living really has the time to seek truth, except if related to his or her job, like people in research; and even then if they come up with the truth, they have to deal with the weight of belief, sometimes generations of belief, which those in power may not wish to change. So a struggle starts and it then becomes a matter of whom to believe: the powerful and foppish Brits who tell us that we are inferior; or the small inner voice that says they're lying and fooling us. Which one? The chap who says miracles don't happen or the one who disagrees?"

"The tendency would be to believe the mightier voice," the Inspector said, "and yet we know in our hearts that many of these things can't be right; we saw so much of that propaganda in the last war. Each one bad talk the enemy; in time truth becomes the victim."

"We are seeing some of that in Georgetown politics; what would British do if violence gets worse?" Jain speculated.

"They send troops to put it down, and shoot a few of us to remind us who's boss, like they did in India and Africa. They'll use war to teach us to keep peace, they always do that." Balgobin said cynically.

"Like everyone else the British are a mixture of good and bad, both in ideas and as individuals; they just happen to dominate us today, because they control the resources and the materials. They feel justified and superior because within their system, in Britain, they tell us that any citizen *theoretically* can work his way to gain power through legal and peaceful means; we can call these strategic manoeuvrings or intrigues.

"Thus the violent overthrow of a British system is rarely necessary, as intrigues and suitably placed incentives result in orderly change. Even when change leads to a loss of direct power, as when colonies become independent, the British manage to retain subtle and behind-the-scenes control of sufficient processes, especially financial, to keep their mercantile interests and profits intact. The biggest error the Brits make--all colonial powers make it--is to have too many layers between top and base. So quality of information reaching both ends gets degraded as it passes up and down."

Jain added, "Hierarchical separation results in loss of power when it gets to critical point. Communists think they can avoid it by levelling all people, which is not possible. Human beings are not all naturally equal. Even in families they seek their own interest and will divide instead of join to meet ends. So in time, Commies too will stratify enough to self-destruct!"

"If you tell that to our leaders they'll flay you!" I said, half in jest.

I remembered a spirited conversation on a similar theme at the Junior Common Room, UCWI, one beer-soaked evening, almost exactly ten years back, while I was still an Arts student. A young English lecturer had invited the class to continue informally a discussion on the role of language as a colonising factor.

We had begun with causes and effects of colonisation; various angles were explored and a historical perspective attempted. The group had spoken glibly of "Indo-European languages" and their evolution and spread, and gloated over the marvels of European literature, with English the prince among them.

As the lone Indian and Guianese in a group of mulattoes and three whites, from different islands, I marvelled at the uniformity of our reading and analyses, but it had seemed as if I was the only one who felt the weight of the half-truths of history as told in our British textbooks, which I used to call the *Yesu Das burden.* I was too inhibited to speak. And then we had adjourned to the side verandah of the Junior Common Room, then housed in a low wooden building near the entrance to the campus pending construction of the Students Union.

When the second quick beer had done its job of removing my timidity and fear of ruffling feathers, I began to say what I had in mind about language and colonialism, formal or informal, mindful that at the end they might hate me and never speak to me again.

But now with inhibitions reduced I spoke, as if to the Englishman alone; his mien was kindly and encouraging. I imagined he was Donald Smith, my mentor--the acerbic yet fair-minded New Zealander, former head of English at Queen's College--who had promoted straight talk and had influenced me greatly in the directions of my reading, encouraging explorations far beyond the set books of our syllabus, and had led me to critics of British and American society including the great satirists of the last two centuries. I had with me notes and quotations that I had collected for the discussion but had been too timid to introduce them in the formal session dominated by a garrulous Jamaican mulatto with a slight lisp.

I heard myself saying, "The British used their naval strength and natural duplicity (he didn't wince) to conquer friendly peoples worldwide and then used language as a tool to enslave them, by the simple process of conducting all business in English, and offering education in English only. And when some, like my parents, resisted and continued to speak and educate their own in Hindi, they outlawed languages other than English, denied any validity to religions other than Christianity and in extreme cases, as in North America, imprisoned children in religious schools.

"It was the same as the medieval use of Latin only which Romans had spread throughout Europe and the Near East and even today persists in Catholic worship. The Arabs imposed their language and religion in all conquered lands in Asia, Africa and Europe. Other Europeans did the same as the British--the Spanish in Latin America, the Portuguese in Brazil, the French and Dutch in Africa and the Far East etc.--but I'll focus on the Brits.

"The most egregious example of this conquest is their behaviour in India; in three centuries of tyranny the most inexcusable acts were those instigated by James Mill, Lord Macaulay and others and carried out under Macaulay's direction. Some of you might have read the withering diatribes of Brian Edwards, Ed Long, Carlyle, Anthony Froude, Lord Harris and others against Caribbean Negroes. But even if you know the brutality of British adventurers in India and Africa--Hastings, Clive, Wellesley, Dalhousie, Curzon, Chelmsford, Rhodes, Churchill, etc., massacres and all--you'd have just the victor's view as triumph over savages!"[10]

It had fallen out thus, but there was more...as I paused one of the white male students asked, "What the hell are you talking about?" His tone was rough and belligerent.

It was my turn to wonder who had had suffered the most from beer; it was all so obvious, but one could not underestimate the power of the propaganda that was British colonial education.

"Patience, please, hear me out;" I said, surprised at how controlled I was, as flashes crossed my mind of the numerous conversations on related topics with Ossie Belgrave and John Moses, far into the night, of lectures by Rajkumari Singh and prior lessons by *chacha* Latchman and my parents. I felt briefly cowed, but the smile on the Englishman's face urged me on.

"I doubt whether anyone of you studied the real history of India or read any of its vast literature;" and when no one said anything, I continued, "so what I'll say might be new. Let me back up a bit. Britain, as a caste-oriented and class-dominated society, acculturated and integrated newcomers who were white, and most were able within a few generations to blend in with their class or improve status, even Shylock's kith and kin, who later provided not only a Prime Minister but the dominant financiers of the Empire and all of Europe.

"Non-whites, however—barring a few Indian princes and such, family of the Raj's *Princes Council*--were inserted on the lowest rung of the social and economic ladder, and they too lost *all* their antecedent hierarchy and values in two generations or so, but unlike the whites, their lines became degraded and marginalised because of *colour*, just as those who converted to Islam in Muslim-ruled India, or to Christianity under the Portuguese, French and British.

"For Indians who came directly under British domination the past began to disappear, achievements were forgotten or denied and all their glory threatened or dismissed as myth. In the degrading, kingly clans died out or became obsolete at best, labourers at worst; most rulers chose comfort in subservience or conversion, those who resisted were extruded or sacrificed, like Palestinian leaders after the 30's revolt.

"In an all-white society, serfs with smarts who conquer language--the alert and clever *harijans*, the Ambhedkars of British culture--can climb to riches and even come close to centres of power! For people of colour, however, the road is full of mines. Acculturation is not enough; riches can make us materially independent; but we will forever skirt the rims of power, taste a bit of it perhaps, but never really get to the centre, no matter what our intellect or ability, or mastery of language.

"You see, the white races and their wards today, are historically and culturally immature, still at the predatory and aggressive/acquisitive (householder) phase of human development, having made huge economic gains as a result of piracy, conquest and the industrial revolution, all incidentally on the backs and minds of people like me and my ancestors, Blacks and Coloureds whose knowledge and resources they've exploited and pass off as their own. They'll do anything to protect these gains."

The group was stunned; I had literally spat the words out. I took two gulps of beer to fortify myself.

---

[10] Years later I came across a similar proposition in the writings of Wilson Harris, the enigmatic Guianese poet/novelist.

One of the four girls in the group, a light-skinned Trinidadian mulatto, staring at me, wide-eyed, wondered whether I was the same person who had been in her class for six weeks, especially as we had had several group discussions on literary themes "that were so friendly".

"Eh, eh!" she exclaimed. "But I never; it must be the drink! It's not like you to be rude."

The white Jamaican girl who happened to have been the first person I had met socially from my class during freshman's week, stared at me wide-eyed and quizzically, but said nothing.

The Englishman was patient and addressed me, "Come, come, surely you exaggerate; we're not as crass as that; we're quite sophisticated; we have one of the world's foremost literatures and a model of parliamentary democracy; we've learned, from Grecian times, many virtues and have produced many new ideas and inventions and created knowledge, seminal knowledge, in most spheres of human intellectual and scientific activity. You know the names."

"Yes, I know, that's true but it hides more enduring myths and denials. We can give you the modifying evidence, when you're ready for it. I'll give you a sample; many of the themes in Boccaccio's *Decameron* and in Shakespeare's plays can be found in an Indian storybook, called the *Pāncha Tantra*.

"The longest and greatest literary epics, *The Rāmāyana* and *Mahabhārata* were composed a thousand years before Homer, whose *Iliad* contains the same story-line as the *Rāmāyana*. India gave the world mathematics[11] and made celestial and other discoveries that made our civilisation possible, and for which others have gotten or *taken* credit. One mathematician Aryābhatta in 499 AD proposed the solar system we take for granted today; he was only 22 at the time. A thousand years later Europeans still believed Ptolemy's geocentric flat earth hypothesis, and Copernicus and Galileo did not have an easy time preaching the heliocentricity of our planetary system nor in changing concepts of the Universe. I can spend a day telling you details of Indian achievements and of property seized by the British, including most of the Crown jewels--everyone knows about the *Koh-i-noor*--and before them stolen or destroyed by the Mughals.

"Ironically, your ascendancy and preferments have lulled Indians into forgetting the great achievements of their own ancestors--including the world's first universities, first attempt at a republic and so on, (you give Plato that credit). Today's Indians, especially those educated by *your* curricula, have become toadies; they believe that you're really superior, knowing nothing of their past nor of yours and how young a culture you are. They're impressed with your might, having lost theirs for a millennium or more.

---

[11]There is evidence that the "theorem of Pythagoras" was known as long ago as 3000 BCE in the *Sulbasūtras* of Baudhayana, Apastamba and others. Most Pythagorean geometry is traceable to India and it appears that much of the corpus of Greek, Egyptian and Arabic geometry derived from Indian mathematicians. (See also Ch 15(2), 15).Traces of Indian terminology are said to exist in the works of Democritus (ca. 440 BCE) and other Greek writers (Datta, 1932). Buddhist missionaries travelled widely, reaching the Mediterranean, and some say, the Balkans. The emperor Aśoka (ca. 260 BCE) mentions Buddhist missionaries in Alexandria and Syria. Geometry in India was linked to religious practice, particularly the construction of religious vessels. In *The Birds* by Aristophanes the character Meton sings: *"With the straight ruler I set to work / To make the circle four-cornered."* To this the leader of the birds Pisthetaerus replies mockingly, *"Verily, the man is a Thales (an Indian)!"* This is quoted by van der Waerden, who muses, "Is it not marvellous that a scholarly problem was so popular in Athens at that time, that it could be made a source of amusement in the theatre?" (van der Waerden 1951 (1950):130).

"And what of the Africans? So much is unknown about them or suppressed somewhere. But I believe that they are in decline, a stage ahead of us perhaps, their societies crumbled after some great cataclysm, whatever it was that created the Sahara, Sahel and Kalahari, dried up their rivers and starved or scattered them to seek new lands and start afresh in forests and plains of middle and southern Africa, where first the Arabs, then Europeans found and enslaved them, and took their lands for the diamonds, gold, copper and forests. The people are, as it were, recycling without knowing whence they came. So may we all become--those of us who survive the next catastrophe!"

"I think you had too much beer; Indians don't hold their liquor well, and Red Stripe is strong," said the Jamaican, who had spoken earlier, cackling derisively, with arrogance. I winced.

The Englishman, however, smiled and astonished the others by saying, "No, no, let's hear what he has to say; he didn't have his say in class; he has a point; let him pursue it. I can see relevance to our theme."

I hesitated, seeing the frowns all around and a gesture from one to keep quiet; he surely would have left had the tutor not been there. But, encouraged by the latter's smile and evanescent nod, continued, hardly recognising my words in the state of release and heightened excitement that had overtaken me. This was the first time since starting classes that I had found an ambience that fed the urge to say things to strangers that Ossie, John, Shah and I (among others) had dissected, analysed and debated the past three years, and which the pretty Mary Durham, herself a pale-skinned mulatto (what the Americans call a quadroon), had quietly encouraged in long evenings listening to my "strange beliefs". Even as I started to speak, I could see her smiling face and hear her injunction, "Whatever you do, don't change; don't be afraid to speak your mind; you can offer so much to us, to me."[12] Thinking of her animatedly, and pleased then that one of the upper class had chosen me, handing me her handkerchief as in times of jousting, lance ready, with her photograph evocatively signed, "tearfully yours", I ploughed on.

"Let's go back to Macaulay and the weapon of language. On Feb 2, 1835 he is alleged to have said this in Parliament, after visiting India; I read from my notes, *'I have travelled across the length and breadth of India and I have not seen one person who is a beggar, who is a thief. Such wealth I have seen in this country, such high moral values, people of such calibre, that I do not think we would ever conquer this country, unless we break the very backbone of this nation, which is her spiritual and cultural heritage, and, therefore, I propose that we replace her old and ancient education system, her culture, for if the Indians think that all that is foreign and English is good and greater than their own, they will lose their self-esteem, their native self-culture and they will become what we want them, a truly dominated nation.'* After the War of Indian Independence failed in 1857…"

---

[12] Ossie Belgrave, John Moses, Shah Khan were among my closest teenage male friends. Ossie was four years my senior, born and raised in India, the son of Christian missionaries, and had through study and experience acquired an ecumenical view of Hinduism and Indian history. He was familiar with much of the material relating to Harappa and Mohenjo Daro, then filtering into the western news as pieces of curiosity, not "real news". John was coloured, my age, the son of a Christian minister and teacher, and on the verge of deciding on a career. Shah had started in his uncle's business. Mary, four years older than I was my constant companion and worked with the Telephone Company as an operator. We were all disciples and admirers of Rajkumari Singh and her handsome husband Harry of the BG Dramatic Society and had played parts in plays under her direction. Harry was a superb actor. His interpretation of Shakespeare's Hamlet rivalled Laurence Olivier's of 1948.

"This is bilge! I never heard of that! It's not in my book!" the rough white one expostulated.

"We called it the Indian Mutiny," the tutor said, "right oh, carry on."

"After the failed War of Indian Independence, British authorities—egged on by Macaulay, Carlyle, Tennyson, Monier Williams and others--employed Max Müller, a German Sanskrit scholar, to translate and interpret the *Vaidas*--the Hindu revealed scriptures--as a major tool to *de-educate*, if I could coin a word, Indians on the things that made them so resolute: the scientific origins and bases of their culture, religion and spirituality. Without ever visiting India--just like James Mill who in 1815, I think, had written an insulting fiction styled 'history'--Müller produced a translation and decided on a chronology of Indian history claiming that it was supported by linguistics, and "proved" that the *Vaidas* were *not* written by Indians.

"Müller was a *good* Christian, believed literally in the Bible and in the Genesis account that creation occurred in 4004 BC. The *Vaidas* however *told* us that the Universe was over 1.5 *trillion* years old, not a few thousands. So to make *Vuidic* history *fit* the Old Testament account, Müller compressed the last 12,000 years of Indian history into just over 3,000, which many regarded as an exercise of evil stupidity; but a more serious intellect, Vaidic scholar, Shri Aurobindo, described it as *'conjecture supported only by conjectures'*. At this time ideas on eugenics and white supremacy had become fashionable in Europe and USA and merged with language to become powerful weapons for global propaganda, to justify colonialism and British India policy, and eventually led to Kipling's notion of the white man's burden that plagues us to this day[13]."

"Where on earth did you get that bunch of drivel?" The mouthy Jamaican mulatto again exploded, his brow creased in a tight frown, his lips wet with slaver, as his eyes darted at the Englishman, for support and direction, I suspected. So much of this challenged the values and knowledge he had so far learned and taught, having been a high school teacher, and which he had expounded earlier in class in relation to the Jamaican dialect.

"I'm from Trinidad, and we have Indians there, I never hear any of that; it sound like nonsense for true," a black Trinidadian said.

Their reaction stirred deeper memories on this subject, which I had explored at some length with my friends after reading texts on *Eugenics* by Havelock Ellis, and by others given me by Tulla, and on *Comparative Religion* by various authors, eastern and western, a gift from Mr Mattai, whose pre-teen sons I had tutored. These had supplemented the numerous lectures by *chacha* Latchman and Donald Smith and conversations with Cameron Tudor, among others. I had studied my essays and memorised passages in preparation for this colloquium. The question and the attitude brought out all the animosities I felt about race supremacists and the atrocities of colonial regimes. I became angry.

"You think that's nonsense! Okay, here's more drivel for you," I said with some venom, and ignoring them and the shuffling, as if they wanted to leave or perhaps punch me in the face, but noting the Englishman's faint smile and raised eyebrows, carried on. "Lord Harris, a 19th century Governor of Trinidad, your homeland, said of non-whites, that's you: *'The only independence which they would desire is idleness, according to their different tastes in the enjoyment of it; and the higher motives which actuate the European labourer…that to be independent in circumstances,*

---

[13] See also Chapter 2 and 5, relevant sections.

whatever his station, raises a man in the moral scale amongst his race; and that his ability to perform his duties as a citizen, and, we may add, as a Christian, is increased by it. These, and such motives as these, are unknown to the fatalist worshippers of Mahomet and Brahma, and to the savages who go by the names of Liberated Africans…'

"I never heard that;" the black Trinidadian, taken aback, said irritably, "did you make that up?"

The white one snarled, "You're nuts! Where in hell did you get that crap?" He had asked that twice. The Englishman looked at him and frowned briefly, as if the white student was letting him down, should know and speak better and be less emotional. I smiled inwardly, oblivious of their remarks, and encouraged by the Englishman's reaction, I blurted,

"Okay, you've heard of David Hume – he's in your books; Harris may not be." I saw several nods, one vigorous from the white Jamaican girl, whose look by this had changed from puzzlement to wonder.

"In '*Of Natural Characters*', he wrote: '*I am apt to suspect the Negroes to be naturally inferior to the Whites. There scarcely ever was a civilised nation of that complexion, nor ever any individual, eminent in action or speculation. No ingenious manufactures among them, no arts, no sciences. On the other hand, the most rude and barbarous of the Whites, such as the ancient Germans, the present Tartars, have still something eminent about them in their valour, form of government, or some other particular.*' You can check that piece of drivel; the book's in the library. And check US Sen. William Jennings Bryan who styled the British in India as '*relays of carpetbaggers*'!"

I thought of Cameron Tudor throughout and his many lessons on biased British aristocrats. The look of consternation and silence was broken by the Englishman, who said, "But do you deny the efforts of the many – Clarkson, Wilberforce, Pitt the Younger, Buxton and others--who believed the opposite and worked to free slaves? The Americans, with Tom Paine, like the French based their republic on Rousseau's *Contrat Social*, on equality; the American constitution states that all men are created equal. The US under Lincoln fought a brutal civil war for liberation of slaves."

"No, sir; no denial! I accept that. But Thomas Jefferson, a lead author of the US Declaration of Independence, and US ambassador to the new French Republic, also said, in the context of equal rights to freedom and all the things Rousseau had talked of, '*I advance it… as a suspicion only, that the Africans, whether originally a distinct race, or made distinct by time and circumstances, are inferior to the whites in the endowments both of body and of mind.*' The French were perhaps a bit more generous in admitting Africans of proven ability into their society, despite their rejection of Haiti's declaration of independence, but they did come closest to establishing a populist state, accepted Josephine, a mulatto, as Empress only to revert later to a traditional hierarchical state despite the title, *République*. Cecil Rhodes in 1887 told the Cape Town House of Assembly, '*We must adopt a system of despotism in our relations with the barbarians of South Africa...I prefer land to niggers*'!"

The black Trinidadian cast me a look of pure hate but said nothing.

The Englishman reflected, "The notion of white man's burden did drive some to excesses. I'll add to your narrative a quote from Albert Beveridge, U.S. Senator from Indiana, who said in 1898 in support of the US invasion of the Philippines, '*God has marked us as His chosen people, henceforth to lead in the regeneration of the world,*' because the Filipinos '*are a barbarous race. It is barely possible that 1,000 in all the archipelago are capable of self-government in the Anglo-*

Saxon sense'." And Cornwallis did say of Euro-Indians: *'...on account of their colour & extraction they are considered in this country as inferior to Europeans.'* I daresay you may have something there. "

The silence from my tormentors reverberated through the verandah. I felt elated and justified, and almost smothered my words through emotion, "So, sir, it seems that equality is for white races and white cultures only. Why else would the US and Canada imprison native children in unilingual English religious schools? Or missionaries impose European norms on Guianese natives? Why would Macaulay insist on replacing the language of India with English? Language preservation is the most powerful form of resistance to oppression.

Several years after he had persuaded the British Government to force British curricula throughout British India, and having denied the existence of any Indian literature and reduced what little he knew to the status of English schoolboy stuff, he reported to the House of Lords, *'Our English schools are flourishing wonderfully...It is my firm belief, that, if our plans for education are followed up, there will not be a single idolator* (sic) *among the respectable classes in Bengal thirty years hence. And this will be effected without any efforts to proselytise, without the smallest interference with religious liberty, merely by the natural operation of knowledge and reflection. I heartily rejoice in the prospect.'"*[14]

"But you have to admit that the British did educate Indians and tried to rid India of the horrid caste system," one of the other mulattoes observed, speaking for the first time.

"No, sir! Indians had a solid educational system for millennia; the Mughals started and the British completed its ruin. It excelled in math, languages and sciences and had roots in the village structure. The first comprehensive treatise on Grammar was written at least a millennium BC by an Indian named Pānini. It still stands as a textbook in Vaidic schools and is extensively quoted by European grammarians. Donald Smith, my English teacher, knew and referred to it in class. Numerous treatises on Astronomy, Geometry, Arithmetic etc. have survived, often buried in religious texts. As for caste, the British and organised Church maintained an impenetrable caste system for centuries. It was a serious belief styled *A Chain of Being* and promoted by Church and monarchies; it was lampooned in Elizabethan cartoons, one showing the human part as a pyramidal tree with different folks sitting on branches from lowest to highest. E.M Tillyard wrote about it in his critique on Shakespeare's historical plays. The British promoted and embedded this strange view of caste in India which was a distortion as Vaidic thought went far beyond this simplistic view of order."

The Trinidadian mulatto girl's eyes brightened with recognition; nodding vigorously, she said, "You know, you're right; my English teacher did show us a copy of a cartoon, with different ranks of people occupying each limb, the king at the top; we thought it a joke, but Shakespeare did describe the Elizabethan chain in Troilus and Cressida."

"If there's something to this diatribe, I've yet to see it; what is it?" the mulatto Jamaican asked, condescendingly, ignoring her remark. Again I was surprised how little of what I had argued seemed to have reached them, although I was fully aware that I had opened a Pandora's Box of uncomfortable issues and utter darkness that colonial students who aspired to high office in the

---

[14] Macaulay, 1876, 1:398-99; see also Ch. 15(2) 46 et seq. for more of his earlier statements; there is some doubt about the validity of the quote two pages back, but in 1951 it was widely accepted as correct.

Colonial Services would rather deny than explore.

"The point is--and I think it obvious from the examples I gave--that language is control; there can be no colonisation without language domination. Look around you: you're African or mixed and I'm Indian; we all speak English; I can handle my ancestral language; can you? All of Latin America except Brazil speaks Spanish; the Goans of India are more pukka English than you sir, pardon the expression; the world is divided by language blocks; when colonial powers made treaties e.g. the 1904 *Entente Cordiale* which gave Britain Egypt and France Morocco, and later divisions of the Ottoman empire, the mandates soon spoke the language of their rulers, and so on. English will soon dominate the world's languages. Not a single freed colony will give it up, not even India, as the US takes over."

The Englishman clapped his hands, in mockery, I thought, but then he said, "Very refreshing, although a trifle overstated, but your main points are valid; we Europeans have been rather aggressive and dictatorial, and particularly evil in India; we do preach one thing and practise another; we are, after all, human beings given to self-interest and not above dissembling or frank wrong-doing to achieve our aims. I take it you know all about Clive, Hastings, Rhodes, Curzon, and their ilk?"

I nodded, adding, "And about the infamous half day session of the British India government that finally ruined India and brought it to its knees."

"I fear I don't know that one."

"The Governor-General and his Council--in 1892, I think--decided to close the Indian silver mints, which for millennia had been the repository of Indian savings and wealth. The mints' closure abolished the silver standard and ruined hundreds of millions of people whose only savings lay in silver. The act coincided with a famine; together the lack of money and the food shortage killed over two million Indians. Senator William Bryan quoted this from a report in a newspaper: *'One can obtain some idea of the evils of irresponsible alien government when he reflects that an English Governor-General and an English Council changed the financial system of nearly three hundred millions of people by an act introduced and passed in the course of a single day.'*[15]

British agricultural policies beginning with Hastings had replaced Indian food farms with cash crops—cane, opium, cotton, dyestuffs--abolished village granaries, extorted high taxes that ruined farmers, leading to famines in times of drought, killing millions. In a similar show of cruelty Churchill denied assistance to Bengal in 1944 during another money famine, which dear Winston called *'the*

---

[15] US Senator and Presidential candidate William Jennings Bryan said of this, "No matter what views one may hold upon the money question, he cannot defend such a system of government without abandoning every principle revered by the founders of the republic (USA). Senator Wolcott of Colorado, one of the President's commissioners, upon his return from Europe, made a speech in the Senate in which he declared that the last Indian famine was a money famine rather than a food famine. In that speech Mr Wolcott also asserted that the closing of the Indian mints reduced by five hundred millions of dollars, the value of the silver accumulated in the hands of the people. If Mr Wolcott's statement contains the smallest fraction of truth the injury done by the East India Company during its entire existence was less than the injury done by that one act of the Governor and his Council." and "As I have often said in public, India is, in fact, now governed by successive relays of English carpet-baggers, who have as little sympathy with the natives as they have any real knowledge of their habits and customs." This remains true today. (1968).

market at play', and waited until 4 million had starved to death before allowing aid offered by others to enter India. And you all condemn Hitler for the *Jewish* holocaust!"

By this time my colleagues had heard enough to know that there was a huge world of intellectual darkness that their focussed education had left intact, of knowledge unlearned which was crying out to be explored. The Englishman paused, looked at his watch, smiled and said, "Enlightening; we must do this again! And by the way, are you sure you want to switch to Medicine, and not do the triple greats?"

For a moment then he sounded so much like Donald Smith; I in turn smiled and remembered Cameron Tudor's identical advice.

"You know," I said, feeling more expansive and confident, in which I saw only him and the two approving women, the Trinidadian mulatto and the white Jamaican, the others blurred, "in preparing to switch Faculties I started to read a bit of biology, evolutionary biology. Seems that peoples and civilisations evolve just as species do. The British seem to be a prime example of Darwinian survival and selection theory. Queen Elizabeth promoted the naval predator in a way that made her predecessors look like children. Her warriors were selected from those with more than an ordinary capacity for bravery, greed, plunder and cruelty to others, even to their own—Drake, Frobisher, Raleigh, for example--and their actions were justified and honoured as long as they fetched a profit for their backers and a hefty share for the Crown!

"Thus were bred three centuries of British pirates who recruited others like them to roam and plunder the world. In doing so they conquered peaceful and welcoming nations in America, Asia, Australia and Africa. This culture of piracy, that made you rich, is the same as that practised by the Arabs who lived by the *razzia* (or raid) and when they became Muslims applied its techniques to conquer the world and hold it for over five centuries."

"You're right to an extent," the Englishman interrupted. "But you must know that those were centuries of free-rolling discovery and conquest. How many think of Puritan American states as sponsors of slavery, for example? The port of Newport, Rhode Island was one of several on the East Coast that traded slaves, as plentifully as the Europeans. Or of the Jewish money-lenders who financed the trade, while complaining of anti-Semitism. For Britain foreign mercantile adventures in five continents did make our aristocrats rich, while their lowlier fellows at home and abroad remained in dire need while basking in the propaganda and aura of national superiority that raised self-esteem but kept them poor; they were content to wear rags and live in filth with pride and give blind allegiance to their warlike superiors in a system that kept lords lords and serfs forever serfs!"

I was astonished that he had bared his stance to us so openly, silencing the others; I was content to conclude what I had to say.

"They were at all levels kept ignorant of the value systems of other nations and taught instead to denigrate them, and despise those who looked, spoke or behaved differently, especially by custom or religion. The hierarchy was even more rigid and impenetrable in the colonies with the added policy of *'our own kind first, other races last'*, a source of huge injustices. Colonial subjects came to believe that everyone in Britain and Europe was well-off, smart and powerful, until the 20th century revolutions in communications and transportation changed all that.

"British rulers made a fine art of the abuse of language to misinform, indoctrinate and subjugate. But I must say that they also made it possible, at times of soul-searching, to relent and give something back, this College for instance, and you chaps; you're fair and likeable; you're not devious aristocrats. I have a quotation to show the vicious levels that language abuse can reach.

"The early 8th century governor of Iraq, the cruel al-Hajjaj ibn Yousef dealt extremely harshly with the defeated. The 11th century Uzbek historian Abu Rayhan al Biruni, in his book *From The Remaining Signs of Past Centuries*, described al Hajjah's methods; here's what he said (I read from my notes): *'When Outaibah bin Muslim under the command of al-Hajjaj ibn Yousef was sent to Khwarazmia[16] with a military expedition and conquered it for the second time, he swiftly killed anyone who wrote the Khwarazmian native language or knew of the Khwarazmian heritage, history, and culture. He then killed all their Zoroastrian priests and burned and wasted their books, until gradually the illiterate only remained, who knew nothing of writing, and hence their history was mostly forgotten.'*

"How interesting! Isn't he the same one who described the heliocentric universe?"

"He and previous Muslim writers used information from Indian mathematicians and scientists from the previous millennium as I said earlier. Aryābhatta, in 499, was the first to propose a heliocentric universe and taught math on a tour of the Middle East, sponsored, it is believed, by the Indian Emperor Chandra Gupta II Vikramaditya. Al Biruni wrote about Indian math in his book *Ta'rikh al Hind (Chronicles of India)*. His rendition of Aryābhatta and others' work reached Europe in Latin translations, hence the credit given to him for the descriptions."

I paused, and finished, "Thank you for hearing me out, sir; not too many people I know are open-minded enough to look dispassionately at what they're learning, and sift truth from untruth."

He chuckled, downed his beer, and said, "And to think I had qualms about coming out here. No, it is I who must thank you. Good luck, and think again of where you want to go."

An awed silence followed. Ossie Belgrave and Ben Yesu Das would have been delighted to see the stunned faces of my colleagues. I hastily gulped the last of my beer. I was overcome with emotion and by his kindness and I felt a curious exhilaration, as other thoughts and distillations of my reading came to mind, not in any order, but vaguely relevant. I thought of William Jennings Bryan (see footnote previous page), who had opposed the US invasion of the Philippines in the late 1890's, and of Edmund Burke's remark on Clive's corruption of an Indian general:[17] *"All the acts and monuments in the records of peculation; the consolidated corruption of ages; the pattern of exemplary plunder in the heroic times of Roman antiquity, never equalled the gigantic corruption of this single act. Never did Nero, in all his insolent prodigality of despotism, deal out to his praetorian guards a donation fit to be named with the largesse showered down by the bounty of our chancellor of the exchequer on the faithful band of Indian sepoys."*

But instead of some acknowledgement I received the cold shoulder and something akin to permanent shunning from all save the two women who had made a point of promising to explore the themes I had raised, and to look at Indians beyond the cane plantations and fields of rice.

---

[16] Greater Iran, modern Uzbekistan; home of al Biruni
[17] This refers to Robert Clive's bribery of Suraj ud Dowlat's second in command.

A week later I moved to the pre-medical class where my virginity in sciences would confront challenges that seemed so remote from language and philosophy; and yet as I tackled them I would marvel how closely and ineffably the volumes of new and perplexing information and concepts relied for order, organisation, expression and clarity on the disciplines I had studied all my life and had just left behind, and how efficiently they would help me to fill the void in my grasp of "science" so that in just over two terms I would learn enough to confound my teachers and classmates and move on with them and without impediment to the next phase of medical studies.

Back on the banks of the Barama I reflected on that seminal "conversation" with fellow students who were bright and steeped in English literature, but like Macaulay had no clue of the immensity and age of Indian literature, and knew little about African history and cultures and the massive exploitation of their own and other peoples by the British aristocracy. When I had urged probing beyond their learned stereotypes, quoting Keats, *"...open thine eyes eterne and sphere them round, upon all space..."* I was talking to a wall, a painful entreaty none had contemplated, least from an Indian!

From my reading of British history, always presented in schoolbooks with a positive and fulsome pro-English bias, (though later I would find Arnold Toynbee a bit more credible), the struggles to unite the British Isles had established an enduring hierarchy of people with more layers than the Hindu caste system, infusing in each layer a strong sense of loyalty, to preserve the homeland from foreign invasion and to maintain their standards. The fact of being islands helped Britain's leaders to create and maintain the fable of her superiority in every respect over Europe and all other nations, especially after the end of the Napoleonic wars.

This--plus the explosion of extravagant construction in the time of the two Georges, made possible by the industrial revolution and income from Empire, chiefly India--inculcated in Britons a love of self and an arrogance and disdain for others that would keep the majority contentedly at home, incurious and dismissive of other lands and cultures. A more formidable and protective wall around the nation could hardly be imagined. This attitude hardened over the decades, and thus preserved the hierarchy. Today it expresses as intense competition among commoners to achieve so as to climb the ladder in the hope of impressing enough powers to merit an elevation to the peerage.

I recalled Mr Yesu Das lecture on the topic, "In 1215 AD, Magna Carta gave rights to aristocrats and later benefited wealthy commoners; these two groups fed off each other in a symbiotic relationship that occasionally elevated a commoner to the peerage. Henry VIII's break with Rome added religious independence to the options. By the time Elizabeth appeared, the scene had been set for exploiting the religious schism and by abjuring the Papacy act freely to indoctrinate to the new realities and to replenish and enrich the treasury, drained by the continual wars which England had waged for two centuries with her neighbours in Europe.

"Elizabeth's endorsement of piracy and support for adventurism began for Britain 400 years of expansion that made it overlord of one of history's largest empires. Barring a brief flirtation with popular democracy under Cromwell, Britain maintained its autocratic oligarchy--governments elected by qualified citizens, but run by autocrats–who, by intrigue and trickery, and other abuses of human interaction, oversaw the colonising of America, the wholesale theft of native lands there, the endorsement of slavery to enrich herself and her colonies, and finally the major conquests of India, Australia, New Zealand, Burma and much of Africa. It mattered little that in the process Britons committed unspeakable horrors on other human beings, enslaved millions, forced untold numbers to make the gruelling *middle passage*, and sacrificed them in every corner of the globe.

"The British left, as markers of their presence, graves filled with the bones and teeth of their victims, scattered wherever they went to seize wealth. For a brief time some men of conscience emerged, for example, William Pitt, a visionary; who held the notion of a state in which the principles of liberty would prevail. But soon that changed as Avarice returned to guide the nation. Wolfe's 1759 defeat of Montcalm in Quebec, followed by victories in Montreal, changed the scene completely, and laid the foundations of the British Empire by seizing America from the French. Continuing wars against France changed it from seeking liberty to become a massively armed state, relying heavily on taxation of subject states, until the Americans rebelled."

"Taxes!" he had exclaimed again, writing the word in bold letters on the blackboard.

"Taxation had caused the earlier Scottish revolt against Walpole. America resisted the stamp tax. Franklin's cartoon of a dismembered Empire caused protests that led British soldiers to kill five Bostonians in front of the public buildings. Pressures led to cancellation of all tax except the tea tax. Bostonians protested loudly, yet were not *brave* enough to storm the ships as themselves, so they dressed as Mohawks! The British closure of Boston harbour united the American colonies, which chose *'poverty with liberty to gilded affluence'* and thereafter hung on to every word that Jean Jacques Rousseau had penned in his *Rights of Man*. Britain subdued and ruined Indians by taxes!"

A few years later Cameron Tudor commented on the same theme, "With America lost, Britain added conquest to trade as her reason to be in India, and as the Mughals weakened began rapidly to gouge Indians and transfer their country's wealth to London. The Mughals had taken India or most of it and made it their home, and kept the accumulated wealth right there, while the British seized spoils, which they promptly transferred home. How little do native English know that the treasures they claim as their own were really wrested from the maharajas, princes and sultans of India or taken from conquered Africa!

"The *nawabs* who ruled the northern regions had foolishly given full trading authority to the British East India Company (BEICo). The French in Pondicherry, South India, had made a similar deal with the local *nawab*. Robert Clive, a young extortionist expelled from Britain, became a servant of the BEICo; he was a carousing opium-smoking criminal who turned opportunistically into a rambunctious militarist; he became very successful, adding wealth to the nation through sudden conquest, and was rewarded with a peerage!"

"Clive exemplified political cunning and arrogant adventurism which the British exploited to seize the wealth of others." Mr Das had said years earlier. "Battling Suraj ud Daulah, a brave and noble leader, and with no hope of winning, he bribed ud Daulah's second in command Mir Jafar, with £250,000." (See Ch. 5 and Burke, above). Clive's victory secured Bengal for the Company, and enabled it to increase revenue enormously by adding punitive taxes to its considerable business profits.

"The British never had it as good as they had in India, squeezing it dry of its wealth and carting it off to Britain. They abused Indians, already softened by Muslims for 700 years, and many brazenly lived with Indian women, to flaunt their disdain for local customs and culture. They seized the best areas of cities, and transformed them to their own liking. Even cemeteries e.g. Park Cemetery in Calcutta became a showplace for their dead, celebrated with grand monuments.

"In south India, Tippu Sultan almost succeeded in ousting them, until defeated by Richard Wellesley with a huge army ironically made up mostly of native Indians *(sipahis, sepoys)*. Wellesley announced grandly, *'I am about to arrange the affairs of a conquered country,'* and proceeded to build a palace in Calcutta. So the notion of the Empire of *liberty* that 18th century Britain had courted came to an end, which ironically would mature in the minds of the French, their long-time enemy."

Dr Brahmam had amplified, "The British became more greedy after Clive; they began to squeeze the *zamindars*, the landowners, who in turn increased levies from their tenants and the peasantry. Warren Hastings had ordered plantation farming with heavy taxes to prevent food farming; the taxes made many lose their lands and become serfs. *Before that India had no serfs, unlike Britain*. Food shortages led to several serious famines, causing millions to perish in Bengal and Bihar. Hastings acted scandalously and was eventually impeached in London. And though found guilty he was forgiven because he had *secured additional territory for the Crown!*"

To these and many other scoundrels the British gave honours, regardless of treachery and criminality, so long as they had enriched the realm. Later Macaulay and Victorian eugenics would conquer and enslave the minds of aspiring Indians, as noted above, so that even today Indians remain subservient, however exalted their position in society. Thus did the British secure economic sovereignty and enrichment for her own people, at every level, at the expense of the colonised, by devices varying from preferential business practices, elaborate tax schemes that favoured British businesses to simpler ones that assured individuals a cut of national trade.

In colonies like BG local British were allowed to extract a generous fee for simply sponsoring imports, styling themselves "commission agents". Their signs were everywhere, you could not buy a thing from overseas without paying one of them, anything from 1 to 10 per cent, for which they did nothing that you could not have done more efficiently and promptly. They were just another useless layer sponging on the public. Even the British Crown indulged in the practice, by setting up the "Crown Agents" which by mandate bought everything that any branch of the Empire wished, from a paperclip to a railway locomotive or steamship, but declined to procure any items of *machinery* likely to create unwanted competition with UK enterprises.

Europeans had practised this type of *apana jaat* from the earliest times to promote conquest—Greeks, Romans, Charlemagne, the Popes, and their successors down to the modern era. The main differences seemed to be that early conquerors were willing simply to extract tribute and to leave the people their ways, their property and their way of life, much as some Muslims did later on in the Mediterranean and in India.

The British instead wrested everything--from land to culture--in an arrogant belief in the superiority of their ways, and finally imposed their own language and customs, on pain of death, on all those they had subjugated. They massacred dissenters and opponents, jailed pacifists and exiled some while murdering others; no one was left out of the general purge.

In that European environment the mass philosophy of Paine, Kant, Marx and others matured and enlightened millions, although it required a high level of schooling to grapple with the language and the concepts. Thus relatively few came in contact with them except from the many interpreters who preached and passed on the doctrines, such as they understood them, like pundits, priests or imams trying to interpret Krishna, Christ or Mohamed.

From the colonies, only the suitably indoctrinated--by chance contact with enlightened or dissident European teachers in such institutions as Queen's College and other grammar schools established throughout the Empire--would be allowed to penetrate sensitive layers of British society, and even so, would pierce it only peripherally, as Mr Tudor used to say, unless thoroughly tested and found loyal and better than the British in devotion to the Crown and possessed of the aggressive cupidity needed to aggrandise it, at any cost, like the conquerors of India and thousands of others before them in America.

On a lesser level were Indo-Guianese lawyers Lionel Luckhoo and Sonny Ramphal, who some would see as "betrayers" of their people, the former to the Colonial Office in the fifties, the latter to Burnham a decade later. (Both men would be knighted by Britain, the typical reward for loyalty to the crown-- "sucking up" as Balgobin had scoffed!)

Bacchus was saying, "I met many Africans in England; they're proud people, not at all like what the English say, though some of them are just like we here, they copy Englishman even to the top hat and cutaway coat! I used to laugh whenever I see an African man in morning coat and striped pants and top hat. But those who dressed in their tribal costumes and head dress, with strong patterns and colours, now they looked impressive; they were the real Africans, but in my time not many did that, only the rebels, to show their own people that they should respect tribal culture."

"I can't see Nkrumah going around Accra dressed like a penguin!" I said. Everyone laughed.

"Yes, those people really foppish, they got morning coat, evening coat, smoking jacket, bowler hat, top hat, different style cap, some kinds of clothes only the upper crust can wear." Balgobin said.

"Or afford." Jain said. "To them the appearance was more important than the substance of a person. If you look good, you are good. They still behave that way!"

"It's a colonial thing; very Victorian, we still follow it, even though we want independence."

"Politicians might want independence, but see how many people running away to England, even some who with PPP, and I know several families breaking up over this." Balgobin said.

There was a murmur of agreement; everyone knew someone who had left or was planning to leave, from all walks of life. The brain drain that had started in earnest in 1953 was clearly threatening to become a flood.

Chapter 4

Another frustrating day on the river, this one marked by an accident in which the Corporal and Jain, our scientist, were thrown into the current; the Corporal could not swim and was fortunate that Jain was close enough to initiate his rescue as others moved in to complete it. Later we carry out a daring if unorthodox manoeuvre to traverse a cataract which a week ago had been less treacherous. Jain and the photographer, Brewster, suffer injuries in the manoeuvre offset by the courage displayed by the young policeman, Rod. A fuel shortage looms. The incidents and the difficulties brought the men closer in a way the two main racial groups would not have thought possible in such a short time and unlike the conflicts found among rodents in confinement experiments. Later we meet a native hunting party smoking their game; in the tradition of the forest travellers, they give the policemen a hind quarter of *capybara*, which provides them a welcome feast and satisfies a craving Brewster had from the start. After dinner we probe into social and racial realities; the officers agree that peaceful co-existence demands that people be informed about one another's culture; they admit that they, like other Blacks, know nothing about others including their own ethnic background; we agree to give them a brief tour of Indian history and culture.

Day 11, Part 1: Rescue, ingenuity, taming a cataract; the blush of
inter-racial harmony

"…although we are of different individualities, different in ideas…let us strive like flowers of the same divine garden to live together in harmony. ... Become as waves of one sea, trees of one forest, growing in the utmost love, agreement and unity
Abd ul Bahá

"The farmer was easy, the artisan encouraged, the merchant enriched and the prince satisfied".
--a succinct description of Bengal before Plessey, by Harry Vere lst Senior Officer of the East India Co.

"There (in India) it is only the business of the people to pay taxes and to slave; and the business of the government to spend those taxes to their own benefit."
Sri Naoroji, an Indian dwelling in England, late 19th century

All religions have common basic tenets; they differ only in their rituals and their prejudices.   Author

We awoke in the grey dawn well before the sun could tint the visible wedge of sky. The forest was wrapped in stillness broken only by the steady swish and gurgle of water twisting along the rocks in the river, and lapping gently on the edges of those obstructing the flow. Since leaving Cokerite ten days back, I had marked the river level, at each campsite, on a rock at the edge of an eddy.

My mark here showed no change, which, although disappointing, was not as bad as a drop would have been, at least to our morale. I washed in the cool water, which instantly banished with a shiver any residual sleepiness. Everyone got busy to prepare, but did so less enthusiastically than in previous days. My group breakfasted sparingly on dry biscuits, stale cheese--from which we had to pare away the surface mould that had begun to colonise it for the past few days-- and coffee. The feelings of everyone could be summarized in one word, frustration; the addition of low-grade hunger did not help.

"At least we 've plenty coffee, Doc, and enough tea for a week or more," Balgobin said encouragingly.

Rodriques had sent two of the natives to scout the river ahead as he had done each day. The stream was narrowing as we began the fairly long passage through the low hills along which the river would drop about a hundred feet, gently and imperceptibly at first, then ending in a series of rapids. The roughest of these had provided some excitement on the inward journey a week ago. Benn had said that the descent could be a lot trickier and the boat may not be able to negotiate the channel fully loaded.

"I don't want to get into that unless I'm sure that we safe from the rocks. Dem is big rocks!" Benn was ever respectful of the river, took few chances. Each morning he would intone his short orison, half Christian, half pagan, known to foresters and river men, with the deep reverence understood only by those who had come to know the treacheries of life on the water. Here the river was everything--transport, communication, food and drink, the very lifeblood of forest communities.

The natives had given names to the spirits (or gods) that ruled the streams; (porknockers were terrified of *massacouraman*, the mythical hairy water monster who ate humans, and yet could be generous to porknockers); you shared their bounty at the spirits' indulgence. In return you showed respect and did not abuse them. How many have lost their lives not heeding this simple principle!

I took photographs of the campsite, the riverscape and my rock marker, as I had done on previous days. The forest remained dark and brooding, an enigma, the river an innocuous-looking skein of thread snaking its way through it in quest for the sea. A low hum emanated from the forest. Was it the sound of the forest spirits communicating as the natives believed, or was it the silence reverberating in my ears that created that hum? I could not tell; I felt it strongly among the trees and on the river while listening to the forest. The murmurs of the wakened morning began to intrude. Voices from the camp were issuing instructions in two languages, and everyone got busy preparing to leave. Camping gear and other baggage were briskly stowed. The equipment, forensic material and my notebook were wrapped in rubber and cellophane sheeting, secured in a canvas rucksack tied to the gunwales. For the return journey we had begun to secure stuff instead of the carefree approach of the inbound journey, when we simply piled everything in the boat. Balgobin meticulously checked the forensic material.

"Even if we capsize, these won't get lost or damaged," he affirmed. Although the routine was by now familiar, it had taken on this day a more sombre countenance, reflecting perhaps the doubts and concerns playing on our minds. But each kept to his task and completed it in silence.

The boat rocked and pitched gently as each one moved in, wobbling to steady himself as the craft swayed sideways under his weight. Benn repeated the cautions for this leg of the journey, the expected turbulence, reminding us to avoid unnecessary shifts of position and weight distribution over rough water. The boat eased into the channel and found a wider smoother passage as we rounded the curve.

The conditions were as the scouts had reported, very little different from the previous day. We would be lucky to cover ten miles, which meant that we would not reach Cokerite that day. A slow return being inevitable, we concentrated on personal safety and preservation of all materials. Should conditions remain the same we would be on the river for up to four more days, reach Barama mouth by day 14, and soon after could contact Georgetown to arrange our pick-up.

The morning sun was warm and the customary light mist hung over the river. I studied my companions. What a dishevelled bunch we had become, all with beards in stubble, except Inspector Bacchus, who had shaved that morning, and presented a face as smooth and clean as a baby's cheeks. Rodriques had little or no hair on his face, a genetic feature of the native side of his heritage. He did have a few follicles as shown by sparse black spots on his moustache and chin. "I wish I could grow a proper beard," he once said ruefully while the rest of us were commenting on our unkempt look. Jain was quite hairy and had begun to clip his hair with a pair of scissors. The rest of us kept our faces unshaven.

I refused to look at my face and accepted the taunts of everyone on the irregular growth above my lip, where strands of hair had begun to overhang my upper lip in an uneven fashion and beard growth was obscuring most of my face. "You look like Fu Man Chu," someone said to me, referring to the movie villain of the forties in *The Drums of Fu Man Chu*. The pesky itching of early growth had become a nuisance, thankfully lessening as the growth got thicker and longer.

I had decided I would keep the beard after returning home, for a little while, at any rate, as a kind of memento. I could already hear my mother admonishing, "you should shave off the beard; you look like a *mullah* (Muslim cleric)!"If my face looked like Balgobin's, it must be very scruffy indeed.

We continued for a while in silence broken only by the calls from Rodriques at the prow to alert Benn on what was ahead: "Rocks, right and left, water rough," or *"tacuba"* or "slow" or, rarely now, "clear". They were alert and cautious. Everyone else looked jaded. Stories abounded of boats traversing rapids coming to a sudden end by crashing against hidden rocks, renting their sides or keel and foundering, sometimes with loss of life, as was the case with Zeke.

Benn was not a worrier, as Doris was, but did not minimize the dangers. He had been in accidents and had investigated others. Few, he felt, were true "accidents"; most were due to carelessness. He was determined to avoid that label. He would maintain tight control of his boat and keep it intact. The craft was sturdy, but had been around for many years. The timbers were seasoned, but however cured and set, could be no match for the big black rocks that littered the river, so ominously visible now in the low water around us and ahead.

"Is not the ones you see, but the ones you don't that is the big headache," Benn said, as if reading my thoughts. This river was more than a match for his skills, he said, but he would have to learn from it how to conquer.

It is difficult to convey the feeling of subdued excitement at that time of entering this dangerous stretch of river. Benn simply called it tricky, but every man was cautioned to a state of high alert and would maintain that faithfully. The sense of danger united the group and each one carried out assigned tasks, however simple, with great care. The boat proceeded gingerly, the engine putt-putting in protest at being so restrained. Once in a stretch of open water it broke out into a smooth even whine as its speed increased, sending a refreshing wave of cool air across our hot faces. The exhilaration of such transitions was brief as more turbulent conditions returned, calling more for caution than experiment. All eyes peered ahead, on the lookout for danger. Tension grew as the boat twisted this way and that, skirting the obstructions and shallows, sometimes perilously close to a looming rock, feeling its way down channel. The uncertainty and the tension became oppressive.

The big worry for Brewster as he sat there ruminating was not his hunger, but the torturing doubt that the police planning process--which he had believed in implicitly and had defended when other officers had criticised it--had proved flawed and negligent suggesting carelessness or authoritarian egos within the Police administration upsetting his faith in the Force He wished he could discuss his feelings with Inspector Bacchus, sitting a few feet from him, especially as this casual setting would give him the confidence to be frank. The Inspector was an approachable man, one of the most likeable at Central Station.

But Brewster stalled, not wanting to air criticism of the Force in the presence of outsiders, even though by now he was beginning to regard us as part of his team. His concern was deep and worrying; if the senior men could make errors on a simple trip like this against the advice of men on the spot, would they not make similar errors dealing with the serious and complex problems they were now facing daily and the aggravations expected in the immediate future? Doris had more or less said something similar when commenting earlier on the advice he had given.

I lit a cigarette, near nine o'clock. I had been in the habit of smoking ten cigarettes or fewer a day, usually between noon and midnight, rarely so early. I had brought a carton each of Rothman's and Benson & Hedges Gold, intending to share and had passed some around in the previous days. Balgobin and Inspector Bacchus did not smoke; Jain occasionally would puff on one when offered, Brewster, Benn and Rodriques ten or so, mostly Lighthouse or Four Aces. Doris, by contrast, was hardly without one, usually a stub of Lighthouse, much of the time held unlit between the lips, and lighted periodically for a few puffs then snuffed out between thumb and forefinger and returned to its parking place at the corner of his mouth or perched behind his left earlobe. I had found this habit amusing and Bacchus had asked him about it, "Old habit," Doris had replied, "seems I always did that, not conscious of it now."

His cigarette-smoking style had reminded me of Dr Subryan, who had been the Deputy Director of Medical Services (Preventive) during my time in the Civil Service 10 years ago. I had never or hardly ever seen him without a cigarette at the corner of the mouth, its long trail of ash curving to the tip, waiting anxiously to fall. Yet it had never managed to, no matter what he was doing. I recall asking several of the clerks if they had seen the ash fall; none had, nor had any seen him lighting a fresh cigarette. I had even imagined that he had specially made cigarettes that came with the curving ash built in and already smouldering! In an expectant atmosphere such as we were in now, I tended to smoke more. I had left three packs with Hari: "I have one now and again," he had said in thanking me, "these will last me a long time." Not many in his village smoked; those who did smoked ceremonially the dried leaves of a plant, which I thought looked like tobacco, but was told that it was different. I have now forgotten the Carib name like so many others I had briefly learned.

Benn liked my cigarettes: "clean and smooth, not like Lighthouse," he attested. But at 9 am the cigarette tasted awful, yet I held on to it. Thin plumes of blue smoke curled up into the air joining the stray mosquitoes and flies that rose as we passed sensing and homing in to feed on our bare sweating flesh. Soon the mist had vanished and the water shimmered in an incandescent dance ahead; the brightness, though pretty and allowing striking silhouettes, obscured the view of the water and slowed us down even further. At times Benn would cut the engine to conserve fuel and would let the current carry us at its own pace; but then he would lose control and restart to use the engine as a brake and restore his control of forward speed. Slowly the sun rose higher and it became hotter. Soon we came to an obstruction, which took about ten minutes to cut through.

"If I knew I was coming to chop wood, I would ha' bring me own axe; at leas' it sharper than these two. And, to besides, we don' even have a file." Balgobin's bluntness lightened the atmosphere.

"What I would like right now is a warm tennis roll, just come from the bakery, smelling fresh, with a spread of butter melting in the middle, and a long glass of cold vanilla milkshake." Brewster broke a long and withering silence when the sun had risen high and sharp in the morning sky, and beads of sweat had begun to wet his forehead and armpits.

His wide-brimmed straw hat shielded his forehead and nose. Strands of straw had come loose from the edges of the brim and sought release from the maker's curved design and had straightened themselves. A few had broken and a small hole, half an inch or so in diameter had formed near the crown. From time to time he would poke a finger into it to scratch his head. As the journey progressed, other strands had unravelled, some dangling from the sides and dropping past the right ear so that he looked like he was wearing a long straw earring.

It was comical in that at any moment you might expect him to jump on stage and do a slapstick routine in the manner of a popular Jamaican comedian whose stage name was "Bam" and who invariably appeared in just such a fraying hat with his partner "Bim".

Brewster's "tennis roll and shake" had been his favourite snack when funds permitted. His round face and chubby body attested to that. Of all in the group, he had complained the most eloquently about the shortage of food, and had not ceased to chastise himself for not heeding his wife's advice that he provision for longer than the police had recommended–a gut feeling, she had said, smiling at the pun.

"The Police scouted the area a'ready; is only a five day t'ing. Besides, we could always catch a labba or fish in the river," he had reassured her confidently, ending discussions on the topic with the thought of the labba delicacy lingering in and clouding his mind. And so he had left behind six large cans of corned beef and a bag of potatoes (the cans were very heavy and the potatoes would rot in the heat, he had told her). Now the words haunted him, and ideas of weight or threat of rot seemed so irrelevant; he would have to suffer her taunts.

"If the worse happen, you can feed off you own fat; you have plenty!" she had concluded, laughing heartily, as she began to respond to his sexual advances. Remembering that, and perhaps as a result of the conversation the previous night he began to reminisce about his wife. She herself was a plump though shapely woman his own age, whom he had known since childhood. She was quite dark, though actually Indian, with long straight black hair and thin lips. Her family was one of several who had settled on land at the edge of a predominantly African village. As time passed their Indian neighbours had moved on, and houses of new families filled in the land beside them leaving her family surrounded by Blacks.

Her father was a tinsmith and had a good business; he got on well with people, bought the adjacent property and rented it to the Brewsters. Her eldest brother, then 18, along with a few of the neighbourhood youth, had joined the British Army's West India Regiment in 1941 and shipped out to the USA for battle training. She was then 10. Brewster was 11. They had married nine years ago, despite some opposition from her family. She was Hindu, though her family did not actively pursue religious practices, being content to attend functions and thereby kept in touch. Her friends in school were mostly black and Christian.

Brewster himself was a passive Christian and as easy-going as any man could be. His familiarity with her family had been taken for granted, and his race had become an issue only when marriage was proposed. After initial objections, her parents accepted the reality that the couple was seriously in love. The marriage had so far been a happy one in every respect, though it was the wife who had adopted the ways and practices of the husband, except for her food preferences, which he had welcomed heartily, having developed a taste for spicy curries and the myriad sweet foods that were made on Hindu feast days.

Her race was a secret carefully kept, which her dark complexion and the head tie she wore in the fashion of many African women facilitated her 'disguise'. He did not wish to be teased as a "coolie"; his old friends had done that enough; he did not wish for his newer neighbours to pick up that refrain. Doris was dumb-founded.

"You wife is a Hindu coolie? Maan, I would never think that!"

He was pondering whether he should say anything now or wait for more privacy when a cry from Rodriques stopped him as we turned a bend and came upon rougher water with spirited wave motion and white caps. For a brief spell we had passed over deep water running smooth as glass and fast with hardly a swirl disturbing it. Then suddenly there was turbulence everywhere and shouts of "Rocks, big ones, straight ahead!"

Benn cut engine speed and deftly swung the boat to the right into what seemed the main channel. The manoeuvre plus the strong current made the boat lean sharply sending loose luggage scurrying across the floor, unbalancing it. The current carried us further to the right than the steersman intended and before he could bring it around it had brushed the side of a large black rock on that side of the channel. The contact jarred the boat to an abrupt halt, tilted it awkwardly, tipping some of the baggage and sending Doris and Jain flying into the stream. Balgobin, sitting in front, clutched a rope tied to the gunwale and avoided being pitched overboard also. As the boat canted, Bacchus, Brewster and I sitting on the left side reflexly threw our weight to the right while the natives jumped off and held on to the prow; these actions prevented the boat from capsizing.

Doris could not swim; in his panic he went under and inhaled water, but before he could be swept away, Jain who had surfaced a few feet away, quickly swam to his aid, grabbed his shirt and pulled him to the surface. Doris thrashed around, gulping water, his arms flailing in panic; one of them caught Jain on his forehead, but Jain managed to hold on to him. I hastily undressed to my underwear while Rodriques, travelling in shorts only, dived in and with powerful strokes reached them as they drifted with the current. Doris continued to thrash about as the two men dodged his flailing arms as they trod water and valiantly stayed afloat with him, oblivious of where exactly they were heading. There was no time to think of that, Jain said. "All I wanted was not drown with him."

Shouting instructions for them to subdue Doris with a knee in the solar plexus (as my lifesaving tutor had taught), I jumped into the stream carrying a rope and soon joined them. Rodriques managed to subdue Doris and was holding him from behind by an arm tightly around the forehead keeping his head above water while he pulled away from the current with his free arm and I struggled in the mêlée to tie the rope around Doris' hips. These actions relieved Jain, whose sodden clothes were impeding his own ability to stay afloat as we all drifted downstream at the edge of the current.

On signal those in the boat pulled Doris in while we steered him free of the current, head bobbing like a cork, to the safety of the offending rock. Jain, spluttering and coughing, was out of breath, but not really harmed; his boots squished soggily as he stepped on the rock. Doris was a heavy man and would almost certainly have drowned in the deep channel but for Jain's quick action and Rod's help. How sudden this incident was and how similar to the one that had ended the life of Hari's friend Zeke and that of the many men who could not swim yet dared to challenge these rushing waters following the call of duty or seeking fortune.

Once we reached shallow water and while Rod supported him from in front I let go the rope and performed two Heimlich manoeuvres with immediate expulsion of water presumably from the stomach and probably some from the oropharynx which would have obstructed air entry; we laid him prone and I pumped his chest rhythmically and was relieved that he responded quickly by frothing copiously at the mouth and nostrils. Bacchus looked at him apprehensively, "Doc, he need mouth-to mouth?"

"No, he'll be okay. But I'll do it if he needs it." I draped a towel over him, save for his head.

Doris was semi-conscious, breathing shallowly, his tongue bluish, but his pulse was good and his colour began to improve. He had a fit of coughing and brought up some more water; he made snorting noises, his body shook briefly, like a dog getting rid of wetness after a swim; he turned over, rose abruptly to a sitting position, looked around as if unseeing and called, "Where, what…?"

"You're okay, everything's fine," I reassured him, "we hit a rock and you and Jain were pitched overboard." He looked around and saw Jain sitting to one side, smiling, soaked.

"Jain saved you, with Rod and Doc." Bacchus added.

Doris' lips moved wordlessly, but his eyes showed his gratitude, and Jain squeezed his extended hand, while Rod, now standing behind him for support, patted his shoulder. Later he would hear details from Brewster, including my willingness to do mouth-to mouth respiration had he needed it: "…and Doc was ready to kiss you even!" Brewster joked; he had viewed the whole thing transfixed, but not immediately registering, so he said, the gravity of the situation.

"Never seen anything like this befo'. Everyt'ing happen so fast, I missed the photo," he complained.

"Now it's over and I see that I coulda drung, me legs tremble; now I feel the fear." Doris was coughing again.

"The fresh water in your lungs," I told him, "you'll cough for a while, helps to clear whatever's left, it's a natural reaction."

"I feel cold," he looked around him and added, to no one in particular, "Yuh got a cigarette?" "We got you a blanket and some dry clothes, but you mustn't smoke until your lungs clear."

He looked at me ruefully, silent for what seemed a long time and at last found words.

"I nearly drung, Doc," he said, with uncharacteristic meekness, "now yuh goin' punish me?"

"It's for your own good, a cigarette now will add to the damage from the sweet water; hold off for a while. Not long." I said as soothingly as I could.

He looked at me squarely, then said, "I thank everybody and God for what you all did. Especially you, Mr Jain."

"No 'thank you' nercessary, I already have this leetle present from you,"

Jain rejoined, laughing, pointing to a small bump just above his left eye. Everyone laughed, relieved by the levity, and turned attention to the other casualties: the boat and the drowned baggage.

While the drama was playing out in the water, the boat had remained unsteady, tossing in the turbulent eddies. Together Benn, Joe and the others had moved it clear of the rock and guided it towards a safe spot near the bank. It was uncertain whether any damage had occurred. Now we had to recover the baggage. Adam and Joe had already entered the water and located the bundle near the narrow channel in about four feet of water. Joe tied a rope around it while the others perched on the rock dragged it back there. The bundle was the last one put in the boat that morning and had not been tethered to the gunwale, as it should have been. It contained a miscellany of utensils, a lamp, our camp stove, a stack of blankets and a box with technical supplies. Fortunately the waterproof wrapper had held firm and on opening it, only the surface showed wetness; most of the blankets were spared.

Our dependence on one another and the drama of the incident gradually eased the tension that had followed the discussion on politics. Conversation became easier again, as it had been before. Perhaps we had spoken freely then because we had come to understand one another and could see that we could *live* together, accept open disagreements, since there was already ample evidence from the society at large that we could *work* together. Even Doris appeared to relax his sullenness and the enforced politeness in dealing with us Indians that had been so painfully obvious, to me at least, from the start. I had thought it a feature of his personality until I got to know him better. Benn, who knew him the longest, used to tease him for being a "sour puss." The need to avoid the perils of the current phase of our journey focussed our behaviours and for the time at least we forgot our differences and concentrated on teamwork.

Doris became quite subdued, physically shaken by the accident and humbled by the spontaneous and brave actions taken by an Indian to save him. "You would do same, Corporal." Jain reassured him.

We spread the wet stuff out on the rock to dry while Benn, Rodriques, Mike and Joe scoured the boat's keel for damage. The rest of us just sat there staring emptily at the surging waters ahead, criss-crossed by fallen trees, a familiar scene that was becoming increasingly distressing, if that were possible. But we felt better for the unplanned and cooling swim and thankful for the outcome.

About fifteen minutes later Benn announced that he was satisfied that the boat was intact, save for a surface bruise, and we resumed our journey. Doris said he felt better and to us appeared none the worse for his adventure save for a residual cough. I advised and Bacchus ordered him to rest for the remainder of that day. "And remember: don't smoke, at least for now." Doris grimaced, pained at the thought of abstinence, but a short bout of coughing helped to boost his reluctant resolve.

"There should be a life jacket on board for people like him," I said, almost pointlessly, knowing full well that no one would wear one in the kind of humid heat each day brought.

We had entered the roughest stage of the rapids and would soon come to the point where the river dropped three or four feet in three short steps over a five to six-yard distance. On the upriver journey the passage had been tricky, but it would be tougher going downstream. The sun had risen high in the southern sky by the time the boat steadied itself in the main current among eddies that warned of hidden obstacles.

The reflection of the trees on both sides of the river rippled as the wave from the boat rolled towards the banks. Ahead we could see a clear smooth stream meandering through rougher water strewn with *tacubas* and boulders, giving an illusion of a stream within a stream. We aimed for the smooth water, which was flowing faster than it looked, foretelling the drop that lay ahead. We too had begun to move faster than the slow putter of the engine suggested, and Benn warned us to be prepared for the descent, adding in a mutter something about "luck and the angels". Fortunately the rapids were near the centre of a straight stretch. This would give us time to spot it and prepare to deal with it.

We proceeded gingerly, keeping to the middle of the channel, pausing to clear debris and thankful that we had so far escaped a major obstruction. The passageways cleared a week earlier had remained patent and still negotiable, thus preventing additional delays. The boat was at times doing an exhilarating 5 or 6 knots and significantly better than the previous day. The steady pace lifted spirits somewhat and in a sense prepared us for any delay that the imminent rapids would surely cause.

We had gone about an hour under the blazing early afternoon sun when we noticed a change in the pull of the current and more pronounced swirls; foam flecked the surface increasingly, and as we rounded a bend, we could see in the middle distance the configuration of boulders that marked the menacing cataract that would challenge our collective ingenuity to prevent serious damage to the boat, avoid being stranded or worse, suffer injury here in the middle of nowhere.

Benn advised that he would berth above the rocks and scout the site before attempting to cross. We might have to unload the boat, he said, park the baggage on the big bare rocks above the rapids near the bank, remove the engine and move the boat over with the help of ropes. The process would be slow, but safer than trying to cross with the load. In either case all persons would disembark, save Benn who would steer the boat and give instructions, and Rod to man the prow.

From a hundred yards off we could hear the low roar of the mainstream as it hit the rocks and see the iridescent spray that rose from the foot of the cataract.

"Water still low, worse than last week; it don't look too good." Benn observed, while the rest of us just stared and listened as he manoeuvred the craft close to a cluster of rocks on the left bank of the stream, still in full sun. Rodriques, Joe and Mike took to the water, each with a rope, two tied to the stern and one to the left side of the bow. A fourth, tied to the right side of the bow was untied and secured to the left side also. The men were soon in knee-deep water among the rocks. The current was even at this distance strong enough to pull the boat sideways and it took the combined efforts of the three men and Benn's rudder to hold its course and ease it safely to a berth in the shallows.

The engine died with a shudder, the anchor was released, and the long pole plunged against the right side into the river bottom so as to prevent the boat from swinging out towards the nearby rocks. From here it was a short walk over rocks and shallow water to the main drop, and most of us went, Doris remaining safely and meekly stretched out on a large flat rock while Mike and Joe held on to their ropes to ensure that the boat remained safely berthed. Voices rose in curious chatter above the noise of the water. Soon we were close enough to see the cataract.

"Not good," Benn confirmed.

The water cascaded in several stages, the first a fall of about two feet between two rocks six feet apart, the one on the right set about a yard in front of the other. The space between them seemed to carry the bulk of the flow, and was the source of the loudest roar and the tall spume created when the jets of water hit the lower rock. On the right smaller rocks more closely placed dotted the river to the bank. No chance of a crossing could be seen there. Near to us and to the left were more rocks where the water tumbled and played in foaming swirls and deep gurgling calls, fell a foot or so onto partly covered rocks then ran to the right sharply and tumbled again over a ledge for about two feet. Foaming and bubbling, the water hurried downstream to join the main flow. In the distance the stream widened and the turbulence eased, persisting only in the shallows near the banks.

The left side looked much more treacherous than the right. So we were back examining the central zone and the flow between the two large rocks. Once past the second rock the water smoothed out somewhat for about four feet then tumbled, frothing and fuming noisily as it fell another two feet, but gradually over several yards, steadied itself and headed forward, pausing only to complain at several tree trunks, up to a foot diameter, that were stuck in its path. It was clear that the central section was the only one deep enough to take the boat, but the force of the water could dash it against the second big rock and perhaps wreck it. We could try to portage the boat, but it was too heavy to carry and in any case there was no path along either bank, to take men or rollers, which we could have obtained from fallen trees. But the banks were steep and moss-covered, and as rocky and uneven as the riverbed.

After considering the alternatives, Benn decided on a plan, "Inspector, I think the best way down is to empty the boat. I will paddle it into the current; Rodriques will come with me an' take the pole. Two, three, four of you will hold de boat back and de rest must stand on that rock," he paused pointing to a flat one just below the one we then occupied, "hold de lines and only release when I say so. Once we cross those two," he pointed to the major threats, the rest should be alright."

"But what about the second drop?" Inspector Bacchus asked.

"The water look rough, yes." Benn replied, "but it deep enough; that's why we have to go down slow and make a quick turn to the lef'; to do that I need yuh all to hold the prow straight and pull hard once it reach close to that rock," he pointed to the second rock, smooth, black and menacing, against which the water pounded.

"I will start to go down from the right; that will give me room to clear both, but I can't steer it clear, me alone." He looked around. After checking that we all understood he said simply, "To besides, Inspector, that's the only way. It tricky, but I think we can make it; we have the manpower; is up to you." The Inspector considered briefly, then nodded

"We have no choice; we can't walk, we can't stay here. Let's go, then."

It must have been near two o'clock when we finally emptied the boat, placing everything on dry rocks by the bank; Benn had completed his preparations, making sure all lines had been placed securely where he wanted them. He, Joe and Rodriques had collected a quantity of wattle, each cut about three feet long which Moses lashed to the right side of the prow with vines and flexible bark Adam had cut, to cushion any impact that might occur. "Better put some on the lef' side too, to balance it," Benn said to Rodriques, "it might help to slow us down too." That done, we rehearsed our roles and responses to Benn's commands.

Two teams were arranged: Bacchus, Jain, Adam, Moses and Doris (he refused to be left out) would hold the boat back on two stern lines, while Brewster, Balgobin, Joe, Mike and I would work the prow lines. Because the prow lines were not long enough to span the distance from our action station to the boat's anchoring position, it fell to Rodriques to throw them to us when the boat neared us and for me to catch them and pass one to Brewster who would man it with Joe, while Balgobin and Mike would grab the second one which I would retain.

Rodriques practised his throw a few times and I my catching and passing. Having grown up on a farm managing cattle I had learned early to throw and catch rope, and as an active cricketer and a good catcher of the flying cricket ball, this was not a big problem, even though the flying object was a rope; so much depended on direction and timing, not so easy in a river, and following through that we spent some time practising until we were comfortable.

I chose my final position on the rock and Rod threw the coils of sodden rope in a long arc. The ropes behaved well each time, and arrived like two snakes about to pounce, swishing through the air, trailing water and curving in such a way I was able to grab them each time and pass them on smoothly. The men took the passes easily after initial fumbles. But I remained fearful that at the critical time something might go wrong.

The practice enabled me to place Joe and Brewster in the best position to receive the pass and Mike and Balgobin to successfully grab the rope I retained. It was essential that I catch both at once, as Rodriques would not have enough time to throw the ropes individually. Joe was positioned also to catch one should the lines separate too much for me to grab them at the same time. Meanwhile the other team tested how much force was required to hold the boat back. All actions would be carried out on Benn's signals. Thus prepared, we took up our positions.

Rodriques stood at the prow, bare to his shorts, his bronze skin glistening, two coils of rope in front of him; he leaned against the pole and slowly moved the boat into the current, while Benn steered with the paddle. The rudder had been removed for fear it would be too long to negotiate the drop, and perhaps impede rather than help, or get broken. The paddle would have to do. It was a large heavy and broad object and quite effective ordinarily; Benn was cautiously confident that it would work well in the conditions; we would soon find out.

The stern lines held the boat to a slow even pace as it worked its way over to the right, then turn left, Benn pulling hard on the oar and Rodriques steadying with the pole. In the middle the water was about eight feet deep, a good sign. Presently the prow came within thirty feet of the rock, Rodriques stowed his pole, and picked up the lines to toss over to us. He shouted, "Ready!" We stood tense, praying that the throw be successful, for the practices had been done from a more stable stance. Rod was powerfully built and had shown his strength on a number of occasions. But this was critical. The help from us was crucial as the rightward sweep of the current was too much for Benn alone to counter. At the stern the lines were taut as the men strained against the force of the current.

Suddenly, like swimmers at a starter's pistol the lines from Rodriques flew in the air across the foaming hurry of the stream but just before reaching me one snapped on itself and fell in the water. I caught the other and Balgobin grabbed hold of the end. Quickly Joe jumped into the shallow eddies and grabbed the wayward rope just as it was about to slip over the edge of a rock. Brewster grabbed Joe's outstretched hand and helped him clamber on to the rock. But as Joe stepped onto the rock, Brewster, holding his left hand and moving backward slipped on the smooth surface and fell hard on his ample behind. But he held on to the rope, wet in his hand, got up with Joe's help, moaning in pain. But we had no time to think of consequences.

"Is okay," he said, hesitantly, as I shouted, "Hold steady."

We braced against the ropes becoming taut as the boat, now firmly in the clutch of the current moved ominously into the passage towards the rocks and threatening to take us with it. Benn was working his paddle frantically; Rodriques had resumed poling on the starboard bow as the boat lurched forward and downward in a great splash. The motion jerked us forward and all nearly fell but I had warned the men and we had taken positions rather in the fashion of a tug-o'-war, hands draped in kerchiefs or towels. Feeling the weight of the boat as it lurched forward in the strong current the five of us were hardly a match but we leaned back and held the strain. We lost sight of the boat momentarily and instinctively I called to the others to "pull hard". No noise of crushing timber reached us.

We strained as hard as we could, with grunts and groans and slipping feet, until the forward lunge of the boat as it bolted down the second drop tore the lines from our hands and sent them flying like kite tails down the stream.

For a moment we saw nothing and heard only the roar of the opaque water. Then through the thick spray we could see Rodriques crouched at the prow on the right side of the boat, and Benn emerging like a ghost from the drenching spray, his black skin shining wet, and small rippling rainbows over and around him like coloured halos and streamers.

It was quite a sight. But he was still furiously working his paddle, struggling to regain control to guide the boat to a safe place, and avoid damage from other unseen menace. The rest of us stood expectantly, watching the craft carried sideways by the current and already some fifty yards downstream. But it was staying afloat, not listing and the two men were frantically pumping away with oar and pole to bring it under control. Soon they were pointing it prow first although heading a bit too quickly, it seemed, for a huge trunk that obstructed half the river about a hundred yards further away.

"Oh shit," Brewster said, above the pain of his bruised coccyx, "he gwine crash!"

"Oh, rass," came from Balgobin, simultaneously, "look, 'e going straight into the tree!"

And so they were, and fairly quickly too, in the swift current, despite their vigorous reversing moves. We watched with nail-biting anxiety as the boat's pace slowed yet the fallen tree appeared to be rushing to meet it.

But with Rod's spirited use of the pole to turn the prow to the left and Benn complementing that with the paddle, they managed to steer it out of the current, slowed its pace further and guided it towards the smallest branches of the tree with which it collided with a crash of splintering wood, and came to a halt like a leaf caught on a rock, Rod jumping clear while Benn in the rear crouched low to avoid being speared by breaking boughs. The boat rocked to a stop, its prow high, and listed to starboard; Rod grabbed hold of the boat to keep it from capsizing, though that was not likely because of the steadying effect of low submerged boughs to the right of the craft.

"Geeez us!" Brewster exclaimed, "they friggin' lucky!"

They had stopped perilously close to the huge trunk. Gingerly they tied up to the trunk, examined the boat as well as they could, grateful that the tree had acted not only as a brake, but as a dock. Slowly they made their way to the bank, stepping first on the tree and wading from rock to rock to reach the ledge, mount it and walk--visibly shaken and exhausted-- to where we were. As they neared us, we gave them a loud cheer and congratulatory remarks, and in the fashion of school boys at a victorious sporting event would have fetched our heroes "home" on our shoulders, had the setting been favourable.

Responding to our congratulations, Benn said, "I thought we gone! I nearly shit me pants when ah see that big tacuba rushin' to catch we!"

Rodriques smiled briefly and in his taciturn way simply said, "Maan, that was close; I didn't think the two ah we could ah turn she 'round."

Benn gave him a look that was at once grateful and admiring.

"Boy, you really strong. Anybaddy else besides you with me there today, and we dead!" He paused dramatically. "You use that pole like an engine. Boy, you good, you good as gold!"

He put an arm around the younger man's shoulders and squeezed him affectionately. If Rod or any of his race needed any proof of fitness to serve, as had been questioned, his performance in this mission should be evidence enough to remove stereotypes and quell doubts.

Benn admitted, "And to think, when ah first meet you, ah say to meself, 'what de hell they send me this time?' Boy, I so glad today it was you! I hope they keep you at Mabaruma, and not send you to Pomeroon!"

That was high praise from Benn whose reverence for engines was a legend in his unit.

Inspector Bacchus was concerned for his men.

"You chaps okay?" he asked, after congratulating them.

"But for the drenching and some water that went dung the wrong way, I okay," said Benn, coughing lightly as Rod nodded assent.

"How about the rest of you?" he continued, looking around. Thus he learned of Brewster's fall, and that Jain had stripped some skin off his right hand, abraded by the rope. Most of us had some degree of hand soreness and bruising, but Jain had substantial tears on the palms of his hands. He had neglected to wrap them the way the rest of us had done, and was unfortunate enough not to get away with it. I examined the injuries. Jain had already washed off strands of fibre from his wounds, the cold fresh water causing him to yelp with the sharp burning pain.

He had suffered a transverse three centimetre excoriation mainly on the two eminences on either side of the hollow of the right palm, rather angry-looking, with full-thickness skin loss from a patch at the inner side of the base of the left thumb, consistent with his stance on the right of the rope, right hand forward. It continued to smart and he winced at the sight. He took two aspirins and I applied an antibiotic ointment from our meagre store and dressed it with a leaf that Hari had given me, one customarily used by the natives for skin wounds, and smilingly endorsed by Joe with "Good, good." (I had taken several of the leaves and pieces of bark with the intention of getting them identified at the Ministry of Agriculture in Georgetown, and somehow get them tested. There was no information on how effective the leaf was when dry. But Hari had been effusive about its properties when used freshly picked.)

"Put this on, let's see how it works."

"So I must be your guinea pig?" he queried, half serious, and I nodded. "No better chance!"

Within a few minutes of applying the dressing Jain announced, "This leaf seems to work; the pain is less and the hands feel cool."

He would later repeatedly voice his relief. Brewster willingly lay on the rock face down in his underpants while I tried to assess the damage from his fall. His clothing had prevented bruising and he had a tender coccyx; I could not be sure whether he had fractured the tip. In any event there was nothing we would do for that beyond providing pain relief. He swallowed two aspirins.

"This is one time that extra padding on the rear comes in handy, but the bruised fat and muscle will be sore for a while. The major hurt, Constable," I teased, addressing him with mock formality, "is to your pride." For some reason the Inspector found that funny. "Inside joke," he explained.

For the remainder of the journey Brewster would shift his weight from one side to the other of his ample buttocks, and stand whenever the opportunity arose. His pain gradually eased.

"How's the boat?" the Inspector asked. We had been lucky indeed and Benn would periodically shake his head in wonderment that we had gotten off with the hull virtually unscathed. No appreciable damage could be seen on the prow where it had made contact with the tree as the impact had been absorbed by the padding of green wattle that had been tied there. A few scratch marks scored the surface where the boat had dragged along the sharp end of a broken branch.

"We'll take it easy and watch for leaks; we goin' slow enough anyway." Benn said.

While these things were happening Rod had left to supervise Moses and Adam as they carried the engine back to the boat; he felt revived from the brief rest and his spirits warmed with a nip of *highwine* the Inspector had given them as they shivered from the drenching they had sustained. When all was ready, Joe and Mike were backpacked and with each of us sharing the rest of the load, took off along the craggy bank, slipping and sliding on the mossy rocks, sustaining knocks and bruises, but luckily without serious accident, and reached the boat.

The advance group had managed to haul the craft past the tree along a narrow shallow lane of smooth water barely deep enough to prevent grounding, and had tied it close to a large flat rock on which we deposited everything for reloading. Benn placed the engine in its cradle, muttering his gratitude to the legendary river gods and to their great Master above. On the far side of the big rock the water was deep enough for safe starting and the manoeuvrings needed to turn the boat around. That done we embarked and Benn eased the boat downstream into the fast flowing water; everyone resumed his vigilance for obstructions. Joe took over from Rodriques at the prow with pole in hand after Benn suggested in a noticeably gentle way that the younger man "have a little rest".

The need to cooperate to ensure success of the manoeuvre and the drama of the incident dispelled any residual tension.. Balgobin had earlier observed that the boatful of us was like laboratory rats in a cage, expected to attack each other and behave frenziedly in circumstances of stress. Instead we were behaving cooperatively; indeed, our mandate did not allow us to behave discreditably, but none of us analysed it thus at the time.

Doris became more relaxed and soon was initiating conversation and exchanging banter with Balgobin, who sat closest to him and remained his good-natured foil throughout the journey. Doris actually smiled briefly in some of these exchanges, the first time I had seen him smile, a nice smile that lit up his face.

"You have a nice smile Corporal;" I complimented him; "you should use it more often."

He looked at me like an urchin caught in a naughty act. I was pleased to see his face relax, and he smiled fleetingly once more, and said, humbly, "You got me there, Doc."

Presently we came to a point where the river received two tributaries but each had been reduced to a mere ten feet width of foot-deep water (while the watermarks on their banks showed that they could be four feet deep and fifty feet wide). Gradually the turbulence lessened and we soon entered a stretch, where but for the threat of sunken logs, the going was the easiest we had had for two days.

Rodriques had been listening to the natives' conversation. From time to time they would look at us and laugh, and on occasion laughed heartily. It turned out that this was the first time they had seen a boat such as ours shoot those "rapids", in fact the first time any of them had seen any kind of boat there with water so low. A canoe would have made the passage more nimbly and with less dramatics, but may just as easily have been swamped by the turbulence. But then a canoe, especially a woodskin, would have been portaged! The amusement was the natives' way of expressing their surprise at the feat they had witnessed and the laughter approval of the way it had succeeded and of those involved, themselves included. I had seen this reaction before and would see it later on returning to Cokerite, the shy smiles of approval and admiration that illumined their faces. It was a pleasure to witness their show of emotion, accustomed as we had become to their impassive faces.

Joe related stories of coastal folk shooting rapids on the upper Cuyuni, the larger river thirty or so miles to the south, on which he had travelled for several years as a guide. The boats were generally smaller than ours, perhaps 16 or 18 feet long, and lighter. If there were enough men and the terrain suitable for portage, that way would be preferred as it almost guaranteed the safety of the boat (he had seen a boat slipping down a ravine and cracking its keel on impact with hard rock). Portaging was a tedious undertaking, involving unpacking and repacking the craft, and much to-ing and fro-ing to get that done.

An ingenious way of doing the same was to erect stilts and hoist the boat on them, then attach levers made of stout saplings to pass the boat from one set of stilts to another and so traverse the rapids. The method was useful where the water was shallow enough for men to work in and handle the contraptions. In shallow water too, men would sometimes pull boats upstream or restrain them on a downstream run, in much the way we had done, and facing the same risk of damage from precipitate movement against immovable rocks. The upstream task was generally safer. Lives had been lost in these exercises, and much injury suffered from falls and other mishaps, from minor wounds such as Jain's and Brewster's, to broken bones, crushed limbs and near drownings.

The afternoon was going fast, and everyone was getting hungrier. We had spent over two hours preparing for the traverse of the cataract, and had had a meagre snack before. Cigarettes had kept my hunger at bay, and sips of coffee from my thermos plus occasional handfuls of the clear river water, which we all drank copiously, filled gastric spaces from time to time. I wondered what wondrous parasites we might be drinking, and so retained samples labelled as to precise time, date and place of collection as identified on our map, for later testing. We did, of course carry boiled water, but it was soon exhausted and it not always possible to avoid drinking from the tasty stream.

Jokingly I said that a simple steriliser would be a shot of rum in the water, and the men were willing to seize on this until I pointed out that the dilution would reduce the percentage far too low for use as a steriliser. In any event the high wine they carried was at most 60% alcohol, and my brandy 44%, neither a steriliser, though the former, undiluted, might with prolonged contact deactivate or denature bacteria and viruses. Spores, protozoa and other parasites would be more resistant. Hypochlorite would have been preferred. In the ten days since we had first drunk the water, thankfully no one had reported any symptoms. But a lengthier period of observation was needed to clear us of any ingested parasite.

These rivers were not known for harmful parasites, like Guinea worms in West Africa, though leeches were plentiful in the shallow streams, and species of Schistosomes had been identified in at least one canal in a coastal sugar plantation. My water samples would hopefully give us some insight into any pathogenic life forms.

We kept a steady pace, pausing from time to time to clear obstructions, and once to chop a path through a newly-fallen tree. In most cases we were able to find the openings we had made on the upstream journey, but shifts and unknown other occurrences had displaced or obscured several. I read a little, napped a few minutes and conversed on various things, mostly the state of supplies and speculations on how we would make contact with Georgetown, and what our families were now thinking, or were being told by Police authorities. We were running quite low on fuel for the boat, and Benn nursed what little he had by pacing the engine at the lowest throttle needed for control. The fairly brisk flow of the current was a welcome help, but its speed had slowed considerably since we left the rapids. Thus we coasted along, at three to four knots, under the sharp and shining sky, now picking up a few wisps of cloud from all the moisture that had risen during the hot morning.

We all prayed, I'm sure, as I did, for some rain, any amount, any time, but none had come. The few clouds that did form in the afternoons would stream off to the west, there to linger and thicken, then gather some spectacular colour in the later afternoon, with soft merging feathers of gold, orange and crimson against a pale blue sky. But no rain fell. And so it was in the mid-afternoon, around three thirty o'clock, as we began to scout for a place to camp, that we came to a point where the river widened, its stream split by a sand bank, an islet really, thick with trees, which had narrowed the channel on either side. The right looked safer and deeper, and as we rounded its curving bank we saw a wisp of smoke rising from the edge of the water and smelled the smell of smoking flesh, seconds before Doris's sharp eyes saw them, and he exclaimed, "Bucks! An' they have meat! They smokin' meat, Lawd help us!"

They were about a hundred yards away to our left, their two canoes beached, the smoke rising from two spits in the sand. They must have gotten there no more than half an hour earlier as we would soon find out. Two men, a youth, two women and a little boy could be seen, "Caribs," said Doris. "From the look of it they went hunting, and got meat. Maybe some fish too. I'll see what I can get from them. Let's go easy. Rodriques, Joe and me will go bargain with them."

The natives watched our boat approach, and looked at the tall men and the four natives, apprehensively. The child ran to one of the women squatting on the beach fanning a fire, clutched at her and almost bowled her over burying his head in her breast; she sat back on the sand and hugged him. They were short, small-boned people of the same pale yellow complexion as our porters. Caribs were said to be of ancient Mongolian origin, after all, but coastal Chinese did not consider them kith or kin. As we came alongside, the men stood together facing us and partly obscured the spits.

"I know that one!" Doris announced as he waved to the men on the beach, "I met him on my first trip to Wappai. I believe his village is south of here, some miles, up that creek we passed a while ago, or maybe the next one down." Then he said to Benn. "Tie up ahead. I'll talk to them. Maybe we could get a share of their hunt."

It was a custom on the river to share supplies with travellers in need of food. Each situation was assessed and appropriate action taken. Refusals were rare.

Doris debarked and with Joe and Rodriques, walked back along the narrow beach to the campsite. A few minutes later, curious as to what was going on, I followed the path they had taken around the bend until I had a clear view of the campsite nestling cosily under a canopy of low boughs and protected on three sides by thick bush flourishing on the bank against a backdrop of taller, more stately trees. Doris was off to one side with the men, speaking to their leader animatedly, mostly with his hands, while Joe and Rod translated, both haltingly, as Joe had first to get the gist of what Doris was saying, and Rod was only vaguely familiar with the particular dialect of this group.

Doris towered over them. Rodriques, the tallest of the rest, was 5ft 6ins, a good two inches taller than the other natives. The women, squatting, were almost invisible in the background. The negotiations were a slow process with much repetition and correction. Nevertheless they eventually seemed to understand one another, as there was much nodding, vigorous dissenting and head shaking, punctuating periods of non-committal and motionless attention. From time to time one of them, Doris mainly, would gesture and point to the objects that occupied the centre of the camp.

The two holes in the ground were overlain with a low frame of fresh-cut wood covered with green leaves through which the smoke filtered and rose straight up in thick grey and black plumes. One hole was oval, three feet long, the other a narrow rectangle seven feet long, like a shallow grave. On the first was a black shape looking like a pig and on the other a six feet long caiman, its jaws bound. Off to one side were two closed straw baskets. I caught Doris's eye and pointed to my camera. He spoke to the men, signalled all clear but the men turned away while I took two or three shots of the camp.

I walked back to the boat and related what I had seen. Balgobin and Brewster wanted to see the crocodile smoking in the deep shadow of the tall trees, so off they went, peeked, and soon returned. Presently Doris, Rod and Joe in tow, came back smiling, holding aloft a large leg of meat.

"Watrash!" he announced jubilantly.

"Great! Oh, man, great! How did you get so much?" Brewster, thrilled, wanted to know. He had been so disappointed that the watrash had so far proved elusive, not the daily fare he had anticipated.

"He good at beggin'," teased Benn as he started the engine and prepared to leave.

"I told him I wanted a piece of croc tail, that's how." Doris replied.

"I don' get it; you ask for a piece of crocodile tail and you get a whole watrash leg; how come?" Bacchus was puzzled, as was everyone else.

"He always get a nice slice of thigh whenever he ask for a piece o' tail!" Benn could not resist the jibe as everyone laughed and Doris pretended he didn't hear it.

"Is like this," he explained, "they will never give 'way crocodile tail. Is de sweetest part of the beast. I know them. If you push for tail they will give you what you really want."

"Especially when you is police," Balgobin chimed in, jokingly.

Doris grimaced, but continued, "Is de watrash I did really want, not crocodile; never eat the thing. Anyway I sweeten the deal; I give them one of my long knives, and my last pack of Four Ace. Doc, you will have to help me out with a few; I hope you have some left." It was gratifying to see how genial he had become and I gladly said "yes, but you should hold off until the cough really clears".

While he spoke he took care to put the meat safely away, and by his animation you could guess how anxiously he anticipated dinner that night. His bright mood was as comforting to us as his apparent return to physical health. He hadn't coughed for over an hour.

Brewster said, "Now that was a sight; I never before see or hear 'bout alligator or crocodile on a spit. I didn't see it too good from where I was, Felix, what it look like?" he asked with interest. In truth Doris had hardly looked at the beast, but Rod and I had.

"Is not alligator," Rod said; he spoke so rarely his voice attracted immediate attention. "Is really a *caiman*, a type o' crocodile that live in these parts. You can tell from the wide dark and light stripes 'cross the back. The coast people in Venezuela, the Warrau, call it *baba*."

I had seen those wide black stripes and the snout before. Caimans were fierce and would attack humans, but their main food was small animals and fish. Rodriques went on to explain that when the river was "high" the caiman was not that easy to catch, but at low water, starting late in the year, they often got trapped in the shallower streams in pools isolated from the main stream making them vulnerable to their main predators, man and the anaconda. He added with irony, "They like to go to those pools to feed on trapped fish, make nest nearby to lay eggs and that's the time to catch them."

"In India, in Ganga River, the big gharial is 15, 18 feet long, like I said before." Jain said, "though I nevair seen one. I read somewhere that the longest one known was 23 feet."

"They're different from these; they have a long narrow snout and crawl on their bellies. We had nests of caimans at DeHoop just like the one I saw back there."

Bacchus turned to Benn, "I'm jus' lookin' at the map here. If the river don' get worse, we should make Cokerite tomorrow, early afternoon. We should stop a little early since we have the meat to cook, and with all the injuries the men need a little rest. What d'you say, Corporal?" He smiled, not wanting an answer, knowing how much his men were looking forward to a good meal.

Doris nodded vigorously, and said, "Sure, sure."

"First good spot I come to, I'll dock." Benn agreed

The river widened a little and though littered with fallen branches and trunks, presented a navigable zigzag path through the debris. Minutes later we came to the sandy beach, just west of the *Wiamu* River, where we had camped that first night out from Cokerite nine days ago. Spirits were high, fuelled by the improved mood of the police at the prospect of a square meal, as they set about preparing their dinner. In quick time, the "leg"--a hindquarter really--was skinned, the meat salted and spiced with condiments from Balgobin who proceeded to make our dinner of canned sardines and boiled rice.

It had been a rough day for everyone. The sky was still bright; we had a good two hours before dark. Inspector Bacchus rummaged through his pack and found his bottle of highwine, offered it around and poured himself a drink. I brought out my brandy bottle. The two bottles stood there perched on the rock we had chosen as both chair and table.

The others not involved in the food preparation, Jain and Brewster joined us. It was pleasant to sit in the glow of the sky and not rush through the preparations for the night. Each day we had pushed our slow and cautious travel to the very edge of night then hurried in the closing minutes to establish camp, wash off the day's sweat, dine sparingly and dive into our hammocks under the cover of nets to escape the bombinating hordes that descended as soon as the light had gone.

Today in this calm afternoon, hot with the sweat that would like a magnet bring out the insects later, we had ample time to cool down in the fresh water, then sit, or lie back, as I did, under the canopy of turquoise sky, watch the streaks of cirrus that had formed like veils across the dome, hardly moving. The forest closed in on either bank and ran thickly forward and back in diminishing lines, which merged low and innocently on the horizon. Close to us it looked so menacing, but in a curiously paradoxical way, so fragile, unable to prevent the death or downfall of its members littering the stream in both directions. Shades of Hari's thinking, I mused.

What would it take to harvest these fallen giants, to use them for some noble purpose, to spare the living ones that stood tall and reached so bravely for the sky? The lines of a song came to me: *Two things that I would never see, A poem lovely as a tree, A tree that looks at God all day, And lifts its lonely arms to pray, A tree that may in summer bear A nest of robins in her hair* … (Here it would be parrots, macaws or toucan more likely, or a cluster of rare orchids.)

Looking around I saw a cleared area at the forest edge extending for about a hundred yards from the far bank and covered with a disorderly growth of shrubs and other young growths almost obliterating split shattered trunks, standing and fallen, now bare and dry and scattered higgledy-piggledy through the area.

It was an unusual sight, as if someone had some time ago thrown a bomb among the trees. This was not the orderly clearing of a site to prepare it for cultivation. No habitation was even close. Nor was there any trace or history of one. Even the natives were perplexed. Perhaps it was lightning, someone suggested, but the area affected was too large.

As I stared at it I recalled a scene in Erich Maria Remarque's book *All Quiet on the Western Front* in which he described troops under fire near a wood, crescendos of noise swelling, thundering as shells burst ahead of the men. Then a second mighty explosion was heard to one side of their position and as they watched they saw a part of the forest slowly rise up into the air, the trees fractured and tossed about, appearing to float an instant then crash to pieces in an irregular heap, sending clouds of dust and debris into the air. The scene before us looked like the aftermath of such a debacle, but no such thing had happened here.

Was it lightning as suggested, or as I preferred to think, had a meteor struck this place? In 1935 one had landed in the Rupununi creating a comparable destruction and repair. If indeed a meteor had landed here, which one of the huge rocks in the area was it? It was a fascinating thought. The similarity to the devastation Remarque described was uncanny.

A few birds, too far for recognition circled to the west, as if seeking the sun, perhaps attracted by the smell of meat rising from the hunters' camp. I sipped my drink, even as Jain did his, while Bacchus and Brewster threw their first abruptly down their gullets in the popular fashion, followed immediately by a large swallow of water, then a satisfying cry of "aaahh" to signal that the feeling was good.

The highwine was strong and I had wondered for years what practice it took for men to drink in that particular way. Sure, I knew it was the fashion among men in several countries, but I had not learned it, having developed what little drinking skills or tastes I had, on a University campus where I nursed my drink of beer or booze to savour the taste, or make it last, since more often than not, one drink was all that I could afford.

I asked the men about this style of drinking, compared to sipping. "The highwine must hit the back of your throat and warm the gullet down to the stomach; it's a good feeling, wake up your appetite," Bacchus said. "This is how we always drink. Not that I mind sipping after downing' the first snap." ("Snap" was the colloquial name some gave to a drink taken at a gulp (a corruption of 'schnapp').

"Ever tried it?" he asked.

"Yes," I said, "once, by force."

"What happened?" I told them my story.

I was living with the Latchmans, and had gone one Sunday morning with Sukhdeo, then 17, on an errand to Vryheid, about three miles south of town to see Mr John, a black farmer friend of Mr Latchman's with whom he exchanged vegetables for ground provisions and bananas. After exchanging baskets, he brought out a bottle of crystal clear liquid announcing, "Befo' you go you 'ave to share mi 'ospitality."

He sat us at a small oblong cedar table filling one corner of the narrow gallery that formed the back section of the house, carefully removed the metal cap from the bottle, sniffed it, smiled, saying, "ah, good, good!" smacking his lips. The smell was sweetish, but pungent, and almost overpowering. It looked like Bayrum, which many rural households used as an antiseptic and contained methanol, which we had been warned never to drink. Mr John ignored my discomfort, asked my age, and when I said I had just turned 11, he remarked, "You old enough to take a drink now and then; you got to learn; soon you goin' look woman!"

He thereupon took three shot glasses from a shelf on the wall above the table and poured a glass for himself and Sukhdeo, and half for me. I winced. I had never drunk alcohol, nor wished any, and had no desire to "look woman".

"It will make me blind," I protested. Besides, my mother had given me strict injunctions not to accept drinks from strangers, mindful of what had happened to her father so many years ago in India.

He looked sternly at me, "You t'ink me go give you bad drink, baye? This is pure liquor, the purest cane liquor you can find in all Berbice; even the police buy from me. Now drink up."

He then showed us how to drink and insisted that we follow and "down de drink, like a man!"

And so with great trepidation we did just as he had shown us. My mouth and throat and soon my whole body caught fire, which the companion shot glass of water and additional dousing with a full glass of water failed to put out. Both of us went home tipsy and I felt nauseous, my head swinging. Thankfully Mr and Mrs Latchman had gone out for the day and would miss the deep sleep into which we both had sunk for several hours, and I felt stale even after a shower.

Inspector Bacchus related a similar initiation by his own father when he was twelve; his reaction was similar, and taught him to handle alcohol with respect. He did not have another drink until he was 17, at Christmas dinner that year! Some discussion of alcohol use followed; and of the preventive value of a "scorching introduction" to liquor such as we had had. Bacchus noted that the Irish would take their pubertal sons to the local pub and initiate him by repeated exposure, which enabled the lads to develop a tolerance for the stuff. We traded Police and medical experiences with drunks and addicts; few policemen cared to arrest drunks, as they often had to do, and dealing with addicts was a sobering business. The talk of arrests and police work led the Inspector to a point of increasing concern for him and his colleagues.

"I'm really worried about what's happening in town; I don' like the way politics is shapin' up." His deep baritone faltered as he wrestled with his thoughts, wondering, I suspected, how much he could say. In fact this was one of the first occasions that he had broached a political topic; but, as he said later, he had come to regard us all as confidantes. He took a drink.

"You know, Doc, I don' talk about these things. As a policeman, I do my duty; I try to be fair. I have a brother in the Force, a detective sergeant, a good one, a real crime fighter; he likes the big cases, the worst ones that nobody want; he 'fraid o' nothing. He spend his time in the streets, much more than me, among the people, all kinds, poor, rich, black, brown, white, Chinese. The day before we left for this trip to Wappai he told me that he was getting afraid for people, for the ordinary people who use the streets every day going about their business, bothering no one. He feels real trouble coming, and soon. He's now chasing a major group doing crime all over town, while sheltering under all the political protests we have to deal with."

He paused and sipped his drink. I twirled my cup tentatively.

"It's very worrisome," he finished.

The slanting sun was bright in the afternoon sky and directly visible over the stretch of river curving to the west. A broad band of gently rippling gold ribbed by silhouettes of fallen trees reflected from the surface, gave the scene a tigroid look, which ended abruptly some distance away. It was an unusual scene, which Jain photographed from various angles. A thin wisp of smoke rose from Doris' fire and spiralled straight up in the still air, taking with it the odour of roasting meat and smothering all others. It continued warm and humid.

"Your brother's right, of course; he sees it first-hand. If you go to our

Casualty department you'll see the results of the violence, a lot of beatings, mostly bruises and knife cuts, from fights, mainly street fights, some gang beatings, mostly Indians seem to be getting punched up and black guys in company of Indians or speaking up for them; bad wounds used to be few but are increasing; and broken bones."

"How do you know this, Doc?" Brewster enquired.

"Hospital statistics and talk among the Casualty officers. Each evening we, I mean the resident doctors, meet at a lounge in the doctors' quarters for an hour to relax, unwind, play dominoes or cards, and talk about things, discuss cases, especially the tough ones. Once a month Dr Stanley Luck and I represent junior staff on the Hospital Management Committee, where we give and get various reports including the ones from Casualty; they're not good. We've been watching this one and the kind of cases is changing; more personal injury, many serious, especially from gang beatings and from the 'choke and rob' thieves. They're getting more than the fevers and accidents."

"That's what bothers the Police; yesterday was fisticuffs, today it's weapons; what next? We can't just sit idle; we can't take sides. And yet we're only marking time." Bacchus was reflective and genuinely concerned, yet sounded resigned and helpless. This was quite different from the non-committal face he had presented to us so far. Perhaps the discussions we had had and the events of the day had brought us closer still, and he felt more secure in baring his true feelings and doubts.

"I don't know if I can ask you this, Inspector, but what would the police do if this agitation leads to real fighting, not just in the ugly parts of the city, but everywhere, or looting?"

"Well, you know, a lot of people asking that, especially businessmen. They're afraid of arson, break-ins, looting. The police have plans to handle them, like we always do. But we don't have the manpower or equipment to deal with gangs that now spread and operate all over town, in several places at once, as if by plan. If general violence come to pass, we're in trouble; we'll be like Chicago or New York with their Mafia. And worse, it will look as if we're letting it happen."

"The first thing that's likely is a strike, maybe the stevedores or sawmill workers, one of Burnham's unions, or the TUC even; that's what my friends say; you agree?" Jain said.

"Well, I'm not sure," he said, a bit defensively, "GAWU is muscling up, we hear, so we're watching all of them."

"But it's not likely Jagan's union will go out against him." Jain said, more insistently.

"You never know what politicians would do." Bacchus countered.

"Realistically," I said, "the opposition controls Georgetown and New Amsterdam. They're the threats to law and order, not Uitvlugt or Albion. But Sawmills is Jagan's union."

"You're right, and the trouble will be in the towns. And the Mayors are anti-Jagan."

"And most of the aggression will come from the opposition ranks, don't you agree?"

The question remained unanswered. Inspector Bacchus looked as if he had gone too far along that road with us; any further exploration would be within the Police Force, or so it seemed. Here it might open a can of worms. Any assent now would inevitably lead to the question of what preventive actions were contemplated by the Police. Clearly that would not be a matter for open discussion at this point. Police strategy would remain secret until put into effect. But the Inspector did concede that Police had been alerted to trends in politics and were paying close attention to the public pronouncements of political leaders, and trying to separate rhetoric from intention.

"Is it true that some Ministers are tailed and spied on, and everything they do reported to the Governor and leader of the Opposition, people like Chandisingh, Mrs Jagan, Ramkarran, Beharry, Moses Bhagwan even though Moses is not a Minister?" Jain asked, rather too pointedly. "That's what the British did in India, from the time protests started, nearly a hundred years ago."

"Naresh, you can't ask the Inspector that; he wouldn't tell you even if he knew!" I cautioned.

Inspector Bacchus smiled, "It's okay, Doc, I can deal with that. Other people ask us the same thing. Some even feel we taking the side of the Opposition. Our job is to protect everybody."

Jain laughed and said, teasing and without malice, "Oh, good, Inspector, you could be a politician." Then he added, "You know, there is a rumour that the PPP spying on their own Minister Balram Singh Rai; how about that?"

"In times like these rumours fly and cause a lot of harm." Bacchus remarked, a bit lamely. But Jain was on a roll, perhaps impelled by the three neat warm drinks he had had in less than thirty minutes, on an empty stomach. It was clear that his inhibitions had been released as he continued the recitation of the many rumours of what the PNC was planning and how the Police would not interfere in whatever action Mr Burnham might order to disrupt the Government, as he had clearly said he would. He asked eventually, "Tell me, Inspector, Burnham is committing sedition when he preaches violent overthrow of Government. That's illegal, right?" And before Bacchus could say anything, he challenged, "If tables turn, and Jagan is Opposition, doing and saying the things Burnham now doing, would the Police sit idle and do nothing? I bet you a hundred to one not! See how quickly they threw him in jail a few years ago just for going beyond his restricted area!"

He ended dramatically, rose, took his clothes off and waded into the cool river, kicking vigorously to churn up the water as if to scare away anything lurking in its depths. Presently he returned, dried himself with his towel, sniffed it and announced, with a guffaw, "I have to get home soon; this towel smells awful!"

"Why don't you wash it with the soap you brought and leave it on the rock to dry overnight?" Brewster asked him. He muttered something about humidity and sat back, watching the closing stages of dinner preparation. Balgobin had decided to cook a good pot of rice to go with the can of peas and sardines with onions and canned tomatoes, our last can, which we shared and had decided to feast on it since we were so close to Cokerite and could get some grapefruit and peppers there.

"How can we go into independence with all this racial strife, Inspector?" I asked after a lull.

"You know I was going to ask the same question, in fact all of us should think about that seriously. We have to find a way to live together, you and me. That calls for respect, me for you and you for me. We must be comfortable with one another at home, at work, at play."

"That's what everyone says, but nobody does, why not?" Jain returned to the fray, his speech slurring slightly, and exaggerating his epentheses, as I had heard before as his alcohol level rose.

"Respect, yes." I agreed. "But we have to go deeper to establish a basis for respect, and that means we have to know one another in a way we don't; we have to know one another's customs, belief systems, food, religion; then you can talk of accommodation, respect and co-existence, not before. Right now the mainly African PNC rejects a mainly Indian PPP government, even though the PPP is more pro-African than pro-Indian. And yet PNC says Indians should accept African rule! Both have to learn tolerance and rule of law. We have to live together; we depend on one another."

"How we gonna do that, doc?" Brewster asked, and added, "Nobody teach us that in school, that's where you supposed to learn those things, right?"

"Right; the school curriculum has to include them, which it doesn't."

"Well how come you know 'bout them, you learn that at Queen's?"

I laughed at Brewster's naiveté. "Sure as hell not, Constable; I learned that at home, in the country, from my mother, my family and as part of our cultural upbringing, and from my own study. Queen's is a British Grammar School, there to train people to be loyal Brits; QC did teach respect, discipline and duty, but that's no different from what I already knew from our own culture and holy book, the *Bhagavad Gita*; we can't forget that the British used schools to indoctrinate the young all over the Empire and convert them to become good *coconuts* and *bigan* when they grow up!"

"What d'you mean by *coconuts* and *bigan*?" Bacchus asked, puzzled.

"Indian joke, *coconut* is brown outside, white inside; *bigan*, eggplant, is black outside, white inside."

After the laughter subsided, Bacchus said, chuckling, "Good one, I like that."

"Then how come Queen's put out two rebels, Jagan *and* Burnham?" Doris asked derisively.

"Even the best schools, in Britain and the colonies, produce mavericks. The majority of students simply want to graduate and find a job they like. Those two went to QC as senior students; they didn't spend long enough as youths to get properly conditioned; besides they are the anomalies, ambitious radicals, what the statisticians call the outliers; for every one of them, you have a hundred slogging away in Government offices, including Police, all over the country; these hardly care about understanding; they care about their work, promotion, paid holidays abroad, pensions, and following rulebooks at work, and those books don't have a thing about social issues. I was in that Service, for fifteen months, didn't like the condescending attitude at the top nor the slavish mentality behind it."

"I agree Doc, we got to do better; but we've been trying as best we could." Bacchus was plainly on the defensive, though he did not have to be. He was as much a victim as anyone else; he too had joined the Force as a young man believing that what he had learned--in knowledge and attitudes--were the standards of the society and would remain so, and continue irrevocably. The political rhetoric of the past ten years had brought him doubts, but they did not affect his functioning as a policeman. He had done his best, as honestly and fairly as any man, perhaps better than most. He had an exemplary record and was respected and admired.

But he had to admit that he knew little about more than half his countrymen, not, at any rate, the way he now felt that he should know them. It was simply that he had not had any prior reason or opportunity to speak on these things with anyone. Nor even to think that that segment of the population deserved some special or different understanding and attention. And in the Force the subject was hardly touched on at all, even among the Indian officers, most of them city men who also shared the prevailing prejudices including a condescending attitude to their own people.

"Frankly, Inspector," I said (I suspect with some release of inhibition by the whisky, but in a low key), "the way I see it is this. Any attempt among us to learn about one another has been a one-way street so far. This society placed us Indians at the bottom of the heap, as you know. Ironically this works in our favour, though most of us don't see ourselves as being at the bottom of any heap. Indians are usually very respectful and that can be misinterpreted as fear or cowardice. We face unfair hurdles at every level but that challenges us to strive harder, not slack. That's how it is with any suppressed people. That's what made the Jews so powerful.

In Montreal last year I noticed that the French people nearly all spoke English, but hardly any of the English types spoke French. They're breeding the same problem there as we have here. Just as the French people there know about the English we Indians know more about you, your religion, your food and so on, than you know of us; some of this we learned in elementary school. When we played with you or socialised with you we learned about you, but you didn't learn much about us. Why?

Because most (and thank heavens for people like you who are different) followed what the British taught and therefore ridiculed our way of life, our religion, our music, our cinema; you called us nasty names like 'heathen', 'savage' and 'backward', just as Brits did in India, when in fact our civilisation is probably the oldest, our people the first scientists and educators and our religion the first and still the most tolerant.

"The number of black people who know beans about Indian history and culture is vanishingly small. QC historian Cameron Tudor was an exception. But we know you. That's why we can reach you, and you can't reach us. By reach, I don't mean the few Indians who have joined in with the PNC, I mean the ordinary Indian. Look, if a black man marries an Indian, she becomes a Christian if she wasn't one already; their children grow up Christian. If a black woman marries an Indian man, he becomes a Christian, too, even if he was a Hindu or Muslim before. That's how it is.

"Few black folks would ever accept the Hindu religion. And I don't see why. They accepted Christianity, Judaism and Islam, but rejected Hinduism and Buddhism because the Europeans told them so. Black folks would do anything for a white man, follow, obey, serve, but not for an Indian, however gifted or well-meaning.

"This is the bias of your upbringing, bias, pure and simple, not the result of study and analysis! Not your fault, really, you were slowly sucked into this situation, from the day you entered school, you were hit by a powerful and impressive British propaganda machine, that did the same to people all over the world, and Indians are first among the brain-washed! There's an African saying, *'when the British came to Africa, they had Bibles and we had land, today we have the Bibles and they own all the land!'*"

Bacchus and Brewster sat silent and looked stunned. Had I gone too far, and misread their willingness to have a serious discussion of a burning issue? I pondered whether I should say I'm sorry, but I did not feel so. My inhibitions were too far gone, my tongue oiled! These men, after all, were policemen, a specially privileged group, who should be among the first to reform their knowledge and attitudes and begin to understand the people they were policing. I had said this very thing before, in the past ten years, and often enough in "bull" sessions at the University College, and somehow each time it had seemed as if I was the one in error and out of line, maligning the sensitivities of the innocent; it was incredible.

I had felt optimistic about the country's prospects a year ago when I had to return regarding my mother's illness, and later in April '61 on meeting Dr Brahmam at UCHWI where he had come to work for a month in the Department of Medicine. We had spent many evenings discussing a broad range of subjects: literature, archaeology, history, mythology and the British period in India, of which he had insights and data new to me, prompting further explorations.

He had come to BG from India on a three year contract and was sufficiently impressed that he was on the verge of renewing it. He had met Jagan and Burnham and was satisfied that Jagan had softened his leftist agenda and would work with his moderate advisors and detractors even to create a fresher and more inclusive, less doctrinaire policy line.

That view had persisted up to the time of Jagan's recent visit to the USA, but since then the tensions had begun to rise alarmingly. I could hear Brahmam's soothing cautions of a scant few weeks ago, but it was Jain who broke my reverie with his hearty laugh and comment, his epenthetic "r's" rolling into the cool waters of the river, stirring the evening and echoing from the dark depths of the forest beyond.

"*Vāh, vāh, Mohanji,*" Jain teased, disinhibited, lapsing into Hindi, "*Yeh raaste hain gyaan ke.*" (These are the paths of knowledge) "*Upna khyal rakhna.*" (Take care).

He sang a few bars of a popular Bombay movie song and added, feelingly, "*Mein bukha hun.*"

"What the hell's that?" Brewster asked.

"Words from a song. He's just making fun of me. Says he's hungry. Too much booze!" I said.

Bacchus was more serious. Finally to my relief, he said, "You're right, but we're not all delinquent. Even if we don't know your story, we can accept that there is a story we need to know; we should correct that. Perhaps that is one of the things that should come with independence, and be compulsory from early childhood that we learn about one another."

"Right, but it should be in place *before* independence, in school, among Government workers, in the Force, in the press, on radio, wherever education can take place, like right here. We can't go into Independence carrying a baggage of misunderstanding. It won't work. Sorry, chaps, I'm not railing at you personally, you know that. God knows you're all decent men, and people like you are our only hope; it's the system that must change. We should begin in a positive way. If I had my way I'd make it compulsory for us to learn about one another's ways, starting now. I don't see Jagan or Burnham doing that. Why? Because that might bring us together and interfere with how they want to indoctrinate us!"

"You can't force people to learn that stuff." Doris was waiting for his roast to finish and for the last few minutes had stood nearby, behind me, listening. Startled by his voice, I spun around. He had a cup in his hand and had, after speaking, swallowed the drink.

"You're right Corporal, not force, promote and encourage. Start in primary school. There are many enlightened teachers who would be pleased to teach it. I had a few in my school: George Forsythe, the head teacher, who even knew some Hindi, his sister Hennie, his wife Maud, Georgina Thomas and Clement Blackman, some of the finest teachers you'll find anywhere; they're African, like you, and ranked among the most highly respected people in a largely Indian community. They accepted the fact that they'd become Anglo-African and told us about it.

"I remember Mr Forsythe telling a group of us in 4th and 5th standard that he coached on Saturdays, '*From the earliest days of slavery, our ancestors began to lose language, names and customs because British overlords and teachers were teaching them their ways, as they did all over the Empire; they spread their customs and practices, their manners, religion and everything, while at the same time told our forefathers how backward, miserable and savage they were, and how "civilised" the British could make them.*'

"That set your basic values for three hundred years. Today British ways are your parents' ways and your ways; and what you learn from your parents gets reinforced in school, where they teach negative and biased views about everyone else, including your ancestors; today you believe that is the truth. You even believed the silly *sambo* stories and how savage the Africans were. It's only today that some of you are discovering some virtue in Africa, especially now that Ghana and the French colonies are independent and Nigeria and others have enough oil to make them rich. Tell me, Corporal, have you ever seen anyone here playing the Ashanti talking drum or Yoruba drum, the ones that look like an hourglass? Or the *djun-djun* and *kpanlogo* which look and sound like the Indian *dhol* that we call *baydam* here. And how would you react if you saw a black man playing one of them here?"

"We've all seen and heard the Indian drums, but I don't think any of us has seen the African ones here." Bacchus replied. "I saw them at the British museum! The practice is lost. Colonial policy separated us from our culture and was meant to integrate us into British society but without true equality. We as slaves had no choice; the Portuguese and Chinese accepted but you Indians held out and kept your culture; although you're criticised, many of us respect you for that."

I welcomed that. We talked then about West Africa which had begun to creep into the news in Georgetown but had been more prominent in UCWI debates, especially as European imperialists were slowly granting independence to their colonies; one wondered what relationships would develop between the new nations and the African Diaspora especially as West Africa had been the source of slaves for the Western Hemisphere. I felt bold enough to ask, "Do you know that it was your fellow Africans who sold your ancestors into slavery, and the trade made many West African chiefs rich?"

"Don't know what you talkin' 'bout, Doc." Doris's voice had regained the old defiance, but his face showed surprise.

So I continued, "What about the Ghanaian, Benin, Sierra Leone, Mali and other civilisations from West Africa and Sahel -- the lands of your ancestors? A thousand years ago they were civilised and rich, rich with gold that they traded with Arabs and others. Hundreds of years ago Europe bought gold from that area to pay for Indian and Chinese goods. The British wouldn't teach you that. Do you know where *you* came from?"

He was defensive now.

"No, I don't, none of us know. They didn't give slaves passport and citizen papers when they took them, you know!" His sarcasm was surely justified.

"Touché, Corporal. But do you know that records exist, that very few, if any bothered to check and that after emancipation your people were pleased to go after the jobs opening up as postmen, clerks, policemen, etc. and those of you who stayed on the estates kept the best jobs, the ones in the factory, the shovel gangs and so on. And that your former owners taught you how to be loyal to them, to look up to them, thank them for little handouts, to dislike or even hate other people, even some of your own kind, painting them as people who would steal your daily bread. The Brits forced us too, with the help of your people, serving them as teachers, clerks, policemen, especially policemen, to stop using our language, to change our customs and to adopt theirs. They did the same to the natives of America and tried it in India and all over Africa. And English became the common language of the educated!"

"Mr Doris," Jain interjected, "The Brits come to nations to trade, America, India, Australia, Africa but soon abuse friendship and agreements; armies follow and seize best lands, share them among generals and lords, take away peoples' trades and jobs; then they force their products and religion on them and tax them for everything while their own pay little or nothing; this way they keep the native people poor and dependent on them; when you poor you can't fight; at same time they select some natives, educate and pay them well to keep others down and so divide people by spreading suspicion and hatred among them. Both Jagan and Burnham complain about these things. Bauxite and Bookers don't pay as much taxes as you, and Bookers own the best farmlands in BG and don't use it all."

"You see, Corporal, things are not as PNC propaganda tries to make out. *We* are not your enemies. The gulf that separates us is a knowledge and culture gulf. We Indians know where we came from; we're proud of that and who we are, even though our own greedy people sold us out as yours did by falling for British bribes and propaganda; so those became rich. But most defied the British even to getting killed because we had something stronger and better in terms of culture, cuisine, religion and so on, than what they offered. If they'd learned about our culture they would've seen its strength, but they simply dismissed us. Those things we learnt in secret almost, at home and in 'illegal' Hindi night schools, while your people jeered at us for what we were and what we did, especially our customs and rituals, shaming many as children to believe that the British ways you followed were better, more modern. So we lost property, but gained knowledge of the Brits, and we learnt about you. Think of that whenever you want to rail against us or jail us, but also if you want to understand us and to live together in harmony."

"That may be so," he conceded, "but you have to know that we don't worship idols or sacrifice animals like your people do; those things not right."

"Like the watrash you're so nicely roasting on that spit? Isn't that sacrifice? Come on, man, examine yourself. That's a British line. Your ancestral religions include a lot of the things you criticise. What you say about idols is only half true, a distortion; we have symbols, yes, representations, just like other religions, they're called *murtees*, but we don't worship *them*."

"Wait, how's that again? You tellin' me you don't have all kinds of Gods and Goddesses?"

"Not in the way you think. It's very involved. Our religion, Hinduism— that's not its real name--is very old, at least twelve thousand years in recent history and likely much much older. Hinduism evolved from thousands of years of study of the visible universe, not just earth; sages, with divine guidance, developed a philosophy that is still *the only one* that accepts all views and all forms of spirituality.

"We believe in a *single* creative Force; you call it God, the Muslims Allah, the Jews Jehovah and so on; we call it *Parabramha* or *Brahman* in Sanskrit--which by the way is the parent of European languages. In English *Brahman* translates as *Universal Presence* that created the universe by various intermediaries called gods or goddesses. The process might be compared to the way an architect creates a plan and a team of engineers and builders complete it. Hindu literature will tell you who did what. Other religions simply say that God created all things and don't tell you about these intermediaries.

"The scholars who developed the philosophy were the leading thinkers, writers and rulers in the world at that time; later teachers found it difficult to explain to ordinary folk in different languages and at different times the abstract spiritual concepts and entities involved; even today these still puzzle people. So they devised symbols to represent them and much later the symbols acquired the names of the 'gods' and 'goddesses'; these were in time passed on to other cultures--Egyptian, Roman, Greek, Mesopotamian, Parsee, the Norse people, Celts, Goths and so on. Images are common in religious worship. Even Christianity has its images: Angel Gabriel, Christ on the cross, the Virgin Mary, the saints, the cross itself, the Last Supper; the pictorials and so on."

"But we church don't use images like you do; the priests condemn them." Doris observed.

"That's your choice; but note that condemnation by priests doesn't mean they're right; I can say the same against them. Muslim and British conquerors of India knew that the only way they could conquer Indians was to destroy their source of strength, their religion and their language. Hindu symbols provide a focus for spiritual concentration by worshippers; they do not replace God; each symbol is best regarded as an attribute of God, and altogether they add up to the qualities of the Super God, *Brahman*, no different from other religions. Hinduism does not pretend to be simple; it cannot be reduced to a simple catechism, like Catholicism and it does use various ways to get its message across."

"But your religion looks so strange to us; and the *fullamaan*[18] too."

"I can see why you say that, mainly because they're conducted in a strange language. All religions have common basic tenets; they differ only in their rituals and their prejudices. Those who want to vilify Hinduism will continue to misinterpret it, no matter what; it's become a power play. An educated person of your group can spread the most vicious lies about me and my beliefs among those who know nothing of me or my beliefs. Troublemakers have done this in every period in history and will do it in the future as their bias or maybe madness impels them. The missionaries focus on Hindu images to advantage to

---

[18]Muslim

vilify us, as your remark just showed; it's the one thing they teach you about Hinduism; they don't dare teach you the essence of it; you might like it."

He was dubious; other stereotypes and personal observations contradicted what I had said.

"Hey, doc!" Benn emerged from his silence, "I saw this feast in Canje where a woman dance and get high and chop off a goat head. What is that?"

"Yeah!" Doris added, "that not pagan?"

"What is pagan to you may be essential ritual in some other faith. Every religion has its off-beat sects. That sacrifice is peculiar to a sect that prays to a goddess Kali. Look, Abraham was prepared to sacrifice his son to please God. When Catholics or Anglicans take weekly communion, they're sharing the *'blood and flesh'* of Jesus Christ, not for real of course, but as a symbol; they learn this from childhood. When you talk of Father Christmas, or Santa Claus, that is a pagan belief; and many Christians celebrate Hallowe'en, not in BG, but that too is pagan, from pre-Christian Germans, Celtic and Wikka. You know every religion and people have some form of practice or beliefs that critics can call deviant; look among Christian sects and you'll find some far more startling, and Mormons have some strange beliefs and practices, with multiple wives even child ones, not legal here; the Muslims celebrate the end of Ramadan, the month of fasting, with a sacrifice of lambs; so don't tell me about paganism; after all, religion is a human invention and there are many deviants among humans."

"Shabash!" (Very good) Jain said, and before anyone else spoke, Balgobin called, "Let's eat."

The chatter continued through dinner, animated by the liquor. It was more than we had had before on any single sitting. Before this we had had from none to a single drink after dinner, as a nightcap. We touched on many things, and I noticed that Doris had quietened and become more thoughtful, less hard-line, or was it the way the alcohol and fresh meat affected him? I knew how variable the effects of alcohol were; some people quickly became aggressive and quarrelsome, others docile and sociable; perhaps he was one of the latter.

But more than that, it was undoubtedly the effect of the spiced roast that he had just demolished that changed his mood. He had eaten heartily as had the others of the generous slab of meat, which we had politely declined, even though the smell of Balgobin's spices in which it was cooked whetted the appetite and would have well graced a leg of lamb or a breast of chicken or fish, or solid vegetables.

It was still light after dinner and wash-up. The insects had not yet descended. A light wind floated in from the river. It was a serene setting, in which the babble of flowing water provided a soothing yet sensuous melody that inspired contemplation. We lounged, in pensive satiety, smoking and sipping drinks. Cpl Doris was saying something in a low voice to Brewster while whittling on a slender twig fashioning a toothpick with which he began removing fragments of his meal from his teeth, recycling some and spitting others away, in between drags on his cigarette, one from the half-pack I had given him ("I didn' take to filters, I prefer to taste the tobacco," he had said). He coughed a little from time to time as he inhaled smoke, and would look at me each time; I kept a straight face.

Jain sat one leg stretched out, the other bent at the knee around which he had draped his arms, sparing his bandaged hands and rhythmically rocked back and forth. Brewster sat with his legs extended and arms straight back relieving the side on which he had fallen, and now more sore than before. His frayed straw hat was pushed back on his occiput. Inspector Bacchus left briefly for a visit into the bushes. The natives were either busy preparing for the night or else lounging in their hammocks, chatting, as were Benn and Rodriques. I sat at the water's edge, my feet dipping in the stream, creating a minor turbulence.

Brewster leaned forward and said, "Doc, what you say about knowing who you are is true. I always wonder where we came from; I don't just mean the slave story. I mean place and time and who those ancestors were, and never know where to look. Nothing in any schoolbook and none o' the teachers know either, at least, not at elementary school. Then we grow up and get busy trying to make a living and have no time or desire for those things. We stop wondering and get on with life. You know, I think most people don't care.

"My wife know more 'bout she father and she people and where they come from, and that made me think. So I asked around and read a little; got a book from the library. I surprised to find out that the Dutch did come here first and built a post in Essequibo to trade with the bucks. But the trade was slow, so they decided to plant tobacco and did well until sugar became the big thing; so they shifted to that, but found labour cost too high and they couldn't compete with the Portuguese in Brazil or the British in St Kitts and Barbados, who used slaves. So they too brought in Africans and sold them to farmers and into households; I di'n' know *anybody* could buy a slave; some homes had several. They said that the first lot, two barracoons full, according to the book, came in 1672 to a plantation in Essequibo. So we were here 289 years."

"I read a PNC paper which said that slaves were here for 400 years; if what you say is true, then they can't be right." Jain said.

"True" I said, "the natives, of course, have been here for thousands of years. Not many know what you just said, Constable, and fewer care for the truth. Burnham also claims that Africans came to the Caribbean a thousand years ago; that may be so and I've heard it repeated. But we lack proof or plausibility. The people who want to use us know that, and bank on it, so they can tell us any old garbage, and we believe them, because we trust them and follow them; it's their tests we must pass, until we decide to open our eyes, ears and minds; then we find out different, often too late."

"Like Sidney King; he change his name to an African one, Eusi Kwayana."

"But he's still same Sidney King, Soviet friend." Jain interjected. He might have new name and even wear African clothes; they mean nothing. Until he can wear them with meaning and regain his culture — whatever it is--he's still *bigan*, a Red one!"

Brewster grimaced, and slowly said, as if savouring each word, oiled with the brandy in his hand, "It's funny how things go; it's the opposite with some people. One time I ask my father-in-law about Hindus and Hindu beliefs and he couldn't tell me much; he bin a Christian too long; his parents though, used to take him to Hindu functions, and he was beginning to play *tāsuh*. Then the school catechist got hold of him and told his parents that he had to go to Sunday school; that that was part of the schooling; his old man didn't understand English too well, but he wanted the boy to get an education, so he let him go; he was only six, and one thing led to another and he got baptised; his parents said that was okay but wanted him to keep up with his own religion, but the Church said no, *'you can't serve God and Mammon!'* So since the Hindus do not have service like we do, he didn't keep up. He say he feel embarrassed when he meet Indians and can't converse like they can. So he grew away from his own culture, just like we did; see how quick it can happen; he wife was a girl from the same congregation, same problem." Bacchus had rejoined us while Brewster spoke.

"Common story, especially the bit about forcing religion and language on Indians in school and misleading about the purpose of Sunday school," I said.

"When I was in England," the Inspector mused, "I met people from different parts of Africa, just like me; some thought I was a Tutsi from East Africa; most of the West Africans said that they never heard of African slavery until they met us in England; many didn't even know about Liberia and how that came about. They asked where the West Indies was; they knew about India and its fight for independence, but not about us.

"When I told them there are over 15 million African people in America alone and more next to us in Brazil and other parts of South America, they disbelieved. None of that dark history was revealed to them in their schools. They thought I was joking when I told them that black people had fought in the American War of Independence, and that there were black millionaires and scholars and business folk all across America.

"It was quite a thing to see their reaction; they had wondered about my name, thought that I came from a Muslim family, and couldn't place my accent. It was an eye-opener for them and for me. We take it for granted sometimes that other people know what we know; and I know people here who think that Africa is small place, smaller than England, or how else could England conquer it? Some of them stopped talking to me, others wanted to find out more. But I couldn't tell them which part of Africa my people came from, that I didn't even know then what a Tutsi was; nor before meeting them, any other African name or anything about the thousands of tribes across the continent. It was there that I learned that Africa south of the Sahara, that is about half of the continent, is what we in the West mean when we talk of Africa and African heritage."

"Why is that?" Doris asked, "why the difference? Africa is Africa; is the same all over, after all!" He stated the last as a fact, nicely illustrating the points re deliberate misinformation.

"Not really." The Inspector replied, "Sahara runs right across the widest part of Africa. North of it and in it you find all Muslim countries except for Abyssinia; you must have heard of Haile Selassie, he call himself *'Ras Tafari, the conquering lion of Judah'*. But the biggest are Sudan, Algeria and Egypt. You might be too young to remember the North African campaigns in the last War and the battles between Rommel and Montgomery. When I told the West Africans that BG played a part in the North African war they told me they never heard of BG much less any role in the War. So I told them about Atkinson Field and the flights to Dakar that passed through Atkinson and the raids against German subs in the Atlantic. That opened a few eyes."

"Dakar? Where is that? I was in school during that war and used to hear the stories," Doris was more subdued, "we never get newspapers but sometimes I would get a piece from the Chinee shop wrapping saltfish, and would read whatever it had and would come to the best part just where he did tear off the paper; once the story was so hot I took the piece to the shop and asked the man if he could find the other part. He chased me away, saying, 'gwan home, me use up all paper!' I was so disappointed. But I never read about Dakar."

"Dakar is in Senegal, and is the nearest point in Africa to South America, just in range of the DC3's that were being used to carry people and materials for the North African campaign." Bacchus replied. There was a pause, after which Bacchus asked me what I knew of this.

"First I'm surprised to hear that West Africans didn't know about slavery, but it makes sense; with the Europeans controlling all means of communication and education, they could make sure their subjects learned only what they wanted; same here, except that we here knew that the Americans were busy at Atkinson Field. We could see it. The Muslim religion came to North Africa by conquest and spread south by trade, to states like Mali, Chad, Niger, Mauritania, North Nigeria and elsewhere, what they call the Sahel region. The northern people are light-skinned Mediterranean types, though with quite a mixture with dark Africans; same in Egypt. They speak Arabic."

"How so, Arabic is the language of Arabia, not Africa?" Brewster asked

"Same as us; we speak English, not one of us is English; the Arab Muslims conquered all of North Africa, East to West, 1200 years ago and made their religion and language the official ones."

"More than enough time to plant anything;" Jain said, with a chuckle, "you can change language in two generations, look at the Indians here; in a hundred years most have changed, even the ones who still speak Indian languages."

"You're right. Anyway, although the Europeans controlled those states, they did not colonise them the same way they did south of the Sahara, barring the French in Algeria. Historically those nations looked to Europe for their trade; that goes as far back as Roman and pre-Roman times. One of the great Roman wars was the series with Carthage (today's Libya). The Arabs also traded south of the Sahara and crossed the desert in several places. Besides goods, they traded slaves, perhaps some of your ancestors. That's how so many places became Islamic."

"Hold on a minute; just now you said the Arabs are Muslim, now you say Islamic; which is it? They the same?" Brewster asked.

"Yes; the religion is Islam, the followers are called Muslims."

"Right; so that means that there must be a lot of black Muslims, 'cos some of those countries have a lot of people, like Nigeria. I met a few in England." Bacchus said.

"Yes. The Muslims spread their religion wherever they went and gained control of the Sudan, Somalia, North Africa and most of northern Nigeria; they're also in other countries of central and East Africa, like Zanzibar but not many in South Africa."

"Recently I read about sects growing up in the States calling themselves 'Black Muslims'. They may be the same thing, but they sound more like a fringe group." Insp. Bacchus observed.

"They're really part of organised negro revolt, which began some time ago. A Jamaican in the USA, Marcus Garvey, began a serious attempt to repatriate Africans 30 years or more ago and actually started the *Black Star Line* to do that. It didn't get far but the *United Negro Improvement Association* developed to seek better rights for Negroes. In the forties various groups sprang up --many because of Communism and to deal with the racist Ku Klux Klan -- but with a religious agenda.

"One prominent group is the *Nation of Islam* headed by a man who calls himself Elijah Mohamed, a curious mix of Hebrew and Arabic. He has no connection with mainstream Islam, ignores Islam's race neutrality and preaches

Black supremacy, the superiority of Islam over all other religions and Allah as the only Saviour who will save only those who follow *his* path of righteousness. Some prominent Blacks have joined with him, as well as a few militant younger men, the most prominent being Malcolm X..."

"X, you say, why X? Haven't seen anything about him in the papers." Brewster said.

"I was in New York last year and the press and TV were full of him. His real name is Little, and he changed it in protest to X because in Maths it means "unknown quantity" noting that the slavers had separated Africans from their roots and none could find their true identity. He had just left prison after a 7-year stay for armed robbery and in jail had studied to become a preacher. He joined the *Nation of Islam*, just under 10 years ago, and soon became their most influential speaker.

"He hotly condemned whites and white racism, advocating a separate Black state, by whatever means needed, and in one speech I witnessed mocked the Civil Rights movement led by Martin Luther King, the high priest of the NAACP, who wants to end segregation Gandhi-style. Malcolm X denounced racial prejudice, which he says is everywhere in the States, even the north. He's right at least in New York where it's plain to see; whole sections of a borough would be Jews only, Italians only, Irish only, Blacks only; it's incredible when you see a person, obviously white to look at, who calls himself black, and an Italian darker than me who is 'white'; they've taken this race and colour thing too damn far; a black man, however good, cannot move into a white neighbourhood because he's seen as a threat to property values; a white criminal can move into a high class black neighbourhood and he improves it; ridiculous!"

"That still happens?" Brewster asked, incredulously, "I thought segregation was illegal."

"In theory, not fact; that struggle is just starting." I opined. "Things won't change easily in the States: too many ignorant people with far too much money; they have no respect for anything, even knowledge sometimes, and push their selfish values over everyone else's. Sure we'll see some token Blacks in high places, but real equality is a grass-roots thing, a high-minded feeling that doesn't come naturally; it has to be learned. Many rich Americans are just rednecks who aren't getting better, and with trends in US education, so-called liberalising, things will get worse as schools teach less and less about the world and youngsters grow up richer but ignorant of geography and history and full of old biases. Hopefully as travel gets cheaper with the big jets now flying they will spend sometime discovering the world, not just sight-seeing; I hope that they learn something from that, though I won't bet one of their dimes that they will see anything beyond the big hotels and ritzy tourist places!"

"That's strong language, Doc," Bacchus said." You really believe they're that backward?"

"We haven't begun to see what their ignorance and highhandedness will do to the rest of us. There are many good decent Americans, of course; but they don't have a voice or a platform; my friend Stanley Luck, who teaches me a lot, keeps saying that decency is not a political virtue; it's not as catching as bigotry, and doesn't earn you a lot of money in a country brought up on the power of money. So far as I've seen, money is the American religion. It's the religion of the big wheels and shysters: the corporations, financiers, Jews, politicians and organised crime, who run the country; it's not the religion of the majority, not the religion of thinkers or statesmen."

"How so?"

"Simply because in America you have to buy your way into political power; no one without a huge 'war chest' as they call it, can have a hope in hell to contest, much less win, an election. If you're very rich, you can do so without strings; if you're not you can only do so with many strings tied to you so that when you get there you're nothing but a puppet made to dance as the strings dictate. That's the American way. You should have seen the money flying in the US presidential race last year; enough to transform BG into paradise, just for one election!"

"And the money that supports one man, that same money can destroy his opponent, however worthy he is, with just a false rumour or two, especially if you can drag sex or some other prejudice into it." Bacchus said, a bit incautiously, considering his position, but by now satisfied that he was among people he could trust and be himself.

A pause followed, in which Benn's heavy breathing came almost as a signal to cease or perhaps a commentary on the futility of discussing things over which one had no control; to be aware of one's limitations and of the prevailing state of affairs seemed enough of a guide for personal action, within the bounds of legality and morality.

I sipped my drink and shuddered slightly as a little wind blew up from the river. Cool. Invigorating. There was a brief pause in the pace of the greying of the evening, as if the day too had decided to take a breather. Suddenly Doris asked, "I have to clear up something. You all t'ink black people will get fair treatment under Jagan?"

"Why not? Jagan has made no moves to change the balance of power in the country. All government services are still staffed mostly by Blacks, and I bet will remain so under Jagan."

"You're right there!" Jain exclaimed, "I will stick my neck out and say that black people will be far better off under Jagan than under Burnham."

I had heard this debate before, briefly at the Doctor's Lounge. Doris raised his eyebrows in disbelief, and protested, "Aw, Mr Jain, you exaggerate."

"Corporal," I said, "I believe him, and go further; if Mr Burnham ever gets to lead this country he will ruin it, chase us away and turn all of you into his slaves and put you out there to rob and kill, to make him rich. Mark my words."

"Come on, Doc, you losin' you' balance, that's not like you!" Doris said, with less vehemence than I had expected, "that's not what everyone say about Forbes. Besides, the PPP already trying to take away we jobs, they want to make us in the force lose we jobs."

"Where did you get that particular piece, Corporal?"

"I hear all the talk about Rai trying to bring coo.... I mean Indians into the Force; if he do that, we lose; that's how I hear it." He had, I noted, stopped short of using the derogatory *coolie*, for which I mentally thanked him. It was a start.

"It's amazing how distorted a simple thing can become when the stakes are high. Minister Rai wants to hire Indians *to fill vacancies in the Force, and for new positions, not to displace anyone*. The Police claim that they are short-handed, to explain why they can't cope with all that's going on, right Inspector?"

Inspector Bacchus nodded, and was careful, "Yes we've had a number of vacancies for some time. We can't get enough people to apply, and yes I have to say that we should cast a wider net."

"So you can't fill all the openings with black men, and you have a serious imbalance and let's face it, Indians don't trust the black police, at least not in the countryside, not on the sugar estates. All Rai wants is a meagre increase to 20%, still way below the 50% Indians represent in the population. And most of those would serve in Indian areas. What do you think of that?"

"I don't think we ready for that. I don't think they can do it." Doris said, weakly.

I asked him why. He fumbled and gave the stock response about physical requirements.

"There may be a place for tall burly men in the Force," I said, "but where's the evidence that such a man is a better cop than someone smaller? Look at Rod. Is he a good cop or no, Corporal?"

Doris mumbled, caught off-guard.

"What do you say, Inspector?"

"No question, Rodriques is a good man. We are looking at various proposals, which I can't talk about here."

"Some of the toughest cops you'll see anywhere are right next door, in Venezuela, and most of them would call me tall!" I was reminded of the several times I had been through the airport at Maiquetia and my one trip to Caracas, each time marvelling at the small men with tall rifles and their almost invisible ubiquity. None lacked authority.

Jain chortled and said, "You know Inspector, India has millions of policemen, all Indians no bigger than me or Balgobin or doc there; they don't import Africans to do their policing! Some Chinese and Japanese police are even smaller," he chuckled again and added, with sarcasm, "you know, big fellows make better targets for crooks than little ones. Good thing BG crooks don't carry guns."

"The police have to be fit to deal with criminals. That's why we have standards for height and weight." Doris insisted.

"But height and weight don't make you fit." Jain said.

The Inspector emphasised the visible nature of the Force, the fact that most of the men were unarmed except for club and whistle, and thus the outward show of strength and fitness were desirable.

"At the present how could a small man cope with a six-footer weighing 200 lbs?" he asked.

"With martial arts training! You can make a small man challenge a bull!" Jain announced. "Look at me. I am 5ft. 8 inches; I weigh 155 lbs; I can take on anyone of you, taller and heavier than me. The heavier, the better!" He paused, stood up and swayed a little, struck a martial pose, skipping lightly, beckoning with his bandaged hands, "Anyone want to take me?"

I thought he must be thoroughly drunk to do such a thing, but Balgobin, who had joined us having completed his chores, humoured him, "Mr Jain, you drink too much, to say a t'ing like that. If Mr Brewster sit on you he will flatten you, and Cpl Doris long reach will floor you before you get close!"

Jain's ringing roar echoed through the forest and must have scared all the night creatures preparing to leave their lairs for the nocturnal hunt about to start with the waning sunlight, and given them second thoughts.

"Ohr, nore, Bal, I might be a small man, just like Doctor Mohan here, but I can do it, I tell you I can do it."

"How you gon' do it? You not a magician, Mr Jain!" Balgobin persisted with his teasing, smiling wryly as he spoke.

"Martial arts, Balgobin, martial arts; you know, like jiu jitsu; you've seen that here."

He danced a little, like a boxer, and threw a few punches at the air with the flat of his hand, his fingers apposed, but extension restricted, and kicked the air deftly, snorted a few breaths, then relaxed; it was quite impressive and silenced everyone. He then described his training in one of the Indian traditional arts which practised both defensive and offensive tactics, and had reached a level of skill just one step removed from the top, which he could attain in the next six months if he could put in the practice. Doris listened with sceptical interest. Balgobin looked at Jain with new respect.

"I have to see that first! Anyway we don' have facilities for that." Doris said, defiantly.

"Facilities!" Jain was even more scornful, "all you need is a mat and some cheap gear. What you really mean is that you want to stick to your monopoly and you shelter behind present rules. That's okay. But Government can change those rules. Which is what Minister Rai wants to do, but is getting big resistance, mostly from his own Premier."

"And what about the estates? At training school they tell we that the Police do a great job of keeping peace there; what about that?"

"Sure, like at Enmore in '48, right?" Balgobin queried, sarcastically and without waiting for a response, added, "They teach you what they want, their side only."

"But Bal, those people were rioting. The police had to shoot." Doris emphasised.

"That's not what the Commission of Enquiry said; I don't mean Boland, I mean the British one, Venn," I offered. "That is one of the beefs the estate Indians have. They don't see it your way. They see you as the *bakra* tool. It's the history of India where millions were slaughtered; Brits think you glad to shoot Indians because of grievances, so they use you to do their dirty work. It's our history."

"You mean, besides Enmore? We never hear 'bout others; what you talking 'bout?"

"Man oh man, that's exactly what I mean; we learn what we're taught; we're not taught what we should really know; we're taught nothing about the many shootings of Indians in the last 80 years, all over the country, starting in Essequibo, Devonshire Castle. But we know about Kofi (Cuffy), Accabre and Akara! Every schoolchild knows about those three. Why is that?"

"I never hear about any coo....I mean Indian shootings. What about them?"

Just then, someone slapped at his arm, squashing a blood-filled mosquito. The biters had arrived, with the last of the light rapidly dying. We hustled to the shelter of our nets, and continued the conversation.

In his book *A History of Guiana* P H Daly recorded the revolt of the African slaves Kofi and Akara, but gave little attention to the struggles of Indians on the sugar estates or to the heroes and heroines who had emerged from them. He totally ignored the fact that Indian workers had in 100 years engaged their oppressors in over 600 encounters over grievances, far more than the Africans had done in their 275 years (at his time of writing), and had lost about 60 dead and ten times that maimed, including women. Even today few even among Indians know much about those brave men and women who gave their lives to improve the lot of their fellows. Those who have moved into the middle classes, either as independent farmers, men of property, businessmen or professionals have put that part of their history behind them, some denying it altogether. But many remember.

Denial has penetrated so deeply that some successful Indians, especially Christian converts, have gone so far as to disavow personal connections with recent ancestral indenture, seeing that background, like counterparts in India, as an embarrassment to upward mobility. They have not only distanced themselves from their kith and kin in the estates, but have shielded their children from this past history, encouraging them in the pretence that they are different from, and superior to the rough and simple folk who still labour on plantations. As a result recent generations have grown up to believe that the Indians of the estates are a lower class than their city look-alikes, different and perhaps retarded and quite remote from them, and lacking in the confidence, initiative or ambition needed to leave those "awful" sugar plantations. This attitude is not uncommon among Indians born and bred in the city, who have come to adopt many of the same beliefs, attitudes and loyalties of the blacks and creoles with whom they grew up and shared classrooms and playgrounds, despite the enduring clashes that have marred relationships between the races ever since the Indians showed that they knew how to work, worked well and long, and saved the sugar industry from bankruptcy a hundred years ago.

The sugar industry, however, repaid that dedication with increasing coercion and by throttling Indian leadership and initiative, denial of education and other services to workers that ultimately hindered their development. The industry, like other British colonial agri-businesses, has religiously taken great pains to spot potential leaders (or "trouble-makers", as the managers called them), and used various devices to identify, then neutralise or discredit them. A minority was promoted to supervisory positions, thus separating them from potential followers; others were "deported" to far-off estates where no one knew them.

Smear campaigns, false charges and convictions were the most common devices used, and penalties harsh; a few of these could totally ruin a man, especially one hoping to rise above the crowd, or to return to India. Besides, other measures helped to thwart protest: unfair laws that permitted detention of workers or imposition of fines for minor infractions, evictions and other legalised harassment, overt threats and the infamous "pass" system which prevented free movement outside the confines of the worker's plantation and thus reduced opportunity to meet and organise. Thus to escape into the wider freer world Indians had to accumulate capital and do it guardedly so as not to attract attention, so that in due course they could cut ties with the estate with a clean slate.

Many obviously had done this but the process often diminished the Indian by changing him into a secretive and suspicious person eschewing the honesty, openness and straight dealing that were the hallmarks of those called 'trouble makers'. To escape with their worth intact therefore many had to stoop to finagling, bribery and subterfuge, and the better they were at these the richer they could become. Some even ratted on their fellows to authorities while others gave false testimony in order to win favour[19]. Thus it was unlikely that a leader

---

[19] Chapter 5 gives examples of betrayal that changed the course of Indian history many times.

could emerge from *within* the system and when Jagan appeared on the scene he was greeted as a messiah.

One wonders whether the caginess and shady dealings characteristic of a subset of the modern aspiring generation, and their subservient attitude to authority might have had their origin in the anxieties and troubles of their forefathers that were passed on to them as a survival tactic. Certainly the obsequiousness of many of today's prospering Indians in the presence of light-skinned authority is matched only by the arrogance of their offspring and disrespect for poorer Indians, perhaps to maintain a safe separation and to enable the erection of walls of class that could become a feature of the new society; in time no one would suspect that the rich and poor had once trodden and shared the same inglorious ground. Thus today it is not unusual for an Indian, usually one with a modest education, to adopt a conspiratorial manner when dealing with another Indian or have no qualms suggesting a shady or illegal way of operating, or openly to dissemble, seek preference or favour even when due and open process would give him exactly what he wished.

Because of this reality, this suppression (or rejection) by Indians of the sordid elements of their history in BG, few Indians know anything of their local heroes, those men and women whose striving and sacrifices have helped change the prospects of their people. I have mentioned Bechu, a contemporary of my *nana* and of Hari's father, who still remains unknown. He could easily have made his fortune outside of the estate, like the Indian gentleman who called himself Samuel Johnson in the 1850's. Instead Bechu chose, against great odds, to fight the indenture system, in press and in public; in the dying years of the 19th century he submitted a reasoned memorandum and gave testimony to the West India Royal Commission that was investigating problems in the sugar industry.

He exposed the flaws and malpractices of indentures, the injustices, exploitation, cheating by supervisors on the estates, their immorality and sexual abuse of women. He endured and for a time survived the harassment and threats of the plantation managers and owners whom he was castigating. And when they failed to seduce him to their cause, or to deport him to India, they sued him twice and twice lost. Then he disappeared; my *nana* maintained to the last that he had been killed on planters' orders, like so many in India.

Those daring and conscientious men who found a way to pursue the cause of justice and fairness for their comrades knew the hurdles they faced. But they pressed on, some fell, some stood, each adding to the mounting momentum that would eventually scuttle the indenture program. It remained for those who followed to make the final journey away from the unremitting squalor of the estates which colonial mercantilism had diligently nurtured and protected, at great profit.

So although an end to Indian immigration came in 1917, the conditions of employment did not change and all the nefarious practices, universally condemned, continued unrelieved. Protests and strikes were frequent, some planned, some spontaneous, all acrimonious. Some were short and relatively uneventful, others bitter and dramatic, and rife with incident, many culminating in death of men and women, usually shot by black policemen.

In Feb 1939, there was a protest strike at Leonora, on the West Bank Demerara, where previous strikes had taken place. Without reading the riot act, police fired into a crowd of resisting workers, and killed four people including a young woman Sumintra. I remember my mother and others talking about it when I was a child barely able to comprehend the gravity of the act, and the gloom at school the day when the story was first publicised under a picture of the fracas in Mr Forsythe's copy of *The Daily Chronicle*. That incident had a desirable outcome; it led the Sugar Producers Association (SPA) – the *de facto* government of the colony--to recognise the Manpower Citizens Association (MPCA), the first sugar workers union, headed by Mr Ayube Edun, and which Dr Jagan would struggle to displace 10 years later, when it was discovered that Mr Edun was on a retainer by the SPA. The 1930s had seen strikes across the Caribbean as the effects of the depression took their toll on wages and jobs. The Leonora strike was probably the last of that series.

That was not the first killing of Indians by police, however. In April 1924, 13 workers were killed and 77 injured at Ruimveldt in the incident that Hari had described. (Ch. 10, p.45). This incident was noteworthy in that it was one of the first instances of joint industrial action by Indians and Blacks. In Rosehall, Berbice, 13 workers were shot and killed in 1913 during a protest against a variety of seething ills including poor labour conditions, long unpaid hours and high rents extorted by the Estate for use of idle land to grow rice. Ironically the angst was directed against a head driver named Jagmohan who was himself Indian (and some said a friend of Dr Jagan's father, who was a driver in adjacent Port Mourant).

It had been for years common practice for the estate managers to pick as drivers--the men in charge of work gangs--either tough Blacks or ruthless and aggressive Indians, the latter tending to be rougher and meaner to their fellow countrymen than the Blacks, perhaps to ingratiate themselves more firmly with their overseers and managers. Ten years earlier at an estate not far away, ironically called Friends, six Indians were killed. In 1896, at Non Pareil, Demerara, five were killed in a protest over wages and to denounce the acting manager for "taking away" and co-habiting with a married Indian woman. The husband was killed in the gunfire. Was this deliberate? Zeke's mother had witnessed this incident[20]. I concluded my summary, saying, "Twenty years or so earlier five workers: Ackloo, Baldeo, Beccaru, Kowlica and Maxidhari were killed during a protest at Devonshire Castle, Essequibo. And of course we're all old enough to know about the '48 Enmore massacre. Over sixty Indians were killed by Police fire in the past hundred years or so, and this in a country at peace. I doubt that more than a handful of blacks were similarly killed in the nearly 300 years they have been in this land. Dr Jagan is fond of pointing out that in France at about the same time as the Enmore killings in '48, a much worse situation of strike and actual rioting was quelled with tear gas; nobody was killed. In BG Police shoot Indians. So Corporal, you see that Indians have not had it easy, or been unreasonable."

"Everybody hear 'bout Kofi and Akara, but who hear 'bout Bechu, Doc?" asked Balgobin.

"As I said, Mr Daly, who wrote the official history book, did not think to include these things; and even Guy de Weever in *Children's Story of Guiana* did not include them as a story. But they are part of local newspaper and Colonial Office records, and available to Civil Servants; that's how I got to know; also my *nana* and my parents told us some of these things, and as I said, Hari's father knew Bechu."

---

[20] See also Book 1, Ch. 10, p.35

"But it's only Indians involved in these things;" Doris said, "I hear people say that it's because only lawless Indians come here."

"Some might have been, but most were peaceful hard-working people. And what about other people who came, Chinese and Portuguese; they were not lawless, too?" Jain asked.

"No, those people come here as shopkeepers and businessmen," Doris replied, "they don't live in sugar estates."

I was again stunned that he did not know what I thought was common knowledge, "Don't you know, Corporal that Portuguese, Chinese, Blacks and some Whites even were brought as labourers under the *same indenture system as* Indians. The Portuguese and Whites were brought before Indians. Africans and Portuguese battled it out in 1856 and 1889. Chinese went to estates all over BG."

"But that's not what we learn."

"Not news! These British distort and divide us everywhere they go; when they teach they leave some things out and invent others, what suits them," Jain said sarcastically, in a voice that seemed too low for him, "I told you what they did in India. Here I think they don't pay attention to Chinese and Portuguese in politics because they're too few and all already British. But they love us or they hate us; they like to kill Indians they do not like; during War they killed at least four millions in Bengal by starving them to death, and tried to hide it. *We should do like the Jews and call this Indian holocaust,* [21] and build big industry 'round it. Then everybody will notice. But Indians not pushy enough to do that! Churchill is every bit as criminal as Hitler but he got honours not hanged like Hitler's people!"

"Four million? You joking!" Brewster cried. "That's more than Hitler. That can't be right."

"I didn' know 'bout that one; what happened?" Balgobin asked, stunned by the number.

"Absolutely true; those poor people were disposable;" Jain spoke in a subdued tone, hiding the emotion he obviously felt. "They were Bengali villagers mainly and poor people from cities who could not get rice from Burma because Japanese took over there. British merchants seized all India rice stocks, releasing only a little at a time which made price too high for most people; at same time production fell; British ignored people dying every day, children so thin they were only bones, like Hitler's Dachau or Buchenwald; the British killed them just as Hitler did the Jews or when they massacred them at Jallianwallah Bagh in 1919; that was with guns, noisy and sudden; this one was silent and slow and made huge profit; Indians starved to death, over 4 million."

"And that bastard Churchill had the gall to claim that England sheltered

---

[21] This refers to the loss of over 4 million Bengali lives from starvation that followed the rice shortage during WWII caused by an artefactual escalation of prices which made the commodity too expensive for rural folk, compounded by the conscription of boats that could have brought in rice from other parts of India. Churchill's animosity for Gandhi led him to deny aid even though people like Viceroy Wavell, Louis Mountbatten, and Indian leader Subhash Chandra Bose pleaded on the peoples' behalf. This holocaust echoed previous atrocities beginning with the first great Bengali famine of 1769-70 which had taken *10 million* lives. Tens of millions are said to have been similarly wasted in the two hundred years of British hegemony, of which little can be found in main-line texts. Similarly little is said of the untold millions (50-100) killed systematically by Muslim rulers in their 750 years. Contrast the continuing strident global reportage and memorials of the Jewish holocaust of WWII, an estimated 6 million, a fraction of the total Indian loss at British and Muslim hands, for which neither apology nor compensation has been made or claimed.

India from the ravages of war," I hissed. "Total allied casualties were six million, and included hundreds of thousands of Indian troops that were among the first to fight in Europe and the Middle East and yet few know about them! Churchill's accounts of the war exclude that murderous Indian famine."

"Not surprising; he hated Indians, he called Gandhi a naked fakir!" Bacchus observed.

"Four million!" Brewster reiterated, in continuing disbelief, "and the whole world giving Hitler and Germany hell for starving and killing same number of Jews. It's not a fair world."

"The Jews claim it's near six million; they have ear of world because they control world's money, newspapers, radio and Hollywood; now they grabbing TV." Jain added, gloomily.

Brewster shook his head reflectively, "In all my life I never thought much about politics. I take my work seriously and try to be fair. Me wife is full Indian; she's Hindu turned Christian, and it never was a problem; I never even think of that. Not even when I first hear 'bout *apana jaat*; I ignored all that stuff and used to walk away from politics and racial talk, until this trip, hearing you all talk. And I was trapped; I couldn't run away. Now I realise we all have to do something to prevent serious strife. I'm like Felix, I don't know much about Indians, even though I married one."

Brewster admitted that he and his generation had believed all the stereotyping of Indians he had heard since childhood; his own wife, despite her Indian origins, knew little or nothing about Hindus or Muslims with her secular upbringing, and believed them also. "Now I have something to tell her!"

In his police years, however, he had been puzzled by the huge difference between the stereotype and the many Indian lawyers, magistrates, doctors, dentists, engineers, businessmen, teachers, policemen even, and others whose behaviour was no worse than any other race; in fact Indians had fewer brushes with the law than Blacks, even though there was the prevailing notion among Indians that policemen treated them more harshly than Blacks.

"You know, Doc; we all been putting aside for too long learning the truth about one another; we still live with and believe all the biases we grow up with 'gainst you people." Brewster said with sincerity. "It's a shame that we don't try to learn the facts 'bout one another; especially we in the Police Force, cos we got to give everyone the same protection."

The Inspector and Doris both looked sharply at him, then at me; the former spoke aiming to conciliate. "The Police don' take sides, no matter what people say; Indians say we biased, but we try our level best to follow procedures that have nothing to do with race."

"What I think in private don't interfere with what I do in my police work." Doris added.

"Don't you think it would be easier on you if you knew something solid about the people you have to police? I tell you as a doctor I want to know as much as possible about people, what they do, how they think, what they believe, what they eat, how they live and so on. You never know which of those pieces of information would help in a particular case. I'm sure that works for all professions."

"The trouble is that we all proceed as if everyone cut from the same cloth; now common sense says that is not so, but in daily life we so busy we don't find the time to find out. It's not in our curriculum, sad to say." Bacchus paused, and then asked, "If you had to give a crash course in your culture that would help in the days to come, what would you do? You think you all can give us a sample of what you would do?"

It was an incredible request even though it had come from a man who could be a prototype for reason and moderation, and therefore would show that kind of interest. But in BG?

Brewster nodded, "Anything would help; we bin talking about it and we think it's something we should take on in the Force. I don't think we would get another chance to hear from the three of you. I know it would help me. Maybe it's something we can take back to the Force. I respect you all; even Balgobin I come to know as an intelligent man; don't get me wrong Bal, you know how it is; you judge people by the work they do, by what you think they are, and that is so often wrong."

"So true," Balgobin said, "I learn to deal with that all the time."

"Well, I don't mind; we can try. What would you like to know?"

"Oh, I don' know exactly; tell us 'bout your people..." he looked at Bacchus, then at Doris; both nodded; "whatever would help us to understand and relate better."

"It's a long story, but we could give you highlights, and hopefully cover the basics. But be prepared for some shocks, I have to say. Luckily, you ask at the right time; I've been studying this for the past year with Dr Brahmam's help; he's the chap who should be talking. First an observation: Brewster said your people were here 289 years. The first Indians came here in 1838, May 5th actually, in two ships, *Whitby* and *Hesperus*." Doris' eyebrows rose, but he said nothing.

"Hesperus, you say, Doc?" Balgobin intervened. "The same Hesperus in the Royal Reader?" And he went on to recite the opening lines: *"It was the schooner Hesperus/That sailed the wintry seas/And the skipper had taken his little daughter/To keep him company....'"*

"I don't think so, since that was only a schooner."

"So your people have been here about half as long as ours." Brewster calculated, "Long time!"

"Yes, and yet not so long, a mere 1% of our present historical timeline when you consider that it goes back over twelve thousand years, and in that time our ancestors made huge discoveries and advances in religion, mathematics, language, astronomy, agriculture, commerce, government, architecture, music, arts, peace and unity promotion, name it, almost every sphere of human activity, making it the richest nation in the old world, until the Muslim and British came and in time conquered it and stole its wealth. Both of them were welcomed as traders to India, a big mistake. They not only stripped India of its wealth, but worse, degraded its people, forcing many, like my grandparents, into bondage, and finally left it with the problems it's battling today."

"And India was as rich and developed, attracted many, as America today, long before Europe came out of Dark Ages." Jain said.

Eyebrows were raised with expressions of surprise and even negation. Bacchus said, "But all that you saying India did came from the Greeks; we learned that in high school."

"Greeks, Shreeks!" Jain exclaimed, "Most of their teachers at that time were Indians, same as how your first teachers were Brits; they came to teach you, and later you went to their country to learn. Same thing then. Three thousand years ago the only Universities in the world were in India; scholars from everywhere—Chinese, Greeks, Persians, Egyptians, Mesopotamians and many others, even Jesus--went to India and several wrote about their experiences."

"The Greeks, you say? And Jesus? Don' joke! You can't be serious! You taking this too far!" Doris expostulated.

"Not really," I said. "Megasthenes,[22] a Greek ambassador to India some 300 years BC wrote a lot about India in glowing terms and about its form of democracy, long before any democracy ever existed in the West. Buddhist and other records clearly show that Jesus spent his "missing" eighteen years there among Buddhist and other religious scholars."

"There's a Muslim sect in Kashmir, most northern state of India, called Ahmadiyyas," Jain added, "who believe that Jesus did not die on the cross and that he survived, went to India to find the lost tribes of Israel, found them among tribes in Afghanistan and Kashmir, conducted missions and died there. There is a grave in Srinagar, identified as his and looked after by them."

This was greeted uniformly with shock and disbelief. I recalled Dr Brahmam waxing eloquent on this subject as we talked through several evenings during his stay at the UCWI. His iconoclastic account of Indian history negated with facts and cool reasoning the propaganda of British historians of India (including their Indian students and successors, especially secularists and Marxists), who he said had almost to a man distorted Indian history and denigrated the Indian people and their culture to promote imperialist ends and to justify to the ordinary British people back home and to the international community actions that were brutal, rapacious uncivilised, tyrannical and evil.

I realised that we had forced our listeners into the deep end without properly preparing them to consider the account of India's history and culture that we would prefer them to have. We would have to do better, if we wished them to understand us and to recognize our authenticity, not just as fellow countrymen but as descendants of an intellectual, economic and civilising force that had once led the world but had come upon hard times, just as the Romans and other great empires of old.

"I'm sorry; we got there too fast; we should back up a bit and go more slowly; it may take a few evenings if you wish."

"We're stuck here; can't go anywhere; might as well hear something new; what you say chaps?" Bacchus asked encouragingly.

"Okay with me," came the uniform reply, Doris adding, with unexpected accommodation, "I won't remember all those funny words and names you people use."

"You don't have to, but we must use them so that next time you hear them, they won't be a surprise. To appreciate this you need to know a little about India and Hinduism; by the way its proper name is *Sanatan Dharma*, which means 'the Eternal Way of Righteousness' or its variant *Arya Dharma*."

"Wait, I know those names; isn't that the one called *'Ma Sabha'?*" Brewster asked; "my father-in-law explained it to me once, but I forgot what he said, some political group?"

---

[22] The Greek emperor Seleucus' ambassador to Mauryan India whose book *Indica*, 302 BC, paints India as a wondrous and opulent society made up of 7 "castes": farmers, soldiers, philosophers, herdsmen, artisans, magistrates and counsellors with abundant agriculture, irrigation and other engineering works. Kautilya (Chanukya), Chandragupta Maurya's Prime Minister wrote his rules of governance, *Arthashastra,* at about the same time.

"More cultural although there was an Indian political party called that. The one he meant is *Sanatan Dharma Maha Sabha*, which means 'Grand Assembly of the eternal way of righteousness', or simply 'Eternal Religion' and is something like a synod of an archdiocese in Christianity."

"Except that they have no control over priests or religious activity;" Jain explained, "they organise functions and hold discourses, more like religious or social club. Hinduism is not priestly religion; it's not based on church or compulsory assembly; it's personal and based on values of *eternal Truth* and *eternal Law*, which the scriptures express in two Sanskrit words *satya* and *rta*."

"You have scriptures? Written down like our Bible?" Doris asked in disbelief.

"Yes, several from different periods, called the *Vaidas*, plus two huge epics, the *Rāmayana* and *Mahabhārata*. These are the world's oldest and some of its best literature."

"I've seen those names, they hard to pronounce, like all Indian names; my father-in-law says we distort them a lot. So you goin' tell us from the beginning?" Brewster asked.

"We'll try. First of all, India's traditional name is *Bhārata Varsha;* today it's the world's most populous federal democracy with over 400 million people, and several million Indians live outside India. It's the 7th largest country, over a million square miles[23] and up to about three, four hundred years ago it was probably the world's richest country.

As you know it's separated from the rest of Asia by the Himalayas, the world's tallest mountains. As we'd expect for a large country the climate, geography, agriculture, industry and wealth vary, just like customs, manners, rituals, ceremonies, cuisine, dress, ways of thinking and education, according to evolutionary and regional factors.

Indians were originally the people of the Vaidas (Hindus) but are today — due to invasions and migrations--a mix of ethnic, linguistic, social, economic and religious groups. Hindus make up 80% and Muslims 12%. Christians, Buddhists, Parsis, Jews, other faiths and agnostics or so-called secularists make up the rest. There are 15 major languages. Most of the people are brown-skinned; ranging from very light to very dark, and there are tribes in the off-shore islands in the Bay of Bengal (Andamans & Nicobar) who look like East Africans..."

"You mean black, with crinkly hair?" Brewster asked, surprised.

"Yes."

"Don't forget the music. That's what everyone hears and identifies us with." Jain advised.

"Besides curry, like we jus' had." Brewster said, with relish.

"India's music and its instruments are unique and known worldwide. It complements the religion and grew with it and became, as here, a socialising force. So music is as old as, or maybe older than Hinduism; its scriptures go back at least to the end of the last Ice Age."

"Ice Age? When was that?" Doris asked.

"It ended 12 to 14 thousand years ago and lasted about 65 to 70 thousand years."

"But that can't be; our church says God created the world 4,000 years before Christ came on earth." Doris was puzzled.

---

[23] 1,222,243 sq. miles to be exact, excluding another 46,976 under dispute; population over 1.2 billion today (2010)

"Now, there's the first big hurdle. Hindus believe differently; and I have to warn you, this is the part that baffles most but at the same time fascinates open-minded people. Our religion is based on Science, man's search for explanations of Nature. From the beginning wise men, in every culture, have wondered about Creation, when and how it happened, as the Bible says; Indian seers looked at all the objects in the Universe, the vast sky full of dancing and moving stars dominated by the sun and moon, and they came to the first fantastic conclusion that everything was part of one grand scheme, physically related and that the earth was a part of this and also floating in space. This is so vastly different from what everyone else felt that the earth was the centre of things. In their struggle to understand they were shown the "truth" by messengers of the Creator, what Jain said as the Eternal Truth and Eternal Law, *Satya* and *Rta*.

"The message was that the entire Universe was created instantly and is growing; we mentioned earlier that this was done on the call of the Supreme Being, also called *Universal Presence* or *Ultimate Reality* and in the original language Sanskrit *Parabramha*, or simply *Brahman or God. Brahman* is the essence of all things, permeates and encompasses all things, that is, each created thing has an element of the Creator in it. That's why Hindus hold all life as sacred."

"So where all the idols fit that we hear 'bout; who are they, what do they do? You did say something about representation; how's that?" Bacchus asked.

"It is as if Brahman delegated tasks to a series of subsidiary forces or powers, just as you would do in the Police Force, from Commissioner to constable or in any organisation. The interaction of primal female and male forces produced subsidiary forces or powers each with a particular function and matching name that created the universe of infinite elements, shaped and moulded them, preserved their integrity and got rid of excess, waste or what's worn out, just as we might do at a building site. The three major functions of creating, preservation and removal, are under the Trinity of Brahma, the Creator, Vishnu the Preserver and Shiva the Destroyer. Thus Creation is linked in a cycle with Destruction, almost like birth and death; each cycle spans billions of years."

"Billions?" Brewster exclaimed. "That's incredible. You serious?"

"If you find that incredible, it gets more mind-boggling. So brace yourself. Hindus view time as cyclical, not linear, and Einstein was one of the first moderns to acknowledge this. Our scriptures say that the universe is 155 trillion years old..."

"You said trillions Doc?" It was Doris this time who expressed disbelief.

"Yes, trillions! This period is divided into various eras which have special names. But life as we know it did not appear until 1.973 billion years ago; that length of time is called one *Kalpa* or *Sristi* Era; life is said to have started as elements in a primitive soup and slowly evolved over this time to what we have today; this is same as British science accepts; in that time numerous species have come and gone. Help me with these names, Naresh."

"Each *Kalpa* is divided into 16 periods of about 120 million years (120,533,107) called *Manvantaras*)." Jain began. "You see how Hindu numbering system could handle huge figures since so long when no other culture could; even Rome, most developed old culture had trouble once you get past a thousand, which is nothing. *Manvantaras* are divided into *ages*, (or *yugas* in Sanskrit). The year 3102 BC began *Kali Yuga*, the Iron Age, last of four in this cycle and starts period of decline that would end in destruction of mankind."

Brewster's comment was inevitable and understandable, "I can see this calls for a whole course by itself; no wonder nobody teach it. How you remember all those names?"

"We grow up hearing them every time we go to puja, from pandits." Jain replied.

"These time spans are incredibly huge;" Bacchus noted. "Of course no scientist takes the Bible creation literally; it's an allegory, really. I see your religion also preach some kind of doomsday."

I took up the story. "According to our scriptures God has intervened to stay the doom by sending prophets and messiahs, or *avatars*, just like Jesus Christ, whenever mankind came too close to the brink; their coming had all been predicted by sages many thousands of years before.[24] Ten major ones, nine of whom have already appeared, were recorded and another twelve or so with more limited regional impact.[25] We accept Christ as one of these and also as a student of Buddhism and the *Vaidas*.

"The creation theory had emerged from study of celestial objects by astronomers and mathematicians who gave them names, grouped and classified them and eventually placed Earth in the Milky Way, and this they did, remember, long before man invented telescopes, suggesting the divine inspiration of this knowledge. Eventually 1460 years ago and over 1100 years before Copernicus and Galileo, the young scientist Aryābhatta described the solar system we know today with the earth as one of several planets orbiting the sun with the moon following it."

"I remember reading 'bout Galileo." Brewster cried in amazement. "The Pope cited him for heresy because they believed that the earth was flat and everything moved around it. And you people knew that the earth was round a thousand years before? Unbelievable!"

"So how d'you deal with the time concept; you say Einstein agree with you?" Bacchus asked.

"Yes, he does, as far as I understand him. Indian philosophy sees time as astonishingly limitless and our world as a tiny particle in an infinite cosmic space populated by galaxies with millions of suns and planets, and realised that Earth was a tiny speck on which man fought to dominate everything and seize power and control, all for the duration of less than the blink of an eye, far too short for us to even contemplate a cycle of billions of years."

Jain continued the narrative, "*Universal Presence* is source of all things,

---

[24] *"Bee chakram prithoi aishai ta khestraaeh Vishnu mansai das sayaan throvaah so asaya keeryo janaas oeroo khashatra so janama chakaar (8)"* meaning "Whenever sinful ways rise up in the world and noble behaviour vanishes, just as the moon disappears on the darkest night, there will appear Vishnu as a prominent Prophet from the Kshatriya Clan and will manifest in consecutive form through 10 Prophets to restore the ways of virtue to the ailing world." *Rg Vaida (i): Mandala 7, Ush 5, Mantra 5.*

[25] The *major* Prophets are, in order of their coming: *Matsya*, fish; *Kumura* tortoise; *Vahara* boar; *Narasimha* man-lion; *Vamana* dwarf; *Parshuram* an imperfect man; *Rama*, (4,000 BCE) physically a perfect man; *Krishna* (circa 3100 BCE), the son of a Virgin; *Buddha* (circa 600 BCE); and *Kalki*, who is yet to appear, though some claim that he is today's Satya Sai Baba of South India. Some Baha'i claim Baha'u'llah for this role and Ahmadiyyas propose Ghulam Ahmed. Hinduism recognises several others as prophets, including Jesus Christ, Mohamed and Nanak. *"In this list of avatars we can trace the gradual evolution and transformation of all species out of the ante-Silurian mud of Darwin to the zodiacal beasts of the Babylonian god Oannes. Beginning with the Azoic time in which Brahma implants the creative germ, we pass through the Palaeozoic and Mesozoic period, covered by His first and second incarnations as the Fish and Tortoise; and the Cenozoic which is embraced by the incarnations in animal and semi-human forms of the Boar and Man-Lion; and we come to the fifth and crowning geological period, designated as the "era of mind," or "age of man," whose symbol in Hindu mythology is the Dwarf – the first attempt of nature to create man."* From *The Secret Doctrine.*

living and non-living, so everything includes a little element of God. The concept emerged of *dharma* and its loss, *adharma*; *dharma* means the righteous way of life in all its manifestations, scientific and intuitive. Our purpose is to live full life, develop ourselves through four stages or *ashrams*[26], express the best of God-like qualities we each have, realise that we are part of God, so that when we leave this existence we might qualify to reunite with God. This attainment may take one or more lifetimes or cycles of birth, life and death (known as *samsara),* and is governed by *karma,* an accumulation of all good and bad deeds which contribute to rate us, as it were. Selfless acts and thoughts as well as devotion to God help us to be reborn at higher level, while bad deeds and thoughts will achieve opposite, even bring one back as lower life form. These are things around which much of rituals have developed and are performed in different Hindu services."

"Every civil society is regulated in some way, and each person finds a role in it." I remarked. "The revealed texts describe man's growth and responsibilities as a moral member of a harmonious community in a complex physical environment. They also deal with the nature of the universe (cosmogony); the behaviour expected of us at each stage of our stay on earth; discuss morality, role in community, government and domestic affairs, and detail rules of conduct in all situations in daily human life, just as the Bible does.

"Much of this literature is preserved and is one of the most extensive in the world even though a lot was destroyed when Muslims destroyed Indian universities and temples in their 700-year rule over much of India. Some collections of *Laws* remain; the best known are the Laws of Manu (*Manusmriti Manu Dharma Shastras,* written in 2,685 verses) which is a sort of guide to contemporary living and is not scripture but includes comments on religious practices. Manu, by the way is a father figure of mankind, like Adam in the Bible.

'There are many similarities with Biblical references. One obvious one is Christian *Holy Trinity* which we think is based on the Vaidic *Holy Trinity---Brahma, Vishnu and Shiva*[27]. We also believe that many of the civilised races of Asia and Europe had Indian origins or religious connections and took *Vaidic* culture and teachings with them wherever they went, although modified by many factors. The flood story with Noah is also similar."

Doris remained sceptical; he said simply, "'Nancy story! How many million stars you say? And prophets? And all those ages with tough names I can't even say much less think how long that is?"

"You're not alone; but it's not really 'nancy story, when you think of it;" Jain said, "already space exploration supports *Vaidic* theories, and that's just beginning. In twenty years so much more will become known; my guess is that you will change your mind."

"Maan, I still can't figure out anything that old; those numbers give me a headache." Brewster exclaimed.

"Much of what you say is not just new, but incredible and different from what we learned." Bacchus said, amazed. "So what about the history; you said India was great; what made it fall?"

---

[26] See Ch 7:35
[27] *Brahman* or Brahma is derived from the word Brih, "to grow" or "to expand" and the name Vishnu is rooted in Vis, "to pervade," to "enter in the nature of the essence"; Brahma-Vishnu being infinite space, of which the gods, the Rishis, the Pitris and all in this universe are simply the potencies.

Chapter 5

I rely heavily on accounts from my friend Brahmam, my first guru Lakshman, and former teachers Ben Yesu Das and Cameron Tudor (see also Ch. 14) for a tour of Indian history to inform our comrades, an epic saga without end, spiritual and secular; it reveals many absorbing sights, from the zenith to the nadir of human achievement and behaviour, from grand to shameful, from tolerance to bigotry --tales of freedom and conquest, wealth and poverty, valour and cowardice, trust and deceit, and the whole panoply of human experience in vibrant colour, from pre-history to the present. There are many surprises: India is a crucible of creativity in agriculture, religion, sciences, mathematics, grammar, medicine, engineering, transportation, government etc. which attracted conquerors, the last the British, who not only continued Muslim aim to destroy Indian religions and massacre tens of millions of Indians but worked to distort and destroy Indian history and create the religion of secularism that rules and threatens India today. The partition of India could have been avoided but for Muslim ambitions and British biases, self-interest and falsification. Our team's discourses fill empty evenings. The material is challenging and most of it radically new to our Police friends; our account is brief, touches major features and calls for added study. Our listeners are puzzled but come to agree that shared knowledge of cultures is essential for race relations in BG. Comparison is made with 19th Century European scramble for Africa including the way Africans, like Indians, were persuaded to fight for Britain in two world wars but remain largely unsung.

Day 11, Part 2: India: A Short History

"We owe a lot to the Indians, who taught us how to count, without which no worthwhile scientific discovery could be made."
Albert Einstein

"The science of yoga was born at a time when mankind was more enlightened and could easily grasp truths and ideas for which our best, our more advanced western thinkers are still groping"
Anon

"India was China's and the world's teacher in philosophy, religion, imaginative literature, trigonometry, quadratic equations, grammar, phonetics and chess. India inspired Boccaccio, Schopenhauer and Emerson".
Lin Yutang (1895 – 1976)

"As I have often said in public, India is, in fact, now governed by successive relays of English carpet-baggers, who have as little sympathy with the natives as they have any real knowledge of their habits and customs."
Hyndman, quoted by WJ Bryan 1898

Section 1: Introduction

I t's a terrible deception!" Dr Brahmam pounded his clenched right fist into the left palm. "What British taught us as history of India are *criminal* omissions and distortions and what's worse, eminent *Indian* professors today still teach this stuff from the same old textbooks and pass it on in their own work! Most don't know Sanskrit yet dismiss *Vaidas*[28] as myth. They're worse than the Brits who brain-washed them; those history books *are* the real myths!"

"That's what Mr Yesu Das told us at Berbice High seventeen years ago; he refused to teach it."

We were at his flat at Taylor Hall, UCWI, sipping "white ladies" made to his personal recipe, and had drifted to the subject on a casual comment I had

---

[28] The **Vedas or Vaidas** (meaning *wisdom* or *knowledge*: **Rg, Atharva, Yajur, Sāma)** are our earliest literary and philosophical works; they deal with spirituality and man's yearning for enlightenment. They are internationally renowned for the depth and breadth of coverage, beauty of language and imagery, and originality. The inspirational style and universal appeal of the spiritual and scientific message have influenced later religious philosophies. *Sāma Vaida* is written as a song and represents the earliest form of music known to man. The *Vaidas* detail methods of worship and actions to safeguard civil life, communities and the environment and to ensure health, prevent and treat disease, and are a model for our own age, but unfortunately suppressed by invaders and religious fanatics for a millennium and remain largely unknown to modern secular Indians.

made about the aloofness of expatriate Indian businessmen--mostly Sindhis--who dominated Kingston's Club India, which he had visited but had not returned as he found them empty and clannish except re business and although he tried he could not find common ground for discourse. Being South Indian didn't help.

That had spurred him to trace our historical evolution, and warming to a subject that fascinated him, he continued, "We don't know for sure how old our civilisation is but it seems reasonable that when the last ice age ended we lost a lot of developed areas along the coasts from flooding, and maybe people too especially when the great rivers were formed from snow and ice melting.

Those who survived must have picked up the pieces by memory and simply started 'new' in India or they took what they knew to foreign places where they'd fled. But the way things developed up to the time the Muslims invaded and from the literature that survives, Bhārata did make great strides in recouping the lost knowledge. But who knows what we lost when Muslims destroyed those old Universities at Nālandā and Taxila? Or when Romans destroyed library at Alexandria or when Popes burned books and held Inquisitions and Hitler burned books?"

"I've always marvelled at the descriptions of flying machines in the *Rāmāyana* and *Mahābhārata*; they sounded just like helicopters, VTOL's and conventional planes, or even flying saucers. I remember specially the one about Bhīma in his shining aerial car, perhaps because I have a cousin named Bhīma, and I was an impressionable six when I heard this, and had not yet seen an aeroplane. So I imagined him in a boxy old Austin with wings, but now I see it as the clearest description of a space rocket."[29]

He chuckled and chanted verses in Sanskrit, the ringing consonants precisely mimicking the thundering sound of a soaring machine. He added, "*Vaidas* also refer many times to flying machines. Bhavabhuti, in millennium before Christ, quoted older references to *Pushpaka*, an aerial chariot, which carried people to Ayodhya, where he said sky was full of awesome flying-machines flashing yellow lights. Your teacher was right; you won't read these things in British textbooks. They worked very hard to twist peoples' minds to believe that Indians were illiterate until they brought schooling and today their disciples still pass on that lie! James Mill perfected that tradition with his book of half-truths."

I was excited and delighted to hear finally this affirmation of a view that had haunted me from the time when I first heard it, which had steered me away from anglophile accounts of India presented in my schoolbook *History of the British Empire* by William Wilberforce whose chapter on India Mr Yesu Das had condemned as British 'mythology'! What I had learned instead were the stories my parents had told us and the accounts given by *chacha* Latchman from his study of the *Vaidas* and the classics (Vyāsa, Vālmiki, Manu, Baudhāyana, Sushruta, Tulsidās, Chanukya, Charaka, Aryābhatta, Brahmagupta etc.). More recently I had read accounts given by or about Sir William Jones, Asiatic Society founder, and Indian critics of British occupation like Bāl Gangādhar Tilak, Swāmi Dayānanda Saraswati, Sri Aurobindo, Swāmi Vivekānanda, Rabindranāth Tagore, Sarojini Naidu, Subhās C. Bose, the Mahātma and others including Tulla,

---

[29] "Bhima flew along in his car, resplendent as the sun and loud as thunder... The flying chariot shone like a flame in the night sky of summer ... it swept by like a comet... It was as if two suns were shining. Then the chariot rose up and all the heaven brightened."

whose father had met members of the Arya Samaj mission to BG.

"The best name is Bhārata; remember that!" *Chacha* Latchman had cautioned, "'India is a corruption of Indus or Sindhu by foreigners and Hindu is a corruption of Sindhu, because those Persians and Muslims apparently couldn't pronounce letter 's'. You must be careful with what British say. After they conquered Mughals and realised that Hindus will not become Christian they set out to ruin us by destroying all rural industry; they turned food farms like mine to opium and cane plantations; they destroyed village economies, health centres and worst the Hindu schools; they called Vaidic learning slavery and teachers tyrants!

"Then they ordered schooling to be in English only, just like here, but built no schools. That left millions of children without schooling and not even charity could help when the famines came. I teach today just like old gurukuls; I am breaking their law; they can jail me! If you must learn what they teach about India learn it to pass exams but understand most are lies. Yesu Das is right. And don't forget, Vaidic religion stresses *learning*; all *varnas* had to learn, even Sudras."

"But where do you get something reliable?" I asked Dr Brahmam.

"There are many books, in Hindi, Marathi, Tamil, Bengali and other major languages. Tamil is the only one remaining of India's classical languages, although Malayalam contains Sanskrit forms. Some books have been translated; some were written *in* English. Read Swami Dayānanda–you have his name, I see. There's Munshi Premchand, his real name is Dhanpat Rai Srivastava; he wrote about the common people and their troubles; British banned his 1910 book *Soz-e-Watan* (Nation's Lament), calling it seditious and burnt all copies, just like Popes and Hitler! And Vinayak Savarkar, PB Desai and of course Gandhi, Nehru, Tilak, or better yet, go to *Vaidas* directly."

He rocked his head from side to side as he spoke. "*Vaidas* are oldest original books of knowledge in this world, twelve thousand years old at least; without philosophical change, scholars say, although some feel that insertions have been made in *smritis* especially *Manusmriti* by British to paint Hindus in bad light, also prophesy about Muhammad[30] *is* an insertion. Original Sanskrit versions are still intact. Gandhi translated *Gita* into Gujarati. Germans loved *Gita* and *Upanishads*; von Schlegel and Humboldt and Schopenhauer called these *'the production of the highest human wisdom'* with superhuman ideas. He called Sanskrit literature *'greatest gift of our century'*. But not Mueller; he distorted and mistranslated Vaidas.

"A scoundrel, British stooge!" he spat that out. "Today everybody reads Nehru's book but he repeats British propaganda. He's pro-British, I think, more Muslim than Hindu, probably anti-Hindu; his Muslim son-in-law insulted Gandhi in taking his name; they and their associates are new breed of 'secularist'; they want to reform or even ignore Hinduism. But they leave Islam intact, at least for now, I think because Marx wrote 100 years ago, 1853 I think, that villages based on Hinduism and caste must be destroyed to 'cleanse' India, and secularists will do that. British destroyed villages and promoted caste to divide more easily. Today many Indian intellectuals demean Hindus because British educated and brain-washed them to hate India and treat Hinduism as petty

---

[30] Muhammad Umar, Muslim scholar, in *The Review of Religions*, May/June 1993. Vol. LXXXVIII No. 5/6 names the source as *Bhavishyat Purana* Vol. 3, verse 3. *Puranas* are collections of old tales of gods and heroes from different ages.

myths and us Indians as primitive tribes; British tried to convert Hindus and bribed them with jobs. You know, the Brits only promoted some Hindus mostly those who observe caste *rigidly*; just look at how they strut in BG!"

"I know about British caste, only they call it *hierarchy*; we used to joke about Elizabethan hierarchy in school, in our Shakespeare classes. There was this picture of a tree, bearing each rank on a branch, from serf to lord. Caste at its best, we said. I told that to some students here when I was in Arts; they didn't like it at all" (Ch. 4). "I reminded them that many of Britain's aristocrats were middle or lower class folk who got titles by military deeds, like Clive, or money, like Rothschilds, or rarely by marrying higher caste partners with contacts."

"Yes; and Indian caste system also *allows* lower classes, the Vaishya and Shudra, to do business, trade and commerce and get as rich as they want; rulers can then prey on them for taxes! Caste does not close door to enterprise. India is full of rich Shudras and untouchables but they need to be socially uplifted. Indeed some people say that one of India's greatest dynasties, the Mauryan, was founded by a lower class."

"But what does Nehru hope then that secularists will do that can't be done by Hindus? India's past greatness came from Hindus and Buddhists, not communists!"

"He and his people think Hindus will oppose socialism, reject caste reform and women's rights, without discussion, and reject education aimed to address those issues," he observed.

"But I thought it was the orthodox Muslim who rejected education of women! Caste as practised now in India *is* a burden; it's not Hindu, not the way *we* learned about Hinduism. We learned about *"varna"* from the *Vaidas* and *Bhagavad Gita;* I can still hear *chacha* Latchman and later my mother's guru Pandit Daulat Ram reading passages describing *varna* as four divisions of labour based on qualities and abilities of persons and *not* on birthright or any rigid scheme; one can move from one *varna* to another depending on circumstances, abilities, and so on, just as Jagan moved from a *shudra* (labourer) to a *Kshatriya* (administrator) or my friend Sharma from *brahmin* (teacher, which he's not) to a trader (*vaishya*)."

"The Mughals and British and before them Brahmins, when Buddhism fell, distorted concept and used caste to make divisions they could pass on and keep permanent. British favoured Brahmins and Kshatriyas gave them new powers over others and employed them as Sepoys *(sipahis);* this made caste rigid. Brits passed off *Smritis* as scripture and authority, but *Smritis* are works of man *(purusheya)* which deal with human aspects of society and rules for living at specific periods, and are not *Shruti* – which is *apurusheya,* not made by man! Some claim that British suppressed revisions of *Manusmriti* to hide regular changes and updates that kept up with new laws and changing customs."

"In BG and Trinidad we got rid of the worst aspects of the British brand of caste although some survive. What's often denounced as caste are social and economic imbalances found in all societies. It's sheer ignorance; British suppression of Hindi language and *Vaidic* education led to this."

"Right!" Dr Brahmam affirmed. "Indian government should tackle caste head-on and not ignore it or continue to punish *all* Hindus like British and Muslims did. British were confused by India; they found a society with huge economy, advanced philosophy beyond their own, math outside their grasp that only a few like Newton could understand, ideas they'd never had, but stole them, and an enterprising people. They didn't know how to manage it, whose advice they should follow, whether to act as trustee as per Burke, or merely to play role of guardian, utilitarian or even despot; none would have worked. Then they seized idea of religious conversion to destroy power of Hindus. That is today's *secularism!*" He sounded vehement, his head wagging, and continued. "Socialist Government and Marxists made secularism upper and middle class city religion, dressed it up with big words and fancy concepts and imaginary fears of Hindutva; they forgot that we Hindus and Buddhists rescued the tormented and persecuted from everywhere--Jews, Christians, Parsis, Muslims and others. They forget that Ashoka Maurya created world's first socialist government with full control of all means of production, *2000 years before Marx*; but he also limited the emperor's powers and fully supported peoples' rights; in this he was democratic.

"Muslims and British stole our land and lived the high life. Secularism is fashionable because it allows 'modernisation' which only means freedom to flout social and religious discipline and morals that the *Gita* teaches; that will only degrade India and make it easy prey to new western conquerors, USA or USSR. So blind they are; they're raising people, especially privileged women, who do PhD's in psychology or sociology, history or politics, and litter our literature with condemnations, neologisms and obscure phrases that require further papers to explain! In this way they ensure academic tenure while degrading their people and heritage; they take themselves so seriously they don't realise how ridiculous they are. They're the new quislings, like Qasim, Jafar, Jaichandra and their kind, some before, some since; they do more harm to India than British; US and UK love and honour them and will use them to conquer India once more.[31]"

"I've met some who fit that description." I said, thinking of Jagan. "They don't hear the ridicule or see the derogatory smirks. Even from the little I know those Indians are ignorant when they attack Hindus who quote the *Vaidas,* and wrong to dismiss *Vaidic* history simply because it's Hindu, while they slavishly accept other views just because they're non-Hindu or trendy, especially the new powers."

"Yes, indeed! Secularists ridicule study of Sanskrit, don't study *Vaidas,* or *Rāmāyana* or *Gita* yet dismiss their content, accept European versions of everything, and give Hindu scholars dirty names, in true colonial style, attack being the best form of defence. Because they're anti-religion, they accept Darwin's evolution hypothesis, quite ignorant of the fact that this is in keeping with *Vaidas,* which speak of ten major *evolutionary* avatars[32] in Hinduism. So they look stupid when they deny or downplay anything that glorifies India's past greatness as if progress to the point of great wealth that attracted invaders happened by chance or in vacuum. Also they miss how closely the avatars match the morphology of species from the dawn of life, from the seabed to land, and from fins to feet!"

"My old Bio Prof. Millott would love this! He's the Brit who trashed doctors as greedy and upbraided me for switching from arts to medicine; he tried to fail me but Dr Taylor nixed that."

"I've met some like that and of course he's partly right. But he must know that British propaganda brainwashed middle class people all over the Empire

---

[31] R. Thapar, an Indian secular historian favoured in the West, seems to fit this description.
[32] See also 15(1): 35, footnotes 6&7: *Matsya, Kumura, Vahara, Narasimha, Vamana, Parasumana, Rama, Krishna* and *Buddha.* Later *Kalki* would follow.

and that they educated us mainly for government jobs, and Indian students faithfully crammed false British version of 'facts' to pass examinations? Indian scholars still believe these British teachings, even what's proven wrong, and continue to teach them, with great force and passion, condemning anyone who disagrees. Some even call themselves scientists, yet fail in the first task of scientists, which is to be objective and consider *all* evidence. They fear Hindus educated in Sanskrit and versed in *Vaidas*, belittle those who demand change in these old curricula when they should be fearing Muslims who are much more sinister and militant; they forget that Muslims have let them down again and again; it's very fragile religion, easily driven to senseless violence by anarchists; I'm afraid that Wahhabi doctrines from Arabia will spread."

"Wahhabis? I haven't heard this before. What are these?"

"They follow doctrine of Mohammed ibn Abdul Wahhab who in middle 18th century proposed strict interpretation of Sunni Islam which restricts it to teachings of first three generations of Islamic leaders, called *salafi*, who had direct contact with Mohammed. *Wahhabism* is fundamentalist sect of *salafis*. Wahhab was expelled from one Arabian tribe for extremism but went to east Arabia and made pact of mutual support with tribe leader Mohamed ibn Saud, ancestor of family that rules Arabia today. Chief danger is that oil will make Saudis rich and give them lots of money to take over *madrassahs* in Arabia, Middle East, Pakistan and beyond. Soviets will keep them in check, but I fear for India under Nehru's blind pro-Muslim leadership since Wahhabis believe that Muslims must reject and even destroy all non-Muslim ideas and beliefs; they even condemn Muslim groups like Ahmadiyyas, Shi'a and Sufi. Wahhabism is big threat to India and to whole world if it begins to spread."

"Wow! That's frightening. Extremism is a danger in any religion but worst in Islam which seems free with *jihad* and *fatwa* and promise extremists great rewards in heaven for acts of murder or suicide done for 'religion'. There are some radical Muslims in BG but I've never heard of any Wahhabis."

"They won't spread easily until they get big money; so far they're only in Arabia, even though you'll find *salafis* in Egypt and other Muslim countries; they're stable for now. India will avoid these fanatics only by asserting *Vaidic* strengths, which are many, especially with *ahimsa* in Hinduism, Buddhism, Jainism and tolerance of religions and peoples. You know, India spread culture over most of Asia without making any big enemies. They did this because after a conquest they adapted to local customs and let people choose, whether in China or Bali or Indonesia. Gupta King Vikram brought Vaidic culture and education to Arabia; some say he made Ka'aba a Hindu temple, which might explain Mohammed's reference to destroying idols. Vikram created a prosperous province and was well liked according to pre-Islam poets. So when nations invaded India it was not to punish but to rob her!"

"I have to thank my parents for their knowledge and insight and my teachers Yesu Das and Latchman who opened doors for me and others who cared. Mr Das gave us a choice of what to study, where the facts were not so badly distorted or contested, and steered us in the direction of tolerance and neighbourliness. I think he was unique and rather brave among teachers of that time."

"In India we had only one syllabus and most of our teachers were already two to three generations brain-washed! French and others were more open to India and gave fairer accounts. Read Louis Jacolliot, who was French envoy in

India, or Madame Blavatsky, Annie Besant, or American Will Durant's *The Story of Civilisation*; better, get Hindi great literature besides Tagore; read poetry of Subhadra Kumari Chauhan and others not available in West. If you want truth and inspiration you *must* go outside British and righteous seculars and Marxists who are plentiful among Indian historians.

"Most of them today merely echo old British propaganda, gang up on anyone who is Hindu and generally know too little about religion, much less Hinduism, to be fair. If they have any religion it's a sanitised view of Islam. You must go to India and see for yourself. India cannot be taught; it must be experienced! And yet your people have a much better understanding of Indian history and heritage than most people in India!"

"I wondered about that; I know about the British: Jones, Hastings, Clive, Mill, Wellesley, Macaulay, Muller, Monier Williams, Kipling and that lot. And I've read Americans Mark Twain[33] and William Jennings Bryan. I suspect that some of the doctors here, Grewal, Stracey, Shenolikar, Bhattacharya and others know only the British version of things and are proper secular Indians. That would explain why they're shy of talking with us; I heard they were shocked to find that the two senior hospital administrators Balkaran Singh and Indar Persaud were staunch Hindus, like Balwant Singh, the lab director and Nehaul, the Deputy CMO."

"Balkaran took them to a *Maha Sabha* function." Brahmam recalled, chuckling. "That was awkward; I'm afraid my colleagues had no clue what was happening. They didn't go back! But the ordinary Indians still treat these fellows like gods."

"I noticed that. But tell me about Nehru. Is he Communist, like Jagan?"

"Not really; he's Attlee-walla, *vaampanthi* (leftist). His policies make many best-qualified Indians leave India. British voters rejected socialism ten years ago, but it *survives* in India. *Everything British survives in India*," he said regretfully. "We celebrate British instead of Indian heroes in street and place names. You'll see Victoria, Shakespeare, Nelson, Newton, Clive, Dalhousie[34] etc. rather than Aryābhatta, Pānini, Bhāskara, Bhikaji Cāma, Lakshmi Bai, Tantia Tope, Madan Mohan, Tilak, Banerjea, Rai, and a million others. Libraries still promote British, Greek and Roman literature and science, even Arabic, but where do you find Sanskrit epics and classics, which came before all these and gave rise to them? Shri Aurobindo felt that *Sanatan Dharma* must return to India if India is to survive. I agree with that."

"British historian Toynbee said something similar; but are the secularists so brain-washed that they don't know the best of India's heritage? Even Nehru admitted India's past greatness.[35]"

---

[33]*"This is indeed India! The land of dreams and romance, of fabulous wealth and fabulous poverty, of splendour and rags, of palaces and hovels, of famine and pestilence, of genii and giants and Aladdin lamps, of tigers and elephants, the cobra and the jungle, the country of a hundred nations and a hundred tongues, of a thousand religions and two million gods, cradle of the human race, birthplace of human speech, mother of history, grandmother of legend, great-grandmother of tradition, whose yesterdays bear date with the mouldering antiquities of the rest of the nations – the one sole country under the sun that is endowed with an imperishable interest for alien prince and alien peasant, for lettered and ignorant, wise and fool, rich and poor, bond and free, the one land that all men desire to see, and having seen once, by even a glimpse, would not give that glimpse for the shows of all the rest of the globe combined."*   Mark Twain, *Following the Equator,* 1896

[34] After1947, Dalhousie Square was named B.B.D. Bagh - after martyrs: Benoy, Badal and Dinesh.

[35] Despite his secular politics J. Nehru recognized India's Hindu heritage without allowing himself to use *"Hindu"* or *"Vaidic"* when he lamented: *"How few of us know of these great achievements of our past, how few realize that if India was great in thought and philosophy, she was equally great in action. Most*

"They don't! It will be long struggle to restore primacy of *Vaidas*, but we have to do it. What I fear most is that secularists will enrich themselves, condemn Hindus in books and publications which West will gladly print and circulate, and fail to educate villagers; *India's strength is in villages, not cities; cities suck its blood*. Coming to BG I expected to find lost people, in spite of what the recruiter said. But I found instead that he understated the incredible preservation of *Vaidic* wisdom, which most Indian cities have lost. I even see things from *Atharva Vaida* which we ridiculed in medical school, but they work: for fevers, injuries, mental health, arthritis and so on. The loyalty of Indian migrants to their heritage in these European colonies is truly amazing and shames us in India. This is partly why my colleagues cannot relate to your people. Also, your relations with Muslims prove *Vaidic* life style is not anti-Islam, as some say; in fact its tolerance is its strength, as Swami Vivekānanda so nicely proclaimed many decades ago.[36]"

"I believe you'll find the same in Trinidad, Mauritius, Fiji, and in Suriname where Indians did better and preserved language; the Dutch were not as vicious as the Brits were in banning studies in Hindi. With regard to Muslims a few have begun to distort history, claiming origin from Pakistan and presenting it as an ancient entity! So soon, they're only 12 years old! This is sheer ignorance. Some even pretend to be Arabic, especially the radical ones. All sensible Muslims I know are embarrassed by this."

"There is so much ignorance even among the educated. You must tell them that there is no need to pretend; an interchange of peoples took place for millennia along the trading cities of the Arabian coast. Arabians and Yemenis resemble Indians and vice versa. "

And so we had talked at great length of how India (Bhārata) had founded an advanced civilisation many millennia before Christ, and had become the leading power in the ancient world, with, as Dr Brahmam asserted, his sing-song tones accentuating the points, "almost perfect language and most tolerant and peaceful religions, which Congress leaders today are afraid to explore or accept; instead they condemn anyone who does these things as fanatic, and claim that Brahmins will obstruct measures to erase caste, religious militancy and so on. Utter nonsense! Secularists are greatest danger to Indian culture. We want *weakness* out, not strength, which lies in *Vaidas*. We must preserve that!"

Section 2: From Origins to the Saraswati-Indus Civilisation

The culture of India is very old and at various times had included most of South Asia, parts of Indo-China, Indonesia, Afghanistan and parts of Iran. Since 1924 excavations and reconstructions of ruins along the Sindhu (Indus) River confirm that Indian civilisation is much older than is currently taught in the west and in many Indian schools, and more closely matches accounts and dates given by *Vaidic* (Vedic) seers than those in the revisionist propaganda of the British and their Indian sycophants.

The first hominids are said to have originated in East Africa 2-3 million years ago and spread to Asia leaving traces which can be used to characterise

---

westerners still imagine ancient history is largely concerned with the Mediterranean countries, and medieval and modern history is dominated by the quarrelsome little continent of Europe."

[36]*"I am proud to belong to a religion that has taught the world both tolerance and universal acceptance."* Swami Vivekānanda (1863-1902) I chose the spelling *Vaida* instead of *Veda* as it more closely matches the Hindi and Sanskrit sound.

and age them.[37] It would take most of the subsequent 2 million years for various evolutionary human forms to develop, including *Homo erectus* and *Homo sapiens* until about 100,000 BCE when *Homo sapiens sapiens* emerged in East Africa. Stone artefacts 2 million years old have been found in northern India, and evidence of elephants and other animals; hand axes and other tools 0.5 million years old have been found in Punjab and Tamil Nadu, and a culture known as Soan was defined 0.4 million years ago similar to other cultures in African and Asian sites. In the interim hominids in Northern India had learned to use hand tools and by 470K BCE could be found over much of India, from Punjab to Tamil Nadu.

Homo erectus appeared around 360K BCE; this species learned to control fire, like their Chinese counterparts; their successors *Homo sapiens* became dominant in Africa and Asia until *Homo sapiens sapiens* spread and, like their fore-runners, mingled with earlier species. They were hunter-gatherers similar to the Barama Caribs we had just met. Their advance could have been affected by the ice age, which began ca 75,000 BCE, changed the world, and perhaps cleansed it. The deep freeze and lowering of sea level exposed land masses in various shallow seas worldwide.

East and south of India a vast area is said to have appeared that came to be known as *Sundaland* incorporating all of Indonesia, the Philippines and Indo China, which with India formed a contiguous land mass (a Greater India) stretching from the Himalayas to the western edge of the Pacific Ocean. The relative warmth of the subcontinent had kept the land healthy and habitable throughout the Ice Age. But the massive Himalayan glaciers so locked in the enormous volume of moisture that early Vaidic scholars likened the phenomenon to a giant serpent that had ringed the Himalayas and barricaded its life-giving waters.

When the globe thawed the melting ice and increased rainfall -- from convection and from wind movements that sprang from the warming waters -- raised sea levels over 300 feet drowning all lowland, converting rivers to seas and creating the topography we know today. Melting Himalayan snows gave birth to or enlarged the many rivers that feature prominently in the Vaidas that converted arid northern India into a fertile and productive land. The major streams were the massive *Saraswati, Sindhu, Ganga and Brahmaputra* in the north and the Deccan rivers in the south. The extensive consequential flooding of low coastal lands by high seas and interiors by river courses destroyed much, including accessible evidence of antediluvian civilisations.

Indian peoples generally survived the ice-age. During this period people remained mainly hunter-gatherers but gradually developed various skills in their individual ways for which some tribes and groups would become known. (This specialisation would in time facilitate the classification of labour–the caste system--used by many north Indian kings). Painted-rock shelters of ca. 40,000 BCE have been found in central India and primitive cave art including a hunter on a horse. Coastal tribes learned navigation which led to marine exploration and eventually migration to Australia and the Pacific islands. Later others left and settled in Europe about 35,000 BCE; this roughly coincided with the migration of various Asian tribes to the Americas across the frozen Bering Sea. (Some believe that migrations also followed natural sea routes as determined by

---

[37] The science of dating artefacts is still imprecise but estimates will bear a fairly stable relationship if measuring errors are skewed all in the same direction.

winds and ocean currents)[38].

By the time the ice age ended, Indians -- then totalling about 1,000,000 people out of an estimated global population of 4 million -- had begun to cultivate grain, domesticate animals, build cities, study the heavens and to refine their philosophy that became crystallised in the following millennia as the four *Vaidas*, which represent not only original and unique spiritual and intellectual insights but some of the most sublime and riveting poetry in the world, written in Sanskrit, then the *lingua franca* in India.

Prosperity spawned larger and more complex communities and dominions along the fertile banks of the rivers that flowed from the Himalayas to the Indian Ocean: The *Rg Vaida* gives accounts of peoples who had established kingdoms along two western rivers, the huge *Saraswati* and the lesser *Sindhu (Indus)* and the region of their five major northern tributaries[39] *Shatadru (Sutlej), Vipasa (Beas), Asikni (Chenab), Parosni (Ravi), Vitasta (Jhelum)* – *sapta sindhu*. This region is mentioned in great detail in the *Vaidas* and epics; it influenced settlements along the Ganga, Brahmaputra and their tributaries and replicated on riverain lands of the Deccan in middle and southern India.

Saraswati-Indus Civilisation: religion, commerce and growth of cities

The Saraswati River once flowed from the Himalayas to the Arabian Sea through the lush grasslands and forests of northern India east of the Indus and almost parallel to it, with the Yamuna among its tributaries. West of the Sindhu were the dry highlands where Baluchi, Pashtu, Afghan and other tribes roamed to the borders of Persia. These peoples have remained in tight clans, which rarely shared in the social and economic growth of the settled kingdoms to the east, south and west. Some assert that they may be the lost tribes of Israel.

The sub-continent was heavily forested, rich in animal life, with numerous rivers and fertile ground along their banks and estuaries. Each tribe held territory jointly, exploited its resources communally and defended it. Geographic features of mountain, river or forest created natural boundaries and provided security; yet weaker tribes often fell to expansionist or greedy neighbours. (Marriage among ruling families was a more civilised way of acquiring territory.) As morality, virtue and ideas of justice matured with the intercession of divine guidance (*avatars*) violence would be scrutinised and its use as a tool in civil life censured, but at times it would erupt with regrettable results.

The settlements, though often far apart, showed common features united by commerce, religion, language, and other beliefs and practices. Those best known today – thanks to excavations of recently discovered ruins of ancient cities – are Mehrgarh, Harappa and Mohenjodaro, while Rakhigari, Dholavira, Dwaraka (the great port at the mouth of the Saraswati at the Rann of Kacch on the Arabian Sea,) and others mentioned in Hindu texts, remain to be researched. Cities had paved streets, laid out in a grid pattern (like Georgetown or Manhattan, New York), large brick buildings, granaries and other warehouses, piped water, indoor plumbing, sewage disposal systems and other features.

Many homes had brick altars as used in *Vaidic* ceremonial worship of Lord

---

[38] The dates are approximate and roughly coincide with modern estimates of the disappearance of large animals in several continents; did man, the ultimate predator, bring about some extinctions as he is causing today and do these migrations represent his search for new sources of food? We'll await the verdict of palaeontologists.

[39] In Hindi, *paanch ab* means five rivers, hence the rendition Punjab.

Shiva, and female clay figurines probably representing *Shakti*. Of note is the exactness of the dimensions of the vessel used for the ritual fire and the composition of the herbs *(sāmagri)* used to create the fragrant and health-giving vapours. The people raised cattle, sheep and goats, domesticated the horse, grew barley, developed pottery and crafts, worked with copper, precious stones and sea shells, and later made coiled basketry, trading these with one another and in foreign lands, by road, river and sea, often long distances away. Their agriculture and manufactures expanded and made them wealthy.

Semi-nomadic tribes were each led by a *raja* (king) with administrative guidance of *Brahmins* (learned men) and frequently raided one another's livestock. For nomadic tribes the size of the herd expressed their owner's wealth, and it seems certain that early conflicts might have erupted not only in response to raids but over grazing rights. As settlement consolidated along the great rivers, rules and conventions were framed to control land use and minimise conflicts, but the opposing positions of grain and stock farmers would remain an enduring challenge, here as in other regions of the world.

Development had reached a high level in the city states of the Saraswati-Sindhu civilisation by the time it abruptly ended ca. 2000 BCE. The excavations in the Indus valley that began in 1924 at Harappa following Sir John Marshall's discovery of relics and later findings by Mortimer Wheeler began the slow process of identification. This has tended to confirm *Vaidic* accounts and their extensive commentaries, which the British have worked so hard to dismiss as mythology.[40] Harappa was some 5-6,000 years old, and its excavations show features of *modern* industrial cities, related farms and villages had complex irrigation and fire and flood control measures.

Cotton formed the basis of a textile industry that traded widely among sister cities and as far as the Middle East and Egypt. The civilisation expanded, prospered, and population increased. Population pressures and periods of weak leadership led to lowering of building standards and a decline in civil society, making it more vulnerable to human foibles and natural disasters, and leading to its eventual extinction. (This cycle of events, coinciding with natural disasters, could bring an end to any civilisation in any age that ignored warning signs. Many feel that today's world has already begun the urban growth explosion and ecological damage that presage the terminal decline in our current attempt to elaborate a "western" civilisation).

The Search for Answers: Science, Religion, Language

From the earliest days of Indian civilisation scholars had marvelled at the richness of life, the myriad forms of living things, animal and plant, that covered the land, how they inter-related, propagated and survived. They pondered the meaning of life, and probed its origin, purpose, rhythms and cycles. The sun and moon and other heavenly bodies with their unique periodicities had always been a source of wonderment and speculation. In due course reaction moved from mere awe to scientific examination and determination of the properties of physical and metaphysical phenomena, which led to the concept of an inclusive

---

[40] Today's Indian secularists – most of whom are either atheists or communists, or both, who became enmeshed in the waves of Marxist fervour between the world Wars and especially after WWII, as decolonisation became a reality -- come from the 15% of urban or privileged persons educated in the British tradition, and continue a campaign to denounce Hinduism or any notion of *Vaidic* rebirth or attempt to recognise the reality that >85% of Indians are Hindus, and that *all* indigenous Indians share a Hindu ancestry.

and extensive, eventually limitless universe. Above all, they puzzled over who had created all the wondrous complexity and diversity they saw each day.

By study and contemplation the sages[41] of that era – among whom were the wandering wise men (scientists) who communed among many tribes -- developed theories of the nature of the universe and of its creation as a coherent whole, one that saw the universe in each person and each one as part of the ultimate "Creator". They integrated the wisdom and observations of their forebears who had noted the succession of *avatars* who had appeared to guide living creatures at critical stages of evolution, and who had eventually revealed to mankind this lineage and thereby some of the mystery of Creation, including concepts of the Universal Presence or Supreme Force that made it possible (*Brahmān*), and with which they could reunite through good works. They recorded this knowledge--from the end of the Ice Age, when Manu led their ancestors towards high ground and away from floods--kept it sacred and passed it on down the generations, with names for each function and functionary, and for each attribute.

The *Taittriya Brahmana* (a segment of the *Vaidas*) is believed to have appeared ca. 10,000 BCE--one of the first religious treatises, if not the first by a human in our civilisation--contained observations of celestial bodies that allowed fairly accurate dating. It confirmed the inquisitive nature of the people and marked the emergence of a religious philosophy and of social norms that would develop and endure.

Seers (*rishis*), enlightened by deep meditation and revelation received the sacred scriptures, the four *Vaidas* (from *vid*, to know)--*Rg, Sāma, Yajur* and *Atharva*--the quintessential wisdom of Creation and the foundation of the religious philosophy called *Sanatan Dharma,* later Hinduism. These they organised as four major religious works (*srutis,* meaning *what is heard,* since early transmission was entirely oral), as follows: *Samhitas,* hymns to praise and glorify God and sounds to invoke His presence; *Brahmanas* to describe ways of giving thanks and rituals for worship; *Aranyaka,* records of the philosophy (literally *in the forest,* perhaps a reflection of the environment of their elaboration); and *Upanishads* (interpretations, literally "at the side of" a teacher).

Sanskrit was perfected in the process and enriched with words and phrases to describe living things and their attributes; physical and social entities; objects; actions or abstractions--thoughts, concepts, moods, emotions, behaviours and so on. They were used in song to express views on the weighty matters that troubled people. Centres of learning developed and temples for assembly, knowledge-sharing, discourse and worship. Heads of governments and administrators thus acquired tools to codify human behaviour to avoid personal or group conflict, and to order and manage the activities of rulers and citizens to promote growth of peaceful and secure communities while preserving autonomy, whether as tribes or kingdoms.

By this time Indians probing astronomical and mathematical themes had begun to elaborate on the nature of time and of civilisations and the influence of natural forces on their many iterations. The current cycle of development had accelerated with the end of the ice age. Research into mathematical puzzles resulted in a unique understanding of natural phenomena, for example, the

---

[41] *Saksat krtdharmanah rsayo babhuvuh* (Nirukta, 1:20), that is, *"Rsis were born who visualized universal laws of nature in the form of the Vaidas."* (Trans. by Prof. Satish Prakash Arya, Indian Foundation for Vaidic Science, New Delhi).

movements of galaxies and their component stars and planets and phases of the moon (which they correctly related to movement of the earth around the sun); expression of abstract concepts like infinity and zero (the keys to all science); and solution of mathematical problems necessary to explain natural phenomena, concepts and features of religion and to perform *Vaidic* rites.

Thus Hinduism's roots in science spurred research into astronomy enabling scientists to document and name solar systems, constellations, galaxies etc. and suggest the size and age of the universe[42] despite lacking the sophisticated telescopes of today. Time was conceived as cycling over four eras called *yugas* and 3102 BCE marked the beginning of the fourth, *Kaliyuga* or Iron Age, a time of regression when ignorance increased, culture decayed, spirituality declined and society generally became selfish, covetous and corrupt.

To facilitate dissemination of Vaidic knowledge the sage Vyāsa put the four *Vaidas* in writing and wrote a simpler version, sometimes called the *Fifth Vaida* to which other writings were added and together formed the *Smriti Vaidas*. These were quite extensive and advanced knowledge or simply recorded it, and covered considerations of human character and behaviour, good and evil, histories, and attributes of stable communities and orderly societies. The Sanskrit language spread from north to south, among all peoples, facilitating communication and study and gave rise to the Indo-European group of languages as people moved for various reasons to the Middle East and Europe.[43]

An unknown part of the vast accumulated knowledge has not survived, due to the destruction of temples, libraries and universities by Muslim invaders and rulers and the undermining of Indian education by the Mughals and British. The efforts of Swami Dayānanda and others in the late 19th century to restore study of the *Vaidas* marked the beginning of a rough road to restore that knowledge base, ironically resisted today by secular Indians who wish to deny their Hindu roots and simplistically denigrate as "fundamentalists" those who seek a revival.

Dr Brahmam was scathingly critical of these, their distortions of Hindu beliefs and practices and false use of Hindu holy terms. His father had told intriguing stories of sunken cities off Andhra Pradesh and of the older *Rāma Empire* which had developed air and possibly space travel as we had earlier discussed; that civilisation might even have discovered an anti-gravity power and use of solar energy for propulsion. They had commerce worldwide and contact with Atlantis. What calamity ended it is still subject of speculation.[44]

Section 3: Kings and Avatars

Commerce, Trade, Migration

The kingdoms had advanced over several millennia through religious, technological and agricultural discoveries in many fields, including commercial

---

[42] See Ch. 4, page 42.

[43] Sir William Jones, one of the first late 18th century students of Indian culture, founder of the Asiatic Society, noted "... *a stronger affinity* (between Sanskrit, Latin and Greek) *than could possibly have been produced by accident; so strong, indeed, that no philologer could examine them all three, without first believing them to have sprung from some common source...The Sanskrit language is of wonderful structure, more perfect than the Greek, more copious than the Latin and more exquisitely refined than either.*"

[44] The recent finding of a script resembling Brahmi on Easter Island supported the idea of foreign contact.

developments such as product preservation and warehousing. These stimulated trade with neighbours in surplus and in specialties derived from various arts--including healing arts[45]---and crafts, and from agricultural, engineering and other practices and products. By this time too rulers in *Vaidic* societies had found it necessary to classify citizens according to their abilities and occupations; this was a useful inventory of national skills, classified as four large groups, or *varnas* as previously noted; in time the system became a hierarchy. Much of this was codified in the Laws of Manu (*Manusmriti*) which remains a singular historical document, which many still use despite outmoded rules and need for modernisation and reform.

It is oft-quoted as authority, ironically by foreign critics of Hinduism who erroneously assert that the "Laws" are "religion" and enforceable exactly as written millennia ago; thus they judge them and the society that spawned them by far stricter standards than they would their own ancient works.

Development was not always smooth. Tribes and kingdoms have from time immemorial clashed over "rights" of one kind or another, and it seemed that humans -- especially their leaders -- could not remain for long in tranquillity or contentment, but displayed anger, hatred, greed, envy and other base characteristics. These were the antithesis of what were deemed laudable human traits and of the Hindu principles of *sat, chit* and *ānanda* --existence, conscious intelligence and bliss--inherent qualities of *Brahmān,* the Universal Presence.

Settlement of differences by negotiation did happen but those that resulted in war got more publicity and provided much material for all kinds of artistic and other expression. The **Rg Vaida** records many conflicts that have influenced the direction of Indian and world history, for example, the **War of Ten Kings** ca. 7200 BCE[46], resulting in the exile or migration of many of the defeated rulers and their retinue, who went west and founded kingdoms from Persia to Europe[47].

Rice cultivation began in eastern India and by 5000 BCE had spread to China. Trade with the Middle and Far East and with Indonesia was evident by 4000 BCE, when India's population had reached well over a million. Many became wealthy and **influential.**[48] Dwaraka most likely developed at this time as a major seaport for trade south and west with neighbouring kingdoms and further afield with Persia, the Middle East, Africa, the Mediterranean and Europe via the Persian Gulf and Red Sea. Many of these contacts seemed to have been Indian migrants who had established settlements and kingdoms in foreign

---

45 The theories and practice of Ayurvedic system of health promotion and general medicine

[46] See S.D. Kulkarni: *Shri Bhagavan Vaidavyasa Itihasa Samshodhana Mandira* Bombay, India, 1994 (now Mumbai).

[47] The losers in this and other struggles either migrated en masse or were exiled, taking their customs and practices to places as far as Europe, in much the same way that recent Indians have established their religions and traditions in the Diaspora, despite changes of language. These and other massive movements took place over several millennia and spawned cultures with linguistic and religious similarities to their parent in India complete with the pantheon of 'god' and 'goddess' figures that are found in Hinduism. These émigrés are said to include the peoples of the Mediterranean and Middle East, the Druids of northern Europe, and German, Finnish Scandinavian, and other tribes. Studies of M-DNA in various Europeans would be very helpful.

[48] "*Peaceful lived the righteous people, rich in wealth in merit high, /Envy dwelt not in their bosoms and their accents shaped no lie,/Fathers with their happy households owned their cattle, corn, and gold,/Galling penury and famine in Ayodhya had no hold,/Neighbours lived in mutual kindness helpful with their ample wealth, /None who begged the wasted refuse, none who lived by fraud and stealth!*" The *Rāmāyana,* ca 4000 BC, trans Romesh C. Dutt, 19th Century CE.

regions.

Vaidic philosophy spread with the migrants, a logical inference from the similar names of "deities" and forms of worship in Mediterranean countries such as Anatolia (Turkey), Crete, Greece, Rome, Egypt and others, which also displayed a matriarchal order and multiple 'deities'.

By the 5th millennium BCE, north Indian kings and rulers, in craving power, had begun to show intolerance, envy, greed, hate, lust, ambition, despotism, and so on, in breach of *Vaidic* principles and conduct, deviating so much from the path of *dharma* or righteousness that *Rāma*, the seventh avatar of God in His role as preserver (Vishnu), was born in Ayodhya into the Raghu clan with a mission to show mankind, by precept and example, how to regain *dharmic* focus and live full and just lives.

His story is beautifully told in two classic epics, one by Vālmiki, in Sanskrit called *The Rāmāyana*, the other much later in Hindi by Tulsidās, generally known as *The Rāmacharitmānas*. They describe India of that time, highlight the decline in human morality, and relate the life and work of Rāma and his mission to eliminate evil and establish a code of interpersonal behaviour that reflected the best and noblest of virtues. These included altruism; respect for others and security of their welfare; goodness; fair and just dealing; and rightness, within a social, economic and religious framework throughout the land, that respected and had a place and a role for everyone. The events of the *Rāmāyana* took place hundreds of years before the date given for the "Creation" according to the Jews, Christians and Muslims[49]!

At this time India extended from the Persian border to the Bay of Bengal organised as tribes, principalities and kingdoms, which flourished in well-built cities and related farming districts along the great rivers, the Saraswati, Sindhu (later called Indus by invaders) and Ganga in the north, Brahmaputra in the east and Narmada, Godavari and others in the Deccan and south.

Barley, rice, cotton, other grains and grasses had become major agricultural industries along with cattle, sheep, goats, camels. This was well before the Egyptians had built their first pyramid circa 2600 BCE. Indians traded among themselves and externally, some to distant areas east and west, having developed expertise in agriculture, astronomy, mathematics, sciences (pure and applied), religion, architecture, crafts, and promoting scholarship, the arts, especially music, dance and song, poetry and writing.

The great Sanskrit grammarian Pānini composed the *Ashtadhyāyi*, the world's first treatise on grammar and language. The *Vaidic* religion spread and was rendered in many languages throughout the land, with formalised worship that applied science e.g. *Agnihotra* to preserve health, air quality and Nature.

As the kingdoms along the great rivers prospered and expanded over the next millennium they drifted inexorably into the state of *Adharma* foregoing Rāma's principles, and ignoring the precepts recorded by *Manu.* Driven by self-aggrandisement and the lust for wealth and power that grew with corruption, families fractured and societies deteriorated morally and spiritually. With internecine war threatening the northern region of the upper Ganga Lord Krishna, the 8th avatar of Vishnu, came on earth to restore moral and spiritual

---

[49] *"It does not behove us, who were only savages and barbarians when these Indian and Chinese peoples were civilized and learned, to dispute their antiquity."* Voltaire, French Philosopher, (1694-1778)

order. Krishna was the hero of the *Mahābhārata* and author of the *Bhāgavad Gita*--which forms part of the major work--and guru to Arjuna, its hero.

The *Gita* records Krishna's explanation of man's role in the universe and his duty to ensure that right prevails over wrong. *Krishna's* advent among men restored their focus on *dharma*, and after a great cleansing of the forces of evil, honour and morality prevailed for a time. Krishna "died" in 3102 BCE, the beginning of *Kaliyuga*. The ancient Indian calendar began at this date, thus making 1961 the 5063rd year of *Kaliyuga*. The *Rāmāyana* and *Mahābhārata* are generally included among the *Smriti Vaidas*.

Many heroic tales are told of the wise and not-so-wise who came to the thrones of India. By 2000 BCE many Europeans of presumed Indian origin--Celts, Slavs, Lithuanians, Ukrainians—the Akkads of Mesopotamia--founded by Sargon--the Kassites, the Babylonians under King Indatu (a contemporary of Varanasi's Divodas), were following patterns and practices similar to those in *Vaidic* India in areas of cosmology, astronomy, theology, marriage and other sacraments and social practices. The world population had reached 27 million, of which 5 million (22%) were Indians (note that throughout history Indians would comprise roughly a fifth of humanity; today it is one-sixth).

By 1900 BCE the drying up of the huge Saraswati River and flooding of the Sindhu from increased flow as it acquired the Punjabi tributaries of the Saraswati forced the evacuation of millions; survivors of the doomed cities migrated in all directions. They are said to have become (or joined with) the Chaldeans, Akkadians, the Mitanni of Syria and other groups in central Asia, the Middle and Far East and possibly Eastern Europe, whose deity and practices were the same as those described in the *Vaidas*. For example at Boghaz Koi in Turkey, stone inscriptions include such names as Mitra, Varuna, Indra and the Nasatyas (Ashvins)--all *Vaidic* deities.

In India the centres of civilization moved to the Ganges valley, even as other Hindu kingdoms in the south: Chola, Pallava, Pandya etc. were developing and establishing trade and other relations with countries of the Middle and Far East where Indian migrants or exiles had settled and established colonies – in much the same way as modern migrants keep contact and carry on trade with their country of origin[50]. In Egypt the Valley of the Kings was becoming a major cemetery and in the Pacific Polynesians were spreading throughout the archipelagos, and Mayan and other tribes were advancing their cultures in Mexico and adjacent lands.

Universities and Governance:

Knowledge accumulated as time passed and crystallised in diverse fields, fuelled by the need to understand and explain natural phenomena, to guide spiritual, religious and scientific exploration, and to organise society in its various sectors and improve government. Sages and teachers found innovative ways to store the knowledge gained, conduct studies to obtain reproducible results, compile analyses and reports and exchange information. By the end of the second millennium BCE intellectual ferment had led to the establishment of many centres of learning throughout India, prime among them the world's first residential universities at Nālandā in Bihar and at Taxashila (Taxila), Punjab.

---

[50] This is also illustrated in the story of the Caribs told by the shaman of Cokerite, see Ch. 6, 17-20

In the two millennia between the end of the Saraswati civilisation and the Mauryans, India was a complex of tribal settlements each with roots in a particular riparian ecosystem, often separated by dense forest or broad rivers that provided abundance and protection for inhabitants, but sadly cover for invaders also. Some had developed further than others, involving alliances and cooperatives that achieved high density, to become kingdoms or principalities united by religion each pursuing a wide variety of economic activities based on agriculture, education, skilled trades, mining, metallurgy, defence, warehousing, merchandising, transportation and the panoply of endeavour to be found in any evolving state, including highly organised governments and a unifying Vaidic religion.

Among them sixteen great realms (*Mahājanapadas* -महाजनपद्- *janapada* = "tribe's foothold") had developed by the time of **Rāma** (4th millennium BCE), spanning the territory from modern Afghanistan to Burma (Myanmar). From West to East these realms were Kamboja, Gandhara, Kuru, Panchala, Kosala, Malla, Kashi, Magadha, Vrijji (Vajji), Anga, Vatsa (Vamsa), and-- south from Kuru--Shurasena, Machcha (Matsya), Avanti, Chetiya and Assaka. They lay along the great central rivers (Ganga, Yamuna and their many large tributaries), and on the great Deccan streams, the Arabian Sea coast and Bay of Bengal.

In this period the major kingdoms had seen steady progress economically and in religion, mathematics, astronomy, engineering, language, agriculture, medicine, crafts, commerce and governance. In politics and government the world's first democratic federal republic was formed in the last millennium BCE –Videha, Magadha and neighbouring city states of Bihar—and lacked in one particular: the enfranchised did not include the lower or poorer classes, and prosperity did not filter down to all who may have contributed to individual and national wealth, even though schooling was conducted in each village and had advanced with the establishment of universities, where students from all over India and many foreign lands including Greece and Rome could acquire higher learning in both secular and religious subjects: astrology, astronomy, grammar, language, mathematics, medicine, metaphysics, science and religion (Hinduism and its offshoots Buddhism, Jainism), philosophy, logic etc. Indian states differed in language but shared *Vaidic* traditions and traded extensively.

Regional customs and practices including dress and cuisine developed according to geography, climate, social and economic factors some of which have persisted to this day and are identifiable among Diasporal Indians worldwide. The most distinctive feature was the variety of languages. ("You all don't have same language?" Doris puzzled. "Nor do Africans, Asians or Europeans," I replied)

Varanasi, the holy city of the Hindus on the sacred **Ganga River**, rose to greater prominence. Scholarship flourished even among the ruling class. For example, **Shuchi**, the King of Magadha, wrote about his studies in astronomy in a book titled the *Jyotisha Vaidanga* (1255 BCE). Elsewhere about this time Zarathustra founded the Parsi religion in Persia.Its scripture, the *Zend Avesta*, contained passages identical to those in the *Rg* and *Atharva Vaidas;* the stress on good versus evil established the dualism of this and other religions that emerged in western Asia.

Further west Egyptian pharaohs of the 18th dynasty took their armies south to quell the rising power of the Nubians and indoctrinated them to their way of life, which they adopted and maintained. More than a century later Moses led

600,000 cantankerous Jews out of Egypt (circa 1250 BCE), and Greeks battled Trojans (1200 BCE) over a kidnapped woman Helen (who seemed rather fond of her kidnapper). In 1124 BCE Nebuchadnezzar I, the Elamite emperor, moved his capital to **Babylon**, then the largest city in the world. By 1000 BCE world population was 50 million and Europe a collection of numerous primitive, unlettered and warring tribes.

By this time trade had developed between India and the Middle East; the port at Supāra (Ophir) on the Arabian Sea near today's Bombay traded with King Hiram of Phoenicia and with Jewish King Solomon and soon after (950 BCE), India accepted Jewish settlers who would make a name and fortune for themselves in the spice industry in Cochin. Many intermarried with Indians to create the "black Jews" who endured the discrimination of later arrivals, the white Jews who were escaping various calamities especially the Muslin-Christian wars. By this time too, Indian technology in transportation, e.g. the spoked-wheel chariot and horse-drawn freighter--widely used in India for over two thousand years--had become established in central Asia, the Ukraine and other regions in the west where Indians had settled. Later these would reach the Mediterranean and become adapted to its societies: Turkey, Greece, Rome and North Africa (Maghreb, Carthage, Egypt, Nubia, Ethiopia etc.).

About the same time as **David** had established his reign over the region that is today's Palestine, Lebanon and Israel, the Greeks began to use iron to replace bronze, which had gotten scarce due to a shortage of tin, thus consolidating the western Iron Age (begun in 3102 BCE in India). In this era the Chinese adopted the Hindu *jyotisha* (zodiac) system calling it *Shiu* (850 BCE). In the Middle East Phoenicians had dominated sea lanes of the Mediterranean and thereby the sea trade. The Greeks held their first Olympic games in Athens (776 BCE), as Pharoanic Egypt devolved into a series of fractious entities under Libyan and other warlords.

The armies of **Nubia** (Kush) under **Piye** (he later adopted the ancient name of Thutmose III) invaded Egypt and held Memphis; his brother Shabako extended control over all Egypt and soon restored Egyptian values and culture, just in time to face the Assyrians under Sennacherib pouring bloodthirsty armies into Palestine. Sennacherib poised to sack Jerusalem then under Hezekiah in the early 7th century BC but retreated on learning of the Nubian advance to assist the Jews. But though Hezekiah saved Jerusalem and Jews he would succumb to the westward expansion of Babylon's **Nebuchadrezzar II** in 597 BC and be destroyed ten years later along with Judah when citizens rebelled; survivors were exiled to Babylon. The subjugation of Phoenicia followed.

At this time the major kingdoms of India were prospering and had advanced in learning, spurred by the universities at Nālandā and Taxila. But as in all human endeavours this progress did not bring benefits to all. Exploitation of the underprivileged had become systemic. Once again the disparities in living standards and the plight of the poor became a principal social concern, and as the number of the oppressed increased and rulers continued waging inter-tribal wars, two avatars, **Siddhartha Gautama** (*the Buddha*) and Jainism's **Mahāvira Vardhamana** rose to prominence (perhaps a century or more apart;). They preached against the evils that permeated human society and expounded philosophies that emphasised respect for life in all its forms, proposing that each individual could achieve an enlightened state by eliminating greed, corruption, enmity and delusions--the plague of nations. They supported other religious figures who were warning against specific evils such as gambling as people seemed taken with *ashtapada*, a board game played with dice. (In deference to the Laws of Manu--*Manusmriti*--the socio-cultural and general guide, dice were discarded and the game evolved into the two-sided strategy game *shaturanga*, the forerunner of chess.)

Mahavira was the 24th in his line of prophets *(tirthankaras);* like Buddha he and his predecessors stressed the principle of *ahimsa* (avoidance of harm), vegetarianism and asceticism (Mahavira) in the search for righteousness and ultimate union with the Universal Presence. Their teachings updated and amended the *Manusmriti* adding values and new frames of reference for human interaction, thus enriching the **social** and spiritual spheres, but a gradual breakdown of Sanskrit as a spoken language began as both movements took to writing in Prākrit, especially Pāli, the vernacular of the common peoples which Buddha used; Sanskrit evolved into a refined priestly language, and has remained so.

But not all reacted favourably to the teachings of these two prophets. One Ajit led a vocal sect of ascetic atheists, the *Ajivika*, in the south; he went about naked for the most part, cursed a lot and believed in the inevitability of everything. Their influence lasted for a millennium in a small section of Mysore. At the same time Lao-tze **Tao-te Ching** established Taoism in China; his emphasis on simplicity and selflessness shaped Chinese life and spirituality from then on and spread to adjacent countries. Later Kung Fu—Confucius--would emerge and enunciate new principles that attracted the powerful and the ruling class and became a blueprint for upper class Chinese education and conduct.

Other great works of that time included some of the **Upanishads**, and an amazing textbook of **Ayurvaidic medicine**, focusing on prevention and holistic cure, by the physician **Sushruta**, of Varanasi, the acclaimed "father" of surgery. His curative work encompassed the broadest range of subjects such as the diagnostic process, medical ethics, toxicology, psychiatry, surgical anaesthesia, midwifery, embryology, cosmetic surgery, antiseptics, use of styptics, surgical implements, and specific topics such as hernia, fistulae, classification of burns, cataract extractions, the pulse, therapeutics of garlic and others.

The spread of Indian philosophy, education and their consolidation in centres of learning and excellence attracted students and visitors from all over the world. Scientific achievements in agriculture, engineering (e.g. irrigation and drainage projects) and in meteorology became widely known and inevitably attracted foreign invaders who coveted India's wealth and resources, both human and material.

The Parsi king Darius I invaded the Indus Valley in 518 BCE. This was a kind of homecoming for his people who had originated there over a millennium earlier. His stay was soon ended and he withdrew. India's population reached 25 million and the world's 100 million (probably the highest percentage India has achieved), reflecting the high standard of living and no doubt also the poor life expectancy elsewhere.

Sometime after, ca. 478 BCE the Gujarati King **Sinhabahu**, exiled his son **Vijaya**, who sailed to Sri Lanka with 700 followers and settled Sri Lanka, while in Greece Socrates became famous, his disciple Plato would advance to start the Athens Academy, and Hippocrates develop the code of medical conduct still in use. He is said to have studied at the Sushruta School of Ayurvaidic Medicine.

Section 4: Dynasties, Invaders and Conquerors

As Darius before him, **Alexander** of Macedonia reached the Punjab in 326 BCE, defeated the Puru king but could not advance further. He withdrew; many of his troops deserted to remain behind, but not before he had massacred thousands of children and women, in addition to an excess of a hundred thousand killed in the war—some say his homosexuality had made him cold to them and thus easy victims--in retaliation for each of the two wounds he had suffered, one a thrust to his chest that was stopped by his sternum, thus saving his life.

Failing to advance beyond the Beas River in Punjab he took his army down the Indus and captured several cities including Multan. At the delta he split his army into three and led one group across the Gedrosian desert to Babylon. A year and a half later, on the eve of his invasion of Arabia in 323 BCE, he developed a febrile illness, almost certainly the cerebral form of falciparum malaria and died within two weeks. His companion and deputy Hephaistion had curiously died earlier of a fever contracted in the mountains north of Babylon.

The Macedonian Empire fractured on Alexander's death and the eastern part came under one of his generals Seleucus Nicator who failed in attempts to retain or expand his Indian holdings and came to a truce with Chandragupta Maurya ceding all Indian and Afghan territories, and a daughter in marriage. He received 500 elephants, which would prove a vital asset in his defeat of Demetrius of Macedon later at Ipsus in Phrygia. Formal relations developed between these two Empires, previously established at an academic level, and ambassadors were exchanged as with other Mediterranean states including Egypt, spreading new awareness of India[51]. Megasthenes served Seleucus as ambassador.

Mauryans: The Mauryan dynasty started when **Chandragupta** deposed King Dhana Nanda of Magadha, in 321 BCE. It lasted until 184 BCE. Chandragupta was an astute general and ruler who came under the influence of two commanding personages, first Prime Minister **Kautilya (Chanukya)** of Magadha whose book, *Arthashastra*[52], written in 302 BCE, described the art and practice of government and gave details on administering an empire. The second was **Jainacharya Bhadrabahu**. Jainism emphasised respect and preservation of all life, vegetarianism, and asceticism to attain *moksha*; the king was so impressed with the doctrines that he abdicated and became a Jain monk! By then he had extended the Empire to most of India, Gandhara and parts of Persia and Central Asia taking advantage of the destabilisation of north Indian kingdoms by the Greek invasion. His son **Bhindusara** pursued Indian unification by conquest of the remaining kingdoms and smaller tribal chieftainships. His Empire extended from the Indus to Burma and Gandhāra to Mysore, except Kalinga and the Chola kingdom at the extreme south.

The Mauryans reached the apex of their power and influence under

---

[51] "But [India] has been treated of by several other Greek writers who resided at the courts of Indian kings, such, for instance, as Megasthenes, and by Dionysius, who was sent thither by Philadelphus, expressly for the purpose: all of whom have enlarged upon the power and vast resources of these nations." Pliny the Elder, *Natural History, Chap. 21.* (Ptolemy II was dubbed Philadelphus on marrying his natural sister Arsinoe II, who in fact was the proper *philadelphus*, having previously married her brother. Ptolemy II is mentioned in Ashoka's *Edicts* and may have been introduced to Buddhism.

[52] Machiavelli is said to have drawn heavily from this text in composing *"The Prince"*.

Ashoka, Chandragupta's grandson who ruled from 273-232 BCE and. Overcome by the horror of his victory over his neighbour Kalinga in the seventh year of his reign, he renounced invasive war, converted to Buddhism and began a period of consolidation of empire, initiating administrative reforms, establishing the world's first socialist democracy in which the state controlled all means of production, long before Marx proposed this. He placed curbs on royal powers, assured citizens' rights, reformed taxation, expanded infrastructure and improved diplomatic relations with neighbours. He sent peace missions as far as the Mediterranean countries and religious missions to China, Sri Lanka and Southeast Asia, his son Mahendra leading the mission to Sri Lanka.

The result of this attention to the spiritual was that Buddhism became the most renowned religion, spreading to China and SE Asia. Ashoka's name and work became the most celebrated in the civilised world. His injunctions and messages to his subjects were carved on stone pillars and erected in major centres of population; perhaps the best known being the pillar at Sārnath, whose lion capital was chosen as modern India's national emblem. The Chinese at this time were building the Great Wall, one of the world's marvels of engineering. Many today feel that a study of Ashoka's edicts might guide our generation towards a more caring political philosophy that could elevate man above and away from the twin dangers of communism and corporate capitalism.

A change in building materials from wood to stone occurred in the Mauryan period after the destruction by fire of the wooden buildings of **Pataliputra**[53], the capital city (today's Patna). Kautilya had described various advances in his book: air conditioning (*variyantra)*, advanced metallurgical methods to extract metals, prepare alloys and assay metals for purity, skills that were based on data and practices that had survived the fall of the Saraswati/Indus civilisation 1500 years earlier.

Under the Mauryans new skills and industries developed in metallurgy, tool- and die-making, cement manufacture, construction design, engineering techniques, masonry, transportation and haulage to create the buildings, dams, canals, bridges, sculptures and monuments that improved the land; many of these structures survive to this day. These had heavily relied on advances in Mathematics and Sciences.

The life of dynasties is invariably limited. But the fall of the Mauryans came rather suddenly in 184 BCE, felled by weakness that comes with intrigue and internal conflict as the dynasty decayed from undermining of its structure under tentative successors to Ashoka.

Four decades later the **Chola Empire** was founded in Tamil Nadu and became noted for its sound government, artistic achievements and agricultural enterprises with some of the most impressive irrigation and other water management works of that time. Besides art it produced numerous religious dissertations on various themes in Hinduism and Buddhism; it thrived for 1445 years, one of the longest in history, until broken up by invading Muslims from the north in 1300 CE.

The *Vikrama Samvat*[54] Hindu era and calendar started in 57 BCE.

---

[53] Half of Tokyo was destroyed in one major WWII raid by incendiary bombs because the city was wooden.

[54] This marks the triumph of Vikramaditya over the *Sakas*, who had ousted his father, Gardabhilla, king of Ujjain.

The Kushans, a Mongolian Buddhist group began their assault on India in 50 BCE, and succeeded in annexing northwest India, Afghanistan and parts of their northern neighbours which they held for 270 years.

Early in this period a bright young Jewish student of religion **Yesu (Jesus)** from Bethlehem and Nazareth, Judea, Palestine, arrived in India to study with Buddhist, Jain and Hindu preceptors at Nālandā and Taxashila Universities He stayed for nearly eighteen years and travelled widely on religious missions after completing several years of study. He was of humble birth but traced his ancestry to Jewish king David.

Back in Palestine his mature teachings were not surprisingly closer to those of Indian philosophies than Judaism, incorporating many Buddhist and Jain principles, especially *ahimsa*, which he preached, much to the discomfiture of Jewish high priests who had waited for a person with his charisma to lead them in war against Roman hegemony.

He completed three years spreading his contrary doctrine of peace and love captivating audiences throughout Palestine, but the Jewish hierarchy rejected him as *the* Messiah, the promised one, and given the choice to save one man from crucifixion at a certain Passover, chose the convict and rebel Barabbas. Jesus *was* crucified, but taken down from the cross after just a few hours--too few to cause death by this method--and was released to Joseph of Arimathea, a man of some wealth and influence; Jesus survived to return to India[55].

Meanwhile, his twelve disciples in Palestine had accepted him as the Messiah and were preaching his doctrine throughout the Roman Empire where it became the official religion after Constantine's Edict of Milan in 313 AD. Christianity thus displaced all other religions there, often with violence, as for example Emperor Theodosius' destruction of Greek temples in 391CE. In time it grew to command the largest and most powerful following in the western world. The Romans used Christ's birth to mark the start of a new calendar era, AD.

India then had about 35 million people, a fifth of the world's population. She had established Shaivite colonies in Funan, on the Mekong Delta--where Kaundinya, an Indian Brahmin, became the first king--and others a century later in Cambodia[56] and Malaysia. Funan thrived for centuries as a business and trading centre, attracting shipping from China in the north to Persia in the west, especially under the Sassanids. Further south prince Ajishaka of Gujarat had invaded Java and founded colonies. A few years later China's Emperor Ming Di (ruled 58-76CE) converted to Buddhism and brought the religion to China where Indian monks directed the erection of a temple in Hunan.[57]

The Chinese leader Zhang Qian led the development of the "Silk Roads" to

---

[55]The *Ahmadiyyas* of Kashmir show proof that Jesus of Nazareth (4 BCE-? CE) had come to India in search of the twelve lost tribes of Israel, had studied religious philosophies with Buddhists, Jains and Hindus and undertaken at least four missionary journeys and pilgrimages throughout India during a period of eighteen years -- the "missing years" of the New Testament -- before returning to Palestine. His *Beatitudes* and other teachings bear striking concordance with those of Indian religions. He returned to India after his "death" to preach and live in Kashmir, married and had children. The Ahmadiyyas claim partial origin from him and protect a tomb in Srinagar said to be his (see *Jesus vivio y murio en Kachemira* by Andreas Faber-Kaiser, Ediciones Roca, Mexico, 1976).

[56] A variant of Kamboja, an ancient region of Northwest India, Afghanistan and Iran whose people are said to have migrated to surrounding lands and settled in Funan, which included the area of modern Cambodia. King Norodom Sihanouk had acknowledged his ancient bond with Indian Kambojis on a visit to India in 1955.

[57]Name changed to Henan Sheng.

the Middle East and Roman Empire, then nearing its zenith, just a few years before Zhang's contemporaries invented paper in 105 CE. Across the Pacific, in the western hemisphere, the population of Teotihuacan, Mexico had reached 100,000 and the city covered 11 square miles.

Meanwhile the **Kushans** had been storming India's northern door since the collapse of the Mauryans. They had little success until the reign of **Kanishka I** (100-144 CE), son of one Vima Kadphises, Kanishka expanded his empire along the Indus into northern India, (Kashmir to Gujarat) and into Central Asia to the Tarim Basin, including parts of western China. He promoted *Mahayana* Buddhism and its architecture, and built a huge *stupa* in Peshawar measuring 286 feet diameter and 591- 689 feet tall. (The building of shrines had been a common practice among warriors of that time, usually to commemorate an important victory, and explains the large number of stupas, temples, mosques and so on).

He supported the Greco-Buddhist (Gandhāra School) and Hindu art (Mathura School). He followed the Persian cult of *Mithra*. At the start of his reign Kanishka facilitated the spread of Buddhism by convening the 4th Buddhist Council in Kashmir with 500 monks under **Vasumitra**, who eventually produced an extensive commentary on Buddhist psychology known as the *Mahā Vibhāśā* or Great Exegesis. (Of interest is that this led to the rendering of the Pāli text into Sanskrit -- the language of Hinduism--as Sanskrit allowed wider dissemination of these writings). Missionaries spread Buddhism throughout the Empire and beyond, especially China, in whose capital, Louyang (in Henan province), Kanishka established a translation agency. A monk, **Lokasema**, translated several texts into Chinese.

The Kushans were a tolerant people; their coins showed Hindu, Buddhist, and Persian deities. They adopted Indian customs including Ayurvaidic medical and health practices, which **Charaka** (ca 80-180 CE), physician to the Kushan king, promoted vigorously with his textbook of medicine, the *Charaka Sāmhita*. The work included a code of conduct for doctors[58].

Many treatises on various religious subjects emerged and led to formation of many sects. Religious discourses flourished in many parts of the country and new commentaries (*Samhitas, Agamas etc.*) on ancient treatises revived interest in them or created new personalities and movements e.g. Shandilya[59] and followers who wrote on the *Pancharatra* and stirred a renaissance in the worship of Vishnu.

Commerce grew internationally, expanding as new routes to China, the Middle East and the Mediterranean were established, including the "silk roads" developed by **Zhang Qian** by 100 AD. The invention of paper affected every nation, as did Rome's expansion which reached its zenith in 117 AD. In time paper replaced palm leaves used by Sinhalese Buddhists.

Towards the end of their rule the Kushans came under increasing influence of the new **Sassanid** regime that would dominate Persia for over four hundred years. In India the Shaka reign over Gujarat came to an end at the hands of an Andhra prince **Shatakarni**.

---

[58] It includes this timeless advice: "*A physician who fails to enter the body of a patient with the lamp of knowledge and understanding can never treat diseases. He should first study all the factors, including environment, which influence a patient's disease, and then prescribe treatment. It is more important to prevent the occurrence of disease than to seek a cure.*"

[59] He promoted *Pancharatra* doctrines and *Bhakti sutras*, on worship of *Vishnu*. The central teaching that the deity manifests in five forms: *Para, Vyūha, Vibhava, Antaryamin,* and *Archa,* which show how *Parabrahma,* the formless God can be brought into interaction with humanity.

The Greek astronomer Ptolemy visited India (where he was called *Asura Maya*) near the end of the second century and lectured on solar astronomy (*Surya Siddhanta*) to University students. He taught that the earth was flat and at the centre of the Universe; he had noted the changes in the heavens, but his hypothesis could not explain them; he thus invented explanations including reverse motion of some bodies; his ideas would be definitively debunked by Aryābhatta in the 5th century AD (see below), but surprisingly retained within the Roman church which declared as heresy all things eastern.

In the 3rd century CE **Plotinus**, an Egyptian-Greek philosopher and religious scholar, was teaching "ahimsa, karma, vegetarianism, reincarnation and belief in a Supreme Force, both immanent and transcendent," all basic Hindu tenets. His work influenced later Islamic and European thought. At this time the Pallava dynasty (ca 250-885) was established in Tamil Nadu; it built monuments and temples, including the *Kailasa Kamakshi* Temple complex at Kanchi, the capital.

Guptas: The fourth century CE dawned with the rise of the Imperial Gupta dynasty in the north (320-540), which replaced the Kushans, and India began a period of renewed strength, unity and prosperity recapturing much of the glory of the Mauryans. This period is regarded by some as the "Classical Age" since it established norms for architecture, literature, art and philosophy. All religious Hindu and Buddhist groups were accepted and the regime exerted control over most of India. The founder, Srigupta I (270-290 CE) was a petty ruler of Magadha (modern Bihar), who went on to establish the dynasty with Pataliputra (Patna) as its capital. He and his son Ghatotkacha (290-305 CE) have left very little to show for their respective rules, unlike their successors, each of whom minted individual coins.

Ghatotkacha's son **Chandragupta I** (305-325 CE) strengthened the kingdom by marrying princess Kumaradevi of the powerful and prestigious **Lichchavi** family, the rulers of **Mithila**. Mithila was the capital of Videha, ancient home of Sìtā, wife of Rāma. The Licchavi dynasty later established a Hindu kingdom in Nepal, which ruled for 550 years to 900 AD and became the major intellectual and commercial link between South and Central Asia. Chandragupta's marriage increased his power and resources enabling him to gain control of the entire Ganges valley and to be crowned Emperor (*Maharajadhiraja*). He quickly extended his sway over most of India. Religion prospered and Vaishnavism, Saivism and Buddhism grew.

However it was his son Vikramaditya, or **Chandragupta II** (375-414 CE) who became the best-known of the Guptas (more tales are told of him than of any other ruler of India, some regarding him the greatest of the Hindu monarchs). He consolidated his father's gains and during his reign and that of his son Kumaragupta India reached a peak of prosperity, opulence and prestige that extended northward and westward beyond the Indus River and internationally to the Europe, Africa and the rest of Asia.

Thus began a long period of political stability, economic expansion and prosperity. Trade and religion expanded west by sea and land into the Sassanid Empire and thence to Arabia, North Africa, the eastern and northern Mediterranean, Europe and Central Asia, even as Attila the Hun (died 453CE) was plundering Europe. The spread of Christianity throughout the Roman Empire inevitably led to clashes with *Vaidic* doctrine and what some believe were its expressions outside India e.g. in Greece, Anatolia, the Middle East, Egypt and Arabia e.g. reincarnation.

In 391 CE, Theodosius, the Christian Roman Emperor, destroyed Hellenic temples in Greece and elsewhere. And although the Greeks adopted Christianity, they still celebrated their pre-Christian heritage, complete with gods and goddesses, unlike Indian converts to Islam living in today's Pakistan and India who, Dr Brahmam said, *"pretend that the world began with Islam and that Hinduism and all its complexities did not exist before Mohamed, yet they reach into the Puranas to find a prediction, an insertion, I think, to justify Mohamed's place in the line of prophets! In same way, many modern Indians do not want Indian or foreign Vaidic scholars to correct our history as British taught it. These critics,"* he sneered, *"forget that it was British educators who planned curricula and wrote textbooks which they used to turn us into coconuts! You know, Qutb Minar was built by Guptas, not Muslims, to celebrate Arab connections made before Mohammed's time! There is evidence (coins, mural inscriptions, ceramics etc.) to show that ka'aba at Mecca was pre-Islamic Vaidic shrine set up by Guptas. You know, Romans did not lose their Empire; they gave up a crumbling militarist one for one based on faith, not might, and for this Constantine must be seen as a seer, to recognise the power of faith as a greater and cheaper tool of conquest than arms and armies!"*

"You have an original thought there, Doc, at least to me; I know that later Popes would become militarists and fight or support wars to conquer territory and to destroy opposing beliefs, especially Islam, which they still do. But they lost eventually to Henry VIII. The Roman Church is larger and more powerful than Roman Empire ever was."

Leisure activities developed in all India as industrial and agricultural prosperity increased. I have mentioned the evolution, centuries earlier, of *Ashtapada*--the four-handed war game played with dice--into *shaturanga*, the two-person forerunner of chess. At a more intimate level another two-person game benefited enormously from the publication of Vatsyayana's *Kāmasutra*, a treatise presenting human sexuality and physical love as essential for married bliss and success. *Kāmasutra* described details of sexual intercourse and the numerous positions in which the act could be consummated, many possible only by exponents of Yoga in its many forms, thus justifying the practices of this branch of Medicine!

The Guptas supported learning, from research to dissemination--in mathematics, language, art, culture, and the sciences, pure and applied. They promoted agriculture, commerce and trade, local and foreign.

The best known paintings of this period can be found among the murals in the Ajanta caves, noted for rich and detailed depiction of nature, people, dress, atmosphere and mood, including the rich and sensuous life of Gupta India. The frescoes also show Siddhartha (Buddha) dressed in the style that Nehru has made popular today, called the *chudidara pyjama*. Gupta styles influenced Buddhist art all over Asia. Indian epics literature such as the *Panchatantra*,[60] a collection of fables--have inspired centuries of European and West Asian writers like Boccaccio, Dante, Chaucer, Shakespeare, Ibn Sena, Omar Khayyam and countless others to this day. Books by **Kalidāsa** *(Meghaduta, Kumarsamhita, Shakuntala etc.)*, the Sanskrit dramas *Mrichchhakatika* and *Mudra Rakshasa* were written in this period. Many new works were added to the religious library and

---

[60]Burzoe, physician and vizier to Khosrau I, a 6th century Sassanid ruler, translated *Panchatantra* into Persian; this version was translated into Arabic by Ibn al-Mafuqqa under the title *Kalila and Dimna* or *The Fables of Bidpai* and became the greatest prose classic of the Arabs.

the law books of Brihaspati were composed at this period. Architecture flourished and several major temples were built, lavishly outfitted and embellished. (They would be looted and destroyed in later years by Muslim invaders).

After the third century Indian trade shifted from emphasis on the Roman Empire to South-East Asia and China. Elsewhere developments were taking place in various ways that would affect India and Asia generally. In the northwest, Hunas (Hephtalites) and Sakas (Scythians) continued to harass border areas. The Guptas repelled the invaders, and established good diplomatic and trade relations with their neighbour, the Sassanids[61] of Persia, whose borders extended east to Baluchistan.

The Buddhist patriarch **Bodhidharma** (450-535) of South India founded *Ch'an* Buddhism in China (*Zen* in Japan). Christianity spread throughout the Roman Empire and developed the structure it would retain to this day, dominated by the authority of the Vatican. Popes assumed the role of Christ on earth and issued periodic edicts, some after due reflection, others unsupported by Christ's teachings, but perhaps based on statements by disciples or their successors or on temporal/political expediency. Thus Catholicism acquired accretions over time. One was the rejection of the idea of reincarnation by the Council of Ferrara-Florence (438-445), and affirmed by the Council of Constantinople a century later which stated categorically that the "soul" did not exist prior to conception, a claim no more valid than its opposite. (The Council of Lyons II repeated this in 1274 CE).

Far away Polynesians were crossing the Pacific in open outrigger canoes to Hawaii and Easter Island, while Peru completed the 150-foot high Sun temple of Moche.

Spread of Indian Sciences: While Gupta armies were repelling Hephtalite forces at the borders, universities were being established in the heartland to advance and spread knowledge, especially in Mathematics and Astronomy. In 499 CE, **Aryābhatta I**, (476-ca 550 CE), a youthful mathematician and astronomer wrote his astonishing work the *Aryābhattiya*, the world's first treatise on arithmetic, algebra, plane and spherical trigonometry. Aryābhatta was probably born in Ashmaka, SW India (Kerala), and studied astronomy at Nālandā University, then over 1000 years old. His achievements included description of *sine*; rendering *pi* as 3.1416, the value usually used today; explanation of eclipses; and revelation that the earth was continuously spinning on a north-south axis, each rotation taking 24 hours and that it orbited the sun in 365.3586805 days, the duration of a solar year. He showed that earth was one of several spherical planets in parallel elliptical solar orbits, which explained gravity and the "dance" of celestial bodies.

Aryābhatta was barely 20 when he made these stunning discoveries, without a telescope, and over a thousand years before Newton described gravity

---

[61] The Sassanid Empire or Sassanian Dynasty (226–651) was a Parsi kingdom established by Ardashir I on the defeat of Artabanus IV, king of Parthia. It ended when its last ruler Yazdegerd III lost his 14-year struggle against Muslim invaders. At its height the empire, which was named the *Eranshahr* (dominion of the Aryans or Iranians) covered modern Iran, Iraq, Armenia, eastern Turkey and parts of the Middle East, Arabia Central Asia and Pakistan. It practised a caste system similar to India's and strictly enforced, under the supreme ruler or *Shahanshah*. The layers were hereditary and consisted of *Priests, Warriors, Secretaries and Commoners*, with little mobility between them.

and the Vatican denounced Galileo and Copernicus for solar theory. Western cultures credit this pair with Aryābhatta's astronomical discoveries and others, including Arabs with his mathematical achievements, despite the clear attribution of that body of knowledge to Indians by Muslim scholar **Ibn Sena**.

Europeans outside the Mediterranean accepted the wealth of knowledge in science, language and mathematics that Arabs brought and uncritically credited them as originators. Their lack of language skills and innate biases kept them for nearly a millennium from discovering the fountains of knowledge and culture that lay east of Arabia; they have yet to acknowledge their debt to the writings of Aryābhatta, his predecessors of previous millennia -- **Āpastamba, Baudhāyana** et al -- and his successors like **Brahmagupta** (598-665 CE), **Bhāskara, Rāmanuj** and the many other Indian luminaries in mathematics, astronomy and grammar who had enlightened the ancient world.

In 499 CE, **Aryābhatta**, then 23, toured the Middle East and Arabia to teach Indian numbers, script and mathematics and their application to accounting practices presumably to facilitate commerce and trade by establishing a uniform system and language of accounting (India then had 50 million people--26% of the world's population and dominated culture and commerce). His book, *Aryābhattiya*, comprising 121 rhyming stanzas, was translated from Sanskrit into Latin and thus became available to Roman and Arabic scholars and eventually Europeans enabling them finally to accomplish complex calculations such as fractions, decimals, square and cube roots, areas of triangles and other geometric shapes, volumes of spheres, relationships, trigonometric functions etc. Other mathematicians of that period included Varahamira whose treatise, *Bhrihata Sāmhita*, dealt with the decimal system.

(Their work would be extended by many brilliant successors down to the present day and be consolidated in the new **Indian Institutes of Technology** (IIT's) that the Indian Government has begun to establish as superior places of learning and research. "Just this year (1961) the fourth one was opened in New Delhi." Jain informed us. "The first Institute was founded in 1950 at Kharagpur, 75 miles from Calcutta; at convocation in 1956 Nehru promised to recapture the past glory of Indian mathematics and technology, and said, *'Here in the place of that Hijli Detention Camp*[62] *stands the fine monument of India (IIT) today, representing India's urges, India's future in the making.'"*)

The influence of **Chandragupta II** reached the Middle East, Egypt and Arabia, where his emissaries were a dominant presence in Mecca (some assert by conquest). Meccan Qureshis adopted Indian mathematics after Aryābhatta's lectures, and applied it to achieve consistency in the division of spoils after raids (*ghazw* or *razzias*). Dr Brahmam had speculated that the **Ka'aba** was reorganised as a Hindu shrine and place of pilgrimage, with many jewelled *murtis* (statues) and *mandalas;* the annual pilgrimage boosted city revenues, even as it does today. It became a Muslim shrine on Mohamed's conquest of Mecca, a model of conquest and conversion that has characterised Muslim approach to Hindu

---

[62] The former Hijli Detention Camp, which the British had built in 1930 to house Indian freedom fighters, became a University just as the former WWII Gibraltar Detention Camp in Jamaica for citizens of Axis countries became the site of the UCWI. Kharagpur is famous for having the world's longest railway station (> 1km). Hijli's inmates included Mahatma Gandhi and the youth Bhagirath. It was here that the British murdered two unarmed detainees Santosh Kumar Mitra and Tarakeshwar Sengupta in 1931, one of the numerous stains on the British in India.

temples ever since. The great Sanskrit poet and dramatist, Kalidāsa, lived at this time.[63]

By the end of the fifth century the Empire was in decline, in spite of heroic efforts of the later Guptas--Skanda, Kumar, Buddha, Vainya and Bhanu--to repel the relentless **Hunas.** Indian resistance was weakened by internal dissension and scheming among subject rulers whose forebears had united with the Guptas to achieve a strong Empire and who now wished greater individual control; they underestimated however the harm that divisions would bring and realised this only too late when the Empire finally fell to Mihirakula. He held north India until expelled ca. 533 CE by the armies of Rajas **Yashovarman** of Malwa and **Ishanavarman** of Kanauj. Persians and Turks later crushed the Hunas. By the middle of the sixth century CE the Gupta Empire had disintegrated and India came under individual kings, great and small.

Chalukyas: The following centuries saw the emergence and flowering of the Chalukya dynasty in Gujarat and adjacent regions of western India (two eras: ca 543-757 and 975-1189CE), begun under **Pulakeshin I.** In Japan Emperor **Kimmei** officially recognised Buddhism, and in Arabia Mohammed (570-632CE) was developing the religion of Islam. At this time Brahmagupta, the great astronomer, wrote the 25-chapter *Brahma Sphuta Siddhanta* on Hindu astronomy, gravity and complex mathematics, extending the work of Aryābhatta. Soon after, the Buddhist king **Harshavardhana** (ruled 606-44) regained control of India north of the Narmada River, south of which the Chalukya Empire prospered under **Pulakeshin II.** Learning flourished throughout the land, centred at Nālandā, Taxashila, Pataliputra, Ujjain, Madras and a dozen other cities. Nālandā was estimated to have over 1,500 teachers, some 10,000 residents, and thousands of manuscripts. Many prolific writers emerged, prominent among them **Banabhatta**, author of *Harshacharita* (story of King Harsha) and *Kadambari*. Vagbhata, a physician, wrote the *Ashtanga Sangraha* on Ayurvaida and a succession of religious writers centred in Tamil Nadu composed thousands of songs and poems in praise of Nārayan, Rāma and Krishna which were collected as *Nalayira Divya Prabandham.*

The Gupta period had seen enormous strides in applied sciences. One example was the unique metallurgical innovation, rust-proofing, shown in the 23-foot high iron pillar at Delhi, which has survived rust-free for some 2000 years[64]. This technology matured in the following centuries and was used to construct rust-proof iron beams, posts and girders for large buildings such as the temples at Puri and Konarak. From earlier periods -- Kushan, Harshavardhana -- India had become widely known for the very high quality of its steel and had developed a method to extract zinc from its ore and make an alloy of copper, lead and tin (*bidari*). In his book *Science in Medieval India*[65] A. Rahman noted that India was making the best cannon in the world; the leading factory was located at Jaigarh[66].

---

[63] Some recent scholars, including Professor Subash Kak, Louisiana State University, have proposed circa 50 BCE as more likely.

[64] There is doubt as to the exact age of the Delhi Iron Pillar; some assign it to the Gupta period of Chandragupta II Vikramaditya, but others place it in the century before Christ.

[65] Quoted by Dr Brahmam.

[66] The Rajputs of Jaipur were said to own the world's largest cannons at the time of the 1857 War of Independence from Britain. Yet, none was ever used against the British who "succeeded in conquering the sub-continent without ever having to fight the country's best equipped armies, thus

The Chinese pilgrim **Hiuen-Tsang** (Huan Zang) toured India and wrote about his travels. By the mid-7th century more than 60 Chinese monks had travelled to India (courtesy of the hospitality of the Buddhist temple that the **Pallava** King, Narasinha Varman, had built at Nagapatam for Chinese merchants and visiting monks); 400 Sanskrit works had been translated into Chinese, continuing the work of earlier Kushans, of which 380 survive today. Meanwhile Hinduism had spread to Indonesia and Buddhism to Indochina, Afghanistan, Central Asia, China, Korea and Japan.

Section 5: The Muslims

At this time the Arabs had begun their conquest of their neighbours, had occupied the Middle East, Egypt and Persia, and were moving west around the Mediterranean. They took with them--wherever their raiding armies went from their bases in Damascus and Baghdad--Indian knowledge of mathematics, sciences and medicine, gleaned from *Aryābhattiya* (499 CE), *Brahma Sphuta Siddhanta* of Brahmagupta (598-665 CE) and other works.

By the end of that century the Arabs had advanced west to Spain, and had begun to arrive by sea at the mouth of the Indus, settling at a point upriver, ostensibly as a base for trade, but soon switched to the true purpose of their coming, namely to establish bases from which to conduct raids *(razzias)* on their wealthy neighbours--a matter of pride, custom, challenge and high-spirited living that fell in nicely with their new-found faith, Islam. As early as 636 CE the Caliph Omar had ordered the first assaults against India targeting Thana on the Maharashtran coast. Their naval attacks continued for the rest of the century but were repulsed by Hindus well into the caliphate of Al Walid I (705-715 CE).

By the early eighth century the Muslims had expanded their control of territory from the Afghan border to the Mediterranean, from Portugal and Spain in the west to the lower Indus valley (Sindh) in the east through a succession of holy wars *(jihad bin saif)*. Thus began the bitter assaults by Muslims against Hindus in India and against Christians on many fronts, from Spain to all points of the Mediterranean and Middle East, until Pope Urban proclaimed the first Crusade to drive the Muslims out of Europe and regain Palestine -- declared Holy Land by Christians – and especially Jerusalem, which the Muslims too regarded as their third holiest place.

The governor of Iraq, the cruel **al-Hajjaj** *(bone-crusher)* **ibn Yousef** had failed in late 7th to early 8th century attempts to capture Gandhara and faced hostility from non-Arab Muslims in Persia, whom he had antagonised by his brutality. According to **Tha'alībī** in *Laṭ'āif* (142) al Hajjaj was one of four men known to have killed over 100,000 men; the others were Abu Harb, Abu Muslim and Babak!

Al Biruni in *"From The Remaining Signs of Past Centuries"* gave this example of how al Hajjaj treated the defeated:: *"When Qutaibah bin Muslim under the command of al-Hajjaj ibn Yousef was sent to Khwarazmia (greater Iran, modern Uzbekistan) with a military expedition and conquered it for the second time, he swiftly killed anyone who wrote the Khwarazmian native language or knew of the Khwarazmian heritage, history, and culture. He then killed all their Zoroastrian priests and burned and wasted their books, until gradually the illiterate only remained, who knew nothing of*

---

demonstrating that technological progress is not an end in itself." It also underlines the divisions and rivalries that have plagued the rulers of India for a millennium.

writing, and hence their history was mostly forgotten." [67]

But the regime's desire to gain control of the Indus River, its wealth and its peoples spawned new campaigns. A sea venture then was fraught with difficulty due to the ruthless and ubiquitous Míd corsairs who roamed the Arabian Sea in their *bawarij* boats harassing all ships.

In 712 CE al-Hajjaj, having failed earlier to take Sindh by the overland route from Makran, sent a much stronger force under his 17-year-old nephew (or cousin) Muhammad **Bin Qasim** who captured the coastal city of Daybul, slew all defenders, collected the women and children as hostages and slaves, and sent a fifth of the total booty to al-Hajjaj according to *razzia* rules. He garrisoned the city, *destroyed the temple and built a mosque on the ruins.* [68] He then moved north along the river subduing towns all the way to Multan, meeting little resistance from the predominantly unarmed pacifist Buddhists and Sindhi Hindus.

When he was opposed later at Brahmanābad and Multan he dealt harshly with the people, killed all fighters, enslaved civilians, desecrated or destroyed temples and replaced them with mosques. Multan was known as the *House of Gold*, home of the great Sun Mandir with capacity of some 6000 persons; it was looted and destroyed. Thus was the pattern of looting, razing and replacing of temples by mosques consolidated and would reach new excesses of cruelty and barbarity under the Mughals.

Once settled on the lower Indus, Muslims began regular plundering of settlements along the river and by 712 had established a stronghold in Sindh, whence they raided Rajasthan and Maharashtra, but Chalukya's armies defeated them at Navasari (739 CE), seven years after the French had stopped their European advance at Poitiers, but both victors would regret their failure to eradicate the threat.

The richness of the prize continued to attract the Muslim hordes, seeking like parasites to fatten themselves off the wealth and labour of others much as the Romans had done until their demise as the greatest power. Muslims persisted with greater resolve to seize Indian wealth and for three centuries battled with fanatical zeal seeking plunder in the *razzia* tradition, before any serious inroads were made into Indian territories. This occurred at a time when the region had become weakened and divided. By then Islam had long split into two factions, Sunni and Shi'a, and multiple splinter groups that would be a source of lasting internecine conflict. The pattern set would smoulder through the centuries and erupt into extraordinary violence up to the present time, even during the fairly subdued period of Ottoman rule.

Haroun al Rashid became the 5th Abbasid caliph of Baghdad from 786-809 and was known for tolerance, promotion of culture, religion, science, music and the arts and a more civilised approach to conquest. The caliphate extended from Persia across North Africa to southern Spain; the Byzantine Empire became his tributary.

In Europe **Charlemagne** had become king of the Franks in 768 CE, and coming to aid **Pope Hadrian**, had conquered Lombardy. By 800 he had annexed Corsica, Saxony and Germany. **Pope Leo III**, Hadrian's successor in 795, dubbed him Emperor Augustus. By 800 he had united France and Germany. He

---

[67] See also Ch. 3, *Language as coloniser*
[68] Similarly Roman Emperor Hadrian rekindled the wrath of the Jews by planning to build a temple of Jupiter on the ruins of the temple of Jerusalem.

respected Haroun and the feeling was reciprocated; they exchanged many gifts notably Haroun's novelty clocks and albino elephants to Charlemagne. Haroun had diplomatic and cultural exchanges with his neighbours and other powers including India and China. When he became ill an Indian physician named **Mankah** arrived in Baghdad to treat him.

The northwest Hindu **Shahi kingdom** of Gandhāra and Punjab was prosperous and self-sufficient and had remained aloof to the trading ventures of Turkic Muslims from cities along the silk route that altogether did not constitute for them a large enough market. Seljuk Turks had by this time integrated with their Persian conquests, adopting language and had eliminated the Hunas after their expulsion from India to gain control of most of Central Asia east of Anatolia, and had made inroads into the decaying Byzantine Empire.

Traders, including Ghori slavers, eyed with envy Indian wealth, agricultural plenty and large population—a source of high taxes and slaves-- tempting *razzias* into the Shahi kingdom whence a conqueror could invade and perhaps subjugate all India by *jihad* (holy war).Various rulers had maintained their assaults on the region for nearly 400 years, from 636-870 CE against Gandhāra and from 870–1030 CE assailing the Punjab. North Indian armies, like those mentioned above, repulsed waves of invaders for centuries until finally in 1001 **Mahmud**, son of the expansionist **Sabuktigin of Ghazni**, a central Afghan state, after 17 attacks in 30 years, entered the Shahi kingdom with a strong Turkic force and overwhelmed **Raja Jayapala's** armies at Peshawar and later defeated his son **Anandapala.**

Ghazni had followed the same route used by Darius in 512 BCE and later Greeks under Alexander in 326 BCE, but these two had failed to hold on to their conquests. Ghazni however soldiered on. He had weapons and a purpose -- beside cupidity -- that previous invaders had lacked: *religious fanaticism and the belief that "all lands belonged to Khuda!"* With Shahi conquered, Ghazni waged *jihad* plundering cities on the northern Indus, including Muslim Multan, suggesting that prey and booty were prime objectives-- although some have suggested that eradicating Sufis, Shi'as and Ismailis might have been a more compelling drive.

He created vassal states along the way to be governed by vanquished Hindus, Buddhists or Jains and reduced the population to *dhimmis*—people who could retain their religion, rights and privileges but at a cost of the *jizya* or poll tax, unless they converted. Thus conversion was forced and occurred among the backward classes or the poor who with few exceptions remained underprivileged since Turks did not observe the Islamic principle of equality among Muslims and in fact practised a more rigid casteism than then existed among Indians. Princes who converted retained caste and other privileges; those who did not were invariably murdered.

From Punjab Ghazni moved south and east, through Punjab and Rajputana and in 1017 sacked Mathura, birthplace of Lord Krishna. Seven years later he destroyed the Shiva temple at Somnāth after seizing its riches and killing 50,000 defenders; he thereon built a mosque.

This success initiated a series of raids and stimulated other Muslim leaders to seek their fortunes in India. It was the game of *razzias* on a grand scale by zealous raiders now fired by the reality of untold wealth, gripped by a militant religion and under the spell of "holiness" and promises of pleasurable rewards if martyred (heaven and 72 virgins). Hundreds of thousands of civilians and children were slaughtered; numerous others enslaved, especially artisans and labourers, and sold into Asian markets hungry for skilled workers.

Meanwhile **Raja Bhoja** of Dhar-Malwa (1018-60 CE), had entered an uneasy alliance with southern allies in a campaign to annex **Chalukya's** Gujarat kingdoms but heavy resistance eventually forced him to return home where he regrouped and drove the Ghazni forces from Somnāth back to the Punjab. In 1031 **Sayyid Salar Masud**, 16 year old nephew of Mohamed Ghazni, born in Ajmer and already a 6-year war veteran, led a large army to recapture cities his uncle had lost.

Realising the threat and strength of the Muslims, Raja Bhoja forged an alliance of Rajput Hindu states which succeeded in driving Muslim forces as far north as Lahore after annihilating Salar Masud and his army at **Barraich**, Uttar Pradesh. Set to take **Lahore**, the last stand of the fleeing Muslim forces, Raja Bhoja's allies squabbled over division of conquered lands and reaching no agreement defected leaving Raj Bhoja to carry on alone. He was forced to split his armies to fight erstwhile allies and moving to defend his capital was killed by an Indian opponent's arrow.

Bhoja was a polymath: poet, engineer, military strategist, philosopher, temple builder, a good ruler and founded the fair city of Bhopal. His mistake and one of India's greatest regrets was to prosecute a war of expansion when powerful and fanatic marauders was already threatening the northern approaches to the rich cities of the Yamuna-Ganga valleys close to his. A culture of divisive internecine war had developed since the fall of the Hephtalites (Hunas) as Indian kings had jostled for power, each perhaps craving the glory of the Guptas or Ashoka Maurya. Thus engaged, they overlooked or misjudged, until too late the power, fanaticism and unorthodox character of Muslim warriors that propelled them to victories which would have been near impossible against alert unions like the Mauryas or Guptas.

Bhoja had made a strategic error in underestimating the strength and resilience of the Turks in Central Asia and in failing to form an alliance to drive Ghaznavis out of India (and Gandhāra) when he had Ghazni on the run from Somnāth. It is arguable whether such an alliance would have had any better outcome than the later one against Salar Masud which fell apart on the brink of a final and decisive win when the endemic rivalry and hunger for possessions rent the alliance and allowed India's major enemies to go free and regroup for re-invasion.

It is not difficult to imagine the resulting carnage at Lahore had the tables been turned with Hindus fleeing. India would blame the alliance to this day for failure to protect her from destruction as waves of frenetic Muslims began to storm across the Punjab to seize, pillage and desecrate the heart of the country and work to end its culture and civilisation.

Muslim brutality: The brutal treatment of civilians as booty by Muslims shocked Hindus. Many thousands of people from Rajasthan and Sindh fled the Muslims and eventually settled in various European countries where they became known as "Roma"; some adopted a nomadic life-style and are generally reviled by host nations. Hindus witnessing Muslim carnage were shocked not just by its intensity, but that it was happening at all.

The Hindu warrior class (*kshatriyas*) waged war against *soldiers* and *armies*, not civilians, among whom casualties were largely incidental, not the result of vengeful and deliberate killing as if targets in a blood sport. Muslim writers of the time marvelled at the lack of "messianic zeal" among Hindu fighters, and socially at the way the men treated women as partners to be consulted, unlike the savagery shown by Turkic Muslims, who treated them as chattel.

Hindus were astounded and repelled by the difference and began to resort to various stratagems to protect their women and children. **Al Biruni** had travelled with Ghazni as his chronicler and wrote: *"Mahmud utterly ruined the prosperity of the country and performed those wonderful exploits by which the Hindus became like atoms of dust scattered in all directions...their scattered remains cherish, of course, the most inveterate aversion towards all Muslims. This is the reason too why Hindu sciences have retired far away from parts of the country conquered by us and have fled to places, which our hand cannot yet reach, to Kashmir, Benaras and other places."*

The loss of Northern India would be complete with **Mohamed Ghori's** victories in Punjab and part of the Ganges Valley between 1175 and 1206 CE. The prolonged period of continuing warfare by Muslim zealots would be but the first major phase of the decline of India that would continue until 1947. The long years of war attest to the determination of the defenders. But had they possessed the Muslims' fanaticism and philosophy of *jihad* or less of a philosophical split between Buddhist pacifists and Hindu defenders the conquest of India would hardly have occurred. Even though constrained by *ahimsa* north Indians held out for 570 years from the early eighth century. The Rajputs, Marathas and southern kingdoms would stem the Muslim tide for another 400 years.

Difference between Hindu and Muslim warriors: Pre-Muslim India was undoubtedly the most advanced country in technology, agriculture, politics and economics, all coveted by Muslims. India lost most of its glamour and wealth as the contest shifted from *kshatriyas* who observed traditions of honour, even when engaging enemy forces that were crude, mercenary and brutal, not the types that fought a "gentleman's war", as al Biruni had noted.

To illustrate further, the 12th century Indian writer **Chand Bardai**, court poet and companion of the Ajmer King **Prithviraj Chauhan**, reporting on the defeat and capture of the Turk Mohamed Ghori at the first *Battle of Tarain* in 1191, wrote: *"Muhammad Ghori was brought in chains to Pithoragarh, Prithviraj's capital and he begged his victor for mercy and release. Prithviraj's ministers advised against pardoning the aggressor. But the chivalrous and valiant Prithviraj thought otherwise and respectfully released the vanquished Ghori."* A year later the tables turned at the second Battle of Tarain and Prithviraj was taken prisoner to Ghori's capital in Afghanistan. *"Ghori ordered him to lower his eyes, whereupon a defiant Prithviraj scornfully told him how he treated Ghori as a prisoner and said that the eyelids of a Rajput king are lowered only in death."* Ghori responded by blinding and torturing Prithviraj who salvaged his honour by committing ritual suicide.

The defeat of Prithviraj illustrates the risks of divisions among Indian kings, occasionally fickle but often quite deep-seated and related to tribe, caste and other loyalties. It shows the ethics of war cherished by Kshatriyas which forbade injuring non-combatants or wounded soldiers; fighting after sunset (warriors needed rest, like everyone else); or involving women unless they were fighting as soldiers.

They abhorred raids and stealthy actions such as Muslims carried out and followed strict rules for guerrilla warfare, treated all opponents alike even kinsmen who fought for the foe, and executed traitors. They took their role seriously, fought valiantly and expected a reciprocal standard of behaviour from their enemies. But they had not reckoned with the different ideology and fanaticism of Islam.

Ajmer and neighbour **Kanauj** were traditional allies and the two strongest Rajput kingdoms of northern India. An enmity had developed between them because 17 years earlier, Prithviraj had eloped with Sanyogita, the daughter of **Jaichandra**, king of Kanauj at her *swyamavara* (ceremony to choose a spouse). It is said that the irate king shunned his son-in-law and stood aloof while Prithviraj faced the invaders alone.

Jaichandra put peeve before regional security and may have helped Ghori militarily. He soon regretted his folly and treachery when Ghori attacked and conquered Kanauj. This was a replay of the schisms within the Raja Bhoja alliance where self-interest had led to a ruinous defeat.

Mohammed Ghori had crossed the Himalayas and conquered Punjab in 1185 CE and eight years later **Qutb ud-Din Aybak** founded the first Sultanate of Delhi and set up the Mameluk dynasty that would rule for ninety-seven years. The Muslims extended their reach across North India gaining control over the Gangetic plain by 1200 CE. On their way they plundered and destroyed great Hindu and Buddhist institutions of learning and culture.

Ikhtiyar ud-din supervised the destruction of the **University at Nālandā**--one of the worst examples of barbarism in human history, on a scale above other atrocities such as the Roman burning of the great library at Alexandria, Egypt, a thousand years earlier, which had destroyed much of the recorded knowledge of Romans, pre-Roman Jews, Egyptians and Mediterranean peoples. (Later other tyrants--from the Popes who authored the Inquisition to Hitler--would similarly burn books and other stores of knowledge.) By his act Ikhtiyar had joined the ranks of the most loathsome of men, those who had destroyed, not structures nor life alone, but *knowledge,* the very foundation of civilisation, and the expression of man's loftiest and most illustrious attainments.

Having completed the plunder of North India and established the Sultanate of Delhi as the major force in northern India, Muslims, under **Ala-ud-din Khalji**, looked south, but apart from a group reaching Cape Comorin at the southernmost tip of India in 1300, they had little success. The wealthy Vijayanagara Empire of South India, which was established in 1336 and lasted through many vicissitudes, held the Muslims in check until it ended in 1646 CE; some princes however managed to sequester wealth in ancient grottoes below less accessible temples.

Dr Brahmam had emphasised, *"I always stress this history because that was when this country, which was so powerful and almost impregnable, lost focus and allowed her wealth to fall to enemies--Muslims and British--because of egotism, hatred and disunity. When Ghazni tried to take Punjab Pālas and Chandellas were major northern powers and could easily have repelled invaders with united defence, like Gupta or Ashoka. Later Kalachuris, Chahamanas, Parmars, and Gahadvalas also failed to take combined action against Ghazni's successors. We didn't just lose territory; we lost our heritage, our command of science, our direction and the momentum to excel. We lost respect, our soul. We became slaves."*

His regret was all the more poignant as he painted an impressive picture of society and the forces that guided its development. Indian science and religious insights had addressed community issues and problems of the day in each region of the country. The range was wide, from Kashmiri philosophical treatises on aesthetics--such as **Abhinavagupta's** nine flavours *(rasa)* of responses to art, music, dance[69] etc.--to such pragmatic economic activities as development of improved textiles e.g. light muslins for clothing, architectural and engineering innovation to counter heat and humidity, manage water in the Rajasthan desert, build reservoirs in Kathiawar, artificial lakes in central, south and western regions, and expand research in astronomy.

New observatories were built in Ujjain, Mathura, Varanasi, New Delhi and elsewhere, to improve the data base for determining times for various royal and community functions and predicting the weather.

Increased agricultural output spurred research in food preservation, with discovery of pickling and other techniques. Progress in medicine and allied sciences such as pharmacology extended the work of Sushruta, Charaka and their successors with new discoveries that placed India at the van of medical sciences. Textbooks on Ayurvedic medicine were well-known locally and abroad and covered studies of the natural history of diseases, their prevention and treatment; use of autopsy to describe and classify them; anaesthesia to facilitate surgery such as cataractectomy, craniotomy, fracture repairs, caesarean sections, plastic and other procedures; technology to devise suitable tools, medicines, disinfectants, dressings, ointments and cleansing agents; and promotion of medical education, quality of care and ethics[70].

Along with scientific advances came--inevitably and from the earliest days of the civilisation to this day--the "science" swindlers, sooth-sayers and dream-peddlers, assorted con-artists and others hawking superstitions and myths, which tainted the practice of medicine and the sciences even as they do today worldwide. But their activities did not prevent the advances in science and technology. In every region of the country scientists were busy in various enterprises.

Chemists refined sugar, produced glass, acidic and alkaline substances for commercial and industrial use, extracted oils, compounded spices, cosmetics and beauty aids. Agriculturalists raised farm animals, created a huge dairy industry, produced varieties of rice, wheat, other grains, barley, corn, pulses, peas, beans, lentils, a wide variety of vegetables, fruits and roots, spices and the finest dyestuffs, which became major exports. Artists expressed the spirit and reality of progress in paintings using materials that have lasted to this day.[71] Miners found the best sapphires, rubies, diamonds, silver and gold; silver became the basis of Indian coinage until terminated by the British.[72]

---

[69] **Abhinavagupta** proposed nine flavours (rasa): abhuta (awe-inspiring), bibhatasa (unappealing), bhayanhaka (terrifying), hasya (comic), karuna (compassionate), raudra (angry), shanta (the peaceful), shringara (erotic) and vira (heroic). To evoke a flavour a work must stimulate and the viewer be sophisticated enough to receive aesthetic stimuli. Thus an experience of art in any form is an interaction between viewer and the art.

[70] "A physician who fails to enter the body of a patient with the lamp of knowledge and understanding can never treat diseases. He should first study all the factors, including environment, which influence a patient's disease, and then prescribe treatment. It is more important to prevent the occurrence of disease than to seek a cure". Charaka Samhita.

[71] Wall paintings in the Ajanta caves have survived for 1500 years, exterior paints on temples at Ellora have lasted over 1200 years. Indian miniatures have maintained their richness for many centuries. Dyes were exported to the Middle East and Roman Empire.

[72] In 1893, the British Governor-General and Council closed the Indian mints to the free coinage of silver, a single obscenely brief moment in history that ruined hundreds of millions of India's peoples. WJ Bryan remarked, in the US Congress: "Mr Leech, former director of the US mint, in an article in the Forum, declared that the closing of the mints in India on that occasion was the most momentous

Indian technology took directions from the support provided by the rulers of its kingdoms. Many from the earliest Vaidic times were enlightened men who supported science and technology, mathematics, religious studies and learning in general. Several were distinguished scientists, such as King Shuchi of Magadha, already mentioned, and Rāja Bhoja of Dhar-Malwa who achieved great engineering successes in his reign, including an artificial lake, roads, iron and steel structures, town planning, and mechanical inventions such as chronometers. His *Somarangana Sutradhara* is really a textbook of engineering. Others supported research and manufacturing of prestige articles, arms and luxury goods, including jewellery, fine fabrics and furnishings, and built structures and monuments, often of great size and complexity, as were many of the temples, palaces and government buildings.

Each region could boast of centres of excellence in manufacturing, which made their owners and regional rulers prosper, developing a considerable middle class of artisans, professionals and other specialists whose skills sustained the success of Indian industries.

But this was a two-edged sword as industry became complacent and overly reliant on skilled labour--because it was plentiful and produced enough for its privileged employers to maintain a healthy profit and lavish lifestyle—and did not see the need to spread prosperity to those less privileged, even as they neglect to do today. A factor in the complacency of Indian manufacturers was the benign climate, with a year-long growing season that allowed the general populace to obtain food, clothing and shelter quite cheaply.

The mass of peasantry survived stoically at a basic level while the elite lived in luxury, a situation promoted by the "caste" system which became more complex as conquerors e.g. Turks and British, added layers.

In temperate zones the pressure to provide for and cope with seasonal changes was a strong stimulus for innovation and growth, even though religion, especially Catholicism, had convinced a large sector of society, the poor, as did *karma* in India, that their lot should be endured for the greater comforts that awaited them in the "other" world.

Indian industry was more developed than most at this early time and relied heavily on the skills and knowledge of its workers and managers. It could have taken greater advantage of expanding external (and internal) markets by increasing production and reach.

This required substantial additional investment in special education to increase the work force, and research and experimentation to develop a wider range of products and more, better and cheaper devices for mass production. But with the smugness that came from success of their traditional methods too many Indian business and political leaders seemed to have forgotten that competitiveness required innovation, and that called for diligence, special insights, research and cultivation of new skills. Because India stopped short of broadening its industrial base by exploiting its scientific knowledge, and expanding education India was ill-prepared for the contest with the heavy mechanisation that transformed Europe during the industrial revolution a millennium later and sent Europeans scouring the world for markets. Yet in some fields, notably the textile industry, Indian machinery, although manually

event in the monetary history of the present century. In that speech Mr. Wolcott also asserted that the closing of the India mints **reduced by five hundred millions of dollars**, the value of the silver accumulated in the hands of the people." Senator WJ Bryan, 1897.

operated was among the world's best and was copied by European "inventors".

The spread of Hinduism and later Buddhism between 1500 BCE and 1000 AD through Lanka, Indonesia, Indochina and southern China--with establishment of Indian colonies in several of them--created a demand for Indian products, spurring international trade, again mainly in goods for the wealthier classes. The huge demand for exports stimulated shipping, ship-building and packaging industries (by the 18th century the Wadias of Bombay would become well known for the quality of their ships), and Indian ports were indeed among the busiest in the world. Even though one could with hindsight clearly see that India had missed an opportunity for worldwide expansion of its industry, the fact is that its standard of living was the envy of the old world, and made it a target for every warlord with a craving for luxury and power.[73]

But India repelled invaders for a millennium or more until the decline of Indian kingdoms and their failure to re-unite as a strong and true *nation* allowed central Asian invaders to triumph--first the Kushans, then the Hephtalites followed by Muslims. Finally the British, who had come as traders, overthrew the decadent Mughals, seized and exploited the country in a way that made their predecessors look like amateurs, and further retarded Indian religion, education, science and technology that the Muslims had already savaged.

Indian trade with the West and East continued despite the changes in governments. The decline of her strength coincided with an explosion in knowledge that came to Europe with the Reformation and its spread by secularising and commercial forces that challenged Rome's hegemony. Gradually the knowledge of India and China flowed to Europe in translations — especially Arabic and Latin--and was taught in Europe's first institutions of higher learning such as the Salerno Medical school, the universities of Cordoba, Bologna and later Paris, all of which thrived on classical Roman, Greek and Arabic learning and their renditions of Indian teachings, especially in the sciences, mathematics and literature.

Unlike Hindus, who were greatly influenced and constrained by the teachings of the Gita and the Buddhist and Jain precepts of *karma* and *ahimsa*, Europeans had transformed Christianity into a militant force and an excuse to conquer the world, having grown tolerant of continuous fighting among themselves for a millennium. They used the new knowledge that came from Asia to make tools and weapons[74] that facilitated territorial expansion, and later industrialisation, which enriched the victors and helped them to reverse the negative balance of trade with India and China that had been an initial stimulus to explore so far away from home.

Major social and political changes took place in Europe starting with England's Magna Carta in 1215 CE, which although benefiting the nobles only,

---

[73] Harry Vere, lst (Senior Officer of the East India Company) described Bengal before Pilashi (Plessey) quite succinctly: "*The farmer was easy, the artisan encouraged, the merchant enriched and the prince satisfied*"

[74] In the mid-11th century the Chinese had invented the compass and moveable type and had refined the use of gunpowder which the Indians had much earlier invented as a mixture of saltpetre, sulphur and charcoal and used in small arms and artillery. Neither major power exploited these innovations in the way the Europeans did when they came to know of them following Greek excursions and later Marco Polo's epic journeys to the East. Note that the Greeks in 678 had used the same mixture, to which they had added petroleum in their successful defence of Constantinople against the Arab Muslims.

did provide a benchmark for those pursuing the slow, plodding and incomplete process of relief from serfdom that would take several centuries to reach a stage where the lower classes could aspire to a modicum of the foreign luxuries flaunted by aristocrats and merchants. To do this they had first to be delivered from the European brand of casteism and gain access to education and equal rights before the law. The process was a long and fierce struggle of the masses versus the rich that brought out the best and worst in humankind. European aristocracy opposed reforms and notions of fairness and equality for the masses and what measure was eventually achieved came only after murderous civil wars and revolutions in Britain, France, Russia and Spain.

The 1272 CE visits of Marco Polo to the Orient had profound effects, not only on Venice, but on Muslims and on India, as he described the opulence and culture of the East to his Venetian sponsors. The consequent trade arrangements established Venetian monopoly over the spice and silk trade with Europe which flourished for centuries while the rest of Europe battled among themselves, pausing briefly to mourn the death of millions of their citizens--among the 75 millions who died worldwide--killed between 1347 and 1351 by the Black death, the plague caused by the bacterium *Pasteurella pestis*.

Europeans had traditionally paid for Indian and Chinese goods with gold and silver, which were becoming scarcer and more expensive and the goods dearer as Venetians tightened their grip on Oriental trade. The layers of intermediaries ramped up the price of Asian goods, to a point that influential and wealthy European consumers and businessmen felt pinched enough to desire direct trade with the East.

They lobbied governments to find an alternative route to India to avoid the routes controlled by the Venetians. Up to the sixteenth century Europeans had neither the scientific knowledge nor indigenous capital to do this and had to purchase gold from West Africa to pay for oriental goods. Advances in navigation, shipbuilding and exploration led to the discovery of gold and silver in the Americas which paved the way for colonisation, seizure of American wealth, and decimation of American natives.

The Spaniards had led in this massive holocaust and seizure of mines throughout Western America; a single mountain at Potosí, in what would become Bolivia, produced enough silver to enrich all Europe. Drake's 1588 defeat of the Spanish Armada off Plymouth unleashed a free-for-all on the Atlantic Ocean, with royal assent to piracy. Atlantic plunder provided capital, first for trade, then for the eventual conquest of India, once England had established naval supremacy over all Europeans in two centuries of bitter fighting, culminating in the defeat of Napoleon..

A Sea Route to India: The race to find a sea route to India made names for Christopher Columbus, Vasco da Gama, Magellan, Amerigo Vespucci, Henry Hudson, Francis Drake, Martin Frobisher and many others. While India welcomed the traders the Chinese reacted differently to commerce with the West by banning travel there in the 1430's--pulling down the first "bamboo curtain". Just before that century ended da Gama discovered a sea route from Europe to India via the Cape of Good Hope. Indian traders welcomed discussions and sought agreements.

Twelve years later a Portuguese force overwhelmed the surprised people of Goa and seized the area, with much carnage, as a base for trade and religious proselytising that became the model of conquest in the cause of mercantilism and Christianity that other Europeans would follow for the next four and a half centuries, and modern multinational corporations would pursue today, a bit more cunningly perhaps, but no less brutally. The Portuguese dominated the 16th century spice trade by sea.

The major development that would eventually threaten this control and despoil India was undoubtedly the desire of English King Henry VIII for grandeur (believed due to the effects of tertiary syphilis, which is known to induce delusions of grandeur); this spurred him to create the best armed navy of the time which his daughter Elizabeth used to good effect. Henry's engineers had succeeded in building cast iron cannons that were far cheaper than bronze and enabled him to equip his fleet, first the *Mary Rose*, each with more guns than other nations' warships.

One of the outcomes of the Muslim presence was its influence on Hindu thinkers, among whom was the Hindu Kshatriya religious thinker **Guru Nanak**, who simplified Hindu beliefs and practices, preached in favour of unity among Hindus and Muslims and against caste and needless rituals and habitually mingled with poor and low caste persons. All of these were quite revolutionary at the time and crystallised as the **Sikh** religion. He attained a just fame throughout the subcontinent and over the next centuries was succeeded by 10 gurus, the last being the *Granth Sahib* or Holy Book. Sikhism had a mixed reception among Hindus and Muslims. The 10th Guru, Gobind Singh, reacting to Muslim aggression and murder of Sikhs including his father, the ninth Guru, developed the *Khalsa* which is the dominant form of the religion practised today.

In the 16th century a major change occurred in the Muslim hegemony over India. In 1526 **Babur the Mughal** (1483-1530) conquered the sultanate of Delhi, which had been from its foundation a centre of intrigue, and initiated the dynasty that existed for the next two and a half centuries. In 1528 he destroyed Hindu temples at Ayodhya and Mathura where avatars **Rāma** and **Krishna** were born respectively, and at Varanasi, and outraged Hindus by erecting thereon Muslim *masjids*.

He built a retreat at the bird sanctuary of Sultanpur, my *nāna's* village near Delhi. His grandson Jalal ud Din Mahammad **Akbar** (1542-1605) became Emperor at age 13, on the death of his father Humayun who had lost control to the Afghan Sher Shah Suri and his adviser **Hemu Chandra** for 17 years from 1540-57. Hemu had earned a fearsome reputation in war and conquered Delhi in 1556, having succeeded Adil Shah, the last of the Suris, and was crowned king (*Vikramaditya*). Several weeks later he was killed in battling Akbar and his regent **Bairam Khan** at Pānipat (the second battle). Hemu had reformed the administration and cleansed it of corruption throughout the Ganga-Yamuna valley, restoring Hinduism and dealing fairly with all religious groups.

Akbar became the best known of the Mughal rulers and a polymath. He professed a love for jihad and used all means to expand his kingdoms. One unusual device, a peaceful one, was his success in "persuading" **Bharmal,** the Hindu Rāja of Amber (Jaipur) to allow him to marry his daughter **Harkha Bai** (Rajkumari Hira Kunwari) with whom he had fallen in love on sight. The Rajput king became his army commander and his Rajput successors then fought for Mughals for 150 years—an incredible alliance considering Muslim cruelty against Hindus such as the looting and destruction of temples, the practice of beheading Hindus and building victory pillars with heads of the slain, and the imposition of punitive *jizya* tax on Hindus, which forced the poor to convert to Islam or be executed for debt.

Akbar's marriage to a Rajput princess and close relationship with her father exposed him to Hindu beliefs and practices and for a time he was less cruel in treatment of Hindus, abolished *jizya* and engaged Hindus, Sikhs, Jains, Parsis and Jews in philosophical discourses. He started a new religion *Din-ilahi* which included the best features of all religions and proclaimed that *"No man is to be interfered with on account of religion, and anyone is to be allowed to go over to a religion that pleases him."*[75] Many today believe that his alleged fairness in dealing with Hindus and his attempts at tolerance and separation of religion from government were exaggerated. Although he did encourage art and literature, the emphasis was on things Persian, not Indian and he did choose to expand Islamic influence proclaiming himself a *ghazi* (slayer of infidels).

His armies in 1565 CE destroyed the city of **Vijayanagara**, which had long withstood Muslim attacks, paving the way for the fall of that empire 81 years later. He and his successors extended their long campaign of conquest and three years after Vijayanagara, the fortress of Ranthambor fell, bringing Rājputāna to the Mughals and thus control of northern India from Sindh to Bengal. The Vijayanagara Empire had also become known for its patronage of fine arts and literature which reached new heights in the major languages of the south: Kannada, Telugu, Tamil and Sanskrit, while Carnatic music evolved into its current form. The Vijayanagara Empire occupied an epoch in South Indian history that transcended regionalism by promoting Hinduism as a unifying factor.

The excesses of Akbar's successors angered the country, but the loyalty, strength and religious fanaticism of the Mughals and their armed forces--many led by Hindus--and with the regular conflicts among Indian kings, kept the population underfoot. Then came the wastrel **Shah Jahan** who squandered a fortune to bejewel the "peacock throne" and build a mausoleum (Tāj Mahal, or *Teju Mahalaya*, completed in 1647) for his favourite wife, on what seemed to have been a Hindu palace or temple; he then finished the Red Fort in Delhi. After him came the zealot **Aurangzeb** (1618-1707), the last of the major Mughal Emperors, whose cruelty undid whatever gains in goodwill Akbar had won among Hindus. He expanded the Empire by invasions south into the Deccan and east to Assam where the **Ahom** army defeated him in 1682. He maintained the *jizya* tax on 'non-believers', largely Hindus--already suffering tremendous hardships--executed Sikh Guru **Tegh Bahadur** in 1675, and by 1688 had razed all temples in Mathura, said to number 1,000. Muslims destroyed over 60,000 Hindu temples in India, and built mosques on 3,000 of them. They annihilated a vast number of Indians[76]

---

[75] V.A. Smith: *Akbar, the great Mogul*, Oxford, the Clarendon Press 1917.

[76] In *The Growth of Muslim population in India*, Prof. K.S. Lal noted that the Hindu population *decreased by 80 million* between the invasion by Mohamed Ghazni in 1000 AD, and the battle of Pānipat. Another 20 million Hindus were killed by Mughals in the north and central India and other Muslims in the south. Koenrad Elst pointed out in his book--The Negationism in India--that the assassination of about 100 million Hindus is perhaps the biggest holocaust in world history: *"Nadir Shah made a mountain of the skulls of the Hindus he killed in Delhi alone. Babur raised towers of Hindu skulls at Khanuaj when he defeated Rana Sanga in 1527 and later he repeated the same horrors after capturing the fort of Chanderi. Akbar ordered a general massacre of 30,000 Rajputs after he captured Chitoor in 1568. The Bahamani Sultans"* (who had revolted against Mohammed bin Tughluk and taken charge of a large area of the Deccan and Central India) *"had an annual agenda of killing a minimum of 100,000 Hindus*

including many who refused conversion to Islam.

Aurangzeb's rebel son had fled to the safety of the Marātha Empire which Shivaji had founded by retaking Vijapur (see below). Aurangzeb invaded the Empire to punish it, beginning a 27 years' war ending in 1705 with his defeat by **Rani Tarabai** at Malwa heralding the end of Mughal power in India.

In 1708, a year after the death of Aurangzeb, **Govind Singh,** the militant tenth and last Sikh guru, was killed, presumably at the command of the new Mughal emperor, **Bahadur Shah I**, (formerly Prince Muazzam, eldest son of Aurangzeb, who had defeated his brother Azam in fighting for the throne). He was a weak ruler and presided over the disintegration of a vast Empire that had expanded beyond its resources and the vision of its rulers. It had become weak, fractured and crippled with intrigue and conflict among the many aspiring princes and foreigners. The centre had become increasingly reliant on regional governors or Nawabs, making it easy prey to the machinations of the wealthy Arabic **Sayyid brothers**, long influential among Mughals (by claiming descent from Mohamed through Fatimah and Ali). They quickly moved to fill the power vacuum and played king-makers in a fragmenting Empire, instigating five changes in 12 years until their last pick, **Mohammed Shah**, organised their execution!

Meanwhile Nawabs had begun their own intrigues to secure full control of their kingdoms and by 1720 **Asaf Jah I** had declared himself the independent Nizam of Hyderabad in the south. In the East **Alivardi Khan**, a deputy governor of Bihar became Nawab of Bihar, Orissa and Bengal after deposing Sarfaraz Khan with the Emperor's approval; soon he too asserted self-governance. These developments had left the Emperor with Delhi and surroundings only and at the mercy of his Nawabs.

Nadir Shah, a Persian robber, had risen to the throne of Iran after boldly driving Afghan occupiers from Khorasan, the capital, in 1725. He had become regent to a boy king whose convenient death left Nadir at the helm. In 1738 he invaded and captured Ghazni and Kabul and moved into India where the Afghan ruler Nasir Khan had been on an expedition.

Khan was easily defeated and Nadir Shah advanced across north Punjab to capture Delhi in 1739, and seize the treasures of the Peacock throne including the *Koh-I-Noor* diamond. He returned to Afghanistan with thousands of captive young men and women leaving a trail of horror and atrocities against opponents. (For this, Hindus of the later British period would say his first name Nadir was well chosen!) Sikh defenders trailed the departing armies and were able to attack their rear, re-capture much of the treasure and release large numbers of captives. Mohamed Shah was reduced to a tributary of Nadir Shah's. The region remained in a state of anarchy peppered with skirmishes led by Afghans, Mughals, Sikhs and Marathis.

Following Rani Tarabai's victory, the **Maratha Empire** had consolidated the gains previously made by Shivaji. By 1760 they had regained all of central India. The Marathi military Commander-in-Chief **Sadshivrao Bhau** had

---

every year. The history of medieval India is full of such instances." (Anon) A similar bloodthirstiness and behaviour making pyramids or columns of skulls of their victims were key features of Assyrian armies in their campaigns of expansion throughout the Middle East in the 8th to 7th centuries BC. India's population had risen to nearly 30% of the world's by 1000 CE but fell to 17.8% by 1900 and remained there. India's population growth fell from 58% in the 500-year period 500-1000 CE to 33% in the next period--1000-1500 CE--the years of Muslim expansion.

prepared in 1760-61 to retake Gandhāra (Afghanistan), which had been part of the Gupta and Shahi Empires. But once again internal dissension and jostling for conquered territory among regional kings led to logistic and support failures at the most critical point in their 1761campaign. Although favoured to prevail over advancing Afghan forces of **Emir Ahmad Shah Durrani** (Abdali)—the Pashtun who had succeeded Nadir Shah and founded Afghanistan--the Maratha forces fell at Pānipat due mainly to failed delivery of supplies to troops and horses that were too exhausted from hunger to complete the final decisive assault against the beleaguered Muslim forces! In the final battle lasting eight horrifying hours as many as 200,000 Hindus are said to have died.

Durrani reinstated **Alamgir II** as Emperor and left Delhi for Afghanistan two months after with a loot of 500 elephants, 1500 camels, 50,000 horses and ovef 22,000 women and children. This was not his first such trove. Five years earlier he had invaded India, established his rule over the Mughals, sacked Delhi, removed tons of valuables, installed Shah Alam II to the throne as puppet and on his way back to Kabul had raided the Golden Temple at Amritsar and filled its sacred pool with the blood of humans and cattle. Sikhs have not forgiven this abomination. The victory heightened Sikh-Muslim tensions and did nothing to improve the chances for restoration of the Mughal Empire and placed India once more at the mercy of the most resolute among those battling for her hand.

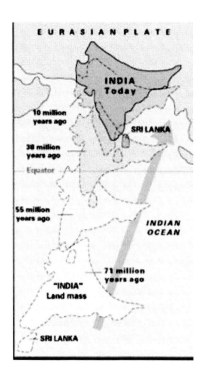

130 or more million years ago, the ancient continent of Gondwanaland was rent apart in a monstrous convulsion of the earth's crust and chunks of that huge continent began to drift away, floating northward; one large block that would become India moved northeast through the vast ocean that would later be called the Indian Ocean and eventually, after shedding fragments that became the islands of the western Indian ocean—Madagascar, Mauritius, Reunion, Seychelles and other tiny ones--finally collided with the southern edge of Asia creating the lofty and rugged Himalayas at the line of impact and south of that the land of India.

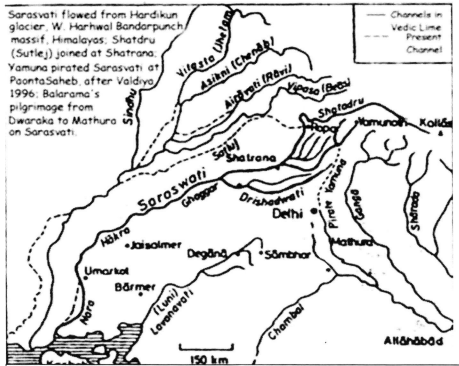

Saraswati/Sindhu (Indus) civilisation ended ca. 1900 BCE. Numerous sites-- found along the line of the ancient Saraswati and in coastal seas of Gujarat since the initial surprises at *Harappa* and *Mohenjo Daro* -- remain to be excavated. The findings so far support Vaidic accounts of ancient Indian societies and show the implausibility of the Aryan Invasion theory of Indian civilisation –the myth popularised by the British to promote the cultural conquest of Hindus. Today many influential Indians still believe the fable much to the surprise of objectives scholars. *Credit: Indian Archaeological Inst., :Rajaram, Frawley et al*

Lothal, Saraswati/Indus civilisation 3rd to 45th millennium BCE (*credit Rajaram &Frawley*)

R: Raj figure Mohenjo Daro (Saraswati-Sindhu
civilisation (National Museum, Karachi,
Pakistan: author Mamoon Mengal) Mengal.)

Major Pre-Christian Religions of India

L to R: Shiva, one of Hindu Trinity; Mahavira, avatar of Jainism; Buddha

Shiva temple at Varanasi

Guru Nanak, founder of Sikhism

Sushruta, father of Surgery, at work, with students; note female associate

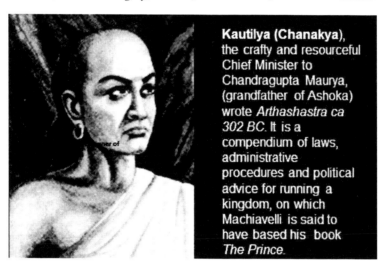

Kautilya (Chanakya), the crafty and resourceful Chief Minister to Chandragupta Maurya, (grandfather of Ashoka) wrote *Arthashastra ca 302 BC.* It is a compendium of laws, administrative procedures and political advice for running a kingdom, on which Machiavelli is said to have based his book *The Prince.*

The main *stupa* (reliquary) of Śāriputra, a disciple of Buddha, in Nālandā University, Bihar, India. This and Taxashila, north Punjab were the first University centres for religious and academic learning in India and the world; they attracted students from many countries, especially China, Middle East, Greece and other Mediterranean states.

View of the Shiva Nataraja Temple, Chidambaram, South India. The evidence provided by ancient engineering works like this is sidestepped nimbly by the massively funded Western missionsaary efforts to inject Christianity into every important landmark or literary/religious work done by Hindus, ancient and modern. Christ was born far too late to have influenced Hindu , Buddhist or Jain thought; evidence suggests the opposite.

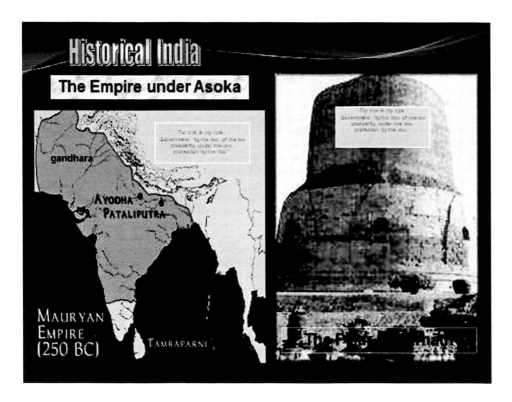

The Empire under Asoka

MAURYAN EMPIRE (250 BC)

Top L: Ashoka's Empire. Ashoka (290-232 BCE), was Mauryan Emperor of India from 273-232 BCE; he was known for erections of many message pillars all over India to ensure that his edicts reached all citizens. This one at Sarnath is one of India's Independence symbols.
The text reads:
"esahi vidhi ya iyam: dhammena palana, dhammena vidhane, dhammena sukhiyana, dhammena gotiti".

This translates to:

"For this is my rule: government by the law, of the law; prosperity by the law,

The Iron Pillar, Delhi, rust-free after some 2,000 years, provides irrefutable evidence of the advances made by Indian metallurgical science when most others were in their infancy. In the 20th century Christian missions would seek to credit foreigners for such work.

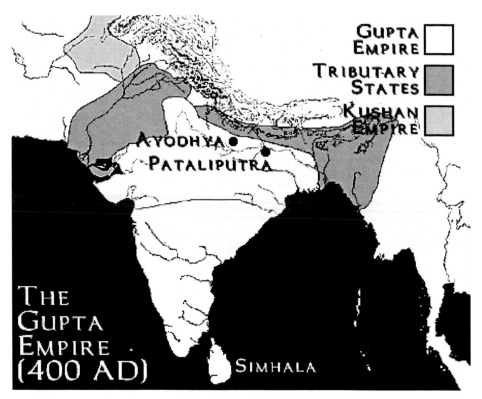

GUPTA EMPIRE

TRIBUTARY STATES

KUSHAN EMPIRE

AYODHYA
PATALIPUTRA

THE GUPTA EMPIRE (400 AD)

SIMHALA

L: Akbar's 3rd wife Mariam uz-Zamani (Harkha Bai), daughter of Rajput Raja Barmal
R: Mural Sculpture, Khajuraho

Section 6: The British in India--From Traders to Raiders

The subsequent capture of India had been charted, unintentionally as it were, a century and a half earlier. In 1600 Queen Elizabeth I of England -- flush with Drake's naval triumph over Spain, the act that fulfilled her father's dream of English naval superiority-- and wishing a steady supply of India's finest opium, granted a group of 216 merchants headed by the Earl of Cumberland a Royal Charter to trade as a monopoly in the vast region between the Cape of Good Hope and the Straits of Magellan under the rubric *Governor and Company of Merchants of London trading with the East Indies* (the East India Company, EICo, British EICo after 1707[77]) initiating a series of events that ultimately led to the brutish subjugation of India, and the seizure of Indian assets that spared few, even the poorest from the fury of British greed, which lacked none of the nastiness of the Mughals' that it replaced. The Queen's Charter was to have lasted fifteen years, but so promising had the Company become and so quickly that James I in 1609 granted the Charter "in perpetuity"! [78]

Meanwhile several Dutch merchants -- in the wake of hostilities between Holland and Portugal/ Spain[79] which had disrupted their supplies of spices from the former to Antwerp--had already realised astronomical profits from pilot ventures trading directly with Indonesia (one trip returning in 1599 realising 400% profit). This and other factors led to the formation in 1602 of the United Dutch East India Company *(VOC Vereenigde Oost-Indische Compagnie)* which obtained a monopoly Charter to trade with Asia and behave independently even to wage war and establish colonies, in the European fashion. Soon they set up quarters in Batavia (Jakarta) finding it more suitable than Bantam further west that had also become home for the EICo. By this time Java had come under Muslim influence.

European companies vying for monopoly fought one another frequently in the Indian Ocean to eliminate rivals; the EICo failed against the Dutch in Java but defeated the Portuguese in 1612 in the *Battle of Swally*. After appropriate diplomatic agreements between King James I and the Mughal Court of Nuruddin Salim Jahangir, mediated by Sir James Roe, EICo received a generous permit to establish an exclusive factory at Surat, Gujarat, where they had visited since 1608. In 1611 EICo set up a trading post at Masulipatam at the mouth of the Krishna River on the Coromandel Coast of the Bay of Bengal, and soon after was granted the right to trade. By 1652 EICo had grown to 23 posts (factories).

---

[77] The first known joint stock Company was the *Muscovy Trading Company* that grew in Moscow in 1555 from the *Company of Merchant Adventurers to New Lands* formed in 1551 by English adventurers wishing to profit from new land discoveries and a Northeast Sea route to China. It was granted a monopoly of trade between Moscow and England and a whaling monopoly off Spitsbergen by Elizabeth I in 1577; the trade monopoly ended in 1698 (cf. *below*).

[78] This was annulled in 1694 under pressure of merchants wishing to compete with EICo. In 1698 an *English Company Trading to the East Indies* was formed but EICo quickly bought a controlling interest and the two merged in 1708 as the *United Company of Merchants of England...Indies*, after years of squabbling. Contrast this with Marathi disunity and the failure of Indian leaders generally to expand education, reform caste issues, involve more people in government and unite against invaders.

[79] Northern Holland had successfully rebelled against Spain, beginning in 1568 and established the Dutch Republic, finally recognised by Spain by the Peace of Munster in 1648. The Dutch West India Company *(Geoctroyeerde Westindische Compagnie or GWC)* was formed in 1621 with a charter monopoly over the slave and other trades, including piracy, and forming colonies, in the Americas and Pacific. It failed eventually and was bought by the Government in 1791. Dutch settlements in the Americas fell to the British and Portuguese.

In 1662 King Charles II of England received Bombay as a gift from the Portuguese on his marriage to Catherine of Braganza and in exchange for a large sum, granted the Company wider latitude -- beside trade in textiles, dyes, spices etc. -- authorising it also *"to make peace or war with any prince or people not being Christian."* Six years later he leased Bombay to the EICo for £10 per annum.

Some years later the Company developed a post at the site of a village on the Hooghly River after failing to hold on to the port at Hijli about 80 miles west which its Capt Nicholson had captured in 1687, and regained by the Mughals.[80]

Lacking competitive sea power the Mughals had come under pressure from the Portuguese and from Shivaji, the first Indian king to build a navy, and had therefore granted the British increasing trade and military concessions in exchange for naval protection. Weakened by conflicting ambitions and infighting, the Mughal Empire was unable to police the English traders who, with new charter powers, openly courted Indian princes, while backing each side in the clashes among Mughal heirs vying for power after the death of Aurangzeb in 1707. In 1708 Raja Jai Singh II began building observatories in Delhi, Ujjain, Varanasi, Jaipur and Mathura.

Rise of the Marathas: The rise of Aurangzeb and the many excesses and rigidities of his rule began the decline of the Mughal Empire. This coincided with major changes that had begun in west, central and north India with formation and expansion of the Maratha Empire and its successor Confederacy (1674-1820), which by 1760 would develop the strength and leadership to rid India of all foreigners, but would fail through squabbling, disunity, intrigue and betrayal. The change had begun with the establishment of the Maratha kingdom in the Deccan by **Shivaji Bhosle** (1632-1680), with capital at Raigad, later moved to Sātārā, thus restoring Maratha sovereignty over ancestral lands which had become a Muslim sultanate.

Shivaji had succeeded his father **Shahaji Bhosle** who, like so many kings and princes who had lost their kingdoms, had had a long and brilliant career as a general in the armed services of Mughals and Nizams of south and west India-- Vijapur, Ahmednagar, and Golconda. Some had converted to Islam; others had given their daughters to Muslim rulers to curry favour. Characteristically no Muslim ruler was ever known to have returned the favour.

Shahaji Bhosle had nursed the ambition to recapture Marathi lands from the Mughals, restore the Hindu kingdoms of India, curb political meddling by foreign merchants and restrict them to their trading posts. He had passed on this ambition to his sons **Sambhaji, Shivaji and Venkoji** and had maintained the family base at **Puné**. From here Shivaji and brother Sambhaji (killed in battle of Kanakgiri, 1654) and their dedicated forces of hardy warriors set out to conquer the sultanate of **Vijapur** which had usurped Marathi lands.

Shivaji's reign began when he was ten years old, by which time, like most

---

[80] The new site grew to become the city of Calcutta and the Company's Bengal headquarters, and became the capital of the British Raj until that was moved to Delhi in 1911. Calcutta grew as two cities: a white Calcutta of fine homes, parks and clean streets and a brown Calcutta of crowded squalor and deprivation sprinkled with a few nice neighbourhoods, not unlike the colonies. The palace of the Governor General was built in 1803 by Richard Wellesley who did not think Belvedere House opulent enough, allegedly proclaiming," *India should be governed from a palace, not from a country house."* The palace became the Governor's mansion when the capital moved to New Delhi in 1911-2 specifically designed as the nation's capital with wide tree-lined streets crowned with a vice-regal palace (*Rashtrapati Bhavan*) and supplemented with luxurious summer lodges in Shimla.

Kshatriyas, he had observed military action. At twelve he went to Bangalore for two years of formal training then returned to Pué. At age 16 he led the first assaults against **Vijapur** with a series of daring raids using guerrilla tactics (*Ganimi Kava*)--which he is said to have innovated--and succeeded in capturing Fort Toma. After a long and arduous campaign, with many ups and downs, acts of daring, including near-death events, in battles that have become legendary, he triumphed over the much larger forces of the **Sultan Adilshah.**

He reorganised the army, developed a navy that challenged the British and Portuguese, established a **Council of Ministers** (*ashtrapradhān mandal*) and encouraged public participation in government. He became a popular, virtuous and exemplary ruler, inspiring his people to greatness, placing him among Maratha and India's greatest rulers. **Swami Vivekananda** called him *"the very incarnation of Lord Shiva."* Shivaji eschewed religious bigotry and the crude behaviour that Indian rulers had adopted under Muslim tutelage. Once when one of his generals offered him a Muslim princess after a victory over a Muslim force he rebuked the general making the offer and forbade such actions thereafter.

He was crowned king in 1674 with the title of *Chhatrapati* (king of the Kshatriyas). When he died in 1680 of a febrile illness, thought to be Anthrax, control shifted to the *Péshwé* (Prime Minister) in Puné--a position Shivaji's father Shahaji had created in 1640, which would become hereditary in 1749. His fort at Raigad remained impregnable for years after his death and fell only when Suryaji Pisal, a Maratha defender, betrayed the defence by opening the fort to Aurangzeb's forces in 1689.

Soon after Shivaji's death the Mughal Emperor Aurangzeb began a series of frenetic invasions of the Deccan with the largest army the world had yet seen– 500,000 men and some 400,000 animals--to destroy the Marathas and capture his rebel son Akbar who, aged 24, had defected to the Rajputs who had arranged for him to be given asylum by the Maratha king **Sambhaji,** son of Shivaji.

Many battles followed with fluctuating fortunes in which Sambhaji and his talented generals led by **Hambirrao Mohite** and Péshwé **Moropant Pingle**, harassed Mughal forces, waged successful wars against **Chikka Devraj**, Wadeyar of Mysore and punished the Portuguese in Goa for assisting the Mughals. On the eve of an offensive against the Mughals in the Deccan in 1689, Sambhaji was betrayed by a brother-in-law **Ganoji Shirke**, captured, tortured for forty days and executed by hanging and quartering.

His younger brother **Rajaram** succeeded him and with outstanding generals **Santaji Ghorpade** and **Dhanaji Jadhav** withstood another decade of Mughal assaults. Rajaram died in 1700; his widow **Rani Tarabai** carried on and defeated Aurangzeb (90) in 1705, expelling the Mughals from the Deccan and signalling their fall. Aurangzeb retreated to Delhi broken in health and in debt, and died soon after. India's population in 1700 was 167 million.

The decline of the Mughals ushered in a period of intense political and military activity, initiated by the British in the East and South to achieve control of larger territories, and Marathas in the North, West and central India to regain Indian control. For many decades of the 18th century, it had seemed that the Marathas--a community of warriors and cultivators with a feudal social and economic organisation similar to Britain--might succeed in regaining India especially when the efforts of **Bajirao I** had brought under their control all of the former Empire of Harshavardhan plus the Marathi lands of the western Deccan.

Shivaji and his successors--**Sambhaji, Rajaram** and his wife **Rani Tarabai, Shahu** (Shambhaji's son) and **Rajaram II**--and their appointed Péshwés, enlisted *sardars* (generals) and princes from all over India. The most dynamic of the Maratha commanders, the most expert after Shivaji and perhaps the first to really believe that the conquest of the Mughals was imminent was **Bajirao I**, the fourth Péshwé at Puné, appointed in 1719 when he was only 20 years old.

He fought the Mughals continuously in 41 battles[81], winning all, until his sudden death in 1740 of a fever (cf. Shivaji). By then he had put the Maratha Empire on a solid base, barring one major lapse which might have been corrected had he not died prematurely. He had appointed local generals as rulers of conquered lands but had not set up a coordinating and controlling government to regulate and supervise their actions, as Ashoka had done, and to prevent power struggles, subversion, backsliding or treachery as profit dictated.

With Bajirao's death regional governors and urban chieftains were left, "on their honour", as it were, *without* his strong central control, free to indulge whims and make alliances to gain personal power even before they had expelled the foreigners. Some of this narcissism and self-indulgence derived from individual military prowess and reflected the same mentality that had allowed Muslims to conquer India. Most leaders had limited geo-political background and lacked the vision of a larger India shared by Bajirao I and Shahaji.

With Maratha victories power devolved to the **Shindes** centred at Ujjain and Gwalior, **Holkars** at Indaur, **Gaekwads** at Baroda, **Bhosles** at Nagpur, and **Pawar** (Parmar), a Rajput chieftain--the five major commanders in the Empire beyond Puné. Allied with other leaders from Rajasthan, Maharashtra and Central India--**Pandit, Sardar Panse, Parshuram Pant Pratinidhi, Patwardhan, Pethe, Phadke, Purandar, Raste, Vinchurkar** *et al*--they served the Péshwé well and by 1760 had captured most of the Mughal-ruled territories except those under British control, amounting to over a million square kilometres.

British Wars in India: While Marathis were building an Empire amid fears of dissension and rivalry, including the alliances that had been forged between Hindu princes and Mughal rulers, the British had clearly shown their intent and had begun to behave more like swindlers than traders and had thereby achieved far more freedom than in China where, for example, the trading season was regulated and merchants, confined to three cities only, were not allowed within city walls and had to leave at the end of each year.

In India however they had ingratiated themselves with Mughal rulers at all levels and used the resulting influence to "assist" local and business favourites. They seized on the chaos among Aurangzeb's successors and influenced the succession. By plotting and other devious acts they acquired territory and *diwanis* which allowed retention of tax collected. One major success was the grant in 1717 by the frail and submissive Emperor **Farruqsiyar**, Aurangzeb's grandson, of tax-free trading rights in Bengal for a mere 3,000 rupees subsidy per year.

In both major trading areas, Bengal and the Coromandel Coast, the French were the BEICo's main rival and had built trading posts and forts at Pondicherry

---

[81]"Remember that night has nothing to do with sleep. It was created by God to raid territory held by your enemy; the night is your shield, your screen against cannons and swords of vastly superior enemy forces," Bajirao to his brother, Chimaji Appa. "The *Palkhed* campaign of 1727-8 in which Bajirao I out-generalled Nizam ul Mulk is a masterpiece of strategic mobility."
-- Field Marshal Bernard Montgomery 1972, *The Concise History of Warfare*, 132

on the Coast and at Chandranagar in Bengal while the British were ensconced in Fort George, Madras, Masulipatam and other Coromandel sites, and in Calcutta and Dhaka in Bengal. The Bengal trade focussed on cotton and the fine cloths made from it enriched with vibrant colours that flowed in profusion from the sophisticated natural dye industry (indigo) of Bihar and Oudh.

The outbreak of wars in Europe–*Jenkins' Ear*, *Austrian Succession* and the *Seven Years War*--occupied that continent from 1739 to 1763, barring a few short breaks, and extended British-French hostilities to Asia (India) and America (including Canada and the Caribbean) and wherever they met on the high seas, creating a virtual world war. The rivalry between the two nations had existed for a millennium or more; in India each plotted against the other recruiting to its cause local chieftains, whether Hindu Kings or Muslim rulers, by various stratagems–bribery, deceit, treachery, breach of contracts, coercion etc.

As the wars raged in Europe each developed a metastasis in India manifesting there as three *Carnatic Wars* between 1746 and 1763 and the first *Mysore War* from 1762 to 1764, and the later Maratha wars. At the outset France had captured Madras but released it in 1748 when the *Treaty of Aix-la-Chapelle* ended the *War of Austrian Succession*. By 1750 the Mughals had lost much of the west and northwest to the **Maratha Confederacy**, the east to **Nawab Alivardi** and his successor **Siraj ud Daulah** and south to **Nizam ul-Mulk** (later of Hyderabad) and the **Raja Wadeyar** of Mysore[82] and his commander **Haider Ali** who later became Nawab of Mysore.

The crumbling Mughal Empire thus provided excellent grounds for shysters and opportunists who materialised like flies from a faecal dump, led by the British and French, the Dutch having been relegated to an outpost at Negapatam and to Ceylon--after ousting the **Portuguese** at the request of Kandy's King **Rajasinghe**--and restricting them to the Arabian Sea coast of India at **Goa, Daman** and **Diu.** Anglo-French wars in India lasted over six decades, each using their standard tools--agreements, intrigue, bribery and other chicanery, as appropriate--to exploit the ambitions of Indian princes and Muslim nawabs to lure them into conflicts, which allowed the European victor to gain Indian territory and usurp Indian rights.

The wars also forestalled Indian unification aimed to prevent political and territorial expansion by foreigners. By the time the first Carnatic War had started, the Marathas had gained control of the west and north and Nawabs the east and south. Here the Nizam ul Mulk in Hyderabad had begun a series of skirmishes against its southern neighbour Mysore, allying with the British Company after initial flirtation with the French who had sided with Mysore, and Shinde, a Marathi confederate. Anglo-French hostilities inevitably became a contest for control of South India and thus untold wealth.

In the *First Carnatic War* the English roughneck **Robert Clive** had emerged as a natural soldier. He had come to India as a Company clerk, was imprisoned by the French in Madras in 1746 and came to the notice of army commander **Major Lawrence** by escaping to Fort St David, which earned him a commission as *ensign*. This lapsed with the 1748 *Treaty of Aix-la-Chapelle*. France saved some face in regaining Louisburg on Cape Breton Island, Canada, in exchange for Madras (today Chennai).

---

[82] **Mysore was o**ne of several regional kingdoms that had emerged from the collapse of the Vijayanagara Empire.

Returning to the Company Clive took up its cause in the conflicts among the Indian rulers of Hyderabad in which merchants jostled for the huge spoils of war and the revenues from monopoly and territorial control. In 1751 Lawrence gave his Clive, then 26, the rank of Captain; he distinguished himself as a military leader capturing the fort at Arcot that year. He was honoured in England, stayed two years and returned as governor of Fort St David.

Meanwhile in Bengal **Siraj ud Daulah** had succeeded his grandfather **Alivardi Khan** as Nawab. He protested British expansion at Fort William and elsewhere, their shielding of treasury thieves and resented the tax-free status given them by a naïve Emperor ignorant of British duplicity and their disinterest in Indian welfare. The British responded to Siraj's order to stop illegal property seizures by waving the Emperor's *firman* affirming its legality in *British* law, and continued as before. Siraj, deciding to expel them from Bengal, captured the fort at Calcutta and held some prisoners overnight in a small room where some were overcome by heat. The incident received exaggerated publicity in Britain with an inflated number of victims, as told by a captive, Howell, enough to fire the British with revenge. Clive was sent to Bengal to oust the Nawab.

In 1757 his combined army and naval force regained Calcutta and took the French post at nearby Chandranagar, ostensibly as an expression of the war in Europe. From there he moved to attack the Nawab at his capital Murshidabad.

Meanwhile Siraj had led a force out of the city, having arranged with **Mir Jafar**, his granduncle and head of his main army, to flank Clive and attack upon his signal. Siraj met Clive at **Pilashi** (Plessey), unaware that Jafar had conspired with Clive to betray him, in return for the position of Nawab of Bengal, Bihar and Orissa. On Siraj's signal at a crucial point in the battle when poised to rout Clive's army, Mir Jafar led the main army *away* from the fray instead of attacking the British force. Siraj lost and was later captured and murdered.

Mir Jafar would earn the opprobrium of history and the label of traitor (*gaddar-e-abrar)*, joining the parade of Indians like **Jaichandra** in the north 500 years earlier, and many since who had sold their country for brief personal gain. Thus Bengal fell to the Company with Clive as Governor and Jafar the Nawab; his treachery was bitter-sweet, however; Jafar had to pay the Company compensation of £3 million sterling, £1.5million for military expenses plus other large settlements totalling an additional £1 million; he was deposed three scant years later (in 1760) in favour of his son-in-law **Mir Qasim** by Clive's successor, **Henry Vansittart**. By this time the Mughals had lost most of central, west and north India and Orissa to the Maratha Empire, restricting their control to the region of Delhi and Oudh.

As the *Seven Years War* intensified the French had planned to invade England, having abandoned a similar plan in 1744, (ironically from Dunkirk where WWII allies would later land an invasion force to liberate France from Hitler's Germany). France laid siege to Madras late in 1758-9 but retreated on the arrival of a British fleet, giving Britain a victory, one of a string worldwide that included Wolfe's seminal defeat of **Champlain** in Québec and naval victories near Lagos, Portugal and Quiberon, Bay of Biscay, and others in Europe and the Caribbean. Elated Britons dubbed 1759 *Annus mirabilis* (the Wonderful Year), much to the joy of PM **William Pitt** the Elder. The defeat of France in Canada and India gained Britain two rich prizes and led to the *Treaty of Paris* ending the War and France's overseas power.

Bengal was the richest province of India then with a large population of some 30 million who bore the burden of paying the oppressive taxes levied by Company and Nawab. Its capture laid the foundation on which Company agents: **Clive, Hastings, Cornwallis, Wellesley** and others, indemnified by the Crown, would begin to subdue the rest of India, by arms, conspiracies and treaties, for the next hundred years. Clive and Hastings were the first amoral Company leaders among many who broke trade agreements to gain Indian territory from unwary rulers, replacing trading pacts with outright conquest.

This type of behaviour was already well-known and lauded in Britain where intrigue and in-fighting among aristocrats had become an art form, titles a coveted end for the middle-class and the majority poor left to rot in the slums of London and every major British city--exploited like colonial slaves--providing the material that Dickens would find appealing and exploit quite profitably. Many of the Company's officers earned titles and extracted great wealth from India through grave dishonesty yet surprisingly most were spared the ignominy of seeing their dirty work dragged into the limelight, saved by ten thousand miles of buffer and threatened only when honest men sought justice. Hastings was impeached for treason but acquitted, earning British praise and the hatred of India's millions. Clive earned a peerage.

While **Clive** schemed with Indian nawabs to dispossess the Mughal Emperor in the east, **Hastings** sought the same in the **Ganga** and **Yamuna** valleys and central India. In 1764 he defeated a disorderly alliance of Mughal Emperor **Shah Alam II, Mir Qasim** of Bengal and the Nawab **Jala-ud-din Shoja** of Oudh at Buxar in Bihar which gave the Company control of the lower Ganga River; Hastings extracted from Shah Alam the *diwani* of Bengal or right to levy land and business taxes which allowed the Company to fund military adventures and send remittances home to satisfy the lavish lifestyles of Company owners.

The Mughal Emperor **Jahangir** had oddly and with foolish generosity agreed to this export in writing to King James in 1615: "... *I have given my general command to all the kingdoms and ports of my dominions to receive all the merchants of the English nation as the subjects of my friend; that in what place soever they choose to live, they may have free liberty without any restraint; and at what port soever they shall arrive, that neither Portugal nor any other shall dare to molest their quiet; and in what city soever they shall have residence, I have commanded all my governors and captains to give them freedom answerable to their own desires; to sell, buy, and to transport into their country at their pleasure. For confirmation of our love and friendship, I desire your Majesty to command your merchants to bring in their ships all sorts of rarities and rich goods fit for my palace; and that you be pleased to send me your royal letters by every opportunity, that I may rejoice in your health and prosperous affairs; that our friendship may be interchanged and eternal...*"

The effect of this fulsome generosity was to impoverish rural India, and by extension cities, by gutting the system of local government that had developed to a high degree over millennia (described in *Smritis* and *Mahābhārata*) and which the British proceeded to destroy. Pre-Mughal India had a well-developed system of self-government. Each village was governed by an annually elected *pānchayat* (Council of Five) which had evolved from individual *sabhas* (assemblies). **Panchayats** were responsible for all village affairs including land allocation and other executive and judicial functions including tax collection for the Rāja. Regional and municipal councils (*janapadas* and *nagar sabhas*) with appropriate supervisory and executive functions intervened between the village and the central government. The Mughals dismantled this structure and created governors or large landlords (proprietors with or without ownership) to collect taxes from the villages, and reduced the authority of the local councils (*panchayats*).

This system was prone to corruption by officials; Hastings allegedly gained from it and on his departure Pitt's India Act of 1786 enabled **Cornwallis** to create the system of "permanent settlements" which vested property in landowners (*tehsildars* and *zamindars*) at a fixed rate; they in turn taxed individual holdings (*ryotwari*), districts (*mahalwari*), and remitted the appropriate amount to Government. Police, judicial and other services were provided from a central or regional pool, as appropriate.

The British destroyed all local land registries and substituted an official (*patwari*) who kept records for several villages and found it easy to falsify these to his advantage especially when he had an equally crooked buyer and magistrate to legitimise his land deals. These actions crippled villagers reducing them to virtual slavery with no political voice; thus the British avoided the situation where political power in the hands of the poor might lead to conflicts and even insurrection. The system had removed a known area of official corruption among Company officers, but created another far more vicious as it enabled the Company and landowners to acquire and use lands to maximise profit regardless of the people's food needs. Thus cash crops supplanted rice and wheat, the major food grains, placing millions at risk in times of drought, yet gave no relief from taxes. Zamindars became rich and soon found ways, with the help of officials, to acquire and trade in land — a new development for Bengal

Meanwhile the Marathas had advanced far into the north, to Multan, Lahore and Kashmir, incurring the wrath of the Afghan leader **Ahmad Shah Durrani** who declared jihad and sent a large Army against them in northern India. In the final thrust to meet **Durrani's** invading forces in 1761--almost coincident with the Anglo-French war for domination of the Coromandel Coast, the Indian extension of Europe's *Seven Years War*--the Maratha army, led by Commander **Shadshivarao Bhau,** fell to the invading force which they had almost routed just before Durrani's reserves arrived. (*Dr Brahman had fretted, "How humiliating and how insulting to the memory of Shivaji, his vision smeared, labours denigrated, aims dishonoured! It made the Confederacy the laughing-stock of the world! The Péshwé had chosen the wrong leader, good fighter, but he didn't know the north; Malharrao (Shinde) was better choice; bad planning allowed Durrani to box them in and starve them of supplies for months and weaken them and their animals; even so they almost won, but made some serious errors late in battle and allowed weaker army to defeat them."*)

It showed BEICo generals that the Marathas could be taken as easily as the Mughals, once the prime British "diplomatic" cards had been played: promises, secret agreements, espionage, treachery and bribes to split alliances, which the BEICo freely used and recouped many times over from subsequent taxation of the long-suffering poor.

The Maratha fracture at the brink of victory recalled earlier catastrophes of Raja Bhoja, Prithviraj, and others since, underlining a recurring theme in Indian history of alliances failing at the edge of final victory. This failure had followed a familiar and predictable route: the personal ambitions, cupidity and internal jostling for power that attended the deaths of kings especially when pretenders-- by their very nature suspect--sought to displace legitimate heirs and sold their souls, often to an invader, to win. This weakened, and at a critical time in Indian history, fractured the Maratha Empire, which had stood poised to regain the glory lost for over a millennium and attained by Shivaji and Bajirao I, had its leaders been less self-willed, more cooperative, prudent and far-seeing enough to rise above differences to promote the national vision, and negotiated a true and binding federation. Enough time and events had passed to show that the independence of action in guerrilla warfare had to give way to generally agreed military strategies with strong and disciplined infantry support to make gains permanent. Hindus had for decades regained the upper hand but lacked the unity, discipline, diplomacy and loyalties that the British generals enjoyed, facilitated by the Company's decision to allow its troops to plunder at will.

Indian failures had deepened cynicism among a populace suffering in want amid glaring excesses of rulers; few believed that any of them would work to remove the burden of excessive taxation by successive Governments or the harassment and extortion by tax collectors, agents and police, which kept them in poverty and serfdom, notwithstanding the efforts of Bajirao and his son **Balaji Bajirao** (Nanasaheb), and after Pānipat **Mahadji Shinde** (1730-92), **Tukojirao Holkar** (1723-97) and later **Yashwantrao Holkar** (1776-1811). Some recalled with nostalgia Shivaji's cancellation of the *jizya* tax when he took Vijapur.

Many turned to scripture and history to find models, paying homage to gurus and past heroes-- Rāma, Krishna, Buddha, Mauryas, Guptas, Gurjara-Pratiharas, Shivaji and others--while seeking solace in religious immersion, the doctrine of *karma* and praying for deliverance. Thus with the loss at Pānipat Indian leaders missed their best chance to win back the country that they had carelessly allowed to fall to a more resolute and forceful invader.

Anglo-Indian wars: The three Carnatic Wars had ended in 1763 with the French restricted to merchandising at Chandrānagar (Bengal), Pondicherry, Karaikal, Yanam (Coromandel Coast) and Mahé (Malabar Coast) although they maintained connections with individual rulers, especially **Tippu Sultan** of Mysore and Raja Shindia of the Maratha Confederacy. The Nizam of Hyderabad was fattened with additional lands taken from the Marathas in the west and Mysore south and would remain unswervingly loyal to the British until 1947, having been sweetened with the title of *Most Faithful!* [83]

By 1758 Mysore had come under **Haider Ali**, the hereditary Raja Wadeyar's military commander, and an ally of France. Aided by the Nizam of Hyderabad and initially the Marathas, the Company had begun a series of actions, the four Mysore wars, against him and his son **Tippu Sultan**. Ali had a cancer and died suddenly in 1783 at the cusp of victory in the second war, which Tippu carried on to win, but at the cost of abandoning a winning campaign on the Malabar Coast. By the *Treaty of Mangalore* in 1784 each side returned seized lands. The **3rd Mysore War** saw action by Lt. Gen Charles Cornwallis, Governor General of India who had in 1786 replaced Hastings, and "fresh" from his 1781 surrender to George Washington at Yorktown, Va., which had ended the American War of Independence. He took charge of the war from the British commander and with the help of Hyderabad and Maratha Péshwé **Bajirao II** besieged Tippu Sultan's capital, forcing him to sign the *Treaty of*

[83] The Nizam made TIME cover in 1937 as the World's richest man. In WWI -- with millions of his subjects in poverty and lacking education -- he had financed an air squadron for the British forces and later purchased a destroyer, which was turned over, fully equipped, to the Royal *Australian* Navy!

Srirangapatnam which cost him half his kingdom, shared among the three victors. This was an incredible event, where two major Indian kingdoms had allied with a foreign invader to defeat a third Indian kingdom to assist the invader's agenda of Indian conquest! Indian rulers were behaving just like Europeans!

In 1773, following revisions to the Company Charter by the British Government, Hastings was made Governor General of territories in India which then comprised Bengal, Bihar, parts of the Carnatic, and lands around Bombay in addition to the tributaries of Oudh and Benares. On acquiring Bengal the Company raised taxes from *10% to 50%* of the value of produce. It also diverted agriculture to commercial crops like cotton, indigo, opium, and sugarcane, instead of grain. Food shortages resulted, aggravated by Hastings' prohibition of the Indian practice of storing a portion of annual harvests. A famine followed reaching its peak in 1770 and lasted several years killing some 10 million people, during which Hastings raised taxes an extra 10%! He did little--other than for Company staff--to help the hungry masses clamouring for aid, their lands seized in lieu of tax, and dying of starvation[84].

Needing money to pay for the southern wars Hastings extorted huge sums from **Prince Chait Sing** of the prosperous Benares kingdom and from the **Begum of Oudh**, also under Company protection. Benares seemed attractive as a new territorial acquisition, so, backed by his army, he craftily, if not ruthlessly, took advantage of the confusion generated by the decline of Mughal power and the breakaway of kingdoms, to seize rich territories and create vassal states or outright possessions. Even before actual conquest the relationship was unscrupulous and dictatorial in which Hastings claimed unjustified payments to the Company[85]. By repeated demands of higher cash sums he planned to force a Raja or Nawab to reach a point where the demand would force him to protest; Hastings would deem protest as criminal non-compliance punishable by territorial seizure. He firmly believed in the primacy and right of force to settle disputes and on absolute rights to lands seized by conquest!

In Bengal he was implicated in the death sentencing of one **Nanda Kumar** who had accused him of corruption. In 1773 at Puné **Nārayanrao**, youthful *Péshwé* and nephew of **Raghunāthrao,** was murdered, an act instigated by **Anandabai,** Raghunath's wife. Raghunath displaced the natural heir, **Madhavrao,** Narayanrao's infant son, and ruled for a year until deposed by a Council of Twelve (*Barbhai mandal*), led by Maratha Finance Minister **Nāna Phadnavis**. Raghunath fled to Bombay and signed the *Treaty of Surat* with the BEICo by which he would regain the Maratha throne as a subsidiary in exchange for Bassein and Salsette, near Bombay, and accept Company control of Maratha lands. About this time Phadnavis gave the French access to a Maratha port, which the Company resented. Calcutta rejected the *Treaty of Surat* and a new one was signed which Bombay rejected, and sent Coronel Keatinge to seize Puné. A Maratha force under **Haripant Phadke** stopped him; Hastings seized the opportunity to move against the Marathas.

This was the first **Anglo-Maratha War;** it ended with a Maratha victory and the British in Bombay had to return all lands previously annexed. In waging

---

[84] See also Ch. 4, footnote 4.

[85] "I resolved to draw from his (Raja Cheyte Sing) guilt (for attempting to break away) the means of relief of the Company's distresses, to make him pay largely for his pardon, or to *exact a severe vengeance* for past delinquency."

war Hastings was merely continuing the campaign of intrigue, discord and bribery that had gained the Company Bengal and was in use in the south and Ganga valley to acquire more and hoping to complete the east to west conquest and control.

Financial difficulties from plotting, war-mongering, a trade deficit with China and a lull in the European economy forced Parliament to pass the **Tea Act** in 1773 which allowed the Company to sell tax-free tea to America without restriction; the taxation provisions led to a revolt among American merchants, the *Boston Tea Party* and three years later the American **Declaration of Independence.** British losses in America pushed expansion in India facilitated by French distraction by **Rousseau's** *The Rights of Man* and the abrupt suspension of royal wars as France's peasant multitudes finally rose in hungry revolt.

Following **Pānipat** the Marathis had fallen further into disarray and the "big four" generals--**Shinde, Holkar, Gaekwad** and **Bhonsle** (no relation to Shivaji)--maintained their rivalries and resistance to the Péshwé at Puné. The Empire thus weakened and became a fragile Confederacy which did rally briefly and effectively against Warren Hastings in the first Anglo-Maratha war; later individual members did succeed in extending their boundaries and maintaining control of territories, leaving Punjab to the Sikhs who had taken control of the region after Pānipat. **Mahadji Shinde** had seen service from age 10 and was the last and only one of five sons of the founding *sardar* **Ranoji Shinde** of Gwalior to survive Pānipat; he assumed Shinde leadership and regained lost northern territories for the Péshwé. In 1766 **Malharrao**, founder of the Holkars, died and was succeeded by his daughter-in-law **Ahilyabai**. She was ably supported by her commander and adopted brother **Tukojirao**.

The *First Anglo-Maratha War* had involved the combined forces of **Mahadji Shinde, Tukojirao Holkar** and **Mudhoji Bhonsle** and forced the *Treaty of Salbai* in 1782, returning to them all Maratha lands. This inaugurated two decades of peace. Hastings was strongly criticised for his various actions, leading to his impeachment in 1786, a year after his forced resignation. He was accused of injustice and oppression, maladministration, receiving of bribes, etc. This celebrated trial, in which **Burke, Fox,** and **Sheridan** thundered against Hastings, began in 1788, and terminated in 1795 with his acquittal, but cost him his fortune.

The Marathas, while remaining poised to attain supreme power, unfortunately drifted into the same inter-regional squabbling that had led to their defeat by Durrani and given the British an opening for their coming assaults. Fighting developed between rivals Shinde and Holkar, two of the four strongest kingdoms of the Confederacy, each of whom wished to dominate a new India, promising their citizens progress and plenty and enriching themselves from an expanded tax base**. Tukojirao Holkar** lost to **Mahadji Shinde's** troops in 1793 under General **Benoît de Boigne**, a French mercenary hired by Shinde to train and lead his army, European style. Although not an officer in the French army he had proved quite proficient and was titled General. A year later Mahadji died and was succeeded by his brother Tukaram's 15 year-old grandson, **Daulatrao Shinde**. On Ahilyabai Holkar's demise in 1795 relationships deteriorated, aggravated by the covert actions of British emissaries who offered sweet deals to each regional leader driving deep wedges among them, and reducing them to a number of weak and malleable forces instead of the powerful army they were as a Union.

The events of the three and a half centuries following the British arrival in

India illustrate the evils of human behaviour when one nation or group seeks dominion over others. The worst emerges when the targets are deemed to be an inferior colour, race or religion. The conduct of the British in India belied the teachings of **Christ** whose name gave them purpose and excuse just as Muslims had invoked Mohamed! A few acts of compassion and kindness, usually outside of government, were excessively glorified while the masses suffered.

The hegemony of the BEICo expanded with conquest, often against the wishes of Parliament--such was the power and stature of the directors. The Company savaged the land further, exploited ambitions, caste and wrangling among Indian kings and regions, led by ruthless colonisers--Clive, Hastings, Cornwallis, Wellesley and other adventurers who systematically looted Indian kingdoms and *transferred their wealth to Britain*. Not content they imposed heavy taxes on Indian production, enterprise and labour, dispossessed millions, impoverished a hundred times that, and began the importation of Britons to do the work of Indians in *India's* civil and military services at rates of pay far in excess of any in Britain or in India. And so, these chosen British--the generations of carpetbaggers--were fattened and on retirement would sponge on Indian peoples almost in perpetuity.[86]

British administrators exploited the fickle and corrupt behaviour of some Indian rulers, and generally reviled all Indians as perfidious, characterising them thus in Britain to justify enforced changes to Indian society and education e.g. closing village schools. **Sir William Jones** made telling remarks in 1786 re Sanskrit that forced serious attention to India's treasury of learning, science, religion and literature: *"The Sanscrit (sic) language, whatever be its antiquity, is of a wonderful structure; more perfect than the Greek, more copious than the Latin, and more exquisitely refined than either, yet bearing to both of them a stronger affinity, both in the roots of verbs and the forms of grammar, than could possibly have been produced by accident; so strong indeed, that no philologer could examine them all three, without believing them to have sprung from some common source...both the Gothic and the Celtic, though blended with a very different idiom, had the same origin with the Sanscrit; and the old Persian might be added to the same family."*

Charles Watkins' ground-breaking translation of the *Bhagavad Gita* in 1785 astonished European **scholars** and spread the book to America, exciting some but earning the wrath of merchants. Its unique philosophy exposed the futility of mindless materialism then governing European actions globally, and would later empower Gandhi in his freedom movement.

During his term which ended in 1793 **Cornwallis** reformed taxation and administration eliminating certain corrupt practices of company officials and gave some small aid to the working class, but he was openly racist.[87] While Robert Clive had won Bengal and Warren Hastings had consolidated the British presence in India, Cornwallis had added to British-controlled territory and alliances. Following him, **Richard Wellesley**, Lord Mornington--who succeeded Sir **John Shore** in 1798--promptly set about to remove all traces of French

---

[86] "Wherever it was possible to put in an Englishman to oust a native an Englishman has been put in, and has been paid for from four times to twenty times as much for his services as would have sufficed for the salary of an equally capable Hindoo or Mohammedan official."

Sen. WJ Bryan, US presidential candidate,1903

[87] Cornwallis wrote of Euro-Indians, "...on account of their colour & extraction they are considered in this country as inferior to Europeans; I am of opinion that those of them who possess the best abilities could not command that authority and respect which is necessary in the due discharge of the duty of an officer."

political influence and to subvert the rule of Indian kings, with considerable and decisive help from the Indians themselves! Traditional tribal ambitions, inter-regal rivalries and the valour of the hundreds of thousands of Indian professional soldiers (*sipahi*) helped his cause.

Wellesley started the **fourth Mysore War** in 1799 by sending General Harris and his brother **Arthur Wellesley** (later Duke of Wellington) to attack Tippu Sultan, who had been negotiating with Napoleon, then in Egypt, but this ended abruptly with Rear Admiral Horatio **Nelson's** victory over the French fleet at the *Battle of the Nile* ending the formal French threat. Nevertheless Harris and Arthur invaded Mysore and besieged the capital.

Tippu was betrayed in this war by one of his commanders, **Mir Sadiq,** who, bribed by the British, removed his forces from the defence of the city wall sending them at the height of the battle to collect wages instead! This enabled the invaders to breach the wall and pour in. Rushing to the defence Tippu was fatally wounded. His death gave the Company control of South India directly and through forced treaties with confused, divided and weak Indian princes. Thus Indian states began to fall victims of Richard Wellesley's scheme of *"Subsidiary Alliances"* for conquered states whereby the native ruler would in humiliation continue his rule, disband his forces, accept a British resident, pay tribute and maintain a Company army! On Tippu's death Mysore reverted to the submissive **Wadeyars**.

By the end of the century the British under **Wellesley,** flushed with the capture of Mysore and still aiming at the French (or perhaps finding it a convenient excuse for war against Indians), decided to open another chapter of the Napoleonic wars by moving against French ally **Raghoji Shinde**, whose French general had defeated the Holkars. Wellesley exploited the schisms among the Marathas but was cautioned by the resolute way in which **Yaswantrao Holkar** had since his ascent to the throne in 1797 tried to dislodge the British from Delhi, earning the Mughal Emperor's admiration and a hefty title. In 1796 **Bajirao II**--son of Raghunathrao whose treachery had caused the first Maratha war--had become Péshwé. He was mean and weak, yet crafty--traits perhaps inherited from wicked and covetous parents and a deprived upbringing. As Péshwé he had the support of the youthful **Daulatrao Shinde** and the prudent influence of finance Minister **Nāna Phadnavis**, who unfortunately died in 1800, aged 58.

Yashwantrao Holkar believed that Bajirao's brother **Amrutrao** would be a better Péshwé. He also resented Shinde who had suddenly attacked him and his brother **Malharrao Holkar II** in 1797, killing the latter. In 1801 Yaswantrao and brother **Vitthojirao** decided to move against their tormentors, but the latter was captured by the Péshwé's forces and executed. Yashwant then moved against the Péshwé, won many battles and finally defeated him and Shinde at Hadapsar, near Puné. **Balaji II,** fearing retribution, declined Holkar's request to return to Puné, and after a delay during which Holkar announced that he would install Amrutrao as Péshwé, Balaji fled to Bassein and concluded a treacherous deal with Richard Wellesley to save his position by ceding the Empire to the Company and becoming a *"subsidiary ally"*!

Bajirao II's defection heralded the *Second Anglo-Maratha War*. He had played directly into the plans of the Governor General, whose great fear of the French influence on Shinde had prompted him to war. His first "victory" was a treaty with **Gaekwad of Baroda** in 1802. The following year he ordered attacks on the remaining Marathas led by **Lord Lake,** the Commander in Chief from Calcutta, and **Arthur Wellesley** from Mysore. They exploited the schism between Shinde and Holkar, and used spies, paid Indian informers and traitors, plots and other forms of "British diplomacy" to secure secrets and advantages that ensured victory. In 1803 Lake defeated Daulatrao Shinde and Raghoji II Bhonsle of Berar at Kol (Aligarh) and Delhi, while Arthur Wellesley achieved the same at Assaye and Argaon.

Throughout 1804 **Holkar** had fought **Lake's** armies with much success until failing to take Delhi he retreated to friendly **Bharatpur,** having received news that an Anglo-Indian alliance including the Péshwé had seized some of his territory and that the British had promised to share his lands among their allies. He and Lake fought to a stalemate at Bharatpur in 1805. In all the battles other treachery beside Bajirao II's and Gaekwad's premature surrender was critical to British victory over the Marathas in the second war, whether fighting separately or together. For example, by 1805 **Alwar** had unexpectedly helped the British against Marathas at Aligarh; **Deshpande** released secrets to Wellesley before Argaon; **Cuillier Perron**[88] abandoned his strong Shinde army and defected to the enemy; **Mohamed Khan** and **Bhawani Shankar Khatri** betrayed their leader Holkar. Of interest is that Holkar, the most vigorous and nationalistic of the Marathis, the closest in talent and character to Shivaji and Bajirao I, or Mahadji Shinde, played little part in the Shinde wars having heard of plans by the other Maratha chiefs and the Péshwé to betray him. The subsequent treaties left all beside Holkar under British control. At home the British painted him in very unflattering colours.

Holkar despised the British presence and overlordship. He continued a campaign to re-invigorate the Confederacy and tried to recruit Indian leaders to new alliances. He received promises of help from various princes but was rejected by Sikh and Kashmiri kings while others balked, on threats from the British. He wrote defiantly to Wellesley: *"Although unable to oppose your artillery in the field, countries of many hundred miles in extent will be overrun and plundered. British shall not have leisure to breathe for a moment; and calamities will fall on the backs of human beings in continual war by the attacks of my army, which overwhelms like the waves of the sea."*

Both Wellesleys left India that year; Richard was replaced by Lord Cornwallis who ordered an end to the wars but died suddenly before his order was implemented. The new Governor General **Barlow** promptly denied Holkar any chance of re-energising the Maratha alliance by concluding a hasty treaty with the capricious Shinde. Nevertheless Holkar stood firm until the British offered an unconditional Treaty of *"Peace and Amity"* which he signed on Christmas Eve 1805.

Six weeks later Yashwantrao wrote Bhonsle: *"The Maratha state had been grasped by foreigners. To resist their aggression, God knows how during the last two and a half years I sacrificed everything, fighting night and day, without a moment's rest. I paid a visit to Daulatrao Shinde and explained to him how necessary it was for all of us to join in averting foreign domination. But Daulatrao failed me. It was mutual*

---

[88] Perron, Shinde's French commander succeeding Boigne, seemed to have been an untrustworthy officer who accumulated wealth, lodged in British banks, yet preached anti-British rhetoric to his employer and army, and at a critical moment defected to Lord Lake and abandoned his army, bribing river transports to deny it passage across the Yamuna, thus ensuring a Shinde defeat. The British gave him safe passage to France.

cooperation and goodwill which enabled our ancestors to build up the Maratha states. But now we have all become self-seekers. You wrote to me that you were coming for my support, but you did not make your promise good. **If you had advanced into Bengal as was planned, we could have paralysed the British Government** *(emphasis mine). It is no use now talking of past things. When I found myself abandoned on all sides, I accepted the offer which the British agents brought to me and concluded the war."*

Despite Shinde's duplicity Holkar continued talks with him and came to a secret agreement on points of defensive and offensive action. Shinde promptly gave it to his British resident! In frustration Holkar decided to fight the British alone. Recognising their superiority in artillery, he proceeded to manufacture his own cannons at a factory in Bhanpura; 200 long and short range guns were made and an army of 100,000 assembled in preparation to attack the British headquarters in Calcutta. Suddenly in 1811 he died of a "stroke"; he was just 35!

The resulting increased influence and control by the British brought increased suffering to Indians especially Hindus, but ordinary Muslims, previously lightly taxed by Mughals, now began to appreciate, slowly and belatedly, the misery Hindus had endured under the Mughals. Appeals to London generally were slow to arrive and fell on muffled ears as the rich spoils from India transformed and enhanced the architecture of London and other cities and dulled the edge of upper crust conscience, which by its close and long connections with power ensured no more than a token response. **Edmund Burke** had labelled Hastings, among other choice terms, a *'captain-general of iniquity'* who never dined without *'creating a famine'*! Such were the blatant excesses and immorality of BEICo executives in India. Subsequently changes occurred that brought slowly increasing oversight by the Government in London, especially after loss of the American colonies, and as controls fell to the Company in each region, by conquest or treaty, London asserted its sovereignty and political authority by various Acts, and had even criticised Bombay's over-reaching in Maratha affairs–a criticism the Company's Bombay directors ignored.

The **impeachment** of Warren Hastings had failed to impress the British public with the perfidy of BEICo's and its officers, even though Parliament had disapproved of the Company's monopoly and had to confront the throne to secure competition and prevent the continued annihilation of traders reaching India. The clergy had kept silent. After all, Charles II had granted the Company wide latitude, including *"...to make peace or war..."*

In the late 18th century a new force had entered European politics, the Rothschild money-lending dynasty--which stood head and shoulders above the regular court Jews-- whose acumen and strategies in financing conflicts and industrial development would soon create empires and make it the world's most profitable and richest private Corporation, with global reach, Indian, Middle East, African and US footprints, and easily dwarfing its imitators.

Advances in British Mercantilism: The dawn of the 19th century had found Europe in unremitting turmoil. The continent had hardly seen any real peace for a millennium. European nations had become known for national and international instability largely due to the dominance of oligarchies, despite claims to democracy, and their obsession with monolithic expansion of possessions and power influenced by imperialism, mercantilism and the imperative to promote themselves under cover of their adopted religion, Christianity, locally and internationally. This was compounded with the absurd notion that skin tone would define the chosen and that the world outside Europe was unschooled and backward, of no account and therefore theirs for the taking. For more than a millennium European imperialists have disagreed, quarrelled and fought one another, each seeking European and eventually global domination. The 16th and 17th centuries raged with wars of expansion and suppression among British, Bourbons, Habsburgs, sometimes Ottomans and Eastern monarchies like Poland, Russia and others. The 18th century followed with some 40 conflicts and the 19th was no better. Nehru would later call it *"a quarrelsome little continent."* But it was not alone.

South America experienced successive revolutions for Independence from Spain while in Brazil the Portuguese Emperor who had ruled from Rio de Janeiro during the Napoleonic Wars, returned to Lisbon leaving his son **Dom Pedro** as Regent of Brazil. In 1822 Pedro declared Brazil independent of Portugal and after a brief war became Pedro I, head of the Empire of Brazil, a constitutional monarchy. The British wormed their way among the new countries when the *Cisplatino War* ended between Brazil and Argentina (1825-8)--fought over the region that became **Uruguay**. The British had gained a foothold in **Guiana** and mediated the *Treaty of Montevideo* August 27, 1828, which created Uruguay. Brazil and Argentina gained peace and lost ownership of the Rio de la Plata which was declared "international" allowing British free access for its mercantilist goals in South America, to complement its gains in India.

Britain was also busy suppressing dissent at home and abroad for the rest of 19th century and up to today. The **Napoleonic Wars** lasted from 1792 to 1815. The Poles fought the Russians in 1830-31; the Hungarians rebelled against the Habsburgs 1848-9, the Danes fought with Schleswig-Holstein and directly with Prussians in 1848 and again in 1864 losing control of the duchies. Between 1848 and 1866 Italians fought the Austrian Empire for unification and independence that brought renown to Italy's **Giuseppe Garibaldi**. In 1854-6 Russia fought and lost the Crimean War against an alliance of French, Ottomans, British, Germans (Nassau) and Sardinians ostensibly squabbling over control of Palestine's holy places. The war brought peace to the Ottomans briefly and achieved unforeseen benefits to the care of sick and wounded prompted by two enterprising British nurses, **Florence Nightingale** and **Mary Seacole**[89], the latter a coloured Jamaican volunteer who performed great feats despite racial prejudice and the animosity of Nurse Nightingale. For the Russians it spurred the abolition of serfdom while the British had to live with continuing fears of Russian expansion. Soon Russia did enter central Asia and made treaties with various rulers including Persia.

As a sop to Indians, London in 1813 renewed the Company charter for 20 years only, restricting its monopoly to the tea trade and to trade with China and requiring separate commercial and territorial accounting. The Act also opened India (and colonies) to missionaries, chiefly **the London Missionary** and other Christian Societies then campaigning to convert "heathens" and to end slavery. The Slave *Trade* had already been abolished but slavers had continued to trade with the USA. In 1812 Americans had been driven from Canada, freeing British forces and army resources. British views of Indians were influenced by **Charles Grant**, a dissolute man turned religious, who had served as Chairman of the BEICo in 1805 and earlier under Cornwallis, sharing the view that Britain had a

---

[89] Honoured by the naming of a student residence at the *University of the West Indies* plus statuary in Britain

duty not just to secure India for merchandising but to rescue its inhabitants from Hinduism, civilise and convert them by allowing Christian missions to operate (see Duff below); this the Company had long opposed as a distraction from business! **James Mill** and **Thomas Macaulay** would take these arguments further in the next decades.

Napoleon's fall brought Britain colonies in the **Caribbean** and **Guianas** and accelerated British expansion in India by the hallowed method of coercion, bribery and deceit. Holkar's sudden death in 1811 leaving a child as heir had energised British preparations to tackle the Marathas a third time, coinciding with the publication of James Mill's *History of British India*, a review of Company documents, since he did not know India or any of its languages. Despite ignorance, he trashed everything about India: history, literature, culture, religions, social customs and even the climate. Mill's motto seemed to have been: *"What I don't know doesn't exist!"* And while attacking Indians he ignored the misery and hopelessness of Britain's landless poor--over 80% of its 14 million population. Mill's denunciations were a godsend for imperialists even though he had also criticised several Company actions; the book was widely circulated and was used to justify abominable British behaviour in later years, including war.

The Third Maratha War began with the British-instigated murder of the **Holkar** regent **Tulsibai** on 20 December 1817 followed immediately by a huge and rash invasion by Sir **Thomas Hislop** to start the *Battle of Mahidpur*; which ending with the surprise defeat in 1818 of the Maratha Confederacy, despite its fractured and weakened state, giving the Company--then headed by Lord Hastings (no relation to Warren)--dominion over most of India either as direct colonies or subsidiary alliances. Hislop would have fallen to the Holkar forces led by 11-year-old **Malharrao Holkar III**, 20-year old **Harirao Holkar** and 20-year-old **Bhimabai Holkar** had treachery, so common in Anglo-Indian wars, not supervened. This time it was the critical defection of **Nawab Abdul Gafoor Khan**–a commander in the Holkar army appointed by Yaswant in 1808--who, like Mir Jafar at Pilashi, Bengal, and Mir Qasim in Mysore, pulled out his forces then poised to deal a decisive blow to the British army, and scuttled a crucial part of the battle plan of the youthful Holkars; they had trusted their long-time commander and had no inkling that he had sold out to the British, which in retrospect explained Hislop's bravado. The Péshwé, who had belatedly realised past errors, especially his lack of vision and misjudgement of the heroic nationalism of Yashwantrao Holkar, had fought with Bhonsle alongside Holkar's children, almost as a penance.

The treaty was signed on 6 January 1818 at **Mandsaur**. Khan received Jawara as reward for his treachery, a mere pittance for having dealt India the *coup de grâce* that ended the Maratha Confederacy and gave India to the British. Bhimabai rejected the treaty, and continued guerrilla attacks against the British. Thus the BEICo came to dominate India except the Northwest and Nepal, reducing Indian *rajas* to "subsidiary allies". The Holkars lost territory, some to the Nizam of Hyderabad and other British allies, retaining only the princely state of **Indaur,** the rest subsumed into the Company's **Central India Agency**. The Péshwé was banished to **Bithoor** and the once proud and expansive Marathi realms were reduced to the small princely states of **Kolhapur** and **Sātārā**. Puné came directly under Bombay. In a form of poetic justice the traitors who had sided with the British–Shinde and several Maratha sardars–lost their best lands, much to their surprise, and were allowed to retain restricted holdings as subsidiary allies. Yashwantrao Holkar and the others who had pleaded for unity were amply vindicated.

The Maratha victories had shown how relatively easily India could have expelled both Mughals and British by the mid-18th century, had the Confederacy survived and Indian Rajas inspired their people with nationalism, self-respect and confidence by reverting to pre-Mughal education, expanding it to all classes and to higher levels generally, taking advantage of technological developments in the wider world, and eventually involving the people in government, regionally and nationally. An appropriate legal and representative structure was already known; individual empowerment by enfranchisement within the rule of law would propel the drive to social equality and justice. Governments would be structured to abide by an agreed constitution with a code of moral conduct, responsibility, accountability, and standards. It is doubtful however if any more than a handful of Indian rulers had a national outlook or democratic feeling, having been nurtured to promote and expand clan holdings and interests, which had kept them at war with neighbours. *Thus the combined might of Indian armies was never used against invaders.*

The **Gupta Empire** had fallen through internal strife. This singular inability to escape tribal confines would dog India to this day and keep her at the mercy of sly foreign "diplomats" schooled in the art of deception and "divide and rule". India's collective military skills were enough at all periods in history to prevent inroads by foreign armies, despite the force of *jihad* that fired Muslims and the strengths of the British: the navy, as Haider Ali had noted, disciplined forces, artillery, greed and its most powerful weapon, bribery. Shivaji had effectively begun to counter them at sea as did Bajirao I and Yashwantrao Holkar on land. Sadly for India these three undefeated champions had each died at the height of his powers.

As a piece of poetic justice, however, India, the land, if not the people, exacted a toll; a cholera epidemic starting in Bengal in 1820 soon affected the whole country, killing some 10,000 British troops and numerous unfortunate Indians. It is said that only one in ten employees of the British Company survived their tours of duty. As for the Indian masses centuries of foreign domination--heavy taxation and dispossession--had impoverished and subjugated them to the point that paid servitude seemed like a reward. Systematic denigration of Hinduism set it against Islam, widening divisions that Akbar had tried to bridge. As facts contradicted James Mill's guesses and denunciations--echoed even today by Indian Marxist historians writing about Vaidic India--the British began to dismantle Hindu village education and malign Hindu scriptures to make its vast literature look petty despite high praise by Company officials like Sir William Jones, co-founder of the Asiatic Society and **Charles Watkins**, translator of the *Bhagavad Gita*. Mill's book, later modified with corrections by Sankritist **H.H. Wilson**, remained a reference for the British as its arguments fell in line with British aristocratic thinking and their *"Subdue India"* and *"Forward"* policies. Despite Wilson's editing, Dr Brahmam had likened Mill's approach to an account of the Jews written by Adolph Hitler, or vice versa!

As the British consolidated gains educated Indians sought accommodation to the new hegemony. One early and determined activist was **Ram Mohan Roy** (1772-1833), a Bengali scholar and religious iconoclast, founder, with Devendranath Tagore, of *Adi Brahmo Sabha* in Calcutta, which aimed to incorporate Islamic and Christian ideals, using a common language, noting that the many languages of India hindered easy communication and united action, even though many Indians were polyglot. He then appealed to **Lord Amherst** to *compel* learning of English as *the* lingua franca! In 1817 he founded, with David Hare and Radhakanta Deb, the *Hindu* (later *Presidency) College,* **Hare School** and **Vedanta College** in Calcutta. Indian education had been changed drastically by the Muslims to studies of Arabic, Persian or Sanskrit and basic arithmetic, quite unlike the curriculum they had replaced. Roy wished to change that introducing science, humanities, English and mathematics. After debate girls were excluded. Roy had campaigned against *săti,* which was banned in 1830. He remained Brahmo Hindu and published extensively. He died in England in 1833 of meningitis having travelled there in 1831 as emissary, with title of Raja, of Akbar II, the Mughal emperor, then reduced to a mere pawn of an Company owned by aristocrats that functioned through control of Parliament. In pushing English, Roy had joined Thomas Carey's Mission and anticipated Macaulay by 20 years. His death prevented any application of disquieting new knowledge gained, specifically the realisation that Britain was an oligarchy, and that the British in India were of classes that did not represent their people at home, who in fact faced as great a tyranny as the people of India, and that the British, having exhausted their islands, were then plundering the world, not for Christianity, but to satiate and aggrandise the aristocracy!

Baptist and Anglican missionaries had set up girls' schools a year or so earlier targeting the lower classes to teach them basics plus needlework and the Bible; the schools were small and increased to less than 500 students in 20 years.

British plebs repressed – what troubled Roy: At the time of Roy's visit Britain was involved in a debate on human rights that confirmed its domination by an aristocratic oligarchy, which dismissed domestic dissidents and the poor as swiftly and summarily as those in the colonies. Authorities in 1819 sent a yeoman cavalry rampaging with swords drawn hacking their way through a crowd gathered in **St Peter's field** in Manchester to protest unequal representation in Parliament. All Lancashire, including its major cities, had only two representatives while a few **"rotten" boroughs**, some with hardly a dozen or so people each, enjoyed one or two; there were over 50 of these in the UK, all controlled by the gentry and through them Lords could exert strong influence on the Commons! But the protesters were merely seeking what the British were boasting to the world: representative government, and even used the word "democracy" to describe it! The Lancastrians called the episode their *Peterloo!* Swift repression cooled protests, but opened eyes.

Dissent did not stop however and ultimately mass action forced Reform in 1832 but the Bill had rough passage, virulently opposed by Lords who nursed fears that the revolutionary fevers of France would consume England and topple their mansions, castles and elegant townhouses built on the backs and with the sweat of slaves and minions; this fear continued for a century and guided London's policy overseas. The rich saw their wealth as sacrosanct and should only change by addition or multiplication. They felt that the small plots of land, the labouring and domestic jobs and other minuscule concessions were enough to placate the plebs; surely they would not know what to do with the vote, or worse with education! Thus, the Lords, lay and spiritual, twice defeated the Bill despite large Commons majorities.

It was finally passed in a weakened form on the third try but only after

King William IV had privately urged Lords to come down to earth and see reality. The Bill's first passage had defeated Wellesley's conservative government but briefly restored him when Earl Grey resigned as Prime Minister after the second rejection.

Once in the House **Wellesley** made the following arrogant and ignorant remarks, (quoted here as it appeared in the formal third person, emphases mine): "He (i.e. I, PM Wellesley) was fully convinced that the country possessed, at the present moment, a legislature which answered all the *good purposes* of legislation—and this *to a greater degree than any legislature ever had answered, in any country whatever.* He would go further, and say that the legislature and system of representation possessed the full and entire confidence of the country. [...] He would go still further, and say, that if at the present moment he had imposed upon him the duty of forming a legislature for any country [...] he did not mean to assert that he could form such a legislature as they possessed now, for *the nature of man was incapable of reaching such excellence at once.* [...] [A]s long as he held any station in the government of the country, he should always feel it his duty to resist [reform] measures, *when proposed by others.*"

Two weeks later he lost a non-confidence motion and was gone! The Bill was passed but had an unfortunate consequence for the proletariat whose members had given their lives in the struggle. Enfranchisement required £10 worth of property which few labourers had; this effectively split the reform movement. (This problem of expanding the franchise would become an issue later among Indian National Congress members). In practice the First Reform Bill had failed the poor but left them grounds for continued agitation. Labour unions awoke, formed alliances which were promptly deemed illegal, but they supported the poor in protests. In 1838 *The Peoples' Charter* was published initiating the *Chartist* movement which has ever since exercised social historians and dispassionate academics. It led to many demonstrations including the huge Kennington rally one of whose organisers was a black Englishman named **William Cuffay**, whose father had come from St Kitts to London presumably as a house slave. Like his father, William was a tailor and had previously led a failed protest to improve wages to six shillings a day. Under repressive laws passed to curb and punish dissent (as in India during the century of opposition) he was falsely convicted of planning armed uprising and sent to Tasmania where he continued in labour politics and died in 1870.

In May 1842 Parliament rejected a **Chartist** petition on representation. The Chartist paper, *The Northern Star,* made this comment which would have resonated with Indian and colonial peoples: *"Three and half millions have quietly, orderly, soberly, peaceably but firmly asked of their rulers to do justice; and their rulers have turned a deaf ear to that protest. Three and a half millions of people have asked permission to detail their wrongs, and enforce their claims for RIGHT, and the 'House' has resolved they should not be heard! Three and a half millions of the slave-class have holden out the olive branch of peace to the enfranchised and privileged classes and sought for a firm and compact union, on the principle of EQUALITY BEFORE THE LAW; and the enfranchised and privileged have refused to enter into a treaty! The same class is to be a slave class still. The mark and brand of inferiority is not to be removed. The assumption of inferiority is still to be maintained. The people are not to be free."*

The Chartist movement declined by 1850 after attracting the sympathy of the popular **Richard Cobham**, a wealthy capitalist and politician, then campaigning for free trade under the banner of the *Anti-Corn Law League* to repeal the *Corn Laws*. He was believed when he said that their repeal (1846) would lower food prices. Some say the ACLL actually hijacked Chartism! Cobham pushed mercantilism in the guise of Christianity, saying: *"We advocate nothing but what is agreeable to the highest behests of Christianity — to buy in the cheapest market, and sell in the dearest."* With repeal of the Corn Laws, British manufacturing saw a rise in productivity, while British agriculture ultimately went into decline due to import competition. Cobham had condemned the 2nd Opium war and the pointless destruction of Chinese property.

The Second and Third Reform Laws (1867, 1887) gave the franchise to males and again created a split among the agitators, this time between men and women! Some of the Lords' justification for this make distressing reading!

In 1832 the British population was 17 million and the first Act increased total voters from 440,000 to 717,000 males with conditions of residence and employment. The subsequent Acts added about one million middle class voters, but still excluded women. Queen Victoria announced: *"The Queen is most anxious to enlist everyone who can speak or write or join in checking this mad, wicked folly of 'Woman's Rights' with all its attendant horrors on which her poor feeble sex is bent, forgetting every sense of womanly feeling and propriety."*

Trade Unions were made legal in 1871 but women had to wait until 1918 for the vote.

These events and conditions in Britain clearly showed how unrealistic Indians were to expect any goodwill, honest dealing or justice from it; those who lived there for a while came to know details but the first Indians to go to the UK were from the wealthy or ruling classes few of whom would have spontaneously exercised either mind or body for the plebs, and would change only when harsh repressions began to affect them.

Contemporaneous with Mohan Roy's lead other groups became active, especially in Bengal, initiating **the *Bengal Renaissance*** which saw a scintillating succession of bright minds who began at last to see beyond their own interests. Early among these was the *Young Bengal*, an eclectic mix of Hindus, new Christians and atheists. It was dominated by the half Portuguese anti-imperialist and proudly *Indian* youth **Henry Derozio**, who wrote fairly mature poetry in the romantic style of Lord Byron and precociously taught English at the *Hindu School*; he influenced many students to examine their beliefs and political attitudes, and to speak for women's rights. His group was styled *Derozians* and adopted the motto *"He who will not reason is a bigot, he who cannot reason is a fool, and he who does not reason is a slave."*

Derozio died prematurely aged 22 but his students became a lively group of movers and shakers in Bengal who influenced the rest of India. They became teachers, writers and businessmen who called for expanding education and social reform and addressed certain issues such as *săti*, female education, widow remarriage, child marriage, polygamy, the erosion of Indian values by missionary teaching and the oppressive nature of the government which was eroding old nurturing values and placing people at permanent risk. Issues were spiritedly debated in papers such as Devendranath Tagore's *Tattwabodhini Patrika* (truth-seeking newspaper), which also discussed science and non-religious topics, and the need for patriotism; its variety attracted a wide audience.

Pyari Charan Sarkar, like Mohan Roy and colleague Vidyasagar before him, promoted education of girls and in 1847 started the first of several schools, including an agricultural and technical school. He wrote textbooks in English for the new schools which made him wealthy when they were translated into major languages. (It is said that Macmillan & Co unethically obtained the revisions prepared for the local printer, who had already begun printing, yet published the books and forced a settlement with the bilked publisher!) Leading educators included **Ramtanu Lahiri**, who saw the opening in 1848 of the private *Krishnanagar College* with Capt. D.L Richardson as head. The writer and businessman **Ramgopal Ghosh** helped to establish the *Bethune School* for girls in Calcutta in 1849. Indian women would become the world's first medical doctors, the first a Bethune graduate trained in Calcutta, the second in Pennsylvania.

But there was much anguish before that point was reached and much after. Journalist **Harish Chandra Mukherjee** earned the wrath of British plantation owners for championing in his paper *Hindu Patriot*, the cause of small farmers and workers who had been forced to plant indigo for negligible returns under slavery conditions (cf fellow Bengali E. Bechu in British Guiana in late 1890s. Incidentally the manager of Bechu's estate, Enmore, was a Mr. Bethune).

In 1831 a group of Bengali **zamindars** formed the *Landholders Society* (acting it seemed out of self-interest and doing so only when their interests were threatened, caring little for the millions of *raiyats* (tenants and cultivators) toiling for them—a situation similar to the British hegemony that inspired the Reform movement (see above). Their names, like *Young Bengal* are famous in Indian historiography--**Dwarkanath Tagore, Prasanna Kumar Tagore, Radhakanta Deb, Ramkamal Sen, Bhabani Charan Mitra** and others—who described a formal constitutional path to protest and assert rights; it was overtly *zaminadari* but it was hoped that any gains it made might trickle down to their *raiyats*.

The BEICo received a new Charter in 1833 giving it political and governing powers for 20 years with **William Bentinck** as Governor General subject to a **Board of Control,** which was specially charged with codifying the laws of the land. The Company lost all commercial monopolies as the industrial revolution created a need for large markets which India provided and China promised. Indians were desegregated from holding Company positions but in practice few "qualified" (see Bryan, Footnote 45).

Conquest by Language--The creation of *Coconuts*:   Thomas **Macaulay**, an ardent Christian with a Presbyterian father and Quaker mother was a parliamentarian, writer, classicist and literary critic who served the BEICo in India from 1834 to 1839 as President of the Supreme Council of India under Governor General William Bentinck. He was aware of the prevailing opinion as expressed by previous Company executives--Lord Cornwallis and others--that Indians were *inferior* to Europeans (see footnote 53 above) and may have exploited Ram Mohan Roy's adverse views of Indian education. Macaulay had already noted the obsequiousness of the subjugated Indian maharajahs and could be forgiven his lack of sympathy, blaming their plight on failure to teach modern science and technology.

He already had fixed views on governance and did not believe that India was ready for any form of democracy, since it lacked essential and stable representative institutions, including a national language, laws, suffrage or unity (Brahmam's *"fatal princely flaw"*). He marvelled that *"a handful of adventurers from an island in the Atlantic should have subjugated a vast country divided from the place of their birth by half the globe . . . a territory, inhabited by men differing from us in race, colour, language, manners, morals, religion..."* This justified his unshakeable belief in British superiority and underpinned his actions and proselytism.

He admitted however to some reassuring quality in the native: *"That the average of intelligence and virtue is very high in this country is matter for honest exultation. But it is no reason for employing average men where you can obtain superior men. Consider too, Sir, how rapidly the public mind in India is advancing, how much attention is already paid by the higher classes of the natives to those intellectual pursuits on the cultivation of which the superiority of the European race to the rest of mankind principally depends."* He then outlines his tactic.

"To the great trading nation, to the great manufacturing nation, no progress which any portion of the human race can make in knowledge, in taste for the conveniences of life, or in the wealth by which those conveniences are produced, can be matter of indifference. It is scarcely possible to calculate the benefits which we might derive from the diffusion of European civilisation among the vast population of the East.

It would be, on the most selfish view of the case, far better for us that the people of India were well-governed and independent of us, than ill-governed and subject to us; that they were ruled by their own kings, but wearing our broadcloth, and working with our cutlery, than that they were performing their salaams to English collectors and English magistrates, but were too ignorant to value, or too poor to buy English manufactures. To trade with civilised men is infinitely more profitable than to govern savages. That would, indeed, be a doting wisdom, which, in order that India might remain a dependency, would make it an useless and costly dependency, which would keep a hundred millions of men from being our customers in order that they might continue to be our slaves.

Are we to keep the people of India ignorant in order that we may keep them submissive? Or do we think that we can give them knowledge without awakening ambition? Or do we mean to awaken ambition and to provide it with no legitimate vent? Who will answer any of these questions in the affirmative? Yet one of them must be answered in the affirmative, by every person who maintains that we ought permanently to exclude the natives from high office. I have no fears. The path of duty is plain before us: and it is also the path of wisdom, of national prosperity, of national honour."

His views are contained in a Minute dated Feb 2, 1935 to the Commission. He decided that moneys spent on educating Natives in their historical/cultural language reaped no practical or uplifting value, Concluding that these were Sanscrit or Arabic, and taught to all scholarship holders, he asked rhetorically, *"Why then is it necessary to pay people to learn Sanscrit and Arabic?. We have to educate a people who cannot at present be educated by means of their mother-tongue. We must teach them some foreign language."*

To justify this conclusion he invokes the "support" of "orientalists", a term then used for European scholars of Eastern studies. *"I have never found one among them who could deny that a single shelf of a good European library was worth the whole native literature of India and Arabia..."* With this he proposed the elimination of all scholarships and substituting English as the language of instruction, stressing, *"The intrinsic superiority of the Western literature is, indeed, fully admitted...It is, I believe, no exaggeration to say, that all the historical information which has been collected from all the books written in the Sanscrit language is less valuable than what may be found in the most paltry abridgements used at preparatory schools in England. In every branch of physical or moral philosophy the relative position of the two nations is nearly the same. The claims of our own language it is hardly necessary to recapitulate. It stands preeminent even among the languages of the west."*

The tenor of this diatribe was no different from that of James Mill, who had cobbled together his *History of India* without any direct knowledge of the country or its history.

From this one would conclude that Macaulay, the classical scholar, had extended his study, as any objective intellectual would have done, to these two languages, if only to recognise them in print or by ear. Macaulay however proudly proclaimed, *"I have no knowledge of either Sanscrit or Arabic."* And so he had denied himself knowledge of the great Shastras of old India, the knowledge hardly fully used.

This and following paragraphs are a fine example of hyperbolic linguistic chauvinism easy to achieve when extolling his specialty in favour of another of which he knew nothing and got so carried away as to lose the objectivity he had invoked as a prime virtue. His Minute includes these gems:

"We are not content to leave the natives to the influence of their own hereditary prejudices..."

"It would be manifestly absurd to educate the rising generation with a view to a state of things which we mean to alter before they reach manhood." (See also Al Hajjaj re Khwarazmians above p.23)

"Yet an intelligent English youth, in a much smaller number of years than our unfortunate pupils pass at the Sanscrit College, becomes able to read, to enjoy, and even to imitate not unhappily the compositions of the best Greek authors. Less than half the time which enables an English youth to read Herodotus and Sophocles ought to enable a Hindoo to read Hume and Milton." (Is this not a compliment to Indian students?)

His summary defined the program for the **Committee for Public Instruction** *"...we ought to employ them* (funds) *in teaching what is best worth knowing, that English is better worth knowing than Sanscrit or Arabic, that the natives are desirous to be taught English, and are not desirous to be taught Sanscrit or Arabic, that neither as the languages of law nor as the languages of religion have the Sanscrit and Arabic any peculiar claim to our encouragement, that it is possible to make natives of this country thoroughly good English scholars, and that to this end our efforts ought to be directed.*

"...We must at present do our best to form a class who may be interpreters between us and the millions whom we govern--a class of persons Indian in blood and colour, but English in tastes, in opinions, in morals and in intellect. To that class we may leave it to refine the vernacular dialects of the country, to enrich those dialects with terms of science borrowed from the Western nomenclature, and to render them by degrees fit vehicles for conveying knowledge to the great mass of the population."

His final dismissal of Indian education was vehement: *"We* (Board of Public Instruction) *are a Board for wasting the public money, for printing books which are of less value than the paper on which they are printed was while it was blank-- for giving artificial encouragement to absurd history, absurd metaphysics, absurd physics, absurd theology-- for raising up a breed of scholars who find their scholarship an encumbrance and blemish, who live on the public while they are receiving their education, and whose education is so utterly useless to them that, when they have received it, they must either starve or live on the public all the rest of their lives. Entertaining these opinions, I am naturally desirous to decline all share in the responsibility of a body which, unless it alters its whole mode of proceedings, I must consider, not merely as useless, but as positively noxious."*

Macaulay had made serious blunders in allowing his megalomania to blunt common sense and good judgement. Like James Mill 20 years earlier whose book was being "modified" by HH Wilson that very year, Macaulay had proudly announced his ignorance of India and Indian literature yet proceeded to treat the country as if it were one nation, failing miserably to realise that a more apt comparison would have been with Europe with its many nations, all *white* where he would not dare to reduce any of their languages to mere dialects as he did to those of India, stupidly assuming that Arabic and Sanskrit were *the* native languages!

As a classical scholar he had failed miserably in not rising above crude bias to examine these older languages and so failed to discover that their role in religion was the same as that of Latin in Christianity, even in his time. So besotted with narcissism was he and so cowed was Bentinck with his credentials that Macaulay was allowed to perpetrate an unprecedented and swift rape of Indian languages, culture and literature. Bentinck's endorsement silenced the Committee; all criticism was inadmissible and Macaulay's position became the basis of British educational policy in India.[90]

At the same time Macaulay chaired the Commission to establish an India-wide penal code, many of whose clauses he personally drafted and perfected. The model followed two principles: crime suppression with least agony and determining truth in the shortest possible time and at the least cost. This Commission's work was applied throughout the Raj although Muslim rulers could follow *Sharia* **law** as before. Throughout the exercise he maintained his trenchant and derisive attacks on Hinduism.

By these two major thrusts: **education** and **law reform**, Macaulay launched the mission to transform India's urban middle class into a group loyal to the British crown, and in every aspect Englishmen (see above) save for the small detail of the colour of their skin. This would never become an issue since they would remain in India to propagate their new learning and behaviours, always under the direction of *proper Englishmen* and at arm's length from them. There would be no socialising or intercourse. Macaulay's plan was diabolically simple: educate the Indians to University level, according to a British curriculum, and make the graduates a dominant social and business elite, but always subservient to a British chief.

Three flagship universities were built in Calcutta, Madras and Bombay and soon became the prime ends of Indian educational ambitions. Today several hundred exist. By the 1870's their graduates had, like religious converts, become British proselytes and indeed began to exceed Macaulay's cherished hopes. Indian aristocrats were isolated from meaningful contact with citizens; their children were brain-washed, many in British public schools. They became *coconuts.* (One early success was the father of **Sri Aurobindo**, Dr. Krishna Ghose, who was so anglicised that he took excessive care to make sure his children were raised free of any Indian influence; two of the three became militantly anti-British!) In 1841 the first award of Fellow of the Royal Society to an Indian went to a Bombay Parsi, **Ardaseer Cursetjee Wadia**, for marine science having built a ship, the *Indus,* at age 25 and later fitted it with a steam engine of his own design. In 1834 he had shown how gas could be used for public lighting.

---

[90] It is said that he had "reported to Parliament" in Feb 1835 thus: *"I have travelled across the length and breadth of India and I have not seen one person who is a beggar, who is a thief; such wealth I have seen in this country, such high moral values, people of such calibre, that I do not think we would ever conquer this country, unless we break the very backbone of this nation, which is her spiritual and cultural heritage and therefore I propose that we replace her old and ancient education system, her culture, for if the Indians think that all that is foreign and English is good and greater than their own, they will lose their self-esteem, their native culture and they will become what we want them, a truly dominated nation."* I have not been able to verify this quote and it is not in his Minute of Feb 2, 1835.

British Push Opium Addiction: In 1839, with India subdued, the British ironclad *Nemesis* sailed up the Yangtze River to "coax" China into formal acceptance of the opium trade (***First Opium War,*** 1839–1842). Seven decades earlier Warren Hastings, on becoming Governor General, had exploited the Company's monopoly on the trade with China to increase export of opium whose cultivation he had decreed in Bengal and Bihar. India's Ayurvedic physicians had for millennia used a weak decoction of opium to treat diarrhoea and impotence. Chinese rulers had rejected the import of opium when Arab traders had brought the Egyptian (Theban) variety to China in 400AD, and reaffirmed the ban when the Portuguese in 1500 AD had tried to induce the Chinese to *smoke* it.

To maximise revenues and to avoid shipping risks and clashes with the Chinese, Hastings had decreed that all opium contracts must be auctioned in Calcutta; buyers would pay the taxes and ship the goods to China on Company ships. Soon the sales enabled the company to pay for Chinese tea, prized in Britain and very lucrative. The Chinese required payment in silver but with rising costs for the metal and an official end to piracy of Spanish ships in the Atlantic, Britain had to find new funding sources.

The opium trade quickly attracted smugglers including several Americans, some famous like **John Jacob Astor** (American Fur Company, NY), **John Cushing** (J & T H Perkins Co, Boston), creating multi-millionaires and large commercial houses, many extant today. Perhaps the most prominent original was **Dr William Jardine**, a founder of *Jardine, Matheson and Co.*, a leading Hong Kong firm and one of the world's largest today. Dr Jardine was ironically a Company ship's doctor charged with preventing and treating illness! Like other officers, he was allowed the space of two tea chests—together 0.4 cubic metre—for personal business cargo, provided it was "local" and did not compete with the Company.

In 1802 Jardine quickly discovered that smuggling opium to the Chinese brought him far more wealth than practising medicine. On one voyage his ship was captured by Napoleon's Navy and its cargo seized; Jardine lost his chests but met and soon partnered with a fellow passenger, an Indian named Jamshedji **Jeejeebhoy** nicknamed *Bottlewalla* (bottle merchant); Jardine campaigned relentlessly against Company monopoly, which Parliament was forced to end in 1834. Two years earlier Jardine and business associate Matheson had formed the Company, in which Jeejeebhoy, one of modern India's wealthiest names, had a substantial interest.

Meanwhile Europe had seen the plethora of opium abuse: it was chewed, imbibed, inhaled and later injected, and popularised by writers like **John Keats, Thomas de Quincey, Elizabeth Barrett Browning** and **André Malraux.** BEICo users included Clive, Hastings, the Wellesley brothers and other Indian adventurers; British generals regularly fed it to Sepoys. **Bonaparte** is said to have indulged as did **Rhodes** in Africa.

With the *Second Opium War* British gunships finally overcame Chinese resistance to the opium trade. The *Treaty of Nanking* in 1842 ceded Hong Kong Island to the British. Eventually over 120 million Chinese would become opium-addicted, eliminating 25% of China's population and ending the **Qing** dynasty in Nanking. (*"BEICo was crooked, like all monopolies!" Dr Brahmam had said sadly, "principals, officers, generals—all crooks; it pained me to know that a doctor was so* *selfish, so heartless and so greedy."*)

British-Afghan Wars: At this time Britain moved to secure the NW frontier by turning Afghanistan into a "friendly" buffer zone against Asian invaders. British imperialists had long viewed the imposing Hindu Kush Mountains as a natural protection from northern invaders and had conceived the *"Forward Policy"* to seize all lands between Delhi and the mountains--which included parts of Afghanistan — to gain control and thus security.

When Napoleon fell, the likeliest threat became the surging **Russian Empire** with whom Britain played the **"great game"**, as British writers dubbed it, to win the Middle East and Central Asia. In the 1790s Russian **Emperor Paul** had allied with Britain against Napoleon and in 1801 sent an army of Cossacks on a mission to conquer south central Asia and perhaps India. With Paul's assassination the mission aborted near the Aral Sea less than a thousand miles from home; but the fact that it had taken place heightened British paranoia and led to further cooling between Russia and Britain, which eventually led to blows.

Russia had already penetrated the regions south and east of the Aral Sea and **Amu Darya River**, and had formed an alliance with Persia. To deal with Afghanistan Governor General **Lord Auckland** arrogantly issued in 1838 the *Shimla manifesto* detailing the conditions to be met by Afghanistan. They needed a malleable and greedy strongman as their puppet and chose **Shuja Shah Durrani** as ruler, while the Afghans generally preferred **Akbar Khan**, son of Emir **Dost Mohamed**. Auckland sent an army, mostly Indians, under two William's--**Elphinstone and MacNaghten**--which had initial successes and later captured the fort at Ghazni by the sure-fire technique of bribery of an enemy officer (euphemistically called "strategic alliance" or "sharing the trough", a potent universal tool today)!

The corrupt Afghan enabled the invaders to blow up a city gate. However the battles see-sawed and came to a stalemate. After two years of skirmishing and negotiations, all in bad faith, MacNaghten tried to bribe Akbar into letting the British remain by offering him the position of Afghanistan's vizier, while spending lavishly on potential traitors to assassinate him! How typical of British double-dealing and immorality and their penchant to undervalue non-whites!

Akbar found out and attended a planned meeting where the plotter MacNaghten and three officers with him were summarily executed! Poetic justice, you might say. His body was paraded through Kabul streets and in the ensuing flight of army and civilians only a few (all captives but two) survived the harsh winter's trek to Jallalabad, India. The dead included families that had joined the troops in Kabul in the wake of initial British victories, so confident had been their commanders. This defeat undermined the fearsome reputation of the Company and the British lost considerable face. Their failure to take Afghanistan was a sober lesson in resistance hardly heeded by Indians; someone should have reminded them how feuding Kalinga and Magadha had allied to repel Alexander's Greeks two millennia ago.

Anxious to protect western India from the Baluchi allies of the Afghans the British proceeded to invade and conquer Sindh in a bloody campaign in 1843. (*"Peccavi!* — I have sinned--General **Charles Napier** punningly telegraphed Calcutta. When Queen Victoria got the news she is alleged to have said *"Get the poor man a priest!"*)

In the north Maharajah **Ranjit Singh** had created a Sikh kingdom composed of Punjab, Multan, Peshawar, Jammu and Kashmir. His death in 1839 left the state at the mercy of factions and weak successors, whom the British attacked and eventually subjugated in two wars between 1845 and 1849, led by Sirs **Hugh Gough** and **Henry Hardinge**, Bengal's Governor General. Sikhs lost Kashmir and other territory to the British, who exacted steep tolls. When the Sikhs failed to pay, BEICo sold Kashmir to Jammu's Raja **Ghulab Singh** for £1 million. Sikhs should have won the first war but were plagued with incompetence and divisions and the seeming yet familiar treachery of their commanders Lal Singh and Tegh Singh who "allowed" the enemy to win key battles! Under the Khalsa, Sikhs had lost the sympathy of their neighbours barring a brief alliance with Afghans under Dost Mohamed Khan.

The **Sikh Wars** illustrated once again the failure of Indian rulers to recognise the costly weakness of insularity, disunity, internal squabbles, personal over-ambition and the stupidity of self-centred and opportunistic responses to foreigners who wished to gobble up the country and pillage its wealth.

In the four decades after the last Maratha war the British expanded relentlessly, seizing lands worldwide, by treaties, stratagems, chicanery, deception, criminality and war, plundering countries shamelessly, just as English colonists in New England had done two centuries earlier by cheating the Natives of their lands. This behaviour stemmed from the conviction that mercantilism was good for rulers who could share in the profits, while overlooking the shameful fact that merchants would simply gouge the populace to maximise profits. (Sociologists ponder the magnitude of plebeian poverty and the rising concentration of extreme wealth. It's simple, really. The total populace produces the wealth; 90% is grabbed by 10% to make them prosperous; a tenth of these acquire enough to become wealthy and a tenth of them so rich as to control nations and the souls of people, using that wealth to assure survival and ascendancy when current empires collapse, as they inevitably must.)

Mughal rule disintegrated over several decades by intrigue and attrition, the process showing the contrasting styles of two brutal conquerors, one erratic, violent and idiosyncratic, the other, their successor, more devious, organised, greedy and bullying. For the Mughals India had become home; they were finally secure and settled in a land of plenty and luxury with a sophisticated and accomplished society beyond anything they had known. Hindus and Buddhists provided economic power, social stability and progress, knowledge and skills, but Muslims held the higher executive positions, thus inducing many Indians, including royalty, to convert. Wealth remained in India enriching the rulers while the majority was taxed into serfdom; skilled Hindus kept their jobs and trades, albeit at a down-graded level.

Mughal rulers enjoyed this symbiosis for seven centuries until chauvinism and religious zeal led them to destroy the very things that had made them so prosperous. Akbar had recognised this when he tried to accommodate Hinduism by separating government from religion. But his success eventually dissipated in his murderous approach to the peoples of non-Mughal India, mainly in the south, creating another line of division among Indian peoples. By contrast the British in a cold and calculated raid over three and a half centuries raped the nation and transferred its wealth to Britain where much of it still lies in the hands of aristocrats and royal families.

Not to be outdone, Indian merchants seized opportunities for profit-making by serving the invader as diligently as the defender, in the way the patriarch of the Rothschild fortunes had advised his sons, i.e. never to favour one side in granting loans to warring kings and governments! Profit flowed whether the borrower won or lost; the wars profited both Indian moneylenders and the Rothschilds.

The Creation of an Indian Diaspora: British oppression took on a new and crushing face under Governor General **Dalhousie** (1848-56). The harshness and excesses of British hegemony had increased steadily since the fall of the Maratha Confederacy and Britain was flexing its muscle in Europe, Australia and Africa. India seethed for forty years before a rebellious spark was lit. In that time the inroads of British imports into India's heartland had ruined its artisans and heavy taxation was ruining farmers. The dispossessed soon became desperate enough to cross the *kāla pāni* (dark waters, associated with the trip across the Bay of Bengal to the infamous British prisons of the Andaman Islands). First it was to Mauritius and Reunion in 1834, then British Guiana in 1838; Trinidad and others followed steadily establishing the global Indian Diaspora.

On Dalhousie's arrival he proclaimed the autocratic *Doctrine of Lapse* whereby entities which had become *Subsidiary Alliances* would fall to the Company if the ruler died without a direct heir or were deemed incompetent. He promptly began a tyrannical programme of annexation of princely states and subsidiaries, ignoring past agreements and custom. He took **Sātārā** that year, **Jaipur** and **Sambalpur** (1849), **Nāgpur** and **Jhānsi** (1854) and **Oudh** (1856), all for base reasons that no court in Britain or Europe would have upheld e.g. *late* payment of tribute! He divested the ruler of **Tanjore** of his title in 1855 in breach of agreement and denied **Nana Bithur** a pension inherited from his father!

University construction began at Calcutta, Madras and Bombay in line with the Macaulay plan and in 1853 a campaign of railroad building and installation of telegraphy for rapid military and commercial transport and speedy communication that with the isolation of *rajas* ended notions of military revolt. Two hundred miles of railway track were completed by 1858, 5,000 by 1869, 25,000 miles in 1900 and 35,000 miles 10 years later. The network would expand steadily and reach over 50,000 miles by 1950 to become the world's largest.

The railways quickly reached the smaller villages, destroyed immense acreages of India's forests, and devastated the environment, destroying much local industry and agriculture. Even though new kinds of jobs and opportunities were created, they were regrettably at the lowest levels, substituting poorly-paid labour for artisans, small businessmen and aspiring administrators. The British could have made some amends for the job losses their policies had caused had they given the displaced any worthwhile positions with the railways. Mass migration to cities and overseas began, chasing crumbs from British factories while Indian rulers remained softened and the dissolute or impotent. Did any ponder as Macaulay had criticised, how they had missed chances presented by the industrial revolution to build new industries and perhaps internal alliances to resist invaders instead of squandering capital in opulence and squabbling? Some, especially Parsis of Bombay and a few brighter members of royal families and intellectuals did pursue new opportunities. But the spirit of the Mauryans, Guptas, Hemu, the kings of Vijayanagara, Chalukya, Shivaji, Bajirao I, Mahadji Shinde, Yashwant Holkar *et al.* was smothered by disunity. But while princes saved their skins and continued to live well village artisans and farmers—80% of the population-- suffered immeasurably and at times of famine or disease millions would lose their lives.

British harassment, bullying and contempt for Indians (see Macaulay in *"The Impeachment of Warren Hastings"*) raised increasing alarms among Indians and even stirred critical responses at home, mostly from missionaries who came to India to proselytise, concentrating on key figures and the poor. Ram Mohan Roy was an early link. (An associate of missionary Thomas Carey's tried to convert him but instead became a Hindu!). The Missions established Christian schools in many parts of India. In the period to the war of Independence various attempts were made to improve the lot of ordinary citizens but the Associations formed, some with English lead, only belatedly addressed grassroots issues and faltered until **John Drinkwater Bethune**, a lawyer and member of the Governor General's Council, proposed a law to bring British subjects under Company jurisdiction.

White objections to this, which they called *Black Acts*, forced Indians to more profound introspection especially as the Company Charter was due for Parliamentary review in 1853. The Renaissance leaders grappled with the complexities and contradictions, the need to place Indians in a civil and just society with guaranteed rights, especially equality of treatment, regardless of wealth, ethnicity or class. Vaidic scholars knew that there were four intercommunicating *varnas* but Brahmins had introduced a fifth, the untouchables, for narrow sectarian reasons, with elaborate circumscription of what they could do or claim in Indian society; in short they were shorn of rights. Now that the British had reduced all but the wealthy and indispensable to the level of untouchable leaving only a few cracks to allow squeeze-through passage for the inventive and resolute, Indians had to decide how to reconcile potentially divisive reforms of Hinduism or piecemeal adoption of western ways with the need to form a unified force against tyranny.

They enlisted British Unitarians who sought similar goals and seemed kindly and understanding. But these posed two hurdles: Christianity (as most were missionaries) and loyalty to the Crown, neither of which was acceptable to the majority, for the tyrant needed to learn that his time at the helm was limited. The British would depart; the only question was when and by what means. Sober minds conferred and formed successive Associations to bring together the thinkers to fashion a plan that would see transitional devolution of decision-making; redress of imbalances e.g. UK citizens were paid 5-10 times what Indians earned for an equivalent responsibility and had no chance of promotion to the highest ranks in spite of talent; or to improve education, health and job opportunities; relieve taxes; give women rights and freedoms; stop abuses of plebs by landlords and plantation owners, the military and police; and correct a multitude of other social ills.

Ram Mohan Roy had approached reform by joining with Scottish Baptist missionary **William Adam** to form the *Calcutta Unitarian Society*, but this failed and Roy had switched attention to Hinduism forming the *Brahmo Sabha* as a reform vehicle. In 1839 a delegation of *Landholders* led by Dwarkanath Tagore had visited the **British India Society**, an anti-slavery UK group to study their programme. On return in 1840, with **George Thompson**, an English abolitionist, in tow, they joined with *Young Bengal* to form the *Bengal British India Society* led by Thompson, **Tarachand Chakraborty**, **Ramgopal Ghosh** and others to address issues on a Pan-Indian basis while remaining loyal to the Government. They publicised Indian conditions needing redress in the UK paper

British Indian Advocate. It is uncertain whether their message went beyond intellectuals.

Meanwhile **Rev. Alex Duff** had started the Scottish Church (Presbyterian) College in Calcutta in 1830 with the aim of inducing high caste Indians to accept Christianity, having persuaded his home Church to fund education on the theory, later promulgated by Macaulay and Muller that when Indians were educated in science, western humanities and the Bible they would abandon Hindu "myths". By educating the higher castes knowledge would "filter" down to those below.

This of course did not happen and only exposed the ignorance of an alien nation that did not have the collective wit to suspect that an old and accomplished culture must have had some scientific basis for its growth and prosperity, to sustain hundreds of millions, and must be capable of reform intrinsically, not by foreign censure. His elitist approach to conversion-- and his belief that dull Hindus would see the shining Christian light--led them only to snigger and scoff. What Duff failed to see was that Hinduism was not doctrinaire, was inclusive, tolerant of diverse religious views and could lay claim to have helped to educate Jesus Christ! This was anathema then as it still is in Christian societies. This amazes me as I fail to see what Christianity would lose in the long term. Indeed I see only gains towards shedding ill-founded biases and moving closer to true ecumenism if not a common faith.

The *Brahmo Sabha* had languished on Ram Mohan Roy's death, until **Debendranath Tagore**, the co-founder's son, a religious man, founded in 1839 the *Tattwabodhini* (*Truth-seekers*) *Sabha* (TS) attracting the polyglot **Akshay Kumar Datta** and the polymath **Ishwar Chandra Vidyasagar**, a professor at Fort William College. They taught and wrote, including textbooks, and promoted female education nationwide and attracted reformist members of the snobbish Kulin Brahmins, dipped into Christianity and Unitarianism and adopted faith in God and public worship as adjuncts to Hindu standards. This inevitably angered Kulin Brahmins leading to more schisms. TS merged with the Brahmo Sabha in the 1860s to form the *Brahmo Samaj* and spread the reform throughout India while each religion could devise its own ways of expression. It maintained support for the Raj, a position Akshay did not share.

Section 7: The British Raj

The War of Independence: The seeds of political rebellion matched the religious ones in number and had been widely sown but Indians remained divided by an unscrupulous and cunning merchant-oppressor before whom they had become cowed, powerless and subdued. Scattered skirmishes did occur across the land, only to be hastily punished, most often with hanging someone, anyone, more to terrorise than punish; prosecution in each instance seemed so easy as eye-witnesses cropped up everywhere, even in pitch blackness!

Suddenly a catalyst for rebellion was supplied in 1856, somewhat callously when the Company introduced a new Enfield rifled musket whose cartridge casings were greased with animal fat—beef or pork—which the soldier had to bite off to access the powder. Sepoys refused to do this, Hindus rejecting beef and Muslims pork. The army's cold and unsurprising response was that the soldiers could supply the fat, clearly a mean, impractical and cruel suggestion certain to inflame anger and conflict.

The resulting **mutiny** began in Bengal in 1857 and fuelled the wider War of Independence, perhaps prematurely. Certainly there were grounds enough and forces enough had Indians decided to unite for once against a foe that had become increasingly coercive, aggressive and dictatorial.

The Sepoy uprising followed the annexation of Oudh where many had their roots and lands and feared loss of perquisites and overseas service bonuses, plus heavier taxes from colonial rule. Many had served in the 1856 Anglo-Burmese War. At that time the total army under direct Company command was 350,538 -- including 38,977 military police, probably all Indians.

The Bengal Presidency had 159,003 troops (cavalry, infantry and artillery) of which Indian nationals were *137,571* or *86.5%*. Interestingly 14% of British troops were in artillery compared to just over 3% of Indians. Bengalis comprised 44% of Indians in the Company's total army and almost all joined the revolt. However the **British Indian Association** and Bengali upper crust, the armies of the Madras and Bombay presidencies, the Nizam's troops and Punjabis--including Sikhs whom the British had humiliated earlier--stuck with the Company, the Punjabis outdoing their counterparts in fighting for the British much to the dismay of Indians who had hoped at last for unity against a vicious occupier. Indians behaved true to form, subdued again by treachery. Influential Bengali Associations and reformers sided with Britain.

The insurrection involved many brave and talented men and women, old and young. They achieved early success, capturing Kanpur and Delhi, but failed to hold them largely through disunity and the British stranglehold over Indian kingdoms and states. **Nāna Sahib of Bithur,** an adopted son of Bajirao II, **Tantia Tope**, son of a nobleman in **Bajirao's** court, and **Rani Lakshmi Bai** of Jhānsi became the major leaders. They fought valiantly, scored initial victories but were let down by rajahs who had grown soft with British sinecures and brain-washing. Tope was a brilliant guerrilla fighter but was betrayed by an associate **Raja Man Singh** of Narwar and eventually executed on April 18, 1859 in a brutish act, contrary to accepted canons of "rebellion against an invader". Earlier **Lakshmi Bai** had also met death along with thousands. Begum **Hazrat Mahal** of Lucknow had proudly led rebels and when Lucknow fell, spurned British terms of surrender escaping to Nepal where she died in 1879. They are known today as martyrs despite British smears and efforts to erase their names from popular memory and degrade the rebellion to a simple mutiny[91]. Sepoy leaders were hanged and others were sentenced to *transportation* to indenture in British Honduras.

My mother's *aja* (paternal grandfather) had secretly given time and money to the independence struggle in the action against Delhi, and his son-in-law (my grand uncle) had as a youth joined protest rallies in Gurgaon, Firozabad and Delhi, running confidential errands for local rebels. Towards the end he narrowly escaped identification and capture by the British, around the time the sad news arrived of **Lakshmi Bai's** murder and the British recapture of Delhi. This saddened everyone in the region and put whole villages and towns into a

---

[91] M S Gill in *Trials That Changed History* quotes T. Foryst, a British chronicler: "It is true that Tantia Tope was responsible for waging war against the British government, but, it was no crime to fight against a foreign government." In *Revolt in Central India,* British writer W. Milayson noted: "It is doubtful whether the succeeding generations will accept the verdict as correct, the verdict of a British War Tribunal. Tantia...was not bound by the legal dictates of foreign occupiers who had deprived his Peshwa (sic) of his estate and ruling power."

state of high alert especially in view of the tempting rewards offered by the British for information on rebels. Many civilians were accused. Thousands of *sepoys* were exiled to British Honduras.

British success was due as much to the ease with which they exploited internecine rivalries as to the quality of their armaments and naval strength. They suborned Rajputs to stay out of the conflict, who it was said, had some of the most powerful cannons in India then. Decades earlier **Haider Ali** of Mysore had ruefully noted that it would be difficult to defeat an enemy that had a strong Navy, and had hoped that the rockets[92] he and his son Tippu Sultan were developing could change that. They were too late. Britain would later achieve the acme of world power with the suppression of the Indian rebellion of 1857, and capitalising on the scientific, industrial and commercial changes brought on by the Industrial Revolution.

The search for dissidents and revolutionaries continued, punctuated by periodic disappearances of young men and women. However admirable the rebels, they--perhaps caught unprepared by the spontaneity of the uprising--had failed to engage the public at large, whose historical memory may have been far superior to that of their leaders. The populace may well have seen the revolt as merely the efforts of the dispossessed elite to regain their former fiefdoms, with no real concern to improve the lives of the needy masses. A great irony and error was the rebels' hasty choice of 80-year old, politically emasculated *Mughal* "Emperor" **Bahadur Shah** as an icon of freedom; he had been confined to the Red Fort for 20 years, and was unlikely to rouse Hindu and Sikh support!

The revolt quelled, the British government replaced the Company and the Mughals with the even more oppressive and extractive **British Raj** that lasted 90 years and made Victoria Empress of India when Disraeli became Prime Minister in 1874. Britain then claimed Bengal, Bihar, Orissa, Oudh in the east; Punjab, Multan and Sindh in the west; Nagpur in the centre; the Malabar and Coromandel coasts; Carnatic and Sarkars; and Ceylon. Rājputāna, Gujarāt, Mysore and Hyderābad and the former Marātha kingdoms of central India and a number of principalities across the country remained subsidiaries to the Crown as they had been since the last Marātha war in 1818. Only **Kashmir, Nepal, Bhutan** and the north-east remained independent. The French and Portuguese kept their trading posts.

Many have marvelled that so many Indians had been recruited to fight for the British—the **sepoy** armies--almost from the first year of the Company's arrival in India, despite meagre incomes and discriminatory selection criteria, favouring the so-called "martial races"--Kshatriyas, cultivators and certain Brahmin groups--who had no qualms fighting fellow Indians. The poor among them were believed to be the bravest and thus good cannon fodder. They were held by petty gifts of land or small favours and by pitting them in war against traditional rivals, usually under the influence of opium; loyalty was also ensured by coercion and threats to family. (Following the war the British recruited *sepoys* mainly from Ghurkhas, Sikhs and similar groups to ensure a division between soldiers and the people they served.)

Sepoys generally gave loyal service despite harsh treatment by cruel leaders. There is evidence of secret episodic planning for revolt that could not easily mature into concerted action because of communication barriers, lack of

---

[92] It is said that the Congreve rocket used by US in the War of 1812 was of similar or identical design.

leadership, and inter-tribal animosities which the British exploited and nurtured to keep the groups apart. This applied even at the highest levels. For instance Hindu Rajput kings of Jaipur were staunch allies of the Mughal Emperor, a relationship rarely displayed towards other Hindu sovereigns.

One must recall that whatever unity existed among Indians was based almost entirely on religion—Hinduism, Buddhism or Jainism—and that Indians were never ethnically homogeneous any more than Europeans, nor any less prone to bickering! Indeed French, Dutch and even English soldiers had fought for the Mughals, Marathas and for Tippu Sultan against the British. It is said that Hitler would not have found it difficult to raise a British battalion to fight their fellows given suitable incentives. Regional rivalries are the rule, not the exception among peoples.

The Müller Hoax: As efforts to convert Hindus lagged the British sought an Englishman, knowledgeable in Sanskrit, who could render the *Vaidas* in such a way that the Indian, newly educated in English, could be led to discard them in favour of the *Bible*. They found none but in 1854 came upon Frederick Max Müller, ardent Christian and German nationalist, unemployed linguist and Sanskrit student who eagerly accepted a grant of £10,000 from the British East India Company (of which he actually got only £3,000) to show that all of India's past achievements and advances, the *Vaidas* included, were the work of foreigners or else mythical. This he dutifully did, dressed in suitable academic clothing. And confirming Mill to an ignorant and biased audience, it was disseminated world-wide by British power.

In 1866 Müller wrote, *"This edition of mine and the translation of the Vaida will hereafter tell, to a great extent…the fate of India, and on the growth of millions… in that country. It is the root of their religion, and to show them what the root is, I feel sure, is the only way of uprooting all that has sprung from it during the last 3,000 years."*

The rebuttal and censure -- presented mainly in Indian languages and papers--hardly made the western press. The effects remain manifest and dominant, chiefly among Indian secularists and anglophilic Indian university graduates who even now repeat and promulgate Muller's flawed hypothesis despite retraction of his original stance: *"If I say Aryas, I mean neither blood nor bones, nor hair nor skull; I mean simply those who speak an Aryan language…To me, an ethnologist who speaks of Aryan race, Aryan blood, Aryan eyes and hair is as great a sinner as a linguist who speaks of a dolichocephalic dictionary or a brachycephalic grammar."*

Müller was a philologist, not a scientist; his translation and discussions reveal several errors in astronomy and mathematics. Main examples were the capitalizing of the Sanskrit adjective *"aryan"*, meaning *"noble"*, with no specific racial or ethnic significance, and by so doing *invented* a Central Asian *"Aryan race"* which he claimed was nomadic, which colonised India and composed the *Vaidas*, all in an incredibly short period. Knowledge of astronomy and mathematics would have shown this to be impossible, according to references to time in those same *Vaidas*.

As a Christian, Müller believed the Bible literally and thus made his notion of Indian history fit the Old Testament account of creation which is said to have occurred in 4004 BC. Thus 10,000 years of pre-Christian Indian history, consistent with *Vaidic* texts, were compressed to 2,000. He also ignored *Vaidic* references to ocean or sea, neither of which is to be found in Central Asia. His error was made at a time of rising of German nationalism and the search for identity, and

German unification under Bismarck. His hypothesis was used to "prove" their belief that German peoples had migrated west from *Sogdiana* in Central Asia.

Müller's retraction had come too late. Germany had already developed a keen interest in Sanskrit and Indology following the teachings of French scholar Joseph de Goubineau (1816-1882), who in *The Inequality of Human Races* proclaimed the "Aryan race" as superior above all and of aristocratic hierarchy; a later outcome was Adolf Hitler's "Aryan" racism and his adoption of a mirror image of the *Vaidic* Swastika as its national symbol. His use of "cephalic" reflects the beliefs of that time re phrenology and Caucasian racial superiority.

Müller thus contributed much to the project of transformation that Macaulay had started. As the products of the experiment emerged, Macaulay wrote, *"Our English schools are flourishing wonderfully....The effect of this education on the Hindoos is prodigious... It is my firm belief, that, if our plans for education are followed up, there will not be a single idolater among the respectable classes in Bengal thirty years hence. And this will be effected without any efforts to proselytise, without the smallest interference with religious liberty, merely by the natural operation of knowledge and reflection. I heartily rejoice in the prospect."*

Armed with Müller's myths the British systematically peddled untruths about Indian culture and denied Indian heroes—military, intellectual, recent and remote--their achievements in agriculture, religion, history and civilisation. They debased Hindus and Hinduism, and altogether succeeded in destroying the self-esteem of educated Indians, especially urban, and consolidated this by curricular indoctrination into British ways at all levels. Macaulay's vision of turning the educated Indian middle class into English toadies became a cruel and persistent reality. (Today, the chief opponents of *Vaidic* culture and education come mainly from the Indian middle class—British-educated[93] pedagogues, journalists, politicians, secularists--most of whom ironically claim to be Hindu. Meanwhile the West today is turning more and more to *Vaidic* and other ancient philosophies in search of answers to the complex social puzzles that it daily confronts.)

Expansion of the British Empire: The establishment of British schools was accompanied by the vigorous imposition of English as *the* language of India and of the Empire; this segregated and emasculated all but the small mainly urban moiety of the huge population--the WOGs *(Western Oriental Gentlemen)* and *coconuts*—rewarding them with small benefits, bribes really, like recognition, social position and a few titles, which Anglophiles value to this day.

The spirited activities of Christian missions globally led to many conversions which enhanced the status of some converts. At the same time the rise of Christian fundamentalism and race superiority theories made bureaucrats and Army officers more arrogant, oppressive and dismissive of Indian values--including religion and culture which their predecessors of the pre-revolutionary period had found as mystifying as they were uplifting--and ultimately treated Indians more cruelly. To consolidate this, the British began to classify society using many attributes that Hindus had not traditionally used e.g. religion. This served to segregate people further and facilitated their conquest and exploitation. (In like manner the descendants of the Mughals, Arabs and Turks were in the next century allowed to carve East and West Pakistan out of India and hold on to

---

[93] Modern Indian curricula have remained largely unchanged from those developed by the British Raj, as noted by Swami B.V. Giri in *Early Indology of India* **Part 2**, and disavow attempts to reinvigorate Vaidic studies.

their converts.)

Thus did the British, by the fruits of the industrial revolution, subdue and hold a population ten times their size. They were however assisted by Indian history. From earliest times India had been a complex of tribes, races and cultures united by rule, religion and commerce, but separated by distance, language and customs until brought together by **Mauryas, Guptas, Gurjar-Pratiwalas, Gahadvalas** and **Marathas**, but easily reverting to original rivalries, even to tribalism, steered by opportunity, temptation, stress and weak leadership, no different from today's Scotsmen wishing to secede from the British union, or the northern Irish wishing independence. But India was unlucky to have two ruthless and greedy invaders in succession zealously exploiting and fomenting these divisions to ensure rich profits.

Territorially Britain by the end of the Napoleonic Wars had eclipsed other Europeans, establishing numerous colonies, acquiring others, and had begun to surge ahead of rivals as it reaped economic and social advantages from **the industrial revolution** and victory in the Indian War of Independence. France, Britain's traditional rival, and also a major colonial power, had become distracted by revolution and philosophical debate at home while fighting Britain, changing from a monarchy to a Republic following Rousseau's doctrine; it reverted to a monarchy under Napoleon Bonaparte which lasted until a second revolt against Napoleon II in 1848 briefly restored the Republic, only to lose it to Napoleon III who would keep the monarchy until 1871. He built the **Suez Canal** in 1869, much to Britain's dismay as it seemed to threaten Britain's Middle East and Indian interests but this diminished six years later when the Egyptian ruler **Ismail Pasha** sold his 44% share to London for £4 million. The Canal was deemed neutral territory by agreement reached in 1888.

By this time defining conflicts had occurred between the Prussians and Austrians in 1866, and France 1870-71, Prussia winning both; as a result a unified Germany roared into the limelight, attributable to the machinations of the Prussian triumvirate **Otto von Bismarck, Albrecht von Roon** and **Helmuth von Moltke,** led by Bismarck as Prussian Chancellor from 1862. Meanwhile the Dutch plodded on dourly profiting from colonies and avoiding wars except by duress.

Even volatile Italy achieved a measure of unity at the expense of the Austro-Hungarian and Ottoman Empires whose decline was eyed by various powers, principalities and surrogates--Serbs, Greeks and others--as opportune to start wars of secession and independence as the century came to an end. Europeans referred to the crumbling of the Ottomans dismissively as the "Eastern Question", as it also involved religion: Christianity vs. Islam. A brutal civil war and Lincoln's murder would afflict the USA in the 1860s.

Soon the mercantilist race—promoted by British free trade advocates like Cobham--intensified as continental Europeans moved to compete with Britain in the new industries that science and engineering had made possible. The USA too had forced its way into trade with Japan and was building at home, with British financial partners, a vigorous industrial infrastructure: railway and telegraph networks, roads, canals and power grids. They focussed on continental expansion, what **John O'Sullivan**, New York journalist and Democrat had dubbed America's "manifest destiny", namely, to see America controlling all lands to the Pacific and even, as republican democrat **Henry Clay** envisaged, including Canada.

Britain by then was drunk with military and industrial strength and the headiness of colonial conquests. It had experienced an economic downturn in the 1840s, and Ireland had seen its worst potato famine, killing many and forcing millions of plebs to emigrate to the United States, Canada, Australia and elsewhere, facilitating cultural and linguistic expansion while relieving pressures at home. The subjugation of peoples "not Anglo-Saxon" had brought Africa in British gun-sights partly as a solution to the land needs of migrants.

South Africa, where the colony of Natal had been started, received few of these migrants, largely through fear of the Zulus on whose territories they would be squatting, despite inducements to build up the critical mass needed for a viable colony. The Dutch had colonised the Cape but as the Napoleonic Wars started yielded control in 1806 to Britain and it was from the eastern end of the Dutch colony that Natal had developed. Both the Cape and Natal relied heavily on enslavement but the trade was banned in 1807 affecting supply and farmers' profits! The British had responded by driving the Xhosa people from their homes west of Zululand and in so doing had also inflamed the Boers who had craved the same lands.

Whites only Migration Policies: The discovery of gold in 1851 in Victoria and New South Wales had attracted over 40,000 Chinese migrants to the goldfields where they competed directly with the locals. The inevitable clashes developed, facilitated by the obvious physical differences between the opposing parties. But if that was not enough the work ethics of the two groups differed enough to make the Chinese more successful in alluvial mining. Agitation by white miners gave rise subsequently to legislation restricting Chinese migration despite breaching British-Chinese agreements following the Opium Wars and the need elsewhere in Australia for plantation workers. *"It is not the bad qualities, but the good qualities of these alien races that make them so dangerous to us."* **Alfred Deakin**, a future Australian Prime Minister observed, *"It is their inexhaustible energy, their power of applying themselves to new tasks, their endurance and low standard of living that make them such competitors."*

Edmund Barton, Australia's first Prime Minister, agreeing with the move for racial exclusion, said, *"The doctrine of the equality of man was never intended to apply to the equality of the Englishman and the Chinaman."* In 1895 a British Colonial Premiers Conference agreed to ban non-white immigration generally; two years later **Joseph Chamberlain**, the Colonial Secretary conceded in a comment on the **"White Australia"** legislation of Australian colonies that *"…there should not be an influx of people alien in civilisation, alien in religion, alien in customs, whose influx, moreover, would seriously interfere with the legitimate rights of the existing labouring population."* Incredibly these same people had failed to see themselves as *"alien in civilisation, alien in religion, alien in customs"* when with consummate hypocrisy they imposed their will on Indians, Chinese and Africans, all with *"legitimate rights"* of nationality!

Britain exploited advances made in Europe, America and elsewhere in science, engineering, technology to revolutionise printing, the textile industry, transport (railways, iron ships, Suez Canal, city underground rail), utilities (electricity), communications, (telephone, telegraph, radio), economics, education etc. all of which helped it to retain its Empire and expand colonies. Social reform (secret balloting, 1872, free primary schooling, 1891) relieved pressure on Parliament. Britain became master of the seas with **Brunel's** launching of the *Great Eastern* in 1858, the largest ship built up to that time (18,915 tons, 32,000 fully loaded); it came into India's history as the cable ship that laid the undersea cable between Aden and Bombay in 1869-70 that facilitated and speeded up British business and government communications to control India.

British commercial profits improved as railways flooded India with cheap British goods replacing Indian industries, as already noted. By the 1870s Britain had the largest unified market which **Benjamin Disraeli** on becoming Prime Minister wished to enlarge by reviving the defunct *"Forward Policy"* in India to subdue Afghanistan and Burma and win more territory in South Africa. Other Europeans and the USA were competing industrially, sought new markets and jostled for empire.

The Scramble for Africa: In 1878, a remarkable year of discovery and invention, **King Leopold** of Belgium *bought* a major share of the huge **Congo.** The year saw changes in society as radical as the railways (with Rothschild and other funding) and soon matched by the perfection of ironclad ships, the naval screw propeller and the internal combustion engine. North America achieved major breakthroughs with **George Eastman's** development of dry photo film, **Alexander Bell's** telephone, and **Nicola Tesla's** many inventions which made others possible including Edison's gramophone and electric light bulb, and Westinghouse's transmission of electricity.

In 1879 while famine was killing millions in the Deccan and central India, the British gave grossly inadequate relief despite recommendations of their own medical experts and the Famine Commissioner **Robert Temple's** experience of a more humane handling of relief that had averted significant deaths in the Bihar famine of 1873-4 and for which he was castigated. His stinginess this time stemmed from fear of renewed criticism for *generosity*, and he not only reduced rations to a fifth but allowed free exports of grain by British merchants! This was the eighth major famine in India since the British occupation in 1769 which altogether had taken about *43 million* lives!

William Digby, a British journalist in India estimated that this latest had killed *ten million* people. Governor General **Bulwer-Lytton** maintained a hard-hearted stance and chose instead to make demands on Afghanistan which were promptly rejected and the British repelled. The loss, although not quite as humiliating as **Chelmsford's** losses in Zululand (see below) was an added shame for Britain. Bulwer-Lytton resigned, showing more character than Chelmsford, and Disraeli's government fell. Once back in London, Lytton churlishly attacked new PM John Gladstone's somewhat less inhuman approach to India.

The resulting economic activity brought some peace to Europe but sadly not shared elsewhere. In South Africa the British clashed repeatedly with Boers. **Lord Chelmsford**, Natal's governor, sharing BEICo's Lord Auckland's arrogant dismissal of natives, decided to rid Zululand of its rightful owners, whose **King Shaka** had generously donated to the British nearly 3000 sq miles of land south of the Tugela River for a farming colony. Coveting Zulu lands north of the river Chelmsford invaded the kingdom early in 1879, casually remarking -- in the true spirit of British immorality that would find a high priest in Cecil Rhodes a few years later--that it was a *"simple campaign of expansion!"*

The Zulu king **Cetshwayo**, grandson of Shaka, was not amused. Despite his professed admiration for Queen Victoria and the British and dislike for the Transvaal Boers, he sent an army under his brother **Dabulamanzi** which annihilated the British assault force at **Isandlwana**, a remarkable feat considering their primitive weaponry. But what they lacked in armaments they made up in strategy and ferocity. Sadly the Zulus and later other native groups would succumb to British guile and military might. British cupidity increased with Chelmsford's destruction of the Zulu capital Ulundi.

Annexing Transvaal they assumed Boer claims to Zulu borderlands and soon reached the acme of cupidity with **Cecil Rhodes**. It was Rhodes, too, who in 1887 told the House of Assembly in Cape Town that *"the native is to be treated as a child and denied the franchise. We must adopt a system of despotism in our relations with the barbarians of South Africa"*. In less oratorical moments, he put it even more bluntly: *"I prefer land to niggers."*

Three years earlier, to avert another European war, this time over ownership of the remaining free world, Portugal proposed and Germany hosted the Berlin Conference to discuss Africa, the last "unconquered" continent; the meeting was styled *The Scramble for Africa.* Most of the participants already had a foot in Africa and when the meeting ended the flags of many European states would be planted somewhere on African soil creating Belgian, British, French, German, Italian, Portuguese and Spanish colonies/spheres of influence, with King Leopold as personal owner of the Congo Free State! This left, by 1914, only Ethiopia and Liberia free. British, French and Portuguese had tried to hog all lands for resources and markets. Bismarck-- represented by explorer Carl Peters-- was not as fond of colonies as some German mercantilists were. In fact he traded a prime interest in East Africa for Britain's tiny North Sea island of Heligoland which gave the British territorial continuity from Uganda to the Indian Ocean north of German East Africa (Tanganyika).

The British were thus in the van of mercantilists raiding the world's wealth outdoing the Muslims for tenacity, efficiency and zeal. The failure of the 1857 War of Indian Independence had brought reprisals. British spies were everywhere, terrifying people with capricious and false charges and arrests, coerced witnesses, kangaroo courts and hangings, to the point that fear ruled and deep divisions and suspicions were amplified among them, even within families. Injustice ruled. It was not unusual for an Indian to be hanged for a peccadillo while an Englishman would be freed despite having committed a witnessed murder. The strictures effectively halted any attempt to plan an insurrection so tight were controls over movements of people and goods and so pervasive the use of bribery and paid informers by the British.

Section 8: The independence movement-Indian national Congress

My nāna recalled this period as one of great privations faced by Indians in all the villages of India, aggravated by the demands of zamindars and their *tahseels, naibs* and village watchers (landlords, collectors, deputies and assistants). Drought, unemployment and food shortages had reduced families to penury. The drop in value of silver, the monetary standard, had reduced the savings of most Indians. Artisans and farmers--the economic backbone of many villages-- were unable to compete with cheap British goods made cheaper by exemption from customs duties, which, coupled with new taxes on local industry, had made local produce *expensive*. Heartless Indian merchants made handsome profits selling British imports and cared little for the millions of their countrymen ruined, or the wholesale suffering and lasting social divisions created. The poor grew desperate enough to move to cities while others accepted indentures overseas.

Nāna was 22 in 1878, with family responsibilities and a growing interest in social and economic problems locally and nationally and the eastern famine that had killed millions. Issues were discussed more intensely among older relatives especially his brother-in-law, who spoke of joining a national self-rule organisation. Since arriving in BG he had developed a better grasp of problems having directly suffered British coercion and cheating. New migrants told sad tales of India's continuing shame, its divided leadership, scattered voices of protest and rumours of a self-rule movement. Some new arrivals were actually returning, driven by recession, famine, British seizure of family lands, punishing taxes and lack of opportunity in the villages, which many said made struggling in the swamps of BG preferable, despite the abundance of natural hazards and, most cruelly, pushy and thieving white men!

This appraisal of India was something of a shock, as he had expected conditions to have improved. He despaired for his lost family as returnees repeated the superior prospects of staying in BG to join the many Indians who had become established and free in the villages, some owning shops and big houses, many with fine clothes, their own equipment and conveniences, bicycles, mules, dray carts and several with fine carriages drawn by horses. Yet all were eager for continuing news of India particularly the state of the economy and their prospects should they choose to return as most still yearned to do. Those who chose to stay reasoned, *"Here I can have as much land as I can manage if I work hard and save; there I have to fit in; that would be okay but for the oppressive demands of the British fearing a new rebellion, so they're suspicious of anyone who look half competent or prosperous; the war in 1857 really shook them. Now they see everyone as a revolutionary and they hang you for stealing bread!"*

Nāna pondered this position, but coming from a family with strong bonds, substantial holdings and connections he decided to return home when finances allowed, praying that the *Swadeshi* leaders would soon succeed in uniting India into a strong and independent nation.

Dissent grew also among the middle class, especially educated and wealthy as they began to face the barriers already familiar to the working classes. If the Mughals were barbaric and cruel, there was no condemnation strong enough for British rulers. The feelings in time intensified as men of intellect from Calcutta, Bombay, Varanāsi and elsewhere joined in the demand for economic fairness, justice and an increased say in central and regional government. Nana's father had grown up with scorn for the British, describing them as "pushy unprincipled thieves". He was cautious in any contact with their military, which although disciplined was as ruthless as Mughals, dealt harshly with civilians and had no qualms about brutalising or killing Indian men and corrupting women. Even before the 1857 war, skirmishes had erupted in various places to protest British breaches of agreements, atrocities against civilians and sepoys, and excesses--especially the desecration of symbols and monuments of non-Christian religions, including the abomination of holding dissolute dance parties at the Tāj Mahal. One Governor looted marble from the Agra fort and considered demolishing the Tāj monument to sell its marble to British scrap-dealers!

The atmosphere darkened for Indians and the grassroots economy worsened. By the time of my grandfather's kidnapping in 1878, the raging and deadly famine that killed millions helped dissenters by attracting attention to the brutality of the Raj.

Dissent, Actions and Official Despotism: On the 31st of October, 1851, the *British Indian Association*[94] was established by the union of the *Landholders' Society* and the *Bengal British India Society*. It was welcomed and had the potential to unify the nation but from the start it was hobbled by its name. Its founders were among the elite of Bengal and all well-known conservatives, except for the more progressive **Ramgopal Ghosh** and **Pyari Chand Mitra** but even they supported the pro-British political agenda. The Association set up branches countrywide for a national stance on petitioning Government, but each retained the right to approach its regional authority independently. Apart from strong support to the British in the War the group attended to *Brahmo* activities until 1870 when a motion from the *Adi Dharma* faction was carried to address Government on issues of inequity, employment in the Indian Civil Service (ICS), and political representation and empowerment. The opponents joined the *Indian Reform Association* led by Keshab Sen (see below).

While Bengalis and the *Brahmo Samaj* flirted with Christian ideas on reform and correctly trashed the corrupting of Hinduism by orthodox Brahmins, the continuing disputation did the latter no credit, painting them as obsolete, misguided and overly dependent on ritual rather than principles clearly expressed in the Vaidas.

Swami Dayānanda Saraswati (1823-83), a Gujarati by birth, emerged from his long training in 1875 and founded the *Arya Samaj* in Bombay to engage in social service, pursue the education of women and their release from the Muslim veil and other non-Hindu restraints asserting that this hobbling of women had led to India's downfall! He showed that Hinduism had been degraded by many accretions and practices not sanctioned in the Vaidas and should be changed.

Thus he advocated an end to caste, idolatry, child marriage-- placing a minimum age of 16 for girls and 25 for males--and to mandatory dowry. He toured India urging princes to support reform and reinstate and expand the *gurukul* system that had served India well, before the Mughals and British. The subsequent growth of Arya Samaj and gurukuls in the north was heartening.

A disciple **Swami Shraddhānanda** established the famous gurukul at Kangdi which produced many Indian nationalists including **Lala Lajpat Rai** and **Ram Prasad Bismil,** both of whom were staunch Samajists. He was aware of various Associations that had been formed including the latest *Indian Association* and saw that Lord Ripon might be too well-meaning for the local British. With the British so recalcitrant and oppressive he supported those who thought of renewing armed struggle, among whom was his disciple **Shyamji Krishna Verma** (see below). Dayānanda was approaching the height of his influence when on rebuking the **Rāja of Jaipur** for his dissolute ways a concubine **Nanhi Jan** poisoned him at a Diwali festival.

Dayānanda's ministry overlapped that of other giants of his time, including two Bengalis, the mystic **Ramakrishna Parahamsa** (1836-86) and his disciple **Swami Vivekānanda** (1863–1902); they propounded the scientific basis

---

[94] The first committee: Raja Radhakanta Deb, President; Raja Kalikrishna Deb,Vice-President; Debendranath Tagore, secretary; Digambar Mitra, Asst. Secretary; members: Raja Satya Saran Ghosal, Harakumar Tagore, Prasanna Coomar Tagore, Ramanath Tagore, Jay Krishna Mukherjee, Asutosh Deb, Harimohan Sen, Umesh Chandra Dutt (Rambagan), Krishna Kishore Ghosh, Jagadananda Mukhopadhyay, Sambhunath Pandit, Ramgopal Ghosh and Peary Chand Mitra.

of Hinduism, its logic, spirituality and accommodation of secular views and its lack of bias based on caste, race or gender and thus welcomed all ideas. Vivekānanda said, *"All differences in this world are of degree, and not of kind, because oneness is the secret of everything."* (He is famous for his rousing speech in Chicago in 1893 extolling Vedanta; it educated listeners about true Hinduism, not the British or Brahmin version in vogue then, and attracted world praise and a vigorous following.)

The *Indian Reform Association* (**IRA**) was formed in October 1870 by **Keshab Chandra Sen** (1838 –1884) and pro-British former members of the *British Indian Association*. In the same year **Lord Mayo** (1869-72) by resolution, sought to devolve certain funded responsibilities to local government such as elementary education, medical care and public works to be financed by local taxes.

But the scheme languished as villages had long lost their political base--the *panchayats*--and the British was unable to quickly supply a reliable and honest mechanism to establish one. They had never paid any attention to the Indian system of local government, perhaps because one did not exist in Britain and the whole idea of local authorities ran counter to their purpose in India: trade and profit, whatever the cost. Indian leaders were no real help as most hailed from the upper and least humanitarian classes, which had little contact with the plebs, and were also experiencing doubts and seeing changes.

Sen was a religious worker associated with Unitarians and had been a member of Tagore's *Brahmo Samaj* until 1866 when Tagore objected to his see-sawing on and eventual espousal of Christianity leading the former to rename the original group *Adi (First) Brahmo Samaj* when Sen formed a group also called *Brahmo Samaj!* Meeting **Queen Victoria** earlier in 1970 he had affirmed his secularism and loyalty. He was enthusiastic about the Unitarian gospel, which he saw firsthand and seemed convinced that British Reforms could be duplicated in India. The Association would therefore advocate *"the social and moral reformation of the natives of India"* and promote change through *"cheap literature, female improvement, education, temperance, and charity."* His weekly paper *Sulava Samachar (Cheap News)* costing only one paisa brought news to the street and was a welcome innovation at that time when the underprivileged had little or no access to news and the gulf between the **Kulin Brahmins** and the plebs was deep and wide. The changes following the War had created a morass of controversy and restlessness at all levels of society especially as more educated youth were emerging from schools seeking jobs and gravitating to religious or political groups (their numbers are large and their identities, roles and intricacies are beyond the scope of this essay.)

It is sufficient to note that Sen was controversial and at times contradictory, perhaps understandable in someone with deep religious roots struggling to reconcile different doctrines especially the very dogmatic Christians in India, the equally dogmatic Kulins, the mix of objectives in Brahmoism which he was trying to meld together into one rational statement or universal religion. In this he was not unlike his contemporary **Lalon Shah**, the Bengali poet, who was then probing Hindu, Jain, Buddhist and Islamic traditions to find a coherent thread to tie his art together. Sen came close after his encounters with Ramakrishna whose unrefined appearance had put him off at their first meeting. Ramakrishna's message to him was simple: *"Worship God as Mother"* and *"All religions are true"*. Sen lost face and his organisation when he went against Brahmo principles and gave his 9-year old daughter in marriage, by tradition, after which he was left to his personal projects and writing.

In 1876 **Surendranath Banerjee**, producer of *The Bengalee*, and **Ānand Mohan Bose** formed the nation-wide *Indian National Association (INA)*--incorporating the Brahmo Sabha and other groups mentioned above, including Sen's after his death in 1884--to promote *"by every legitimate means the political, intellectual and material advancement of the people"*. This was easy to say but tough to envisage considering the pervasive divisiveness among Indians—a trait that seemed unusually deeply ingrained and easily exploited by any power determined to subdue the country. Earlier the first results of higher education for women appeared when **Chandramukhi Basu**, a Christian from **Dehra Doon** and **Kadambini Ganguly**, a Bengalee Hindu obtained BA degrees from University of Calcutta in 1882. Basu earned an MA in 1884 and later became Principal of Bethune College, the first female head of a College in South Asia. Ganguly[95] became the first female graduate in Medicine in 1886; **Anandi Gopal Joshi** studied Medicine in Pennsylvania graduating in 1886, age 21, the first female Indian with a US degree.

Lord Ripon (1827-1909) served as Viceroy from 1880 to 1884 following Mayo's assassination in the Andaman Islands and resumed the issue of decentralisation of power by changing Local Boards from large nominated units to smaller elected ones; British citizens—the main beneficiaries of Board appointments--opposed this on the grounds that natives were not yet ready for an electoral system! How ironic that the British first destroyed the Indian electoral system then less than a century later had the gall to suggest that the ones deprived had no knowledge of what they had been deprived, showing how little they knew of the ways by which knowledge was transmitted among Indians and to posterity! Their objection forced Ripon to accept partially elected Boards. He addressed serious abuses of farmers and introduced the *Tenancy Acts* which surprisingly returned to *raiyats* land lost under Cornwallis's *Permanent Settlement* legislation.

Ripon supported education at all levels (*Education Commission* of 1882), and he prevailed in granting freedom of the press by repealing the **1878 *Vernacular Press Act*** which had muzzled criticism of Government. His attempt to reform the judicial process, the *Ilbert Bill*,[96] was opposed in Parliament. It sought to ensure equality of treatment of all accused thus removing the preferential treatment accorded whites and rendering them liable to appear before Indian judges. The House debate on the issue had painted bizarre pictures of Indians, British women claiming that Indians were unsuitable as judges as they were loose and fickle because their women were ignorant and allowed such behaviour! Bengali women in turn ridiculed them as hypocrites and showed that British husbands kept Indian concubines and no British woman in India had a college degree while the University of Calcutta had graduated two females in 1882, years before any UK university! The main opponents of the Bill were plantation owners who feared that Indian judges might not overlook their many

---

[95] Dr Ganguly's father was Braja Kishore Basu, Brahmo activist and advocate for women's rights, one of six female delegates to the 1889 session of the INC; she organized the Women's Conference in Calcutta in 1906 in the aftermath of the partition of Bengal. In 1908, she had also organized and presided over a Calcutta meeting for expressing agreement with *Satyagraha*.

[96]C.P. Ilbert wrote a *Government of India* in which he said that the post-1857 period of Crown governance, *was followed by... "an era of peace in which India awakens to new life and progress."* This MUST have been said tongue-in-cheek!

peccadilloes! The Bill was watered down but did allow trial by Indian judges in district courts except that whites were allowed a jury of equal numbers of Indians and whites.

Ripon gained the respect and admiration of Indians as no other Viceroy or Governor. Most were insensitive and dismissive and his successors undid the goodwill he had earned. The controversies and recriminations surrounding the overdue reforms he had tackled reaffirmed the raping of India, shamed some British civil servants and inspired the formation of the **Indian National Congress in 1885** (INC भारतीय राष्ट्रीय). The Congress was a natural development of a national voice uniting the regional forces that had by then become active in all regions of India. It was a union of Hindus, Muslims and a few Europeans to promote self government.[97] At its founding it merged with the INA. The leaders were **Allan Octavian Hume, Womesh Chandra Banerjee, Surendranath Banerjee, Manmohan Ghose, William Wedderburn, Dadabhai Naoroji**[98]**, Dinshaw Edulji Wacha** and many others. Their first meeting was held in 1885 in Bombay, organised, ironically by Hume, a Scottish ex-BEICo official with a conscience and a passion for birds.[99] Most of the founders were intellectuals, businessmen or bureaucrats who were actuated when their heads began to butt against the white ceiling restricting their social and political development (**Ramesh Chandra Dutt** of Bengal was the first to achieve Executive status in 1882, some said as Queen Victoria's token Indian to keep her 1858 promise of "equality"). The 1886 meeting launched regional committees and debated WC Banerjee's dictum on limiting the Council to politics, not social issues.

As to strategy some proposed armed struggle but earlier **Justice Mahadev Govind Ranade** (1842-1901), an eminent scholar, like many of his colleagues, argued for moderation and a measured approach to self-rule, working to preserve the tenets of Hinduism with dignity while promoting reforms especially the elimination of caste and certain social prohibitions e.g. widow remarriage. As a respected member of the Bombay legislative council and a judge of the Bombay High Court Ranade's prestige lent weight to his optimistic view that political progress was inevitable, without force, but Indians needed to modernise and could do so by education without losing their traditional values. He joined the Bombay-based *Prarthana Sabha* (prayer group) that had been formed in 1849 following Brahmo principles. He and others started the *Puné Sārvajanik Sabha* (Public Society) in 1870 to represent the people's interest to the Government. But they had failed so far to build the nationalist spirit required to oust the British.

The reform movement gained strength as voices coalesced across language barriers, ironically aided by the enforced spread of English as the *lingua franca*, and abetted by the pens of S. Banerjee in Calcutta and from other cities **Gopal Krishna Gokhale** (1866-1915)**, Lala L. Rai, Bāl Gangādhar Tilak** and **Bipin Chandra Pal** (*lal-bal-pal* trio) They led the militant and more insistent group which unequivocally condemned the British for their ignorance about and denigration of Hindu culture, and their rulers for brutality, but at the same time recognised and commended those more humanitarian British who sought to improve Indian education by incorporating appropriate "western" methods.

Tilak and Gokhale shared heritage and education (both were mathematics

---

[97] Its first meeting was held on Dec 28-31, 1885, chaired by W C Banerjee.
[98] Later became the first Indian member of the British House of Commons.
[99] My grandfather knew that Hume had often visited his village Sultanpur near Delhi, home of a bird sanctuary.

professors) and helped Ranade to found the **Deccan Education Society** in 1884 in line with commentaries on India's education which Lord Ripon had explored. They established a Western-style school in Puné in 1880 (later called **Ferguson College**). Like Ranade, Gokhale was a moderate and emphasised social reform to uplift ordinary citizens while Tilak was militant and insisted on expelling the British, by force if necessary. He also reminded readers that the *Bhagavad Gita* had described the conditions under which righteous men were obligated to fight an oppressor. The British had amply fulfilled those. The differences between the two grew between 1891 and 1897, particularly in the *Sārvajanik Sabha*.

When a famine and plague ravaged Maharashtra in 1896 Tilak--then a member of the *Bombay Legislative Assembly*--chastised the Government for mismanagement. Protests and reprisals followed. In one confrontation with citizens an Army officer and head of the plague relief committee were killed. Tilak was arrested for inciting murder and jailed for 18 months in 1897 (he served 11 months), and again several times after. His slogan, after serving his first jail term, *"Swaraj (Self-Rule) is my birth right and I shall have it"* made him a hero, but the British called him the *"Father of Indian unrest"*.

The Militants: Inevitably British excesses in all spheres of life–political, physical, financial, moral — and the increasing penury of the Indian masses led to persistent calls for autonomy and met needlessly violent reprisals in the manner of authority without intelligence. The INC had achieved little in 20 years considering its huge and expectant support base. Some said it was too passive and cared little for rural folk. The frustrations invigorated militant individuals and groups who resented the new **Viceroy Curzon** who, hardly arriving in Calcutta in 1899 moved to achieve "English" dominance in the **Calcutta City Corporation** by cutting 50% of the number of elected Indians and curbing the autonomy of Indian Universities.

The British hegemony and the atrocities it engendered were aided by stiff laws introduced after the 1857 war aimed to curtail gun ownership and to license owners. Legitimate protest was ignored. Organised militancy began to appear near the turn of the century among Bengali Hindus. They operated cautiously, always mindful of the ubiquitous informers and spies and the violence of British retribution; as one wag said, *"Even the bhagi must be carefully searched before eating!"* Although many incidents had occurred in the last decades of the 19th century the first organised movement advocating revolution to achieve independence was *Anushilan Samiti*, founded by men of intellect, who had despaired of any reforms noting the pro-government stance of the INC and its failure to press for the masses and despite S. Banerjee's efforts and his work as an elected member in the Calcutta City Corporation. He had founded the INA and had vigorously opposed Curzon's arbitrary cuts in the elected membership of the City Corporation, playing Muslims against Hindus, calling the latter a Brahmin clique remote from *real* Indians.

The leaders of *Anushilan Samiti* included **Jatindra Nath Banerjee** (later Niralamba Swami)), vice-presidents **Aurobindo Ghosh** and **Chittaranjan Das** (CR, Deshbandhu), treasurer **Suren Tagore** and famed activists **Jatindra Nath Mukherjee** (Bagha Jatín), **Bhupendra Nath Datta** (Swami Vivekananda's brother), **Barindra Ghosh**, Aurobindo's younger brother and many others who formed units in almost every state. Aurobindo established contact with **B G Tilak** and **Sister Nivedita** (Margaret Elizabeth Noble), a disciple of the late Swami Vivekananda and strong advocates for independence.

Anushilan Samiti spread quickly through Bengal, especially after its partition and on Aurobindo's writings, in one of which he summarised frustrations with the INC: "... *that its aims are mistaken, that the spirit in which it proceeds towards their accomplishment is not a spirit of sincerity and whole-heartedness, and that the methods it has chosen are not the right methods, and the leaders in whom it trusts, not the right sort of men to be leaders; in brief, that we are at present led, if not by the blind, at any rate by the one-eyed.*" The movement soon spread across India. In Bengal it spawned the *Yugantar* (New Age) party in 1906 led by young men, chief among them Bagha Jatin, a martial arts expert and briefly civil servant, Aurobindo and Barindra Ghosh.

The militants targeted known British tyrants one of whom Judge Kingsford, a Calcutta magistrate who was unduly harsh in punishing young activists. A bomb hurled in his carriage by 18-year old **Khudiram Bose** and **Prafulla Chāki** killed two women. Kingsford was unaccountably not in the carriage at the time. Khudiram was a strong believer in justice and had been impressed with the lessons of the *Bhagavad Gita*; he saw the British as more villainous than the Kauravas and himself as a warrior in Arjuna's army. Prafulla's suicide and Bose's hanging attracted many admirers and new recruits to the movement which maintained guerrilla actions against the British and Governor General Curzon's policies. Many activists were arbitrarily imprisoned in Port Blair, Andaman Islands.

Boosting Muslims--the Division of Bengal: In 1905, **Curzon** divided Bengal into Muslim and Hindu sections, clipping off pieces to Assam and the Central Provinces. The only ones satisfied by it were Muslim political aspirants of East Bengal headed by the **Aga Khan** who obtained separate representation and an enhanced share of India in exchange for fealty to the British. Even the English administrator of Assam, **Henry Cotton**, opposed the plan. The act was condemned by all Indians and was perhaps the most perfidious and ill-conceived of all autocratic acts in India as it set the stage for Hindu-Muslim division which the **Morley-Minto** "reforms" of 1909 would place beyond redemption and throttle the quest for unity among all Indians, regardless of religion. This Act did however make some useful changes such as devolution of a few powers to provinces and increasing elected members of governing councils but left government firmly in the control of the Viceroy and his executive. The religious fracture of Indian peoples and awarding of additional privileges to Muslims would haunt India from then on and subject Bengalis and Indians generally to great harm. Eventually the Bengal split was reversed in 1911, the year the new capital was built in New Delhi.

In response to Curzon's policies the INC changed its goal to self-rule. Tilak and his followers began the *Swadeshi* (self-sufficiency) movement to boycott British goods and restore traditional Indian products. Articles in *Kesari* promoted these activities but lack of political progress and disagreements in the INC on method led Tilak and his militant followers in 1907 to split the INC into two camps, dubbed the *Garam Dal* ("hot faction") led by **Tilak** and *Naram Dal* ("soft faction") or moderates led by **Gopal Krishna Gokhale**.

Tilak propounded the philosophy of *Swaraj* in his paper *Kesari*. Banerjee in *The Bengalee* had for years exposed the inequities and prejudices of the British, and criticised Curzon's high-handedness and flawed reasoning, so much so that friends and readers feared that the writers and editors would be arrested in reprisal on some fabricated charge or perhaps through some instant or capricious law that criminalised their actions; indeed subtle changes to sedition laws had been made near 1900. Tilak was jailed for 6 years for sedition for articles defending Khudiram Bose's revolutionary activities. On conviction he told the jury: *"... I maintain that I am innocent. There are higher powers that rule the destiny of men and nations and it may be the will of providence that the cause which I represent may prosper more by my suffering than by my remaining free."*[100] Gokhale meanwhile founded the *Servants of India* in 1905 based in Nāgpur. Its English paper *The Hitavada* started in 1911.

The **British Raj** was then directly ruling three-fifths of the subcontinent's 350 million population and the rest--over 560 states of all designations--as subsidiary alliances, each of which provided and maintained a part of the British Army which far exceeded the number needed for India's defence and was used for aggressive wars and suppression of local dissent. By 1901, the British had transferred over £1,000,000,000 of Indian wealth to the UK, including the **Koh-i-Noor** and numerous similar gems and precious objects, culled from palaces and temples and enriched with the addition of the giant *Star of Africa*, decorating the necks and appendages of monarchs and the British royal crown, sceptre and orb! The rape would continue to the last days, when even the tiny gem inlays on **Tāj Mahal** tiles would be looted.

The spirit of revolt was assisted ironically by the new universities in India plus access to the best British schools—Oxford, Cambridge, LSE, London, Inns of Court etc. where students absorbed liberal political views on morality, ethics, equality and ideas, methods and other virtues from **Locke, Johnson, Ruskin, Spencer, Bentham, JS Mill, Blake, Marx, Hyndman, the Fabians** and a host of others, literary and philosophical, including continentals from the later 18th century like **Rousseau, Kant, Kierkegaard, Nietzsche, Descartes** and others. On graduation Indians discovered the colour bar to employment and promotion in the Indian Civil Service,-for which they had prepared so assiduously, the huge salaries paid to British recruits and other forms of bias more virulent than casteism at its worst.

At the end of the 19th century several wealthy Indians in London--**Bhikaji Cāma, Shyamji Krishnavarma, S.R. Rana, Vināyak Sāvarkar and others**--had formed the *India Home Rule Society* and published, with British sympathisers, a paper, *The Indian Sociologist*. Earlier Shyamji had founded **India House** as a student residence. When British authorities threatened arrests they moved to Paris forming The *Paris Indian Society* in 1905, a branch of the IHRS, under the patronage of Bhikaji Cāma, Sardar Singh Rāna, **B.H. Godrej** and included at various times **Virendranath Chattopadhyaya, Har Dayal, M.P.T. Acharya** (founder of the Indian Communist Party), **Lala Lajpat Rai, Sāvarkar, G.S. Khaparde, Rambhuj Dutt and Bipin Chandra Pal**. In 1907, Bhikaji, along with other IHRS associates, attended the Socialist Congress of the Second International in Stuttgart. There, supported by Henry Hyndman, she demanded recognition of self-rule for India and in a famous gesture unfurled one of the first Flags of India. In frustration and in a spirit of revolt Sāvarkar and other students in London had formed the *Free India* Society and a London unit of the *Abhinav*

---

[100]This is carved on a wall in the Bombay High Court. On release from prison he became less militant, supported Gokhale's advocacy of constitutional approaches to self-rule. With Jinnah, Khaparde and Annie Besant Tilak formed the *India Home Rule League* backing a federal system with equal states and Hindi written in Devanagari script as the common language. At his death Gandhi called him the *"Maker of India"*.

Bhārata (Young India) Society in 1904, who swore:

> "*In the name of God, In the name of Bhārata Mata, In the name of all the Martyrs that have shed their blood for Bharat Mata, By the Love, innate in all men and women, that I bear to the land of my birth, wherein the sacred ashes of my forefathers, and which is the cradle of my children, By the tears of Hindi Mothers for their children whom the Foreigner has enslaved, imprisoned, tortured, and killed, I, ... convinced that without Absolute Political Independence or Swarajya my country can never rise to the exalted position among the nations of the earth which is Her due, And Convinced also that that Swarajya can never be attained except by the waging of a bloody and relentless war against the Foreigner, Solemnly and sincerely Swear that I shall from this moment do everything in my power to fight for Independence and place the Lotus Crown of Swaraj on the head of my Mother; And with this object, I join the Abhinav Bhārata, the revolutionary Society of all Hindustan, and swear that I shall ever be true and faithful to this my solemn Oath, and that I shall obey the orders of this body; If I betray the whole or any part of this solemn Oath, or if I betray this body or any other body working with a similar object, May I be doomed to the fate of a perjurer!*"

Although the fate of the would-be betrayer was undoubtedly an anticlimax, the zeal was unmistakeable. The Society expanded by 1906 and paralleled Tilak's activities; Sāvarkar allied with the *Garam Dal* faction of the INC and wrote many revolutionary tracts and a book titled **History of the Indian War of Independence** which the British promptly banned but thereby made more desirable when it was published, through Bhikaji Cama's intervention elsewhere in Europe. Sāvarkar was imprisoned in 1910 for involvement in armed opposition to the Morley-Minto Reforms. In jail he and Tilak came to experience, almost simultaneously, the punishing life of India's crores[101] of downtrodden people—described by my grandfather as worse than hell--but ignored by their so-called "betters", especially the Brahmins.

Prisoners, like indentured workers, awoke at 5am, toiled all day at heavy manual labour under duress and in silence, even at mealtimes, and were manhandled and tortured for minor breaches. Prison allowed them ample time for reflection, which gave Sāvarkar ideas to reform Hinduism which he presented as *Hindutva*. The *Akhil Bhārata Hindū Mahāsabhā* (*All India Hindu Congress*) adopted it, along with his rejection of the *Naram Dal* stance in the INC. He proposed a union of all Hindus (using the term to include Buddhists, Jains and Sikhs) as inheritors of the entire sub-continent, there to establish *Akhand Bhārata* (*United India*) as a **Hindu Rashtra** (*Hindu Nation*).

While leaders argued, the poor, disenfranchised and dispossessed masses had become inured to oppression even by their own people; Hindus and Muslims sought solace in religious activities, in temples and mosques where spiritual leaders were often their only advocates. **Ramesh Dutt**, a founder of the INC, came to recognise the centuries-old problem of injustice and crimes against rural Indians who bore the brunt of British atrocities, often with the help of upper crust and urban Indians. The village administrative *panchayats* had secured the land and its productivity through millennia of dynasties and empires. He now observed that tenants had no assured rights of any kind, paid exorbitant taxes and that since people had no political representation bureaucrats had no way to assess their concerns!

That applied equally to the British or Indian officer; but while the one could be excused by his position as ignorant conqueror, Indian leaders must be

---

[101] One crore equals 10 millions.

blamed for being distant and haughty and participating in the continued subjugation of their peoples whose ancient rights and practices to deal with local problems had been brutally taken away. Indian leaders over the centuries had profited from this and had become the go-between for the conqueror, first the Mughals, then the British. They also kept aloof, maintaining strict class and tribe distances that he despaired of ever seeing improved unless the British commanded it! That was unlikely as it provided pliable middlemen and lackeys to collect taxes and do other "dirty work". Back in Britain the aristocracy that supplied the rulers of India generally behaved the same with scant care for the masses; small wonder that they would care at all for the reviled Indian.

Despite agreement in Ripon's time to regenerate India's *panchayati* raj, progress was snail-paced perhaps because none in the INC or other groups had any real contact with rural people; but did they not read, these learned men, of village organisation and government in the Hindu classics? In the two decades to the end of WWI in which the problem had languished, reviews identified the same problems, the same abuses, the same miscreants and the same remedies. These included the 1907 *Royal Commission on Decentralisation* chaired by **C.E.H. Hobhouse**, undersecretary of state for India, affirming the need to reconstitute *panchayats*; **the** *Government of India Resolution* of 1918, which said the same, urging strengthening of local government; and the 1919 *Montagu-Chelmsford report* which passed the issue to provincial ministers but failed to empower *panchayats*. The *Government of India Act* implementing the M-C Reforms endorsed expanded provincial councils and transferred them to ministries of education, health and agriculture. Centrally it created a bicameral legislature with a lower house of 144 seats, 104 elected and an upper Council of States of 60 members, 36 elected, but nothing was done to restore village-based self-government as it was not in the interests of British business and seemed a trivial or even vexed one for the Government. Curzon for one had no patience for local government and saw his role simply to promote *"the interests of government and the English (sic) in Calcutta"* and to *"cut the Babu down to size"*; both would be achieved by shrinking legislative bodies and not by creating more layers. And so the issue languished until Gandhi began his campaign.

The formation of the Congress had an impact beyond Indian politics. It was warily welcomed by many Indian émigrés whose families had suffered losses due to British policies. In the continuing protests for self-government many were arrested and imprisoned without trial, or simply disappeared. My grandfather agonised that his family might have been among them, betrayed by some simple act, even though he knew how vigilant they were, schooled by generations of silent protest and having geographically been in the thick of major wars of that millennium, including three at nearby Pānipat. Caution was in their blood but they remained at risk. Nāna remained sceptical seeing in the names of those involved a curious mixture of *bhadralok* (westernised upper class), intellect and business. (Dr Brahmam had agreed and felt that the Indians were not unlike American businessmen who had craftily promoted the War of Independence as a means of expanding business and growing profits! *"Indian upper class and some middle class moved only when directly threatened and most prosper under British."*)

Disunity and the absence of true nationalism continued to dog India and hobbled progress, its security, integrity and obstructed determined action for self-rule. Self-interest, not unity and purpose or principle or strategy governed majority actions despite hostile responses from Government. The divisions were overt and pervasive, the voices strident on each side and concerned mainly with wealth and privilege and scant thought for the masses. Schisms worsened as more Indians became anglicised and many of the privileged adopted pro-British attitudes, values and behaviour to preserve businesses or rank or to prevent too rapid a shift of power from the upper crust to the masses.

The Diaspora: The repressions, dispossession and hunger following the 1857 War and subsequent famines had led to the development of a **Diaspora** that by 1961 numbered over ten million people, mainly in Mauritius, the East and West Indies, Malaysia, Africa, South East Asia, Hong Kong, South Pacific, a sprinkling in the UK and USA, and an enclave of Sikhs in Canada. Indians had become a majority in BG, Mauritius and Fiji and a third of the Trinidad population. By 1890 many had achieved enviable success in agriculture and business, and had begun to educate their children in professions such as medicine, engineering, accounting, teaching, law, agriculture and politics.

But as the self-rule movement grew and called for representation, it demanded, *inter alia,* an end to emigration and indenture, largely due to Gandhi's experience at Champaran *(see below)*. That was not likely to happen until the British monopoly--then crippling India's industry and continuing to extort and export its wealth to Britain--was brought to an end and measures taken to deal with burning issues, for example, the disenfranchisement of villages, the ruin of rural Indians and the conversion of individual and family food farms to commercial plantation crops like cotton, opium, sugarcane and tobacco. (This practice continues in India unchecked today, and the players have changed only slightly).

The issue of contract migration was controversial and, as noted, opposed by the INC. The British Raj "studied" it and decided to allow it to continue as long as contracts were legally done and their terms observed to the letter, noting that many had renewed contracts. Nāna recalled the argument for declining repatriation: *"In Demerara I have the same conqueror, but I can't start a rebellion here, so they leave me alone, considering me too humble and passive to trouble them; that allows me to do business and keep out of their way until I get big enough to deal with them on my terms; so I will stay here and build some wealth, as my karma dictates, and hope to reconnect with my family in India as opportunity allows and when I have something to offer."*

Race and Politics: With the formation of the INC the Raj tightened surveillance of dissident activities. By 1900 the British Empire had reached its zenith. The larger white colonies had already achieved a measure of self-government and colonies in Canada and Australia had federated (1867 and 1901 respectively) while South Africa was close to it (1910). The United States had adopted aggressive mercantilism conquering all of America to the Pacific Ocean, defeating Mexico, "liberating" the Philippines and the Spanish Caribbean, holding Cuba and Santo Domingo in fief and Puerto Rico as a colony. Earlier in 1854 Admiral Perry's warships had convinced the Japanese to forego *sakoku* (isolation) and accept US trade; by this time the British had already smothered the out-gunned Chinese with opium.

The policy of the INC before the end of the century was still to achieve equality of opportunity in Government services, desegregation of public facilities including vehicles such as railway carriages and elimination of the many barriers to promotion of Indians who often had to tutor superiors recruited from Britain at hugely inflated salaries paid for by Indian labour and taxes while business profits were banked in Britain. By 1883 Francis Galton's ideas on *eugenics* had become popular in white circles, attracting racially bigoted European and American politicians and giving susceptible whites a feeling of superiority and excuse for boorish behaviour, prevalent in India, Africa and the West Indies.

The INC announced its plan for self-government within the Empire while India's sister states in that Empire were planning to pass discriminatory legislation denying Indians equality and the right of free movement within the Empire. This principle had allowed the British to move freely across the world and was an implied if not stated guarantee in treaties signed with Indian rulers ceding territory to Britain or swearing allegiance. On this understanding, groups of agricultural Sikhs and Hindus had entered America and Canada, attracted by the wide plains and valleys that Punjabis were craving as famine, adverse weather, land use policies and political developments had threatened their livelihood at home. Diasporal whites were not all racists, but those who favoured racial segregation won key elections--defeating forces of morality and fairness in Australia, South Africa and Canada--that led to the "White only" immigration policies adopted by them.

The British had come to India with a firm purpose to trade and make profits and cared little about Indian people or customs beyond what either could contribute to fatten the British purse. They thus dismissed Indians without consideration, superimposing their own beliefs and practices and sparing no effort to divide them into small malleable units. Hindus and Muslims had accommodated to one another over a period of several centuries, and the vast majority lived in integrated communities, rural and urban. Muslims had accepted the anthem *Bande mataram*, knowing its Bengali origin and that most Bengali Muslims shared heritage and language with Hindus and Buddhists. Hindus regarded the Muslim man-in-the-street as a victim and ally, but generally judged Muslim administrators and the military who were mostly of foreign origin--Mughal, Persian, Arab, Turk --as self-seeking, ambitious, unreliable, devious and insecure; they had abruptly decried the anthem as too "Hindu". (Afghans were of mixed Indian and non-Indian heritage and often not considered "foreign".)

Reaction to British narrow-mindedness, arrogance and the dismissal of INC, perhaps because of its internal disagreements, led to activities which resulted in the arrest of **Lala Lajpat Rai** and **Sardar Ajit Sing** in 1907 and their deportation to Burma. Convinced of British invincibility, **Lord Montagu** in 1908 fulsomely proclaimed, *"The British Raj will not disappear in India so long as the British race remains."*

The *Morley-Minto Act* spread religious divisions down to the lower classes and rural populations previously living in harmony. With the formation of the **Muslim League** in 1906 it made Muslims believe themselves entitled to more of India than their numbers or importance justified; the British might have regretted this outcome but Muslim leaders, who feared loss of power in a unified India grabbed it and promoted it vigorously until the partition although the idea of separate states did not gel until WWII. The *Prevention of Seditious Meetings act, 1911*--Act No. 10 of 22nd March, 1911-- awarded six months in jail +/- a fine in breach of it and effectively shut down meetings. It remained in force until 1927, by which time it had enabled many arbitrary incarcerations and seen another pointless but predictable INC split. No wonder people like Montagu were so convinced that the Indians were too easily divided to ever succeed against them.

British Columbia and **Canada's** abominable treatment of a shipload of Indians (340 Sikhs, 24 Muslims, and 12 Hindus) who had arrived in Vancouver in 1914 on the Japanese ship *Komagata Maru* has become a symbol of the most objectionable elements of racial bigotry and breach of trust as expressed by Canadians and British during and after the event, clearly showing that the phenomenon had existed for a very long time. Two months of imprisonment on board ship at Burrard Inlet, BC and denial of food and water were followed by forced deportation, reflecting the callous disregard for even elementary decency by the highest levels of the "civilised *Christian*" governments of British Columbia and Canada.

Antagonism to brown folk had developed before that. By 1900 there were merely 2000 Indians living in Canada, mostly Punjabis, proud of their British citizenship and more loyal to Britain than to India. As numbers rose and began to include more Hindus (Canadians called all Indians Hindus with generous injections of the epithet "savage") one **H.H. Stevens**, on becoming head of the *Asiatic Exclusion League* in 1907explained the League's mission to keep Canada white, pontificating that *"the destiny of Canada is best left in the hands of the Anglo-Saxon race"*. Exclusionary legislation followed as did sanctions against domiciled Indians, some of whom were Canadians by birth. (They would have to wait nearly fifty years for any semblance of fairness, but equality would elude them to this day.)

The *Komagata Maru* and its passengers were forced out of Burrard inlet on July 23, 1914, except for 24 passengers who were allowed to stay in Canada, because they were returning residents. As the vessel entered Indian waters heading for Calcutta, the British seized and diverted it to an off-shore island. A simple protest on board led to the summary execution by gunfire of many unarmed passengers followed by imprisonment of survivors!

The Revolutionaries: By the time the **Great War** started there were many nests of anti-British revolutionary activity world-wide. The groups included the **Ghadar Party** formed in the USA and British Columbia; the **Hindu–German Conspiracy** in WWI; the **Indian Home Rule Society** (IHRS) in Britain; Japanese and others groups, all seeking Indian independence. The Germans were willing to commit arms in WWI when Indian activists seemed to grasp at any helpful military hand, Germany's foremost; however it petered out. These supplemented civil disruption on Indian soil and attacks on the British with loss of life on both sides. However vigilance by the British and their crafty exploitation of treachery and betrayal by many Indians impeded protests and led to major arrests, imprisonment and execution of revolutionaries including the respected young intellectual leader **Bhadra Jatín** in 1915, age 35.

The Ghadar movement had started among Sikh Punjabi members of the *Hindustani Workers of the Pacific* led by **Har Dayal** and **Sohan Singh Bhakna** to seek Indian independence, by armed revolt if necessary, and urging Indian soldiers to mutiny. The war provided a convenient milieu to canvass support in the USA, India, Germany and elsewhere, through the publication *Hindustan Ghadar* and contacts with prominent militants such as **Rashbihari Bose** and **Taraknath Das** (MA Berkeley, PhD Political Science University of Washington.

Das was a Bengali revolutionary and scholar who had earlier organised Indian migrants on the West Coast in favour of Indian independence.

Once a professor of political science at Columbia University and visiting faculty in several other American universities, he had formed the *Indian Independence League*. Hyndman, Shyamji Krishnavarma and Madame Cāma encouraged Taraknath in his venture. *"To protest against all tyranny is a service to humanity and the duty of civilization."* He had added a strong academic input to the independence struggle and had had discourses with Tolstoy, already well-known for his ideas on non-violent resistance as discussed in *The Kingdom of God Is Within You (1894)*, an exposition of Christ's non-violence. Gandhi too had read this book in South Africa and had discussed ideas and methods at length by correspondence with Tolstoy before his death in 1910.

The **Ghadar Party** (GP) viewed the Congress-led mainstream movement for dominion status as modest and its constitutional methods as soft and ignored Tilak's moderate arguments in favour of the middle ground. The Party preferred a campaign to entice Indian soldiers to revolt and to that end established in November 1913 a press in San Francisco to produce a newspaper and other nationalist literature. Afterwards it established contact with prominent revolutionaries in India. But the group was infiltrated by British spies, especially one Sikh "activist" and when members tried to carry out projects in the Punjab they were quickly arrested by the British and GP was effectively neutralised. At War's end it split along ideological left/right lines and eventually died with India's independence. It was however a valid quest for independence which ran parallel and often counter to the later **Non-Cooperation Movement.**

At this time there were many small groups agitating for Indian independence in Europe and Japan similar to the activities of the Ghadar Party. One, the **Berlin Committee,** had several Indian pro-independence activists including **Maulavi Barkatullah** and **C. R. Pillai** who had teamed with **Kazim Bey**, a Turk, German academic **Oskar Niedermayer** and diplomat **Werner Otto von Hentig**. Led by **Raja Mahendra Pratap** they visited Kabul in 1915 to induce King **Habibullah** to declare independence from Britain. This failed when Habibullah, having accepted a large money grant and arms for an attack against the British, schemed with the latter to resist the attack in exchange for full independence, which was duly granted in 1919.

When the **Bolsheviks** took Russia they too plotted with Indian communists--*the Kamlyk project*--a military assault on the Northwest province of the British Raj to destabilize the area and promote Bolshevism in India; this also failed. These coincided with the rise of **Mahatma Gandhi** and the Khilafat movement which was started by Indian Muslims to protect the Ottoman Empire from dismemberment at the *Treaty of Sèvres* when WWI ended.

It failed and the Ottoman Empire was divided into multiple areas of influence: Britain, France, Italy, Greece and Armenia, while the region around Istanbul and the Bosporus was placed under international control. Turkey was left with the central part. Britain and France secured the lion's share. The seeds of future conflict were thus well sown. In time Turkey would regain most of its territory from Greece, Italy and Armenia and some from France and Britain.

The *Komagata Maru* massacre had been publicised and condemned in India. Yet despite the horror and injustice of these actions the INC at the outbreak of WWI that same year, agreed to support wartime austerities and the recruitment of Indians for the war in exchange for **British guarantees** of constitutional reform, a decision based on an oxymoron widely condemned.

Tilak too had "forgiven" the British and had written King George in support before WWI. But there was no general support for the British commitment of Indian soldiers in WWI. As it happened, over a million Indians fought bravely in many major campaigns in Africa, the Middle East, Italy and France. They distinguished themselves in Ypres, in Flanders, and in Mesopotamia where the foolish Townshend led 12,000 to their deaths against the seasoned Turks. Altogether 36,000 were killed, and 100,000 others injured. India contributed, in cash or kind, some £400,000,000 to Britain for WWI, yet merited barely a footnote in British accounts of that war. Punjabis, who comprised about half of the British Indian Armed forces, were disillusioned and hurt to find on demobilisation that they had reverted to their "native" status while their white counterparts were honoured in many ways.

Gandhi (1869-1948) returned to India in 1915 after years of activism and peaceful protests (*hartal*) in South Africa punctuated by jail terms for civil disobedience (ironically, he was decorated by the British for humanitarian work during the 1899-1902 Boer War and Zulu Rebellion). He had made gains for workers, which he would repeat in India, where he soon became involved in helping rural workers, peasant farmers and urban labour to organise protests against discrimination.

The problem of low prices for produce, poor wages, violence from enforcers working for British landlords, over-taxation and other impositions was then particularly burdensome in **Champaran**, Bihar and **Kheda**, Gujarat, both afflicted with famine, the inevitable consequence of diverting farmland exclusively to the production of commercial cash crops like tobacco, indigo, cotton and opium as dictated originally by the BEICo and continued by the Raj. Indentured workers barely subsisted on eroded wages, in filthy huts in unhygienic villages, riddled with disease, alcoholism, and casteism. Champaran had seen two revolts, both brutally quelled, but public outcry had been ignored.

Gandhi and co-workers in 1917 waged a campaign (*hartal*) of refusal to pay taxes or submit to legal and other threats. They were harassed, assaulted, jailed and otherwise vilified. But resistance did not waver and in time forced the governments of the affected regions to sign agreements suspending taxation in times of famine, allowing farmers to grow crops of their own choice and get increased pay for crops. Political prisoners were released and all seized property and lands returned. It was the biggest victory against the British since the American Revolution. Gandhi, although Gujarati, had cleverly left his Gujarati colleague **Sardar Vallabhbhai Patel**, to lead the Kheda action; Patel proved an excellent choice and later became Gandhi's closest associate. Champaran and Kheda were the first major breaks in the post-Tilak period and propelled Gandhi to forefront[102]. Grateful farmers dubbed him *Bapu* and *Mahatma*. Gandhi joined the INC and persuaded it to non-violence and non-cooperation.

---

[102] Gandhi was influenced by Jain and Hindu values and ideas of foreign forerunners in this movement, from antiquity, and more recent exponents, including PB Shelley and HD Thoreau. He often quoted Shelley, who, appalled by the British massacre of peacefully assembled citizens at Manchester's St Peter's field in 1819 immediately wrote a stark condemnation in this poem on Passive Resistance *The Masque of Anarchy* 1819 ending segments with *"Ye are many, they are few."* The following stanza succinctly reflects the doctrine of peaceful defiance, which must have been in Gandhi's mind as he rallied his forces: *"Stand ye calm and resolute/Like a forest close and*

Jallianwallah Bagh Massacre: By this time the **Indian National Congress** had existed for over 30 years; it had reunited moderate and militant factions and expected the British to keep their promises of reform. But when the War ended they added salt to Indian wounds with the passing of the *Rowlatt Act* in 1919, despite opposition, which extended the 1915 war emergency measures, a shameful and treacherous imposition that postponed indefinitely any discussion of plans for Indian self-government. It is claimed to have become a necessary security tool because of the threats of military uprisings in India.

But the Act suppressed legal protest also by jailing leaders and "wrong-doers". In one incident in Amritsar on April 10, 1919 two Punjabi leaders **Drs Saifuddin Kichloo** and **Satyapal** were seized and deported by a deputy district commissioner **Miles Irving**. Gandhi had travelled to Amritsar to join the protest but was arrested at the provincial border and ordered back to Bombay by the lieutenant governor of Punjab, the hated despot **Michael O'Dwyer**. The followers of the arrested men marched to Irving's camp to demand their release, but met fire from British troops; several were killed. This led to a riot in which several British men died, two women were attacked and banks burned.

At this time the city of Amritsar was busy preparing for the annual *Vaishaki*[103] and Sikh *Kalsa*[104] celebrations and thousands had come to the city to participate. On April 13th nearly 10,000 people had assembled in Jallianwallah Bagh, an enclosed square, and co-incidentally became part of a peaceful protest against British action against the Indian leaders.

On Sunday April 13, a few days after the riot, **Gen. R. Dyer** arrived from Jullundur with a brigade to assist O'Dwyer and without warning or reason penned the essentially peaceful crowd in the Bagh and ordered his men to open fire "to preclude the spread of mutiny", having decided to shoot even before he had reached the Bagh! Dyer admitted to this in hearings of the **Hunter Committee,** and **Churchill** confirmed it in a speech to Parliament in July 1920.

The number killed varies from a minimum of near 400 to thousands. The British physician on the spot claimed the number to be 1,800, including women and children, and over 1,200 wounded.

This act was condemned worldwide, but hardly fazed the British Raj. But it left indelible marks on the tender minds of several youths who had joined the *Non-Cooperation Movement,* among them **Bhagat Singh** and colleagues and **Udham Singh**, who would go on to become martyrs in the cause of freedom, Udham by killing Gen. Michael O'Dwyer on March 13, 1940 in London having stalked him for years. It is clear that O'Dwyer was fully aware of Dyer's plan to shoot without provocation having said earlier that it was time *"to teach the Indians a lesson, to make a wide impression and to strike terror through-out Punjab"*.

The Hunter Committee in 1920 censured Dyer for a "mistaken concept of duty". Parliament fired Dyer but a London paper, the *Morning Post,* declared him

---

mute,/With folded arms and looks which are/Weapons of unvanquished war." Gandhi was followed by many in Europe, America and Africa; little has changed in human interaction and tyranny gets worse, at times more subtle as mercantilism spreads.

This account re the Gandhi era is drawn from experiences of Indian physicians at the Georgetown Hospital, who hailed from all major regions of India and had anecdotal or direct experiences of the events.

[103]This is an ancient harvest festival marking the first day of *Vaisakh*, in the *Nanakshahi* solar calendar, (April 14th).

[104] *Kalsa* means "Servants of God", founded by the tenth Sikh Guru Gobind Singh in 1699.

"the saviour of India" and raised £26,000 for him, a third coming from India! By Christmas a group of Anglophile Indians formed the *National Liberation Federation*, which soon failed. The Raj created and maintained to the end a consultative **Council of Princes**, whose members generally favoured the Raj in their roles as impotent subsidiary allies.

In 1920 **Chakravarti Vijayaraghavachariar** (1852-1944) — a Tamil politician, friend of Allan Octavian Hume and a founding member of the Indian National Congress--became INC President. He helped draft its constitution, and felt that the Congress should be political with economic and general social aims, while others opted short-sightedly for politics only. He helped frame the *Swaraj Constitution.*

In 1921 Gandhi became head of the INC with the goal of *Swaraj* (self-rule) by the process of *civil disobedience* or *Satyagraha* (soul force), which he had used in South Africa and the Egyptians against the British in 1919 to force independence (1922). Gandhi soon began to attract members from the ordinary citizenry thus changing the character of Congress from an elitist to a mass movement. He spread the resistance country-wide aiming at several goals: national unity and solidarity; religious tolerance; reduction of poverty; restoration of individual self-reliance and of Indian village life that had once made the nation prosperous; expansion of women's rights; an end to untouchability to bring dignity and rights to those affected, whom he called *harijans* (God's children), much to the displeasure of **Dr. B.R. Ambhedkar,** a Dalit member of Congress and a highly respected lawyer and economist.

Among many nationwide rallies one at **Chauri Chaura** ended badly. Protesters were stirred up by police assaults and shooting of stragglers dispersing from a rally; the crowd ahead saw the carnage and turned on the attackers who retreated to their station *(chowki)* which was then set afire; 23 men died, either from burns or from attacks while trying to escape. Gandhi concluded that the deaths would weaken the philosophical basis of his protest (truth and non-violence) and called off the *Non-Cooperation Movement* which had been in place for two years, had attracted a wide following and had put great pressures on the government to the extent that many saw imminent victory.

Moreover the NCM had taught discipline, solidarity and sacrifice as tools in resistance and showed that the masses had high motivation, stamina and courage; NCM had taken politics from upper crust city parlours into rural huts and villages. But the suggestion has been made that the Chauri Chaura affair had been engineered by British Police to frame Indians and provide the excuse for reprisals against leaders, the enabling legislation and a justification to Parliament. British tacticians frequently used this type of trickery throughout the Empire to embarrass or quell opposition.

Militants also pointed to the brutal suppression of Ghadars and Sikhs, wholesale imprisonments and unknown losses of lives in jails, secret places by firing squads, the rape of the Indian economy to help finance WWI and the Jallianwallah Bagh massacre of innocents. Infuriated leaders organised many protests including a "*hartal*" on April 6 when Indians stopped all business and fasted in protest (Rowlatt *Satyagraha*). Protests increased and resulted in several incidents of fighting, in breach of the principle of *ahimsa*. The British responded in character, killing many, jailing more, including Gandhi.

Motilal Nehru criticised the suspension of NCM as it effectively relieved the British, and members demanded a change in policy. With Gandhi imprisoned a split developed between those who wished to continue passive resistance ("no-changers" R Prasad, V. Patel and Gandhi) and the more militant members who wished change ("pro-changers" M. Nehru and C.R. Das). The latter started the *Swarajya Party* to contest elections in accordance with the 1919 *Government of India Act*. M. Nehru opined, *"The truth is we cannot get anything from England except by proving our strength,"* suggesting that the British would only yield to military defeat, and citing their continuing treachery, plots, spying and breaches of agreement.

Disagreeing with the idea and not wanting to appear to be cooperating with the oppressor, Gandhi resigned to allow room for free debate among the disparate political and economic camps, from conservatives of all kinds and bureaucrats to socialists, labour unions, student radicals and communists. By this time the Bolsheviks had taken control of Russia and socialism was spreading across Europe. Many younger Indians, INC members and other militants, had made contacts with Marxists and studied their philosophy and methods and keenly promoted the armed overthrow of the Raj: in this spirit they carried out actions like those of the *Anushilan Samiti* and Punjab's *Ghadar Party*.

Gandhi was released from prison in 1922 because of appendicitis. He remained irrevocably on the side of non-violence just as Motilal and Das were diametrically opposed. Responding to criticism and pressure the Viceroy's *Repressive Laws Committee* in March 1922 repealed the Rowlatt Act, press censorship and over twenty other pieces of legislation, perhaps goaded by the Chauri Chaura incident of the previous month and the festering discontent everywhere and periodic outbursts of frustration or rage. Regrouping quickly and deploying forces of the Raj or a subsidiary, Police began reprisals against Indian leaders. The retaliatory militancy was not surprising and might have been what the British wanted, and Gandhi rejected. The *Swarajya Party* contested elections in 1923 and became the opposition facing a majority of British appointees and bureaucrats. But they only managed to delay finance and a few measures.

In Bengal the *Hindustan Republican Association* (HRA) was formed as an offshoot of *Anushilan Samiti*. Among the leaders were **Pratul Ganguly** (later a member of the Bengal Legislature), Narendra Mohan Sen, and Sachindra Nath Sānyāl, who famously argued with Gandhi opposing his gradualist approach to independence. HRA's manifesto noted *"...Official terrorism is surely to be met by counter terrorism. A spirit of utter helplessness pervades every stratum of our society and terrorism is an effective means of restoring the proper spirits in the society..."* but promised to refrain from terrorism for terrorism's sake, and use it only *"...when expediency will demand it..."* Its aims included universal suffrage and religious freedom. It had a socialist orientation and drew inspiration from Bolshevism.

Chandrasekhar Tiwari (Azad, 1906-31), his close associate **Bhagat Singh** (1907-31), a militant Sikh and others changed the HRA into the *Hindustan Socialist Republican Association* **(HSRA)**. Bhagat, although a Sikh, was educated in a Vaidic school because his father, an Arya Samajist active in the *Ghadar Party* along with two brothers, rejected the pro-British education of the Sikh school for his son, as so many other Indians had done in response to Gandhi's call. He later attended a high school founded by **Lala Lajpat Rai.** Bhagat later studied communist writers and became an atheist.

Frustrated with the lack of progress and needing money to purchase arms several HRA members organized a train robbery at the town of Kākori in 1925.

The incident is notorious for the publicity, the excessive severity of the sentences: five executions--**Swaran Singh,** uncle of Bhagat Singh, **Ram Prasad Bismil, Ashfaqullah Khan, Rajendra Lahiri** and **Roshan Singh--** and several life sentences, and the involvement of most of the leadership of the INC in their defence, headed by **Govind Ballabh Pant**, later Chief Minister of the United Provinces. The Viceroy, **Lord Irwin**, denied many appeals for clemency. **Jogesh Chandra Chatterjee,** a member of *Anushilan Samiti,* received a short sentence of ten years. (On release, he became an INC member, left to form his own Party then re-joined and became a member of the Rajya Sabha, serving until his death in 1969).

The *Simon Commission* had been appointed in 1927 to probe Indian political reform, yet without a single Indian member and incredibly denied any testimony from Indian politicians! Its boycott was understandably countrywide, supported by Jinnah, and provoked demonstrations. Police in Lahore attacked one of these in 1928 and beat **Lala Rai** to death. **Bhagat Singh, Shivarām Rājguru, Sukhdev Thāpar** and **Jai Gopāl,** in seeking to avenge his death, mistakenly killed a deputy superintendent named **Saunders** instead of the target, Police Chief Scott. They escaped. Sometime later Bhagat was arrested and sentenced for life after a bombing incident at the Central Legislative Assembly in New Delhi. When Police arrested others from the HSRA for bomb making, some among them identified Bhagat as Saunders' killer which led to his conviction and execution along with Rajguru and Thāpar.

Motilal Nehru, President of the INC in 1928, headed a group whose draft constitution demanded Dominion status such as Canada's within one year. In the previous year Jawaharlal Nehru had moved a motion demanding "complete national independence", which Gandhi had opposed because he did not require full independence. The Muslim league and the Liberal Party rejected Motilal Nehru's report. Jinnah's 1929 report was also rejected.

The **Raj** justified most of its rejections claiming wide support from "responsible" Indians; these were nearly all self-interest groups dependent on British favour or cash such as the *Council of Princes*, businessmen, industrialists, zamindars, Christian converts, Anglo-Indians, a few intellectuals, British residents, officials and others with scores to settle, exploiting the British propensity and willingness to pay for alliance and loyalty. Most had organised in 1910 as the pro-British *Liberal Party* although some of its key members supported independence within the Empire and rejected Partition. Most of the Indians had broken away from the INC when Tilak and colleagues had begun to talk in radical and militant terms.

Zāmindars and city employers fattening off low-paid labour felt that empowering rural folk was a mistake as the masses were ignorant (meaning unschooled, not stupid, but that was quickly changeable) and might expect more from a vote than just the emotional agreement to choose someone they liked whether able or not. For this reason, they said, olden democracies had enfranchised only those with something to lose: property owners, the educated and the aristocracy.

These men feared that rural folk taught to protest effectively in the promotion of *Swaraj* and to seek restoration of the *panchayat raj* (village governing councils) might believe that success would free them from taxation (cf. Jagan's following among BG estate workers). Others believed that it was essential for persons to own property in order to safeguard the condition of the masses.[105] By this view every farmer should regain the vote, which ancient Indians had at their village councils. An education programme could supply the knowledge base to change perceptions, broaden horizons and inculcate in people *critical thinking* on political issues without which the franchise is a waste, despite wealth or status.

Jawaharlal Nehru, a charismatic and radical leader, had become fully established as in the van of the left wing of the Congress Party, and had risen under the mentorship of Mahatma Gandhi to the position of Congress President in 1929-30, (also 1936-37 and 1951-54). He had opposed his father's acceptance of dominion status and willingness to seek office in the Central legislature, advocating instead complete independence from British Imperialism. His main rival as successor to Gandhi was Vallabhai Patel, the ailing but to many the superior candidate. Throughout his life, Nehru was also an advocate of **Fabian socialism** and saw the public sector as the means by which an impoverished nation could address and overcome chronic economic exploitation and under-development. His appreciation of the virtues of parliamentary democracy, secularism and liberalism, coupled with his concerns for the underprivileged and poor are recognised to have guided socialist policies that influence India to this day (1964).

On Dec 23, 1929 Viceroy Irwin met with Gandhi, Nehru, Patel, Jinnah and Tegh Bahadur Sapru (Liberal) to develop a plan for Dominion status which by this time was rejected by all activists and only considered as a last resort and even then a *very last* resort. The Government ignored the INC position, buoyed by the support of their toady, the *Council of Princes*, the minority *Liberals* and the *Muslim League*. However, Indian independence was inevitable, regardless of how many favoured the British. Only the path and method to sovereignty remained undecided. Dayānanda's critique of the Maharaja of Jaipur could have applied to any prince! The Nizam of Hyderabad (dubbed "The Faithful" by Victoria and given a plaque) basked in the positive publicity he received from the British on whom he lavished gifts in peace and war, including planes and a warship, spending millions that were diverted from the education, health and infrastructure for the poor mega-millions under his rule (see footnote 55). Most others had lost lands, prestige and power--only 120 of the 570 or more headed *"salute"* states i.e. meriting a gun salute between 9 and 21-- and commanded little more than local traditional allegiances. Few had shown either interest or vision to throw off their yoke. By 1900 they had become mere lackeys of the British.

Eight days later, at midnight on December 31, 1929, the Congress, led by Gandhi and Jawaharlal Nehru, raised a national tricolour flag in Lahore and published the **Declaration of Independence (Purna Swaraj** or complete self-rule) on January 26, 1930. The declaration included, inter alia, the readiness to withhold taxes, defy forest laws and stop doing business with the British etc.

The declaration included this statement: *"We believe that it is the inalienable right of the Indian people, as of any other people, to have freedom and to enjoy the fruits of their toil and have the necessities of life, so that they may have full opportunities for*

---

[105] In *Rerum Novarum* (1891), *paragraph 16* Leo XIII "the main tenet of socialism, that is community of goods, is directly contrary to the natural rights of mankind...The first and most fundamental principle, therefore, if one would undertake to alleviate the condition of the masses, must be the inviolability of private property."

growth. We believe also that if any government deprives a people of these rights and oppresses them the people have a further right to alter it or abolish it. The British government in India has not only deprived the Indian people of their freedom but has based itself on the exploitation of the masses, and has ruined India economically, politically, culturally and spiritually. We believe therefore, that India must sever the British connection and attain Purna Swaraj or complete independence."

Satyagraha: J. Nehru became INC President in 1929. The Working Committee of the INC assigned Gandhi the decision to choose a protest action. He decided to galvanise and unite the independence movement on a *Satyagraha* basis and chose to assail British hegemony by marching 240 miles from Ahmedabad to Dandi beach on the Arabian Sea in Gujarat. Gandhi's choice of *Salt Satyagraha* mystified his colleagues, even his closest comrades Patel and Nehru who were perhaps too polite or shocked to question his sanity as many did; Viceroy Irwin scoffed, declaring that he would lose no sleep over it and the pro-British press and Liberals openly chuckled. Patel wondered about boycotting land revenue instead.

But Gandhi had chosen well. Indians had never been forced to pay for salt or denied its harvesting; it was freely available in Gujarat as a "gift from God". Everyone used it, every day, from the lowliest to the mightiest among all people and all religions. As Gandhi said, "Next to air and water, salt is perhaps the greatest necessity of life" in a climate that sweats!

The **1882 Salt Act** was one of Lord Ripon's negative achievements and sullied his rule. The Act made it suddenly illegal and criminal for anyone other than the British Government to harvest and sell salt, which was then taxed and brought in 8.2% of the British Raj's total tax revenue, a huge amount "stolen" from the poorest Indians. The Act was seen as denial of a common birthright and turned a natural resource and a free general necessity into a trading commodity, whereas *before* only the labour to harvest commanded a price. Salt manufacture as a cottage industry abruptly died and workers became employees of the state under conditions of near slavery and earned much less than they had done as independents. Many defied the ban, were arrested, fined and/or imprisoned; some were even killed.

This shameful extortion of a poor man's resource had lasted nearly four decades, impoverished the coastal people and had been almost forgotten among the numerous similar seizures of Indian sources of living. Salt manufacture was not an occupation for Brahmins nor princes! Gandhi's unique perspective on people and his place among them allowed a superior appreciation of issues. He was one of them, not above them, a position that seemed to have obscured the vision of Motilal with all his heart, Tagore with his intellect or Jawaharlal with his conscience. None of the proffered alternatives had the same high impact. To their credit the INC Working Committee allowed the March despite doubts and soon enough was singing an opposite tune. Gandhi's entourage swelled with each mile. The March took from 12 March to 6 April 1930, by which time hundreds of thousands had joined him. "It seemed as though a spring had been suddenly released." J. Nehru remarked.

C. Rajagopalachari understood Gandhi's viewpoint. Publicly he commented, "Suppose a people rise in revolt. They cannot attack the abstract constitution or lead an army against proclamations and statutes...Civil disobedience has to be directed against the salt tax or the land tax or some other particular point—not that that is our final end, but for the time being it is our aim, and we must shoot straight." The British were dumb-founded. Lord Irwin not only lost sleep over it but came close to losing his seat! Britain responded by arresting Gandhi and imprisoning over 60,000 people!

The Committee concluded plans for follow-up and Gandhi's replacement as his action was under current laws punishable by imprisonment. In those tumultuous years it seemed that the British would hastily pass knee jerk laws banning every criticism or right an Indian citizen had, blissfully abandoning the principles of fair play and justice in society and freedom of speech and association which Englishmen were wont to tout as their unique inventions that they claimed had made them a superior nation; but in India such rights were applicable only to whites! Surprisingly the British detained Nehru in March, Abdul G Khan in April and Gandhi only after skirmishes had taken place in Peshawar, Punjab and Chittagong, Bengal. Each was jailed for six months.

The following extract from **Hansard,** July 1930 is instructive: *"The chief event of the week has been the declaration of the All-India Congress Working Committee as unlawful association under the Criminal Law Amendment Act. The Committee consists, at full strength, of about 15 persons. For a considerable period they have been playing a prominent part in organising and directing the civil disobedience movement. Not only have they passed a number of resolutions urging the public to defy the law and to refuse payment of taxes, but they have circulated widely an incitement to the troops and the police to fail in their duty in dealing with the Civil Disobedience Movement. Simultaneously with the notification of the Committee, the President, Pandit Moti Lal Nehru, and the secretary, were arrested, and were subsequently sentenced to six months' simple imprisonment each. Following on this action there were hartals in various towns, but many of them were incomplete and there have been no clashes between the authorities and the public. Popular demonstrations have been most marked in Bombay City, where conditions continue to be unsatisfactory, and the mill-hands suspended work for two days. The day before the Committee was notified a meeting was held, the results of which have now been reported in the Press. A number of resolutions were passed, the general sense of which was to urge the continuance of the Civil Disobedience Movement with increasing vigour. The Committee confirmed the resolution inciting the troops and police to fail in their duty, reference to which has been made above, and they urged all Congress organisations to give the widest publicity to it, in spite of the fact that the resolution had been proscribed under the Criminal Law.*

§ *"During the week the Governor-General promulgated an ordinance for the purpose of controlling effectively the seditious bulletins and news sheets which, since the issue of the Press Ordinance, have been published in many places in deliberate defiance of the law. These bulletins consist largely of falsehoods and misrepresentations, and their object is to stir up racial and anti-Government feelings. In spite of the vigorous activities of the Congress, the situation shows distinct signs of improvement in several directions, as already noted. The position on the frontier is rapidly returning to normal. In parts of Gujarat there are indications that the movement is losing some of its vigour, and most of the Provinces report a slackening of effort. The conviction that the Civil Disobedience Movement cannot succeed is growing and commercial and industrial circles are showing increasing concern regarding the dangerous consequences of its continuance. There is an increase in constructive effort towards a constitutional solution of political problems, and Muhammadans (sic), in particular, are devoting much thought and attention to the presentation of their case at the London Conference. While the situation, therefore, has still many unstable elements, these are not so numerous or so pronounced as a few weeks ago."*

Motilal Nehru died on February 6, 1931, gratified that Jawaharlal and Gandhi had come to see him in his last days. A month later Viceroy Irwin met with Gandhi and agreed to free political prisoners once civil disobedience was halted, and allowed Gandhi to attend the *Round Table Conference* on India in London, but this failed to address major issues, and did little for constitutional advancement. Irwin gave way to **Lord Willingdon** who, when Governor of Bombay Presidency, had met Gandhi in 1915 and had called him a *Bolshevik*. He immediately turned the clock back by re-arresting Gandhi but failed to deter him or the inexorable *Swaraj* campaign; three attempts were made on Gandhi's life, of uncertain instigation.

When the **Government of India Act, 1935** granted Indians limited self-rule INC won a majority of seats and formed ministries in six provinces, initiating **Congress Raj**. Bengal was the only province with a Muslim government secured as a coalition with a pro-British group. Gandhi returned to active politics in 1936 with Nehru as president and head of the parliamentary majority. The intractability of the Muslim position led Congress--itself prone to factionalism--to decline coalition governments with AIML in several provinces.

Subhas Chandra Bose became President in 1938 and clashed with Gandhi over policy regarding the path to independence, Gandhi insisting on non-violence while Bose had more faith in armed alliances then being pursued with Japan and Germany. As war began Bose and the Congress government resigned *en masse* over Britain's unilateral decision to drag India into the war without informing Congress. They accused the British of hypocrisy in declaring Nazis tyrants when they were just as tyrannical or worse in India and had already been responsible for killing scores of millions of Indians. Refusing India its independence, while "fighting for democracy" in Europe was disingenuous and disgraceful, not just a paradox. Gandhi had earlier given Britain qualified "non-violent" support but sided with the INC and withdrew it. The AIML remained solid in Britain's support.

Gandhi intensified the call for independence and in 1942 the INC passed a *Quit India* resolution to which Churchill responded by arresting half of India, killing thousands and imprisoning *hundreds* of thousands, refusing even to allow relief to reach famine-starved millions of eastern India (see Ch. 4, footnote 3). Gandhi replied with a "do or die" declaration to gain freedom. He and his Working Committee were imprisoned-- interestingly enough at the Aga Khan's Palace in Puné--from 1942 to 1944, along with his secretary, **Mahadev Desai** and his wife **Kasturba Gandhi.** Desai died from a heart attack six days after entering the prison and 18 months later Kasturba also died in prison. Gandhi fell ill with fever, probably Malaria, soon after and was released to undergo surgery later that year.

That same year talks with Jinnah led nowhere despite Gandhi's offer to the Muslims of 25% of the Indian constituencies although they comprised less than 15% of the populace; relations hardened despite many efforts to regain unity. Jinnah remained adamantly opposed to the *Quit India* ideas and a **One-India** solution, contrary to the position of the influential *Jama'iat e Ulama Hind*, the highest-ranking Islamic religious body in British India but obviously without the same clout as Jinnah's pro-British team. *(Jain snidely remarked that Gandhi should have taken Jinnah to a high-end pub in Mayfair, London, for the crucial talks,)*

Partition: WWII ended with a Labour Government in power in the UK thus assuring India imminent independence. Britain was broke and had mortgaged India and the entire Empire to the Rothschilds' delight! Gandhi ceased *Quit India* actions; INC leaders and over 100,000 political prisoners were released. Churchill had lost to the "naked fakir" after all, and he did preside over the Empire's trip to the brink, leaving Attlee the final pleasure of pushing it over in three segments! He however did have a revenge of sorts in supporting the creation of Pakistan by combining India's Muslim majority regions, east and west.

India's division was not a surprise. After years of working with the INC, a few powerful Muslims, led by **Sir Sultan Mohammed Shah, Aga Khan III,** had formed in 1906 the *All India Muslim League* **in Dhaka (AIML).** As President he declared the League a political party seeking only Islamic interests to counter the united pan-religious stance of the INC, of which Muslims remained members.

Unrest had been building since 1930 since **Iqbal's motion**[106] for a separate state. It is possible that the future of the sub-continent had already been decided in 1909 with the Morley-Minto "Reforms" when Minto, an anti-Hindu demagogue, allowed Muslims a separate electorate and other favours to Shah including legislative nominees and a disproportionate number of seats in future governments. But Jinnah had remained overtly in favour of "One India".

However his antagonism to Hindus that had increased through the previous decade was difficult to understand, despite his back-sliding over the years on issues previously agreed with his INC colleagues. He was an early member of the INC and in 1913 he and GK Gokhale had journeyed together to Britain and founded the *London Indian Association*. He did not join the AIML until 1915 and almost immediately moved to establish a joint committee of Congress and the League to bring about Hindu-Muslim unity. The result was the *Lucknow Pact* which brought the two organisations together, credit to Tilak and Jinnah, to pressure the British.

The Pact healed many breaches between Hindus and Muslims until the twenties when various forces worked to weaken and ultimately destroy it. Differences with Gandhi on the *Non-Cooperation Movement* led to Jinnah's resignation from the Congress in 1920, some alleging that he was pressured by Anti-Hindu Muslims who would benefit from further favoured treatment through the *Montagu-Chelmsford Act* of 1919, and resented Gandhi's Indian-ness, his simple clothing and life style, in stark contrast to the highly Westernised Jinnah and other AIML officials. The AIML at its 1929 Delhi session adopted Jinnah's views and rejected M. Nehru's critique of the Simon Commission. Relations further soured when the INC failed to endorse Jinnah's position, the so-called Fourteen Points. Rifts developed in 1929 between Jinnah and the Nehrus over the *Simon Commission*, which both organisations had boycotted as it excluded Indians. The religious groups which so many had worked so

---

[106] On a visit to India and Bangladesh in 1974 (as a Commonwealth Fellow) I met many officials and ex-officials, one--a retired Muslim physician in Dhaka who had been in the All India Muslim League and had treated riot victims-- gave me this quotation from *Speeches and Statements of Iqbal* A.R. Tariq ed. Lahore, 1973: *"I would like to see Punjab, North-West Frontier Province, Sindh and Baluchistan amalgamated into a single state. Self-government within the British Empire or without the British Empire, the formation of a consolidated North-West Indian Muslim state appears to me to be the final destiny of the Muslims, at least of North-West India."* Iqbal, whom he knew well, really wished a Muslim state in the northwest as a self-governing *part of a strong federated India*, perhaps a buffer from new invaders, not a separate nation. Tara Chand's *History of Freedom Movement in India* Vol. III, 253, New Delhi 1972, corroborates this.

diligently to unite were now targeting each other, some say surreptitiously organised and facilitated by British commercial interests, using the resources of the Raj. Jinnah's subsequent 1934 election as Permanent President of AIML cemented his withdrawal from the INC and the League's position against a unified India.

Jinnah's speech at the League session at Lahore in 1940 argued for separation, based on the irreconcilability of the two *religions*. In 1943 he presided over AIML's Karachi session and fired up the crowd, saying: "We have got millions behind us; we have got our flag and our platform; and what is more we have now the definite goal of Pakistan." His tour of India raised a storm, a proper jihad!

Jinnah and AIML may well have been puppets manipulated by an entrenched Islamic aristocracy. Division can be traced in the writings and career of **Saeed Ameer Ali**, a Muslim jurist who had founded the ***Central National Mohamedan Association*** in Calcutta in 1877 urging Muslims to take advantage of English education then becoming available as Hindu leaders established schools (*see above*). Like the Aga Khan (Sultan Mohamed Shah) Ali was staunchly loyal to the British, perhaps recognizing in them the same acquisitive qualities possessed by his own ancestors who had also come to India to pillage, get rich and spread Islam at the expense of Hindus. He was instrumental in securing separate electorates for Muslims and was active in the AIML until his death in 1928.

Before him **Sayyid (Syed) Ahmed Khan** had urged Muslims to secure a British education and had founded a college in Allahabad which would become **the Muslim Aligarh University**; he vigorously promoted the cause of Islam, supported the Muslim League but hypocritically suggested that the Indian National Congress--a nonreligious body led by tolerant Hindus--was not to be trusted! To his credit he did blame the British East India Company for the 1857 war accusing them of arrogance and failure to study Indian culture, understanding which might have spared them needless blunders and bogus conclusions in their administrative orders. For this the Secretary of State for India reflexly wished to cite him for sedition, even if he had to pass a new law to do that! Khan was perhaps the earliest influential voice for separation of Muslims from Hindus. **Mushtaq Hussain** (1841-1917), Nawab Waqar-ul-Mulk Kamboh (Kamboja), was a founder of the AIML and credited with inducing Jinnah to join. **Khwaja Salimullah Bahadur,** a contemporary and fellow founder supported the partition of Bengal.

These were a small though powerful sample of the many rich and well-placed Muslim relics of the Mughal past who, as the AIML, led the move to fracture India. They were landowners, lawyers, bureaucrats, businessmen and military officers nurtured by the **Raj** and paraded conveniently at *durbars* as representatives of *Indians*. While the majority of Muslims were Indian converts these men were largely of remote Mughal, Arab, Persian, Turkic and other non-Indian descent with privileges under the Mughals and British and eager to maintain or gain high office after independence.

Fearing dilution of their powers in a free India they had begun a campaign of intrigue and civil destabilisation currying favour with successive Viceroys of India, gaining preferment from the more virulent of these, notably, Curzon and Minto. The schism they promoted was a disappointing development for the beleaguered forces of Indian unity and a sad prelude to the intrigues that had led to Mohamed Iqbal's 1930 proposal for a separate Muslim state, which Jinnah, up to then a promoter of a *One India* policy surprisingly and suddenly, or so it seemed, enlarged to mean **Partition** in 1939, which he promoted with vigour and achieved with threats and a bloody *Direct Action* program.

When asked to explain Jinnah retorted: "*Go to the Congress and ask them their plans. When they take you into their confidence I will take you into mine. Why do you expect me alone to sit with folded hands? I also am going to make trouble.*" Earlier he had argued that India was not *a nation*, thus invoking a nationalist feeling was irrational; India was several distinct nations and cultures, socially, spiritually and by religion; they must find unique solutions which could only happen peacefully in separate states. The pros and cons are buried in time.

Between late 1945 and Feb 1946 the British court-martialled three members of the armed forces--Colonels **G.S. Dhillon, Prem Sahgal** and **Major General S.N. Khan** who had joined the INA and fought with Japanese forces. National protests had united Hindus and Muslims giving some hope of political rapprochement. Although convicted their sentences were commuted in fear of an Army-wide revolt especially when the Royal Indian Navy mutinied in Bombay and Karachi against poor conditions and racism of white officers. But the unity quickly dissipated in the terrors of *Direct Action* Day.

Inflammatory press reports stoked violence much as they had done in BG in 1962, except that in BG the reports were largely one-sided. The Muslim President of Bengal declared the pre-determined *Direct Action Day* a holiday which Muslims observed but Hindus did not, thus laying their businesses wide open to the goons, men with grudges, religious fanatics, and assorted riff-raff wielding *lathis* and other weapons, fired up by the exhortations of **Jinnah** and other partisan demagogues. They terrorised urban and rural areas creating bedlam that ran the gamut of violence from personal attacks to looting, arson, riot and murders; In Bengal word had leaked out that the Police would look sideways! When a lull came, the Hindu press placed the dead in thousands but the Muslims denied any fatalities!

Lord Mountbatten with Attlee's approval had supervised the debacle and ignored the entreaties of strong delegations opposed to partition. **Attlee** as Prime Minister had shown little interest in India beyond its socialist leaders. When unrest among militants was growing in Indian cities he had chosen to withdraw troops from the country leaving a mere skeleton to deal with the disasters that followed. At about the same time he withdrew troops from Palestine leading directly to the success of Zionist terrorism under the Irgun, Stern Gang and other groups and could be blamed for the bitter feuds between Palestinians and Jews that shame humanity to this day.) Attlee had claimed that the cost of maintaining troops in these areas was too high, blithely overlooking the fact that India had contributed more than enough in the past and to the Allies in WWII, and did not merit desertion at a time of crisis.

It helped little that Attlee had sent **Sir Stafford Cripps** as head of a rather lightweight delegation[107] to conduct the crucial negotiations among the parties. As Chair, Cripps spent more energy at meetings grandstanding instead of diplomatic negotiation. His approach ridiculously followed British policy of

---

[107] Gandhi, addressing a youngish British delegate, marvelled sarcastically that such an untried mind could deign to carry out policies that demeaned and exploited people, "not in any subtle way, you understand, but overtly".

'divide and rule' at a time when unity was sought. His actions, Attlee's apathy and British lack of a strong policy allowed divisions to deepen between Hindus and Muslims, despite Gandhi's agreeing to a guarantee of excess seats in the Indian Parliament for Muslims. The Muslim League had demanded a third while Sāvarkar had insisted on one man, one vote. It is said that partition suited British policy as it created two entities which could, for trade and aid, be played one against the other in the up-coming jockeying for bilateral preferences. By see-sawing support, the British could keep India and Pakistan on a leash. Stafford Cripps (parodied then as *Stifford Craps*) may not have been that crass after all.

Partition was not easy for India because Hindus and most Muslims shared original Hindu roots, and while those who historically had resisted conversion to Islam might have resented their fellows who did, relationships had largely survived by virtue of traditional habits, occupations and practices. Yet partition led to a holocaust of murder and pillage which was largely avoidable had the political forces been less inept. The decision cost millions of lives in senseless massacres mainly in Pakistan where a strange madness plunged people into a frenzy of religious chauvinism as leaders uncertain of their positions fumbled and failed to stem the fury they had unleashed.

Gandhi's insistence on placating Muslims, his failure to recognize Pakistan's territorial ambitions and failure to heed advice and swiftly repel its advance into Kashmir were seen as grave oversight and a weakness and he was assassinated on January 30, 1948 by a disgruntled journalist, **Nathuram Godse**, allegedly to support the militant views of **Sāvarkar** who had advocated armed rebellion against the British and had supported Indian recruitment for WWII as it would allow men to be trained in the use of modern arms, so far denied them in India. Indians he argued had become too soft. By the time India counter-attacked in Kashmir and a cease-fire was agreed, Pakistan had occupied the key northern parts, yet India accepted an unfavourable new line of control in 1948, supervised by the UN[108]. A stale-mate resulted and tensions have remained high along the line. Jinnah died on 9/11/1948.

Shortly before Gandhi's death, Nehru had become the first Prime Minister of independent India. Nehru's appreciation of parliamentary democracy coupled with concerns for the underprivileged and poor enabled him to pursue an essentially moderate socialist agenda and one of *"positive neutrality"* as the **Cold War** raged. He became a key spokesman for the non-aligned countries of

---

[108] The British Minister in charge of Indo-Pakistan affairs in 1947-8 Philip J. Noel Baker took an anti-Indian stance in the United Nations contrary to instructions from Attlee's Government. The Americans, led by Secretary of State George Marshall, were pro-Indian and accepted Kashmir as legally part of India. Noel-Baker, however, misrepresented the US and Indian positions to his Government while persuading the US to float a UN draft resolution allowing Pakistan to send troops into Kashmir if India agreed. He was reprimanded by Prime Minister Clement Attlee in a remarkable "Top Secret and Personal" telegram: *"I find it very hard to reconcile the view which you express as to the attitude of the Indian delegation with the representations I have received through the High Commissioner from India here. It appears to me that all the concessions are being asked from India while Pakistan concedes little or nothing….The attitude still seems to be that it is India which is at fault whereas the complaint was rightly lodged against Pakistan."* Zafarullah Khan, Pakistan's legate, had argued that Pakistani raiders in Kashmir were not "raiders" but seekers of justice, peace, and the people's will (which he was reminded had already been expressed by Kashmir's choice to join India)! In November 1948, the acting leader of the US delegation in the Security Council, John Foster Dulles, complained to the State Department that the "present UK approach (to the) Kashmir problem appears extremely pro-GOP (Govt. of Pakistan) as against (the) middle ground we have sought to follow." (From *War and Diplomacy in Kashmir 1947-48* (Sage) by C Das Gupta)

Africa and Asia, many of which were former colonies that wanted to avoid dependence on any major power.

The Muslim League that had promoted partition and fomented divisions and bloodshed ironically disintegrated in 1953. While India moved to create a stable yet vulnerable democracy with a socialist, non-aligned agenda under Jawaharlal Nehru, Pakistan speedily became a military dictatorship in 1956 under **General M. Ayub Khan**[109]. Jinnah would mercifully not live to see how quickly and brutally his exchange of wisdom for ambition would prove a calamity.

Section 9: Summary and comments

British policies in India had created divisions more menacing than the tribal enclaves of primitive peoples, preventing social integration that was deemed essential to unite the nation and accommodate its many ethnic and linguistic groups and to secure its well-being. The same effect was seen in every country of the Empire with a multiracial or multi-religious population. Even if wiser management had prevented internecine strife--which many feared that partition had entrenched--India would need much thoughtful and painstaking work to purge its social and educational systems of two centuries of intensive disinformation that corrupted Indian history by turning ancient facts into 19th century myths.

Painful though it may be, the only way for Indians to regain their self-esteem and pride is to reclaim their culture and heritage. India must bring its peoples out of the morass of mutual suspicion, antagonism and rejection in which generations had been nurtured, and strive to regain the wisdom, wealth and respect that had made her the hub, if not the cradle of world civilisation, the originator of higher learning, of contemplation and of grass roots democracy *(panchayat raj)* crystallising in the Mauryan and Gupta periods and solid enough to survive the vicissitudes of dynastic change until dissolved by intrigues, rivalries and conquest, first by the Mughals, then the *coup de grâce* from Britain.

By this destruction the British impoverished India, decimating its population through a series of holocausts on a far greater scale over 200 years than the little one which the Jews have made into a profitable industry and a flail for Germans; the Indians have so far failed to inform the world of their losses to conquerors. The British achieved this killing of Indians by a farm policy that substituted commercial export crops of no food value, with enslaved labour, for one developed over millennia that had always adequately fed the vast population and provided surpluses for storage and export. British greed and profit-seeking extorted excessive taxes from the dispossessed poor, corrupted officials, drained India's wealth to support British lords, forced subjugated princes into further taxation to support large armies for British, not Indian needs, gutted its coinage and destroyed individual savings, neglected infrastructure and reinvested minimally in India the fruits of Indian labour.

Most execrably, they destroyed Indian village education, and spent an enormous amount of talent to distort, debase and deny Indian history and religion, and its scientific, mathematical, linguistic, astronomical and other achievements. They exacerbated social divisions and exploited them to create greater rifts that perverted society at large by empowering a subservient fraction

---

[109] It would remain so for most of its existence punctuated by short bursts of corrupt civil leadership.

of converts to their cause *(coconuts)*, who then aided the suppression of the majority. In this way they brutally maintained a Raj that is the shame of history. Their depredations have not ceased, only changed in expression and direction.

In the course of three centuries many British Indophiles or at least people of conscience, did emerge. Some are named above. One of interest and poles apart from the Lords who trashed India was a parliamentarian **Charles Bradlaugh**, a railway contractor whose support for the Freedom movement and Indian self-government earned him a cancellation of contracts and expulsion from India! **Annie Besant, Madame Blavatsky, Bertrand Russell, Octavian Hume, Charles Wedderburn** and many thousands—teachers, administrators, clergymen, physicians, writers and the vast unnamed and unsung contributed just as much as the major names, for without them--the Vaishyas and Sudras of society--the more pretentious and forward Brahmins and mandarins would not have achieved much.

India was massively supported by the weak and lame and poor who among them gave more in proportion than all the wealth of the mighty who have seized the nation, fattened themselves and continue to do so at the expense of the downtrodden, just like the British! Who among India's growing wealthy will lift a finger to help their fellow citizens retain what little they have squeezed from a greedy and ungrateful ruling class? The INC has drifted back to its elite roots and forgotten the power of the mass argument that Gandhi so ably and tellingly showed would eventually free India. To say that Independence arrived with bloodshed is to accuse those who failed Gandhi, not *Satyagraha* or *Purna Swaraj* or *Quit India*.

It amazes me that British Governors-General and administrators for whom Macaulay had claimed such sagacity and honour could each ignore the simplest connections between their oppression and the reactions: hatred, protest, revolt; and so profound were their blunders that even when a half-decent one among them, Lord Ripon, tried to do one humane thing and correct a great wrong he would be promptly replaced. And as for Clive, Hastings, Wellesleys (Mornington and his brother Arthur), Dalhousie, Curzon, Minto and the rest in India and Chelmsford, Rhodes, Kitchener and others in Africa, the honours they gained were truly *"rooted in dishonour"* as **Tennyson,** one of their ilk, whose pen was his sword, has said, *"And faith unfaithful, kept him* (them) *falsely true* (to the Throne)!"

Dr Brahmam was deeply cynical that India's leaders would acquire the wisdom needed to guide and protect the country, especially from laissez-faire mercantilist US pitfalls. Already Pakistan and China have each clipped a piece off her boundaries, just like thieving money-changers of old who would or shave thin strips from the margins of smooth-edged gold and silver coins, until milling and wordage made the act not just detestable but detectable!

Jain had concluded from a comparison of his Indian upbringing with his experience in BG that India could benefit from emulating diasporal Indians if she wished to regain her individuality in the world, noting how well Indo-Guianese, despite their status as underdog and separation from the motherland--or perhaps because of it--had nurtured, shared and preserved culture and traditions. They had accepted certain new and innocuous social practices of other cultures, for example, forms of casual dress and observance of feast days, while spreading some of their own virtues, especially religions, cuisine, agricultural and medical systems, and philosophy of peace, accommodation and universality.

This process had eliminated from the Diaspora the worst aspects of caste and ideas of untouchability. Unions of caste and tribes are rare in India, but were a means to achieve inter-tribal cohesion needed for formal political trust and unity to overcome isolationism, language, cultural and other barriers which had stymied past efforts to unite, e.g. Yaswantrao Holkar of the Marathas, the rebels of 1857, Sri Aurobindo and *Anushilan Samiti* and others, and to restore past strengths, e.g. in local government. With the insights that come from positive examples and universal education India could begin to integrate socially and become a nation, in heart as in the head.

Caste as practised hobbles the nation in its search for a way to promote the interests and secure the constitutional, moral and spiritual development of *all* her peoples, and to create a model of equality that promote rights and reward ability regardless of one's birth--thus sparing the many Ambhedkars[110] of India the humiliation that could have soured lesser talents. Passively condemning caste practices is not enough. Hindus who fail to agitate for change risk losing adherents to the blandishments of proselytising religions that are active among them and to the increasingly powerful commercial interests from overseas entities seeking its huge market, so far excluded by Nehru's heavily regulated but faltering economy, the same force that had driven his countrymen overseas a century ago and was repeating that today, mainly of professionals and businessmen, heading to the capitalists' mecca, the USA.

Change for the sake of change is not a worthwhile objective if it diminished in any wise the strong foundation of learning, tolerance and altruism that characterise Hinduism, India's founding philosophy, despite the taint of greed, selfishness and corruption that has challenged its mercantile and ruling elements throughout history. A way must be found to avoid past errors, choose better paradigms and adapt them to local customs and practices to advance the nation socially and economically, while preserving the mores and spirituality-- the tradition of rectitude, of *dharma* as the guiding principle to the attainment of *moksha*--for which India is rightly paramount, and avoiding the decline of morals and behaviour that threaten western societies awash in crass and egocentric materialism.

But modern India's early adoption of a heavily bureaucratised USSR-style central planning, while pragmatic in some ways, and designed to prevent the hegemony of large corporations, is seen by diasporal Indians as retrograde and ill-advised, as it seems merely to replace private corporate domination with inefficient and equally corrupt state monopolies and worse create a minority out of the majority Hindu rural peoples, who remain isolated and powerless and without education or land. Critics of India, particularly in North America-- consumed with **McCarthyism** and the **Cold War**, and as allies of **Pakistan**--are less generous, and view these as evidence of a backward people unfit to govern themselves.

Many Americans still feel that, given time, India will disintegrate into chaos, and threaten world stability and peace. This negative appraisal has become a popular stereotype of all Indians and in the Diaspora has tended to increase their feeling of isolation and subservience among peoples of the West.

---

[110] BK Ambhedkar, Marathi lawyer, one of the framers of the Indian constitution, was born into a low caste family; a gifted student, he faced harsh discrimination and endured terrible hardships to achieve a good education.

This changed somewhat in 1948 when India established a consulate in Georgetown, and began to offer West Indians scholarships to several of India's 200 universities and technical colleges.[111] To his credit Nehru has remained neutral and is slowly working to build capacity for his people. He has recognised India's need to regain technological and scientific excellence. She had never really lost her mathematical and agricultural skills although the one had been suppressed somewhat and the other diverted to a foreign agenda. India remains vulnerable to its neighbours but more ominously to US corporatism. That is the turf on which India will have to defend herself!

Section 10: Adapting in the Diaspora

The recitation of the above had taken several sessions, in less detail, of course, than this written account, but the highlights and enough details were given to provide a framework for reinforcement. I had concluded saying, "To begin to understand Indians in BG, Trinidad and Nickerie, you have to appreciate something of this history, chaps, not the details, but the idea that we are not what British smears say we are, largely to hide their own weaknesses and inhumanity; sugar workers see their true colours every day and give Cheddi and others food for protest. Most Indians know about the Raj, the independence struggle and the religious and social history; those educated in villages were spared much of the distortions that the British taught which Hindu scholars are now trying to correct against opposition and name- calling."

"Indenture was act of desperation for Indians," Jain added, "they knew that when British took them on ship it was to jail in Andaman Islands. They didn't know they would travel for three-four months, to unknown and stressful place far from home, over-worked, cheated, jailed in hovels, hearing a strange language, frightened, among people of different races, most of whom looked hostile, and the majority, Africans, totally new."

"I can see how frightened most people can get in those circumstances; but the slaves had the same problem and they didn't choose to come." Bacchus observed.

"Exactly; this is why we should come together in a constructive relationship, sharing beginnings, not as two poles never to meet; we're heading there, I think, thanks to the Brits!"

"I agree fully. So what about the folks who came? How did they fare with others?"

Indian-African Relationships

Much of what I know derived from tales told by elders--especially my grandfather through his extensive conversations with my mother--and from direct experiences of studious people like Mr Latchman, Hari, various pandits and our Hindi teachers and friends. In BG, as in Trinidad and elsewhere, no closeness could develop naturally or easily between Indian workers and Afro-

---

[111] Several Blacks benefited from this including a Barbadian who studied Medicine, now speaks fluent Hindi and became his country's Minister of Health in 1971. In the nineties India shifted to an open economy allowing more freedom and fewer regulations that lay the foundations for its current advances, but brought prematurely the very challenges that Nehru and others of the past had fought against and hoped to avoid. India now must fend off a US Corporate take-over.

Guianese because the two were so different socially, culturally, linguistically, by religion and mythology.

From the outset the Africans had resented their presence, seeing them as new competition, hard on the heels of the Portuguese, not as victims like themselves, not knowing their history. Indians on the other hand soon saw that Africans dominated police and public services and generally belittled them and provided biased, reluctant and inferior services, despite some gentler hands. Thus from these early negative experiences Indians developed ambivalence and caution in their relationships with others, especially Police. Much later Indians seeking jobs at any level of the Public Services began to face systemic discrimination. For rural Indians the divisions were often insurmountable.

Most Indians had never seen Africans before arriving in BG, and had not been told that they were already there, freed earlier after two hundred years of slavery. Nor had they known of their struggles towards emancipation, much less their background, religion or culture. My *nāna*, for instance, had met black men in books, described in derogatory terms, the most familiar being a reference in the *Rāmāyana* in which Hanumān, using a flame-thrower type of weapon in battle, had singed the hair of some of his foes; thus emerged the myth of the origin of kinky-haired peoples! *Nāna* therefore avoided them as much as he could or approached them with great caution. His reaction was also conditioned by stories he had heard from British sources on the ship of the strange and primitive peoples inhabiting the continent of Africa; indeed when he saw them toiling as stevedores on the wharf where his ship had docked, he had concluded that he had been brought to some part of Africa, to which thousands of Indians had already been taken (Réunion, Mauritius, South Africa, Kenya etc.). Their speech was strange, and it took him some time to realize that they were speaking the same language as the white overseers, only differently accented.

Everything was new to him then. He had read and heard stories dealing with slavery, practised from time immemorial among nations, especially Muslims and Europeans, and knew of Indians enslaved after defeat in war, not as an item of trade by peace-time merchants. He had no knowledge that trading in slaves had provided workers worldwide, was widely practised by conqueror nations, from ancient times to the recent past, and that it was the abolition of that trade by Europeans that had led to Indian recruitment by British farmers in the west and to the bloody Civil War in America.

In time African bias against Indians had reached ridiculous levels of contempt for and vilification of the Hindu way of living, far in excess of British attitudes. For instance Hindus customarily conducted religious services in their homes and openly celebrated major seasonal and religious festivals, according to a solar or lunar calendar, with song and music, alien to and different in style and presentation from those of the Blacks. Non-Indians never tried to understand these practices, copying the British stereotype of scoffing at and dismissing things Indian as "heathen," "primitive" or, least charitably "barbaric".

At religious services, called *pujas,* Indians would squat comfortably on floors covered with white cotton sheets, mats or blankets to listen to the pandit's (priest's) homily, participate in the *ārti* (the terminal devotional song and ceremony), receive and consume the *prasād* (blessed food offering, similar to the Roman Catholic *host*) and the *bhoj* (meal) that followed each service. These above all other practices were derided by non-Indian witnesses, *"Wha' happ'n, baye, ahyou na gat chu'ch?"* and *"ahyou cyaan afford chair? Ha, ha!"* were questions that had become absurdly familiar to me by the time I was six. Spat out in the vernacular they sounded even more spiteful than they might have otherwise.

In elementary and high schools, I had been alternatively teased, criticised and castigated for our social and religious practices, and I felt shamed and hurt. It might have scarred me were it not for the knowledge and wisdom of my mother (and my father before his untimely death) and later *chacha* Latchman who chose each rebuff as an occasion to tell us some fine story, of which they were many--deep, uplifting, distracting and ennobling--from Vaidic texts and from Indian writers, especially **Tāgore**, who had made the world notice India by winning the Nobel prize for literature in 1913. We knew, from a local jingle praising her, of the outspoken nationalist **Madame Cāma** who had reviled and embarrassed the British in a spirited campaign and had planted a prototype Indian flag at a conference in Germany in 1907. Earlier she had chastised Egyptian men in Cairo for denying their wives a role in running their country!

Gandhi was a household name in BG; his *Satyagraha* pictures were everywhere as well as other leaders'. Sarojini Naidu had become famous for her verse and politics; other literary and spiritual voices had risen from all classes of society. This had come up in relation to the charge of suppression of Indian women. Jain had added briefs on several outstanding Indian women warriors e.g. **Rana Tarabai** of Malwa had defeated Aurangzeb in 1707 to begin the Mughal collapse; **Bhimabai Holkar, Lakshmi Bai** of Jhānsi and **Rani Avantibai,** Begum **Hazrat Mahal** and others had led armies against the British and fought valiantly against great odds. Contrary to stereotyping women dominated Indian family and religious life.

Mr Latchman's illegal *pāthshala* in New Amsterdam was dedicated to teaching Hindi and Sanskrit to sceptical youngsters who would rather be playing; one or two took great pains to avoid being seen entering his premises by non-Indian classmates, and dreaded the teasing if caught with Hindi textbooks. His son Sukhdeo and I served as teachers. One day, Mr Latchman overheard Uday Jairam, a classmate, who had just started Hindi classes, asking me about our Geometry homework, a rider to a theorem. We thought he would scold us for the distraction, but instead gathered the group--seven or eight students--and, in Hindi, as was his practice, for he believed in immersion, announced, "The problem you're discussing is *Baudhāyana's* theorem; you see this *hawan kund* here," he pointed to a copper vessel--a square truncated pyramid resting on its narrow sealed side and occupying a corner of the room--and spoke with great stress on the key words, "that *kund* was designed by our ancient priest-scientists to precise measurements so that it could be made in quantity, all same proportions, whatever the size. To do that, they had to solve many math riddles including properties of triangles, rectangles and circles. *Asvalāyana, Baudhāyana, Āpastamba* and others solved many, including what your teachers call **Pythagoras'** theorem, over five thousand years ago, when *Kaliyuga* began, long before the Greeks. Later on I will tell you about the *Sutras* concerning these things, and who taught them to Persians, Egyptians, Greeks, Romans, Arabs and later Europeans. They don't teach you that in school!"

We were stunned and knew enough then to marvel that this thing we had learned as a Greek invention of 2500 years ago had been around for twice as long.

"I will tell you about great mathematicians and astronomers: Aryābhatta, Brahmagupta, Bhaskara, Mahādeva, Rāmanuj, and so on. Did you learn that the world is round?"

We nodded in unison, wondering why he had asked something known for over 300 years.

"Well, **Aryābhatta**, a young astronomer of the late Gupta period, over *1400* years ago, taught that the earth *was* round, turned on its axis and circled the sun. You all know that the Pope wanted to kill scientist Galileo, just 300 or so years ago, for saying that same thing; so don't believe that all you learn in your school is true. You have great scholars in your ancestors; be proud of them. Ask questions."

At another session, sometime later, he asked us, in relation to a piece of translation, "You learn Chemistry?" We nodded and Uday told him that Mr JJ Niles had just begun classes in Atomic theory. Mr Latchman was as usual expansive.

"*Nahi, nahi!*" he exclaimed. "You remember I told you that Vaidic scholars believed that all the matter in the world was made up of five elements (*pancha mahabhootas*): earth (*prithvi*), air (*maya*), fire (*agni*), water (*apa*) and ether (*akasha*). A young student named **Kashyapa,** son of a philosopher named Ulka, who lived well *over 2,500* years ago, was one of the first, if not the first to propose that all this matter was made of minute parts, *kana* (grains) which could be divided until you come to the smallest indivisible entity, called *parmanu*, literally "beyond the atom". It's so small that we can't appreciate it with any of the special senses we're given to perceive each element of matter: smell for *earth*, feeling for *air*, sight for *fire*, taste for *water* and hearing for *ether*. He included time, space, mind and soul as important as the physical elements in nature and creation. **Kanadā** described how atoms joined to form compounds (*dwinuka*) of the same or different classes explaining the variety of matter and suggested the physical forces that made reactions possible. You can find this in the *Vaisheshika-Sutra* (peculiarity aphorisms) which deals with this science and philosophy far deeper than Greeks did; yet two Greeks, Democritus and Leucippus get the credit, *as indeed the Greeks do for all things Indian*. He says, 'Every object of creation is made of atoms which in turn connect with each other to form molecules.'

"The *Vaisheshika* School also believed that atoms were points in space. The sage **Muni Soma Sharma** gave Kashyapa the name **Kanadā** to celebrate his observation about *kana* and *parmanu*. So you see Kashyapa, or Kanadā, was the real father of Atomic Theory. Another sage, **Pakudha Katyāyana**, had come to the same conclusion in Buddha's time, and should share that credit. When Alexander came to India he took Aristotle and other philosophers who must have taken all this exciting theory back to Greece. Remember that **Krishna** was born of a virgin in Mathurā, and Christianity repeated major themes in the lives of both him and Buddha such as Immaculate Conception, a star marking the birth of the avatar, twelve disciples, several of the miracles, parables and so on."

We were fascinated. But none of us dared to mention this information, much less use it.

"I think our guru's lessons[112] can get us expelled from school!" Uday said, insightfully.

---

[112] A.L. Basham, an Australian Indologist, commented thus: "*They were brilliant imaginative explanations of the physical structure of the world, and in a large measure, agreed with the discoveries of modern physics.*" On the other hand Thomas Macaulay had sought to obliterate all Indian knowledge .

Most Indian migrants had had a fair level of native education which had prepared them to self-learn from continuing readings and discussions of whatever subject matter they had covered. Most families had passed on this education to their BG children of whom *chacha* Latchman was one. He had excelled in primary school and continued personal study of Sanskrit, no doubt stimulated by his own father who had discoursed on the revival and preservation of Sanskrit with members of the Arya Samaj mission early in the century. Because of British embargo on books in foreign languages most teachers were confined to the epics and other religious writings. I recalled my primer in Hindi and Sanskrit by my father who used to read to us at night from his collection. (A year after his death I had come across an official English document that had described him as *"illiterate"* without specification!)

Mr Latchman was an encyclopaedia of *Vaidic* lore, not just in story, but in the deeper meanings and extended philosophical reasoning of the nature of the universe and all it contained. The vision, the wonder and the complexity of the *Vaidic* concept of creation, and of the role of man and all things in that universe stirred the imagination more than any other story I had heard or read. I wondered why no one at my school, not even Indians, spoke of them as Mr Latchman did, nor of his stories of great discoveries in science, astronomy and mathematics that ancient Indians had made, and inventions such as flying machines and missiles, much as we have them today. I was too young to worry about the silence on such matters, but I had noticed the turmoil in Sukhdeo's mind and how plaintively he sang; his songs were all sad or so complex that I didn't try to understand them until he would explain, and then only in terms just as complex. I was only ten.

I distinctly recalled years earlier when my ailing father, sitting on the sofa in our living room after the first American aeroplanes had appeared in our surprised skies, reading a few *shlokas* from the Rāmāyana and explaining, "We knew that one day these flying machines would come again, when mankind learned enough of the knowledge that was lost." He told us about the scientist and Ayurvaidic scholar **Bharadwaj** who lived in **Prayag** and described three kinds of flying machines: those that flew on earth, those that flew between planets and those that flew between universes. His treatise is called *"Yantra Sarvasva"* Much later my mother would tell me that when the first cars came to the colony, Nāna had talked of flying machines and other space lore, saying that "one day you will see flying cars, like giant eagles, *just as in ancient times."*

At school none of us mentioned these things; we would be chastised, for sure, for heresy, doubting our lessons and Christian precedents or some such equally dreadful religious crime; after all, our teachers were educated people with college diplomas and teaching certificates; they taught what they had learned and what was in the curriculum. Mr Latchman was a farmer whose formal British schooling was to the sixth standard elementary level, the highest, and home schooling, India style. He had become a Hindi teacher, a good one; he spoke English well, not with a rustic accent; he taught two foreign languages and constantly studied Vaidic and other Indian books, thick books wrapped in red cotton, just like my father's. (All pandits I had ever seen kept their books the same way). He had acquired a huge fund of Indian lore, from which he would draw and recite to the class each session. Pandits often consulted him for clarification of tricky points in the Holy Scriptures.

In a sense the mocking and antagonistic attitude of Blacks helped to stoke our interest in, and consolidate learning of Hinduism, by backlash, quite apart from the lessons learned from its routine practice within our community. But even though our self-esteem was thus strengthened at home many maintained a degree of doubt, wondering why most educated coloured and Black Christians, barring a few open-minded men and women— neighbours, friends, teachers, co-workers--whom we knew well, had so little curiosity about our customs and practices.

Were they right that we were pagan dreamers, of no account, an inferior people—"idolaters" as Macaulay had called us--and were our parents and elders misguided? Youthful distractions protected us from further exploration of such a weighty issue; I simply accepted the assurances of my elders.

Our versions of timing, events and accomplishments were simply not important to others; their derogatory opinions were firmly entrenched and gratuitously expressed. Their misspelling and mispronunciation of our names seemed so deliberate and belittling, distorting their meaning. They remained as dismissive and cruelly critical as the ruling British and their "high-coloured" sycophants. And yet those same British had been less than kind in their opinions of black folk.[113] What added to their ungenerous view was that most Indians who were advancing socially had begun to do so after adopting Christianity, giving weight to the view that there was no intrinsic merit in being anything but Christian. Little did ordinary Blacks know that most Indian converts had done so to gain jobs, social positioning and a chance to advance.

It is a marvel and testimony to the strength of Indian culture that more people did not capitulate under the relentless pressure and damning criticism, so glibly repeated by fellow citizens. Despite a thousand years of assault in India by two militantly evangelistic religions, and despite scores of millions murdered by Muslims and British, Hindus had prevailed; less than 2% had become Christian in 200 years, and about 10% had been coerced into Islam in the previous 750 years, by economic or caste forces, not religion or spirituality; the great Akbar had failed to persuade Islam to incorporate Hindu values.

Hinduism

Most Indian immigrants were Hindus. Christians and their missionaries misunderstood and religiously misrepresented them from the very beginning of their association, an attitude begun in India in the 19th century that spread throughout the Empire and persists to this day. They ignored or denigrated Hindu religious authorities, the pandits, however knowledgeable or prominent in their communities, because they were not full-time priests presiding over a congregation and had to earn a livelihood in the regular lay economy.

They ignored the fact that Hinduism, unlike Christianity, did not have a clergy and thus they misunderstood the role of the pandits in Hindu society. In turn the BG pandits did not effectively counter Christian criticism and ignorance. While practised in the rituals many did not have the depth of academic training, English language skills, nor indeed free time or media access, to present confident and convincing discourses to explain and illustrate their religious principles.

Pandits--and, to a lesser extent imams, who had a greater control and more defined role in Muslim society—needed to improve their grasp of scripture, comparative theology, English, and of the techniques of effective

---

[113] See Ch. 3, 12-14, and read Thomas Carlyle and his contemporaries, rich with denigration.

debate and communication. What failings they showed reflected the lack of opportunity and facilities for secondary and higher education in the colony. Besides, their knowledge of literary Hindi and Sanskrit, and in the case of Muslims, Arabic or Urdu, was limited to rote learning of scriptures and commentaries. The British banned importation of Hindi literature since so many of the most erudite scholars and writers were also staunch nationalists who uniformly condemned British policies and practices.

Migrants learned colloquial Hindi, Brij Bhasha, Bhojpuri or other language from their parents or at Hindi school conducted by members of the community, but were hampered by lack of books and teaching materials; thus few could take students beyond an elementary level. (The Muslim League had unsuccessfully objected to British recognition of Hindi as an official language in India in the run-up to self-government, preferring Urdu, which is Hindi peppered with Persian and Arabic words, few of which were unique except those naming religious, military or local geographic entities.)

The lack of a **School of Hinduism** (or Religion generally) has for the past century led BG pandits to concentrate on mastery of rituals and tried-and-true homilies rather than of fundamental principles and religious philosophy; they have generally not become familiar with the tenets of other religions, knowledge that would have expanded their repertoire, enabling them to deal effectively with frequent and unschooled attacks on Hinduism, including Dr Jagan's. The sons raised into panditry (or banditry, some say) by their fathers have generally followed the latter's practice. Although a few more scholarly pandits have begun to appear, most deal poorly with the issues of polytheism and *murti* worship, waffling and fumbling for words rather than providing clear explanations and scriptural references.

Jain nodded in agreement, and asked, "Why are Roman Catholics allowed to get away with that criticism, when it practically flaunts idolatry and symbolism? This slander is very harsh and offensive when made by Muslims of Hindu ancestry; this includes *all* Guianese Muslims; they forget they too use symbols and abstractions, just like us, although different in style and looks, to show many faces and elements of deity. They deny all other knowledge and keep repeating in India that Islam is 'last and final version of *three* great monotheistic religions.' It is pretentious, very pretentious!"

"I suspect that Islam was attractive because of the spoils from *razzias* and also Hindu rituals couldn't really be done in a desert country so far from sources of all that stuff that the pandits use. So getting rid of them saved everyone a lot of expense and difficulty."

"Of course; that could be true," Jain said, "but you don't need all those rituals and fancy murtis; they're toys of wealthy; better to spend it on poor. See what Guru Nanak did and simplified worship; and *Arya Samajis* even simpler."

"I must repeat this; the Gita says that worship can be simple. Hinduism is the oldest and most open religion, inspired by *Parabramha*, the Absolute, formless, the Universal Presence, or God whose power created the *entire* Universe in which all objects have a relationship; living beings are allowed to evolve, man as latest and highest form with responsibility to live righteously and preserve Nature. When man fails badly *(adharma)* avatars are invoked to guide him back to the path of truth and peace. It's a continuous process. The priests, the Brahmins, chose to introduce images fairly late in the history of Hinduism to represent the various manifestations of God, a perfectly sensible device, like drawings, to explain the complex workings of an abstract Entity.

"Christian churches also have their *murtis* and other symbols: the Christ figure nailed to the cross, photos, statues and statuettes of Mary and many murals of *Madonna and child* and other motifs. Indeed some Christian sects, notably Roman Catholics, don't require their flock to study the Bible, but teach dogma and various creeds only, stressing absolute faith as the way to God; these are regurgitated, in Latin, at each mass. Islam uses verbal images, calligraphy and rituals and expresses God in several dozens of these."

The lack of formal religious education exposed Guianese pandits to the criticism by Christian priests, often arrogantly stated "that any Hindu can don a *koorta* and *dhoti*, wear a *pagri*, give himself a likely name, carry a few dog-eared books wrapped in red cloth and proclaim that he is a man of God." Surely one doesn't have to go to school to be a "man of God"!

This type of unkind exaggeration has been repeated so often that Hindus simply ignore it and prefer a positive approach. Their organisations have long recognised the need for a College of Hinduism similar to Christian Colleges such as Codrington in Barbados. Official response has been antagonistic, and the apparent lack of a plan to raise the needed funds has not helped.

"But, you know, the UCWI will become the University of the West Indies next year and plans to build a campus here as soon as our government agrees; one of the new Faculties to be based here will be **Religious Studies**. That will help. The British *Government* would not sanction a Hindu or other Religious College on its own as that would go against their historical stance; Jagan seems to agree; so neither will help. So any College will have to be privately funded unless we go with the UCWI."

"Is that so?" Bacchus asked. "I didn't hear about that. But Jagan is hinting at his own College."

"That's the fear. We're hoping that he changes his mind and stays with UC. BG couldn't possibly on its own afford to do this plus the others planned: Geology, Law, Mining, Forestry, and Basic Arts, Natural and Social Sciences. I hope he sees that. "

Hindu Celebrations *(Sanskars)*

Brewster said, "I know 'bout weddings, but what are all those others, like the one with red water?"

"That's *Phagwah*, Spring festival," Jain replied, "Red water is *abeer*. Others are Diwali, festival of lights, birthdays of avatars, like you have Christmas, change of seasons and other cosmic changes, birthdays, weddings, coming of age, death and so on. They vary from simple *puja* (prayer), *katha* which is reading from religious work or even whole *Rāmāyana*, which could last up to a week and is called a *Yajna*. This is the most taxing and expensive of all. Yet every Hindu hopes to host one in his lifetime."

"My sister Mahadai and her husband Tulla did an eight-day *Yajna* in July 1952. That was brutal, a real sacrifice; used up my College money! We must have served 5,000 meals, not counting other costs."

"Incredible! How so?" Bacchus asked.

"Well, it's virtually open house for meals; we served all comers three meals a day, and over two hundred at each sitting. Nights were busy with cooking; we hardly slept. A lot of friends helped; that is the custom. Jagan, Burnham, Janet, John Carter, Dan Debidin, CV Wight, John Fernandes, JB Singh, and a lot of politicos, civil servants and big shots attended the opening and closing ceremonies. *Yajnas* attract pandits from all over. And young folk get to see or meet the opposite sex; quite a few matches often follow."

"Is it true a wedding last two-three weeks and the couple don't sleep together that first night?"

"In strict tradition, yes, especially with child weddings when it could be years before they sleep together. We don't do those here and they're no longer legal in India." I answered.

"Marriage *(vivāha)* is major *sanskar* among Hindus," Jain began, his epenthetic "r's" adding weight to his words; "it's usually arranged to find a good fit and usually couple are young virgins who will now begin *grihaspati* (household life) and start family. Folks hold short services in two-week period before wedding, both sides; rural folk are stricter, especially with delaying sleeping together. Ceremony discusses vows and responsibilities; each promises to support the other at all times, and share things. Marriage is the most elaborate ceremony where families show off their wealth and influence. It's often performed at night, especially in rural areas, perhaps with more pomp here than in India, with big dowries before wedding; rich people give gifts at ceremony-- jewellery, equipment, utensils, cash, livestock or land. Hindu marriages usually endure for a lifetime, if matchmakers did a good job."

"I've heard of some of this and went to a young constable's wedding last year. "Bacchus said. "You're right about the pomp, and the gift giving. I liked the music and the singing and dancing."

I added, "It's common to find people marrying here from widely separated regions of India and from different castes; indenture brought them closer here than they might ever have been back in India. That's true integration and also good for population genetics. It usually makes Indians less clannish, more unified and understanding of one another.

"About the sleeping issue some require that the bride be chaperoned on the night of her reception at the groom's family and to return home to her parents' next morning for a week. This is said to allow them to back out, since with arranged marriages the wedding might have been the first time they saw each other. The groom will come to take her home and she will finally part from her parents; this marks the beginning of their honeymoon and life together."

In answer to other questions we noted that marriages among estate workers were quite stable and families held to their traditions as they did in Indian villages. Indo-Guianese have long abandoned child marriages and do not object to widows remarrying or inheriting their husband's estate. Marriages between mature persons, whether on board ship during migrations or on the plantations, did quite well, although a few did end in separation, often amicably. In most instances if reconciliation did not take place, the separation was socially accepted and respected as permanent and each was free to form new links. Such secondary liaisons, if stable, carried no stigma as long as it conformed to local style and religious norms. Divorces were rare.

Separation due to adultery or among the wealthy was often rough and contentious. At times, the aggrieved party, especially the male, would resort to violence, even murder, to assuage the wrong. Rarely women committed suicide, and some have been known to poison their husbands. Such sensational events would bring a swarm of black policemen directed by a white man in khaki and a peaked cap, into the couple's premises, and the ensuing trial, conviction and punishment--by hanging if guilty — fed media biases and brought great notoriety to the Indian community quite out of proportion to the frequency of the occurrences. Those were often the only times Indians would get publicity prior to the advent of popular politics![114] In the early decades of Indian migration there were far fewer women and each was therefore highly prized,[115] (a situation similar to that of the first slaves).

At the turn of the century there were 50 women to 100 men among Indians in BG overall, and 40 or so per hundred on the estates. The shortage persisted well into this century. Women migrants were generally courageous and independent, by the mere act of accepting recruitment as single persons; they did not readily accept a subservient role. Some men might not have been prepared for expressions of free will from their wives, and when that happened conflicts arose with potential for disharmony and breakdown. Most reasonable men adjusted but there were those who stuck to tradition, became disgruntled and even beat their wives in anger, having learned to fortify themselves first with cheap rum, which seemed ubiquitous at shops on the fringes of sugar estates, and nearly always owned by drivers or overseers. Women still bound to estates had no recourse and suffered in silence; free women however sometimes escaped their private hells by seeking work and refuge in some faraway place.

Non-Christian weddings were not registrable in BG; so Government regarded children as "illegitimate". But Indians accorded them all rights and privileges of inheritance, unless challenged in court. A second marriage was rarely allowed under Hindu rites, and was usually a civil one and thus registered and "legal". This had inheritance implications for the ex-wife and any children of that marriage. This was a source of contention, acrimony and even violence in the settlement of estates. For this reason, those separating after Hindu marriages were urged to establish the legitimacy of their children, protect their rights, and not to legalise a second marriage until they had settled inheritance issues.

Both married and single women were often forced into liaisons with estate staff especially the white overseers and managers, as I've noted earlier. Near the end of Nāna's first contract an incident occurred in which a young married woman delivered a fair-skinned first child; the husband promptly disowned it, accusing his wife of infidelity, having heard that an overseer had regularly put her to work in his house while he was toiling in the fields. In the ensuing quarrel he rejected her pleas of rape and in a drunken rage chopped her with a cutlass inflicting a serious wound which nearly severed one of her arms; her life was saved by intervening neighbours who applied a tourniquet to her arm, which soon after was amputated as an emergency in the City hospital, fortunately not too far away.

Conversions

Up to the 1940's, Hindu converts to Christianity, especially in towns and villages, were mainly for jobs, especially teaching in denominational schools and

---

[114] *They did however attract criminal lawyers, among whom Mr Lionel Luckhoo, Jagan's nemesis, stands tallest, and holds the Guinness Record for the world's longest sequence of murder acquittals, 245, awarded in 1990.*

[115] Many early male migrants remained single for lack of women or took Negro or other mates and thus added to the mixed section of the population; many disappeared phenotypically just as their migrant counterparts had done in the Antilles; one would be hard put to find full Indians in the Leeward and Windward Islands.

in Government Services, or from lower castes who had seized the opportunity to escape caste boundaries, as has happened in India for millennia, by converting to Buddhism, Christianity, Islam, Sikhism etc.

While converts often gained what they sought they were often shunned by their fellows, not as often now as long ago. Many of these would become the first to move to towns and large villages and have inter-racial relationships, including marriage. Lower caste folk did not embrace Christianity in BG as eagerly as has been made out, for caste reasons alone, since the caste status allowed certain lines of access and protected economic activity within the Indian community wherein specific occupations were left to the appropriate caste and no extraneous competition occurred, as happened outside the caste structure.

Indians, like the Africans before them, saw the teaching profession as the first rung on a ladder of progress for good students who wished to leave the farm. Such departures were often part of an overall family plan, which identified children for different careers to broaden the family's income base, secure its independence and improve its role and influence in the community.

Music

"Indian music and dance vary from group to group, region to region, and from classical to popular, folk, dance and other forms, just like Western music." Jain said. "The instruments go back thousands of years--flute, sitar, drums, sintoor and tanpura, harmonium, cymbals--form roots of classical music. Drums and harmonium are popular for religious services, folk music and dance; we have many more instruments."

I recalled the first time I had seen a classical concert. My mother had taken us, as a great treat, to the Mahaica cinema where classical musicians played the most exquisite music with *sitar, tabla, harmonium, sarod tanpura* and *sarangi*; I was mesmerised by the skill of the *tabla* player and for days after tried to imitate — on any hard surface--his rapid yet delicate and precise finger movements and the flourish of his head as it moved in time with the melody; how beautifully he made the *tabla* yield its harmonies on which the plaintive notes of the *sitar* soared as if reproducing the music of the universe, the sound of the great Brahman thinking. But when I heard a *sintoor* expert I knew that I had finally heard something heavenly.

With the introduction of battery-operated radios rural Indians could finally hear popular songs that Station ZFY aired on two Indian "hour" programs (each a half-hour only). One of the first was hosted, starting soon after WWII, by Dindyal Singh, a family friend who gave me my first taste of broadcasting when I read the commercials and announcements between songs. Non-Indians generally pooh-poohed the music and made fun of us, the songs and the unfamiliar language, making no appreciable effort to understand our point of view.

In Georgetown Indian films from the prolific Bombay studios were shown regularly, but only at the Capitol cinema on La Penitence St. in Albuoystown, the southernmost ward of the city, thick with Indians and a staging point for their advance into more prestigious neighbourhoods in the city's north. The shows were on Friday and Saturday nights. Occasionally the Olympic Cinema on Lombard Street would show an Indian film. Indian films were commonplace in rural areas, however. But the highbrow Georgetown cinemas like the Astor, Metropole or Empire would hear nothing of it. Their owners considered it *infra dig* to put up a poster in Hindi characters on the posh billboards decorating their facades.

Thus it was a moment of great triumph when the plush Astor Cinema decided in late 1949 to show an Indian film, *Barsāt,* (Deluge) with Raj Kapoor and the lovely Nargis who had the audience drooling with desire. The film had won international acclaim, soon after India's independence. It was a major social affair, attended by the Governor, the Indian representative, and dignitaries. The cinema overflowed with Indians pouring in from the countryside, giving reporters a chance to ridicule their lack of city-wise comportment. The Astor had never done so well; yet it would take many years to show Indian films with any regularity. Even the Plaza on Camp Street, owned by Indians, would initially show only token Indian films. To these no Blacks or other races came.

Muslims

"You sure Muslim religion did not start in India? You say they Arabs and force you to convert?" Doris asked, puzzled. "But you all look the same. And we hear that when you got independence you all kill millions o' one another. Some people here scared of what you all will do when BG get independent, that you all will murder Africans. Didn' Jagan talk about his own Police?"

Jain could hardly contain his mirth at the misrepresentation, admitting that the carnage did occur and repeated what he had said earlier about the killings. I told the story of one Indian victim.

A Sindhi Hindu of *Ahir-Arora* lineage who managed a furniture store on Regent Street had fled Pakistan to escape murdering squads of Muslim *muhajirs.* His forbears had preserved Hinduism in the face of increasing Islamisation of Sindh that had by 1947 reduced Hindus to 25% of the population. Yet they had hoped that the good relations that had existed between the two religions in the preceding 200 years would sustain co-existence and preserve the urban prosperity that Hindu commerce had brought to the Sind. But at partition, which few Sindhis wanted, hate-mongers sent hordes of *jihadis* prowling streets, ripping apart whole communities, looting businesses, raping and murdering hundreds of thousands of Hindus in Karachi and other cities while Muslim Police stood by and watched or joined in; Hindus fled, abandoning all possessions. His family was among them.

"We hoped that Pakistan Government would stop killings and help us return to our people and business. After all we give the most to economy of region and nation too; but they curse us, call us Jews of India and give away our property to looters. But we are resourceful people and will make good wherever we go. See how well we do here. But we will always mourn those we lost, family and friends; we had community that our language, customs and heritage had made one. Now gone! Invaders took all. Sindhis who became Muslim now get more rich; some we know stole our business; others took what little we had with us when they chased us away. Not one rupee they left us!"

He paused, choking on his words, recalling the losses, the bloodshed and wasted lives. "It's our bad *karma.* It was same long ago when first Muslims came to Sindhi Jāts; they were like us, merchants and traders; some of us were Hindu, some Buddhist, few Jain, all living in peace. Muslims came with horses and camels, weapons and swords. They say *'pay taxes and become Muslim, or we kill you and take your women.'* Our people split; some become Muslim, others, especially Buddhists, accept terms; they are allowed to live and work; only few resist in our small town and all are killed, their bodies defiled, their heads piled in a mound. Our people are very unhappy when they hear how many thousands were killed in Multan, and how many *stupas* and temples they destroyed. But *Sindhiyat* stayed strong in our blood, to this day. It is essence of our culture, our bond with our land, *dharti māta*, Mother Earth. All gone."

"Sad but very human story. Man is his worst enemy, especially when fired up by religion." I said.

"You know, when I look at what's happening here I think same thing will happen;" Jain said, unusually sadly; "and what's worse because I'm Indian I will be hit again, only this time the Police who will watch me burn and bleed will be African, not Pakistani. Many people now agree with Subhas Chandra Bose that pacifism, Gandhi style—he was Jain like me--allowed Islam to destroy India in the same way that pacifist Buddhists allowed Islam to enter in 712."

(Dr Brahmam and other historians he knew had suggested that Buddhist and Jain philosophies with their potent message of peace and tolerance and the sophistication of society from Mauryan to Gupta times had softened Indians who then expected foreigners to be impressed with peace and behave in a civil and principled way. They had forgotten the inhumanity that hunger, greed, tribal and religious bigotry can breed, and how great states can be crushed by ambition and the lust for power).

Muslims make up less than 10% of India's population and about the same in BG; here they support the three political parties almost equally, following economic lines. All Muslims in BG are ethnic Indians, but have begun to show an emotional connection with Pakistan based on religion, and some even claim that their ancestors originated in Pakistan even though they know that the majority of migrants had come from UP and Bihar up to a century before the birth of Pakistan and descended from Indians converted to Islam during the seven centuries of Muslim rule. There were no migrants of Sindhi origin to the West Indies, prior to recent advent of Sindhi businessmen, all Hindus, who had fled the carnage in Pakistan.

BG Muslims, like Hindus and natives, have been the target of Christian proselytism, with some conversions, as in India. In BG, their small numbers could have threatened the survival of Islam, but in 1908 the moderate and mystical Ahmadiyyas (a benign form of Islam founded by Mirza Ghulam Ahmad in Kashmir, who claimed to be the resurrected Christ) established a mission in BG, which rallied support and restored confidence and focus.

Muslims and Hindus have coexisted from the beginning in BG with little or no friction. Few Muslims today know or care whether they are Sunni or Shi'a, but most must be Sunni or Ahmadiyya, the main Indian groups. Politically, prominent Muslims have aligned themselves with the United Force, largely because of its anti-Communist stance (despite USSR support of Muslims in the Middle East). Those who support the PNC are largely city working class and trades people with union affiliations. Rural Muslims support the PPP. The UF and PNC have promised to recognise as holidays two Eids – *ul Fitr* and *al Adha* – and the *Yaun an Nabi* (Mohamed's birthday). The PPP government had declined to grant holiday status to the holy days of both Muslims and Hindus (*Diwali and Phagwah*). The *Sadr Anjuman e Islam* is the major Islamic organisation in BG.

Need for Indo-African Cooperation

Responding to a question on tolerance, I said, "Indians have learned much about their African neighbours, and realise that no peaceful political progress can be made without mutual cooperation. The notion of acceptance is inherent in Hinduism; we do not proselytise and each of us is free to follow our conscience provided we pursue peace and goodwill to all. Hindus recognize the need to bring all racial groups to the same table in order to create a peaceful and prosperous society and a well-meaning and honest government. This is one of the big messages of the Holy Book, the *Bhagavad Gita."*

The thrust of past BGEIA activities had been to foster unity among Indians as a prerequisite for linkages with other races, especially Africans. It was essential to pursue unity among Indians to counter their innate clannishness which has gradually changed in BG as people of necessity learned about one another and developed a wider more tolerant social basis for trust and interaction than mere blood ties. Resurgent tribalism, family and business hierarchies which the British encouraged divided India and would delay the unity she needs for balanced development and to advance her reputation.

"Nobody more snooty than Indians from India," Jain joked. "It's a curse."

"It's a serious problem they must solve quickly; my friend Ossie who grew up in India had explained this to me years ago. It could ruin India, especially if they continue to be *coconuts*. We see some of that here still, and directed at everyone. It's made many Africans believe that Indians are their foes," I said. "But look at Jagan; he does far more for Africans than for us; we don't object as long as there is some balance. We know that Indians and Africans can work together and live together. What hurdles exist are mostly in towns and big villages, and due to misinformation, but they can be cleared. Africans have much to gain with good Indians in charge of the economy.

I don't mean by that that Africans cannot take charge of the economy. But in today's conditions and the very nature of Hindu beliefs--especially the organisation of life's journey -- keeps us focussed on learning and achievement as the basis of developing our society and sustaining it. Those who say otherwise are generally those who know us least. I grew up in a community with African neighbours and teachers and had more issues with Indians than them; sure there were instances when we fussed or teased one another, but that was at a childhood level; adults and families were always cordial. I can't see any one of us taking up arms against you chaps; besides you're the ones with the weapons. The British denied us shotguns for a century!" I ended jauntily; the men chuckled.

Reactions

"I met Indians in England, competent men; but did notice how different they looked and spoke; a few even looked like Chinese. Of course we didn't talk of past history. I knew India was complicated, but this is one heck of a story; is all that you say really so?" Bacchus was sceptical.

"I too never hear this before; how come we never come across this stuff?" Doris asked.

"British kept these from you," Jain said, "otherwise you might respect us; they don't really want that! They helped us to hate each other, to rule us both more easily. Divide and rule! That's the story of Brits in India. They're past masters at bribery and corruption, but quick to condemn if you do it."

"True!" Brewster noted. "We learn what they tell us, and that don't include you at all."

"It's partly our fault. Indian culture is knowledge based; we have always wanted to set up schools to teach these things but no money; years ago a BHS teacher wanted to start Indian studies, but war nixed that and after the war he went to England! Indians don't know enough either and many city Indians, as Jain said, tend to belittle those from the countryside, like they do in India."

"Maan, I agree that was a lot of heavy stuff, most new to me. I hope I remember some." Brewster said. "I went to an Indian picture a lil' while ago with me wife; I din' understand a word, but I got the story; now I hear what you say it had to do with one of those Muslim invasions, don't remember the name , but the costumes were terrific and the action great; first time I see elephants in an army. I get the gist but not the same as when you know the language. Pretty girls though. Pretty girls."

"The older folk understand; most young people understand only a little, but they memorise the songs and dances, and do good imitations in local shows and parties."

"I think Bombay will change and use subtitles if market outside India gets big. They don't have to now because 95% of market is India, and subtitling is expensive." Jain explained. "That film sounds like **Mughal-e-Azam**, about that king named Prithiviraj, the one who released the captive Muslim king."

"Even if they do subtitles, I don't see African people going to see Indian pictures. The styles too different; besides they don' respect us enough; it needs lots of education." Balgobin suggested.

"You're probably right, for most people," Bacchus said, "however cosmopolitan people will investigate and take an interest in new things; the process might be slow."

There were nods of agreement. He continued, "Doc, clear up something for me. You say you had this terrible war between armies of the same family and your God came down and advised the commander of one side to fight against his family? How then you say Hinduism is peaceful if God advise killing? Christ said to turn the other cheek."

"War was a last resort; all else had failed, starting with turned cheeks! The good were doomed; war was fought to restore the good and righteous from the evil. The armies were led by first cousins who had grown up together. The commander you refer to, *Arjuna*, could not bear to fight them, however wicked they were; all he saw were familiar faces not the evil they did; not stopping them would harm millions. Krishna explained to him right and wrong, duty, loyalty, morals, and all good qualities a person must have to live and share with others in a just society and the circumstances when a person has to put right, good and duty before feelings and kinship. The *Gita* is the record of his advice."

"It is one very complicated story, no, many stories," Jain amplified, "large family, very rich and powerful ruling millions of people; one side of family with many ambitious and powerful members get greedy, use tricks to seize government from rightful king--Arjuna's eldest brother--by winning bet; he agrees to go into exile with his brothers for so many years, after which they would get their kingdom back. The wicked cousins exploited and oppressed people, lived lavish lustful lives, enriched themselves; life became unbearable, with hunger, poverty, disease and no hope. When the exile was up the king and his brothers returned, their cousins broke agreements, rejected them and continued to rule. When all negotiations failed war became the only way."

"The doctrine of 'turn the other cheek' is part of Hindu, Buddhist and Jain teachings called *ahimsa* and was the basis of Gandhi's struggle against the British." I added.

Some discussion followed on the concurrence of various tenets and teachings among religions, their practice and applicability in modern times. We agreed that many virtues and principles were timeless, transcending religion. Rituals and beliefs however varied with time, place and conditions but were often set in stone by those who profit from them and thus could impede understanding and progress if the perspective were distorted.

"Doc," Brewster asked, "going back to what you told us about your religion and scriptures. They that old? Older than the Bible? And the British really corrupted your history like that?" Brewster, with his marital link to this past was more curious than the others and open-minded, but was finding it hard to believe that his mentors could have been so callous and deceitful.

"Oh, yes, all true," Jain said, "Brits believe their old story-tellers but they call ours childish! And much worse; changing our history is one thing, but they wrecked our economy, stole our reserves and killed millions of our people. Much of India's poverty you hear about is due to foreign rule, Mughal and especially British; Mughals made India home but Brits took all wealth to UK and built fancy buildings in London and other big cities. I have to say though that they got great help from greedy Indians. Here you get little or no real news about India. By 19th century Brits controlled news with telegraph and thought they could change and erase India's memory and get away with lies; millions of Brits died believing those lies."

"Many died because they didn't!" I added, "Brits also addicted 120 *million* Chinese, don't forget that. We still have old Hong Kong and Canton addicts on Lombard St on daily opium quotas. India lost over 100 *million people* between 1770 and 1944. Europeans tend to forget how young they were, barely four centuries out of the dark ages, when they entered India, then a mature and complex civilisation, and marvelled in the same way a child marvels on entering a toy store or someone from Bush Lot on first seeing New York!

"They grabbed the toys, just like children would, all the toys! What followed was predictable: covetousness and greed and the bravado of a young and martial people who had nothing to lose, much to gain and used their great talents of piracy and seamanship and belief in divine right of kings, where lords expect to be obeyed to the letter and be served by lower classes, who would slit the throat of their neighbour to gain a pittance. Dickens tells that sordid side of Britain, which rulers tried to hide, even as the French people, the proletariat *sans culotte*, were rebelling and showed how fed up they were with their rulers.

"In Germany principalities struggled in vain against one another while in Italy Popes, regional dukes and duchesses fought one another with sword and poison for territory and power. Europe from the 17th century was a mess of surging humanity, in social and religious terms, and almost broke. So they turned to piracy and raiding, like the Muslims before them. Henry VIII began to build a great navy to pursue his syphilitic delusions to rule all nations. His daughter continued that work."

"When Muslims lost Europe they went east and seized many lands," Jain noted, recalling the accounts he had given, "until they became strong enough to take India, then the land of wealth and beauty. No, we gave it to them through conceit. We had enough chances to expel invaders; we failed not because our soldiers were weak; we failed because our rulers were selfish and found it hard to unite; it's our disgrace."

"If you look at Africa, the story is just as shocking, and I mentioned the

Zulus." I said. "Cecil Rhodes stole the diamond- and gold-bearing parts of South Africa, by trickery, forcing contracts with Natives written in English, fought wars against Africans and Boers, and gained lands, for which Britain rewarded him, as they had done Clive, Hastings and all the other thieves in India.. France and Spain took West and NW Africa that Brits didn't snatch. Germans took parts of East Africa, but lost them to Brits in WWI. The Portuguese were vicious in India, and still are in Angola and Mozambique, while racist Boers claim to 'civilise' South Africa! So when Macmillan talked of *wind of change in Africa,*[116] it was just a big fart!"

The hilarity subsided, Jain exclaimed, "Pure hypocrisy! His speech was racist and gave European thieves credit for founding African nationalism, while what they did was steal South Africa and India's best lands and give them away to English farmers. He's hypocrite when he speaks of freedom and dependence; he must learn some history. Theses peoples had survived well for many thousand years before British made them dependent. Only thing they can teach is how to lie, cheat and steal. Verwoerd ignored him and after one month massacred many Africans at Sharpeville. Portuguese will not release colonies without fight."

"Yes, all over the world it was a European grab-fest." Bacchus agreed. "At Police College the tutors refer to this with great pride. Even Yanks joined in and took the Philippines and Cuba from the Spanish. Now they control all of America, north and south, economically if not politically."

"If Yankees could get away with colonies, we would be one; Puerto Rico would be a slum if not for Munoz Marin; besides US still has to treat Africans as people just like whites."

"The African missed his chances to succeed in Haiti," Bacchus observed, "and here Kofi and Akara could have won out, but they were immature, had no resources, no guidance or experience. And worst of all they were disunited, just like your people, loyal to tribe rather than nation. Yet under strain Africans *have* done well. Take the **West India Regiment**. In England I visited Windsor Castle and saw their colours in St George's Chapel, and learned about their exploits."

"Yes," Brewster said; they disbanded years ago, 1927; we learnt about them in training."

"They gave 132 years of proud service." Bacchus added. "Do you know how they came about?" Heads shook and Doris said, "Vaguely."

---

[116] Harold Macmillan, Feb 3, 1960, to the South African Parliament, "*...No one could fail to be impressed with the immense material progress which has been achieved* (in South Africa). *That all this has been accomplished in so short a time is a striking testimony to the skill, energy and initiative of your people. We in Britain are proud of the contribution we have made to this remarkable achievement. Much of it has been financed by British capital. ... In the twentieth century, and especially since the end of the war, the processes which gave birth to the nation states of Europe have been repeated all over the world. We have seen the awakening of national consciousness in peoples who have for centuries lived in dependence upon some other power. Fifteen years ago this movement spread through Asia. Many countries there, of different races and civilisations, pressed their claim to an independent national life. Today the same thing is happening in Africa, and the most striking of all the impressions I have formed since I left London a month ago is of the strength of this African national consciousness...The wind of change is blowing through this continent and whether we like it or not, this growth of national consciousness is a political fact. We must all accept it as a fact, and our national policies must take account of it...Well you understand this better than anyone, you are sprung from Europe, the home of nationalism, here in Africa you have yourselves created a free nation. A new nation. Indeed in the history of our times yours will be recorded as the first of the African nationalists. This tide of national consciousness, which is now rising in Africa, is a fact, for which both you and we, and the other nations of the western world are ultimately responsible....*" (also said in Ghana, Jan 1960)

"Fighting against France in 1790's, the same wars that went on in India," he continued, "Sir Ralph Abercromby developed quite a reputation and became head of British Caribbean forces; he captured Demerara and Essequibo from the Dutch, Grenada, Saint Lucia, Saint Vincent and Trinidad from French. He was the first British governor of Trinidad. He was a fair man and treated people well - - slaves, soldiers and public. He praised African workers for *'fortitude, loyalty and physical robustness'* and because malaria and dysentery were killing off English forces his superiors authorised twelve black West Indian regiments to replace them. But planters objected; they were scared of armed Africans, no matter how loyal, but truth is they didn't want to lose their best workers.

"So the army recruited West Africans and formed the West India Regiments (WIR). These chaps gave first class service and they captured St Martin in one of their first outings, then Dominica. They fought in all the Islands, went to the US in 1814, and to Gambia where private Samuel Hodge of Tortola in 1866 and Lance-Corporal William James Gordon of Jamaica in 1892, won Victoria Crosses. Their commanders gave them high praise and that was a time when white superiority was the rage in Europe and America and practised by island governors and local elite; few Blacks got any honours."

"We see that even today, though perhaps not as bad," I said.

"They disbanded some battalions before the Great War," Bacchus said, resuming his narrative. "The rest served in Palestine under General Allenby against the Turks and one contingent served in East Africa. The Regiment saw its last in Kingston, Jamaica in 1927. It merged with the Jamaica Regiment. They get confused with the *Caribbean Regiment*, which was formed later, in WWII, and served mainly in POW camps in Italy and to escort prisoners from one location to another."

"About 3,000 West Indians, mostly Africans, including Guianese, joined the RAF in WWII," I added. "Some served in the air but most were ground crew. One of my wife's in-laws was in it; he saw the ugly side of racism, American style, when he trained in Georgia and the funny side of it at his base in England; he found the English more tolerant and married one. Errol Barrow the up-and-coming Bajan politician served as a rear-gunner in a bomber crew and flew over 40 missions over Europe.[117]"

"Some of our current officers fought in the War and lost several of their comrades. Sometimes we forget the people who served and died in our name," Bacchus said with regret. "The British have never given coloured troops the honour they deserve, and so many died in the two great Wars fighting for Britain. White, Black, Brown, and Yellow: we were in it together; just like your *Gita* war. I can easily believe your story of British deception, fabrication and suppression in India. After all they broke so many conventions that Europeans dubbed them *'Perfidious Albion'*!"[118]

---

[117] He was a socialist verging on Marxist; realising his tiny country's situation he changed and became the highly respected and successful Prime Minister of Barbados with whom I would have a mutually respectful relationship when I became Dean of the Medical Faculty at UWI, coincident with one of his terms in office. The Barbadian economy remains one of the healthiest in the Caribbean.

[118] Augustin, Marquis of Ximenez seems to have been the first to use the phrase in writing in 1793, although another Frenchman: theologian Jacques-Bénigne Bossuet used the phrase "perfidious England" a century earlier and the idea of British perfidy has a much older history among Europeans. See Schmidt, H.D. *'The Idea and Slogan of "Perfidious Albion"'*, Journal of the History of Ideas, Vol. 14, No. 4 (Oct., 1953), pp. 604–616

The Chain of Being

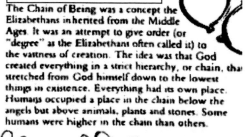

in general, much
most everyone
to heaven or hell
kill his
is praying,
, heaven.

t country - it had
rch of Rome.
ment called the
attacks on
nd led to the
nt, churches.

olies, was
in 1581.

ne of
en as
were

The Chain of Being was a concept the Elizabethans inherited from the Middle Ages. It was an attempt to give order (or "degree" as the Elizabethans often called it) to the vastness of creation. The idea was that God created everything in a strict hierarchy, or chain, that stretched from God himself down to the lowest things in existence. Everything had its own place. Humans occupied a place in the chain below the angels but above animals, plants and stones. Some humans were higher in the chain than others.

The monarch was the highest, with nobles and churchmen below. Then followed gentlemen and finally commoners. All women were considered to be inferior to men, with the obvious exception of Elizabeth I. Her position as monarch outweighed the fact that she was a woman.

Accepting one's place in the chain was a duty that would be rewarded by God in heaven. Disrupting the chain was thought to lead to chaos, but of course many people still did challenge their position in society.

The "Great Chain of Being":
God
Angels
Kings/Queens
Archbishops
Dukes/Duchesses
Bishops
Marquises/Marchionesses
Earls/Countesses
Viscounts/Viscountesses
Barons/Baronesses
Abbots/Deacons
Knights/Local Officials
Ladies-in-Waiting
Priests/Monks
Squires
Pages
Messengers
Merchants/Shop-keepers
Tradesmen
Yeomen Farmers
Soldiers/Town Watch
Household Servants
Tennant Farmers
Shepherds/Herders
Beggars
Actors
Thieves/Pirates
Gypsies
Animals
Birds
Worms
Plants/Rocks

The Elizabethans inherited the belief that this **"Chain of Being"** or order was divinely ordained, as enunciated by Thomas Aquinas. They and their descendants practised this casteism as it obviously was very advantageous to aristocrats (barons and above) giving them the authority to exploit and abuse the rest (commoners). A secondary heirarchy existed by religion, race and colour, with ignominy heaped on Jews "heathens" and Blacks. The Commoners, not to be outdone, had their own levels, as Tomas Nash in 1593 said, *"The Courtier disdaineth the citizen;/the citizen the countryman;/the shoemaker the cobbler./But unfortunate is the man who does not have anyone he can look down upon."*

Lack of education and the Ptolemaic view of the Universe favoured by the Vatican allowed the system to flourish and continue for centuries, even after Galileo (Europe did not know about 5th Indian astronomer and mathematician Aryabhatta—see Ch 5). The "Chain" belief allowed enrichment of the aristocracy and their protégés, and permitting atrocities such as slavery and the brutality of colonialism as seen in America, India and Africa. Attempts by equality advocates to change it have been partially successful-- as education reached the lower levels—especially in areas of personal freedoms, for example, to seek education, housing, employment and start businesses etc. but the mass of humanity remains trapped in its grasp. Similar hierarchies existed and still exist in other countries and among non-Europeans. Apologies for poor reproduction; text accessible today on internet

Shivaji, founder of Maratha Empire

Features of Jantar mantar 8th C. Delhi Observatory. These are precision astronomical instruments constructed by Raja Jaisingh and were remarkably accurate.

Bajirao I, the invincible, Péshwé of Marathas

L: Mastani (died 1740) wife of Péshwé Bajirao 1. R: Rural young woman, one of majority of modern Indians from families whose lands were seized by the British and given to their minions. This continues today as foreign corporations, mainly US, seize rural India with the help of local raiders and an inert and corrupt "secular" government, deaf to their pleas; they have divided India into rich and poor, urban US-oriented coconuts and rural Bhāratiyas, the real salt of the earth that Gandhi worked to elevate socially and economically, and to restore their lands; instead India is being conquered again; politicos and the rich fatten while farmers commit suicide!

Yashwantrao Holkar and sons, all of whom (including Holkar's daughter) fought valiantly against the British and would have driven them off but for Indian divisiveness, bribery and corruption by the enemy and treachery to their "allies"—a recurrent theme in Indian history, that dogs the land to this day.

India Gate, Delhi

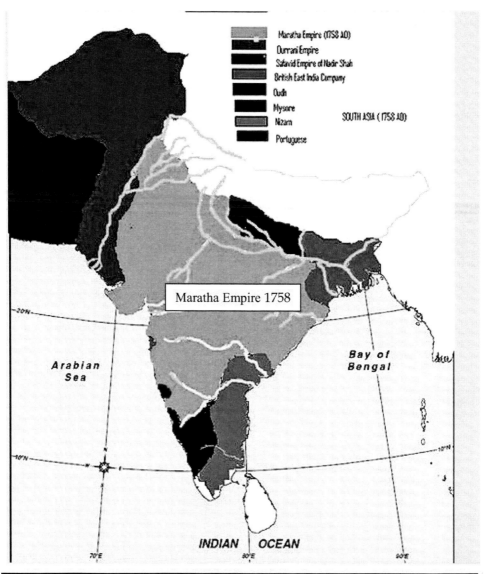

Maratha Empire 1758

Legend:
Maratha Empire (1758 AD)
Durrani Empire
Safavid Empire of Nadir Shah
British East India Company
Oudh
Mysore
Nizam
Portuguese

SOUTH ASIA (1758 AD)

Arabian Sea

Bay of Bengal

INDIAN OCEAN

Many languages are spoken in India, a fact that confuses those ignorant of the country which means most westerners. Hindi is the primary spoken language of 41%, Bengali 8.1%, Telugu 7.2%, Marathi 7%, Tamil 5.9%, Urdu 5%, Gujarati 4.5%, Kannada 3.7%, Malayalam 3.2%, Oriya 3.2%, Punjabi 2.8%, Assamese 1.3%, Maithili 1.2% and others 5.9%. These 15 plus Kashmiri, Sindhi and Sanskrit are official languages. English has "associate" status but remains the a language for higher education and for national, political, and commercial communication (2001 census). In the past fifty years since independence India has come under intensifying attacks by rich religious fanatics, especially American Christian evangelists and the Vatican, seeking to subvert Indian culture and convert Hindus especially Dalits by repeating the "aryan-dravidian" distortions Muller and the British had made a century ago. South India has become the preferred battleground using minority rights, caste, dowry etc to militarise gullible youth, and the Thomas myth to base myriad presumptions of the role of Christianity in key features of Hinduism; Sanskrit is assailed and even the "best" US universities are guilty of plotting its demise. NE India has already fallen to Christianity as the attacks continue and the INC government seems powerless to stop it, terrorised by minorities, racial and religious, falling to US corporate greed and quite willing to see the majority emasculated and country balkanised. (2007)

Clive, Hastings, Cornwallis

The impeachment of Warren Hastings in Westminster Hall, 1789. Engraver; Pollard, R.; Jan. 3 1789. Downloaded by Fowler& Fowler" Talk, 22:04, 23 March 2008 (UTC) from the British Library Web Site

Sepoys (Indian infantrymen) of the East India Company line up outside the north entrance of Tippu Sultan's Palace, Bangalore, 1804. The Company had followed a strict hierarchy in its use of native staff, as in the home country, and used a system of minor but prestigious awards, medals, ribbons etc to maintain divisions among natives and ethnic groups, to consolidate the divisions, ensure loyalty and reduce chances of their realising that they were being duped and used to fight, for small gains, against their countrymen and to support the seizure of native lands and otherwise enforce policies to enrich the invader.

The Rape of Indian Industry: Mellor cotton mill in Marple near Stockport (1802) exemplifies this: it was built in 1790-93 by Samuel Oldknow, England's leading manufacturer of muslin, which had previously been made only in East Bengal. The building was six stories high, and the mill was powered by a waterwheel fed from a nearby river diverted into a series of mill ponds.

British offficers executing captured Indians by blowing them from guns! This had taken on the aura of a sport, as brave as hunting tigers from the safety of an elephant's back!

"And England, now avenge their wrongs by vengeance deep and dire,/ Cut out their canker with the sword, and burn it out with fire;/ Destroy those traitor regions, hang every pariah hound,/ And hunt them down to death, in all hills and cities 'round." Martin Tupper, stirring bloodthirsty hate in Britain, *Wrath of the Lion*, NY Times reprint, 1857

British Reaction to 1857 War of Independence, a sample. You would think India had invaded the UK!

"... All the city's people found within the walls of the city of Delhi when our troops entered were bayoneted on the spot, and the number was considerable, as you may suppose, when I tell you that in some houses forty and fifty people were hiding. These were not mutineers but residents of the city, who trusted to our well-known mild rule for pardon. I am glad to say they were disappointed." *From a letter published in the "Bombay Telegraph"; reproduced in the British press, 1857.*

"It was literally murder... I have seen many bloody and awful sights lately but such a one as I witnessed yesterday I pray I never see again. The women were all spared but their screams on seeing their husbands and sons butchered, were most painful... Heaven knows I feel no pity, but when some old grey bearded man is brought and shot before your very eyes, hard must be that man's heart I think who can look on with indifference..." *Edward Vibart, a 19-year-old officer"*

"All honour to you for catching the king and slaying his sons. I hope you will bag many more!" *General Montgomery to Captain Hodgson, on his massacre of Delhiites, 1857*

"With all my love for the army, I must confess, the conduct of professed Christians on this occasion, was one of the most humiliating facts connected with the siege." *Capt. Hodgson, British Army in India, 1857*

British soldiers looting Qaisar Bagh, Lucknow, after its recapture. The steel engraving depicts the Time correspondent looking on at the sacking of the Qaisar Bagh, after the capture of Lucknow on March 15, 1858. ***"Is this string of little white stones (pearls) worth anything, Gentlemen?"*** asks the plunderer. Who's the barbarian and thief?

L: Begum Hazrat Mahal, 1857
Patriot, escaped
R: Tantia Tope, betrayed by a friend and executed by British, contrary to "rules of war"

The War of Independence had smouldered for a century since the days of Clive as India teetered between the excesses of the British and the disunity of Indian rulers. Mangal Panday, the young soldier who fired the first shot in outrage against his Sgt. Major and adjutant, finally showed what must be done but mercifully did not live to see the carnage that reprisals brought. The British press gloated and screamed for blood, praising the brutality of their own and condemning Indians even the many civilians killed. Britain proceeded to gut India, seize its industries, scuttle its state-of-the-art manufactures, replace them with shoddy goods, destroy peasant farming, bribe its rulers or else "legally" eliminate them, plotted to undermine India's major religions and transferred her wealth to Britain--the most egregious example of international theft in history, eclipsing the Romans. The US, it seems, is aiming to outdo the British in rapacity.

JUSTICE.

1857 *British Justice* Punch Cartoon- John Tenniel

Lakshmi Bai of Jhansi

Sipahis(sepoys) in action in Indian War of Independence 1857

1876 *Punch* cartoon captioned *"New crowns for old ones!"* PM Disraeli (1804–81) making Queen Victoria Empress of India!

Residence of successful businessman Sir Jamsetjee Jejeebhoy (bottlewalla), 1st Baronet, 1858, notable for his alliance with Dr Jardine in trade with China. His palace is lit to welcome the British monarch

The free market viewpoint understands economic liberty as the freedom to produce, trade and consume any goods and services acquired without the use of force, fraud or theft. By this definition the Brits did not practise economic freedom in India or Africa or anywhere in the Empire.

Staff and students of the National College, Lahore, founded in 1921 by Lala Lajpat Rai to train students for the non-cooperation movement. Standing, fourth from right, is Bhagat Singh, later to be executed by the British and martyred for his revolutionary activities.

Above: Gandhi at Salt Satyagraha, 1930; *Below:*Nehru and Gandhi at INC opening 1937

Ruskin, Savarkar, Tagore

Nehru: Independence Midnight "tryst with destiny"

M A Jinnah: Muslim nation (fragmenting India)   Independence Day for 2 nations

Rashtrapati Bhavan, New Delhi

Bene Israel family, Bombay 1906

Drs Brahmam and Walter Singh during a discussion

Chapter 6

Finally a shower of rain fell, only too briefly to do more that cool us down. We are delighted on finally reaching Cokerite to find our patient fully recovered and almost unrecognisably vivacious. The Chief and Shaman were not surprised at our delayed return but were close to sending out a search party. I was made an honorary villager and Mike, the child's father, presented me a ceremonial arrow, one of the first he had made; in return I left him all my writing materials; he had shown a knack for drawing on sand everywhere we had stopped. I learn the legends of the Barama Caribs and a fascinating story of their belief that they originated in Atlantis, which they assert was flooded many millennia ago. They also bemoan their decimation by Europeans and their subsequent humiliation by missionaries and coastal people, and threats to their culture. In our group we note that our talks seemed to have eased tensions and created a lasting camaraderie; conversation has become easy and more intimate; daily greetings "feel" as if they came from the heart, not from habit.

Day 12: Return to Cokerite, legends of creation

That's the error of the missionaries who come here: they preach to the natives, but never listen to them. Hari

A thing is not true simply because it is believed by many, not even if it is of some use. Anon

The camp was busy by the time I emerged from my cotton cocoon, which had trapped an array of small insects, mainly mosquitoes, within its folds; I squashed them all reflexly and noted that a few contained blood. We hustled our preparations in anticipation of an early arrival at Cokerite. We had biscuits and coffee and by the time I made my way to the boat, Benn was already crouching in the rear whistling while he readied his engine for the journey.

Doris stood in erect silhouette on a rock at the edge of the camp surveying the scene while puffing on an early morning cigarette, its blue plume rising lazily up to the still grey sky. The men busily stowed the baggage and prepared our departure. The scene looked the same as on any of the previous days anywhere else on the river. The sameness was now so familiar that details became the only noteworthy things. The sky looked heavier this morning, the humidity more oppressive and more haze above the early mist that capped the river and hung like cobwebs between the trees.

The tarp was moist with overnight condensation, which made it swish as it was folded. Beads of moisture rimmed the leaves along the bank. The sun had yet to rise beyond the eastern trees and the hum of the forest silence announced the retirement of all the creatures of the night. Here and there a bird wheeled in the sky sensing some fallen animal and seeking out its early meal. The river gurgled at our feet as we hurried our departure; we got underway just as the changing colour behind the eastern forest told of the sun's new rising.

The 14-mile run to Cokerite was slow, hardly a run, more a crawl through the familiar gauntlet of fallen trees but we were relieved to find that the path we had cleared on the upstream journey had remained clear save for scattered driftwood stuck among partially submerged branches. It continued to amaze everyone how crowded the river was when viewed from a distance, almost like a road made of stout crisscrossed logs, with all filler lost, and how surprising it was that there was enough uncluttered room between the logs for the boat to zigzag its painful way through them. It brought to mind moments from my childhood when we would try to coax a *corial* (dugout canoe) through a stretch of canal choked with a plethora of water plants, from reeds to lilies or water hyacinth and half-submerged mosses, and how delighted we would get when we came upon a stretch of open water. It was the same feeling whenever the engine revved above a low putt-putting.

We paused several times for broken pins, and after an hour or so Benn casually told the Inspector that we were down to our last bottle of gasoline, four pints. Fortunately we were going with the current, and he was running the engine at low revolutions; with luck we should have enough to take us to Barama mouth. Beyond Cokerite the river was deeper and wider with fewer obstructions, none major, but would probably be just as slow as on the up-river journey. Some fuel conservation would be possible further downstream. At the very worst, we would have to finish by paddling a few miles.

At mid-morning we had been on the river for two hours and came upon a flight of crows circling the forest just off the south bank of the river. From time to time groups of slender gnat-like insects could be seen hovering erratically a few feet over the water. The atmosphere was steamy and the early morning haze had given way quite quickly to a mantle of cloud, hiding the sun for the first time on this trip. Doris, Ben and Rod were shirtless and frequently drizzled water scooped up from the passing wave to cool down.

"I wish we had a sunshade on this boat," Inspector Bacchus spoke for all as we both pulled soggy shirts from backs sticky from hours of perspiration. "This fella was meant for short quick trips, not long slow ones like this."

I wet my face and head frequently with the cool water. Today was particularly uncomfortable. The cloud build-up continued fairly rapidly and changed colour from milky white to grey cumulus. The air smelled differently and a little cool wind sprang up from the river, welcomed by all.

"Look like it goin' rain," Balgobin said, "I better make sure nothing get wet, especially the food," and busied himself with impedimenta at his feet, pulling the tarpaulin this way and that to make sure that it covered everything.

We were paused to clear some branches which had freshly fallen into the channel when the rain started, at first a fine spray rather like the one that came up from the prow, then larger drops that hurried across the air above us from north to south and came down in a thick drenching sheet, the coarse drops sputtering on the surface of the river, each sending an inverse cone of spray rising an inch or more.

A crashing noise came down from the treetops as the big drops hit the leaves, dispelling the brooding silence that pervaded the scene whenever the engine stopped, and we would hear again the ripple of water flowing and the hum of the forest--the voice of nature as its elements conversed with one another--or else the howl of "baboons" in distant treetops.

The raindrops stung where they hit bared flesh, but their cooling effect was welcome. The shower lasted about fifteen minutes and relieved the searing heat of the day, leaving us drenched and cooled. We watched the shower as it coursed across the sky, its chatter on the treetops fading as it went.

"We need a day of that to raise the water level." Benn said ruefully. The sun emerged almost immediately and soon the day had resumed its sultry course. Before long all traces of the shower had gone save for the lingering dampness of our clothes.

Two hours later, we passed three small streams joining the Barama from the south, the *Ourabaru, Enamu* and *Tenambo*, all reduced to rivulets just a few feet wide. At 1.35 pm we rounded the bend that took us in sight of the dock at Cokerite. Children on the riverbank and those cavorting in the water nearby saw us first; those on the bank began to jump up and down excitedly, alerting the village. Some of those in the water swam feverishly to both sides of the boat, their heads bobbing up and down and calling out greetings. As we eased alongside the dock some clambered onto the boat and as quickly dived off into the water, repeating this manoeuvre in a show of welcome while continuing to squeal and frolic with unabashed delight even after we had docked. Still, they kept a distance from us on the shouted cautions of the women supervising their swim.

Throughout the morning, as we neared the village, my concern for the baby with pneumonia had increased steadily to a nagging fear and several of the men, including Joe (who had seen similar illness in the past producing a fatal outcome) had doubted that the child would recover. Mike, his youthful father had maintained a straight and stoic face, perhaps not understanding the concerns expressed or through natural fatalism. Twice I had dreamt about the child. I kept seeing his pale, hot, limp body clasped in his little mother's arms, herself so delicate, childlike and still, enigmatic like a porcelain figure or sphinx. I had prayed for his recovery, encouraged in this outcome by his initial response to my makeshift dispensing. How I regretted not bringing along more antibiotics.

Our briefing had not alerted me to the possibility of having to treat an illness except among our party, nor to the possibility of having to stay for any length of time in a native village other than Wappai. Both oversights expressed the prevailing ignorance on the coast of the realities of life in the forests. The sight of children frolicking in the water made me automatically search the group closely, not that I expected to see him among the swimmers. On our approach the children--other than the daring ones who had climbed on board--had scurried out of the water, splashing, like four-eyed fish riding the crest of waves as they rolled ashore, a sight I had become used to in my years criss-crossing the Berbice River or surveying that great stream from the long pier of the New Amsterdam Market where I would spend Saturday mornings helping Mrs Latchman at her stall.

The two women keeping watch over the swimmers at the water's edge were young, each minding a naked toddler, who kept running back and forth between them and the river's edge, picking up small objects and throwing them a few feet into the water. The women, on seeing us land, had called out cautions to the children in the water, hastily picked up the toddlers and darted up the path to the cluster of huts beyond the rise. We were too far away and the action too quick for anyone to be recognised, except perhaps by the natives.

The show by the children was as much for the returning fathers as for the visitors. Joe pointed out his two children and one each for two of the others. I searched Mike's face for emotion or sign that he had recognised his son among the children on the beach. It looked impassive, no hint of the concern he must surely feel as he scoured the scene and not finding what he sought. Joe said something to him as the boat tied up, and they began to unload the baggage.

In a few minutes the boat was emptied and we followed the porters up the narrow path to our logie. Just then the village chief appeared, holding a staff in his right hand and wearing a headdress. The shaman followed close behind. They greeted us warmly and the Chief came up to me, smiling, said something which I did not understand, and walked back up the path, gesturing for Joe and me to follow with the baby's father close behind as we meandered along the narrow sandy path bordered by tall grass. (I had thought that Mike was baby's father until I met his pregnant wife and the baby's father)

"We go see baby!" Joe said. I felt immediate relief, interpreting the Chief's welcome and smile as good news. I imagined what I would see, but on arriving at the hut, there was no mother and suckling baby in a hammock, the last image I had of them, but an empty hammock and the two women, mother and daughter, whom I had met with the sick child. They smiled, but said nothing. I wondered whether the baby had died a propitious death, but even so their behaviour was paradoxical, although I had heard that under certain circumstances death was greeted with relief and celebration.

The Chief asked a question, which needed no interpretation as the younger woman reached behind her; finding nothing, she turned and went to the far end of the room, reached behind a large covered barrel (which incidentally held a supply of *cassiri*) and emerged with a kicking, squealing child. This was my patient, fully recovered, golden brown, not the ashen pallor I recalled. It was an astonishing transformation. Not only did he look good, he was unusually full of energy fighting his way out of his mother's restraint to drop to the floor and scurry off to his hiding place. Enquiring how much of my antibiotic concoction the child had been given, I was shown the empty container.

I went off and returned with my stethoscope—I didn't really need to, but they expected it--and verified that the reluctant squealing examinee was structurally fully recovered. Later when I returned to our now familiar billet, Mike came to me, all smiles, saying many thanks in his own language, and presented me with an arrow, from the first batch that he had made by himself years ago. With sign language and Joe interpreting, he told me that he would be forever in my debt and that he and his baby would be like family since I had saved his life. I was deeply moved by his sincerity and assured him that I would have done the same for anyone in the village, and that I would do whatever I could to help them. Searching my mind for something of practical value I could give him, I recalled his frequent doodling on the sand, in the few quiet minutes we had at the end of the day, while his co-mates carried on a conversation, sometimes about his pictures. He used a stick or lengths of stiff grass tied into a broom, and often drew elaborate pictures of animals, canoes and what looked like hunting scenes. He was also known to scratch images and forms on rocks at the river's edge, using sharp stones, nails or arrowheads. So after consulting Joe about protocol, I gave him my pencils and my last pad of plain paper, which pleased him enormously since he had no media. I undertook to send him a supply via the visiting sicknurse/dispenser. Jain and Brewster took photographs of the presentations and of the group, including Mike's wife.

The Chief invited us to share a drink of *cassiri*, once we had settled in. The shaman accompanied by an ageing man with a shock of grey hair and wizened face, came to escort us to the Chief's tent. There we exchanged pleasantries; I noted that the shaman spoke quite good English, and told us how pleased they were that we had returned safely, and had begun preparations to send a scouting party upriver; they had decided to wait one week based mainly on their confidence in Joe as a forester and hunter and on the news of low water in the river; five days earlier an airplane had circled the village then headed downriver.

The drink he offered was this season's; (it was rare for any to carry over into the next year, anyway); it had a taste and kick not unlike sugarcane highwine, though, I guessed, at lesser alcohol content, perhaps about 30%.

The shaman explained the process of making the stinging sweetish drink first from fermenting the cassava, and finally colouring the strained liquid with sweet potato peelings. The liquor was drunk communally at ceremonies, especially after the harvest, and to welcome important visitors. It was often served with new cassava bread (biscuits really), which they would dunk in the liquor to soften them and improve the flat taste.

Later the shaman pointed out the hut where the stock of liquor was stored in large earthenware containers. This surprised me as I had heard that this store was jealously guarded, especially from strangers. In a nearby hut women were busy processing mounds of freshly reaped cassava. Each was busy at a particular step in the process, working like an assembly line, hardly pausing between stages. Two pounded the roots to a pulp; one poured the crushed roots and aliquots of water into the *matapi* then turned it screw-like around the fixed top end to squeeze the milky eluate containing the poisonous cyanide, which was collected in an earthenware vessel.

The elution was repeated several times to extract all cyanide leaving a flocculent residue, the flour which two women were busy kneading and rolling out into flatbread. The bread was dried on the roofs of the huts. Looking up I could see them, white circles eight to ten inches in diameter with edges curling as they dried giving them a scalloped look.

We were shown the citrus grove, well, not really a grove but a few scattered but lush grapefruit and lime trees laden with fruit, which someone-- possibly a missionary or someone returning from the coast--had introduced to the village sometime past. We were given grapefruit, the first fresh fruit we had had in ten days. I took the opportunity to explore the part of the village I was allowed to and observe how they provided for themselves, a fact of which they were very proud. Their cassava fields were rotated from one area to another, every two or three years, and they had ample acreage for this. There was one large field, with stalks about four feet tall at the front and three feet at the back due to staggered plantings. Bare areas indicated reaped sections. The dying stalks lay randomly on the ground, wilted and pale. Two young women were tending the field, hoeing and weeding. The moist packed sandy soil gave testimony to the rain that had fallen there earlier. The air was fresh, though still and had the clean smell of citrus, heavy with humidity. My clothes were still sticking to my body, and patches of perspiration had soaked the armpits.

To the south, a quarter mile or so away, the clearing gave way to forest, through which ran the trail to the Cuyuni River 50 miles south. This narrow and unimpressive path—access to which was closely guarded at Cokerite--allowed only single file passage and had in times past been trod by men seeking fortunes in gold or else by agents of lumber companies scouting the forest for the most valuable commercial trees: greenheart, purpleheart and wamara.

In the section near Cokerite the trees were not as tall or stout as we had seen in the upper Barama. The underbrush was thicker and encroached on the path. This traverse definitely required the assistance of a stout stick and machete, at least for the mile or so that we explored. Further south, we were told, the forest became taller, the trees further apart and at ground level less bushy. But even as we entered we were promptly caught in the grip of its power and infused with that awesome and magical hum that had become so familiar, indistinguishable to me from the powerful Vaidic *Aum* slowly intoned.

The villagers, we learned, were worried that the increasing interest shown by lumbermen in this area might change the character of the forest and affect their way of life. Their concern was aggravated by the fact that although most of the northern part traversed by this trail were in their traditional territory, no one had consulted them on further use of the forest. They had assumed on our first arrival that we were representatives of industry, until they recognised Doris, and our mission was explained.

Back in the village we were not allowed to go beyond the riverside fringe of peripheral huts nor to approach or photograph the larger huts deeper in the village where the chief, the shaman and other elders lived. The peripheral huts were smaller and housed the younger couples and their household, which could include one or both parents. As children were born and the parents achieved more seniority (and, I think, higher risk of injury or death), they moved inwards to more protected locations as young couples took over their former residences.

In our meeting with the chief and shaman, the former thanked me formally for "saving" the child, and made me an honorary villager, with the privilege later in the afternoon of seeing more of the place than I had seen earlier. He also informed me of the illness of an elder's wife, and asked that I see the couple. They were some distance away. He would send for them and have them come early the next morning. He could not say what symptoms the lady had, so I had to keep guessing until I saw her.

How different the residents of Cokerite seemed from those at Wappai; although they had maintained the customs and trappings of Carib village life, they seemed less independent and less self-confident. They had periodic dealings with St Bede's mission, 30 or so miles downriver, and with Government workers, particularly the sicknurse/dispenser, who visited fortnightly. But with all the mission's presence and efforts, pitifully few of the villagers could communicate effectively with the outside world except for those who had actually spent a long time on the coast. Those who had done so, however, had invariably stayed away, so changed had they become in their ways, likes and dislikes, and grown "soft" with absorption of the habits and impedimenta of the coastal peoples.

Several of the older men of Cokerite had been to Mabaruma and environs during World War II, having first travelled upriver to Towakaima then trekked north overland to Arakaka or to Port Kaituma, attracted there by paid work at the manganese mines. When the mines closed after the war, fewer and fewer had made that trip, since it was not part of their hunting grounds. None of the young men we had met had gone there, but some were curious and would visit if the opportunity came. They had heard also, somewhat vaguely of the "big city" to the east where fewer yet of their people had ventured, but the stories of a place so bright that night became day, fascinated them, and I had heard Joe asking Balgobin about the lights. For a time he had been puzzled as to what was meant by "the lights" and only after some thought and talking to Rod that he finally understood. It was an interesting insight into relativity, not Einstein's perhaps, but the relative value of an object in the eyes of different beholders.

Those living in the city would take their lights for granted and might even consider them dim. The forest dweller, to whom a candle seemed bright, and exterior standing lights were unknown, would see those lights as something awesome, captivating, dazzling, until the passage of time and visual accommodation dimmed that view.

I recalled the awed reactions of the children to some of the things we had brought into our assigned hut that first day we had come among them. The strange, crackling high-pitched sounds of my pocket radio had brought the children in to investigate. How curiously they had peeked, keeping a discreet distance, brown eyes hiding behind the tall grass that covered much of the ground. (I would not venture through that grass, for fear of snakes that might lurk in such cool and secret places, but we were told that it was rare for reptiles to wander far onto the site or reach the centre where the huts were placed.

Incidents had occurred of children from time to time picking up young snakes, which hadn't yet learned to stay away from man. Once or twice, the last time a year or more ago, a poisonous viper, probably a *labaria*, which though fully grown, is barely one or two feet long, had bitten the hand of one unwitting child killing him almost instantly, the snake itself immolated by a swift blow from the distraught father.

Most of the objects we had brought were quite familiar to them, the hammocks and the lanterns, rope and twine, and the tools. But when I had shone my pen light in the baby's tent they had watched me from afar, eyes keen and wide, following the dancing light that seemed to turn itself, now on, now off, as if by magic, like the firefly that flitted among the tall grass at night. My stethoscope was another wonder, like the radio. Yesterday, seeing me using the stethoscope on the baby once again, they had asked if they could see and touch the magic tubes that healed the sick, and wanted to know what had silenced the little box that spoke and sang.

Wearing two masks to protect them, and wiping with 70% alcohol each object I handed them, I showed the children (who would have been in school were they living on the coast) how the flashlight worked (its light now dim from failing batteries), the radio that barely crackled, and the *pièce de resistance*, my stethoscope. I would have given anything to capture the wonder in those chubby round faces when they heard their heartbeats--*lub-dup lub-dup*--and their reaction, withdrawing in startled awe while their companions laughed and teased. I wish I knew their comments, flowing thick and fast, with wide-eyed smiles, what they felt, how they chose to relate this experience, and that I could witness their reactions, were they to see the pictures that Jain had taken of them.

We showed them other things, the tools mainly; they squealed in delight on recognition of something, pointing and clapping, their naked bellies heaving, or else they looked puzzled, with index finger holding down the corner of the mouth or lips parted in awe of the strange new things they were seeing. My mask was a puzzle—not unlike the reaction of Hari's wife at Wappai; some tried to tug at it, but stopped as if they understood my "No" and upraised hand, open palm forward. They were fascinated by my matches and stepped back when it flared, and gingerly touched the cold metal of the cameras Brewster, Jain and I carried. The instant prints of a Polaroid Land would have been a sensation among these bright-eyed and curious children. Adults too were as curious, but the women kept their distance and few came close except the mothers of the ones to whom I was then speaking.

At Cokerite--as in other native villages--children were integrated very early into the life of the tribe. The women supervised and taught them in groups, introducing them gradually, by age, to the activities and responsibilities of the village, so that each child could learn and develop the skills needed for survival and prosperity. In time they learnt the looks, sounds and smells of different animals and plants including the kinds of soils supporting different species and thus where to find them; early lumbermen were quick to capitalise on this talent to find choice hardwoods. It was amazing to see how much a six year old was trusted to do, how confidently he went about his tasks.

(It had been the same with us as children on the farm and I daresay every other rural district; we were given tasks to master and then carry out on demand almost from the day we could stand unassisted and express ourselves. I learned later when I was nearing eight that city folk on the other hand could hardly tie a knot, or fetch a pail of water, or control a wayward calf, or tend a younger child. Nor could they swim, fish, or play the games we played, or make a kite that could sing in the wind. What did they do all day, I wondered?)

The children looked fit and well-nourished and created as much play and games as any cluster of children would anywhere, using and improvising on what was available. The hemisected calabash covered with a piece of skin became a drum, the hollow reed cut from the water's edge a pipe, the *awara* nut the basis of the spinning top -- we called it a *bucktop* -- that was popular among older boys who loved to hear it play its soaring high pitched whining tune when it was pulled into motion.

The children loved the water and had learned to swim almost from birth. Once a few months old, the child would be put into the river--Doris said "thrown"--in a body harness, tied to a rope. Its "puppy" fat and primitive reflexes would keep it afloat, spluttering and coughing, occasionally crying out when it inhaled water, but generally the screams soon subsided. After a few immersions the infant would paddle itself without fear and consistently stay above water. Soon thereafter it would propel itself in random directions. The harness would be removed at this stage. Thus a baby could move in water long before it had acquired the strength and nervous connections to support itself on land and creep confidently. A throwback to our watery origins? Perhaps.

The shaman, with a flourish of his six foot staff *(baculo)*, explained their belief that man had developed in stages from an original fish-like form (snakes and caimans were also classed as "fish"), evolving into a land animal that walked on four legs and later stood upright, balanced itself and walked on two limbs only. This was an amazing thesis, almost identical to that described in the *Vaidas*, where the avatars of God took the form of the creatures of the corresponding evolutionary period. Was Darwin then so original?

The natives had many beliefs about animals that could live or feed in water and on land, like the capybara, manatee, frogs and reptiles. Reptiles with legs, like the caiman, were regarded as a class in transition to an upright life on land and in folklore were assigned various attributes of good and evil. Carib tradition included tales of huge animals: lizards as tall as trees, boas and anacondas thick and long as a mora tree, flying creatures whose wings blot out the sun. When first heard a century or more ago these accounts were regarded as the raconteur's hyperbole, but the discovery of bones of mammoths and dinosaurs has validated these beliefs.

Observing the children was an enlightening experience, matching the lessons learned from our four friends on the trip to Wappai. They were so natural, curious, lively and entertaining! A far cry from the people on the coast! What had made them change? My prior knowledge of natives was a mix of misrepresentation and stereotypy, and some casual direct contact with villagers at Biabu on the Mahaica River, workers in Georgetown and patients in Hospital. We knew that children had been removed from villages to the missions for immersion in English and Christianity, but they learned only enough to make them reject their culture, religion and people as "primitive" or "unsophisticated", in much the same way as Jain had said the Christians of Goa or Cochin or Bombay had learned ages ago to belittle non-Christian Indians. A standard evangelical mantra, universally applied!

Those who converted as adults often bore a greater burden. They tended to embrace the new doctrines with such fervour that they became less tolerant of their people and scornful of their old ways. The burdens of the new religion and adaptation to a different way of living have proved too heavy for those not possessed of insight to assess the nature and meaning of conversion, or to reconcile a promise of salvation with the reality of a wretched and dishonourable life among Christians who had not been educated beforehand to accept native converts with kindness and compassion instead of the customary ridicule.

I have seen several of these perplexed and piteous folk, small men and women of indeterminate age, languishing in persistent isolation on the compound of the Mental Hospital in New Amsterdam, labelled adjustment failures with "mental breakdown", repeating their confused perceptions of good and evil, past and present, shaman and priest, not stupid enough to accept change without question, and not smart enough to reconcile their wretchedness and loss of dignity with the fact of conversion and failure to fully understand and assimilate the new values. They were almost all too proud, and too shamed by their failure on the coast, to return to their own villages and admit error.

It was easy to understand this mental torture. By accepting the new doctrines without assessing their merit in practice, they had openly rejected the validity and worth of their own culture, a denial of their entire hierarchy of ancestors. They had become the end of a long and proud line. This was a sin against their forebears and their children too, for what could they pass on now? They could not in a trice, in the short span of a human life acquire enough insight and knowledge of the new beliefs to pass them on to their children, as their parents had done for them from the day they were born. Though humble in their forest fastnesses, the natives were proud, stood straight, each with a respected place in tribal society, each honoured for his or her work.

Out among the alien peoples they were nothing, knew less, did not speak the language, were treated like serfs, idiots or mendicants, scorned and distrusted as thieving and unreliable. Everyone else was so much more attuned to things, the names of places, actions, objects, knew what to do, where to go and when, and most important what not to do.

All was new and strange to them, and not what they had envisaged when the priests had talked of heaven on earth, of blessings and goodwill among men. Where would they find these things? The stark truth about conversion was that it tended to lay waste whole cultures unless great pains were taken to shepherd the converted through each scenario of life in the new culture, to explain it, or explain it away.

I have also seen a similar distressed reaction and outcome in Hindus rejecting their religion for Christianity (not among those simply engrafting Christ onto Hinduism for social and economic reasons). Those too naïve to deal with the deep philosophical burdens of change, but not simple-minded enough to accept the new tenets easily, often developed deep moral and mental rifts, which fractured personalities, creating dualities often too complicated to master or control or explain. It was like reconditioning an old room rather than building from scratch. The new coat of paint is superficial, the foundation hidden, but still remembered and not eradicated. Yet by virtue of speaking English, these would become the spokesmen for their kind.

This fracture of the native psyche, the enforced adoption of an alien way of life has had grave impact on native communities. Envy, greed, malice were human traits which seemed to gain new strength in direct proportion to European influence. When natives eschewed their own norms and adopted, half-wittingly, those of others, they set the stage for internecine conflict, which threatened the life of a tribe. This was a sad thing and obstructed any reform in the way the tribes were treated, and more importantly, in the management of native lands.

Native life and living were in every detail affected by the decisions of a government that excluded them and failed to recognize the legitimacy of their concepts of habitat and lifestyle. Hari had eloquently complained of Government's apparent disinterest in the threatened losses of natural vegetation and the increasingly indiscriminate use of resources that traditionally sustained the native population. Over the centuries tribes had lost their fishing grounds, their freedom to use the lower riverain plains, had seen the loss of species of wild life and had had to migrate further inland for survival. Today there was hardly a trace of the ancient coastal Caribs.

In the faraway Pacific, the same issues had dogged the Polynesians with the coming of the Americans. The Hawaiians had for years struggled against the Americanisation of their country. Their priests held steadfastly to their traditions of "Aloha" and the rituals aimed to induce success and dispel negativity. Although they failed to expel the Americans (sharing that fate with other Polynesian and Pacific island peoples), they have managed to cling to "Aloha", although its influence has remained less than its priests would have wished.

Even worse examples were the intrigues and double-dealing of the British in their treatment of natives of Australia and Africa, tribes probably at the same level of development and natural expertise and adaptation to environment as those in South America and the Pacific. At least for some of the North American tribes subjected to the same blind and bigoted policy of identification and transformation, melding with the larger society was possible, for some of mixed blood, like the Métis of Canada, although that integration had not always been made easy by mainstream society. In BG, however, the racial traits were so starkly different that such absorption was well-nigh impossible. It remains for me a mystery that church and state authorities would allow this tragedy to continue for so long and still encourage it today.

Indians in BG and elsewhere have been similarly bombarded by the forces for conversion, oiled by the promise of personal advancement in a society where Christians controlled the economy and all the financial and other structures that made business possible. But they managed a compromise, adopting some of the ways of the overlords in order to get ahead, while retaining the sustaining nexus to the huge fund of written and oral tradition that was India. This buffer was lacking in the history of the natives of America. They had not found a balance between their excellent spirituality and the human need for exploration, expression and creativity that had made the Hindus dominant in the pre-

Christian world. Was it because they had not developed writing and thereby a written record that was less capricious and more easily shared than the oral one? I pondered these things as I walked with the Chief and his small group.

It was not unexpected that they would want to discuss health issues as the case of pneumonia had occurred so stealthily and almost lethally but for the accident of our arrival. Their susceptibility to serious infections, especially of the respiratory tract, had remained a major problem among natives, and usually followed contact with outsiders. Influenza, pneumonia and tuberculosis were especially deadly.

The shamans had made the association fairly early but were powerless, except by religious coercion, to restrict close contact to the extent needed to avoid the many thousands of needless deaths, but they did eventually establish a process of restricting contact with strangers like us, except in emergencies.

The church authorities (and, to a lesser extent, the state) nevertheless continued to resist this, arguing that denial of or impeding access to young people interfered with the educational and other work of Christian missions. In answer to his question I told the Chief (or Captain as he was called at Cokerite) that I agreed unequivocally with the policy of quarantine. Quarantine and isolation had served us well in controlling infectious diseases all over the world, I told him, by gestures and words which the shaman translated.

In the forest setting, leaving strangers separate in a visitor's logie, with limited and controlled contact with the villagers, was clearly a simple and safe way to protect the tribe short of wearing masks and other clothing barriers and avoiding avenues of disease transmission. At the time of our visit the elders were allowing only persons who had survived prior contact with strangers to get close to, and have dealings with them. It was most important that strangers with evidence of skin rash, fever, colds, coughs and sneezing, regardless of cause, be kept away from the villagers. He nodded in vigorous agreement. I emphasised too the great value of hand washing especially after toilet.

With regard to disease transmission, it was quite possible that those villagers, who might have acquired some immunity by previous contact, particularly those returning to the village from the coast, had also transmitted disease. Strictly speaking, I told him, they too should be quarantined. But that was not done, largely because they had no concept of the nature of infectious agents and ascribed infectivity to "foreignness" rather than to living organisms, as I tried to explain, which were much too small to see, and which could be carried by anyone. That last concept of living things invisibly small was new to them, even though they knew about magnifying glasses. But to take the idea of magnification that many hundred times greater was another dimension, mind-boggling, another trick or lie, the shaman felt, of the deceiving foreigners.

With my language deficit, I could not get very far into an explanation, even with the translator there, since their language lacked the words to convey the basic concepts. But in the end he did seem to grasp the idea that even their own people could acquire the qualities that made them carriers of lethal alien diseases. It had been so much simpler discussing the same issue with Hari. In a sense the shaman's position was no different from that of the sophisticated European physician of a century or so ago who had stoutly rejected the germ theory of disease. I was pleased that he was willing to accept the ideas. Perhaps Hari might consider a role as teacher. I would put the idea to Dr Nehaul.

One of the paradoxes that continued to trouble them was that the missionary, who claimed to be the spokesman for the Great Spirit on earth, was himself able to transmit disease to the natives. Was that the Christian God's way of punishing defenceless natives? And for what wrong? Not wearing clothes? It was incomprehensible and the priest had given no answer except that they must have faith, that God knew best and worked his will in ways mysterious and wondrous, that they must be patient and forbearing, since rewards for faith would come in their future heaven.

All of this was a meaningless abstraction; their culture focussed on the present and did not store their history, except by memorisation and oral transmission to each new generation (I did notice two silent youths trailing and paying close attention to the shaman and chief wherever they went). The future was an enigma and life in a heaven after death alien to their philosophy. How could the preacher, this agent of death, deign to claim to be a messenger of the Great Spirit and one blessed to interpret or preach His wisdom and goodness?

The missionaries had brought their own medicines and foisted them on the natives. Initial resistance eventually gave way to acceptance especially after antibiotics became available and made a dramatic difference in the treatment of infectious disease. Achromycin and Sulphonamides (which everyone knew as Sulfa) were handed out by priests, often indiscriminately, in remote villages like Cokerite, since medical help was not readily available.

Their rapid effects impressed many natives, who began to lose interest in time-honoured remedies, preferring the ease of swallowing a pill to the more tedious task of gathering fresh bush, often from a great distance, and preparing the required concoction. This was a major factor in undermining discipline within a tribe and the authority of the shaman, who could rarely perform the magic of the antibiotic, which I too had shown them so recently and so dramatically. Already concerns had been expressed at Cokerite and elsewhere that the knowledge of the older folk, transmitted down the ages through word and example, might well be lost since no written record existed, and practices had been changing. There was a real fear that that knowledge might not survive intact beyond the present generation.

These same fears were expressed a few years ago also in Surinam, where missionaries among the *Tirois* tribes had run into trouble for telling people to discount or ignore their traditions and customs and follow only the new doctrines and practices that the missionaries preached.

The success of the new medicines had indeed lessened the authority of the shaman in health matters; many of the more truculent tribesmen came to believe that the reality of the magic cures of the strangers gave them a corresponding superiority in all aspects of life, and they began to defy tribal rules. Claims for sanctuary at the missions increased steadily, now that the villagers knew that contact *per se* was no longer potentially lethal. Notwithstanding the efficacy of the new medicines, the sporadic nature of the medical services, as provided currently by an itinerant Sicknurse & Dispenser, allowed cases such as the child and woman I had seen to become easy fatalities in the interval between medical visits.

I was puzzled why the missionaries, from accounts I had heard, had seemed to be unaware, here as in the rest of the Americas, of the deadly hazard the European posed to the native peoples, from the days of the first Spaniards. The donning of the long black robe did not exempt the clergy from responsibility for the carnage brought on by deadly diseases. How then, and why, did they do nothing to curtail direct and close contact with the natives? Cynics might say that the decimation of native populations by disease, once it had been recognized as an outcome of contact, had become part of the European strategy to conquer the continent!

The fortuitous discovery of the simplicity and efficacy of humans as vectors had given the conqueror the first major weapon in germ warfare, which the Spaniards, and later the British, French and Dutch, had used so effectively, from their earliest periods in the Americas. Disease brought in by the Spaniards had destroyed whole complex civilisations in Mexico, Central and South America, and many of the epidemics were initiated by the clergy.

An early catastrophe in the 16th century was the loss of over 50,000 souls in one incident in Baja California. No one really knew the extent of the total casualties suffered; conservative estimates have placed the total loss of native lives in the Americas at hundreds of millions in the four and a half centuries of contact, a scale of human destruction matched only by the decimation of populations in India and elsewhere in Asia, Africa, Australia and Europe by a millennium of Muslim and Christian slaughter.

In the Barama region head counting was difficult as the people were scattered over a large area of dense forest; some of the men who contracted diseases from visitors would often sicken and die during a hunt deep in the forest and be buried there alone and unmarked. The priests who did the counting would hardly find out about these.

It would be safe to suggest that the loss over the four centuries of contact between Europeans and Caribs would be at least fifty thousand. The Chief told stories of populous villages with fields of cassava and sweet potato, and of rivers crowded with canoes, and plentiful fish, watrash, birds and crocodiles to provide delicacies for the table, and everywhere abundance in everything they needed for daily life. In those days there were, of course, periods of natural difficulty, floods and drought, sometimes prolonged, causing hardship and fatalities, but generally the population was contented, healthy and prospered.

Of the Guianese peoples the Caribs had been the least eager to accommodate the foreigners. From today's perspective it was a pity that they had not kept their distance. Even the isolation and relative inaccessibility of the Caribs of the upper Barama had failed to spare them the effects of the foreign plagues. They were a small group much dependent on interchanges and trade with the tribes downriver; that contact did result from time to time in disease and death, though much less impressively than had occurred among the natives of the lower riverain villages. Today they were still heavily reliant on quarantine to protect their children from strangers, but they allowed certain adult males the freedom to make contact with outsiders, little realising that the men could thus become intermediaries and carriers of disease into the village.

Before leaving Georgetown for Wappai I had been briefed by Dr Nehaul, the Deputy Chief Medical Officer, on health conditions in the "interior". Needless to say little was known about the Barama, much less Wappai. There was the standard caution about Yellow Fever, Leishmaniasis, Malaria, and information on hookworm and other infestations that arose from walking barefooted on damp forest soil or from drinking contaminated water or eating undercooked fish or meat. And yet I had seen little evidence, and heard no complaints suggesting hookworm infestation among the children of either village. Natives regularly treated their children with a cathartic infusion made of a certain bush, which they claimed kept the children from getting any worm-related disease. Hari had assured me that he had seen only one instance of a villager, a child of about 10, with anything resembling anaemia. He had been cured with a three day course of the cathartic, followed by a daily drink of a tea made from another bush culled from a copse near the Cuyuni River.

This reminded me of certain practices common among Indians in rural BG, likely of Ayurvedic origin and rigidly adhered to in most households, whereby children were given a laxative for one day during each school holiday and twice in the summer, to cleanse us, we were told. The substance used was usually castor oil, mixed with sweetened orange juice which one drank, under the most anguished protest, first thing on the chosen morning, usually a Saturday, fasted and spent the rest of that day in or near the outhouse, competing for the space with the other victim of the treatment, since no more than two of us were treated at the same time. We had only one toilet and the two treated were withdrawn from chores that day. For complying we were rewarded with a favourite food when the ordeal was over. There was hardly an instance of worms in those who observed this practice. The native ritual was similar, but used more often, with a milder laxative, akin to *senna*, certainly not as strong as castor oil.

The threat of loss of an important archive--and of the Caribs' sense of history and their traditional health practices--was unquestionably a serious matter for the Government. I planned to raise it with the Premier when I saw him next on his monthly visit to my sister's store and I would emphasise in my report to the medical authorities the need to study the natives' choices and use of medicinal plants--properties, efficacy, toxicity and other features--their time-honoured methods of extraction and use of curare, and their experience with naturally resistant food crops and their conditions of growth.

As the conversation plodded on the Chief and the shaman began to speak more freely, encouraged perhaps by the interest I showed in their position and my new status as an honorary villager. I had spoken directly to the Chief, allowing the shaman to pick up on cue and translate. The Chief would crane his neck, this way and that, and make darting movements whenever I turned to address the shaman. From time to time he made approving or contradictory grunts, which you could decipher after a few false starts. The shaman was always attentive and made few comments, but as the dialogue developed he began to unburden more of his feelings than I suspect he had done before to a stranger.

He wondered why neither the priests nor Government people had so far told them the things I was now saying, adding that his distrust of those two groups, especially the priests, had made him believe me, and that I should learn their language and come back to work among them, the way the white doctor had tried twelve or more years ago. This was a clear reference to Dr Jones, whose work had been terminated in the spring of 1951, and which had set out clearly the threats to native survival and suggested measures to contain them.

The shaman proceeded to describe his frustrations with the missionaries and the strained relationship that persisted between them. He was sceptical and did not think much of their claims. He had heard the chants and incantations and seen them swing censers to drive away bad spirits, just as he was wont to do. He liked that act, but after the wisps of smoke had danced by, there was nothing left to impress anyone, except, of course the tasting of the wine. However the mere sip offered was not enough for him to get the taste right. He wondered why the priests were always so stingy, especially as his own people, who had none of the wealth or fineries of the aliens, were generous and would offer a cupful of *cassiri* to the priest whenever he visited. He had also puzzled that the priest chose "really big" words to express himself, words for which there was often no equivalent in his language; that suggested to him that such strange words could not have come from God (for God communicated in simple universal terms).

He noted too, that after the priest had swallowed enough of those big words; they would turn into vapour in his belly and come out of his lower end as bold airy statements! At the thought his serious set face broke into a thin smile, as evanescent as the thin green flash that the setting sun emitted as it sank into the ocean, a sight that fishermen would pause at their nets and wait to see.

The shaman's scepticism was echoed by people sympathetic to the natives who felt that the missionaries were intruding too much into village life and were confusing villagers and alienating them from their traditions. He believed that missionaries should occupy themselves with harmless and helpful work like comforting those in distress, supporting them in their intercessions with the authorities—whose rules and regulations often confused them--and praying to *their* God. Except for learning the foreign tongue the children could do with less intensive and more relevant schooling since much of what was taught was foreign ("English") fare, which had limited value in their tradition.

Day-long classes and rigid hours at school interrupted the more serious lessons about tribal life and practices the children had to learn each day. Nor should the missionaries spend so much time distracting or removing the men from their crafts and responsibilities—hunting, fishing and cultivation -- that had sustained their people for millennia.

Natives generally had been brought up to be self-reliant and to work cooperatively within the tribe to meet each day their bodily and spiritual needs and obligations, and to live unselfishly. The shaman's task was to ensure that these qualities were inculcated in each one by careful adherence to ceremonials and practices that had been handed down from the ancient past, from long before the time of the great floods. By following them they had avoided disasters for all the time they existed before the coming of the white skins.

They could thus be spared the irrelevant, unattainable and impractical life style and strange belief system that their Jesus seemed to have taught these pestilential missionaries. The shaman had noted inconsistencies in the foreign ways of doing things, and was especially upset that they were frequently in direct conflict with those of the natives, and threatened destruction of their life style. His reaction to them was therefore one of rejection, irritation and powerlessness.

It was easy to sympathise with the shaman. The Bible was, after all, an allegory and should not be trusted in the hands of evangelists who tended to interpret its passages literally. What value in the Guianese forest setting were idioms and metaphors derived in a Palestinian desert landscape, or protocols that had evolved in mercantile Europe? And yet they were being spread uncritically among the natives of all South America through the deepest Pakaraimas, the Rupununi and along the Orinoco and Amazon Rivers, a terrain vastly different from anything in the Bible.

Even the reference to the great river Nile was restricted to the episode re Moses in the basket, and in that story the river is made to look insignificant and benign. To him the "basket" was a ridiculous idea as a safe place for an infant; every native, however young, knew that a basket leaked and could hardly float for more than a minute, and had been the object that the ancient First Chief had ordered the errant monkey to use to fetch water as punishment for molesting the other animals! As a child hearing the story of Moses, I too had been mystified that someone could place a baby in a basket, and put it a river.

I had pictured the Nile then as a little stream, certainly nothing bigger than the Mahaica River, in which we all knew a basket with a child in it would not have lasted five minutes. The shaman complained that the priests' activities and proselytising had split loyalties in the village, and affected its discipline, efficiency and morale. He worried about the unreal expectations many had come to have and the damage to human health when these were not realised. Drunkenness, dereliction of duty, thievery and prostitution had all followed.

The priests' reply had been unvarying: they were bringing light to an area of darkness and grave ignorance, and God to the ungodly. In the culture of the Caribs (and all native peoples) the shaman was the learned one who by long training and special intellectual insights communicated with the Spirit World to learn its divine secrets; he was the intermediary between his people and the *Great Spirit*, their guide away from evil in all its forms, including sorcery.

His tasks included rooting out evil, healing the sick and troubled, and advising the Chiefs on any tribal matter. The missionaries were, of course, aware of all this and that the shaman was responsible for all spiritual matters among his people and to ensure proper observance of the ancient rituals.

But they called them irreligious, their history a fairy-tale; they condemned and dismissed the traditional practices as barbarous and profane, an idea that confused the villagers, who began to doubt their beliefs especially when the medicine brought in by the missionaries could cure illnesses the shaman had not been able to manage. The latter did emphasise however that those illnesses had mostly been the strange fevers that the foreigners had brought, and that the people who had survived them following native practices had gained resistance and could face the foreigner afterwards. Those who died had been mainly the frail and careless. The fittest survived. This Darwinian argument coming from a 'savage' would long continue to baffle the priests.

Most adult villagers maintained their traditional beliefs and practices, though many did attend the services out of curiosity or coercion to hear the exhortations from the pulpit. It was an odd scene, first to hear the harangue in a foreign tongue, then the echo of it coming from the soft hesitant voice of the native translator. The effect was surreal.

The missionaries seemed oblivious to this, and ploughed on with their homilies, even though their translators often failed to find the words to convey meaning or as often did not understand the complex argument being made, and from time to time would tell the audience just that, the priests interpreting their reaction as an expression of interest in his message. But the translators did a yeoman job and passed on the gist of the messages--reduced to simplicity and dogma, according to their grasp of the meaning -- to everyone's satisfaction, or so it seemed. In time the priests learned enough of the language to speak directly to the congregation.

Some of the natives were baptized with great ceremony and given Christian names, chiefly those of major Biblical characters, including the disciples, though for some reason Jonah seemed popular. Because the priests pooh-poohed native ways and saw the villagers only on Sundays, they were easily duped into enrolling and thus protecting errant villagers--those being disciplined or punished--or those avoiding daily spiritual or other duties, or in the case of brides, failing to conceive.

It was rare for priests to admit to being conned when the truth was brought to their attention; they would instead claim the defections as evidence of success, and refuse to release the miscreant to face native justice. This action tended to increase animosities between the tribes and the missionaries. The shaman maintained that Christianity was thus a corrupting force, raised false hopes among his people, lured them with false values and would ruin them eventually if not curbed.

Hari had described these very issues, his reaction and the frustration of many villagers, their chiefs and shamans expressed at annual tribal gatherings. Their view of forest life remained seriously at odds with that of the missionaries pursuing the dubious global aim of converting all to Christianity and seeking to establish "new Vatican or Westminster satellites worldwide". They had set out to "civilise" natives, already steeped in millennia of sylvan culture by luring them into a commercial agrarian way of life unsupportable within the deep forests.

Pity their zeal had not included a systematic or consistent study of the environment, nor of the natives' *raison de vivre,* to understand why they had not "advanced", as native peoples had done elsewhere, and developed a *formal* religion and distinct elements of "culture". Natives were soon aware that the "civilised" races of Europe had no respect for people who lived or believed differently, least of all for non-white natives who "did not have the wit to clothe themselves", or otherwise show some modesty and decorum, as the priests would often say. They could not understand why natives seemed so satisfied with their primitive physical surroundings and lived so frugally. Development for the European was a matter of increasing one's personal wealth and for the missionary the elimination of heathens and the expansion and glorification of the Church.

Although the pursuit of a religious objective was notionally the opposite of that of personal (and national) wealth, Hari and his colleagues saw the two as complementary, mutually dependent and equally destructive, one wasting the environment, the other plundering the souls of men. He had seen this in the arrogance of missionaries he had met, who had immediately labelled him an imbecile. Yet they were so obsequious when dealing with those of wealth or of light skin--the Portuguese men, all Roman Catholic Sunday-givers--who had set themselves up along the rivers as venture capitalists, grocers, brokers and moneylenders to the gold-seekers, balata bleeders and lumbermen.

His personal rejection of the message of the missionaries had been absolute. Instance the degradation at Cokerite, where the natives, he felt, were neither sylvan people nor a coastal one, torn as they had become between dissatisfaction with the promises of the missions, and nostalgia for their own disappearing way of life.

The missions had curried favour among the natives by periodic handouts of clothing, toys and domestic articles, emphasizing that these gifts from God – like the fruits of the tree of life--would flow continuously to those who adopted and faithfully followed Christianity. In all the time these men in black had preached among them, no sign of heaven had been seen by anyone, and much was either wanting or confusing in the messages and injunctions. Young people would return from the missions from time to time acting and speaking and behaving strangely and asking questions that had no native answer.

A recurring problem was the insistence by the "black coats" that native women selectively cover their breasts and genitals, and the men their penises, when these things were just parts of their bodies, like eyes and fingers; why not cover those? To the natives covering up was done for occasion and decoration, not false modesty. The sight of breasts evoked no thought of lust in men, who had grown accustomed to the naturalness of those structures just as penises did not all go stiff at the sight of a naked female.

Custom and upbringing had conditioned them into modest responses just as much as in civilised society those same factors had made men behave indelicately and stupidly in the presence of bared bodies. Adaptation was not something amenable to dogma. Those priests who had learned this -- there were a few who did--kept it as a personal secret, allowing the native converts to dress "their way" in the forest, but declined to tell of their leniency to the bishop or other higher-up for fear of censure.

It was said that Christian missionaries in Africa believed that Africans were the descendants of Ham, one of the three sons of Noah, who had been charged with the task of repopulating the world. This belief stemmed from the incident related in Genesis, Book 9, in which Ham found his father drunk one day and naked, laughed at him and left him in that condition. His brothers Shem and Japheth came on the scene but covered their father's nakedness and when Noah became sober they told him of Ham's wickedness.

Noah responded by cursing his son and damned all his descendants to perpetual slavery. In time--so the Biblical fable goes--the burgeoning generations of Ham dispersed afar off, mostly to the south and became progressively darker with each generation, while the opposite happened to the offspring of Japheth, who became the progenitor of the Europeans. Shem and his descendants remained in the Middle East and gave rise to the Jews and Arabs.

Missionaries used the book of Genesis freely and literally in their proselytism, and would harp on the theme of nakedness, the cause of Ham's downfall. This justified their insistence on clothing all heathen natives throughout the forest, and they themselves would go about in full regalia, though they sweltered in the humid heat, and secretly envied the freedom of the natives including their ability to cool themselves at will in the clear brown waters that were everywhere. They chose, however, to pretend never to understand or justify how anyone but the most primitive and degraded could ever flaunt the imperfections of their nakedness!

The Chief of Cokerite, throughout his years as head, had been troubled, saddened even, like the shaman, by recent changes and their erosive effects on the verbal history of the tribes handed down from their predecessors and through them to the people, of how numerous and thriving their folks had been long ago. I asked them to tell me some of these as Joe and Hari had referred briefly to several beliefs and practices but had not had the time to relate the history. The Chief smiled at my interest and nodded to the shaman, who went on to recite in his slow deliberate English-- to which I occasionally supplied a few words--some of the legends that had given birth to the principles by which they lived and the deep spirituality of their culture, which bore a strong resemblance to similar aspects of Hinduism. A profound nostalgia and rapture permeated the recitation and I listened spellbound.

When the worlds and the universe were created out of darkness and peopled[119]*, the progenitors of the Caribs were placed on the beautiful bright side of the moon. As time passed they pondered the changing darkness of the earth below and decided to go down and clean it up so that it could shine at all times like the moon. And so they left their bright homes, floated down to the earth on white clouds, and once there they worked with great diligence, and brightened the earth; when finished they tried to return, but the clouds were nowhere to be seen. And when they failed to find them, they prayed to* Tamosi Kabo-tano*, the Great Spirit, the Ancient One, to help them find the lost clouds. But in vain.* Tamosi Kabo-tano *did not hear them. Aimlessly they wandered the earth, and wandering became tired and hungry. And finding no food they started a fire with coals on which they baked cakes from clay. But the cakes of clay were not edible. And they languished further. But* Tamosi Kabo-tano *did not forsake them. He showed them a flock of birds feeding in a tree and they copied the actions of the birds, savouring the nourishing fruits even as the birds had done, and so they were saved.*

But it is the nature of humans to tire of the same food day after day, and knowing not where to find variety, they pined even more for their bright homes on the moon and wished that they had not thought to change the earth, and had kept to their own land, with all its comfort and plenty. Tamosi Kabo-tano *heard their pleas, and pitying them, raised a magnificent spreading tree, one that had not been known to man before, nor has one been created since. Each branch bore a different fruit, and in the shade below, all manner of tasty roots and fruitful plants abounded. He brought them cassava, potato, yam, banana, plantain, corn, vines and shrubs such as feed the earth to this day.*

Now it happened that when the Great Creator had made all living things--large and small, even as the hills and mountains, and of great variety, each suited to its place, with feet or without--he had given them the gift of speech in a single language with which they communed, both animals and plants. And he had sent them a Chief to rule over them lest any disharmony spoil their daily lives. Among the many kinds of animals on the earth was Maipuri*, the tapir, and the people could tell by what road he travelled by his footprints, four toes in front and three back;* Maipuri *found the fruitful tree, tasted of its fruits and ate his fill, for he loved them instantly, and he grew fat, sleek and contented, losing his lean and hungry look. The people noticed this and asked him what had caused such a wondrous change, but* Maipuri *did not reveal his secret.*

So they sent the woodpecker to spy on him, but the woodpecker was not wily enough and passed his time noisily tapping each tree, alerting Maipuri*, who thus avoided scrutiny and exposure with great ease. They turned to the rat, who knew the footprints of the tapir, and followed them to the great tree, and he too found the fruits tasty and ate his fill. At first the rat professed failure to the men who had hired him until he too began to change and the people noticed. Speaking to him one day after he had returned from his searches and again hearing his denials, they saw traces of the fruits sticking to his whiskers. Thus they discovered his deceit, and they made him reveal where he had found the food. And when they found that it was their tree they sang praises to* Tamosi Kabo-tano*, the Great Provider. Abruptly His voice was heard in deep tones saying 'Cut it down! Let each one take a piece and plant it near to his dwelling for his sustenance.' They*

---

[119] Compare the *Ṛg Veda* on *Creation: Nāsadāsinno sadāsit tadāning./na mrityur āsida mritang na tarhi./Tama āsit tamasā gulhamagrē (Sanskrit)* In English: There was neither non-existence nor existence./There was neither death nor immortality. / Darkness was hidden by darkness.

hastened to obey and began in awe to fell the great tree. It was a slow and arduous task almost beyond the capability of their primitive stone axes. They had grown idle, unwilling and unable to fend for themselves needing only to pick the fruits of the tree. The task taught them patience, persistence, how to organise themselves to carry out a difficult task, to make tools, to take responsibility and how to work together for a common purpose. It also taught them faith and the power of belief, for many doubted the wisdom of wasting the abundance that the tree provided and indeed had grumbled and faltered at the task. Ten months they laboured, and finally the great tree leaned and slowly toppled to the ground with a mighty crash. Then each man was instructed to take cuttings from the trunk, the branches and the roots, and to plant them, each in his own plot near his home, and to nurture them. The transplants flourished and bore fruit in plenty and sustained them. And in like manner have they cultivated their food for the many millennia that followed, and learned to live at one with the plants and animals, as Tamosi Kabo-tano *had willed.*

Now beneath the great tree was a cave, which contained a sacred pool of sparkling water that was the place where the water-Mama bathed. And one of the tribe ventured there lured by evil spirits; and as he gazed with rising lust upon her naked form the waters began to rise. Scared, he hastened to warn everyone, every man, woman and child, and they all ran to the summit of a nearby hill just in time to see the waters drown their homes and threaten the very summit upon which all had gathered. They prayed fervently to the Great One for help. For a while nothing happened and the water rose steadily. Scouring the surroundings for some sign of hope, they suddenly saw a huge rock emerge and slowly move to block the entrance to the cave; abruptly the waters ceased to flow.

Time passed and the waters receded; they approached the rock, which had saved them, to pay tribute and give thanks. And the rock said, "I have indeed saved you from the great flood, as God willed, but take heed, if you and your offspring wish to live a long and healthy life, to gain perpetual youth and not perish by drowning, listen not to the spirits that dwell in the woods, who will tempt you, to gain your soul."

As it is with men they soon forgot misfortune and the good advice of their Saviour and began to yield increasingly to selfishness and the tempting blandishments of the wood spirits, which came to them through the friendly monkey Yarrekaru chattering and performing great antics, distracting them so that they failed to see him reach the rock and start to dig around it. And by nightfall the rock cried out in dismay, "Waters covering me," but the people heeded not the lament and slept instead, and did not hear the final warning, "Soon you will all be covered even as I am and I can help you no more, for you have ignored my words and have been faithless." Too late they scrambled out of drowning hammocks and climbed trees but all perished save four who had managed to reach the top of the cokerite (komoo) palm.

As the floods receded there came from afar the wise one, Amalivaca, *riding on a large and strange craft, a canoe such as they had never seen before; on the way he passed through the canyons of the rivers and would pause to carve numinous signs and enigmatic figures on the rock faces, and these remain to this day, their meaning still obscure. He also smoothed the hillsides that seemed to him too rough, and all men were in awe of him and listened to his words. "Each of you must clear a piece of land by the river, and use the river to visit one another so that you can speak with all your people and live in harmony." But they hesitated, not knowing how to do these things. So* Amalivaca *taught them to make canoes, each a small one that could carry himself and his wife and children, and made for each a paddle and showed them its secrets. And soon they took their canoes and paddled downriver, to commune with others. But when they tried to return they found it harder to paddle against the current. So they asked* Amalivaca *to make the current flow upwards on one side of the river. He tried to please them but this was not a thing that he could do without causing great changes over all the earth; instead he asked the ocean to send a tide upstream but the tide raised the level of the water as it came in and flooded the banks and would have drowned all the settlements had Amalivaca not stopped the tide. And so today the tide flows only so far up the rivers, and men have learned how to use it for their good. And when he had done this and seen the people settled and in good understanding of how they must live, he left the Caribs to take care of the lands. From that time many generations came and went and their numbers grew greatly and the settlements stretched to the sea and over the snowy mountains to the lands of other tribes and nations.[120]*

The theme of recurrent flooding and escape to far off lands seemed a dominant one in Carib lore. The Shaman agreed and said, "For good reason." Then he gave a different less allegorical account of their past. He seemed convinced that his people, now a mere fraction of what they had been, did escape their original homeland far to the northeast of BG, how long ago none today could accurately tell. "Perhaps the answer lies in the stars." His account amplified and agreed with what Hari had told us.

Deep in antiquity his remotest ancestors lived in the land of Atlantis whose rich red soil stretched in all directions: north to the cold climes, and south, east and west to the great oceans and lofty mountains. Schooled by the great Creator (whom their brethren the Akawai called Makonaima) and his emissaries, the people multiplied, prospered and built large villages and filled them with buildings and other public works. They became so pleased with their ingenuity that arrogance overcame their leaders. But then the northern climes grew warmer; the vast snows and ice that covered them melted sending a great flood south that drowned vast areas of the continent and thousands of hapless people who had failed to heed the word of the Great Creator, and were lax and unprepared.

Those survived who reached high ground, but countless others fled the land fearful that the waters would surely cover the highest points even, and knowing that there were taller mountains to the far west. Thither they journeyed, seven fleets of the largest canoes with seven tribes; after many weeks they reached the high mountains with their steep slopes, broad valleys and rushing waters. There they settled and rebuilt their homes and their villages. In time they forgot past misfortunes. As they learned more and more some among them were seized with greed and a powerful desire to control the rest, both the animals and the plants, to gain free labour, as some men of other tribes were wont to do, even as the white men do today. So strong was this urge that it became a disease, a pestilence that blighted the land, and brought great grief on the people.

Then the ocean and the rivers began to swell again, as if the Great Creator wished to cleanse the land. Once again they made long and stout canoes as their ancestors had done before, and seven fleets of these took leave to seek new lands still father west. And so it was they came upon the land to which they gave their name, Caribia, and its great sea that bordered it. Some built new homes, grew crops in valleys and up mountainsides on winding terraces and they began to prosper once again. One tribe went north where a great river penetrated deep into the land as far as the icy north[121], and had found the land so tempting they settled along the river banks.

But others of the seven did not like the lofty mountains nor the cold north and chose instead to journey south, to warm and unknown climes; these were his ancestors. They traveled for many a moon until they came upon a gently undulating land, lying low, with large rivers running through thick forests where no man had ever dwelled, with

---

a surfeit of animals on land and in water and birds of wondrous bright plumage such as they had never seen before. And the sight gladdened them, as they had grown tired after the long voyage and rough seas, weak, hungry and nursing those who were sick or dying. They paddled wearily along a brown river with plenty of fish and bird to sustain them, so some stopped and made settlements, and started their crops.

But others--less content or with a different vision--took to the ocean once again and ventured further south seeking higher ground, for fear of the flood that they knew might come again someday and drown the low-lying land; after many weeks they came upon a mighty river, so wide its shores were lost in mist; it was the mightiest of rivers, whose waters were cool even in the heat of the noonday sun; surely, they reasoned, it must flow from the tallest of mountains. Soon they came upon a range of hills which they explored and some found to their liking and went no further. Some, more fearful of the wrath of the great floods, sailed their canoes up the great river, whose banks were still obscured one from the other, reasoning that they had not yet reached the tallest mountains. They were gone many moons and only a few returned to tell of their fortunes and of the endless forests where no man dwelled, and of the multitude of animals and plants that could sustain them forever, they and their children's children. Thus it was that their ancestors became scattered over a million square miles of the strange, new and fertile land, thick with the tallest trees that they had ever seen and rich with life.

But the tribes longed to see their kin and so they agreed to hold a great reunion at a central site once in every 104 moons, where representatives of all the tribes would renew ties, update their calendars and share experiences and knowledge gained. Some relocated, just as people do to this day. But as time passed and the waters continued to rise and the seas became rougher and wider, their children and their children's children lost first their closeness, then their knowledge of those that went before them, ceased meeting and became as strangers. So they have lived ever since, in tribal isolation, one from the other, acquiring many new family names, new words and ways of speaking them, thinking to be different, despite a common origin from the same large root now buried deep in antiquity.

As their numbers grew some moved further inland, each tribe choosing a place at will from among the many choice locations, even as Amalivaca had shown their ancestors. These too like others of their kin before them lost the immediacy and power of personal memories soon lost contact with their kinfolk. However they continued to live in freedom and simplicity as they had done before their migration, as small separate tribal groups that helped one another. They built homes among the forest trees or beside the streams; they fed from the land and from the rivers, some of which were mighty and flowed like thunder through the thick green woods, fresh and full of life, of fish, of fowl, of animals. And they grew roots, potato, cassava and maize for their yearly food and brewed a liquor for the feasts in much the same way as they do today.

And through the long years of their history the men hunted and dug the ground, and defended the tribe; the women raised the crops, and taught their offspring the arts, crafts and techniques of survival and prosperity, sometimes inventing a new tool or process, and if it worked better, passing it on to replace the old. And so they lived, progressed and grew in number forming large families that spread up and down the great rivers and their tributaries, from the first great one called the Orinoco to the greatest of all, which we call today the Amazon. And in between, in Guiana, the land of many rivers, they had flourished on the banks of the lesser streams and their numerous tributaries that ran from the highlands, tumbling down in mighty cataracts to cross the great flatlands to the Atlantic, their own ancestral ocean. Their people had founded many settlements on these--from the Orinoco, Waini and Barima in the northwest past the Essequibo, Berbice, Corentyne and Paramaribo to Cayenne in the southeast. But here some had made homes in the Cuyuni, Mazaruni and Potaro in the south, where their *brethren the Akawai, Arekuna, Pemon, Macushi, Wapishana and many more could be found. And even beyond the great Kaieteur, the Old Man's Falls, mightiest of the cataracts of thunder and mist, other tribes--perhaps their forgotten brethren from antiquity--the WaiWais live in the high Tepui and in the savannahs even onto the mountains of the far Akarai, where the great Essequibo rises in the mist of the mountain tops and collects its myriad streams, great and small and flows to the ocean. "And if you journeyed even farther away into the territories of the limitless Amazon you will come upon our Carib families, called today the Guarahi, Tupi and Ge and others whose names I do not know, waiting for the great reunion that we've craved so many thousand years."*

Guianese have been brought up to believe that natives were primitive and almost mindless. This astonishing and epic tale was so incongruous with this characterisation that I felt ashamed once again of our biases, as when I came face-to-face with their talents and Hari's studied appraisal of their worth. How amazing it was that millennia of belief and narrative could have survived in such detail in the shaman of a remote and forgotten forest in a hostile land.

The Shaman at Cokerite believed sincerely that the natives of South America descended from survivors of the deluge that drowned Atlantis and had settled the Western Highlands. Later their ancestors had broken away and escaped, rejecting the elitist and acquisitive values of those who had become leaders and priests. Having escaped they had bravely set out in search of more congenial lands to the south and east, where they could live free from the shackles of the arrogant and powerful. Thus they, like the later pilgrims of Europe, had fled their new settlements to avoid persecution, enslavement or death at the hands of a capricious class of rulers and priests, their kith and kin, who had developed an ideology which allowed no room for disagreement or opposition, and unsuitable for tribes that were of an independent mind but small and powerless.

The legend of Atlantis had fascinated me from boyhood and I had read all that I could in the meagre library available then. Hari had confirmed that several shamans and chiefs including his father-in-law held the same belief without using the word Atlantis, but referring invariably to the land of "red earth" lost in a "great flood".

Plato in ca. 350 BCE had written about the continent of Atlantis, which sank in the western (Atlantic) ocean without a trace about 10,000 BCE when the last great ice age ended raising the level of the Atlantic by over 350 feet. This mass of water drowned the huge landmass — which was separated from Europe and Africa in the east and America in the west by large seas--reducing it to a few islands in the mid-Atlantic (the Azores, Madeira, Canaries), and creating the large archipelagos in the west, the Bahamas, from the flooded Bahama Bank to Turks and Caicos islands and those of the Caribbean Sea. Jacques Cousteau provided some evidence of this when he filmed a grotto at a depth of 165 feet in the sea near Andros Island in the Bahamas group. It contained stalactites and stalagmites and its walls showed evidence of having been above water 12,000 or more years ago. Plato however had identified Atlantis with Crete, where recent archaeology has found evidence of a palatial structure attesting to an old and accomplished civilisation.

In the Caribbean Sea many small islands formed where once there were fewer but larger ones or perhaps even a continuous land mass from north to south traversed by large rivers and it seemed that up to then one could have travelled overland from North to South America by an eastern route. It is said that the natives of Atlantis roamed and settled this entire area beginning with the first signs of a rise in the ocean thousands of years before the final migration. Some went east towards Europe and North Africa reaching as far as Egypt while others went west, taking their religious practices to their new homelands.

Edgar Cayce, a student of Atlantean 'mythology', adduced some evidence to show that people had settled in Belize before 9,000 BCE where Anna Mitchell-Hedges in 1927 found a skilfully carved, life-size crystal skull, under the ruins of a Mayan temple. She thought it had originated in Murias, a city in Bimini (Bahamas) that had been the capital of the region and the site of a large temple containing similar crystal objects, associated with youth and with beliefs and rites of rejuvenation. The priestesses in the temple brewed potions from flowers, herbs and other plant materials, which they used to treat disease and 'restore' youth. Some believe that these potions might have been identical to those concocted by mythical Greek personalities--Calypso, Circe, Medea and others, supporting the Platonic connection between Atlantis and Greece--and that the temple had become famous as a Fountain of Youth, which later would lure European adventurers, including DeSoto and Ponce de Leon.

The reference to "the old, red land in the sunrise sea" is used not only among Caribs. The Toltecs, predecessors of the Aztecs in Mexico, characterize the homeland of their ancestors as the "old, old, red land". (During glacial times red clay was more abundant in the area above the surface in the Atlantic Ocean than it is now, and persists in Prince Edward Island in the Canadian Gulf of St Lawrence, and in parts of BG).

The settlers dwelt happily in *Caraiba* for a very long time and grew in number. Visiting priests from Atlantis taught them the religion of *Tupan* and gave them the name Tupi, "the sons of Pan", another name for "the old, red land" (The Tupi live in the southern Amazon; their language is said to contain idioms similar to those used by the Basques of Spain).

Having chosen the land of the Guianas Carib settlers had roamed the forests and explored the headwaters of the many rivers. In time they found gold in the highlands and in the streambeds during the dry season, and finding it smooth, shiny and easy to work with, but too soft for knives or arrowheads, had fashioned it into fine ornaments, which they used in trade. The people all loved the ornaments; in one place remote and far away they had found a way to turn the metal into dust, which their Chief at times of ceremony sprinkled over his body to make it glow in the sunshine, like a god's. And that had pleased him, so his tribe had given him the name *'the golden one'*.

When the white men came and saw the ornaments they became extremely excited and sought instantly to know where to find the gold, and 'the golden one'—in their language *'el dorado'*--and would have killed all the tribes to get it. The Caribs were amazed at their cupidity and willingly traded gold for the long sharp sticks they carried tipped with iron, for cutting tools and shovels, marvelling that the gold should be so prized by these strangers that they would part with such rare and precious tools. But when the Caribs showed the white men the riverbeds that gave them the gold, they became displeased and aggressive, and wished to find the "mine" of which they had heard. In their greed they tortured many men to no good purpose, which angered the nations that had received them in friendship and had helped them in many ways to settle believing that they too had fled from some calamity of nature, perhaps another flood. And when they did not cease their terror, the nations rose, joined hands and drove them off the land.[122]

The shaman's family, or tribe, had built many villages on the Barama and its tributaries, and trails to connect them to the rivers north and south. They had roamed the Kauramembu mountains nearby by many trails, most of which have now disappeared into the fastnesses of that rugged place. Today only one of the long trails remained of all those they had trod through the centuries --the lonely trail from Cokerite that ran to the Cuyuni many days journey to the south.

"Those were our ancestors," the shaman said. "We are an ancient people, God-fearing; we live as God willed, not by the rules of man which seem to dishonour God and the land He gave us, and deny his creatures their rights; but we are few now, too few to prevent the destruction that your lowland people will do to us, our animals on land and water, our forests and our rivers."

When the "white foreigners" returned after many decades, they came in trickles, befriending the Warrau and the Arawak, the people of the swampy estuaries, and rode in their canoes. These were new and spoke a different tongue and wore different clothes. They brought strange new weapons, new tools and trinkets that dazzled the people, "and fooled them", so that almost to a man they brushed aside the shaman's injunction to stay away from the strangers. These too, like those who had come before, wanted only to find the source of gold, and 'the golden one' in his 'golden palace' in the remote mountain forests beside the lake. The Caribs knew of no such place, and so informed them.

They paid no heed, these white men, for they were races of tormented egotistical men from across the same great ocean the Carib ancestors had crossed in the forgotten past, but these were not driven to the Carib lands by floods or other calamity, as the Caribs had assumed when the first ones had come, but by an enormous materialistic appetite, who, like the Hebrews in the Bible whom the missionaries disparaged so much for their greed and arrogance, also wished to own the world!

From far off these savage men had come, not for help, but to steal and plunder, covering their white skins in strange garb as if hiding their blemishes or their shame. They had come as far as their long boats could take them, carrying sticks that exploded with a fearsome noise and puffs of smoke that could strike a man down. And they used bribes and threats and torture to impress many Caribs in their search. And there were those among the tribes, weak and troubled men, who listened and turned to serve the foreigner, oblivious of their selfish and cunning ways; and many who did so, and heeded not the shamans, suffered gravely and many died, even the very young. But no one could find the mythic palace of gold that they coveted so much, and for which so many had perished.

As the years passed and as contact increased his forefathers had sickened in increasing numbers and most had died, men, women and children, killed before their time, not by weapons but by all manner of sicknesses that the tribes had never seen before. Some had died quickly, their skin burning with fever, panting for breath and their insides coughed up in bloody phlegm. Some had broken out in the most vicious pox, with angry blisters covering their bodies, and

---

[122] This refers to the first and only attempt, by the Spaniard, Pedro d'Acosta, to settle the Barima area in 1530.

wracked with pain, dying after weeks of agony. But there were others who lingered longer, wasting away in a slower suffering, coughing and in pain, their chest heaving, spitting blood, their bodies withering in fever, drenched with sweat each night until the end came, or else covered in blemishes and bumps and dying in slow madness.

Failing to find *'el dorado'* the 'white-skins' had settled the swamps of the coast and grew a long grass for which they brought many slaves with skins shiny and smooth as glass, the colour of the huge black rocks that littered the upper Barama; these were fearsome men, never seen here before.

In the nineteenth and twentieth century more and different kinds of swampland people invaded their forest abodes; there were the missionaries who settled at strategic sites along the rivers. Others were the black men who, like the whites before them, had come in search of gold. The Caribs had been much puzzled by their skins, thinking them to have been painted, or else charred, but finding the colour natural had viewed them with greater awe, then as now, dreading as much their colour as their size. As more came and contact increased, tensions lessened, but native reticence persisted. An exchange of views and beliefs did take place, but the flow was heavily one way, from the "sophisticated" Christian blacks to the "ignorant bucks".

And so to today as tensions raged among the coastal peoples, he dreaded the fate of his people, seeing how many were defecting, lured by wild and heart-breaking promises of a better life and a greater God that were not theirs to claim, and when they had lost their way of life and become as slaves how sad that they would never know how wondrous it had been to live in plenty, to have communion with the trees and birds and fish and animals and all of life and be at one with nature.

I felt humbled and deeply grateful for the unique lesson and their trust in me; I thanked them profusely, knowing that any sentiment I expressed could not match the profundity of what I had heard.

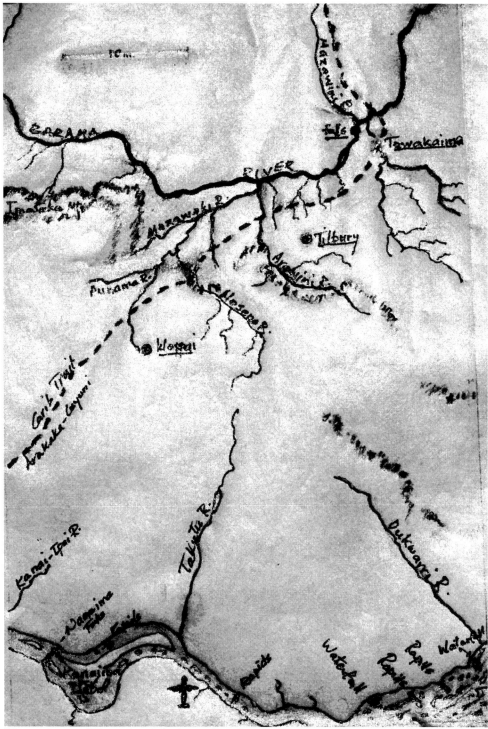

The environs of Wappai and the immediate hunting/farming territory of the local Caribs. The Cuyuni River runs across the lowest field. The region is densely forested, hilly with the lofty Imataka and Pakaraima Mountains nearby, rich with fresh water and restless streams; it is largely unexplored and poorly documented, but rich in life and promise.

Return to Cokerite: Balgobin, Mike's wife, Jain, Mike, Brewster

At Cokerite, return journey: Balgobin, Jain, Mike'swife, Bacchus, Mike, author; Bacchus is holding the bow I had been given.

Cartoons of passage through twins rocks composite of Mike's sketches and photo

The BG coastal and Sand and Clay belts form a roughly 40-mile swath parallel to the Atlantic shore; the coast has 95% of the population and economic activity, primarily business, farming and fishing, while bauxite is mined in the S&C belt. The map shows location, at lower left, of Mts. Roraima (Ror.) and Kukenaam (Kuk.) and Kamarang (Kam.). At lower right PM is Port Mourant, Jagan's birthplace; .Burnham's is Kitty, a Georgetown suburb. Mabaruma is at extreme north. Most of this half of the country, except for the Coast, is very thinly populated and remains mostly pristine forests at risk of evisceration for gold and diamonds or deforestation for hardwoods.

Waini River

Bearded Author, day 17,

Chapter 7

I see another case of lobar pneumonia at Cokerite, this time in a middle-aged adult female, wife of an elder of the tribe; I give her the last of my antibiotics; her husband takes her off to the nearest hospital at Mabaruma about 10 hours away by motorised canoe. We leave after him on the last leg of the Barama River journey, prepared for further hardships. In quiet moments I recalled childhood encounters with Warrau natives at a reservation on the Mahaica River and the poor opinion the British had of them, which their neighbours did not share. I review what we've heard of encounters between Natives and missionaries and the poor opinions they still hold of these resourceful people. An evil omen, according to local legend, greets us at the Barama Mouth as a snake crosses our bow. Police are disappointed that no message had been left for us at Cokerite or at the Rest House, but the caretaker informed us that the plane had come on schedule. We review Burnham's progress, slavery and Christian attitudes to Indians, conversion failures, social decay and British acculturation..

Day 13:   We reach Barama Mouth

A leader is a dealer in hope.   N. Bonaparte, *somewhere west of Moscow*

"There is no cause for which I would kill anyone, but there is a cause for which I would die!"   M. K. Gandhi

"…we should have an adequate and objective understanding of the way our people lived, thought and acted ….for what is a people or a nation that has no history or that has lost its history?... the past furnishes us with an organic connection with what we are today; it can tell us how, when and why we came to be what we are. The history of our people may also serve as an inspiration to us and a spur to future conduct and activity."
B.S. Rai – PPP Minister of Education, BG, October 18, 1959

Early in the morning, hardly awake, I was summoned, with great deference, asked to fetch my "doctor" instruments, and escorted to a hut close by. An older man dressed in khakis and a peaked cap was standing near the entrance, and seated in a hammock within was a woman of about 50 looking tired but alert. The man spoke enough English to be clearly understood. He had spent time on the coast, at Mabaruma, and had worked on the Kaituma railroad during WWII. He told me his wife had come down with a fever, chills, and considerable coughing, which hurt her chest. Just then she threw a fit of coughing and produced a wad of sputum which she held in her mouth, got up from the hammock, went out of the hut and unloaded it at the edge. Part of it hung on a leaf where I could see it clearly, dull greenish brown and thick.

Before I could say it he asked me if I wished to examine her. I nodded. He said a few words to her and she took off her blouse. There was no brassiere; there had never been a brassiere since the tell-tale marks were missing. Five minutes later I was explaining to him that she had a right lower lobe pneumonia, and needed antibiotics. I had four capsules of Achromycin left; I gave her two immediately and advised him to give her the rest at eight hour intervals, but she needed more. He understood quickly, asking questions and offered suggestions.

The district Sicknurse & Dispenser (S&D) would be visiting in a week's time, but that was too long a wait even if her resistance was better than the rest of her tribe's considering that she had lived on the coast. He thought that he could get to Mabaruma by canoe in two days if he started promptly. He had a small booster engine with enough fuel for three or four hours, and he could do eight or 10 knots or better since the entire journey would be downstream with the tide and could reach or come close to Baramanni. There perhaps he could get medicine or get a ride on a speedboat to Mabaruma. If the latter he could get there within eight hours. Failing that he would remain there overnight and paddle to Mabaruma next day; if so we might meet and help him get there. I was worried at the thought of a sick woman in an open canoe for even a day but saw no alternative to his plan, since there was no emergency medicine at the village. I scribbled a note to the government doctor at Mabaruma, and another to be handed to the S&D, in case. A third was written *To Whom It May Concern*, asking for help in providing more antibiotics and/or transportation.

Doris and Benn agreed with the plan, and felt that Baramanni or the nearby mission might have an antibiotic, perhaps a sulphonamide. (We learned later that they kept quinine--which they dispensed for all fevers--aspirin, some mixtures for cough, diarrhoea and pain, zinc paste, and glycerine and ichthyol ointment). Meanwhile the man quickly prepared to leave, settled his wife comfortably in the canoe, covered her shoulders with a shawl and her limbs with a blanket against the chill of the early morning, then went back to his tent.

The others of our party had in the meantime completed preparations for our own departure. Soon the man appeared on the path leading to the water's edge carrying a long bow and two steel-tipped arrows in one hand and a knapsack in the other. I thought nothing of this, considering the weapon as a necessary part of the equipment for a trip on the river. But instead of heading for the canoe he came straight up to me and without pausing or ceremony, simply said, "Doctor, this bow, arrows, for you! Please take."

He extended the arm holding the objects towards me, and briefly looked at his wife; she nodded and smiled. I hesitated. Cpl Doris said, "It's a big honour, Doc; you can't refuse."

My mind held conflicting thoughts of gratitude versus appropriating instruments of someone's livelihood. But the look on his face was so sincere, his stance so dignified, imperious almost, that I quietly, though reluctantly, accepted the gift and extended my hand. He took it, smiled, let go, and briskly walked to his canoe. We watched, standing there at the river's edge, my eyes watering shamelessly. I waved as he deftly swung the canoe around, caught the current and headed downriver. Soon his engine spluttered to life, whined then settled down and whisked them into the mist that clung heavily to the river and obscured its surface.

By the time we left, the village was fully awake and busy with its quotidian chores. I paid a visit to the Chief and to Mike and his son, thanking him again for his thoughtful gift. He signalled me to wait, ran to the back of the hut and came out with the pad I had given him. He handed it to me, bowing; two hurried sketches showed our boat in troubled waters with two figures and the third showed figures as yet undefined sitting in it on calm water, the hats and the positions occupied clearly identifying us. He had an excellent sense of proportion and perspective, but he had not gone far enough for me to judge lighting and detail. Nevertheless to me it was astonishingly good, judging from the work of talented artists I knew. I was certain that he could benefit from training in the arts, but how? The cultural transition had proven deadly for many of his fellows. Bringing the arts to Cokerite would seem a better way than the unacceptably high rates of failure that faced those who tried to make it on the coast. The culture shock might ruin this fine young man. It seemed possible that he could develop on his own and with a steady flow of art supplies could go well beyond the rock carvings of his ancestors, such as those long discovered in the Pakaraimas. It should not be too difficult to keep him supplied.

We parted, rather emotionally, from the four men who had helped us so diligently and expertly; and made completion of the mission possible; their natural stoicism gave way too to sentiment despite the language barrier. We left with them the tools we had brought, and what supplies we had left, including four of the storm lanterns and residual kerosene, retaining only what we kept in the other lanterns. The villagers mustered on the riverbank to watch us leave, perhaps still perplexed by our visit and waiting to quiz the men about their adventures; the whole scene had a quiet dignity, in which even the children participated as if stage-managed.

From Cokerite the river ran north for about 45 miles to reach the Waini, snaking its way through dense forest where hardly a sign of civilization disturbed the brooding tranquillity of the scene. The river got gradually wider but the hazards, floating and fixed, remained much as we had seen them on the inward journey. The path we had cut through the *tacubas* was retraced, although delays did occur at some points where the passage had refilled with flotsam.

We were able to maintain a brisker pace than we had done since leaving Mazawini, though now restrained by the desire to eke out the maximum mileage from what little fuel we had left, and by caution to steer clear of visible and submerged obstructions, especially fixed objects like rocks, the most feared threat in these low water conditions. Our boat's shallow draught was somewhat reassuring, and we were lighter by the weight of the four men to whom we had bid goodbye at Cokerite, plus the exhausted supplies. Nevertheless Benn took no chances and placed everyone to assist Rod and Doris on lookout. It helped that we were going with the flow hence floaters were less likely to do serious damage. We missed the men, who had been so close to us for ten days, and half expected to see them at any moment filling the empty spaces they had left, and Rod particularly would look to his left imagining Joe to be at his elbow.

We were at this point unsure of where this leg of our journey would end. We had expected a message of some sort at Cokerite, and were very disappointed that, although we were six days overdue, Police HQ had not appeared to show any interest in learning our whereabouts. The policemen shared our surprise, and Inspector Bacchus voiced his dismay, "I can't figure out why they would not at least try to reach us. Somebody slacking!"

"Or too busy keeping order." Jain chuckled.

"The best we can hope for now is a message at the Rest House. If nothing there we'll have to head for Mabaruma." Bacchus concluded.

The town was about 65 miles north of Cokerite as the crow flies, but 135 or so miles by river. Our main problem would be gas; there was a small cache at the Rest House, hopefully enough to spare us a gallon or two.

I was poring over a map reminding myself of the landmarks we would pass along this segment of the river. The main ones were the tributaries that joined the mainstream from north and south, forming a pattern like the skeleton of a fish. Ten miles downriver was *Torubaru*, a northern tributary, then the *Asowari, Diarundu, Amoyakamu, Ipotaikuru, Asawini, Muri, Arisika, Amaturi, Sawarikuru*, and so to St Bede's Mission, 25 miles from Cokerite. Beyond were the *Kurasan*i, followed by an unnamed tributary from the south, then *Wanaparu, Ebini, Kuruwani, Waiwa,* and *Kurupanna* just before the Barama reached the Waini. The tributaries all flowed through dense woods with hardly a sign of habitation except for St Bede's Mission. Their names evoked mystery -- I wished I knew their meanings, what stories each might tell. I knew only that *Cokerite* was a type of palm found in the North West District and elsewhere in the sand and clay belt.

A huge *tacuba* which spanned the entire stream stopped us. The opening we had made on our upstream journey was blocked by a thick tangle of flotsam, which Doris and Rod proceeded to clear. The sun shone harshly from a cloudless sky. The humid air was still. It took almost an hour of sweaty chopping, pushing and heaving wood onto the bank nearby to clear the opening. Balgobin, Brewster and Jain assisted in stacking the wood on the bank, while Bacchus and I retreated towards the far bank after our help was declined. From time to time the men would drench themselves with the cool water to get relief from the stifling heat. These were conditions for siesta, not heavy manual work. The Spaniards had avoided labour at this time of day, but the British had firmly rejected the notion. *"Mad dogs and Englishmen go out in the mid-day sun"* Noel Coward had sung.

I sat on the *tacuba* in dappled shade, fiddling with my camera. Inspector Bacchus joined me, contemplating the flowing water as it made burbling spirals around the branches that dipped below the surface, and the eddies and foam that ran along the shallows. The exposed surfaces of the *tacuba* were many degrees hotter than those in the shade. You had to be careful where you touched or sat.

"Well, Doc, we'll be home soon. All the talk we had was eye-opening."

"For both sides, I think." I replied.

"We appreciate what you and Mr Jain did to inform us," Bacchus said. "You gave us a lot of new and strange things to chew on. I for one will follow up on this, but you know people believe what they grow up with; we'll see. You should do this kind of thing more often. It would be good to talk again and discuss questions. This was the first chance I had enough time for a long conversation, and certainly the first time I ever spend more than a few hours with East Indians, much less talk seriously or find out anything about their history. That's a big black hole. Same for the others."

"I had no such luck," I joked. "Both at Queen's and at University, I've had more than ordinary contact with black and other folks, all kinds. Many of my best friends are not Indians, chaps like Earl John and Neville Linton; Earl is with Bookers and Neville's abroad; you might know one of the very best, Leslie Romalho, head of the Licensing Office. We've been best friends for nearly 20 years, since Berbice High."

"Yes, I know him quite well. Nice chap. Speaks fast."

"That's him; and you know, my wife is mixed race: Indian, Caucasian and African. And Christian; her mother is half Jew, so her family gatherings are a racial soup. And they all get along quite well."

"I didn't know that." He sounded genuinely astonished. "I thought she was one of those rich folks, Hanuman or Maraj or Sankar--from Middle Street or Lamaha St."

I laughed. "No, she's Jamaican, but she looks Indian. If you saw her you'll call her 'coloured' or *dougla*."

He paused, not knowing what to say. His eyes darted at mine for an instant and I sensed that he was seeing me suddenly differently, that here was a man who was not just talking about the two most difficult human issues: racial tolerance and religion, but who knew what it was like to live life intimately in different racial and religious camps. I allowed him the time to absorb this news. His face regained its composure. Then he said, as if nothing had changed, "I think even Doris learned something; he wouldn't admit it though. You have to see with him, He sees things differently, like so many of our people. And he feels strongly. He never mix with East Indians, grew up in a pure African village."

"Well, Inspector," I said as respectfully as I could, "if we don't find a way to live together, this country is dead! It will be taken over by the worst elements among the politicians. And unfortunately I think that's Mr Burnham and the racist clique he leads. I know him fairly well. Followed him and Jagan since I was a teenager. Have you ever looked at him close, looked at his eyes? They're mean; they have no compassion; they look evil!" I realised that this might be a *faux pas*, but in the conversations we have been having on this trip, *faux pas's* had been the order of the day, at least for me. "He will collect and breed evil people, who will terrorise future generations, yours and mine, like Stalin or Hitler."

"No, I never look into his eyes; I only met him once, and that was across a picket line, and he was screaming at the Police!" he paused, as if wondering whether he, like me a moment earlier, had said too much. But he continued, "We're speaking privately of course."

"Of course," I nodded.

"I worry about his tactics; so many undesirables following him, you know, tough guys, with police records. I see them in the streets, marching. We can't arrest them unless we catch them red-handed. It's hard. It's very worrying to me. But some officers don't see it that way."

"I hope we can find some way to discuss our positions--needs, wants, agreements, differences, you know what I mean--like we began to talk about on this trip. If things are left to happen naturally, all of us will slip back into our routines, fill up our days as before, and forget this whole episode. We would lose so much understanding."

"That would be a pity," he said, "maybe you should start a social group or club to bring people together who want to understand one another, and learn how to get along."

"That would help; maybe you could help organise such a group. That's how Jagan started."

"In my position I have to stay clear of politics, but I can help in other ways, yes, I believe such a group without fixed political affiliation can help, a sort of *Citizens for Fairness* group."

"But don't you think people have already made up their minds and that they don't want to change? Each day I feel the tension between groups growing, even among the doctors at the Hospital and in the BG Medical Association, as if the sides could never meet. I see how the voices drop whenever I walk into a conversation among Blacks, and I'm sure the same thing happens when a black doctor comes among Indians, no matter what they're talking about. That's new and very worrying."

"But now that we're near Independence, next year, or the year after, what will happen? Confidentially, Doc, I see big trouble coming."

"You're right, but it's we Indians who would be in trouble. We're not militant, at least not yet, and even those who are will have to face black policemen carrying rifles, as they've done before. Remember Jainarinesingh and the march after the Enmore massacre? The Indians have no firepower, so you won't get any real trouble from them. But watch your own folks. Have you seen the types shadowing Burnham these days? A few Americans among them, tall black guys, some say they are CIA, who knows? I fear more from them than from the local people, bad as our folks can behave. The Americans know little or nothing about Indians, nor of India, for that matter, and if they're told that that's the enemy, they'll see wigwams and Tecumseh, Cochise and Geronimo all over again, and we'll have a lot of dead brown bodies in the morgue."

I had laid it on thick, but I did not think I would have another chance to speak like this with a ranking Police Officer. What I had to say might influence this one officer, as we had developed a mutually respectful relationship. At worst, it would do nothing. So I continued, "You know, Inspector, if I had to decide, I would not choose independence now. It makes no sense from either the economic point of view, or social."

"What do you mean?" he asked, almost harshly, "Everyone wants it!"

"Economically, we lose all clout," I replied, in as soft a voice as was audible, "we can't afford independence; for ten years various sums had been earmarked for development, and nothing substantial has been done; the interim government was given something like $40 million for development and hadn't a clue how to use that money properly; they underspent, apart from some housing, and wasted much, contracts for friends. It's as if the Brits wanted to prove we couldn't do big things. Truth is, a lot of skilled people have left; who will carry out the big projects that this country needs, like the Hutchinson scheme they've been ignoring for over ten years?. That's what the Interim chaps should have started – they had enough money to do a substantial part. Income generated would have added capital. We'd be well on our way to being a major agricultural nation, and keep our people here."

"But people don't want to work on farms; they prefer office or service jobs, or trade; farming is long hours and uncertain."

"That's true for town people, not where I come from; those who know will tell you that water control is our greatest need and saviour; mixed farming Indian traditional style can make us rich. I haven't heard a single politician discuss this, not even the old PPP; instead they offer freeness!"

"Right! They say only independence can give the control for that kind of decision."

"Don't believe it; they have the wrong ideology for this country; people don't know enough to disagree and instead suck up to Jagan and Burnham. It would be cheaper for us to opt for internal self-rule only. Let the Brits bear the other costs. God knows, they owe us. Socially if we go independent, we'll only be exchanging 'black dog fo' monkey', as the Jamaicans say."

"What d'you mean?"

"We'll be exchanging the British dictator for a local one. Independence will only give us the right to choose our oppressor! At least the British seemed somewhat responsible in judicial and fiscal matters, if not in social or economic ones. Burnham says that this Jagan government should not take the country into independence, even though he had agreed to independence during this term. The Americans were led to believe that Jagan would lose this round. Now they're almost frantic. They have a blind hatred of Communism and will upset a Communist state if Jagan goes the way of Castro. Jagan did not convince Kennedy that he was merely a Socialist and not a Communist. Many of Kennedy's advisers are thoroughly against Jagan, even though Kennedy himself and at least one major adviser, Schlesinger, as well as Melby here prefer him over Burnham, and are willing to give him the benefit of the doubt, at least for the time being. The Americans don't trust Burnham, but you know him, he will not stop until he gets his way. And he's smart enough to fool the US. If it comes to an election as a condition for independence, as Burnham now demands, Jagan will win again. And that will start the real trouble. Burnham will not be satisfied with a loss. He has a strong lobby in Washington, which Jagan does not have. In fact his name is becoming mud there. So his best bet is to stall, make peace with the Americans, and let the Russians go. If he does that, I bet you, in five years we'll be well on the way to progress such as we've not seen before. But Jagan has to act smart, which he's not done so far. None of this is new; my brother-in-law laid out all of this to him ten years ago, in detail, with figures."

"Really? Do I know him?"

I gave him details. Yes, he knew the family name and the store, a few blocks from Police Headquarters and in fact had shopped there on occasion. But he had never met Tulla Hardeen, and remembered that one of his senior officers, a man named Sutton, had spoken well of him and attended his funeral, along with other senior officers.

"You know, I always keep away from these things; ten years ago, I was in the country and knew little about politics. In '53 I was a corporal in New Amsterdam and heard Kendall complain that Jagan wanted to replace the Police with his own *People's Police* to support dictatorship. That didn't go down too well and I believe it put the Police on guard against the PPP ever since."[123]

"That was unfortunate; he's not biased; my brother-in-law chastised him for loose talk; Jagan had this awful habit of speaking from emotion, expecting listeners to pick up his true meaning."

"So your family was with PPP from the beginning?"

"Yes, behind the scenes, not party members, but as friends and supporters; my brother-in-law was close to Jagan and a key adviser; he gave him money and helped raise campaign funds."

"So he had ideas of what it would take to develop this place?"

"Better than most; he spent a lot of time trying to let Jagan see things as clearly as he did, and in a moderate light, but although Jagan agreed with his arguments, he didn't follow through."

"But if Jagan changes that way, and join hands with the Yanks, he would have to do things their way, I'm sure he wouldn't like that. Look at the stuff he writes about them. On the one hand he asks them for aid, and on the other he blasts them. Even the toughest skin would chafe with such needling. And one more thing, wouldn't they try to come in with heavy machines roaring and destroy all the things Hari was talking about?"

"Sure the risk is there, and we have to make sure everyone is clear on that. I believe we can develop agriculture on the coast starting with infrastructure. That means roads, drainage and irrigation works which is what Hutchinson proposed, with enough power to process our products cheaply, and bargain for markets. Mr Crum Ewing, a white farmer neighbour, convinced my father back in the thirties that he could get all the power needed on the coast from wind and

---

[123] Jagan had argued that the Police were not men of the people but *"recruited from people who cannot find other jobs. They are displaced workers. We told them we sympathized with their cause. We were fighting for the policemen and they were in sympathy with the P.P.P. Police in the past had to obey instructions of white officers. I am not talking about racial hatred, but the planter class and the sugar-bosses. When it comes to strikes or quelling disturbances the police are sent not because of law and order, but to carry out commands of officers who are sympathetic to reactionaries. A great deal has been said about a statement of mine torn out of context that the police were used before to shoot workers. They shot at workers who tried to run away. We don't want police like that. When I speak of 'people's police' I mean police that will not act in that way. But my remark was torn out of context."* (Caribbean News, Nov 1953)

water, as he had done. The West Indies can use all the rice we can sell them. We don't produce enough reliably; our rice lands are either too wet or too dry.

"We need water control. Investment money – local, American, British, whichever--can do that for us. Farmers from Mahaica-Mahaicony-Abary area feel that local sources should be tapped first, not foreigners; that way the profits of investment stay in the country. I know for sure that a group of MMA landowners had offered Jagan in 1952 to raise financing for the first phase there of Hutchinson's polders, provided that they received Government guarantees and market support, *which foreigners get as a routine*, but Jagan, or perhaps his wife and her far left chums, hooked on Soviet data, did not accept it. Those folks include some of my in-laws and friends and had approached Government in the late thirties. That's another sad story. Without markets though, we're strapped; no one will invest or risk their money in loans to this Government, not a communist government. And these chaps were willing to do that."

"That's incredible! Now Jagan says that Russia can buy all our produce at a profit for us. He quoted some fella from England, I forget the exact words.[124] Anybody else believe that?"

"The Communists do; the only way that Russia can make trade profitable at this costly distance is from heavy subsidies, as they already doing with Cuban sugar, or as the Yanks do with US Sugar and Dominican Republic to screw Caribbean producers."

"But that will only come at a big price."

"Absolutely."

"I read Jagan's Chile speech this last May; he claimed that central planning of the economy is the superior way, that even the Americans make plans and don't rely entirely on the market."[125]

"My brother-in-law was quite a smart businessman, ahead of his time, at least for BG. He used to tell Jagan that the state alone could not create a prosperous economy, unless wealthy or lucky or both. An economy needs people with ideas, and the knowledge and guts to strike out on their own, in other words free enterprisers, a term, like entrepreneurs, that both Jagan and Burnham dislike. And even if you have those in plenty you need a lot of savvy consumers to grow your business. But of course, US business brainwash and herd their people into categories worse than the Soviets to get them to buy all the manufactured goods they make, from cars to hair spray and packaged food. It's the combining of those elements that made the US so successful."

"If that is so, why haven't the Americans tried to help us before?"

"It's a complex story. The best sources of money would be private investors or government. Rule out the first since Jagan is against private enterprise. As for the US Government, I know for sure that Melby has

---

[124] "If Russia were to make use of her superior industrial productive capacity to obtain raw materials and food by exchanging them for industrial products, the terms of trade of the primary countries would violently shift in their favour, and these countries would have considerable benefit by trading with Russia. At the same time, Russia, far from suffering a disadvantage from such exchanges, would also benefit as she would obtain food and raw materials on far more favourable terms, by concentrating her own efforts on industrial expansion, than she is capable of doing at present. Thus, Russian self-interest and the interest of the poor countries would coincide. This is an extremely menacing prospect for the industrial countries of western Europe which depend on the import of primary products and export manufactures". *(Thomas Balogh, Economist, Balliol)*

[125] *"There is need, as we all admit, for rational economic planning. We cannot afford to leave development to the vagaries of chances. Planning is required to maximize returns from limited resources."* CB Jagan, Santiago, Chile, May, 1961

recommended aid, and President Kennedy and his advisors, especially Schlesinger, agree. That's what our friend Steve so much as said, promising us some good news. But I don't think they can approve it just like that, nor in the amount Jagan wants, or the country needs. The Hutchinson scheme alone was costed at £30 million 10 years ago. The US government is hobbled by rules; all foreign aid has to go through USAID, which is strict and can even go against the wish of the President. That is one big hurdle. The other is that BG is a colony that they deal with through Britain. They can't favour BG over Latin American states. Besides everyone thinks Jagan is Communist and no one wants a Castro-style government in South America, and the US cannot look as if they're rewarding known Communists. It's a tricky position for them.

"The Brits, I suppose, could interfere, but only if there's some gain for them. They're struggling and wouldn't mind if the Yanks took over in the Caribbean, which is now costing them more than they're willing to pay. They've already milked us almost dry, just as they wanted to do forever to India, and still doing in Africa! The main thing is that they still hold the reins; the Americans can't just come in unless they're invited. Jagan's been pushing the Brits hard. You remember a few months ago he had the House pass a resolution requesting the British Government to fix a date for independence next year. Just about now he's to meet with the Colonial Secretary, Reginald Maudling to fix a date for the independence conference. What Maudling does will likely depend on US wishes; if so, Jagan might well come back empty-handed. If that happens the grapevine says Jagan will appeal to the UN in view of their de-colonisation position."

"But if he tries that, the Brits and the US will use the veto." Bacchus suggested.

"I'm sure you're right. But remember in 1953 with internal self-government the Governor wasn't willing to veto any measure passed by both houses; it's preferable to give the impression of orderly change, not chaos. Personally I think Jagan and Burnham crave independence purely on ideological grounds; we're not economically ready for it, and despite three elections under adult suffrage, most people don't understand the issues and are politically naïve; they blindly follow the leaders, like the rats and children followed Browning's Pied Piper. Remember him?"

"Yes, we had that one in our Reader."

"Also we have no popular basis to support the structures needed to maintain a democracy. We don't have enough trained people; we can't guarantee an independent Police Force--no personal offence meant, because I feel officers like you are in the minority--we cannot guarantee that we'll maintain an independent judiciary; any armed forces we develop will easily be manipulated by a strong-arm man like Burnham, largely because of racial politics, and Jagan is no better, though not as ruthless, but the Soviets will lead him by the nose.

"The other big thing is money. Here the best sources of money would be private investors or government. Rule out the first because of Jagan, and no one trusts Burnham. All the bad examples of business exploitation Jagan quotes are foreign companies, like the Demerara Electric Co., Canadian, and a particularly bad one. The truth is that there is still considerable wealth in local hands, which has never been tapped, because it's in hands that do not trust local governments or local banks. Jagan was advised over and over again in the last ten years to develop confidence in local institutions and shed the colonial habit of running to the same masters he bad talks. Instead he put politics ahead of economics and threw out the wealth creators from around him and most of the local wealth is already in British banks. That's why I'm so pessimistic about our future."

"But then if we delay independence we'd still be a British colony; and if the Brits can't afford to pay, won't we be worse off?"

"Not really, the present constitution gives us internal self-government, which gives us the freedom to make deals with anyone. The Brits would not object to any modest American initiative. And the Brits would still be responsible for foreign affairs and defence, the two costliest things for an independent nation. Don't forget that Venezuela and Surinam both claim big pieces of BG. We should insist that UK settle that finally before independence. Also, those outstanding Colonial Office plans for specific works in BG, a new hospital, the railway and roads, sea defences and others, have been around since the late forties. If the Brits really wish to get rid of us, they should carry out those works before they go. Jagan should insist on a revival of those plans."

"You said that before; what plans are those? I can't recall seeing anything about that. The ones I know are what they gave the Interim Government between '54 and '57; World Bank had a plan which Savage claims Jagan ignored in '53. Is that what you mean?"

"Those and others that CDW had proposed since 1947; the Interim government spent money on them to get architectural work for a multilevel hospital, and survey for an inland East Coast road. I'd seen those plans in detail in '51 when I worked in the Medical Department; the Colonial Office had stalled them almost from the day Jagan won his seat in '47. Funny, eh?"

I told him the rest of what I knew and quoted sources. Hardly had I done this than it occurred to me that I had been reckless, but I trusted the Inspector. "That's between us, okay?"

"Okay. That's some story. The press must have had it. Lethem did start a series of social works in the forties under the same scheme. How far did he get?"

"Not too far because of the war and not enough technical people. What intrigues me is not so much why Jagan doesn't pursue that line--if he did and the Brits came across with some funds, even part of it, Jagan would lose much of his ammunition, and won't be able to complain so much--but why didn't the interim government seek to implement those plans between '54 and '57? They weren't just rough drafts! They knew about them. Their supporters in the Service did and I can't imagine them holding back such crucial information. Was it because the Brits who appointed that Government put a muzzle on them, having already decided to scratch BG from the list of CDW beneficiaries of capital *grants*, and replacing them with *loans*? Or maybe those all got absorbed in World Bank and the later five year plan? Moneys were allocated, much unspent."

"Burnham knew about this?"

"Sure he did, and must have thought of it tactically; that information went to the PPP in 1951. Forbes doesn't miss a trick; I'm sure his contacts in the Service would have reviewed the status with him. But it seems to me that he would give up pressuring the Colonial Office to gain the bigger prize of the Prime Minister's job. If that's what it would take to buy out the Brits, Forbes would do it! The Brits love their bribes! Remember the Indian stories?"

"My God, Doc!" There was consternation in his look. "I can't imagine anything so harmful to this country; you really don't like Burnham, eh?"

"Liking him is not the issue, Inspector; Burnham is who Burnham is. He's ruthless, ambitious and selfish. It's plain for all to see. I know quite a few things about him that are not complimentary. Some of which you chaps might well have on record."

The Inspector looked up at me sharply, then just as swiftly looked ahead, paused, just noticeably and said, "When the last elections were held, we all understood that the next step would be independence in the middle of 1962. If this unrest continues that might be a problem."

"Precisely. That's Burnham's tactic, to create enough of a disturbance to show the world that Jagan cannot keep law and order here; therefore it would be reckless to grant independence under his leadership. His followers are too mesmerised to realise that he's using them."

"You really believe that!" It was not a question; it came out more as a discovery. "I had my doubts when the first incident happened the day the house convened after the elections. But I gave them the benefit of the doubt. By habit we have to avoid taking sides, but then keeping law and order often means taking sides. It's a big stress for our ranks to deal with the conflict; most are decent and law-abiding. But we have our position and we trust leaders to do the right thing."

"That would be nice, Inspector. But just consider all that's happened since the elections. Burnham's been agitating all over the country not on policy or programs, but on claims that Jagan will favour Indians only and trample on the black population. Jagan will trample on Indians, *never* Blacks, but Burnham keeps saying it. You keep slinging mud on a smooth wall eventually some will stick. That's the rankest form of politicking, appealing to people's worst fears. That includes the Police Force; he knows he has great sympathy, if not open support there[126]. Why else would he lie down on High Street at Brickdam intersection, in front of a heavy police vehicle, and dare anyone to move him? Certainly no black policeman tried. Remember that? I felt sorry for you guys to be put to that test. "

"I did hear about it and it really bothered the officer in charge."

"But Burnham couldn't give a hoot for how policemen would feel. He already has ex-policemen forming a terror squad and training people in use of arms and teaching strategy; I hear he's gone so far as to have those guys force their friends at Eve Leary to give them rifles, revolvers and grenades for his coming fear campaign. You watch; he gets to lead this country, he'll turn the Force into his doormat, and everybody else; next he will create a loyal bodyguard, like every other dictator, past and present, Batista, Duvalier, Nkrumah, great examples. They already call Burnham an *obeah* man. He'll find the most crooked cops to head the force and the good guys like you will leave. Or be forced out. I'll bet anything on that!"

---

[126] At a public meeting in the 1957 election campaign an Indian heckled Burnham, "You keep talking about workers' rights. What d'you know of what it takes to work, the hot sun and sweat, the bullying overseer and foreman, the low wages? They dock we pay, they have favourites; we try to get 'way from there; you t'ink an Indian worker can get a job at Transport and Harbours Department?" Burnham frowned, but said, "Good point, comrade, come up here and say you' piece."
A few men grabbed him roughly. Burnham scolded, "Easy, men; don't hurt my friend."
Once on the podium, away from the microphone, while a lieutenant spoke to the people Burnham said to the man, "You say another thing like that, I'll have them break your neck." Then into the microphone he said, his arm tight around the man's shoulders, "This is a man with insight. This is the kind of man we want in our party. Give him a proper introduction to the party; give him a membership application." The next day he was admitted to hospital unconscious with severe head injury and fractures of three ribs and an arm.

I was astonished at how casually I spoke, but before he could react, I quickly added, "Nothing personal, Inspector; that's the Burnham I know; it's honesty and honest guys like you I'll be sorry for." Bacchus was sufficiently aware of these things not to take offence.

"We're almost powerless there. I hate to say this, we're under big pressure right now, and we don't know who stands where; we're in a real bind; most officers are good, decent men, do their job without fear or favour, but things changing, too fast for most, and bring confusion. Loyalty to the crown was easy; the white officers controlled everything; indiscipline or dereliction of duty was promptly and decisively punished. Sad to say, I'll worry when they go and we're independent; we really not trained mentally to take over in a mixed society like this. Ten years ago I wouldn't have thought of race as a big thing here," he concluded ruefully, "but today, it's everything."

"That's why I feel we don't need independence yet; Burnham's actions will buy time, which is what we need, some time to think, but his way will not allow us to think in peace; it will be violent and only split us more and buy us his version of independence with dictatorship, not democracy, and the Americans will support him just like Duvalier, murders and all."

"What I hear people are really frightened of is that Jagan will bring in Russian troops to take over and get rid of the local police force until Jagan can set up his own trained by them."

"That's the wildest speculation, D'Aguiar's stupid harangue that embarrasses smart people in UF; it will only play among the uninformed; Jagan will *not* get independence under a Communist ticket; the US *won't* allow it; the Russians *won't* risk a confrontation with the US; they're ahead in space already which pisses off the US. Nixon went over there and had good discourse including showing off a typical American middle class house complete with shiny appliances. When Khrushchev went to the States he was snubbed and Disneyland did not allow him to visit; he was mad that he did not get to visit an aerospace centre, but he did get another blast of US materialism and Hollywood glitz. When he agreed this year with Walter Ulbricht to build a wall dividing East and West Berlin, he was widely criticised and yet our two leaders said nothing about this. Khrushchev's collectivisation of agriculture is not the miracle he thought it would be and Jagan is bluffing when he tries to ignore it. Even if by some miracle Jagan got independence, the police will sabotage him as long as Burnham controls the opposition. *The only thing that will save this country from future dictatorship and corruption is if Jagan drops his Communist policies and steer a middle course*; that in itself will be a miracle and even so he'll have to work hard to convince people that he's changed."

"You think his wife will let him? Everyone says she's the boss of the PPP."

"That's the big question, Inspector; I used to think that she's the hard-line leftist and brains of the movement, and he the mouth, the front man, with Burnham. But now I'm not sure."

"And what of the PYO?" He asked more to find out what I knew, not for information for it was well known that the Police had agents among them.

"I know that they have goon squads and are learning how to wage civil strife; but they're small fry compared to the expertise the PNC has; especially now with CIA funding Ishmael and D'Aguiar people for destabilisation. You have to watch the UF; they have spies in the PNC and PPP camps, people on their payroll who regularly hang out with PNC guys. If a street fight happens, the PNC is clearly better prepared and armed."

He said nothing for a while, staring in the distance, then said, "We're in for troubling times. Look, the chaps are ready."

We soon passed the last of the major obstacles on the river and continued cautiously to St. Bede's Mission. The ping of a dislodged or broken propeller pin had punctuated the journey in a way as distinctive as the ululation of the 'baboons' in the treetops or the steady whinnying of the outboard. I did not know too many specifics about St Bede's beyond what the natives had said or inferred. The mission had a long history and had been "guilty" of all the things already noted, the most telling being the decimation of the coastal Caribs by disease. It maintained a school and had natives on staff. It was small as missions went; the population did not justify anything more ambitious, especially as the unit could not be self-sufficient, and would need external funding into the foreseeable future. There was the real fear that a socialist government might not fund or subsidise its activities.

The United Force had campaigned among the natives with promises to respect and guarantee their rights, and supported funding for unspecified "interior enterprises". This had pleased the natives, but few of them, not even the UF politicians could elaborate on the meaning of "interior enterprises". One uncharitable critic had suggested that they simply meant "interior stuff, bedrooms you know, whorehouses. That's what they do; they fool the young Arawak girls, promise them all sorts of things, convert them, then take them to Georgetown, screw them and put them out to 'pick fare', even if they get pregnant! Some lucky ones, the prettiest, find husbands and make nice children with Portuguese or Indians."

The remark brought back memories of native men and women whom I had known in Georgetown, two of whom had worked for my sister and brother-in-law. They were Arawaks from the Pomeroon region or Warrau who had been the main targets of the early missions established in the lower reaches of the main rivers, and most of the bovianders were mixtures of these people with Portuguese or Blacks. The first native I had seen or heard speak was Warrau from the Biaboo reservation on the Mahaica River about 15 miles from its mouth.

The Mahaica River arose in low hills of the sand and clay belt and wriggled downgrade north by east for about 40 miles then turned abruptly ninety degrees east flowing for about five miles before turning north again to twist and turn like a restless sleeper until it reached the Atlantic Ocean at the village called Unity. Along the way, about 23 miles from its mouth it yielded part of its waters to the Lama canal. The Lama canal took off from its west bank and ran due west to the Greater Georgetown area, emptying into the Demerara River at Plantation Providence. A few miles before reaching this point a branch canal, protected by a sluice gate, ran north to the Georgetown waterworks, which supplied the city with fresh water.

The Lama canal drained all the land, including several major sugar estates starting with Cane Grove, which was situated directly on the west bank of the Mahaica River. But the wide expanse of flat, low-lying land on the river's east side which extended for up to fifteen miles from its mouth, remained flood-prone and forlorn until the Indians came, released from indenture, in search of farmland. The first settlers included the parents and family of my second brother-in-law *(bunoye)* Bāba, who had come into the area early in the twentieth century and thought it suitable for rice and cattle, if they could control the flooding and deal with the reptiles that infested the waters. They soon came into contact with the local native tribe at their reservation at Biaboo, fifteen miles from the river's mouth, where they built boats, especially canoes and flat-bottomed boats. They were master fishermen and quite willing to work on cattle farms, but cared little for the sugarcane fields.

Bāba's large family had come to own much of the land, about five water-logged square miles at a site called Number 10 District a few miles north of Biaboo. Bāba was married to Pampat, my second sister; he had inherited a share of about 1000 acres about three miles east of the river and had erected a house on built-up ground—to avoid flooding, the earth coming from three deep trenches, each about 70x30 sq. feet and 10 feet deep. These served all purposes, although he had installed a large vat to collect rain water from roof run-off for cooking and drinking. They farmed cattle, grew rice on the fertile soil and prayed for nature to cooperate. In a good year they did well, hoping to save enough to finance drainage and irrigation, acre by acre, or so it seemed. This was part of the huge area that the *Hutchinson scheme* was designed to protect, support and enrich.

I was eight years old when my mother sent me to spend part of my summer holidays with them to help with their three children 4, 3 and 1+ as she was about to have a fourth. Heavy rains had flooded the area for miles around and Bāba had become quite busy moving cattle to higher ground a mile east of the homesite and securing them there. Only those with milk were penned near the house. I was to help him with the milking and tending the calves and in-between mind the children. Their home was the southernmost in a row of half a dozen homesteads separated by barbed wire fences. From the house you could see Biaboo, a thin line of houses silhouetted against the clear horizon about three miles due south across the flooded plain.

When my sister told me who lived there, I became interested and asked her if I can visit the place with their corial (a dugout canoe). She smiled, "You want to go there alone?"

I nodded vigorously.

Then she said, "Too far for you; your *bunoye* has to go there soon; I'll ask him to take you."

We set out early one morning on a circuitous route covering nine .miles to complete a three mile walk if the land were dry; this alone told the entire story of the hardships of rural enterprise and the courage and faith of those involved. First we set out across the sodden muddy fields north for half a mile to reach the main Fairfield dam[127] where it made a right angle turn, one arm leading north for three and a half miles to Fairfield on the main East Coast Road, crossing the railway as it went, the other swinging west for three miles to reach the Mahaica River. The dam ended at the river in a T-junction; where we could see the black water through the trees ominously swirling and rushing as the tide flowed in. We took the turn south along the riverbank and could have walked the remaining five miles to Biaboo, but the recent rains and high water had created breaches and soft spots, deep sink-holes of loose mud that posed a sudden

---

[127] Dams were everywhere in coastal BG; they were ten to twenty feet wide hard packed dirt roads created by the digging of canals to empolder land for flood control which drained into a river and/or the ocean.

serious hazard, especially for a child, acting like quicksand, trapping people and animals, sometimes with tragic outcome.

I had already become familiar with that phenomenon and recalled several incidents at De Hoop, involving humans and animals. Twice our donkey, Filly, had gotten stuck and was in danger of slow drowning; each time several men had come to the rescue with ropes lassoed to the animal's neck and dragging him out of the quagmire. Once found such spots were marked, and gave proof to the injunction of parents, "Never go where you don't know!"

I was once sucked down in one such sudden pit in the bed of a foot-deep clear water channel that traversed the open pastureland and ran for a mile stopping at the public road splaying out into a four-foot deep "estuary". Looked at in perspective it looked like a miniature river, complete with tributaries. The system had been created as paths along which cattle were herded home and over many years the pounding hoofs had destroyed the vegetation, and created a rut that became wider and deeper as it neared the road. In the rainy season it filled with water and acted as a drain for the surrounding pastureland and in time had become–save for a few occasions of severe drought--a constant watercourse one to four feet deep, which would rise by a foot or more after the heavy rains.

After one such deluge, I was at the back of our herd trudging home single file along the flooded main track. Ordinarily the water was clear and cool, and at a point where it widened to about ten feet and deepened to about three feet, we would begin to swim and intermittently hang on to the tail of a cow and be towed. I had just grabbed the tail of one of our gentlest cows, *Lāli,* when I almost disappeared as the ground gave way below me and I was sucked down below the surface. How deep the sinkhole was or how wide I could not tell but I held on to the cow and she dragged me clear. Perhaps the hole was not too wide and the cow had either missed it completely or if one of her feet had stepped in it, the other three had easily pulled her clear.

After walking half a mile we came to the home of *bunoye's* older brother. There we borrowed a corial and paddled upriver with the tide for four or five miles to Biaboo. At the time I enjoyed nothing more than playing in water and with boats and corials. We did not have one but *bunoye* did, but he said it was big, slow and clumsy, built for carrying heavy loads along the main canals, not for running around or as a pleasure craft or one that a little boy could handle alone. He needed a smaller, swifter craft to take him around the flooded ranch, hence the trip to Biaboo.

It was late morning when we got there and the village was busy; a line of low buildings occupied the river bank for about two hundred yards; some had verandah-like structures overhanging the water's edge constructed of *manicole,* a palm that grew quite plentifully on the sandy soil further inland where the ground was higher. Two centuries earlier, the Dutch settlers had farmed sugarcane on the lands north between Number 10 and the ocean shore and had built an elaborate system of wide trenches and dams to empolder their cultivations. The vicissitudes of time and European history had displaced the Dutch in favour of the British, who created British Guiana in 1831.

The Dutch settlements on the east bank of the Mahaica River were abandoned family-owned farms bankrupted after a particularly severe economic down-turn at the end of the 18th century, the end for others coming as a result of ruinous flooding by sea-water after a shoreline dam had given way.

We found the boat builder, busily at work on a sleek canoe chipping away at it with an adze. Two children about my age were playing in the yard. I thought they looked like Mrs Balkaran Singh's youngest child, who, though Indian had Chinese eyes and thick lips, not at all like any of his older brothers or sisters who looked more like us. Only much later would I learn that the boy had Down's syndrome (Mongolism), a genetic defect that gave him an extra chromosome, which changed his looks and retarded his development. But at eight I did not know these things and simply thought that the natives must have all had mothers like Mrs Singh. *Bunoye* was in luck; he could have the *corial* the man was working on, which was the type he wanted and it could be delivered in two days; they soon negotiated a price and we returned home the way we had come. We were offered lunch (or breakfast as the noon meal was called) at his brother's place and after some small talk and an opportunity for me to pick mangoes and *jamoon* from their trees, we returned home the way we had come.

Chatting later with my sister he had told her how impressed he was with the friendliness and industry of the people of Biaboo, in spite of the restrictions the nearby Cane Grove estate owners had placed on native activities on estate lands (which ironically had been traditional native lands). The white colonists had labelled them as lazy, ugly and something of a menace. But they had retained their dignity despite this grave and undeserved maligning; they remained proud in their humility, and far different from the ugly, jealous and thieving little men that their oppressors had made them out to be; they had endured this malignancy bowed down by its weight, but not defeated.

As time passed and contacts with others increased, with resulting cross-breeding, they had acquired a cadre of new offspring who attended the mission school on site and began to learn, along with their half-brothers, the ways of the white man and gradually merged their interests with those of the wider society. But in the 1940s they were still largely detached from the main mass of coastal peoples despite the commerce between them. They were the same tribes as inhabited the lower reaches of the BG rivers and populated the Orinoco delta.

We came to the Barama Mouth at about 5.30 pm just as the sun had begun to dip behind the trees; the inshore waters assumed a chocolate hue, clear and cool, ominous and smooth as glass. The far shoreline became a black haze streaked with sunset gold. Closer towards the middle of the river the surface of a circumscribed area of water was suddenly thrown into ripples, which moved fast in one direction, then abruptly reversed themselves creating a collision front which rapidly dissipated; the likely cause was a localised movement of air prompted by the rapidly changing temperature; it was an odd phenomenon that I had seen before at dusk on open water at DeHoop; it was as intriguing now as it had been when I first saw it. "It's the water spirits playing," someone had explained, and forever after I would avoid entering such areas lest I disturb those invisible powers.

We rounded the southern lip of land and entered the Waini heading for the Rest House another 15 or 20 minutes away. The boat was gliding along like a sled on ice, its high-pitched whine putting to flight some of the crows assembled on the treetops along the banks, while others ignored our intrusion. A light cooling breeze came up from the water to greet us, strengthening as the boat accelerated with the boatman's willingness to drain his tank on this last extravagance at full throttle. We had sped along for about five minutes when

Rod at the prow called out in warning, "Snake" just as the sleek swiftly sliding creature, about six feet long, scurried across our bow not five yards ahead, the boat barely missing its tail.

"Bad luck!" said Doris, instantaneously, almost to himself, but clearly audible in the still, darkening eve. "Bad luck to have a snake cross your bow," he repeated with authority, and looked around as if to ensure that the message was received.

"Go on, man, damn superstition!" said Benn, half-heartedly, as if he did not believe what he had just said, but felt he had to say something to allay anxieties.

"I hear something like that before I lef' town!" said Balgobin, "a buckmaan told me that; he work at the hospital." The rest of us said little. I asked Rod what kind of snake it was.

"'Bout six feet long and black," he said, "I not sure; it move too fast; maybe a black back; they poisonous."

Ten minutes later, just before six o'clock, in the crepuscular light of eve, we were tying up at the Guest House pier.

The caretaker and his wife greeted us warmly. He had no news for us other than that the plane had arrived on schedule, and that the pilot had told him he would conduct a search along the Barama to the extent of his fuel reserve. He had despaired of seeing us return as the days grew to a week and fearful speculation had replaced his natural optimism. He had heard nothing from the authorities. He was therefore glad to see us alive and well, introduced us to a young Arawak man awaiting to be picked up next day, and saying "you all must be hungry, you know your rooms," he hurried off leaving us to unload, find our quarters, and freshen up, while he and his wife prepared dinner.

Inspector Bacchus was quite perturbed that no attempt seemed to have been made to contact us, perhaps with a message left at Cokerite, or at this Rest House, after the plane had returned empty. He sat in silence with his head bowed, his hands cupping his face.

"I'm sorry, chaps; Brickdam let us down;" he said presently, "I expected better but as an officer I have to accept their decision and share their blame."

I tried to make light of the matter, notwithstanding strong feelings of let-down and loss of honour and reliability by the Police, but Jain was the first to comment, "At least, Inspector, we'll get good meal tonight and can have happy party today."

"I guess we'll find instructions at Mabaruma." Doris said resignedly, avoiding any new attempt to vilify Brickdam in deference to the Inspector.

"There must be some good explanation;" Bacchus said finally, "a lot could happen in two weeks. I'll talk to the caretaker; you chaps freshen up."

It was an unusual feeling to be indoors; I expected at any moment to hear the ripple of the river and the night sounds and be on full alert for the unknown, trusting that when sleep came we were under Nature's care, and the protection of our relay of guards. The first few nights in the open were tense with the visions from all the yarns of the hinterland that had been spun in imaginations fired by fear and wonder. The visions had given way to objective awareness of the strange and wonderful panorama of trees, air, light and water and the life they sustained, and the unique environment created of which we could become a part, like the Caribs, and not disturb its rhythm or its character. Soon, especially after meeting Hari, I began to take things for granted, and was thus able to learn more from the night and the forest. Now we were suddenly half way out and separated by the comparative safety of four walls while the forest outside was beginning its nightly hum as its denizens emerged for their customary hunt.

We freshened, had a drink while the smells of cooking seeped in from the kitchen, whetting appetites, reminding us how frugal we had been with food. Soon we were dining heartily on spicy fish with rice, vegetables and fruits, and Indian flat bread, *paratha* style. We talked casually in the relaxed way of people who knew one another and I was delighted to note how different the atmosphere had become, compared with our first meeting in this room. Soon the caretaker brought in tea and cake and joined us enquiring into our adventure, which Bacchus summarised. (The caretaker kept a diary of visitors, their mission and any information that could assist future travellers.) His wife came in briefly then left for the kitchen.

"It was slow, as you know, but we got there and everyone did his bit; we had a few tense moments but no major mishap. No *massacouraman!*"

"I'm not so sure; I nearly drowned, remember?" Doris supplied reflectively, sipping his drink. "And Rod got pitched over; good thing he can swim. And the snake cross we bow."

Bacchus and the others briefly described the highlights, emphasising the difficulties due to low water and the need for an adequate food supply and medicines. Afterwards, we had cigarettes and a nightcap (we left the last of the bottles with the caretaker). Jain began to tell jokes and each one contributed, including brief personal anecdotes, further illustrating how comfortable each felt in the company and the camaraderie that had developed; even reticent Rod felt free to describe his reaction when he fell into the river and joked about the end he had imagined while briefly stunned in the deep. Balgobin looked thoughtful and summarised the disposition and spirit of the group.

"Who say we can't live and work together?"

He was right, of course. I ruminated over this in the hour before sleep and of the main characters-- and features-- in the drama now on living stage in city streets who at this very moment might be plotting to confound and agitate the multitude of simple people whose major crime had been to allow their leaders to bamboozle them.

Burnham remained for many the quintessential knave, the end of peace and hope, something like Herod Antipas of old, as one evangelist sadly described him; his record so far of scheming, cheating and political wheeling-and-dealing was second to none. His sister Jessie had told how he had modelled himself on Machiavelli, his hero. He liked to jump into neatly made-up political beds, which he then seized, like a crow raiding a robin's nest.

Thus he had left the LCP to join the PPP because it brought him support of the majority Indian working classes already allied with Jagan. Parachuted into the fledgling PPP as Party Chairman—which immediately impressed his followers as they considered *that* the top position in the Party--he had little work to do to gain his objective: a little scheming here, backbiting there, playing favourites with some, spreading damaging rumours or framing others. In this way he had "stolen" the black and coloured poor to create the Burnhamite faction of the PPP when his attempt to seize the Party failed.

In 1957 he made his second major political shift. He remained however a "socialist". Yet he somehow persuaded the middle class conservative UDP--a party of mulattos, blacks and a few East Indians, dominated by lawyers--to join with him to form the PNC, the UDP acting simply out of ignorant fear of a government by Indians. To make the union possible Burnham showed what an accomplished chameleon he was by assuring everyone publicly that the new party would follow a right of centre line in politics, and thus would be the natural choice of "thinking Indians". But that sop bothered many who knew of his unswerving resentments against Indians for reasons no one could explain or he himself clarify. Somewhere deep in Burnham's mind was a sere black world which he ruled rigidly according to personal norms of ethics and morality, where his power would remain paramount long after his death, but even that he would somehow manage to prevent indefinitely or work to his advantage!

The rise of Indians in business, farming and the professions did not sit well with Africans, most of whom had gravitated to towns and large villages, and preferred to find paid work; many were often surprised that Indians had done so well, having swallowed the prevailing British colonial propaganda that the Indian was backward and uncivilized. Africans who operated farms or businesses generally got on well with Indians. Burnham did not see this side of Indian-African co-existence and claimed instead that Indians had wrongfully acquired African land, which he would promptly restore to them, once elected, and settle "old scores".

When Indo-Guianese observed India's independence in 1947 Burnham was not there to see how confounded Africans were by the jubilant display of allegiance to a "strange and backward" country and the expensive celebrations that had followed. They had begun with a parade through Georgetown along Camp St from Broad St to Thomas Lands in which cars bicycles, motorcycles and people numbering thousands participated, carrying posters of Indian heroes, especially Mahatma Gandhi, dressed in his loin cloth and carrying a staff, taken on the march during the *Salt Satyagraha*.

Most Africans were content to snicker at the image and mention of the name, thinking of him as the supplicant Churchill had refused to meet in his simple costume, derisively calling him a naked fakir. However, there was hardly an Indian anywhere in BG who did not know about him in detail, nor display his picture on the best wall of the home. By reviling Gandhi in this dress Churchill was echoing the puritan disparagement of bare skin as some kind of primal sin that tortured the Christian mind wherever he met tropic natives. And when they succeeded in converting people Christianisers would fail to recognise that the winning argument was economic, not the spiritual or puritanical. Burnham had also missed the contemporaneous 1947 election victory of first timer Cheddi Jagan.

Gandhi had eventually eclipsed Churchill and his ilk in human greatness and, to Churchill's chagrin, had brought the great British Empire to its end without war. In the long years of Gandhi's struggle, his detractors (and some of his followers as well) could not fathom his steadfastness in the face of continuous abuse, aggression and murder. The British Army had seemed to welcome the flimsiest excuse to shoot down Indians and their leaders; indeed several massacres had taken place after the Indian Rebellion of 1857 (which the British had dubbed a mere 'mutiny'), one of the worst being the Amritsar massacre. In this century Indian militants like Subash Chandra Bose had wished to mount a military campaign to oust the British and had even proposed an alliance with Hitler to achieve that end. Gandhi's response was *"There is no cause for which I would kill anyone, but there is a cause for which I would die!"* This epigram would become etched in the memory of Indians worldwide.

The British were perplexed and did not know how to deal with Gandhi and would have preferred a conventional insurrection, like that of the Boers. Gandhi's weighty philosophical position, after all, was not what they were taught to expect from a mere heathen. The missionaries in India, who in a real sense were a British fifth column, were further nonplussed by the fact that Hindus generally were cordial and welcoming, engaging them in discourse in a way that was puzzling. They heard principles of Hinduism explained and questions asked about perceptions, which they could not answer, weighed down by the rudimentary and dismissive notions of Hinduism they had learned from those conducting their briefing for the mission in India.

Instead of lost and troubled souls the missionaries had found an intelligent, industrious and ambitious people eager to learn, a people whose culture and traditions were already millennia older than those of the proselytes, highly inventive, and sophisticated to boot, with a rich literature, and command of mathematics, science and astronomy far beyond their own. They were staggered to discover that the so-called "Arabic" mathematics was entirely Indian in origin, from Āpastamba and Baudhāyana to zero and the zodiac.

This contrasted dramatically, Burnham had noted with chagrin, with the dearth among West Africans of any major indigenous literary, cultural or philosophical achievements at the time Europeans made contact with them. Yet significant civilizations had flourished centuries earlier in Benin and Ghana, but had declined for obscure reasons and reverted to a more primitive and fractious tribalism, one of the factors that had made large scale trading in slaves possible.

 The majority of African slaves traded to the Americas originated in the West African Coast between the Volta and Niger Rivers (the Slave Coast) and further south to the Congo delta (one derogatory term in BG for the African was *cungoh* also meaning "a foolish person").

After centuries of slavery few identifying features survived for the African beyond traces of a lost cuisine like *fufu*, stewed meat, *ackee*, words and phrases like *backra, cocobey, quashie* "*cut you eye 'pon me*", *day-clean* and *forceripe*, and spiritual beliefs like *obeah* (when one dies his spirit returns in fearsome form to inhabit trees etc.) and *Jonkanoo*. They were therefore fertile ground for the new and convincing doctrines of the London Missionary Society, the Diocese of Rome and later the Canadian Presbyterian Mission.

By the end of the nineteenth century Blacks had become Christians, both Protestants of every denomination and Roman Catholic. Many had become deacons, priests and theologians, while others had broken away from their initial allegiances to found fringe or special purpose religious groups in the fashion of their American brethren. The most unusual and interesting of these were the *Rastafarians* of Jamaica, who claimed precedence in the Coptic Church of Ethiopia and viewed Haile Selassie as *"Ras Tafari, King of Kings and conquering Lion of Judah"*, a Messiah, or God on earth. They used marijuana, "the mystic weed", in social and religious congress, and for medical purposes, as tea, smoke, balm, and combinations of these.

Social and educational changes created new expectations among people and many were easily led to believe in the promises of politicians. As schools expanded throughout the country most children could expect eight years of a good elementary education that emphasised the three "R's", Geography, History, Art, Music (some schools) and other basic areas of study such as Nature (plant and animal ecology), Home Economics, Hygiene and Health. It included the opportunity to qualify for scholarships or for entry into training programmes for teachers (elementary level) and technicians. However the opportunities were limited, stimulating intense competition, with attendant fall-out, disappointment and frustration which politicians exploited to the full.

Conversion to Christianity opened avenues for Indians but rewards did not flow as easily as they may have been promised, by-passing some altogether, who perhaps had forgotten that success lay in ideas and hard work. Since it was almost impossible to tell a Christian Indian from a Hindu or Moslem, unless specifically costumed or otherwise identified many Indian converts continued to experience the discrimination of their non-Christian fellows. Some suffered a form of self-loathing that often broke families apart.

Others who had moved to the towns but unable to make ends meet, regressed to illicit or demeaning activity, often too shamed to return to their rural homes, especially those who had rejected their heritage or entered mixed race relationships. In the towns the norms of behaviour had changed enough as time passed to countenance mixed marriages especially among urban Indians, Chinese and Portuguese. Coloured and black men found Indian (and other non-African) women quite alluring, and many would "give my eye teeth" to get one. They loved the long straight hair, the modest lips, small nose, slender bodies and bright eyes. But unions between Indian women and black men were less frequent than between Indian men and black women.

Compartmentalisation of fragile Guianese society would fuel the plots of the two protagonists waging political war despite its threat to destroy the very thing that could make the country unique: harmony among a multi-racial, multi-religious population with such varied and interesting cultures as to be an example of what civilisation could achieve in an increasingly complex and divisive world.

As noted earlier Hindus and Muslims had accommodated to one another over a period of several centuries, and the vast majority lived in integrated communities, rural and urban. This was not the case for the majority of BG Indians and urban Blacks. The initial thrust of politics to bring them closer had failed and both leaders, despite the racial polarisation, were pushing headlong for self-determination without first settling the relationship issues in all sectors of social and economic activities, including the crucial and pressing one of law and order. The perspectives differed considerably, not so much on ideology but on who would lead the country into independence. Members of the BGEIA had advocated satisfaction of conditions needed for viable and peaceful independence, and preparation of the population for it by education and social services, not the mindless agitation that the politicians were waging.

The movement to the cities had accelerated during WWII by both "push"--from myriad hardships and loss of jobs due to the effects of the war—and "pull", the lure of the city, where a certain sector of the economy had blossomed, and could absorb many recruits. When American soldiers came to billet in

Georgetown in WWII, they mixed with what women they could find. Prostitution, at that time of general want and increasing poverty among the masses, became a good source of income, for pimps and their charges. Recruiters soon fanned out among the plantations and villages, advertising "jobs in the city", and luring gullible young women -- eager to leave a depressing sugar estate enclave or poor family setting -- with generous offers of paid work, room and board. Most were virgins, who would, within a week of leaving home, begin the formal life of prostitution. Some actually went with the blessings of the family, as recruiters were careful to send matronly representatives to the homes oozing charm and substance, suggesting without saying so that the level of material prosperity they enjoyed could be shared for the asking.

Some married women chose the opportunity to run away from a bad relationship, or might already have escaped, but could not find enough regular work to make ends meet. Few were trained in anything other than housework for life as a wife, the dominant role for women touted in glitzy US magazines. There was a limit as to how many could find positions as maids, cooks or housekeepers. Few, if any, had the skills or means to advertise or register with employment agencies, if indeed any did exist at that time.

What few charitable groups there were did try to help single women in distress, but these too did not have the capacity for the numbers displaced; besides, recidivism was high as few of the women would adjust to the strictures of these homes. Pimps would scout these places as well spotting women who looked unsettled or "in business" and made them job offers. Prostitution often came to the rescue in poor economic times, some starting casually in the hope of quitting as soon as they had achieved a financial goal. These women, however, quickly became known by their work, and would be trapped by their lack of skills, poor education and general shortage of legitimate jobs. The influx of soldiers in the 1940's and in later waves in the fifties made business boom.

The relationship with early soldiers produced some poignant stories, which the newspapers and magazines largely ignored. But the smarter "girls" learnt much from their customers, some cultivating regulars who told of a more satisfying role for women in foreign lands, the USA or Britain, and "opened their eyes" to this other unknown world. With the end of the war and the departure of their source of livelihood, many of the brighter "girls" gave in to the lure of opportunity to start anew, and emigrated, primarily to Britain.

As a teenager working for my brother-in-law after school, I would overhear "man-talk" among the hired help, talk that included mention of which "rat" or *"baad gyaal"*--slang terms for prostitutes–had "disappeared". That meant they had somehow found a way back home (rare), or were eliminated for unknown reasons and unlikely to be searched for, much less found ("fed to the fishes", tied naked to a stone and dumped into one of the great rivers, or disposed of in some other way that the generally inadequate police force would hardly discover, in a land so full of secret and remote places). Besides, the Police had better things to do than to "chase after lost trash!" But increasingly hard evidence emerged of many of the missing resurfacing, usually somewhere in Britain.

A government lawyer just returned to BG after completing his bar finals at Lincoln's Inn, London, was talking to a friend who owned a shop and was notorious for the stable of prostitutes that he regularly patronised.

"You know who I saw in London? Lin! You know, the one that used to come here for a *freck* (tip), you' midday sport!"

"Oh, she! The girl disappear suddenly so! I thought she dead; whey you see her?"

"She working in a fancy store named Selfridges in Oxford Street. I had to look twice. I had to make sure, so I pretend I want to buy a gift for me wife, to speak to her. She din' recognize me; after all is only a few 'short time' we had and so many pass through her. When I call her Lin you should see how she face fall! As luck would have it nobody was near enough to hear. She try to pretend I wrong, and if she wasn't working there, I sure she would 'a walk away. Then I call your name, I tell her I'm your friend. Then she relax and give me her real name, Vidya. She tell me she life change; she in England now three years, married and just starting a baby. She looked nice. Her husband is an English guy--a salesman in the same Company-- just got promoted to Floor Manager. They make good money."

"Rasshole! Lin? one of the best you can get; her ass was so busy I din' think it could settle dung! I glad to hear that, man, everybody t'ink she dead. Wait till Sunny hear."

"Do me a favour, don' tell anybody, not even he; you never know who or what little slip can mess it up for her. She deserves a break; I promised her!"

Another example of this change involved a prostitute who was one of the many oppressed by low self-esteem who felt that her Indian-ness had been a hindrance and a sign of what she had termed "low-classness". Vera (all the 'girls' had assumed simple English names) was a handsome lass from the Corentyne (a favoured recruiting area) who had entered the trade specializing in Americans, from her base at the upscale Grand American Hotel at High and Regent Streets, an elegant building owned or managed, or both, by Mammas, the most famous of all Indian madams. Her fortune was largely venereal, and she had a stable of the best Indian, Chinese and high coloured girls--no blacks--including the beautiful Omar sisters. Vera, once immersed among the Americans, disdained her own people, and following the colonial practice of shunning those considered low class--perhaps to presume a higher station or greater ambition-- she soon shunned all Indians, including her own family.

In their turn some of her kin had begun to move up in business, and her profession, known only to a few of them, would have been a grave embarrassment; how relieved they were that she never visited! And when someone told them that she wished to go to Britain to change her life they bought her a ticket and were understandably delighted when she accepted it and left the colony in 1949 on a Booker Line steamship bound for Liverpool, hopefully never to be seen again. Once there she had gone to London, enrolled in night school and taken courses in "beauty care" and "social behaviour" to prepare herself for a career as a beautician. Being quite pretty, (pretty used too, as one unsympathetic cousin had ruefully remarked), she had found admirers in the circle in which she now moved and worked.

She eventually met and married a beauty products salesman, who was taken by her demure behaviour in public, her smooth skin, and then completely overwhelmed by her rapacious sexuality in private. He had served in the Far East during WWII and had "known" women of various races, but none who could transform into a sexual machine and elicit such performances from him.

By 1959, they had saved enough for him to suggest an overseas holiday, insisting on taking her for a visit to her "home", more so that he could experience this BG that had produced his remarkable wife. There was no thought of family reunion, as she had told him she was an only child, her parents were both dead and that two uncles and aunts had all migrated to the United States to run away from Communism! Indeed she did not wish to return, with all the turmoil she had heard of from the many Guianese coming to Britain with every plane and ship, some very wealthy who had begun to buy up rental property in various parts of London: Streatham, Paddington, Kentish Town, Maida Vale, Brixton and in upscale areas including Hampstead, Chelsea, Hammersmith, Kensington, Notting Hill, Park Lane and others. Some were settling in other cities: Southampton, Bristol, Birmingham, Sheffield and Manchester, while others had gone north to Edinburgh and even as far as Aberdeen and Dundee.

Belfast in Northern Ireland attracted many, as did Dublin in Eire. Her husband, however had insisted on the trip; he had done some reading about the British colonies, and wished to see one before they were all given up, so why not the one she had come from? Besides, they would not need US dollars as currency restrictions did not apply to the colonies; this would allow them greater freedom to spend, and perhaps see the great mountains and waterfalls.

In Georgetown they had stayed at the Tower Hotel, which at one time admitted no Indians as guests, not beyond the bar, anyway. In the bar an old Indian customer from her earliest pre-Mammas days of 1942, when she was barely 18, who had been her steady for two years until the Americans came and swept her away, recognized her, despite the many changes that time, hair-styling and affluence had visited on her, seized a moment when the husband had gotten involved in animated chatter with some other Englishmen, and spoke to her just mentioning his name, hers, and the place they had shared for a while.

True to her new identity and station as the wife of a white man, she looked sternly at him, and in her best British accent, said, "I beg your pardon. I don't know who you are. I am not this Vera, whoever she may be. I'm Mrs Bumford, of London, England!" And as she made to walk away, he said, slipping into dialect, "And ah suppose Mrs High an' Mighty, you ent tell the bum you used to pick fare in High St! Fo' me, yuh is still a coolie rat!" Then he turned, stooped to reach his drink on the low table, and sipped, his back to her, as she stood rooted to the spot. No one had heard the exchange. It was too early for the cocktail crowd.

She came over and apologised, pleaded that she had long ago left her old life and asked that he help her, that she would do anything to prevent exposure; she had not wanted to come, but after ten years she didn't think anyone would remember her, thinking she was dead.

"Woman,' he scolded, "you is a coolie, respect you'self, and you will get respect, you won't have to pretend. All I wanted was to make sure it was you. You din' have to pyass and get so blasted piggish. I could expose you right here for stupidity, but I am your brother's best friend, as you know. If anyone know his sister was a rat, it will embarrass him bad, maybe even ruin his business. He get big here now, in business and in politics! Everybody think you dead. If dat is how you behave now, you might as well be dead. Now go on back to you Mr Bum!"

Chapter 8

We cruise down the Waini River to Mabaruma, administrative centre of the North West District, and learn quite a lot about the area geographically and economically from its two most prominent citizens, Al Chin Sang and John Mohamed. The latter had built the 35-mile railroad from Port Kaituma to Matthews Ridge during WWII to carry manganese ore for an American Company. Our tour of his lime estate was interrupted by the Corporal bringing tragic news of the murder of the Inspector's brother, a city detective, by criminals he had cornered to arrest. The snake omen takes on a bizarre significance. We hear of Al's dilemma in choosing a leader, caught between two disagreeable choices: an avowed communist Jagan whom he likes as a person and his trustworthiness with public funds and Burnham, a leftist of uncertain ideology, probably Marxist and not known for trust. The choice is plain.

Day 14: To Mabaruma and the snake omen

For it is in giving that we receive; it is in pardon that we are pardoned; and it is in dying that we are born to eternal life. St Francis of Assisi

Truth is the last end for the entire universe, and the contemplation of truth is the chief occupation of wisdom." Thomas Aquinas

Man, biologically considered, is the most formidable of all the beasts of prey, and indeed, the only one that preys systematically on its own species. William James, Memories and Studies

Nine miles north of the Barama Mouth the Waini River is joined by small tributaries, the *Kumaruwa* and ten miles further on by the *Baramanni*; these two drain the southern part of the triangle of coastal forest formed by the Pomeroon River system south, the Atlantic coast to the east and the Waini to the west. Several Arawak settlements have existed along these rivers and the larger Pomeroon for a millennium and were now threatened by timber companies gradual encroaching deeper into the forest combing it for its valuables, especially greenheart, purpleheart and wamara.

This area, like the Barama, has seen intensive RC missionary activity with several missions, the Santa Cruz across from the Barama mouth and further east Santa Rosa and others on the Moruka and Pomeroon Rivers had succeeded in "taming" the Arawaks for general labour. Several temporary lumber camps have been established in clearings along the rivers and one semi-permanent installation near the mouth of the Baramanni complete with its own electric power supplied by diesel generators whose pounding could be heard for miles.

The noise had become part of the scene and hardly disturbed the crows that peppered the treetops along the river. From the west the *Sabaina* flows into the Waini 16 miles from Barama Mouth and connects with a little tributary of the Barima called the *Koraia*. The Arawaks have used this waterway to access the Barima and thus points west as far as Arakaka.

From Baramanni the *Waini* runs north by northwest with barely a wiggle — emphasising its youth--almost parallel to the Atlantic coast to empty into the ocean 58 miles away at the southern extremity of the Amakura delta (mouth of Orinoco River) and close to the Venezuelan border. Three short and narrow tributaries *Luri, Mokoboina* and *Kuberina*, almost equidistant one from the next, enter the Waini from the east between 12 and 25 miles from Baramanni.

From the air the Waini looked more like a lazy anaconda, in contrast to the serpentine Barama with its numerous tributaries on each side giving it the look of a tightly twisted millipede in free motion. About 6 miles short of the Venezuelan border the Mora Passage linked the Waini with the Barima River. Two and a half miles south of this junction the sleepy village of Morawhanna nestles on the east bank of the Barima River. Four miles further on we came to the Arouca river, a western tributary of the Barima and coursed along it for four miles to reach Mabaruma, the administrative centre of the North West District, the large triangle of land formed by the Atlantic coast on the east, the Venezuelan border on the west and the Barama River to the south.

The Barima arises near the Venezuelan border from northern spurs of the Imataka mountains and flows east parallel to the Barama, picking up many tributaries, some deep and navigable like the Kaituma and Arouca. About half way along its course it veers abruptly north, flows parallel to the Waini, unobtrusively crosses the Venezuelan border to empty into the Amakura delta.

As I look out over the broad expanse of the Waini, I realize how its mere size could make one forget that this great river was a sort of slave, ecologically speaking, of the lower reaches of that grander concourse, the Orinoco, the great river of Venezuela. The regions of the lower Orinoco and adjacent northwest Guiana north and east of the Imataka mountains form a lowland tropical forest ecosystem, which merges to the south with the tablelands *(tepuis)* that occupy south-eastern Venezuela and west central Guiana, that Hari had explored with the "British surveyors" twenty-two years earlier *(Bk 1, Ch. 9)*. The mountains were known to contain a variety of commercial ores especially iron, and gold. But the land was inaccessible except by river or air and this had prevented exploitation, thus fortuitously saving the forest so far. This situation was changing unfortunately, from the native and ecological point of view.

Although located entirely in Venezuela (save for contributions to its estuary by the Barima and Amakura Rivers), Orinoco could have a marked impact on the peoples of North West Guiana. By the time it reaches Ciudad Bolivar, the Orinoco is several miles wide, but here it has to squeeze through a narrow gorge barely a mile wide, a convenient circumstance that allowed engineers to bridge the river and thus open the southern hinterland to development. Lower down, the river widens steadily across the plain to Barrancas, the apex of the delta, where it is fully 13 miles wide. Here it fans out into an intricate network of streams that form the delta, whose base stretches some 200 miles and extends from the Gulf of Paria in the north to Punta Playa in the southeast, the northernmost point on the BG-Venezuelan boundary.

The main stream through the delta follows an eastern course and before emptying into the roiling Atlantic, gobbles up volumes from the Amakura and Barima rivers, which drain the northern end of the Guyana shield; their waters are fresh and cool, hiding, some say, millions of dollars' worth of suspended gold dust that no Raleigh will ever see. So much silt is poured out of the Orinoco that the ocean shows a palette of colours, from muddy brown at the river's mouth through various shades of brown increasingly tinged with blue and green until the deep blue-grey of the ocean is reached beyond the continental shelf sixty miles from the coast.

Columbus sighted the estuary of the Orinoco in 1498. His reports to Ferdinand and Isabella of Spain reached the rest of Europe and fired the imagination of adventurers who for the next century would explore the river seeking the gold of *El Dorado*, the fabled king of the hinterland who they were told would frequently bathe in gold dust. As noted earlier the best known of these adventurers was Walter Raleigh, who chose in vain to explore the Essequibo River in Guiana *(see Bk 1Ch. 2)* since many Spaniards and others had failed to find it on the Orinoco. But the legend lived on. Today it is widely known that there is much underground gold and some diamonds in Essequibo, and in the adjacent Venezuelan province of Guayana, which shares its geological and topographic characteristics.

The Venezuelans have started to develop the province by exploiting its mineral and forest resources. A new city is being built, Ciudad Guayana, where the Caroni River meets the Orinoco some 60 miles down-river from Ciudad Bolivar. This new city will be a major port, an expression of a will to conquer and exploit the vast wild land, and take its treasures, to enrich and glorify the nation. The city will serve as a base to populate the east and renew claims to Essequibo. Such is the Venezuelan vision, and is held in check only by the need to keep peace with the USA, its developer, and respect for the *Alianza.*

In a trice, if the US agrees, however tacitly, Venezuelan forces could swarm like wild bees into BG, by land, air and river and overrun the area claimed within a month. The treaties signed so far have enough ambiguity to keep their claim alive. Their own maps that I had seen recently at La Guairá clearly claimed their eastern boundary as the Essequibo River which receives via the Cuyuni the drainage from a large tract of south-eastern Venezuela, the lands of the Pemon-speaking tribes of Caribs, a fact usually down-played by the UK.. What can BG do but be prudent, know the pros and cons, and act smart?

By 1961, Ciudad Guayana already had a population of about 10,000, most of them new settlers. The Caroni River's several waterfalls were powerful enough to provide hydroelectricity for heavy industry and for a city of half a million, and plans were far advanced to harness those falls.

Initially the port would ship iron ore and bauxite until the hydroelectric stations were built, when secondary processing would be started to add value to the raw materials, and spawn the growth of technical and other skills, and all the paraphernalia, human and other, that accrue, like warts, to grow a city. Already the damage to the Orinoco has been considerable--the water polluted with waste and effluents from construction--and the once pristine Caroni shows an increasing milkiness.

The first victims of this development have been the forest and its wild life, not to mention the native peoples. Fears that this type of damage might spill over into British Guiana had become more manifest, with daily examples that caused increasing concern among the forest people, hunters, fishermen and the farmers who had begun to make the District a major agricultural area, with plantations of citrus, pineapples and other crops that could be easily expanded.

The Waini pours its muddy emulsion into the Atlantic precipitating a broad band of mud flats on its eastern bank while the deeper part of the channel hugs the gentle curve of the western side as it aims for the ocean. Along the eastern shore and on the flats we saw several flocks of flamingos serenely feeding, hundreds of them, their pink feathers set against the blue of the midday sky. They stood tall, as if on stilts, some erect and still, one leg bent half way, the other taking the weight, others with long necks craned, poised, still as silence. Suddenly, silently, a neck would dart forward snake-like in a lightning strike to come up with a wriggling catch held across the body, which the bird promptly turned around and devoured; its head and long beak bobbing up and down for a while; then she settled as if in a doze. Another moved cautiously among the group to a fresh spot and resumed her vigil.

"These are fat birds; can you eat them?" Brewster was curious.

"Some people do. The Warrau eat them. Some people stuff them for decorations. I don't see why." Doris replied frowning. "It's so much prettier to see them like this." This was a soft side to this complex man that the detachment of the moment bared and allowed us to appreciate.

As if to illustrate Doris' view a few took flight as the noise of the engine got louder. What a grand sight, that take-off, like a fleet of show aeroplanes carefully synchronized for timing and symmetry. They made a slight swishing sound that lingered on the wind and slowly faded as they curved to the right, became smaller until swallowed in the silence of the distant sky. I had seen them in plenty, a smaller strain perhaps, bright red, taking off just like that, in the Caroni swamp in Trinidad. Doris was so right. How could we be so cruel as to waste these wondrous creatures? I had heard that a hundred years ago they were as plentiful on the coast of Demerara and Berbice as the plovers that graze those beaches now. Where have they all gone?

In my early years in New Amsterdam, I used to admire the colony of flamingos feeding on the eastern mudflats of Crab Island, which stands like a dark sentinel in the middle of the Berbice River obliquely opposite the mouth of its tributary, the Canje River. They had become fewer, I was told, as the human population increased. Will we lose them forever? I wondered. And if we do lose them by our acts of selfish greed, what will take their place in the grander scheme of nature where each life form has a role to play? Our ignorance of that role does not mean that it does not exist. The Warrau fishermen have noticed the relentless decline in flamingo population mainly from injudicious hunting but recently from spontaneous death ascribed by some to contamination of the fish that feed them.

"They safer here. The bucks shoot them with arrows, one at a time, only what they need; they don' stuff them. Is we people who do that; we not supposed to, but we people shoot them with guns, with scatter shots that kill one or two but injure more; the wing break, they can't fly, they die in the mud, or else crocodile or snakes eat them." Doris spoke disapprovingly and in plaintive tones that seemed out of character with the gruff and rigid stances that he had presented so far.

"What does the law say about killing the birds?" I asked.

"I don't think it say anything special, but we charge people under the firearms law; they need a licence, and most don' want to pay the fee. Besides we can't patrol the whole place, and many of the shooters are Venezuelans; they poach a lot over here. Over there, they got plenty police with guns and speedboats, so the thieves come over here!" With that the harshness returned to his voice.

We approached the Mora Passage just before noon, and entering it Benn remarked that it was built when WWII started, and ran from the left bank of the Waini due south for about three miles, then turned west through a deepened tributary of the Barima to end in the latter thus allowing ocean going vessels to get from the Barima to the Atlantic without having to traverse Venezuelan territory. At one time the Barima River was entirely in BG, and shipping could go directly down it to the Atlantic. At that time the north-western BG-Venezuela boundary was formed by the mainstream of the Amakura River, a tributary of the Orinoco which in its terminal 45 miles flows about 12 miles to the southwest of the Barima and parallel with it.

A boundary conference between Britain, Venezuela and Brazil ceded to Venezuela about 750 sq. miles of land lying between the Atlantic coast and the terminal 45 miles or so of the Amakura River. This immediately placed the last 40 miles of the Barima in Venezuelan hands. The new boundary was drawn from a point on the great westward sweep of the Amakura northeast to the corresponding curve of the Barima then straight northwest to Punta Playa on the Atlantic coast. (At the same time the British ceded to Brazil just under 5,000 sq miles of the south-western portion of the Upper Essequibo at the western end of the Akarai Mountains).

This realignment terminated all Guianese shipping from the Atlantic directly into the Barima to points inland. It also brought Venezuelans within 6 miles of Morawhanna, a small town on the right bank of the Barima River, then the administrative capital of the North West District. Almost immediately delta Venezuelans began to visit, mostly illegally, "savages disrupting the serenity of the small town" (as one report put it) and straining the resources of the small police detachment there. The threat of a European war in the 1930's and consequent demands for increased regional security, the neutrality of Brazil and the suspicions that senile Juan Vicente Gomez in Venezuela would deal with the devil for a fat reward brought quick completion of the canal. The capital was relocated to the village of Mabaruma on the north bank of the Arouca, a tributary of the Barima about three miles south of Morawhanna, which retained its function as a border post and a trans-shipment point for ocean cargo.

On entering the Barima, and a few minutes later the Arouca, I was immediately struck by the speed and restlessness of the waters. They flowed deep and fast and with much fanfare created a great display on the surface with colliding swirls, eddies and menacing whirlpools that filled me with awe and brought to mind the stories I had heard of the many dangers lurking behind those signs. I became absorbed in studying the waters and as we approached the pier at Mabaruma, the busy river traffic of small motorboats and paddle canoes, filled with ordinary people pursuing their daily affairs, and including round faced women and children, who seemed to treat the river as I would a city sidewalk. And when I expressed my awe to Benn, he said, matter-of-factly, "After you're here a while, you don't notice it. Rivers are the roads here."

"But this one looks pretty angry; is it always like this?"

"Arouca make you take notice. She is swift. Only about 30 miles or so long, comes down from the hills near the border, due west," he pointed towards the sun, "she come in a rush, but slow down when the tide come in, like now it turning, that's why you see all the swells and whirlpools."

About four miles south of the Arouca the Kaituma River, a larger tributary enters the Barima River. Kaituma is navigable by freighters for about 35 miles west to Port Kaituma, whence a 35-mile railroad connects it to Matthews Ridge, via Arakaka, which is half way there. Matthews Ridge was a hive of manganese mining during WWII, and now scaled down lies like a neglected bride who, after a passionate courtship, had been left waiting at the altar for her groom, and years later, her beauty fading, she groped for a groom, any groom, to show up and take her hand. The railway, like some spent umbilical cord, was virtually withering away waiting for the surrounding jungle to reclaim it for her own.

At the pier we were introduced to two prominent townsmen Messrs John

Mohamed and Al Chin Sang, both farmers and businessmen. I soon discovered that we had mutual acquaintances in Georgetown and that Mr Chin Sang had done business periodically with my late brother-in-law during the fifties. He, and it seems everyone else in the town were at the pier to greet the steamer from Georgetown, which had come in minutes before our arrival. On arriving we clambered up the steep gangplank, dishevelled and generally scruffy, and attracted the attention of the townspeople. They all knew Cpl Doris and Constables Benn and Rodriques and must have wondered what those three scruffy Indians had done to get arrested!

Doris introduced us to several of them including the two businessmen. A few were taken aback by the mismatch between our titles and the unkempt faces and crumpled sweat-soaked clothes, but Mr Mohamed was unfazed; he invited us to his house for a welcoming drink, pointing to a typical Guianese bungalow, painted white, raised on eight-foot stilts, with a red metal roof and located on a low hillock a hundred yards away overlooking the pier. Mr Chin Sang invited us to lunch the following day.

"The government Rest House got a good cook, but we don't often get good company; besides it's Saturday tomorrow and she wouldn't mind going home early. We will have plenty time to look around, and have a good lunch and good *gyaaff* before you go. Besides everybody gettin' ready for Christmas."

"My gosh, it's next week; in the bush I just didn't think of it." Brewster exclaimed.

"You'll get home with days to spare." Benn reassured him

The spontaneity and genuineness of these greetings and invitations were a characteristic Guianese response to travellers. I used to boast about it among my non-Guianese friends at University, and had been pleased to note that people who had visited the country had been uniformly impressed with the hospitality. This reflected both the character of the people in general and the fact that BG was not a tourist destination as say Barbados or Jamaica or the Lesser Antilles, and therefore reactions to strangers tended to be more sociable than commercial.

Doris went off to the Police Station, Inspector Bacchus, Brewster, Jain and I went with Mr Mohamed to his house, while Balgobin stayed with Rodriques and Benn to safeguard the equipment and other baggage, which were still in the boat, now safely moored; they would join us after everything had been off-loaded and secured at the police station. Doris would contact the Government Rest House, to make sure of accommodations, then return with the Police Land Rover to take us and our paraphernalia to there; the scientific and evidentiary material would be kept in safe-keeping at the station. Doris had planned to welcome the Inspector as an official visitor with all the applicable fanfare.

The traditional inhabitants of the lower rivers and delta region were the Warrau, who called the area *Shiba,* meaning *a place of rocks.* No one is sure when the name was changed to Mabaruma—a word that in the Carib language meant *"my grater"*-- nor is the connection to "grater" clear. The town as we saw it then consisted of a main street, a straight narrow paved ribbon undulating for about a mile and led out of town to run for several miles through farm country. Short dead-end streets ran off it on both sides, like ribs off a backbone, ending on the riverside at the edge of a ravine, and on the other in fields, some cultivated, mostly in citrus. The Government Rest House was a two storey wooden building of Edwardian style, located on the main street a short walk from the pier. The

Court had recessed for the term so we had the place to ourselves except for the lone resident, a government agricultural scientist doing botanical surveys in the area.

Mr Mohamed had obviously had several drinks already. He was a voluble man of stocky paunchy build, short with prominent hairs growing on his ear lobes, bushy eyebrows, bloodshot eyes and full lips. He was dressed in khakis, short sleeves and short pants, exposing his hirsutism, his head shielded with an American baseball cap. His facial jowls rippled as he spoke. He spoke intently and fast, his words tripping on the heels of the ones barely ahead. He spoke with authority, like one accustomed to giving orders. He told us in quick succession of the geography and economy of the North West District, "the best damn part of this country", and then warmed, almost to the point of anger, on the economic slowdown since the closure of the manganese mines at Matthew's Ridge. He was the contractor who had built the 35-mile railroad from Port Kaituma to Matthew's Ridge, and freely boasted that he had made a couple million US dollars, which he had put to good use and multiplied a few times in the past twenty years.

"Is the damned Government fault, for not goin' ahead with the power project! This place would be buzzing now. You not drinkin', Doc!" He had poured each of us a whopping drink of whisky, nearly half a glass, pulling a fresh bottle of Dewar's from a case that stood at the top of a stack of four at the far end of the gallery. I had barely sipped half an inch and had enough left to anaesthetise a horse, while he had finished his. He looked dubiously at me when I made an excuse. Policemen were known to be hearty drinkers. The two did much better than I, and had almost halved their drink. Jain also drank sparingly. Mohamed was disappointed, but excused us.

"Well, you only just get back from the bush. I see with you."

He recharged his glass, pointed out a few features of the waterfront that could be seen from the windows, then took us on a walking tour through his lime orchard, which adjoined the house on undulating land that fell away from the house, rose a hundred yards away only to descend again out of sight. A separate building sheltered the press that produced the oil which he sold on contract to Bookers' Drug Manufacturing Co. in Georgetown for the manufacture of a cooling skin lotion called *Limacol* ("the freshness of a breeze in a bottle"), one of the few totally Guianese products.

Mr Mohamed was born and raised in the Vreed-en-Hoop area of West Demerara, and after 7 years in elementary school and a Primary School Leaving Certificate, had landed a job as a "casual contactor" with the Public Works Department fetching burnt earth from the "*bu'n-heap*" to the work sites. He used his family's donkey cart, loaded the cart by himself and made six trips each day travelling a mile each trip. It was an exhausting day for a 14 year old, even though he had a stocky, muscular build. But he was paid two shillings each day, six days each week. That money fed the family and the donkey, and maintained the cart. His father was deeply grateful for the financial support from his sons; the older boy rode an old bicycle two miles each way to work at a rice farm during the planting and reaping season and at the factory owned by his employers when extra help was needed after the harvest. He minded the two cows they owned and milked them each morning. The boys helped their mother tend the family patch at the back of their small yard, where they grew all the vegetables they needed and sold the surplus in Vreed-en-Hoop. The four youngest children, all girls, between twelve and seven, were in school.

Mohamed was given the name John by the foreman, a large big-boned black man with thick pouting lips continually dribbling past the unlit stub of a hand-rolled cigarette, its limp *papier du Maroc* wrapping stained brown from burnt nicotine and tars. The stub seemed to be a permanent part of his lips and moved with the bottom one as he spoke. He was rough, always wore the same faded khaki clothes, covered in red dust and heavy with acrid body odours. His blue cap held islands of the dust, like little dunes, in its folds.

His fellow workers were mostly black, as in any government construction or maintenance project; the only other Indian in the crew (they were called "gangs") of seventeen was another youth called Gobind, then twelve, who also fetched and carried. The black men called him Singh, complaining "Why you coolies na get real names?" Like most Blacks they had difficulty pronouncing Indian names, even the simplest phonetic ones.

Mohamed and Gobind took this philosophically, conditioned to forbearance by their parents. After a few months Gobind left, presumably to go back to school but John soldiered on. The gang was engaged in maintaining a five-mile section of the main road. Guianese main roads were then constructed on a foundation of packed clay mixed with varying amounts of rocks and logs then covered with layers of burnt earth strewn evenly upon the surfaces and compacted by a heavy roller. Each layer was treated similarly. With usage the surface packed smooth, but the surface pulverized under heavy traffic in the sun's heat and, with rain, washed away in red rivulets leaving grooves on the surface like gashes in raw flesh.

In dry weather passing traffic started clouds of red dust swirling in the air, which the wind carried into every nook and cranny of any structure in its lee. Heavy downpours further scoured and broke the surface allowing seepage to undermine the surface, creating areas of weakness, which collapsed under the weight of heavy truck and bus traffic to form potholes. Hence the need to maintain permanent repair crews on site, especially close to the city where the traffic was heaviest. The crews tended simply to pack the potholes with fresh burnt earth, tamp it down and leave it up to the traffic to act as final roller. The ruts easily recurred. In severe cases they went deep enough to reach the clay base creating a sticky mess that often trapped wheels or even wrenched them from their housings.

Mohamed was tough and single-minded; a quick learner, he soon outgrew the road gang, at about the same time the work was finished and his "contract" ended. His foreman had liked the way he worked and recommended him to a friend, a maintenance supervisor on the railway that ran from Vreed-en-Hoop to Parika who put him to spread ballast between the sleepers.

In time he learned railroad construction when a spur line was put in to a sugar factory. He saw how sturdier the foundations had to be on the railroad for the heavy rolling stock, with no room allowed for differential settling, as was accepted on the roads. In the next years he would work on the East Coast Railway extending his reputation for hard work and no nonsense. Then, at age 25, he got his big break. He was sent to head the gang working on the Wismar-Rockstone Railway that linked the Demerara and Essequibo rivers sixty miles inland. A few years earlier he had enrolled in evening classes at the Government Technical Institute; he learned the elements of land surveying and, following that, studied maintenance of road machines even though few of these, other than earth movers, graders and rollers were in regular use in BG.

Soon the noises of another European war reached BG. Photographs of Nazi rallies filled the newspapers. There were several reviews and commentaries on Hitler's career; the authors quoted extensively from *Mein Kampf* and described his rise to power in 1933 when he became Reich Chancellor; soon after he sanctioned the burning of books by Jewish intellectuals, such as Mann and Freud, who were well known outside of Germany. One column was a reprint from a British paper which castigated a German filmmaker, Leni Riefenstahl, the best known female film director of her time in the world, whose filming techniques had been designed to make Hitler look imposing, and superior to other men; she defended these long after the horrors of his administration and his personal weaknesses had become widely known. Mohamed read the papers avidly and absorbed it all, and kept many, *in toto* or as clippings.

British inertia had troubled observers even as Roosevelt's New Deal had begun to revive economic hopes in the Americas; his 1933 *Glass-Steagall Act* had established oversight over certain financial dealings that had contributed to the depression and with other measures promised stability and to curb over-zealous and greedy financial adventurism that while enriching the predator vanguard, tended to ruin small players especially emerging nations and their fragile economies. Mohamed saw that these would change things even in BG–the backwoods of Empire--but had no way of knowing when and how.

He believed that private entrepreneurs could enrich the country and felt strongly that a railway system would be a better way than roads to probe the interior of the country and spur its development. He envisaged a line that ran south from Rockstone through the Potaro above Kaieteur Falls and on to Orinduik, Lethem and Dadanawa. The savannahs and their food potential would be opened up and cattle that now walked the long journey to Ituni, only to arrive emaciated and in need of expensive rehabilitation and fattening before journeying the last legs by river and rail to the abattoirs of Georgetown and New Amsterdam. They would move more swiftly and cheaply by rail, retain their flesh and save on rehabilitation costs. Building it would not be cheap, but similar gambles had paid off in America, in India, and more recently in Africa and South America, especially in South Africa and Argentina. The railhead at Lethem would place, not only the Rupununi but the entire neighbouring area of Brazil-- much bigger than BG--within reach of an ocean port at Georgetown. To him the potential was endless. First you build the railway!

A year-long study and practical course in the USA supported in part by the Bauxite Companies and the Government, taught him practical roadbed construction. He had developed a macho image, helped by his stocky build and bulldog face, and among the men at least, his ability to hold liquor was awesome ("Muslims drink too, y'know, never mind what they say in public!").

He had gotten married, and years before the war started, had become the father of two girls, who would jokingly and behind his back be described as "spitting images of their father"--not a compliment. When the African Manganese Corporation began operations at Port Kaituma and invited tenders for the construction of a railway from Matthews Ridge to Port Kaituma, he used his contacts to find out how things were going, and his attractive bid won.

Everyone agreed that the railroad was well built, though many criticized his ruthless use of unskilled labour, particularly native, to reduce costs. He made further profits on the maintenance contract which ran for the duration of the war and up to the closure of operations a year or so later. His detractors would assert that he had profited far more than he should have, and much of that on the "backs of workers".

Others appraised him differently, noting that he had kept investments locally and in Georgetown unlike the white foreigners. He had put some of his money into the expansive farm in Mabaruma, having decided on fruit. He methodically determined that the area and the entire North West District were suited to orchards and had already shown success with citrus fruits: oranges and the hardier limes and lemons, which the natives had grown for over two hundred years.

He had lobbied the Government since the early 1950's, but had become disillusioned with its failure to respond. He rued the fact that BG could not access US institutions since it was still a colony of Britain. He recalled with envy the news the Inter-American Development Bank had provided funds to irrigate the Lorenzo Valley in NW Peru to create a now thriving community of fruit farmers, growing limes and mangoes--the very things he had planned to grow, as well as pineapples and potatoes–but BG could only look, almost in vain, to cash-strapped Britain for development funds.

"We got lots of good ideas heah, but we don't have enlightened leaders. All that we hear every blasted day is this shit 'bout Socialism. Blasted Communists, with their backsides in Georgetown, they know nutting; they do nutting while all the good and smart people leave, and take their money with them. I used to do different; but now most of what I got is safe in London; I ain't stupid. If the Government was serious, if they was smart, I would put all I have into this scheme. It would be more than enough, I assure you; this country don't realise how much money was here and already gone. But I don't trust them. I just marking time. Those rasshole civil servants Jagan got in charge don't know one shit 'bout business either. And he rass want Government to take over and run business? He must be sick! And Burnham worse; everybody I know say he t'ief. If I was a white maan, I de get the okay long time once you know the ropes! But now wid these Communists who know shit, that won't happen easy."

"What about mining?" I asked as softly as I could to soothe his ire.

"We don't have the power to mine manganese cheap. Besides, mining is only so good as the ore is cheap, and the ore don't last forever. Mining here make big profits for foreign companies; they bring in their white people who live like kings---you should see them strut at Mackenzie and Kaituma and mos' o' them don't know shit, we people got to tell them what to do, it make me sick; the workers live separate, in filth, and can't go near the white man quarters. They dig out what they want, clean you out and leave you to clean up! They give back nothing to talk about and get by with bribes. I was one of the few locals that made a lot of money from the mining company, an' fret and cuss when they left. And I work hard. But since I go into agriculture I realise how mining destroy everyt'ing, the land, the water, the fish, even the people. With all the years the Company operated what they leave? Nothing! With agriculture, if times go bad, like now, we can still eat what we grow or preserve what we can't eat."

I was astonished to hear this ecological lesson from such a rough and fearsome source.

Just then we saw Doris and Balgobin crossing the field in a tearing hurry, wearing long faces. Doris beckoned to Inspector Bacchus, who went over to speak to him. Mohamed was in the middle of a sentence when we heard Bacchus exclaim, "Oh, God, no!" and while Doris held him we heard sobbing, and rushed over to find out the cause, and thus heard the stunning news that Inspector Bacchus's younger brother, the detective, had a week ago been shot dead by black gangsters whom he had cornered while investigating a series of violent robberies and killings in Georgetown and environs. His funeral had taken place three days ago, since the family could wait no longer for the Inspector's return. Police reported that they knew his killers and arrests were imminent.

It was distressing to see the look in Bacchus' face as it changed from one of utter disbelief to one of horror and grief, as he tried to deal with the news. "Oh God, no! No!" he repeated; tears filled his eyes, spilled over his eyelids and ran shamelessly down his cheeks in little curving rivulets which he wiped away with the back of his hand. We tried to console him, expressing sympathy and rallying to touch and otherwise show the grief that we all instantly felt, impotent to help and as shocked as he was by the suddenness of the terrible news. In the gloom and loneliness of our outpost situation there was no genteel way to break and deal with bad news. The Commissioner of Police had sent an emergency message to the Inspector via Radio Demerara, but we were then well out of range of the broadcasting station, and with failing batteries. Doris had delivered the news as compassionately as he could.

We remained for a while motionless around Bacchus, hardly speaking, too overcome to speak until Brewster found a tremulous voice and spoke for all, "Inspector, it's like we own brother gone! We grieve for you; we grieve with you." He said a short prayer for the deceased and asked Christ's compassion to relieve Bacchus's pain. Then he too turned away and sobbed unashamedly.

Suddenly Doris exclaimed, his voice trembling with anger and frustration, "The moment that frigging snake crossed the bow, I knew something bad goin' happen to one of us!"

Mohamed led Bacchus to a seat on a field bench, of which there were several that he had placed in the shade of trees, at vantage points to enjoy the restful view of the gently undulating meadow as it fell away to the river in the distance. Tears welled in the Inspector's eyes, and as he sat there he looked so vulnerable and not the commanding figure we had known over the past two weeks. It was so sad to see this tall, dignified man suddenly reduced to tears; his bowed head propped on hands spread along the sides of the face, while his body shuddered from time to time. We all stood by him, helplessly, trying to share his grief. I stood behind him and put my hand on his shoulder and Brewster did the same.

Mr Mohamed had become quite sober and very solemn, and uttered a prayer, in Arabic and English for the departed. (Several of his workers had died during construction of the Kaituma railway from a variety of accidents, one or two of which were questionable, in which rumour even implicated him. He was quite practised in giving condolences). His expressions of regret sounded very genuine, however. And why not? He had no reason to be other than sorrowful at the sudden and shocking loss suffered by his guest.

He came over to where Bacchus sat and solemnly put his hand across Bacchus shoulders, Brewster and I giving way.

"I sorry to hear this dreadful news, maan;" he repeated, the feeling piercing the normal gruffness of his voice, "I am really sorry; we all so sorry." He paused briefly and said, "Let's go back to the house. I have a radio telephone there; you can call anyone you like; time like this, you need to be with fam'ly; you can't be with them today; talk is de next best t'ing. Come, le' we go."

Doris said, "It's okay, Mr Mohamed, I already arrange for a call from my station, so we will go straight there; but thanks a lot for the offer."

Bacchus got up, composed himself, and began to walk slowly off, Mohamed to his left, his hand flat on Bacchus's back, and I on his right. We walked slowly, the others following in tandem, as if in a funeral procession. I felt dejected and shaken by the abruptness of the change. Others voiced the same feelings. Less than ten minutes ago, the Inspector was joking and at ease, enjoying a respite, knowing that Doris would have informed Central Station in Georgetown of our whereabouts and that someone would even now be calling the families, easing their minds.

How cruelly fate had changed our outlook and our very lives in a direction and manner totally bewildering and devastating! It was as if the trauma, though his alone by blood lines, had passed over to the rest of us by invisible bonds forged in the past two weeks of contiguity, as if the process and manner of our relationship had made us one. As we comforted him, each one in his unique way, he kept repeating his distress and disbelief, through tears that made his eyes shine and his voice falter.

"And I wasn't there to put him to rest, or say goodbye; his poor wife must be facing hell."

As we recovered composure we talked a lot about death and the anguish it brought to loved ones, yet as rational humans we had the resilience to bear a loss, accept it and eventually recover, but forever there would remain an empty place where the lost one had resided in our hearts, and the rekindling of a memory of him or her would always bring new tears and a new lump in the throat.

I thought at this moment of the losses that had made me suffer: my father, before I was old enough to understand it fully, but which I would feel more and more as the years passed--so many sharp memories of this fine man seen through a child's eyes and enhanced by the tales of my mother and others who could speak of him from an adult experience. Even now I can think of him only with wet eyes. Then there were my cousin Jit, who was a young father figure after my own had died, and Lena, who was somewhere between a sixth sister and a lover in my youth (she in whose memory I had kept the name she had given me); my brother-in-law Tulla Hardeen, who had been one of my mentors and guardian, the envy of his peers and generous in his help to them, lost in the prime of his life; and Evelyn, dying in lonely agony in an English hospital far away, her ruptured appendix festering while incompetent physicians wondered what obscure tropical disease she had brought them.

Sad memories had a way of rushing back, at times unexpectedly, to revive the hurt and bring fresh tears. At times like these, or even at movies or even when someone got deserved praise for a kind act my eyes would swell with tears; I would struggle to hide them as all males had been schooled to do even in childhood, since tears were viewed as a sign of weakness, a thing that women shed; but I had always had great difficulty in hiding mine, and would sob internally, my voice and my eyes together betraying my sensibilities and my weakness.

We went in deep gloom, hardly speaking, to the Rest House, where others had gathered including Rod and Benn. Doris told us that the message from Georgetown had indicated that the Inspector should fly home if we arrived in time for the flight, which as it happened was the following morning, and that the rest of us would take the steamer that left the day after. Vouchers would be brought to us in the morning.

We held an impromptu service in memory and said appropriate prayers. Balgobin offered an incantation and mantra in Sanskrit and translated it. It was all very moving, though simple. The general dejection was pervasive. But it was good to see the Inspector begin his grieving in a positive way. He recalled shared moments of their boyhood together, their decision to join the Force, he as the older one enlisting three years before and feeling very proud and pleased when his brother decided to join.

"He was always solving puzzles; reading *True Detective* magazines when he was young, and when he got into the Force, reading cases and judgements, analysing everything, looking for clues everywhere, talking about his cases, very thorough in whatever he did, a real professional; you know he always say that if you want to solve a criminal case you have to think like a criminal; he would say, 'if I want to kill that man, how would I do it so that I wouldn't get caught?'" And with each recollection new tears clouded his eyes and his voice failed.

Brewster was the only other one there who knew the deceased and had worked on some of his cases. He did an impromptu eulogy, recalling the zeal and commitment of the man and his very positive attitude and fairness. "He had a lot of Indian and Chinese friends," he concluded, looking at me, standing on Bacchus' right, my hand on his shoulder.

"We face death every day we leave home, but we don' think of that," Benn said, in one of his rare interventions. "It wasn' like that before, but now people getting revolvers so you don' know who you stop can be carryin' one."

"But you can't get guns to buy," Balgobin said.

"They're smuggled in from Venezuela; from here those guns can go anywhere." Benn replied.

"Up to now most murders are done with other instruments: cutlass, knives, and what we call blunt instruments, the gun will get more popular though, because we don't have enough men to patrol the border properly," said Doris, "And it will get worse after independence, because the Venezuelans respect the British, but don' have respect for us."

The shift in conversation diverted attention to a police issue that had been gaining increasing attention in the city and other dense concentrations of population. Crimes against persons had been increasing and city streets had become risky. The change had begun to occur concurrently with the rise in political agitation in the mid-fifties, at first imperceptibly, but escalating during strikes and political marches, which criminals would choose as a cover for their varied activities. The failure of Police to put a quick end to these had allowed the crimes to move into daylight and from poor and depressed neighbourhoods to hitherto untouchable middle and upper class enclaves. Increasingly criminal weaponry had moved from simple pocket knives and coshes to more lethal automatic firearms. The trend had bothered the Police brass and affected the policeman on the beat. Policemen had of course been hurt in the course of their work, but rarely murdered. The murder of a detective was even rarer, and the way in which Detective Bacchus had met his end presaged a new era in criminal behaviour.

We had arrived at the Guest House in late afternoon. The sitting/dining room windows looked east, west and south. The orange glow of the setting sun dimmed to a mere tinge then quietly and swiftly disappeared leaving a rapidly deepening grey. The gloom of the silhouetted hills in the distance intensified until all was black. The sound of crickets chirping rose all around us and we could hear and see hordes of crepuscular insects as they recklessly threw themselves against the screens that barred their access to the lights within. The caretaker had hastily prepared dinner, but no one felt particularly hungry.

Bacchus recovered his composure and urged us to have our meal. We hadn't had anything decent for over a week, but for our dinner at Barama Mouth. He would join us, and treat the meal like the offerings of a wake, in memory of his brother. "Daniel would want that." After listening to the Inspector's reminiscences and further consoling thoughts from everyone, Doris, Benn and Rod exchanged goodbyes with much handshaking, each of us making a little speech with expressions of camaraderie and goodwill, and they left to return to the station.

The little farewell party we had planned had been of course cancelled. John Mohamed and Al Chin Sang came in to commiserate with Inspector Bacchus as did several local government officials, a clergyman and ordinary citizens, all total strangers to him but that only increased the sincerity of their expressions of sorrow. As one older lady said to him, holding his hand, while her husband stood by, his head bowed, "I feel as if it is my brother dey kill. We share your grief Inspector, and you' family grief; we sympathise with you all."

The priest said a prayer and soon after the visitors left, one by one, followed by Chin Sang and Mohamed. It was now night and a moon was out. The sky was clear and the stars shone brightly despite the moon. When the policemen got up to go I went to the door with them and stepped outside into the cool night. Insect activity was high, so I repeated my good wishes, including those for the Christmas season now a week off and thanked them again for our time together. I accepted Doris's offer to show us around the next day after the Inspector's departure.

A little while later we retired, but I was not sleepy and spent the next two hours reading and making notes, but other thoughts kept intruding bearing on the events of the past two weeks and the misfortune that had marred its end. The policeman's murder was a bold and ominous announcement of a new, higher level of criminal activity, a stern warning certain to exacerbate the climate of fear that would work in favour of the more militant elements among leaders of the PNC and UF who had begun to show signs of increasing and reckless contempt for law, order and life.

Chapter 9

We bid a solemn and emotional farewell to the Inspector after a short memorial to his slain brother and see him off boarding a Grumman Goose amphibian on its scheduled flight to Georgetown. The rest of the city group will travel next day by coastal vessel *SS Tarpon*. We keep our luncheon appointment with Mr Chin Sang as the Inspector had insisted and learn more of the region's agricultural and mineral potential and difficulties with transportation, communications, British neglect and border breaches. Now political instability and indifference in the city was adding to their burdens. The Force is five full-time officers headed by Cpl. Doris covering some 16,000 square miles, numerous rivers, over 250 miles of border and inadequacy of every resource. They are highly respected and do not let political bias affect their work. Cpl Doris in an impulse poignantly admits that he has begun to look differently at Indians since our talk; we thank him and urged education of all peoples.

Day 15: Mourning In Mabaruma

If you can snatch a jewel a crocodile holds in its teeth,
If you can swim across the ocean, while the tempest roars,
If round your head, unruffled, you can wind a poisonous snake,
You still can't hope to change the stubborn mind of a born fool.

Bhartrhari

"I find it the greatest irony is that Indians should be fleeing to Britain, the country that cruelly suppressed their ancestors, enslaved their parents, taught them to hate themselves and their heritage, and robbed them of all self-esteem!"

Author

We were up early, and had a cheerless breakfast, which was finished by 7.00 am, Inspector Bacchus eating hardly anything in his state of silent anguish. Alvin Chin Sang ("call me Al") would be coming to pick us up just before noon. I suggested that we call off the planned lunch in view of the tragedy. But before any of the others could respond, Inspector Bacchus shook his head, saying, "No, I don' think my brother would want that; life goes on; he believed in carrying on, regardless. We pay our respects, we mourn, we remember. But we must resume life; I am still on duty and will do what I have to do. You must do the same. You all must do the same."

"I appreciate that, and agree, but still, I don't think anyone feels like celebrating." I looked around at my companions; they nodded.

Brewster said, "I agree with Doc, I don't feel like celebrating."

The Inspector took a few steps towards the windows that looked out to low hills in the distance, with residues of mist still hanging in layers in the still air veiling the trees at the horizon; he gazed silently at the view, then turned around and spoke with emotion, his eyes wet.

"I didn't think I would be leaving you all like this; I still feel numb all over; but I have to thank you all for the sympathy; no one could have given me more comfort and support; you're real friends, I will miss all of you; we now go our separate ways, I today, you tomorrow, back to our routines; those routines did not bring us in contact before, but I hope we can get together some time back in town."

He paused, looked around at each of us, and continued, his deep baritone filling the room, at times hesitant as he fought with his feelings, "You know, the two weeks we spent together changed us from strangers to a small family; at least that is how I see it; that is how I feel. When I left town, this was a simple routine assignment, even though it was into deep bush; but it was almost boring the way I was given it, almost like a punishment, taking me away from bigger challenges. But I was so wrong, not because of what the job really was, but because things didn't go right, and when that happens, my experience is that men start to behave different and show their true colours; many become less human, more selfish, but some become brave and noble, like you all. For me these two weeks opened my eyes, taught me something about being a leader, being responsible for others, working under pressure, dealing with the unknown, with only ourselves to lean on. We all learned a lot. And we learned from one another too. It made me realise how little we know 'bout one another although we all live in the same place and have to get along.

"Doc, you show me things I did overlook, just never thought that Indians had grievances against we black people, specially Police. And I never thought that Indians seriously thought about *our* welfare as you organised your lives and went about your business. I see how easy it is to misjudge one another and how much we have to learn about one another if we going to avoid serious trouble. If we could force people to share hardship they might learn to live together in unity. I will pray on my way home for many things, and I will pray not only for the soul of my dear brother but for peace to take the place of strife and hate everywhere."

His voice trembled and broke as he said this and tears overflowed his eyelids even though he fought them off, wiped his eyes and added, his voice tremulous, "We're in times of trouble and we're not getting better; the only hope for us is to work together even though we have differences; those differences don't prevent us from 'give and take'; I still go by the motto I learn in school: *"damus petimusque vicissim"*, we give and take in return; it's a good one for us now to live by, and I mean that in the best sense.

"Now as I said yesterday, my brother would not want to stop the flow of life's twists and turns; he used to say that was what made it worth protecting. For his memory you must carry on and visit Mr Chin Sang and treat the living with the same respect you feel for the dead. If I did not have to leave today, I would have gone with you. I hope my brother did not die in vain, that what happened to him will tell the politicians that they too should come together, and settle matters in a friendly way, instead of fomenting more trouble. When we catch the men who killed him, I will feel at peace."

We were sitting in the drawing room, in reverence, as in a church. Brewster got up and walked over to the Inspector, took his hand, held it and said, "With all respect, Inspector, I hope you will forgive me for breaking rank, but I hope and I know we will get those bastards; your brother was a good man; I take off my hat to him and will pray for him and the family. I want to say something to you, chief; you know I didn't want to come on this trip either, but I feel different now; I'm glad they sent me. I will have a story to tell my children." And then he added in a way that was unusual for men in the Force to speak to superior officers, "I feel that your style and personality made the difference; helped us, made us all strong to bring out the best in us; left to me we would ha' turned back at the first big *tacuba*. And I never know anybody coulda get me to walk so far through bush." His remark lightened the scene; even Bacchus smiled as the rest giggled briefly.

"I agree with that," Balgobin said, "if I ever get in trouble, is you I will come to, Inspector!"

Then he went over and shook Bacchus' hand, which we all did, endorsing or adding to what Brewster had said and expressing good wishes on his journey. In my turn I held his hand and said, "We are brothers at heart, children of the same soil. This is a terrible tragedy indeed, not only for you and your family, but for the country; it shows a level of lawlessness that is a new low, and gives you a bigger challenge; I had looked forward to the chance to talk in a more relaxed way on the boat to Georgetown; there is so much left to say; so much to do; you are one good man, sir; if there are more officers like you in the Force we have nothing to fear. I offer you all condolences, for myself and family, and wish you God speed."

"And I will add, Jain said. *'Aum shanti, shanti, shanti.'* Peace, in the name of the Almighty."

I gave Bacchus a manly hug in the style of the Spanish and he responded in kind. Just then Doris arrived--wearing a long face--to take him to the pier. There we said a final goodbye and he was taken by water taxi, a motorized dinghy, to the Grumman Goose leaving for Georgetown at 10.00 am on its regular scheduled flight. He waved briefly as he stepped into the aircraft, the last of the passengers, a wan smile on his face. The door closed and presently his face appeared at a window, and his right hand moved a few times across it. We all waved back and watched the plane move slowly off, rapidly gain speed and rise into the sun now high in the cloudless morning sky. That was the last I saw of him.

Years have flown by since and I have thought of him often, especially at times of reflection on things that were bothering me and I wanted to talk to someone strong who could listen patiently and share confidences. Each time I think of him the first image in my mind would be that of a tall man with a sad face crouching to enter a small seaplane bobbing gently among the eddies of a fretful river.

Al understood our reaction but adopted the same stance as Bacchus that life must go on and that the performance of the various acts of daily living was compatible with mourning. What was most impressive to me was the depth of feeling for Bacchus' loss and for someone only Brewster had known two weeks earlier. Such was the respect and camaraderie that had developed in the short time that we had spent together in the deep forests. In the same vein all of Mabaruma had heard of the Inspector's tragic loss, and had turned out to pay their respects at the pier, a moving tribute to a man none of them knew, a telling commentary on their own humanity, and an extension, I sensed, of their respect for their district policemen.

Doris, like every one of us, stared at the sky until nothing could be seen.

"I wonder if I'll see him again; he's a good man; he listens and you can disagree with him." Doris said, and turning to Al, added, "Al, we have to check in at the Station, see you after."

"Okay."

Al swung his Land Rover around and turned into the road, heading home. The vehicle filled the narrow paved portion. Another crossed us on the way, and the driver waved; each had to take to the grassy shoulder to allow the other his half of the pavement. At home, he gave instructions to some workers who were finishing up for the day. Then he gave us a tour of the premises. The house sat on ten foot tall pillars, open below (the bottomhouse) except for an enclosed area occupying about a quarter of the space. An orange "sorter" in the shape of a large tray occupied the rest of the space surrounded by bins laden with oranges. Similar bins, some empty were in the yard not far from a parked Ferguson tractor and a large cart. The rear fence was of chicken wire stretched taut and attached above to a line of horizontal one-inch lead pipes supported by wallaba posts. On the fence sat a stately macaw, its long and colourful tail draped elegantly on the house side of the fence. It stood, head erect, oblivious of the intruders; from time to time it would preen the under surface of its wings, and when I came near to take its photograph, looked at me with a haughty gaze and wagged its beak.

In his living room Al introduced his wife and seated us near a row of casement windows that formed one whole wall giving a panoramic view of the landscape beyond. The panes were of muranese glass, thick and opaque with an intricate and popular pattern of leaves (of what kind I knew not, probably olive), with frames of pine imported from the USA, flaking paint and cracked putty, the hallmarks of life in the tropics, all reminding me of my sister's house in Hadfield Street, which had exactly the same windowed wall down to the last specks of white oil paint inadvertently left on a pane or two. He saw me staring at the windows.

"Maan, those t'ings always need paint." It was more a statement than an apology.

"It's not that," I smiled and explained. Then on a whim, I asked, "These made in Georgetown, not imported, right?"

"Yes," he answered, adding, "You know, we got the wood to make these things, windows, doors, floors, trim, everything, right out there." He pointed to the forests in the distance. "But no power; we can get the machines, but the power too dear, and in any case, not enough; we have barely enough for the houses."

"You got them at Vigilance factory, at Sussex and Camp?"

He looked surprised.

"Yeess," he strung the word out, "how did you know?"

I told him that I knew Mr Vigilance; his shop was a block and a half away from where I used to live in Albuoystown, and that they had made windows for my sister's two buildings, all exactly like his. His son had been a classmate at Queen's College.

The group was subdued throughout Al's introductions. He suggested a drink, a libation as it were to the departed. As we responded to this toast and sipped the drinks he told us he had heard the news items concerning the detective's murder and the radio messages sent by both the Police and the family to the Inspector. Everyone had known of Doris' departure but did not know his destination. That had raised no queries since the territory was large, the Police detachment small and Doris was constantly on the move. The news had not mentioned Doris but he had surmised, on hearing "somewhere on the Barama River" that Doris' mission had something to do with the Inspector's trip. Now he felt the man's loss.

The killing of a policeman was a rare thing. He had read various articles recently in the three dailies (which came to him in weekly batches): several dealt with the changing circumstances and behaviours of people, especially in urban areas, that had led to many killings, and now that of the policeman. Rural populations were getting frightened that the lawlessness might spread to them. Politics was changing behaviours in a way that was polarising people and enabling ruffians to carry out antisocial acts that varied from the simply illegal to the bizarre and evil. Those things were having an effect on the economy yet

Government did not seem to know enough about the country nor what it could do or should do to bring enlightenment, social stability and progress to *all* people. The parties seemed interested only in one sector, labourers and their unions. He gave as an example the attitude of Government to the North West District.

"The land here is great for fruits and vegetables. The future could be bright but only if we can get cheaper freight to Georgetown. You know the boat charges 2 cents a piece to transport oranges to town? Even the ones that rot. They don' have cold storage on the boat, so we lose a lot. The Government Produce Depot in town sells oranges from the coast for 2 cents each. They sell ours, which are bigger and sweeter, for 4 cents each, 40 cents a dozen. How can we compete? We, all the growers here, we petition the Government to charge six cents a dozen for freight; if they agree our fruit can sell for 30 cents a dozen; we'll make a little, the government will make more. They bin considering that for two, three years. I thought they were waiting for the elections to come and go then they would do it, but months gone by and nothin' yet. You know, Trinidad grapefruit come into Georgetown cheaper than mine. The freight is cheaper and those bigger ships have cold storage."

"What about juicing, here? Would that help?"

"If we had cheap power, like Florida. Florida can sell me juice cheaper than I can make it. Even if I had power, I'd still have the problem of freight costs."

"What about air freight?"

"Worse. More expensive still even though we wouldn't get the same spoilage."

"So what can you do if you don't get the subsidy?"

"Keep pushin'; we have to get some relief or the industry will fold. I don' see why they can't give the subsidy right now. Cheddi say he's in favour. But he can't order T&HD (Transport and Harbours Department). In fact it wouldn't be a true subsidy. You see, the rules those people follow go back to the time when the boat was mainly carrying out Government business and moving mail and a few people. That boat sails whether or not they have freight. We pay to get the stuff on board, so their expense is small. They can carry these oranges to Georgetown for nothing! If they don't help out, they will kill the orange and grapefruit here. Like Mohamed over there, I will switch to limes, put in a press and sell the extract to him.

"Mohamed has the contract now with Bookers *Limacol* Factory but he can't produce enough to supply the market. I sell my limes to him now. And that's another thing. We can export lime extract and concentrate, but to do that we have to ship to Georgetown, then export from there. Port-of-Spain is two hundred miles from here. Why we can't get a service there, like we had when ore was shipped out of Port Kaituma? Even once a month would help! A schooner would do, we don' need a bigger boat. But they can't get the damn export status! Now, you tell me why! They say that all exports got to move from an international port. And BG got only one, that one is Georgetown. But that's nonsense; Kaituma was one. So why can't Mabaruma or Morawhanna be a port for foreign trade? They say the business is not enough for them to put the staff in. Now which come first? The trade can't build until the port status change; they won't change until the trade build up. Now, what you call that?"

"Catch 22," I said.

"Catch 22? What's that?"

I told him.

"That's exactly what it is. I mus' remember that. You know, I don't think the Government--and I vote for Cheddi--I don't think they really interested in business or in private development. Everybody here try to tell me he's Communist, but I never believe. He come here and siddung, right whey you sit now, and we talk and I t'ink the maan understand. I'm not so sure now. If he wants to be Prime Minister in an independent country, he got to understand the country and make sensible decisions, not just follow ideology. Look, I gripe enough. You know, is not often we meet new people here, especially from Georgetown, so we talk a lot. Have another drink, chaps. I see the wife signallin'. We soon ready to eat."

The smells that floated in from the kitchen were enough to divert any attention and I suspected none of us paid much attention to all the facts about the North West that Chin Sang was giving us. We were accustomed at home to savoury fresh-cooked food and had been reduced to dry biscuits and bits of canned food for the last ten days. Chinese food was the next choice for most Indians after their own, regardless of all the rumour and jokes about the fate and destiny of canines in the Chinese quarter. Mrs Chin Sang and her staff had prepared a table as generous and inviting as the mind of the "starving" man could have imagined, as Brewster later described it. The favourites were all there--shrimp fried rice, curried fish (*"morocut, the sweetest fish in the world"*, Rod had said), vegetable chow mien, chicken in soya sauce, sweet and sour shrimps, plain rice and for the non-Indians who savoured it a slab of roast pork which had been cut into thin slices and served with a soya dressing.

We ate heartily and silently for several minutes while Al took his time and talked on about the area, encouraged by acknowledging grunts from us. He told us of the prosperity and wealth that manganese mining had brought the District until it folded a few years ago and of the consequent loss in population especially from the Port Kaituma-Matthew's Ridge area of the Barima River.

During WWII this region of BG had seen considerable development while the manganese mines operated. The ore was strip-mined in the area around Matthew's Ridge, and shipped by rail to Port Kaituma, thence by ore carriers downriver to Morawhanna and on to the USA. The exploiter was the African Manganese Mines Limited, which, despite its name, was entirely American and based in Montana or Wyoming. With the end of WWII and the consequent reduced demand and lower price for manganese on the world market, the mining had ceased and the company withdrew. The installations remained but the government has not so far been able to attract a successor industry. Forestry products were considered but the energy requirements were high and called for considerable capital to develop hydropower from one or more of the waterfalls on the Barima or Kaituma rivers. Goring Falls was studied but the result had not been released.

The property in any case lay at the edge of the Arakaka Indian reservation and the natives have renewed their objection to the type of callous destruction that the African Manganese Mines' stripping methods had wrought despite their continuous complaints, objections and protests. Such were the power of the USA and the exigencies of war not justified in peacetime. The energy needs for the mines had been met by petroleum-fired generators at an unprofitably high cost and with harmful ecological side effects that were barely justified as the price of war. The high cost was the main reason for the cessation of mining. The manganese was said to be of a very high quality and its mining could be revisited should cheaper power become available. Before it left, the AMM had surveyed, among others, the Towakaima Falls as a possible source of cheap energy. The results of that survey also remained locked in secret Government and Company files. Mr Tilbury had tried in vain to get them.

"There's a lot of energy in those Falls, even though the river is not so wide, but the falls are over a mile long and the total drop nearly 100 feet. You should see the water bursting down the big rocks when the river is high!" Tilbury had enthused.

But Hari and the natives had not been pleased at the prospect, however remote it might have seemed at the time. In fact the Barama Caribs have maintained their uniform opposition to any harnessing of waterpower in their ancestral lands, which they reminded us were protected by treaties. Natives wished to continue using the forest the way they had always done, with discriminate cutting and extracting, but not destroying--no fire, no big machines that ruined the ground, no chemicals that poisoned the water and killed the fish, a major source of food! They knew they needed political strength to do this, just as the hustlers--lumbermen and miners--had. How could they get this?

They could not read, nor write, nor argue in the manner of the coastal folk. The Barama Caribs had turned to Hari and men like him, whom they trusted, to articulate their fears. Beside Government inaction, they had to deal with threats to the native leaders from those who saw the trees and the ground as purely sources of quick profits. Even the otherwise benign Tilbury was viewed with suspicion because he was a miner, and might have been scared off, had he not agreed to show tangible respect for their concerns.

Native leaders, Hari had told us, had already noticed that developments along the Orinoco River in Venezuela were polluting the river and creating ecological changes that would impair the quality and range of life downriver, even the waters of the North West District. Observers in Mabaruma agreed and predicted that the changes would first spread through the entire Amakura (Orinoco) delta and thence into the two large rivers, Amakura and Barima, which arose in the Imataka Mountains. Amakura formed the boundary between the two countries while Barima flowed through the middle of the NWD, first east, parallel to the Barama, then swinging abruptly north and northwest to empty in the southernmost arm of Amakura delta. It would not be long before pollution reached the more eastern and larger Waini River, which emptied almost into the lower lip of the Orinoco mouth.

Venezuelans claimed that it was not likely that Orinoco pollution would significantly affect the Waini since the north westward sweep of the Atlantic's south equatorial current would tend to push the Orinoco outflow away from the Waini mouth. But such was the volume of the Orinoco and so often was debris with Spanish markings found in BG waters in border areas--and, increasingly, further inland--that local residents were convinced that pollution in the Orinoco would affect the Waini contrary to Venezuelan claims. Besides, the force of the south equatorial current was not fully felt along the coastal waters, and from the evidence of flotsam in the Waini, the force of the Orinoco was considerable enough inshore to push huge volumes of water and silt southeast beyond Waini Point and thence into the Waini River.

This siltation has given rise to numerous islands in the Amakura delta all rich in mangrove forests, home to numerous species of wild animals, birds--

especially cranes and flamingos--and fish. In this environment the Warrau nation has dwelled and prospered for millennia building their houses on stilts in the shallow waters at the river's edge, and feeding on the plentiful fish and game. They joined the houses to one another with bridges made of longitudinally hemisected trunks of *manaca (manicou)* palms. These trees grew absolutely straight up and tall, to about 200 feet. The trunks were water-resistant, split easily, were fairly brittle and their convex surface smooth, black and though not very strong---crushing easily under heavy weight-- were cheap and plentiful and easily replaced when damaged.

The Warrau have used them in construction for ages and in recent times young non-native rural homesteaders on the coast have copied their methods to construct *manicou* bark flooring for their first house. I recall the smooth sheen of a manicou walkway in our yard between the outhouse and the foot of the staircase that led to the main floor of our house; it was a great convenience during the muddy rainy season, and how I liked to jump up and down on it and watch it spring back into shape with a creak. In time with much punishment of this type the bark would crack longitudinally and settle down a little flatter, less curved, and stop creaking when jumped on. We missed that.

The Warrau people live on fish. Fish are plentiful now but biologists have already warned that even small amounts of poisons like mercury, lead, cyanide and sulphur would be enough to seriously endanger the fish and bird life of the lower Orinoco, and thence the Amakura, Barima and Waini for as far upstream as they are tidal. Venezuelan authorities pooh-pooh the fears of ecologists and have branded them as alarmists, asserting that the huge volume of the Orinoco was sufficient to dilute any pollutants that industry at Ciudad Guayana might now and in the future produce!

The Guianese Warrau--kith and kin to those in the adjacent Amakura delta of Venezuela--have repeated the concerns of their Orinoco brethren. I doubt whether any politician or civil servant living on the coast of British Guiana, or in Caracas, has any feel for this particular problem, and so far the BG government has been silent on the issue, despite repeated representations from those close to and threatened by it. Recent rumours of proposed offshore exploration of the delta and the nearby Guiana continental shelf for oil have added to the concerns of those who wish to preserve the local habitat.

"For what?" some government officials and businessmen ask. "What is there to preserve? There is nothing there; nothing! Only bush! The economy of the area couldn't be worse. The only hope the people there have for prosperity is new industry; they need new capital for development. And so what if a few fish and birds die?"

Al pointed to a low cone-shaped hill in the middle distance. "That's about seven miles from here. You can drive there on a dirt road if you take a jeep or tractor. When you get up there, you can see all round you for miles and miles, nothin' but trees, a lot of *awara* and *cokerite* and other palms that grow wild. People pick the fruit to sell. The palms give palm oil. In this area they used to grow cocoa and at Hosororo; it's a very old Arawak village, they say the first place cassava grow in this country nearly 4000 years ago. Imagine that.

"There's a Catholic mission, been there years; a lot of the natives get converted but that don't help their pockets; they lose contact with their tribe and culture; many live hand to mouth. The Church don't do a damn for them. With money this place can turn like Florida. Now that Cuba gone we can take its place in trade with the States. But it need money, maan, more than we got, we have collateral to back loans but the banks in Georgetown don't want to hear from us. We don' even have a bank in this town, only the Post Office Savings, and that's for jills only. If I was in the States, I'd get a loan, jus' so. On the value of my land alone. But here, that tradition don' exist."

He paused. "It's the same all over in this country. The two banks, Barclays and Royal, don't even know we exist; not only they don't have branches here, they don't have branches in no small town or village in BG. I ask them for a loan to buy machinery; they turn me down, say they don't deal in that kind o' business, and in any case I'm too far from town for their likin'. Yet they want my deposit! The truth is that they won't give seed money to local people, even with collateral and guarantors; you know how many first class ideas the banks turn down every day? Even though all the managers at Royal are local Putagee, people that we know, who come from indentured stock, like all of us, and should know that we didn't get here by lazing around. They worse than the Canadian boss if you ask them for a loan. Is like they jealous to see their own make good.

" They only interested in Alcan and Sprostons. They like lick white ass, even the most junior ones! They think lickin' dry shit will give them promotion! It's disgusting!" He sounded very bitter and brutally critical at that moment. As if surprised by his eloquence, he paused and swallowed his drink.

"That's the crux of the matter," he went on, noticing the impact of his remarks, an edge to his voice. "Jagan don' want to ask the banks to change their ways. He think the Government can do all the development. Nonsense! He go to Kennedy and ask for $6 million for development. Chicken feed for the US! What you think he going do with that money? Waste it! He don't have the people with the business smarts to do things right. They have commie book knowledge and plenty commie talk, but not one clue what to do, in a place like this, or any place past their desk. Talk 'bout potential, this place got it.

"This North West and lots of other parts o' Guiana that I been to. All we need is finance, and a little help from Government with transport and the proper laws, and some protection. Our people are enterprisin' enough to do the rest. And to besides, we people will pay taxes, not like the foreigner who won't even spit on you without all kinds of tax breaks and guarantees. The last thing we want is for Yanks to sweep in here; they will turn us into slaves again.

"American business ain't got heart; they all run by Jews who want everything for themselves and to help out Israel and to hell with you coloured people!" His bitterness was infectious; he spoke from long acquaintance with them and a deep belief in their insincerity and greed. "Cheddi fooling with Russians; he got no experience to deal with them; he got no experience in business. Look what happen to Hungary in '56. We ask him at the time if he think tha' was right; he say that Imre Nagy was a US agent and Hungary was Russia neighbour and part of USSR, so Russia had to do what they did; no different from what US did to Arbenz in '54 and will do here. All cold war. Tit for tat. He going make a mess, and you watch; the way he going he going let Burnham run away with the country."

His voice had risen in pitch as he spoke; he stopped to sip his drink and swallow some food; he looked around to gauge our reaction. Brewster chose the pause to refresh his plate. Everyone was listening keenly, like students at a key lecture. Encouraged, Al continued.

"Cheddi think he is Che Guevara and he following Castro example. Everybody will be equal yea, but all poor. BG is not Cuba. We don' have no American Mafia heah, no big rackets, no big beaches, no big whorehouses to entertain Yanks, even though Mammas did a good job building one when the Yanks had Atkinson." He giggled briefly at his own joke, and with a wave of the hand continued, "The only communists we got here are bums and drunks. One maan the other day, drunk like hell, wobbling on he bicycle, call out to me, 'Missa Chin, Missa Chin, as soon as we get independence, you will have to gie me half yuh land.' Is when they drunk you know what going on in their heads, and what the party hacks telling them. I would gladly give him half my land if the bastard knew what to do with it!"

He paused long enough to sip his drink and chew on a shrimp, then continued, "It makes me sick to see how Cheddi wasting his chance, third time. Mark what I say, if he don't change his tack this time, he boat sink! This is he last chance. Yuh know him, you boys got to get to him and show him. The maan so stubborn, or else he stupid!" He spat out those last words.

"Yes I know him, that's why I don't think he will listen to me, or to anybody else." I told him of our relationship and of the failed efforts of my late brother-in-law from 1946 to 1956 and of his death in 1959.

He looked dejected, and exclaimed, "What, you say Tulla was your brother–in-law! Oh shite, small world Doc, I really sorry to hear that he dead; he was a good maan, and smart. I used to stay at he hotel whenever I go to town in de early fifties; that's where I met him and we used to talk; he liked his Scotch, and his women. He was one of the people who got me to look at Jagan seriously; he was thorough. I din' know all what you tell me. Shite, Jagan don't have no excuse for de mess he getting us into. Every time I hear stories of people who work they ass off to help him I feel sick. Still we have to keep trying. Things changing, specially with the Yanks, with Kennedy. That gives us a last chance. Cheddi got to see that the US serious and won't let him fool around with Russia. You got to talk to your friends, talk to him. Try again. Tell him if he make sport with this Commie stuff, Burnham will whip him, and you know what that mean!" He was emphatic rather than questioning.

"I will try." I replied, uncertain of what I could do or whether Jagan would even see me. Perhaps this Wappai mess-up might get me an audience. I told him of my minor role on an advisory committee and that Jagan still visited my sister's business place for a chat and her monthly contribution, and I did know several of the party brass.

"I have to say, he still comes personally, and my family still rejects anything critical of him even though his policies are crippling their business. That's how loyal they are to his *charisma*. Also how much they fear a Burnham takeover!"

"*Charisma*? What is that, Doc?" Balgobin asked.

"Hindi word," Jain said, "means 'magic' or 'miracle'."

"I never hear it before."

"Well, now you know why, it's because politics now squarely in the hands of magicians."

After the mirth subsided, Al went on, "You know, even though I criticise him baad, I still have to support him. Or else D'Aguiar, but that man is a fool as a politician; he does politics like he does business, by pushing people around. He won't get anywhere! All he'll do is split the Indian middle class; if all of them turn PPP they might force Jagan towards the middle."

"That's what my brother-in-law tried to do; it's where they might have gotten if the extremists, Janet, Westmaas, Carter and a few other hard-liners weren't so powerful, and rich Indians so blind."

"Now I have no use for Burnham; he too damn crooked. I hope what I say don't upset any of you, but if you don't know already, you will find out that what I say is true. You all remember how last year he took several thousand false signatures to the London conference in favour of PR? That was the first time anybody hear of that particular 'poll'. He fool Cheddi and JN Singh, make them look stupid and both o' them ignore his sister Jessie's warnings. Up here only black people that work with Government support him. He worse than Cheddi, maan, he lie, he thief. He thief baad!"

Al downed his drink, sat back in his chair and rocked reflectively. Brewster winced at the last comment, but agreed with the political analysis, as did everyone else.

"What's in the future for the North-West, then, if things don't change?" I asked him.

"In a sense it's a good thing we don't have the money to spend on big development. It might save us in the long run." Al said as he surveyed from the comfort of his chair the sweeping view across undulating groves of oranges that he had just begun to reap."Cheddi know that the Colonial Government had development plans since the 40s–I know 'bout the CDW and World Bank. Col. Spencer was up here in 1948 looking at manganese and citrus; as far as I know he recommended help to us farmers with transport, and for Government to change policy and *promote*, not just *tolerate* cultivation here. Nothing changed in 13 years.

"The World Bank team did come here before PPP won in 1953. And when they win, instead of talking about economics and development Cheddi start to push legislation about freedom of movement of two Commies from Jamaica, Ferdi Smith and Richard Hart, that their own party, the Peoples National Party did expel! Imagine that, Jagan and Burnham fighting for a couple of Jamaican communists and forgetting we Guianese; he says it was big principle; what principle? And I back him. Shite, I ain't got no one else to back." He sounded resigned, harping on it, even as a hundred thousand other voters might have sounded just then.

"We're in a last ditch stand there, you know;" I mused, "Jagan or Burnham. It's come down to that. Jagan will not see other people's point of view. He's not in the real BG as we see it. He's in some Communist paradise that exists only in the imagination. And he thinks that he can make that imaginary land come alive and real if only he had independence. He thinks that the mere fact of independence will solve all. This is stupid and blind idealism."

"But look, he already blow two chances to become great. He and the rest make fools of themselves, twice, the first time in 1953. That was a comic scene; I was there in High Street and watch them, all dress up in new white sharkskin suits strutting like turkey down the street to the Public Buildings to open the House; they make history and they turn it into a joke. It was a big day, and a big achievement for us, the first popular government, rich and poor alike put them there; you would think they would want history to respect them, instead they come off like clowns. Then this other fiasco. Rudy Luck and Rory Westmaas made a lot of noise, Burnham and Cheddi sounded off in the House. They call themselves intellectuals. We don' need intellectuals like those; we need practical people, not talkers who don' have to do a day's work. Even the books they use they borrow! As to Rudy, his sister got a whole bookstore full at Central High; he should go back to those and read the pages he missed out first time 'round!"

"I was away, then; didn't Cheddi bring an expert of some kind from England, an economist, I think, from Cambridge? A man named Burrell?"

"Yes, the fellow name Ken Bernell; and he was an economist. Everybody say he was a Communist, but Cheddi say no. I don't know maan, everyone he bring since he start either pink or red. Why he so stubborn, and can't see BG reality is real hard to understand. You know how much we talk to him. I go to town specially to show him things; we tell him that he starting the wrong way; he and his executive can't decide what political system best for the country without really knowing the country, and the people he talking to don't know a thing about what he's saying, all they see is a handsome fellow, with a nice set of teeth–good ad for a dentist--telling them what wonders he will do after independence.

"But he fooling himself if he think communism will cut it; on the other hand, I say again, a middle course will lead the way to prosperity. I tell him the same thing I know Tulla did tell him; that plan still suits us best. Our people are hardworking, and enterprising; I keep sayin' that; they don't want hand-outs; they *will* develop the country, once Government put in the basics. Instead he talking about taxing people to give Government money for development; that's the worst thing he could do; people need to keep their money to develop their business; that will create jobs. He says instead that government will run the businesses and make sure everybody has a job; private enterprise don't do that; they only exploit. And his only example is the sugar estates. But I show him that government does a lousy job of business, and he must stop judging businesses by the standards of the sugar estates. He sit down, he listen and agree; make me feel good. Then I leave and he forget every single damn thing I tell him; he go off and do something else. And I'm not the only one he fucks up!"

"Some people say that Janet makes the decisions, that he can be convinced to be moderate, but Janet won't let him change, and that Westmaas, Bhagwan, Carter, Chandisingh and the other Communists are solidly with her. So even if he wants to moderate they won't let him."

"You believe that, Doc?" Al sounded surprised.

"No, I don't, because I know how he operates; he listens to them, but he makes the decisions; everything has to go past him."

"What about those other guys, like Rai, and Ramsahoye and Nunes? They're all Ministers and don't behave like mad commies; don't they have any clout?" Al asked.

"Rai is good man," Jain said, "not commie; he's smart, he is good Minister of Home Affairs and Janet does not like to see how popular he's getting; they have party elections soon and he could become Chairman. That would be good fight to watch. Jagan will not like him to compete."

"I agree with Jain; Jagan will want a black candidate, no offence meant, chaps, it's just his way; he calls it equality to balance black with white, but then he should find black talent equal to the Indians in his party; Burnham took away many of the smart Blacks. My info tells me Rai will have a tough time ahead; he's the only one with independent brains, although at times Nunes makes good noises; Ramsahoye will do what it takes to get ahead, even shift to another party; we'll see."

Brewster recalled something he had heard his father-in-law say during the last election campaign, after listening to one of Rai's speeches. "He's Rajput stock, higher class than Jagan, who they say is a *chamār*, so things may not work out between them; what's this, Mr Jain?."

"They also say Rai is *banjārra*;" Jain replied; "a Rajput is anyone of a number of tribes from the state of Rājasthān, which used to be called Rājputāna; some tribes are known by their trade; *banjārra* are travelling salesmen and artisans, another one I see here are *Gadia Lohārs*, they go from village to village, make and repair agricultural and household implements. *Chamār* is leather-worker, in the lowest caste."

"That's right," I observed, "my mother used to deal with one *lohār* man and his teenage son; they regularly visited DeHoop for work, mending pots and pans, leaky milk cans, and taking orders to make utensils of various kinds."

"Rajputs are tough, brave and enterprising people;" Jain added, "good businessmen; some tall, some short, some light skinned, some dark; each tribe has name of occupation or caste; one of oldest Indian tribes is *Bhils*, famous archers. You wouldn't see them here, but now you have bow and arrows, you can become one, Doctorji!" He giggled. "Caste is still strong in India, not so much here."

"Without doubt Jagan rejected all that, and Rai being a practising Hindu doesn't help, so we'll have to wait and see." I said.

"They better settle their inside stuff and understand where they leading. They frustrating a lot of good people who support them; I don't have to tell you how many already pull up stakes and gone to England, and how many with real money put it all in Lombard Bank in London!"

"I know a lot of ordinary people, workers, teachers, craftsmen, even businessmen who right now packing up to go." Brewster confided.

"Several of my family have gone; others are planning to go," I said. "It must be bothering the Brits to see all these coloured people. But you know, the Guianese exodus is a drop in the ocean compared with that from Jamaica."

"Why the Jamaicans leaving? They don' have a communist threat."

"Well, not yet. Different problems, same result. There's a lot of poverty; Guianese haven't seen anything like that scale of need, at least not yet. Also they fight a lot. The two parties, the JLP and PNP have frequent shoot-outs, like cowboy movies; I hope that doesn't come here."

"But we not far behind," Balgobin said. "You watch what come to pass when Burnham turn up the heat; you hear all the fiery words he spitting out, like de devil 'self. We in fo' some rough times! The man talking treason, or worse, he stirring up civil war!"

Balgobin had been uncharacteristically silent, apart from nodding agreement from time to time as Chin Sang spoke, and echoing some of his thoughts, for example, "Dr Jagan frustrate all o' we in the party; then he come and give sweet talk and make you forget what you want to complain 'bout. He always fire first, always say everything is so because he ain't got the power yet to do what we want, and that the Americans holding him up. Then he leave and everybody realise that the meeting di'n get to discuss the real problems. Sometime he bring other people to talk who take up all the time and we don' get into de meat of the matter. We get mad with he, but we cyaan stay mad; he still the leader, and we got to listen to him; me son say I is stupid to stay in the party, but who we got to turn to? So he too lef' an' gone to England."

"I think you're right. People will leave and go wherever; you should see how many lining up to apply for US visas. The smart ones are going to England before independence. I believe that's why the Brits are so anxious to give us independence, to stop all this flow of coloured people; it's creating social problems, not much right now, but if this continues from all the countries nearing independence, Britain will shut her door. If Cheddi would only listen he could use that as a bargaining chip to get proper aid from UK. My brother-in-law laid out a great plan for him ten years ago and showed him how delaying independence and getting essential works completed would benefit everyone. He and JN Singh wanted independence next day, but Tulla told them to go slow and smart and they'll get the works and independence in 10-15 years. They said no way. Now look eight years later, they have nothing, everything crumbling, the Party broke up, no independence and people hustling away!"

"He's not even thinking of that. He probably says good riddance since most of the people leaving don't want nothin' to do with Communism. Like Castro and the Cubans he hustlin' to expel to de States." Brewster said.

"But the people leaving are the ones with skills or brains or money; the very ones we need to develop this place." Al stressed, punching his left palm with the right fist. "What the politicians doing now, both Jagan with communism and Burnham with violence, is to chase away our own good people, and lose the talent they need for development; remember the Interim government couldn't spend the money they got, because they couldn't find enough skilled people. Now it's worse. They will have to import foreigners to fill their place; but for a foreigner they will have to pay at least double. That make sense to anybody?"

"Yes, to the Brits. They encourage Jagan to drive off all the talent, which they collect; then they sell Jagan expertise later on at twice or thrice the going rate which Jagan will gladly pay with low interest loans from those very people! That way they get rid of a liability and make a bigger profit in servicing the transaction! That's made the British financier so very wealthy and powerful. We're just pawns!"

Later in the afternoon Cpl Doris gave us a tour of the area and for several miles further along an undulating road to Hosororo and a few other sites including a little waterfall on the Hosororo Creek which flowed into the Arouca River at the village. He proceeded until the road ended and became a trail, which ran on into the enclosing forest. Once there he asked to speak to me alone. He was making the best of a bad time, clearly quite saddened, and his subdued mood reflected both the death of the policeman and his own vulnerability.

He knew the danger inherent in his work, especially here where his staff was small and daily faced the challenges of a border area with too many avenues for infiltration and smuggling by armed Venezuelans, a problem not sufficiently appreciated in Georgetown. He had not thought of personal accidents; risk was inherent in his work, but the near drowning was beginning to be replayed in his mind causing something like aftershocks, with momentary trembling and a cold sensation. So far he has maintained his functioning and hoped he was not becoming like soldiers in war zones who developed battle fatigue.

He was quite astute to make the comparison as the condition of stress had been receiving increasingly rigorous attention and seemed as real as physical injury, and not as General Patton had dismissed in WWII as a sign of being "yellow". We briefly discussed what was known about it as a sequel of trauma and well-recorded in medical literature under names like *traumatic neurasthenia*, shell shock, combat fatigue but doctors had been seeing it in people who were not soldiers and in relation to other shocking events such as his.

At this time it seemed that psychological support and open discussion with trusted people would help and that the temptation to overuse alcohol to relieve unwanted feelings could harm. Generally it was felt that with a positive attitude to life, work and with family support most eased in time. There was no professional source of psychological support in Mabaruma but the priest at the mission, even though not of his denomination, could be consulted if the need arose for a professional ear. His main need was to understand what was happening and after hearing even the little I had to say on the issue he felt he could "shake it" and thanked me for the information. In reply I offered to reply promptly to any correspondence on that or any other matter.

On the way back he related his reaction to the things he had heard, especially the signs of imminent rough politics and did not want internal strife added to his problems. He remained loyal to his political affiliation, unofficial and private though that was, and strove to keep his work and political beliefs separate. His personal motto was "duty first". He had sworn to keep the peace and that would be his focus.

He ended the tour back at the Rest House where over tea he told more tales of his clashes with Venezuelan smugglers and his mood lightened. But in the ensuing silence he began to fidget a little, then got up, crossed the floor to the windows overlooking the broad expanse of forest to the hills in the distance; he stood there staring intently at the scene and said, to no one in particular, "All this country out there, pretty but empty and everybody say it got riches. If it got so much riches, why nobody there?"

He returned to the table and sat obliquely across from me, sipped tea and engaged in casual police and other talk with Brewster, including jokes, which we found quite interesting and would make comments, some also funny.

After a pause in the exchanges, Doris changed the subject, looked more serious and said, rather poignantly, "Something I want to say before you all go back home. And don' get me wrong. You know this is the first time in me life I ever spend any time, much less so long, with East Indian people, and I never know a doctor or a scientist, much less travel and discourse with them, except for my medical. I don' have no East Indian friends. I see East Indian people in the street and I think all of you de same, we hear you all come here jus' the other day from India with nothing, that you all heathens and dacoits, wild and dangerous and don' wear clothes over there! And here you all makin' progress and getting rich at we expense!" He had blurted out the last and looked relieved that he had unburdened himself of the thought. "But now I stop and wonder these last few days since you all tell us this strange history; if that is the truth, we living a lie here; we turning 'gainst you all for no reason; you're victims same as we."

"Hooray!" I cried, "that's great! It's wonderful of you to say so; it takes courage, which we all know you have! We need to tell that to one another more."

"I feel the same," Brewster said, "and I thank you Felix for saying it so well. I want to know what's true; I never give these things any time 'till now; so why Dr Jagan don't tell people these things? He tell us instead not to believe the pundits, and that the East Indians here are Guianese, not Indians; they have nothing to learn from India. Don't sound so from what you tell us."

Jain chortled "Dr Jagan is not Indian indeed; he only looks so; he's just brown Guianese, like some Portuguese people; he knows no more about his roots than you do or Chinese or Portuguese! In India we have many people like that; cities full of them! They too don't know the history we told you; they follow British teachings and deny their own, especially city people and Christians from Portuguese Goa; Muslims say history start 1400 years ago; Jews and Christians say that Creation take place in 4000BC. Hindus welcome these people and others when they came, and rescued Jews and Parsis from persecution."

"Now all these converts who used to be Hindus curse their own. Imagine that!" Balgobin said. "My neighbour is one of them."

"You're joking." Jain said.

"You see, Corporal, we're not the only ones who struggle with wrong information; all races need to know the truth; that way we *could* work together, respect one another whatever the outcome of the political tussle; we can't if one thinks he's superior and can abuse the rest."

"This trip teach us all a few things; it sort of bring us together," Doris' eyes shone brightly with a new recognition if not appreciation. "I din' know what to expect at the start when I see you all. But you all surprise me and I come to respect you; that's why I tell you how I feel; I still have to digest all that I hear; it's the strangest story."

"What we said is true;" Jain said, pensively. "Alas, what you get in your books is propaganda British spread to make us look like savages and dacoits and not able to govern or look after ourselves. We had huge empires size of Europe when *they* were savages! They treat Africans same way. Your story too should be corrected and told. As for India this civilisation does go back at least 12,000 years, further back than any other we know so far. Mr Doris, we are blood brothers now, and I am glad for that; you taught us many things on this trip and I'm glad to do anything in return to help my brothers."

"Hear, hear." I said agreeing fully, and Bal added, "Me too."

"So why you people not doing something to spread the truth?" Brewster asked.

"Good question." Jain replied, and as he spoke I recalled an almost identical statement by Dr Brahmam on this question. "We Indians have been slow to get up after taking so many blows. We goofed. We allowed a thousand years of Muslim and British rule to break our spirit. Indians are diverse people; we don't all see eye to eye. We're strong individualists, many peoples and many languages, and the country is huge. We still suffer hangovers from past; main one is British rule and caste system which they made worse; it's better here, but still big problem in India although outlawed in constitution; British left communities very divided, destroyed local government; it's only 14 years since independence and there is Cold War; India is leading non-aligned movement. Not easy as Pakistan already steal piece of Kashmir and wants all of Kashmir and more. Indians must become Indians. But history must be corrected."

"India is in trouble and has to shake the colonial past but is cautious and makes mistakes; it too chases away its bright people who need a fair chance; same danger we face," I continued. "Here before the War the city and country people were making good headway to get together, to provide better education and teach people about their heritage. The War slowed things down. Then Dr Jagan came and before you know it everything began to spin around him, and he got ahead by denouncing all previous and current Indian leaders as uncaring, selfish, untruthful, corrupt or exploitative. Those criticised should have responded strongly, but they felt the accusations were so outrageous the people would reject them. That was a judgement error. There was some truth in what Jagan said, but you know what they say about half-truths. Your Police colleagues did him a huge favour in 1948 when they foolishly killed those strikers at Enmore; those killings were a godsend for him. He blamed Indian leaders for letting them happen and hijacked the Indian cause right then and merged it with Communism. At the same time he pooh-poohed religion and brought down old stalwarts like Dr J B Singh, a good humanitarian.

"So the plans to educate people properly stalled, first, by the British Government who before this did little and now even this Indian one would not introduce these studies in school; second, the political party structure benefits a lot from dividing people. In Ireland they use religion to divide people; here we use race. If both sides were properly educated, which they won't be as long as these two demagogues are around, we might be spared a lot of future grief."

In the ensuing discussion we agreed that it would take an enormous act of goodwill to halt the political wrangling that was threatening to bring the Indians and Blacks to a head-on collision, two "races" with profound and almost irreconcilable local differences. Yet these factors need not impede or frustrate the development of a cooperative *modus vivendi* in which each could keep and express its uniqueness to add lustre and variety to the emerging society. As a start we needed to become informed, to dispel untruths and put myths in their place.

The urgency and desperation of the afternoon's conversation weighed heavily on us, already saddened by Bacchus' distress. Though I did not know the murdered man, I felt that I had known him as an extension or alter ego of his brother. Doris had brought us a newspaper photograph of the slain detective showing him in an action pose in which he looked invincible; this added to the tragedy, like that of a fallen Samson. Inspector Bacchus had looked so frail and vulnerable as he waved goodbye on his way to the Grumman bobbing on the river as small craft cruised or raced around it.

The river had been alive with morning traffic, with boats of different sizes, from pleasure craft to small freighters. The steamer, the *SS Tarpon*, which would be taking us the next day on the overnight run to Georgetown loomed over the other craft, and from time to time strained at her moorings with loud groans. Sailors were busy hosing the decks and preparing to load the cargo stacked high on the pier. Passengers were expected to board from 10.30 am.

The trip, its purpose, its uncertainties, its dangers had accidentally brought us close together. We had relied heavily on one another and shared food, supplies, work and knowledge. Doris owed Jain his life; both sides had learned that there was no inherent barrier to working together, while observing personal tastes and practices and preserving their individuality, but willing to sample and acquire something new (as Brewster had observed, salivating, "You know, the labba seasoned with Bal's spices was the best I ever taste!")

Co-operation had been spontaneous at all times once the difficulties of our situation had become clear; each man had put trust in his comrades to achieve the aim of the expedition, and no one had behaved uncivilly; even the so-called "backward" natives had been indispensable in getting us to our destination, and had been an example of friendliness, decency, discipline and teamwork.

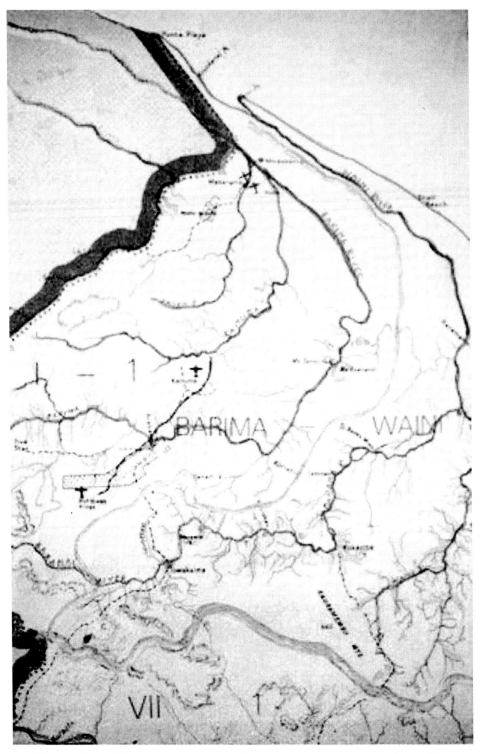

The Northwest District; inset shows northern extension towards Amakura delta

Chapter 10

We return to Georgetown by the slow coastal ship, a 26-hour journey, and learn something of the geography of the coast, the internal politics of Government transportation, and hear more tales of smuggling along the poorly defended border waters between BG and Venezuela, and the dangers posed to coastal fish stocks by indiscriminate trawling for shrimps by an American company. I observe the passengers noting racial peculiarities in provisioning for this trip. The captain is a seasoned sailor who prefers to stay out of politics but is concerned about security of his retirement benefits. I again receive the honours of colonial hierarchy but find an inviting and privileged perch on the prow of the ship where I spent time in silent contemplation, and thoughts of the new widow and her family.

Day 16: Depart Mabaruma 12.30 pm

Prince, would you milk this bounteous cow, the state?
First, you must let the people drink their share:
Only when calves are fed, will Earth's tree bear
Fruit, like a cornucopia, for your plate.

                                                                        Bhartrhari

We slipped out of Mabaruma on the afternoon tide. I stood between Brewster and Balgobin as we waved goodbye from the upper deck to people in general assembled on the wharf, and in particular, to Cpl Doris, Constables Benn and Rodriques, and Mr Chin Sang, who had driven us to the wharf. I had spent an hour before the sailing with Mr Mohamed, who had invited us for a drink before leaving. The *SS Tarpon* was one of a small fleet of coastal steamers acquired after WWII from British surplus stores, and had been plying this route for over two years.

I watched the lush green banks of the restless Arouca River slowly recede as the ship sought the main channel. The low bushes arching to kiss the water's edge bobbed rhythmically up and down as the waves set in motion by the ship rolled to the shores, almost in tune with the throbbing of the engines as they picked up speed. How different was the vegetation here, luxuriant mixed growth, the tallest trees reaching up no more than sixty feet, about a third the height of those giants among which we had walked but a few days ago. Here and there a tall erect palm, *troolie* or *manicole* rose above the rest.

The journey from Mabaruma to Waini Point took about 3 hours, helped by the tide, which had begun to ebb soon after our departure. I was amazed at how quickly the water flowed and how much the level was dropping as we moved along. What the ship gained in speed was somewhat offset by the distance it would have to travel into the Atlantic along the deepest channel to avoid the banks and shallows, especially at Waini Point and beyond.

It was a clear bright afternoon. The river was alive with swirls, some of which were large enough to make the ship shudder as she crossed them, like a car going over a rippled road surface. Soon we were out of the Arouca River and into the Barima en route to the Mora Passage, which would take us into the Waini River to near Krunkenal Point on the West Bank of the Waini estuary, a few miles south of Punta Playa, the northernmost point in BG. From its mouth we would make a long slow turn northeast into the waters of the Atlantic, where the strong eastward flow of the Orinoco effluents would collide with the northern flow of the south equatorial current to create one of the roughest seas in the western Atlantic whose effects were felt in the shallow Gulf of Paria between Trinidad and Venezuela. In antediluvian times Trinidad was connected to the

Venezuelan coast and Paria was a shallow swamp forming part of the delta of the Orinoco.

Once into the ocean we would swing south to follow the coast about ten miles off shore to make the slow choppy journey to Georgetown in the teeth of the countervailing current. The distance from Krunkenal south to Shell Beach was 43 miles, Point Kokali 58, Moruka River mouth and Waramuri Mission 93 and Pomeroon estuary 97 miles. Here we would begin to meet rougher seas for the next six miles or so as the Pomeroon, the first substantial outflow into the Atlantic on our way, poured into the ocean. But this would be nothing compared to the buffeting we would receive from the much greater turbulence of the wide Essequibo starting off Hampton court (30 miles from Pomeroon estuary) near Anna Regina and extending for 30 miles to Tuschen[128] on the West Demerara coast, 20 miles from Georgetown. Out in the choppy waters of the Atlantic the *Tarpon* creaked and shuddered.

In this vessel, as at the rest houses, government protocols prevailed. As the highest-ranking Government officer on board, I was given one of two "first class" staterooms located amidships on the upper deck behind the bridge. A bunk bed occupied one side of the room across from a chest and cupboard. We stowed our baggage in the chest along with the scientific material and sample bag. Jain and Balgobin were given a room with two bunks across the narrow corridor from mine. Brewster occupied a room similar to mine.

It was hot in the rooms during the daytime. An oscillating fan in a stout wire cage mounted at an angle on the ceiling pushed air across the room tainted with the smell of diesel fumes; its hurried whirr seemed to complain against the slower rhythmic growl of the diesel engines coming up through the floor, somewhat muffled by insulation. On entering the Waini we had headed into the cooling northeast trades, a welcome respite from the sultry heat of the afternoon.

I roamed through the ship noting that there were about thirty passengers, most of them seated or stretched out on rows of benches on the lower deck. Jute bags filled with produce were stacked on the covered portion of this deck and crates of oranges spilled into the open area, where two Government Land Rovers were parked. From the bridge the sides of the ship curved gracefully forward from left and right to meet at the prow now rising and falling to obscure or alternately reveal the encompassing sweep of grey-green ocean.

In the foreground two steep flights of stairs led from each side of the forward end of the lower level to the upper deck on which stood two box-like flotation devices with slatted tops, coils of rope, capstans and assorted *bric à brac* all lashed securely to the deck.

This was the most inviting area of the ship, and out of bounds for departure and arrival. Access was restricted but allowed to VIP's. I took full advantage of this and spent most of my time there well into the night, seated on one of the large floats, enjoying the enormous sweep of sky bejewelled with stars that danced while the engines drummed and the waves swished in harmony. In this setting it was soothing to revel in the music so unconventionally created;

---

[128] The official width of the Essequibo estuary is 20 miles, but in reality Parika, the eastern point usually quoted is too far inland to be on the Atlantic coast. Tuschen, Verginoegen or some point a little west seems the most likely eastern boundary. The distance from Anna Regina to Tuschen is 28 miles.

was this not a corollary to the *'music of the spheres'* that so attracted the romantic poets and made them ponder its genesis, and dominate all Sanscrit chants?

The captain invited us to join him for a cup of tea on the bridge as we rounded the headland forming the right bank of the estuary of the Waini. I watched from this vantage point the flocks of pink flamingos stretched out on the mudflats. In studied nonchalance, they ignored our passage, serenely erect while contemplating the next morsel, or like voyeurs, waiting for the next exciting thing to happen. A sailor brought us tea, sweet biscuits, saltines and triangles of Gouda cheese. We talked briefly of our experiences. The captain was a shade taller than I, and a well-built man of mixed race, thinning wavy greying hair and brown complexion. He spoke easily and commented carefully on the news circulating among his friends.

He reflected on the prevailing concerns about the mounting political instability in Georgetown. As a Government worker he was careful to be neutral in his opinions. He had already served twenty-five years in the Transport and Harbours Department, and had another five to qualify for retirement. He was concerned what would happen to people like him if an administration were put in place after independence that did not respect the current conditions of service. That seemed a real possibility and bothered the men and women in the T&HD, whose standard displaying these initials in bold blue lettering on white ground was even then waving proudly in the breeze. The Trades Union Council advocated on behalf of the subordinate staff while officers like him were among the Civil Service ranks, and hence not formally unionised; they belonged to the British Guiana Civil Service Association, of which Dr Balwant Singh, our laboratory director, had just been elected President.

I asked him about the costs of freight along the route. He didn't know much about the business side of the service. The accountants handled that. But he did confide that the T&HD, as an arm of Government, was run as a service to facilitate Government work, not as a business. "Not like the buses on the coast roads." He agreed personally that they could do more, and certain things differently, for example, actively promote the North West District, but those were issues of government policy and T&HD management, from which he had long ago learned to steer clear.

"No, sir, those are rough waters; you can drown in them! Out here I feel much safer."

In the brief silence that followed, the rumbling of the engines below and the thrashing of the waves against the sides of the ship seemed to become louder and more insistent. I pondered the portent of the remark, and Brewster, as if reading my mind, asked, "Why is that?"

"T&HD is almost independent among Government services; and the boys in Georgetown want to keep it so. The politicians eyeing it and nobody want that. So everyone is being coy. Everything is stalling. Same thing with the trains. The service needs to expand, to grow to meet new challenges, but that means listening to the new boys, Jagan and Burnham, and allowing them to affect policy. T&HD managers don't want that; they want to keep full control, they will work with Burnham, because he is one o' them, but Jagan is another story; they don't see eye to eye. I don't have the stomach for that kind of wrangling, so I keep away. And then the TUC got their own ideas…"

"And they too in bed with the PNC." Jain said off-handedly, while biting deep and noisily into cracker and cheese.

The Captain changed tack and asked about our mission, and Brewster gave him the official line.

Spread out in the shallow water to our right were the nets of half a dozen or so fishermen, their open boats, hardly bigger than dinghies, tethered to the same tall poles that anchored the nets. I watched them through the Captain's binoculars. Further in the distance other flocks of flamingos were no more than specks, which rose to vivid life in the magnifying lenses. A scattering of small grey birds scurried along the soft mud. They looked like plovers such as we used to see so plentifully on the DeHoop foreshore mudflats, but some were different, with long slender bills curved at the tip like those of sandpipers.

The fishermen were busily preparing to pull up stakes. Their boats bobbed gently, their outboard engines rising high up from the deep, as the waves from the *SS Tarpon* rolled by from several hundred yards away. Most if not all of the men were natives of the Warrau tribe; one or two waved as we passed by. They could be Guianese or from Venezuela.

"Now see, there's a problem that should be settled before independence, because I don't see lil BG dealing with big Venezuela and winning. You see those boats?" He pointed to a group winding up activities further north on the left bank. "I would bet they all come from 'cross the border; it's only a few miles away, 'bout the same as from here to Mabaruma. They come every day and fish over here."

"And nobody stop them?" Brewster enquired.

"No, not as long as they stay peaceful. You see, these folk here are all Warrau; this whole area all the way to the Orinoco and Amakura delta and beyond is their traditional land; they don' know boundaries laid out by foreigners. They go by tradition and historic landmarks; they don' read maps, and probably wouldn't know one if they see it. Officially, of course, they poaching, but it's not a big problem," he paused and added ominously "yet!"

Brewster's policeman's instincts were aroused, "Why is that, Skipper?"

"Well, you see, the Venezuelans claim all this area; in fact I understand they claim all of Essequibo County. So if we let their people run free in our territory, and we do nothing to stop them, they can claim traditional usage, and" his voice rose to a higher pitch, "we might have trouble getting them to leave. They clashin' already with our people, and the police got involved. Those Venezuelans carry guns. Our side not allowed to. Doris din' tell you?"

"He did touch on it, but were taken up with the Inspector's tragedy; what happened?"

"Some of those boats came to Waini Point early one morning–you know, they set up their seines overnight and generally follow the tide. Seems these men had done that, then left and went to Morawhanna, as they always do, to pass the time; they had a few drinks in a saloon, and got into an argument. You know, they like we rum and they will come over here for that alone; they do it all the time. Some have friends and family in Morawhanna; and stay overnight or for days sometimes. The border post at Morawhanna check their papers, and search for guns and so on.

"Anyway, this time, the saloon keeper din' like their behaviour so he got his bouncer, a big Warrau man, to talk to them and get them out. They left, but got into a fight outside and were beaten up because several more people joined and double-banked them. They got away before anything serious happen, and somebody sent a message to the police. By the time a policeman come, everybody scatter. Early in the morning, those same men raced their boats over to the Guianese side and shoot up the nets, badly damaged one boat and wounded one of the fishermen. Luckily he was the only one they could see near the boats, how the other six or seven escape I don' know; it was still too dark, the men must ha' hide in the bottom of the boats. Doris spend the next fortnight hiding with two men in a cove near Krunkenal waiting; the last night, in foreday morning, they came back and do the same thing. Benn moved he boat to cut them off and Doris fired a warning shot. He say he never see manoeuvring so! They din' know how many policemen were there nor how many guns; the river at that hour still misty and you have to know it well to fool around on it. So they hustled out, but one of the boats in trying to spin round, turned too fast into the wash of the one in front and got swamped. So Doris was able to arrest the two men in it. He locked them up in Mabaruma and sent a telegram to Georgetown for instructions. This was now an international incident, and you know the Venezuelans very touchy, very volatile; they blow up at the least thing! If this did happen the other way round, I t'ink those two would be dead by now!"

"My gawd, Skip!' Brewster exclaimed. "So what happen?"

"A week or so later, Doris get a message from Georgetown to escort them to the border at a certain time and hand them over to their own authorities, who would be waiting.

"It was a big thing here, but I don' think it made the Georgetown papers."

"When was that? I don't remember hearing or seeing anything 'bout it."

"A year or so ago. You know, a lot of things go on here and you don' hear 'bout them. The papers in town only print what suits them; nobody up here is news. This one could have caused bigger tensions; the Guianese was not seriously hurt, but the boat had to be laid up for repairs. So I suppose it was wise to let it go with the five days they spent in jail. The hand-over was friendly, with handshakes and all that. Nobody knows what the Venezuelan Police did with those men. They can be very harsh, or soft, it depends on the politics; you never know."

"Then there is the smuggling; nothing much comes this way, some cigarettes and guns, but a lot of Guianese rum move across, and the Venezuelan police don't like that."

"You know Cap'n, it could be that the Governor in town didn' want to raise any fuss with Venezuela." Brewster suggested.

"You're right." I said, "President Gallegos is renewing claims on Essequibo and he thinks USA will stand off and let him slug it out with UK. Gallegos hates Communism and Castro; there's a report of Castro beginning to stir things up there. He also thinks that with Jagan being Communist and close to Castro US would look aside and let Venezuela take Essequibo."

"Why is that?" the Captain asked, "I thought the boundary settled over 60 years ago."

"Why they have a claim anyway?" Bal asked "Jagan don't say anything about that".

"The claim goes back 400 years when the Pope divided the New World between Portugal and Spain; Guiana came under Spain but they made only one attempt to settle it and the Natives expelled them. The Venezuelans raised the claim after they became independent and when the Brits published the Schomburgk boundary they protested; a settlement was reached with the Americans as referees with the understanding that neither side would try to develop the land. But when gold was found in 1850s and the Brits moved to exploit that the Venezuelans protested. The Brits ignored them until US intervened and a settlement was reached with BG yielding territory at the Orinoco estuary. The Venezuelans were never pleased with this but did nothing until now, with the threat of Communism. This one is still a UK responsibility as it is comes under foreign affairs, so Venezuela is dealing with the British Foreign Secretary. Jagan will have no real say except to insist that they settle it before Independence."

"I think you're right about that, Venezuela wants full control of all these waters and access to the Atlantic without hindrance." The Captain said. "Right now with Trinidad on one side and BG on the other side of the Orinoco estuary and Gulf of Paria their free passage is not so free. Even this isn't on radio or in the paper; at least not so far."

"Looks like you're right Constable that the Governor doesn't want people to know about this." Bal said.

At that moment the "remote" North West District with its scattered exonyms, most of which had failed to take root, suddenly seemed more real and more connected to the arrogant city that ruled it from 170 miles away. But the distance, the expense of travel, the lack of interest by the media in rural and hinterland happenings, however significant or important, created a physical and ideological divide that existing politicians and media owners found unwilling and unable to bridge as the rewards would not match the energy needed to do that.

Before the advent of universal suffrage and party politics, Georgetown and New Amsterdam were the only places one heard of on radio, or read of in the three daily papers. They did, of course, report the occasional rural sensations like strikes and killings, presenting them condescendingly, with a distinct anti-rural bias, as if those areas and the persons concerned were of no consequence, or had never existed before and were newly erupting, like recrudescent Krakatoas, to sully the placid national scene. Even disasters such as floods, drought or loss of crops, however punishing to those affected, got short shrift.

Nothing must appear to criticise the British Government. Ignorance and neglect of things rural, from place names to activities, were worn by city folk and their publicists as a badge of virtue. With increase in popular politics the two towns and the Georgetown-based media slowly and grudgingly began to pay heed to rural events and issues; even so, they picked and promoted favourite areas, such as Buxton and Mackenzie, with positive comment but continued to make the sugar estates their whipping posts. Independent agricultural regions — broad swaths of the country — were areas of darkness in the eyes of media and city folk alike. Coverage of rural events remained rare, sketchy, superficial and biased.

So deep was the ingrained prejudice and stereotyping among the literate classes that ran the country that many thinkers, especially those in remote areas, like Hari, had, in consistently decrying that attitude, remained pessimistic of the chances that even the leading public figures-- media, politicians and bureaucrats--would change appreciably. Sooner or later, however, these authorities would have to include--in their policies, programs and publications--strategies to inform all of their readers, listeners and followers, about the economic and social conditions of the whole country, not just those of their narrow centres of interest, whether local, party, constituency or department. Rural dwellers empathised with those feelings, for they knew that to the city folk Novar was just as remote, insignificant and uninteresting as Wappai. How our problems and official neglect of them do unite us! Both Mohammed and Chin-Sang were right in condemning that attitude as a significant barrier to development; although Mohamed had profited considerably from the very disinterest that characterised his compatriots on the coast, he knew that it was an obstacle that Government must recognise and remove, since it was unlikely that anyone would consider careers in areas which were disadvantaged by ignorance or negatively affected by bad or no publicity. But significantly neither had considered the border issue nor the attitude of the parties concerned.

The tea interlude ended and the captain excused himself to attend to his duties. He went over to where the helmsman stood at the wheel. The chart spread out below a thick pane of glass screwed down to the table showed details of the shoals and bars, the safe channel marked by buoys. Still the captain took care to verify the exact location of the ship and confirm the position of the buoys, leaving nothing to chance; buoys had been known to "move" in the night. The ship had begun a wide right turn to enter the Atlantic and travel east into deeper less choppy water about 15 to 20 miles offshore, where she would cruise south east for the remainder of the journey to Georgetown. Reaching there it would overshoot the city by about six miles to escape the turbulent cross currents produced, especially at the height of the ebb, by the combined waters of the Essequibo and Demerara Rivers as they flowed across the shallow continental shelf to merge with the deep ocean farther off.

The silt deposited on the shelf from these and all the other rivers of the Guiana coast from Punta Playa to Cayenne and North-east Brazil provided nourishment to plankton, which fed a myriad of life forms, producing one of the richest fishing banks in the tropical Atlantic. This fact was common knowledge among fishermen, a few having ventured far out into the ocean in their small craft, although not intended for such use, and tasted the rich prize that was so easy to catch, but none could remain off shore for more than a day in those boats; and tragedy did befall several who had dared to go too far or for too long. A rich folklore of fear and lament had developed around these tragedies, creating legends of life and purpose deifying the many natural marine forces, with resulting rituals among the seafarers to placate them.

Few local fishermen had the safe size of boat to venture into rough seas thirty to a hundred miles off shore to cope with the conditions and take advantage of the plenty there, and even those few did not possess the gear or refrigeration equipment to bring in a catch of sufficient size to justify the costs. Besides, cold storage facilities on shore were insufficient to handle large catches, and the one large facility that existed, Weiting and Richter's Cold Storage, was expensive and near saturation. Despite excellent and convincing representations, Government had been lukewarm to the repeated proposals for infrastructural support, put to them by fishermen and their local financial backers, starting in the fifties and continuing well into the Jagan years. And yet by 1960, Jagan had allowed Georgetown to become an extension of Florida- and Texas-based shrimping fleets, which locals have since consistently criticized as 'raping the fledgling Guianese fishing industry' and 'snatching the livelihood of thousands'.

The foreign trawlers came with a foreign crew, and only after protests did the Government require local employment. Among these few was Basdeo, my second cousin, who became the head of the Texas company's motor pool; from time to time he would bring me quantities of excess or unwanted catch retained by the fishermen for their families and friends on shore. This represented one to two of the catch discarded as being of *no* commercial interest to the trawling fleets! He told stories of the enormous waste that took place each day, to the great distress and annoyance of the local fishermen working the trawlers, among whom were some of the same men who had failed to get the backing of the Jagan Government for a deep sea enterprise!

The major criticism of the Americans was their use of trawling, a method of bulk fishing in which huge nets--often miles long and weighted with steel rods--were dragged by the trawler across the ocean floor, scouring it and picking up everything in their path. The drag was facilitated by heavy steel bars placed at the front of the nets to act much like a rake in a farmer's field. The Americans were interested in shrimp only; everything else was discarded, including, as Basdeo would relate, substantial catches of good commercial fish like snapper, grouper, sea bass (*cuffum*) and mullet that many of the local fishermen would have been happy to get if they had the means to fish that far out. The trawled fish were almost all killed in the manoeuvre and many tons of them discarded at sea. Another problem, recently examined by a Government Fisheries Officer who chose anonymity for fear of repercussions, was the likely destruction of both fish habitat and the food chain by what he called the "indiscriminate reaping and wholesale murder" of the stocks, including their places of spawning, and the wanton sacrifice of young fish inevitably caught in the nets. The Government had been content to accept assurances from the fleets that this would not be allowed, that the destruction was exaggerated and the news fomented by "reactionary elements among locals jealous of the fleet's success, and opponents of economic progress and job-creation." They produced figures to show the "many jobs created, noting that the fishing crews and shore-based employees were all Guianese". Jagan (I would say, since no one in the PPP could have made an announcement without his approval) completely buried the fact that he had exchanged short-term gain for long-term loss, and against the interests of his own people, a thing the Americans and Russians would never do, in similar circumstances.

The fishermen's proposal had sought help for larger boats and cheaper refrigeration facilities, not the more expensive and destructive trawlers, and would have become the nucleus of a local industry supplying an important element of local diet, reducing dependency on imports of salted, canned, smoked and pickled fish that, although established in the Guianese dietary, should, for health reasons, be replaced by fresh catch and local preserves. But as one critic observed, "if the Government can't do the fishing, Jagan will give it away to a foreigner for a small tax; the man can't stand the thought of any local people making a profit; it's okay to be a worker, beholden to him and voting for him, but not an employer, who *might* vote against him. He can't understand that the local guy will pay taxes and spend his money here, while the Yanks give him a pittance on the raw material, add value back home, not here, and spend their profits *there*, and leave a lot of dead fish in our ocean!"

I spent the rest of that afternoon lounging on the forward deck ruminating. Jain, Brewster and Balgobin joined me for a while; we were by then in the open Atlantic about 15 miles offshore heading southeast along the coast, which could be seen as a faint line on the western horizon. Brewster had a queasy stomach, which was not helped by the greater movement and slight roll at this end of the ship. The wind was brisk and cool, coming out of the northeast and blowing into our backs across the ship from left to right. Feeling nauseous, he had left followed by Jain, similarly afflicted. Balgobin and I stayed on until he began to shiver in the cool wind, and left, explaining that he would see to our supper. Snacks were available on board; tea, coffee and soft drinks could be purchased; many passengers had brought their food for the journey, as was customary among Guianese travellers. Several could be seen exploring their food packs and bringing out various items, some easily identified as fried fish or chicken or cassava by the smells that soon filled the air and even before that the tell-tale oil stains on the wrappers.

Even here you could see the distinct cuisine of the Negroes and Indians and the overlaps. Travel food for the Indian was invariably puri, roti, bakes or *daal-puri*--each a flat bread, the last containing a fill of pureed split peas or other pulse—biscuits and cheese, while the Blacks carried root vegetables, fufu (roasted plantain mixed with oil, seasoned, mashed and rolled into balls), fried cassava, roast pork and black pudding (spiced blood sausage). Both groups might also have fried fish--and the more affluent, chicken--oranges and other fruit in season, especially bananas. In time the varied smells would carry with the wind and reach me lying on my back studying the motions of the few clouds in the fading light of the evening sky.

The swish-swish of the water against the steel sides of the ship was a soothing sound. I watched the waves coming out of the wide sweep of ocean, running between one and two feet, and striking the ship, every so often sending upwards a small spray that reached me as a fine mist, and occasionally mixed with a few droplets of water. The water remained a pale green tinged with brown, the first time I had seen ocean water in BG any colour but brown. As evening fell the setting sun turned orange and the sky, now streaked with brighter high strato-cirrus clouds, glowed light orange along the cloud lines, mimicking the sun. A long swath of silver lit the waves from the ship to the western horizon and disappeared into a broad sheen of light in the haze of sky around the setting sun. The sky brightened briefly then quickly turned grey as the sun disappeared. The ship lights were all that remained to illuminate the waves as the night closed around us.

Tilapia a recommended protein source, easily farmed, and a cash "crop"

St Andrews Kirk, Georgetown, across from the Legislature scene of daily mob scenes; D"Aguiar's HQ and mustering place is directly behind the building; the school is to the right out of the photo. Thus children were able to watch the mob activity

Police launch, a luxury, on the Mahaica River; Mahaica became a hideout for Black anarchists involved in anarchic activities; the launch policed areas upriver, all Indian.

Chapter 11

Our return is as silent as our departure despite the anxiety of eight families and a major Government error due to ignorance and overconfidence of the planners. The disinterest of media raises concerns and matches their inability to conduct scholarly analyses of issues and changes in development trends, preferring to focus ingratiatingly on petty foreign visitors and stoking fires of political partisanship. Their neglect to recognise graduates of the UCWI adds unwittingly to unfair Government criticism of the College and hides inept recruitment practices that favour foreigners, deter applicants and create inordinate delays in filling Government posts, allegedly to secure proper ideological matches. Details are given. Press handling of issues also favours foreigners, illustrated by its handling of the visit of a British physician to whom I am assigned as counterpart and liaison. We discuss the influence and cost-benefit of the UCWI and other systemic issues. The press also toadies to visiting American physicians the last a group arriving as an epidemic of polio rages to field-test a vaccine they could not ethically do at home.

Day 17: Arrive Georgetown 4.30 pm.

"But don't let that scare you too much. If you can succeed in marrying a man of good family you'll be alright, because I'm white, an Englishman, and I'm no pauper. That will count heavily in your favour. Mother will be forgotten and overlooked in the general reckoning."　　　　　Edgar Mittelholzer, *Sylvia*

"To keep up we must be far ahead"
"A man all wrapped up in himself makes a small package"
"Where the whole person is involved there is no work."　　　　　Marshall McLuhan

"The good life is just beginning."　　　　　CB Jagan, Victory Speech, Aug 2, 1961

I woke up in time to see the sun rise out of the eastern ocean and immediately brighten the whole sky; its warmth beginning to dispel the chill of the night air. The water was choppier now, as cross currents raised the waves several inches higher, sending them slapping against the sides of the ship. I wondered about Brewster; he was rolling fitfully in his bed when I last saw him, but his malaise had not increased beyond nausea. Neither he nor Jain was interested in the spectacle of the dawn at sea, and could muster no emotion for the sight of the great orb rising effortlessly from the bowels of the ocean to dispel the darkness, a sight that had fired so many myths of bygone times. Instead they complained that this little ship was too damned slow. And so she was, in relative terms. Doing 10 knots was good; with currents against her, seven or eight seemed pretty acceptable. Faster than walking a forest trail, or boating among tacubas on the Barama, I teased, but they remained unmoved.

The morning was clear and the coastline remained a thin dark line on the western horizon, with no detail. Somewhere on that line was the estuary of the Pomeroon River, the source of the cross currents, which we passed in a few minutes, and the ship settled down in calmer water. The wind was light coming off the land from the southwest, blowing into our bow. As the sun got hotter the wind died down leaving a period of calm, which was soon dispelled by the sea breeze that came up blowing from the opposite direction. I joined the Captain for breakfast, but the queasy stomachs of Brewster and Jain declined the invitation. "Some high wine would soon settle that!" the Captain teased amiably.

From the forecastle of the *SS Tarpon* I watched the distant coastline, barely visible in the brilliant morning sunlight now slanting across our bow from left to right, and glinting off the crests of the waves. Soon a buffeting began as the ship entered the cross currents created by the outflow from the broad Essequibo that would stretch over the next forty miles of sea. It was an uncanny feeling, as if the deck underfoot was experiencing clonic spasms with a high frequency, interrupted at regular intervals by other sounds, lower frequencies, people sounds, all against the deep throb of the ship's engines. In an odd way there was music in the overall effect, not displeasing to the morning ear. I recalled a quatrain from Byron's *Don Juan*, which seemed to fit the moment perfectly, and which I had always thought so reminiscent of a sonorous Vaidic verse that Mr Latchman loved to chant, whenever he sat in the shade of the large mango tree beside the garden hut, paring his shallot bulbs for the planting:

> *There's music in the sighing of a reed*
> *There's music in the gushing of a rill,*
> *There's music in all things, if men had ears:*
> *The earth is but an echo of the spheres.*   (Lord Byron, Don Juan, XV)

After breakfast Brewster joined me though still feeling queasy. We sat on the prow looking at the broad expanse of dirty green water all around us and listening to the rhythmic slap-slap of the waves battering the hull while the bow cut its slow way forward with a swish-swish-swish in slower tempo. The slow hours passed and the day grew warmer under a cloudless sky.

By mid-morning the buffeting grew more intense as the ship encountered heavier currents where the Essequibo collided with the western fringe of the south equatorial current flowing northwest. It was an eerie feeling to be trapped on the little ship uncertain whether she could survive the relentless pounding, and yet the decks seemed steady enough to walk on and stable underfoot, despite the side to side roll that made some nauseous.

At 11.30 am we had lunch with the Captain, which Brewster's nausea did not tolerate; he chose to lie down instead. Afterwards I went to the foredeck where Balgobin and I sat on a raft under the open sky; Balgobin dozed and I read a little or napped or scanned the distant shore, read and napped again.

By mid-afternoon we had cleared the roughest waters and were heading towards the Demerara River overshooting its estuary by a few miles to reach the main channel where the ship made a wide turn to the right that led uneventfully into brown water and past the hulk of the *Keyholt* to Port Georgetown. We were welcomed back by our families escorted by a Police Superintendent and Inspector Bacchus, who greeted us very warmly. I was pleased to greet Mrs Brewster who looked just as I had pictured her.

Our return merited a line or two in the papers, a mere copy from the Police blotter: *"Police Party Returns from Jungle Mission"*, and named Inspector Bacchus "with party of seven" (only four had left with him from Georgetown) but no story told, nor did anyone seek any. It did mention Bacchus's tragic loss of his brother and his misfortune in missing the funeral. A line was given to the fact that the party had taken 10 days longer than planned for the mission, but neither details nor comments were given nor questions raised.

Neither press nor radio interviewed any of us, even though both radio stations had broadcast Police messages to us on several occasions in the past ten days, and had commented on the unusual delay and lack of response from us, noting the remoteness of the area to which "the Police Party" had gone. Also they had sent specific notification to the Inspector of the murder of his brother.

Yet on our return they were incredibly incurious as to what had kept us. No bureaucrat nor politician called in the days that followed, except perhaps to offer condolences to Inspector Bacchus. Astonishing as it seemed, we were simply not news. My co-workers however feared that we might have met some grave danger, had an accident or had gotten lost. Our failure to return on time had prompted questions to the "authorities", but no one among them seemed to have known anything specific about our destination nor of the terrain we had to traverse to get there. None had apparently ventured much beyond the well-travelled coastal or riverain routes. All had seemed blissfully ignorant of the actual conditions in the hinterland, and quite content to remain so. At the Central Police Station, the only reaction had been one of optimism and "wait and see".

The Laboratory Director, Dr Singh, and the Deputy Chief Medical Officer, Dr Nehaul, had conveyed their concerns to the Police authorities, and from the guarded response received had concluded that no one among them had much of a clue what could have happened to us, and worse, did not seem to know where or when to start a search, should one become necessary.

Ministry of Health and Police officials were relieved that we had returned safely. Ours had been the longest impromptu foray into the deep forests, 'wilderness' in coast-speak, and had raised all sorts of issues. I suspected that they had begun to talk embarrassingly of sending a search party into the foreboding wilds that at least one of them, Dr Singh, had avoided by sending me.

Hearing in brief my story and gauging correctly that I had enjoyed the experience and learned something from it, they were relieved and Dr Nehaul expressed his pleasure that I would not complain; he showed great interest in the material, agreeing that I include the non-forensic issues in my report, as a way of getting them on somebody's agenda. Dr Singh had done his best to placate my distraught wife, who had begun to worry after the tenth day.

The general lack of media curiosity was surprising, although on reflection, should have been expected, given their narrow-mindedness. No one, it seemed, wished to explore that vast area of ignorance; the press and radio had no hinterland experts, and in any case, could not be distracted from the more stirring developments in political opposition strategy, and the pursuit of scoops.

At the same time government officials responsible for the trip did not wish their ignorance and incompetence revealed. And chief politicos saw no benefit in exposing their own indifference to an issue that had no coastal resonance whatever, and could well be a hornet's nest. Balgobin succinctly opined, "None o' we important to any o' them!"

"We were so worried; ten days passed and no word," my wife said, "and they wouldn't tell me anything; your sister called a Commissioner she knew; all he did was get someone to call back to tell her everything was OK. Dr Singh called me every day and Dr Nehaul a few times. They told us the same thing each time. No news is good news. None of them sounded as if they knew anything, really. I was sure you were lost or dead; people kept telling us jungle horror stories. Phillip and Peter ask if it was true that you're not coming back, and Ranji, poor thing, kept waiting at the door for you, and crying."

At the cultural-educational level, neither the Library nor the Museum nor the Ladies of Charity, or whatever they called themselves, made the slightest effort to court any of us for a talk or interview about that unknown quarter of the country, as was their wont, and as they had done recently when they buttonholed a white Christian evangelist college *student* from Mississippi, USA, who had "braved the wilds" of the upper Demerara River (populated) to volunteer for a week at a religious mission close to the bauxite mining *town* of Mackenzie. The poor thing was embarrassed and had nothing to say other than how polite everyone had been to her and how impressed she had been with the

Mission and the great work it was doing for the "backward people of the jungle, healing them physically and spiritually, and rescuing them to be brought into Christ's kingdom!"

The paper had presented the student as if she were an expert; the mulatto interviewer had been solicitous and deferential, and had sought her opinion on everything including inanities, with generous space given to the student's impressions of the natives, the country, its readiness for independence, how the "outside world" saw it, its people, its politics, the river, the hospitality of her hosts, the sanitary arrangements, the food (*'did you like our casareep? It's native, you know!'*), omitting nothing and enquiring whether she had partaken of the obligatory *'labba and creek water'* to guarantee her return for further knowledge-sharing and displays of white altruism and superiority!

The report had concluded with an apology for the colour of the river water, the heat of the sun (the student had remarked on the humidity), the lack of a first class hotel in the upper Demerara forests, and other amenities to which "you are so accustomed", and thanks for the time she had "so generously given to help BG to modernise and acquire the latest in Science, Health, Information and Technology!" To the embarrassed girl's credit she had claimed no conquests.

Contrast that example of toadying (usually called *'the colonial mentality'*) with the lack of interest shown in graduates returning from London University's new College in Jamaica (UCWI). I was the College's first Indo-Guianese graduate in Medicine, and the first and youngest to obtain a specialist appointment in the BG Medical Services. Each in itself was encouraging news in a small country starving for higher education, since the purpose of the new College--soon to become the independent University of the West Indies--was to meet the needs of the Commonwealth Caribbean for post-secondary education, and to train professionals, starting with medical doctors, graduates in sciences and arts, followed by engineers, agriculturists, lawyers and others. Training in the Caribbean setting would enable graduates to deal competently with local issues, from the beginning, and avoid extra years spent currently to educate those who had studied European or American models and had to adjust their thinking, knowledge base and technological expectations to be of any real use in the tropics and places with limited resources. Some failed to make the adjustment and returned to their places of training[129].

The establishment of the UCWI had been a major recommendation of the Moyne Commission, but postponed by WWII. Responsible media should have been more curious to follow the progress of what was conceptually a unique institution, supported by fourteen colonial governments with high expectations and therefore at high risk. Clearly for BG a study of the UCWI's Guianese graduates would help to assess institutional performance and product value, and to address Jagan's claims that the College was not worth the expenditure. I've always wondered at this media omission since a thorough examination of the College's performance and its graduates would have provided enough material to deal with Jagan's polemics. Regrettably BG media lacked the capacity for, or

---

[129]Many in BG were astonished that we did not have to spend extra time in the UK to "finish" our training. Twenty years later there would be similar doubts when as Dean I led the establishment of postgraduate medical education in the Caribbean as part of UWI activities, a programme that still stands as a unique and highly successful example of a single University supervising the education, training and examination of medical specialists.

interest in scholarly analysis and preferred to spend their efforts on stoking fires of political partisanship, to increase tensions among the relatively naïve peoples of the country and rip them apart in a way that would be almost impossible to mend.

For most of the period since WWII, the dominant local intellectuals were considered to be those tutored by whites and included coloured Christian educators, the clergy, journalists and a few others in the professions and business, among whom were several Christianised Indians. Those with a university education were virtually revered.

A Queen's College graduate from the sixth form could command a good position in the Civil Service, business administration--especially at Bookers, the two banks or the large estates--a teaching job in a secondary school, or a position as a journalist. All except Indians. For them, especially non-Christians, change and acceptance were slow. Perhaps the media, in overlooking the performance of the UCWI, were merely projecting their adherence to Victorian attitudes and biases; their failures to recognise, report on and examine trends in social movements--including higher education- were the unspoken anguish of a group unwilling to adapt or contribute constructively to the changing social and intellectual scene.

The College had opened with a batch of 33 medical students starting a 6-year study programme of London University, adding a similar number into each of the Faculties of Arts and Natural Sciences a year later for the regular 3-year Bachelor's degree programmes. The first graduates emerged in 1952 from the Arts and Science Faculties and from Medicine two years later. By 1961 several Guianese graduates had become established as teachers and scientists, mostly in Government institutions. But it was plain that BG media did not see any glamour in the UCWI graduates to compare with those returning from the UK or USA, unless they were from "socialite" families.

This neglect bothered many, including prospective students. Some of the early returnees, e.g. Pat Dyal, the first Indian graduate, a historian, had commented on the prevailing snootiness of the local intelligentsia---mostly British-educated or -trained, and peopling the Civil Service, the media and the professions. They tended to dismiss anyone or anything outside their immediate ken, many doubting the ability of a tropical institution like the UCWI to produce graduates of any depth. They were amazed however when its graduates showed skills and knowledge far surpassing those from temperate institutions, and its medical graduates were being lured by US and Canadian hospitals and graduate schools; even in Britain they were often landing positions ahead of local rivals.

But in BG of the early sixties, it was very much that "a prophet was not without honour save in his own country!" It was ironic that the media, which generally opposed Jagan and favoured Burnham and D'Aguiar, helped Jagan's anti-UCWI stance by not publicising the excellence and reputation that the College had already gained, presumably because media supported Burnham who shared Jagan's criticisms of the UCWI and the directions he wished to take to establish an independent "socialist" university for Guianese.

Part of the problem of BG and its media's disregard of the UCWI was that its base in Jamaica was seen as inferior to Europe or the USA as an environment for higher learning. One wonders what their attitude might have been had the University been sited elsewhere as several islands and BG had been postulated as suitable centres. The Jamaican government had smartly come up with a grant of 680 acres of developed land and temporary buildings at Mona, just released from housing the WWII Gibraltar Internment Camp[130]—named after the rock from which most of the internees had come.

It was a splendid choice, nestled in a gently-sloping field above the Hope River with Long Mountain to the south separating it from Kingston; to the north spurs of the Blue Mountains rose abruptly from the eastern bank of the Hope River in steps to the highest peak of over 7,500 feet; the campus thus provided breath-taking views of the foothills and of the main range. I have seen many campuses in many countries and have yet to see one more naturally attractive.

In the early years the new College had attracted the more studious types (among whom were older students—teachers and government workers-- sponsored by their employers to complete degrees) rather than the merely young, aimless, radical, rambunctious and politically aspiring. While its geographic location and political development might have posed a prestige issue--since Jamaica itself was a colony and not foreign enough for the Guianese colonial mentality--PPP (and later PNC) politicians had never accepted the educational biases or directions of the new College.

Even family members thought most of us daft to go to an unknown, start-up institution, ignoring the fact that it was run by the University of London--one of the world's most prestigious institutions--which was not about to hand degrees willy-nilly to any colonial jack or jill unless merited, and it proved quite tough, as we found out. Indeed more was demanded of us in those pioneer years, to establish "the highest standard" within the London complex of Colleges. Successive lines of British examiners would later record their pleasure with the quality of the graduates; offers of postgraduate training came to many from both sides of the Atlantic hardly had the first few batches graduated.

And yet I found myself defending the institution to family and friends, who had difficulties shaking the powerful biases they had acquired in their early education. PPP politicians (with Burnham as their spokesman on Education) were well aware of the solid reputation that the College had quickly acquired and, despite a Caribbean-wide consensus to the contrary, wanted it to be more "progressive and radical" in its curricula, whatever that meant, and gaining no support, not even from the Social Science faculty, revived and exploited Guianese biases to justify the decision to withdraw from it.

The clash of ideology had been evident from 1953, when Burnham as Minister of Education had met with Sir Thomas Taylor and Hugh (later Sir Hugh) Springer, Principal and Registrar respectively of the five year old University College, impressing both with his arrogance and ambivalence.[131]

---

[130]The first Indian Institute of Technology campus established by Nehru was at Hijli, Bengal, also an internment site-see Ch. 5,

[131] Springer revealed this privately, observing the irony, when Burnham in the late sixties was seeking to have Guyanese medical students admitted to the UWI, having agreed to pay for five annually, and argued for special admissions criteria, which, as Chair of Admissions and later Dean of the Medical Faculty, I rejected; Senate affirmed the practice of a uniform medical admissions policy, but left final choice from among the qualified to the Guyanese Ministry of Education. Later Burnham asked for a list of all qualified Guyanese applicants in rank order; invariably the top five included at least three Indians; we usually got one, but only if the Indian happened to come from a PNC-supporting family. The worst case of bias was when young Drepaul (son of CML Chief Technologist Joe) won the Guyana scholarship in 1972 and Burnham's government denied him a place at the UWI!

A definitive clash, predicted by the UCWI resident tutor in Georgetown, was forestalled by the premature end of the first PPP government. A more positive and supportive relationship developed between BG and the UCWI from 1953 to1958, the year that the second PPP government renewed its iconoclastic sparring with the College, totally ignoring the fact that the main strength of the College lay in its ability to withstand pressure from individual governments, as proven by his failure to downgrade admissions policy and "socialise" curricula. Each member remained free to raise issues in Council and to persuade colleagues to their point of view, where the majority prevailed.

Independence from individual lobbying, even from Jamaica, the largest financial contributor, allowed UCWI to develop as an academic engine for the region, to power programmes as diverse and innovative as the region wished and its economy could support. But what the PPP wished was to see a less "elitist" admissions policy that would enable *even* the more mediocre of its protégés from the PYO to gain entry, and provision for pre-admission courses or a preliminary year to qualify them for matriculation.

But the College was not funded for this; Council correctly pointed out that such courses could be given more cheaply in up-graded high schools for which the UCWI would train the teachers. The problem was not that the University standards were too high but that there were too few schools in the Caribbean colonies with the capacity to prepare students for matriculation, especially in the Sciences, and for a time the College did run a first year upgrading programme until expanding capacity in its contributors--made possible by the College's science graduates who had turned to teaching--made that unnecessary.

One of the BGEIA's Centennial resolutions (*see Bk1, Ch. 5, p.31, footnote 12*) had called for Government to expand rural education, to enforce the terms of existing Education Acts and to prepare the inexperienced majority for responsible use of the vote they would shortly be given! In the early 1940's, the Colonial Office had released funds for colonial development but the BG Government had not produced a high school plan beyond modest expansion of Queen's College and additional funding for Berbice High School, instead of several new high schools, one in each large centre. Public frustration and demand propelled entrepreneurs and religious groups to start a number of private secondary schools in Georgetown.

By the late forties high schools had begun to appear in the larger villages, facilitating rural students. But for higher education one still had to go to Europe, North America, India or elsewhere, until the establishment of the UCWI in 1948. And what Jagan envisaged there was something more like a populist US College with its elastic admissions criteria, a grass-roots institution rather than one occupying the top of the academic ladder. This was an unrealistic and retrograde expectation as most of the contributors to the UCWI quickly realised, and agreed to the original charter of the College and accepted its policies.

When BG finally expanded secondary education it was dismayed to find that many of its own gifted teachers had slipped out of the country for peace and security in other lands, including Caribbean islands, and that most UCWI graduates were reluctant to serve a communist agenda.

If Jagan or Burnham had a valid criticism it was that too many of BG's best had not yet returned to work in the country. But that was no mystery. Tulla and Ramroop had told him why years earlier. The first medical graduates (1954), 13 in number, included one from BG, Michael Woo Ming, who had remained in Jamaica to specialise in Surgery, married a Jamaican and never returned except to visit family. Keith Tang graduated the following year, married a Jamaican and also stayed in Jamaica to specialise in Obstetrics and Gynaecology. Stanley and Donald Luck graduated in 1956, both starting on specialist paths and also married Jamaicans.

Stanley returned to BG in 1960, to begin a career as a general duty medical officer. In 1957 Wallace (Bud) Lee, Jimmy Munroe and I graduated, Bud the fifth Chinese, Jimmy and I the first Black and Indian respectively. Bud married his Guianese sweetheart and returned to BG after completing postgraduate training, in the UK, in general surgery, as did Jimmy, who remained single until the late sixties when he married an English nurse, and returned to Georgetown for a brief tour of duty. I studied Surgery and Pathology, married a Jamaican, and had planned to return to BG on completing training in orthopaedic and reconstructive surgery. My mother's near-death fight with typhoid fever in 1960 changed that, and I returned before I could complete my surgical training, accepting a position in Pathology which allowed me to be close to her.

1958 was a bumper year for BG medical graduates: Emran Ali, Zatul Amin, Walter Chin, Charles Lewis, Neville (Bunny) Lowachee, Quintyn Richmond, John and Honnett Searwar. All save Richmond and Lewis returned (both wed Jamaicans), Chin and the Searwar brothers permanently. They were followed by Harold Chan, Punraj Singh, Ramnaraice Bissessar, Hardutt Sukdeo, Lloyd Kerry, Yvonne Harding, Krishna Persaud, Sydney Wong, A. Mekdeci, Alwyn Egbert, Andy Joaquin, Vasil Persaud, Raj Ramphal, and a few others by the time Jagan severed ties with UCWI[132] in 1963. Of these only Ramphal, and K. Persaud, returned for a spell. Jagan used these data to blame the University for failing to "return graduates to their countries of origin!" The UCWI deemed this conclusion naive and unfair.

While marriage to Jamaicans was one reason for some not returning, the outstanding reasons were the opportunity to specialise and the *failure of the BG government* to provide adequately for interns or put in place a plan to recruit graduates (not just in *Medicine*), in contrast to Antigua, Barbados, Jamaica and Trinidad. Stanley had started specialty training but an accident changed his direction and he returned six months or so before I did.

Medical graduates from the UCWI had begun to trickle in and a few from other colonies or islands had by 1960 served internships in Georgetown. In 1961 there were eight of us on the General Hospital staff: four generalists--Stanley Luck, Bunny Lowachee, Honnett Searwar and Zatul Amin (predominantly in Anaesthesia); three interns--Raj Ramphal, just ending his term, Krishna Persaud and Jan Evertz (Curacao); and I, the lone specialist; a ninth, John Searwar, was in private practice. The first three would remain for the long haul, joined in later years by surgeons Bud Lee and Emran Ali, paediatrician Walter Chin and internist Sat Doobay.

Between 1955 and 1965 the quality of BG graduates had given them ready admission into specialty training programmes at UCWI, and in North American and UK hospitals, and was the most important reason for their remaining

---

[132] Rabin Sahoy, Boodh Doobay, Ummul (Shirley) Amin, Joanne Jaggernauth, Joy Forsythe, Sat Doobay, Ranjit Singh and a few others would complete their training after BG withdrew from the UWI. Of these Jaggernauth, Forsythe and the two Doobays would return for varying periods. Sat would stay on to become a senior internist.

overseas. A close second was the BG Government's failure to meet its decade-old commitment to provide adequate facilities for internships, anticipated to be four annually, starting in 1954. By 1960 barely two were accredited; thus the Service was not seen as a favourable environment for interns and could not compete for the best graduates--among whom were most of the Guianese--who sailed easily into choice internships at the UCHWI or Kingston Public Hospital.

Although the increasing turmoil in Guianese politics had begun to discourage many from returning home, it was not as daunting a factor as the unacceptably long wait between application for a position with the BG government and acceptance even though the vacancies were there. It did not help that the Civil Service hierarchy took the position that all trained Guianese "owed a debt of return to serve their country", regardless of conditions of service or quality of the practice environment, or whether the country had fully supported that training. They were expected to suffer happily and negotiate all the absurd obstacles that would be placed in their way, as if a long trial of suffering and proof of stupidity---to endure such duress--were necessary qualifications to work in the Guiana medical and other professional services!

Approval of my application took *nine* months, like completion of human pregnancy! I had applied directly at the Ministry of Health in Sept 1960 when my mother's illness decided me and had received written acceptance by the MOH within a month "pending completion of formalities".

The main reason for the extended delay was that neither the Hospitals nor the Ministry of Health had the authority under Government regulations to employ staff directly. Physicians and other Government professionals were automatically part of the BG Civil Service, from the most junior and undifferentiated to the most specialised, and were put through the same laborious process as dictated by the Public Services Commission (PSC), whose head in 1961-63, Lyle Harewood (with whom I had worked in 1950-51), was himself a critic of the ponderous grind of its entrenched and seemingly irremovable succession of checks, double checks, buck-passing, inter-office minutes within the Commission and memos between the Commission and the target Ministry. It stalled for comments from other groups as to suitability (often for no good reason), Police checks, family interviews (why this, no one knew), requests for lost testimonials (originally supplied with applications) and other impedimenta of the PSC appointments process as recently embellished by the PPP Government, with PNC support, peppered with periods when the file would slip its routing tethers, take a break from this hectic odyssey and hide in a limbo land until fully rested or inadvertently awakened!

Ironically the Colonial Office in London could recruit someone, whether from Britain or a colony, for any colonial posting within a few months--much of that time spent waiting for mail to cross the Atlantic Ocean, now considerably speeded up with the advent of air mail. The Guianese process, although Colonial Office based, took a year or sometimes longer to get the same recruit. Had it not been for my mother's illness and the incredibly supportive University College Hospital at Mona, Jamaica, and its Pathology Department's head Gerrit Bras, that kept me on staff for nine months on a month-by-month basis until the slow wheel in BG had turned its circle, I would not have survived the frustrating process, with a family to mind.

Most of us were willing to face a certain level of instability and inefficiency, and to work to reduce it, each in his/her own way. So while Jagan complained that doctors in particular had not returned from the UCWI as expected, and in general that Jamaica was swallowing up the best graduates, he appeared oblivious to the ineptitudes in his own administration, the same one that was to take on his centralist responsibility for industrialisation! (I could hear Tulla laughing.)

No one could explain to me why it took nine months for the PSC to complete my recruitment even though I had appeared in person at the Ministry of Health, been interviewed by Dr Nehaul, the Deputy CMO, who had endorsed my application all in two weeks! By contrast it took the Barbados and Trinidad governments less than two months to get a graduate appointed, and the University College Hospital just a few weeks. When I told Jagan these things, he recalled that my sister had told him of the delays and he had referred the matter to the Minister of Health, who simply passed it on to his CMO and Permanent Secretary, all of whom were also waiting for Jagan's approval!

I put this position to Lyle Harewood; he astonished me when he affirmed that many 'improvements' had been made but the lower costs achieved by centralising appointments and other functions of government (which all parties favoured) had been offset by new inefficiencies in cases of professional (and other, as I would find out) appointments, stemming from the need to consult every department that might, however remotely, be affected by the candidate, in addition to all concerned with approving the appointment, including the Ministries of Home Affairs (the Police), Housing, and Public Works.

I knew, from my stint as a personnel officer in the British Colonial Service 1950-51, that the process--put in place in all the colonies, to favour the employment of UK nationals and ensure loyalty to the Colonial Office--had been modified in places that had achieved internal self-government, except, it seemed, in BG, which instead of developing systems to improve internal administration, appeared bent on making it more cumbersome, complex and self-defeating. In my case the file had languished for *seven* months *in Jagan's office*, and was there *at the time of my sister's enquiry*!

To make matters worse Government Ministries often failed to meet contract obligations as promptly as they should or could. My almost bitter struggle to secure housing as agreed illustrates. Having waited nine months for confirmation of appointment I decided to travel alone to BG on the advice of my brother to make sure that conditions were satisfied before committing the family to join me. I stayed with my sister for two months awaiting allocation of a flat or house, as agreed. Finally, I was called to the Ministry of Health's Personnel Office to review and sign my contract, having twice delayed it pending assignment of housing.

The Chief Personnel Officer was a former acquaintance from my time in the Civil Service, who empathised when I told him, as politely and as firmly as I could, that having waited *two months* for a flat, knowing there were vacant ones at the hospital, I would not sign the contract unless, within 24 hours, I had a key in my hand to suitable accommodations, and that I was prepared to cancel my family's travel from Jamaica and quit. I still had a standing offer of a residency in vascular surgery at the University of Miami School of Medicine.

He went to see the Housing Officer next door while I waited. Since the wall between the two rooms was a partial one, I easily overheard their conversation. He started by telling the Housing Officer in a low voice that I was in his office, but that did not affect the latter's tone or manner.

"You finalise his housing yet?" he whispered.

"No decision on that one." The Housing man was emphatic, speaking in a normal voice.

"You joking, two months gone already, maan! What's the hold-up?" He was again careful to speak in a whisper.

"Ragbeer is from heah, who 'e think 'e is?" his voice carried easily and sounded resentful. "Because he's a doctor he think he can demand anything. Why he don' go live at he own house in Hadfield Street? He family got a big place dey; why he don' go dey? Luck live at he fada place in Smyth Street, why Ragbeer cyaan do de same?"

"Keep you' voice down, maan. Is different, you should know; Luck renting, not bunking, like Ragbeer. That Hadfield Street place is he sister's; he don't have a natural right to live there."

"So wha'? Is he family, he close family; we got to keep de flats dem for people coming from abroad who ent got no family heah."

"But that is *your* problem, not the doctor's. You still have to find him housing; his family comin' in a week and he just tell me that if he don't get a place to stay by this time tomorrow latest, he won't sign de contract and he'll tell them not to come. I have to agree with him; he already wait *two* months while you make styles. DCMO and PS pressing me on this and Gool Khan, the Lab Manager, keep calling. Settle it today, maan!"

"What I gon do if I give him a flat and a foreign doctor come and I have nothing to give him?"

"When you expectin' de next one?"

"Ah don' know, four, six months; we negotiatin'."

"How many empties you got?"

"We got two flats, and two houses."

"Four empties?" He asked incredulously, and exclaimed, his voice raised. "Four empties! You must be nuts! He only need one, and you have nobody else in sight! What in hell is wrong with you? What you waiting for? Jeesus! And I'm the one they pressurin'."

"He contract is Registrar; he only entitle to a flat; he not entitled to house...."

"But the contract *says* we have to provide *housing* or pay rent; it don't say flat or house; it just says standard housing. The man got nearly four years' experience; he has a family of five; Government give engineers who just graduate a house; you have four premises, two flats; what preventing you from releasing one to him?"

"I still think he can go live with he family."

"That's unreasonable, and everybody from PS to me agree with the doctor. You better move you ass on this. If they come and we have to put up he family, five of them, in a hotel, while you play the ass, you might end up paying the bill. How you like duh? Come on, maan, ease up and don't let you prejudice show. It look like you don' like him, something personal? I notice you frown the first time I give you his name; wha' happen; you know him? From school?"

"Nooo; he went to Queen's, I was at Central; but same time. I never met the man; all I know he was the big language star; even JC was saying he would try to get him to teach at Central."

"Now I see; that was the job you di' looking! But he wasn't the one that take it from you."

He frowned, lowering his gaze. "What I don't understand is how he turn doctor and specialist so quick. He like me, never do science. How so?"

"Lemme brief you a little." He lowered his voice almost to a whisper but the thin wall failed to stifle the words and by now I was really listening. "The guy for real; he bright no rass. You know he did this same job I have now in Personnel. Was his first posting. He was 18. Charlie Petrie say he learnt everything in three months and took over the desk when he went on long leave. Imagine a Class II Temp filling in for a Class I and soon after doing confidential work for the DMS. And the only help he got was his friend Neville Linton, another clever one. Everybody in the office shocked and they had good people, Lyle Harcwood, CO Joseph, Massiah, that Mittelholzer dame, the one with the body, and then Yvonne Eleazar, Joe, I forget he last name, the Indian chap, you know de one who was in the Chief Secretary's office."

"You mean Leila, I hear he resigning and going to England."

"Well, maybe; you remember Miss Gravesande, petite and pretty, she and Eleazar did like him bad; they said he and Neville were the nicest fellows, easy-going and friendly. When he left for University, the office staff gave him a going-away gift, a nice blue and gold Waterman's fountain pen, engraved with gold, real nice. The DMS Dr Eddey, Chief Clerk, Lewis — what we call PS today--his boss C O Joseph and Yvonne all made speeches. When Yvonne handed him the pen he kissed her, then went 'round the room and kissed every female even the three old virgins, the two Lewis women and Olga Dempster — they called her the fortress--she turned purple; the oldest Lewis, Elsie I think her name was, giggled and blushed like a teenager with the excitement."

He chuckled as he recalled the scene. "Rumour had it that she'd never been kissed; I don' believe that. Then he shook every man's hand and said he can't ever forget them because he would be holding them close in his hand for every note he took. Sweet talk, like somebody high, he had them eatin' out of his hand that day. I met him first when we debate against one another years before, and then at cricket, and we talk a few times at the Y when I was at Lands & Mines; he quite regular; not the pushy type. So I think you're wrong and you holding a bad grudge--your fault, not his. So cool down and do right. Gi'e the man his flat today, tomorrow latest, because if you don't, he will go back where he came from quick as that," he snapped his fingers, "if everything we hear about him is true; and you, my friend, *you* will be in real shit!"

I would spend many hours urging PSC officials — and party brass in the committee on which I later sat — to accept the devolution of most appointments to the responsible Ministry, leaving the PSC to set guidelines, advise, oversee, audit and arbitrate. Harewood, perhaps the most respected civil servant then, wished the same, but diehard civil servant that he was, he could only advise and not agitate for change. In any event he was near retirement and would not be there to argue for the long haul. Mohamed Ali, an old friend and one of Harewood's deputies, probably his successor-in-waiting, would only recite the appropriate regulations, and agree that some changes would be good, but like his boss concluded that it was a matter for the Executive Council, of which Jagan was Chairman or Co-Chairman and was fully aware of the difficulties!

Again, it seemed, the ball had been fumbled in Jagan's court, or had he and the ExCo been deliberately stalling appointments? Stanley Luck, from conversations with his contacts in the PPP and drawing on experiences of others, produced evidence that Jagan *had* endorsed the unwieldy process to centralise control of appointments and to ensure by "close scrutiny of credentials and affiliations" — as one PPP official had put it--that decision-making in Government Services was not in the hands of "undesirable elements". Moreover, enough and critical room had to be left open for those for whom the Party had secured scholarships to Soviet bloc universities, a few of whom had begun to trickle back fresh with their communist credentials. It was essential, too, to have positions and housing available for known sympathisers and activists who could help to further the "socialist" cause.

The appointment of Jack Kelshall, a Trinidadian communist, who had no knowledge of BG, had been one of the latter. Even though not strictly a Civil Service appointment, his designation as Personal Secretary to Premier Jagan had put him in direct contact (and conflict) with the heads of the Civil Service, including the Clerk of the Legislature. Such contacts had hitherto been seen as the privileges of position, usually restricted to senior civil servants. It was said that he knew Kathleen McCracken, wife of Harold Drayton, the alleged BG communist expelled by UCWI. The appointment dismayed many PPP supporters, infuriated the Service and tended to confirm the extreme left course that Jagan had set.

Kelshall was obviously bringing nothing to BG beyond being non-Indian and an experience as a communist organiser among youth in Trinidad — that much was plain from his *curriculum vitae*; it rankled that there were many Guianese with superior education and skills, in and out of the Civil Service, who could have served admirably as Jagan's private secretary.

Among emerging nations of the Caribbean it was highly unlikely that Eric Williams, Norman Manley or Grantley Adams would even *think* of appointing a non-native to such a position, and any leader crass enough to do it would succumb quickly to the political fall-out. Many, even within the PPP, saw it as a slap in the face of the qualified people already within the Party ranks. Jagan, on the other hand, saw it as an expression of the 'international' scope of his thinking, and vigorously and blindly defended the embarrassing appointment, much as he had done his choice of Burnham in 1950.

It was amazing that Jagan could ignore what was plain for all to see; I know that he was advised that his actions, including the courting of Castro, were leading to increased isolation and rejection by Caribbean leaders, who were far more attuned to the realities of the region, socially and economically, and to the power of the USA and what McCarthyism had done there to leftist causes in the fifties. It was incredible that he could so unalterably fail to note that Caribbean politics, Cuba excepted, had shifted away from the totalitarian diatribe of the fifties towards middle-of-the-road policies shorn of the litter of extremist ideologies. Changes, many induced by the Cold War, had forced leaders to pay attention to human nature, desires and behaviour to gain and hold the support they needed from their own citizens and from the West, once independence was achieved.

The Barbadian Errol Barrow had returned home in 1950 after distinguished WWII service in the RAF, joined Grantley Adams' party to push for independence, but split to form a socialist party similar to Jagan's; but after coming to grips with reality, he had slackened his pace and moderated his socialism on discovering that the majority electorate, nearly all black and spared racism, were ideologically moderate; he would later become Prime Minister of a stable and relatively self-sufficient and progressive country.

Even Jamaica, in many ways identical to Cuba, and perhaps the best candidate for Communism among the British colonies, had begun to steer clear from Cuba and had openly rejected Castro's style of government, even though there was widespread admiration for the man and for Che Guevara (almost a household name in Jamaica) and for their achievements. But Jamaica had not been a dictatorship controlled by the American Mafia, though it had strong elements of British paternalism and segregation still. The socialist PNP under Norman Manley had looked at the reality of Jamaica's position and relationships, and, despite strong nostalgia for past leftist activism, had moved towards the ideological middle[133] carrying its support along that path, and in the process had dismissed communist elements including Richard Hart and Ferdinand Smith.

Jagan was quick to blame the UCWI for anti-communist attitudes and used them as an argument to set up his own University on ideological lines and under his control to train his sycophants. He had candidates enough in the PYO. What he had overlooked in puzzling over Jamaica, was the positive influence of the United States on the country, many of whose citizens had relatives there whose remittances added considerably to family fortunes in Jamaica or helped to get qualified members there.

This was almost the opposite of the trenchant analyses and justifiable condemnation of US brigandry by Hart and other intellectuals whose essays were widely read and provided material for many a "bullshit" session at the Students' Union or in the Halls of residence. In recalling this I would hear again Al Chin Sang's distressed comment, "Eight years ago he tried to get Hart and Smith, both Jamaicans, to help him agitate, and lost a government for that; today it's a Trinidadian, Kelshall; tomorrow we'll all be speaking Cuban; what that tell you? We Guianese are not communists; we vote for Jagan in '53 to get us to run our own affairs, not to import Communists to do it! Today Jagan eight years older, but he not one day smarter; and still I vote for him!"

Guianese media had done little to inform its audience of the major changes taking place in Education and ignored the many UCWI graduates in several disciplines contributing to strengthening national manpower and reducing reliance on foreigners. The media did pay some attention to some medical graduates. They had noted the return of Bunny Lowachee, Stan Luck and the two Searwars in the past year or two, but had failed to invite any of them to review or explore the role of the UCWI in BG's agenda. Hublall, Chetram and others like me slipped in unnoticed and not a word was spent, such as *"BG Welcomes New Doctor (Lawyer, Engineer etc)"* with sub header, *"So-and So returns after ... years abroad"*; that was the template for such notices in the social pages of each paper and the "social" hour on radio.

---

[133] Pressured by moderate partisans who were in the majority, by the pro-US Jamaica Labour Party under Alexander Bustamante, externally by the British, and by the US under Truman with its heavy investments in Jamaican bauxite and tourism industries, and the edicts of its "wise men" — lawyers and businessmen who dictated US foreign policy to favour business and post-war reconstruction in Europe — including heavyweights Dean Acheson, George Kennan, Averell Harriman and John McCloy.

As a teenager I used to read the papers from front to back, including, on a rainy or slow day, the advertisements, notices of births, deaths and anniversaries. Every coloured or white civil servant returning from overseas *leave* was duly met and his/her argosy graphically chronicled and posted. None of us, however, got that attention from the press, Keith Tang excepted, who had returned after graduation in 1955, not to work in his homeland, but for a Christmas holiday! And he had rated a two-column headline. Was it because he was a city Chinese and his father owner of a popular sports goods store, with radio and press advertising, who would never miss a chance to promote his cause, his business and his family and had made sure the press knew of Keith's visit?

The subject made for lively debate at the Doctors' Lounge. Someone — Hublall, I think-- suggested that we who had chosen to come back and stick around for a while had qualified as "nuisance, not news". We were not foreign enough, nor members of the favoured set, nor unusual. Indian professionals had become commonplace and perhaps too numerous to be given further publicity. Besides we were widely regarded as additions to Jagan's machine. How different from the occasion, in December 1899, when Dr W H Wharton had returned from Edinburgh as "the first East Indian medical doctor" from BG. That was momentous news and he was suitably greeted by a delegation of prominent Indians of that time who presented him a signed address of welcome; all this was amply reported in *The Daily Chronicle,* and in the *Argosy,* then a weekly (*Daily Graphic* and *Post* came later). It must have been the same when Joseph Luckhoo qualified about the same time as the first Indian lawyer.

However we were trendsetters of a different kind--pioneers of medical education in the British Caribbean-- which colonial experts had declared as problematic and not feasible. Yet these very colonies had been training grounds in Tropical Medicine for the British Colonial Medical Services, and might have remained so, uncluttered by locals trying to muscle in on hallowed territory, had not two world wars and their effects on the manpower pool in Britain added to social and nationalist pressures to change that trend.

Indeed, prior to WWII newly qualified physicians returning to BG had been routinely denied paid positions as Government Medical Officers, which would have given them access to hospitals and rotational training in different specialties to prepare them for general practice or for specialist appointments. Many new doctors had to resort to volunteering to gain local experience (for no British school could really prepare anyone properly for the practice of medicine in the tropics). Dr Nehaul, the Deputy Chief Medical Officer in 1961, had been one of these volunteers 25 or so years earlier. Others rejected by the Government had simply started a practice and ploughed on, unsupervised, neglected as it were, learning by their mistakes!

There was no doubt that the media had indiscriminately taken sides in politics and had already put everyone into stereotypic dossiers. Thus to the press elite the doctors back from the UCWI were just four Indians and three Chinese, all potential Jaganites. Who among them would want to noise it abroad that so many Indians were earning London University degrees? Certainly not the stalwarts of the PNC and UF who controlled the media and would denigrate everything Indian to the point of preaching racial discrimination. Graduates from the Arts and Sciences faculties had preceded us, entering the teaching profession and Government services, and were uniformly highly regarded and had largely steered clear of political parties. PNC racism, PPP communism and the colonial mentality so ingrained in the Guianese middle class constituted the three big strikes that would guarantee the sidelining of talented Indians, especially those who refused to subscribe or kow-tow to the prevailing political and bureaucratic stereotypes

Between 1960 and 1961 one black and five or six other Indian doctors had returned from Universities other than UCWI to work in BG, adding to the small complement of young men and women who could form a nidus for the much desired local medical professional force. The black doctor, Gordon B..., an old QC friend and cricket team-mate, received a pleasant press, while the others were altogether given a line or two at the foot of the article on Gordon, no names mentioned. Gordon, like Dr Jagan, had studied in Washington DC at Howard University, that bastion of higher education for Blacks in the US, and was well-connected, his father having been the popular head teacher of an elementary school in the city. He showed none of the biases Indians feared and was always objective and fair in his judgments. The Indians were all from rural areas and their families unknown to the establishment; they had studied in Europe (UK, Ireland and Germany) and India.

This treatment was one of many illustrations of the role of the major media in perpetuating and perhaps intensifying the divisions among the major races in the country, by ignoring some and openly favouring others creating lingering stereotypes that fed the diatribes of political campaigners. Even high achievers were overlooked, or rarely featured and then given only jealous praise or treated as an exception or circus freak, a few honest appraisals notwithstanding. This was in stark contrast to the attention given to the accomplishments of those whose families were "society" people, regardless of the quality of the attainment or the value of any intrinsic personal story.

As an example Trevor..., one of my classmates and son of a socialite, got a fulsome welcome in the press when he returned to BG with "an engineering degree" after only two or three years study beyond his QC School Certificate (today's "O" levels) at some unfamiliar college in the southern USA. An engineering degree from a British University required four years minimum after the Higher Schools Certificate (today's "A" levels). That meant six years after School Certificate, assuming no obstacles or interruption. In most US universities, it required four years post BSc. On returning to BG Trevor became Georgetown's deputy City engineer while I was just finishing my first year in medical school. Yet he regularly made the press, photo and all, no one wondering how come. (I believe he did attend the College, and that he did get a diploma after a two-year course in *engineering technology*, not Civil Engineering, which is how it was publicised in BG.

To be newsworthy, you had to be white, rightist or well-connected, as Trevor and Keith undoubtedly were. Trevor's father was a well-known solicitor and member of the Interim Government after the PPP debacle of 1953, and, like Tang's, in the eye of the press. Faces like Hublall were not light enough to be white and not dark enough to be black, definitely not the stuff that speaks to the privileged Ladies of Charity, nor to the staid high-coloureds who attended and supported Mr Roth's gatherings at the Georgetown Museum. Hari's doubt was well-founded, after all.

It was slightly better in sports, then dominated by the whites, coloureds and blacks of Georgetown. Few others made national teams. This had led

Thomas Flood earlier in the century to donate a cup for competitive cricket among Indian teams in the three counties. The BGEICC played in Garnet Cup until their move in 1929 to their present site on Thomas lands --obtained in 1926 by Indian envoy Kunwar Sir Maharaj Singh--which gave them a ground large enough to qualify for the higher level Parker Cup, having produced talented players like K Ruhoman and BK Persaud who had had a record partnership of 491 for the 2nd wicket against the white Georgetown Cricket Club (Ruhoman 319). C Pooran and B. Saddick played for BG in 1929; in 1934 Pooran scored 174 in his first appearance in the "Triangular" Tournament (BG, Trinidad, Barbados).

K Ruhoman also played in 1934 against Trinidad and Barbados. It was great news when Ganesh Persaud was selected to play for BG in the Intercolonial Cricket series in the late 1940's, but when Baijnauth, the left arm medium-paced swing bowler from Berbice made that same team a little later the press was harsh and decried his naiveté wondering whether he could mix with the more sophisticated members of visiting and host teams. They ridiculed his rural background, his discomfort with shoes, his rough manners, especially unfamiliarity with cutlery and inability to speak Standard English (most rural Indians ate with their fingers and spoke the local dialect).

But he proved his worth by performing well enough to be included in a subsequent overseas touring team. Yet the Guianese press kept the adverse spotlight on him, demanding a level of perfection at each appearance that certainly affected his performance.

He was left out of later teams but his emergence was the first of several talented Indian cricketers from the same area of Berbice, Port Mourant, Jagan's home, who came to dominate for several years the national and later West Indies team and English League cricket (Rohan Kanhai, Joe Solomon and Basil Butcher).

Rohan Kanhai would rise to great heights and create records as a batsman. The Guianese press would be late or grudging in acknowledging his great talent, flaunting instead their non-Indian favourites from Georgetown and Garfield Sobers of Barbados. In the pre-war era it was more common for Indian players to be criticised for failure than congratulated for success.

Baijnauth was not allowed to grow his talent in the way Jamaican Roy Gilchrist did. He was a very rough diamond discovered in rural Jamaica in the mid-fifties. An excellent fast bowler, he became a fixture and an embarrassment on West Indies Cricket teams until persistent uncouth conduct led to his downfall. Throughout his career, despite recurring misconduct, the Jamaican press dealt leniently with him. Baijnauth could have done with such empathy.

In politics as in sports, the same scrutiny and response obtained. As Chin Sang had pointed out, Jagan's failure in 1953 recalled the previous 1928 "failure" of a democratic government in BG. In 1891, BG and a few other colonies had been ruled under a relatively advanced "self-governing" constitution, which had by the 1920's engendered enough trust and confidence among the local population that they and their representatives felt comfortable and mature enough to pursue a populist agenda. Enough local (creole) legislators had emerged with fresh ideas and a distinctly local perspective to want to implement changes. As bad luck would have it the reigning planters did not share popular enthusiasm for the changes and engineered a suspension of democracy in 1928, which put an end to thoughts of reform.

People like JB Singh, who was politically active at the time, quickly learned the dangers of going too far too fast, and devised a strategy to achieve positive political progress by first gaining economic and social strength, and a broad base of educated and skilled people involved in viable activities---farming, trades, commerce, professions--to create a significant electorate to dilute the influence of the planters and their ilk. Unless one could repeat Castro or revive Bolivar.

Barring that approach one had to make haste slowly, to achieve a sort of social epeirogeny. This line of thinking was clearly not as appealing as the more animated campaign to overthrow the long-standing oppressor, led by two charismatic young men with none of the wisdom, inhibitions, tact, patience or experience of the older and more reserved generation, and spurred by the rosy possibility of immediate power and material gain. In 1952-3, arguments against the PPP tactics of bravado and extravagant promises would be ignored and criticized as the feeble last ditch stance of city slickers who were no longer insulated or protected by a franchise restricted by property and literacy qualifications.

The orientation and attitudes of the Guianese press and people were nicely illustrated by the treatment given to visitors. We had a succession of medical visitors in the two years I was there, especially after the unexpected PPP victory in August 1961.

A few weeks later, Dr A B Raper came from Bristol, England; I had the duty of squiring him on his official tours of places and major institutions. Locals were expected to and generally did defer to foreigners, who usually arrived in the colony with haloes, especially those who came for short "expert" stints under sponsorship by agencies of the British Government such as Dr Raper's sponsor, the British Council, or by other foreign agencies.

Besides Dr. Raper two groups of high ranking Americans attracted attention. One was a pair of physicians from California's Loma Linda University, Drs John Peterson and Robert Soderblom visited the Georgetown Hospital. Reasons for their visit were vague and not shared with us. The hypothesis that the US needed to understand our medical capabilities in the event of serious civil strife gained ground when later the same day Dr R.A McComas from the US Public Health Services Division of Foreign Quarantine toured the Hospital accompanied by David Hughes, a US vice-consul.

Almost exactly a year later, in July 1962, five months after terrible acts of violence, looting and incendiarism against Indians, we hosted psychiatrists Drs F. McCandless and Philip Serge from the University of Albany, New York, also on a vague mission; a snide rumour spread that they were sent to ascertain the mental status of the major party leaders in view of the general state of insanity into which they had so far succeeded in bringing the country and to suggest a line of treatment and prognosis for the guidance and entertainment of the US State Department and, by the bye, the CIA! Later we heard that they were actually finalising a student externship program with our Internal Medicine Department. (Dr Hamilton, the head, used the occasion to have them interview Stanley who was then having a relapse; nothing new came of this, to no one's surprise).

In December 1962 a group of US virologists--Drs J. Witte, M Page and H. Gelfand--came from the CDC, Atlanta, Georgia during the epidemic of Polio that hit BG, killing 9 children (whom I autopsied) and maiming many. The epidemic provided the CDC a timely opportunity for the world's first large scale use of the Sabin (oral) Polio vaccine, which undoubtedly lessened the burden of illness during that terrible outbreak. The CDC physicians had little clinical interest having come to identify the strain of the virus for epidemiologic purposes and to study the body's response to the vaccine which they had not been able to do ethically in the USA. I coordinated our Laboratory's role and supervised city immunisation teams.

Dr E.S. Tikasingh, a virologist from the Trinidad Regional Virus Laboratory was the first scientist to answer our calls for help, as BG had no virology laboratory; he arrived without fanfare and directed the collection of samples for diagnostic studies; his contributions were invaluable. I was assigned to liaise and squire each of these groups and thus saw first-hand the obsequiousness with which the media greeted and treated the Americans, elevating them to celestial pedestals, as they had done Dr Raper in 1961. But they hardly noticed Dr Tikasingh's seminal and superior clinical work.

Dr Alan Raper

Dr Raper was a Bristol haematologist, touring the Caribbean giving a lecture or two at each stop and, purportedly, assessing the medical laboratory capacity of the colonies on behalf of the Colonial Medical Services. Why this in 1961, on the eve of the British departing seemed suspicious, especially as the CMS had delayed and almost certainly abandoned the rebuilding of the hospital, and no one seemed to know exactly what the outcome of the mission would be. Dr Nicholson, the CMO, did not seem to know when he summoned me for the briefing, nor did Dr Nehaul, the Deputy.

The ungenerous teased that Raper was a low level spy sent to find out how doctors really felt about Jagan, by listening to their off-the-cuff remarks while discussing cases, facilities, needs, government responses to health care issues, and so on. Plausible, but was this believable? Certainly in those crucial years we did see a procession of British Council 'experts'. (Later on rumours were strong that the two US psychiatrists were working undercover for the CIA, which seemed likely in view of their seeming lack of clinical skills.)

During his two-week stay we visited Bartica Hospital, the Reynolds Bauxite Co Clinic at Everton on the Berbice River, the New Amsterdam Hospital and several medical facilities in Georgetown. I organised "rounds" with staff at which he was shown clinical cases in his field, but uncommon in his country. He was deeply appreciative and thanked the staff for "expanding my horizons". After each trip he met with Ministry officials.

Raper avoided the limelight and was embarrassed by a spate of private invitations to a meal somewhere, every day, and worse when the press sought him out for an interview each day of his two-week stay. Mercifully we were able to refer them to the British Council, which they knew was the proper channel, but were trying to circumvent. I told him that was the price he had to pay for being a white Englishman and a doctor at that, in the colonies, where people like him were few and fawned on, viewed by the local society types, the 'wannabees', as a sort of messiah, with something between envy and veneration. The press in BG flattered celebrity--any foreign white face, especially if a professional, was, *ipso facto,* a celebrity, with Englishmen at the apex of the heap. Hostesses, fed on British lore, pounced on them eager to feed them and hear their accents and their lectures ad lib., preferably without understanding a word they had said.

How different their dealings with locals, especially Indians, no matter what their credentials. Professor Harry Annamunthodo, a former Guiana scholar, who had by then achieved a deserved fame in London, at the UCWI and in the Caribbean for his brilliance as a surgeon and teacher, was adamant that he would not work in BG. He resented the blatant displays of snobbery, hypocrisy, indifference towards local achievers, barring scions of prominent and influential families; that reeked of racial bias and denigration.

This biased attitude to him and other local sons and daughters of humble birth had kept many gifted scholars out of the country. A family acquaintance, Dr Chang, a bright Chinese man of modest Albuoystown parentage, had made quite a name for himself after qualifying as a public health physician and gone on to lead an expert group at the WHO in Geneva. His mother gave us news of his progress, and bemoaned the fact that despite his high achievements, he had to remain away from family in a distant land because "the BG Government has no place for him; he keeps writing them!"

The intellectual divide was clear to me in 1961. People like Harry Annamunthodo or Stanley Luck or Lowachee or me were judged to know too much of the Caribbean and were of the wrong stripe; we were thus anathema. Besides, we were insiders, with interests more enduring than transient. We wanted more than the daily fare of crass, repetitive and stereotypical accounts of issues facing the new nation. We expected more from the media than the hollow reportage of national pastimes: social events of the ruling class (*gubernalia,* I had dubbed it), party politics, trade unionism, cricket, and the personalities involved.

Although they considered themselves intellectuals, few reporters or columnists then had more than a didactic high school education and the mere ability to put sentences together with proper syntax was enough to qualify. Critical or in-depth thinking--although intuitive in many--was inconsistent, and indulged it seemed only at the whim of owners. Triviality prevailed, embellished with clichés, stereotypes, journalese and pedantry. Most media folk were people like us, locals, and seemed uncomfortable with the fact that their own kind did include many with superior talents and learning more often than not eclipsing those of foreigners. To acknowledge talent in a non-white would mar the myth of the superiority of those from "away" so carefully inculcated in them over the past two hundred years by those from "away"! So locals who had risen above the crowd were largely ignored. They were anomalous, mysterious, threatening.

Dr. Raper noted ruefully how I was ignored in all the joint interviews with the press, when what I had to say might be more relevant and important than his fleeting view of things; he said this once to a well-known coloured reporter, unsettling him—but he was too ungracious or inept to apologise. Later he said the same thing to the Minister of Health, Ranji Chandisingh, who responded in silence with a drunken sphinx-like gaze. Again I had to bring Dr. Raper down to BG earth. Here it was not how right you were, or what you were or knew, or contributed, but how *white* or *red* you were, especially if the *red* was indelible!

I told him of the racial and colour hierarchy pervading Caribbean society, even predominantly black societies like Jamaica, where he would see the same reverence for the foreigner and some subtle variations on the theme of regard for gradations of skin tone among the population, engendered by his own people as a controlling tool. In a spirit of camaraderie we discussed on several occasions informally with others after concluding formal sessions, oiled with a drink or two, the pressing issues of colonial existence, new and fascinating to him.

Raper had expected the media to be more sophisticated and to adopt a constructive role in nation-building since they were in a position to stimulate the positive thinking needed to unite the different interests to work to a common good. Instead they seemed "shallow, obsolete and parochial", promoting barriers and divisions hostile to developing or advancing a progressive national agenda. He was surprised that they were obviously overlooking the rapidly changing face of talent in the country, and denying the reality of rising numbers of brown and black faces qualifying to fill positions of responsibility and authority in most fields of endeavour.

In his discussions with "authorities" he had been pleased to learn that those educated with a Caribbean orientation had gained insights into regional issues beyond those that could be gained from training in Britain or other temperate country alone. The new scholars were able to debate a wide range of subjects with members of the media elite and the older "intellectuals" who instead had retreated behind traditional class barriers to safeguard their primacy.

Thus the new voices were not given a proper hearing from the general media, especially the newspapers and their conservative owners. Since labour had flexed its collective muscle and put a socialist government in power, prudence would dictate that media efforts be directed to win them over by overtures of moderation rather than conflict and insistence that popular rights and choices be summarily condemned and rejected.

We who had come from the UCWI were even more of an enigma. We were seen as definitely a rung or so below our European trained peer, especially if he had attracted a white wife–in which case the focus would shift to the wife, whose colour would justify and excuse any attention paid to him, often much to the poor woman's dismay. The fact was that pride in local things and people did not exist. The British had seen to that. Worker education had to improve and self-esteem nurtured if the aim was to develop an informed and confident new nation, regardless of who governed it.

The politicians were going about it the wrong way, and encouraging, by obfuscation and harangue, divisions and enmities that would destroy rather than build. Raper agreed also with the need to develop a *secure* cadre of natives with expertise in every field of endeavour, real expertise, not just copy-cats of foreign models that often failed badly in unfamiliar settings. The UCWI was created to avoid this and develop training models based on local issues and situations; it did this surprisingly well as its British and later American peers readily and at times effusively acknowledged.

Raper met with a group of UCWI graduates for a perspective on their training and views on the outlook for the College preparing for its weaning from London, in view of Jagan's statement that UCWI was not meeting "Guiana's needs for dynamic socialist thinkers". Stanley, Bunny Low-a-Chee, Zatul Amin, Honnett Searwar, Jan Evertz and I met with him at the Interns Quarters over tea. The group affirmed their satisfaction with their training and would choose UHWI again, recognising its shortfalls, especially in facilities for all subspecialties, and need for expansion to take more students. We did not support the idea of a separate BG university because of the controls and costs involved; besides, the UWI due to be chartered in a year or so was slated to establish Colleges in BG and Trinidad.

The rest of the session dealt with local research opportunities which Stanley outlined were numerous in almost any field of study, not only infectious diseases, (noting that a WHO unit was studying typhoid vaccines and a few itinerant groups were collecting data on malaria and various vector-borne conditions including filariasis and its association with tropical eosinophilia). We identified other topics prominent in BG such as native issues, poisoning, diabetes, strokes and heart disease which were showing unique variations worthy of study especially as we had a racial mix that would add new perspectives to disease incidence and expression. Our problems were lack of funds, facilities and time. Funds could buy technical assistance and field help; government provided hardly any and we had, unlike developed countries, no philanthropic foundations to finance research.

Raper had discussed research with senior physicians and surgeons who had also identified similar conditions for study to amplify medical databases and enhance care internationally. He was impressed with the opportunities he had seen in his brief stay and the general grasp among doctors, young and old, of problems and how to solve them. Although money for objective medical research was a universal shortage, he had formed the impression that we were particularly under-served here, and would convey that to both Jagan and the Colonial Office. He repeated the lack of medical news and discussions in the local media and wondered about links between the profession and media.

This opened a spirited critique of the major press, which Stanley began by accusing them of neglect, bias and politicising of all issues. He noted that apart from overlooking achievements and exploring problems in local medicine, the oldest and once respected *Daily Chronicle* had become stridently "anti-PPP to the point of degrading the quality and reliability of its news and reducing its editorials and general bias to a level below shame and contempt!" It was widely seen as an agent of rebellion.[134]

The *Argosy* had struggled to balance its anti-communist stance with objectivity, but under pressure from its owner, a creole white businessman had also degenerated to an anti-PPP organ sacrificing its reputation and quality and risking its financial viability. The *Guiana Graphic* had maintained near neutrality but one sensed the struggle in its boardroom. The latest entry, the *Evening Post* had promised fairness and accuracy but it too clearly struggled to steer a middle course. None of these papers had an Indian investment, neither in money nor in tradition. More often than not they misrepresented that population.

Since Jagan's supporters were mostly Indians, all Indians by the logic of the media became suspect Communists, especially those with a University education. They advanced the hypothesis that the UCWI had imbibed the blandishments of Karl Marx, since many of Jamaica's early advocates of self-rule: Hart, Smith and others of Jagan's friends — had been Communists; even Norman Manley had distinct socialist leanings. And because the UCWI was located in Jamaica, its students had curiously been identified with the philosophy of these prominent men, none of whom was on the College Faculty! In fact the opposite was true; there were "pitifully few militants" and "radicals", to use Jagan's words, at the UCWI. I've noted elsewhere Jamaica's expulsion for Communist activities of Harold Drayton, a creole white Guianese who had entered the College in 1950, and banned from re-entry. So the red paint used to smear us had two baseless origins: being Indian and studying at the UCWI!

---

[134]In 1962 the Commission of enquiry into the 1962 riots would amplify this criticism and almost accuse the paper of fomenting anarchy and for routinely overlooking the terrible acts perpetrated against law and order by Jagan's political and civil opposition.

A more substantial concern was emerging. Jagan had repeated his intent to develop tertiary education in BG to produce graduates "appropriately oriented" to the needs and realities of BG's "special situation", *viz.* its struggle against imperialism! Jagan asserted that UCWI graduates were not, as a group, as "progressive" as he had hoped. In a speech at a 1960 UCWI Council meeting in Jamaica he had criticised political inertia among students and had hoped to see them "agitate more" for "radical change". Instead they seemed keener on study and on aims to secure stable careers and to gain material success!

Students, he complained, were too conservative! It was small wonder that he paid little attention to their quality and achievements--barring those of a few leftist graduates--tolerating them for their technical or professional skills, but preferring to nurture his own kind in schools of the Soviet bloc. His speech to students impressed only the few known communists; his agitation to change the thrust of student thinking gaining no ground, he left in a huff and shifted his direction to the creation of his own Guianese university.

The establishment of the UCWI had highlighted BG's neglect of financial support for gifted students. It offered fewer full scholarships and bursaries and fewer first class high school places per head of population than most UCWI contributors; its high schools however were among the best in the Caribbean, as reflected in the high rank held by Guianese students in all faculties. Barbados and Jamaica had the highest number of high schools capable of taking students to matriculation and were more generous with scholarships to their students.

The PPP did not increase scholarships. This was surprising as education had been a major plank in its original platform and the first Education Minister had been Mr Burnham. Both leaders had frequently spoken in support of teenagers seeking affordable higher education and had reiterated this position in my interviews with them for the *QC Lictor*.

The following dialogue on the subject had taken place in mid-1950 in Dr Jagan's dental clinic. He was attending to a political crony when Mrs Jagan went into the surgery and told him I had arrived. A few minutes later the drilling stopped and he came to the door and summoned me inside.

"You know this man?" he asked, as I entered the room.

I nodded, recognising Rudy Luck, in the chair. The Lucks were well-known as a talented family, who shared an uncanny resemblance, as if they had all come from the same egg, and released piecemeal at yearly intervals--as I would tease Stanley when I met him two years later at the UCWI. JC, the father of the tribe, was a gifted teacher who had started the Central High School on Smyth Street near Hadfield Street, a few blocks from our home. Central had rapidly become quite popular and had about 400 students. Jagan continued, "Tell him what you told me about the Guiana Scholarship," which Rudy's youngest brother, Donald had just won, having taken two Maths (Pure and Applied) and Latin. I was shy and hesitated.

"You 'fraid of him, because of this Fu Man Chu moustache, or because his name is Luck? Go on, tell him, he's one of us and has good ideas. He's our Education man and might work on this."

I recited the points I had drafted for an article in the inaugural edition of the *QC Lictor* and as I spoke waxed warm on the subject of cramming versus learning to think critically--which Donald Smith, the head of English, had been at pains to drill into us--and weaning from reliance on teachers who "taught" instead of creating the atmosphere for self-directed learning, where teachers were guides, as expected and practised in Universities. The Guiana Scholarship rewarded the former.

I argued that there should be at least four scholarships, two for boys and two for girls, increasing to ten in ten years, with separate awards for Arts and for Sciences, as were offered in Barbados, Jamaica and Trinidad. The single scholarship placed an unfair burden on Arts students whose tests emphasised critical commentary of reading material, analysis or detailed knowledge of context, as well as memory work, which was the major component of science and math tests. In Math particularly, a good student would in the two-year programme be drilled in the common themes and could complete and repeat the favourite problems sufficiently to do them in sleep. Thus it was possible, especially for someone taking the popular trio, Pure Math, Applied Math and Physics to get full marks, an unknown in the Arts. The combination of the two Mathematics plus Latin was considered the "easiest", because the limited scope of the Latin syllabus gave the student ample time to really master it, especially those who did not play representative sports.

At this level tests in the Sciences (Chemistry, Biology and Physics) and Maths were almost entirely quantitative--written and practical--and capable of "yes" or "no" or purely factual answers. A correct answer was not subject to examiner bias. Not so in the Arts (Languages, History, Geography) where tests were mostly qualitative, interpretative, with quantitative features limited to aspects of Geography (among the four subjects I had taken) and much memory work, requiring discursive essays and elaboration of ideas for which there was no single set of references or standards.

You gave your views and were marked on the strength of your arguments--supported by the literature and the work of the specific author(s) studied--and the quality of your compositions. You were very much at the whim of the examiner as to whether he could empathise--sitting in London, Oxford or Cambridge--with the perspective of someone in a remote tropical colony.

The scholarship went to the student with highest aggregate, whatever the subjects. No account was taken of extracurricular activities. (This experience did influence my later concerns for rigour in scientific measurement of performance, to ensure that like was compared with like, to prevent the drawing of erroneous conclusions.) None of the winners of "the Guiana" in the past four years had been a member of a school's sports team or other major extracurricular activity.

Rudy Luck said nothing, could say nothing until Dr Jagan had retreated from his mouth. He rinsed, leaned over the little round sink with its continuous swirl of water that disappeared down the spout, spat a few times into it and rinsed again, wiped his lips dry, then turned in the seat and said, "Boy, you talk like a lawyer, I suppose you going to study Law."

"No", I said. "Geology; I got a scholarship to do Geology."

"Maan," he said, "you go and study Law, and come back and work for us. I suppose he belong to the Party?" That last was directed at Dr Jagan.

"I told him to join whenever he feels."

Rudy asked, "You think anybody in this Government will listen to your argument?"

"Capt Nobbs says that the present way is unfair, and he's a scientist."

"That don't mean a thing, you know that! You have to get the Ex Co to agree; that means the Governor; or McDavid or CS. Tell me, you say you took the scholarship in Arts?"

I nodded.

"What happened?"

"I tried twice. I lost both times to science students."

"So how did you do?"

"Fifth or sixth overall on the first try and I think third second time."

I told him I had assumed that my work would be compared to that of all Arts students and not with that of *all* Arts, Math and Science students, that any comparison would be by *rank*, not marks. For what it was worth I had the consolation of receiving a commendation from the English Literature examiner and had won the Sixth Form Prizes for General Knowledge and Geography for 1949 and 1950 and in 1950 English and French also. The Geography prize was by default since I was the only student at QC doing it at that level. Mr Beckles, our form master had said it was the first time anyone had had four in the same year.

"You know, I agree with you about separate scholarships; if they do it in Barbados, Trinidad and Jamaica, we can do it here. Barbados got half our population but *four* times the scholarships!"

At that moment I felt quite thrilled that a political voice would be raised in support of an idea I had championed. Rudy Luck said, "You should study Law, boy, you really going to do Geology?"

"Yes."

He shook his head. "Who you family? They agree with that?"

I hesitated as usual whenever faced with that question. Should I say DeHoop and give my mother's name, or simply say Georgetown and my sister's family name. City folks did not know rural places and handled Indian names very poorly. In the pause, Dr Jagan said, "You know his brother-in-law, Tulla."

"Tulla? Tulla? Tulla who?"

"Hardeen, man; Magan Hardeen, you know; Hadfield Street; you practically neighbours."

"Oh, Mrs Hardeen is your sister? I know she; great lady, smart; she get rich yet?" I said nothing; then he added, "The new QC soon finished; looks spacious; what you think of it?"

I started to answer, but just then Mrs Jagan came in and ended the conversation by pointing to her watch, saying to me, "You're next," and ushered Rudy into the ante-room.

Earlier that same year, Capt Nobbs had arranged for me to tour the new QC building then under construction at Thomas Lands adjacent to the school's playing fields. It was a good site, cool, and memorable for the pleasant sweeping view of the brown Atlantic from the third floor. The wooden structure rambled over several acres; the superstructure was almost all completed and work was proceeding on the preparations for painting and completion of electrical and other service installations. I was shown details of the building plans and given a tour of the special function rooms, the offices, laboratories and library. Several detached bungalows were being built for the Principal and senior staff on the south campus perimeter.

I wrote almost ecstatically of the modern facilities for learning, and the promise that the new building would realise for so many students qualified to enter; but I did wonder whether more of the structure should have been of hollow brick or similar material that was less flammable and cheaper to maintain. Capt Nobbs had often complained of the high cost of maintaining public buildings, especially those made of wood. The British architect who escorted me through the premises looked searchingly at me when I asked the question, and said something about cost and availability of materials, and the "laudable" desire to use local materials!

In my inaugural edition of the *QC Lictor* the main articles would have been the one on Jagan, the Guiana scholarships, and the review of the new building-- as a follow-up to an article published in the 1949 *QC Magazine*, of which I was associate editor with John Adamson. I questioned the wisdom of constructing science and other technical units out of wood, especially when gas would be piped throughout those rooms, all of which were on the ground floor. Economising on safety and foregoing low cost maintenance did not seem wise, and was certainly not in the long-term interests of the school or nation. This conclusion was not entirely original, and had emerged after discussion of my doubts with people I knew then who were experienced in construction: my sister, brother-in-law Tulla and Mr Hackett, the contractor who had just completed their Hadfield Street building. Friends at school, including Mr Cameron Tudor, history master, and Captain Nobbs, Principal, had agreed, but the Colonial Secretariat censored the *three* articles.

A year later as a civil servant I would discover that London had reduced the budget on capital projects in various colonies and postponed others. The much-delayed QC building had been approved finally on a much reduced budget and several structural features had been downgraded. At the same time the new Georgetown Hospital construction had been postponed, 'pending further study'. The reasons had been shared with a few local politicians, and certainly not with the anti-British neophytes of the PPP agitating for power in 1950. But in 1957 two British officials, E. Davis and A. Stokes, had visited the Hospital along with two medical consultants and on leaving Stokes had commented "We hope to return soon to start building a new Hospital." That did not happen.

We informed Dr Raper that nothing more had been heard of this new hospital which the entire country had expected since 1947. He confessed he was puzzled by all this and agreed that we had a broad basis for complaint; he then summarised his impressions. He had met many technicians and professionals who would "grace any institution in my city of Bristol, and elsewhere in Britain, I'm sure." He had admired their work under conditions varying from the simply difficult to the primitive, noting the outmoded buildings, the limited facilities, especially for emergencies, the high maintenance features and evidence of neglect and want in the Government hospitals he had visited in Georgetown, Bartica and New Amsterdam--clearly a Colonial Office matter--while the private St Joseph's Hospital in Georgetown and the Bauxite Co. clinic in Berbice were well-appointed. He felt that our physicians' ideas on physical facilities, staffing and organisation--as it emerged in discussions--had seemed "right, realistic and proper" and should be implemented.

He confessed that until I had taken him to a sugar estate and he had seen the conditions of work, housing and social life he had assumed that the coal mines of Wales and other parts of Britain were the worst exemplars of human exploitation and degradation. Later he had met with a group of nurses who had trained in Britain, at a social hosted by the British Council. He had been impressed with their grasp of wants and needs for the Nursing Services, and had undertaken to seek equipment and an expansion of post-graduate training for them, one of the things that Leila had talked about, supported by Matron Marion Harding and the Deputy CMO, both in attendance.

They had talked frankly and he was "pleased indeed" that no attempt had been made to stifle free expression. Even so he could sense a tension between the Indians and Blacks. He admitted that until this trip he had thought of all Indians as natives of India and had only a sketchy idea of the extent and duration of indenture, "as I'm sure is the same for all people of my upbringing and education". He was aware of the press-ganging of locals but had thought that confined to service at sea. Extensive and systematic indenture was not a learning issue in provincial schools. It was generally felt that the abolition of slavery had ended that form of labour. This was a shocking admission, as we had uniformly assumed that *all* British folk knew of the indenture programmes and of the horrors of colonial life that had made their higher standard of life possible! His discomfort was obvious and his apology on behalf of his countrymen genuine.

He remained troubled by "the bias and negligence of the press" despite the British Council's warnings of what to expect. But the reality was worse and bias had been reduced to pettiness that "is almost pathological and a bad omen for an emerging society." As an example he noted that he and I had travelled together for the entire period of his visit and each occasion had been reported, yet no mention had ever been made of me or who I was or what role I played on these trips and visits.

He told me that Dr Nehaul had proudly said that I was one of the "new young men who would be taking the Services into the future." He had therefore seen me not just as his escort and medical liaison but as a person of trust and promise whose ideas were worth examining. For this reason the press omissions had bothered him, one in particular where I had been trimmed out of a newspaper photograph illustrating our visit to Everton where issues on industrial health had been discussed with the Company's American physician and nurses and with Raper's prompting I had contributed the views of our doctors (we had aired the issues in the previous week knowing of the upcoming visit). The newspaper photograph showed only the pilot and Raper beside the chartered four-seater Cessna airplane that had taken us there, while the two prints given to him had shown the three of us. The article omitted any mention of me or the substantial contribution I had made to the meeting; he felt that my views were part of the story whether they agreed with them or not.

I had not seen him betray his emotions until then: he shook his head in disapproval, his forehead creased, his lips set, verging on anger. In answer to his question, I confirmed that I had not been given a copy, but I assured him I had expected none and did not mind. I had been seen as one of "Jagan's boys", and thus deserved no support or publicity. But how insensitive, presumptuous and stupid of the paper to assume that Raper would miss the difference between the two versions of the picture, or the poor reporting, or worse, that in spotting it would not wonder about the omission!

The paper had cast Raper in its own bigoted light, concluding that he would not object to the biased presentation, nor discuss it with me. Raper apologised as if it had been his error and indicated that he would present the "proper" photograph to Dr Jagan, and make sure that "he understood the invaluable contributions you have made throughout my stay". I assured him that I was inured to the antics and foibles of politicians and press, and expected no fairness from them. As to our local politicians I held no real hope of reform. But perhaps in time the press might improve and achieve its potential for spreading truthful information and fair comment but I would remain a sceptic.[135]

I was glad to meet Dr Raper; he was a simple and kindly man, quite straightforward in his ways, and genuinely enquiring and helpful. He agreed that the Hospital should be replaced and geared for a teaching role. The CML appeared self-sufficient as a basic laboratory, but should soon be given the resources to expand into specialised testing, forensics and virology, as the poliomyelitis epidemic at the end of that year and later deaths from Parathione poisoning would underline.

He praised our laboratory effusively, assessing our staff as well-trained and highly skilled and "every bit as proficient as any in my own University laboratories". High praise indeed. When he asked me what I should like him to say to Dr Jagan, I hesitated, then urged him to say exactly what he had told us in his final talk, that we were doing as well as anyone could with the inadequate resources given; that we were under-equipped and could not introduce efficiencies nor do tests, like electrophoresis (to study blood proteins and diagnose certain disorders prevalent in the black population), nor intensively investigate the high diabetes and heart disease rates in Indians; and that the peripheral laboratories needed radical upgrading to save Jagan's index "ordinary man" time, inconvenience, expense and anguish because most tests had to be referred to the city.

The New Amsterdam and Suddie laboratories, we had agreed, should be developed as full service laboratories, each with a pathologist, or at least a chief technologist as head.

Research was essential for every health service and professionals should be expected to engage in it and be given the capacity to do it systemically; he would have no difficulty emphasising this to Dr Jagan and in his report to the British Council. He had taken his assignment seriously, confessed his inadequacies and thanked us for "your many courtesies, not the least being your open sharing of views." In turn we were pleased he had visited and had so quickly become one of us to the point that we could trust him with our frankness in reciprocating his. We shared good wishes and gave him names of UC graduates he might meet in his travels to the islands. If he *were* a spy he was a damned clever one!

---

[135] A year later one paper, the *Guiana Graphic,* would interview me and carry a photo of three technologists and me on the eve of our departure from BG. I suspect the prominence was the paper's way of making a political statement adversely critical of a government that would stand by and watch the depletion of its technical staff but poised to replace it with others more "politically palatable". The reporter did not go into the training and staffing issues I had raised with Government; the item merely showed the photograph and caption without comment! I was hardly surprised.

Chapter 12

I return to Mabaruma in the New Year for the murder trial; the accused is convicted for manslaughter. He has already been banished by the tribe. The Corporal shows my wife the sights; he winces a little at her criticism of political leaders, including Burnham; he reveals something of his early life and development of an aversion for Indians based on "heathen" religious practices, which he understands better now. We see an ugly side of Mr Mohamed. I reflect on meetings months earlier with the American agent, Steve, which allowed Shah and me to critique extremism – USSR Communism and US corporatism finding Steve out of his depth (a local incident is cited which had fuelled rage against the US) – and gain insights into US views on BG which we had given to Dr Jagan before his trip to Washington; he is also reminded of predecessors and contemporaries whose ideas he had adopted and urged not to discard wise counsel nor bury BG deeper in the Cold War. By year end Burnham amplifies anti-PPP rhetoric, urging mobs to continue harassing civilians and openly carry out daylight robberies by the "choke and rob" technique; Indian women and men walking alone are prime targets. The Minister of Home Affairs, Mr Rai, wishes to add Indians to the Police Force to improve its range and credibility. Jagan objects.

The Trial; Espionage and "Choke and Rob" in the Capital

The difference between a caprice and a long life passion is that the caprice lasts longer; simple pleasures are the last refuge of the complex. Oscar Wilde, *The Picture of Dorian Gray*

It disturbs me no more to find men base, unjust, or selfish than to see apes mischievous, wolves savage, or the vulture ravenous. J. Sartre

The trial lasted less than one day. The circuit judge had arrived by plane several days before my wife and me, and had been busy trying the accumulated cases. On the fourth day he dealt with our case. The evidence was straightforward; the prisoner, a slight young man, seventeen or perhaps eighteen, who resembled Moses from Cokerite, sat impassive in the dock through the recitation of his crime and the events that followed.

A translator carefully relayed to him each sentence. His defender was a young Indian lawyer appointed by the Court, and not much older than I, who went through the motions to satisfy the procedural requirements, and little else, although he did ask me a few questions. Doris, led by the prosecutor, gave the court details of the investigation which the court reporter dutifully recorded in shorthand, and the translator relayed to the accused.

I told the court what I had found and why the victim had died, and satisfied it that the process and all documentation had been properly completed. I was cross-examined on my youth and experience or the lack of it, and on the effects of time on the accuracy of assigning cause of death. I admitted my relative youth and that this had been my first exhumation, but could see no reason why youth would taint my testimony any more than it would discredit his role as defender! I told him I would leave it up to the Court to decide whether inexperience had affected the quality or completeness of the data we had collected and their interpretation.

The judge smiled surreptitiously. To the defence's second question, I described the autolytic process and how it might vary under different conditions. I showed what it had done in this case and concluded that it did not affect our main diagnosis, pointing out the main features on the photographs, which I had already described in my evidence. Though slowed by the need for translation, the matter was despatched within the day.

The young man was found guilty of manslaughter and sentenced to six months in jail, in addition to time already spent, a far more lenient sentence than he had gotten at the tribal trial. There, as Hari had told us, he had been banished from the village, left to fend for himself, and enjoined from coming within contact range of the village or any member of the tribe. Now no one in Mabaruma would answer with any conviction what would happen to the wretched man on release from jail; his dejection was plain to see and he hardly spoke to anyone, not even the interpreter. Doris had thought that arrest had been a relief for the young man and had for a while improved his mood visibly. Perhaps the dejection had returned with the knowledge that he would soon have to fend for himself again in a difficult and strange environment since his sentence of banishment from the tribe still stood. Perhaps the missionaries at St Bede's might agree to supervise his recovery, but for the time being no one seemed to care or know what to do.

I felt sorry for the youth and shared with Doris my fear that he might drift into a depression and do harm to himself. Doris asked me to write a note to this effect which he would pass on to his guards and use as a reference to the medical officer in charge at the hospital; I admitted that mine was a concern, not a diagnosis. In concluding the case the judge, on "releasing" all participants, confessed that he had not expected much, having never heard of me, but was pleasantly surprised at the thoroughness and quality of the presentation, and hoped to see me involved more often in criminal investigation; he wished me good luck. I left feeling elated. But I wondered about the defender whom the judge dismissed as having *just* satisfied the minimum required by the brief!

It was interesting and instructive to compare the justice and ethics of the native peoples and that of the prevailing "western" civilisation. Both outlawed killing of another human being; both punished the guilty; but they differed on punishment, and on perceptions of responsibility and therefore culpability. Even in a closed community with clear rules of interpersonal behaviour and community relationships, passions can make the weak commit the most awful crime. In this case the killer was well aware of the futility of his suit for the girl.

Custom had dictated a marriage outside the clan of which he was a member and he was well aware of this. His act would unfortunately be mitigated by his drunkenness in the eyes of British law, which in any case judged the native under a different set of criminal laws from those in general use, on the premise that natives were inferior and poorly developed morally and spiritually, "wild", "savage" "primitive" and therefore naturally volatile and prone to violence--a mere cut above the animals. The alleged cannibalism of Caribs was often quoted in mitigation of acts of violence done by them. Thus the law considered twelve months in jail a stern punishment compared with life imprisonment or hanging for others.

Yet when one spoke to natives about right and wrong, one quickly learned that their codes of conduct were just as moral, strict and binding as any on the coast. Carib law prescribed banishment for the crime that was committed and this decision and reasons were made known to other clans; that was a fate worse than death in a society that relied on community action to assure survival.

By killing his "rival" he had doomed himself to a life without a mate, perhaps forever, for the social structures would deny him access to other persons in the villages; the ostracism was for good. He might ironically escape his loneliness by fleeing to the nearest Mission, and there convert to Christianity. The Missionary greeting him at his doorstep, without knowing his background, would proudly claim a convert.

We were there for three days and were taken on the same tours as before, for my wife's sake. Cpl Doris was distinctly more solicitous to me having met my *dougla* wife. He took great pleasure showing her the sights in Mabaruma--not much to see, mostly views far less picturesque than those in her native Jamaica, but it was a wild and dramatic place beyond the cultivations. He took her to Hosororo, an ancient Arawak village on the Arouca River, 7 miles on the narrow road from Mabaruma and said to be the oldest cassava cultivation site in South America, some 4000 years old; currently it was the site of a Mission and cocoa plantation.

We toured the site and saw cocoa plants and types of palm new to her. I took photos and he described the various features to her. I became engrossed with the broad expanse of treetops, not the most spectacular view that I had seen--certainly the rugged volcanic islands of the Caribbean were much more arresting and the *tepui* of the Pakaraimas by Hari's description would exceed this in grandeur, but there was an ineffable allure in the endless rolling carpet of green extending to the horizon interrupted only by the scattered taller palms that altogether gave me the feeling that I could see the soul of eternity.

Her pleasure delighted him; for the hours we spent together she had him literally licking her hands. He had taken instantly to her, and he seemed to have seen in her all that justified his devotion to his beliefs and allegiances. She was an attractive woman (easily the most arresting in court that day), elegantly dressed and a fine figure that showed well especially as she walked; and I saw that he had noticed, so I was sympathetic.

He told her she reminded him of Dorothy Dandridge whom he had seen and admired in a recent film. He told her "what a good person Doc is, how informed" and how "Mr Jain saved my life", reciting the incident--which she had heard related before, from my perspective—but now in a way unique and revealing as could only come from the victim and told with deep feeling and professional detail. He had shown her instant respect and spoke easily and deferentially to her purely on the basis of her appearance and responses for he could not know anything about her upbringing, her attitudes or interests, except perhaps to have concluded that she looked "lovely, sophisticated and privileged".

It was characteristic of him that he would do this. Brought up in the thick of Negro ferment near Buxton at the edge of a sugar estate, where frequent confrontations took place between white and high coloureds (management) and the "coolies" (labour), he had grown to believe that the Indian was a lowly, disruptive and acquisitive person guided by strange beliefs and weird customs.

One of these he had witnessed each year in March when crowds of Indians from the estate would parade on the dam on their side of the "forty foot"[136] canal prancing and jumping to the frenzied beat of drums and clash of cymbals, holding high and waving bottles of a red liquid which they would periodically sprinkle through perforated caps all over one another in great jollity.[137] Some

---

[136] *"Forty foot"* is the colloquial term for the wide canals that empoldered the sugar estates.

[137] Phagwah, *or Holi, is the major Hindu spring festival celebrated each year in March at a particular phase of the moon. March corresponds to the second half of the Hindu month of* Phalgun *and the first half of* Chaitra, *hence* Phalgun-Chaitra*; April is* Chaitra-Vaishaakh*, May is* Vaishaakh-Jyeshta *etc. (Note that India as a secular republic follows the international calendar for government and business). Hindu New Year starts on March 25th, the birthday of* Rāma*, and initiates nine days of* **observance** (**naurātri**) *ending with the April 2*

carried bottles of cheap white or dark rum. Several of the older youths and young men were "high" on the drink. He couldn't see the point of anyone ruining perfectly good clothes with such pagan excesses, as the parson in his church had described their festivities.

"The coolies will be at it again," he had warned; "watch out for them and their red water; they call it *abeer*; it's the blood of some cruel sacrifice; stay away from them, or lose your soul to the pagans. *Blessed is he that heedeth the word of the Lord.*"

He recalled it as if it were yesterday, and the hatred he had developed for the event and its celebrants. He would invariably join Negro teenagers assembled along their side of the canal who made a great show of caricaturing and jeering the merry-makers. Sometimes stones would be thrown and verbal warfare engaged. Once, a group of enraged revellers had stormed across a narrow plank footbridge spanning the canal; it wobbled spiritedly as they ran, and on an upswing had tossed a couple of them into the water. Further enraged by the ensuing ridicule they had swum over to join the others in the altercation which rapidly deteriorated into a fist fight in which several of them were bloodied, and one Indian slashed with a knife across his chest, fortunately only skin deep. More sober minds on both sides had interfered and stopped the fracas, but not before some of the Negro parents had added insults of their own.

The police, two Negro men, arrived on bicycles, and proceeded to threaten everyone with jailing. Grumbling, both sides settled down. Doris was impressed with the authority carried by the blue uniforms and brass buttons, and that just two men could command over twenty to their will. His future was decided then, though he was barely twelve at the time.

Then in 1948 he had witnessed the Police shooting into a crowd of Indian demonstrators at the estate killing five of them and injuring probably another twenty. The protest had been peaceful enough, though a bit noisy, but threatened no one, and like all mass gatherings, was viewed as a kind of show, a masquerade, and when the police contingent responded he and other villagers had followed to "see". When the volleys started and men and women began to scream and fall his feelings had been, not with the unarmed victims whom he had just found amusing, but with the men in uniform with rifles at the ready, and bayonets attached.

That was the year of his acceptance as a police recruit, and he was eagerly anticipating his departure for the Eve Leary Barracks in Georgetown to begin training. The commotion before and the sensational events after the shootings

---

celebration of Rāma Naumi *(nau in Hindi means* nine*)* Phagwah *is a colourful and festive event of considerable religious and social significance. It celebrates the victory of good over evil, spirituality and faith over tyranny, exemplified by* Rāma's *triumphant return to his city of* Ayodhya *after defeating the evil* Rāwana, *and by the legend of* Prahalad *whose father King* Hiranyakashipu *had sentenced him to death for not worshipping him as God, so powerful had the King become. When other methods failed to destroy his son, fire was tried. One early spring day the King ordered his sister* Holika, *whom Nature had made immune from fire, to take* Prahalad *with her into a fire, and sit there until he was reduced to ashes. The fire consumed* Holika *instead! The King again ordered the boy's death, to no avail, the King perishing instead. The ceremonial burning of the* Holika *at* Phagwah, *(Holika Dahana) commemorates this event, and honours faith and the power of the Divine.*

In another aspect *Phagwah* celebrates Spring. As Nature revives the earth, families reunite, attend community *melas* (fairs), share in material things, in song, dance and food and give gifts *(daan)* to those less fortunate in the community. Symbolically celebrants splash red-coloured water on one another.

had rattled him a little, but he had no qualms about what he would have done had he been in that Police rifle detachment that day. He had finally chosen the Force over the Post Office because he wanted to be a man of authority standing behind a gun when the "showdown" came with the Indians, which everyone in his village was sure to take place soon.

I was pleasantly surprised at the change in him, from the acerbic, truculent man I had met at the Barama Mouth, at the start of our trip to Wappai, to one who was pleasant and charitable. The change, perhaps his epiphany, had begun to take place after his near drowning, and had come so far that I hoped that he would begin to look at Indians not as objects to be derided, but as people with the same needs, fears and ambitions as Blacks, and a deep desire to live peaceably with their neighbours, in a climate of understanding and tolerance. It was important that the two races rise above the political divide, which he had described once as "insurmountable", adding a quote from a harangue delivered by Burnham during the 1961 election campaign. Failure to cooperate would rob them of the chance to see the broad vistas beyond the cultural barrier, and trap them, forever perhaps, in opposite camps, imprisoned by the narrow rhetoric of their idols, doomed to pursue separate visions through others' eyes.

Now before him was a foreign woman, a Jamaican, a people about whom he knew little, brought back to the colony the same way other strange women had been brought, as wives from Europe, USA and Canada, and more recently from communist countries. But this one was different; she was a *dougla*, yet clearly a "lady", a person of culture and sophistication, the first foreign-born wife of a man of "high position" that he had met.

Moreover he had had the pleasure of her company for a whole day, this "beautiful lady who turned heads" wherever they went, whom he clearly admired, who spoke so acceptingly of people he had shunned all his life, had fallen in love with one and married him, borne his children, and who showed a curiosity to discover more about the peoples of her husband's country, and had none of the blinkered and intense racial animosity that drove the followers of the two parties to hurl brickbats at one another.

She had stunned him with remarks that she had seen no real differences between the two peoples in terms of what they wanted from a government, and criticised them equally for slavishly following boastful leaders who were not as interested in the people's welfare as they claimed, but were merely using them as stepping stones to power, "just as they do in Jamaica". She hoped that the people in both Parties would "smarten up" and see their leaders in their true colours!

Doris had winced and been left speechless; she had expressed the profoundest sympathy for his views, but had shown none of the prejudices that he had expected. Her sincerity was obvious. Was she an anomaly, or did she represent a significant body of opinion among people of her class? How would he fit her into the PNC scheme of things, especially knowing who her husband was? Unhappily I would not last there long enough to find out.

On the second day we had lunch with Mr Mohamed. He was attentive to Carol and paid her an excess of compliments. She did look lovely in a print dress that again showed off her figure, and her hair was nicely done. As he quaffed drink after drink of Johnny Walker Black Label whisky he spoke on his favourite themes of opportunity and industry, the decline in manganese production and the continuing problems of transporting farm produce to market. As he talked and drank, he changed from the suave host who had just served and shared a sumptuous meal, to an irritable man with too much saliva in his mouth and a multitude of sprayed complaints.

He had been polite and entertaining, regaling her with stories of his life in the North West and the building of the railway, about his wife and two daughters who lived in a big house on Waterloo Street in Georgetown, just across from the Parade ground, he said, where Burnham made all his speeches. His unmarried daughters were in their mid-twenties, had returned from school in Britain and both had learned to fly his single-engined Cessna. He spared no details of their generous, perhaps spendthrift ways, especially with people they loved.

He had provided each with a trust fund of a million dollars and either would therefore be "a good catch for any man". He spoke easily about this and suggested to me—I thought casually and in jest that "for a nice young man, somebody like you, my young one would make a good wife!" I told him I'll check among my friends. Then he said, not stopping to think, and his speech quite slurred, "so how about you, you would be perfect, I can arrange to get rid of obstacles," he paused, nodding in my wife's direction, "no one would suspect a thing–up here anything can happen, and the rivers deep and rough."

I was caught flatfooted by the sudden change in his tone and the horror of his meaning; I laughed with embarrassment at his remark, regarding it as a drunken joke. He was all this time slobbering, spraying saliva as he spoke and at first she too dismissed the remark, but it festered in her consciousness; but when he repeated the whole thing I suddenly realised that the alcohol had quickly changed him from polite casual talk to a loose threat of murder. She looked stunned, and I felt the same, but dismissed his behaviour as drunken bravado, which I have seen often enough. Abruptly she got up, looked venomously at him and without a word walked to the door, turning only to ask, anger in her voice, "Aren't you coming?"

By 1961 the US had resolved not to countenance a second communist state in the Americas; to this end, the White House maintained pressure on Britain to withhold independence from BG and began covert activities aimed to depose or eliminate Jagan if he continued to build communist alliances and reject moves toward a moderate political position. Cuba was already a big headache; the State Department had goofed there, because of "flawed intelligence" (in White House jargon).

Their researchers among ordinary Cubans had been content with superficial appraisals of both Castro and the rank and file in Cuba. In BG they knew of the Jagans' Marxist orientation but little about the people or the country beyond the extractive operations of American bauxite companies, whose interests alone could give the US Marines an excuse to seize Georgetown--as another expression of "the white man's burden" which the oppressed interpreted as greed, but the oppressor claimed as the more honourable duty to protect democracy from abuse, a concept which US Senator William Jennings Bryan had eloquently criticised at the end of the 19th century but British writer Rudyard

Kipling had extolled to justify America's seizure of the Philippines from Spain to install a "democracy"[138]

Although disappointed with the results of BG's August 1961 elections and the failure of the Burnham-Lachmansingh coalition to defeat the PPP, Kennedy was willing to work with Jagan, and give him the opportunity to come over willingly to the US side and not follow Cuba. He, (or possibly Dean Rusk, US Secretary of State), had said, *"The United States supports the idea that every people should have the right to make a free choice of the kind of Government they want.... Mr Jagan who was recently elected Prime Minister in British Guiana is a Marxist, but the United States doesn't object, because that choice was made by honest election, which he won."*

This had defined the US attitude to BG in the immediate post-election period. However, it was unlikely that this soft stance would continue as several key advisers to Kennedy were convinced that the Jagans were insincere and inextricably linked with the USSR. However much the husband might be dangling a foot in the Western camp, they argued, current attempts to change his political philosophy and focus were fruitless, therefore he must be neutralised. The White House, although united on a policy regarding BG's place in the world as an independent non-communist country, was split on the strategy to achieve that, given the hold the country's two majority leaders had on an electorate they had divided racially, and the tenuous difference in their political philosophy.

In due course Jagan's fiery pro-communist speeches and blatant anti-Americanism cancelled the early White House preference for him. In any event he might have succumbed to the rising tide of Black Power that had effectively begun in 1955 with Rosa Parks' refusal to give up her seat in an Alabama bus and the fillip that gave to the Civil Rights career of Martin Luther King, not unlike the Enmore killings on Jagan's.

Burnham had been a bit more circumspect than Jagan. Having been rejected by the US for his known duplicity and his anti-US ranting, he had begun to heed the advice of friends and cooled his anti-American invectives, as Jagan's waxed warmer on that front and watched as his fortunes waned. Burnham studied the advances being made on Civil Rights in the US, and the favourable views of JFK and his brother Robert, the Attorney General, regarding those rights. The White House needed to confirm what was suspected, that the local Guianese population was hung up on personalities, not ideology. It was the task of Steve and a few others in the US consulate to research this and report ASAP.

It was a fine early September day. We were sitting on the seawall in West Demerara one Sunday when we had taken Steve on a rural tour; we watched the small party of Shah's niece, Fawzia, two nephews and Steve walking toward us the narrow stretch of beach laid bare by the receding tide. The sea breeze was a cooling welcome in the bright afternoon sun. Great wads of cloud like cotton wool brought islands of shade as they hurried past the sun. They were out of earshot. I asked Shah, "You've followed things over the past years more closely than I; where's all this heading? Is Cheddi willing to bend? He was never flexible, and he waffles a lot still. My brother-in-law died trying to change him."

---

[138] Take up the White Man's burden –/In patience to abide, /To veil the threat of terror /And check the show of pride; /By open speech and simple, / An hundred times made plain, /To seek another's profit /And work another's gain.   *R. Kipling*

"We try; we all believe in creating a humane and caring state; we're small, we can do it, and do it well; we need benevolent and understanding guidance, wise guidance; if you're asking me if Cheddi has that, my answer is no, but what is the alternative? There is none. We are caught, no, trapped; we have no room to manoeuvre. Yet we must try. That's why I see some hope that Steve here might give us a lead to US thinking, which we can use to get to Cheddi. He's CIA, of course!"

"Yes, I had begun to think that." I replied.

"That's why I encourage him on these excursions, to meet real people."

"I'm trying to be positive but you know how pessimistic I've become; I see no encouraging signs since returning; Cheddi remains authoritarian, self-centred, as bad as Burnham; I'm sure he'll try to set up a totalitarian state, and screw the economy; he's placed too much of a damper on enterprise already; people screaming but he's deaf; all the businesses and skills I know are bleeding; we're such a small population with lots of talent and ideas, liberal in outlook, and nothing to gain from communism."

"Absolutely, my uncle sent money overseas instead of investing it here, and he had plans that in this year alone would have employed ten more people; instead two will lose their jobs. And he's smaller than many I know, including your family."

"It's an illness, I'm sure, an obsession; this cold war spawns extremism on both sides."

"Fearing what's coming, I've been looking at authoritarian states, Haiti for example, with far too many people for its economy, one of the poorest on earth, just as its neighbour, Santo Domingo and until two years ago Cuba. All have servile populations; all are Roman Catholic with strict taboos on birth control. The dictators exploit them and prosper by simply creating well-paid and elitist security forces whose only loyalty is to their paymaster. It's funny; all dictators do it, whether they're capitalist or communist, or claim to be democratic, like the US, which is nothing more than a *commercial hegemony*. Look around Latin America; the formula is simple; if the US is on your side, that means if you let some US company control your economy, like United Fruit or AT&T or Alcoa, you could be the very Devil you'll be safe from opposition, unless your country can find a Castro."

We paused as the others got closer and called for us to join them; they were now strolling barefooted along the water's edge, the ebbing waves low and softly breaking against their ankles as they moved along.

"It's nice and cool, I feel like jumping in," the girl said, gathering her shirt about her knees as she moved further into the clear brown water.

"Can you swim here?' Steve asked, eyeing the shapely legs now innocently bared before him.

"Yes," she answered, "but the water is too low now; next time you come, bring your swimming trunks."

"He talks a lot about her, from that first day he met her; he keeps bugging me to bring him back." Shah whispered confidingly.

"You better watch out; you might end up with an American in the family."

Shah laughed showing his even teeth. He was a handsome man with a thin moustache and a goatee beard, elegantly combed and trimmed. He looked like one of those actors in Indian movies who played the role of the rival for the heroine's love and who clearly attracts her with his dashing looks, but is not of a caste or profession approved by the girl's parents. Or like the Hollywood actor, Douglas Fairbanks Jr. I used to tease him about that and his only response had been, "I wish someone from Bombay or Hollywood would hurry up and discover me soon!"

Later when we returned to the house for lunch, Fawzia disappeared briefly and returned holding a slender pink object in her hands.

"What on earth you got there?" Shah asked his niece; from the angle where I stood it looked like an elongated partly inflated French letter of a type I used to retail on the UCWI campus for pocket money (Dr Jagan had quipped "better than my snake oil business" hearing that I sold a gross monthly).

"It's a doll."

"A doll? What kind of doll can that skinny thing be?" he asked teasingly.

"It's a new kind of doll; we don't have them here. It's called a Barbie."

"A Barbie? Never heard of that; where did you get it?"

"Steve brought it for me, a present, isn't it nice?"

"May I see it?" I asked

She handed it over, this fresh symbol of American innovation and concept of beauty, another weapon in the conquest of woman; Steve looked at it a bit sheepishly as it changed hands, its pert breasts suggestive, but I was taken by its long skinny thighs and legs which seemed so bizarre anatomically, and the shock of "hair" the colour of a ripe paddy field which caught the light and reflected it sharply.

"It must have been designed to be dressed up, like those skinny models you see in magazines." I handed it back.

"I'm going to dress her up in a sari," and with that she left swinging her own shapely form up the short flight of stairs from the deck into the house, disappearing through the door. I watched Steve's unabashed admiration, or was it lust? I did not blame him, but then felt sorry for him, knowing how strict though low key the chaperoning of this 17-year old was and that her parents had already begun the process of arranging her marriage.

She had pleaded with them to postpone it until she finished the School Certificate examination, which she had not been able to do, as there was no secondary school in her area; she had therefore enrolled in an external correspondence program with the added help of an uncle who was a schoolteacher. Shah had interceded on her behalf and there the matter had rested. That was six months ago; in two months she would be taking her examinations, and soon after celebrating her 18th birthday; her prospective fiancé had agreed to wait until then. Steve would no doubt be invited to the wedding.

Half an hour later she reappeared and ran down the steps holding the doll aloft for all to see. She had dressed it immaculately in a resplendent maroon and gold *sari* with a band in her hair fashioned from a piece of gold edging. Everyone clapped.

"I can just see someone collecting a bunch of those and dressing them up in the costumes of the world. That would be spectacular," Shah said.

We met with Steve at his request a month or so later on his return from a short visit to the USA, presumably Washington. We sat on the wall facing the ocean as we had done before; it was a serene setting, far from the troubled city, seemingly detached and yet vulnerable, like peripheral cells that depended on the heart for their sustenance. A train rumbled by on its way to Parika, the children gathered on the beach waving, as they did each time a train or bus passed by.

It had not taken us long to learn to read Steve's code, feeling some excitement that we were involved in an intrigue; we played the game, and so learned Kennedy's view that Jagan's majority position, his solid organisation and discipline, however capricious, and the loyalty of his following merited US attempts to pull him back from Communist USSR, and bring him into the hemispheric economic fold that the US dominated. They had reasoned that when he came to confront the economic consequences of independence, he would see that there was really no future prosperity in being a satellite of either Cuba or the USSR.

And if by then he had failed to change, the final solution would be applied, as with Patrice Lumumba. In this JFK had the support of Arthur Schlesinger, a moderate man, and Consul Melby; and so overrode the position of the hawks in his administration who had proposed that should Jagan win the 1961 elections, he be dealt with summarily as a Communist going the way of Castro, and that a scheme be put in place to select a successor. Jagan was aware that the CIA had operatives in BG and that Melby--and probably Hughes, his vice-consul-- was kindly disposed towards him, assuring him at the minimum a friendly greeting at the White House. But he was not aware of how extensively they had begun to study his support base[139]. US officials, it seemed were also concerned about Jagan's views on individual rights, and how he might apply them in an independent Guiana with regard to business. Would he enforce communes as Mao had done, or cooperatives in the Russian style, or nationalise business?

---

[139] Recent access to US official documents confirms this summary. The following excerpts illustrate:

"Ambassador Caccia felt that the Jagans provided the most responsible leadership in the country and they would be difficult to supplant. Mr White stressed that we ought to work in the direction of getting the people in British Guiana interested in British Guiana's joining the Federation. Lord Home agreed and said the UK would like to see British Guiana in the Federation." – *Meeting of Colonial Secretary MacLeod and Under Secretary Fraser on the British side and Ambassador Bruce aided by Ivan White and Jack Bell on the American side.*

"Senator Dodd's request Alex Johnson is seeing him Monday with respect his August 3 letter addressed to you expressing hope 'some action will be possible in this situation before we have another Castro regime in Latin America'."

Rusk fumbles Ball: Aug 5-11, 1961 concerns re CBJ and open threat from Rusk to Home.

"Arthur Schlesinger, jr. to Kennedy: Sep '61: 'State also recommends a covert program to develop information about, expose and destroy Communists in British Guiana, including, if necessary, *the possibility of finding a substitute for Jagan himself, who could command East Indian support'.*"

"The idea, in short, is to use the year or two before independence to work to tie Jagan to the political and economic framework of the hemisphere, while at the same time reinsuring against pro-Communist development by building up anti-Communist clandestine capabilities."

"The covert program proposed might conflict with the friendship policy proposed in .... This means that the covert program must be handled with the utmost discretion and probably confined at the start to intelligence collection. "

"Dean Rusk Sep '61: 'However, it is our judgment that an across-the board effort to salvage Jagan is worth attempting. *A factor in our conclusion is the unattractiveness of the available alternatives.* (emphasis mine) Clearly, the closest Anglo-American cooperation is essential. We also hope to bring in the Canadians and possibly others."

"We would like to see the following emerge from your talks with the British: 1. A brief, agreed intelligence assessment; (2) British acceptance of the general concept of our action program; (3) Agreement ad referendum on a coordinated aid program; (4) *[1½ lines of source text not declassified].* The covert program described in the enclosure is only a basis for planning and discussions at this time *[less than 1 line of source text not declassified].* Specific actions under the program would be subject to further high-level U.S. Government consideration and approval.

"Agreement on tactics."

Would Indians accept a communal or cooperative state? Steve asked to be frank, "no holds barred; in confidence."

Shah said, "Okay; the answer to your questions is both yes, and no; for most endeavours our people would prefer individual enterprise; for some, example large scale commercial farming or fishing or lumber, cooperatives would offer advantages as we're already seeing among Mahaicony Creek rice farmers with regards to transportation. By the way, the natives in the interior live in communes as they've done for millennia. And they never heard of Marx. We don't all see a single best approach or solution to all economic problems; circumstances, for example resources, skills, market conditions will influence choices. Government has a role, just as it does in your country."

"Individualism has served us so well, and created huge enterprises: Bell, Carnegie, Edison, Ford, Rockefeller, Vanderbilt, Mellon, Morgan, Roosevelt, Kennedy, and numerous others – they are the bases of our prosperity today, just 175 years after independence. A strong man of ideas and action began each one, and grew it into the corporate giants they are today, providing millions of jobs and the world's highest living standard."

"True," Shah acknowledged, "and mountains of waste; the industrial revolution was a triumph of individualism; like Europe you had energy resources to power it; and the capacity to build the skills needed. Don't forget that those magnates dictated the policy and direction of your government. They skirted even the few restraints you had to protect people and those same events produced Marx and the revolutionary themes that make you tremble today. "

Steve winced.

"In our time the rights of the individual have been taken too far," I said, "it has corrupted people widely, and made the US the mecca of all those who wish to accumulate material things in whatever wanton free-wheeling way they may choose. You call it the American dream. Poor folk call it a nightmare! The notion of individualism is attractive and useful in many ways, as we agree, but it's been corrupted by the unscrupulous and now threatens our civilisation."

"That's a revolutionary thought," Steve said, surprise etched on his face, "pardon my asking, but are you a communist?" Shah laughed knowing intimately my views on various "isms".

"Far from it," I rejoined, "that's typically American; you see only black or white! I come from a fiercely individualistic family, but I'm not greedy; I won't grab other people's assets; we're here because British aristocrats seized my family property and took all India, ruining local industry and forcing theirs to gain from the industrial revolution after US seized independence. You've become like that, blinded by the rich few; you don't see the millions of poor that barely subsist all over America and the rest of the world dominated by your businesses. Communism is no better; it's done exactly the same as you. I am a concerned human being who dislikes the seamy side of individualism, which has reached the status of a cult, at least in America and parts of Europe, and I do not wish to see the excesses of the 10% rich and powerful, stealing from the weak e.g. Aborigines, and leading the rest of us to Armageddon. That is a legitimate fear, and not only among Communists."

"That's strong talk; have you no sentiment left for individuality?"

"Naturally, I do--didn't you hear me?--if appropriately and honestly pursued, not to create new tyrants and aristocrats; in some situations I believe that the rights of the community — and that does not mean communism, as some of your people naively believe — their rights should take precedence."

"How so? Can you give me an example?"

"Yes, if one is accused of a crime, one should have all the rights under the law to self-protection and a fair trial. All the principles of individual rights should apply so that the community does not become a lynch mob, like your KKK. But on the other hand the community's rights should override those of the absentee mining magnate whose enterprise is poisoning the community's water supply and sources of food. Right now the US industrialist can do pretty damn much what he pleases anywhere and his government would back him, however miscreant, and wherever in the world, in his right to pursue his personal affairs; the US supported a cheating United Fruit against Arbenz in Guatemala. The US behaves as if it is overlord of the universe, and freely tramples, and allows its citizens to trample on the rights of others, just as the British had done so shamelessly all over the globe."

"Wow! Tough talk. That's what Commies say, but why do *you* say that?"

"That's the false indoctrination of Americans which I saw up close last year; any critique of the US is swiftly labelled "Commie" as you just reflexly did. Just as a Jew cries 'anti-semitic' each time someone criticises Israel. Look around you, my friend, the reasons stare you in the face; United Fruit literally owns Central America and hogs the best agricultural land, like SPA here; natives starve. Your oil companies dominate Arab nations who ape everything you do. The State Department supports a dictatorship in Pakistan, and created Castro's communism; AT&T runs Chile; the bauxite companies have a heavy hand in Jamaica, here and Surinam; the CIA killed Lumumba on a whim; the US created a monster in the Middle East by splitting Palestine to create Israel for Zionists. You need more? We can go back a bit to show that this is not just recent history. The US government itself has breached its own vaunted Constitution around the globe; it won't get better, as the Cold War heats up. That's why people follow Jagan and Burnham, because Jagan dwells on these abuses, telling people that Americans don't criticize Government policies because they don't know these things or simply ignore or worse, condone corporate wrongdoing because it seems each of you wants to be a millionaire. The other thing is that few in these colonies can see a good side to America. Individuals yes; businesses nearly always no."

"Hold on! It took the US just 175 years to become the world's strongest nation; it takes private enterprise to create wealth; what's wrong with that? D'you think governments can do as well, the USSR, f'r instance?"

Shah and I had discussed this issue several times.

"Wealth is one thing; trampling your fellows, bribery and greed are something else," he said. "The US government is an instrument of US corporations. The USSR is a major corporation; neither is a good model; we prefer Sweden or Finland. US style entrepreneurship is destructive. A century ago, the US fought Japan for free access to its markets, sixty years ago they fought Spain; meanwhile the British and other European powers kept competition out of their empires by levying duties on others' goods. Their competitors cried foul, especially you Americans who openly complained about the duties, and whined until GATT opened doors in '48.

"These same whiners today buy *our* raw materials at prices *they* control, dump their manufactures on us at *inflated* prices, but won't let us sell our value-added goods in their markets, just as the British and other Europeans had done to them! That's fair? Look at sugar, your government subsidises US Sugar whose products cost more than ours to produce but the subsidy plus punitive tariffs on ours make your sugar cheaper than we can sell it to you. And worse the USSR is buying Cuban sugar at higher prices than we can ever get, so every small country sugar producer wants some of the same treatment. You blame them? Now your corporations have gotten so big by using repressive and monopolistic practices and bribery that reach so deep, into the White House even, that a single one can own a small country by controlling its economy. That's what we're against. Here you own bauxite, the British sugar, and both of you looking to loot our forests and minerals."

Steve looked stunned. Recovering he asked, "So you think central control of all aspects of the economy will protect you? Would that not be restrictive or even obstructive to those with ideas?"

"My! You're missing the point. We're not talking of unbridled central control," I took up the issue, "there is a middle ground where both concepts have a role; you use it but you don't say it out loud; your democracy had controls at the start which put you on a good footing. FDR brought you out of recession with central policies. Extremism is not acceptable, neither yours nor the Soviets'; your corporate executive is probably worse than a Soviet commissar if only because you know where the commissar stands. Your guys are plain crooks; I don't suppose you know about that Monsanto fellow who swore DDT was safe. People like that are criminals and your corporations are full of them. We believe that individual enterprise must be encouraged but subject to some regulation to curtail wrong-doing, like FDR did in the thirties to restrain banks; that's government's role, and to provide for law and order and other infrastructure. I believe government should be at arm's length from business. In your system business *runs* government through lobbies that fatten politicians and pay their election expenses; that is your cycle of corruption. Elections should be paid for by Government to release the elected from having to 'pay back' sponsors.

"Communism is just as crooked in the opposite way; they say Government *is* business, and government, the abstraction, will ensure *all* are looked after, unlike privateers who only fatten themselves. I believe in the middle ground as shown by Scandinavian countries, not that they're perfect, but they'll outdo you in human rights and quality of life. They don't stifle enterprise as some of you think. But look, this is a tiny country and a tiny economy by any standards; the population is just that of a medium-sized American city. We know we have resources; some are already exploited, but in a predatory way, like manganese in WWII, leaving desolation when the US exploiter quit.

"Your corporations barge in, destabilise if necessary, buy out locals so no social measures creep into contracts nor remedies for deliberate defaults or spurious bankruptcies. They pay fat bribes locally and no real royalties, so natives bleed. Jagan offers honesty — not that he can guarantee that--but he seems free from money taint, unlike Burnham, and that makes people believe him. He is unfortunately blinded by ideology, not pragmatism.

"You Americans are too emotionally against this kind of talk, and so quick to apply labels that you ignore your own thinkers who advocate a better approach in poor countries instead of just preying on their weakness and gouging them. If you really believe in free enterprise and want us fully on your side you should forget Ayn Rand and other demagogues and help *our* entrepreneurs by ending tariffs that block our goods from your markets. That's true free enterprise! Not monopoly! The American Revolution started as a protest against taxes. That's what you fought the Brits for; remember the Big Tea Party?"

Steve winced and said nothing, his eyes questioning. Had I gone too far beyond politeness, I wondered, and had he been serious in asking for frankness? Before I could test these, Shah added, almost without mercy, "When Americans push their weight around in poor countries and create dissension, and should be restrained your Government blindly takes their side and does the opposite. The pattern is that US investors move in, bring their own staff, who know nothing about us or the place, act on stereotypes, take what they want and leave a mess for us to clean up; we have no one to appeal to. So to go back to your question we would like them to do their homework, come in as partners, whether with government or a private company, employ local skills as much as possible, and carry on the activity to the full extent possible here; that way they will help develop our infrastructure, preserve the asset base, and make a profit, and not lose it by ignorance or neglect, as has been happening so far everywhere since the industrial revolution. Companies should do this for self-interest if not the general good, and they will become economic assets for the long term, not just fly-by-night thieves."

"Look," I said, when Shah paused, "right now there's talk of mining; if an American company wants only what's in the ground they'll destroy the forests and all their treasures to get it. This country is one huge forest. Its intrinsic value is largely unknown, but I'm sure there's a dollar value to each tree, each vine and shrub, to the rivers and waterfalls and mountains, to the wild-life and life style of the peoples who live there, above and beyond mere land price. If we think that way we will be less cavalier about disturbing the forest just so as to get at minerals in the ground, which in any case should not alone decide the fate of the forest or of the country. That way creates deserts; the prosperity is brief and only to a few of you. We get shit! So some study is needed, before you bring in the power shovels."

A pause followed; Steve silently passed around a pack of Marlboros, lit one, dragged in and exhaled the smoke in two streams through his nostrils; I watched the smoke curl upwards, as I lit mine.

"But don't you have lumbermen and miners who are just as likely to trash the land?"

"Of course," Shah said, "but so far they don't have the capital to be really destructive. And there's regulatory oversight. Most mining is placer type with panning or sluicing in boxes or trommels; in fact from what I've heard, not too many have these, even though they're simple to make and are not as destructive as drilling or tunnelling with heavy equipment and hydraulics. The fear is that your folks will swarm the country at the slightest smell of gold with heavy equipment and careless methods that *your* states outlawed in the last century.

"Same thing with lumber; you clear-cut and leave a barren waste behind; that won't work in a tropical forest, but Brazilians have begun to do that, egged on by you to raise beef for hamburgers, and will destroy it. Problem is that poorer countries copy the worst of American behaviours in business and socially. Your people tend to forget ethical practice when they leave the States! And you're all so sanctimonious and over-bearing and believe even your biggest flaws are virtues."

Shah smiled, his teeth sparkling. "Don't get me wrong; you're a great guy, we both think so; that's why we're saying all this. US is a great country, not because of mottos and slogans, or politicians and corporate giants but in spite of them; I don't see you as a symbol of equality; in fact the opposite: your rich and powerful crush the rest and more often than not deny them a chance to achieve the American dream — that's all it is, a dream. Your greatness is in your institutions and in the promise you give ordinary folk that they too can reach high, with or without uppers and downers, evangelists or shrinks. You don't have real national friends; you don't seem to know how to make friends; you have sycophant nations who are forced to be your allies and people afraid of the sudden punch you're so quick to throw, like in the movies. In short your image needs work; Kennedy is trying but I don't think Republicans will let him succeed." Shah took a long drink, and smiled again at Steve.

"Wow! I asked for frank talk, and got an earful. They don't teach us *that* in States-side schools! But I see your point. It's good to hear it from people who clearly have thought through the local situation. It's not often we have a chance to hear directly from regular and thoughtful citizens who can see both sides; our lobbies are so weighted to influence voting on issues, a dispassionate examination of beliefs doesn't happen often enough; we're hoping President Kennedy might change that. We're at the mercy of our information sources, and of biases; the big lobbies that populate DC add fluff, not clarity. We should clear the air and spread the net for facts more widely. You guys have been straight. I need that. But tell me, what's this about British stealing Indian property? Never heard that! I didn't study India in College, but the general view is that the British civilised India, like Africa; is that not so? I didn't know any Indians back home; there were some in Seattle, mostly traders."

I almost exploded, and might have were it not for the others there; Shah was dumbstruck to witness this level of darkness about an entire subcontinent and the culture of its huge population twice that of the United States. It took me many seconds to compose myself before I could answer.

"The British went to India as a trading company owned by aristocrats and royally chartered; they found much of it under Muslim domination; after much fighting with the Dutch, French and Portuguese they were permitted to establish trading posts on the West and East coasts, eventually with headquarters in Bengal. By the end of the 17th century the Mughals had begun to disintegrate; the British seized the opportunity to make deals, facilitated by a strong Navy, a series of bribes and betrayals, and gained territory on both coasts, centred on Bombay in the West and Calcutta in the East.

"Meanwhile Hindu kingdoms had reinstated their hold on the North and central India and parts of the West. They fought wars throughout the 18th and the first six decades of the 19th against the Mughals and British ending the rule of the former but succumbing to the latter finally in 1857 when the company gave way to government by Parliament.

"Two decades earlier Macaulay had proposed a strategy to displace Indian education by English and finding a way to distract Indian students from the study of their own literature and culture to that of English. To achieve this they employed a German Sanskritist to create a fake version of Indian *Vaidic* texts complete with erroneous dates devised to fit biblical accounts and to show that the Vaidas had been brought to India by conquerors as myths. Having gained control of most regional governments by coercion and trickery it was an easy step to design curricula at all levels to promulgate this. Macaulay's plan produced brown Englishmen who were given preference for jobs and promotion up to certain ceilings in that society. An *English* education became *the* requirement for all government jobs.

"With control they took full charge of the economy by completing the destruction of its village base which the Mughals had started. They imposed a pattern of agriculture by switching from food to plantation crops, mainly cotton, dyestuffs, opium, sugarcane and levied exorbitant taxes on crops. Failure to pay led to confiscation of lands which the state made available to local landowners and princes who supported them.

"Before mass communications Brits dominated the media; it was all print then. To this day those falsehoods remain a divisive element in Indian society as even Indian intellectuals believed the British version, having been prevented from seeing much less studying Indian texts.

"Indian culture goes back at least 12,000 years to the end of the Ice Age; that's longer than any other known civilization and India made the first great advances in mathematics, language and sciences. Your government heavily influenced by British positions have kept Indians out of the US and it was only during World War II because of Indian performance in the war on your side that FDR allowed 7,500 Indians to enter the USA. Even so they were not allowed to vote or to become citizens. I can go on and on to enlighten you so that you may shed those obnoxious biases you've inherited, which had led British aristocrats to seize that rich land, just as your ancestors trampled all over America believing the notion of racial superiority and the teachings of eugenics.

"I have the greatest respect for you or I wouldn't be sharing any of this. You may wish to verify what I've said but you won't from Anglophone sources, including your universities, but there are genuine Indian and other sources you could tap. I'll send you some material for a start, but I stress again that British and US sources are uniformly anti-Indian. The French have done a much better job of setting the record straight. There are Indians in Georgetown who might be willing to sit with you if you're interested.

"Indians had developed an excellent system of governance based on local councils at the village level, and lived morally and spiritually, largely free of domination by business interests. The system the Brits imposed was almost designed to be corrupted by officials and enriched many for two hundred years. Where do you think the tea came from that was dumped at the Boston tea party? Who were you paying taxes to for that tea?"

As if to underline this critique an incident occurred in Georgetown, which embarrassed US officials. The BG Government Pharmacy had just purchased from Italy a generic brand of tetracycline at a price several times lower than a US quote. Lederle, the makers of *Terramycin*, a variant of the same drug, protested the purchase alleging Italian infringement of US patents but failed to mention that those patents were not recognised in Italian law, nor did we purchase Terramycin. The US Consulate's commercial attaché promptly and publicly announced support for Lederle and began to apply heavy pressure on the Government to cancel the deal. In this and similar issues, the US was widely seen as a bully, very much the elephant threatening the mouse.

The pettiness of the Americans and the victims of their outrageous and ill-timed complaint--public patients who could hardly afford to buy tetracycline, let alone Terramycin--was a God-sent example of the rapacity of US business that the fair-minded had been condemning throughout the country. This sore in canker-ridden American-style capitalism allowed critics to give *all* private business a bad name and justified the Government's leftist condemnation. By ignoring the fact that the drug purchase had been made by open tender and decided by a Board strictly on satisfaction of criteria, the Americans had exposed themselves to the criticism of slavishly placing a US company's interests before a country's fair practice rules and the public good. It was bad enough that the Company had complained but it was downright immoral in most people's minds--even among those who were unabashedly pro-USA--that a Consulate official should have supported it so blatantly. It was as if there were no bounds to American bullying and greed, and the entire US government took the heat for it.

The BG Government did not capitulate, affirming that its purchase followed international law, and indicated that it would not only defend its position, but claim court damages from Lederle and the US consulate for false prosecution, misrepresentation, and mischief. This did not become necessary as Melby intervened and apologised, dubbing it all a mistake. Lederle continued to grumble as the matter receded from the news. For long after *Terramycin* and *Lederle* became terms of abuse in the country, and few doctors ordered the drug. Lederle had given Jagan a perfect example of vicious US business and what poor countries could expect from the US and its corporations. The incident fuelled his raging vilification of capitalism.

On his return from Washington in October 1961 Jagan vigorously pursued domestic legislation aimed at government control of production, higher education, and re-alignment of economic policies along communist lines. Burnham and D'Aguiar vigorously opposed these, much to the delight of their American lobby in Washington, or perhaps because of its advice and continued to confound the populace with word games. In the closing days of 1961, in a verbal clash with Jagan after his return from the USA, Burnham proclaimed, "I am not saying that you are wrong, what I assert is that you are not right!"

His followers were elated at the put-down and began to use it freely to taunt Jagan and his kind. Later in an impromptu speech, Burnham stirred them up further when he intoned into his megaphone at a street-corner rally in Charlestown, referring to their election performance, post-election tactics and Jagan's failure with Kennedy.

"We may have lost this round, but we will not go down like slaves! Remember *Calabari,* where our people in Basutoland trounced the white invaders from Cape Colony. That was 70 years ago. How many of you are 70?" A single hand was raised above the small crowd.

"You are the victor of that struggle. We, your sons and grandsons, we will win again!"

A heckler — a skinny black middle-aged man, well-informed, with a deep voice, one of the many regulars who had made my attendance at street-corner meetings worthwhile, and one of the few still left — shouted, "But we not from there, we from West Africa; Basutoland is South Africa!"

Swift as a ray of light at the break of dawn his slight frame was levelled to the ground with bloodied face and pinioned hands, a streak of blood from a cut lip running down his neck and staining his white shirt collar bright red. He strained weakly against his two burly assailants. The speaker held his hand high, "Why do you do this, comrades? let him speak; even if he does not speak truth;

we are free to speak; the country I want is a free country, so let him speak today, but let all who wish to speak falsely know that the punishment will be swift, and sure!"

It is not known what happened to the luckless man, as they led him away into the night.

In another escalation "choke-and-rob" style robberies by street hoodlums moved into main streets, often in broad daylight, emerging from PNC and UF agitation with the help of the CIA; they began to sully the Georgetown scene, and started to destabilise the Government. The attacks grew and were coddled until fully blossomed, then spread to other towns and villages, inducing many, especially family of victims, to flee the country. The thugs were exclusively young black men, and the victims nearly all Indians, mostly older women from the country on innocent and routine visits to the city to see relatives, to shop or seek medical help at one of the Hospitals, or to conduct other business or social activity. Indian women were wont to display jewellery on social occasions, including travel.

The streets of the city had been traditionally noted for their safety, even at night. The robberies shocked the populace and were the first major assault on social peace and the first major step down the path to lawlessness that would soon turn the once serene city of Georgetown, the flower of the Caribbean, into a mecca for brigands and cutthroats. The friendliness of people turned inexorably to suspicion; the cheery greetings of yesterday were replaced by scowls, the *joie de vivre* by worry, bitterness and anger. The police claimed they were powerless, but no one believed them.

It was widely believed that the policeman on the beat was turning a blind eye to these crimes because the perpetrators were members of various PNC and UF destabilisation brigades. In one incident outside the Hardeen store a black youth assaulted one of my sisters visiting from the country grabbing at her bangles in full view of two men whom my brother Buddy later identified as policemen. She resisted and fended him off just as Buddy came out of the store hearing the commotion; the thief ran off with one bangle and when Buddy asked the men why they stood by and let him get away with assault and robbery, one replied, "We're off duty!"

Jagan's opponents were quick to point to his failure to do his duty to protect his own people. Here, the PNC and UF said--in condemning the attacks-- was a man who placed ideology above law and order, whose actions had alienated the Police and the Civil Service, an impulsive man whose leadership would inexorably take the country to disorder, lawlessness and anarchy. They asserted that "none of this lawlessness" would occur in a non-communist regime.[140] Jagan, in turn, made the right condemnatory noises, and re-stated his faith in the integrity of the Police, his commitment to securing law and order and the democratic process, and his right to govern. PPP supporters countered the opposition message by taunting "Yeah maan, soon as Burnham turn Premier, he goin' put all he 'choke and rob' friends in jail!" and "If PNC turn government, Burnham will have to hold all his meetings in jail!"

---

[140] Contrast the speed and assertiveness with which the same Force responded to PPP protests in 1964 and later years to ensure law and order when a PNC-UF coalition assumed power (See Epilogue).

Meanwhile the Minister of Home Affairs Mr Rai, a moderate man, a lawyer, repeated his view that law and order could only be achieved by an impartial Police Force, which was more likely to develop if the character of that Force was changed to reflect the make-up of the population. Indians were 51% of the population, yet less than 10% of the Force; Mr Rai had a plan to change that by immediately recruiting Indians to fill vacancies as well as for new positions. If all such positions were so filled the percentage of Indians would rise to just under 15%. Even the Press had relaxed its normally strident anti-government stance and grudgingly admitted the wisdom of the move both to preserve law and order, and to begin the road to equality and fairness in employment.

Mr Rai also wished to remove certain traditional barriers to recruitment: such as height, weight and religion in favour of ability, agility, aptitude and physical fitness. Dr Jagan surprisingly vetoed the plan and almost simultaneously a rumour began to circulate that he would oppose Rai's nomination for the position of Party Chairman in the elections set for April, 1962. He favoured Brindley Benn, declaring that at no time should the top two positions in the Party (or in any Government enterprise or organisation) be held by Indians, regardless of ability or suitability[141]. And since Jagan saw himself as Leader to the death, there was no place at the top for another Indian. By this egregious dictum did Jagan sow the seeds of his own downfall! He would consistently condemn the questions and the questioner who asked: "How can any talented Indian rise in the PPP and bring new ideas or ways to solve old problems if only you can dictate what policies we must follow?"

Upper Mazaruni River to show source, Kamarang vicinity (arrow) and varoous gold-mining sites (See also map p.654)

---

[141] See Footnote 2, page 6

This map is repeated from p. 39 for ease of reference. The dark line is one of the alternative boundaries of the proposed partitioned British Guiana

Chapter 13

Early in 1962 I am assigned to exhume and examine a probable murder victim in the hinterland at Kamarang, a Government post and mission on the Mazaruni River. My escort is Superintendent McLeod of Brickdam Police Station, the designated head of the fledgling Forensic Unit, which he outlines to us on the journey. Kamarang is a one day trip by DC3 airplane, which allows me and Balgobin to see the *tepui* panoramically--including the tallest of them and the broadest table, Roraima and other *tipus* nearby--and their myriad waterfalls. We meet a notable Guianese writer and poet at Kamarang who joins our flight back and gives a commentary on the geography below that he had helped survey during his career as a Government surveyor, including spectacular views of the Mazaruni River as it cuts a deep A-shaped gorge through the Merume Mountains, a section of the eastern Pakaraimas. Back in Georgetown people are terrorised by violence fomented by opposition to Government's new budget. We eavesdrop on a secret meeting between Burnham, the PNC leader, and a confidante, and learn about the seditious activities of US agents and agencies. Riots erupt in which many are injured and my new friend Superintendent McLeod is killed, and arson destroys a huge chunk of one of the city's main business districts; my family barely escapes. I stand mesmerised by the conflagration. The senior pathologist conducting McLeod's autopsy recovers the rifle bullet but loses it! The hospital is abuzz with the scandal; my wife reacts to the worry and the heavy emergency load by urging me to complete the US qualifying medical entry examination (ECFMG) which I pass. I report on the fears of physicians, entrepreneurs and others. Politicians remain obdurate.

A Killing in Kamarang; tumult and fire

Man, biologically considered, is the most formidable of all the beasts of prey, and indeed, the only one that preys systematically on its own species. William James, *Memories and Studies*

"Chronic wrongdoing or an impotence that results in a general loosening of the ties of civilised society…may force the United States, however reluctantly, in flagrant cases of such wrongdoing or impotence, to the exercise of an international police power." Teddy Roosevelt to US Congress, Dec 6, 1904

"National independence. This is the basic thing. As long as you do that, we don't care whether you are socialist, capitalist, pragmatist or whatever. We regard ourselves as pragmatists." Ascribed to John F. Kennedy, 1961

There's a Police Officer on the line, wants to see you; he says it's confidential and urgent." Marian said into the intercom, a tremor in her voice. I immediately thought of Inspector Bacchus, with pleasure.

"I can see him this afternoon, any time after 3.00, or tomorrow morning, first thing."

At 3.05 he was in my office. It was not the Inspector, but Superintendent D. G. McLeod, a stocky creole white man in his early 40s, about 5'10" and around 210 lbs. He was dressed in a khaki uniform, summer issue, with shorts, long cream socks and green tassels, regulation shoes and peaked cap. In his left armpit he held a short tapered mahogany staff with a brass cap at each end.

He told me he had come straightaway because he needed me to "do an autopsy tomorrow in Kamarang". A plane could be available at noon; to get it he had to confirm by 3.30 latest. Kamarang was a government post and mission on the Mazaruni River high in the Pakaraima Mountains, nearly 200 miles due west of Atkinson Field. The trip would be under an hour in either direction.

"Why me?" I asked, wonderingly, (silently pleased at the thought of another trip into the hinterland) and thinking that he really didn't need my agreement, except perhaps for the timing. But it was good of him to say so.

"Brickdam told me to get you. Seems you've made an impression there. Remember Inspector Bacchus?"

"Yes, a real gentleman, and smart, too."

"That I agree."

"How is he? I'd hoped to keep in touch, but things got so hectic here, haven't got around to it."

"It's the same with the Inspector, as with the rest of the senior staff. He's been out of town for some time on another assignment." Then he asked, "Is it okay, you'll go?"

"Sure; I'll go, unless Dr Singh says no. You cleared with him?"

"MOH approved it and is contacting Dr Singh. It's either you or him."

"Then it's me; what's the story?"

He looked at his watch, "Let me confirm with Airways, and then I'll brief you. Can I use your phone?"

"This one can be slow, it's a hospital extension; let's go next door; Marian's phone is on a direct line. She'll get the number for you."

I left him briefly with Marian Kissoon--the beautiful doll-like secretary I would have for just a few more months until she left for Russia, to everyone's amazement, on one of Jagan's scholarships ("I'm a socialist, not a communist," she had told me)--and got on to Sumintra to make us some tea, which she brought in while McLeod was briefing me. We thanked her, and she left, smiling, as she usually did, in the presence of "authority".

"The case looked straightforward at first. A man shot another with a shotgun; he claimed he had loaded the gun with buckshot, had fired a single round, and that it was an accident, that he was about 50 yards away. At that distance the type of shot shouldn't kill a man; we know the place the man was shot, but unfortunately our people weren't the first to get there. We secured it as soon as we could. There weren't any witnesses; there seems to have been some bad blood between the two."

As he spoke I realised that I had to brush up on gunshot wounds, shotguns and other firearms just in case that came into question. He summarised the flight and on-site arrangements, which would be done by someone from the District Commissioner's office; I suggested a few changes and additions, which he would transmit to Kamarang by radiotelephone. He finished his tea, selected a folder from his briefcase and handed it to me.

"You'll find the relevant information here. I'll come for you at eleven tomorrow."

"I'll bring Balgobin with me, my right hand; he went with me to Wappai."

"Yes, of course, the famous Balgobin; they talked of him too. I'll be glad to meet him."

The 26-mile road trip to Atkinson Field took almost an hour, through two large sugarcane plantations close to the city and ribbon-built villages and fields beyond. The road ran along the east bank of the Demerara River and ended at the airport. It was rough going, a succession of jolts, due to the poor condition of the road, something which had become a bone of contention for users of all roads in the country. Never very good, BG roads had deteriorated considerably in the past few years, through neglect, especially on the East Coast Demerara, where a recent trip to my mother's had ruined two of my tires. New rains had made things worse, as if that were possible. It was a relief to get on the BG Airways DC 3 and onto the smooth tarmac for the take-off. I had a healthy respect for the plane and still think it one of the most reliable flying machines ever built. She rose gracefully, if noisily, into the hot afternoon air, made a wide slanting loop and soon we were crossing the Demerara at Sand Hills on a course due west over the thick dark green blanket that hid the ground.

The great rivers greeted us, first the Essequibo, then the confluence of the Mazaruni and Cuyuni, wide and sparkling as we flew along it at 5000 feet to Bartica, nestling in the angle between the Mazaruni and Essequibo rivers (how forlorn it looked, this small town with its little grid of streets and houses with steel roofs glinting in the sun, as if sending SOS signals to anything that passed by. Beyond Bartica the flight took us briefly along the southern bank of the Cuyuni towards the northern bank of the wider Mazaruni angling off to our left and partially obscured from view by heavy forest and low cloud. The unending carpet of green, a rare peek of the skinny trail that ran for thirty miles west of Kartabo Point (where the Cuyuni and Mazaruni met), or a clearing—things that marked the passage of men seeking timber and gold--and small snaking rivers were the only features until we came in full view of the Pakaraimas.

Supt McLeod took advantage of the scenic monotony to describe the elements of a proposed Forensic Sciences unit in the Ministry of Home Affairs, which his Minister Balram Singh Rai had fully endorsed. He had just completed plans for a preliminary meeting of those who would be involved, mainly the pathology, chemistry, legal, pharmaceutical, agricultural and other services. These would contribute their skills as consultants to the unit, which would have a nuclear staff under a director, coordinator and "general dogsbody", tentatively himself. The first meeting would be a fortnight hence, in early February, and would include administrators, (the Permanent Secretaries or delegate) from the Ministries concerned. He gave me a copy of his draft, which, apart from a statement of purpose and a catalogue of existing resources, human and other, and administrative structure, consisted of blank chapters to be contributed by the various services. The Ministry of Health had referred him to Dr Singh for the technical input, and he had suggested that McLeod brief me on this trip.

"Why the wry smile?" he asked, noting my response.

Balgobin, who had been paying careful attention—which McLeod had welcomed, since he would be part of the unit—responded in his direct way, "Doc is the lucky one; he get to do the work after everybody else turn it down."

We laughed it off, and I agreed, if it came to that, to write the pathology proposal. (I could draw much from the work of Dr Deepan, a Trinidadian pathologist, whom I had met in July '61 on my way to BG, who had gone through a similar exercise. I had a copy of the proposal he had put to his government, which remained unfunded, as the Williams government seemed quite enmeshed in a characteristically Trinidadian thing, *buhbul,* a complex blend of vices, from delay, through neglect to the grossest forms of corruption.

Deepan's proposal was his initiative, not that of his mulatto department head, Jack Arneaud--who had been a lecturer at the UCWI--nor of the Police, and issues of class, colour, race and authority loomed large in the approval process in that racially divided land, where Indians formed 34% of the population, and, as in BG, were economically strong and seen as a rising threat to the status quo. At least two good novelists, Sam Selvon and Vidia Naipaul, had begun to express the legitimacy of the Indian position, to balance the stridency of CLR James.

The Pakaraima Mountains burst on us suddenly; the eastern fringe of that remarkable and vast expanse of tall flat-topped mountains *(tipu* or *tepui*) that ran from BG deep into Venezuela, which Hari had described so vividly (*Book 1, Ch. 9)* They did not look like the mountains one saw in pictures—cones of jagged rock soaring in the air, like Everest or Matterhorn or McKinley; these were huge, solid cylinders of stone of varying height that rose abruptly from a flat or undulating plain, like massive silos, out of the forest, taking clumps of thick growth with them, like a school of dolphins rising from the deep with spumes of water clinging to their tops and sides. Some of the thickets of growth were quite tall and sturdy and clung stubbornly to the sheer cliffs.

"That's the beginning of mountain country, the Pakaraimas," the pilot's voice broke in suddenly on the intercom just audible over the drone of the engines; "this formation goes hundreds of miles far into the Canaima region of Venezuela; they call that huge area beyond the tallest tepui *La Gran Sabana*. It's a very pretty area, full of great scenery and wild life, including people, mainly Pemon, just like the ones at Kamarang and around there." He paused, static filling the air; presently he resumed, "Look down below; we're crossing the Puruni River, and you can see a round island in it just to our right; it's called Jackass Island--love to know how it got that name. Look ahead; those falls will give you an idea of how tall the cliffs are; these coming up are about a thousand feet, further inland and to the south they get up to three, four thousand until you get to Roraima which everybody knows is over 9000 feet."

The panorama was wonderfully new and breath-taking, so different from the North West District. Several cascades, up to fifty feet wide, fell off the edges straight down floating like sheer silver veils stirred by a zephyr. The largest of these fed tributary streams of the Puruni, which ran south to join the Mazaruni. The falls on our right was on the *Kamawaru* River near the *Warupina* peak; that on the left was on the *Tiger*. The cliff-face made a wide curve to the west just beyond Kamawaru, falling a thousand feet to the valley of the Puruni; the river, too, followed the same curve and changed to an east-west course. Just hearing the succession of strange names reminded me of Hari's accounts of native lore, his vivid descriptions of the tepui and their waterways, and the significance of the names.

We were now over the first large tableland, a thousand square miles of rocks, stones and trees, with secondary rises like clumps of careless surplus bricks left at a building site. Rain had just fallen and thick vapour closed in to obscure the view.

"Put on your seatbelts, gentlemen, it'll be bumpy for the next few minutes."

We came through the bumpy clouds at seven thousand feet, and into clearer air where a peak taller than any we'd seen before appeared on the horizon.

As if in answer to my silent question, the pilot announced, the speakers crackling, "We've just left the tepui and soon we'll cross the Mazaruni, but you won't see it: too much low cloud and mist filling up the valley. The mountain in the distance is called *Tomasing*; it's about three thousand feet, one of the Merume Mountains; we're just north of the middle part. In a few minutes we'll see the tallest peak, 3500 feet, but look to your right, it's not very clear but you can see three waterfalls; they're narrow, but I swear that the one in the middle is as tall as Angel Falls; it's on the *Eping* river; the one on the right is *Perenong* and on the left *Taureneiro*, which runs near Kurupung, (everybody in Georgetown know about the Kurupung gold rush long ago). I can't tell you how long it took me to remember all these names," he paused. "Actually," he chuckled, "I have them all on my flight map, so I ain't that clever after all."

The falls were indeed narrow--at this distance mere strings of white mist dangling off the cliff's edge. But they were quite a sight, dissipating into spray before they could touch ground, where they would be noticed as a gentle spray from heaven that continually wetted the forest and kept it lush and very damp.

"When the rains come," the pilot called out, "those cascades really begin to show; they get wider and fuller at the height of the rainy season. The region is famous for them but the best ones are far south; everybody know Kaieteur, at least the name."

The Merume Mountains occupied much of the Mazaruni enclosure, a large triangular tableland contained within a sharp curve of the river. We passed just north of the source of the Mazaruni, near a peak called *Partang*, almost in the centre of the Merume *tepui*. From there the Mazaruni flowed south across the forested plain (the top of the table), descending steadily, and after thirty miles or so took a U-turn to the west to gain the western edge of the tableland where it cut a deep gorge that ran north and downgrade for about sixty miles before curving abruptly like a hairpin to rush south-east through rolling hills in a canyon carved between the Merume *tepui* and its eastern neighbour; the river descended in cascades to its southern extremity, then again curved abruptly, this time northeast, to hurry on to join the Essequibo 150 miles away.

"We're coming in to Kamarang; tighten your seat belts; weather clear; the ground's a bit damp; they had showers earlier; this time you'll see the Mazaruni."

The unpaved runway lay on a picturesque plateau, one of several near tall peaks; it was smooth, composed of hard packed clay and grass in good repair and ran east-west parallel to the Paruima River just south of its junction with the Mazaruni. We landed with a bump and taxied smoothly to the terminus, one of several metal- or thatched-roof bungalows that housed Government services.

Three men emerged to greet us. One was the airways agent, a young Chinese man, the second a coloured officer from the office of the district commissioner for the interior, who had organised the autopsy, with the help of the third man, the local sicknurse/dispenser, a native Pemon, age 35, one of the few natives trained in this field. While the DC officer conferred with McLeod, the nurse briefed Balgobin and me as we changed and prepared our gear. He gave me a carefully hand-copied set of his notes, identical to one sent earlier to the police. I was amazed at the precision of his written work, and complimented him; he asked for permission to view the autopsy.

"Sure," I said, patting his back in a friendly gesture, "you can help us; we'll learn together."

"Come, I'll show you what we 'ave to do." Balgobin encouraged.

We joined the others at the southeastern edge of the runway, where two Black workmen had assembled a makeshift table at a point which commanded a sweeping and dramatic view of the mountains on all sides, and of the Mazaruni River about a hundred yards below in its deep gorge curving gently to the right through the side of the tepui on its course north.

A male relation of the deceased was there to identify the body, which had been interred about a week before. With the aid of a block and tackle erected over the grave, the crude wooden box was brought to the surface, and opened to reveal a shrouded but well-preserved adult male body in early stages of decomposition, slowed by the cool sandy sediment in which it had been laid.

The smell was pronounced but less penetrating than the one we had met at Wappai and easily kept at bay by Balgobin's rose oil. As he started the incisions I glanced at the assembled group, and was immediately struck by its composition: two Blacks, two Indians, two mulattos, one Chinese, one white, one native; add the Portuguese pilot and we were another microcosm of the BG population working without fuss or fury, together, to complete a task!

This is what we could achieve as a matter of course, if the politicians would only allow goodwill and cool heads to prevail. Mc Leod had noticed it too, and remarked on it later on, when we met in the city. He had commented then on Bacchus's glowing report on the way in which men of different races, including natives, had worked together on the Wappai trip.

"He even mentioned the long discussions you chaps had. I envied him the experience; said he came out a wiser man, praised the group to the last man; won't be surprised if he's promoted soon."

"He was perfect for the situation and kept us encouraged." I said. "I learned a lot about life and living together and about native peoples; pity about his brother Dan; that killing really shook him."

"A great tragedy; he was a fine detective." He paused. "I gather you two have much in common."

The deceased was a thickset mulatto man of about 45, who had been shot in the back; we counted twenty-two puncture wounds covering his trunk, occipital scalp and buttocks, the furthest 41 inches apart. The centre of this line was over his left kidney, where three entry wounds were seen.

Most of the pellets (they were two sizes, about 4mm and 6mm), had struck bone--vertebrae, pelvis, shoulder bones--or were embedded in the thick muscles of the buttock, upper thigh, shoulders and back while a few near the centre had penetrated the thinner flank muscles and entered the viscera; three of these had torn a hole in the left kidney between its hilum and the adjacent adrenal gland, shredding the veins and creating a large peri-renal and retro-peritoneal haemorrhage, which had tracked up to encase the pancreas, and down lifting the peritoneum along the course of the ureter and descending colon.

Another had lacerated the back of the liver, causing a lesser haemorrhage into the peritoneal cavity, which had about half a litre of degraded blood clot, riddled with air filled sacs from bacterial action. A few pellets in the left lung caused minor bleeding into the thoracic cavity. The heart and brain were not injured. Elsewhere we found no major damage or disease. We concluded that he had died from shock (peripheral vascular failure) due to blood loss. This was consistent with his mode of death. McLeod took photographs of each feature.

The shooter had found him conscious, dragged him out of the wood, then hurried to the airways agent for help. He, in turn, had promptly radioed the news to his office in Georgetown, and was told that a plane could arrive, if approved, early the following morning, as it was then near dusk, and air regulations demanded at least one hour of clear daylight for any flight from an unlit airfield. They had brought the victim to the emergency hut, where the nurse had given him whatever aid he could, kept him warm and forced oral fluids for as long as possible, but the victim had become paler and weaker, drifting into sleep and by nine that night could not be roused. The agent then informed his office, which relayed the news to CID, Brickdam.

We were through by 3.30 pm. The body was wrapped, placed in a cedar casket provided by the family and brought in by our plane, and placed in a special bay in the cargo hold. The victim's relative and the man from the DC's office joined us for the return journey. While we were busy, the pilot had supervised the loading of cargo consigned to government and private persons in the city. He was joined by another mulatto, a small man my size about 40, who looked almost Indian, but for his shock of curly hair; he had been staying at the Government rest house, a few buildings removed from the edge of the airstrip; he had heard the plane land and had wondered what unusual circumstance had brought it in that day. He had come over and had decided to take the opportunity of the fortuitous flight to advance his return to Georgetown, and had greeted the pilot knowingly. He introduced himself to us as Harris, whom McLeod immediately acknowledged, pumping his hand enthusiastically, saying, "Glad to meet you again, didn't know you were back." Then seeing the quizzical look on Harris's face, added, "Sorry, did I...?"

"I had hoped to complete this little escapade incognito," Harris interrupted affably, "but I see I'm revealed; I trust you will keep this to yourselves, at least for a while." He paused, his brow knitting, then asked enigmatically, "And where did we meet, if I may ask? I don't recall an encounter with the Police."

McLeod laughed briefly. "No, no; you mightn't remember; Carnegie Library, poetry reading, some time ago, just before you left the colony."

"My word!" Harris exclaimed. "Was my poetry that inciting? To summon the Police brass?"

Mc Leod laughed, this time more heartily.

"I'm sorry; I was off duty, in mufti, nondescript; don't expect you to remember me. Three years is a long time."

"They say we lose a million brain cells every day; I must have dropped the ones that held you; such a pity." He sighed, realistically, or was he just play-acting? He gave us no clue.

"I'm reading your book, *Palace of the Peacock,* challenging, slow going for me, but I enjoy it; have you been up here long?"

"Not really, just a few days, a stolen trip, as I hinted, securing a few neglected ends; time has a way of fulfilling itself; besides this is an energising place, one of nature's excesses; look at the spectacle around us; *formidable*, the French would say. It's nice to meet with you again, Superintendent; I'm pleased that you have the time to read what I write; so few do. By the way, may I join you on the flight back? The agent said I should clear with you. I'll pay him the fare, of course."

Mc Leod answered, "Yes, yes, no need to do that, from my point of view." He then introduced the rest of us adding, "Mr Harris used to be a government surveyor, until he left for England a couple years ago."

Harris nodded, said thanks, and as he shook my hand, he enquired, "And you're the pathologist solving the riddles of man's chicanery? You look awful young for that sort of distraction. And a bit gaunt too, I might add, but then gaunt is good, is it not?" His eyes twinkled.

"Good Lord, no, I mean 'no' to the *riddles* part. I'm just ambling along, trying to pick up as much information as I can." I tried to match his banter.

"Information? Or knowledge? They're different things you know; knowledge can spring from good information but we can be knowledgeable about misinformation, and proceed vigorously with that imperfection; that's called politics! But wait, I must get my bag."

He set off briskly, like a seasoned hiker, in the direction of the Rest House, leaving us agog, and was back in five minutes. Balgobin meanwhile had assembled all our samples--which McLeod and I had checked—packed his case and gone to the plane. While we waited, I savoured the clear fresh air as McLeod, citing the autopsy and related investigations, described the last elements of his concept of the Forensic Unit, specifically the role of our laboratory and the form of governance. He had obviously put much work into it, and his presentation made the whole project sound so exciting that I began to imagine myself in it, and liked the thought of becoming its chief medical sleuth—a far cry from plastic and reconstructive surgery, but reconstruction of a different kind.

At the steps, the agent stood with the pilot, writing on a clipboard. He tore the page off, handed it to the pilot, and said, "That's all done; till next time; have a safe flight."

We shook hands, thanked him and boarded the plane.

"Have you ever seen Roraima?" the pilot asked, looking up at the changing skies; (Harris had, as a government surveyor, and had been almost everywhere in the interior); when the rest of us said no, the pilot added, "it's about 30 miles south, less than 10 minutes away; I can take the little detour if it's okay with you, Super; we're within our fuel limit." Mc Leod hesitated briefly, looked at each of us in turn, saw the obvious approval and pleasure in our reaction, and nodded.

"You won't regret it; it's clear now; not much cloud; you'll see it from the right side; we'll pass about 10 miles east. It'll be the longest and tallest of the range. I'll break in and point out the sights."

As he walked off to the cockpit, Mc Leod said, nodding at Harris, "Or maybe Mr Harris might do that; he knows the interior better than most of us."

"Ah, flattery; 'twill get you everywhere." Harris said, his face mock serious, a wrinkle on his brow.

The plane taxied down the runway into the afternoon sky, its twin engines throbbing noisily; the weather had cleared nicely, the heavy grey blanket we had passed through two hours earlier replaced by fleecy white clouds that sailed sedately across the deep blue sky. The drone of the engines reduced conversation; besides, the sights distracted us, and I moved from left to right and back again to take photographs of features as the pilot recited them over the intercom and Harris shouted details from his long and intimate knowledge of the geography. We flew south following the line of the Mazaruni gorge, the western edge of the Merume Mountains to our left and the Kamarang plateau to our right. Ten miles on, we came to the *Kako* River, a tributary of the Mazaruni which rose from the northern edge of Roraima, and followed it south, as the main river veered to the east skirting the northern rim of a tall peak, part of a long range that ran north to south, on our left, a few hundred feet below eye level.

"That's *Karowtipu*, over 4,130 ft. tall," the pilot said, the intercom crackling, "and the next one a few miles south is *Hiamatipu*, 3745 ft.; it's on the same plateau as Karow."

"That's *Kako* speeding in that gorge below, almost straight down from *Assipu* near Roraima," Harris pointed, "it's turbulent, tumbles over three thousand feet before colliding with the Mazaruni and seems to push that great stream abruptly north off its western run; we'll probably see at least two spectacular cataracts, one just about now on *Arabaru*—there, to your left--falling off *Karowtipu* after carving a path down from the eastern plateau to join Kako."

We had a fleeting view of the distant falls glistening in the afternoon sun too shielded in mist for identifiable details from so far off. The pilot broke in.

"Our flight path will take us over the *Kako* gorge south to within 5 miles of Roraima; the forest is quite dense and the gorge usually misty but you might still see the *Chinakuruk* Falls."

We missed that sight as the river was lost in trees and mist; this after all was probably the rainiest region of BG. Almost immediately a tall tepui appeared on the southern horizon. The pilot made a slow wide turn to the east and announced, "There it is, Roraima, on the horizon, to your right: that long tall oblong; 9,094 ft.; it's partly hidden by cloud, but you can see the Guianese part quite clearly. You're getting an oblique view, as the long side runs roughly north south. We're at 10,000 ft. and about 5 miles north northeast; we're leaving the *Kako* and will soon cross the source of the *Arabaru* as we bear east. "

"From here Roraima looks like a fist, palm up, the knuckles facing us" Harris added, making a right-handed fist, then pointing to it, explained, "the wrist is in Brazil; the thumb is actually a second peak, the *Wei Assipu*, entirely in BG, like its three brothers we're now passing to the east of it: *Appokailang, Yakontipu and Maringma*. How I love the energy and rhythm of those names!"

"They sound like Sanskrit words." I observed. "You're part Indian, right?"

"Perhaps there's a linguistic connection; bears exploration as everything does here. But I fear I know naught about that ancient tongue or all who played a role in my genesis."

The mountains looked surprisingly close, especially *Yakontipu*, 8,050ft. tall, a T-shaped table that projected towards us. Seen through binoculars, they were similar to the picture I had formed in my mind from Hari's recent description of the *Kukenaam*: flat, brown, mysterious, and covered with rocks and low vegetation, their sides partly bare, partly festooned with tenacious trees. As a child, seeing mountains only as pictures in schoolbooks, I had imagined these as cones, not the solid oblongs or variations thereof that they were in reality, although their bases, lost in dense greenery, must be much wider than the summits. A most unusual sight, these truncated cones, stout and silent sentinels, as brooding, mysterious, compelling and inviting, as any of the world's wonders.

Within a minute, as the pilot completed his turn, we lost sight of Roraima but retained glimpses of its 'brothers' to the east, and then they too were behind us as the plane veered northeast over a thick carpet of green interrupted by white clouds. Soon we crossed a small stream running north, more forests, a second stream, and immediately over an airstrip, the *Kikui* River and Pipillipa airstrip, the pilot said. Crossing dense forest we came to a wide valley traversed by a stream into which several others flowed down on both sides.

"This is Mazaruni country;" the pilot intoned, "that river collects all of the streams that flow east and west off Merume; you remember we flew past Partang this morning, where Mazaruni starts; now we're passing it again about 15 miles south. The river makes a U-curve as it swings from south to north, so we'll cross it twice."

As we came to the first arm, Harris pointed, "There's a beacon almost directly below here; in the distance you'll see the airstrip at Imbaimadai, which is 15 miles north and perhaps Partang, if the clouds would let us. There you'll find many miners, mostly pork-knockers, chasing rainbows, but politicos vainly talk of getting heavy stuff, big pumps, drills, rock-crushers; UF assemblyman Eugene Correia, wants that, claims Americans will come with bags of money. 'Twill be a sad day if that happens; those men use mercury in goldfields; mercury is deadly for fish; fish is food which keeps us healthy. And any arsenic in the soil is turned into a deadly poison–your field, Doc. I won't be here to agonise over it; my views are known, but not heeded."

I recalled that an ansenopyrite is a component of many gold-bearing soils; when crushed and treated it releases the arsenic which reacts with atmospheric oxygen to form lethal arsenic trioxide. Mining companies often break agreements and neglect to clean-up this unwanted by-product and are known to declare bankruptcy even to avoid the expense, especially in small countries.

Suddenly he pointed to the northwest, "There, the *Chi-chi Falls*, not a great one, but very picturesque from the ground."

We crossed the Mazaruni again, at a point where it fell over a cliff, its spray glistening.

"We're now flying over the southern edge of the *Karanang* Mountains," the pilot advised, "the peak will come into view soon; it's 2,245 ft. high; a few minutes later we'll see the river again, only much wider, where it makes a sharp V-curve then settles in a northeast course to Bartica. It'll curve as we go along but we'll see it most of the time. We should land at Atkinson on schedule at 17.14."

"Mazaruni is shaped like a hairpin held curve up," Harris added, "with the left arm folded two-thirds the way down in a U to the right; then you bend the bottom end of the right arm to the right at a 60 degree angle and that gives you its line of flow from here to the Essequibo. With a little imagination you could find better analogies," he grinned, "but this will do for the moment."

As he finished, with a slight flourish, the river reappeared, indeed much wider, perhaps up to a mile, having completed its long hook-shaped turn around the Merume Mountains to begin its northeasterly flow, skirting the southern slopes of the *Sororieng* and *Banakaru* formations, the last of the tepui, which occupied the area between the Mazaruni and Puruni rivers, the eastern boundary of the Pakaraimas.

"I see the river fascinates you," Harris said, "that is treacherous water, brooding, at once a lifeline and a threat to life." He pointed into the distance, " just about now it will turn sharply northeast and run up to there," he pointed to the green hazy distance beyond the left windows, "then make a perfect half-circle, like a virgin's breast, and as pristine, before turning northeast."

Soon we left the Pakaraimas behind and there was nothing to see except the river completing its main downhill rush to enter a broad valley several miles wide where it spread out releasing megatons of pent-up silt to form numerous islands. These we would see peppering the river to within twenty miles of its confluence with the Cuyuni. It was an unusual sight. Among the islands the river flowed as a leash of narrow channels separating the islands and, descending to the valley floor, gave rise to stretches of white water, which we could see clearly. We flew along the southern edge of the valley; at times it was difficult to tell which of the dark skeins of water represented the main stream.

"You can take your pick and make a case for it; elsewhere it's easier." Harris said.

Ten minutes later we came to the confluence of the *Puruni* and Mazaruni; there were several points on both rivers where the water was white with foam from rapids, cataracts or waterfalls. As we got closer to the Cuyuni junction, the stream re-formed in time to throw itself successively over the Mora, Kuname, Mampa and Crab Falls. No sign of habitation was seen anywhere, other than a few narrow trails through the woods.

"The water is rough;" Harris broke in, "rough she is, like all the upper reaches of these rivers; they drop down from the tabletops, hit the floor either in one drop or after several steps; each stream has its array of waterfalls, cataracts and rapids; Kaieteur, the most impressive, is known widely, but they are all like family, different, big and small, yet alike, all wonderful to see --*miarbile visu*, as Horace Taitt would say--you must have had Horace in Latin, he's been at Queen's since time began—but these waters are perils, like the proverbial sirens, the bane of boaters; even the corials have to pick their way with care."

Then he drifted, almost trance-like, into an even recitation, on a theme he must have mulled over many times in the solitude of night and reflection, "Mazaruni is notorious for her unforgiving waters; they give life and they take it back. Mazaruni expresses the incorrigible persistence of nature, its refusal to give up even in the face of man's most abusive and grotesque actions.

"Look at that tapestry below, exquisitely designed; don't let its tranquillity fool you though into believing that the serenity is real; it is of the utmost moment for us as humans to study and appreciate that tapestry, and let its elements work its magic in our minds: the river, the forest, the mountains, all orchestrated and enlivened with sounds and shapes—mystical and real—of man and animals, trees and shrubs, and wild flowers. All so fragile--though tough they may seem-- because we know enough to destroy, but not enough to preserve them.

"You Hindus are smart; you retained your myths; you have separate gods to preserve and destroy. Would that we had that! Have you yet seen an orchid brightly viewing the world from its perch high in its host tree or a lone native in his placid canoe gliding on glazed water, silhouetted against the setting sun? Or a rare dragonfly hovering over water while the sun plays with its diaphanous wings and the minute tree frog that defends herself with killing fluid? Or thought of the clever Arawaks and Caribs of pre-Columbian times? And what of the night that brings the stars down to kiss the black treetops?"

Recalling my years of schooling in geography, I had learned more from him in that hour and better than in days spent poring over descriptions and landscape photographs. Even my widest angle lens could not reproduce the panorama of Roraima and the peaks due east; or of the bent hairpin shape of the upper Mazaruni he had so vividly fashioned; or the immensity of the green carpet through which tumbling brown waters snaked and over which scattered white clouds roamed, and in which a myriad of life forms lived and died.

Nor could I capture the enthralling imagery his intelligence had shaped from years of intimacy and bonding with fearsome Nature creating a mystical ethos that sustained him however removed he was from its energising force, and carried lessons for everyman. Was this why he had returned? Like someone in need of a booster dose of vaccine? Yet he exuded strength and piety -- though I doubt whether he would have called it that--laced with excitement that approached bliss, as if celebrating his epiphany (what Hindus called *darshana*) and the gift of enlightenment.

My last recollection of him was what he said, somewhat enigmatically, when I asked him why he, an artist of great promise had left a land of which he was so clearly fond and the many roots from which he had sprung – making him an archetype of BG's racial intermixing.

"Emotional and genetic attachment can be a heavy load to bear. But I must write. Who do I have here to read me if indeed I can find someone to publish what I write? My task here is done. I want to preserve these memories and not witness the stain that will overtake them if I stay to watch the scenes of pending grief unfold, so I've chosen exile. Escape. I have faced my oppressor head on; I understand him; I have chosen to live with him, yes! Years past he merged with his slaves and I'm the product of his adventurism and lust. I learned and absorbed his ways; he was good to me; he educated me, showed me light to relieve a curious darkness I had known in youth. He helped me to learn the secrets of this strange country, which few of my people on the coast can comprehend. Their indifference pains. My brother is less than kind. But most of all, he's consumed with ego and ignorance. He wants to rule me and bend me to his will, whatever that is. He's cruel and selfish. He does not just exploit, he smothers, he debases, just as my remote ancestor did, with none of his ancient virtues. I have seen the light. And the light led me to a cold and distant land--like Denis Williams, Vid Naipaul and George Lamming--that I might pursue my art and breathe without fear. Art and life are two sides of a coin. BG has a unique coin, the silver fourpence, our own symbol. The politics of BG will dull the sheen of both sides--art and life--and blunt, control and debase expression. I cannot abide that."

The police concluded their investigations, read the details of my report and laid no charges; I didn't query the decision, as I had no hard evidence to challenge it, even after the victim's relative, whom I had met at Kamarang, sought me out and bared his suspicions that bad blood had existed for a long time between victim and shooter, the nature of which was unknown beyond a passing hint. McLeod was aware of this, had researched it, but came up empty. I heard no more of the case.

McLeod moved swiftly on his Forensic Unit project. It was almost as if he sensed an accelerated need for the unit to begin its work, in addition to his stated fear that if the momentum were lost, the country might forever miss the opportunity to assemble the state-of-the-art equipment and technologies (and associated training), firmly promised by various US-based forensic units and the Colonial Office[142].

Hardly had we been back a few days than I got a phone call from Rex Woo Ming—a contemporary at QC and UCWI, now a senior chemist, or perhaps head of the Government Chemistry Laboratories, and in charge of Toxicology--asking for details. By early February McLeod had gotten each of us to describe how and what we could contribute to the unit, now becoming an urgent need as the mounting political unrest ushered in by the budget had clearly begun to show. We detailed current capabilities, limits, shortfalls and our individual needs. With Ken Eyre, Rex's classmate, now Government Pharmacist, we attended a meeting at the Ministry of Home affairs on Brickdam a few days later.

---

[142] McLeod knew of our attempts to develop a cheap and reliable test for blood alcohol, for both medical and forensic reasons, which Jain was working on; alcohol was a dominant factor in domestic quarrels, anti-social behaviour, from fist fights to murders, and increasingly in traffic accidents on land and water. He also wished early expansion of techniques of human identification, from trace to whole body samples, and a push for more comprehensive forensic data banks. I contributed to this from a number of case and group studies.

The Minister, Balram Singh Rai, a man my size, about 40, strikingly handsome and very self-assured, attended for about half an hour, greeted each by name, heard our points, indicated his wish to move quickly to develop a "strong independent unit, second to none, combining sciences and law to serve the public good; we will get substantial foreign aid and institutional support for this work if we can put a solid proposal in place." He wished us to support Supt. McLeod who had his confidence and the authority to do whatever was needed to get the unit started.

"In the present unsettled times we may have to move more quickly and likely before we have all things in place in the way you may wish. Cabinet understands the need; the Police welcome this action; so cooperation among Ministries is to be understood. We hope that we can do this right and in the best way, to give our country a solid base, and a model for others, for this aspect of law and order. I know that even before that, should there be an emergency, God forbid, I know I can count on you to do what has to be done with present resources to make sure that justice is fully served." Rai concluded his remarks and planned to follow up on developments.

His reference to "emergency" was the threat of political agitation already begun by the opposition to protest the introduction of strict currency controls starting soon after our return from Wappai. This caused resentment among business and professional classes--not because of controls *per se*, as they were common tools of poor countries--but because they were done without prior discussion with the Eastern Caribbean Currency Board of which BG was a member and its dollar fully convertible thereby to sterling. Controls effectively stopped currency export but it was "a little too late" as by September what little liquidity anyone had had already left. Further unrest--this time extending to labour--was expected to follow Finance Minister Jacob's budget presentation in the Legislature in January.

Jagan's performance in Washington had disappointed many and had given Burnham an excuse--however tenuous legally--to challenge Government's legitimacy. When the Legislature convened in January 1962 he refused to attend Parliament and defied orders to disband mobs agitating with him at the Public Buildings. The tension rose inexorably, as young demagogues denounced and issued deadly threats to Government and its workers in blind support of their leader. Later, hordes of protesters obstructed streets and defied police.

Violence and looting erupted, sporadically at first--by Black mobs shouting PNC and UF slogans and attacking any Indians who came in their way--then systematically, with news of the approaching budget, hardly had its author Nicholas Kaldor arrived. Failure of the Police to stop the disorders emboldened the anarchists.

Kaldor was an experienced and reputable left-leaning Cambridge academic, who had advised the Governments of Sri Lanka, India, Ghana and Mexico, aside from service on the United Kingdom Tax Commission.

It was postulated that he would introduce unpalatable fiscal measures to deal with declining national income, high unemployment and deteriorating social conditions that threatened the once peaceful, optimistic and vibrant city and country. Some fiscal strictures were probably justifiable and acceptable if there were political peace and stability, or at least the promise of them; or if the people had confidence that the leadership could be trusted to bring together all sectors that contributed to the building of a sound economy. That included the neglected and oppressed small businesses and farms and the middle class in general--in aggregate one of the largest employers.

But it seemed that Government focussed on "big" businesses--the two largest industries, sugar and bauxite--and was aiming to become the third, and ominously, the only industrial power, claiming to address a need avoided so far by investors, ignoring the fact that the social and political unrest over the past decade did not encourage investment. Rather it had already driven the bulk of Guianese capital overseas. Political stability had to be in place before financiers would commit the large sums needed to build a sound economic base with enough flexibility to adapt to changing needs without undue strains.

In plain words, the budget had to be timely and the government trustworthy. But there was little trust in the word of Government leaders, least of all Jagan, especially after his visit to the USA, doubts on the question of his personal political philosophy, and the seeming threat of a Castro-like take-over.

The disappointment had become foreboding, and Kaldor's budget was anticipated with some resistance, if not dread. When it was introduced in the Legislature on January 31 it could not seriously be called "a communist budget", as it contained some reasonable elements, but it was premature, heavy-handedly presented and consolidated distrust already simmering, and threatened small business activity; many said it seemed more suited to a developed economy, noting that while it did not affect the labouring class directly, it would by contracting the pool of employers!

The main features were a personal capital gains tax of 45%; property tax of 0.5% of net wealth over $35,000; taxes for any business declaring a loss would be calculated on a minimum profit of 2% on total gross annual sales; advertising deductions limit of 0.5% of total sales (these two to catch businesses with persistent annual "losses"); compulsory deduction of 5% from personal salaries in excess of $100 per month--the National Savings levy--which would purchase 7-year bonds yielding 3.75% free of tax to provide a fund for 'industrialisation'-- the most contentious of the measures, all of which had set "wealth" levels too low. Other measures were exchange control, gift and various other tax increases, including "luxury" taxes on tea, alcohol, tobacco, soft drink concentrates, motor spirit, perfumes, cosmetics, the more expensive dress fabrics, footwear, glassware, chinaware, jewellery, radios, refrigerators, motor cars and on imported food for which there were abundant local substitutes. An increase in excise duties on beer, rum and other spirits was included.

Although endorsed by sober analysis the measures contained enough and accumulative new impositions that any critic could twist to his/her own agenda. Senator Tasker, head of Booker Bros in British Guiana, the largest plantation owner in the country and a hated name in Labour and PPP circles, assessed it as *"a realistic attempt to grapple with the economic problems of British Guiana."* His UK boss, Sir Jock Campbell, declared it *"a serious attempt by the Government to get to grips with the formidable economic problems of the country by a hard programme of self-help"* and suggested that the Guianese people had nothing to lose. The *London Times* called it *"courageous and certainly not far from what Guiana must have"*, and the *New York Times* said something similar. (In a sense these did not help and were often quoted as "big business" seeking to position itself for future favours.)

But what caught on and hit the terror trails were the screaming headlines in local political papers especially *The Chronicle* and *Argosy* and the truculence of their originators: *"Tax Avalanche..."*, *"Slave Whip Budget"*, *"Budget is Marxist"* etc.

Finance Minister Jacob exacerbated these harsh reactions by reminding people of his warning delivered a few months earlier in the House on the rosy future of Marxism in BG: *"My honourable friend, (Mr d'Aguiar) who is a member for Georgetown Central has attempted on the floor of this House to refute Marxism. This is a futile attempt. Learned university professors, of course of the bourgeois tradition, professional mercenaries, politicians, common vilifiers, have all tried to refute the unassailable logic of Marxism. They have all failed. ...We will attempt to build a new society, a society which exists in more than one third of the world today, a society in which there will be freedom and plenty for everybody. That is a genuine socialist society."*

In a display of uncommon naiveté blended with arrogance, Jagan piled error upon error justifying the proposals and actions as party policy endorsed by the electorate, but many saw them as incautious, whimsical or self-indulgent, serving only to feed opposition ire. As previously noted several actions seemed not only premature but insulting, e.g. the appointment of the bumptious and opportunistic neophyte, L. Mann, to a new and sensitive headship of Jagan's new Import/Export Control agency.

This office was itself controversial and severely criticised by the Civil Service and a perplexed business community, the UF asserting that it would merely be an instrument to facilitate PPP's business arm, GIMPEX, as it established trading links with the Soviet bloc. Jagan glibly dismissed this and other contentious issues in addressing adoring followers asserting that the measures were part of "the mandate which you the people have given me". These were the same folks who, in the privacy of their homes and to confidantes like Shah, often admitted that they hardly understood a word of his jargon-filled and long-winded diatribes.

The budget was grist for the opposition mill. In the deteriorating political climate, Burnham and D'Aguiar harangued their followers, D'Aguiar proclaiming, "*...show your mettle, buck up and kick off the braces, unite and fight to break this bare-foot, bare-back, bare-faced budget...Oppose, expose and depose"* the government. Meanwhile Burnham told his people that the government *"cannot be removed by mere slogans;* much more *was needed!"*

Their lieutenants: Ptolemy Reid, Robert Hart, Hamilton Green (PNC), Egbert Bolton, Rahman Gajraj, Richard Ishmael, "Nasty" Nascimento (UF) and Party hierarchies down to the man in the street used these leads uncritically to fuel fears of totalitarian control. The city was thus poised for serious conflict. No one beside the PPP planners believed, for example, that the National Savings levy (NSL) would be used wisely for its stated purpose, since everyone knew that the government did not have the experience and expertise to invest in gainful enterprises, even if its philosophy favoured such things[143].

Thus the levy was seen as just another tax grab perpetrated by a gang of the untried and incompetent, led by a demagogue. The opposition parties and trade unions generally, including the Civil Service unions, the press, business and commerce, not to mention many individuals had all slammed the proposals for new taxes. Businesses, small and large, condemned measures aimed to raise general revenue while imposing stringent new controls on prices and profit

---

[143] "The intelligent use of visiting experts depends upon the presence of a well-trained planning staff. Without it the expert comes, spends a long time searching for the most elementary information, makes a report which inevitably raises a series of new questions, and the bulk of his work is quietly forgotten when he leaves." Raymond Smith, 1961

margins that many small businesses showed would be too low to cover costs and thus cripple many and lead to further loss of jobs.

Political protesters, organised by the PNC and UF, continued to terrorise the streets in large gangs, crippling business on the city's main commercial thoroughfares. Indians, including small businessmen affected by the measures, stood dismayed, yet stuck with Jagan, the "devil", already fearful of the "deep blue sea" that was now displaying its tsunamic rage.

Enter "Singh", stage centre

In mid-February 1962 Burnham had one of his regular meetings with a friend and adviser, whom he called simply "Singh". They had met for many years behind-the-scenes discussing Indian relations, starting with briefings on the BGEIA and expanding into the customs, motivations and philosophies of Indians. He was of rural origin, had joined the RAF at age 19, and served on its ground staff in communications, at a base in southern England. There he had met and been impressed by a Barbadian, Errol Barrow–his first Black friend--who served as a gunner and by war's end had completed 45 or so bombing missions over Europe.

Barrow was a keen leftist with definite ideas on decolonisation and the directions West Indian colonies should take towards federating. At war's end they had joined the mass of demobbed young people entering British universities to complete degrees. Singh studied politics, economics and history at the London School of Economics (LSE), and finally took law. Barrow also did economics at LSE and law, but concurrently. At LSE he had also met Michael Manley of Jamaica, Pierre Trudeau of Montreal, both keen and voluble socialists, and Lee Kwan Yu of Singapore, who helped to mould his views.

They were fascinated with Soviet victories over the "brown plague" ("Nazi" sobriquet), and contrasted the coming excitement and promise for social change with the repressive capitalist hegemony and excesses that had led to the Great Depression. All agreed that it would be foolish for societies to return to those wretched days, and perhaps the Soviets might have some promising alternatives. None was ready to adopt Communism without further study. Singh was attracted to Trudeau's notion of *"personalism"* which saw the socially conscious individual operating symbiotically within communities and helping the economy, on a basis of justice and free choice.

He wished to debate the concept and the manner in which a society can achieve justice and fair play, especially in access to economic activities in underdeveloped colour-afflicted states such as the Guianas. Trudeau seemed to be well off despite his spare life style and was planning an extended study-travel trip overland to the Middle East, India and China and invited company. Singh dearly wished he could have said yes but finances and family commitments determined otherwise and Trudeau went off alone. He hadn't seen him since.

Singh had met Forbes Burnham at meetings of the West Indian Students Union (WISU). Regarding his rhetoric as shallow and bombastic he remained unimpressed and aloof and avoided him until they both attended a World Youth Festival in Paris and were billeted together. Burnham was impressed with Singh's sharp intellect and fair-mindedness and despite an inherent resentment of Indians — which to his surprise was not reciprocated by those he met at the Festivals, nor by Barrow — he covertly courted Singh's friendship and used him as a sounding board for his plans to play a lead role in BG's politics, and hoped to continue the relationship on Singh's return to the colony.

Singh had returned to BG late in 1956, settling into a quiet business law practice under a company umbrella with major clients including Bookers Bros, the sugar giant, which suited his talents and self-effacing personality. He maintained a small farm near his Ogle birthplace and took the train each day to his office in Georgetown, or else on fair days rode his bicycle along the train tracks to Kitty and thence to his office via Lamaha and Main Streets.

When Jagan won the 1957 elections he had offered—with the encouragement of Bookers--to contribute anonymously to the Government's planning and policies. After initial private meetings brain-storming fiscal matters Jagan accepted his offer to prepare appropriate guidelines for the first budget, but Jagan rejected them as *"too bourgeois, and while they might be okay for Bookers and corporate exploiters, they did not fit in with the thrust of my socialist government!"*

Singh's arguments showing the long-term benefits of the strategies outlined and how they would uplift the masses had impressed several of the Ministers and officials present, but Jagan was adamant in his rejection, and soon ended the relationship, despite covert approaches by Bookers to reconsider.

Burnham contacted him some time after, but once bitten Singh was reluctant to deal with politicians although he knew that his proposals were moderate and eminently suited to BG. Indeed even the Sugar Producers Association (SPA) was in favour although its members stood to lose considerable tracts of land, then idle and unlikely to be brought into cane cultivation. He eventually and cautiously began a non-partisan relationship with Burnham, which both wished to be a discreet and private one. He had direct access to Burnham but no links with the PNC Executive[144], and would meet secretly with him for "strategy sessions".

On that day they discussed the tactics of confrontation and violence against Indians which Burnham had already sanctioned. Singh disagreed with the tactics and told him so, asserting that he could win over Indian support by cooperating with Jagan's government, and using the house to point out Jagan's weaknesses, his extremism, *anti-Indian* activities, and to show how PNC policies would empower Indians in the real sense. He urged him to consider Jagan's power-sharing offer.

To this Burnham scoffed, "Maan, you joking! Empower Indians? We're not going to do that. We can't do that. All my people will go over to him; you know he does more for black people than for coolies," (Singh winced), "but my people don't see it; I don't let them! I can't let them!"

"Nevertheless, call off the hounds and give up the policy of violence against Indians," he urged, "stop robbing, criticising and targeting Indian businessmen; they're not the enemy, the enemy is the ruling elite, the hegemony of whites, Portuguese and Chinese who dominate trade and commerce. Indians

---

[144] He later regretted the secrecy and anonymity when Burnham became Premier--much more quickly than he had expected, as he said, due to Jagan's "intransigence"--and initiated repressions against Indians which Singh condemned. But he could not credibly make his role public; as Burnham said when he summarily "dismissed" him, a year later, "you don't exist." His life threatened, he chose a business visit to the Skeldon Estate to quietly slip over to Surinam, escaping to England via Holland, like so many other Guianese. His place was taken overtly by Sonny Ramphal, a lawyer and Burnham sycophant who is said to have helped design the Constitution Burnham would later impose on the country, transforming it from a democracy at its founding to a constitutional dictatorship.

are peaceful people; their religion, at least Hindus, is firm on that, and violence is frowned on except when all else fails and even so they will defend, not attack, so no fear there."

Burnham was sitting in a cane rocking chair; the low table that separated them held a bottle of J&B Rare whisky, bottles of soda and an EPNS ice bucket. Whiskies of various brands stood on a portable trolley near one corner of the room. He stopped rocking, swung his body around.

"Careful! That's bold talk, maan. Indians can get along with us?"

Singh said quietly, "Yes. I'm trusting my intuition that you want it straight, no soft soap."

Burnham eyed him briefly, quizzically, then nodded. Singh continued, urging him to change his policy and approach and to push for increasing the number of Indians in the Police Force and Civil Service. Indians were more loyal anyway, especially good Hindus.

"Give them the job, pay a decent wage; you don't have to bribe them."

"How's that again?"

"Well, the revered Hindu sacred text, the *Bhagavad Gita*, dealt with the precedence of duty over emotional attachment to kith and kin, the very opposite of your doctrine. You know well that your own black supporters are fickle and have to be bought, and are only loyal if you feed them or capture them, as you did, in fief, by rhetoric and charisma, and now they know they're protected when they rob Indians and that you or one of your legal mates will defend them if caught, for free. So they do it. But believe me, they'll drop you if someone richer or nicer comes along.

"Good Hindus will keep their loyalty to duty, which means Police and service people will be far more likely to do a good and fair job than Negroes. Also Hindus are tougher on their own kind than on Negroes and Portuguese or Chinese, because they don't want to show favouritism. You blacks don't feel that way. So recruit for the Police and Security services from good religious Hindu families, incorporate *Bhagavad Gita* principles and teachings into PNC literature and openly acknowledge the teachings and religions of the Indians."

Burnham stopped rocking, leaned forward and exclaimed, "You must be crazy, Singh! What's all this fool talk of *Bhata what,* whatever? Look, we're not here to joke!"

He sounded irate, but Singh stuck to his point. He said, "I'm serious; it's not a joke. The *Bhagavad Gita* is a holy book for Hindus. They try to live by its principles."

Burnham looked sharply at Singh, gulped his drink, smacked his lips and said, after a pause, "If I do the things you say, remember, a big IF, how long will it take for me to get power?"

"One full term, two at most."

"Too long."

"Well, even though the Brits are keen to get rid of us, you have to allow time for Jagan to screw up, which he's doing fine! He will forget the Indians and go after the Georgetown Negroes, as he's always done, no matter how badly they treat him. While he's doing that you remind the Indians of his neglect, and show them how *you* support them; the middle class will listen and come over, especially when they see no progress in fair employment practices and increasing strictures in business legislation. Also Jagan is more and more in bed with the USSR, now that Cuba is their satellite and getting aid. Castro will be

Jagan's mentor now. The Yanks don't like that. Also, as Jagan continues to cuss the pandits and mullahs, you do the opposite; don't make it too obvious; make a few practical gestures, like attend a service at a mosque or *mandir*, and follow the proper religious practices. Lastly, hold out the olive branch, act as if you *really* believe in unity, and you'll get the US to see you differently. You know they don't like you and as we speak are busy trying to drag Jagan out of the Soviet camp into theirs."

"The US! Those greedy hypocrites? They're not smart. They'll have to come to *me*, on my terms, you watch! What you say, my friend, make sense as usual, but I can't do what's against my blood. I already have all I need to take over, and I won't wait a whole term; Cheddi makes it easier for me every day, like he was my lieutenant." He grinned ominously. "Two years at most. Cheddi is too blind with ideology to see my trap. Besides, he picked the wrong side in this Cold War! He's not a practical man."

"Two years? Jagan has four years to go. He's taking Jai's independence motion to London soon."

"That's his big mistake. But I want to tell you a few things. It's true that the Indians are not the real enemy now, not in economic terms, though a few of them, a hundred, maybe two hundred families, are quite rich; others are well-to-do, but you know they are the perceived enemy of my people and in a sense robbed Negroes of their birthright, the country lands..."

"Sorry to interrupt, you always say that, and it's not true..."

"What is truth? It's enough for me to believe that that is true, because all black people believe that that is true, rightly or wrongly. What the mass of my people now see is numbers; you people are too many; the number scares us, because we don't have your culture, your dedication to work and duty, your philosophy of non-violence, your rich history, your views on life. I saw that up close in '54 when we toured India. My people are generally lazy; that suits me They still believe that Government is responsible for them and will provide; they think Jagan will send them back to cut cane and haul punt. They are also British, black Brits, they have nothing of Africa; none of us has. Look at Sydney! Fooling himself that if he change his name he will become African: Eusi Kwayana!"

He expostulated with derision and venom, "I didn't really want him to join me, but he's useful; he embarrassed Cheddi and swelled my membership by a few thousand. With all his pretensions, what's his reference? What African thing will he bring to our hungry ignorant brothers? Which one has ever heard of Gorée, Dahomey, Ajaland or the other Black West African kingdoms that sold their inland ancestors into slavery, coffled by the neck like swine to market? If you tell them that their own people sold them like meat, they'll kill you. We are not a culture here; we're displaced Africans with no language, no law, no literature, no religion, no architecture, no medicine; all that we have is British.

"We're four hundred years removed; we have no common ground left except our colour. Sure there is some art, music, clothing, jewellery, food, all lost tribal stuff of no great moment, but I can exploit them, as Haiti did, from Dessalines to Duvalier. I now lead a tribe! You can't have a tribe that does not share blood lines. I cannot be the leader of your tribe. No Negro can look at an Indian, however dark, and say, 'that's my kith and kin'. That sentiment is what determines their loyalty. I am their Chief, their shaman, their medicine man. I am their provider. I hold the power of life and death over them. They all know it. So I must look after them. I can make them do anything, *anything*!"

He spat out the words, paused and took a long pull at his whisky, and ended expansively, "I can make them go wild. I can make them keep the peace, but I cannot make them accept you all the way you'd like, Hindu or Muslim. To do that I would have to send every man jack of them through a liberal University, or at least QC or Bishop's! No, no; each must stand alone, to me subservient!" He paused again while Singh stared into the distance as if seeing the shape of a future he dared not contemplate. His eyes closed, while Burnham, oblivious, took another pull at his drink. "No Singh," he resumed, "I have to say that what you propose sounds excellent, but it won't do…"

Singh interrupted, knowing full well that Burnham would bristle, but he trusted his judgement, "It will, as long as you explain it to them. Look, I accept the tribal part–some are already calling you *the witch-doctor*--and that's just the point. The hold you have over them is strong enough to hold them back from violence, which, by the way you encourage and promote in all your speeches, however conditional, Mr Machiavelli! Or should I say Chanukya? I may have told you about that Indian genius who laid it all out long before Machiavelli."

Burnham guffawed, "You getting close to danger, Singh!"

It was difficult to interpret how much of that was jest, but they had set the rules that the talk would be open and frank, brainstorming, in fact, and Singh felt he had to say it as it came. He had had enough of the Jagans' obduracy, but then had questioned his sanity in deciding to deal with Burnham.

"In the next week or so when you raise the issue, you remind them that Indians and Negroes have co-existed reasonably well in country areas for a hundred years, that the rise of Indians was due to hard work, that Indians in Georgetown and New Amsterdam are major employers of Africans, that many have black friends, and some relatives even; Indians and Negroes play together, cricket, football; they represent BG internationally. They swim in the same ocean, catch the same fish, eat in the same restaurants and read the same papers; they go to the same cinemas, date one another. You tell them that it is fine to be loyal to the tribe, but co-existence is possible and *is* a superior concept.

"Tribalism is the way of blood, but every tribe admits new blood if it wants to refresh itself; here we can refresh by extending our hand in acceptance and moving forward to a common goal. They will do what you say. Instead of destroying the place to achieve power, get them to help you build, help you work for unity and mutual strengthening. Remember the BGEIA resolutions? That's precisely their thrust still. They want to work with you, gain your trust."

Burnham turned aside, as if unable to counter the power and logic of Singh's monologue. Slowly he got up and walked across the room and turned into the corridor that led to the bathroom. He pissed loudly and long. Singh looked at the bottle of Scotch, 40 ounces. He had had two drinks; the bottle was half gone. Burnham had had some twelve ounces of liquor, yet seemed unfazed. Or was he?

He returned, belched loudly, resumed his seat, rocked squeakily and leaned forward to pour a drink, saying as he did so, "You know Singh some of my people thought this J&B was made 'specially for Cheddi and me. Incredible! But maybe I could use this to sell your idea."

He guffawed and finished pouring; Singh smiled and accepted the proffered bottle, pouring an inch into his glass. Meanwhile Burnham leaned back in his chair, rocked a few times, as if contemplating. Sipping his drink, he started to speak through it, sending a spray across the table, falling short of Singh.

"Sorry, maan, sorry," he paused to dab at his lips with a handkerchief pulled, like a gun, from his hip pocket; the movement was swift and startling; he grinned, or rather leered, as that was the structure of his face that it produced sometimes unintended appearances, which worked more often than not to his disadvantage. He noticed Singh's reaction.

"Frighten you, eh? It's jus' me kerchief; but to go back: you know what you say is, as I said, eminently sound and workable, it took the Indian Congress over 60 years to get rid of the British. The way of peace and the strategy of harmony are fine in a mature society like India with an old culture and lots of highly educated people. But let's face it, we don't have that in Guiana; we're dealing here with rabble who are normally docile but once fired up—as we've made them by promises of freedom, independence and plenty–they cannot understand the language of patience, understanding and forbearance. They think independence will mean freeness for all.

"Many Indians think the same way, too. I hear Cheddi or maybe it's just his agents, telling people that when independence comes they will get many free things: ploughs, tractors, sewing machines, the three things allyuh *coolie* will kill for." (Singh, the quintessential urbane Indian, again winced visibly).

"Cheddi is promising Government control of production and of the means of production, but they don't know language enough to understand what he's saying. So they believe each will get free tools to do what they like with, instead of state ownership of everything, even their labour. That's the mentality we're dealing with. Primitive. Almost bestial. We know it, we exploit it; but the poor suckers don't know it. Look, in Jamaica Manley the intellectual lost to a clever joker, Bustamante. Why? Busta's people toured marginal areas and handed out free saltfish–the Jamaicans love their ackee with saltfish.

"I promise the people independence since 1953. They already marked time. They're fired up; they're hot; they're ready now! Your plan as you rightly say will take five years, likely ten. If you can see five maybe I'll think about it; maybe I can wait, but will they?"

"You must think of your place in history and not allow the charge of rabble-rousing to develop and take hold, no matter how well you believe you can control press and radio or change things later on. Information passes down the generations in powerful and enduring ways and is preserved; we can't control that information, neither its flow nor content, much less ignore or erase it, unless we all die childless, or society disintegrates."

Burnham laughed heartily.

"Oh, Singh, Singh, my friend; you are serious! Don't fret about that one! Once I'm in charge of Government, I will have wealth *and* power; I *will* control tomorrow!"

Singh sighed; he knew full well that Burnham's response indicated that his mind had been made up, even before the meeting, and that this sounding out was more for a social and intellectual purpose than as guide to political strategy. He returned to Burnham's point re a guarantee.

"No, I cannot give time guarantees, you know that; who knows you might achieve it in four, if the momentum picks up, as well it might. We won't know unless you give it a try. The difficulty is that too much has happened these past eight years to polarise people and keep them so."

"Water under the bridge, and all that! How do you see us proceeding?" He humoured Singh.

"Well, You can try what I suggest, gauge the response of the US and UK, and retain your right to shift tactics. As you know the US slammed Britain and other colonial powers in the UN, but the US Secretary of State holds the contrary and hypocritical view that Britain should *not* grant independence to BG as Jagan is considered Communist and another Castro. You know that US is pushing London to delay independence. In fact we now hear that a group headed by one Bill Burdett within the State Department is forcing Dean Rusk to formally press Alex Douglas Home to even *deny* independence under Jagan. But I doubt that Home can deal with BG separately from other colonies; given that, I believe Rusk will have to do better than just push and must come up with a sweetener; an easy one in this hemisphere would be to have their Guatemalan puppets dismiss their claims on British Honduras."

"And we look good helping our BH friends. Smart. You're sure of your sources? The Burdett thing is highly charged, I'm told, and can embarrass Kennedy."

Singh nodded. "The US has serious domestic problems with civil rights, and externally with Latin America — that includes us--but the worst is with Khrushchev over Berlin and that could mean WWIII, even with the Wall penning in East Berliners. In that context BG and Jagan are small painful burrs on their behind, and taking up more time than they wish, but their obsession with Communism magnifies it just as it does Cuba. Don't forget that in Uruguay a few weeks ago, the OAS declared Marxism-Leninism and Cuba under Castro as contrary to the "Inter-American" system. Jagan will *not* change. So you can forget independence under him.

"If the CIA finds a genuine alternative in the PPP, he would go the way of Lumumba, or at least Guzman. Or if he was a money hound, they would already have come up just so," he snapped his fingers, "with a nice Swiss deposit. But he's there, and will be for a long time, as he keeps Indians pacified. That leaves you as the only alternative. We can forget, and although difficult, forgive that simpleton D'Aguiar except as a convenience you can use as you like."

"You know, of course that he's retained me to defend him before the courts?"

"Yes, and that might make the US pause to reappraise you. The US doesn't trust you--we already said that--but distrust never stopped them from convenient alliances. See how they courted Duvalier to get the vote on Cuba at that OAS meeting! So if you give them something they will have to return the favour, or look mean. So you should change tack, go easy on Indians, hold out the olive branch, soften your attitude to D'Aguiar and with the strength and rise of black power in the States and a strong black lobby in Washington, you'll have the US looking at you differently. So slow down the rhetoric on independence. Tell the people you have just found out that the Brits have been withholding development money since 1947 and that Jagan knew about that since 1953 and did nothing to expose this fraud, yet he's attacked the Brits for failing to develop the country, ignoring all the excellent advice he's had from the earliest days and more recent open secrets of exchanges between here, Washington and London all saying more or less what we have said.

"He's too quixotic, doctrinaire and indecisive to lead an independent country. What *he* hopes to do is to go for independence, negotiate a release of development funds as a kind of parting gift and then come home and tell the people that he got that all for them, 'see what a great chap I am' sort of thing.

You can do much better; your socialism isn't yet the baggage his is in the eyes of the West."

"You trust your US sources? Melby here not on my side! Who you got?"

"Bookers is an international sugar company and exists on the quality of its information. US Sugar is owned by the Mott family, friends of Eisenhower who pushed through various anti-Cuba measures since '58 and now cancelled US sugar imports of nearly 2 million tons yearly; we want some of that quota, but Communism could block that. Also with Trujillo killed last May, and Joaquin Belaguer now starting a democracy in the Dominican Republic, *they* might get the quota boost; it's quite fluid; Cuba remains a major headache for Kennedy and he doesn't want another; Jagan's not helping himself, our sugar industry nor the interests of the people he wants in his sugar union. So I pay attention."

Burnham sipped contemplatively, praising Singh for his ideas. "I can see why you pushing me in your direction. You have balls, I say. None of my people would dare suggest I accommodate Indians. Hammy's eyes will pop out his head if you talk peace; and Ptolemy, he's a vet with a hard head; he does what I say, but he too will quail. He's a Director at Bookers and doesn't seem to know this inside stuff."

"If any director knows this it would be from hearsay."

"OK, Singh, I tell you this. I'll think on it. Research the timeline a bit more; what you say widens my options; we'll talk again."   ·

On February 12th I hurried to pick up Phillip near noon on a call from his school, St Andrews Kirk & School, at the intersection of High St and Brickdam, across from the Public Buildings. I had taken my camera having heard a radio broadcast describing the intense street activity near the Legislature that had forced the school to close. While waiting outside the school I was standing perilously on the small oval traffic island in the middle of High Street at Brickdam aiming my camera at a boisterous mass of black men in tattered khaki shirts or white singlet vests who had mustered on Brickdam in front of D'Aguiar's Imperial House just past the Kirk. They were brandishing sticks, hoes, bicycle chains and similar "arms" as they shouted in response to a harangue by Peter D'Aguiar whose white shirt and red tie gleamed in the full sun striking the north sidewalk of the Legislative buildings; a cluster of black men surrounded him, among them Burnham's deputy, Dr. Ptolemy Reid.

A passing truck with an Indian store logo screeched to a halt as it neared the crowded intersection almost removing my bent elbow and spoiled my picture. It rolled on a few feet past me, to be hammered by the tail of the irate mob; its black driver was impulsively dragged out of his cab and pummelled before someone shouted with authority, "leave him alone, is one of we!", and allowed him to move on, wiping blood from his frightened face.

Looking up I saw Steve standing close to the iron railing that framed the yard of Phillip's school just then disgorging hundreds of children for pick-up. I was concerned too for my sister's building and business located on Hadfield Street a block away across the south face of the Legislative Buildings. So far the action had concentrated on Brickdam where the main gates had been locked to prevent ingress by the mob. Jagan and some ministers including Jacob had received threats from unnamed sources. The PNC and UF leaders had billed the raucous and unlawful assembly *a spontaneous and peaceful popular demonstration*". At that moment it seemed more like preparations for a battle with much shoving, shouting, waving of sticks and bicycle chains (and God knows what other occult weapons) with insulting and belligerent name-calling of the Premier closeted somewhere in the Building. At the fringe of the crowd Indians straying too close were pounced on; one was led away bleeding from a wound on his forehead, another had his bicycle smashed. The few policemen at the scene looked pitifully inadequate. (Later the Chief of Police would tell the public that the Police were "on top of the affair" and had many plainclothes men in the crowd, presumably to protect the mob, as one of the injured ruefully remarked to a reporter!

But officially he had asked the Governor for army assistance, which did not appear for several days.) When the worst actions occurred Burnham denied the Governor's request to intervene saying, *"The man who calls off the dog owns the dog!"* D'Aguiar responded by asking for protection for his wife and family from the dogs he had himself released! I had no doubt that had this occurred on a sugar estate the Riot Squad in full gear would have already shot the ringleaders as soon as the Act was read.

Steve was clicking away at the scene unmolested at the edge of the surging crowd, the only white face visible there; I quickly crossed the street, avoiding close attention lest my camera be seen by the mob, and went to the padlocked gate of the schoolyard, now manned by a guard. I told him that I had come in response to the broadcast alert to take my son home. He hesitated seeing my camera, "You a reporter?" he asked suspiciously.

"No," I said, "I'm a doctor at the Public Hospital."

He looked even more sceptical, but just then I saw Gaitri with Shanta, holding hands, and Kip (three of Buddy's children) with Phillip and a group of boys racing across the schoolyard towards the fence nearest the commotion, their school bags bouncing on their slim hips as they ran. Phillip heard my third call, stopped abruptly just short of the fence that angled away to the right along Brickdam, not twenty yards from me. A fight broke out on the street and two women standing on the sidewalk, suddenly lifted their dresses, and with deeply flexed hips and knees aimed bare arses towards the Legislature, shouting at the top of their lungs, "Hey Jagan, you coolie dawg, come lick duh!"

They straightened, guffawed to vociferous approbation of the men close to them whom they had briefly distracted from the serious business of rioting, one offering, "Keep it warm dey, gal; ah goin' ketch you laytuh!"

Just then the mob marched off behind their leaders and headed north on High Street to the Parade Ground where they assembled for further haranguing. Steve came over as I collected the four children and held them in the compound, waiting for the mob to disperse. We exchanged small talk about the children and when the road cleared we parted.

The iron folding gates of my sister's store were barricaded and manned, and the plate glass windows covered with tightly-woven steel mesh shutters, as if under siege. People had begun to come out from hiding to resume their life, with much regretting and wonder at what they had seen and heard. *"Dis na nottn; it gwine get mo' baad! Fire dey fe come!"* a skinny well-known thirty-ish black waif in shirt-tails announced as he sailed past on the sidewalk, right arm swinging to its full extent, his left cradling a large brown paper bag with his customary daily receipts of food collected from businesses on his beat, *none* of which was African-owned!

Some of the gangs had earlier rattled the gates and shouted threats of arson and murder, but no breach had occurred. As relative calm returned my brother Buddy concluded a roll call of family, employees, visitors and customers. His oldest daughter, Savitri, 11, was "safe" at Bishop's High School, on a quiet street, half a mile away, but not far from the Parade ground.

My sister Mahadai had remained in the store despite advice to join the others upstairs in the locked house: Lily (my fourth sister) and her two children, Khemraj and Atma, Betty (Buddy's wife), Baby, a niece (one of my second sister Pampat's daughters, who lived with them). They could evacuate by rear accesses to the yard or into the back of the warehouse section of the store. Access from the street to the stairs and yard was protected by a sturdy locked metal and greenheart gate, which however would yield to the pressure of the mob.

The children had seen the whole thing, and described it to parents far more frightened than they were. To them it was a curiosity and an exciting change from lessons. With the profound insight and frank innocence of a six year old Phillip would later relate the incident to his mother as if it were a huge party, dwelling innocently in his narration on what had impressed him most, "Mummy, they didn't have no panties; you wouldn't believe how black and round and *biiiig* their batties were!"

While the government pondered its position and Jagan broadcast his condemnation of the undemocratic and violent tactics of the opposition, emphasising the legality of his actions and willingness to discuss concerns, Burnham urged his followers to move "from slogans to action". That evening he spoke at length; he affirmed his undying support for independence, condemned the tax, and accused Jagan of preparing to bring his rural army to Georgetown to provoke a fight with them.

He ended with this exhortation, *"Comrades! The fight starts now. Tomorrow at 2 o'clock in the afternoon there is a demonstration organised by the Trades Union Congress, a demonstration against the harsh proposals of the budget, which will make all life unbearable. No doubt the Riot Squad will be there. Do you still want to go?"* The mob roared *"Yes, Yes"* ... *"Comrades, remember that tomorrow Jagan's army is coming in from Cane Grove and Windsor Forest. Do you still want to go?"* Again, with a mighty roar, they cried, *"Yeess, Yeeesss!"* *"Comrades, I will be seeing you tomorrow at 2 p.m., when we will all join the demonstration. Thank you and goodnight."*

On February 13th, riots, looting and attempts at arson erupted as massed gangs paraded the main business streets, concentrating on Regent with its half-mile long stretch of predominantly Indian businesses. The Civil Service Association and TUC had condemned the National Savings Levy and announced a strike to start at 1.00 pm. That would add a new dimension to the reigning chaos, already beyond the control of the Police. Gov. Renison denied Jagan's request for army intervention. The Police appealed for general calm and urged people to stay off troubled streets and felt they could cope.

Hospital activity, especially the Casualty services, reflected the social unrest. Policies were revised to deal with increased injuries and each physician, regardless of location or assigned service was on call for the Casualty Department. My surgical training came in very handy and the steady stream of injuries pushed us to the limit of resources and often exceeded both human and material ones. All elective in-patient work had ceased for several days, clinics curtailed to essentials and extra supplies ordered. On Feb 13th the Civil Service struck; when the "big" riots erupted, I was working in Casualty, and soon saw a succession of injuries, thankfully mostly minor or manageable moderate ones.

There was some black humour in the events. A young black man with a wound in the leg was brought to my cubicle frantically complaining of pain and "bleedin' to death from a broken leg"; I found a trickle of blood coming from a neat hole over the middle right tibia and probing gently extracted a shotgun pellet from the periosteum. He had no fracture. He said he had been "peacefully walkin' in Regent Street mindin' me own business" when a policeman shot him "for no reason". I reassured him, treated him appropriately, notified Police and put him in a holding bay.

Three hours later I was just finishing a scalp suture when the triage nurse called me to look at a man with a bad scalp wound that had covered his face with clotted blood and drenched his shirt; prompt pressure bandaging had stopped the bleeding. Removing the facial 'mask' I was astonished to see that he was my man with the pellet in his leg, whom I had last seen in the holding bay! He had slipped out of custody and gone 'home'. This time he said he had been casually "walkin' by a store in Regent St, mindin' me own business" when a pane of plate glass inexplicably fell on him. "And is your business looting stores?" I asked.

This time he was not so lucky. A policeman had arrived, identified him as wanted on several counts of wilful damage and looting. We mended him and released him into Police custody. Some others were hilarious. One victim was cut on the back and neck narrowly missing the right external jugular when he tried to exit via the shattered plate glass window of an appliance store, with a small refrigerator on his back. He had earlier stolen another appliance from the store, but his wife was not satisfied and had sent him back for the fridge of her choice! Another was similarly injured when he too was sent back by an irate wife for records, having already stolen a player! And so on.

Hundreds of gory tales were told that evening by our small group of anxious young physicians assembled as customary on the verandah of the Interns' Quarters, hoping that the calls would be fewer and manageable, as already the surgical units had issued warnings of overcrowding and were busy setting up extra beds in corridors and discharging anyone who could even remotely be allowed home. The rising tide of violence had already brought us, in that second week of February, waves of new trauma cases of increasing severity — fractures, concussions, deep lacerations, gunshot wounds, knife and machete wounds etc. Most of us working that day had spent ten to twelve continuous hours, mine in a small operating room seeing some of the wounded, suturing, setting fractures, starting IV's for those awaiting admission, and so on. The nursing staff was incomparable, handling an unruly and demanding horde with patience and despatch, knowing when to be stern and when to be gentle. Many of the injured simply clamoured for quick attention, eager to return to the fray. By evening the pace had slackened allowing the regular shift to cope without extra help.

On the 14th half the nursing staff and 28 of 36 orderlies stayed away. The Red Cross, League of Friends and St John Ambulance Brigade helped us out.

One of the Casualty physicians, John Prashad, operated a small clinic a stone's throw away on Thomas Street, at which he would provide his off-duty services for private fees. This was against Ministry appointment conditions, but officials turned a blind eye to it, as he dealt with some of the non-police cases. We had witnessed that day some appalling examples of human aggression under strong and intemperate influences, and worse was expected in the days to come, as McLeod had feared. And yet opposition leaders continued to push their followers to extremes, urging actions that came close to sedition. Inevitably we questioned Jagan's contribution to the deterioration. The timing of the budget measures was supported by only one person in our predominantly pro-Jagan group, and that only half-heartedly.

Stanley asked, somewhat rhetorically, "About the budget, one simple observation, you can't mobilise capital from a communist perch. How can you drive away entrepreneurs, then try to raise capital for entrepreneurial efforts? That might make sense to doctrinaire communists, but not to the ordinary man who wants to do business and live a free life, and not under government orders. Socialism is okay, but not totalitarianism, which is Jagan's line. So I blame him."

"You're right; people associate communism with confiscation of property, arbitrariness, heavy-handedness, waste, oppression, police state—all those terrible things, not always true." Hublall said, harking to his European experience while in a German medical school. "But all those things are capitalist virtues too, as Jagan rightly tells people! In Europe after the War communists were romanticised for helping to crush the Nazis."

"Our people not sophisticated enough to understand those paradoxes. They stay simple." Stanley observed. "Budget defenders say that it did not cause the rioting; the principles were sound in shifting development to local hands. But what they overlook is who's in charge. Opposition would not have been so hot if people trusted the government. Our leaders lack insight; and I include all parties; PPP philosophy is unpopular, despite their majority. I feel the Government should've been more restrained and patient, not picking fights. Look, the whole thing is nothing more than a struggle for the top job between two egomaniacs, and the way Cheddi behaving, Burnham will win! You with me?"

"Yes!" I agreed. "Jagan insists that his majority gives him absolute right to rule and carry out his wish to industrialise, whatever that is, regardless of other opinions or ideas, and few of his supporters understand it; Burnham and D'Aguiar say that he got in with a minority: 42.6% versus 57.4%. UF with 16.4 % or one sixth of the votes got one ninth of the seats (4) and PNC with two fifths got one third. Jagan stupidly didn't run any candidates in town so his supporters voted for UF or not at all. Burnham doesn't let him forget this; claiming constitutional rights won't make it go away. What's worse for us, Jagan's already rejected mountains of good advice, particularly to back off from the USSR and to stop needling the US if he wants their aid. Yet he continues to preach and teach Communism and waste time and money chasing mystical foreign "experts", instant leftist saviours, like Kelshall et al., now Kaldor, when any one of us can tell him what to do. Look at this shithead Chandisingh we have as Health Minister. When we meet with him he's on a different page from the rest of us."

"Not surprised; he's probably stoned and three pages behind you," said Cecil Appadu, an interne, also from Port Mourant. "Corentyne people say he drinks a lot."

"That might explain some of his behaviour." Gordon said. "This trouble we're going through should open Cheddi's eyes. It's bigger than local politics. I don't mind the man, I like his style. There's nothing basically wrong with the ideas in the budget or his intentions. But it's too much for people right now. We don't have the industrial base for this kind of budget and in any case he has no trained people to do what he wants. If he wasn't a commie, US would back him; and we too. No matter what he does now, he *will* be opposed. I'm telling you, maan, he got to ditch this Commie stuff. Rags, you can get to him, he's your friend; he still look after you' teeth? Tell 'im, if he don't change soon, he dead! Politically."

"Right on, Gordon," Stanley said, "Odo will wipe the floor with him, and the CIA will help! Even Rudy of all people leave him. I don't think he's got more than a year, at this showing."

"And I tell you all if Cheddi leave Communism today, Odo is history, no matter how many black people, or Rudy or anyone else, stay behind 'im." Gordon asserted. "The Americans don't like him. They say he's dishonest and a scamp. You know what the hot rumour among our guys in DC is right now? They say that UK Ambassador Caccia told Secretary of State Dean Rusk, that Jagan is the most responsible leader in BG, has a good organisation and would be hard to replace. So they'll stick with him. They think Rai is OK, yet they trying to link him with Odo. Odd!"

"Indeed," I agreed (though none of us had heard of Caccia). "Shows how desperate they are to find a way to oust Jagan and get around Odo. Jagan's been told that a thousand times in the last ten years; once or twice he even admitted that it was practical, if not wise to be pro-US, or at least not so pro-USSR; he knows he could do that now, with Kennedy, without losing his soul. Both he and Odo know that; Odo supports Jagan's communism, privately, when they meet as friends. Don't look so surprised, Gordon; you know they're both communists, fighting this game to be number one, like chess players. But notice that only Jagan plays it straight, like support for Castro; Odo is cagey, smarter, buying time, fomenting unrest, laying a trap; in a year or two he'll seize the upper hand. Right now he downplays his commie views, while Jagan prattles on insulting the US. The US will lose patience soon and let him go, one way or the other, and Odo will make sure he's the one to pick up the pieces. It's a game to them; but it's our future. I don't think Rai would team up with Odo, even though I hear that Odo is willing to serve under him if he leaves Jagan and links with PNC."

"Good opposition tactic; that would leave Cheddi with a minority." Gordon said.

"You know, my friend, we did try to sway him before he went to the States, but obviously our arguments failed. As for dentistry, Jagan's not much into practice right now, except that the cavities he has to fill are those big ones he's making in the economy; that will take one hell of a lot of amalgam! And an eon of time! We have the materials here but he didn't learn *that* skill. So I go to Dr Dean."

"Good metaphor;" Stanley observed. "You sound frustrated. But things will get worse. Burnham behaving like someone who already has his army of enforcers and it looks like rank and file police are with him, even though he cusses them. D'you think Jagan and D'Aguiar have the same?"

"Of course they do; all those fuckers have their goons!" Jan Evertz said suddenly, emerging from lethargy to pour a drink from his gallon jug of Russian Bear. "They would be stupid not to."

"If they do, we're going to have a three-way war, right? What do you chaps think?" Hublall asked. "I'm not hopeful; we'll see worse tomorrow."

"Two commies and one capitalist, fighting it out; interesting to see; Burnham and Jagan behaving like Bakunin and Marx," Stanley said. "D'Aguiar posturing like McCarthy. His 'Highway to Happiness' led to a forest of jibes and ridicule and into a silly dream; even a fool would be embarrassed. How odd, to find that losers from the world's strongest powers have counterparts in this little backwoods."

"A three way fight is not likely," I said, "I don't think Jagan would confront Burnham or the PNC physically. D'Aguiar and UF have too small a following to amount to anything, unless the US installs him, by putsch, like one of their Latin American puppets, and that won't happen, as long as Kennedy's in the White House; they don't even mention him as a runner. Anyway that's how I read the things Steve says. The Portuguese and Catholics solidly back D'Aguiar even if his highway is a mud dam, but all have visas ready to run to Canada. Only the few too rich to leave will stay."

"Canada Immigration won't accept people like me." Hublall said. "Too brown. You have to be black or white."

"Another set of hypocrites!" Stanley exclaimed, his ire rising. ".Look, the crux of the shit we're in is this; we argue it with Rudy all the time, and his best answer was to jump from Cheddi to Forbes, like a rat from a burning ship into a stormy sea. What all these communists doing is simply copying what Attlee, Bevan, Wilson, Gaitskell and the rest of the British Labour Party preach, and Harold Laski taught them, Manley and a lot of Indians who busy screwing up India; now they parrot that crap all over BG: *'the public ownership of the means of production, distribution and exchange.'* But that is not for us as Rags with his farming connections keep saying *ad nauseam*; that could work in a heavily industrialised nation, not one of hard-working, entrepreneurial farmers and shopkeepers; look at how we Chinese—from the poorest beginning just a hundred years ago--are now nearly all middle class, some quite rich, but we're too small in number, like the Portuguese, to make a big statement at the polls, like we used to before universal suffrage. Enterprise and hard work developed us, Africans, Indians, whoever, and will continue to do so; only then will socialists have something to take over and waste!" He laughed briefly, hollowly.

"Good one, Stan," Gordon said, and everyone shared the nervous mirth.

"That will take twenty, no fifty years." Stanley went on, "I don't mind social spending, but right now we're too poor for Marx. And if they get their way, we'll be worse off in thirty years than today; if we do the opposite, we'll be well-off, damn well-off, all of us in that time frame; in other words levelled high instead of levelled low. These guys are not thinkers, they're copycats; the thinkers are in this room!"

"Then we should take over. And you can be Premier, and Rags take over Finance." Honnett, who had maintained his usual reticence, said with mock seriousness. "Doctors replacing dentists and lawyers. We won't do worse than this government, that's for sure. They're making so many mistakes we'd have to govern for a lifetime to match what they've done in just a few years!"

"Good thinking, Honnett, and we'll bring the politicians to deal with Casualty." Hublall said.

"Naw," Stanley drawled. "They'll kill everyone! Me, I just want to practise good medicine, not the shit they goin' to reduce us to. Besides, they say I'm crazy, so they leave me alone. What you say, Rags?"

"I agree with you, not the crazy part." I said. "The sad thing is that we have no choice. Burnham will be even worse. When those two talk about socialism, they're dreaming in ideological terms, mainly Russian, not ours. Like you I want to practise good medicine, not politics in medicine. These chaps have no interest in good health care; left to Chandisingh all we'll get are 'barefoot doctors', 'feldshers', or any low life Cuba or Mao can give us."

"They don't want the best medicine; minimal incident care is enough." Hublall said. "We need to research this environment and develop our own data base; right now we using Britain's, which is okay in principle but not in reality. The natives for example do things we need to explore."

"How right you are!" I agreed. "We can learn much from native practices. One example: at UCH we saw *Chromomycosis* and its treatment failures…"

"What's *Chromomycosis*?" Cecil interrupted. "Never heard of that one."

"That's your European education, my friend, that the locals think is so superior! It's a deep skin infection, very destructive, caused by *Phialophora*, *Hormodendrum* and other genera of wood-associated fungi.[145] The Barama Caribs treat this awful infection with a local 'bush' and the shaman in Wappai healed the rotting legs of at least two porknockers. Both of them refused amputation in Georgetown, and now have useful legs. The Brits called it *Leishmaniasis*; but the natives know both cause and cure. I brought back samples of the fungi, and would like to research the cure."

"Precisely! I came back here hoping to do local research because I know how many unknowns we can tackle from this angle." Stanley reflected. "Like *Chromo*, and many others. We all have ideas on health and some could make a big difference in BG and elsewhere. Rags and I worked in Microbiology for a while and he was typing rare *Strept.* and isolating and identifying the fungus causing Jamaican *Chromo*…"

"While Stan was getting worms like *Strongyloides* to grow in unique ways." I interrupted.

"As an aside, why do you want to do that?" Gordon asked.

"For positive i.d." Stanley advised, animated by the subject of his aborted research. "*Strongyloides* looks like Hookworm; many say that it doesn't cause disease; but Rags just finishing a paper documenting fatal cases of Strongyloidiasis[146]. By growing the eggs found in the patients we can positively identify genus and species. Those worms are widespread here, but you won't find more than a brief note in your textbook. Same for *Chromomycosis*; the texts even call it a '*blastomycosis*' which it isn't."

"Another one Hari told me and you might know, at least my mother and others in our country district knew about soursop tea which they use to treat a variety of illnesses: fever, insomnia, nervousness, spasms, high blood pressure, worms, lice and they feed it to young mothers to increase milk. Although they prefer the tea, the whole plant is a medicine."

"You're right," Hublall said, "our neighbour had a soursop tree and would give us fruit in season or maybe my mother bought it and fed us to get rid of worms. I didn't really like it, too stringy."[147]

"And we haven't begun to look at the big diseases, heart and stroke, diabetes and cancer, the maimers and killers. You think you can get Jagan or

---

[145] See Ch. 9, p.5-6

[146] Published with others in1964, Lancet, II, 1257

[147] The antihelminthic properties of fruit and seeds are said to be due to acetogenins which also kill lice. The other medicinal properties—sedation, secretagogue, hypotensive etc. reside in the roots, leaves, seeds and bark,

Chandisingh, Charlie Nicholson and that crowd at the Ministry or Legco to hear this, to fund any research?" Hublall asked. "Those buggers won't listen!"

"What's worse, Malaria resurfacing; just saw a case from Vreed-en-Hoop area." I said.

"Even that won't shake them; they're all crappy politicians, rabble-rousers, full of communist shit! Odo too!" Stanley exclaimed. "Jagan secretly says that it's a war; cold or hot, we have to take sides; so he chose the Ruskies; they give him propaganda; he slams Uncle Sam from the left side of his mouth and begs him for money from the right, to show that he loves Uncle; only an idiot will try that."

"It's like a spoiled child playing one parent against the other." I said with some venom; "Jagan feels he is the only one who can bring about unity, but doesn't realise he's the one destroying it with crappy policy, immature attitudes and wasting money on useless foreign advisers. Who needs them? There's not a one who has come so far that's any better than any of a hundred here. The real experts are those who live here, work here and succeed here. They're the ones he should listen to, not some nose-picking professor or fellow-traveller from yonder-land! It's not that Jagan's wrong and the US right, but that the US is strong and Jagan not so bright."

"Ha, ha! Right. He has the same biased mentality he condemns; if it ain't white it ain't right; so he brings white communists for double duty; the white part to impress colonial rabble, the commie to make sure they don't rock his boat; meanwhile UF doing the same except his imports claim to be Christians come to help their local brethren, the good guys; sad eh?" Gordon's sarcasm was palpable.

Nervous laughter relieved some of the gloom we had noted spreading inexorably through the city and captured in discussions, deepening when Chet arrived with news of continued violence and mob disturbances downtown. "The situation is real bad. Burnham's nuts! What the hell next?"

"Chaos!" Stanley exclaimed. "The TUC is in bed with PNC and UF; both Government workers unions, CSA and FUGE, are with them; TUC will get support from CIA via the US unions AFL-CIO. All will combine with the Opposition to nix the budget. The streets will become a slaughter-house!"

"Gloomy but realistic," I said, "I believe we're near, if not at, the point of no return; from here on it's a steep roll downhill, with Jagan in front, and Burnham on his tail, poised to overtake!"

"And the *white* man will pick up the winnings, whoever wins." Evertz, the white interne, laughed, accidentally spraying Russian Bear droplets from the mouthful he had just imbibed.

The Government responded to the riots by declaring the vicinity of the Public Buildings a "proclaimed area", thus barring unauthorised entry and assembly. Jagan announced a modification of the National Savings Levy (NSL) to start at $300 per month instead of $100 to placate the unions and Civil Service, but it attracted little attention. The opposition was on a roll, intent, as D'Aguiar kept urging his audiences to *"oppose, expose and depose"* the government. D'Aguiar broadcast his opinion that Jagan's NSL amendment amounted to a budget defeat, forgetting that parliamentary practice allowed changes between the first and second readings of a bill. Nevertheless, he maintained, Jagan's failure to resign demanded swift and decisive action. Both he and Burnham repeated the call to arms at rallies and on February 15th led their troops in a defiant march through the proclaimed area, mustering thereafter at the Parade Ground and Bourda Green for the customary tirades.

I had a busy morning and would not find out until much later what had happened downtown. The tension had risen palpably as the day wore on. Walking across the broad paved breezeway below the Obstetrics block--beyond which were the laboratories, fronting on Middle Street--I came upon a knot of Black nurses and other ward staff lounging on the rows of benches used for teach-ins, as was their wont during breaks. This time they were speaking animatedly, with much arm-waving and histrionics.. They had become for me a barometer of interpersonal relations in the hospital. I did not work with these women, but I knew them by sight and two of them by name. In the past weeks I had noticed a distinct cooling of their responses and an increasing vexation. On this day I saw deep scowls on their faces and for the first time they ignored my greeting.

I pondered the reaction in the light of the overt racism sweeping the city. More and more groups at the hospital, especially among the nurses and subordinate staff, were becoming openly polarised in their social relationships; where they had to work together they seemed to disagree, argue and even quarrel for trivial reasons (a development that Leila had anticipated and wisely left, before it could ruin her idealism or scar her in other ways forever). As I crossed the area several others, male and female, mainly Blacks and a few Indians joined the group and engaged in the discourse. I paused to listen, no one seeming to mind, wondering what portent lay in this gathering.

One worker was leading the discussion. She repeated the condemnation of the press of the budget "tax-grab" and call for Jagan's resignation. The headlines had become hysterical and misleading.

"He want to take $5.00 from me poor $100 and I got four mouth to feed and rent to pay! Is wha' this maan think? Alyou better tell me. An' to think I vote PPP! The maan mus' be maad!"

She was a black maid with over 25 years' service in the hospital and had started to work for $15 per month. She recited her story of loyalty and good service shared by many there. Two laboratory workers on lunch break, attracted by the crowd and having heard the rumours of greater trouble planned for that day, joined me at the rear of the gathering.

"Eh, eh, me gyul, you gat something to cry fuh. I don't get that much, but if I did I wouldn't give one red cent to any communist, no matter how he nice," pronounced another.

"Is Russia he gwine bring here; you think is anybody good? I read 'bout them in me son school book; dem bad fuh so; dey say that one o' dem name Stalin he one kill one million people!"

"Ah what you say, gyul, one million? You na hear right!"

"One million, one thousand, no matter; is plenty. You want dem so people to come hey? We na gat one thousand much less one million fuh them to kill."

"That not gwine happen hey; we Forbes gwine see to dat! You hear 'bout the meeting at the Parade Ground? I going; alyou coming? We can see with Dora; leave her to think; she will change and come over to we; after all, we kith and kin."

I asked my two colleagues, "What do you think of all this, the budget they talking about?"

"I don't see anything wrong with it," the tall elegant one said, "it's ironic though; I just got the Guillebaud increase, Cheddi yanks it out of my hands. But I'm single and I suppose can afford to pay but so many people can't; they're not prepared; they're confused; they see Jagan as a nice-looking man, who everyone says is a wicked communist. I like him, but I think he has to change or this racial violence will get worse. The PNC is using the budget to create strife."

"True; my brother and I are with PYO;" the other girl, our strikingly pretty and petite secretary, Marian said, "we're worried, because the ordinary members don't know what's going on; we get orders what to do and no reasons why; we toe the line or get out. We can't afford that; we're hoping to get scholarships soon to study in East Germany."

"I'm sure you'll get it, my dear; just pray they don't send you to Moscow," the other cautioned her. "This is Burnham's crowd mainly; I know Dora, the old one, she worked with us for a while; didn't know she was PPP, must be from Sidney King days; she's from near Bel Air, in Mr Rai's district. These people know her, so they leave her alone; all of them were PPP until Jagan and Burnham split; now only a few of the older ones remain, mainly because they all love him — 'pretty Jagan or ugly Burnham' they used to say. But boy they give us Indians a hard time; even Jagan treat us like dirt! Isn't that something? He comes to us for votes, then swats us because we're Hindus."

"What do *you* think of that? You hate Hindus?" I asked the pretty communist, herself Indian.

"Religion is the opiate of the people; Dr Jagan wants to emancipate poor Indians; he says dialectic materialism will bring them out of squalor and bondage."

"Wow!" I exclaimed, stunned by the disconnect between the beautiful child-like face and the weighty words. Recovering I asked, "Out of or into? That line is pure bull, my dear; fools only the fans; you're a smart girl; your parents are Hindus, not swine; don't believe that they are because Jagan tells you so. He's never read the *Gita* nor the *Vaidas*, nor have you, I suspect, but he's quick to condemn Hindu values, his own birthright. If you must condemn do it from knowledge, not ignorance or prejudice. Even *chamars* have a duty to learn and be fair." I felt bitter.

"He has a huge chip on his shoulder where Hindus are concerned," the tall one, Jinni, said, ignoring the discomfort of the younger girl, and the flush in her face. "The pandits say his actions flow from his *karma* and his low birth; it's true, he never took the time to study his own religion, even a little bit, even though his mother is staunch Hindu, and he says he cares for her."

"Anyway, we mustn't harass you," I soothed her, feeling suddenly a kindred urge to rescue her from certain damnation, but mindful of my position, I spoke more formally, "but at the same time, don't become slave to a doctrine that has no place in this country, not now or ever. Communism will destroy it. Think for yourself; if you let Cheddi or Janet do your thinking, you'll be just another cipher."

"Why do you say that? You don't know them; you were away."

"Oh, but I do, I do, only too well, better than you ever will! You see, you're mesmerised by them; I was too, but grew out of it." She looked surprised. "They're long-time friends of our family." I explained simply. "We helped them, from the very beginning. I was perhaps his first teen-age fan."

She looked away, not knowing how to deal with what I said; she had never met anyone who knew the Jagans outside of the PPP. She looked so frail then, her almost perfect form vulnerable and crying out for protection. She turned to me, and with a smile that would amply advertise Jagan the dentist, said with open adulation, "But Dr Jagan is so smart; he knows everything; we love him; don't you like him?"

"Yes I do; as an ordinary person outside of politics; he's a great dentist, and could make a more useful mark on our health than he ever would through politics. But he loves to talk, especially to hear himself talk; he reads a lot, has a greater breadth of knowledge than those around him, so he impresses them, confounds them with data they don't know and can't assess. But a lot of what he spouts about economics and politics is plain communist dogma, like a cow bringing up its food."

"You sound as if you don't like him," she said, without malice, almost a conclusion.

"That's the trouble with our people; they believe that you cannot like people you criticise; I can like a person without liking his politics. I like you, you know that, even though I'm now hearing you're a Marxist. I won't change towards you unless you try to stuff it down my throat."

Jinni looked pensive, and turning to me asked, "And what do *you* think of the budget?"

"In other circumstances and in another place, okay; but here and now, inappropriate and premature; it's tough and will be labelled communist, which it isn't; opposition would be weaker if Jagan were not communist. So it'll be used to try to bring him down. In any case, he's history, if he doesn't declare against communism. We don't need communism here; we need people with ideas and enterprise; sadly Burnham's worse, a dictator and also a communist; the choice is 'black dog or monkey' as the Jamaicans say; our best hope is to change the black dog, Jagan."

A look of consternation creased Marian's face, and her eyes said that she might have said something scathing if I were not her boss. Or maybe she was willing to consider my point of view.

"You don't look like a communist." I teased her, "you look so benign and nice." She blushed.

"I believe in Marx...."

"Not Gandhi? Not solid Hindu values? Not duty, not *ahimsa*?"

"Gandhi was okay for India; Marx has more to offer us."

"So a German Jewish theorist of another age and culture who never ran a country or even got elected anywhere has more to offer Indians in BG today than a modern Indian of their own heritage? More of Jagan's rubbish! What's this wondrous thing that Marx will offer?"

"*The greatest good for the greatest number.*" She parroted the timeworn slogan warily, but somehow coming to me from her gentle face and in her soft voice it seemed instantly achievable.

"And what is that *good*?"

"What do you mean?"

"Exactly that; where will you find the greatest good to pass on to the greatest number?"

"From wealthy people, who control the commanding heights of the economy."

"That's bloody jargon, sweetheart; Jagan told me that when you were so high." I held my hand at her chest level. "I believed him; he sounded so sincere. But it was nonsense then; it's more so now; besides, the few rich birds we had have flown. Well, not quite, their money has flown." She looked mystified. "Into British banks, love! Look, Communism works in the USSR only by repression and strictures; the 2 million members of the Communist Party live in privilege while the remaining 200 million slave for them. That's 99% enslavement; think of that. It not the way Cheddi and Janet and Chandisingh tell it. Keep your eyes open, if they allow you to, when you go there."

"But that's western propaganda; the USSR is well run and powerful; Russian science is far advanced and put a man in space. And see, the Americans missed the moon!"

"Yes indeed, but both used *German* science captured in 1945, when you were, what six, seven? USSR maintains them at great cost to the proletariat, the greatest number, remember? The ones who do without proper housing, get poor food, low wages; and they can't get even what little they can afford to buy; and they can't leave; you see that they're now penning them in East Berlin like sheep behind a wall because so many have slipped out. The serfs of ages past are alive and suffering in Communist USSR."

"But our texts say they're free of Czarist yokes. And Russia just made a trade pact with Cuba that will give Cuba a sure market and a high price for their sugar; and Albania is now ally of Mao Tse Tung. Communism is helping poor countries more than the West is."

I felt the weight of heavy propaganda and a great pity for this gullible youth, seven, eight years my junior and yet suddenly child-like and vulnerable. "Did they tell you in what country Marx achieved his 'greatest good'?"

When she couldn't' I told her of dissent and ambition among the founders and preachers of Bolshevik Communism. I told her of Stalinist murders, Gulag, their re-writing of history to suit current norms and acts to malign previous party bosses and enforcers by removing memorials e.g. Molotov and Kaganovich who were blamed for famine that killed millions of Ukrainians due to crop failures from forced collectivisation. I told her of other weaknesses in the Soviet economy and its social failures despite the promise of improving the majority, while what Jagan called their "common man" took second place to a massive military build-up and Khrushchev's recent concentration on ballistic missiles.

"All that is not true!" she sounded exasperated. "And look USA banned trade with Cuba. Why?"

"You poor thing! Tell you what; I'm sure you'll get your scholarship, for learning your catechism, and for loyalty if for nothing else. When you get there, hopefully Germany, not Lumumba U., and find out the truth; will you write me a letter? Watch out for the censor, though; I hear all foreign students' mail is censored. So write me in code. We'll make one up before you go. And you'll give me one dollar for everything I said right; I'll give you *ten* for everyone I got wrong. Okay?"[148]

I made light of it; she looked so sincere, it was poignant; besides, I had to work with her. The tall one, Jinni, had kept quiet, studying the small crowd, which had maintained its dissection of Jagan, his wife and the PPP; the gathering resolved finally to join the strikers at the Parade Ground. As we walked to the

---

[148] Two months later, at a time of relative calm, she obtained a scholarship to study economics in Moscow and after a few weeks was gone; I've always wondered what became of her.

laboratory the tall one said, "You know, people say something terrible is going to happen. That grand conjunction ten days ago of eight heavenly objects: the new moon, the Sun in eclipse, Mercury, Venus, Earth, Mars, Jupiter, and Saturn is not a good omen. Do you believe in these things?"

At the rally Burnham commended the mob on the "success" of their defiant march that morning through restricted zones and their embarrassment of the Government and Police. He urged them to move to the next stage beyond slogans and condemnatory placards. *"Comrades!"* he declaimed, *"First of all, let me say this that the People's National Congress sees the way clearly, step by step and phase by phase. All I can tell you is this, that it is no sense taking part in this explosion which has happened at this moment if you are going to peter out or turn back half-way. You have to see it through. I believe that the PNC knows what we all want and knows how we will seek to achieve what we all want; but one thing I know you do not want, one thing I know the PNC will not countenance, and that is violence. Comrades, violence we shall never start because we are a peaceful people. If there is to be violence, let others start it, not the People's National Congress; but comrades, they shall not pass."*

He then suggested that they rest from their labours for a day. The mob responded with frenzied calls to maintain the pressure next day, to which Burnham replied, rather conspiratorially, and ominously, *"I have heard what you have had to say, and I have noted very carefully what you prefer and want, and therefore, Comrades, you will be informed what exercises may be necessary tomorrow. Comrades, you will be informed. I do not want to make any suggestions here tonight what that exercise should be. You will be informed through the usual channel which has proved effective in spite of the fact that our comrades, the Post Office workers, are on strike, and tomorrow we shall meet again some place, somewhere, somehow!"*

Friday February 16th, 1962 dawned clear and cool, and before long white fluffs of cloud were scudding across the sky. It was a beautiful day, but tense. I felt the tension as I walked to my office and saw it starkly in the faces of the crowds milling around the Hospital's Newmarket Street gate just outside the Casualty Department. The previous day's events and mounting injuries had unsettled everyone.

My flat was on the fourth floor of a block of flats situated obliquely opposite the hospital entrance. From several windows, at this high vantage point, we could clearly see the entrances, adjacent structures and access paths to the buildings on both sides of Newmarket Street, and watch the passing parade of patients, visitors and staff. (It was from one of the kitchen windows that our housekeeper Beatrice had seen the thief wearing my pants, which, a month or so earlier, he had stolen, along with several of my underpants, from her laundry line on the enclosed rear landing. This had made me the butt of some jibes as a reporter had written a short news item titled "Man steals Doctor's underpants!") Since the unrest had begun I would watch from a south window and note everything that came and went -- cars, bicycles, trucks, people -- and would take random photographs of the crowd that inevitably collected at the two gates on either side of the Street. I had even shown Phillip and Peter how to shoot photos from the window in any unusual circumstance.

In the escalating challenge to authority a PNC mob that morning had carried the fight to the government, setting fire to a pole in Kingston near the Electricity Corporation, where they had assembled ostensibly over a labour dispute. In the *mêlée*, Police under Supt McLeod used tear gas to clear the crowd, now including onlookers. A child affected by the fumes was brought away by its mother screaming that the child had died. The child was in fact quickly resuscitated at the nearby St Joseph's Hospital. However D'Aguiar noised it abroad that the Police had killed a child, exacerbating the tensions and sending a mob gathered at the Parade ground rampaging through the streets, screaming, robbing people, beating others, as they marched to Robb Street congregating at Freedom House, the PPP headquarters, resisting Police attempts to disperse them. Farther off in Camp Street a store was set on fire but the Fire Brigade quickly responded and quenched the blaze.

At Freedom House, McLeod's contingent faced the mob now brandishing several illegal weapons including an army type .303 rifle. The mob got rowdier and more belligerent, accused the Police of murder and advanced on them, despite timely correction of D'Aguiar's malicious rumour. In response to tear gas shells bursting among them mobsters under cover of a vehicle, fired at Police, hitting Asst. Commissioner Phoenix and more severely injuring Supt. McLeod, who was rushed to the Hospital, bleeding internally. Surgery and multiple transfusions kept him alive that day.

The first explosion came on the afternoon of Mc Leod's shooting with a mixture of disbelief and relief: disbelief that the threats had actually been carried out and that the egotism, ambition and ineptitude of political leaders had brought the unprepared country to this sorry pass; relief that it was somewhere else, not "our" building. The explosions were loud enough to be heard in my office at the Hospital nearly a mile away. I was just packing up to leave for the Casualty Department and looking from my office window in the direction of the sound, saw a plume of black smoke rising in the south-western sky. Whatever "relief" I felt quickly turned to concern for my two sisters and brother and their families, all of whom lived and worked in the Hardeen Building just opposite the Legislature. I phoned but the line was busy. I rushed home, but Carol had taken the car, leaving Ranji with Beatrice; he had had his first birthday party just two days before, on Valentine's Day.

I ran to the taxi stand near the hospital gate and hurried the driver who sped frantically towards the smoke, west along Middle Street then south on Main, the while protesting my crazy act. New and louder explosions rent the air as we neared the scene, which was closer than I had thought. I was not prepared for what I saw. A policeman was stopping all traffic near the Carnegie Library, where Main, Church and High streets converged on the Cenotaph roundabout. The driver pulled over and parked. I paid him. Hurrying south on High Street I came face to face with a thick suffocating black wall of hot smoke that had blanketed the south-western side of Regent and High Streets, smothering the Bank of Baroda, Kirpalani's and adjacent stores, and obliterating the sky. The smoke rose in giant billows rushing and tumbling, their fury growing as each mass collided with the one just above. The white and ivory-coloured buildings that fed them looked so forlorn--like ghosts or condemned men chained together, unable to move, awaiting a firing squad--silhouetted against the black wall of rushing smoke. Plumes of fire tore off from the main blaze and rose swiftly from multiple foci, arcing as the wind took them, like flaming torches hurled at an unseen enemy. I stood frozen despite the searing heat, even as the hundreds standing there seemed transfixed by the horrible beauty of the scene. The High Street canal glowed eerily in the light of the flames, reflecting the scene beside it in blazing shades of orange, grey, red and crimson against a turbulent coal grey sky, something that William Turner might have painted, like *The Fighting Téméraire*.

The firmament and all it contained were lost to view. The brightness of day had turned into an eerie dark dusk. Nearer the ground everything on Regent Street between High and Water Streets was ablaze, with flames in bright rainbow colours licking at walls, swallowing roofs and bringing them down crashing, one by one, with astonishing speed and vigour. And then came the loudest, most terrifying boom of all, as several 40-gallon drums were tossed through the blazing roof of a paint store and rose up thirty feet or so through smoke and fire like launched rockets. They twirled as they rent the hissing air in quick succession each trailing thick streamers in brilliant hues of green, orange and blue set against the churning mass of grey and black smoke. For a moment each drum, its surface glowing, stood silent at its zenith, frozen at an awkward angle, silhouetted against the smoke, then fell abruptly with a horrendous crash. The others rose, paused and fell in like manner, each bursting as it hit the ground sending brilliant rays of elemental hues to mingle with the dense grey of the deadly suffocating smoke. No painter's palette could be more colourful. None of the mighty engines I had ever seen huffed and hissed so powerfully.

One by one in swift array the buildings came crashing down, each crash sending showers of sparks flying high in all directions; many fell into the High Street canal, hissing loudly, mercifully quenched. Kirpalani's crumbled quickly into ashes, then others in that block west and south. The intense heat kept firemen from getting close enough to the blaze to do any real good, and the low water pressure in the hoses was barely enough to reach first floors. So they used what water they had to cool adjacent buildings as yet unharmed. A light wind blew towards the north but it did little to influence the spread of the fire. At least not at first. Even as far away as I was from the blaze, the searing heat jammed my camera. I retreated even further as embers sprinkled on the roadway a few feet from the numbed and moaning crowd, some raising small popping blisters in the asphalt.

I wanted to leave and go south to my sister's place, but was stopped at a Police cordon. I stood on the sidewalk outside the premises of the Crown Life Insurance Company and surveyed the line of structures on the east side of the High Street, elegant buildings of Edwardian style: Demerara Life Insurance, the Town Hall at High and Regent with its tall tower looking sombrely and anxiously at the scene--although for the moment safe by distance and by politics--and further south, the Law Courts, a splendid example of Edwardian architecture, all just across the canal at risk from the raging flames.

Other fine buildings stood on the west side of High Street, about a hundred yards to the windward side of the inferno, including headquarters of the Hand-in-Hand Insurance and the British Guiana & Trinidad Mutual Fire Insurance Co--the most attractive of the group, fine examples of late Victorian architecture -- and the loftier Central Garage, its white façade dominating the scene just across Regent Street at High St closest to the blaze. Firemen wetting its southern side looked so ineffectual as the sprays they poured vaporised and disappeared into the heated air.

Two blocks west of High Street Regent St intersected with Hincks St and continued to end at a T-junction with Water Street; on the far side the JP Santos building stood between the street and the river: three floors of proud concrete, the flagship of Portuguese business in the city and a bastion of anti-PPP activism;

close by to the north was the Headquarters of the Bookers Empire, hidden from view. But I could see JP Santos clearly from where I stood. Its second floor balcony was occupied by a group of Portuguese and coloured men drinking beer and cheering the fire on, waving and gesturing, from their seemingly safe vantage point. Two wide streets separated them from the blaze raging between High and Hincks and spreading south to Commerce St, paralleling Regent, where firemen were busy wetting, as best they could, threatened structures. Among the merry-makers was a UF activist called 'Nasty' widely "credited" with organising this bonfire party to "teach the PPP a lesson" at the expense of East Indian businesses.

But Nature has a way of creating impressive ironies. We watched in awe as the flames against all expectations fanned north, crossed Regent Street and quickly engulfed buildings on the north side, first Thani's store, then the big Central Garage beside it, and began to threaten others further north along High St: Humphrey's, Hand-in-Hand Insurance, BG&T Fire and the Portuguese Pawnbrokery.

Later fire investigators would say that Thani's had succumbed to spontaneous combustion from the intense heat that had raised the ambient temperature of its painted walls beyond the flash point. It would also come out that the perpetrators had grossly miscalculated the combustibility of the painted wooden structures, and overestimated the heat resistance of concrete and metal. The air temperature had risen high enough to threaten buildings as far away as I stood. Our continuing retreat and my frequent wetting of my face and handkerchief in the warming waters of the canal attested to that. The buildings beside us shone pink with reflections of the blaze. The walls were uncomfortably warm.

One business owner stood beside a barricaded door, not twenty feet from me, and chewed on his fist until blood flowed and yet he continued, as if in a trance, tallying losses. The faces of the crowd, from black through shades of brown to white, glowed, transfixed, with a peculiar eeriness, mouths ajar, jaws drooping, a few supported by flexed arms reaching up. Their silence was broken only by periodic gasps and the shuffle of feet as they retreated from the surging heat and the roar of angry flames.

In an incredibly short space of time I saw "Nasty" and his group of revellers scurrying from the balcony of JP Santos Ltd, as flames headed their way; they entered the building and disappeared from sight. The scene changed, the people became more agitated and soon low groans and exclamations punctuated their silence. Voices could be heard, bemoaning the scene, protesting, condemning, cursing, while others, eyes closed, prayed loudly in fear. One woman, wearing a pink apron over a floral dress and white head tie, clutched a rosary and loudly told her beads, alternatively clasping her hands and genuflecting.

The Garage burned briskly, its wooden superstructure of three floors feeding the flames, now hotter than before, and noisier, abetted by the flammables within. The flamingo trees that lined both sides of the High St canal, partly protecting us, had begun to wilt, leaves curling ominously as if in death. We could see past them through the Garage windows to the multihued flames that engulfed the repair shop, whence the fire caught and ran along lines of combustible waste curving and zigzagging like a snake escaping in fear. The building's many windows shattered one by one sending sharp hot shards like miniature rockets in all directions. Many fell into the canal sizzling loudly, others were trapped by the trees, searing branches, while some flew far enough to land in the street, shattering as they fell, except one, a foot long red hot triangle, which landed intact point first, embedding itself in the asphalt, not five feet from where I stood. Startled, we all retreated jostling one another to the far sidewalk under the building's metal-clad awning.

Women screamed "Oh, Gawd, Oh Lawd!" and beat their breasts, some wailing loudly as if they had done some wrong. Children cried into their mothers' skirts, and held on tightly, hiding their faces. Some people stood, unspeaking, shaking their heads. Black people were in the majority, with Indians, Chinese, Portuguese, a few whites, all staring in awe, uncomprehending, mesmerised by the tragedy before them. A few men hurled imprecations at the politicos, some even showing their partisanship, the most vocal a wizened black man who kept repeating, "Is Jagan cause this; why he ain't give up communism? All ah we done dead now!"

Finally a stocky Indian removed the wet kerchief from his face long enough to say, "Yuh wrong, maan, is nah Jagan do this. Is Burnham do this, with all de hooligans he got followin' he. You na see them every day trampin' up and dung the street dem, wit' bicycle chain, beating up people, stealing, harassing women and dey children; ah you na see them? All o' them is black man!"

I feared for him where he stood almost surrounded by Blacks, mostly older men and women with strained lined faces such as I had seen at PPP meetings, people who had remained with the Party; many of them were followers of Jessie Burnham, who had left her brother's PNC. Perhaps the people around him were not opponents of the government after all. I had put his lack of caution to extreme duress. Be that as it may, he was voicing what the majority knew to be true, that the PNC had encouraged and condoned anarchy and riotous behaviour, and its leaders had failed to criticise any of the acts of brutality and lawlessness that had made city life a fearsome hazard.

"Na forget the UF and D'Aguiar," someone said, with a rural accent, probably Indian, "me na trus' dat maan dey call Nasty, he nasty fo' true; dey say he work fo' D'Aguiar; you see how he run 'way jis now from JP Santos? Why he stap drinkin' beer, why you t'ink he stap drinkin' D'Aguiar free beer? Dem dey in this, t'ick and t'in. Dem ah panic, da store go bun dung tonight. Da is why 'e run, de ugly skunt!"

Astonishingly the crowd allowed this blatant criticism of the political opposition to go unpunished. I was prepared for the worst, and looked around to map my escape route, but no retaliation took place, other than from one sullen black youth in tattered khaki shorts, and naked from the waist up, standing a few yards from me, who simply said, to neither speaker in particular, "Ah you gwine get what you lookin' fa; dis na nutt'n yet," and ran off up Robb Street, followed by a few who looked and behaved like him.

Meanwhile the crumbling of the garage proceeded swiftly. Most of the cars had earlier been driven out of the building but a few that could not be moved in time had quickly caught afire. They burned briskly, releasing foul vapours from smoking upholstery and as gas tanks exploded, sending red-hot fragments and plumes of fire flying in all directions. Thick black smoke streaked with rainbow hues filled the building and billowed through the shattered windows rushing with incredible speed into the black sky. With a horrendous noise the building imploded sending a cloud of sparks and burning timber mushrooming up into the air. Several tongues of flame and glowing dust fell on the building next door but a group of fire fighters pumping water from the High Street canal doused them and continued to spray the building. This plus a miracle of Nature saved that and others, including my sister's four blocks south. A wind sprang up and began to blow south, sending the licking tongues towards the structures on Water Street—against all the expectations of the arsonists--and soon JP Santos and its Portuguese neighbours including Bookers, John Fernandes, Fogarty's and Bettencourt-Gomes, had become united in the inferno. Mr 'Nasty'--if indeed this had been his doing--had miscalculated and had clapped too soon.

As I stood there, numb with fear and tension, I recalled as a child standing on the roof of the band stand at the New Amsterdam Esplanade on a fair February day just like this in 1945, the 23rd, with several schoolmates and two teachers staring in awe at a huge orange flame that had lit the sky 62 miles east as the heart of Georgetown burnt to the ground, just blocks away from the current disaster.[149]

When all had quieted down, the steel roof of the Stabroek Market had saved it and structures beyond, from the embers, heat and flaming debris that had rained upon it, the same that had ignited its vulnerable neighbours with their freshly painted walls and flat or gently sloping roofs. Slowly the fire calmed its fury as it consumed all structures to Croal Street at the edge of the spacious Market Square, empty save for the petrol station that stood ominously silent near the centre, across from D'Aguiar's Imperial House, where four days earlier D'Aguiar had stood whipping up crowds into a frenzy.

The activity at my sister's had been frantic and had begun with the first explosion. Carol had joined Buddy in a desperate effort to move valuables, records and the children to my brother Deo's home in Campbellville, three miles east, a task that took most of the afternoon. She drove ahead of his laden van and through mobs that stopped and threatened them but backed off when she boldly came out of the car and told them the two vehicles were PNC and working for her. Being a *dougla* saved her that day, but for one frightening encounter as she made the last trip alone at dusk, with failing visibility, and dim street lighting. As she slowed at the intersection of Camp and Hadfield Streets, a burly black youth at the back of a gang of about twenty crossing in front of her, paused, peered into the car and shouted, "is a woman, is a rich coolie woman, get she!" He grabbed the locked back door and held on to the car as the others swarmed behind and beside it. In slowing she had geared down to second; instinctively she floored the pedal; the car lurched forward into the intersection, narrowly missing a lone cyclist and sending the assailant spinning to the pavement while

---

[149]In 1947 at QC I befriended Derek Adamson, son of the Bookers pharmacist in whose *Limacol* plant the 1945 conflagration had started. It was a revelation of how Bookers exercised power in the city; they broke many by-laws in designing and constructing the factory as an extension of their "Drug Houses" and had gotten the City Council to overturn the denial by the City Engineer of a permit for yet another unsafe addition, just three years before the fire. Three careless employees were publicly blamed, one Ivan Morris, who failed to secure an alcohol pump, turned it on and sprayed himself and the floor with 68 over-proof alcohol, the second Desmond Nightingale, a solderer--what irony in the name--who lit his blow lamp and ignited the alcohol, and I.G. Carpenter, an Assistant Manager who permitted the dangerous apposition of flame and alcohol. The corruption of public officials by corporations knows no limits. It has existed from antiquity and continues blatantly today, dominating the governments of powerful nations and is the root of most environmental disasters, notably in mining—all forms—and construction.

several others hung on to the sides and rear bumper; she almost ran over another who fell as the car finally pulled free.

It was just as well that Buddy was not on that run as the gang would surely have attacked him. He and the rest of the adults were busy dealing with threats from the simultaneous fire that had been started on Lombard Street a few blocks south and had raged north towards Hadfield Street driven by a southerly wind. Flurries of sparks had fallen on walls and roofs which the defence team doused with buckets of water as there was virtually no flow in the pipes, but not all embers were within reach.

When the water pressure was restored it was enough for hoses to reach the first floor only, but that was easier than buckets, which were still needed to quench those that could be reached from the upper floor windows; the rest, they consigned to "God's will" and whatever resistance the metal and slate roofing offered. And thus they had toiled—as had everyone on that block between Lombard and High Streets—until evacuation became a real alternative. They had kept a discreet watch over the riotous crowd tramping the streets shouting anti-Indian slogans. Suddenly the wind changed direction to a northerly dramatically reducing both smoke and sparks allowing them and the firemen to get closer and fight more effectively from street level, and bringing to the threatened intense relief and for the first time that day hope of survival.

Fire-fighters, responding promptly to the earliest blaze, had been hampered by low water pressure, courtesy of waterworks staff supporting the anarchists. When the fire had exceeded the limits expected by the arsonists and turned on them with celestial vengeance, the miscreants tried frantically to have the water pressure restored, but messages did not reach the Works soon enough and one by one their precious properties caught fire. By the time the pressure and flow rate had improved, it was too late for too many in the doomed area. The biters had been severely bitten! Meanwhile water pumped by firemen from the river had helped those buildings along the waterfront by cooling the sizzling roofs and keeping the vital Market wet. But they were unable to save Bookers which swiftly fell to the flames; nearby Barclays resisted and was saved, like my sister's, when the wind changed direction.

Five blocks of prime commercial property—56 buildings and goods had summarily disappeared; 87 were badly damaged and most looted. The loss was estimated at US$25,000,000; insurance covered one-fifth that. The area became a wasteland of smouldering ruins, jagged remnants of wooden walls, steel and greenheart struts, posts and beams, twisted corrugated metal roofing and crumpled woodwork that would for several days defy the daily dousing by weary fire fighters, and would from time to time burst into flames that fluttered gaily and hungrily then died with a great sizzling rush of smoke as the weight of water drowned their hopes of regeneration.

A few sad and disembodied staircases stood as if suspended in air inviting the intrepid to climb surreal steps to nowhere, while the earth below them crackled with resurgent flame. The air was thick, acrid and dense, unfit to breathe, shunned even by the masked police and firemen who maintained watch at the site, patrolling its perimeter trailing turgid yellow snake-like hoses to douse the smouldering ruins. Men and women, many weeping unabashedly, wandered aimlessly around the site, despite the police cordon, or else stood transfixed, numb, with heads shaking in disbelief, staring at their lost livelihood in the hot stinking air, wondering in the darkness about tomorrow, uttering intermittent cries of anguish, seeing nothing for their children in the desolation that a scant few hours earlier had been a vibrant hive of human endeavour that employed, housed, fed and sustained thousands.

Nearer the Market where the flames had eventually been subdued, Fogarty's and Bettencourt-Gomes—victims of the terrible arson by a divine expression of poetic justice--retained fragments of their skeleton and façade, within which remnants of their rich contents, charred bolts of expensive cloth, furniture and bric-a-brac lay bare and exposed to whatever trespass or evil any one might wish, notwithstanding the proclamation hastily issued by the Premier and Chief of Police banning access to the area, and finally endorsed by the Governor and Commander of the British battalion that had belatedly arrived to support the Government against threats of further civil strife and anarchy.

On Carol's return home she responded to an appeal by the Hospital Matron Harding to "special" Supt. Mc Leod post-operatively; she was an accomplished RN and spent the night at his bedside but as she reported, his blood pressure kept falling despite transfusions, medications and other measures, indicating continuing blood loss. A second exploration revealed oozing from multiple rents in the deep pre-sacral venous plexuses not noticed at the first surgical exploration, when a ruptured external iliac artery had been ligated stanching the blood loss. No doubt the shock and hypotension at that time had obscured the tears in the deeper veins. But as his blood pressure and circulation recovered with use of inotropic agents the venous ooze had begun and his blood pressure fell dangerously low. Multiple transfusions of banked blood were needed to maintain a viable pressure, and resulted in a defibrination syndrome; he succumbed two days after the injury. He had not regained consciousness during that time. Asst. Commissioner Phoenix and some 40 other wounded policemen and scores of civilians survived.

On the night of February 16th, the flames barely cooling, soldiers shot three young men, two Negro, the other Portuguese, caught looting the ruins at Bettencourt-Gomes; they had defied an order given through a loud-hailer to "come out with your arms raised." Two died on the spot; the third was rushed to hospital bleeding from leg wounds. It fell to me to conduct the medico-legal enquiries and autopsies. The two British soldiers concerned were no older than their victims, barely 20. Both were devastated and related the circumstances in tears when their commander asked that I speak to them.

They were in a patrol truck parked on Water Street near the north end of the Stabroek Market and the entire square had emptied quickly as loud-hailers had poured repeated warnings of the curfew. As darkness fell a searchlight played across the Market Square and the nearby smouldering ruins of Bettencourt-Gomes, Fogarty's and other businesses on Water Street. In one pass the light picked out several men rummaging in the first store; the patrol leader called on them to halt and come out with raised hands; they didn't. He repeated the call and gave two soldiers an order to fire warning shots; this they did, two rounds, but the looters ran instead ignoring the repeated halt order; the riflemen were then ordered to shoot at their legs which they did, each one discharging several rounds, aimed low. Three men were hit, two of whom had dived while the third had kept running. Shadowy others had escaped in the dark; the police were notified and a nearby patrol responded, arresting some of the escapees.

When the deaths were publicised both opposition parties denounced the army as trigger-happy murderers using coloured people for target practice. Mobs gathered in further defiance, ignoring the official version of events and many intemperate things were said. Burnham called the shooters "white beasts" who had fired on men who had stopped with arms raised. With mounting concern at the possibility of mobs disrupting our part of the investigations Dr Nehaul called from the Ministry of Health before the autopsies and assured me of full military protection. The hospital grounds had a six-foot perimeter fence of iron railings or sheet metal, with heavy gates at each of four street entrances, three of which were in daily use. Middle Street was the southern boundary of the premises and gave access to our laboratories, which stood about 80 feet from the street across a courtyard and directly opposite the gate.

On the morning of the autopsy the gate was closed and manned by police guard and one of our porters who saw to the needs of incoming patients. A military truck with about ten soldiers on deck at the ready was parked in the street outside the gate, barring access from the street. Infantrymen were posted at intervals along the perimeter. Middle Street was eerily silent as access to the hospital segment had been closed. Soldiers reinforced guards at other gates.

Balgobin had concluded preparations when I arrived. The autopsies were witnessed by the customary police investigator, a superintendent, police and army photographers and two military officers. Dr Nehaul came in for the start and watched the first examination. At this time all I knew was that the men had been shot by soldiers. I took care to identify the wounds on each body, trace the paths of bullets and secure fragments of any that had not exited the body, and define the injuries. One squashed bullet was found embedded in the left chest of the Portuguese man after it had tracked from his right armpit through the right lung, pulverising two vertebrae leaving a gaping space, fractured a third, torn the aorta and then passed into the left lung to settle against a rib. His chest was full of blood.

In the other the bullet had passed cleanly through after entering the upper back of the liver, mincing it, the portal vein and inferior vena cava, the distal stomach, hitting a vertebra before exiting through the spleen. I was thus able to define the line of fire from the evidence provided on the position of the shooters and posture of the victims, concluding that they were prone at the time they were hit. We secured all samples for forensic and routine examinations and after studying the police documents including photographs before and at the autopsy I reported that the findings corroborated the soldiers' version of the incident that the deceased had both run and dived and so received in the upper body slugs that had been aimed at their legs. This refuted Burnham's widely dispersed and inflammatory claim that the men had been shot while standing with arms raised.

A check of the surgical report on the third victim verified this; he had frozen on hearing the halt order then panicked and ran as the roving searchlight fell on him. He was wounded in the legs, one tibia shattered while the other leg showed a neat track of a bullet which had pierced the interosseous membrane bruising the outer coat of the anterior tibial artery and leaving it with a small haematoma and miraculously intact. He had fallen clutching a bolt of singed tweed and a handful of trinkets, cuff links, tiepins and a grey Stetson. The Portuguese youth was handsome, muscular and well dressed, his pockets stuffed with expensive pens and tie clips, and costume jewellery of marginal value. The black deceased had a few items of cheap jewellery, a watch and a bolt of tweed, half burnt and blackened with soot at the edges, and probably of little worth.

The two soldiers involved were devastated by the deaths and the early reaction and name-calling. Their commanding officer came with them but stood down during the interviews. They had received counselling to help with feelings of guilt. One of them was especially shaken, despite their Commander and the Governor's soothing assurances that he had merely done his duty and properly followed orders, and had therefore done nothing wrong.

"Nothin' wrohng?" he asked plaintively, tears in his eyes, "Oi joost killed a mawn, suh!"(Were there any like he at Jallianwallah, I wondered?)

I explained the autopsy results to them, with diagrams, and answered questions related to Burnham's allegations, and confirmed that my report would support their version of events, not his. They were young and clearly shocked at the outcomes, but were consoled by hearing of the relief their presence had brought to ordinary people just like them who had endured terror from mobs, one of whom had shot a friend, a Police officer. He had just died in hospital despite intensive care, and had been nursed by my wife who had earlier that same day escaped another mob. The soldiers could have had no idea whether the looters were armed and could have just as likely been shot at; death is never acceptable especially if one caused it but is easier to handle if understood. It was reasonable for them to feel guilt and grieve and seek emotional support. I was pleased that after an hour their composure had improved, but I doubted they would ever fully recover.

In the next several days the arson site would continue smouldering and occasionally break out in flames, which, catching the breeze, would flicker and dance only to be squelched with loud hisses as the monitoring fireman aimed his hose at them. An army truck full of soldiers was parked at the southern access to the site blocking Water Street at the point near the Market where Jaikaran's Drug Store and Kawall's had burnt to the ground.

Further north the Portuguese had also suffered major losses on the west side of Water Street, with the razing of John Fernandes Ltd and the proud JP Santos general store and a few lesser businesses, all sacrificed as if by divine punishment, as these were not targets selected by the arsonists who had so brazenly displayed their UF and PNC colours while the fires were consuming the livelihood and investments of those whose only error, if one could call it that, had been to be of the same race as Premier Cheddi Jagan. Before the crisis ended two other looters were killed.

Feb 16th 1962 thus became another "black Friday" for the city, plunging people into deep fears and a maelstrom of new activities to protect life and property, personal and public, with an attention that was new, unproductive and burdensome. Suddenly people were looking backwards and sideways wherever they went, cautious, careful to recognise each strange sound or sight. Children, oblivious of the lurking menace, carried on while parents sweated their return from play or school or from a routine local errand. In the weeks that followed, the population seemed numb; people spoke in whispers, or not at all. The spontaneous and cheery morning greetings of ordinary people were muted to a low mumble or fell silent altogether. Blacks appeared chastened, and the middle class moved around with tails firmly tucked between their legs, cautious, apprehensive.

At the hospital black doctors were apologetic and commiserated with Indians, some of whose relatives had lost all in the inferno. The news of Portuguese involvement briefly halted the destructive venom of those people and cooled their powerful presses for a spell. Indians, inured to mistreatment and social injustices, beat their breasts in disbelief that they could be so hated as to be so viciously treated by fellow citizens. The air was thick with apprehension, disbelief and sorrow. In rural areas, from Essequibo to the Corentyne, as well as in the hinterland, peoples' reaction mirrored that of the DeHoop man, who lamented, *"We never know man could be so savage. We read 'bout Hitler, and all the terrible things he do, but this worse! And worse, we hear Americans help the savages who did this!"*

It was obvious that Jagan's earliest request for troops would have been answered had the US and UK been on his side. Were they trying to prove to him his inability to maintain law and order? In April, 1960, the Police Council had emphasised the urgency of the need that the BG Police Force represent "a reasonable cross-section of the community". Would such a representation have helped to forestall the disaster? And again, since the likelihood of such disturbances in an independent Guiana under Jagan was extremely high, would he have asked for Cuban help to quell them? And what would American reaction have been? I have no doubt that the delayed military response helped to "prove" Jagan's inability to maintain law and order and led to the postponement of independence that year to keep the British in charge and avoid a communist intervention. US national newspapers with typical hubris gloated.

The Washington *Evening Star* of the 19th February said: *"So it is an irony of sorts that free Britain which has no love for the man, has responded affirmatively to Mr Jagan's cry for help. Almost needless to say, there are many reasons why the ouster or sudden downfall of this pro-Soviet troublemaker would be good, but the mob cannot be allowed to take charge. Accordingly, with British military intervention, Guiana is quiet at the moment, and London can be counted upon to postpone the grant of full independence until there is a Georgetown government competent enough to insure that the place will not become a red satrapy or sort of Congo in the Western hemisphere."*

The *Baltimore Sun* echoed that: *"At best, the trouble may postpone the constitutional conference scheduled for May, and so delay the establishment of another Marxist state in the Americas."* Such was the shallowness of the senior American press on colonial issues and the huge blind spot it shared with its leaders on the negative side of Capitalism and its refusal to entertain anything more human or liberal.

The *New York Times* was more forthright: *"One result is obvious - British Guiana is in no condition for complete independence for many months and perhaps for several years. Prime Minister (sic) Cheddi Jagan's Government has shown its lack of wisdom and what is more its inability to maintain law and order. Dr. Jagan would now be in exile if he had not been able to call on the British for military help. The events provide a classical example of the gap between economic theory and practical politics... The destruction of Georgetown was a fearful blow to the already weakened economy. Thanks to the British, the disturbances are over, the constitution and internal self-government remain in force, and a new start can be made."*

A peculiar incident occurred at Mc Leod's autopsy, which left a sour pall over the investigative services and was a sorrowful irony in that it let down the slain McLeod, the very man who had been pushing hard to establish a first-rate forensic service. The laboratory director, Dr Balwant Singh, who was on autopsy duty that day, conducted the investigations. A crowd had gathered outside the building, buzzing, as Police secured the site and their top brass attended the examination. It was crucial to find and identify the bullet, and thus the weapon.

The bullet was found as expected, on probing in a straight line from the entry wound, past the ligatures in the lacerated iliac arteries to the sacrum, where it was squashed and embedded in the bone. Dr Singh removed it with customary care, then incomprehensibly placed it on the table beside the body--instead of directly into a specimen jar--where it got caught in the stream of water that continuously bathed the table and was swept away into the drain. Frantic attempts were made to dam the effluent at the nearest access point, which would have narrowed the search of the drains, and allowed almost certain recovery, but the flow of water had not been turned off soon enough. Two days of painstaking search and straining of all contents of the drain and its connections for several hundred feet to the point where they joined a major sewer line, failed to recover the bullet.

Dr Singh's embarrassment stayed with him throughout the enquiries that followed (and perhaps for life, since the killer was never brought to justice). Efforts to shift blame to the autopsy assistant Mahabir did not help, while in private Dr Singh's detractors—there were quite a few--snickered and accused him of collusion with, or bowing to the threats of those responsible for Supt McLeod's murder. PNC activists were concerned that the bullet would clinch suspicions re the identity of the gun, thus the murderer, and finally force an arrest.

The killer was never charged, even though a hundred or more people had seen him and his colleagues at close range, nor was the gun retrieved, although its identity and that of the murderer were known to many and from the fact that the death instrument was a rifle bullet, not pellets from a shot gun, which was the weapon carried by other armed mobsters except that one rifleman. (Another sad irony for me--knowing how urgently and diligently he had planned to investigate this very type of crime—would occur in just over a year's time when I would be facing the same firearm and rifleman demanding to end my life).

Excuses, explanations, recrimination, justification; the politicians exploited them all; they had a field day, every day, for months. Lies, more lies; blame, more blame, the cross- and counter-currents of political chicanery, finger pointing and infighting. The Governor pontificated, the Police Commissioner grandstanded while Jagan issued platitudinous remarks from which few could conclude that the targets and victims were Indians. Those directly affected by the fires moved around in a daze, or else were struck dumb and totally broken, many driven to deep shock or near madness by the sudden and final enormity of their loss. Quietly, without fanfare, multitudes of young and old took flight to England, bleeding the wounded land of what assets still remained.

Slowly, inexorably, life returned, as those whose job it was fell among the ruins to remove the debris, leaving silent and lonely remnants of once proud and bustling structures: broken, charred posts, rising straight up from the coals and ashes, half-burnt splinters and twisted metal that covered the ground haphazardly. One forlorn staircase that had borne the busy weight of many in the discreet hotel that it once served rose incongruously angled, leading up to nowhere. Here and there runs of concrete walls with jagged outlines and blackened facades stood precariously where they once joined with others to enclose a storehouse of paint or cloth or machinery or other merchandise. Grim-faced men searched cautiously among the ruins, mindful of hidden embers and the weakened remnants, knowing that even a puff of wind could send structures crashing.

But as it is with humans, calamities are mourned, regrets expressed, some restitution follows along with accommodation to the new *status quo*. Life plods on. Temporary premises rose hastily at the site of the major stores, but several owners moved to new locations or else resigned and left the country. The arson site remained largely ruins and modest new structures temporised for years.

Just after the incident, Jagan commented, inter alia, *"A country of the mind not of the soil, of the intellect and of the heart, not of the arm; that is what we want. We were created by geography and history, we were created by accident. Our opponents would want you to believe that we are men of violence; there is nothing further from the truth. Just look at the events of the past week; who burnt down the city of Georgetown? Whose followers rampaged through the city in gangs of chain-reeling bicycle thugs? Who stood on Bourda Green and the Parade Ground and preached to his followers to agitate and defeat the legitimate government, to defeat my government? If you ask yourself these questions you can easily answer them. They say we are communists; they say all sorts of things about us; they even say that we are violent. Ask yourself again, who is violent?*

"Despite the passion behind the observation and condemnation Jagan received scant sympathy and soon the brief period of public mourning and soul-searching among the anti-Jagan businessmen who had suffered unexpected and punishing losses gave way to renewed calls from an unrepentant PNC and UF for his removal. But Jagan remained steadfast to his principles and his position.

The effects on the health services soon spread from the palpable decline in morale to loss of scarce professionals. One day several weeks after the fires I ran into Dr Nauth-Misir, the dermatologist, as he came down the steps of his clinic — a building located across from the Laboratories. His head was covered in his perennial safari helmet -- a vestige of his QC days, and the "saviour of my scalp", as he put it, pointing to his thinning top; he wore a frown on his face.

"Did you hear that Dr Murray leaving?" I hadn't. Dr William Cawas Gilbert Murray was our head ophthalmologist; I had met him in 1950 when I was a fresh personnel officer at the Medical Department (the forerunner of the Ministry of Health), and had been intrigued by his unusual second name.

"And I hear Stracey, Grewal and Das Gupta thinking of leaving soon. Did you know Rayman, the obstetrician? He was still here when you came."

I nodded.

"He went on leave to Saskatchewan in Canada; you know how cold that place is! He's not coming back even though he's facing some racial prejudice from the white doctors there! Things real bad when you see Rayman decided to stay away, with all the property they have here and the race bias in Canada."

"That's serious; with Shenolikar already gone to St Joseph's, we won't have any surgeons left." I observed.

"And nobody will come here to replace them; the word's already out that only black people safe here. And they don't have black doctors; and even if they had, they won't come to work for Jagan."

"I heard them say that Nehru will help, and that Mao will send them plenty doctors."

"Only the barefoot kind, I'm sure; who tell him China has doctors to spare? Mao killed off all of them that didn't escape to Formosa; they still rely on Bethune, you know, the Canadian communist who trying to teach western medicine there. I can't believe that a dentist would be such a poor judge in medical matters; maybe it's because they un-learn how to listen; you know, they talk and even ask you questions, when they have your tongue immobilised, your mouth open, a drill running in it and it's full of water and a suction tube. I suppose they don't really want to hear what you have to say." He clearly enjoyed saying this.

We both chuckled; how often had I felt like asking Dr Jagan, 'Why do you pick just then to ask me that when you know I can't reply?'

"Well, Chandisingh's not helping either." I told him, ".he says we're overpaid; he said the porters do as important a job and make less than we do; so we shouldn't complain."

"What an ass! When was that?"

"At a meeting the junior doctors had, you remember, a few weeks ago, we threatened to stop working overtime. Stanley told him he would be glad to take less if the Ministers led the way, and level their salary with the porters, and give up their perks. Besides, we emphasised, nobody will miss the Ministers, but people will miss us if we're not there in Casualty to help them with all the troubles the politicians bring them."

Nauth-Misir laughed, "I wish I was there to see his face. Was he sober? He drinks a lot, you know. So what happened?"

"Nothing! The guy's a sphinx; didn't bat an eyelid, just asked what's next."

"Must have been plastered. You got what you wanted?"

"Practically, yes."

"I don't know 'bout you, but I'm worried like hell; the place looks a little calmer now, but more violence is just 'round the corner. And the PPP holding elections soon. I hope Rai wins the chairmanship; he's the only level-headed one in the Party! And you know Balwant is dead set against them. So much politics screwing up Medicine, pushing and pulling, it's a tug-o-war."

One by one the incidents had brought the dangers closer to home. Reacting to my wife's disquiet and the prodding of Jan Evertz – who had been a good friend from medical school, with shared loyalties to our Hall of Residence -- I decided to take the US ECFMG examinations to qualify for licensing there.

For this I went to the US naval base at Chaguaramas in Trinidad, and examinations apart, saw first-hand the similarities and differences in the approach Dr Eric Williams had taken to independence, then just months off. Like Jagan, Williams had begun by engaging in a series of informative open air lectures which were held in Woodford Square beginning in the mid-fifties. They drew large crowds and the place was promptly dubbed the *'University of Woodford Square'*. Williams, an economist, had become known for his thesis *Capitalism and Slavery* arguing strongly that slavery was a necessity for agri-business success and growth and that freedom had occurred only when industrial capitalists opposed it as unfair labour competition!

Unlike Jagan, Williams had adopted a moderate platform for his Peoples National Movement (PNM), similar to Tulla's ideas, with ample room for free enterprise and a strong role for government. I was disturbed however to note that he had made few efforts to engage Indians (who comprised over 35% of the population of a million) despite having Indians as first Chair of the Party and Assistant General Secretary.

I attended two of these meetings; the square was quite close to my Bed & Breakfast hostelry on Abercrombie St. The methods—decrying colonial history, slavery, neglect of education, exploitation and disenfranchisement of Africans, and promoting their "natural" right to the succession and to lead into independence—were the same as I had heard in BG. There Jagan wooed minority Africans, while Eric Williams pretended that minority Indians were invisible. (He became the power in Trinidad and would dominate its politics until his death, achieving personally what Jagan would fail to do in BG. An interesting note is that Jagan and Williams had each consulted Jamaica's Norman Manley in framing his Party's constitution.)

I completed my examinations (successfully, as I would learn a few weeks later) and went to Tobago for a few days visiting with classmate Glenn Nymm, a handsome black man and his wife, a Jamaican nurse of Indian ancestry. They showed me the prime sites on the picturesque and tranquil island including the incredible Buccoo Reef where the marine life was as close as an arm's reach and even with just a snorkel you could see an astonishing variety of fish, shellfish, little turtles, sea horses and a host of other life forms, small and large, plain and colourful, known and unknown. The amazing clarity of the water allowed one to see great detail to a depth of over six feet with the naked eye.

Reflecting on Tobago's pristine natural beauty and its idyllic separation from bustling Trinidad, Williams' politics seemed quite remote. But in discussing it Glenn agreed that the PNM must make an even-handed and honest attempt to incorporate Indians into all aspects of civil society and recognize the unique contributions they could make, especially to culture. This would almost certainly place Trinidad at the van of Caribbean nations, as it worked to establish a model of peaceful and cooperative multi-racial function. This would require however that Williams and his cohorts abandon the notion of Coloured/Black primacy and accept the reality that Indians were in Trinidad to stay. This incidentally was Jagan's philosophy for British Guiana but unlikely to bear fruit under a communist umbrella. Sadly the actions of the PNM were not reassuring and I feared that Indians would have to fight for rights in that promising land with oil reserves and the largest deposit of pitch in the world to fuel their economy.

The US presence was obvious everywhere, from the WWII naval base at Chaguaramas to the oilfields near San Fernando. The ordinary citizen identified with Americans, aped every aspect of their dress, behaviour and noisy entertainment, coveted US products and swarmed its movies. The spirit of the late forties calypso was flourishing and the emblematic tune of that period remained popular:

> *Drinking rum and Coca-Cola/ Down Point Cumana*
> *Both mother and dawta/ Working for the Yankee dollaaaa…*

It was clear that US dominance in the island's economy would not tolerate any threat to industrial stability, yet unions in Port-of-Spain and San Fernando were constantly ruffling that calm, chief among them the Oilfields Workers Union headed by leftist John Rojas, whom Jagan claimed as his friend.

I returned home to relative quiet which lasted through most of the second half of 1962 and seemed to have lulled us all into believing that perhaps Melby had been able to bring Jagan around to his side--especially after US envoy Hoffman had visited and made encouraging comments—so much so that I made the commitment to buy a nice plot of land on the ocean front six miles from the city, at Courida Park, a block away from the place where I had met Leila in 1961.

Here I would build a home; the sweeping views of the Atlantic would be an inspiration; from there I would develop a career, raise the children, and do good works, as Hari had wished for me, in partnership with Stanley; I would travel the country and build a little hideaway in Kamarang, or at the top of the Kaieteur gorge (unlikely there as it was a national reserve), or Towakaima, and work in Mabaruma for a while which would expose me to the realities of the frontier, a thing that no political leader had done so far, and yet they pretended to understand how to rule in such a place. And later, *perhaps*, I would enter public service.

Stanley had similar ideas, fought front-line battles during a posting at Bartica, and returned to his father's spacious apartment atop Central High School. There he suffered an exacerbation of his post-traumatic behavioural problems. I tried to help by responding to calls from his forbearing and beautiful wife Ivy, who had become close friends with Carol, sharing Jamaican roots. Those visits had taken place during his worst period of about a month. I would sit with him, listen and converse as if nothing untoward had happened, recalling our time at the University and his re-telling of the night when he had had too much to drink and wrapped his car around a utility pole! He was particularly critical of the way the physicians had handled the behavioural aspects of his head trauma and the use of ECT by the psychiatrist which might have helped behaviour in the short term, but had placed a label of "madness" beside his name instead of an organic syndrome due directly to the accident.

Usually he settled after these sessions as if the retelling had been a catharsis, and would often fall asleep; at other times he would send me home, saying, "I know what Ivy's going through, and the children; it's not easy for them, especially when I tell them I'll jump out that window." He would laugh at that point and add, "This house full of windows; they can't mind them all." And Ivy would say, "That's the kind of thing he says that makes us all worry, worry, worry. I'm terrified and can't sleep; and with all that's happening outside, things here getting worse; even bad Trench Town in Jamaica not this bad!"

Stanley retained a remarkable insight into his condition and in one bad episode Hamilton and Brahmam looked after him, since the nearest psychiatrist was at the Mental Hospital in New Amsterdam seventy miles south-east. At Ivy's request I gave them all the background information we had, and both agreed with Stanley's assessment but were unable to suggest what beyond psychotherapy and sedation could do any good. He was home a few days later controlled by heavy sedation and proved a real challenge to his wife, and the children, who, despite their youth, were remarkably supportive and developed novel ways to deal with his difficult moments. The relapses occasionally became violent but no personal injury resulted. In general they lasted a few days, after which he was quite lucid and able to function normally. His reliance on aspirin for headaches gave him a stomach ulcer, which posed its own challenges. The political situation upset and absorbed him and contributed to the exacerbations. But abruptly his behaviour improved, he returned to full duties and we began to plan our ultimate health facility.

Mazaruni River at Kamarag; Airstrip is behind photographer (from a postcard received in 1955, photographer ? L.Witt)

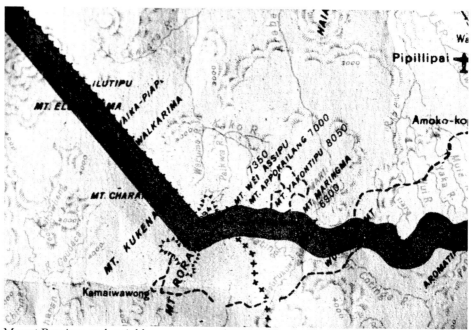

Mount Roraima and neighbour summits along the Venezuelan border. Most of those east of Roraima are in Guyana; as the map shows Roraima extends into Brazil and Venezuela. Note the course of the misty Kako River and its steep descent as the contour lines show
See also map on page 309

Typical slogans in D'Aguiar's *Ax the Tax* campaign at time of Prince Philip's "Trade" Mission, Feb 12, 1962

"He doth bestride the earth like a colossus!" Wm Shakespeare

JFK and associates, 1962; his administration was intimately involved and directed British policy towards British Guiana, however much the British claimed to have been the main player. It was inevitable from their history that British rulers would disappoint the majority of the six peoples of the country.

Central Garage, High Street at Regent, Georgetown, wide angle view; all buildings in photo were destroyed by fire, Feb 16, 1962; the canal dividing the street is at left.

Hand-in-Hand building, on High St, near Cenotaph, Feb 12, 1962, spared in fire 4 days later; Central Garage in middle ground, was destroyed; Town Hall tower at left, escaped.

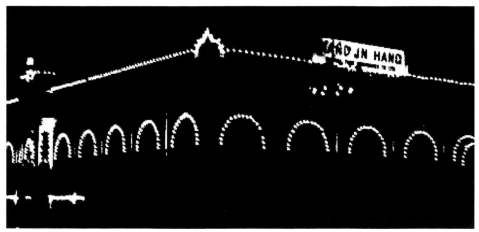

Hand-in-Hand Insurance Co offices lit up for Prince Philip's "Trade" visit on Feb 12, 1962

A Portuguese bicycle store, one of the arson victims of Feb 16, 1962

Steel roof of Stabroek Market--with ferry and Demerara River in background in this wide angle view--the final barrier to the conflagration of Feb 16, 1962. Pumps on fireboats on the river kept this roof and adjacent buildings from overheating.

Town Hall, reflected in High St Canal, lit up for Prince Phillip's visit, Feb 12, 1962

Water St looking north from Stabroek Market (bottom left), before loss to arson; JP Santos and Bookers, the white building and one beyond on left, middle distance

Panorama of area destroyed, view from Stabroek Market tower, 1961: Market Sq. where South St ends is in foreground; Town Hall tower in rear centre. All the structures in this photo in front of the line of the town Hall were destroyed or seriously damaged.

Above, Top down: Bookers HQ, Fogarty's Department Store, Barclays Bank, all on Water St. The Bank escaped damage from fire whose smoke is seen in background

Feb 16, 1962: An unintended victim on Water St.: ?J P Santos; charcoal sketch

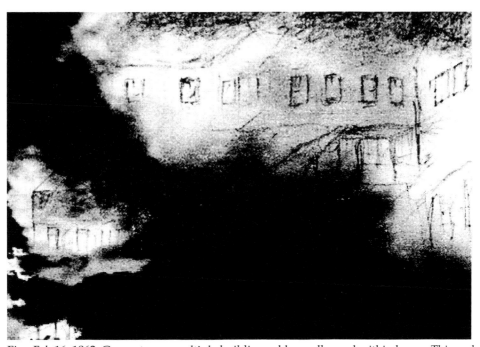

Fire, Feb 16, 1962, Georgetown; multiple buildings ablaze, all razed within hours. This and
the two following are charcoal sketches of the disaster area.

Another "accidental" victim on Water St.:-- Bookers HQ

Skeletons of two structures after the fire

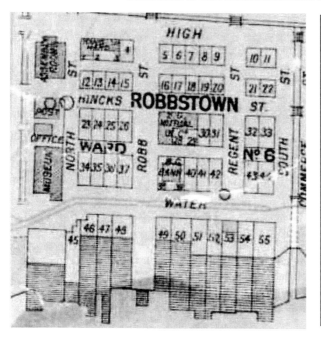

The area burnt down was bounded by Regent, High, South and Water Streets, plus lots 8, 9, 20, 31, 42 and 52-55; other fires were set half a mile away on Camp St near South. Church St is at extreme left; the Demerara River is at bottom (docks shaded). The area contained many commercial and Government buildings, including the country's two banks, Royal at Water and Robb, and Barclays obliquely across on Water St.

Chapter 14

A defeated candidate, a long-time political opponent of the Premier, reflects on opportunities lost to explain the franchise to the unschooled and vulnerable early enough to forestall the debacle into which naiveté has taken them. The moderate Mr Rai is elected to the Chairmanship of the PPP but his election is arbitrarily overturned by a Jagan putsch and the incumbent retained. The Premier—as party leader—and his wife, party General Secretary, are accused of highhandedness and election rigging. He vetoes a Rai plan to make the Police Force more representative of the population. My colleagues discuss the deterioration in society. I finally get a chance to speak frankly to the Premier and angrily accused him of betraying his supporters.

Post-mortem at the BGEICC

"Dr. Jagan has made his greatest political blunder…he has cast aside moderate Indians in favour of rabid communists. He has exchanged competence for incompetence."

Sunday Graphic, June 17, 1962, re Rai's expulsion.

To paraphrase John Dewey, we could accept ignorance if clothed in humility, but not when it manifests itself in a mere repetition of catch phrases, an arrogant assembly of obtuse terminology that provides a thin veneer of learning. Such conceit only fools the perpetrator and coats his mind with varnish impervious to the cleansing waters of real knowledge… Anon

But I can assure Honourable Members that as long as we are in office, this country will be industrialised.

CB Jagan, Budget Speech, April 1962

We were sitting on the spectator benches at the EICC one spectacularly beautiful afternoon in April after a game of tennis, enjoying the ambience. The clear sky of an uncommon blue colour forecast a night of the brightest stars; the gentle Atlantic breeze seemed specially scented that day; the murmur of conversation in the background was muted and merged with the click of billiard balls, punctuated by periodic exclamations or thumps of cues on the floor when a good shot was made. My children, Phillip 6½, Peter nearing 5, and Ranji, 14 months were frolicking on the tennis courts just below where we sat, squired by their mother. My friend and tennis partner Rudolph, at 36 head of his family's haberdashery business, joined us, handing out drinks.

There was BK Persaud, an acerbic older man, twice my age, short, average build, and as agile and crafty a tennis player as he had been in his heyday as a club champion and colony representative, and once a first class cricketer. Mohamed Rajah, his colleague and foil of the same vintage, a slim tall man owned a thriving sports goods store on Regent Street; thirteen years ago, he had donated a trophy for third class cricket, the Rajah Cup, drafting me as Secretary of the Organising Committee. Dan, a lawyer and politician, had just come in, straight from his office, and two others, Parcotan (Dhanpaul) Dookhie and JP Prashad, both young businessmen, who like Rudolph, were all brimming with ideas to expand their business operations, like so many others we knew. Parco-- we called him Dan, but I've used Parco here to avoid mix-up with Dan the lawyer—was a relative by marriage, doing well in Insurance, whom I had invited over. From time to time others would join us, say hello, and stay or leave as their interest in the conversation dictated.

"You need to work on your service, Doc." Rajah said, abruptly, light-heartedly in his hurried way of speaking that often clipped the ends of words and could be baffling.

"Yes, it's awful; never get a chance to practise. Work eats up the time."

I thought of the challenges identified by Walter Singh in Paediatrics, and by Stanley with his keen eye for research possibilities, and of the material awaiting analysis from the recent Parathione poisoning outbreak that had left many crippled, nine dead, and others in hospital.

"Looks to me like other things eat up your time, Doc." BK observed, slyly, his high-pitched voice breaking into my brief reverie, as he nodded towards the mother and her three children playing on the court; she had just then, as if cued by BK, bent down to pick up the wailing toddler and so displayed her perfect form straining against skin-tight white sharkskin pedal-pushers. They giggled, sheepishly.

Rudolph, sensing my discomfiture, changed the subject, "You know Ivan packing up to go 'way?" he asked no one in particular. Ivan was a club cricketer, and a middle grade government administrator of some promise.

"He's not the only one; *all* qualified young people will disappear from this country if we don't stop it." Dan said.

"True," Parco said, "we need them to fill needs after independence."

"You damn right and we got to stop it; who in his right mind would leave a place like this?" BK waved expansively, taking in all the elements of that gorgeous afternoon.

"How do we stop it?" Rajah asked, "Cheddi got us in this mess, and he still don't see he's the cause of all this uproar, the riots, the looting — I lost nearly half my stock, like every other businessman, and so much business lost — then the fire, now he fighting with Rai, the only smart one in the whole damn government; Cheddi will destroy us all."

"He sounded like he cared for Indians, in the beginning when he was with us here," Dan said matter-of-factly, "but we soon found out, didn't take a year to show his colours."

"But you all, we all, went about things the wrong way." BK said, "It is we who let down the Indians. A few people like Rai tried to change things, but got nowhere. And before that you remember Tulla and his brother-in-law, what's his name, the soft drinks and theatre man."

"Ramroop," Parco said, "my wife's *mousa* (father's sister's husband)."

"Yes, the same one; they were big behind the scenes trying to shape him up; he should have listened to them, smart businessmen, good ideas, but the Commie pull was stronger."

"You're right; and I'm partly to blame," Dan said, in measured tones, enunciating each word, as was his style, "I used to be with those men too, and didn't listen either, I the smart lawyer, and they with sixth standard only; the arrogance of the merely erudite versus the smarts of the truly intelligent. They warned us to get out into the country, since '40; Jagan did and we," he paused, "*we* left the country people, in all their innocence and hunger for change, we left them wide open to his rabble-rousing."

He shifted in his seat, loosened his tie, sipped his drink delicately, and continued, musing self-deprecatingly, "he was a show, and they enjoyed him, as if he was Ashok Kumar, and Janet was Devika Rani; that's what they saw, and loved, two entertainers, two stars, and Janet being white, clinched it. Especially when she ate at weddings with her fingers from *kamalgatta* leaf, and Cheddi slammed us for using knife and fork! When I was campaigning on the East Coast I realised that independent Indians did see through them; they knew that what Cheddi said wouldn't work, because they had been through that already, and here, in this very pavilion, we fooled ourselves into thinking that every Indian would just as easily see through him. Instead we should have gone out long before he did, at War's end, before the Enmore killings, and raise hell, and recruited bright young people of all races, from town and country, do the bottom-house meetings to prepare them for self-government. But we stood aloof, as if paralysed; we betrayed them; we gave them no facts, no alternative; we were so taken up with the rightness of our own views and interpretations, we forgot to tell the people about them, especially the estate people; we overlooked them in a way and missed the fact that most of them had no daily news, no papers, no radio, only word of mouth from unionists or local leaders, and no concept or experience of independent life, whether in farming, or in business."

"Life on the estates was slavery, denial, and ignorance; it demeaned people. They lived in the dark. So they couldn't see much beyond better pay and cheaper rum, and Cheddi promised that."

"In Jamaica Bustamante won with food, ackee and saltfish; here it's rum!" I complained.

"He beat us badly there." He resumed. "We were more ambitious for those people than they were for themselves; they didn't want independence, they don't know what it is; but handouts they know. They bought his propaganda and his ridiculous promises of free this and free that, so when we started to tell them the truth, they dismissed us; Cheddi had already warned them we would come 'to fool them', that we city types were on the side of the estates and wanted to keep workers down. So he used their ignorance and innocence to beat us. Now that he's Premier, they feel good; they hold their heads up, share the limelight; they feel the power he talks about, but don't know enough to realise he's ruining them, and that they have no one else to turn to, if they stumble on the truth. The sad thing is that Burnham will soon take over. And no matter how you put it to Cheddi, he still refuses to see that he's the one that's handing us over to that tyrant. The man can't change. He's not smart enough to change. It's like he's fixed in formalin. Right Doc?" he tittered wryly at his quip. Sadly, I nodded.

"Why didn't all of you just join the Party, when you saw that you couldn't take him from outside, and create a force for change, from inside like Rai trying to do?" JP asked.

Dan shook his head, "Too many stubborn weak people; too opinionated, too much self-interest; too much blindness. And I'm one of the guilty ones. Some tried, like you said, Tulla Hardeen back in the very beginning; but after he died, no one had that kind of interest or knowledge or perseverance to try, until Rai."

I had discussed the same question recently with Shah on one of our trips to Leonora and later with Parco and Zaman on a trip to Mahaicony.

"Isn't there time? I saw politicians in Jamaica pull back from the brink; why not here?"

"Everybody's black in Jamaica, well over 90%; they don't have *our* racial divide;" he answered. "That is the cross we bear, our big obstacle. Ordinary people can overcome it; but it's honey for politicians; they savour it, they stoke it, they exploit it."

"But look at Trinidad," BK said, "we were way ahead of them in politics; they didn't get off until Albert Gomes came on the scene, and fired Eric Williams from his Caribbean Commission job in 1955; Williams was hurt and started to make speeches in Woodford Square; he insulted and threatened Gomes but didn't speak against Indians then as Burnham doing here. One of the founders of his PNM was Indian, Kamal Mohammed, and I think Dr Mahabir also joined.

But Bhadase (Sagan Maharaj) had been on the scene there since the thirties; he had little education but was smart and tough; he stood up to Gomes and to Williams too. He united Indians into the best organised group in Trinidad from the late thirties on, and included rural Indians, getting them to build schools and showing them to take pride in themselves; it was the opposite of what happened here; Trinidad Indians didn't take to Communism like this; and yet you know that Cheddi asked Bhadase for money to invest in *Thunder*; isn't that ironic?"

"True; he did, and he even said that BG Indians not business-like--or something like that--typical of him! But nobody here goin' invest in a communist paper; so he choose his usual to bad talk us." Rajah's felt righteous anger. I looked at Parco whose loyalty to and defence of Jagan had begun to wilt.

"We have to be more vigilant now that Jagan seeing Castro as his hero. The CIA would have killed him, like Lumumba, if there was a plausible alternative." Dan observed gloomily.

"Rai could be that person, if he becomes Chairman of the Party," I said. "But I understand that Kennedy's advisers still think they can win over Cheddi; they promised him aid, and Jack Melby here is still pro-Jagan, and can't stand Burnham."

"But I hear Melby is losing patience and may change after the hearings of the Commission of Enquiry into the riots. It's sad, but Forbes will take over, Cheddi or no Cheddi, this year or next." Dan opined.

A long pause followed, emphasising the general pessimism. Parco broke the silence.

"Dan, you were on the Association's executive when Jagan became Secretary; what did you think of him then?"

After a pause, and sipping his drink, he replied, measuring his words.

"That was in '47; he was fearless, full of fire and brimstone, almost suicidal; we liked that; we thought his US experience and wife would help us at a practical level to deal with the US, but within a few weeks we found he knew more about damn Russia, where he'd never been, than the US, where he lived for seven years! And Janet hated the US. It was as if he had moved in and assimilated an imaginary level of US life with none of the familiar places, characters or institutions. Like a dream. It was a big disappointment, as we realised that his far-left thinking would make us lose political and economic momentum, and worse, discredit and sideline us. You see, we had a good plan, starting back in the thirties; but war "security" set us back; we were too slow off the mark when it ended, and as soon as Cheddi saw our plan he took it and ran away with it, lock, stock and barrel, changing the words to suit ideology. Or so it seemed. At first when he was simply harassing the colonial government and the estate monopolies, we egged him on to do that because it was nasty, crude and undignified, and he suited it so well, but that was, as I said, our big mistake." he ended unhappily, taking a mouthful of his drink, and savouring it before he swallowed.

"But if the Association realised that he was Communist, why didn't you all go after him from the beginning?" Parco asked.

"At first we thought his thick skin and manic behaviour would be great to whip up support and he wouldn't be put off by criticism and name-calling as more sensitive persons would be — and you know how most of our best thinkers can't face a heckling audience--not so Jagan; his tirades woke people up, which was good, especially for rural folks; they listened to him and we hoped they would join our cause." He paused, sipped again, and shook his head sadly, "but we were wrong to think that they would vote against him when they found out he was Communist, because by then he had turned Marx into God and he the Messiah."

"Was that in the '53 campaign?" Rudolph asked. "Is that when apana *jaat* slogan was used? Did you start it, as Jagan says? Was that a problem?"

"Some said it was; more so since PPP split, but campaigning ten years ago we tried to explain Communism to people, that it was not a Christian or Hindu or Muslim concept, nor was it an African thing. So we reminded people of their culture and what was foreign to it; to explain it for the majority of Indians we used *apana jaat* to mean their familiar Indian culture as distinct from an alien Communist one. It had nothing to do with race; we were fighting Jagan, an Indian and we were Indians too; only fools or mischief-makers would call it racial. What we didn't reckon with was how hungry estate folk were for hope and deliverance and how desperate for a leader and how deeply entrenched Cheddi and Janet had become among them. They were prophets."

"The estates as private property did not allow meetings; to his credit he took on the estate managers and was one of the first to take serious politics to the estate people. They love him." Parco said, having witnessed first-hand Jagan's superb massaging of people's emotions and sharing the élan, feeling it even.

"It would have happened anyway;" Dan replied, "all the unions were there and getting more active as universal suffrage became a surety. Some of our people were too aloof, almost snooty in dealing with country people, as if they felt shame, even though some of them were only one generation removed from plantation life. Estate folk hated that attitude, and Cheddi exploited it to divide us. Even so, we could have beaten *him*, but we had no weapon against *Janet*. She is his juggernaut."

"You're right," BK said, "but *apana jaat* took on a racial meaning in '57, and Burnham used it hoping to get Indians to vote for Jainarine and Latchmansingh."

"And when they campaigned in Negro areas, they called for support of '*kith and kin*'," Rudolph recalled. "They came through the Market saying so and rubbing forearms as a sign."

"How short memory is!" I said, "or maybe just convenient; PNC going around claiming that PPP started racial politics. Can PPP rise above that?"

"We'll see soon; they're holding elections for the Party exec this week at Guiana Oriental College; that will show which direction they're heading. I worry for the future."

"Well won't Rai will be made Chairman?" Parco asked, innocently.

"I fear not. He's not communist. A lot of us thought and hoped he could take them from inside; he has a good following and even Janet praises him as a Minister. But that's PPP politics; her remarks are for public consumption; pure hypocrisy! Privately they're planning to ditch him," Debidin contended. "Those elections are a non-event, a play to distract from the real mess we're in. Benn will remain Chairman. Cheddi and Janet will simply tell the delegates to vote for Benn."

"Don' joke, Dan!" Rajah exclaimed. "After how Rai handled the school situation, and his take on police recruitment, he's the only bright light in the party, even counting Nunes and Ramsahoye; he has lots of supporters; even the opposition treats him with respect."

The idea of another term for Benn offended him considerably, giving added intensity to his remarks. He had in the past supported the PPP but like others opposed to Communism had shifted to the United Force.

"My guess is that even the opposition would like to see the last of Rai; he's a moderate, he holds different views from the Marxists; he has strong principles. Rightness, *dharma* and *karma* are his guides, not communist ideology; he joined the party to moderate it, move it to the centre; we had hoped Ramsahoye, Nunes, and a few others might join with him; but even there we misjudged the tight controls the PPP Exec has on its member cells; the top--and for all practical purposes, that's Cheddi and Janet—tells everyone else what to do. None of those chaps would get elected on their own. Their internal elections are a lively and contentious process stirring up the grass roots, who feel empowered because they get to choose delegates, but democracy ends there; Cheddi and Janet then tell the delegates how to vote. You have any friends as delegates? Just ask them."

Dan's cynicism was infectious; I thought of Dayla from DeHoop, and Shah's friend Bashir, from Leonora and two of Buddy's Black friends--all honest men and regional PPP officials and activists; all were delegates; what might they say? Then there were other delegates I knew, among them my secretary and a young Caribbean Atlantic Life Insurance Company agent who sold insurance and communism at the same time, without acknowledging the paradox; he did not see one, explaining that when true communism came to be—and "there's no true communist state today"—all would be totally equal and no government would even become necessary, since each one would be his brother's keeper, a government of the people by the people. That, multiplied globally, would eliminate all enmity, competition, greed and covetousness; each one carrying out his tasks will contribute to the general good of society. He resisted questions on how to get there, how to accommodate or eliminate differences ("we'll get there in time") or to give an opinion on where we stood in that paradigm.

No one said much for a while. Small talk from the bar drifted down to where we sat; they were talking about cricket and women, and laughing at one another's quips, unconcerned, or perhaps the opposite, too powerless to change anything, and burying their fears in drink and casual talk like ordinary folk everywhere.

"That's one reason why I quit PPP." Rajah said, his words racing, "they tell you how to think; you can't have a contrary opinion or another way of getting a job done, especially if you're Indian; if you do, they treat you like pariah, and throw you out. The only Black person I know that they threw out was Bowman, in '59 same time as Edward Beharry."

"I heard of that in '60, when I came home to look after my mother, but didn't get the chance to get the full story; I know Edward well; he's a family friend; his store was just round the corner from my brother-in-law's depot in the Market; what happened?" I asked.

"Well," Dan started after a brief silence, "after his surprising win in '57 Jagan put a lot into plans for development and later into the '59 budget; he desperately wanted money for his favourite theme *'industrialisation'*, which has a powerful meaning for Marxists. He went to London looking for $200 million for a new plan to replace a $91million 5-yr plan previously prepared and considered inadequate. He tried everywhere to raise funds. A Swiss bank offered to lend him £6 million subject to British backing. London declined and referred him to the World Bank, which he immediately contacted. That was August '58.

"He also approached Washington's Development Loan Fund and there got a run-around because he did not follow US procedures, which are quite rigid; they told him to go to the Import Export office. Near Christmas a World Bank economist John Adler visited us and endorsed Jagan's plan. At home here he had a running fight with Renison about those same plans and about taxation and appointment of an economic adviser. Jagan wanted a socialist, and the head of the India Statistical Institute—I forget his name[150]—had recommended a fellow named Charles Bettelheim. He was not available, nor were other favourites like Gunnar Myrdahl and Tom Balogh. Eventually he got Ken Berrill of Cambridge University, who visited early in '59 almost colliding with an American economic team. Berrill watered the plan down from $200 million to $110 million saying that future interest cost would be too big a burden for a small economy.

"That made Cheddi really see red, claiming Berrill underestimated the revenue from the new 'industries'. Delegations visited Canada, the US, Germany, France and Italy. No luck. He blasted them all and claimed he could get cheap money from Russia just as Nasser had gotten for the Aswan dam. Renison relented on the tax issue. Nobody except D'Aguiar minded the excise tax on beer; but the potato tax of 3c/lb hit Indians hardest; Jagan claimed that it was to protect ground provision producers, most of whom were Blacks, even though production would not match need, so he was bringing relief to them at Indians' expense--as Indians would have to switch their food tastes—all this to show he was not racially biased! To show more 'even-handedness' he added a tax on wealthy producers by reintroducing the sugar production, acreage and distribution taxes, which had been abolished in 1951. Renison objected but Jagan quoted to him McDavid's original statement about re-introduction of that tax. D'Aguiar greeted that with his *'axe the tax'* campaign. Beharry in his wisdom opposed the taxes, but then it turned out that he'd won a very lucrative distribution agency for Bristol cigarettes from the Demerara Tobacco Company!"

He recounted how Jagan had promptly accused Berrill of following a colonial plot to defeat him; his followers had cheered wildly when told that these obstacles would all vanish once he had secured their independence. He didn't think he was duping poor blind ignorant people, and told them instead that his critics were enemies who wished them to remain poor. He maintained this with great vigour and kept claiming that independence would solve all problems, by accessing Soviet help to get the right people, and to train his own home-grown socialists "right here in Guiana". He accused London and Washington mercilessly of delaying independence for this reason. They returned him to power in 1961.

"But what he didn't tell his voters was that both the UK and USA were in sympathy with the plans but neither could give him special treatment without doing the same for every other supplicant. He must have known this; I know it and I'm not in Government; it's common sense. Besides if your plan is good and the bankers won't fund it, it's usually because they don't trust you to work it. That never entered his mind even though he's been hearing it for ten years."

"And while he saying so," Rajah interjected, "thousands of the brightest people leaving their jobs, families, businesses, and his industrial dream projects

---

[150]Prof. Mahalanobis

and will be walking the streets of cold London, not warm Georgetown. The man's crazy."

"London and Washington know he's driving away talent and money; that's one reason so many ignoring or opposing him." BK added. "You hear all the bloated claims he made about the Hungarian glass plant and how Cuba will give him $32m to harness Malali rapids for electricity, with five million US thrown in for a wood pulp plant and rice bran oil factory from East Germany? Words, words! Cheddi will drown us with words."

"The only reasonable things he's done are the land settlement schemes, the land registry and take-over of the 50 religious primary schools." Prashad said.

"And it was Rai who pushed that one." Rudolph corrected.

"He should ease up on this independence thing; it's not the great idea he says, except to the Communists. To him and Janet independence is a prize for winning a race, not a stage in the maturing of a people, which, by the way, *he managed to delay for over 10 years*! He should have left it to BGEIA; we might have seemed slow, but we weren't climbing on the backs of ignorance; we wanted our people educated first, and we wanted the Brits to pay for that education; they owed us. Now he's lost it," Dan observed grimly. "And what's worse all these rejections have convinced the fence-sitters that financiers don't have faith in him. As Raj said many skilled people even those with good jobs are leaving; and I hear every Tom, Dick and Harry with two cents in the bank withdrawing it and sending it abroad. Don't you see the British bank ads in the papers? Lombard Banking and Rothschilds are doing well."

"One thing that makes our situation so desperate," I suggested, "is that no matter what anyone says the mass of people do not know what it means to have a communist government, so they continue to vote for both major parties, each of which is red, neither having any real economic savvy; their leaders are consumed with theory and personal ambition."

"You're so right!" Dan exclaimed. "We faced a wall of pro-PPP solidarity and deafness to reason that not even appeals to check our facts from any reference of their choice made any impression. The kind ones dismissed all criticism as sour grapes; others less kind pelted us!"

"I prefer eggs cooked, not *ganda*,[151]" BK joked. "Going back to this firing of people, the PPP always did that; from way back in the early fifties; they say it's for discipline, Jainarine Singh was a big early one. Beharry asked for it; he not only opposed the Party budget, but his mates thought the Bristol tobacco deal looked too cosy. PPP leaders don't like questions; they're infallible."

"And almost divine in the eyes of supporters; I was solid Jaganite, like Tulla bunoye and most of our family, like Parco and his folks, but Cheddi afraid of talent in others." I added. "So, many are moving to England."

"Several of my friends also going, and many went before, like Karan who quit before they could throw him out." Rudolph said. "All the smart ones are leaving for true, even some who have a lot of property here."

"You remember Abdul Khayum—he was heart and soul PPP and used to recruit here on cricket days and next door at the Y and other clubs—PPP throw him out; Janet said he was causing 'racial disharmony' because he criticised them for picking mainly black people for jobs." BK noted.

"Oh yes, Khayum was chairman of the PYO." Rudolph recalled.

---

[151] rotten

"If you don't carry out Jagan's orders, you gone," BK said; "that's why Rai is history; Janet praising him is the signal; like Judas kissing Christ; and it's Easter time too! The axe will fall, unless he toe the line."

"You know, a lot of other bright people have dropped out of sight; some of them used to move around with us; you don't hear about them," Debidin recalled. "You remember Karim Juman -- he used to be around here a lot, and Pandit Sridhar Misir? Cheddi threatened to expel them because they too disagreed with the party brass about preferential treatment of blacks, and backed Rai's move to bring more Indians into the Police Force."

"It's true; even some of the black fellas who spoke up were threatened: George Bowman and Pat Alleyne; Alleyne was a sitting member." BK reflected.

"When was that?" I asked.

"Two, three years ago."

"I know Karim well; he never stopped talking about how hypocritical the Jagans were, he feel sure that they giving up the country to Burnham; and when you say that to Cheddi, he gets mad, and you better pack you bags!" Rudolph added. "I can't understand wha' happen to him; he used to come around to the market and we all gaffed; we give him money and now he treat us like dirt and won't listen to anything we say." He was close to tears with hurt. Parco remained impassive, his loyalty threatened.

"You know Bashir Khan from Rosignol?" Debidin asked no one in particular, after a pause, "he has a lot of influence in West Coast Berbice; well, he's come out in support of Rai for Party Chairman; Fenton told me just yesterday that Cheddi chewed him out, and Janet threatened to *kick him out*; but he told her to go ahead; *'do it, if you think you bad!'* he threatened back. We'll see what happens to him."

"So the delegates who support Rai are condemned as being racial? Are you chaps sure?" Prashad asked. "Cheddi talk 'bout democracy all the time."

"Only in speeches, nowhere in practice; Cheddi is all theory, no administrative skill and poor judgement, poor planning, bad political timing; those people are only a sample of the members, mostly Indian, who lost positions or were expelled for opposing the Jagans; it's been their style from the beginning, from the time Cheddi chose Burnham for the Chairmanship, and even when Burnham kick him in the face, he still goes back there for more, but let an Indian go against him, he's history, like Jainarine Singh and JB." He turned to me, adding "Tulla was Cheddi's mentor; Cheddi squeezed money and brains from that man, and then let him down; if he could do that to him, and JB who helped him more than once, what about all these smaller fry? I'm surprised Rai last so long." Dan's bitterness was obvious, perhaps enhanced by the disinhibition produced by the two drinks he had had; his reference to Tulla revived many painful memories; but I kept silent.

"There were many other issues Jagan failed to consider;" I said. "I've heard that back in the late forties some influential people including Indians felt that BG should seriously push to join Britain as a self-governing unit, with seats in Parliament, like some French colonies. That would remove us from the rigid Colonial Office administration and give us equal status with political units there. We would have had greater freedom to develop and take advantage of British institutions, as a means of pulling ourselves up quickly. D'you know about that?"

"That idea came about before the War, the County option, and Tulla and others revived it as a serious option to improve education, business and the economy before independence, like the French islands have; and we would keep access to European markets like those islands and Cayenne. Jagan and Burnham rejected it with no better argument than that the idea showed a 'slavish colonial mentality', totally ignoring its temporary nature and the many merits and benefits for ordinary people. Tulla pointed out very forcefully that we would retain access to all British educational, medical and scientific institutions and to markets. But ideology, ambition and greed--Jagan for power and Burnham for power and money—won out over good sense. We really can't afford independence now; the obstacle *we* saw was that the Brits might balk at the idea, but they couldn't force independence on us if we didn't want it. Tulla had suggested a referendum with all points up for debate."

"I hear Rai favours slowing down; is that so?" I asked. "Jagan's saying mean things about him that sound far from what the man is and does in Home Affairs. What's up?"

"It's not a healthy scene at all. The PPP is now a one man Party." Debidin explained. "Rai is an anomaly; he's not a communist; that by itself is no big problem, because he's a hard worker, and they don't have too many like him, he's smart and organised; in fact he is more on the ball than Jagan and the rest; he looks for tangible results, while Jagan is satisfied with rhetoric and theory and keeping up the heat by always blasting something or someone. After 10 years of his agitation we have nothing good to show, only crumbling roads and unemployment and people leaving right and centre, and even from the left, most of the qualified people either gone or going. The Indian people like the rest of the population want to see positive results and progress; they can't eat words. Rai is a practical man. Also he's a staunch Hindu, an Arya Samaji. If he succeeds in what he wants to do, Indians, Hindus especially, might move away from Jagan; that troubles all the communists in the PPP."

"But I thought that Jagan was backing the changes Rai was making." Parco said questioningly.

"Like which?" Rajah asked.

"The Police Force," Parco replied, "Rai wants to see up to 15% Indians in the Force by the end of this year, and up to 30% by the end of his term."

"That's a reasonable target to me." BK said. "After all, you can't have a majority people without proper representation in forces of law and order and public service; that's asking for trouble, especially in the country areas, where the Police bully the locals, always demanding bribes, money, rum, vegetables, anything; rich people who want favours give them whisky. Besides, there are places which have no police where Negroes wouldn't want to work, like up Mahaica and Mahaicony creeks, too swampy."

"But Burnham and his friends have a playground up the Abary River, where they sport on weekends: women, alcohol, speedboats and such." Parco said. "The front is a big ranch with herds of cattle where people say a dougla' fellow pen other people cattle, almost all Indian property, that he and his negro crew round up at night. Sometimes people hear the noise the frightened cattle make; shots are fired; several people have been injured; they too scared now to complain. When they do, they get in trouble; a lot get beaten up, seriously, a few disappeared."

An exchange of stories followed; names of prominent City lawyers were mentioned and a doctor who had given several of the celebrants penicillin injections after a particular night of partying.

"These people want to take over from Jagan? we in for worse times."

A lull followed in which people retired briefly to refresh drinks or relieve themselves. I asked Dan his views on Jagan's failure to join the West Indian Federation, a decision for which Africans in BG and the Caribbean had lambasted him.

"I don't blame him for that; in fact most people here agree with him, even the Africans, although they may not say so openly. The problem was and still is that West Indian governments have been cool to an Indian-led government here, no matter what the ideology. On our side we want to be sure we won't face hostility, not when we're trying to build bridges."

"We're not alone there," I offered. "Many Jamaicans are against Federation for a different reason; they see 'small islanders' converging on Jamaica already with a big poverty problem. I've been in debates at UC — students, intellectuals, politicians; Norman Manley favoured Federation, but his main opponent Alexander Bustamante does not and will pull out of Federation as soon as he gains power. So it was wrong to view Jagan's position as a racial one. I defended him knowing how consistently and hotly he would reject race as a factor in this or any decision, and I believe him, knowing his fondness for Afro-Guianese."

"The view that religion played a role is even more unlikely, if not preposterous, since Hinduism and its derivatives Buddhism and Jainism rank among the most tolerant and accommodating of philosophies, as India's ages' old record and non-aligned policies in today's world affairs and offer of scholarships to colonial students of all races have shown."

"On this topic of race" BK said, "I just heard that soon after the elections two senior Indian policemen dressed like labourers went secretly to see Cheddi at Freedom House to discuss the Police problem. What d'you think of that one?"

The story was that they presented him figures on the composition of the Force in 1957 (and *1961*, shown here in brackets) to emphasise a difficulty in ensuring proper policing of the country. There were 1519 (*1494*) officers and men, of whom 148 (*203*) were Indians, 1234 (*1157*) Africans. There were 30 (*41*) officers of whom 2 (*2*) were Indian and 16 (*25*) Africans; 3 (*5*) chief inspectors, all African; 52 (*47*) sub-inspectors, 6 (*4*) Indians and 35 (*34*) Africans. The remainder included 8 (*8*) European officers and 129 (*126*) other races, all ranks. They emphasised that the Force therefore was 81% African and 13.6% Indian. Seen as a percentage of the population Indian policemen were 0.07% of total Indians while Africans were 0.6% of their total; that meant *almost ten times greater density of African police than Indians.* So employing additional Indian policemen was not only desirable but just. They had taken a big risk, but they wanted to share their fears and make recommendations.

Jagan instead saw them as interfering and mischievous; he chastised them for racism, saying that the Force could not be called racist since they were Indians and *had* become 'officers'! He ignored the numbers totally and the fact that they had been appointed by the Colonial Office and their number had remained relatively stagnant! Jagan pooh-poohed their fears declaiming that he was without racial bias, trusted the Police and was sure they would do their duty and serve him impartially.

Disappointed, the more senior officer said, "Undoubtedly the officers and senior staff will, at least most will, but Burnham will know Police strategy well before you. No officer can dictate or guarantee the behaviour of constables on the beat; they're fallible human beings. Remember, those men did not vote for you; you did not give them that chance; opposition candidates won; they are not your constituency; you need them; they don't need you. We came to warn you, confidentially. Especially about trouble spots with Indian minorities: vulnerable places like Buxton, Mackenzie, Wismar and New Amsterdam. We don't have enough Indians to post even where there is an Indian majority. Consider what we said. We urge you to increase Indian recruitment into existing vacancies; that'll give us at least a hundred more. There is enough goodwill still among top brass to make it work before it's too late. We don't think you have much time. We're not racist; we're public officers, on the side of law and order, to serve Government. If you insist on having your way, sir, you'll regret it."

Jagan fumed, dismissed them and called Rai, wondering what he had planned or done.

"Yes, that was a strong rumour, but no one confirmed it." Dan agreed. "Rai did begin to move on the recruitment to fill vacancies; Police brass supported him. But if he pushes that one too fast, he could run into trouble with Burnham, and Jagan doesn't really want that so he's soft on the move; for that matter, he doesn't want to move on any of this racial imbalance stuff in Government service, so he will use Burnham's opposition to change to quell Rai and anybody else who wants to support him."

"So you think they will come to a show-down on this?" BK asked.

"If not that, the budget, education, taxes-- almost any major issue."

"You know, a lot of people wonder how come Rai is in this Government. He doesn't fit, not like Ramkarran, who is a union man, straight leftist views, loyal to the death to Jagan." BK observed.

"You're right, he's been an anomaly to me; as a loyal Arya Samaji he has good relations with pandits and he is moderate and straight, not an opportunist, like Beharry. He's educated and a fluent speaker." Debidin continued. "He started out with us by supporting Jagan in the forties in his home area, but he's seen that the other Indian leaders and their parties were going nowhere; Jainarine with his GIM is way out on a limb and he is busy sawing off that limb on the wrong side and will come crashing down. In a sense JN and Jagan are alike, stubborn, selfish, uncompromising, blind beyond today. I'm out of it. Luckhoo and Gajraj are so far right they're useless. So Rai is stuck in a party far too left for him, but he did his analysis, didn't see any hope for a third party with our racial composition and decided to stick with Jagan and work to promote the advantages of a moderation and hopefully to get big and strong enough to pressure the Communists to shift towards that middle."

"If he succeeds, great, but it's doubtful. He's the only one with balls!" Rajah stressed.

"I suspect that the way he's pushing, for example on the Police issue, that he's gone too far too fast and will get slaughtered by the reds in this party election." Dan mused. "He shouldn't turn his back on Mrs Jagan; I think she's the Gestapo in the PPP with Chandisingh and Bhagwan, or I should say KGB. But he knows this; he's been warned over and over to watch his step, toe the party line and bide his time. Rai's getting too much publicity for his own good. He's the best candidate for Chairman but the Jagans want a Chairman they can control, and not an Indian. So it's Benn, or possibly Wilson."

"You're right." I said. "Jagan has a big weakness there, a narcissistic streak, and dislikes competition especially if the person is smart. He feels threatened. I've met Rai and see him as sincere. He has a tough hand to play, especially with talk of coalitions between PPP and PNC but Burnham won't go there unless he's head; he thinks Jagan is woolly and indecisive and a failure as Premier. He will join though if Rai becomes head of the Party, an unlikely situation."

"I agree." Dan said. "You know, although Rai's senior Vice-Chairman, Benn never consults him nor invites him to key meetings. That's scandalous. Rai has good ideas, thinks independently while Benn and Wilson depend on Jagan for their jobs; the other Ministers don't matter; even Ram Karran, Nunes and Ramsahoye are quite insecure and will stick with the Jagans. But for Rai, they could well change the Party name to JPP, Jagan's Political Party."

"We saw that coming," BK said, "good chaps got weeded in the fifties."

"True, and Cheddi broke many promises made to moderates from the very beginning, but people ignored us, called us nasty names." Dan said bitterly. "One good thing though; unlike Burnham he's not racial; militant, yes. You remember how he behaved when the Carters, Keith and Martin, Westmaas and Jeffery--I forget his first name--all Stalinists and looking for blood, demanded that the Party abandon its claim to non-violence; Keith was expelled. Jagan sternly criticised them, in writing, for their behaviour and scolded them for threatening to alienate moderates and right-wingers in the Party! He warned them against left or right '*deviationism and opportunism*'".

"That's the person I knew," I said. "He assured us he would follow the middle road and had a place for different views and would take a stand to protect them. But all that's gone, and Castro's success has pushed him way left. He still favours Blacks. Rai is our last hope. If he goes this country goes to hell! Not because we don't have bright people, but we don't have them in politics."

"Hear, hear! And what about Ralph Grey secretly meeting with different people and talk of bringing Jagan down on this budget?" Rajah asked.

"It's happening; I know he met with Rai, Burnham, D'Aguiar and some others, including Jagan of course; if Jagan loses the budget vote, he could fall and that would trigger an election, which he will win. I don't think he wants an election with the shaky state of finances; we're almost bankrupt; he may wriggle out of it somehow; I hear they're working on a compromise. But more to the point, if Rai doesn't win the Chairmanship he will leave the Party and could sit as an independent or form his own party. If he goes he might take two or three with him, Shaffee and Mackie Hamid and perhaps Ramsahoye. If that happens Jagan loses his majority and the way is open for a coalition of opposition parties to take over. Obviously Burnham will want to lead that, but he says he is prepared to serve under Rai, as I said before."

"I don't think Rai will go for that;" Rudolph opined, "I know he doesn't trust Burnham at all. He doesn't trust Benn either; that's why he's only interested in the Chairmanship."

"Then again, if he doesn't get that he might say he's had enough of politics and retire to practise law. It all hinges on what happens in those elections, and which way Burnham leads his street gangs now that the Brits start pulling out their troops. Indian blood will flow, I fear." Debidin drained his glass, glanced at his watch and got up. "Chaps, I'm sorry, but I must go."

A week later that April the news blanketed the media. Rai had been elected Chairman over Benn, for whom the Jagans had not only campaigned but had *directed* delegates to vote! Thus was expressed the much vaunted "democracy" that Jagan habitually accused others of denying him, and clearly revealed the awful double standard that dominated the PPP. Yet Janet Jagan brazenly declared the elections "null and void", alleging that Rai's supporters were "racialists", had tampered with ballot boxes and perpetrated other irregularities to divide Indians and Africans. Many, including Misir, Juman, Khayum, Shivsankar Sadhu--with the notable exception of Bashir Khan--were expelled in a great show of party cleansing, and Benn was anointed Chairman with ceremony, designed, the insiders said, to distract people from the increasing social and economic degradation that Jagan's far-left policies had achieved, notably the steady loss of constructive Party voices that sought to steer a moderate course. It was obvious that both major political parties had become slaves to their leaders and not instruments to rescue an embryonic nation from drowning in the stormy waters that their methods were creating. It was as if the disasters of February had never happened!

Soon after the announcement of Benn's appointment, reports circulated that Jagan had personally handed delegates a list of candidates they should vote for, minus Rai's name, and that Kelshall, Chandisingh, Annibourne (then PYO Chairman), Janet and members of the WPEO had followed up by lobbying each delegate on Benn's behalf. Most delegates refused to be coerced and restored Rai's name to the list, only to hear, after the counting, that Rai had won but was "disqualified". The hooting that greeted this announcement was unexpected, but it failed to faze the Party brass.

"Well, it was either Jagans' way or no way," one delegate commented bitterly, talking to my brother and others in the store; he had rejected "orders" and had canvassed for Mr Rai, "I thought the PPP was the people's party; that's what the name says, but only now my eyes open and I see, and many other delegates see, what Dr JB Singh used to tell us years ago in West Demerara, that it's really Jagans' Personal Party. And to think I vote for Bowman against the doctor in '53; I feel sick today."

"Can't say we weren't told," another lamented, "Jagan sees the Party the way a child sees its favourite toy, and now bad Mr Rai wants to claim it and deny poor Mr Benn who doesn't have a toy because his own Black people wouldn't give him one." He ended derisively.

The events of April 1962—the PPP election fiasco, the Government's final retreat from its main budgetary thrusts and the departure of British troops—were followed by an uneasy peace that lasted until the year end. But a sense of foreboding remained which became ingrained by the poignant reminder provided by the black charred emptiness of a once prosperous business core and the sad tales of despair among the many who had lost their livelihood. To many these and other portents of Jagan's inept administration and poor political judgement—however well-defended by his wife's blasts in the *Daily Mirror* or *Thunder*—were warning signs of a state failing even before its launch. Much time and effort were spent behind the scenes to address Jagan's weaknesses to which he responded by intense and vocal denials and as a distraction by attacking his favourite target, the USA, whose local Consul—on his side for years—was becoming jaded by Jagan's unremitting intransigence, but troubled that the only alternative was demagogue (or demiurge to some) Burnham, a man probably less competent and equally rash. He was unlikely to become head of government by popular choice, yet was hinting that he *would* go to the polls if voters were asked to choose their leader for independence.

To Jagan's dismay the Colonial Office, prodded by the US, postponed the constitutional conference to the autumn of 1962. That should have given him enough time to assemble the elements needed to improve his administration, the governing skills of his Ministers, especially judgement and decision-making, and to create a viable hierarchy in the party, not just nominally but with people possessing real talent. But he wasted his time in ceaseless and repetitive attacks on the USA and failed to develop and implement a programme to improve relationships with the Services on which Government must rely. Indeed more direct attention was given to divisive Union activity — clearly inappropriate for Government leaders, and viewed as defeating a key theme of democracy that government should address the needs of *all* the people. Clearly the rights of workers were important but should be left to those able to pursue them on a full-time basis. Both Jagan and Burnham rejected this thinking and maintained their union affiliations.

Meanwhile saner heads were studying population statistics, demographic indicators and the evolution of power distribution in the country, and realised that under normal circumstances Indians would remain the logical rulers of the country and probably dominate the economy. Shah and I had discussed this with Steve and Stanley had raised it at one of our discussions. We tried to downplay this fairly obvious fact to avoid misunderstandings or negative reactions since Jagan's record so far had been unsatisfactory and tended to sour opinions on the quality of Indian leadership. Many thoughtful people who voted for the PPP did so, not to endorse Jagan's ideology, but to reject Forbes Burnham and D'Aguiar. Jagan's record did not instil general confidence that Indians could govern *all* Guianese people and had led many instead to label all Indians as "communist". Only a confirmed shift to the middle and acceptance of the notion that the Premier represented the *whole* country, not just PPP supporters, would give him an even chance of leading the country into independence.

And there lay the problem. Jagan was intractable on the issue of ideology. Capitalism was his nemesis just as socialism was a source of comfort. He saw them as mutually exclusive. But could he have missed the import of all the terrible hardships and reverses his policies had brought so far? Surely, no; and yet he behaved as if they had not happened, and carried on like a blind bull in a china shop prodded by his opponents, who were paying closer attention to the signals and thus becoming surer each day of Jagan's imminent self-destruction.

While Feb 16th created new difficulties for the city it brought reminders of rural neglect by successive past governments, which Jagan had continued, and had gotten away with it as race overtook programs as the prime vote-catcher. But it was important, for social and economic stability, that urgent attention be paid to the problems of rural inhabitants, particularly to facilitate their efforts to increase and improve arable land and productivity by implementing initiatives proposed by the people themselves. A road built or improved, water management put in place, extending electrification coverage--begun half-heartedly between 1953 and 1957, the time of the Interim Government, would have done much to wean them from a slavish belief in Jagan's censorious assertions that no development would occur without independence. Unfortunately the Interim Government and its UK-US support neglected rural needs because of a purblind desire to punish rural folk for supporting the PPP, making Jagan's claims increasingly credible. When Jagan won in 1957 he did not get the funds to begin these projects, mainly because he failed to recognise that providers of capital wished political stability, not the volatility his win predicted. However revision, moderation and pragmatism could have changed things in his favour but after five years in Government Jagan had remained inflexible.

In June Rai was relieved of his Ministry, accused of 'racialism' and fired from the Party. He was replaced as Home Affairs Minister by the strong Communist hand of Mrs Jagan who immediately put a halt to the "Indianisation" of the Police Force, softened the Rai plan to increase the percentage of Indians in Government services and to bring equity in promotional opportunities for those already there. The Party brass ignored the general grumbling over these events, and parried Rai's charge of vote rigging with a vicious campaign of character assassination that drew protests across the country.

But the worst outcomes lay in the deep gloom that greeted these actions and the failure of the PPP to investigate charges of electoral fraud despite Rai's impassioned and substantiated account of delegate coercion and the injustices and denial of due process perpetrated by the Jagans. Of Rai's dismissal the *Sunday Chronicle*, June 17, 1962 quoted Burnham as saying *"the Minister's dismissal meant that the last vestige of intelligence was removed from the PPP"*, and the same day's *Graphic* quoted D'Aguiar as saying: *"Dr. Jagan has made his greatest political blunder...he has cast aside moderate Indians in favour of rabid Communists. He has exchanged competence for incompetence."*

Many ordinary citizens with no direct political affiliation expressed their bitterness and outrage at the loss of the one strong voice for good sense and moderation in the PPP[152]. But the Jagans stumbled on oblivious; they could afford to ignore protests, even from their own supporters, as by mid-1962, the country was irrevocably split along hard racial lines, and short of some force silencing the main causes—the leaders of the political camps—nothing would alter the people's voting practices, not even the reality that the country was plunging irreversibly into economic chaos.

The Jagans moved swiftly to obliterate all traces of Rai's Ministry. The Forensic Unit took a back seat somewhere, as Mrs Jagan took over Home Affairs, "to put its affairs in order", her brief speech had put it, and to "redress imbalances"; she thought that Rai was misdirected, and accused him repeatedly of "racialism". Indians dominated the agricultural sector, she observed; why should they want to be in the Police Force also? On that issue she claimed that she had the 'full support' of the Opposition. How nice for a change! A cruel wag in her Ministry said that a Forensic Unit would have had too many political thugs in its sights; hence it was not a good thing to develop at that time in BG!

The numbers migrating increased--from every sector of society, all talents and abilities, all age groups and all races. The diehards and those too rich or too

---

[152] In 1964 Rai formed the Justice party but failed to break through the thick walls around the huge masses of people captured by the PPP's 'politics of popular protest' and the PNC's 'politics of no compromise'.

poor to move or to care, and those rooted to the soil or to their source and means of livelihood or who saw capital in the impending mess would remain to brave or fight it out. For a brief moment, the negative publicity of Rai's loss and his subsequent dismissal from his ministerial post, gave the country a chance to reflect and realign its allegiances, but there was no group credible or strong enough to take advantage of the opportunity; much of the talent had already fled. Increasingly PPP's Freedom House began to recruit young men for 'training' in Cuba. Neither the criteria nor the scholarships were advertised. Young volunteers were trained to spy on politicians, businessmen and visitors to Government House. Many of the youths were members of the PYO rallied under the wings of social scientists Steven de Castro and Ramjohn Holder, contemporaries of Lawrence Mann. They congregated, it was reliably said, at a Freedom House lounge called the *Itabo* lured there by young women eager to contribute to the Jagan machine.

The flight of capital and skills had begun as early as 1950 and in May 1961 Jagan had complained to the *Alianza* in Chile about capital shortage in BG. The National Savings Levy was aimed to correct this, by compulsory contributions. This was widely seen as just another tax, added to all the anti-business taxes then burdening--some said ruining--the economy. The measure deepened the antipathy to PPP policies that had been building even among his supporters and patience had worn so thin that even without the massive destabilisation by US unions and agencies, local tensions and disenchantment would have risen to a high enough pitch that even the deceitful Burnham's militant rhetoric alone would have been enough of a rallying call for "war".

Regent Street is a wide and bustling thoroughfare, running east west and almost bisecting the city. It carries all manner of traffic, from pedestrians, bicycles, motor scooters, donkey- and horse-drawn carts and drays, motorcycles, cars, trucks of all sizes, and city buses. It is a lively street, its western half from Camp to Water Street thick with commerce on both sides, and businesses had begun to occupy buildings east of Camp Street. (The February fire had erased structures west of High St.) In most of the buildings, the ground floor was given over to business while the owner or tenants lived in the apartment above; most had one, several two floors. The overflow of enterprise went to Charlotte Street, one block south, and to the more residential and sedate Robb Street one block north, where one could find a few restaurants and offices that fed off the hurly-burly of life on Regent Street.

It was on Robb Street that Saroop, the cook, and Inshan, the everything else, two peas in a pod, friends and lovers, had set up their restaurant, called simply *Saroop's*, specialising in chicken and vegetable dishes, curries, fried rice, and Indian breads. Its appeal was widespread. On Friday or Saturday nights, Saroop held court to a circle of friends that included several of the young resident physicians at the General Hospital. On these occasions, he would lay out a long table in the paved backyard, between rows of sweet-scented trellised vines that hung languorously from their supports; there he would lay out, with marvellous finesse, a spread fit for the most discriminating of palates, and provided, unless we could persuade him otherwise, an enviable variety of alcoholic and other drinks.

The affair was all male, and meant to prepare the attendees for later dalliance, off premises, of course, each according to his taste. Evertz, for instance, would caress and embrace a brown gallon-jug filled with Russian Bear rum. No one could challenge that, the rest of us feeling content to tackle a girl friend or a wife, whichever was appropriate; such was the light, bantering, carefree, hedonistic spirit that was cultivated on those premises, to ease the heavy burdens that we carried, perhaps more than most people because we saw and agonised with the victims of the political and social upheavals threatening to destroy the city and tried to mend them, despairing with each failure. Saroop's *soirées* were in essence a welcome and therapeutic escape, occasions for the most light-hearted, and at times illuminating of conversations, where all problems were solved or else relegated to their proper place in another dimension, for four hours. Here among the chatter and gossip, we found a curious solace that enabled us to return to our hospital residences to face the tensions that seethed beneath the fragile layer of outward calm and prepare for a new day and new challenges.

Most of the interns and residents at the Hospital were there one Saturday evening during the months of relative calm that had followed the great fire. Although the fury had abated conditions had not improved and it seemed that apart from his insisting that independence would solve all BG's problems Jagan was in a mental limbo as far as action went, and remained immersed in the coming Party elections. Saroop did not often sound off on politics, but he had become frustrated with the unremitting folly of the Party in which he and thousands of others had put their trust. He gave a trenchant review of Jagan's errors, and ended by saying, "Even the country customers are fed up."

"They should be, after leaving *Saroop's!*" Evertz teased, guffawing, through rum-soaked lips.

This lightened the moment but was not enough to distract the group and the knots of conversation soon settled into a single stream.

Someone said to Stanley, "You know, I can't figure you; you criticise Jagan and his wife, yet you sound like a true PPP!"

"PPP, hell! You might take me for *Mad John* or *Law and Order*[153] for even they make more sense right now than PPP. I sure ain't no Commie; my family got this far by hard work, their own enterprise, no bloody hand-outs, independent in all kinds of weather. But we don't believe in payola either; I have no more regard for the dictators of Latin America or greedy Americans than I have for those in the Communist world, Khrushchev or Mao or Trujillo or Duvalier."

"I think BG will end up like Haiti. The fight between Jagan and Burnham is just like Dessalines and Henri Christophe. Did you read Walcott's poem about that?" I asked.

"Yes, I loved it, strong biting language;" Stanley said, "but he romanticised two bullies. Just like we're risking here. But BG is not Haiti. The people there all black and fight among themselves, just like Jamaicans; politicians encourage that to prevent them from uniting and so hold on to power; each one gives his followers regular handouts or steady jobs with a uniform to impress their friends, and because they all black, you can't guess easily who is on what side. So Duvalier and his *Ton Ton M'acoute* can rule forever. In BG--with half the

---

[153] Two of many familiar homeless characters, mentally or physically disabled, who roamed the city and were seen as sources of "fun"; children and thoughtless adults often taunted them to provoke a "cuss-up" or other violent retort.

population Indians--a dictator on either side has to control the Police and armed forces, by padding them with their people; predominantly Indian for PPP and Black for the PNC. Instead, the PPP got it the wrong way round, a mainly Black Police who side with the Opposition. Now that is instability, no, stupidity. But Jagan will not change that even when Police wanted the change. Now Rai's gone. He's playing straight into Burnham's hands. If the PNC subvert the Police fully-- and they've almost done so--Jagan is toast!"

"So Jagan has many strikes against him...." I remarked.

"Good pun, Rags, good pun!" Gordon exclaimed. Everyone laughed, glad for the relief.

"Oh go on with you;" I said. "But to be serious, the man's a Communist, so the US hates him. He's Indian, so the islanders see him as a threat; they want to come here when it's prosperous, as everyone expects it to be; he's stubborn, so he doesn't listen to advice."

"Why should he? He's in Moscow's pocket and forging stronger links there." Stanley said. "He has the balls to keep on praising the Russian economy, quoting unproven Russian figures for agricultural production, when they're importing wheat from Canada!"

"Look, he's been doing that for ten tears and ignores every scientific challenge." I said.

"Nothing new; he always did that." Saroop said.

"So he's burning his bridges at every turn and Burnham keeps up the pressure harassing him here and at the Colonial Office. The Governor is not pleased with PPP policies, but he has orders to give them a fairly free rein, to just this side of the abyss." Stanley said.

"Absolutely!" I exclaimed. "A Jamaican friend I met in '60 at Howard sent me some newspaper clippings on the February riots. One from the DC *Evening Star* pointed out the irony of the Colonial Office sending troops to help Jagan keep law and order even though they'd love to get rid of him. The others from Boston, Baltimore and New York said the same. The *NY Times* was scathing and blunt; it said the riots showed the Government's *'lack of wisdom'* and *'inability to maintain law and order'* and *'the gap between economic theory and practical politics'* and that without British help Jagan would be *'in exile'* somewhere. All concluded that he won't get independence; US don't want a Congo or another red stooge in this hemisphere. But they agree that indefinite postponement is not on."

"He and Burnham came close to exile in '54." Saroop said. "There was a strong rumour then that they would be barred from landing in BG when they came back from India; in fact they couldn't get passage on any airline until Air France helped them and took them from France to Guadeloupe and then here. And even then the governor didn't want to agree."

"This is just what the US needs to hear." Gordon said. "They will use this to push Britain to do something drastic; I can see State Department hawks harassing the British Embassy in Washington to stop Jagan or suspend the constitution again. The Brits might consider it."

"That was yesterday; today if that happens it will only strengthen Jagan's position for the next election; they would have to get rid of him by exile or otherwise, CIA style." Honnett said.

"For sure Jagan won't get any help soon from the States." Stanley said. "He has this thing about 'industrialisation' as a pure Government initiative and under central direction. In his budget speech, he said so in plain words talking about development in Soviet satellite states, but there he's fooling people to compare those places with BG; they already had a long-developed industrial base[154]. Besides he seems to think industrialisation is something you can buy, instantly, in one chunk, like candy. Not so, it has to grow, like a plant; his job is to provide the basics and the nutrients."

He paused, sipped his drink, as others reached for savouries in the many dishes laid on the table, or else got up with scraping of metal chairs on concrete to pour drinks. The brief twilight had suddenly given way to darkness and we resisted for a while turning on any lights as Saroop had begun to do. Two oblongs of dim light from windows next door played on the vines and trellises creating a surreal backdrop to the sombre talk. Someone started to say something, but Stanley interrupted.

"Let me finish this before I forget what I want to say. If Burnham wants to achieve what he keeps saying, he has to do two things; impoverish the Indians and enrich the Blacks. That means spending little on education and a lot on health. Malnutrition as we know is a problem of urban people, and nearly all the affected are black people; if you survive malnutrition you never escape the results: mental and physical weakness. That is not the kind of person who could protect a dictator. So Burnham will have to feed them and take care of the sick especially if he wants them to produce large healthy black families. He can do that at the expense of education; teach them enough to read and write, but no big spread on high school and college, except for an elite, which USSR or GDR can train for him. That will give him a healthy ignorant following, all dependent on his handouts! It's an ethnic thing now. Tribal."

"No, no, he can't be that gross." Evertz reacted to a thought that was not as bizarre as it sounded.

"Oh yes, you watch; we young, we should live to see it, if we survive to the next election."

"There are undoubted elements of tribalism in Odo's behaviour, inherent in what he says and does." I said. "It seems an ethnic thing, a primal way of wielding power--no offence meant, Gord."

"None taken. He's authoritarian, alright. Tribal indeed; he sees himself as the *obeah* man."

"It's like the Haiti situation. You can't change ethnicity; it's inherent. Even that poor demented Cato--who's often hauled up in court for exposing and playing with his cock--knows the difference and has challenged Burnham to protect him from Indian magistrates. Jagan thinks he can erase ethnicity; Burnham knows he can't, and exploits it instead. You can't ignore it. You can integrate people more easily vertically than horizontally..." I said.

"I can integrate with women much better horizontally." Gordon interjected, guffawing.

"Boasting again, eh Gordon?" Honnett teased, as others laughed and made funny remarks.

---

[154] In his 1962 budget speech Jagan asked, "If the Soviet economy is producing factories, complete plants, if former colonies which were in the same backward condition as countries like ours — Poland, Romania, Hungary — are today in a position to develop rapidly in the industrial sector, are we to close our eyes to developments in this sector of the world? If favourable offers of trade and aid are made, must we not accept them?" His critics noted his misrepresentation of the named countries' infrastructure and political history.

"But seriously, you can bring people of different races together of the same intellectual level or social class and they will behave similarly if they're in the same environment." I said.

"But not as easily as if they were the same race." Stanley observed.

"True; but we don't need that; look at the US mix, the colour bar aside;" Gordon observed. "The differences remain, even among people at the same social level; the Italian is not the same as the Dutch or Scandinavian or German; they're all white, but have differences, more often subtle but sometimes easy to see, like some Italians who darker than many of us here, and Pennsylvania Dutch."

"But here we have too wide a spread in education, from none to a lot; so differences are easy to spot; often they're merely social, but if race is involved we call the difference racial rather than social; we don't take the time to differentiate." Stanley replied, to general assent.

"Tell me, Burnham wants to bring in Blacks; what will he give them to do, if he intends to keep them ignorant to suck up to him only?" Saroop asked, reverting to an earlier comment.

"They'll be his bodyguards. A new form of slavery but pays more!" Stanley was biting.

"Stanley, maan, you worry too much. The country is big and the population small. They could raise chickens, and supply Saroop for his Russian chicken or chicken-in-the-rough. Pass that plate, Stan." Evertz quipped, emptying his glass and reaching for the bottle at his elbow.

"At least, Jan, the people in Curacao have no illusions about their economy; here we have a chance to create real independence, economic independence, freedom from sugar and fickle tourists — we don't have them anyway." Stanley replied, rather dejectedly; "when the damn interim government had forty odd million dollars they couldn't spend it; they wasted a lot building a few housing schemes for black people in Georgetown, when they should have brought back the Hutchinson water plan; that would've seen us well on the way to become the breadbasket of the Caribbean."

"So BG missed the boat." Evertz said.

"And the sad part is that Burnham would never build anything that could bring wealth to Indians, even though every smart Black knows that Indian agricultural skills and business enterprise will make us all well off; without them, we'll starve in a Burnham hell." Stanley emphasised.

"Punning again, Stan? What's this about the breadbasket bit? In DC we didn't keep up with home front news, not economic ones, anyway." Gordon asked.

"We have more fertile land than all the British Caribbean islands together. Most of their best lands are tied up with sugar and banana. They import most of their food; we can produce and sell it to them cheaper. We have no hurricanes and no earthquakes. But our arable lands outside the estates are plagued by drought and flood. That's what the Hutchinson scheme would have cured. And provided far more and better jobs than this airy-fairy industrialisation he talks about. " Stanley responded.

"Besides land, we need capital. It's true about the Interim government; sheer stupidity." Chet concurred, "Jagan since '57 did improve some basics: workers conditions, housing, children's crèches, health centres and expanded pure water supply; he took over 51 church schools, and put what money he got from the UN into a few land settlement schemes for rice production, but I don't know about Hutchinson; I don't know anybody who know about it."

"Ask Rags;" Stanley exclaimed, "his family researched it in a big way and pleaded with Jagan to push it. How come you from the country and not hear about this?"

"You know we don't get too many papers where I come from, and Government keep quiet on things that could help us. Yeah, what is this?"

I gave a summary of the plan, and ended, "he should aim to build that grand scheme but won't do so unless he can control it forever; the farmers don't like that idea; they point to Black Bush and think it will fail."

"But he won't get the money for it without a solid business plan, and even then no one outside of the USSR will trust a Commie with that kind of money." Honnett said.

"Cheddi says he could get funding from them. Like Egypt. But without independence, UK and US would block that move." Chet asserted. He had arrived late, but soon picked up the thread.

"What about the banks? It'll be good for them in the long run." Gordon asked.

"You kidding? Banks won't lend Government so much, especially this lot." Stanley said.

"Besides they don't deal with farmers, especially Indian farmers, unless they happen to own a town business or know somebody. We're not in America." I said. "We have four banks, all satellites of foreign corporations; they'll take your deposit if you have social status. But beyond that all they seem to do for local people is facilitate import-export transactions. Barclays is British and Zionist and too snooty to lend except to the rich; Royal is Canadian and seems to back only Canadian enterprises; Chase Manhattan and Bank of Baroda are new; Chase would lend to you or me but we're not 'capitalised' enough; you'd think Baroda might facilitate Indian enterprise but so far they finance mainly Indian traders, the Sindhis. The point is none of these banks finances development; they're not venture "lenders". I used to blame them but not anymore; who would want to lend money to Jagan or Burnham?"

I had heard this complaint repeatedly at DeHoop, from various people and from my second brother-in-law who needed long-term capital to develop his Mahaica River lands, but the banks had turned him down, even the one holding his deposits, claiming they're "not into agri-business".

"But people also need to realise that there is more to work than sitting in a Government office with a white towel draped on your arm and free coffee with condensed milk served at intervals by a maid." Chet repeated an observation I recalled with some amusement from my days as a civil servant. The stereotype was enduring.

"During World War II there was a *Grow More Food* campaign; it worked wonders and gave us fresh food." Saroop recalled. "Farmers prospered; as soon as British imports came back farmers all over the country went broke. So people don't trust Government; the GMF campaign should've continued."

"It's like the fishing situation." I said. "Right now a fleet of trawlers from Texas is pulling in tons of shrimp from *our* continental shelf, like taking sweeties from a baby! Now why Texans? Why not Guianese fishermen? Surely not lack of skill or ambition. Many work the trawlers anyway. But the banks won't lend them money either."

"Fishermen don't have college degrees, nor wear suits and drive fancy cars." Honnett. said.

"Right, they're low class, they smell, their wives smell; but everybody loves the fresh fish they catch and sell." Stanley said, scathingly.

"That's right; nobody respects fishermen, just like farmers. Can't you see the reaction if a fisherman entered a bank in his work clothes? They'll throw him out." I said.

"They respect the suits, though, no matter how much they steal." Chet observed.

"These two problems will kill us, the Banks with their policy of hands-off and the Government for not acting to create markets or correct the financing situation." Gordon observed.

"But that's a capitalist thing, and linked to possible profit; neither Jagan nor Burnham wants any of us locals to make a profit. Okay for foreigners to do that, so they lease to them for a small tax, and perhaps some added kickback to some bureaucrat or Minister, then somehow convert that into a government cooperative or something like that down the road. It's garbage thinking." Stanley said.

"It's not only shrimps; it's the whole fishing industry; we'll lose it all before any local gets a piece of it. Those trawlers scour the ocean floor clean; they kill off millions of fish at all stages of life, every day. They only want shrimp; it's like burning down a whole frigging forest just to make enough charcoal to make dinner!" I remarked, thinking of my cousin Basdeo's criticism of the American Company whose transportation contract he had, and which fitted this perfectly. The only fish saved were the few brought ashore by the men for personal use; I've received crate-fulls of these and felt sad to know that so much food and life were wasted by a foreign business in for the quick kill, not planned to benefit the young nation.

"You right. The whole economy is run by foreigners, bauxite by Americans and Canadians and sugar and lumber by the Brits. We here get the crumbs that fall or the dregs they don't want. And that poverty is what gives Jagan his following!" Honnett observed.

"But even the crumbs and dregs are controlled by the privileged, the locals who think and act just like the foreigners. Business and commerce are open to all of us theoretically, if we don't tread on the big man's toes, or make him think we want to dip into his bowl."

"They keep us out by controlling the money supply, by withholding it actually. Bank profits made here are invested overseas. You have to have your own money to start anything." Chet said.

"Why in hell that? After all these years of talking about it we have not established a bank for development, as Rags said? Is it only because of the Communist government?" Stanley questioned as he stood up, rubbed his forehead and walked in a small circle returning to his chair, leaned on the back and answered his own question, emphatically, "I don't think so; for there is no way that the US will allow a communist Government to take root here under independence. No bloody way! So it's not that. It's merely to starve people of enterprise; that means East Indians; Portuguese and Chinese have no problems accessing bank money. And that has nothing to do with smarts or quality of management. It has to do with starving the Indians in a show of power to break their political support of Jagan!"

"Right, Stan! Excellent analysis! A toast!" Evertz applauded, joined by the rest of us in a toast.

When the applause had ended, Honnett said, "I believe they can do better. Look at the shipbuilding business here. Sprostons have built ferryboats and they and others have for a long time been making schooners that ply the Caribbean. I know one of the engineers there. He says they can build refrigerated ships like the fishing trawlers and coastal steamers for passengers and freight bigger than we now have. They have a design for a safer river craft and for deep and shallow water speed boats. But no government support and no buyers; they all heading north."

"It all comes back to Communism." I said. "My late brother-in-law laid out a business plan to Jagan ten years ago, in detail and advised political moderation. People, local or foreign, don't want to invest in a leftist political climate, even with guarantees; but some don't mind if they can get support. A family friend who runs two small fishing boats has been trying to get $100,000 to get a bigger boat equipped to compete with the trawlers. He can raise $25,000 including the value of the two boats. Friends will back him to the tune of $20,000. But the two banks have consistently turned him down for the rest, even though he has a sound business plan with market guarantees exceeding his proposed catch. He went to the Minister of Trade and Industry and to Cheddi to ask for a letter of recommendation to the two banks, or guarantee to Sprostons; they said it was not their policy to interfere in individual business! And yet they gave a licence to this same Texas shrimp company whose GM simply paid Jagan a visit and went to the office of another Minister. Why the different treatment?"

"He probably handed over a fat baksheesh! Like they do in Curacao to get the best hotel sites." Evertz said. Everyone nodded vigorously sharing a low groan.

"No, I don't believe that Cheddi would accept a bribe, though the licensing officer could have taken something. But I think its PPP ideology." Stanley noted. They had all heard the story of his holiday chalet proposal and novel tourism plan that offered adventure and a stark contrast to "bright sun, white sand and blue sea". "The other thing to remember here is that the banks have no tradition of loans to the locals at large the way banks function in the States or Canada. Here they follow the UK system which does not encourage the man in the street to open an account, much less borrow or invest."

"Until that changes people will scrounge around for backing; those who get it will advance; those who don't, won't, no matter how good their plan. That is the real pity. That's why you hear so many stories of ordinary guys leaving here and soon after making it big overseas, in both US and UK."

Saroop had left the table intermittently to look after business matters and had been present for the last exchanges; he cleared his throat and said, "What you say is so true. When we wanted to start this restaurant, we didn't have a place and not enough money to buy all the equipment and furniture. I was chef across the street there and we were so busy we turn away people; so I knew Robb Street could take two restaurants. Me and Inshan save every cent for nearly 10 years before we could pay down on the place and make a start. I even took a small loan from a moneylender to get those two freezers; the maan charge 1% *a day*! But we had a lot of friends; business was good, some friends helped and we pay the man in ten days. Although we had all we savings in the same bank, they turn we down for a loan."

"We didn't know that; why you didn't tell us this; Gordon alone could have put up all you need." Stanley said banteringly. Everyone laughed at the thought of Gordon the moneylender, a PNC adherent financing a PPP supporter. But it did happen often enough, often the other way around.

"The way things going, those with means will thrive and those without will not. When we have enough without, passions will get hot and politicians like Burnham will use the *have nots* to raid the *haves,* never mind the long labour, scrimping and saving and doing without that they did to get wealthy. That, Gordon, is why your people and mine don't always agree. It's utterly senseless. And we allowing it." Chet said.

"Amen!" Evertz announced, tossing back his drink, beads of sweat forming on his forehead and eyebrows, a thing that happened whenever his alcohol intake reached a certain high level.

"I'll give you an example. Ramroop, a relation, is quite well-off; he has a large family, now divided between BG and England; he has just sent his last son to College there, to prepare for medical school. So he can afford a few things. And I believe most of his money is now in London."

"Is he the chap who owns Ideal Water Factory?" Saroop asked. "He got a son named Sundatt?

"Yes. Now that man started to bottle drinks by hand and peddled them from a dray cart to a few cake shops in Albuoystown, Charlestown and La Penitence; he has 10 or more children; married twice; everyone worked in the business, which started in his bottom house. His oldest son is now a government engineer. Today he has a modern plant, a wide range of drinks; D'Aguiar barely beat him to the Coca-Cola contract, and that I think because he refused to pay a bribe. He has a bakery and two cinemas and several rental properties, here and in England. He's a testimony to hard work. Half of his employees are Blacks. They like the way he treats them. He's now getting restless and insecure. He has guards around his properties, black and East Indian, to protect them from vandalism and sabotage. You should see the security at the Olympic these days. This is the plight of many Indian businesses today. The way the PNC behaves, he's afraid to put black workers on certain jobs, especially security. Only the oldest and most loyal, and that's bad; even the black men come up to him and commiserate."

"Same all over," Saroop said, "what does your family do? They're in the middle of trouble."

"Well, most evenings at times like this my brother takes up a position in the store mezzanine armed with a shot gun, aimed at the big sliding side door that thieves routinely try to smash; they make a loud noise; police often walk or pedal past and hustle away. When they call the police — Brickdam is two blocks away, and Stabroek Police one block--it takes hours to get a response. Lately a long-time black friend, a heavyweight named Crozack, who looks like Jersey Joe Walcott, has come in whenever PNC has a demonstration at the Public Buildings; they close the iron gates of the store and he stands in the doorway, warning mobsters, 'You leave my family alone.' And so far they've done that."

"What Jagan did, in spite of his bumbling and arsing around with Communism, was to improve self-esteem and dignity among us, open doors that people had barred; he gave us a greater sense of worth, to bring us word of our ancestral achievements." Chet said.

"You can't credit Jagan for that; Gandhi did more than anyone to restore pride in your people. Don't forget that Jagan has been cussing your pandits and priests." Stanley replied.

"True, but he learned about peaceful political protest from Gandhi and Nehru." Chet added.

"And some communism from Nehru, too!" Stanley countered.

"I wouldn't call Nehru a communist; socialist, yes." I said. "And I don't think, Chet that Cheddi gives or knows a shit about ancestral Indian achievements--I like the way you put that. Instead his atheism and communism prevent him from exploring Hindu spirituality, which would help him a hell of a lot and probably save BG the horrors of Burnhamism that *will* come. Odo is not even in charge yet and is already creating a little kingdom in the upper Abary."

"And what about the Brits?" Honnett asked. "They influenced him; they took his side, at least in the early days. They're the model we learned and have been following."

I answered thinking of Ben O. Yesu Das, speaking as he might have done.

"The terrible thing about the Brits, and other Europeans--French, Dutch, whatever--is their ignorant arrogance, their brutishness--my mother calls them *barbar,* meaning barbarian. They deny anything and everything outside their experience, distort and degrade Indian history and achievements, preach their flawed versions to justify their own values, based solely on oppressive aristocratic mercantilism which they call Christianity, degrading the name of Christ, and spread themselves everywhere for two centuries. Incidentally Marx thought the Brits did India a favour by destroying traditional Indian society based on Vaidic teachings! Ask Dr Brahmam about this if you want an earful."

"I don't know too much about that obviously," Gordon said, "but I know they knocked off the natives here the same way they did in America — that story just getting known--the Wampanoag, Cree, Iroquois, Huron, Sioux, Blackfoot, Apache, Comanche, Seminole and a hundred others, where the stakes were so much higher, the profits from conquest so much greater, immediate and long-lasting. But for every Iroquois that took the European side there was a nation destroyed, like the Hurons."

"They're destroying native groups even today, and it remains a heinous crime against humanity." I suggested. "Nazis were tried and hung for just that. What the Brits did was worse; but natives have no rich Zion to shout their hurt from the rooftops, nor the financial clout of the Rothschilds to make everyone tuck their tails between their legs and do what Zion says. I saw that native need up close last year and fear they might lose their land."

"Careful; they'll call you anti-Semitic." Stanley said.

"That's criticism, not anti-Semitism," I replied, "surely they're not above criticism, even if they think so;" and returning to my theme, I added, "Remember Dr Jones, the doctor who wrote about those 'beautiful' people in the Akarai foothills — the *Aruma,* likely kin to the *Wai Wai*--who had at best twenty years to go at the time he studied them in 1948; all had tuberculosis and other diseases of foreign contact. The Brits changed those people, as they tried to change us, without notice, without regard for any of the customs or foundations of their lives, denying their history, their authenticity."

"You're right." Stanley concurred. "Colonial bosses often act on prejudice and stereotype; same thing in China; they use ignorance like a weapon, like fire that destroys all before it; they make ignorance into a virtue, destroy knowledge they do not have, the greatest crime of all, they corrupt and destroy a way of life without knowing its virtues, for what? Europeans stumbled on this continent and claimed it as their own, ignoring the millions who inhabited it. I wonder what their reaction would've been if American natives had arrived to settle on a British coast a few hundred years ago."

"They'd have been massacred. Not welcomed!" Evertz said with a deadpan face. "You know when the Vikings sailed into Britain and Ireland they took the women and young men and sold them as slaves and concubines to the Middle East and Asia; they plundered everything, kept colonies and killed all the old people and fighting men. So the locals developed this caution and hate for foreigners. It's a dreadful history and sad because we did the same to the American natives when we found America. Except that the natives did not attack us. You know we Dutch were one of the biggest slave-traders. And the Jews financed us; they built the ships and hired us as captains."

"I didn't know that; are you sure?" I asked.

"Some even say that it was a group of Jews who financed Ferdinand and Isabella and a few of them were on the Santa Maria."

"Wow." Chet exclaimed and raised questions re authenticity; the buzz soon settled.

"Tomorrow those who took this land will be gone and what have they achieved?" I asked. "Some personal wealth, but to their everlasting discredit they leave the country poor, and brought heartache, despair, drunkenness, death to trusting natives! And they call that Christian? In India Brits castigated Indians who resisted their *laudable imperial efforts* to 'civilise' them, calling them 'backward', 'stubborn' and 'ungrateful drunks', when they were the ones who plied them with cheap alcohol. And now they say the same about the natives."

"You really can't force people to accept strange ways, ideas, and practices without showing them clear benefits, no matter how superior those practices may have been for you." Gordon intervened approvingly. "How can you expect people to comply if you force change? Would you comply if the situation were reversed? No, you would demand fairness, accommodation, consideration, trust, sympathy! You would not need to force your ways if they were intrinsically superior and if you brought them on with courtesy, respect and dignity. Cheddi and Odo have not learned that yet!"

"Touché, the conquerors pitied the natives, even as they pitied us in the past. We do not need their pity. They need the pity more!" I said.

Mrs Belgrave threw an impromptu party to honour the Jagans and to deflect from the gloom into which the Party had sunk following the postponement of the constitutional conference and the rumour that Trinidad would achieve its independence in August. She had collected close friends and fellow travellers. Much was being said that was so ingratiating that I felt sick and after a few drinks I approached Cheddi and grabbed the chair beside him as it was vacated; I spoke to him in a conspiratorially hushed voice to conceal the headiness induced by the drinks. The words came easily.

"Maan, they garland you, you eat their food, you hear them praise you and then almost lick your ass, and now you turn round and cuss them, belittle them, call them ignorant sheep? How can you do such a thing, make you look like a fraud. You kiss them to get their vote, but kick them as soon as you get in! Not right, not fair! And look what your Freedom House people did to poor

Jagdish; he gave up his job, worked his ass off for you last campaign, and when he applied for a job with you all in his field, you behave as if you never knew him, and had him kicked out of the place, almost broke his leg. Now he's jobless, near to begging. That's shameful and disgusting. And you all claim to be socialists!"

I was one of few people who still dared to be frank with Jagan, a thing not even Jagan's brothers, Naipaul and Derek would do; they had grown up in his shadow and looked up to him as one would to a god figure; besides they were beholden to him for making their careers possible, Nipe as everyone called him as a dental technician and Derek as a lawyer. Nipe was one of my brother Buddy's close friends and was frequently at our house, venting his views and supplying inside news.

"Now look here, watch your mouth. You know is not them I cuss, as you put it. It's the pandits and mulvis who fool them every day, and get them to do all kinds of stupid things. Remember what I told you, these are simple people, they are gullible; they didn't go to QC or University like you. They don't have your knowledge or insight; that's why you're here and they're there!"

"But you do the same thing to them as those pandits. And those 'fools' might ha' missed school but they not stupid; they might be simple, but they not simpletons; you know that most of the small businessmen in BG, whatever their race, didn't go beyond 5th standard. That's your own statistics. And they are the financial backbone of the PPP, not your card-carrying socialists, who only looking for freeness; left to them you wouldn't have had a jill to run any elections, much less win!"

"You beginning to sound like a reactionary; look, these people don't know what they want. It is our job to show them how, the theory......"

"Theory, hell, and that's just the point, the PPP is all theory and everything it tries to apply fails and gives Indians a bad name. People hate us and think we're all bad. Now don't you see how condescending you sound, Chief?" (I added the last when I realised how disrespectful my words had sounded, but my tongue had been loosened by three of Ronald Belgrave's vodka martinis which I had downed in an hour, much too fast for me. I had become increasingly upset over time how easily Cheddi invoked the welfare of the "ordinary man" yet so swiftly neglected it. Our conversation had at first not penetrated the hubbub of party conversation but the longer I sat there the more interest we attracted and a few close by had stopped to listen; as our voices became more animated they carried to them; soon they began to look at me with disapproval, ordering me to be quiet and "show some respect."

Jagan bristled at my remarks, and scowled, adding above the din and calls for me to shut up while several hands tapped my shoulders with admonitions to go "cool down". But I was fired up. Things I had wanted to say to him for some time were welling up in my mind and screaming to get out, at least he should hear them. I would not have another chance.

(Once when he was visiting my sister's store just after the 1961 elections and my return to BG, we had talked, and bridged the gap of years since I had last seen him at Tulla's funeral late January 1959. The talk had been mainly pleasantries, the one serious exchange having to do with my encounter with Steve, who was doing things and had made remarks, some ominous from the PPP standpoint, some couched as questions like "How long d'you think Dr Jagan's honeymoon will last, before people realise how tied he is to Russia?

Would they care?" Steve had casually let us know the direction of US thinking, given in the form of "I fear that." or "I hope that our government does not…"

This had puzzled us; Steve knew of Shah's connection with the PYO and that his ex-girlfriend was a camp-follower of the WPEO, "Licking Janet and Frances' ass" as he had teased her once too often. Steve had dutifully passed on all the information given.

Jagan had shown no surprise and seemed to know quite a bit about him, and had simply said, "He's one of many running around the country talking to people" He had changed the subject and asked, "What do you know about Cuba?" and I had sailed into an uninterrupted three-minute account of how I had tracked Castro's exploits through the pro-Batista *Radio Progresso* from 1955 to his triumphant march into Havana. RP was abruptly silenced even as I listened to its *News*, never to be heard again; it was replaced by a government station which carried long speeches by Fidel and others, while the vivacious music of RP, the big bands and raucous sexy songs had been banished to Miami and probably playing there for the same mafia Castro had "encouraged" to leave.)

Now as I sat against the wall, drink in hand, other thoughts were racing though my disinhibited head and instantly settled on one that rankled, "You remember Tulla? He died before his time, abandoned by you and your double standard; now you're fooling my sister, who trusts you, squeezing her for what she can't afford to give, thanks to your ruinous taxes on business. You killed him through stubbornness and insisting on a philosophy that won't work here. He told you that a thousand times and gave you good reasons, and he, not you, was the one who cared about the hopes of the Indian people, all of them, not just the few communists. He told you, back in 1951, how you could become the greatest reformer in the Empire and show the rest how to do it -- Trinidad, Jamaica, Ghana, Malaya, the lot. Benign and pragmatic socialism, he called it, remember? Eric Williams trying to do that in Trinidad even though he hates Indians. Like Williams, Tulla knew that you can't turn a colony into an independent democracy without a sound economy. He spent years showing you how moderate policies will help this country grow while extremism will destroy it, kill the middle class and reduce the rest to a collection of helpless serfs under arrogant commissars. What happened? You did exactly the wrong things at the worst times. You've given Indians a bad name; in fact you've been bashing us since you joined BGEIA, took their platform and ran with it into the estates and told them that it was all yours! You stole their ideas! And how come you found time to visit an injured black looter in hospital but not a word to twelve of us, all races, who almost died in a remote wilderness on your government business?"

I was foaming at the mouth, almost screaming though the room had become eerily silent as people stopped their own conversations and, surprised, were uncomfortably listening. These were members of the PPP, financial backers and other supporters including some like me--preferring to work behind the scenes free of Party labels. Few knew the context of the last question. I heard him say, with emphasis, "Boy, you drunk! You don't know what you're saying!"

"Drunk?" I exploded, resenting the dismissal, "You think this is booze talking? Tell these people which of the things I said is wrong; you tell them, or you want me to tell them more, how Tulla warn you about Burnham; he knew that snake better than you did! Remember Rangela and Latchmansingh and their union; they helped you and trusted you. You remember they tell you about

Burnham's shady doings, with diamonds and gold? 'Don't trust that man,' they warned you, 'he will stab you in the back and crush the Indian people all around you.' That's what they told you, but you pissed on them; you and your stooges, insisting that your way, the Commie way, was best. You think that if your 'ordinary' Indian knew what Communism was he would follow you? Even cane-cutters will think twice! And now look what you and Burnham did; you turn this poor country into two enemy camps, a frigging blight; we can't walk the streets anymore because of your damned blindness; soon I won't be able to speak to Ossie or John or any of my coloured friends because our races are stained with your poison; we might as well split the country into two and let us go our own way; you two are worse than the CIA and the Brits you condemn!"

"That's enough now!" the stern but gentle voice of Mrs Belgrave stopped me. "No quarrels tonight; this is a meeting of friends."

"I'm sorry, Mrs B." I tried to sound contrite, amazed that I was allowed to say so much, "but aren't frankness and sharing views what friends do, even with heat? We should handle dissent, right, Chief?" I felt shame for the outburst and tried to laugh it off, but the words were harsh, their intent clear. Jagan was not smiling. He in fact looked ominous in the low light of the table lamps that shed cones of light in the four corners of the room. He tried to make me look silly and deflated by playing up the drink angle, his face relaxing, "Liquor does this to some people; he'll sober up."

Again I got mad, and blurted out, "That's the problem with you; you only listen to yes-men. That's ass licking; you told me once never to do that; no wonder all the good people leaving the Party. Now Rai's gone. You kicked out the last sensible brain you had. All you got left are nonentities and opportunists you use like puppets! You have no thinkers left. Not even you, all your thinking was ready-made by Marx and Hegel and Trotsky and Lenin. There's nothing for us in that world, nothing that could help our people here; you can't eat rhetoric. The coast roads have crumbled into a thousand ruts. Give the people land, roads and drainage, not ideology. That's all they ever wanted for a hundred years. But your ideology will kill them. That big fire? 'Nasty' and the black UF and PNC stooges may have started it, but you caused it. Who lost? Indians lost. My brother-in-law died because you don't give a shit for Indians; you only use them, and if you can't, you walk all over them. You're worse than Burnham! You two really belong in the same bed! You've wrecked it for the rest of us!"

I had blurted it all out and was amazed that I'd said that and no one had shut me up and only half-heartedly restrained me, for they were party diehards, loyalists or sympathisers, or perhaps they were curious to know the source of my venom; what I said was new to most; or perhaps they were simply too deeply consumed with their whisky/sodas or gin/tonics, but Jagan did respond.

He rebuked me, calling me rude, irrational, drunk, a disgrace to my sister and distorting "facts", but before I could respond, giant hands came out of the shadows as it were, grabbed me by my pants seat and shirt collar, dragged me to the door, which another had opened and pushed me out, faltering; I almost fell downstairs. "Go home!" he ordered and shut the door in my face.

"That's all you all know; how to throw people out, like Rai; you rassholes can't stand the truth!" I fired off my last salvo at the closed door. As I walked slowly downstairs, slightly giddy, hanging on to the rails, Ossie came down the back steps, hurrying, asking with a wry grin and a high-pitched voice, "Mohan, what got into you? Never seen you like this!"

We sat at the foot of the stairs. I put my head in my hands, and said nothing for a while, and recalled the scene. I felt sick, water brash souring my throat. But I did not feel shame.

"I don't know, anger was there building up in me, I guess; he's a frigging hypocrite; he's infuriated me so often with this asinine Communist shit which has no bloody relevance to this place, but will for sure ruin the goddam country, even before it gets started. Do you think the British will give *him* independence, or the Americans allow it? I'll bet anyone all I got, a hundred to one, that they don't; and that scunt Burnham will get it all because he's playing the smarter game, you watch."

"No, no, you're upset; Ron's cocktails are rough, man, and you got emotional. I know what happened to your brother-in-law; that was tragic."

"No, you don't, Ossie, you don't know the half of it; Jagan fools you like he does the rest; my brother-in-law gave him what no one else ever did: knowledge, ideas, support, lots of money; that's what all those people in the Interim Government knew and decided to teach him a lesson. So they ruined him. Those nasty crooks and bitches ruined him, because he supported Jagan. One of them told him that since he is such a Commie lover he shouldn't mind sharing the wealth; you know, from each according to his ability to pay!"

"Wait, wait, what was that, I hear that he got sick after he lost his fight with Income Tax, that he was evading tax. That was the story all over town."

"Bullshit! Lookshit bullshit! Interim Government bullshit! Jagan knew the truth, but the bastard never corrected them, although he had over two years to do so. Left to him no one would know Tulla existed, or my sister, yet barefacedly visits her each month for a donation. Still! That's what hurts. Tulla was almost his backbone in the early years; what the Interim Gov. did was to *allege* evasion and demand in 1954 that he produce documents going back to 1945. He produced originals they asked for but papers for four of those years, 1945-48 were damaged from mildew and rat bites while in storage; I saw bundles of them, chewed up at the edges, stained with rat shit, the paper soggy and the ink smudged; we still have them. There was nothing he could do to repair them.

"He showed the lot to the magistrate, another Jagan hater. They didn't care for truth or justice, only vengeance. The Government slapped an arbitrary tax ten times what he had already paid, based on pure guesswork. It was blatant persecution. His lawyer said the appeal would be a piece of cake. But you know what? He had to pay the money or go to jail pending the appeal. The judge hearing the appeal was another Lookshit stiff, and postponed the case three times so that it dragged on for over a year, postponing each motion for a hearing. That drained him, made him more depressed than anything else, that these so-called democrats and fair-minded people, the judges and senior lawyers in this society, could be so crooked, so easily manipulated. If they could do that, what would Burnham do when *he* takes over? And he will! Tulla asked Jagan this question before Jagan went to jail, but Jagan rebuked him for 'naming' his 'friend' Burnham! Did you know all that?"

"No, I didn't; that sounds awful."

"Jagan was in power for a year and a half when Tulla died in January '59. He barely held on to the two properties on the Demerara River, but had to mortgage them and the equipment, sell the engine he had at Sand Hills and the rails from four or five miles of track to pay the tax grab. And when Tulla died no one stepped in to help my sister left holding all that debt, which she dutifully accepted. I heard that Cheddi denied her request for a review. And yet he has the gall to dun her regularly for money! And you know what else? He was the one who held up my job application for over seven months after everyone had approved it, *and told my sister he didn't know where it was*! And once, a few years ago, she asked him to *advise* her nephew how to get a job in government, *advise*, no more, and he rebuked her for asking."

Ossie was silent. The Jagans were close friends of his family, and adored, their philosophy in tune with the thinking and orientation of the elder Belgraves and attractive to the younger. I had jokingly told Ossie that their being creole coloured folk was a big plus for Jagan; he saw them in the same way he saw the Dummetts and his other coloured pals of old.

"Your sister is a saint; I know; she'd be the last person to even hint at anything wrong."

"You know what she said when I told her about his Communism?"

"No, I haven't seen much of her since I got married and Alicia came; she's a real handful and takes a lot of time; Mary works so we're both busy, hardly time to visit anymore."

"That's the modern menace, man, working mothers. Will ruin the society we know and like. But anyway, she told me I was blind to what a good man he was, that he won't harm Indians who show initiative! My sister is the kindliest person, smart, with great insights, except into Cheddi; that's her blind spot. When the last anti-business tax was passed limiting retail profit to 6½ % and wholesale to 5% she blamed Government for the ensuing job losses and other hardships to small business, but excused him! Incredible! How he will ruin them! Yet she defends him, claims I misread him and that he worries that capitalist monopolies will smother true enterprise and he's merely trying to protect us!"

"She said that?"

I nodded.

"But what about her husband; how did she take all that?"

"She's a Hindu; she accepted it all. She told me that he had suffered, not because of Jagan's communism, but because that was his *karma*; or maybe his *kukarma* (sin, misdeed); that he did not have enough fortitude, had neglected the teachings of Krishna and to remind himself of duty by readings of the *Gita*. He had the major scriptural texts and may not have read them since the big *yagna* of 1952. 'You read enough for both of us!' he would tease her, usually with a smile-- he had a beautiful smile, you remember? Better than most film stars, used to send women crazy, his brother Kublall once told me. Now all that's gone!" My voice broke as tears filled my eyes with the agony of recall.

"Sorry, man; I know how close you two were, like father and son. That was a sad thing that happened; he was so young. You know I must go to see her; she must think badly of me."

"No, not her, my sister is, as you said, a saint, the last person to think badly of anyone. She'll simply behave as if she'd never missed you."

"I will, and I'll take Mary and Alicia."

"She'll like that, and will probably want to claim Alicia for Phillip."

"Your son's a handsome boy; that would be a nice bond for our families."

Main coastal road, EC Demerara Dec, 1962, the country's premier economic highway. Its dilapidation typifies Government's failure to preserve and improve infrastructure

1963: Town Hall, where Gajraj, Speaker of the House, berated Jagan

Law Courts, scene of assaults on young women in 1963

i

Searching for gas, 1963 general strike

British Military Trucks, the long strike, 1963

Chapter 15

The country reels in the aftermath of the great fire and the killings of February 1962. Independence talks are postponed five months; the pleasant lull in violence fools many into believing that the worst had passed. The Cold War however reached a critical and frightening stage when the US successfully blockaded Russian ships from entering Cuba after the discovery of missile bases under construction there. The change of Khrushchev's attitude has a small but appreciable effect in reducing world tension and lightened the atmosphere in BG. The delayed Independence conference fails to come to a conclusion. The simultaneous epidemic outbreak of Poliomyelitis emphasised the country's poverty of resources and reliance on foreign aid. This weakness is underlined when lack of basic supplies and equipment leads to a tragedy at Bartica hospital, despite Stanley's heroic efforts, with international repercussions. Agents of CIA are active and perhaps KGB, as rumours fly and the premier admits he's communist and decides to sever links with UWI and establish a University of Guiana.

The March to Perdition

But man, proud man
Drest in a little brief authority,
Most ignorant of what he's most assured,
His glassy essence, like an angry ape,
Plays such fantastic tricks before high heaven
As makes the angels weep.

Shakespeare, Measure for Measure, II, 2

The outward calm through mid-1962 belied the ferment of unpublicised activity aimed to rescue BG from the Soviets even as Jagan sought every means to radicalise his administration and make it more subjective. This irked the Civil Service brought up to be apolitical. But one could hardly ignore the mounting heat that the Cold War was generating culminating that year in the first major direct confrontation in the Americas between the US and the USSR. In October US warships blockaded Cuba barring the passage into Caribbean waters of Russian ships said to be carrying rockets and rocket launcher components for assembly in Cuba. Kennedy's agents had collected convincing photographs that identified the location and nature of bases in central Cuba to be used as missile launching sites. In the thick of the Cold War the intent was obvious and to the US "extremely" provocative, while Khrushchev thought differently, noting that the US had bases in Iran and Turkey which *border* the USSR, a pact with Pakistan and a seat on SEATO. Cuba, he said wryly, was 90 miles from the USA! But he had ignored America's unilateral diktat, the Monroe doctrine.

People who followed international events hung on every piece of news; I chose the BBC and Voice of America both of which could be picked up by my trusted short wave portable radio. I listened sweating that day, hardly able to work, as the Russians came within range of the American ships and received the warning to turn around and go home. The tension was unbearable and the likelihood of compliance seemed less than the showdown so feared for more than a decade. World War III, nuclear midnight, total human desolation--sparing perhaps only those in the most remote and backward areas of the world--seemed imminent. Who will fire first became academic, as was the issue of whether the US was justified in presenting the USSR-Cuba axis as intentionally evil and designed to *attack* the US while US positions abroad were *defensive*. If so USA would have a moral if not political problem to justify such a remote defence line. Neville Shute's *On The Beach* sprang to life.

When the announcer excitedly exclaimed that the Russian ships were turning around the relief was as dramatic and envelopping as the fear it had replaced. At that instant BG's problems seemed trivial, even though BG was a scaled down version of the same ideological struggle, and for its people the incident was an epiphany. The US would do the same anywhere in the Americas to forestall any perceived threat to its integrity, and if Jagan thought there was any bluffing in American expressions of concern over the direction of Guianese politics, Kennedy's resolve and confident use of American power should have disabused him of that thought. Guianese were generally pro-American, if not pro-USA and in particular liked Kennedy; that day we stood elated in his camp and basked in the "victory".

In the aftermath people relaxed and moved about more freely, and in some ways tried to regain the camaraderie that had previously prevailed, but for nagging anxieties over resurging political militancy in the van of the Constitutional Conference slated for October 23rd in London. There the parties fought to a stalemate over Proportional Representation. Duncan Sandys, the Colonial Secretary, ended it by postponing talks for Georgetown in November. The factions remained polarised, Burnham rejecting good offers from Jagan including a coalition government. Sandys returned home in frustration, leaving the city apprehensive on the eve of the year end holidays which it customarily celebrated with style, enthusiasm and energy.

As if to emphasise our vulnerability and inability to meet the costs of full independence we were struck by an epidemic of poliomyelitis that killed nine children, paralysed many. The great irony was Jagan's appeal for US help; the prompt response of iron lungs kept several victims alive and a team of CDC virologists with batches of the new oral (Sabin) polio vaccine helped to stem the tide of disease. Other international help baled us out. I was consumed with the logistics of the immunisation campaign which in two weeks blanketed the coast. It was heartening that people of all races, from workers to volunteers, pitched in to help[155].

That 1962 Christmas holiday season was one of the more trying periods of my life. There was some good news. On Dec 9th, Sister Mahadai's birthday, my daughter was born at the University College Hospital in Jamaica, without fanfare, and no blood group incompatibility. I was sure that Devika was an answer to my sister's prayer hence her birthday gift. Everyone in the family was overjoyed and their reaction overshadowed the ominous portents of worsening political tensions in the New Year. Despite this joy my disquiet remained. Soon it developed into premonitions of doom, of a terrible cataclysmic clash that was about to take place much as the mobsters and rapists had been shouting at each opportunity.

Jagan's bewildered followers would ask, in anxious tones, not wanting or daring to criticise openly and having no way to convey their message to him, no polls, no press, and worse, no alternative, "Is wha' de maan doing wid we, eh?" Perhaps I was most troubled by my knowledge of Steve's admonitions and the equal knowledge of Jagan's unwillingness to yield on any matter of his agenda, however unpopular or inappropriate or poorly timed. It was more pique, conceit and stubborn inexperience than good sense that drove him. He

---

[155] Years later a Latin American physician, after the Allende ouster, asserted that the CIA had introduced the virus to embarrass and re-direct Jagan, win Guianese support and provide a population sorely needed to test the vaccine! Fantastic Cold War product? Possibly.

was harsh, even venomous with critics and any reference to the Cuban missile crisis made him see red.

He did not want to appear to yield to the opposition, for however much he prated or griped about democracy, he believed that opposition should bend to the will of the majority. They had put *him* in power, and thus he *had* the unfettered right to rule! Thus he rejected pleas to slowdown, amend or soften his legislative proposals, or forego or postpone the more controversial ones. There was little really urgent in his plans; indeed many felt that he was putting the cart before the horse, or worse that he had killed the horse and was personally pushing the cart over a cliff! Successive representations fell on deaf ears. Delegations to Freedom House or to his office in the Public Buildings left puzzled and dejected. The failure of the Constitutional Conference to reach a decision rekindled the smouldering tensions bringing them to a new blaze.

The New Year shattered the year-end calm and brought renewed political unrest in the van of fresh and unpopular legislation. Public speeches revived the hostilities and led to heightened anxieties. It was in this climate of tension that my wife returned from Jamaica with the new baby, Devika, the long desired sister to the boys, the *tétar béti*, whose big soulful eyes, round cheeks and bright smile transformed the threatening scene, and brought smiles and hope where none seemed to exist. Babies bring out the best in us; their helplessness, like a magnet, draws us to them to do their bidding, to think less of *us* and *now*, and more of *them* and of the *future*, to make things smooth and fend away harm and danger. Perhaps if Mrs Jagan had chosen that year to have one, she might have forestalled her Party's misfortunes, and changed the future of the country for the better.

In the lone hours of night I reflected on my past and how children had come into my life–long before I had even thought of marriage, much less children—how they had changed its character and direction and how much I enjoyed them. It was early May '62 when Carol announced her pregnancy and within days everyone in my family was offering congratulations, not knowing that we had to deal with a Rhesus incompatibility issue which, because of my heterozygous state, had produced two unaffected children so far out of three (the second had a modest neonatal anaemia). Dr Bhattacharya, the Bengali obstetrician, who had decided to stay in BG, was well-reputed and by my own estimation quite up-to-date and skilled, but had failed attempts at the British specialist examination--the Membership of the Royal College of Obstetricians and Gynaecologists (MRCOG)--largely I suspected, because no one understood what he wrote or said, especially the latter, in English. Perhaps he would have satisfied them in Bengali.

But in June he saw her, three months on, became concerned that this pregnancy was statistically likely to be fully affected, and agreed that she should go to UCH, Jamaica, since our hospital did not have the means to do exchange transfusions and post-exchange monitoring, which such an infant would need. Walter and I set out to solve this problem in May 1962 and by the end of June had successfully exchange-transfused three severely jaundiced neonates and thus established the procedure in the hospital, much to the surprise of the Ministry. Indeed Charles Nicholson the Chief Medical Officer had some much-deserved egg on his face having just told the Minister that the technique was complicated and required "special funding, equipment and training". I left it up to Walter, Bhattacharya and Carol to decide how to manage our situation.

A few weeks later I was delighted to receive a telephone call from Mr Tilbury, and invited him over for dinner. He had come in to collect his claim permit which had been finally approved after an agonising delay of some five months; no explanation was given. He had spent most of ten days getting supplies including a new pump and felt sure that he was close to sizeable returns, perhaps $200,000 or more if the indications held true. He had brought in enough gold to pay for purchases and gave me a "nice little nugget" in its natural state, smooth oval, the size of a kidney bean, almost half an ounce. "It would make a nice pendant for the missus, Doc, or a great pair of cuff links."

We discussed Wappai and the outcome of the trial, of which no news had reached them. He brought a letter from Hari, still awaiting word about the promised meeting with Dr Jagan or his Minister re maintaining Native treaties after independence. I brought Tilbury up-to-date on a few issues not covered by family members; he had been struck by the tension in the air wherever he went and felt oppressed by it; he longed to return to Wappai wondering how his wife and family could seem so nonchalant about the terrible events of the past months and the violence waiting to erupt. "I must have changed a lot, but I've always been a peaceful man; it hurts me to see up close that peace and harmony are so threatened."

I wrote a letter to Hari, promising to get word to the Premier (despite our quarrel) and to the Minister concerned. I prepared a package with writing materials, some photographs and paperbacks for his little library, and some cloth and spices. I gave Tilbury a prescription for common antibiotics to add to his stock of medicaments–antiseptics, multivitamins, ointments, analgesics, antipyretics, antacids, antihistamines, gauze and other strapping, bandages and assorted other common remedies that he kept in his medicine chest.

I gave him two linen bags of self-indicating silicone beads to keep his cabinet dry. His visit and the items of importance recalled the different realities of life in the deep forest; his animation revived the feeling of adventure and the primal rhythms I had regretted leaving on resuming life in the city. The thought of how remote his mine was in real travel yet so close in distance invoked a mysticism familiar to the *sanyasis* of Hindu philosophy; it seemed a great pity that we were so unaware of the marvels of the interior and its many challenges and that we had so misunderstood and devalued its most fascinating inhabitants who could teach us much more about the real meaning and purpose of life and its natural preservation than we could ever show them.

In early August, half way through her pregnancy, Carol decided not to risk the uncertainty of the Georgetown Hospital considering the likelihood of political upheavals as the year wore on, despite the calm that had prevailed since April with resolution of the budget issues. She left with the two younger children, Peter and Ranji, for Jamaica, to see Dr David Stewart, head of obstetrics at the UCH, who had delivered those two. Besides, she recalled, Stewart had suggested that she return promptly to his care, should she start a fourth, to be monitored throughout the event. Phillip remained with me. Beatrice, our part-time housekeeper, came on full-time and my mother decided to come to stay for a week at a time and cook for me, her style, which I had always found a superior culinary experience.

Phillip was nearing 7 and preferred to remain at my sister's during the "summer" holidays, where he had the company of my brother's four children, aged between 12 and 7. That left me time to do additional work after hours at the laboratory on my autopsy studies of sudden deaths for the Ministry of Home Affairs, an outbreak of Parathione poisoning that had killed several people in Essequibo and a study with Walter Singh of what he had dramatically styled *"an epidemic of congenital heart disease"*, a tragic event for a score or so mothers who had within a short span of time produced babies with serious heart defects. I had completed autopsies on nine fatal cases, and we were following others living with poor cardiac function. We puzzled over the clustering and suspected a common and unusual causation, infectious or toxic. We struggled to probe it with few resources until Dr Nehaul, the Deputy CMO, loaned us two Health Visitors to help with the community and family studies.

About the same time Marian, my pretty communist secretary, departed on one of Jagan's Russian scholarships, and it took a week or more before a replacement arrived. Jinni, the graceful poetess with voice soft and smooth as silk, volunteered her spare time for technical typing to help clear my backlog, and often stayed overtime, ("it's alright, I can spare an hour, two or three days a week"). She was an arresting figure, tall and elegant, as already noted, who reminded me of Audrey Hepburn in her portrayals of elfin females sailing demurely through scenes in their lives and I wondered why she had stayed in so prosaic a place as a medical laboratory when she had the attributes to decorate and enliven a stage, as model or actress.

She had a deep interest in Indian poets, and was especially fond of Rabindranath Tagore, Sarojini Naidu, Meerabai and the ill-fated Subhadra Kumari Chauhan-- whose *Jhansi ki Rani* she introduced to me -- and others who had taken part in India's independence movement. Her collection of their works was quite substantial, much of it unknown to me until then and later amplified by Dr Brahmam. Someone had recently given her a copy of Mahadevi Verma's *Sandhya Geet* which thrilled her enormously and occupied many an evening. She had a keen interest in local writers also and would discuss Edgar Mittelholzer, Albert Ferreira, Martin Carter, AJ Seymour, Wilson Harris and others. Harris was "the enigmatic one" who, she puzzled, was "part Indian, looks Indian, but denies that part of his ancestry; why? She felt that the media published their favourites over "better stuff" from new writers. She had a collection of various known and obscure local work going back to 1930, culled from various literary magazines—Seymour's *Kyk-over-al*, *Bim* (Barbados), the *Christmas Annuals* of the three local dailies, and other sources. Her anthology included her poems and surprisingly two pieces—a poem and a short story--which I had written in 1950, taken from forgotten issues of the periodical *The Civil Servant*.

"That was you, wasn't it?" She had asked half surprised. "At first I was sure it couldn't be you, too young, until I got to know you. You're an enigma, at least two maybe three different people." She gave spirited critiques of what she had read, favoured poetry and short stories and liked those of Albert Ferreira, who had died accidentally in his twenties when she was 13, and just starting her collection ("a great pity, a literary tragedy", she had decided. I introduced her to Samuel Selvon, Vidia Naipaul, Derek Walcott and other Caribbean writers, whom she adopted with enthusiasm.

In the months that followed she taught me yoga. The exercises helped enormously to deal with the prevailing tensions and the increasing work volume as physicians and patients came to hear of the changes we were trying to make in the face of a ponderous, detached and insensitive--perhaps ignorant even-- Ministry administration.

In those relatively peaceful months the city and countryside buzzed with cautious resurging energy and we dared to accept the lower level of political grumbling--which had replaced the anger and viciousness of the first months--as a "normalising" development. We talked a lot about politics however and of what we could and should do, how good things could be. We had hoped – the country had hoped--that the relative calm of that period would carry through into the following years. But I had developed an awful sense of foreboding and fear for the future, mindful that Burnham's vexatious pronouncements had not stopped nor his ambitions changed, and that Jagan's brinkmanship and inability to mount an effective counter-strategy was increasing. I told her of the conversations at the Doctors' Residence, and suggested she join in; all would surely welcome the opinions of a thoughtful woman. "On no, I couldn't do that; you won't talk as freely." She said that so softly I almost did not hear it.

Activities at Freedom House had expanded and the PPP had established a business called *GIMPEX* (Guiana Import and Export Corp.) and *The New Guiana Corporation* (which some claimed was a front for espionage and to receive materials and money from the Soviet *bloc*. Its youth centre *Itabo* had been flourishing for some time attracting many angling for scholarships. The USA had meanwhile endorsed covert operations to find a replacement for Jagan despite rumoured approval of finance for certain projects that he had presented, including funding for feasibility studies of hydro-electricity, highway development, soil surveys under a UN plan and, as Indar Persaud, the Hospital Secretary had told us, an Outpatients Orthopaedic Clinic for PHG.

The amounts rumoured came to $1.5 million which Jagan would certainly welcome. This surprised some of us into wondering whether the US was merely temporising to keep Jagan quiet or merely acting to show good faith to whomever emerged to replace Jagan. Could the US now be thinking of backing Burnham with all the negatives they had accumulated on him? If so, they must be getting frantic and so jaded with Jagan as to plunge us again into civil strife, a prospect that was driving anyone with the price of a ticket to seek a UK entry certificate.

In June, at hearings of the Commonwealth Commission enquiring into causes of the February riots, Jagan buckled under intense cross-examination by his nemesis, criminal lawyer Lionel Luckhoo, and admitted that he was a *communist*. This admission finally settled the question he had skirted in Washington eight months earlier and would determine the course and scale of US activities in BG. It made plausible the idea that they were indeed considering Burnham as a replacement since Rai had not up to that time indicated the direction he would take in any future political activity.

It was unlikely that Rai would join with Burnham even though the latter would have welcomed him as a temporary ally to use against Jagan, hoping that should Rai cross the floor two or three others might do the same and reduce the PPP to a minority. The US would no doubt increase pressure on the UK to delay independence since the actions of their agents and consulate gave increasing hints that they *were* giving up on Jagan, convinced of his irrevocable ties with the Soviets. Thus they needed time to put together a plan to prevent the creation of another independent communist government in the Americas. The Cold War was still too hot and Castro's influence increasing.

The doubts and negative experiences of my family members in business and farming and those of their friends in daily dealings with Government departments induced further despair; the deteriorating state of infrastructure, especially roads and drainage, was causing great hardships to all, especially outside the city limits where the main coastal road had become a succession of potholes crudely repaired, often with only roughly cut stones with sharp edges, creating even worse hazards.

On the hustings Burnham continued to harangue his troops and talk of winning the elections that must precede any grant of independence and vigorously promoted a referendum on Proportional Representation prior to that event. Meanwhile Jagan and his Ministers continued efforts to pressure the Civil Service and the independent Public Services Commission in its decisions on appointments and promotions. Rumours abounded of PPP (and PNC) spies in the Civil and Police Services.

In the administration funding problems had escalated, stalling pet projects such as the East Bank Essequibo Road from Parika towards Ampa and beyond to a point opposite Bartica. My friend and classmate Fred Debidin, a road engineer in the Public Works Department had been assigned as liaison to the project contractors, a Venezuelan company; he quit when the project folded and left for the USA then building a network of interstate highways. Jagan's other projects were not started, including the dredging of the Berbice River bar.

The medical services continued to decline for lack of supplies, services and loss of skills. A widely publicised incident involving Stanley illustrated the extent and implications of the neglect. The wife of one of the Venezuelan engineers had died in childbirth at Bartica when Stanley was the Medical Superintendent and the only doctor there. She had presented on a weekend in late stages of obstructed labour, exhausted, with her baby in severe distress. Stanley worked to revive her, with no equipment, no blood for transfusion, no IV supplies, no laboratory for tests, while he improvised to complete a caesarean section with no general anaesthesia and might well have saved her, the baby having died, but for lack of blood.

CMO Charles Nicholson and Minister Chandisingh criticised Stanley for incompetence and poor judgement, and the engineer threatened to "sue and destroy" him until a Venezuelan obstetrician brought in by the Company reviewed the events and questioned witnesses. He exonerated Stanley with effusive praise for *"exemplary conduct and superior medical skills under the most difficult and primitive conditions"*. Once more Nicholson was wiping egg from his face as Chandisingh and Jagan fumbled for excuses.

In his report the Venezuelan doctor related Stanley's desperate efforts to get an aeroplane to come for the patient as soon as he had assessed her. The airline was contacted and would have responded instantly but needed authorisation from the Ministry of Health. The Ministry was closed and both the Airline and the Bartica Matron failed to reach any of the senior officers; precious hours were lost before someone was contacted but he was at too low a level to authorise the plane!

Meanwhile the baby had died and the woman's condition demanded instant evacuation of the uterus, which Stanley did but had no blood or other fluids to complete her resuscitation. Interestingly had the engineer taken his wife the forty miles to Georgetown, perhaps four hours by the same speedboat, she and her baby might have been saved. But how was he to know that the Bartica Hospital, just 45 minutes away, had *no* equipment to deal with such an emergency?

The tragedy had been foreseen. Raper and I had visited Bartica less than a year earlier; his report had incorporated my views which had been formed partly from information from doctors who had worked in Bartica and had long complained of the inadequacies, a situation that had become intolerable by the time Stanley was assigned there. Raper's report had warned of just such a probability and outcome, with no supplies, few trained staff, an unreliable telephone service and uncertain or no fast transportation to the Georgetown Hospital on weekdays much less weekends. Raper had been disappointed in the Minister and CMO's response, but did not tell us what that was, suggesting it would "come to light in due course". Was this perhaps what he had warned?

The dramatic and tragic illustration created a stir yet little action from the Ministry. But the incident had left an indelible hurt on all of us, any of whom could have been in the same situation. Few had the skills, knowledge or courage Stanley had displayed that day. The agony added to the personal pressures he was trying to overcome, threw him into a relapse which his wife Ivy and their sons dealt with bravely and effectively, as noted earlier, with whatever help and reassurance I could give during frequent visits to their home and in long conversations with him, in which periods of lucid and logical thinking belied his mental fragility. In time he returned to work part-time until he was able to take a steady load, barring short relapses.

"What I would give to turn the clock back, even just ten years!" Saroop said mournfully at a week-end soiree in early 1963, while ruminating over his memories of past years. "We worked hard after the war but the place was so peaceful then and everyone friendly. Maan, I could walk all over town, day or night, and feel safe; none of this kind of violence we have today."

"Except Lodge and Tiger Bay, I would say." Inshan said.

Everyone agreed. In my own mind that time was one of languorous sentimentality, with the swooning verses and lilting melodies of Indian musicals filling the airwaves and listening booths of record houses that sold Indian songs. Lata Mangeshkar was just beginning her spectacular career and seeming to sing every song on the air, her exquisite voice probing young hearts and merging with each heartbeat. And there were the Bombay stars Devika Rani, Leela Chitnis, Kāmini Kaushal, Nargis Dutt and many others who, like Hollywood's Hedy Lamarr, Lana Turner, Rita Hayworth and a score of other beauties were raising male spirits and penises in the dark corners of every cinema.

In English, Bing Crosby, Frankie Lane, Nat "King' Cole, Judy Garland, Doris Day, Lena Horne, Connie Francis, Dick Haymes, Frank Sinatra, and others were disgorging wonderfully expressive, often simplistic variations on the theme of love, faith, constancy and duty, and, on the dark side, their antitheses. Turmoil was something other people had, far away, in Jammu & Kashmir, Palestine or Korea. The movies and idols were still there and the musicals had become even better, but their plaintive messages of love and longing belied the violence of our streets and the dejection of the people who used them, with increasing wariness.

We had tried to stay away from two topics: medicine and politics, and generally succeeded, but after several clashes with the Minister of Health[156] and the great fire of 1962, tensions had risen and fear had multiplied in the mind of every Indian citizen, not just among businessmen. Ordinary people felt they were being followed, and anxieties and panic drove people to seek calming medications wherever they could find them. We had suspended the soirees after the great fire of February '62, to avoid attention and targeting, and resumed them several months later when it seemed that some political compromise had been reached and a measure of calm prevailed. That was a time of intense covert foreign activity, mainly peaceful, stage-setting, with promise and hope that Jagan would finally look objectively at the local scene and the reality of America's obsessive fears, and downplay the Marxist friendships and do what was obvious to all as right for BG, not what was right for the Jagans or Communism.

It was Stanley--his hurt still fresh (he had declined advice to sue Chandisingh, Nicholson and senior health administrators, with our help) -- who had broken the political ice, one evening after another frustrating meeting at the Ministry. He had come through a relapse and had been doing quite well, remaining on medications, which his distraught wife Ivy would struggle to keep regular and within limits, and I would visit to spend time with them listening in an almost clinical role as the family shared their anxieties re his behaviours or prognosis.

"Tell me," he said, to no one in particular, "does anybody still think these Commies will get it right? I know Rags doesn't." He paused, and hearing silence, added, "Anybody?"

"Stan, relax; forget those clowns, put your feet up and listen to the music." Evertz advised.

"Jan, it's not easy to relax when things getting so rough out there; this was a peaceful country, like Saroop say; Ivy used to tell the Jamaicans they should come here to learn how to live without fighting; now she's reversing that; I don't think our boys will ever get it right."

"Get what right?" Hublall asked. He had studied Medicine in Germany, was partial to the PPP and a Jaganite, although when he did pause to think, he would entertain some doubts.

"You know what I mean. The news is that Jagan now negotiating with several Soviet bloc states, Czechoslovakia, Hungary, East Germany and a couple

---

[156] Ranji Chandisingh, the Minister, aged 35 or so, was a doctrinaire Communist in the Janet Jagan mould, a stern and poker-faced man whom Stanley and I, representing the "junior doctors" had confronted on his Government's failure to honour its many promises to improve conditions of service, including the sensitive ones of *abolition of the preferences given expatriates*--a carry-over from Britain's over-generous pay scales for UK hires (see Bryan Ch.. 5)--and pay for overtime and on-call services. Our last had been an ultimatum that we would refuse to do overtime after a set deadline. In the week that followed attempts were made to divide us. I was promoted to acting specialist, and thus disqualified from representing "juniors" since specialists were *ipso facto* considered "seniors". I refused and was told my decision would "ruin" my career. "So be it!" I said. Stanley was promoted Medical Superintendent of the Bartica Hospital. Earlier Chandisingh had told us that militancy was unbecoming our profession and would get us nowhere. We reminded him that we were merely following the dictum of his "fearless leader", who heavily promoted militancy as a means to desired ends. Chandisingh recognised the double standard; two weeks later his Permanent Secretary, Ivan Seelig, grudgingly informed us that they would honour Government promises, but hedged them in with conditions, which we rejected. Later they negotiated individually and all except one stuck to our terms until they capitulated. The irony was probably lost on them that we had succeeded against the PPP using its own choice weapon of withholding service.

more to set up industries here. He thinks he's right to join these people, and bring them here because they all believe the capitalist system will fail and the whole world would then become a Marxist paradise."

"But people here see that as selling out to Communists. America won't allow it." Saroop said matter-of-factly. "Never!" he added with emphasis after a slight pause.

"The sad thing is that business needs a stable environment and a moderate government;" I offered, "nothing new; what he's done is to create conditions to frustrate enterprising locals so that he can invite those countries to start his *industrialisation* kick, whatever that means."

"What gets my goat is the pompous way he claims proprietary right to everything!" Honnett expostulated in a rare show of heat. "It's always *my* this, *my* that, whether supporters, party, committee, council, government, country; he doesn't have the guile to use "our", you know, like Royalty; he should only use "*my*" when he talks of his dog or children or wife or house, or mistress; that sort of thing." Hearty laughing greeted this, perhaps to relieve the general frustration, as we acknowledged Honnett's observation with nods or interjections.

"You're so right; he makes a lot of people hot when he does that." Saroop said.

"Fifteen years ago," Hublall stated, "Stalin was sure the Americans and Europeans would fight each other, and destroy themselves; but that didn't happen; you'd be amazed at the pace Europe is rebuilding and things looking up for them. The Soviets were dead wrong there."

"That's the Marshall plan at work. Here we had no bang-bang war," I said, "but we suffered heavily nevertheless because we relied too much, and still do on overseas goods, even for daily food. But that trade slackened since the big fire, and movement of goods and produce locally is not good, what with bad roads, poor policies, like for North West produce, increasing costs, robberies and threats. Yet Jagan excludes self-employed folks from his plans if they're too self-reliant. Communist centralism we don't need; we need enterprising people, the ones Jagan rejects, not serfs."

"Hooray!" Gordon exclaimed. "Strong criticism, Rags, but the big exporters seem okay so their employees don't feel the same pressure that the casual or low level workers have, the ones that small business employs. I see your point but then at the same time, I like what Jagan did last year to make secondary education free; that was long overdue and should help."

"Those kids when they graduate won't be walking into jobs if Jagan has his way unless they join up with him;" Stanley said. "He goes after them promising heaven; those kids want soft jobs, 8-4, with paid holidays and pensions, or else scholarships and professional training. What will they all do without industry? You notice how the PNC ignoring the ones that graduating now; JC (Stanley's father) says they're now up to more than 6000 annually countrywide. The education move was something Rai had started when he was Education Minister in the previous term, not just Jagan's doing; I don't think anybody will disagree with that move unless they think it's because Jagan had a hard time getting an education."

"No harder than me and a lot of people I know," I answered, "and none of us going around frothing at the mouth and fomenting needless revolution to get independence; we'd have gotten it already if it weren't for him, and on better terms. He should copy Williams or Manley instead of Namboodiripad."

"Namboo who? Who the hell's that?" Jan Evertz asked.

"Namboo heads a Maoist government in Kerala, one of the southern Indian states; you must have read about Cochin, Vasco da Gama and the fight for control of the spice trade, old stuff. Even your Dutch ancestors fought for that trade."

"Yeah! That trade is what took *all* the Europeans to India; that's where Columbus was heading." Chet reminded him.

"Which brings up another thing," Gordon said, "we have people from different races and backgrounds here; Jagan doing his best to bring us and Indians together."

"He won't bring them together his way," I said, "and in any case not unless Africans learn something about Indian culture. Even higher education doesn't do that, not here."

"I hear you had a teach-in in the interior, very impressive. What was that?" Gordon asked.

"Who told you that?"

"Confidential sources; but what I heard was good; you should broadcast it, so all can benefit."

"You're serious, right? If you are, that's the most encouraging thing I've heard all year."

"I'm serious; what did you do?"

"Addressed the same issue; you know, we were three Indians and five policemen, four black, including Inspector Bacchus, and one mixed Portuguese/Arawak and four natives. I had blasted something Burnham said which offended one of the cops, a staunch PNC believer. My assistant warned me to be careful, lest we three got wasted and the Police return home claiming an accident! That shows you how much misunderstanding exits. But I had no such fear, because I think I understand Black folk as well as I do Indians, and I know what got me there was information. So I said so to the cops and after a few shocks when I gave facts of Indian history that erased British lies, they were keen to find out more. But what else could they do especially when I accused the Force of policing us from a background of ignorance and slavishness to Brits? We were four days on a slow zigzag on a rough and threatening river with nothing else to do, so I wasn't surprised they agreed to listen; it helped that one of them had an Indian wife."

"So you don't think Jagan's racial attitude is doing any good?" Chet asked.

"His attitude is fine; it's his policies that need work; he abuses Indian history so he's failed to educate Blacks about our culture; I got an earful of what they believe and none flattered me. Marxist indoctrination about comradeship might be okay among the races of north Asia, who share the same beliefs, but they'll do piss here as Africans, barring some rural ones, know little about Indians that's useful. Besides, Cheddi overlooking the other races, or else he lumps them all together as exploiters."

"And the rest, though minority, is powerful." Stanley said. "Some politicians exploit difference when they should take steps to change it. The problem is we all really grow up separate; the social and education systems teach us about Britain, nothing about one another; so we distrust one another. You go in a Christian house; it's the same whether Chinee, Indian, Putaguee, or Negro."

"You think so, too, eh? They all look the same, sort of British." Hublall said, speaking from his European experience. "The Portuguese totally lost their heritage; you'll find traces in some of their dishes, and bad muscatel wine, but not enough to start a restaurant, for example. As to music and dance, *Fado* is as foreign to them as *birahā, choutāl* or *ghazal*. At least the Chinese kept their cooking while the Indians kept everything, but they losing language fast."

"Thanks to Christianisation, compulsory language laws and church schools," Chet said, sarcastically, "but in every race, you find differences; look at Indians from India; they not the same as we here; they standoffish, narrow-minded, arrogant like Grewal; but Brahmam is a gentleman and a scholar, the very best. And Stracey is a nice fellow; Shenolikar should be in politics; the others, Das Gupta, Ghose, Bhattacharya, they do their work but think too much of themselves."

"Boy, how they skin poor people! I see them take their money under the counter, and abuse them still, especially the country Indians, who treat them like gods!" Evertz remarked.

"You're right," I said, having had long talks with Jain on the subject, "they're here for the easy money; things are tough in India right now, with Nehru playing the neutral country game, yet making treaties with USSR, and looking very leftist with his tight central control and restrictions on private business. Besides these guys are not a true measure of Indians; they're city Indians schooled to be anglophiles, they're in limbo--the children of Macaulay; they're WOG's, coconuts, Brahmam a few others excepted!"

"Coconuts?" Gordon exclaimed, much amused. "That's new to me."

"Brown outside, white inside." Hublall said. After the guffaws, he continued, "those guys are gone the moment things get rough."

"You're right. One asked me the other day about the islands." I said.

"They can go, but we're stuck." Hublall said. "They call Jagan a *'spoiled coconut'*."

"Come again; why that?" Evertz queried.

"Brown outside, black inside."

When the laughter subsided, I said, aiming to be serious, while some giggling continued, "It comes down to this. We're agents of our heritage; thankfully our parents preserved ours and passed it on. If I have to live in a country and share it with blacks and others, then I must know them, and they must know me. I feel that I have learned enough about all the peoples of this land, even native tribes now, and know enough of their religions and culture that I can move freely among them and socialise with them in their way, whether white, yellow or black, Christian or Muslim or Nowhereian. I can share jokes, stories, idioms and intimacies…" (Someone murmured, "You don't say?") "Yes, that too, I can share with almost anyone; and, by the way, Gordon, Chinese girls aren't arranged crossways! You heard that one Stan, right?"

They all laughed.

Chet said, "On the serious side, I take your point. Here non-Indians accept you for your smarts. The Indians look for wealth or caste, since these are symbols of smarts and suggest how you might fit into their plans for advancement. Wealthy Indians could help other Indians get wealthy if the cards were played right. Therefore they had to make choices; and to make choices they had to know. So they took all kinds of measures to get that information, at times falling back on ancient tribal customs, which helped them to keep their wealth in tight little circles--which Communism now threatens-- and by wider education. To us in the country, non-Indians knew little of this caste stuff and accepted Indians the way they saw them, rich, poor, in between. An Indian student who was nobody socially but good at schoolwork would find a cluster of eager students--Indian and non-Indian--cribbing everything he did in school, even his mistakes, and the rich students helped him gain social status. That lifted many above caste, like Cheddi. Maybe that's why he shits on rich Indians all the time, and prefer Negroes; and why Balwant and his new movement getting set to spar with him." Chet was often convoluted in his delivery, but this reasoning was good and he got his point across.

"Let's face it, there is no place for communism here, Russian, Chinese, Kerala, whatever; we need people with money, skills, enterprise. D'Aguiar's promising to bring in half a billion to a billion dollars in investment; who's he kidding? That's the foolishness we hear from these politicians." Stanley repeated our experience in trying to get a lease of government land.

I felt the stupidity of that Government decision all over again, and said, "Jagan and Burnham are nuts; these guys want to recoup from the Brits but they overlook a few things: first, there is a relatively easy way to do this, second that the loans and hand-outs they crave from the rich countries, US, Britain, wherever, will give the donors and loaners control over the economy and enslave the people once again; third that even the Communist types would bring a worse kind of dependence. Why can't they see that promoting local talent and self-reliance is the only strategy if they want to be truly independent? It doesn't have to be a strict autarchy." Tilbury's comments came to mind.

"I don't know if the economists will agree with you, since capital is needed for development, and we don't have it; but you're right about pushing local enterprise." Gordon said. "They brought in foreign exchange controls, but by then the major money had left."

"They're still pushing local capital overseas, what little still remains; I agree real liquidity has long gone!" Hublall said, with a sad look on his face. "With all D'Aguiar spouting, his party lives mainly in the *Catholic Standard* and in his mind; and he's so rightist few moderates have joined; he spouts far right crap for the rich 2% when what the public wants is moderate talk."

"The PNC sits by idle; doing what? Hatching plots!" Stanley stated. "They're flooding Georgetown with hate and have the *Chronicle* printing that crap to the point that it's a party rag and not a newspaper; not even fit for cat litter. Odo's main focus is this PR referendum, but he's doing nothing to explain it to rural folk; people in many areas don't know the PNC, but they know the PPP. This is bad news and sows confusion. Those who know them realise their ideology is the same. Odo lets Jagan take the heat for what he himself is planning to do."

"The most serious issue is the increasing brain drain, which benefits the very countries they curse today for delaying independence; tomorrow they will have to turn around and pay these same countries high interest for hefty loans, and big consult fees for the same talent they chased off. Our currency will devalue for sure. What stupidity!" I said.

"All this politics is crazy," Jan expostulated, taking a big gulp of his drink, "how come this country allowed those two commies to screw everyone! Besides, who wants Russian communism, when you can have Russian Bear and Saroop's splendid Russian chicken?"

"Jan, you heard of a fellow from Curaçao named Daniel De Leon? Way back, sixty years." Stan asked.

"No; who's he? That's not a typical Dutch name. Probably Dutch Jew." Evertz said.

"You know I tease Rudy 'bout leaving PPP and he said he had a perfect quote to explain; he gave me this statement." He pulled a sheet of paper from his shirt pocket as he spoke. "DeLeon became an American citizen, joined the *US Socialist Labour Party* and became a powerhouse as editor of its paper. Rudy was reading about him and found this description which he says fits Jagan to a tee: *'...he possessed a tremendous intellectual grasp of Marxism. Those who had suffered under his editorial lashings looked on him as an unmitigated scoundrel who took fiendish delight in character assassination, vituperation and scurrility. But most of DeLeon's contemporaries, and especially his critics, misunderstood him, just as he himself lacked understanding of people. He was not a petty tyrant who desired power for power's sake. Rather, he was a dogmatic idealist, devoted brain and soul to a cause, a zealot who could not tolerate heresy or backsliding, a doctrinaire who would make no compromise with principles. For this strong-willed man, this late nineteenth-century Grand Inquisitioner of American socialism, there was no middle ground. You were either a disciplined and undeviating Marxist or no socialist at all. You were either with the mischief-making, scatter-brained reformers and 'labour fakirs' or you were against them. You either agreed on the necessity of uncompromising revolutionary tactics or you did not, and those falling into the latter category were automatically expendable as far as the Socialist Labour Party was concerned.'*

We were stunned.

"That's perfect." Evertz said. "So we breed Communists in Curaçao!"

"It's true; Cheddi's not after power for power's sake." Hublall said.

"Burnham is the same but *he's* in there just for power!" Chet said.

The dawn of 1963 brought news of controversial legislative measures and for me, the discouraging reality of the PPP's resolve--now public and supported by Burnham and a thousand people starving for higher education, however miserably provided--to quit the new UWI that year, and start his own tenuous socialist *University of Guiana*. This was Jagan's sop to Cerberus Burnham, but it did little to ease tensions or slow his inevitable defeat. The doors of the freshly independent UWI thus closed abruptly to new Guianese applicants. Hundreds of bright students, planning to apply that year for entry into the professional faculties or for one of the various scholarships and bursaries at UWI, were greatly disappointed and mystified by the move; those who could afford it began to look elsewhere, particularly the UK; others left for the USA, just as Jagan himself had done 25 years earlier. A few took to Canada or scrounged throughout Europe for whatever places they could find, regardless of language. Some chose India, especially for Medicine and Engineering.

Jagan's *University of Guiana* plan--as initially conceived and advertised, but later radically scaled down-- had called for the establishment of professional faculties of medicine, agriculture, forestry, geology and mining. But the costs of these were staggering for an economy as small as BG's even at the best of times. Yet, incredibly, the proposal to withdraw from the UWI was approved on the grounds that the local institution would do all that the UWI did, but much more cheaply! It soon became clear that the persuasive estimates of lower costs, and therefore savings, compared with the country's contribution to the regional university, had been put together on the most flimsy and whimsical bases.

The greater loss was that the UWI had planned on establishing a campus in BG, aiming for a thousand acres of land east of Prashad Nagar--Sophia or nearby Turkeyen-- then leased to Bookers Bros and used only for desultory cattle-grazing. Preliminary and secret negotiations between UWI interests and Bookers had been "very encouraging". The primary faculties would be the professional ones of Forestry, Geology, Mining and Law (and probably Religion) in addition to General Arts, Natural Sciences and Sociology. This arrangement would have been far superior to the ill-conceived UG, despite the latter's immediate acceptance by a population starving for higher education but ignorant of UWI's plans; most educators at that time felt that the country would surely have preferred the larger and internationally reputable UWI, had they known of these plans.[157]

I was pleased to discover that my friend Rahim, then an Administrative Assistant to the Minister of Education, Senator Cedric Nunes, had been charged with piloting the proposals through the planning stages. Soon after returning to BG I had joined a PPP discussion group ("think tank") which met regularly at Freedom House--usually at night and occasionally on weekends--to consider various matters: health, education, agriculture, law, engineering, mining, forestry, and other special topics. I attended the sub-group sessions focussing on health and education, and there had met Rahim one night when he came to give us a perspective on his Ministry's projections for higher education, and to introduce topics for exploration. Minister Nunes joined Rahim soon after and spoke generally of the needs for higher education in relation to PPP objectives, as befitting a country nearing independence, but did not mention any plans for a University, except in answer to a question that it was "an option".

Rahim had been a classmate and close friend at Queen's and up to the time I left for University. We had reconnected socially on my return after that chance meeting, and I had met his children (he had married his childhood sweetheart) and in time we had filled in the gaps in our knowledge of each other's interests and activities. He had bought a nice house on South Road with a calming view of the canal and the vista east and west. Although, like everyone else, he rode his bicycle to work five minutes away, he had a polished black car parked in the bottomhouse that would join so many others for the customary family outings to the sea wall, the Gardens and family "in the country". He had advanced rapidly in the Service and had acquired a broad knowledge of the workings of

---

[157]The issue generated much emotion and rested ultimately on the attraction of nationalism and local control. I believe the UWI was a superior alternative. The fact that the UG has since had some distinguished graduates is a commentary on the calibre and maturity of its early students, and merely shows that the bright student could prosper even in a poor environment. The real tragedy is that the full potential of those clever minds could not be realised in a sub-standard learning milieu. Yet the graduates were led to believe in their achievement, and most are unable to appreciate how low the bar had been set, or how superficial was their university education, no better than the lesser US colleges in the more backward states. The UG continues to struggle, with few qualified academic staff while the campus established by the UWI in its stead, at Cave Hill, Barbados, has developed a sound international reputation. If Jagan had critiqued UCWI for elitism and failure to democratise University education it would have pointed out, as the UWI did later, that its students came from all social classes, the majority from poorer parents and were subsidised, the Jamaicans up to 100% by the mid-70's. (1992).

Government departments, more than most at his rank; that had proved an asset to his Minister. But there was one issue on which he had admitted to "big gaps" in his knowledge – this had come up by accident, it seemed, as we talked. At issue were questions concerning the "real" attitude of the Jagans to higher education, which he thought as a foundation for an independent country, should be approached cautiously. Moreover the basis of Jagan's expressed animosity to the UCWI was puzzling and incomprehensible in the face of almost universal praise for the College's achievements in all the research he had done. I told him what I knew.

In 1960, at a meeting with students at the UCWI campus in Jamaica, Jagan had criticised the College for elitism, its lack of a "progressive" philosophy and its adherence to "bourgeois values, programmes and curricula", which he saw as reactionary and irrelevant to the "legitimate aspirations of colonial peoples and to Guianese in particular". He had dubbed the campus a hotbed of "effete conservative values more suited to Victorian Britain and not to the suffering Caribbean nations struggling to emerge from exploitation and subservience". He did not see in the campus the militants needed to take on the real battle to divest the Caribbean colonies of "the long lines of oppressors" who had subjugated them and still held them "in fief". The UCWI was replacing economic rape with intellectual colonialism! If the institution did not or could not change it would fail and thus alternative structures would have to be found to carry out for each new nation what the UCWI had been created to do.

In a speech to Council he had scathingly criticised the "fact that only two doctors had returned home to practise", fewer than had come back from Europe. He had lauded the offers of subsidised and full scholarship places in East German and Russian Universities for "qualified Guianese rejected by the *elitist* UCWI". Why, he had wondered, was there such a difference in the requirements of those ancient and venerable institutions of excellence compared with the exclusivity of the Mona campus, then bristling with new concrete residences, classrooms and offices, a thriving Hospital and "luxurious" homes for an expatriate staff living as they would never be able to do in Britain? Why should "my poor exploited country continue to give aid to the wealthy? What have we gotten from the UCWI in twelve years that we could not have gotten elsewhere at a fraction of the cost?"

He had gone on to show that the cost for each graduate who had returned to serve in BG had been several times higher than had his Government given each a full scholarship to "any European university" in accordance with the practices then in vogue. For BG, therefore, "the returns do not justify the investment", he had concluded. (There had been an understandable ripple of amusement at his unwitting invocation of a quintessential mantra of capitalist thinking.)

Hugh Springer, the Registrar, a low-key taciturn man, corrected him on each of his claims; he showed that four of thirteen Guianese medical graduates had returned for internships along with three from Caribbean islands since 1954 and more might have done so but for the BG Government's failure to upgrade its hospital facilities and levels of supervision which the Government had agreed to do since 1954 to reach the standards required by London University, the degree granter. Several graduates had not returned as they had chosen to specialise in fields sorely needed in BG and the Caribbean. He gave names of a much higher number of graduates from the Arts and Sciences Faculties, including non-

Guianese, who had been serving BG for the past eight years, several of whom were already occupying senior positions in his Government's Clerical, Technical and Educational Services that he had obviously overlooked!

Jagan did not allow facts to sully his argument and resumed his focus on physicians for its high profile value to show his Government's concern for relief of suffering and to bolster his case for his own UG concept at which Medicine would be the first, or one of the first faculties. The only beneficiary of the UCWI so far, he continued, had been Jamaica, where medical graduates seeking to specialise tended to remain at the teaching hospital, while others had married Jamaican spouses and chosen to remain there.

The Guianese students and graduates he had met, he opined, while academically competent, had been "ideologically and politically immature and insecure." Many seemed to have been seduced by the fast pace of life in Jamaica, the higher standard of living and the pleasant and scenic environment, putting sensory pleasure and selfish indulgences before their primary loyalties to their homeland, to which they owed their education. He had urged all Guianese to return and put their "shoulders to the struggle".

Jagan blamed his Government's failure to attract UCWI graduates on everyone except himself, his party's policies and practices, the social unrest and the general disturbing and divisive trends in Guianese politics. He did not appreciate the outlook of Guianese students who had found new understanding of their fellow West Indians creating for some the desire for closer associations while others reacted with increased nationalism or isolation, creating the beginnings of future strife. Jagan was not really interested in these dynamics, finding the idea of "few" returns a welcome bolster to his case for his own *socialist* University. Despite correction Jagan had maintained his argument at home.

A few months later he had begun to accelerate the pace of planning for a university in BG and withdrawal from the UCWI. By his calculations, the money saved would be more than enough to start to produce people with the "right" ideological orientation to match the leftist direction of political activism and join in the "great struggle" in which "*my* people are deeply engaged". In this he had obtained Burnham's tacit, if not open support.

Rahim had been selected to develop the proposal, first as a "secret", later "confidential" project. By early 1962 he had completed the draft and summary of needs, with cost estimates provided by the various relevant technical and administrative groups in Government.

On the evening Rahim confidentially disclosed his role in the plan, I was casually recalling events at the UCWI, and mentioned Jagan's speech, and how it had affected the Guianese present. Reaction had varied from derision (Keith Tang) to embarrassment (Mike Woo Ming, Rudy Collins, Bud Lee, Emran Ali and I), wonder (Ram Bissessar, Stanley and Donald Luck, Quintyn Richmond and others) and praise (Lawrence Mann, Ramjohn Holder, Stephen de Castro and a few other social scientists). I told him how surprised I was that Phillip Sherlock — hearing that I was returning to BG in 1961--had taken time to brief me concerning plans for the UWI's new BG campus in the first triennium beginning in 1963.

I had first met Sherlock on his visit to Georgetown in 1951 with a UCWI team (Philip Sherlock, Eric Cruickshank and Charles Hassall) interviewing applicants for admission. I had applied for a place in the Arts Faculty as my Geology scholarship had been delayed a year, and I was anxious to get back into academic studies. I would lose nothing if I had to transfer later and meanwhile would gain a year of languages. He had read some poems I had written (now sadly lost) and said he was impressed with their maturity and would encourage me to continue. In my first term at the UCWI he, as Deputy Principal, had called me in about my application to switch to Medicine, and had overcome his objection by the end of the interview. Later I came to know him well and to like him from working at the Registry in the summer of '53 and subsequently in my role as a student representative. Thereafter our relationship had remained mutually respectful and he had always supported and encouraged me.

He had invited me to tea for the briefing. He asked my plans and wished my mother well, surprised that I would so radically alter my career plans since my mother was now mended. I told him of the Hindu concept of duty and responsibility, and its reverence for 'mother'. He raised his eyebrows quizzically, as if pondering a new insight, but said nothing. I had by then known of his old biases against Indians, confirmed by his questions to Malcolm Boland and me during our summer employment in 1953.

At tea eight years later we discussed BG politics and my relationship with Jagan (which he had known in 1953); he told me about the UCWI's expansion plans including the campus in BG to house a College of Arts and Sciences, and Faculties of Law, Forestry and Mining, plus a branch of the Trinidad Faculty of Agriculture which would evolve from the coming take-over of the Imperial College of Tropical Agriculture (ICTA), as soon as the UWI obtained its Charter. Could I gather the UC and other graduates to lobby for this with Jagan and his government, and try to sway them from the idea of a smaller and separate national university? "You could be an influential and powerful voice."

I was flabbergasted to be so honoured and thought then that Phillip must be losing his marbles or else leaving no stone unturned to veer Jagan from his path. Once in BG, I had spoken in favour of the coming UWI on several informal occasions to senior PPP politicians, including Rai and Ramsahoye, but had not been able to get enough time with Jagan for a discussion, although I had briefly mentioned the issue. In any event I was not sure how to argue it, especially as no information had yet been released about his Government's intentions, nor did I or the local UCWI Resident Extra-mural Tutor have details of the UWI proposal. Rahim was stunned by this news about the UWI. But he said nothing; after a pause he asked, "Would you like to read the document?" It was my turn to be surprised.

"Sure," I tried not to show the excitement of the moment, to have before me the very thing I had desired to know more about than any other of the recent plans of the PPP.

"Strictly off the record," he continued, "you know, I know very little about this type of thing; what I have is from what I was given plus British government standards for Universities. I wanted to show it to someone I trust and who could be frank. This is a piece of good luck that it just came out. I suppose when I got anxious I would have risked calling you about it."

I laughed and he joined in, both of us feeling a kind of relief that our friendship had regained the easy intimacy of our youth.

"I'll keep it to myself. I won't have much of a clue about British standards though, but I do know about UC, Queen's and some other Colonial Office projects from my time in the Service ten years ago."

With that he went to a desk at the far end of the room, opened a locked briefcase, selected a brown legal size file and handed it to me.

"I can't let you take it home; when do you think you could read it?"

"Now," I said, "it's nine, shouldn't take more than half an hour."

"Okay," he said, "I'll go fix a drink and get a snack."

The document was in standard format introducing the subject, arguing the case, outlining the plan and providing an estimate of requirements for implementation. Costing was based on BG Civil Service salary scales; building projections were a rehash of out-of-date Queen's College building costs; there were gross underestimates in every area, from fixtures to consumables; levels of staffing were unrealistic. I gave Rahim my first impressions, as gently as I could, not wanting to sound adversely critical; we agreed to meet on the weekend and discuss my reaction. I used the time to speak with the UCWI extra-mural tutor who gave me current UCWI triennial estimates and statements and BG's contribution.

In our subsequent discussion Rahim confessed his concern for the inexperience of the estimators, and the resulting inadequacies and omissions in their work, the Government's anxiety to push the plan ahead, and to get agreement on it in the Legislature. He did not understand, except in ideological terms, their unwillingness to conduct a comparison of costs and benefits with the UWI alternative. He was aware that Burnham backed the idea, and that had made him suspect its motives.

In dealing with some operational specifics about which I had some knowledge, he said that personnel currently employed by the Government would be expected to contribute on an overtime basis, but the proposals *excluded* the costs for their time. The University would start with evening classes at Queen's College thus maximising the use of that space. Curiously the only figures given for annual expenditures were those being contributed each year to the UCWI as if they were the sum total of all expenditures by BG in post-secondary education.

The "experts" consulted had all been UK Marxists with a minimum experience in educational planning, and none with direct knowledge of British Guiana or a similar country. Lancelot Hogben, a well-known UK academic and socialist, then semi-retired, had been contacted secretly and had indicated a willingness to assist. The acting Principal of Queen's College, SRR Allsopp, would be brought into the plan at the "appropriate" moment, though it was suspected that he might disapprove; thus the less he knew at this stage the better. Neither Jagan nor Burnham seemed interested in the forthcoming UWI's plans for a campus in BG. But Rahim felt that Nunes would be and should be given all relevant data as soon as possible, lest he be blind-sided by the press when they inevitably learned of the issues. He asked if I would meet with them; he could get me half an hour.

Nunes listened with interest and asked questions, made complimentary remarks about what he had been told by "your superiors" and allowed me to advocate for the UWI alternative. The advantages of hosting a campus of a world-respected regional University, which shared resources and maintained a standard that ensured comparability and portability across the Caribbean, if not the entire Commonwealth, were enormous, and would ensure the autonomy of the institution, buffering it from the narrow or purely ideological pressures of individual politicians and governments. The access Guianese students would have to the specialist schools in Jamaica (Medicine) and Trinidad (Engineering and Agriculture, later Dentistry) would be unlimited and create trans-Caribbean associations to facilitate research and development in the region.

The pool of expertise thus developed would flow freely across the region and obviate the need for the more expensive and often irrelevant North American and European ones. Similarly the BG campus of the UWI would attract a number of students from the other 13 contributor countries to its basic programmes in General Arts and Sciences and all those at the post-basic levels in the specialty Faculties of Geology, Forestry, Mining, Law and later Religion proposed for the BG campus, much as Trinidad would become the focus for Engineering, Agriculture and later Dentistry and Communications. This would contribute to pan-Caribbean rapprochement, University solidarity and independence.

The withdrawal of Guianese students — whose performance had become highly respected, in fact, a shining example among the countries represented at the UCWI--would have a negative impact on the College soon to be the independent UWI, which would thus be born with a limb missing, like neonates whose mothers had taken the drug *thalidomide*. Guianese students, who tended to aim high, would do well in any setting, but confined to a shoe-string University of Guiana, and at risk of academic in-breeding, would be short-changed by being denied resources and the salutary effects of competition for honours with their West Indian counterparts. Exposing the latter to an academic experience in BG would give them a better appreciation of the Guianese people, especially Indians, just as we had learned about Jamaicans and changed our pre-conceptions of them as a people. Indians would benefit greatly from the interchange.

The acculturation of West Indians in BG would carry on the beneficial early experiences of non-Trinidadians at St Augustine (the Trinidad campus of the UWI) and would particularly help others to understand Indians in their national setting as part of a multi-ethnic, multi-cultural nation, although currently under great stress in BG and Trinidad by major political forces. The friendships and allegiances formed and the general mutual understanding would help us in independence as we began to develop and trade more with Caribbean nations.

"You feel strongly about this." Nunes observed reflectively. "You think the UWI could bring us quality, regional integration and social justice, which a UG wouldn't do? Why do you say that?"

I looked at Rahim. We had talked freely about the relationships existing among the races, and as Mr Nunes was a man of mixed Portuguese and African descent, I was unsure of how he might react to what I might say. I glanced enquiringly at Rahim, hoping Mr Nunes would miss it. Rahim nodded ever so briefly. I relaxed and spoke slowly and cautiously.

"Well, sir, it has to do with two main themes, University autonomy and race relations, topics debated almost from the day the UC began. With regards to autonomy, few would leave a University under direct control of a single government, and here I fear that a University of Guiana would be very much just another school, pushed this way and that at the whim of politicians. I heard Dr

Jagan speak at UC and know that he wants a *socialist* university, whatever that is, and will want to dictate programs and priorities. Rather like the *Ideological Institute* that Kwame Nkrumah's started last year to train "socialist" civil servants. I also know that Burnham supports Dr Jagan's UG idea as he would instantly seize control of it, if he takes over, and exploit it to secure his personal agenda. Neither he nor Dr Jagan will stay at arm's length. A UWI campus would assure quality by preserving independence and pursuing generally agreed programmes, despite political ideology and pressures. Contrary to what Dr Jagan said recently, UC students run the gamut of political philosophy, from left to right. Most of us would work to support an independent University, but not likely one run by politicians. For what it's worth, sir, most physicians at the Hospital feel that the way things are going Dr Jagan will lose BG to Burnham, before independence. The signs we feel are clear as crystal!"

I paused, fearing that I had gone too far, but he smiled, pursed his lips and said, "Go on."

I went on to admit that "race relations were much debated at UC where initial reticence and uncertainty had yielded to familiarity and willingness to speak frankly. I have the impression that most, even segregated Barbadians, have become comfortable to deal with other races, but things had gotten hot when it came to the place of Indians. Few outside of Trinidad and BG knew that we were over 25% of the total BWI population, and a major social and economic force in our homelands. While Indians spoke from experience, the others argued from stereotypes, and we had to defend or explain Indians, often in anger at the strange opinions some students and teachers held about us; if these were indeed destined to be the future leaders in the Caribbean, Indians are in for big trouble soon.

What emerged was clear. Centuries of British indoctrination had turned Blacks into *bigans*--copies of the British—after emancipation they had become policemen, government workers, teachers etc, inuring them to duty and loyalty. Blacks greeted the newcomer Indians as intruders and job-stealers, and over the years unto today, encouraged by British divisiveness, had ridiculed us as persons, our dress, our culture, our religions, our very names even, which they mis-spelled terribly, to shame us, to make us lose face and become subservient to their thinking.

The estate system allowed this, but we resisted. I wouldn't want to change my name, which means 'wisdom of the Supreme' to 'John Brown'. Nor would my sister change 'great goddess' to Mavis Brown. These names are spurs to achievement, not just monikers. Some Indo-Jamaicans were sceptical and scoffed at our Indian-ness, denying theirs, even though other Jamaicans uniformly called them 'coolies', a state that most of them had either not known or forgotten or denied.

He allowed me to describe how some Jamaican Indians had heard of large numbers of Indians in Trinidad, but few knew about BG. The older folk, however, had greeted us with something between awe and adoration; we had stirred memories of childhood experiences, now lost or dying, or simply fading into the general shame they had been made to feel about their "heathen culture and religion". It was pathetic to see one community there celebrating *Tadjah* without a clue as to what it meant.

They were stunned to know that we had remained Hindus and Muslims, especially when they heard that we had been in BG since 1838, the first western home of Indians in any large number, years before Trinidad or other Caribbean locations. In Jamaica and Cuba all East Indians had been forced into Christianity, barring a few recent business arrivals from India. It was not that we had had no cultural casualties, we told them; many of our people had changed under pressure.

"But we were too many and the culture too rich, too ingrained in people to become diluted, supplanted or lost. We couldn't be shoved aside, like the poor natives, into little backwater reserves and we weren't hunter/gatherers dragged into a world with H-bombs and sputniks in the sky. Our people invented those things. There is so much about us that the others in the Caribbean, and BG, need to know. I believe we are good enough to take this message to them. But we have to go *among* them; they won't come to BG for it, certainly not to a political University of Guiana."

"I can see your passion and your point; well said; very enlightening; you enjoyed your time there? Made friends?"

"Yes, sir, I did, and now have friends all over the Caribbean."

"Good, you have some other points, I see." He looked at his watch and nodded to Rahim.

I went on to suggest that a UWI campus would expand the work of the Extra-Mural Department and stimulate the growth and improvement of secondary schools in BG whose students would be aiming at a higher standard than the UG would almost inevitably have, for funding reasons alone — no disrespect intended, as I had already heard Jagan make an argument for lowering UCWI admission standards and increasing numbers. Too, it would take care of Jagan's major criticism — made when he last spoke in Jamaica--of the deterrent effect of the high cost of living in Jamaica, many Guianese preferring to send their children to the US where at least they could get jobs to help pay for their education, as Jagan had done. Indians would benefit proportionately more as their expected high performance as students and contact with their wider communities would give non-Guianese a better appreciation of them as a distinct people with a long and exemplary contribution to knowledge generally and to the West Indian economy and variety in particular.

I argued that the Guianese economy was too feeble to sustain a "proper" University at that time and any institution that was hastily established, however welcomed in the short run, might have to struggle under a political yoke that would stymie true learning. Greater benefits would accrue as the UWI introduced the specialty fields of study--Forestry, Mining and Law--to complement Masters and PhD programmes in General Arts and Sciences. None of these was in the UG plan, which envisaged some Technology, General Arts and Basic Sciences only, at Community College level, while the UWI campus would begin as a full-fledged University, equal to Mona or St. Augustine.

Withdrawing from the UWI would deny Guianese students entering the professions a guaranteed place at a university, and put them back in the same quandary as existed before the UCWI. I could not see BG affording professional faculties like Medicine or Engineering for a long time, at least not until it had consolidated its basic studies at the tertiary level, and even then it would need a huge financial windfall. It could of course opt to train various technical grades or nurse practitioners then coming into vogue at the post-RN level. I had been asked about training physicians' assistants, following my experience with Balgobin, and specifically about the *feldshers* of the USSR and China's *barefoot doctors*. These were cadres trained in service by Health Ministries, not Universities and were entry-level workers, trained for specified practical tasks in specific settings through short courses, and a far cry from clinical clerks, much less physicians. It would be invidious to compare them with anything done at UCWI, whose physician graduates, as he knew, had already established an enviable international reputation. A doctor could not wish for a better *alma mater*.

Nunes acknowledged that but questioned the value to BG of any funds spent on a teaching hospital in Jamaica since only Jamaican patients had access to it. True, I admitted, but those Jamaican patients were educating Guianese like me, and would continue until Guiana could afford a medical school. Besides, BG, like all non-Jamaican contributors, was only paying for the education component of the hospital's activities, as per formula--which I understand was negotiable-- and not at all for patient care; that was paid *entirely* by the Jamaican government, which therefore paid 87% or so of the hospital's budget. I pointed out that the mere presence of a teaching hospital had had a positive influence on Jamaica's Health Services, "forcing" Government to upgrade in significant ways, both structurally and operationally.

It was no secret that the BG health services were sorely deficient in many ways, in quantity, coverage and quality. Recent acquisitions of Indian specialists had added capacity and improved care and coverage but that was likely to disappear as social unrest and violence had already begun to scare away physicians and impede recruitment. A University presence could stimulate changes in the Georgetown Hospital, as it had done in Jamaica, and was starting to do in Trinidad and Barbados. If so, the Georgetown Hospital could qualify to take clinical students, as it now had interns. As the UWI expanded its intake, more clinical teaching units would be needed; this would enable earlier return of students who had finished pre-clinical training. Phillip Sherlock had emphasised that this idea had already been mooted by Trinidad and Barbados as an objective for the independent UWI, and I had heard it repeated on my visit to the new Queen Elizabeth Hospital in Bridgetown in mid-1961.

Nunes did not know that Doctors at the Georgetown Hospital (GH) had for several years, despite grave needs, contributed papers to the Medical Research Council's annual international conferences and that the staff and facilities were visited each year by a Council Director (in 1962 by internationally known Dr John Waterlow, Director of the Tropical Metabolism Research Unit at UCWI) to discuss material for presentation. He raised his eyebrows when told that the coming 1963 Conference would see at least four significant papers from GH physicians. These were major bonuses, both for staff and patients.

The conference stimulated enquiry and efforts to improve quality, and was part of the Faculty of Medicine "package" not specifically costed in UCWI estimates. Furthermore several of us were keen to make sure that the GH did qualify for clinical training, and my own role was to assist my colleagues to lay the basis for a first-rate pathology service; I had already assembled a substantial collection of fully annotated teaching material—specimens mounted in display cases, slides, other exhibits, case histories, references etc.

Dr Walter Singh and I had started several research projects, introduced innovations and with Drs Brahmam, Harold Hamilton, Stanley Luck and others had decided to submit applications for project funding through an Indian government initiative to explore integration of Ayurvaidic and scientific medicine for specific health objectives. This included a proposal to the Ministry of Health to investigate native medical practices including herbal cures, which I had seen first-hand, and were well-known in Ayurvaidic medicine. Affiliation with a Medical Faculty would facilitate such applications and field research.

Finally I suggested that the estimates of costs for a separate University of Guiana were unrealistically low and that I could not see how the plan could attract to its faculty any competent academic by competition, from the viewpoint of both salaries and conditions of work, such as the UWI would assure from the beginning. I felt it would be unfair to any good student to establish anything in BG of a standard that no one outside the country would recognise. Nunes smiled, nodded, stood up thanked me and added, "You make a powerful argument. Did you discuss this with your group?"

"Only in principle, sir; we've debated the pros and cons of staying with the UWI. I am not supposed to know any of *these* details."

He smiled. The interview had lasted two hours.

Soon after, the UCWI Principal, Arthur Lewis, called on Jagan and Minister Nunes. Lewis took the time, the evening before, to meet with as many graduates as he could, at a simple cocktail function organised by the Extramural tutor. He briefly mentioned the impending formal inauguration of the UWI, its mission and the meeting he would have the next day with the Premier and Cedric Nunes. No one besides me had any but a basic suspicion of the government's intentions. I kept confidential what I knew. In any case Lewis knew the seriousness of the situation or would not have made this special trip. In a sense his failure to change Jagan's mind was predictable, even if Jagan had been flexible. *And I blame Lewis more than I do Jagan for the eventual withdrawal of BG from the UWI experience.*

Lewis was a mulatto from St Lucia, a respected economist and academician with a supercilious air, who not only scoffed at Jagan's economic plan--much as Trinidadian Eric Williams, also an economist, had already done — but felt that the natural inheritors of power in the Caribbean were people like him, not the upstart Indians they knew little about and had been wont to denigrate, who were now "invading" their "territory". That was the chip that seemed to weigh so heavily on his shoulder. He had grudgingly let slip the observation that "those people"--as he described us--were now crowding the College and wresting honours there, although he had to concede to them the right to be accommodated equally, not just tolerated. But this was the unspoken view. Had he, and for that matter Phillip Sherlock--who despite his affability did not view the Indian as a significant entity in the Caribbean--been sincere in their desire to recognise the Indian and his legitimate place in West Indian society, something good might have come of it, but it was clear in 1962 that the Indian had not "arrived" in the eyes of the creole mulatto, that Jagan's immaturity, egotism, posturing and lack of sophistication and statesmanship had confirmed this, and his bluff could be called. Lewis would show him. The fact that Jagan was an avowed Marxist, and in Lewis' view "a dunce at economics but a good parrot", did not help matters. Thus the two had clashed in Jamaica and would now meet on a background of mutual suspicion and disrespect.

Lewis misunderstood Jagan's intent, assuming that he was trying to achieve an independent University College within the UWI structure, with freedom to innovate according to "national aspirations" in curricula, hiring, research priorities and other academic matters. He told Lewis that the colony was "crawling with students ready for University but unable to bear the cost of education in Jamaica," and in any event could alone saturate the College's present capacity.

Lewis, never fond of Jagan, frowned at his exaggeration and firmly reminded him of Council's plans and that the UWI was ready to start building the BG campus as soon as it received his Government's approval, including the appropriate land grants for the site, hopefully that same year. He brusquely concluded that Jagan should choose either to be part of an expanding UWI under its current charter, free of any single government's domination, in line with the relationship existing with the other contributors, or else go it alone. He also summarily rejected consideration of a linkage between the proposed UG and the UWI, which would imply recognition and approval. Jagan abruptly terminated the interview.

Lewis was nonplussed and for a moment could not accept his dismissal-- he the Vice-Chancellor of a great University dismissed by a peon? But he had clearly overplayed his hand; he had tried to bully a man who had become an expert at that game, and in this he had completely misread Jagan. He was lucky to leave with his dignity intact.

Clearly miffed by Lewis's attitude, Jagan confirmed his dismissal, ignored him thereafter and later gave short but polite shrift to a strong delegation of UWI partners, first Eric Williams of Trinidad, later Errol Barrow of Barbados and his Minister of Education, Hon Cameron Tudor (my mentor for the *QC Lictor* 12 years earlier at Queen's), Carlyle Burton, his Permanent Secretary, Neville Osborne, Financial Secretary and Fred Cozier, Cabinet Secretary. I heard later how discomfited Nunes had been at the treatment of these men, and that he had been swayed by my pro-UWI arguments, and had put them forward as forcefully as he could, raising Jagan's eyebrows at the details in his presentation, making him ask whether he had met with Lewis privately, which he hadn't.

Nunes, of course, as a teacher, saw issues differently from the Jagans. Like him and many others, I concluded at the time that Jagan had allowed his animosity towards Lewis to blind his judgement on the merits and academic superiority of the UWI proposals, and to choose instead a third rate alternative to go ahead with UG. Lewis had of course behaved arrogantly and foolishly and ought to have spent his time wooing Jagan rather than giving him grounds for a divorce!

Later, however, I came to realise that the Jagans did not want an independent University in the strict sense, particularly the UWI with its jealously-guarded autonomy, buffered by its multi-territorial financial base, but instead one whose curriculum and admissions they could control; they were bent, it seems, on copying Nkrumah's "socialist" tertiary education centre. The Soviets and Cuba had promised help with materials and staff.

The failure of these influential neighbours and friends to sway Jagan from his imprudent educational venture stemmed as much from their insensitivity to the deep resentments of Indians for the sustained denial of fair access to Government positions as from Jagan's intransigent and single-minded obsession with creating a Marxist welfare state, which demanded suitably indoctrinated lieutenants and operatives, unblemished by any liberal or conservative thought.

What was also not appreciated was that Burnham shared Jagan's view of higher education seeing it in purely pragmatic and functional terms related to party agenda. Let Jagan take the heat for pulling out of UWI and starting a 'University' on a shoestring. He, Burnham would exploit it in due course! But that was not what Burnham had told Lewis when they met in Georgetown. Back in Jamaica, Lewis, having failed to see that Burnham had duped him, would tell others that he had found Burnham quite "sympathetic" and supportive, and could be his ally in BG!

Before long the UWI was chartered and almost simultaneously the University of Guiana was announced as BG declined to sign the Charter. Lancelot Hogben--the Welsh mathematician known for his book *Mathematics for the Millions*--became the first Vice-Chancellor and endowed UG with some immediate prestige. The rest was a swift slide downhill, obscured only by the quality and poignant enthusiasm of the students striving for knowledge and access thereby to a career. Few were communists; most could not describe one; few if any knew of the alternative University their Government had passed up for ideological reasons so they thanked Jagan profusely and gave him their vote and everlasting loyalty.

They happily enrolled, and went to classes in the evening at Queen's College until the UG campus haltingly began at Turkeyen four miles east of the city. At one point, it was posited that the UG would take over the QC campus, and the latter would be moved to a smaller site at Ruimveldt, near the site of the 1924 killings that Hari had witnessed. It was a stupid idea, if true; the QC site was not large enough for a full university, even with high-rise buildings, but such was the mood at the time that any rumour, however idiotic, did not seem ridiculous enough for the men and women in government, whether PPP, PNC or UF, especially when Government ended the QC tradition that had spurred its students to excel, that is, its choice of the prestigious Oxford and Cambridge Joint Board School Certificate as its badge of secondary school achievement, graduation and eligibility for matriculation.

"Not even Marx would have objected to the O&C in this imbecile way!" QC Acting Principal SRR Allsopp had exploded in these or similar words and promptly left BG for a position at the new UWI campus started in Barbados instead of BG.

Chapter 16

Labour and taxation measures give the Opposition now united on a militant path and openly backed financially by anti-government US organisations--including the CIA, AIFLD--and local trade unions an excuse to foment a strike. When the government fails to change its policies, mobs, incited by the Opposition, take over, rampaging through the streets, terrorising citizens, invading government offices, assaulting staff, and continuing a campaign of bombing and killing. Police raid PNC offices and find elaborate plans to take over the government by force. I am threatened with murder in plain view of a multitude of onlookers and decline permission to carry a loaded revolver; I find other ways to protect myself. A fire is started in my garage which I discover before harm was done. Others were not so lucky.

Civil strife as Cold War heats up; end of the road for Jagan?

"The cure for pride is knowledge.
Who can cure a man who's proud of knowledge?
If the patient should be allergic to ambrosia,
The prognosis is hopeless"   Sanskrit Verse 82 in "Poems from the Sanskrit, trans. John Brough, Penguin Classics, 1968

"We have done so much with so little for so long we can do everything with nothing."   S. Luck, 1963

I f a University was welcomed by those so starved of higher education that anything named "university" would have sufficed, the labour and taxation measures were not. They evoked angry responses initiating the final series of events that would doom Jagan and all Indians and people of any class or calibre to eventual subjugation under Burnham's dictatorship, or face exile. It would become a bitter and murderous path that we would tread, littered with the shattered hopes of a quarter million people, who had laboured to bring the country to a state of readiness for self-direction, but whose enterprise and *modus functionis* were anathema to the surging militancy of the new left, commanded by a handful of dedicated Stalinists in each major party; to them people were ciphers, mere means to an end, to be used or abused as their leaders wished, and able only to say 'yes' and fall in line behind them. And in this they would lucklessly have only two choices, to go far left or to go beyond that.

To compound this and the catalyst for disaster and Jagan's eventual downfall was the *Labour Relations Bill*, almost verbatim the festering legislation that had dethroned him in 1953. In pushing the 'new' bill-- which could have given him (or any Government) control of all organised labour--Jagan claimed that it was his mandated right and a major element of his election manifesto, naively insisting that since Burnham had supported it vigorously in 1953, he would support it now, despite his changed role as leader of the opposition, and the events of the previous year.

On a 'speaking' visit to Black audiences in New York in early March 1963, Burnham alleged that "numerous" applications for vacancies in the Police Force had come exclusively from Indians. He lambasted the PPP, calling it a racist group that was giving all jobs in the Police Force and other Government services to Indians only! This was, of course a blatant lie, as appointments to Government positions, civil and police, were in the hands of Commissions that zealously guarded their autonomy, and brooked no interference from any outsider, not even the Governor, and had already objected to attempts by Jagan and his people to influence their decisions.

It was no secret that the PPP and PNC both wished to have pliant Civil and Police services to adapt to their preferred biases and both had agreed to the creation of a *Press Council* to monitor–or even muzzle–the media or coerce them to party support. The new *Central Planning Division* consisted almost entirely of Indians, local and foreign, whom the PNC had ungenerously labelled party hacks simply because they were Indian; this had become the preferred way of dismissing and condemning Indians of any influence or substance. The PNC had spread a rumour—repeated to me by one of the Black physicians, an ophthalmologist at the Hospital--that a planned National Army and BG Defence Force would be mainly Indian, or if not, communist sympathisers trained by Cubans. Critics referred in support to the collection of Indians in Jagan's office, two consultants from the UNDP Drs Gyan Chand and P N Dhār and several Guianese career civil servants, among them Ram Tiwari, Asst. Secretary to the Premier and Secretary to the Council of Ministers, H R Persaud, and archivist Patrick Parbhu Dyal, none of whom were known to be Communists. Parbhu was the first Indian graduate of the UCWI, a quiet studious academic, who simply happened to be Indian. Also in Jagan's office on the UNDP team was Lloyd Best, a Black Jamaican and UCWI sociologist, usually not named in PNC critiques of Jagan's Development and Planning Ministry.

Back in BG Burnham spoke heatedly on March 17 at a demonstration on unemployment organised by the PNC and the Trades Union Council, presaging further unrest and commotion. Learning beforehand of the demonstration, Jagan's tacticians simultaneously mounted equally mouthy pickets outside the Governor's Office/Residence complex, with slogans proclaiming independence, asserting that colonialism was the real cause of unemployment!

In the near riot that followed the clash between these two, PNC mobs stoned Freedom House--the PPP headquarters--- while Burnham rallied his forces at the Parade Grounds half a mile north, telling them of the power they held in their hands, and how that power could be harnessed for their 'good'. The crowd responded with knowing shouts and raised fists, clenched 'Black Power' style. A week later at another mass rally Burnham accused the PPP of 'planning violence', reminded his listeners of their strength and raised a tremendous alarum when he called on them to *'apply the remedy!'* to cure the ills of the Jagan administration.

The following day, March 25th, the printed version of the *Labour Relations Bill* replaced idle talk and rumour, and the Government announced that they would debate it in the House on April 17th. The condemnatory reaction was immediate and came as had been promised by both PNC and UF, and gave the distinct impression that no one had taken the time to study the document--a replay of the response to the 1961 budget--so determined were they to oppose it whatever its contents. Soon after, various other public groups including the Trades Union Council spoke against some of its provisions, while others—big business, the Roman Catholic Church and the press (and inferentially, the CIA and MI5)--generally castigated it.

The bill sought many things, most of which were desirable elements of labour stability, e.g. secret balloting (already practised in USA, Canada, Jamaica and elsewhere), outlawing of union control by employers (the so-called 'company unions'), and mechanisms to end jurisdictional disputes which tended to hobble workers and their organisers, and foment painful strikes. (Ironically just such a situation would soon develop at the Rice Marketing Board, leading to a riotous clash on April 5th between opposed groups each claiming to represent the workers; one worker was killed).

On March 26th mobs began milling about the Public Buildings, grew larger and more vociferous in the following days, threw up relays of pickets and began to harass legislators and civil servants. One day, groups of black ruffians entered the Buildings and occupied Jagan's office; he tried to pacify them but was abused in return; miraculously they did him no physical harm.

In the tensions and confrontations that threatened and inevitably followed, Jagan repeated the same increasingly tiresome assertions of his right to govern, and to push his personal agenda. In 1962 the clash was blamed on the Kaldor budget, which Jagan claimed would benefit urban Blacks by "industrialisation" rather than the Indians who had voted for him. He had repeatedly over the years used the word "industrialisation" as some kind of soothing slogan with a unique meaning for him that seemed to evade everyone else, as he often used it, not as a generalisation, but as if it were something precise, a discrete entity that could be measured and quantified.

His 1961-2 budget had proposed measures that seemed reasonable for any country poised for development, but while it called for funds for capital, its sponsor was chasing away the very people who could by personal enterprise and risk-taking generate and use that capital to transform and grow the economy. Jagan was blind to the fact that communistic capitalism was an oxymoron, the Marxist dialectic of ultimate government by the people unrealisable-- however sacred it might sound--governmental entrepreneurship a falsehood of his own devising, and to expect civil servants steeped in colonial bureaucracy to run businesses was ludicrous. It was not that people opposed the Kaldor budget; they opposed Jagan's stewardship of any new funds raised in the manner Kaldor had proposed.

Civil servants had objected to the National Savings levy, but reluctantly accepted a modified version of the original. Business people objected to the capital gains tax of 45% and to the development fund even though their contributions would earn 3.75% tax-free and the capital would be refundable after 7 years; they objected, not because the idea was bad, but because the funds would be handed over to Communists! Even his backers balked at the notion of the PPP undertaking and supervising *'industrialisation'*, some terming it fanciful, while others, less generous, called it a looming disaster. And so on for all his proposals. In 1963 the Labour Bill rekindled these objections and would in time undo him.

Jagan never believed nor confronted the reality of the people's ignorance and fear of Communism, and would always bristle when reminded that he had never gone to his electorate on a platform clearly labelled Communist! And while he correctly criticised the Opposition for their violent tactics, he overlooked his role as the prime *agent provocateur* by bringing forward controversial and sometimes harsh measures before he had established support for them or good reasons for anyone but the pure fool to trust his objectivity. Nor did he spend the time to convince the *real* majority, not just plantation Indians, that he did possess good sense and balanced judgement, if not a measure of wisdom. Indeed he had, by intemperate and provocative language, and by the nature and timing of his legislative programme, given ample evidence to the contrary, of being welded to a pre-formed and single-minded agenda that had no room for the ideas of others nor for compromise, hence no chance for success.

His failure to promote a strong agricultural focus to replace increasingly expensive imports and as a means to diversify exports would forever brand him as short-sighted and wrong-headed. He remained, as JB Singh and Tulla Hardeen had warned him fifteen years earlier, the proverbial bull in a china shop, mangling the customers and wrecking the merchandise. His actions therefore were no surprise to us who had known him from the beginning, but came as a shock to those meeting him intellectually for the first time, like Best, and overcome by his charm.

In 1963, Jagan faced the same issues and the same foes as in previous years, now wielding bigger sticks and having garnered more support, including that of the USA, in various guises. Even so, he could have won them over. But he remained arrogant and inflexible, even as his foes were poised to destroy him.

"Jagan claims he can do that because he was 'duly elected'; but that doesn't give him the right to be stupid!" Stanley said, loosening his tie as he sat down at the dominoes table.

"You remember those Americans, Joost Sluis?" I asked. "The country people called him 'just slush', an unconscious and apt pun as he held a slush fund for anti-Jagan activity; he and that other fellow Schwartz were always with the UF crowd; they campaigned against Jagan with a vengeance in '61 and said they were *Christians* working with D'Aguiar's *Defence of Freedom,* crusading against communism—boy, did they say some unchristian things about us! And without knowing one damn thing about us; ignorant hypocrites! Just because they have money! Why didn't they just give it to some of their own poor people in Appalachia?"

"Defence of Freedom was a joke; they defended everything except freedom. You know they stayed on way past the '62 fire?" Chetram asked, adding, "as if to make sure they had done what they came for. Frigging pimps!"

"RC pimps? How cute! Did you know that one of the medieval Popes[158] ordered that all prostitutes give 50% of their property to the Church?" I looked around to satisfy myself that Honnett had not yet arrived.

"You're joking!" Just then Honnett came up the stairs, and asked, "What's the joke?"

"It's about this American with the funny name Joost Sluis; the joke is that when they heard Joost was coming, Jagan thought he was getting real juice, to pep up the economy." Gordon said, with a guffaw. "And when Cheddi tried to evict the guy the Governor declined to sign the order, saying Sluis was "an American" therefore came under "international affairs", and therefore he had to consult the Colonial Office!"

"Then in May '62, a month after Joost left, the US finally sent us Harry Hoffman, an economist from Washington. Hasn't done Cheddi much good, but earned us some peace. A year's gone and Hoffman still hasn't reported. So Jagan wrote Kennedy a long letter complaining about that and about how much aid-- over a million dollars—came from the US to pay strikers and for trips to the US for union and other folk." Stanley recited what most people who got their news from the regular media would not have known. He often heard "inside" stories of political issues at his family's Sunday get-together, especially when Rudy

---

[158] Pope Clement II (1046-7) issued a Bull requiring prostitutes to leave the Church 50% of their property.

attended. Stanley's wife, Ivy had invited me to one, which Rudy had attended; I was impressed by its range, depth and liveliness, with JC, scion of the family, presiding, a grandchild in each arm.

"And D'Aguiar accusing PPP of a double standard claiming they received just as much money from the USSR, and Burnham says that Jagan getting arms from Cuba." Honnett said.

I recalled that Jagan had countered this by charging that the *American Institute of Free Labour Development* had been training operatives including highly placed persons like Richard Ishmael, President of the MPCA and of the TUC, to harry the PPP. He had claimed too that Ishmael had led the April 5th riot and the violence that had started with the picketing of Cuban and Russian ships, then in the harbour. That action had moved to the premises of the Rice Marketing Board, where a union jurisdictional dispute was already in full swing. The resulting mayhem led to rioting and looting, another 'Black Friday'; one looter was killed.

On March 27 & 28 an unruly mob picketed the Public Buildings and attacked Ministers of Government; the riot squad was called out and fired tear gas into the crowd. Across Brickdam the 400 children, aged 4 to 14, of St Andrews elementary school were on their mid-morning break. Naturally the commotion attracted the children who tended to congregate at the fence that protected the compound, like spectators at a soccer match. The teachers hustled to get them away but not before the children had seen some of the action, with the tear gas guns going "pop, pop", and large Black women mooning the police, as they seemed to do at each event, and which the children had come to expect as a key element of the show.

On April 14, '63 D'Aguiar's *Sun* published a story accusing Jagan of planning to put children to work in communist factories--to be installed by the USSR, East Germany, Hungary, Czechoslovakia, Poland and probably other communist states--to make cement, glass, bicycle tyres and tubes, and oil from rice bran. The truth of this story was not questioned; it spread, acquired mass and distortions *en passage* and further rattled parents, especially the middle class, already incensed by all the unwelcome changes, and it goaded the mobs. D'Aguiar himself took to the streets to urge them on. The turmoil thus increased and on April 17th, Jagan met with a delegation from the Civil Service Association, including my senior, Dr Balwant Singh--then President of the CSA-- and other officers, including representatives of the TUC. It was a replay of February 1962; the players had not changed. Jagan was disappointed to hear that all affiliates of the TUC, including the CSA, would comply if the TUC called a strike for the following day.

And so it did; the CSA response followed immediately. Several categories of Government workers had long been designated "essential" and thus could not legally strike. Among them were hospital workers, most of whom supported the PNC. So militant had they become and so whipped up by the frenzy of their political leaders that many abandoned their posts and reported sick or simply did not come to work. In other sectors, more exposed to the public, like the Law Courts Buildings, those who went to work were first harried by roving gangs, and paying no heed to the threats of the protesters, were later assaulted.

One day a gang of screaming toughs invaded the Law Courts, attacked the men with fists and sticks and attempted to rape the women. One petite clerk, an 18-year old Indian virgin fleeing the scene was grabbed by two ruffians, pinioned against a table, in full view of their comrades and other trapped staff, had her skirt yanked from her slender body and was about to be raped when two of her colleagues rushed to her aid and pulled the rapist off her, only to be turned on and clubbed senseless. Another girl trying to flee the scene was struck in the back when her typewriter was hurled at her; she fell to the floor screaming and was jumped by two men, her panties wrenched from her writhing body, but she was miraculously saved by the arrival of the political leader of the group, who called them off.

I was helping that day in the Hospital's Casualty Department, and treated both girls. Both were virgins, had bruises on their upper thighs from the attempted rape but no genital injury. The girl struck with the typewriter had a large bruise and had been spared serious injury by the forward propulsion of her body dissipating some of the force of the missile. She would remain incapacitated for weeks and stressed for a very long time while her co-worker fell into a depression and required continuing therapy. These were two of the many--over a hundred, whom we treated that day--including the young men who had intervened on their behalf, suffering head wounds and concussion, requiring admission. Fortunately no one died, but how long the scars — emotional, physical and mental--would remain was sheer guesswork. I saw the two girls and several others in follow-up over the next two weeks, with members of their family. The intensity of the shock was clear to see, and would take all the compassion and support that their families could give to restore in them a measure of calm and trust. Both spoke of "sending the girls abroad," an option both families regretted having declined earlier.

The strike soon involved all unions, and affected government services and many private companies, including the sugar and distillery operations of the estates. Mail, shipping, airlines, rail and ferry services ceased abruptly; electricity and water--all essential services like the hospital--were threatened by outsiders and by their own militant pro-strike insiders, bent on defying and harassing the Government. Perhaps it was the knowledge that the Police were generally sympathetic with the PNC that underpinned their confident defiance, but it was clear that the mood was blindly anti-PPP and rebellious, to unseat the government, regardless of legal consequences or whom they hurt — the hungry, the powerless, the children, the poor. Clearly political activists had chosen to inflict suffering and chaos rather than tolerate even a hint of communism. Their instrument, the mob, was in it purely for the spoils.

The heavy hand of US intervention, especially the CIA, was everywhere obvious, particularly in strike funding, in training of militants and in providing weaponry. With all these the terror soon escalated and no curfew could have been more effective in clearing honest men and women from the streets at dusk than the spectre of hidden menaces ready to pounce from every shadow; you walked with your head swivelling. Businesses that thrived in the night–clubs, restaurants, musicians, taxicabs, prostitutes etc.--began to lose heavily; many legitimate businesses closed permanently; others braved the threats from the dark, by simply recruiting members of the terrorists themselves as guards.

There is no question that a major instrument in the savaging of Indians and their businesses was the vitriol daily excreted by the increasingly militant press-- two owned or controlled by D'Aguiar, *The Daily Chronicle* and the *Evening Post* while the *Daily Argosy* and *Guiana Graphic* were controlled by other local business elite. All of these supported the UF, ideologically and materially, and helped to make it the richest of the three parties. In a trice, or so it seemed, the country's media had sacrificed news and fair comment in favour of harangue and incitement, using exaggerations, distortions, lies and innuendo, to exact a heavy toll from all those deemed to support the governing party. Small business people whose perennial complaint—ignored by *all* parties—had been against the monopolies of the 'Big Houses' and agencies, mostly British or Portuguese, including D'Aguiar's, that tightly controlled supplies, were made by innuendo and smear the causes of the shortages! From April to July the papers, led by *The Daily Chronicle* produced a steady barrage of anti-Jagan rhetoric exhorting the populace to overthrow him by one means or another including violence, one writer claiming that *"words have failed"* and *"no imperialist guns can hold us any longer. Let us.....show the Bloody British, the TUC and Jagan and his government that the workers will settle the affair."* They accused Jagan of diverting available supplies of essentials to his strongholds and depriving the city of their needs for wheat flour--an imported staple for Indians---while allowing locally-produced ground provisions--the negro staples—although plentiful, to be "made scarce" by traders of all races who sequestered them for purposes of profiteering.

In the early days of the strike the stoppage at the airlines had left travellers stranded, including Walter who had gone to Port of Spain, Trinidad to present-- at the annual conference of the *Medical Research Council*--our work on the outbreak of Congenital Heart Disease, which we had eventually found to be associated with a rash of *Rubella* (German measles) infection in the mothers during early pregnancy—thanks to some dedicated sleuthing by the two health visitors loaned to us by the Ministry of Health. We had trained them to search for any consistent pattern of injury, infection, toxicity, medication or other noxious agent that the mothers' might have contacted during early pregnancy. None of us had so far heard of an association between Rubella, a viral infection, and birth defects, so we were at first sceptical but later quite elated as the association withstood independent review. *We would make medical history!*

Walter's wife, Jacquie, became quite concerned when the strike began on the day after his departure, both for his chances of getting home in a timely way, and for the security of her children and herself, noting the inflammatory rhetoric from the opposed politicians and the simultaneous increase in burglaries and personal assaults in the streets and elsewhere. Her disquiet was heightened that Saturday when she witnessed, from her living room window, the brutal assault, beating and robbery of a swarthy old Portuguese man who was dragged by two black youths from his bicycle while riding on Newmarket Street which ran parallel to the fence that separated her bungalow from the street; he was flattened on the pavement, kicked and punched in the face several times, his pockets emptied and his bicycle stolen. Her screams scared them off, and her son Butch had come racing to get me. They were gone when I got to her side, and tried to calm her; she was half in hysterics, her hands to her head and intermittently pointing to the poor man still lying semiconscious on the road, trying to move. Two porters responded to my call and got him to the Casualty room, where his wounds were treated and he soon revived; after a period of observation he was released home with relatives.

The strike brought shortages of everything; soon there was hardly any petrol, and police would stop vehicles to examine their carburettors; a red stain indicated use of government rations released only to certain government workers whose jobs required travel, or to farmers satisfying certain criteria. I was allowed three imperial gallons per week, for which I joined a long queue at the Public Works Department off Main St, inching along for 300-400 yards and probably consuming quite a few pints of the precious stuff just idling! A relation in DeHoop gave me another two gallons from his farming quota. These enabled me to give my brother two to three gallons each week to supplement his meagre supplies squeezed from increasingly scarce and contaminated sources. To help him I had to decolourise the gasoline, a risky operation which I did secretly in my laboratory. Police foot patrols increased in key business areas; the men were deployed in pairs, and increasingly one Black and one Indian. It was instructive to observe that the one rifle issued to the pair was always carried by the Black policeman.

As the strike wore on, my frustrations with the way Jagan was running (or ruining) the country was matched only by the greater fear that the only alternative, Burnham, was hotly campaigning in the wings to terrorise the population and unseat Jagan, just as he had tried in February 1962, only now more brazenly, and with strong overt American and British allies. The foremost local weapons in Burnham's war—for that's what it clearly was—were the phalanges of men on bicycles who would ride at great speed, recklessly down main streets, including the sidewalks, amid great noise and clamour, swinging bicycle chains in menacing circles above their heads and, at the flanks of the raging columns, lashing out at any one who happened to be there. Many were injured this way and we would see them at the Hospital with wounds, from cuts, bruises and limb fractures (forearm usually) to serious head injury. This technique had been honed over the past year of practice to the point of precision and increasing terror, more befitting, in another theatre, a Roman phalanx or Nazi panzer column.

I came within a hair's breadth, literally, of joining their victim group. The scene was *Saroop's Restaurant*, early one Saturday afternoon. We had gone to collect some chicken, which Saroop had offered to supply us in view of the general difficulty of getting food, whether local or foreign. My family's business connections and our extended family in the farm belt kept us reasonably supplied with fruits and vegetables, including rice and tubers, all of which had become scarce and expensive. Wheat flour, kerosene for stoves and gasoline and diesel for vehicles—all imports-- soon disappeared into the underground, emerging sporadically to face long lines of patient supplicants queuing to get a little. Invariably only a fraction succeeded in getting any.

That day I had taken the family to visit my sister and on the way home had stopped at Saroop's. Ranji, then 14 months old, had fallen asleep in the back seat, so I left him in the parked car, windows part way down, just outside the steel grill gate that shielded the door of the restaurant. We were only stopping for the few minutes it took to collect the package. It had been a quiet day, but Burnham had made another of his rabble-rousing speeches at Bourda Green, at the eastern end of Robb Street and the atmosphere had become palpably tense. We squeezed into the restaurant and the gate was closed and about to be chained behind us.

Hardly had we entered than a great shout rent the air: *"Bicycle Gang! Big One!"* Immediately my wife panicked, "Ranji!" she cried. Swiftly Inshan opened the gate and I dashed out, yanked the car door open, glancing sideways to gauge the speed and fury of the phalanx thundering towards me. I grabbed the child, kicked the door closed and to the shout of "Hurry, Hurry!" I dashed to the restaurant gate, ducking as I crossed the sidewalk and thus narrowly escaped the swinging chain of the hurtling cyclist who slashed at my head with a loud swish taking more than a few hairs with it. The one that followed rattled the steel door with his heavy chain. A group in the rear stopped to assault and rob Indians caught in the open street.

Paralysed I watched the collective menace, at least a couple hundred strong, stretched in a fifteen-man phalanx across the wide street, and one on each sidewalk, racing down it, some wearing only a singlet above the waist, many bare-chested, their eyes intense, their black bodies shining with sweat, as they shouted abuse and threats, swinging chains in wide circles above their heads, and striking at any Indian in their path. Inshan secured the steel gate just as a group, mere teenagers, two quite heavy-set, detached from the main group and threw themselves against the strong barricade, frightening the customers and others gathered inside and cowering behind walls and furniture. They stopped and backed off only when Saroop's guard appeared with a loaded shotgun and aiming it at them, commanded, "Get you' rass from dey or I'll shoot you' fucking heads off!"

Three of them were gone in a flash, one shouting, "we goin' come back, coolie!" The other two were slower; one cowering, crouched and pleaded, "Take it easy man; take it easy; we goin'," and slowly backed away. The last had frozen where he stood his eyes wide in fear, his knuckles tightly closed and pale around the bars of the gate. Presently he began to tremble, wet his pants, the liquid dripping onto the pavement, then promptly threw up as his grasp released and he sank whining into his own vomit, then defaecated.

One day, near the end of April, as the strikers became more frenzied and coercive, a mob presented itself at the gated Middle Street entrance of the Hospital compound. I've mentioned this entrance and gate earlier in relation to McLeod's autopsy of 14 months ago. It gave access to specialty services units within the hospital complex including the laboratory. The mob was boisterously demanding to speak to the head of the laboratory, Dr Balwant Singh, who had stayed home "sick."[159] (He was President of the Civil Service Association, which had joined the illegal strike called by the TUC, and had just refused the Premier's request to order a return to work). I was the next in the line of command at the Laboratory and agreed to meet them. It was 10 am.

At the head of the mob was Dr P. Reid, a PNC deputy to Mr Burnham. He was standing at the edge of the road outside the bolted postern that was manned by our attendant Mahabir. Reid wished to know why I--he mentioned my name-- had prevented workers from striking.

The previous day I had assembled the staff and had read to them a letter from Mr Ivan Seelig, Permanent Secretary, Ministry of Health, informing all staff that since the strike was illegal, all absences would be deducted from leave or vacation entitlements. I had advised them of the action supervisors would have to take in the event of unauthorised absences. Three members of the Clinical Chemistry section, known to be PNC supporters and activists, insisted on their right to strike. I merely stressed that the strike was illegal, that under current

---

[159] Even greater men have been known to default from responsibility. Someone pointed out that Lord Cornwallis had absented himself from the *Surrender Ceremony* at Yorktown on Oct 17, 1781, US War of Independence.

regulations health care workers could not strike, that each worker had to choose whether he or she could morally justify withdrawing services that had been deemed essential for community well-being; failing to report for work would be a matter for their conscience. Finally I advised them to study Mr Seelig's letter and stressed that anyone absent without leave would be treated in accordance with its directives. I was however willing to consider *extenuating circumstances.*

In response to a question from Dr Reid in which he named as complainants Miss Matheson and Mr McWatt--two of the three who had shown the most surly anti-government behaviour in the laboratory--I replied that they or any other worker was free to join the strikers, but should they do so, their supervisors would have to respond according to Mr Seelig's directives. He might therefore wish to speak to that gentleman.

The mob kept striking at the gate that separated us with sticks and chains and pushing and shoving in an attempt to take it down. It was a sturdy double swing structure 10 ft. wide supported on thick posts and was made of stout greenheart with iron reinforcement of the main frame. Each was ten feet tall at the hinged side and twelve at the centre, and was divided into upper and lower sections by a thick 6 inch wide horizontal plank. Vertical 1 inch diameter bars were embedded in the frame, 4 inches apart, and stiffened with diagonal bars. The base was a solid 12 in. wide plank. The gate was closed, each half bolted into a concrete pediment and the two secured at the middle with a heavy chain and matching padlock. The fence that ran off on either side was about 4 inches up from the sidewalk and made of 6 feet tall iron spikes set four inches apart.

The mob was noisy and in a foul mood. It consisted mostly of young Negro men, wearing T-shirts and shorts, all angrily waving fists, sticks, swinging bicycle chains above their heads, and shouting imprecations, anti-government and anti-Indian slogans. Half a dozen equally boisterous women stood tugging at the gate. Several carried placards with the same gory and ominous messages. One, the tallest among them stood about forty feet away holding a rifle braced to his shoulder aimed at me above the bobbing heads around him. (I had learned to recognise various common firearms for forensic purposes and had seen and examined many, and used to draw them as doodles during meetings). The rifle was army issue--.303 calibre--identical to the one that had killed Supt. Mc Leod in February 1962.

Upon hearing my reply to Dr Reid, the tall man steadied the gun and shouted above the din, "Lemme tek 'im, chief; I got 'im; lemme tek 'im! Ah gwine tek 'im." I was staring straight into the muzzle of the rifle, fixed and commanding in the man's hands. Reid's upright hand stayed him; pointing to the chained gate he said, "I see you locking the workers in, though."

The postern within the right hand half of the massive structure allowed people to pass through, one at a time. Mahabir had orders to let no one in without a valid hospital pass or outpatient identification, e.g. clinic appointment card or completed laboratory requisition form. It was he who had summoned me to the gate. He stood to one side half protected by the gatepost and looked terrified. A black staff nurse was at a first floor window in the building a few feet to my right, which housed the Ophthalmology and Ear, Nose and Throat Clinics. I had seen her standing there as I walked into the scene; now she was about eight feet directly over my head.

Across the driveway the Dermatology Clinic was silent, windows closed. I heard the nurse say, in a low voice as if talking to someone near, terror in her voice, "Ohmigawd! Look, that big man dey, he got a gun and he gwine shoot the young doctor! Is wha' this happenin' here today? These people gone maad!"

"We're not locking in anyone; this gate is closed on the orders of the Hospital Secretary. Anyone is free to leave. You can see why we have to keep the gate locked." I was almost flippant as I gestured at the many unruly and hostile hands shaking the gate as if to bring it down and rattling its chain in a most menacing way.

"What will you do if one of your staff wants to leave now?" he asked.

"Nothing," I said. "It's a matter of their conscience, as I've explained to them. There's no coercion. If someone told you he or she was prevented from leaving, that's simply not true. Would you like to come in and ask them, Dr Reid?"

I can still today clearly hear the booming voice of the itchy-fingered rifleman shouting his eagerness to fire, his gun levelled at me, and looming inordinately larger and more menacing by the second, just as the mob seemed to blur, their shouts and execrations muffled.

"But you brazen! You done dead, coolie!" several shouted while shaking the heavy gate, rattling the chain. Reid silenced them and asked, his voice even, "You know who I am?"

"Who doesn't, sir?" I replied.

He paused briefly then said, "I hear a lot about you, young man; you will hear from me if I want to come in!"

And without planning to say it, I said, "It's no fun in here, doctor; all this violence keeps us very busy; people are troubled, confused and terrified. Many have been threatened."

"And your directives not helping them!" And then he asked what I then thought was an idiotic question, "If you were a Negro would you have acted that way?"

Being an Indian, I was automatically assumed to be a PPP adherent, acting on a partisan agenda, and therefore fair game for sniper, arsonist or bomber. Knowing that my stand was based on rectitude, not politics nor in defiance of the right to protest, I replied, "Two things, sir, I know I am not a Negro, and cannot possibly put myself in his shoes, no matter how much I understand his position. Second, by your question, are you saying that a Negro in my position facing this issue would make the wrong decision?"

His eyebrows knitted; someone beside him hissed, "But you got gall; you tongue sharp!"

The rifleman shouted, *"Gi'e me the word, chief; dis one gat to go; le' me tek 'im!"*

Reid raised his hand, lessening the hubbub and said simply, "He would see it our way."

Reflexly, the rifle looming in my sight and my inability to defend against it notwithstanding, I retorted, inexplicably, in a low voice, "And make the wrong decision? I don't think so, sir. Only a scoundrel would do that." The words had slipped out unwittingly, replaced by instant images of a funeral, wailing relatives, sad-looking friends and four little orphans.

I saw his eyes narrow but his lips parted in a slight smile. In the pause broken only by the continuing racket I felt uncomfortable and in a sense numbed by the occasion. A powerful impulse to leave the angry scene at all costs came over me, and I heard myself say, as if from a distance--with the picture of the man with the long gun aimed at me etched indelibly in my mind--something unusual for me, often the last one to end an interview, "Please excuse me, Doctor, if you don't have more questions; I must get back to work." I looked straight at the gunman, turned around and walked slowly back to the laboratory.

The door was a straight thirty yards away. The longest thirty yards I have ever walked. I kept telling myself, "He's so close, if you hear the shot you're probably alright; dive right and roll; he'll probably aim for your back or head." But I reached the door amid the clamour that filled the street and driveway, which my mind had managed by then to reduce to a mere buzz, so dominant was the thought that this could be my final moment.

I entered the laboratory feeling unaccountably exhausted, as after long and arduous exercise or a day of cricket; I leaned against the wall, which ran on the right straight down to the back of the building, bounding a corridor that led to work areas, and off to the left, just within the entrance, to a flight of stairs that led to my office. Staff lined the corridor looking tensely as I came in. Two of the young women, one dressed in a blue uniform, were holding tensed hands to their lips in a gesture of fearful expectancy. A third had fainted and was being fanned back to consciousness while someone else waved smelling salts under her nose.

Among the others, all white and blue blurs according to the colour of their coats, one girl had bitten through her knuckles, blood staining her lips like hastily applied lipstick and drops had begun to fall to the front of her coat. I went to her and calmed her as best as I could and mopped her lip and the bitten knuckle; a senior technologist took care of her, still sobbing.

"Let's get back to work." I said softly, without thinking, the first words that came to my lips. The uniformed girl smiled. The others murmured various things. Slowly smiles began to replace terror in their faces. One shouted to others in the rear of the building, "He alright!"

Balgobin had come in from the autopsy area on hearing the commotion, and had witnessed the scene.

"You awright, doc? I thought the black man woulda kill you."

"Well, I'm still here," I said weakly; then slowly walked upstairs to my office, which overlooked the gate. As I entered the office a group of staff accosted me with warnings.

"They still there, Doctor," Miss Wilson, the daughter of one of Jagan's Black Ministers warned, her voice tremulous with fear.

"Don't go near the window," one of the men added, "what if they decide to shoot? The bullet will go through the wall"

I turned and tried to reassure them. "I don't think they'll shoot now."

I had no reason for this confidence but I felt impelled to show myself at the window, making sure first that I could see the gunman before I got to the window; I could hit the floor in case I was wrong. The crowd lingered noisily but the leaders had begun to move on down the street, taking the gunman with them maintaining his position about fifteen feet behind the leaders, his rifle pointing up, bobbing up and down as he pumped his right arm. Moments later, the Hospital Secretary, Mr Indar Persaud was at the door.

"Someone called to tell me about this terrible thing," he began. "I called the Police; they said they would send someone, and that patrols were on the streets. You okay?"

"Yes," I said.

"What happened?" I told him.

"Write me a brief report; I'll file it with the Police and Ministry."

I went back to my work and tried to bury myself in it, interrupted by others, the heads of sections, individual technicians and secretaries, commiserating, wanting to see for themselves that I had survived the encounter. The ENT nurse, a pleasant, buxom middle-aged lady, came over and commiserated, "I had to see you if you okay, Doctor; I don' know you, but I see what these people doin'; they my people but I don't agree with all this violence; I was so frightened, I prayed for you; t'ank God nott'n bad happen; but you brave fo' true!"

She was standing a foot from me as I thanked her with wet eyes, taking her hand and choked with emotion, merely squeezed it; she followed with a tight reassuring hug, which I returned, then she quickly left. The news spread through the hospital compound, and had a mixed reception; from the predominantly black staff it ran the gamut from condemnation ("they goin' too far") to tacit approval ("e lucky, 'e coulda dead; it no end dey; it gwine get wuss!"). I had become an instant hero and was greeted, wherever I went for the next several days in the Hospital, as if I had won the Victoria Cross.

But the incident, like others, was not reported in the newspapers, nor on radio.

At 4.30 that afternoon an Assistant Commissioner of Police (or Senior Superintendent)--one of the few high-ranking Indian officers in the Force, who I was told had been a Captain or Major in the British Army during WWII—came in to see me. The staff had all gone save for Sumintra and Indar who were cleaning up; Indar brought him in. I felt honoured.

"I'm acting entirely on my own," he confided. "I don't like what I hear, and I'm sorry the Force let you down. I think you need protection, but I can't convince the chief of that. He says we don't have the manpower. So I want you to be protected somehow, as best as we can."

He paused, reached inside his briefcase and brought out a shiny new Police .38 calibre revolver with holster and 20 rounds of ammunition, which he proffered me.

"Can you use one of these?"

"No, sir." I said.

"I'll take you tomorrow to the practice range; you should get the hang of it in a couple hours; you can practise after that, a little each day." He was deadly serious, and yet his face had such a benign look, rather like my mother's guru, Pandit Dowlat Ram. Caring, friendly.

I looked at the weapon, held it, turned it over in my hand, getting its measure, feeling its gleaming coldness and admiring the craftsmanship. It fitted well and felt as if it had always belonged in my hand. I shuddered realising that I liked how it felt, the reassurance it gave. I recalled how I had craved a toy six-gun as a child. This one made its presence felt. I did not think long.

"Commissioner, I can't thank you enough for your concern and this wonderful act; gives me great relief. But I can't take this, I have three boys; they're 7, 5 and 2; they might find this wherever I might hide it, and think it's a toy; my flat has no real hiding place they don't know. You know I did P.M.'s on two children killed in play with guns this past year."

"Yes, I know. But are you sure? I think you should carry this on your person, keep it ready when you're driving. We'll issue the appropriate licence. I hear that your work takes you into Lodge and Riumveldt; those are rough areas for an Indian. Think again. Here, this piece has a safety catch, not easy for children to move, let me show you."

He showed me the mechanism. I was still uneasy. A determined child could eventually work it.

"I'll have to keep it loaded if it's to help me at all. No sir, I better not."

We talked about guns and injuries, the forensic situation and the lack of progress since the murder of McLeod--who had been working with him on the project--and Mrs Jagan's assumption of the Ministry.

"It was such a senseless killing; we've known all along who did it, an ex-policeman working with the PNC, but none of the many witnesses will testify, out of fear perhaps, and we can't force them. Probably the same man who aimed at you. Fits the description. We still hope for a break." He rose to leave.

"I'll i.d. anyone if you show me your photos."

"You will?" He did not hide the surprise.

I nodded.

"I'll pass that on to the officer in charge; meanwhile, the piece is yours if you change your mind. That incident could have been nasty, like McLeod's. It was a very brave thing you did. I heard that the plan was to set fire to your lab. We have plain clothes men among them and on the compound, but the terrorists are many, and we don't know them all yet. And our chaps are few. Be careful; keep your car locked at all times; don't trust anyone, not after this."

"One or two there in the crowd looked like Americans." I said.

"Could be." He said, non-committally, as indeed was appropriate.

As we walked to the side door he admonished, "Be very careful, especially in your work travel. I'm sorry I can't give you personal protection; call me at this number if you need me. It's private. I'll call you if I have any news for you. Keep in touch." He handed me a piece of notepaper and left.

The following day I went home earlier than usual and for some obscure reason varied my routine. Instead of going directly to the entrance to the flats I deviated and entered the carport where my car was parked, front forward, in the right hand slot against the wall; the other two spaces were empty; I walked as far as the left front door and saw nothing of concern. I turned around heading for the entrance and was half way there when I realised that I had not seen the right front side of the car which was close to the side wall of the carport. Hurrying there I was astonished to find, just under the right end of the bumper, a small tent made of thin plywood carefully sheltering a briskly-burning fire just then beginning to char the thin tent roof on the side nearest the car, inches from the front of the engine.

The car was locked and I did not have the keys. There was a fire extinguisher in the stairwell on each floor of our building. I rushed up to the nearest one, grabbed the extinguisher, ran back and emptied it on the blaze, smothering it. The Casualty Department and gateman's station were across the driveway from our building. Soon Security was all over the area and I had to write another report; this time I took photos of the scene. Police arrived and took statements. I heard nothing further from the authorities; it was as if nothing had happened. Again the news spread through the compound. Many on the staff and among my friends that same evening speculated on a connection between the two incidents. I called the Asst. Commissioner; he too felt there was a connection, but feared a more widespread targeting of hospital staff and property because of their failure to stop work *en masse*, and of the mounting schisms between strikers and non-strikers among hospital staff.

The following day, Saturday, on my way in from work just past noon I found a tent and firewood exactly like the one the previous day, wet with kerosene, but unlit, this time near the gas tank of Harold Hamilton's car parked in his carport in full view of any traffic along the broad driveway that separated our block of flats from his 3-storey building (which also housed the internes' quarters and doctors' lounge). His carport was opposite mine. This generated new fears among hospital staff as the attempt against Harold tended to negate the suggestion of racial targeting and tended to confirm attempts to harass certain doctors. Harold had expressed open outrage at actions aimed to terrorise Hospital staff. I called him and Security.

"These people are crazy; they don't like criticism," Harold exclaimed, taking in the scene and speaking to the knot of doctors that had quickly formed at the site. He was a short, stocky Trinidadian, with thinning curly hair, full lips and a pleasant smile, whom I had met in 1957 at UCH when he was Senior Registrar in Medicine and had coached several of us in the months before final examinations. "You know the car wasn't locked; they could have put the fire in there; they must have done it after I left hustling to the ward. But they brazen indeed to do this in broad daylight; someone on staff, maybe; must be the same fellow as yours."

As the violence increased I had to find ways to defend my family and myself, at home and in the street. An intruder had already reached and tried the locked back door, in broad daylight, only to be scared off by Beatrice's screams. Having declined the pistol offered me by the Police Officer, I resorted to making my own defensive weapons, which I carried in the car. First was sulphuric acid, which I placed in an acid-resistant plastic container with a sturdy nozzle, a squeeze of which would send the fluid instantly forward twelve to fifteen feet; I practised secretly until I could control volume and distance accurately, burning a lot of grass and paper targets in the process. The second was a bromine 'pellet' bomb. I had found a litre of fuming concentrated bromine protected in the dark recesses of an unused fume cupboard in my lab, idle and covered with dust. We no longer used it for tests, so I decided to use it defensively as an irritant and deterrent. I charged glass ampoules with the heavy liquid, sealed them with sealing wax or hard paraffin, and found that the thin glass would break easily if thrown against anything, including a padded object, and release the stinging fumes, which lingered at the site. The third was a flexible steel cosh made by folding in two a two-foot length of coiled stainless steel spring an inch in diameter, which we used, laid flat, in a drawer, as slide holders.

I informed the Assistant Commissioner, since they were all illegal. "I see, but I didn't hear what you said," he responded. I kept the pellets in my car, my office and home, gave some to my brothers and taught my wife to use them. The acid was stored in a resistant case fashioned in the glove compartment of my car. I carried the steel 'cosh' whenever I went out on foot. My younger brother Deo was briefed on these innovations, as he occasionally used the car. He was a teacher and lived with his wife, two sons and daughter on Sheriff St in Campbellville, reasonably removed from the main scenes of terror, but with no telephone we had to rely on the "no news is good news" theory as far as their safety was concerned. More often it was they who worried about us in the city, especially the folks on Hadfield St, right across from the main line of fire, the Legislative Assembly.

My bromine ampoules had a live field test once at a standpipe in a tenement yard in Lodge Village, one of the points where I used to collect water samples for daily testing of the city's water supply. I had become known in the past year to most of the residents, all Negroes, and they knew my purpose. A week or so after the fire incident I had just collected samples at the site, and was about to enter my car, engine idling, when two young thugs approached running from about 30 yards behind me, one swinging a bicycle chain over his head, the other shouting menacingly, "Hey, coolie, stop dey! Wha' de scunt yuh doin' in we place?" I had begun to keep several of the ampoules in a tray below the car dashboard and two in my test kit. I reacted as I had practised, grabbed the two ampoules and tossed them on the ground about ten feet in front of them, then reached for the sulphuric acid container when an older Negro man I knew emerged from his dwelling roused by the shouting. He was just in time to see the brown pungent vapour rise slowly towards the two, who hesitated as he admonished, "Leave de doctor alone; 'e doin' we wuk! Go on, doctor!" I quickly got into the car and was off, wheels screaming sending loose gravel flying. Through the rear-view mirror I saw the one with the chain wiping his eyes while the shouter stood staring at the little brown cloud.

The Hospital's specialist staff had begun to thin out after the fires and riots of 1962 and the PPP's unrelenting push further and further to the left. The strike had exposed to the most confirmed doubter the web of connections between the PPP and Communist states. Even formal meetings of the Hospital Management Committee became plagued by clashes of ideology and personality as people began to form or reveal allegiances. Most were sophisticated enough to deal with matters dispassionately, even with vexing issues of low supplies, threats to workers, personnel illegally striking or failing to perform (confident of the protection guaranteed by the PNC). The broader issues--new taxation and other impositions on professional earnings and freedoms, commodity shortages and rising prices, increasing incidence of muggings in broad daylight, burglaries with violence, assaults and murders—weighed heavily on staff. When the security of hospital households and the potential for attacks on family within the hospital compound came to the fore, the grumbling became loud, troubled and insistent. I recall the surgeon Grewal, an imposing six-footer, declaiming in his heavy Punjabi accent, at a meeting when hospital security was discussed in the wake of the fire threats in two garages.

"Who be next?" he thundered. "They will call me one day from theatre to say my house burning?"

The expatriates had been the first to leave, their wives and children slipping away as if for a holiday before the strike had started. Others stayed on merely to complete contracts and were promptly off, first chance they got. Many, like Walter—with Stanley, Brahmam and Gordon, my best friends among the doctors—Searwar, Chetram, Hublall, Narine, Bedessie, Poonai and many of the laboratory staff, were devoted enough to Jagan to argue the merits of his cause. Walter even convinced his Canadian wife, Jacquie -- the belle of the residents that included such attractive women as Mrs Brahmam, Anila Poonai, Mrs Luck and Carol—to stay. Sadly Jagan paid no heed to the disastrous effects of his intransigence on his ablest supporters. He was living his credo oft stated in his harangues and personally to me in his dental chair so many years ago, *"First you must destroy, if you want to build! You must not be side-tracked!"*

Late in 1962 Enid Denbow, an internist at the Hospital and wife of an LCP and PNC activist, Frank Denbow, had shown her hand, previously appearing neutral even though everyone knew how ardent an advocate of PNC policies Frank was, including violence, if needed, to get what they wanted. She had spoken out finally after the 1962 Constitutional Conference held in London had failed to agree on proportional representation as the tool for determining government authority. She had repeated the PNC/UF slogan, *'no PR, no independence'* used to encapsulate their opposition to the transfer of full powers to the PPP government which Jagan asserted had been promised and which Burnham had supported in the past. The Colonial Office was picketed by PPP adherents in London for failing to support the "duly elected" government. The failure of that conference solidified the divide between the two sides and gave the thugs of Georgetown free rein. The Attorney General, Fenton Ramsahoye, pithily and bitterly accused the Colonial Office of sanctioning violence, looting, arson and murder by siding with the opposition.

Frank sought me out to commiserate after the failed attempt to set my car afire. We had previously talked cordially on several occasions about contemporary events, and his wife had been friendly, and supported me in my work, even took my side in criticising Dr Nicholson, who had published my work on Parathione poisoning under his own name at the 1962 MRC Conference. Frank was short, paunchy, about 5ft 5 ins., ebony black with glistening skin and a cone-shaped head topped with scanty grey hair. (Enid was a good three inches taller, slimmer with ample breasts and narrow hips, and fine smooth black skin.) As he spoke he would rub his ample parabola of a belly, from long habit, perhaps.

"You have to use all the weapons you have, man, when you fighting a war," he said.

"What war, Frank?"

"We're fighting for freedom, not slavery."

"Bullshit; it's a make-up war, pure Hollywood! Kids playing cowboys and Indians, with real Indians!" He laughed. "Come on Frank, don't you remember slavery ended for you guys a hundred and twenty-nine years ago? You hear Odo talk you think it hasn't happened; that last speech at Bourda was pure sedition." I ended recklessly, but I did not care, feeling a curious exhilaration in seeing the gunman with steady aim while Frank spoke as if in a dream.

He laughed again, uneasily this time, his bright white teeth gleaming, highlighted by contrast with black skin, "No, no, you misunderstand; it was a rallying call. The rhetoric of the day. Hyperbole."

"You can't speak like Mark Antony or use rhetoric with that rabble! You know this is no battlefield; this is crude and obvious brigandry, to steal a nation before it's born, deliberate infanticide." Although not a physician, he understood and often used medical terms.

"You're being dramatic, man; you're naturally upset because of the incident last week; that was bad judgement and Ptolemy dealt with it on the spot."

"Or I might be with McLeod today," I said sadly, in silent recall of a lost talent. "We were planning to work together, to build a great forensic facility, not to be killed together."

He ignored that, and putting his hand on my shoulder as we slowly walked towards the Doctor's Residence, he said, "People respect you as a bright and honest young man, the whole Hospital say so. Enid din' like you at first, she thought you were one of the Balwant clique, but she soon realise different; she says you fair and straight, you, Luck, Gordon, a good team. Join us, we need people like you."

I felt flattered, but the memory of arson, rape and murder and their many victims over the eighteen months, emboldened me to say, "But you're a racist group, Frank, just the old LCP clique that would burn me as easily as they tried to burn my car. A couple weeks ago your bicycle chain gang almost took off my head. This race stuff is not my style. I have friends from every racial group you can find here and all the combinations. I like them. Do you know I'm also an honourary Barama Carib? I would tell Cheddi the same thing if he played race."

"But he talking about an Indian army when he gets power; we can't let that happen; we been waiting long for this final emancipation. He's building up force in the country districts; Cuba giving him arms. If he gets his way, you, your people will face terrible danger."

"But Frank, we hear the Police raid PNC and PPP HQ a day or so ago; will they find nothing or will they find you chaps loaded with plans, structure and material for war? Will anything happen if they do?" I paused; did I say too much? He stared at me, as if I was drunk or crazy, his face shining, serious. I added, "You're the ones in danger, you know; Odo only needs you to take him to the top. Watch, you'll see, he'll dump all of you when the time comes, unless you toe his line. Look, he even has Mayor Merriman, undertaker and pacifist, promoting this militancy; is that because the violence brings him business?"

Frank laughed, "That's funny. Anyway, we not racist, we just look after ourselves; think about what I said; it's *your* future." He ignored the matter of the raids.

"Then tell me the truth. If PNC takes over, you think Odo will guarantee Indians the same rights to law and order that Jagan guarantees to you? Will all Indians have a place in this country where they were born? Will he get rid of enough of us to reduce our majority? You know that he hates us, barring a few he can use, Ramphal, Sase, Bissember, Jainarine—two opportunists, two hotheads."

"You have a place, of course, like I said; but not all will find it the way they want; there'll be adjustments, just as under Jagan. We'll thrive, man, we'll thrive."

"Did you know about the 1938 Indian Centennial resolutions, how they sought a state in which all races will have a proud place, equal in all respects, pursuing their own way of life, expressing cultural, language and religious freedoms that the British had denied us, a peaceful place like it was twelve years ago when you and I could stroll side by side with our girlfriends on the Sea Wall and no one would molest us? We've lost that as Cheddi and Odo, both too young and too foolish for our good, began to wrestle for the top. They won't help us, Frank; they'll ruin us--Cheddi with Communism, Odo like Duvalier."

"Come, come, Odo not like that. But I like what you say, sounds like exactly what we want: good government, peace and order; Communism won't give us that. About those resolutions, I've heard vaguely about them, years ago; something about joining hands for cooperation and development; our people said that Indians were usurping our position."

"Not so, Frank, I know what the LCP said, but maybe you should read them; I lost my copy with moving around, but the Library has, or borrow Odo's; he has one. I know he studied them. Didn't he tell you?"

He stopped abruptly, looking stunned. Indeed, it *was* his turn to be surprised.

We had completed the examination of a bomb victim and after the Police had left, Balgobin and I turned to a Negro man who had suffered a stroke, a massive intracerebral haemorrhage that had killed him quickly by destroying much of his vital centres. The work now was routine, but in the course of reviewing, at McLeod's instigation, all cases of forensic interest that we had completed in the previous two years I had come to realise that Indians and Africans who died suddenly of natural causes had a different profile of the two major lethal events: heart attacks and strokes. This had led to a research interest in the underlying conditions and associations found in the victims; I was finding that more Indians had heart attacks and diabetes (the lay folks called it sugar diabetes), and more Africans had hypertension and strokes. I was not surprised at the latter, as the combination had been recognised at the UCWI and was being researched there; Dr Hamilton had assisted in that. But much less was known about Indians and not even the doctors from India, including the very knowledgeable and up-to-date Dr Brahmam, could recall any paper or other reference on the matter.

A year earlier I had been made deputy chair of the Hospital's Library Committee under Dr. Hamilton, and with Walter Singh, a Committee member, had spent a considerable number of hours discovering the contents of all the disorderly mounds of journals lying on the floor and in boxes. The room was small and had been reluctantly carved out of the eastern end of the administrative block, which occupied the entire second floor above the Casualty Department, outpatient pharmacy and stores. A part-time librarian, loaned by the Carnegie Library, had methodically listed most of the journals in the room, but not being a medical librarian, she had done this alphabetically rather than by specialty or subject. Thus there was a huge pile under "A" and another under "T". The index and shelving remained to be done and we had agreed to help. She would place piles of journals on a table and one of us would examine and assign them to categories the Committee had recommended.

It was thus that I found a paper in the WIMJ written on the topic a few years earlier by a Trinidadian, Dr Wattley, describing similar ethnic differences in the occurrence of heart disease and stroke. If the sample we had studied reflected the general situation (and statisticians said it did) the results could significantly affect the allocation of resources in health planning, as the two groups comprised 90% of the population. At the Ministry of Health, however, none of the major conditions, arterial disease, which caused both heart attacks and stroke, diabetes, which aggravated both and often led to kidney failure and premature death, and hypertension, received more than a token recognition of their contribution to the total burden of disease, nor to the economic and social consequences of illness and premature death.

Dr Hamilton's interest in hypertension had begun to make a difference there, but that was a mere beginning. I had prepared a paper for the Ministry of Home Affairs, and had planned to send an abstract for presentation at the meeting of the Medical Research Council in Port-of-Spain in 1963, at the same time as Walter was doing ours on cardiac anomalies and rubella. Protocol required that all presentations be sent through the office of the Chief Medical Officer, Dr Charles Nicholson, but he denied approval to send it on unless his name was included as an author, which I refused, recalling that he had submitted my report on Parathione poisoning under his solo authorship! I suggested instead an acknowledgement, which was unacceptable to him. I was not given permission nor financial support to attend the meeting, and found out later that he had substituted his name for mine on Walter's paper and wanted to read it but relented when Walter said, "In that case you must deal with the questions."

Nicholson's academic dishonesty reminded me of Dr Louis Grant, the black Jamaican head of Microbiology at UCWI whose custom it was to insert this name as lead author of all papers originating in his department regardless of any input he may have had. None of the residents had an objection to his name coming after the lead researcher but to claim primary authorship was anathema. In 1960 four of us, Stanley included, suffered this but I managed to remove my drafts from his office, especially as he had no part whatever in the work done, and the only change he had made to the draft was to put his name before mine!. That paper, like the current work on East Indian heart disease did not make the conference.

Balgobin had become a key figure in my work. He had become proficient in dissecting, displaying and preserving samples of small blood vessels from various parts of the body and, even more encouragingly, had begun to read medical essays and texts relating to his work. He asked me one day whether we should not tell people their risks and help them avoid the terrible outcomes we were seeing in men and women, some barely in their fifties. Discussing my findings with physicians, both Drs Brahmam and Hamilton were quick to recall instances of sudden death in Indians from "heart attacks" and Dr Nehaul, the Deputy CMO and former Chief Pathologist, had noted the disproportionate incidence of coronary disease in Indians. The conventional teaching had been that Indians, apart from those with diabetes, were *not* apt to suffer heart attacks. Unfortunately, apart from measuring blood pressure and sugar we had no easy tests to identify those at risk early enough to make a difference, especially in the many Indians without frank diabetes or hypertension who might later suffer a heart attack. At that time these were invariably fatal events and were generally accepted as the consequences of ageing, bad genes or acts of God, dismissed by the medical administrative establishment as the natural unchangeable termination of life and regrettable when it occurred early. Attention was given to more urgent things, like infectious diseases, nutrition and sanitation.

Nevertheless Balgobin had undertaken to tell his colleagues what he knew, and would check with me before he discussed medical topics. On returning from Wappai he had welcomed the suggestion to inform people--starting with colleagues he met daily--on various matters that affected them since the press was biased, the radio unreliable and the political leaders were only trumpeting dissonant messages on health issues. The ordinary people might read a pamphlet but word of mouth, especially when casually given, might help more people to understand especially those who could not read very well and who needed answers to questions as they arose, but this needed many mouths to utter the words; pamphlets were definitely easier and would reach more people, but had to be produced. He carried a notebook crammed with data on various topics, from medical to political, and would share them as occasion arose.

The issue had arisen again when I walked into the sterilising room where three porters were arguing the incident that had taken place earlier involving Dr Reid's rifleman and me. Their interpretations had followed party lines, the two Indians condemning the act, the one Negro excusing it. I had interrupted and suggested that unless they knew first hand what the policies and intent of the different sides were they should not take sides on pure party or racial lines lest they make grave errors or help to commit injustices or harm the innocent. Balgobin had walked in on the conversation, frowned, but had said nothing.

As he was sewing up that day his face looked set — not its customary relaxed look. I asked him what was troubling him. He hesitated, and as if steeling himself to the task, blurted, "Is not my place to say it, Doc, but you wastin' time with these people," he paused, "people like Sumintra and Indar, she fuss with him all de time, he drink the lab alcohol, and get high; then she quarrel with him. And John, he bring his black friends in and they too have their own spree. You t'ink you can get them to learn the t'ings you tell them? You wastin' time, Doc! And when I say anything like we talk about, they ask me if I playing Doctor, and laugh at me."

I was impressed with his earnestness, and asked, half seriously,

"So you don't think they can learn anything new, even about themselves? They're all young, what, late twenties?"

"They only look young, Doc; they got old people brains. And all such like them. The only t'ing they understand is orders and strictness, jus' like estate people that follow Jagan like puppy follow dog; if you try to reason with them and treat them good, they will *eye-pass*[160] you. That's why Burnham will beat we. We people don't know when somebaddy doing' real good for them. We eye-pass them, instead of showing them respect. Promise them some freeness and kick dey ass, and you get them to do whatever you tell them to do; even kill, like how Burnham and Reid a' do'. Ask them to improve themselves and think befo' they act and do the right thing, they just suck dey teet' and say, 'fu wha' or 'who you think you is'?"

"Bal, you overstating this thing; surely they would like to learn a few things, not only 'bout their work or disease but where they came from; their own history, so that they can understand where they are and where they going; and make better judgements of what politicians say; why wouldn't they want that?"

"Because they not smart enough to see knowledge is power; they only understand t'ings they can touch and feel, and you can't touch and feel knowledge, and worse, knowledge won't improve dey pocket; they understand money. Now if you give them money or a case of sardines every week or some ice apple come Christmas, or better, a bottle of rum, then you will get attention."

"That's what Bustamante did in Jamaica to get the poor man's votes; he gave 'way salt fish and ackee." I mused ruefully.

Balgobin looked puzzled. "Ackee? What is that, Doc?"

---

[160] Overlook, disrespect

I explained the fruit and told him there were two trees along the main hospital driveway leading in from Newmarket Street. He had seen the trees with their pear-shaped red fruit that everyone said was poisonous, and so was avoided.

"Yes," I confirmed, "they can poison because they have a chemical that make your blood sugar get so low you can die; but the Jamaicans know when to pick them and how to use them safely. You have to wait until the pods pop open and for the air to act on the flesh; then they're safe. Ackee and salt fish fried with onions and spices is a Jamaican national dish. One of the porters told my wife about the trees and he picked the fruit for her. But tell me more about what's bothering you."

"We people got big mouth; they say yes, yes, to de big man to he face, 'specially if he white or high coloured; behind he back, they cuss him proper and criticise what he do; you ask them to do anything, even to help themselves, and they keep quiet and do nothing; but you do it, and see how quick they find fault."

"You telling me they so petty?"

"They pick sides, that's it, that's all they need; that's how bad it is. Some pick Jagan, some Burnham; and they believe them, no matter what; they grow up loving them; nothing you say will make them think for themselves. The Black people think Burnham is god. Indians from the estates and even in town believe everything Jagan say, and will follow him to the grave, and will cuss you and beat you up if you say anything bad 'bout him, even the truth; and all Mrs Jagan has to do is smile and they melt like ghee on a hot stove. That's why these other Indian parties going nowhere, not even Mr Rai own; I not jokin'; you ask."

"You really believe ordinary people will behave like that, not see what's so obvious, that the trouble is all about Communism, and that PPP leaders are Communist? Why do they think Rai left?"

"They think Mr Rai wrong because Jagan says so. They will never change. Worse, if you don't belong to their clique, they will crucify you. They all looking for freeness that the politicians promise. You bin away too long, Doc! You don' know how these people change these las' ten years; the old ones are bad enough, but I won't trust' the young ones at all; all the ones that grow up since Burnham and Jagan fighting know only how to pick sides, quarrel, cuss and fight, like gangs. Is nigger this, coolie that; even the young policemen them follow what Burnham say. Makes you want to go back to the old days, bad as things were! I di' want to tell the policemen that when we in the bush, but I din'."

By May 17th, tensions had increased markedly and crowds rampaged around the Public Buildings following a barrage of inciting speeches by Burnham and D'Aguiar, and despite emergency bans on gatherings there, PPP Assemblymen George Robertson and Moses Bhagwan were attacked leaving the Assembly, the latter stunned by a blow to the head. Others escaped with torn clothing and vituperation thrown at their fleeing backs. In Wismar, the beleaguered Indian minority continued to be abused and assaulted, capped by the beating of Senator Christina Ramjattan. Sporadic attacks on Indians did occur in the largely African villages of Demerara, especially Buxton, and in New Amsterdam.

A PNC directive sent women to squat in government offices and do whatever it took to harass and disrupt staff. They committed acts of wanton brutality, intimidation and coercion, verbally and physically abusing workers, especially the small-bodied young Indian and other women, pelting and spitting on staff as they turned up for work, provoking fights and other retaliation, and mooning those who had gotten inside, while the bicycle gangs continued to terrorise the business streets as the main weapon to stop commercial activity. These and the daily uprisings went beyond the requirements of "loyal opposition" to the point that they moved even strong PNC supporters like Dr. D. J. Taitt to openly blame Burnham for the violence calling *it 'improvised tribalism at variance with the economic realities of the two major ethnic groups...',* and urged him to change direction. Ignoring such major denunciation from his own, Burnham sent goons to "urge" his critics, including Dr Taitt, to desist or "who knows what might happen in the dead of night?"

As the shortages led to desperation and further anti-social conduct—even among ordinarily law-abiding citizens--Jagan began to scramble for help, ironically first from all the people he had been castigating throughout his political life. The conditions for the receipt of help remained stiff; in essence, abandon Communism and pursue a moderate socialism that would allow the people a greater say in the way their country should be run. Jagan was daily harassed by mobs at the Legislature despite the Emergency status. Yet he tried to carry on as in normal times, writing letters to Kennedy and his friends in the British Labour Party, importuning the Governor and the head of the army contingent at Atkinson Field and making overtures to Burnham. The last remained inflexible. Soon Jagan in desperation turned to Cuba and the USSR for material help. Opposition pamphlets, the press and street propaganda frightened people with lurid descriptions of how it would feel to drown in the "red tide", and warned of the blood that would flow, Indian blood, if that were to happen. *"Free Guiana today or we'll have blood tomorrow"* in bright red paint stained the concrete facade of the Georgetown seawall, as if it had always been there, and dangers littered the streets of the city that had been once so safe, gentle, kind and welcoming.

Forbes Burnham, PNC Leader, the beaming firebrand from Kitty

Mob at a Hospital gate, agitating for General Strike, April 1963: Author under the gun!

Above and Below: Detail from cartoon on previous page: the leader, R arm uplifted

The shooter, itching to fire, egged on by crowd

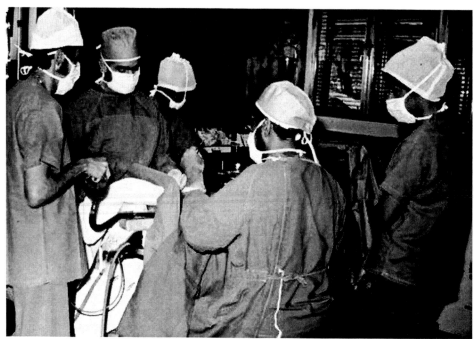

Surgical team at work during emergencies.This is a fairly sophisticated group; more often doctors and nurses worked alone or with scant equipment and material in an overcrowded emergency area but managed to avoid major disasters and did help the majority.

D'Aguiar's Imperial House, corner of Market Square and Brickdam, HQ of a liquor and entertainment complex, located obliquely across from the Legislature; mobs often started their marches here and D'Aguiar rallied groups here for his "ax the tax" campaign.

Any gas?

Scouting for supplies, outside Stabroek Market, 1963

Seeking supplies general strike 1963; store barred to prevent vandalism or arson

No gas! 1963 general strike

Strike: line-up for Government issue of gas at PWD depot, April 1963; (my car is at extreme right)

Hopng to find bread, 1963 at one of Georgetown's largest bakeries.

Crowd at Kerosene Vendor — daily search for fuel

Police patrol, 1963; note who carries gun!

Another side to general strike, 1963, garbage piles on sidewalk

Author's flat at Georgetown Hospital (topmost window) 1961-3

Hospital Gate inside which bomb tunnel was found in late April 1963, left side

GUIANA GRAPHIC   MONDAY, JULY 22, 1963   PAGE 7

LEFT TO RIGHT: Dr. Ragbeer, Mr. Sahai, Mr. Hassan
The fourth (right) is Mr Jethoo. The paper printed the photo of four departing
Indians, to suggest disillusionment with Jagan's government.

Chapter 17

The strike gets more violent; I begin to see murdered victims of political terror and anarchy, while opposition politicians posture and promote violence as society unravels around them. Police find arms caches and riot plans at PNC HQ but no prosecution follows. The withdrawal of the provoking legislation shames the government but fails to end the strike or violence, increasing anxieties and pressures on essential services, which continue to be disrupted. Shortages of essentials reach the point of desperation and Cuban aid provokes further violence. A farming family provides a view of the Hutchinson scheme proposed 12 years earlier and opposed by the Sugar Producers Association (see earlier chapters). Hospital doctors under threat start a vigilante watch over the compound as Police admit inability to cope; our first watch thwarts a plot to bomb the hospital's Casualty department. The press ignores the threat to the hospital and the evil minds that would target the entry point for the victims of terror. The flight of expatriate and local physicians begins in earnest. The public is unaware of the spreading tensions and many in the PNC and UF falsify the news.

Of hope and despair

"Change is a delicate and capricious beauty; you push too hard, she retreats and you lose her; go easy, show her you mean well in thought and action and you'll win as long as your suit is just."

Author, ASCOFAME, Bogotá

"I begin to believe in only one civilising influence – the discovery one of these days of a destructive agent so terrible that War shall mean annihilation and men's fears will force them to keep the peace".

Wilkie Collins, 1870

The shattered body of the plump middle-aged Indian lady lay on the table, still clad in her nightdress, shredded and blood-soaked, a gaping hole with jagged edges where her right chest met the abdomen. Multiple skin wounds radiated from this crater: lacerations of the face, scalp, chest, abdomen, back and right thigh, the right ear and nipple hanging by threads. Her brow was still creased in bewildered anguish and the ashen pallor of her skin attested to the massive loss of blood that had terminated her life. How many more would we have to examine of these innocents caught in the cross-fire of anarchic insurrection? Balgobin was morose and silent as he prepared for his task.

I had seen him with tears filling his eyes during our examination some time ago of nine children who had succumbed in quick succession to poliomyelitis and before that the same number of victims of parathione poisoning. I had on each occasion counselled him and encouraged discussion of his feelings and free expression of emotions, within certain obvious limits, noting that compassion was not a weakness and feeling hurt for someone a noble virtue. He had been concerned about our reaction, but I re-assured him that he was not on trial. But having heard his views on communal violence and inter-racial strife I had some misgivings about his reaction to this event.

"This is the worst we ever had;" he said finally, as if reading my mind; "at least those children had bad disease, or accident, but here we killing we self. Last year we were doing looters, this year it's innocent people."

At about 10pm the previous night this housewife from Howes Street was preparing for bed when suddenly she heard the loud crash of breaking glass coming from her daughter's bedroom, which faced the street. She raced into the darkened room and saw a bright hissing fuse on the far side of the sleeping girl's bed. Instinctively she threw herself over the girl just as the explosion resonated through the room shattering furniture and rupturing a wall. Shrapnel—one-inch lengths cut from 6-inch steel nails—ripped through her ample body from two feet away mincing the skin, shredding her liver, including the hepatic vessels, the diaphragm and most of her right lung, filling the chest and abdominal cavities with instant blood, killing her. Other missiles spread out and made deep and pointless rents in her right arm, neck and much of her right side to her ankle, and split her right ear, right breast and nipple, strips of skin and the nipple dangling like earrings.

She died not knowing what had happened. Her instant sacrifice saved her daughter's life but devastated the youth who remained shocked and delirious, and was even at that moment lying heavily sedated in hospital under Dr Brahmam's care. The family was Muslim and had no known political connections. Their only crime was to be Indian. Some said that she had refused to close her small shop to support the general strike. One of her neighbours was PNC enforcer Hamilton Green, the policeman had said, to no obvious purpose.

Elsewhere, heavy property damage had been done in a similar way to private and public buildings. Indians, convinced of the impotence and/or unwillingness of rank and file policemen to enforce the law, had belatedly begun to arm themselves and do vigilante rounds; in the worst areas serious retaliation had begun against the frequent "cuss-ups", robberies and beatings of the weak by black gangs. In one of these a black mugger was killed in the act, allegedly by a group of Indian vigilantes. To the dismay of level-headed citizens, *The Daily Chronicle* had used this to trumpet the conclusion that "racism was here to stay!" But it ignored the idleness, joblessness, misery, suffering and starvation among Jagan and Burnham's followers! These got no screaming headlines. And while the strikers collected a regular stipend--paid for in part by the CIA and private American agitators and supporters--non-union workers, rural and urban, forced to stop work, went about hungry. The strike exposed the partisanship of the so-called neutral Civil Service.

"I was at this friend's last night." Stanley told me that day, as the news of the bombings and bomb-makers spread, and we became even busier in the Casualty area. "You'd be shocked to hear what senior civil servants were saying, and some QC masters who were there, even calling for Cheddi's head; they didn't even have the facts straight, whether about the budget, or the strike-leaders, or the press, or who stoking the violence; you know few admitted to knowing about mobs at the hospital and none had heard of the one that wanted to kill you; and worse, most pooh-poohed news that CIA was thick in this and one told me I was crazy to say they'd been there for years."

"Didn't you tell him you're seriously crazy, that's why you know these things?" I teased.

He laughed, "I don't think he would have gotten the pun. But still I expected better."

"So, why are you surprised, Stan? Things were bad last year, but now we're in deeper shit with incompetence and ignorance added to bias at every major level of government, and now our one hope for reason and help, the press, has gone totally berserk. How can we get a temperate message out there when everyone is so frigging hot and taking sides by whim not wisdom?"

In May police raided the headquarters of the major political parties. At Congress Place, the headquarters of the PNC they found arms, ammunition, other weapons, training manuals, materials for bombs, the names and secret rankings of the PNC "army" and strategic instructions on how to carry out various acts of terror. The news shocked and horrified the populace, and for a brief spell helped the Jagan government by bringing calm to the streets. The police traced the material to the highest levels of the PNC and promised prosecutions, but surprisingly none came. Soon the mayhem returned as opposition politicians resumed their anti-government attacks, with stirring invectives promising booty, blood and guts to those who "fought the fight" and carried "the battle to the enemy" to "remove them forever and to regain your birthright!" It became plain to even the staunchest sceptic that the strike was entirely political, and the unions had been used once again for a base purpose, and the Police compromised. This was ironically the same union card that Jagan had hoped to play, only to discover at a critical point in the game that he had not drawn any trumps.

On May 24 Burnham in an impassioned speech at Bourda Green pledged his life to his people so that they may live in 'freedom and prosperity'. After having accused Jagan of planning violence, he called on his followers to take action and to shift *'the scene of agitation and opposition from the Legislature to the places where they grow rice'* a clear call for attacks against rural Indians, and *'keep the pressure on them'*.

The day after this salvo, five weeks after the strike had begun, an incredible incident led to the withdrawal of the Bill that had started it. Debate on the Bill had gone on for much longer than the Government party had expected, until that night when the Speaker, Rahman Gajraj, indulging his biases against the Bill, allowed every member of the Opposition to speak until near midnight when the House rose. Jagan was incensed. Outside in the corridor he, his brother Derek, and colleagues Victor Downer and Mohamed Shaffee upbraided Gajraj for his conduct of the debate. Gajraj responded by promptly suspending the four thus placing the Government in a minority position and facing certain defeat if the matter came to a vote. Jagan avoided the threat by proroguing the Legislature! The bill effectively died. The news was all over the country in a trice, some even spreading a rumour that the Government had fallen.

All expected that the strike would then come to an end. But that was not to be. Strike leaders were taken aback--their *causa belli* stilled--and floundered, directionless, until Burnham, D'Aguiar and other forces in the wings found new issues to justify anti-Jagan action: they announced fears that the Bill would be re-introduced, and demanded agreement on strike pay. They emphasised these with uglier and more frightening ways to express their views, aided by generous financing by US-based agencies: Government, union, and private. The tactics adopted included "aggressive de-stabilising" of government, harassment of Indians, closure of businesses and stoppage of government services, in other words, "lethal violence"! By this they hoped to terrorize people to the point of bringing individual and collective pressures on Government, or alternatively change allegiances. But this was a shallow assessment of both the Government and of their voter base, particularly Indians. Neither knuckled under and instead, to the dismay of the opposition and its militant lieutenants, Jagan survived the storm, denying strike pay but promising to stay the Bill for four months.

In an unusual political circumstance that could probably have occurred only in a colony or third-rate republic, House of Assembly Speaker Gajraj had continued to serve as a Councillor on the Georgetown Town Council. He was enjoined by the Constitution to be impartial in the House and refrain from partisan or personal comment on any legislation. However he felt he could say what he wished in the Town Council on any matter that affected the city. A short time after withdrawal of the Labour Relations Bill, he denounced Jagan and the PPP in the Council, expressed grave distrust of their motives and his fears of a sell-out of the gestating nation to Communism. He declaimed that the PPP was a threat to "the liberty of the citizen" and that despite its promises, the Government would reintroduce the Labour Bill as soon as things had settled. This was a highly unlikely outcome, which Gajraj knew, perhaps better than most, but he could not resist the chance of doing what he could not have done in the House, to state his personal opposition to the Bill and to the Government. The press pounced on his remarks and gave them much publicity. Gajraj, a Muslim, spoke to the Muslim Youth Organisation, urging its members to steer clear of communism, as it was anti-religious and against the teachings of the Quran. One youth asked him if that were so why had so many Muslim states in the Middle East aligned with the Soviets, who had been giving them financial and military aid for ten years at least? In fact did the USSR not threaten the UK and France when they moved against Nasser's take-over of the Suez Canal? Mr Gajraj was stumped!

The immediate relief and cautious optimism that followed the withdrawal of the Bill gave way abruptly to suspense then outrage as the strike continued. People were suffering everywhere, from joblessness, hunger, social strife and economic decay. Line-ups for every basic commodity had become routine. It was unbearable to witness children moaning in a bakery queue, and their mothers screaming in anguish when their turn came, only to be told they had arrived too late. Amid the tension and the hate there were acts of uncommon kindness; an old man who had waited in line for four hours tore his small loaf and handed half to a woman clutching her wailing child to her breast. He was Indian; she was black. Not far off at a kerosene pump, a black woman was pouring kerosene oil, the last precious purchase that day, from her half-bottle into that of an Indian boy shedding silent tears because he had none. Similar acts of compassion and sharing were repeated all over that troubled city among those without voices and of all races, the real victims whom the politicians sought out only for the vote, but whose feelings and aspirations had little place in policy or operational strategy.

Although terror had increased with the strike and shortages and suspension of services were ravaging the populace, the real fury and brutality of Burnham, D'Aguiar, their coaches and minions remained to be unleashed. The PPP, in its turn, mounted provocations of its own at a time when Jagan could have shown ideological moderation, if not statesmanship. This phase began on May 30 at the funeral procession of Senator Claude Christian, who had briefly held the position of Minister of Home Affairs, and had died of natural causes. Not to be overlooked the opposition incredibly started a rumour that Janet Jagan had stabbed him!

At the funeral it seemed that the entire PPP had joined the cortège, and Jagan was accused of turning the procession into a political rally unlawful under the Emergency Regulations. Hostile Black crowds surged among the mourners attacking them with stones and clubs, injuring Jagan and a few other officials of Government, then calling the PPP hypocrites and bandits, carried the action into city streets sending scores to hospital, some with life-threatening injuries. Skirmishes with civilians and Police occurred throughout the southern part of the city for several hours. We were kept busy at the hospital, and were hard put, with supplies running low and only a skeleton staff at the Ministry and at our main suppliers, the Government Pharmacy (despite its name, it was our main source of all government hospital supplies, not just pharmaceuticals). Police foot patrols had increased, especially near business centres, and where possible one Black was paired with an Indian, the former armed.

At the Hospital we felt the frustration acutely. The laboratory could not do many tests--including most of the emergency ones--due to lack of supplies--and had to conserve what supplies were left and restrict tests to essentials. Staff were thus idle and took the opportunity to house-clean to distract themselves or else sit in tight anxious knots in their sections, wondering how they would behave towards those who had illegally joined the strike, or if a mob were to invade the premises.

Section heads, meeting to brief clinicians and get their opinion on further emergency planning, expressed their frustrations. Some discussion took place on the work we had hoped to do to follow up on the problems we had unearthed re high heart attack rates and diabetes in Indians. Dr Hamilton was continuing his work on hypertension and strokes and Walter had a full slate with the sequels of polio epidemic and the heart disease cases due to German measles. Everyone knew of the difficulties he had in getting to Trinidad for the Conference and were upset enough with Nicholson's demand for inclusion as an author *and* to read the paper—to which he had contributed little, if anything--that we thought a meeting with him necessary as soon as the strike was over. They knew too that his demand had made me withdraw or rather not submit my abstract of heart disease in Indians although the title had been submitted. This all felt was a serious ethical issue. They also wished to take up the problems of Amerindian Health which I had brought up with the Ministry on returning from the interior but so far the reply had been "no funds", and not even a casual discussion. These long-term issues were now eclipsed by security and shortages of materials.

"They want us to do all things with no supplies." Gool Khan, the Lab. Manager said.

"The legislature prorogued over a week ago and the bloody bill lapsed. Why in hell this strike still on? And all this damned fighting?" Joe Drepaul, the tall lanky microbiologist, asked irritably.

"I don't think Burnham is satisfied with that." Ramjas Tiwari, the heavy-set haematology head said. "You convinced now that the real reason for the strike is to bring Jagan down? You remember all the offers of power-sharing Jagan made since last year? He rejected all."

"Common knowledge. No secret!" Dr Walter Singh, my friend and co-researcher, a staunch Jagan ally, said with some passion. "Cheddi made a big mistake there; it gave Burnham more confidence to keep up the terror; he has nothing to lose. Cheddi complaining all over, to the Governor, the Army, to Police Chief that Burnham and PNC getting away with murder, while PPP activists get arrested for the least thing. And now that two-faced rass Gajraj did not help by speaking in the Town Council the way he did; stirring up more divisions. Speakers should remain neutral, no matter what the platform, or where he is. He rass should resign."

"You're right. With reference to the strike, Balwant says they're arguing over strike pay and TUC wants assurances that Jagan won't bring back the bill." Gool Khan, the suave lab manager said, in his distinct accent honed from years in Britain, patting his brow delicately with a handkerchief.

"That's a nonsense request. Mere provocation." Dr Brahmam--representing internists--declared, rather solemnly. "You can't ask Government not to introduce legislation they told you they will bring on. That's an issue for the next election. Until then we have to live with it if we pretend to democracy."

"Right, but people feel we're not a democracy, have no hope of getting there with the goons we have as leaders," Drepaul said, "and the unions say they don't trust this Government to stay out of unions and that the Bill gives too much power to the Minister and the Commissioner of Labour."

"But they did get some amendments to reduce that." Khan observed.

"Maybe so; I hear the same argument." I said. "Even Frank Denbow said so a few days ago; but they're wrong; when the Bill died, amendments died; so they have to negotiate from scratch."

"In any case they can't re-introduce that legislation for at least four months." Khan said.

"So that's dead, at least for now; but strike pay is still a sore point." Drepaul said.

"And probably will stay so. Jagan is adamant he won't pay wages to illegal strikers." Brahmam said. "The TUC asked the British TUC for help with the strike pay issue, and they sent a fellow named Bob Willis from the Typographical Workers Union to try to mediate."

"So this strike will continue and the violence will get worse until that is settled; I can't see any good coming out of mob rule." Walter said cynically. "Burnham has smelled blood; the strike will continue. He wants to kick Cheddi out! Last year he tried to burn him down."

"Justifying the name Burn'em *Argosy* gave him years ago." I said.

"It's peculiar paradox," Brahmam observed, "like what happened in '47 when Palestinians rejected partition; that was bad mistake which pleased Jews, because Jewish portion then had 45% Arabs whose high birth rate would've quickly made them majority there too. So Jews seized the chance to buy up spare lands, most of which was state-owned, and evicted the unsuspecting Arabs."

"So Burnham is secretly glad that Jagan refused strike pay;" I added, "we felt it was a red herring to begin with anyway, a bargaining chip; Burnham already knew Jagan's response, and that gives him the excuse to continue havoc and put his civil war plan into action."

"You're talking about the PNC war plans the Police discovered recently? Anybody surprised?" Walter asked. "Only problem is they don't have anyone able to organise all that."

"Oh, but they do; the place stinks of outside agencies." Tiwari proclaimed.

"I agree, they're everywhere, CIA and other US organisations." said Brahmam.

"Why are we otherwise intelligent people allowing these assholes to wreck this poor country?" Drepaul asked, in exasperation. "Can't we do something about it? It's plain to see that we have fools in power only interested in themselves."

"They're not wrecking it; they're hijacking it! Like Mafia!" I offered, dejectedly.

"While we stand by passively and watch it happen. Tch, Tch!" Tiwari shook his head.

"You want to take on the CIA, MI 5, which one, or both? And local press?" I asked.

"You're serious, I can tell. I always suspected that those two were directing things; they're the real enemy. Burnham and D'Aguiar are the tools to screw Jagan. It figures." Drepaul nodded.

"The people here have already become so polarised that it would be difficult to bring them together even if this political strike is settled;" Dr Brahmam said, shaking his head from side to side. "That would become permanent sore and this place will be another Palestine."

"We're now a battleground in the Cold War and Cheddi denies it while Burnham revels in it." I said. "He heard of some conciliation efforts we started here mainly to provide proper information on Hinduism and Islam, based on the positive reception we had to this on that interior trip with the police eighteen months ago. I have to thank you, my friend, for all the lessons on Indian history, which I used to explain who we are and what we stand for; they've swallowed the British propaganda and we have not taken the time to correct it. If we don't we can't live together in peace. No matter what, if you waste Burnham today, someone will replace him; there are many just as cruel in the PNC and outside who would murder for a price. Balgobin tells me that the Negroes are already saying that what we say is new nonsense and telling people not to listen. Now if Jagan would only leave Marx in his grave and smell the reality of what his line, now 16 years old, has done and change to a centrist policy we might have a chance to overcome all this. Otherwise it's grief; the poor will suffer most."

"You know, as we've talked of this before, I share your worry;" Walter said, reflecting on possibilities we had discussed including setting up a medical clinic there with Stanley. "I even thought of getting Forsythe–he's our old schoolmaster—to take this on and make DeHoop a centre for inter-racial cooperation and hold weekend workshops there on racial knowledge. It's the money to do it; anybody rich enough to sponsor such a thing?"

"Even if you can find a rich person to do this, I believe Burnham's goons will move in and blow you away." Drepaul said.

"It could work, with enough money, "Ramjas offered, "but Cheddi has to agree and do the right thing; he doesn't lack for telling, but he keeps burning his bridges."

"Makes me want to move to frigging Skeldon, or cold Canada, which would please Jacquie!" Walter said, ruefully.

"Or better, Kamarang, Barama or even the Rupununi." I suggested, half seriously.

"And I can go back to India, even Kerala with Namboo and his Communists!"

"Anywhere except this hell-hole." Khan concluded.

At a street corner near Bourda Market, on a fine morning a few days later, in early June, a young black man in tattered khakis, a short pointed beard elongating his narrow face, stood on a box, a foot high, a megaphone to his mouth, his voice a high pitched crackle as he harangued the small group that had stopped to listen, a few Indians and Portuguese shoppers in a tight cluster off to one side. They, like everyone else were there early to buy up any food item they could get, and searching everywhere for cooking oil, flour and kerosene. He said many things about Black history and African geography, most of it incorrect, but evocative. When he saw that they were listening, he sailed into a "call for war."

"This strike not done yet; alyou t'ink it done? No maan, it jus' start. We kill the Bill. Now we gwine get the rest o' you. You all mus' know that Cheddi building a secret army, but let him, we 'ave we own; we gwine fight him and we gwine beat him; we gwine kill all you coolie, and you Putaguee better keep you' place. You watchin' me? Hear what I say, and we gwine let you go today so you can tell all you' friends and family. We gwine stop all work, and you gwine stop work, whether you union or no union; we will take we licks but we will give it first and last. We will get you, with gun and bomb, we will get you; we not frighten, for everyone o' we you get, we going get t'ree or four o' you. Like Joshua at the gates of Jericho! The day of reckoning is at hand. If Cheddi don't free we now blood will flow, an' is you blood; you watch!" Then he burst into a little ditty:

"Putaguee, metagee,
You white, you right,
You black, you slack,
You yellow, you jello,
You brown, you drown
In a sea of black faaayces."

He paused briefly, then continued, "Hear me, hear me good. Listen to the words. Alyou just come and alyou coolie, Putaguee and Chinee, all alyou tief we land; alyou na belong hey. We belong hey; we dey hey long long time! T'ousand years we dey hey! T'ousand!"

A young Indian man with a cultured look and accent, a teacher perhaps, detached himself from the crowd and fearlessly accosted the speaker, "That's wrong; you here just over three hundred years; you don't have to spread lies. Is true I can't trace my people here more than a hundred and twenty years, but that don't mean I have less rights; neither of us has an ancestral right to this land even though we can claim the rights of birth."

"Oho, you find breath, coolie! You talk refine'! Well hear this, my people spilled their blood here, their sweat and tears."

"And so did mine, in the same fields as yours. Where's the difference?"

"We were promised this land."

"By whom?"

"Queen Victoria give us this land!"

"So, you got it from thieves who stole the land from the natives, the rightful owners! That don't mean you own it; you don't own a damn thing if you don't have title. The white man's laws govern now and that's what we go by. Title! If you want to be fair and decent, you should give everything back to the bucks, and let them decide. I'm willing to do that, are you?" He stared with disdain at the man, his megaphone drooping, his mien quizzical, waited for a minute, got no response, hissed his teeth, turned and walked off.

The black man stared at the retreating back now out of earshot, scratched his head, coughed and spat in front of him, shook himself and resumed his diatribe. A few policemen from the group on regular duty at the market listened impassively, and let him rant on. After half an hour in the same vein, he renewed his threat, saying "Ah you wait; you think we jokin'; see what happen tomorrow!" Whereupon he stepped down from the box, put on a wide-brimmed straw hat, picked up the box, placed the megaphone in it and walked off along the South Road canal, biting into a large mango, one of two that he had casually taken from a vendor's tray without paying, in full view of the police.

On June 10th mobs invaded the Legislative Buildings. We had a great view from my sister's home across the street, its array of continuous windows now closed to deflect bombs and gifts of Molotov cocktails. We peeked from the third floor casements--too far and too narrow except for the most formidable hurler--at the milling throng of sweaty men and screaming women that filled Hadfield Street with a continuous inflow east from Lombard Street and west from High Street meeting in the middle like two colliding currents and erupting in a thunderous roar at the barred and guarded rear entrance to the Buildings. Waving excitedly towards the edifice, they banged the iron fence with staves, pieces of lead pipe and bicycle chains creating a cacophony that filled the angry air.

Their way blocked at the gate, they ignored the armed guards inside and in unison began to scale the fence while the guards looked on, taking no action except to safeguard their persons. Not that they were in any danger, unless they tried to do their duty, as all were black men, perhaps kin to some of those now swarming the premises and racing across the grounds towards the entrances, just as Jagan emerged protected by Police, who escorted him to safety, but not without fierce jostling and dire verbal threats. The crowds grew restive after the target had left, but hurried to disperse as sudden explosions of tear gas canisters sent men and women choking and spluttering from the scene. Many felonies were committed in plain view of the Police, from simple purse snatching to severe assaults and attempted rape of Indians in full public view.

They returned the next day and in the melee crowds assaulted a youth and a girl who had erred in riding their bicycles along High St while the main crowd was at the barricades and fences, and the street quite clear. The youth was dragged off his bicycle and mauled while the girl was grabbed but jumped off her bicycle letting it fall towards her assailants allowing her to run screaming into our yard, the gate guard hastily allowing her in before the gang got there. Even so they began shaking the gate and cursing in the most hateful manner, determined to invade the premises, but desisted when Mr Yhap, our Chinese neighbour, appeared on the scene and talked them out of it; this was providential, as my brother Buddy had hastened to her aid and from a strategic position was aiming his shotgun at the leaders. He told me later he wasn't sure whether he would have fired without warning, but the terrified girl, no more than fifteen, was in hysterics, screaming, cowering at his feet.

Elsewhere Minister Wilson was set upon at the Post Office building on Hincks Street; and at the Stabroek Market vendors had their wares looted, several were beaten and robbed, while struggling others saw their small stands and glass cases of merchandise smashed and destroyed. In one pathetic scene a slender older lady, who--with her case of Indian sweets that she made fresh every night--had been a fixture at that spot for over twenty years, saw her *mithai: payrah, jilaybi, dhnouri* and *badam laccha* spilled on the pavement, mixing there with splintered glass and fragments of orange, tangerine and fig bananas from the stand next to hers, both tumbled and crushed underfoot by the marauders, and mixed into a bizarre salad, as if ordered by the devil himself. The two women--one Indian, slender with fine facial features, a blue knee-length apron over a floral dress topped with a Madras headkerchief, shaking her head in disbelief; the other Black, obese, round-faced, with a blue and white chequered apron over a denim dress, wide-brimmed straw hat, both looking stunned and violated, standing side by side staring at the wreckage — suddenly broke out into a piteous wailing, embraced rocking gently sideways as their bodies shook with grief and consoled each other.

Other major violence centred on the Rice Marketing Board wharf where USSR and Cuban ships had docked to unload relief cargo, and at the Electricity Company, where my friend Rayman Bacchus worked as an accountant. He related the harrowing scene as the mob mauled the guards and invaded the premises, reaching his office, where he was threatened, as the entire staff had been, unless he left. He tried to talk the mob into reason, using all his skills as a negotiator, told them he was PNC, which they believed when they saw on his desk a picture of himself and his coloured wife; eventually he persuaded them to leave just as the Police arrived. Another major assault took place at the Water Works, where a mob tried to shut down operations. The multifocal attacks divided the Police while a contingent of the British Army sat oiling their guns 26 miles away at Atkinson field, and its commander lounged sucking on his pipe pretending nothing was happening. The governor too, despite calls from his own kind, agreed that there was no cause for alarm. Nero fiddled!

"Is what the hell happen to these people? They gone mad!" Zaman rhetorically asked Buddy on arriving at the store after working his way around the belligerent throngs in Hadfield Street. He and Sam, his younger brother (11 years earlier they were almost my brothers-in-law) had come in from the family farm at Bara-Bara, Mahaicony for regular supplies. In normal times they would make the 50-mile trip weekly, but with the shortage of gasoline they had reduced that to once monthly. This was his second trip since the strike began, and although he had heard radio news reports of the tumult in the city, he was not prepared for the almost suicidal abandon of the mobs he had encountered. "They block the road at Buxton and Kitty, shouting and threatening, and so close to the Police Station you wonder what in hell the Police doing. We almost turn back; we might catch hell going back. And the road so damn bad it took nearly three hours to get here."

"You're lucky; that same road ruptured two of my tires a few months ago; it's dreadful." I said. I had arrived a few minutes earlier after picking up my sons at their school, and to deliver two gallons of gasoline I had saved for Buddy.

"What's happening in the country?"

"None of this mess; but a few days ago the Police did find some stuff to make explosives hidden in bush at the Mahaica race track, and they investigating a black gang people saw going and coming. If it wasn't for the shortages, we in the Creek wouldn't know anything wrong."

Our friend, Crozack, in the store at the time, joined the conversation, and said, teasingly, "I can't understand you Indians; you disagree with nearly everything that Jagan stand for and yet you voted for him."

"Same with you and Burnham. If you say you agree with him, I won't believe you." I said.

"Well, they cut from the same cloth."

"Except that Cheddi treat the whole country as if it's one big sugar estate and every living soul a cane-cutter." Sam observed. "So his plans for the country goin' stray."

"That's why he brought in all these bookish foreigners with no practical knowledge or experience of little places like this, like this fellow Kaldor that caused him grief last year. He refuses to see that BG is a great opportunity for local talent to develop local solutions." I said.

"You're right, looks like they took big country situations and scaled them down to fit ours; a bad approach; and then Jagan wonders why people with savvy objected." Zaman said.

"And then he called them reactionary and bourgeois stooges, whatever that is, and chased them away," Buddy said. "And when he comes here, we treat him like a king."

"It's his insecurity." I said.

"When he failed to form a moderate and stable government, he knew he was sidelining local entrepreneurs and setting things up for the state to take over businesses. All the talk about glass and other factories is just smoke and mirrors." Sam said. "And the worst part is that's small fry compared with what he could get from tackling drainage, and going back to the Hutchinson scheme. That alone could make all of us rich."

Sam was an intellectual; his district had chosen him, despite his youth, to form and head the local farm cooperative that had so far reduced cost and increased efficiency of transportation and had begun to tackle warehousing and milling. Bred in the city and resenting the move to the country the family had made fifteen years earlier, he had adapted to rural life, studied its problems and, with his brothers, had brought a scientific and market-oriented approach to farming, engaging the experts at every turn; he had finally declared rural life an intellectual challenge and "the only thing now for me".

"When you ask Jagan about Hutchinson he says the Brits scuttled it, the sugar barons opposed it, and that it's too expensive and too long-term; the people want jobs now." I said.

"But he's missing the point; the jobs begin the day the scheme is approved; a long-term scheme would offer job stability and create conditions for us to plan and expand agriculture in a predictable way and create many more jobs than the airy fairy factories he keeps promising; right now the best lands outside the estates are either flooded or too dry." Sam noted.

"He really has no excuse; it's a blind spot. It simply doesn't fit in with his commie plans." Buddy said. He was quite familiar with Jagan's arguments, from their frequent meetings at the store. "I tell Sister Mahadai that all the time, and you know she agrees with me, and still gives him money every time he shows up. I tell him to come with me into the country any Sunday and see how we have to rake and scrape to make a few cents, and then he turn around and cripple us with taxes and duties. Now with no gas I can't even do that. The man's nuts."

"Incredible; and he talks so much about improving the lot of the people, but does the opposite!" Zaman agreed.

"Now he's stewing in his own juice, he blames everyone else for his failures, while Odo firing up the people to keep pressuring him, thinking he'll give in." Crozack said.

"That's where Burnham is dead wrong; Jagan is too stubborn to do that; besides his mania drives him on and bloats his ego; he won't quit; they'll all have to gang up on him to force him out, by legislation, like in '53," I said. "This illegal protest reach this scale only because CIA stoking it."

"They might do a Lumumba on him." Sam suggested grimly.

"He must know that's a possibility; I can tell you it's not a good feeling to have, to know a gun is pointed at you, even figuratively. He's got to be uncomfortable." I said.

"What you know about that?" Zaman asked.

"Didn't you hear? Few weeks ago, they aimed a rifle at him and nearly killed him; and the next day started a fire in his garage." Buddy explained.

They all looked incredulous, or likely stunned; but then the papers and radio were daily reporting the many instances of violence and even death to ordinary citizens.

"For true? What happened?" Sam asked. "I didn't see anything in the papers, and I read all of them, and listen every night to the news. The papers even inciting hatred and violence. Maan, the *Chronicle* really out for war, and *Post* is not too far behind. But nothing 'bout that."

"If it makes the PNC or UF look bad, they won't print it." Crozack opined.

They knew about the roving mobs that swarmed the streets, disrupting businesses and terrorising government offices to enforce the strike, even coercing those in essential services and those who were not union members. I told them about the mob that had visited the hospital soon after the strike had started, and the exchange of views we had had.[161]

"Good grief!" Sam exclaimed, "and you went back to work as if nothing happened? I wonder what I would ha' done if someone aimed a .303 at me. Maan, I nearly drown a few years ago, and every time I see the river, I get the feeling all over again; it's not too bad now. So, how you feel?"

"I'm OK; but I shudder sometimes when I think of it. I can still see his face clearly."

"Boy, how things can change and a good life snuff out for stupidness." Zaman mused.

"These same leaders incitin' mobs to terrorise people here and every Sunday they have big parties and games up in Abary, with girls from town, lots of booze, speed boat races, and they raise hell; they even have armed guards dress up like policemen stopping all traffic on the dam and the river until they leave."

Sam described the spread where Burnham and his partners, all lawyers, had established a large farm, squatting on government lands, with lots of cattle, mostly stolen from Mahaicony and Mahaica areas. It was managed by a well-known malefactor from Mahaicony nicknamed Dougla Alfred. The place had become the private getaway for PNC leaders and senior ranks and rumoured to attract a guest list of both sexes that would surprise the miscreant rabble that did Burnham's dirty work for the pittance the Party provided and what loot they could capture and retain. Hypocrisy!

When the mobs blockaded the Public Buildings that day Education Minister Nunes was beaten as he left the buildings just ahead of other legislators and tried to make his way through the gesticulating crowd across High St to get

---

[161] See Ch. 16: 7-11

to his office.[162] Inflamed by success of this intimidation and assault, the mob stormed the Public Buildings and with clenched fists, swinging sticks and chains they frightened all those around, in and out of the building, blocking the exits and trapping inside several politicians including Jagan. Traffic travelling South on High hastily turned aside into side streets before reaching Brickdam. The riot squad arrived, cleared the gateway with some difficulty, but hardly contained the excited mob. Asst Commissioner Carl Austin reached Jagan's side, and with pistol drawn, escorted him to his car. But the mob was unrelenting, shouted abuses at Austin for protecting "the coolie", and pressed against the car, which eventually was able to move off, but not before the mob had thrown stones at and into the car, one of which struck the policeman sitting beside Jagan in the rear seat, injuring his jaw. Jagan and his Ministers having left, the mob grumblingly dispersed, leaving a sizable knot of testy men arguing on the sidewalk at Hadfield and High Streets

With fuel running cripplingly low Jagan unwisely sent his private secretary Jack Kelshall to Port of Spain to negotiate an oil shipment. He should have known that the mission would fail. Kelshall was not an elected member of the Guianese Legislature, and had come to Trinidad as the emissary of a man whose remaining days as head of a government were few, and Eric Williams was not the one to do anything to extend them. In fact, anything he could do to hasten Jagan's political demise would help his own cause in Trinidad. Secondly, Kelshall was a Trinidadian and almost *persona non grata* with Williams' government for his role as a pro-communist agitator and member of a group closely watched by the Trinidad Police, and might have been arrested if he did not have "diplomatic" status. There was no chance therefore that a Trinidad official would see him.

Jagan fumed as Eric Williams ignored Kelshall, but Shell Co. sent a shipment, which could not be unloaded at the Ramsburg terminus on the East Bank Demerara, because of strike action and threats. It went instead to the New Amsterdam depot, but that closed as the Company reacted to further threats. A week or so later, mob activities intensified around the Public Buildings, which the Police treated with tear gas, while Jagan told the people by radio of his failed efforts yet again to get the Governor, the police commissioner and the army under Commander Pemberton to work together to bring peace.

In an increasingly tense atmosphere, with opposition militancy whipped up by an intensive campaign of speeches, pamphlets, newspaper articles and letters, the terror entered a new phase. In the third week in June (17-25), bombs lobbed into homes in the night killed four civilians in separate incidents, injuring others, while daytime explosions destroyed sections of the premises of many Government buildings, including the Transport & Harbours Department, the Campbellville Government school, the main Georgetown ferry stelling, the Ministry of Home Affairs, the Ministry of Labour, Health & Housing, the Central Housing & Planning Department and the Education Department. Several were

---

[162] This building, known as the *White Elephant* since its erection in 1947, had been the administrative hub of the US air base at Atkinson field during WWII and had been "bought" by the Interim Government, amid financial scandal, dismantled and re-erected at the High St site opposite the main Legislature. It was companion to the block of flats where I lived, formerly officers' apartments. Both were built entirely of wood, considered fire traps then, and remained draughty, "porous" and otherwise substandard, despite expensive refurbishing. Neither had been built by the US army as permanent structures.

injured, some seriously, at each site but no one killed immediately. Nearly all the victims were Indians.

In one dramatic scene, more like a movie than real life, a huge charge tied to the pilings of the Rice Marketing Board wharf where two ships were unloading cargo, was discovered minutes before the lit fuses had reached the explosives. Another was discovered similarly at the Licensing and Revenue offices that had my friend Leslie Romalho, head of the section, sweating and recounting his story for days[163].

When the bombs began to go off, city Indians sent their wives and children to stay with family in the countryside. There they finally learned at first-hand what it meant to be without indoor plumbing, running water, electricity and learned all about pit latrines and tolerance for the pervasive smells of live animals, human indoor slop and strong disinfectants like *natolean*. The older folk, or some of them, took the deprivations in their stride, some finally understanding why their rural relatives were usually unsympathetic with their continuing demands for this or that 'luxury'. But their children were like fish out of water. One incident highlighted the dangers of unfamiliarity; a child went unattended into a latrine, sat on the adult seat, too wide for him, promptly slid through and fell into the cesspit. His action had been witnessed and an alarm led to his rescue but not before he had inhaled and swallowed excreta. He died in hospital of fulminating inhalation pneumonia.

We met at Dr Leslie Luck's bungalow on the hospital grounds. The escalating violence in the city was threatening the hospital as gangs such as the one that had terrorised the laboratory and taken aim at me roamed throughout the city and sporadically into the countryside. The battle was for Georgetown; you take the capital city, you take the country. Burnham understood that. Jagan seemingly never did. With fires set in my garage and Harold Hamilton's it was plain that the Hospital targets would expand. Surprisingly neither Jagan nor any Minister visited these scenes or talked to those affected. Pipe bombs had already caused four deaths, all Indians, and many injuries. The investigations--after we had done extensive forensic autopsies and recovered homemade shrapnel--were taken over by a unit of the CID and I heard no more of them. Even my file copies of the autopsies were sealed. The tumult continued, and fears multiplied. The bombing of Government offices brought the Hospital back into focus as a probable target; the threats had been plain enough.

The meeting of physicians, which included a senior police officer, discussed the ominous situation and debated possible actions. It was clear that the Police were too stretched to properly patrol the hospital compound, and equally obvious that hospital staff were too partisan, and therefore compromised and untrustworthy, particularly the security staff. We decided to do our own patrols as 'vigilantes' throughout the night, working in pairs, starting immediately. We might have been naïve but there was nothing else we could do.

---

[163] In 1968, I was entertained at dinner by Raymond Smith, a British sociologist and his Guianese wife, at their home in Chicago where Ray had a chair in Sociology at the University of Chicago. He had studied the various peoples of BG, but astonished me with the news that just before the strike started he had visited Georgetown in an effort to get Jagan and Burnham to reconsider their polarisation of politics; he managed to get a meeting, which was held in a car driving around the city, since neither could agree on a venue! The meeting was a frustration. The only new thing was Burnham's amused claim that Queen Elizabeth had offered him the Governor Generalship of an independent Guiana under Jagan, which he had promptly rejected.

Leslie Luck and I drew lots for the first night. Armed with stout purpleheart sticks and flashlights, we did systematic rounds of the compound, gingerly probing dark doorways and alcoves and checking the public areas, noting who was there. The officer had briefed us on what to look for, in the case of bombs, and signs of tampering and intrusion or break-in, what to do, and more important, what not to do. The Hospital administration had issued a directive detailing tighter security controls and enforcing identification rules. It was not in favour of our decision, but did not obstruct it (in fact the Secretary privately endorsed it).

It was a dark night. Circles of light under lampposts provided dim illumination in the state of brownouts then prevailing. We spent two hours on that first round, between 10 and 12 pm and regrouped at 2.00 am for our second. We spent an hour inspecting the southern half of the compound, and noted that the main gates on either side of Newmarket St, which bisected the Hospital grounds, were secure and only the northern postern unlocked, to allow access to the Casualty department just inside the gate. On our second circuit, just before 3 am, we came to this gate and saw a freshly dug hole in the ground about twelve feet from the entrance to the Casualty department where a small crowd waited patiently under the glare of a naked bulb hanging from the ceiling. A nurse was tending a child nestled in its mother's arms, while a man's body, breathing heavily, was sprawled across two chairs nearby; a pregnant woman sat, hands clasped on her swollen abdomen, her head resting on her spouse's shoulder; two older women sat silently, bolt upright with stoic faces, while other shapes loomed in the shadows, some fidgeting, two children sleeping on parents' laps. Altogether there were over a dozen people, all black, in the room, which at any hour in the daytime would have had fifty or more.

The hole was a perfect circle, 2 inches in diameter, freshly dug, with loose soil heaped around its rim as if an ant had dug it, and more brushed aside. My flashlight showed that it was empty but it was difficult to see detail below eight or ten inches. Leslie found the gateman, who had been off his post, on a break, he said, for about twenty minutes, and had seen no one. We recalled the guidance by the police officer and called the number he had given us. In about ten minutes a constable arrived on his bicycle from the nearby Alberttown Police station; he looked at the hole, and straightway ran up the flight of stairs to the telephone operator located above the Casualty Department.

Half an hour later two officers arrived from the Central Police Station Explosives Division; they carefully inspected the hole, which was indeed empty and eighteen inches deep, made with a type of augur used in heavy industry. They concluded that it was meant to carry a substantial charge, like others that they had studied across the city, including a dozen or more that had gone off creating considerable damage, injuries and loss of life. They suggested that we might have interrupted the operation and had it been charged and exploded it would have taken the Casualty department with it. We might even have seen the persons responsible, among those entering the Casualty Department, perhaps with a bandaged head or arm in a sling. As we stood there several young black men had moved past, with head or leg bandages, arm slings, or hobbling on crutches. How many of these were real, how many simply in disguise? The police, we later learned, had quickly identified the source of the bombs, the makers, their affiliations and prime locations from materials seized at PNC headquarters, Congress House, in May, but curiously no arrests were ever made.

Leslie was upset at the revelation; the news spread quickly through the hospital, but to no one's surprise, nothing appeared in the papers about it, just as nothing had appeared about the rifleman and me, or about the threats levelled at hospital workers who refused to join the strike. It was one of those gaps in the coverage of strike events that kept the public from knowing some of the baser tactics of the opposition in its aim to bring down the government; they would not have reacted well to news of potentially lethal attacks against hospital staff who should be there to help when the time came.

One by one, like refugees in the dead of night, expatriate and Guianese physicians quietly left the country, along with thousands of others in a massive exodus of talent. Months earlier, Ghose, the Indian radiologist, Murray, the Antiguan Ophthalmologist had left for Britain and Rayman, a Guianese Obstetrician, for Canada. Das Gupta, the ENT surgeon, also went off to the UK. Leslie Luck left for Barbados. Grewal, Stracey and Shenolikar--three Indian surgeons--left, the last from St Joseph's Hospital. But it was the flight of Dr Frank Chandra–hounded out of his position as a respected leprologist and Head of the Mahaica Hospital--that should have jolted Jagan to reflect on the terrible state to which the people had descended where reason had given way to anarchy and self-destruction. But Jagan scoffed at the departures, even Dr Chandra's, calling the individuals cowards and worthless bourgeoisie and not "relevant to my struggle". He would remain unmoved by the issues of forced emigration and the drain of talent blaming them on everything other than the policies of the PPP.

Chapter 18

Against the background of escalating violence and the prolonged strike a prestigious group of citizens discuss partition along major ethnic lines. Secret talks are held with neighbours favouring the idea with the prospect of forming alliances of like cultures. The hurdles are enormous but negotiable, especially as the US seems favourable, yet the step is too radical for leaders whose soaring ambition is all or none; pragmatism and logical thinking do not enter into the formula, despite the collapse of the WI Federation. Politicians exploit hunger and desperation as tools of protest and anarchy. As fuel and other staples near exhaustion Cuba sends a shipment of oil and USSR sends wheat. They provoke harsh reactions.

Lifeline: partition

"The government of England is as great as, if not the greatest perfection of fraud and corruption that ever took place since governments began. Tom Paine 1792

Reason, recognizing that only that is enduring which is just, asks whether the thing proposed ought to be done; force says, I desire, I can, I will. US Sen. W J Bryan

Peace has no heroes in our civilisation. Nor does harmony and lack of strife. If a leader wishes immortality and he cannot repeat what Krishna, Jesus or Gandhi did, then he must choose some form of anarchy and promote that with all the vigour he can muster. He must! Author

The group of men had gathered almost by accident, hurriedly, at the home of a prominent businessman. But its purpose was deliberate. The men were all informally dressed, though two or three had on light jackets and ties. Introductions were not made, and mostly not needed; by unspoken agreement no last names were used. As they milled around helping themselves to brandy, whisky or tea, and cigarettes or cigars from a bar discreetly occupying a corner of the room, a young Indian man unrolled a map of BG, spreading it across a board resting on an easel at one corner of the room below an elegant fluted sconce that sent an even glow across its face. He secured the map with thumb tacks, and adjusted the angle of the easel so that all could see it. The gleaming greenheart floor reflected the light from three corner lamps. The room was not air-conditioned, but the high ceiling, clerestory jalousies and northern exposure kept it naturally cool. They sat in upholstered chairs arranged along the perimeter or stood at the bar awaiting the last arrivals, and made small talk or smoked in silence. They represented all races, men of property and knowledge, and a few politicians. They looked and were uncommonly pensive, for men like them, accustomed to speak their mind and use every opportunity — this was a golden one — of "advertising" themselves and their businesses. A few lesser known shadowy figures sat silently in the far corner.

Outside in the city, the strike had long taken an ugly turn. Even as they sat there the dull thud of a distant explosion could be heard. For a second all ears were turned in the direction of the sound. Then there was silence. It was just past 7pm. Violence had been terrorising ordinary citizens day and night. The victims were mainly Indians, from slender old ladies assaulted for their jewellery to businessmen in their shops and political personalities at the Legislature and at home. In the past week guns and bombs had been thrown into the fray. Several people had been killed some for no reason other than that they were where the bomb or bullet had struck. The terror had to be experienced to be understood. It was everywhere; it filled the air; it permeated every breath one breathed; it stuck to the skin like sweat on a sticky day that never left, even after a long shower. Whatever emotions they might have expressed most adults had grown up in an atmosphere of law and order, a positive although at times brutal result of heavy-handed British rule to protect the minority whites. It was a British colony after all where, despite bias and restrictions, most ordinary citizens did enjoy freedom from molestation at all hours. But in the past two years, first terror had seized the city, then violence!

When the guests were all assembled and settled, the convenor, a slender black man of about 50 rose, crushed his cigarette, and using the bar as a prop, began to speak, his tone subdued. He said that his name was *Sam*[164], then welcomed them and explained that the session was "a sounding board to examine an idea that had begun to attract many thoughtful and influential people. The nation is now clearly divided ideologically, spiritually and racially. Let it be divided physically, to avoid further harm to our people." There was no surprise as one might have expected. Most remained impassive; a few nodded "You all know our good friend Ram," he nodded towards a younger man sitting on a stool beside him. "He'll now address you substantively, to begin our exploration of the issue. Ram?"

He sat down among them facing the new speaker, an Indian lawyer, about 40, dressed in a light blue suit, white shirt and a dark blue tie. He cleared his throat, took a sip of tea and began, slowly and unemotionally, like a child reciting his ABC.

"Thank you; thank you very much. I'm glad you all could come. This is very informal. What we say tonight should be for our ears only. We shant use any names for obvious reasons. Any personal discussion beyond this should be without reference to this meeting or to the persons here tonight. You probably all know one another, but not all may know the young man with the map; he's an incredible resource, and came to my help almost without my knowing he was there. Maps are his hobby; he became involved with me in an unrelated professional matter; he probably knows this country as well as anyone, and I mean the country, not just the coast." All eyed the slim 30'ish young man in long-sleeved white shirt and grey slacks sitting at the table. In turn he bowed and smiled briefly, with a fleeting flash of gold from an incisor filling.

"The world is in turmoil everywhere," Ram continued, "although we're supposed to be at peace, there is conflict, foolish conflict, induced conflict, provoked conflict, unnecessary conflict. Conflict that has arisen from deep divisions created in our society by external forces, first by European business, now American politics. The British who rule us are a major source of the division that is strangling this unborn nation, like a navel string tied around its fragile neck while in the birth canal. All over the world they invaded continents, drew lines on paper, just as we are doing here," he smiled momentarily, "and sometimes in sand. But they ignored native traditions and treaties, native animosities and native boundaries, and in many places cut across them like a hot knife through butter, creating entities that suited their own territorial and commercial needs. They split nations and brought friend and foe into the same tent; perhaps to unite them? No, to control them, to keep an eye on them, to teach them their ways, to lure each group into believing that it was better than the one next door, fomenting and exploiting traditional differences, sowing new suspicions and hatred among them, rewarding loyalty and creating local elites who would behave to their own people even as their masters had done;. Thus

---

[164] *Sam* and *Ram* are pseudonyms for actual participants; permission was not obtained to use names; the event is factual.

they enslaved the masses, converted them to their customs and religion and cultivated key natives in all groups to be surrogate rulers, and encouraged their ambitions, to what selfish and awful ends we have just begun to see; the now-defunct *Princes Council* in India is an especially egregious example. Now that Britain sees us as a liability and cannot afford to carry us, now that the world opposes colonial hegemonies, now that the colonised themselves are demanding release, we find that we will, in every colony, mark my words, in every colony, inherit a host of animosities that had been inculcated in our peoples fed by generations and even centuries of divisive upbringing culminating in the worst forms of prejudice—race and colour!"

He paused, drank from his teacup. No one spoke. Someone blew smoke in the air. Ram coughed briefly, then continued, "Are we surprised that wherever the British went there is now bitterness and war? People became their victims, not just their tools! In Palestine, Jews have seized Arab lands with British help; in India the Muslims bit off two huge chunks of Hindustan, and in Ceylon, Singhalese fight Tamil; in every nation of Africa, it's tribe versus tribe. I saw this first hand in Kenya, Uganda, Nyasaland, Tanganyika, Rhodesia and more tellingly in Nigeria, Ghana and French West Africa. Each is on the brink of grave internal conflict and faces a grim future, despite their abundance of resources, or perhaps because of that. And the same is true of the Belgian and Portuguese colonies. In Ruanda the Belgians officially segregated Tutsis and Hutus just as the Brits did Indian castes and African tribes. The Congo is in turmoil, highlighted by the Lumumba murder, a foolish piece of evil, for which those in the know blame the CIA. A new form of colonialism has replaced the old, with American and European sponsorship of local dictators in each emerging nation, educated clowns and egomaniacs picked for their greed and the power they hold over their fellows, whether political, traditional or military, and given the means to amass great wealth as long as they control the populace and make it easy and cheap for the foreigner to reap their resources, and so to continue to bleed Africa just as the Europeans have been doing for more than a century; we're well into that era now.

"The British on the eve of leaving incredibly forced the same people they had kept apart for so long to sudden alliances and federations, and expected them to forget old or induced animosities and succeed! How brazen! And now they blame those poor divided people for failure? What fools! And the more fools we! To heed these brutes who talked of a West Indian Federation! What a joke! That was a pre-ordained failure; any idiot could have seen that. There is no unity even among Caribbean Blacks. They're more heterogeneous than any other Caribbean group, from those who think purely in white terms to those in black, from rich to poor, educated to illiterate, urban to rural and so on—all these defining factors that prevent real integration; same for the other races. And when Jagan and Burnham agreed to withdraw from the UWI, they started its erosion as the one unifying force—save cricket—removing from it the leavening effect of Indian presence; Trinidad's alone is not enough, and they too are divided. In time, I fear, this newborn UWI will grow up as racial as those intellectuals in Jamaica who sideline Indians, who pretend we do not exist and would deny us a place in this region's history[165]. How shameful! How arrogant! How dangerous!

---

[165] In *A Short History of the West Indies*, Macmillan, London, 1971, GH Parry and PM Sherlock, both of whom I knew well at the UCWI, dealt briefly and cursorily with Indians, less than a page out of over 300, confirming this assessment!

"In our turn a local University will quiver in the wind as it faces academic isolation and inbreeding at the mercy of a Marxist Nkrumah-style curriculum; our children will lose perspective and the intellectual contact with people with whom they must associate as history unfolds, and the salutary effect of a multifaceted Caribbean presence of the highest calibre, in our midst. Indians are probably a bit better off economically than their African brothers. They can unite around religion and culture, if not ethnicities, and gain both breadth and depth which narrow isms cannot achieve and will not permit; but Blacks, what have they got? They've lost everything. They've become British. And those same British have spent a century to sequester us into discrete competing groups emphasising differences; here and in Trinidad that worked to create huge interracial barriers making virtual enemies of Indians and Blacks (and of others, I daresay) and now they expect that rift to heal by magic as they hustle to leave us to clean up their mess! And sadly, we have two egomaniacal leaders who exploit the divisions and have no real incentive to change; they are unlikely ever to unite in the real sense; if one governs the other will promote anarchy, as now. The Indians are likely to win each election so the current civil strife will only get worse, and as you see plainly, Jagan is incapable of containing violence, since he has no credibility, nor control over the forces of order or anarchy. All the talk we hear of his forming a Peoples' Militia is just that: talk! Where is the money? Where is the popular will? Where are the military men to take charge? Cuba? Therefore I say, for the sake of peace and future progress let us divide this country, so that our children can be freed from the danger of learning and breeding antagonisms and be allowed to develop the mentality and understanding to deal amicably with one another—the way India deals with Kenya or Nigeria. Only then can we federate, from a basis of knowledge and respect, not imposition, not false values nor strange and inappropriate philosophies. This is where both Jagan and Burnham have gone astray, and both are too ambitious and narcissistic to see it, or if they see it, to change."

"Hear, hear!" and "what the hell?" A murmur arose that filled the room. Surprise, agreement, alarm, rejection--the gamut of reaction. A stocky man with an Indian accent started to speak; the rest fell silent.

"I came here to help find a way to unite two major races," he said, "to prevent further bloodshed. But racial divisions are deep here; in India we had people that looked alike–at least at first glance--and we had religious tolerance; we had same idealistic belief like Dr Jagan until that was bastardised to the point that we had no chance to talk of an economic federation even. There the British let us down; you must not therefore rely on them but be warned of their self-interest. I have to agree with what you just heard. You have much potential for economic development, better than most Caribbean colonies; but it will take hard work and cooperation, not energy wasted in squabbling and racial strife. There is already too much bitterness. Technically I am not here tonight, but I will tell those who sent me that there is no other way, if peace and prosperity are your aims. When Mohammed Jinnah spoke to support partition of India he said, *'Hindus and the Muslims belong to two different religions, philosophies, social customs and literature... derive their inspiration from different sources of history. They have different epics, different heroes and different episodes... To yoke together two such nations under a single state, one as a numerical minority and the other as a majority, must lead to growing discontent and final destruction of any fabric that may be so built up for the government of such a state.'* Hindus didn't agree with Jinnah then but those remarks fit your situation. Just change "Hindus" and "Muslims" to Indians and Africans. I am authorised to offer any reasonable help to both sides, including diplomatic, I emphasise *both*, without prejudice, if leaders decide on partition, to make a smooth and peaceful transition. There are powerful forces at large in the world geared to seize resources and newly independent countries are fresh targets; today they want to use their money to press India in a certain direction; so far we have resisted, despite strong criticism from certain Indians, but new ways of spreading news will make it harder to keep their propaganda from reaching our people; powerful moneyed forces of Europe have for nearly 200 years controlled money supply and fomented and profited from unrest and war, lending to both sides. Today they control and even own Israel; tomorrow, who knows? The world maybe. They see India as a big profitable market, but if we let them have sway over our banks, we're once more a colony!"

"We're aware of strangers lurking in the shadows of our nation, not only those involved in destabilising our society; they're busy taking stock, as it were. What can they want from us?"Sam asked.

"Your resources; they know more about you than you yourself, because they've had centuries of access to confidential documents of British government. They know what you have, and what you need. You are very small; they may leave you alone if they see you as no big prize, but nature has given you much. We are willing to share information and expertise and help as we have done with for others and with scholarships."

"We're deeply grateful for your offer and know it comes from the heart." Sam declared. "You're right about us, I'm afraid. I agree with Ram. I too have travelled in British colonies in the Caribbean and in Africa. I've agonised over our situation for over ten years. The people will live in harmony if their leaders will let them. Black leaders cannot ignore the Indian majority as the British had done. Even before the war gentler and wiser voices—Indians and Africans-- had begun to spread a message of respect and accommodation. But radicals, myself included, and all the leaders today, were unfortunately too caught up in the wave of post-war socialism to recognise the wisdom of the approach suggested by a true Guianese hero, the late Dr JB Singh, and his generation who saw a way of uniting our races into a people who could move forward together into peaceful prosperity and avoid the demagogues. Now, as if the scars of slavery were not enough, Africans had to fall prey to the worst form of ambition which has come dressed in compelling language and the rhetoric of brigandry; this in a sad way appeals to our largely uneducated majority. I believe Indians suffer likewise. Now we have no healthy way forward except though separate development. We recall that this land was once two entities until the British acquired them and made them one colony 132 years ago. A terrible error, to my mind, for the people of Berbice, for they lost. There were deep divisions then and inequalities of development favoured Demerara to this day. This young man prepared maps for us and will explain as we proceed. He suffers from the stereotyping of his race, but he's neutral; see how easily we fall into the trap of labelling!"

A rather stern looking paunchy middle-aged black man spoke up, "I share your regrets and wish for signs of better things. I deal each day with people of all races and find it painful to see that we're heading into racial anarchy under present leaders and almost certain dictatorship under whomever wins this game of chicken." He spoke with an ersatz British accent, spreading his lips and pausing to suck on his meerschaum pipe, its bowl cradled in his left hand while his right played around the rim of his whisky glass. His head inclined to one side, as if speaking to his neighbour only. His voice was a mellow baritone. His affectations of speech, dress and bearing would have labelled him an English gentleman were he not black, and totally belied his bohemian early life including his University time on a scholarship. "The British may have set up the conditions but these two players had better and smarter models to follow, from the British themselves. Look at Lee Quan Yew in Singapore; I see good things there even though he might regret joining with Malaya, with his Chinese majority, a situation rather like Trinidad's Indians in the West Indian Federation. The next few years will tell, but he's on the right track for economic purposes, I daresay, having sensibly shed the Communists. I had thought Jagan to be a Fabian and more influenced by Bertrand Russell than by Karl Marx. But he's proven me wrong, sad to say, as Burnham has made it a zero-sum game which he intends to win by hook or by crook. Jagan will not accept loss of face and so continues his headlong rush over the cliff. I refer, of course, to Robert Lindner's book *Rebel Without a Cause*. But I digress; I apologise. Shouldn't we first agree on what we're here for? Does everyone feel the same?"

"Yes, of course; your thoughts are well put, as usual, sir. I thought it was common knowledge among us assembled here. But you're absolutely right." Sam paused, then continued, "I remind you of the conversation we had a few days ago on this matter and you expressed support; in the same way most of you on a one-to-one basis have spoken favourably on separate development. We're here now to consider the partition option as the best and safest way of separate development and to stop the violence that's destroying our two major peoples and sabotaging our country; it suits only those who want to dominate us, each in his own way, especially after independence."

"No doubt the very money men that trouble my Indian friend;" he gestured with the meerschaum, "I know of what he speaks and they have used conflict, often of their own devising, to split and polarise even erstwhile congenial communities, their own even; Palestine is indeed a prime modern example and you might know they funded both Hitler and Stalin, the Russian czar and the Bolsheviks, Wellington and Napoleon etc. They're a sly and universal enemy, a ruthless threat to this civilisation. Very troubling; very troubling indeed."

A shuffle of feet, a rustle of clothing and a few loud sighs expressed the dread he had induced. Sam paused; this was a tempting theme and he wished more but it was at this time tangential to the agenda. "For reasons Ram gave," he resumed, "we must go our separate ways first, if we wish to live in peace now so that we may have a chance to unite later, by a new generation grown up knowing inter-racial tolerance and peace developed at arm's length. In a way we advocate the reverse of Lee, because we too think he will not survive his Malayan link. Here if we separate Africans from Indians, who will they fear or fight? How then can unscrupulous politicians foment anarchy? There will be peace and plenty."

This incredible statement was made in a monotone and as casually as a stray hello to no one in particular passing by.

"That's not so easy to do; easy to say, of course." The stern man said, surveying the awed faces, and anticipating the hum that followed as men pondered the weight of what was said.

"So this is why we're here?" a Chinese lawyer asked, his voice masking his anxiety.

"Yes. You're here because you've publicly condemned the present state of affairs and privately expressed the wish for something better. You're here also because you, like our Portuguese friend here, represent a numerical minority but powerful economically and with equal rights of origin and birth; being in minority is irrelevant really; your views *must* be accommodated." A softer hum of approval from many voices blending hung in the air for a few moments then faded into silence.

"I see." The Chinese man said, "We are a minority yes, mostly urban, christianised, businessmen and professionals; a few of us are in government. This generation believes it's always been so; but we too came indentured, a little more recent than either of you but our roots are no less deep and our stake on a per person basis higher than most, so economically we do have some clout. Most of us now side with D'Aguiar; we supported PPP in '53 but were disappointed when Jagan and Burnham could find no room for people of enterprise and instead drifted into extremism with strange allies that is creating today's problems. Partition in my reading of history is usually a result of war--like Korea in '50 or Vietnam in '54--imposition by a superior power, like British in India, or request by a segment of a state as happened with Northern Ireland, although I may be simplifying the Irish situation. None of these has been peaceful and all inconvenienced or eliminated minorities. Burnham uses racism and violence as political tools openly *and* also in a sneaky way to terrorise people and to silence opposition, even simple heckling at public meetings; we even know of people who have "disappeared" without trace. Fortunately Jagan has not retaliated, but will that last if Burnham pushes the fight? Not likely, which means that the fate of this lovely city will depend on warring and vicious forces that envy all those who have inspired and built it; we've seen *already* what that means. If by agreement, like Luxembourg of old and Ireland or Norway and Sweden, we can arrive at a peaceful partition we will abide by that and hopefully give full inputs on disposition of property and on the treatment of minorities in whatever states emerge. Chinese are adaptable people; we can survive anywhere." He sipped from his glass and sank into thought in the ensuing murmur.

"Hear, hear!" The Portuguese gentleman applauded, "you speak for us; we too came from humble beginnings and have few connections left to the old life; we are now British, with no other point of reference. Secretly we envy Indians for keeping their culture, even though we too, I'm sorry to say, belittle them and condemn their religion, because we've always been ignorant of those things; we've practised neglect and bias, from the cradle you might say; we fear their numbers and worse, their high energy and talent. When we pause to think we marvel how they tolerate and cope with suppression and hardship yet remain basically peaceful; they are perhaps the most tolerant and resilient of all our peoples, no disrespect for anyone here, simply my experience in thirty years of business and mixing with all kinds of people. I respect, we respect, people of all stripe and commend achievements--our public record shows that—but the destruction we've all suffered and will likely see worse if the impasse continues has forced us to consider tougher solutions. We would prefer internal self-governing states, partitioned or not, within the United Kingdom until we can grow cool heads, moderate attitudes and understanding all round. Partition into independent states is less attractive but it beats the chaos we have now and undoubtedly can succeed with goodwill and dedication; if that's what we must do, we're behind it. The material issues are secondary. Our people are resilient and progressive; they will survive and prosper in whichever state they choose to settle."

He continued to nod ever so slightly and heard his colleagues' voices as if muffled by a great distance or coming through glass. He dragged on his cigarette and watched the smoke emerge from his nostrils, as he had done, without thinking, many times each day. At that moment he pondered the act and marvelled at what made it possible. He leaned back and listened attentively as an Indian of about 50--a small man with greying temples and a professorial air, dressed impeccably in a cream serge suit--spoke up with authority.

"Thank you for the very kind words; they give me and those like me even more heart. Partition, as my friend just pointed out, is not a popular tool, but often necessary; Koreans are essentially one race but they fought an ideological war and settled for a rancorous ideological truce: south right and north left. But Palestine is closer to our situation and divided by race and religion which the UN decreed, but the Palestinians declined to endorse it and so far have achieved none of the benefits that the Zionists gained through better organisation and heavy financing from the Rothschilds. Today more and more countries are recognising them and I hear that Japan will soon have an embassy there. The Palestinians were too staid and not driven enough to look at this reality largely because they were misinformed--just as we have been, by a biased British education–and in disarray, made headless when the Brits hanged or jailed or exiled their leaders in the thirties. Hindsight tells me Palestinians got it wrong and should accept partition before the Jews buy up or dispossess them of all their land, God forbid. Zion will get stronger with Rothschilds' money clout and US help. I argue this with our Syrian friends here almost daily since the violence started. Their plight is not the same as India's. India suffered from the exploitation of Islamic teachings by ambitious and powerful Muslims who seized the chance to recapture the glories of their Mughal ancestors; Palestinians suffer and will suffer more from *failing* to separate! Zionists will bring in Ashkenazim from everywhere and replace them; they will have nothing. So I believe we must look urgently at *our* reality, propose partition and seek a consensus."

"That's a strong statement." The Black Englishman said. "Why do you think it must be so?"

"Well," the cream suit paused, "for one we're in a civil war, whether we want to accept that or not and the rifts are getting deeper and violence polarising us which does not bode well for the future under any of the leaders as long as they maintain their current policies. Our infrastructure has crumbled to a state not thought possible; our best and brightest people, the non-political ones, backbone of a country, are leaving in droves; the pace has increased to a torrent already. Partition will stay that to a large extent and will reduce civil strife, restore law and order and allow people to get on with their lives without fear. It will save us from becoming a nation of compliant dunces and slaves once more. I think a multiracial state is possible if each is respected and can pursue its interests without jealousy or fear. So let's look at what's proposed and discuss it." He leaned forward to tap the ash from his cigarette into the tray in front of him and sipped water.

"Yes," said the other, sucking on his pipe.

"Let's see then what this young man has to show us." Sam said.

"Just before we look," the Indian interrupted, "I must make point about Palestine; what's happening there will shake the world". Eyebrows raised but no one interrupted as he continued, "This place is home for three fighting religions; it was ancient Land of Canaan and former Ottoman province on both sides of Jordan River; people today are mainly Arab Muslims, with minorities of Christians and Sephardic Jews; it became British Mandate after First World War when UK and France divided Ottoman provinces. Migrant Jews could make home anywhere in Mandate until 1922 when British restricted them to West Palestine, now Palestine. East Palestine, renamed Transjordan, was given to Hashemite King Abdullah who lost Hejaz province in western Arabia, when Ottoman Empire fell. British hoped that Arabs from West Palestine would all go there, but they didn't. Jewish newcomers were all Ashkenazim from Europe and USSR brought in by Zionists who get money from Rothschild banking giants and American Jews. This brings America to Middle East and makes Soviets nervous. It's part of Cold War now, just like you here. Some say that Rothschilds founded Israel as personal fiefdom, centre of their world empire which means Jews will have unlimited money and Arabs are in trouble. Ashkenazim all speak different languages and are prejudiced, aggressive, intolerant and doctrinaire. In Palestine they clashed with native Arabs and Sephardim Jews, so much so that British accepted Peel Commission proposal in 1937 to partition West Palestine. Arabs rejected it and more clashes happened. Ashkenazim militias were veterans of WWII resistance; they formed Polish and German gangs--Irgun, Stern and others—all called terrorists by British. In '46 Transjordan gained independence. In '47 further clashes led the UN to partition West Palestine. Arabs again rejected partition—bad advice, big mistake--but Jews accepted and migration zoomed. In '48 Ben Gurion declared Israel independent, fought war against Arab states and won. That is Rothschild power. Jews and Arabs now hate one another and each side swears to get rid of the other. The trouble gets worse. Transjordan is fairly well-run and peaceable, but it still has problems with Jewish state. I want to emphasise by saying this thing that polarisation under the same roof increases not releases tensions; better to agree to separate and then get on to build your part."

"Well, thank you for that." Sam said. "Point taken. Analogies and examples are very helpful."

"Permit me to add a few observations which I find *a propos.*" The Black Englishman said. "I thank my Indian friend for his remarks; we here tend to ignore the lesson of Palestine and fail to see the emerging thread of controls by really big power blocks, of which Rothschilds and their Zionist followers are probably the most fearsome. We'll be in their sights only because US paranoia will take us there, and unrest will make us even more attractive and bring out the vultures as it's done in Africa. Here I'm bothered by the pattern of incendiarism and violence, both organised and random, that my friends in the PNC and UF have adopted and promote, not unlike the Palestine experience; you've heard the news of martial plans which the Police raid recently uncovered at PNC headquarters." He paused, sipped his drink and continued more gravely as silence resounded throughout the room. "Some of you know I've been delving into West African history, such as we know it--an ancestral search really, an idea I've picked up from my Indian friends—and have travelled fairly widely through the region, British and French. Like us they're caught up in the independence push and like us they speak with many tongues. This surprised me, as I had absorbed the European propaganda of homogeneity among their African subjects to support federations. Like us the dominant ideology is socialism, some even say communism. But there are exceptions.

"I've met several powerful men, and some not so worthy; I'll comment briefly on three that are relevant because they influence our leaders: Sekou Touré of Guinea, Felix Houphouët-Boigny of the Ivory Coast and Ghana's immensely popular socialist Kwame Nkrumah, who has just survived an attempt on his life presumably instigated by the infamous opposition triumvirate--KA Busia, SD Dombo and JB Danquah--whose NPP had fomented terror across the nation. Danquah had even proclaimed to the 1958 Jackson Commission that he was above the law, boasting that his objective was to make the nation 'ungovernable'. This is the very phrase Forbes Burnham used last year at Bourda Green. Indeed the use of fire, bullets and bombs follow the Ghana pattern of the past few years with frightening similarity.

"I confess I had reacted *against* Nkrumah's socialism until I met Dr Danquah and learned of the abominable behaviour of the powerful group he leads who resent the fact that the "rabble" has a say in governance, and that their children were swelling the ranks of Nkrumah's Ghana Young Pioneers, the next generation of power in a united Ghana, and Nkrumah's ultimate tool of proletariat revolution. The response has been dozens of plots and incidents, with at least three getting close to Nkrumah and youth targets. In one a young girl handed him a bouquet which hid a bomb; the child died as did others and Nkrumah was wounded. In another attempt a policeman shot at him, missed five shots but killed his body guard. We see the same here except that we have three youth groups run on ethnic lines, being schooled into violence, Africans actually getting better practised at it, and thus we're seeing the evolution of a permanent base for discord. I say this as we all looked up to Ghana as the first colony to gain independence despite local chiefs' objections. But power corrupts and absolute power corrupts absolutely, and Nkrumah from all appearances is headed to a dictatorship very soon.

"Touré was a poor man, a fine orator, rather like our own protagonists, who also rose through union activity; he was elected Guinea's representative to the French National Assembly in 1951. In 1945 he had become Secretary-General of the Post and Telecommunications Workers' Union and helped to found the Federation of Workers' Unions of Guinea, linked to the World Federation of Trade Unions, of which he later became vice-president. We too have connections there. He organised the longest strike in French colonial history and got what he sought. Burnham's strike tactics is pure Touré; his lasted 76 days. My guess is that Burnham will want to outdo that. When President Charles de Gaulle in 1958 offered French colonies federalism versus independence, Touré persuaded Guinea's voters to choose independence, thus rejecting de Gaulle; Guinea became independent on October 2, 1958, with Touré its president. France reacted by withdrawing technical and other support which led Touré into alliances with USSR while simultaneously seeking Western money. He even planned with his soul-mate Nkrumah ways to achieve African political unity, but nothing came of that. Is this not Jagan in action?

"Félix Houphouët-Boigny was a physician, planter and son of a tribal chieftain who founded an agricultural syndicate to defend against French settlers after WWII; he became a French national assemblyman and a year later, in 1946, formed the Democratic Party with communist affiliations and supported African federalism. However, as a pragmatist in the face of French anti-communism, he changed tack, broke with the communists in 1950, and painstakingly over the following ten years built his political base as party leader, becoming a cabinet minister in France, president of the colonial assembly and mayor of the capital Abidjan. By the end of the decade his policies had made Ivory Coast prosperous; he rejected federalism as he saw his country subsidising less productive neighbours; his free enterprise policies in cash-crop agriculture had succeeded, where others had failed in attempts to set up centralised state-run industries, such as Jagan keeps pushing here; instead he should follow Houphouët-Boigny's approach to a sound agricultural future, as advised to do repeatedly. Felix became President of independent Ivory Coast three years ago; he's immensely popular and incorporates into his platforms ideas from all sectors of society thus engaging the fiercest opposition and maintaining trust through cooperation and consensus; his government to date is the most stable and progressive among new nations, although it's a virtual if not real one-party state.

"I've taken long, I know, but I had to make sure you have this information; I apologise if you already know it. The situations I describe all sound terribly local and topical. Our leaders know these men and have learned of their circumstances and seem to have copied from some of their less desirable methods; the parallels are striking at least to my mind, and show that race is not the only barrier; class could be just as obstructive and destructive. Blind allegiances to form are not the best model for a start-up; smart pragmatism has more to offer; our leaders should study Félix Houphouët-Boigny, not Marx or Nkrumah[166]."

"So many things we need to know that we don't hear about;" the Portuguese man said, "now most of what you said is news to me; we don't get African news here or even Indian; I did read about Nkrumah, but not the other two; from what you say if we change the names they could easily pass off for politicians here!"

"My very point, and these are only three of many examples from west, central and east Africa; and they don't have an Indian majority to target." the Black Englishman said sadly. He paused, reflecting, his head partly bowed and added, "Here my people are exploiting race in a shameful way, and I was part of that movement before it took this shape."

"I've spent my political life among my people and Indians, almost in equal number and I've crossed paths with all races," Sam remarked, "if I speak of the major races for a moment, their rank and file are salt of the earth, hard-working, tolerant and seeking a better life for their families, just as Chinese and Portuguese continue to do. They don't stir up trouble; sure there are miscreants among them, as in any society. But Burnham and his crew are busy spreading hate against Indians; *I don't hear Jagan telling anyone to hate Black people*; in fact he welcomes us. I want a stable union of peoples, but the rift has widened as

---

[166] In 1964 Nkrumah moved to become President-for-life and two years later, as Burnham was assuming the headship of independent Guyana, Nkrumah was deposed and Touré accepted him in exile. Houphouët-Boigny remained president of Côte d'Ivoire (Ivory Coast) for 43 years until he died in 1993, having seen his country achieve one of the highest standards of living in sub-Saharan Africa, a singular achievement for a nation without oil. He was consistently unopposed in elections for the Presidency until 1990; despite his advanced age he won handily.

hostility increases. Indians I know will work with Blacks, but Burnham has seen to it that Blacks will reject Indian rule."

"I've listened carefully to what's been said and I must accept some blame for the mess we're in." a white creole middle-aged gentleman, with curly hair greying at the temples, spoke up, as he leaned forward on a silver-capped cane; he was known to most present, as his family had been in business and trade in Georgetown and New Amsterdam for a century; he was undoubtedly one of the privileged in society and one of two of his race present. "I say this because of who I am--my ancestry. As a child and youth I accepted the status quo and believed that what I saw was the natural order of things; I believed our ruling propaganda--we didn't call it that yet--and thought nothing of not knowing where my playmates disappeared to after a game. I thought they all lived comfortably and in plenty, like me. But in due course I found out differently, not here as you might think, but in an English university and later in the British army! The revelation was a shock, and for a time, I abandoned myself to War and was surprised to emerge alive with only a tolerable limp.

"When the war was over I thought of hiding in white society and even endured the effects of British damp on my game hip, but my accent kept exposing me and eventually my love of this warm land and the family and friends of all races I had known, now mostly lost, brought me back. That was fifteen years ago and I still ponder our future here. I'm highly privileged and remain free to go wherever I choose; that's the awful hurt of anyone white with a conscience; so often have I wished to be otherwise; no, this is not hypocrisy, although it could be interpreted that way. But I wanted to feel the pain of prejudice. Like those who had suffered it and today fight for civil rights, in the USA or wherever people of colour are made to feel inferior.

"I thought I could play a part to make this small country a just and fair society where race mattered little and talent much, where shame was not for the colour of one's skin, but for being rude and anti-social. I share the views of the newer generation of my race that we *have* done terrible wrongs in the Empire, through jingoism, and continue to make mistakes. But those who feel like me are still swimming against the tide, as indeed we must, so we operate behind the scenes and try to do what's right. The disappointment of failure is hard to take. I did not anticipate this awful turn of events nor did any of my folks, but perhaps that's our delusion; we helped after all to promote divisions among people so that a small force of ours could control a nation. Since it's plain we cannot have one peaceful country here I want to help form two nations which can grow in peace each in its own way, and once weaned of ignorance, suspicion and malice, perhaps come together later in a union to achieve what we long for: an exemplary multi-racial society at peace in the new atomic age. It's hard work; we can see from our Dutch neighbours that the multi-racial experiment is fragile when you have to share scarce resources, and so easily scuttled by greed, hurry and ambition; they've been at it for nearly ten years and I doubt they can make what they have into an independent nation; we must be cautious but decisive; a partition will give us all the best chance of building solid and building well."

"Hear, hear!" several voices said at once, impressed with the sincerity of his tone and stance.

"Nobly put;" the Indian said, "British Indians helped India's independence, notably Allan Hume."

"Yes; it's sad that the innocent often pays for the actions of the guilty." The Black Englishman said. "People of goodwill from all races are the losers here; they're in the majority but will be smeared as racists along with the few who truly are; power-hungry Burnham feeds the ill-educated with biases and misinformation and has spurred those with racial hatred to acts of inhumanity. Jagan consumed with ideology fails to recognise that by muzzling enterprise, he's his people's worst enemy. We must stop that if we are to endure."

And so the evening had unfolded. The meeting lasted until well after midnight. No one except Sam and Ram was ever called by name, as agreed and no record was kept except for what notes the young man scribbled. They debated the pros and cons of separate states, referring frequently to the map, over which alternative sheets of transparent paper bearing coloured lines were placed to illustrate the discussion as it evolved on the issues of boundaries, individual and group choices, rights and agreements, property division, compensation etc.

It was surprising how quickly the notion of partition was accepted, confirming that all present had long considered it. They debated governance alternatives, and variations within each, from the status quo with alliance to Britain, to a dominion or confederacy called Guiana with three or four internally self-governing states or provinces similar to Canada, or two freestanding fully independent republics, as in the rest of South America. The young man with the maps produced on demand figures to illustrate the debate, including rough estimates of the cost of each model, (courtesy of two anonymous accountants, one from Government, the other Booker Bros.). While it was desirable to maintain a single dominion, current events dictated separate development in view of the polarisation of the two major groups. The likelihood that current leaders would initially dominate their state in any partition was accepted; however it was expected that a viable opposition of the *same* race would immediately emerge, and have a good chance of countering current leaders--who relied exclusively on ethnic emotion--and at the same time addressing US fears re spread of Communism.

"I remind you," Sam said, "that PNC is a coalition, some say coercion, of leftist Burnhamites and rightist LCP, opposed to Indians and promoting Africanism. Given their own territory, Blacks will be free to regroup according to ideology and economic pressures and so present a stronger and more viable alternative to Burnham, who as you know is every bit as committed to a socialist dictatorship as is Jagan. Right now our African brothers are blinded by race and easily pushed into anarchy. In such a setting the US will drop him."

Just then the muffled roar of an explosion in the middle distance rent the air, punctuating his remarks. Keen ears focussed trying to guess the target, Freedom House, perhaps.

As the echoes died Ram added, "Most Indians, rural and urban, are entrepreneurs and individualists, not communists, and would oppose communism if they knew what it was; right now that's not an issue for them and they won't listen to any criticism of Jagan; they see him as protection from Burnham and African domination. They're wrong, of course, because Burnham will win in London, unless Jagan changes stripes. So a separate Indian state will allow the same chance for different voices to emerge and oppose the communists. I have every confidence that Indian moderates will succeed if Black violence is removed. *So you see both men stand to gain from maintaining the state of unrest, the status quo.*"

"The Civil Rights moves in the US are all playing in Burnham's favour;" Sam said, "he made much hay with the Alabama arrests in May and the rhetoric of that stupid Governor Wallace."

A flurry of debate followed ending with a general consensus that two separate states had the appeal of promoting moderation in each and thus should attract UK, US and popular support. They touched on the situation in Dutch Guiana (now Suriname) which had begun well with internal self-government in 1954 but soon a multitude of political parties had emerged, largely on ethnic lines with coalitions trying to find common ground. So far there had been no majority Party; indeed the directions taken as judged by their parties' composition and aims would militate against that ever happening. The 1958 elections had produced a coalition of the Suriname National Party (*Nationale Partij Suriname*), dominated by light-skinned creole Dutch, and the United Hindu Party (*VHP*). In 1961 the left-wing Nationalist Republican Party (*Partij Nationalistische Republiek*) was established. VHP solidarity was weakened by internal divisions, some say as a result of "contamination" by Jagan or his lieutenants who were active there and had aligned with the PNR. There was even a rumour of an "action group" splitting from the VHP. Events there would suggest that the East Indians and possibly some of the Indonesians and NPS members were unsettled enough by political trends and the economy to consider an association with Indians in an autonomous state.

They shifted to discussing broad principles, chief among which was the disposition of assets in Georgetown, the wealthiest and most developed area in the country. The man with the map spoke in favour of including Georgetown in Black Guiana subject to compensation for fixed assets of others, noting the likelihood that European, Chinese and Portuguese businesses might choose to remain there. The favoured division called for Indians to receive the eastern half of the country, with the Mahaica River and an appropriate southern projection as the boundary to reach the Essequibo at Potaro, which would continue the boundary and end at Roraima, already a common border. The Kaieteur Falls would thus be shared equally by the two entities, (rather like other major waterfalls: the Niagara between Canada and the USA, Iguaçu between Brazil and Argentina, Victoria between Northern and Southern Rhodesia (today's Zambia and Zimbabwe). The advantage of this division was that Georgetown would become African and thus avert major opposition and bloodshed.

The least favoured was almost the opposite for the Indians, that they occupy the lands west of the Demerara River, mostly undeveloped, with coastal farms and interior forests, whose southern extension would reach the Essequibo, follow it and then the Rupununi River in a straight line to Lethem; thus Black Guiana would receive all of the developed urban and coastal farming areas of Demerara and Berbice, both Georgetown and New Amsterdam, the forested interiors of Berbice and the southern half of the Rupununi savannahs. The potential for conflict in this model was too great, even with the alternative of the Essequibo River forming the boundary to its source, and it was thus down-graded.

Other divisions were discussed. The men became quite excited at the possibilities while mindful of the huge financial and personal effects of resettlement, and the cost of compensation. They discussed variations in boundary lines for each alternative and agreed that a final configuration could be subject to later talks. They also agreed that individuals should be free to choose one or other entity, subject to prior guarantees of minority safety and security, but several were sceptical of creating or perhaps perpetuating an obstacle and source of animosity, especially among those who held major assets.

The division of property was clearly a major issue, and would be heavily resisted by proprietors. But the consensus was that no matter what was done Indians would lose heavily whether the country was divided or not, as shown in 1962. The Indians nodded and agreed, "If that's what it would take, we'll have to bear the loss. We're already targeted and have already lost heavily. Last year's arson was not cheap. Things won't change much if the status quo remains. Next will come massacres!"

Two men, both Indians, who had been almost invisible in the room, spoke briefly to each other and to Ram, "We're with you," one said, in a distinctly Trinidadian accent. Much thought was given to transitional security and policing to avoid violence, and anticipate and thwart criminal behaviour. Acceptance in principle was the current priority. The planning was obviously a start, as much lobbying had to be done, and of course, the major leaders and the Colonial government had to agree. Each of the attendees was charged to open the subject casually among trusted friends. The most common line would be, "Did you hear this rumour about partition; what do you think about that?"

The three men stood at a picture window of the third floor room that gave a panoramic view of the Nickerie River, as it curved right to empty into the Corentyne a mile away; a thin early morning mist partly obscured its turbid brown waters. A manservant and maid were laying four places at a round table for breakfast. The smell of coffee suddenly filled the room as the man came in with a fresh pot, placed it on an alcohol warmer, and politely asked if the men wished to be helped. They declined, the older man replying in Hindi, "We'll wait; he should be here any minute." Then turning to his companions, he asked, "Did you sleep well? Rahman, my guru, likes this place; that I know." He nodded solicitously to the elderly man, 80'ish, leaning on a burnished mahogany cane, who said, in a surprisingly strong voice, "At my age sleep comes easily;" and turning to the Guianese, half his age, he added, "this place is very restful, different from Paramaribo; I'm always glad to come here; to see this delightful view: those long lines of Royal palm and the kamalgatta flowering so plentifully in the canal, remind me of my village in India; I cried when we left; I was so young. I like to watch the river and its traffic, now so silent behind this glass; yes, yes, very restful."

"That scene looks just like a canal in Blairmont, a pretty sight indeed," the Guianese said. "Everything is so familiar; but for language I wouldn't know I had left home."

"I feel the same when I travel to BG, as I often tell our people; I have long talks with my young friend here; I call him my Hindu son; we must stay together, Hindus and Muslims; we are one people, from one soil, Bhārata. All this trouble in Pakistan is a Mughal problem stirred up by Syed Ahmed when I was a child. *Dui jati Bhārata se aye, Hindu Musalmāna kahalaye, Rahi priti dono maim bhari, jaise dui bandhu eka mehatari.*[167]"

---

[167] "Two communities came from India, Hindus and Muslims; between them a strong love existed, like two brothers from the same mother."

"I didn't tell you that Rahman is a famous *munshi* [168] of Suriname, learned in the Ramayana as well as Quran. He's written books and received honours from the Queen. He believes as we do in unity, peace and harmony, and is our most valuable ally. And how was your night?"

"Oh fine, fine; it was good to feel safe and forget even for one night the thought of a bomb coming through the window," the Guianese replied, "but I still feel the rolling waves; the small boat crossing on a windy night was tricky; last night was rough and yet so many seem to be doing it. Corentyne's a big river."

"Ten miles at this point," the host said. "But that's nothing for men of enterprise. Your Essequibo is wider still. Your strike is making many here wealthy; because the river is our territory, all the smugglers have to do is elude your shore Police, which is so easy; they pay them something to look the other way, or simply move the big loads at night from bases on one of the islands. They're innovative and smart. They sell everything. If your strike carries on, everyone here will have a new house soon!" He chuckled.

"If Cheddi carries on this nonsense he will reduce the entire Indian population to smuggling and will corrupt all government officials, especially the Police," the Guianese said, ruefully. "And once they learn the sweetness of that combination, there's no turning back. Corruption will prevail, like in British India."

"I was in India last year," the Surinamese said, in Hindi, "I couldn't believe how bureaucratic they were and how corrupt our people had become from top to bottom; my business friends freely admit to it and add the payouts to the cost of doing business. It's a scandal that embarrasses Nehru and is almost too big and too deeply entrenched for a young democracy to stop. Makes Mao look good; he's popular in Kerala!"

The noise of a motor coming up the long curve of the palm-lined driveway broke the early morning silence and ended their conversation. Presently a heavy-set middle-aged Indian was ushered into the room. The host apposed his hands for the Hindu greeting of *namaskar*, bowed saying *"Namaste"* as did the others.

"Sorry I'm late," the newcomer said in a Trinidadian accent, after returning the greetings. "ALM didn't get in until 11pm, and my charter pilot this am had to wait for the fog to clear."

"No apologies, my friend, we're so glad you could come. You know our Guianese friend, but I don't know if you've met Rahman; he's our local guru, in learning, politics and religion."

"I'm delighted and honoured; we need your wisdom." The other bowed briefly, smiling.

"Come; you must be hungry. Freshen up and we'll have breakfast. The bathroom is across the room." Turning to the servants, he said, "You may leave us now. I will call you."

The table was spread with assorted fruits, peeled and cut — mango, papaya, guava, pineapple, sapodilla, bananas — and standard breakfast fare: roti, several *bhagis*, chutneys, boiled eggs and fried fish. The smell of spices invigorated the air. The host summarised their agenda, "Quite informal, no official record, of course."

---

[168] Teacher.

"The meeting in Georgetown was interesting, and timely," the Trinidadian said, sampling the fruit. "My people would support any move you folks can make to that end."

"Great!" the Guianese exclaimed. "As easy as that? I'm delighted. Now it's up to us."

"Unfortunately, my friend, it's not up to you," the Trinidadian said, "Cheddi will say no, of course. So will Burnham. Williams will condemn us once more as ignorant and dangerous. Neither he nor Burnham can run a country without Indians. We're the future economy. That's not to say the Blacks not enterprising or smart. But they like to get it without sweat; baksheesh, you know. You should see them with tongues hanging out when Eric trots out his promises. And now they're showing us a real hard time, especially with jobs."

The host smiled and nodded, "It's the same here; we make the money; they spend it."

Rahman smiled, "When I came here in 1898, we were resented for competing for labour; now they resent us for being successful. You can't win, not if you want peace. Jagan chose a route that will be painful for Indians; the only hope for us in the Guianas is a state along the lines I see in your partition plan. Has anything changed in Trinidad since Independence? Racially, I mean? I know Williams has been at loggerheads with Bhadase Maraj and has nothing good to say about Indians. Even though he became moderate politically, like Manley in Jamaica and Barrow, the up and coming socialist in Barbados, all smarter moves than Jagan's, he will, I think, continue to deny Indian values or presence even in Trinidad."

"In some ways it seems to us that Williams is deeper into this racial thing we're trying to avoid," the Guianese observed, "at least in BG the Jagans embrace the African and proclaim they're non-racial."

"The problem, if you want to call it that, is that Bhadase was the first Indian to strike out and do something politically useful for Indians in Trinidad, where they have been at the bottom of the social heap, and still are, just like BG but I see less so in Suriname." The Trinidadian warmed to his theme. "What Bhadase did was to mobilise Indians to self-help under the banner of a united *Hindu Sanatan Dharma Maha Sabha,* as you know, which raised many hackles; he formed the *People's Democratic Party* in '53, and with Simbunath Capildeo= and others changed the name in '56 to *Democratic Labour Party*; we narrowly lost the elections that year to Williams' PNM 11:13, and *we* won in the 1958 elections for the Federal Parliament. But when Jamaica's Bustamante dithered, the Federation started to unravel just in time for the '61 elections; we lost badly under Simbu's brother Rudranath Capildeo. You know his choice as leader was a compromise as factions among us couldn't agree. Our weakness; we're still too tribal; sadly the Blacks have even more layers, from Laventille to Tobagonians and Grenadians, up to Diego Martin; all this should teach others something."

"Same in BG; many tribes and every Georgetown lawyer wants to lead his own political party."

"With us the loss was so bad that everyone felt that Williams rigged the voting machines to give him 20 of the 30 seats; he then claimed under the two thirds rule the right to go forward for independence without consulting the opposition. Capildeo dug in his heels and got enough concessions for Williams to sail into independence last year August 31. Since then Williams continues to foment and exploit divisions among Indians by playing religion, putting

Christians and Muslims against Hindus and handing out a few favours, real colonial style. Bhadase left the limelight but he was the one that pushed Hinduism as a uniting force for Indians and other races while Cheddi was belittling Hindus and undermining the East Indian Association, which at least in BG was a non-religious group."

"Indeed we have that weakness, disunity;" Rahman agreed. "I've been preaching unity among our peoples for fifty years or more; it's a slow process; we want peace after all; I support a Hindu party; I teach about Gandhi; our nation must be free. I don't like how some of my Muslim people working to split us more by claiming that they're Pakistanis, not Indians. How quickly we humans distort events to suit us."

"I was *amazed* to read the news of vote rigging in Trinidad," the host said "especially the report that one candidate A.N.R. Robinson won his seat with *more* votes than they had registered voters!"

"Yes." The Trinidadian replied. "We were shocked; but nothing happened."

"Cricket, calypso, carnival, isn't that how Trinidad is painted?" the Guianese asked, jokingly.

"Now you can add another "C" for "crooked" and also our other famous "C", CLR James, our resident intellectual Marxist who hates Indians, including comrade Cheddi, and writes about cricket."

They turned to an examination of the proposal, hoping to arrive at a way to perfect and promote it. "We agree then to a plan that will give us the eastern part of BG as defined and work to federate with a separated Nickerie to create an *Indo-Guiana*. And you will help to lobby the US and UK, and you the Netherlands and France to support it. Rahman's reputation will help us in Europe and India."

"The current feeling in the States is to get rid of Jagan at all costs. Even your consul Melby has turned against him. You know also of the simmering racial conflicts here," the host remarked. "US and Dutch interests are worried; their signals say they're favourable to our proposal; a race war will stall development."

"Melby can't overlook any longer that Jagan is a diehard Communist, not after Luckhoo exposed him before the Commission last year. Yet Jagan still refuses to moderate his policies. That's the problem."

"But what surprises and in a curious way encourages us," the Trinidadian observed, "is that, against his better judgement, he would favour Burnham, convinced that Jagan is beyond redemption, and might therefore swing towards our alternative. The UK will do whatever the US decides, so will Holland. They will want to know where Jagan will end up if this came about. The split will give Burnham his kingdom and you will have to cope with Jagan's stronghold, the Corentyne."

"It's like Israel and Palestine all over again," Rahman observed, with a wry smile, "except that you are the luckless Palestinians facing a far better organised and heavily backed Zion."

"But unlike the Palestinians we won't be caught flat-footed by a better organised invader." the Guianese claimed. "Even if the worst happens and Cheddi retains leadership of what for the present we can call *Indoguiana*, it will be for a short time only; without Blacks he's helpless. Without Blacks threatening them, Indians will look at the real issues, and that will expose Cheddi's many weaknesses, in objectives and strategies, and especially administration. Indians don't see this; they don't really vote for him; most vote *against* Burnham. That's why another Indian party will never beat him, for when it comes to the ballot box Indians will not risk giving Burnham a majority. It's strategy, not platform. So for now Jagan has the solid backing of estate workers, farmers and small businessmen, and the fear votes of others, of any religion or race. As people advance they will leave him. And right now his policies are squeezing everyone who works for himself; few businesses are hiring. So he kills jobs and can be truly blamed for unemployment and migration."

"Seems to me that part of your problem is that rural Indians don't have access to schools like we developed in Trinidad, by self-help, which makes them think for themselves."

"And here in Nickerie we maintained our own language, speak it and teach it. I think if you had a moderate Black leader respected by Indians, Jagan would have been forced to match him."

To begin the discussions the host led them to a map of Suriname on which he had placed a transparent overlay showing a sinuous line running from the mouth of the Coppenaam River, about 80 miles from where they sat following its course to the source of the eastern tributary that arose in the Wilhelmina Mountains (Gebergte), then following the watershed between the sources of the Suriname and Lucie Rivers, to almost a straight line to the Brazilian border, a total distance of 240 miles. He clarified a few details about the northern part of this region, its similarity to BG, and explained geographic features that would dictate the final boundary line, which would be modified as political realities and geography dictate.

"This is the area we want to separate off; it's about one-third of the country; Indians now are roughly 35% of the nation's population and creoles about 30%; they descend from the colonial power and want to continue to monopolise the country; they resisted universal suffrage in 1948, but we work with them now and I'm surprised how they have come to respect our position, although the elite remain aloof. We don't want to create divisions and enmity with the top as BG leaders have done, and hope to persuade them to be inclusive, give a little now to ensure future security, to reach out to people, provide more social services and improve infrastructure. This is our initial position, but we'll concede the southern mountains and Sipaliwini savannah south of Lucie River and settle for a southern boundary at a line from Lucie River to the Corentyne."

"I have a great fear," Rahman said, "that we'll end up with too many political parties. Right now our VHP is in a working coalition with the creole NPS (Suriname National Party); two years ago some militant socialists started a Nationalist Republican Party, some say influenced by Jagan and his Suriname supporters. A group in our Party, called the "action group"-- quite smart but rash people -- is threatening to split off saying we're too slow or that they can do better and quicker by pushing their personal or small group agendas. It's very much like Jagan and your East Indian Association; we advised him then to stay. I see you smile, but we have good and strong contacts, not only through business in Georgetown but from shared families; you would know at least one prominent one, the late JB Singh's wife Alice was from here. And we used to enjoy the songs and dances of Pita Pyaree on tour with her musician husband Pandit Tulsi Ram, until she retired."

"I didn't know that," The Guianese admitted. "Interesting. Alice was very active socially and earned awards; their daughter Rajkumari is doing great things with the arts and helping to break racial barriers I have been to Pita's shows at the Olympic Cinema. You know she was almost ostracised when she began pre-war."

"We need all our talents, on both sides of this great river, in sciences and the arts and we hope Cheddi respects this; he made a bad choice when he left the Association; you see where he is now. We can't stop our members from leaving either, but hope that they'd prefer compromise to radicalism or else play into opposition hands. We're becoming less able to negotiate and follow common agendas. Indians will be hurt most, if politics gets polarised and Marxist, as it is in BG and Trinidad. We want to avoid that. Our destiny is with you; we can make a strong union. Otherwise we'll lose our brightest people to Europe."

"I agree," the man from BG said, "with your numbers and a moderate policy we can beat Jagan in any straight fight; the Indian is basically entrepreneurial; we see that everywhere."

"So also in Trinidad; if we prosper the Black man will prosper too. If he takes over, we're dead!"

They spent hours considering details of the plan and how it might be promoted. None of them had any illusions that it would be immediately accepted, but one could not predict the outcomes of negotiations at this early stage. The hurdles were huge. The Suriname government would reject the proposal outright if for no other reason than that a major asset was the Corentyne River. Mineral deposits were expected to exist in the Bakhuis Mountains south of Nickerie including bauxite and iron ore as a common feature of its age and geology, as yet to be researched; bauxite, mainly from the east dominated the economy; the mines had been active for many decades and reserves are still plentiful. The USA was the main exploiter, as in BG and Jamaica. The case for Nickerie separating was entirely dependent on a partition of BG barring an armed insurrection.

The massacres that had taken place at the partition of India were repeatedly quoted and the recent Israeli-Arab conflicts did not help the partition arguments in either country. But as the Guianese pointed out most Indian leaders had emphasised the differences between these examples and the situation in the Guianas. The American outlook, an essential aspect of any negotiation, was premised largely on Cold War politics, and two new socialist entities so close to the US under-belly were not as easy to manage as one. But there were local issues, particularly the need to secure popular support and to ensure that any action is seen as part of a general plan to achieve peace and good relations with other races, and to eschew the paths advocated by more racist WI leaders. BG's land mass offered the opportunity for separate development which C.L.R. James, Marcus Garvey and others had advocated for Negro self-esteem and advancement, from a Caribbean-wide perspective. But the coloured majority tended to ignore or deny the Indian reality and incredibly, even in Trinidad, was behaving politically as if Indians would in due course disappear.

To the group it seemed sensible that the million Indians in the three contiguous states (and others who might join them) could form a viable small state and with continued initiative and enterprise be an example of progress and stability. None of them thought it likely that coloured Caribbean attitudes to Indians would change in the foreseeable future. Indeed the divisions could harden as coloured governments replaced the British in each of the islands, and lead to worse social unrest and anti-Indian discrimination than currently observed. Migration to Europe would increase where Indians could still go with relative ease, much to the discomfiture of British and Dutch politicians and labour. This prospect could persuade Europeans and locals to support the creation of an Indo-Guiana state by merging Eastern BG and Nickerie.

They would also consider being part of a confederacy of self-governing states, a Federation of Guiana (despite the sorry history of recent colonial federations including the collapsing West Indian Federation), in which foreign affairs and defence were placed in the hands of the federal government made up of an equal number of representatives, no more than three, from each state, with power exercised rather more like Switzerland than the USA.

"The Swiss have a de facto separation of German, French and Italian peoples in their respective cantons, with a low-key but effective central authority having roles as we've outlined. We're nowhere near their level of development, nor favoured by geography and population distribution as they are, but with hard work and patience we should do well." Rahman said.

They agreed that although not solving the main issue of racial animosity, the plan would allow for an interim union more palatable to the US and other foreign relations, while internal changes could accommodate and facilitate a more gradual and "natural" realignment of the population, by internal movements and immigration.

"These are good alternatives to the mess that's inevitable if the status quo remains," the Guianese said. "The proposal has the advantage of restricting Jagan and Burnham to their own ethnic entities. It allows sober heads to come together and develop purely local solutions to regional problems, not the half-assed and ruinous dependence on foreigners for every step of development. How stupid we've been! We chase away our richest then go cap in hand for foreign loans. We chase away our brightest and most able then import third-rate foreigners as expensive consultants to take their place. That's Jagan's policy right now, and Burnham is no wiser; his greed is even more damaging and dangerous. For every dollar that comes in he'll stash away fifty or sixty cents, of that I'm sure."

"Most other political thieves are satisfied with 10 percent; I wonder if there's any place where we can find an honest politician," the elder mused.

"Jagan as far as we know is one of few if not the only one around; many people vote for him just for that," the Guianese admitted, "even his enemies acknowledge that. I'm sure part of the US frustration with him is that they can't buy him out."

"Isn't it sad that we can't find a leader unless we settle for a thief or a communist," the host mused; "and I'm not sure the other communists will settle for nothing as Cheddi does."

"So you have a big selling job to do; we'll help on our turf;" the Trinidadian said.

"We'll use all the diplomacy we can muster to get this one heard. It won't be easy."

The Trinidadian sucked on his cigarette and ruminated, "If all diplomacy fails, which I think very likely, an armed effort might be the best ploy, but to do that you would have to start to organise now, wait for independence and move as soon as you're properly deployed, hoping that in the meantime you've secured US support. It would help too to have Brazil and Venezuela on your side. You can look after Brazil; we'll take care of Venezuela."

"That won't be easy, although if people are sufficiently motivated, and we act in concert defining the new Indian state as pro-US, we could do it," the host said. "A US official, I forget his name, visited us recently and was impressed with what he called our 'progressive Hindustan community' in BG and Suriname. It would help to have such American people on our side. Brazil is not a problem for us. I was in there in '60 for the opening of Brasilia, their beautiful new capital. Stunning architecture, but the idea is even better; move administration away from business centres and regulate lobbies; *everyone* must be able to influence government; that's the US weakness."

"Brazil will be good for us; Rupununi is solidly on our side and will be in our territory."

"Good luck, then, I must get back home before they miss me," the Trinidadian said.

"Goodbye and safe flight." The host replied. "And oh, above all else, this meeting is our secret."

Steve shook his head, in answer to Shah, "Confidentially, off the record, we liked the partition idea here, especially the 2-state federal plan; it needs work as these things always do, although the Nickerie deal might address a Suriname problem as well. We'll see what DC says; it's a political hot potato, which this strike made much worse. And even our own citizens are working in a way our administration dislikes. But that's the American way; as long as what they do is not illegal, we can't interfere beyond advice. And you know Corporations are treated as if they're persons."

"A corporation has the same freedoms as a person?" Shah exclaimed. "Nonsense!"

"That's how they're treated in our law; I know it looks crazy to you."

"That must explain why there's so much corruption in your electioneering." Shah said disapprovingly. "A corporation can donate many thousand times what an individual can."

"Proof that US is run by businessmen." I said "That's plutocracy, not democracy!"

The various separation plans had become drawing room conversation long before the strike ended, and had attracted many, mainly the middle classes, with surprising support from some wealthy Indians (who stood to lose much financially) and from grass-roots workers.

Jagan and D'Aguiar heard the "rumour" independently and dismissed it reflexly, without debate. Burnham hemmed and hawed, pondering the pros and cons and briefly discussed it with a few "comrades", two of whom greeted the idea with enthusiasm, and mentally began to claim Indian properties in choice Georgetown locations. Most saw it as economically advantageous, with huge racial benefits, opining that it would make them more like an African state, or "like Barbados" and give them a freer hand in forging international liaisons and a more reliable basis for them; carrying the Indian "baggage" did create an identity problem, which the Caribbean islands, except Trinidad, did not share. Thus they urged Burnham to agree to partition. Burnham pondered and at first merely nodded.

It eventually reached the press, which debated the idea, speculating, without evidence -- as had become their style -- that the US and UK would "never" agree to it. The momentum slacked off when Sydney King raised the issue and all political leaders united to oppose it. But it was a sound alternative to the threatened civil war or dictatorship and economic slump that would inevitably intensify should either Jagan or Burnham lead the country into independence. It remained drawing room conversation for a long time, until one by one most of the protagonists, quietly or with fanfare, left the country, to make their fortunes in alien lands.

It was said that the failure rested on King and on the "timidity" of the BG member of the quartet that had met that morning in Nickerie in 1963, particularly the failure to take quick advantage of the considerable urban and rural "non-sugar estate" support for the idea, to organise an authoritative pressure group to seek a hearing at the constitutional conference slated for October-November 1963. Steve's indication of US preference for the federal idea should have given momentum for the preparation of a detailed plan for public debate and the collection of signatures to a petition for presentation to the Colonial Office, if needed.

US constitutional advisers were on hand to assist with drafting, but it is unclear whether their help was sought. Instead it seemed that none of the promotion and planning had proceeded with the degree of dedication and speed with which it had begun, the promoters preferring to "reason" with leaders of the three main parties. Eager supporters of the idea waited vainly for the call to meetings from those heading the pro-partition movement. It is said that threats of lethal violence were levelled against anyone publicly promoting partition, and with anti-social acts increasing it was not surprising that the debate was restricted to the drawing rooms of those already on side. With a virulent press taking their cues from the PNC and thrashing the idea, coupled with Jagan's rejection, it languished. Protagonists in Surinam and Trinidad kept the confidence.

Perhaps it was the vehemence of the denunciation by political leaders that cooled enthusiasm for the plan, and the threats of murder and harm to family, but almost certainly, it was the failure to capitalise on and retain the early and clandestinely offered US support, which would eventually fade with the assassination of John Kennedy. With that and changes in US social policy following the campaigns of Martin Luther King for equality and justice and the subsequent focus on Black Power and Black rights, Lynden Johnson withdrew from any matter that seemed to threaten Blacks. It was clear that BG had become in Washington a Black rights issue subject to a vigorous and influential Black lobby, which simply lumped Indians together, dismissing them as misguided Jaganites and Communists who would, out of self-interest and economic pragmatism, have to integrate with or adapt to the inevitable Africanisation of the country.

In mid-1963 the WI Federation finally folded, somewhat vindicating Jagan, but this did not help him as expected. Instead he was blamed in part for the failure for keeping BG out of it, on the hypothesis that BG's presence would have stabilised the union. Fat chance! The seeds of failure had been planted centuries ago by the creation in each island of an intense desire to emulate if not merge with the mother country, and by promoting competition among the islands for her favours. Thus were created the fierce loyalties to London that each showed, and as a corollary, the animosities against one another. All routes led to Great Britain; few existed between the islands other than those carved by a few intrepid traders who sailed against the tide of British control. These were not there to serve the cause of a Federation and those in power were the very minions that Britain had created in the centuries of British rule. The same forces were forcing a collapse of the central African Federation, where it seemed that only Rhodesia wanted to keep it going, while Malawi and Zambia clearly feared that the ruling white party in Rhodesia would thwart development of African peoples. This argument, properly exploited, would no doubt have assisted the pro-partition group in its efforts to get a hearing in Washington and London.

On June 17, 1963, with oil supplies almost spent and Jagan's government on the verge of collapse, a Cuban tanker arrived with enough oil to both rescue Jagan and rouse people from their deep despair. Strikers prevented unloading at the regular terminus, but mercifully the ship was able to off-load into the tanks of the Demerara Electric Company in Georgetown and the Shell Co in New Amsterdam. In later weeks further supplies arrived from Cuba and the USSR, the latter sending a shipment of wheat flour in the freighter *Mitshwnsh* precipitating some of the worst acts of vandalism and hatred in the sorry history of that strike.

Late in June Jagan gave TUC's Bob Willis an offer; he would loan strikers two weeks' pay repayable over six months. The local representative of the British TUC, Walt Hood, advised acceptance, but the BG TUC balked until Willis threatened to return to London and arrange to withhold ICFTU funds. On July 7th, the unions ended the strike, 80 days after its start.

My contract came to an end on July 31st but I was owed casual and vacation leave and decided to depart a week before that. Getting organised to do this had become hectic largely due to the strike. Mail disruption had left me wondering about my Commonwealth Scholarship application to complete graduate studies at the Royal Postgraduate Medical School in London, but thankfully the British Council had received a telegram in May announcing the award and had telephoned me to pick up a copy. But with the Ministry functioning only with senior staff, the end-of-contract paper-work was slow. Eventually as the weeks passed slowly into late June all approvals were completed save signatures. When I attended to sign at the office of a Mr Adams, a senior assistant to Ivan Seelig, the MOH Permanent Secretary--who had earlier told me that all was in order — Adams demanded that I sign an "irrevocable commitment to return or forfeit the scholarship *and* leave pay". Seelig had by then left for an extended leave of absence and Dr Nicholson, the CMO, was no help. Dr Nehaul interceded and supported my argument that the MOH had nothing to do with my scholarship, which had been obtained independently, *ad personam,* and not by Government application or at their expense, and that my leave and termination pay were contractual rights and due regardless of renewal, and unconnected to the scholarship. Adams held that since I was a servant of the Government, I had to be treated as if the Government had applied. He remained adamant.

In those troubled times the telephone was not much help; eventually I decided to go to the Ministry of Education since they had acted as agents for the applications. I managed to get an appointment with the Permanent Secretary, who I found was Kassim Bacchus, the older brother of one of my best friends, Rayman, but I desisted from revealing this. He listened to my tale and agreed that Adams had no jurisdiction in the matter and he would so write him. Adams was apoplectic, telephoned someone, while I sat there across from him, hearing a repeat of his arguments as he tapped on Bacchus's letter opened before him. I could tell that he wasn't winning and waited patiently until he hung up, rather sadly, and sullenly concluded the affair.

That left me with just a few days to ensure all travel arrangements had been made, family notified and domestic affairs settled, including disposal of household items and car. I had also started rebuilding my mother's house whose completion had been delayed by the long strike. Thankfully my family pitched in and my sister Pampat agreed to oversee the completion of the house and take the car.

It was my last day at work. Piles of papers and reports had finally been cleared from my desk; slides collected and filed and a number of notes written to assist anyone who might take over my duties. My last task was the completion of an inventory for audit purposes. I was busy at this in the mid-afternoon when I heard a hurried knock at the door. Jinni stood there looking quite shaken. I had expected her visit as she had telephoned earlier having arrived in the city the previous evening five days later than planned. She hurried in and, unmindful of who might be seeing her, threw her arms around me, voicing distress, with all the drama of a true *tragédienne*, her face pasted intermittently against my neck, her long hair collected in a bun that bobbed up and down and side to side as she kissed my face, my mouth, my neck, and squeezed me with passion. I had expected a warm greeting, and an expression of sorrow at parting, but not this exuberant, almost public release. Surprised, I asked, almost breathless, teasing.

"What happened? I'm glad to see you too!"

"I'm so relieved; I just heard this terrible thing; what happened, are you alright?"

"What terrible thing?"

"They tried to kill you!"

"Oh. That was over two months ago."

Arriving early to visit briefly with colleagues, she had heard, apparently for the first time, about the rifleman and me. Thus I found out how isolated she and the people living on the Essequibo coast had been during the long strike, bereft of any real news, with no paper or mail, erratic radio reception and a dreadful telephone service, dependent on those few who had travelled to and from the city, since transport was at best sporadic and unreliable, relying on the ingenuity and enterprise of those willing to take risks. Even emergency services had been reduced to almost nothing. Sickness and suffering went without relief.

I was aware of the difficulties having had to rely on police channels for communications with our staff in certain areas, including the Essequibo coast. I had by this means sent her a note outlining my plans to leave at the end of my contract, to take up the scholarship. I had arranged to travel via Jamaica and New York. I had not heard from her until the brief telephone call earlier in the day. With the strike ended, essential services had been slowly returning, and she had obtained leave of absence to visit Georgetown for a week before my departure, but had gotten delayed by the late arrival of her replacement.

Visibly upset by the news, she had rushed up to my office worried and anxious, heedless that she was revealing her feelings. Her concern was sincere, even though belated, and made me wonder how she might have reacted had she been there to witness my little ordeal.

"I would have screamed," she asserted, her voice cracking, "and if they had killed you, killed myself, like Juliet." she added, dramatically lowering her voice to hoarseness. I had laughed. She had bowed her head, with a shyness that made her look fragile and defenceless, "I would have, in truth," she murmured, sincerely.

Her tight embrace had revived all the passion of our time together. Her eyes moistened as she rued the fact that there was no time left for us, no time for her to say good-bye "the way I wanted".

She paused in dejected thought, then in a soft voice she said, "My darling, we may not have much time, but can you do me one teeny-weeny favour? You must say yes! It will not harm you in any way and there'll be absolutely no repercussions."

I thought that that was a curious thing even for her to say, although she was given to flights of fancy and devising "games of the mind" as she called them, mostly harmless, and often quite engaging; but there was a new note in her voice, a subdued insistence and urgency.

"I'll try, as long as it is neither public nor illegal." I tried to lighten the mood.

"You're making fun of me." Her eyelids fluttered briefly, her eyes flashed and I thought I saw tears collecting at the nasal corners of her eyes. She walked off to the far side of the room overlooking the yard; she dabbed her eyes with tissue from her bag and blew her nose.

"You're not getting a cold, I hope? It's going around."

"No, it's my allergy," she lied, smiling faintly.

"I said something to upset you, I'm sorry." I walked over to her and hugged her soothingly. "Now tell me what you want me to do."

"Excuse me." She released my hold and walked over to her purse, which she had left on my desk, fished in it, and came up with a sheet of blue notepaper and an envelope. For a moment I thought she was going to ask me to mail a letter for her overseas; I had already collected quite a few from people with relatives abroad. With the Post Office just returning to work after the long strike, no one was putting any trust in the service. The animosities that had developed between Indians and Blacks during that sad period presaged bitter things. The Bill that had been the stimulus for the strike was now withdrawn, but no one was willing to bet that the Government would let it remain so for very long. It was even rumoured that Indian mail would be sabotaged, or searched for money. She handed me the envelope and I was taken aback to see my name on it in very stylish careful script.

"This is for you; it's my final version," then tendering the blue sheet with its prettily-designed floral corners, she whispered, "Please read this; it says what I feel and what I want better than I can."

I was stunned on reading it, and glanced at her questioningly; she was standing erect, one hand lightly touching the edge of the desk, the other flexed at the elbow and pressed across her lower abdomen; she looked like someone posing for one of those formal photos of a decade or two ago.

"This is incredible; will you publish this?"

"No; it's for you." We stood silent for a minute; then she said, looking around the room, "See, I know you have a lot to do; I can help; I have just one chore to do; can I come back later?"

"I'll be in the darkroom when I'm finished here; I have some prints drying and must tidy the place before I go."

"Perfect," she said.

In the quiet of her small town posting she would have forgotten the tensions of the city but for the daily headlines screaming of rising violence. Returning to the city, her home, she had come to agree with other members of her family that the political trends in BG were irreversible and would destroy Indians.

"What Cheddi started, Burnham will finish;" she said sadly, a tear coming to her eyes, which I dabbed as gently as I could with a handkerchief.

"I'm afraid so; I saw that hate up so close, and it hurt. A few years ago, Christmas '57, I was home for a few weeks after graduation; everything looked so promising, even though the political clouds were darkening, but there was energy, and hope, like refreshing rains from dark clouds. The violence had not yet begun, but looking back the seeds were there, subtle changes had taken place in the voice, the attitudes of some of my high school friends, the black ones, guys I'd played cricket with, debated, gotten on well with, many now in the Civil Service or University or law school, or business etc; but in '57 I thought nothing of the change, and looked forward to completing my training and coming back to work among these very people: Indian, Negro, Portuguese, Chinese, White, Natives, all. Now look what's happening. I feel betrayed."

"I'm so sorry for you, especially you who give so easily and ask for nothing in return; you're so vulnerable; you're unique, you know that? All the girls talk about it, the men too. The girls love you, and not just like a brother, I tell you. Only Luke is disappointed, and he was a great admirer. But he feels let-down because of me; he's still a virgin, I think, and believes you've sinned. But Dick and Neville and Eric, your schoolmates say the nicest things, even McWatt, but at first they thought you might be like the other doctors, pompous and posing. Eric says it was brilliant how you dealt with your mother's bacteriology!"

"My goodness; you have these conversations? But I guess it's natural to probe like this."

"The Chiefs will miss you the most; they say that you make their jobs a lot easier and take proper responsibility. Everyone in your position asks for the moon; look at Balwant, he's so greedy, he lets you do the work and he takes the credit…and the cash."

"No, no, my dear, don't be so harsh. There's a lot we can do to make this place great to live in, not rich and bountiful, like New York or Paris, but comfortable and civilised, *better, more humane* that those, kinder and really free. And this lab has potential beyond belief; the staff is as good as UCH, better in some ways. And the doctors are great, Stanley, Honnett, Chet, Gordon—what an exception he is, hasn't changed from our time at Queen's. Stan and I wanted to start a model clinic and involve those guys, as soon as we're settled; we like the challenge."

"I love this place too, its youth, its freshness, and the countryside is delightful, primitive, difficult, so unspoiled, so clean. But the Negroes won't let us live in peace; they won't let themselves live in peace."

She described her feelings for place reminiscent of expressions from many of my family. Theirs was a romantic view nurtured by the broad expanses of fertile plains cooled by Atlantic breezes and home to waving grain or fields of grass where sleepy cows chewed their cuds when calves were satiated. They shared a vision of BG as a potential paradise on earth if for no other reason than their birthright, which gave them a stake in contributing to create that desired outcome after independence; sadly and unnecessarily, political chicanery spoiled it for them.

"I like Suddie and the Essequibo coast but I felt sure I would get raped there one day; I was always looking over my shoulders; all the girls felt the same; that's not living. Burnham wants everything; he's nothing but a bloated egomaniac, a tyrant; that's as plain to see as day. You were right all along; the only way for us is partition. I believe that one of the British colonial officers here has also come to this conclusion. I cannot watch this disintegration; my family talks of leaving soon, if only until politics come to its senses."

"Don't bank on that." I said with deep cynicism. "Yet Cheddi can still swing this around; he has one last chance; all he has to do is say three words, loud and clear, and show that he means it, 'I reject Communism' and cool his passion for the Soviets. But he does not have the guts to do that; he's no statesman, no nationalist, he's too egotistical, too obsessed with ideology, too blind to see that if he rejects Communism he will save the Indians, and the Negroes too, whose welfare drives him so much; if he doesn't, he dooms us all and he dooms himself. And Burnham, a megalomaniac, will oust him. The Americans are so obsessed with Cheddi's politics, out of proportion to BG's size or importance; they're tired of waiting for him to change. Castro has scared the shit out of them, pardon the slang! If the Brits don't come up with a way to get rid of him constitutionally, the CIA will kill him, like they did Lumumba."

"You're right, I'm afraid, slang and all! I think his wife won't let him forget Communism. You were right last year too, when you came back from that trip to Wappai. That was lucky for you; you saw the real land; whatever happened changed you, made you so mature and changed your whole outlook." She touched my cheek, and gently traced its outline. "I wish I could have gone with you," she whispered wistfully.

"What a nice thought, m' dear, but you're much too fragile for that place or for what we had to do. Perhaps you could go when we can make the journey in a less demanding and dangerous way than we did. Yes, a lot did happen, much more than I've shared with you. Now there's no time; and this last strike has damaged relations so much more, I'm afraid for the people."

"Me, I feel violated and cheated; things looked so promising six years ago, the way so clear. I've looked at this from several angles; you know my views; I'd be out there jostling with the rest and seeking office if my remaining lung were more robust. You can't do much with only one lung, even with all the wondrous help I get from yoga. I would fight to my limit if I thought there was hope, if partition had a real chance."

"It's the only hope but I'm afraid that Cheddi has pissed on all who dared to suggest it. You saw how Burnham trounced Sidney King for supporting it. We're dead in either camp."

"Many of my family and friends have already left; it's my turn to go."

There was so much that flooded my mind after, but we were parting, doubtful of meeting again. She had resisted the pressure to leave with relations who had left the country at the first signs of PPP Communism, and had been determined to stay in BG, carve out a career and hope for "stability and good government" to justify and sustain that decision. She was confident that I too would return into such a setting, on completing my postgraduate work. But she had become disenchanted with almost every move that Jagan, her tarnished political idol, had been making, and was now close to her own final farewells.

"So self-destructive! Why is he so stubborn, so blind? Is it for power that he will sacrifice us all? What virtue is there in being a Russian stooge?" she asked angrily, rhetorically, as she prepared to leave.

"Many say what you just said, that Janet is the staunch Communist, the decision-maker. But I don't believe that; they're both the same; she thinks, plans and organises and does the woman thing; he reads, he does the research and makes the long speeches…"

"And the big mistakes!" she added bitterly. She paused, sighed and gently whispered, "And now we must say goodbye until… we may meet again in London, who knows?"

Two days later my family and I left for Jamaica, a bitter taste in my mouth, disillusioned with the behaviour of Guianese leaders and astonished that they could be so short-sighted, selfish and destructive, sullying the air that had smelled so clean and light that morning. Neither Burnham nor the PNC was ever brought to book for allegations of acts of terrorism and sedition, nor for schooling a generation of youths in the practice of anarchy, looting, assaults, robbery, and murder. McLeod's murderer--almost certainly the man who would have shot me in cold blood that fine April day--was never prosecuted although hundreds had watched him squeeze the trigger to kill McLeod, just as they had watched him threaten to murder me.

For a long time after I would try vainly to suppress the powerful images of the encounter. But the entire scene would erupt through the cover filled with scenes of victims writhing in pain and discarded by the angry mob that stood before me rattling the gate threatening to bring it down. The details were even more arresting, the clenched fists, the foul language, the denunciations and cries for blood. I can clearly see to this day even the hot sweat beading creased foreheads and running down the faces of angry men and women, teeth bared, the ripple of naked muscles moving, and above their heads the cruel face behind the long muzzle of a burnished rifle, the sunlight dancing on its barrel, and hear his booming voice as it carried over the heads of the mob urging his leader, *"Le' me take him, chief, le' me; dis one gat to go!"*

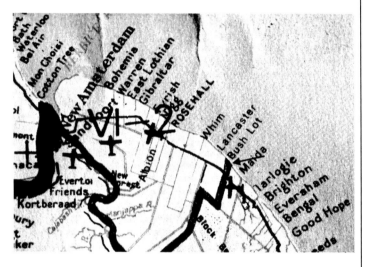

Top:

Map of Coast from Essequibo River, left, to Mahaicony R; Georgetown and environs were the main sites of the destabilization activities: arson, violence and murders, prior to the 1964 massacre at Wismar, 60 miles upriver from Georgetown.

Middle:

The populous Berbice- Corentyne coast, solid in support of the PPP and base of the PPP leader. Arrow shows location of Port Mourant

Bottom:

The Essequibo estuary and adjacent coast showing the settled islands and the relatively narrow strips of riverain settlements along the smaller rivers, Supenaam and north of this the Pomeroon, a piece of which is seen curving across the upper left.

Chapter 19

It is October 1963 and the definitive Constitutional Conference on Independence is taking place in London; Dr Jagan must renounce Communism or risk dismissal; he is on the wrong side in the Cold War; it is clear that the US will take any measure needed to prevent his leading an independent communist country. Burnham maintains his demand for elections before independence, under Proportional Representation, which Jagan rejects. They clash at the West Indies Students Union, London. I meet many young Commonwealth and British socialists who support Jagan and urge him to heed Kennedy's resolve and thus regain his favour and his help. A group of "exiled" businessmen, Commonwealth friends and a senior aide in the Colonial Service--who is fond of the BG hinterland and is probably one of the men whom Hari had escorted into the tepui in 1940--offer him aid and a chance to avert ignominy. The decision is made in favour of PR and Jagan loses his last hope when Kennedy is murdered. I reunite with old friends and debate with new ones the tussle between Jagan and Burnham.

Last Stand in London

"Real liberty is not found in the extremes of democracy, but in moderate governments. If we incline too much to democracy, we shall soon shoot into a monarchy or some other form of dictatorship".   Alexander Hamilton

"You know my views about proportional representation…It is a crooked, rigged system which has been imposed with the object of removing my Government from office, even before the expiry of its normal term. But I have no doubt that in the end justice will prevail. "All of you decent minded people, I know, abhor the crude methods being used in the name of democracy."   C B Jagan, 1964

"Sit still/ For you are drunk/ And we are at the edge of the roof."   Sufi mystic

The scene is London, England; the time autumn 1963, the place the Colonial Office in Whitehall. The British Guiana delegation was meeting with officials headed by Duncan Sandys, the British Secretary of State for the colonies. Jagan was fighting for continuation of his government; he felt violated, terribly wronged, angry and almost disoriented, unsure of the issues and incapable of seeing into the arguments of his opponents. He fell back on his unwavering socialist theories and endless recitation of all the high British authorities who had said a good word about him and his policies. But for each one of these, any dolt could have assembled an army of doubters and frank opponents. Burnham basked in Jagan's confusion and cleverly exploited his familiarity with the city and its denizens.

I met them at the West Indies Students Union, 1, Collingham Gardens, which I had visited a few times after arriving hoping to find a ferment of young minds debating the issues of the day of significance locally and back home. I did find eager young intellectuals, but the place had become a hotbed of trendy radicalism dominated by Black iconoclasts and a sprinkling of other races trying to outdo the Blacks in "Blackness". I had found the place dingy, the atmosphere foreboding and the membership unwelcoming. I had hoped to try out for their cricket team, but meeting Eugene Ward, a Barbadian friend from my UCWI days, decided to play for the team he had joined. In any event only a few weeks of cricket was left that year. The rubric "West Indian…" was singularly inappropriate.

On this day the bar was thick with smoke and its floor smelled of stale ale. The billiards and TV rooms were noisy and even the library looked dishevelled. The hall was crowded on that day and Jagan arrived first, a mistake, but it gave me a chance to speak with him. It was not a setting for conversation but I would not get another chance, and in that brief period I passed on a few messages from Buddy and the information Elizabeth had wished him to have about oil interests.

He was sceptical of both the data and the source, suggesting I might have been too quick to accept "rumour and propaganda", despite my emphasis that she was "part" of the oil lobby in Washington, DC. Nevertheless I urged that if the information were true it was a desperate last plea to moderate his ideological position, "even at this late hour, to fend off Burnham and the Americans or even reconsider partition." It would be a bold move and would surely derail Burnham and his cronies. He frowned fleetingly, forced a smile and patted my shoulder.

Abruptly a horde of supporters surrounded him waving pro-PPP placards. He answered questions, even before the meeting had started, and received noisy accolades. He explained his policies and programmes, listing the derelictions, unlawful and seditious acts of the opposition, led by D'Aguiar, Burnham and the PNC, and of the British and Americans who supported them, or at least turned a blind eye to those things. He thought he was upstaging Burnham. But the latter's entry into a Union that he had ruled as Chair fifteen years earlier[169] and had left with his reputation enhanced, shattered any hopes of Jagan's getting the upper hand. Burnham was greeted with acclamation. Caesar was outdone!

The debate was acrimonious. Jagan ranted on at length, giving dates, facts and figures and quoting references and endorsements. He condemned Burnham's unwillingness to join with "my multiracial government" and informed us that Barbados would be lowering voting age in a year or so to 18, hence his request for the same was not the horror Burnham proclaimed. In response to a heckler he reminded us that the failure of the West Indian Federation was far from his fault: "I wasn't even there!" He thundered.

Burnham ignored all, barefacedly blamed Indians for the violence in BG and focussed on the "rights and plight of the black man", his claim to lands that his enslavement had made "rich", his right of "natural succession above all others whatever claims they might have," and "to reign over all those lands in perpetuity". It was pure demagoguery, tinged with enough truth, like a coating of spice on rotting meat to make it palatable; wasn't this, after all, the original reason the British sought Indian spices? Burnham was smoothest when he was most deceptive. This was the same man who had said informally at a soirée not so long ago that the notion of rights especially individual rights was "unknown" before Rousseau, and his *Contrat Social* an untested hypothesis of no relevance to a new nation, ignoring the question that it had spawned the American nation, now the world's most powerful.

Hoots of approval and clapping greeted his speech. Nevertheless he was heckled by many, led by Winston H, a student from Trinidad, and by several black students, including one who persisted in condemning the many acts of black violence against others—he did not say Indians, but there were no other targets in BG—he gave names and places, and for a while rattled Burnham, creating enough unrest that others began to ask questions, others with non-Guianese and African accents, so that a murmur began to rise up in the room, emboldening the questioners to become more direct and to quote from Burnham's own speeches inciting anti-Indian violence. Shouts arose demanding that the questioners, including a rather serious Ghanaian student from Hans Crescent, be evicted as "he's not one of us!"

In the resulting chaos some heavyweights swiftly encircled the man and, lifting him off his feet, "escorted" him from the room, and threw him

---

[169] The Union met then at the British Council Residence, 1, Hans Crescent, Knightsbridge.

unceremoniously into the street. Luckily he landed on his feet. I was jostled; a fight broke out near me, and a flying fist knocked my glasses off one ear; I ducked another and managed to duck out to a less turbulent spot and found a door that led into the crowded bar. Winston, Ashley--his black countryman--two Nigerians and a white Rhodesian who had gone there with us, found other routes to escape the mêlée and reconnect with the Ghanaian. On stage the chair pleaded for calm, through crackling loudspeakers; whether he got it was unclear. My friends and I regrouped at a nearby pub to marvel at the performance. It was Bourda Green all over again.

"Jagan is dead meat." Winston said simply, his deep baritone adding gravity to the words.

"Not if he drop that Communist crap," Ashley said, his voice a higher pitch contrasting with Winston's. He was a slender man of about thirty-five near the end of his legal training at Lincoln's Inn. He was, as usual, elegantly dressed, and had a long white faux-silk scarf trailing from his neck. "I've seen Kelshall and that crowd at work; for a time I followed them wherever they went; I think nearly all us youngsters leaned to Socialism and got impressed with the language and the histrionics, waving banners, mixing with older people and getting close to easy women and a few Carib beers. We really didn't know much or care about the issues, but the sex was good and easy, even with the risk of clap. They were thick with jargon and all too shallow, man; there was nothing for anyone with initiative, or sense or any feelings for true independence. They packaged stale thought and peddled it like salt fish. That's why we dumped Gomes for Eric Williams--'Uncle Eric', he sounded left, but he acted right, get me pun?" he ended colloquially.

"Good one! I agree with Winston. Jagan is boiled plantain in Burnham's hands; he will pound him into *fufu*, sprinkle a little salt on him and chew him to pieces. Just watch," I said, the mountains of my disappointment peaking, and knowing he would ignore the information I had just given him.

"*Fufu*? You say *fufu*? What you know 'bout *fufu*?" asked Akindele, one of the Nigerians, also about 30, a law student and budding politician, son of a tribal chief; he sounded surprised; but then he had told us that he did not know that West Africans had been enslaved in America until he had read one of Kwame Nkrumah's 1948 speeches, resurrected recently by an "underground nationalist" in Lagos. Ashley laughed and explained his origins, ending with a question, "Where did you think I came from?" Akindele shook his head, as Ashley turned to me, pursuing his earlier thought, asked, "Who is this fellow King? A bunch of us from Lincoln's Inn went yesterday to hear him arguing for partitioning BG."

I explained. "He thinks that the country should be divided into two or three separate states, one African, one Indian and the third for the others, or if two their option to choose. But there are other ideas, like federation. Most prefer two states, which is what he would present."

"They say he's met with one of Sandys' men, unofficial." Ashley said.

"Sandys should seriously consider that issue," I said, "King is a seasoned politician; he defected from high positions in both parties. Jagan and Burnham trashed him and the idea, calling both airy-fairy, as they did in BG. But bear in mind most comments came from politicians with aliases. So if he wants to get anywhere, as many of us hope he would, he should lobby Kennedy instead, because we know that JFK now agrees with his advisers that Jagan is too far in the Soviet pocket to be salvaged. And the news in September that the Russian freighter that ran aground in the Bosporus was carrying arms to Cuba will harden US anti-communist thinking."

"He should do this now as both US and UK will have elections next year. I don't think the Tories will win this time here, but Kennedy *will*, over there." Ashley remarked.

"Seems King would have a better chance if he has Indians on side, in any dealings with the Americans." Winston observed. "Is he alone on this?"

"Hell, no, quite a lot of thoughtful people of all races are in favour; most prefer two states as Ashley said, with minorities free to choose between them. Some would consider a federal arrangement of three or even four states each self-governing but for defence and foreign affairs."

"Isn't that asking for a blood bath?" Ashley asked, "Look what happened in India."

"Undoubtedly there'll be some violence, but in the past 10 years BG politicians have exploited and promoted racial divisions, just like Eric Williams in Trinidad, to the point that blood has been flowing steadily, mostly Indian blood, which will flow even more if Burnham gets his way. And Indians will see their properties and businesses trashed or seized in any state he rules. So they'll give up property in a peaceful exchange."

"You believe that?" Akindele asked.

"I *know* that!" I emphasised. "It's already happened; there are Guianese businessmen, nurses, teachers and other professionals, tradesmen, clerks—all kinds of skilled people--making a new life in this country because of what happened in BG the past few years, especially last year's fire. This year the Police found detailed plans and illegal materials in PNC headquarters for armed insurrection, and so far no arrests. If that had happened in British India or South Africa heads would have rolled. None of the murderers of innocent civilians will ever be brought to trial. Even in opposition Burnham controls the Police. The Police know who killed three of their own, a superintendent, a detective and a constable and one who almost killed me; yet they go free."

"Looks like PNC means *'Plenty Noxious Characters'*" Winston said to chuckles. "Wasn't King with Jagan?"

"Yes, a founder member of the PPP, made a surprise switch to the PNC in '61, now he's left the PNC because he opposes independence at this time, and is lobbying for partition first. And by the way PNC really means *'Please! No Coolies!'*" Winston and Ashley guffawed knowing the context, while the Africans looked puzzled.

"Any Indian politicians of any standing with King?" Ashley asked.

"Not openly; but I know several politicians, prominent businessmen and professionals who are; Rai is almost certainly among them; he's moderate and was a good Minister of Home Affairs until last year when Jagan expelled him; others don't show their hand for fear of reprisals, knowing that both main leaders are opposed and will no doubt retaliate against partitionists."

"So Burnham wants to rule a mixed race state; how can he do that if only one race supports him?" Akindele asked. "We have the same problem in Nigeria and each big tribe, including my own, wants to go its own way. Same everywhere in West Africa. The French gave independence to their colonies but make agreement with them to hold power from behind the scenes, so that they can continue to milk them. They put Félix Houphouët-Boigny in charge in Côte d'Ivoire and Sekou Touré in Guinea; both will become dictators like Kwame

Nkrumah in Ghana and already Dr Danquah tried to have him killed. So if Burnham has a majority against him, how will he manage?"

"He will almost certainly give high positions to at least three Indian lawyers: Sase Narain, who wangled his way to the presidency of the largest Indian organisation, the *Maha Sabha*; Sonny Ramphal, a shifty and more subtle *coconut* who will seize the opportunity to aggrandise--a trait he is said to have shown even in high school--and the third, a sour man called Neville Bissember that the PNC acquired by scraping the barrel for any compliant Indian.

Ramphal is the most able of the three; Bissember is something of a joke, even in his party, which uses him merely for public show. People jokingly call him 'dissembler'. Burnham will I'm sure carry both Narain and Ramphal as his tokens. None of these will get an Indian vote in any fair election, except maybe from family. And of course he will change tack, fall in with Black Power forces and woo the Americans. That's a policy that gained ground in USA and when Kennedy wanted to make an exception and help Jagan beyond AID and OAS norms, he was deluged by letters and lobbyists against Jagan and told emphatically that BG was a black state! Dean Rusk has written him off. So I'm afraid he's Winston's 'toast' unless he does something dramatic here."

Akindele observed, "Since you have agriculture he could follow Félix and be a benign dictator and develop the economy that way; Côte d'Ivoire is doing well and is the most stable state in West Africa."

Various comments followed comparing political styles and experiences in African, Caribbean, Asian and other colonies and the inevitability of independence for all, with or without armed struggle; most agreed that the Portuguese would resist to the last and will only go down fighting. All agreed that the US Black Power wave and the work of the National Urban League will circle the colonial world like a tsunami and cause various reactions depending on the milieu. The wave had already affected BG and the Caribbean and will spread.

At the WISU meeting I had seen several vocal Black left-wingers from UCWI, including Walter Rodney, a bright and articulate Guianese history student, politically inclined. I had previously seen him as an undergraduate at Mona in early 1961 at a meeting of Guianese students. His remarks were typical of a million youths parroting Marx. I thought that this was a treacherous time for anyone in a colony who did not wave the red flag, or now the black one. Who will Rodney join when he returns, if he does, to BG? Jagan most likely, for ideological compatibility.

Henry, our white Rhodesian friend was ordinarily quite outspoken and not afraid to argue; he took correction well, especially when making some stereotypical and usually derogatory statements about foreigners; he was inclined to be fair-minded and unlike most white Rhodesians he sympathised with Malawi and Zambia for wishing to pull out of the Central African Federation.

"I don't support Ian Smith as you know." he said, "but he is right that most African leaders are Marxist demagogues with huge egos and little administrative experience who would ruin the continent and in Rhodesia reverse whatever progress had been made. I don't believe in segregation like South Africa or US South but feel that Africans should generally adopt European education patterns and give up many tribal customs, especially health and social ones, to develop a modern society and benefit from it."

Akindele countered this by reminding us that man originated in Africa and that Africans had highly-developed moral and social codes and concepts of law and order that Western societies were only beginning to study, and quoted the approach of many West Africans to crime and punishment.

Winston described Colonial practices that fuelled rage and resentment. One was the custom of injecting favoured groups ("trusties") into critical positions in colonial governments, e.g. Brits, Parsees, Brahmins and elite Muslims in India, mulattos in the Caribbean, Indians in Burma, Singapore, Malaysia, Ceylon and Fiji and so on, breeding internal conflicts among a nation's ethnic groups that seemed a powerful spur to Marxism and a threat to stability and orderly development. He had done courses in Government and had pondered the "coming racial showdown" as he called it, in Trinidad and BG, and how to avoid it. He thought it unlikely that a multiracial nation in the Caribbean could be a harmonious one given the sour climate that local politicians had established. "You know, your idea of separate ethnic states in a federal construct to preserve ethnic peace is a damn good idea," he said reflectively. "BG would have a better chance of avoiding disaster; look what happened in Burma, a country of many races where the Brits populated business and the civil service with loyal Indians and some Chinese; their political situation was exactly like BG with clashes between two wings of the same communist party. The federation at independence in '48 had five states, and started well under U Nu but in ten years the economy of what in 1948 was the most prosperous state in SE Asia had collapsed and last year after further clashes the Army under Ne Win toppled U Nu--Pakistan all over again!"

In my third week in London—the same week of my orientation at the Royal Postgraduate Medical School at Hammersmith Hospital I had attended a rather impressive welcoming function at Commonwealth Centre in St. Martin-in-the Fields for Commonwealth scholars and certain categories of foreign graduate students--mainly from Europe--studying English,. As a scholar I met and chatted with Prince Philip who had visited BG in 1962 on "a trade mission" to BG, Venezuela and Colombia, but more realistically as a goodwill ambassador to cool the BG conflicts and be a sop to Romulo Betancourt who had been exercised over the border issue and had taken it to the UN. The Georgetown visit was followed by the burning of the city's business centre so that was a failure. The border issue had seethed to the point that Venezuela forced Lord Home to a meeting in November in London, soon after the BG independence conference. Philip regretted the unrest and made some bland remarks, as expected, about the Constitutional Conference. I said that it will achieve nothing unless Jagan agreed to PR or renounces Communism; his eyebrows rose and he smiled the faintest smile.

At the function I met Pat Cacho, a senior civil servant from British Honduras (now Belize) on a bursary; he had travelled on the same ship as I, except in second class so our paths had not crossed. From him I discovered that my friend Hyman (Jack) London--a graduate of JC Luck's Central High School in Georgetown, BG, and of the UCWI Humanities program--was studying Law at one of the Inns of Court and living in South London in a nice flat with his Jamaican wife, Del (Ethley Delores) Harvey, a teacher. Brenda obtained his phone number from the British Council and got us together.

A short time later they threw a first wedding anniversary party with a mixed guest list of old and new friends including some members of the BG constitutional delegation and several Londoners, most of whom were young socialists; some were even *Young Socialists* and emphasised the difference.

The BG constitutional conference dominated the conversation and led me into a brisk and passionate encounter with an intense leftist Jaganite Louise Le Sage, a 30'ish teacher colleague of Del's, who had met members of the BG constitutional delegation at a political meeting called in their honour by the local Labour MP at the request of friends of the PNC. She had spoken to Robert Hart and met Burnham and was impressed with their "strong militant socialism" and "dedication and commitment to peace and tranquillity".

She had concluded from Hart's remarks that he was an active agent in the cause of welding the two major Guianese races into one party, which would bring "the greatest good to the greatest number in the new Guiana"! Del had warned me that Louise was easily swayed by rhetoric and could spread the wrong impression of people or news unless presented with "the other side."

Learning that she might have been fooled and that Hart was a well-known racist and actually opposed to Jagan, Le Sage had become quite upset; she and others there--some outright Communists, who had attended the meeting with Hart--had become hostile accusing me of "bourgeois bias" (having heard that I was a physician) until Jack came to my rescue. Together--during a break in the music for a late meal--we gave an impromptu seminar on Guianese politics, and quickly discovered how easily and completely these impressionable people had been misled to believe a lie.

In the discussion we discovered the distortions about BG that they had heard including "facts" about Indians which Del on hearing them from Louise had found belittling and disturbing; she tried to correct them but had no direct experience of BG and now that I had arrived Jack had suggested that we "talk". In introducing me he had said, "This is just the person for you; he can give you an unbiased comment on the questions that trouble you. Besides he knows the country better than most."

It was instructive for me to hear versions of events I had witnessed told in a way that made them unrecognisable and downright false. For example, the fires of 1962 were caused by Indian arsonists doing them for the insurance! The strike of 1963 was a protest against an anti-social labour law! The PPP had failed to win a seat in Georgetown and thus had no credibility. All Indians were Communists. A referendum on PR conducted by the PNC had resulted in a huge majority in favour. The PNC was the only stabilising force in BG. British commandos had shot and wounded or killed several "peaceful protesters" doing something that "any Londoner was free to do."

When we were through dealing with these distortions and questions, including samples of Burnham's lies to American audiences, I invited them to check my sources and official documents. Louise admitted that her biases had automatically put her on the side of the underdog, but she did not realise that there were *two* underdogs fighting for the same bone, and that the more vicious one will win!

Hart had clearly exploited their naïve allegiance to Jagan to further his own and PNC agenda, creating among them an illusion of a PNC dedicated to togetherness, which could not possibly have survived the scrutiny and publicity given to the Conference, unless these young political activists — few older than I-- had totally ignored press reports of the meetings or of recent events in BG. Hart could not be reached when one of them called his contact number to arrange a follow-up meeting. Later Jack would tell me that he had left London before the Conference had ended.

At the October 1962 London constitutional conference Burnham had advocated Proportional Representation as the electoral system for pre-independence elections. His supporters had since then chorused and bannered the slogan *"no PR, no independence"* at every opportunity and location. In response Jagan had quoted the condemnation of PR by Israel's David Ben-Gurion, who had wanted a reversion to the first-past-the-post (simple majority) system. He had claimed that PR allowed small splinter groups with extreme agendas to wield power out of proportion to their importance, and, by creating *unholy alliances*, became the many little tails that wagged the national dog.

Jagan asserted that PR would entrench racialism and divide the country forever, and endorse the position of the racial and regional clubs that "dotted the land". The failure of that conference to resolve the differences that stood in the way of independence had led Jagan to offer Burnham a share in Government. But just before Christmas 1962 Burnham had responded with the first of several rejections, which had punctuated the months to early July 1963.

Near the end of the strike Burnham had demanded that Jagan call a referendum on PR, claiming that as Jagan did not get a majority of the votes in August 1961, he did not speak for the majority of the population. Jagan bristled and promptly reminded him of the many British governments that did not gain an absolute majority; moreover that point was inconsequential, since the elections were fought to win a majority of constituencies, not plurality.

In any event the constituencies did not have an equal number of voters and it was thus possible and predictable that a winning party might get less than an absolute majority. Burnham sniggered and pointed out that the PPP did not get a single vote in the five Georgetown constituencies[170], the most influential in the country, and that fact had made Jagan's government "illegitimate, a fraud on the nation". "Let's have a referendum on PR, I say!" he had concluded to resounding cheers from an adoring audience.

Jagan's surprised reaction was pure sham. Should he have been surprised? Burnham, animated by the success of the 1963 strike in rattling the Government and frightening the population, had strutted and postured through the sessions. His actions were in keeping with the duplicity and scheming about which his sister and others had warned since the birth of the PPP (see Epilogue, p. 12).

In furthering his new image as a political moderate—some even said "conservative", God forbid--Burnham had decided to exploit the Americans, having concluded that their obsessive apprehensions about Jagan's leftist views (most of which he shared), made them easy prey. In private he would often deride them as shallow, conceited, sanctimonious bullies, who strutted their financial domination of the world, bristling with fears about security, and unfortunately too poorly educated about world history and geography to command respect as global leaders. He was astonished to discover that all he had to do was agree with them, play their game and he could get to do whatever he liked, as long as Jagan persisted in his evangelical infatuation with communism,

---

[170] Jagan's decision not to contest Georgetown seats had been much criticized and many had urged him to reconsider, since it was politically important to show that he had substantial, if not winning city support, especially since his political credibility was bound to be assailed if his win was unconvincing. In 1957, PPP gained 47.5% of the popular vote; in 1961 42.6%, a loss of a shade less than 5%, presumably due to Jagan's lack of foresight.

which he encouraged in their private conversations. Thus he felt confident that the US would support his silent strategy to gain first the leadership, then the ownership of the country! Like the pre-Christian Indian administrative genius Chanukya (Kautilya) or more recently his disciple Machiavelli, he would exploit their Cold War fears and squeeze them financially for sums beyond Jagan's wildest imagination.

In the climate of continuous inter-party wrangling that followed the '63 strike Jagan, Burnham and their entourage had come to London in October where, after preliminary skirmishing in public places, such as the meeting at the WISU, they settled down to business, consuming days disputing proposals and counter-proposals, and meeting supporters and advisers in private evening sessions. The main constitutional dispute was the electoral system for an independent Guiana. Jagan insisted on the existing first-past-the-post system; Burnham remained obdurate on proportional representation.

Jagan arrived early at the plush Hampstead home with two of his associates--without bodyguards, against the advice of his delegation--but the man who had invited him was an old and trusted acquaintance, who had often disagreed with him but never betrayed his trust. He had readily agreed to attend the informal social event, a respite from the hurly-burly of political wrangling, to have dinner in sedate surroundings and meet and hear from former Guianese who had established successful businesses and professional or academic careers in London and other cities. Several now owned substantial property, some in London's prestigious West End. One was said to own an entire street in Kentish Town, and a country mansion fit for a duchy. Similar unobtrusive successes were known in other cities, especially in the midlands.

They had gathered at the request of the owner of the Hampstead home who thought that they should try one last intervention at this critical time in BG's history. Each had in some way tried and failed to steer Jagan towards a mixed economy, centrist politics, and out of the Cold War, so none was optimistic that he would listen. But they had reasoned that he was desperate, just saved from collapse and finally confronting an unyielding foe with colours fully unfurled; he had nowhere to turn to safely; the USA had soured; he might therefore listen. This would be a last chance for Jagan, Indians and BG.

His host had asked him to come ahead of other guests for two secret personal meetings, the first with an unnamed official, said to be from the Colonial Office, who feared a Burnham "victory" in the negotiations, the second with an "agent" of Booker Bros. Upon arrival Jagan was taken directly to the library and there spent twenty minutes in brisk dialogue with the official. Later the host would say that the man had risked his position to brief and warn Jagan on the inevitability of the US position prevailing so that he could plan an appropriate strategy which the assembled guests would outline to him after dinner. In particular he thought that Jagan should know of US interests in oil exploration on the continental shelf, which would certainly harden their opposition. It was also critical that he insist that the British Government settle the border issue with Venezuela before independence, as any prospects for oil would revive Venezuela's claims to Essequibo. He finally urged Jagan to expose Burnham's plans for insurrection that Police had found at PNC HQ and on which BG Government had taken no action so far; he was sure that were the tables turned and Burnham the Premier PPP principals would be in jail!

The official left discreetly a few minutes before the Bookers agent arrived. The meeting focussed on the Company's position on independence; Jagan had from the start of his career blasted the company as a greedy exploiter and had recently made acrimonious comments on its opposition to independence, its intransigent sequestration of the best-drained farmland in the country, including thousands of untilled acres that are denied non-sugar farmers, and its practice of neo-slavery and anti-union activity.

The agent was brief. He did not defend against the accusations except to remind Jagan that he had shown an unwillingness to discuss issues or negotiate and simply expected a commercial operation with deep roots in the economy to change abruptly. Ten years ago a Bookers Director had made overtures through various persons including a business neighbour of Andrew Yhap, a local Bookers executive; Jagan had rejected them. They wished to prevent a Burnham victory and would cooperate with the PPP and assist in social reform and national development, including long-shelved schemes.

He recited the many reforms in Company policies and practices, including training and employment of locals at every level, as detailed by Chairman Jock Campbell and the BG chief, Anthony Tasker, who were seeking common ground free of "ideological burdens". Jagan had indeed met with Campbell who was keen on starting a series of exercises in synectics to arrive at a workable plan but bitter years had passed without a PPP response. An accord was now imperative as the eleventh hour was upon them. He understood the basis of past animosities and confrontation and urged Jagan to bury the hatchet, and remember their willingness to negotiate on a "clean slate" when the meeting with Sandys resumed. But Jagan must take care that he had chosen the *best* ideological ground, as once committed, the road forward was one way only. Bookers was willing to work alone or with one or more members of the Jagan group.

It was an astonishing ten minutes; Jagan listened to it all, staring at the man as if at a ghost. Eventually he acknowledged the offer but not before a swipe at him querying, "Are we dealing with the Guiana Bookers? Our own East India Company of thieves and despots? You're changing your spots?"

The men assembled in the great room were mostly Indians, two Portuguese, a few Chinese and several coloured (dougla) and black gentlemen of Guianese origin, a Jamaican, two Indo-Trinidadians, one Ugandan Indian who had visited BG and had a Guianese daughter-in-law, two white Englishmen and a gentleman from India, unmistakeably Northern but without turban. The buzz of conversation and occasional laughter stopped as Jagan entered.

The Guianese greeted and treated Jagan well, despite sour memories of his anti-business measures of the past two years, their losses from looting and arson in Georgetown and general pessimism that he would at this stage heed their advice. Conversation and pleasantries resumed as he circulated acknowledging those he knew and making small talk with those new to him. A few old faces puzzled him and the names brought a glimmer of recognition but he failed to place them. The evening social went smoothly although one of the Guianese Indians almost lost his temper after a few drinks, wagging his finger at Jagan in recalling what he had lost in the 1962 fire "because of your asinine policies then; and now you come here and make a jackass of yourself at the Students Union and let Burnham wipe his ass with you! When will you learn?" But barring the brief shouting, which hardly fazed Jagan—he had become inured to the most vitriolic of verbal attacks—the evening proceeded much as planned, with commendable civility. Their approach was simple. They had agreed on a business plan and a political position, not linked, and in a suitable moment after dinner the host would take him aside and privately present them, one on one. And so he did.

"We have a suggestion, an offer really; you want investment and *industrialisation*-- whatever that means—we take it that's for factory-type projects to employ city Blacks. Among us we can raise immediately enough to get you started, the same amount you wanted from the Americans." Jagan raised his eyebrows appreciably. "We know your road to Bartica is stalled and that the strike crippled your finances. You're technically bankrupt. You're losing to Burnham, but you can stop that. Unfortunately, the way you're going, you'll go home empty, politically and economically!"

"What are you telling me?" Jagan sounded harsh, confrontational, bristling.

They sat facing each other in front of a crackling fire. The room was large and elegantly furnished with sofas, arm chairs and occasional tables, an escritoire, cream-carpeted floors, scattered Indian rugs, manicured walls with French trim and heavy maroon drapes over sheer hangings at the two windows. Several paintings occupied the squares and oblongs framed by the stained wood trim.

"That English Colonel you met is a confidante," the host replied, "our friend in high places, as they say; we have for good reason distrusted the Brits for generations; the higher up the ladder the worse they are; it's our first reaction, but there are some decent ones. Years ago, at the start of the War this man served on a special mission in BG--relating to Nazi plans for South America--and tells us he fell in love with its wildness and its promise, as well as with one of 'its flowers'--a youngish wife neglected by her much older wheeler-dealer do-it-all, grab-it-all husband, the kind you love to hate; he keeps racehorses; the Colonel would love to see the Anglo-Indian child he left in Georgetown, now a young woman, also a horse fancier, with her own thoroughbred, and had hoped to command the troops that are there, but that didn't happen. He's gone so far as to establish a trust for her, against the day political events might force her to come here, even though her parents are quite well off. But, he worries about them, because he worries about what will happen to BG under Burnham. You see, he's privy to things you haven't heard of yet, transatlantic talk, UK's rush to dump BG, and would like to help you avoid that terrible outcome; to do that you must make the right decisions in matters of PR, Communism versus moderation, and border security; don't rush into independence without at least winning those. He knows that if you stick to Communism you'll lose BG and he too will lose. You see, he dreams of retiring there, deep in the hinterland on a tepui in the Cuyuni that overlooks the *Kanaima Itabo*. Do you know where that is?"

"He must be joking; nobody lives in the bush!"

"Really? Have you been anywhere near there?"

"No."

"Yet you dismiss it; I haven't either, but when I saw the photos and heard his story, I wish I could go there, but my age and diabetes won't let me. Still, as long as we have life we have hope; we'll see."

Jagan said nothing; the rebuke went over his head; he stood up and walked over to a large painting on the wall showing in vivid colours a typical rural Guianese bungalow, on eight-foot stilts, unpainted, of weathered greenheart and dressed with new Muranese glass casements in a setting of tall trees: flamingo, mango, guinep, and a spreading guava tree laden with fruit, with flowering red hibiscus and oleander on either side of the entrance to the yard and a stand of crotons near the stairs; three chickens scratched the earth, and a dog slept at the foot of the stairs that led to the front door; a girl and a boy, perhaps five and six sat on the topmost step peering intently at a picture book. He returned to his seat.

"Where is that place? Anywhere I know?" Jagan asked, the typical edge in his voice subdued.

"It's where I came from; it's where you came from; it's where all the men in that room came from; and look today, they have fancy properties in this the world's most influential city, and thriving businesses, some with US and European branches. How did they do that? Not with your philosophy! And yet there's not a man out there who would forget that past and not go back with you and work to make BG prosper, not for themselves, but for everyone, if you could only absorb and accept what our English friends just told you, that this is your last chance to lead BG into independence."

"So I assume you have a proposal." Jagan said, seemingly ignoring the concern and admonition, harshness, umbrage even, returning to his voice.

"Yes, we do. In your speeches you talk of development and industrialisation as if they can be done by a snap of the fingers; I'm afraid that happens only in fairy tales. Harsh reality calls for vision, talent, skill, determination, endurance and money. The drive must come from within; you cannot legislate or enforce it; you either have it or you don't. The British changed India to their liking by extortion. You don't have that luxury!"

"Yes, yes, I understand that," Jagan said testily, ignoring the reference, his impatience fully restored. His host smiled.

"We hear that you now agree to a mixed economy; that's good. You give us a solid guarantee and we will fund specific projects in BG, through individual companies that we will register there; any assets purchased or profits made will be free of tax for five years; this is no different from what you will give gladly to any US or European financier, under any international bank plan, World Bank or IMF. The difference is that we know Guiana and we, not foreign bank officials, will be totally responsible for setting-up and managing enterprises; we will also *re-invest any profits* in the country and only take out what capital was put in from outside, not like Demerara Electric or Alcan that you rightly criticise for gouging. We'll run ethical businesses and employ our own, both from here and properly qualified in BG. We'll train new staff in BG if we can't induce those already here to return."

"What about my people? The unions? Where do they stand?"

The host ignored the cynicism.

"We want to be free of disruptions; therefore we plan to involve all staff as partners in the businesses, as a condition of employment. Trust me; with us they won't need your unions. In your mind unions are natural enemies of employers; you and others in BG, I'm afraid, only know the oppressive British or Soviet model and don't see workers as partners; to us workers are essential and therefore a logical part of business. We've studied the projects on your shopping list. We can start with priorities. That's it in a nutshell."

Jagan was stunned. After a pause, he got up from his seat, walked towards the opposite wall, stood staring at the painting, his left hand holding up his chin, and without turning, asked, "And what do you ask for this?" Then he turned around and faced his host, with stern eyes.

"Freedom from nationalisation and all forms of government interference for twenty years except your representation on Boards and directorships, and normal processes of law and audit."

"And how do I do that? My government cannot give up its duty to pass laws according to our declared policy and platform."

"That's well put; you *will* govern; what we ask you to do is the only thing that will save you and your hopes: declare against communism at the next session you attend."

Jagan bristled, and blasted "capitalistic reactionaries" and "other stooges"; his host allowed him his rage, having anticipated it, and while Jagan spoke in circumlocutions, he quietly attended to his pipe, methodically bringing it back to life, sucking on it vigorously. Then, blowing smoke straight ahead, he said, quietly, "You're fond of condemning successful Indians as vicious capitalists distinct from lowly and poor exploited workers. But know this; we all came from the same roots; we're small as capitalists go; some might even say we're insubstantial, but on the BG scale our enterprise has improved the lot of many more than *you* ever will. Each one of us employed at least twenty people there, each with a family of four or more. Multiply that and you have several thousand, and only from this small group. Where are those workers now? Either here with us or *jobless in BG*. Left to you we would all remain exploited, subjugated by your philosophy; you've exiled most of your best people already. You speak of capitalism as if all enterprise is *laissez faire* capitalism, which we aren't. We are small business and that is where the economy grows, even in mature countries; what you want is a bureaucratic nightmare, so spare the vitriol. You like to brag about your 'struggle for independence', but that struggle is entirely in your own mind, not anyone else's; know this that independence was there for the asking, and on better terms than you will ever get. *We* worked for that and expected it long before Trinidad. They got there without a fuss in August last year. Your actions took the Brits off the hook for a lot they owed us. But that is neither here nor there now. What matters is that you're in one hell of a pickle; this group represents those who think they can help you, not because of you, but because of their ideas, their people back home and their own self-respect. Me, I wouldn't bet a penny to a pound on your chances…"

"We're not in a horse race; we're here to bring an end to colonialism and exploitation!" Jagan expostulated.

His host shook his head, studied him briefly, ignored the last remark and scolded him, rather gently and paternally, "Quite right; but you've managed to divide the one Guianese horse into quarters; you know that's typically Indian. Look at India; for generations riddled with factions; that's how the Muslims and Brits were able to take over. Is this how you end colonialism, by dividing your people and chasing away your most enterprising, your highest achievers? Come off your high horse and be realistic, man, you're a Pied Piper leading innocent followers to hell as it is; I can't believe you don't know that, after so many years of coaching from Tulla who gave you his life. BG needs Adam Smith, not Karl

Marx! Experience teaches wisdom to those who are able to learn from it. Don't be blind. I say it again. The Americans will never allow a communist government to take charge of an independent BG. You heard that tonight from the horse's mouth, who also took risks to warn you that that's not negotiable. So be smart. You can stop tilting at windmills and take advantage of the American position without giving them your soul. Tulla told you that a hundred times ten years ago, laid it out for you from the day you started and you ignored his wise advice. Had you listened to him then you would have been the envied prime minister of a promising country already, like Singapore or Ivory Coast, or Mauritius, respected by the world, not dismissed as a bumbling Soviet stooge, doomed to create a stifling oppressed backwater for you and Burnham to fight over. This conference is the last chance you have, the last chance for the economy and I'm sure the last chance for all Guianese. If you don't take it you'll live to see the most massive drain of what's left of brains and capital from a small country that's ever taken place. And it won't be Indians only; Portuguese, Chinese and even Blacks will run away from you two. These are the very people you will need for your imagined industries. The people you met tonight include multi-millionaires who began to leave BG from the day you and Burnham took to the streets; here their enterprise and European needs and demands made them rich, so rich they can help you without the enslavement of hegemonies like IMF. The two white men in there were born in BG and are among the most passionately nostalgic; they'd return there with substantial investments in agriculture and oil exploration if you let them."

"We are struggling to create a society based on socialism and the greatest good to the masses, not capitalism and all its evils. These men are capitalist exploiters. We're not alone in socialism; we have powerful friends who will not desert us! They will not turn us down like the Americans."

The host smiled indulgently. "We know you pledged Kennedy a mixed economy some months ago and he hasn't replied; d'you suspect why? He's one side in a vicious Cold War and you're not on his side. You really think the Soviets would give you a $100 million as they gave Castro? You need to cast your mind back. When you condemn men of enterprise willy-nilly and spout your isms, think this that our ultimate ancestor, the hunter-gatherer, was quintessentially an entrepreneur and individualist; when he came up against a mastodon he learned the value of teamwork, just like the first BG Indian to plant rice. When they became tribes they perfected communal living where many remain, as our natives in BG and across America. But some evolved into urban nations by perfecting agriculture, which some say began our doom--the curse of Kaliyuga.

"It would have been fine if all men were endowed exactly the same or if all moral men were more powerful than the immoral; that would have protected nations from aggressive and greedy egotists who joined others like them to overcome and dominate entire regions or even continents, and threaten our world. Today those cartels have settled in the USA, concentrating their capital in Wall Street from which they direct the exploitation of world resources, regardless of isms and boundaries. The US seems to have assembled all the greedy elements of Europe and elsewhere and allowed them to seize native assets to become the fattest nation on earth, where less than 6% of the world's population command a third of global income creating the imbalance that feeds your ideology! On that we agree. You've no doubt heard of the Bilderberg group, mainly Rothschild-led financiers, court Jews and princes who aim to own the world. So step down from your doctrinaire platform and get real, if you wish to succeed.

"The human intellect is very good at devising ways to study and classify things including ideas of social or political organisation. Russian Jews rebelling against their moneyed brethren came up with Communism, to counter Capitalism and that brought us today's simple-minded Cold War between those controlling money, the Capitalists, and those who wish to relieve them of it, the Communists. You must by now know that Wall St is politically neutral; makes money from both sides, in war and in peace and may even foment unrest for profit. Who do you think financed your Bolsheviks? The Great War was prolonged until Wall Street was good and ready to join. And Hitler? Who's gaining most from European reconstruction today? That's the beauty of the formula; you fund two sides to destroy each other then loan them more money to reconstruct; Wall St reaches into every pocket, every life today, as yesterday, and revels in the Cold War and the space and rocket races. We in BG could have largely escaped this conflict, had you not taken sides with Communism; we cannot avoid a take-over now by the very forces you condemn so much, though at times, I must confess, quite correctly. But you have condemned willy-nilly and have no strategy to deflect attention from BG and no plan to improve it, and even if you did, you've scared away and wasted its talent. And when you need it you'll have to pay heavily for it, and you have no money!"

Jagan was livid and forgetting civility, jumped up from his chair and headed as if to the door, but turned around abruptly, remembering where he was, retraced his steps, faced his host and spoke sharply, ignoring the main point of the discussion, "Look here, I hear that in Georgetown all the time. All of you who got rich take away bread from my people. *My* new University will train *all* the people I'll need for *my* development plans; I'll get help from friendly countries--America be damned! The traitors can run away, if that's what they want. For everyone who runs away, I will train ten! Mark my words!"

His host smiled indulgently, and with a soft voice, as if speaking to an imbecile, said, "I'm sorry, I let my feelings get the better of me. I didn't mean to be rude, just frank--man to man. There's so much to say and so little time; it's come down to hours! Consider this; you have winning qualities that will for a long time get you Indian and women votes, and even some from blacks and others, enough to win every *fair* election. But only so long as you have enough people free to vote. People like you personally; most of us do, that's why you're here, but we don't trust your ideology. You've heard that enough. So I will just say this as someone versed in the ways of growing a business. We want you to do well, but you will never do well if you continue to believe your own invective, like the lines you just threw at me. The US *will* give Burnham the country, if only because of the Black Power lobby and the Civil Rights Movement. Did you hear King's speech? And the spate of anti-communist letter-writing to the White House against you? If you seriously think your communist university in BG will fill the gap for trained people, whether or not with Soviets help, you're in for a bigger fall than you know. Sure Burnham supports you there, but only because it fits his plan too. He's another Nkrumah. Now hear me good; if you don't renounce Communism, your hands will be stained with the destruction of BG and the blood of your people, those you call exploited, and whom you claim to represent. That blood is already flowing, and you pretend not to notice while violence and terror confound the people, especially Indian people, and US and UK gang up against you. Much of what they do *is* wrong. But you cannot suppress or escape your role in making that wrong look right, and so you'll destroy your country; they, poor folks, don't see that; they believe every word you say, and now swear by you, totally blinded by you and your wife. And they're passing that passion for you on to their children, your future loyalists, your PYO. You know this and yet you're handing them over, piece by bloody piece, to a harsh and evil man, more conniving and vicious than you know, outfoxing you at every turn, even at this minute laughing at you, like Mephistopheles, while you paint yourself into a corner. Do the right thing, man, for once, for your own sake, if not for the hundreds of thousands who believe you and hang on every word you utter! Take our offer, and don't give in to PR. That will certainly hang you. *Go for partition instead!*"

Jagan snarled, as if to a stubborn pupil, ignored the argument and picked up on PR. "Sandys won't go for PR; he didn't give it to Zanzibar when their opposition asked for it; you forget that it was not an issue last elections; independence was. I heard McLeod say in Sandys' presence that PR was 'rotten and abominable' and Ed Gardiner asserted in a BBC broadcast that PR was a ploy to defeat the PPP."

He paced the room reciting familiar offers of industrial assistance from the Soviet block -- Poland, Hungary, East Germany, Russia and others. His host listened patiently, sucking at his pipe, and when Jagan ended he said, "You must know what happened to Burma. Last year it finally became a military dictatorship, like Pakistan. Except that Burma had twelve years of communist infighting between U Nu and others that ruined a sound economy, drove away productive elements and now faces poverty and dissension--a rich country beaten silly by thoughtless demagogues, not unlike you and Burnham. Learn, man, from the mistakes of others. Copy success, not failure; do like the Ivory Coast, not Ghana."

He paused while Jagan stood silent; then looking at his watch, he added, "The most serious issue you face right now is the outcome of this Conference; I don't have to tell you that. Burnham will not budge from PR, and the US backs him. We have our sources close to him and even as we speak he's meeting with a group just like this, mostly Black, including a US State Department official, several West African and West Indian leaders, including at least one Trinidadian Minister. You must not flinch and you must hold out against PR. Sandys will be under tremendous US pressure to delay independence or grant PR, especially since Kennedy's special visit here in June this year."

"I will not accept PR, nor will I become an American stooge; I leave that to others!"

"Strong words, but your position is weak, as so many have told you. Instead of PR, or if they force it on you, as seems likely, you should introduce the option of partition or a federation of two self-governing states, which you and Burnham rejected recently, rather selfishly and emotionally, we thought. That could still save you, since you also turned down the "county" option, which is how you should have started years ago, like the French West African model which helped your communist friend Touré and ex-communist Houphouët-Boigny of Ivory Coast. As I've said copy him: he saw the real side of Communism, rejected it for *his* country, which is like BG, and now he presides over a flourishing economy. You're aware, I take it, that Touré and Nkrumah are heading for dictatorships and Burnham's been getting ideas from them to blow you out of the water?"

"I don't know about that." He responded, surprised, frown lines on his forehead.

"Study this last strike and compare details with Touré's which lasted 76 days; coincidence?"

"These are colonialist propaganda; I've always opposed colonialism and oppose partition now; I believe even Americans will oppose it. You forgot what happened to India? I don't want to see bloodshed in *my* Guiana. Those who propose partition are thoughtless or don't know history."

The host raised his eyebrows and himself from the chair, said "Excuse me a minute" as he pulled a satin sash cord that hung near the fireplace, its fire still glowing in the dim lighting they had chosen for the discourse. He went to the door just as an aide appeared and took whispered instructions. Presently four men joined them, whom Jagan recognised from the earlier session as three non-Guianese Indians of about his own age, whom he had previously met at a recent Colonial Office reception, and a Black Guianese lawyer he had known for many years. He was puzzled by their selection for this *tête-à-tête*. The host reminded him who the non-Guianese were, that the man in the black Nehru jacket was an official in his country's External Affairs services, and the other two Indians were from Uganda and Trinidad, the former a lawyer and businessman, the latter a scholarly man on the faculty of London University. For drinks they selected water.

When they were seated the host said, "Dr Jagan objects to partition and fears a replay of what happened when India was split, the hatred and loss of life; he blames Americans for interference and for siding with Pakistan so as to get a naval base on the Arabian Sea. He rejects his friend Sydney King."

"Oh no," the Indian said, leaning forward to place his glass on the table in front of him, "much misunderstanding 'bout partition! True that over 600,000 of our people were killed and 14 million displaced, and we lost over 25% of India's territory, but that was plot between small clique of powerful Muslims and British lords; started in 1905 when Aga Khan formed Muslim League for exclusive Muslim interests, while Congress represented all religions. In 1909 Viceroy Minto guaranteed him separate and disproportionate voting rights for Muslims in exchange for loyalty to Raj. Jinnah stayed member of INC and had fallout with Gandhi and later Motilal Nehru over 1919 Montagu-Chelmsford Reforms and other issues. In 1931 Mohamed Iqbal proposed separate Muslim state but he wanted it as part of India. *Jamaiat Ullama-i-Hind*, largest Muslim organisation in India, condemned even this and Jinnah opposed it then, but in 1939 Jinnah and Liaquat Ali Khan surprised us, abandoned unity and joined separatists, for only selfish reasons, under pressure from foreign Muslim upper class. Jinnah did not share Gandhi's *Quit India* movement and instead declared *Direct Action*. Much violence followed; separatists won and gained such power that at independence British Minister Noel Baker took side with Pakistan and when Pakistan moved armies into Kashmir Baker lied to America that UK supported it and lied to London that America favoured Pakistan. In truth US and UK would have taken our side against Pakistan in the UN[171]. Things would have been very different if Baker had not lied."

"I don't see what this has to do with my government in Guiana," Jagan bristled with hostility. "Partition did not work for you, why do you think it would work for me?"

"Because partition was imposed on India, not agreed," the man from India replied, coolly. "There it was religion, for you it's race. So situation is very different; the call for separation in BG is thoughtful call for peace, to allow your major peoples to develop, as each can do better alone than together with so many internal schisms. If you ignore the hate that is brewing, you will in future kill one another from habit, like cat and dog; hate will become a mantra. Children will learn it from birth; you don't want that; we've seen it. India is prepared to help you, to help all her people overseas. Don't forget we still have bruises of wretched past. Beware the British; they are still autocrats; they don't think much of us."

The Trinidadian cleared his throat and spoke softly in his rapid sing-song style, "Your PNC "friends" are consulting with West Africans at this moment; you can make similar liaisons, which is why I'm here as your neighbour and ally, to offer a hand."

"And why I'm here;" the Ugandan interjected, "things are touchy in East Africa, despite the show of unity; it's a sham; our federation will fail just like the WI federation which you wisely avoided. And the Central African one only awaits formal dissolution which will happen by year end. Colonial peoples are too immature--pardon my saying so, but it applies to all of us—all fired up by Communism in youth and too proud to give up for the greater good their present range of power and the promise of much more with independence; most have poor economic foresight and don't know what that greater good is.

"Instead they will simply jostle for total and I might say selfish control. We see Africa as the next frontier as colonies lose the protective buffer of Europeans, horrible though their history, and become prey to wealthy and powerful corporations. But the turning tide favours natives if we can control that tide; right now it's more like tsunami waves powered by leftist passion and wild promises by mostly tribal chiefs who wish to regain what the Europeans took away and don't have a real feel for democracy.

"Africa has rich resources; the industrial powers, especially America, want those resources cheap so will have to find a substitute for imperialism. The models are plain to see. The dominant powers in Africa today–US, UK, France, Belgium, Portugal—will no doubt use the US Latin American model of installing puppet dictators, which has brought them huge profits. Already they're meddling in the Congo and Nigeria and pre-independent states. In your case it's plain that Burnham will win, with US help, and will ruin your country. We were Law students together. He's as communist as you are, I'm sure you know that; he did not hide that from us; we were too distant to matter; he used to tell me that

---

[171] See Ch.5. In November 1948, John Foster Dulles, head of the US delegation in the UN Security Council, complained to the State Department that "the present UK approach (to the) Kashmir problem appears extremely pro-GOP (Government of Pakistan) as against (the) middle ground we have sought to follow." On January 30th Mahatma Gandhi was assassinated by Nathuram Godse, 35, editor-publisher of a Hindu Maha Sabha weekly in Poona, in retaliation for Gandhi's concessions to Muslim demands and agreeing to surrender 27% of India to create the new Islamic nation of Pakistan.

my days and privileges in Uganda are limited; we often debated post-colonialism; he's not interested in economics as he knows Indians will excel if given a free hand; his leanings are definitely towards totalitarian power; he wants to enslave Indians. Today he masks his politics but reveals it through agitation, in the Bolshevik tradition. He'll sacrifice you personally, if it suits him. Take our advice, if you have Guianese at heart, especially Indians. History will not forgive you if you don't, unless of course you massage it."

Jagan's discomfort was obvious, "I'm fully aware of the issues; Guiana is not Uganda. I deal with US imperialism every day; if it weren't for them we would not have had such a long and bitter strike."

The Trinidadian raised his eyebrows and resumed, his tone measured. "That alone should have been warning enough. I need not remind you, sir, how fractured the peoples of our two countries are. The Blacks know nothing about us, while we know them fairly well; they share little of our culture and values; we share much of theirs and have even adapted some to our way of life, the music, for example, and some forms of entertainment. We who are Hindus and Muslims know as much about their Christianity as they do, we sang their hymns in school and church; I was even a choir boy in a Presbyterian church.

"We celebrate Easter and Christmas. How many Blacks have heard of the *Gita*, much less read it; how many do you think can sing a *bhajan*? How many ever went to an Indian movie or read an Indian book? How many will celebrate *Diwali* or *Phagwah* or go to a temple or mosque in BG or Trinidad? Aside from Government and British concerns, how many employ ordinary Indians, and how many Indian businesses, small and large, employ Blacks? They think we're heathen, unworthy, yet because of us the economy will grow and assure their prosperity. But our successes emphasise their failure as businessmen and allow demagogues like Burnham to convince them that we are taking away their bread and butter. *Blacks will not come to respect us unless they're left on their own to solve their problems*. We know we can build a country; I believe mine has no real future for my people unless they integrate physically and culturally and lose their identity like Jamaican and Antillean Indians. I do not see Trinidad changing its racism under Williams, and he will leave a lasting anti-Indian legacy, even if an Indian succeeds him. The future of our people lies with an Indian Guiana, which we can build together, with the help of our people from the motherland and our sister colonies. And don't forget the millstone round your neck: you have two border issues and Venezuela is really pushing, as you well know, and is probably already in town here right now to meet with Lord Home; you must make sure the Brits and US settle that but you're at a disadvantage there: Gallegos is anti-Communist and as anti-Castro as you are pro; so don't expect much from Dean Rusk. And don't trust Sandys or any British official!"

"This is all reactionary and bourgeois theorising; I'm aware of the border issues and will take appropriate steps. On the racial side, my PPP is made up of all races; I intend to remain the head of a multiracial party; I will not stoop to racial politics." Jagan said passionately and dismissively.

"You forget that it was those same bourgeois that brought you into politics. Not a single sugar worker voted for you in 1947. Remember that and don't be ungrateful." The host scoffed, with sarcasm. Jagan squirmed; the host continued, "And what about *apana jaat*, eh? You sir, are in the curious and risky position of having an Indian support base and Black opposition but you pursue a Black and anti-Indian agenda. I'm sure you know that an organised opposition by Indians in a predominantly Indian state will threaten you far more than an opposition of Blacks; your policies will only work in a multiracial Guiana since Indians fear Blacks and will unite behind you hoping you'll keep them at bay. The same goes for Burnham, that's why he too rejects partition. In other words partition will help the ordinary people see the light in Guiana, while for Pakistan partition benefited only the ruling clique. You saw how quickly they sank into military dictatorship. We believe both of you are scared of debating Partition openly!"

The Black Guianese had so far been silent and now spoke slowly, deliberately, his English accent sharply different from the others. "I've had the privilege of studying post-war independence movements, first in the Caribbean and recently I travelled through several countries in West Africa, independent or close to it. Most are socialists. I was one too. Black Africa is burdened by tribal disagreements and conflicts, skirmishes and wars in the making. You and I have disagreed in the past, but I daresay I feel closer to you than to my kin Forbes, not ideologically — you two are the same — but in your desire to see the races benefit equally from your welfare state. I admire this as you know. But, my friend, you are impractical and a dreamer; Forbes is the opposite, focussed and hard as nails, ruthless. You as a communist are no match for him, you're putty in his hands; you already know he has a strike force and that Police raids and undercover agents in the PNC provided details with seizures of plans and weapons.

"The strike should have convinced you Forbes is not joking, but I sense from what you say that it didn't. Here's my plea to avoid a Burnham dictatorship as my friend Nkrumah is planning, perhaps in less than a year. As you know Nigeria, Somaliland and South Cameroons became independent three years ago, Sierra Leone in '61, Uganda, Jamaica and Trinidad last year; Kenya and Tanganyika will follow by year end — all this with Macmillan's support, his *"wind of change"*. You should have been there already; we were ready years ago. But you preferred polarisation and a strict Marxist line. It won't work. We don't know how Home will turn now that Macmillan's going.

"Look around you and see what works. In Barbados Errol Barrow put Marx aside and will lead a moderate party to independence in two-three years. Côte d'Ivoire became independent in 1960 and Houphouët-Boigny did the same, and today his is the most prosperous state in West Africa. And he has no oil or gas or gold. He's like you. But he analysed his situation and put his country to farm and has avoided the hegemony of resource hunters. So take a hint and put Guiana to farm. (Throughout this the others were nodding visibly, at times vigorously and muttered 'yes'.) That way you also save the hinterland of which we know so little. Do as these two did and Lee Quan Yew over in Singapore, Barrow now starting in Barbados and Bustamante and Manley in Jamaica; reject Communism, even at this eleventh hour; make it sincere and US will reconsider; you have a mere flicker left in your political candle. Do otherwise, and you'll drag your benighted followers into a black morass that would make hell look like a holiday. If you visit the villages of Africa — which you unfortunately cannot do as I have done, incognito--you'll understand. Africa is barely warming."

A pause followed in which Jagan was uncharacteristically quiet. He stared at the Black Guianese playing with his pipe, a half smile on his face, as if seeing him for the first time. Jagan was clearly moved by the understated power of his facts. And being Black gave him a technical advantage over the others. Jagan remained silent, pensive.

"These arguments should show you, Doctor, how thoughtful minds have viewed your situation and want to help you steer a safe course," the man from India observed. "I came here to tell you as I said before, that my government will offer help to peoples of Guiana, *all* peoples. We wish to support Indians wherever they are, but we must be cautious and not interfere. We believe in moderate socialism, but we can only advise. We can help you with education, both sides, especially higher agriculture, industrial and technical support; clearly interaction will be simpler, more comprehensive and more focussed when one Indian state deals with another, despite differences in language and outlook due to passage of time. We can help you avoid or ease pitfalls of partition if you choose that route. We know that many of your best people are leaving Guiana.

"You may know that we have applied pressure to US and Canadian Governments to ease immigration and citizenship restrictions against Indians. That will happen next year or latest '65; when that happens your best educated Indians will leave you, if free to leave, same way we expect they will leave Namboodiripad's Kerala and any other place that Communists may rule or likely to dominate, like West Bengal. We won't like that but we have the capacity and will to increase our training and education, which you don't have. We can help you."

The host looked up at the clock ticking away on the opposite wall. He rose as did the others and said, in a rather gentle tone, "Beware lest you turn a potential paradise into a place full of poor oppressed people. You can continue as you have done or take a hint from experienced people including these men who have your people's welfare at heart; I remind you again of the crash of Burma's economy under Communism and the excellent prospects for moderate states as our friend has just described. His commitment to help plan a prosperous future is unquestioned; here's someone who has seen both parties from the inception and the movements that gave them birth; a few months ago he spoke eloquently in favour of separate development and political partition. Such experience should not be wasted. Think on what we've all said. I repeat our offer to give you a start. We backed the Hutchinson Scheme twelve years ago and see it as your gateway to a bright self-reliant future, and could start with that; it needs updating but not by much. Others will follow. It's more than you will *ever* get and on better terms. Your time is almost all gone, I'm sorry to say. I speak for all present. I won't contact you again, but I'll answer any call you make, anytime you want to come off that high horse and get down to brass tacks. Good luck."

In the following days Jagan acted as if the meeting had not occurred; he ignored (or dismissed) the offer, never mentioned it and snubbed other friendly delegations that yet again urged him to rethink his political strategy; he remained inflexible, steadfast to the principles of communism, and mesmerized by its aura. He met secretly with a Soviet group. He chose to ignore the border issue, the PNC arms cache and secret war plans and his failure to prosecute. Thus he utterly lost sight of the fact that by these actions he would forfeit control of government, and be eclipsed by Burnham who would proceed to humiliate him, trash his followers, and seize the country for his fiefdom. Soon he would discover that no moral or other argument that he could make would prevent this.

For Burnham, the prospects had begun to look rosy. The alliance between him and the US was contrived, inevitable and anticipated, even though U.S. Consul Melby, his CIA affiliates and the State Department were aware of his deviousness and despotic tendencies, both of which would enhance his qualification in US eyes. US obsession regarding Communism blunted its vision on foreign affairs. Having confronted the USSR over Cuba it took extreme steps to deter Communism in the Americas, and was prepared to take the fight worldwide. It had already intervened in Korea, the Congo, southern Africa, South East Asia and was studying anxiously the emerging threats in Latin America, of which the BG situation was the most urgent and required swift and decisive action.

By 1963 the Americans had tried for 10 years to bring Jagan to their side, and had exhausted all patience. Too many converging forces had conspired against any further attempts and matters were brought to such a point that even if Burnham had been a serial killer or rapist, Washington would have selected him over Jagan, however benevolent Jagan's Marxism, or non-violent. Kennedy was personally opposed to his removal in the manner of Lumumba, unless as a last resort, had even been willing to risk Venezuela's wrath, but had become convinced of Jagan's intransigence and had therefore deviated from his tour of continental Europe and the Berlin wall to visit London in June 1963. He had informed British PM Harold Macmillan of US concerns re BG's increasing instability and its unsuitability for independence under a government unable to maintain law and order. His press secretary Pierre Salinger had said as much in a BBC-TV interview. Then on June 29th Dean Rusk—aware that Macmillan had supported PR in a 1946 proposal for union with the Liberals--had urged Britain to suspend the BG constitution and hold a referendum on PR in the light of BG Opposition's demand for it. Meanwhile the CIA would continue its work to destabilise BG socially, economically and politically, to create enough havoc to justify Jagan's removal.

In his turn Burnham had devised ways in which he could exploit the properties of PR. He had earlier rejected it on population grounds noting that with over 50% Indians in a racially polarised electorate he would never gain a majority, unless he could team up with the third party—which he had dramatically announced he would never do—or somehow use his contacts in the Civil and Legal Services to so adjust electoral boundaries as to concentrate PPP support in a few constituencies, as had been done for the 1957 elections. He felt he could do either or both and that it would be a simple matter, if the boundary manipulation was not enough to give him a majority, to "show statesmanship by extending a hand of peace and accommodation" to the United Force to establish a coalition (though he would never say this in public, unless as a last resort). Once at the helm, independence would quickly follow. He would "retire" his hooligan army and restore peace and give himself enough time to "arrange matters" so that the next elections would yield him an absolute PNC majority, allowing him to discard allies of convenience. Trinidad's Eric Williams had discussed with him the utility of voting machines, and someone else had given him the idea of calling *"all Guianese, loyal and free, wherever in the world you may be"* to register as voters.

Burnham mused on these things in rosy detachment while delegates droned on settling the lesser issues, but sprang to life to resist any argument against his PR proposal. Jagan had planned to wrap up the conference in two weeks or so, but it dragged on. Earlier in the year, in response to Jagan's request for an advance to cover his annual payments shortfall, the Colonial Office had sent KC Jacobs to BG who had advised that the deficit for 1964 would be $5 million, a sum that would require the UK treasury to assume control of the colony's finances. This was an unacceptable humiliation, amounting to a verdict of failure and no-confidence in his government. It intensified his already high level of frustration and anger over Burnham's entrenched position on the electoral issues, and was too stubborn and shamed to re-consider the Hampstead business offer.

In this state of pique he surprised his delegation and private advisers on Oct 25th 1963 by meekly leaving the decision on the matter of proportional representation in the hands of the Secretary of State for the Colonies, Duncan Sandys, who had chaired the sessions and seemed partial to Jagan's views. He agreed to sign this directive to Sandys as the latter had composed it: "*At your request we have made further efforts to resolve the differences between us on the constitutional issues which require to be settled before British Guiana secures independence, in particular, the electoral system, the voting age and the question whether fresh elections should be held before independence. We regret to have to report to you that we have reluctantly come to the conclusion that there is no prospect of an agreed solution. Another adjournment of the conference for further discussions between ourselves would therefore serve no useful purpose and would result only in further delaying British Guiana's independence and in continued uncertainty in the country. In these circumstances we agreed to ask the British Government to settle on their authority all outstanding constitutional issues and we undertake to accept their decisions.*"

But in choosing PR--to many the weakest alternative, and less favoured than partition by many intellectual observers and students of the Guianese socio-political scene--Sandys merely bowed to the US, which partitionists had failed to fully brief, and so established racial voting and the separation of voters from their "representatives". These would now be chosen by the Party without any requirement for local service or approval by voters, thus shifting political loyalties to Party instead of the people. PR would promote the cause of minority and fringe parties, risk fragmentation of political support (since no elimination was required) and enable a demagogue to seize power and snuff out all opposition. This would leave people as voiceless as they had been before universal suffrage, reward antisocial and violent behaviour, and fail to reconcile differences among the races and their parties.

Sandys, awaiting further orders from the US, did not set a date for independence. However his decision, labelled imprudent by most thoughtful Guianese, relieved both the British and the Americans, who could thus avoid drastic measures against Jagan. The CIA would not have to "do a Lumumba" on him; the constitution and the new electoral system would. Sandys conveyed the decision to the incensed and out-manoeuvred Jagan, and much to the latter's horror, without a date for independence. Jagan erupted with all the fury of a woman scorned. He accused Sandys of breach of faith, conventions and agreements, of neo-slavery, dissembling, hypocrisy, and assorted other forms of wickedness. He accused Burnham of treachery, scheming and breaking faith, claiming that he had not campaigned in 1961 on the issue of PR, but then Burnham accused him of never putting to the electorate a platform of communism! The fact is that both had played the shell game, hypocrite vs. hypocrite; in the end the one with the greater cunning had won. Jagan's imprudence and blind obstinacy had led to his disgrace.

I had tried to see him, however briefly, after receiving a message for him from my brother in Georgetown about the plan by the London group to offer him aid (I heard details later, as above) but Jagan's schedule did not allow anything after the brief exchange at the WISU meeting. I wondered whether he had forgotten or forgiven my outburst at the Belgraves, but his greeting had been cordial.

We were playing bridge one Sunday in the Hans Crescent lounge when the porter brought in the papers. Most carried news of the "successful" conclusion of the BG Constitutional Conference and the decision re Proportional Representation (PR) as the main feature of the pre-independence constitution. Several of us who had witnessed the WISU debacle reacted with disappointment or astonishment; some of the West African students favoured PR and gave reasons. Someone recalled Israel's Ben Gurion's adverse comments on PR and so the conversation went. But regardless of where the voices stood on the matter, all—including the Africans--condemned the manner in which the decision had been made and derided Jagan for being duped in such a simple-minded way.

They blamed him too for his role in what Winston called the "continuing eviction" of Guianese talent from their homeland, men and women who had joined the inexorable flood of migrants from other Commonwealth nations streaming into Britain. So vigorous was the tide that the British government had begun to frame legislation to restrict coloured immigration; yet they were secretly thankful to receive so many skilled and hard-working people for their businesses and industries, at a time when British labour had become known for its laziness, unreliability and waning productivity, captured in the Peter Sellers' film, *I'm all Right, Jack*.

Later that week, I boarded a Central Line tube train and found a seat near someone hidden behind an opened *Times* newspaper. Some unseen force propelled me to break what I had come to regard as a tube convention not to look sideways nor appear to be interested in what the person next to you was doing. "Curiosity killed the cat!" the advice went. But I did look and was astonished to see Dr Frank Chandra behind the paper. I interrupted him with a discreet "excuse me" just as the train reached the station we both wanted. It was an amazing chance meeting.

I had first met Dr Frank Alexander Chandra when he came to Berbice High School to teach French. I was 11 years old and had just started Form 3. He was a brilliant student who had won the Guiana Scholarship that year and was awaiting placement in a British University to study Medicine. He left two or three years later and I heard nothing more of him until my return. After completing his studies he had returned to BG as a medical officer, and after various postings--as was the custom--he was given study leave to specialise, which he had done in Tropical Medicine and Hygiene, with sub-discipline Leprology. In due course he had become the Superintendent of the Mahaica Leprosarium (Hospital), just about the time I joined the Central Medical Laboratory.

The Hospital was governed by a Board appointed by the Ministry of Health with wide representation from the public and the RC Church, which had originally established it as a charity staffed by one of its Nursing Orders, and now absorbed into the Government Health Services. The Government representatives included a member from our Laboratory and I was assigned. The

Board met monthly at the hospital, an enclosed community built on a salubrious site at the mouth of the Mahaica River 22 miles east of Georgetown, six miles short of our family home. The Chair was the RC Bishop, a burly affable hedonist, who, despite his cloth, had a way with such luxuries as milk chocolate, fancy pastry, and round bottoms, preferably attached to nubile Portuguese orphans from St Elizabeth's Orphanage where he visited once weekly to "take tea" with the superintendent, and where, twelve years back, Ossie and I used to visit Angelica, a resident, who had been one of the splendid butts of the Bishop's manual explorations (so she said).

Frank and the Bishop dominated the meetings, Frank with reports on the patients, and the Bishop with his affable and business-like despatch of the agenda, so as to leave good time to indulge in more hedonistic activity, particularly the Nuns' generous high tea—easily among the best I've had in a life of high teas.

I renewed my acquaintance with Frank at the first meeting I attended soon after returning from Wappai and in the subsequent year became friends. He was a veritable storehouse of knowledge, had remained single and probably celibate, and cared for his mother and a fantastic collection of orchids, claiming to own at least three unique species from deep in the forests of central and southern BG. All were meticulously catalogued and maintained under optimum conditions he had established in a fenced area below his house on the Hospital compound, which had a prime location in full view of both river and ocean whose humid breezes were "just right" for the plants.

The leprosarium housed active patients as well as those disfigured with "burnt-out" (non-infectious) disease. Persons in the latter group without disabling deformities were allowed out on day or week-end passes. Frank was widely admired by people in and out of the hospital, and by the workers, more than half of whom were black. His political views were held private, and the only time he mentioned any to me was on that cold platform in London where we sat for an hour sipping tea while he awaited the night train for Scotland.

In the strike that year he had taken the same stand as I in response to the same Ministry of Health circular. Disgruntled workers and gangs from the local PNC chapter, reinforced by activists from Georgetown plotted to storm the hospital and, according to his agitated informant, a black man, to *"teach the coolies a sharp lesson"*; the man was sure that they meant to kill him and his mother. At first Frank shrugged it off as preposterous; he knew those workers; they would not do that. Later that day a police constable visited and urged him to "take a vacation right now" with his mother, and added that his housekeeper, a mulatto hospital employee, who had been absent on "leave" for a week and had returned only that morning, had been giving the mob details of his home and possessions. Again he delayed leaving, but packed essentials, including some of his prized orchids, and informed the Sister-in-Charge that he had to go to Georgetown urgently.

Early the next day, two workers rode breathlessly to the hospital, found him doing rounds and told him that the mob-- armed with knives, cutlasses, sticks and bicycle chains-- had begun to assemble about a mile away, and was mouthing dire threats against him and would most likely start their move within the hour. The nuns on rounds with him advised that he leave immediately. This time, the thought of his mother--confined to a wheelchair--made him move quickly. Arriving home, he found her on the floor, her wheelchair lying partly across her back, the bedroom ransacked, and the housekeeper gone. His mother described how she had been slapped several times for not knowing where "Doctor keep all the money". With the help of two Indian porters, he got his mother, hurt and in shock, into his car, loaded it and drove off, seconds before the mob arrived waving sticks, chanting slogans, then abruptly shouting in frightening unison and bursting into a run as they saw his car pulling out of the compound, heading west away from them. Fortunately they had nothing faster than bicycles, and so he outran them and although they pelted and struck his car with stones no major damage was done. In frustration they beat workers still on the job, some severely, a few suffering concussions and fractures. Both Indian and African workers suffered at the hands of the mob.

Frank sped to Georgetown and a few days later, influential friends arranged to keep his mother while they took him secretly by plane to Surinam. Before leaving he had reported directly to Jagan and to Health Minister Chandisingh, verbally and in writing. The only news release was a brief and incurious paragraph that Dr Chandra had been given "leave of absence to study abroad." Not a word about the assault on his mother, nor the threats on his life by a militant mob that had driven from the country a talented and efficient physician, the only leprologist in BG, well-known and respected world-wide.

"He let me down terribly; I would not have believed anyone who said Cheddi was so callous and self-obsessed, until this thing happened to me," he reflected sorrowfully, his soft voice filled with emotion. "I'm no politician, but I supported him and tried to be fair to everyone, regardless of colour or religion; I didn't believe what people were warning me about, so wrapped up I was in my duties; I didn't believe them until the very last minute. They almost killed my poor mother."

He recalled how freely the Bishop had shared his views of Jagan and of his prospects based on facts and rumours then rife among the people in his social circle, which included D'Aguiar and other prominent members of the United Force. It was as if the Bishop was hoping, by sharing these, to draw him into the UF club. But Frank in his loyalty to Jagan merely played along, listening, at times half-heartedly, concentrating more on his patients especially those whose condition was at a critical stage. At tea after the March '63 meeting of the Leprosy Board the Bishop had casually predicted Jagan's downfall "within the year", noting the recent remark by the US Assistant Secretary of European Affairs William Tyler that he did not favour Jagan as head of the BG government. Frank had dismissed this as UF propaganda, but had said nothing.

But later, in June, he had become aware of Kennedy's London visit. The British press had asserted that the Colonial Office had surrendered to US pressure. Frank reflected on these and on the Bishop's recitation of Jagan's arguments against PR negated by his precarious political position. Foremost was Burnham and D'Aguiar's statement that the PPP had won more seats with fewer total votes than the combined opposition, due largely to Jagan's imprudent failure in 1961 to contest the five Georgetown seats, thus imposing on his urban supporters the choice of voting for the UF or abstaining. Further Jagan had brought in measures unpopular even among his followers: the budget of 1962 and the Labour Relations bill in 1963; who knew what else was up his sleeve, perhaps increased personal and business taxes and widespread nationalisation? It wasn't so much that the measures were bad, but they were prematurely introduced in an atmosphere of hostility and fear and thus their intentions were so easily distorted.

"It's a sad time for me," he continued, "my mother died, you know, and now I'm stuck in this country, looks like forever."

"I spoke to the Bishop after you left; he told me that a PNC clique was threatening to kill you if you returned. All of us are astonished that the people you helped so much could become so ungrateful and vicious. Sister warned me to be doubly careful driving through Unity Village."

Frank was silent, overcome with the sadness of it all. Shaking his head he said, simply, "It's so unnecessary. It's stupid. I can't believe that Jagan let Burnham browbeat him like this. And now he's given up the country at this conference. I had thought he would have seen that the electoral issue was more important than any temporary colonial office take-over of finance control. God knows he could do with the help; it was the lesser of two evils."

"I'm shattered in many ways too, greatly disappointed in him; we were close once, and I could speak frankly to him, as to a favourite uncle, but when they threatened to shoot me in broad daylight, out in the open, he didn't even call, and you know, he made a great show of visiting a black fellow who had been beaten, about the same time, by persons unknown; I didn't really care but others—in the hospital and outside-- made much of it. Life has its great levellers, doesn't let us get too high or too low; I'm not hopeful."

I told him of the help Jagan had been offered, a last ditch effort, by a business group in London just before the conference and we talked briefly of friends and family, until it was time to go to his platform. As we walked he asked, "What will you do when you finish your Scholarship?"

"Hard to tell, I'd like to go back, it's a condition of the award, though not binding except for payment of my return passage, but so much is up in the air. I have a year to go. This PR thing will ruin the country; it'll bring Burnham to power and he's a crook. I don't think I can stomach that. We're not ready for independence, not under Communist Jagan nor Dictator Burnham. I don't think I could survive under either of those intolerant and arrogant bastards."

He smiled ruefully, "I see you speak from hurt. But you're right. I feel the same. They spout democracy, but ignore people who speak from the middle or right—remember the fight he had with the 'young militants' in '54? Both Cheddi and Burnham are obstinate and blindly ideological and have made democracy absurd, opposed both at home and abroad and will destroy us. Cheddi can't achieve his socialist *nirvana* and remain democratic. See what's happening to Ghana. Who would have thought Nkrumah, Jagan's African idol, would go one-party?"

"The Africans at Hans Crescent say Nkrumah will be a dictator. As for Cheddi, PR, from all I hear, will not be changed, no matter what noises he makes and to whom; the US backs it; if he pushes the wrong way, he might not survive the CIA. So far he has Kennedy to thank for his life. But even Kennedy's patience has worn out, and now that Cheddi's ignored the help of wealthy Guianese Londoners he's politically toast, as my friend Winston had concluded after the WISU meeting."

"I know that Sidney King and Dr Louis Bone had tried hard to get partition discussed, but Cheddi refused; I've met good smart people of all races, who like the idea and call it a lifeline. So now he's turned down two lifelines?" his voice low, his eyes wet. "Either would have saved him."

I stood at the door of his carriage as the porter carried his bags inside. The engine tooted briefly, and the conductor waved his light, shouting the all-clear. The sadness of the moment was unbearable, the huge flood of emotion over the awful displacements that two selfish men had already caused for scores of thousands, and that was hardly the beginning. The emotion was choking, and voices faltered. We shook hands, marvelling at the chance that had reunited us, like ships passing in the night, as the saying went, acknowledging each other silently, by symbols.

"Come see me if you're in Edinburgh."

"You have my address here; I hope to see you again. Good luck."

"And the same to you. 'Bye."

Almost imperceptibly the train eased out of the station and was gone.

A short time later, on the evening of November 22, as I entered the Hans Crescent lounge after a blustery cold walk in from the Knightsbridge tube station, the wind eating into my backbone, Winston greeted me with a long face and the news that John F. Kennedy had been murdered in Dallas, Texas, Vice-President Lyndon Johnson's home state. The news shocked me back into the deep gloom into which I had sunk after hearing of the tragic drowning of my brother's only son, Kip, age 12, less than two weeks before, in a boating accident on the Demerara River, which had displaced from my emotions all news of Jagan's final failure. For days I had gone about, in an introspective and philosophical daze, calling on all the things spiritual and transcendental that I had learned or experienced, to explain the cruel end to my nephew's life, and now the atrocious killing of a man of great power and promise, yet to reach his prime, who had begun to put a human face to the bumbling and avaricious American giant.

I held Kennedy in high regard, having closely allied myself with his campaign in 1960 when I spent six weeks in the USA, and subsequently followed his fortunes. In the two weeks I had spent in New York before sailing for England, I had been elated by the optimism and *joie de vivre* among people I had met, most of whom were recent university graduates and young professionals who all saw a hope for a kindlier, gentler, more accommodating America that could share its wealth and expertise with the less developed or needy. Blacks were particularly optimistic and hopeful that the movement for equality--north and south--would pick up pace and grow to provide them finally with a chance for full, unbiased and unimpeded expression of their talents just as whites already had. Would Johnson continue this trend? Most preferred to wait and see.

And more perplexing—who would have killed this man? Who would gain most? Americans were known to be violent and accustomed to settle grievances and dissent by the gun, at every level of society, including the presidency. Indeed the gun seemed as popular a way of making change as the ballot box, and the National Rifle Association was a powerful lobby in Washington, DC, as Elizabeth had informed me just recently. I thought immediately of the CIA, his own agency, for this was their style. No one could casually have had the prescience and the detailed knowledge required to put snipers at the only places on the route from which they could have had clear shots at a moving target. (Wasn't it bizarre that Kennedy was shot in a Ford Lincoln and Lincoln had been shot in the Ford theatre?)

Other speculations abounded, from Cuba, a favourite, to disgruntled businessmen, southerners and republicans critical of Kennedy's civil rights endorsements and "softness" on communism and on to KGB agents of the USSR. As a pathologist I was keen to hear details of the wounds, having fresh memories of my own reconstruction of the trajectories and other features of gunshot wounds. None of us that day in that lounge believed that it was Lee Harvey Oswald acting alone. And when he was promptly executed by Jack Ruby while in police custody, I was certain that it was an inside job with a CIA footprint or Mossad, as one Sudanese army and several Middle Eastern physicians at Hammersmith had promptly concluded. I knew little of this Israeli agency then but heard much that week, with added insights from an English colleague who had served in Palestine and Jordan and had become aware of its role. Some LSE graduate students had even pointed to Europe's most powerful banking family and those behind the US Federal Reserve, as Elizabeth had noted, which Kennedy had wanted to relieve of the task of controlling the money supply and who had determined to end the Viet Nam war, thus threatening to reduce the profits of the large military-industrial corporations and of the banks financing them.

A few months earlier, Jagan had written Kennedy a long letter recounting his frustrations with the slow pace of US aid, stressing his desire to 'industrialise' BG, the level of assistance sought, and his commitment to a mixed economy. That was a refreshing surprise. Although he had not heard from Kennedy by the time he went to London, Jagan had remained hopeful that he might still be received sympathetically--for that was the impression formed from their meeting in 1961 and subsequent remarks by JFK–despite the vituperation he had persistently heaped on the USA since. The news of the assassination put to rest any hopes that he might have had to appeal to a kindly ear in the struggle yet to come: the implementation of the new constitution under proportional representation.

In a way Kennedy's death put out many little lights that had begun to glow in various corners of the world, in the hearts of ordinary people, young and old, who spared a thought and dared to hope for a world of fairness and justice, which had become possible with Kennedy as US President. One of these was Maria, the blonde German Swiss sociologist from St Gallen who had come to London on a three month study bursary for English immersion. She was enamoured of the man, and spoke incessantly of her faith in him. She was a virgin in her late twenties when Jack London introduced us on one of those study-visits that the British Council had organised for foreign students to meet British people in historic places—this one to Banbury, Oxfordshire, in late September. (This was Flora Pierce's home town, but she was away that week-end and I did not get another chance to visit.)

Maria had befriended Del London at a Roman Catholic Church social in Denmark Hill. She thought my English was easier to understand than the Londoners' and I had agreed with her supervisor to help; we had met several times since, on weekends, at a teahouse in Soho. She revealed a surprising knowledge of the Americas, knew something of BG and the Caribbean, and had gone so far as to enlist with a Catholic mission active in the region, but had not yet found the "linguistic courage" to accept an assignment. She was infatuated also with Jagan, the person, "Oh, I so love him to smile!" as she had put it in her way of speaking and disbelieved that he was a Communist, ("but, oh, he is too nice!" she defended him, "communists have thick hair on the lips and fat round faces! They are too mean.").

It took me a while to fully grasp the profundity of her reaction, perhaps because I was unprepared for it, as indeed I had been for Elizabeth's insights. But who would expect a young person from a small town in eastern Switzerland to be familiar with the affairs of a distant isolated British colony that rarely made headlines? She represented that silent and unknown moiety that one knew existed but rarely met, whose interest in human affairs was universal and kindly, but sadly rarely heard above the clangour of self-seeking and demagoguery. Her reaction had induced in me a feeling of warmth and goodwill for my fellows, mitigating my cynicism, for which I thanked her profusely. Like Elizabeth, she was sincere and agreeable with no obvious prejudices, such as one might find among those in a colonial setting.

Maria had visited West Berlin after the building of the wall and had cried on seeing the Unter Den Linden end abruptly at the tall structure and the Brandenburg Gate so forlornly behind it; she had stood at the lookout point where Kennedy had stood and been photographed; she had kept the newspaper photo, now to become a valuable "treasure". She had told me that Kennedy and Jagan personalised her "vision of the angels, one big, one small, but same" who would effect social and material betterment for humanity. She was horrified when I suggested that neither could nor would do that, although Kennedy had the power, but Jagan had so far made a mess of opportunities to better his thin slice of the globe.

She had cried piteously on my shoulders when she came to see me the day after Kennedy's assassination, bringing half a dozen newspapers with full or half page portraits of the slain president and photos of the death scene, sobbing anew as each grisly crime scene was shown. She never quite recovered from the incident largely because she could not picture anyone so horrible as to *want* to kill, much less actually murder such a "prominent, popular president"; nor could she envisage the circumstances that would justify such an act.

I was not surprised by her intense reaction. When I received the terrible news that Kip had drowned in the Demerara River, I had called to cancel a planned theatre visit (a curricular choice), as I wanted to mourn in isolation. She thought the cancellation strange ("not like you, you want so much to go; is it me?") and pleaded for a reason. In the end I told her. She insisted on meeting, ("I must to comfort you!") and showed a level of distress more appropriate to near kin than to someone unrelated and unknown, sparing no tenderness to relieve the hurt and improve my mood. It was a most impressive show revealing--as I experienced it that day and in the weeks that followed, by word, gesture and actions--a genuine and deep concern for others, which at first I had thought contrived.

Now in her grief over Kennedy's murder, she held me tightly, thumping my back periodically with alternate fists, as she reached for release. I steeled myself against this show of emotion, saying soothing things until she became calmer, more accepting of the tragic reality and began to speak of fate and of the inevitability of death--in a surprisingly Hindu fashion--as a step towards immortality, repeating many of the beliefs she had shared with me on Kip's death. She left London for Zurich three weeks later, regretting, "I want to spend Christmas here, and go to Brighton for the holidays; I beg my office, but they want me back, many cases waiting; already I stay away one whole week longer. But you need more, too much more, for you to heal."

I was sorry to see her go, and would miss her sensitivity, fresh sense of humour and always remember her delighted reaction to what she had called her "final surrender". She wrote often in the following weeks from Switzerland describing how busy she had become, with "so many cases....." and dwelled on the Kennedy affair sending clippings from French language newspapers from Geneva and Lausanne ("I know you not read German"), and sounding pessimistic on his successor. She had maintained also her interest in Jagan and wished updates as there was "not so much interest in Switzerland in a small communist."

I had seen her off at the station; we chatted over a cup of tea while animated crowds milled along busy corridors rummaging through stacks of postcards, magazines and books, or stopped to chat and sip tea as we were doing. She had become reflective and concerned about BG and Jagan. By then the decision had been publicised and been examined, supported or trashed by everyone with the slightest political interest in BG. I was, as a Commonwealth scholar, one of a group interviewed by members of the press but nothing much came of that; we were too analytical and did not provide them an inflammatory or catchy headline. Maria had kept up with the topics and assiduously combed papers for news and comments.

"But I worry too much about poor Mr Jagan and what will happen with him. That evil Mr Hart, is he to take over from him?" She too had met Robert Hart at Jack London's flat and had, in her sociologist's mind, assessed him quite differently from Le Sage, labelling him with great insight as "pretending and well in need of friends; this man is not good for politics or healthy society; this man will hurt you and crush you."

"He talks a lot, but I doubt he has the strength or wisdom to do that."

"He is not sincere, I think. He has too much hate." She had emphasised.

"It's not Hart; it's worse, Burnham, the man you met at the Conference in October. He's the tyrant. *He* is the head of the PNC."

"The ugly man with the sneer? He's worse? Worse than Mr Hart?"

Her disbelief was genuine and spontaneous. She paused for confirmation, then moaned, grabbing me by the waist, "Oh, no, noooh! Now I will worry too much more for you when you go back!"

Just then a brief hoot had signalled the train's departure. Tears trailed down from her eyes as I hurriedly kissed her goodbye, tasting their saltiness; she had boarded quickly and waved. For the third time in three months, I was standing once again on a chilly platform and seized with a great emptiness as I watched a friend disappearing into the sombre evening as the train eased out of the station and was soon lost in the gloom of the tunnel that swallowed it. Then all was silence despite the hubbub of traffic and press of people at one of London's busiest termini.

The main gold-bearing areas, also heavily forested, of Mazaruni and Cuyuni basins, the former shown in a little more detail; Kamarang is at white marker. Roraima is due south.

University of Guyana, Turkeyen, early construction

Kassim and Shami Bacchus with daughter Narri, 1968. As Permanent Secretary in the Ministry of education, he had done key work on UG plans

Chapter 20

The Premier protests the Secretary of State's decree of Proportional Representation as the basis of BG's independence constitution. Violence erupts as his union base strikes and clashes with Police and the more prepared Opposition, which escapes charges despite subversive activities and discovery at its HQ of arms and bomb-making material during the long strike; a massacre of Indians takes place at Wismar, near the bauxite town of Mackenzie. An election is imposed for December 1964. The PPP gains a majority of seats but the Governor invites the Opposition parties to form a pre-independence government. The new Government quickly asserts its control of Police; protesters and leaders are promptly jailed for protesting, although far less disruptively than the governing coalition had done with impunity when in Opposition! The seeds of a racial dictatorship are sown.

The End of the Beginning

"If you're so concerned for that worker, teach him to be a good worker, not idle. That good-for-nothing is not a worker; I am worker. I put in at least 12 hours every day, non-stop. You low-rate the meaning of work if you call every hanger-on who vote for you a worker."   Georgetown businessman N. Mattai to Jagan 1954

Sometimes it is said that man cannot be trusted with the government of himself. Can he, then, be trusted with the government of others?   US Senator William J. Bryan, 1898

"I wish they'd make up their mind; which gang of hooligans will run this country."
        Boris Pasternak, Dr Zhivago

"Jagan get shack out[172]!"   DeHoop rice farmer, Dec 1964

Despite all Jagan's protestations Sandys refused to change his decision re PR. In January 1964 the PPP began protests to show pro-Jagan solidarity. In what it called a *'hurricane of protest'* planned to culminate in a Citizens Freedom Rally crowds assembled at each end of the settled coast, from the Courantyne in the east to Essequibo in the west and started to march simultaneously towards each other to meet in Georgetown on February 9th for a grand rally.

Amid clashes with PNC thugs in the major Negro centres and in Georgetown Jagan fired up the huge assemblage gathered finally on the grounds of the Rifle Ranges and condemned racialism, fascism and other -isms arrayed against his "legitimate" government, invited Burnham to join with him and reject Sandys' non-democratic formula and D'Aguiar's rightist extremism ("fascism").

At the same time an intercessionary delegation under a Ghanaian academic, Professor W.E. Abraham, had arrived at Jagan's request made directly to Nkrumah and to counter opposition allegations that his Party was "anti-negro". Abraham sought a workable formula for PR, especially as Jagan had offered Burnham a role in government with a share of Ministerial positions but was understandably unwilling to hand over both Defence and Police to the PNC, as Burnham had insisted.

Abraham's visit coincided with labour unrest in the sugar industry initiating another round of tension and hostility—a recurring and predictable affair since inter-union and union-employer squabbles had become a popular political ploy under Jagan and Burnham, and widely used in the colonies. After talks with both sides Abraham was leaving in frustration on Feb. 19th after ten days of cold shoulder from the PNC and UF but in a last minute telephone call from the airport he persuaded Burnham to accept Jagan's concession of the two Ministries in exchange for a 12% exclusion (minimum vote needed to gain seats) and the Surinam (mixed) model of PR.

---

[172] ejected

Abraham advised Jagan that he wished to announce the agreement immediately to forestall changes, in view of the difficulty in getting to that point, but Jagan demurred, a decision that he would regret for the rest of his life as Burnham reneged on the agreement hardly had Abraham left.

Labour unrest culminated in a general strike on Feb 17th following failure to resolve a dispute at Leonora Estate, West Coast Demerara. The employers responded by employing scabs from Georgetown, mostly negroes, to break the strike, resulting in various clashes and serious injury; for example, on March 6th, pickets at Leonora were assaulted by a non-striker who drove an estate tractor into their gathering, severing the body of one woman, Kowsilla, and maiming three others: Daisy, Jagdai and Sukhram.

Despite this setback, the Sugar Producers Association (SPA)--as irascible and stubborn as Jagan's Guiana Agricultural Workers Union (GAWU) — incomprehensibly and provocatively refused to recognise the union despite its presentation of confirmation of membership by 56% of sugar workers. This intensified the animosities and led to further clashes, often vicious and lethal, with bombs, Molotov cocktails and hand weapons.

The Police unfortunately did not always play a neutral or peace-keeping role, and were seen to be openly siding with scabs or marauding Blacks and transporting them in police vehicles to workplaces on strike. In another incident at Leonora a bomb thrown at the Union organiser, M. Mootoo, blew off his right hand when he blocked it. Many violent incidents of attack and defence punctuated the tense atmosphere resulting in death of a few adults and at least one child, bombed in a bus on the East Coast road at Lusignan.

Negro scabs from Georgetown continually attacked strikers and other Indians well into May and burned their property in a succession of terror not unlike that aimed at Nkrumah in 1962-3 by segments of his opposition United Party. This plus Police bias and use of lethal force at points of confrontation, or at times in the absence of conflict, resulted in many killed or maimed, mainly Indians, in all three counties. For example, on May 21 Police shot three Indians standing on the Public Road at Zeelugt, WCD, killing two and seriously injuring the third; nearby other Policemen beat a man to death.

Elsewhere a few instances of poetic justice relieved the one-sided struggle: a bomb exploded in the hand of a man, blowing his head off and tearing his limbs apart, as he was about to throw it at a group of fellow Indians who were PPP supporters guarding the yard of assemblyman Vic Downer. In another incident a bomb exploded in the hand of a PNC activist while he was assembling it at his home in New Amsterdam. His wife was injured also. Police found bomb-making materials on the premises.

The unrest that began with the rally in February was followed by a strike for union recognition--the very heart of Jagan's Labour Relations Bill — and grew quickly into open racial conflict. By the middle of May the anger and violence had escalated to the point that reprisals had begun to occur with injury to PNC activists and supporters. On May 23rd two Negroes died near Buxton; Indians were blamed. This led to widespread retaliation by PNC gangs, much better prepared, equipped and more practised, who rampaged through town and country killing many, inflicting numerous serious injuries--many life-threatening--and committing multiple acts of arson, looting, robbery and murder along the coast.

In one day sixty people were injured in Georgetown and on May 26th the violence became particularly vicious in the Mackenzie-Wismar area, where the minority Indian population was systematically terrorised, brutalised, raped and killed. In all 2,668 families were affected, 176 killed, 920 injured, many seriously. Scores of Indian women, including girls aged eleven, twelve and in the early teens, were raped and battered. Five blacks killed in retaliation were treated as martyrs in Burnham's speeches and by the press while both dismissed Indian deaths as "casualties of war". Arson destroyed 1,400 Indian homes, the loss totalling over $5 million. The Commissioner of Police ascribed all to "a criminal gang attached to…the Peoples National Congress".

Following the night of the Wismar massacre Janet Jagan resigned her position as Minister of Home Affairs to protest Police and Army failure to "serve and protect" the minority Indians of Wismar-Christianburg. Fifteen thousand people who lost all were eventually relocated to a squatters' settlement on the East Coast Demerara. Jagan condemned the actions declaring them the acts of reactionary and opportunistic politicians against a socialist-oriented national working class; on May 30th he said on radio, *"You know my views about proportional representation. The Government of British Guiana is opposed to it. It is a crooked, rigged system which has been imposed with the object of removing my Government from office, even before the expiry of its normal term. But I have no doubt that in the end justice will prevail. All of you decent-minded people, I know, abhor the crude methods being used in the name of democracy."*

The agitation and seditious violence continued and several vicious murders of Indians were perpetrated that summer, despite the presence of British soldiers, including the massacre of several families—Sooknanan, Jaikaran and others--in Mahaicony, by members of their farm staff aided by a Police sergeant. Despite positive identification and arraignment none was tried. Similarly and incredibly no Police action has yet been taken against the twenty-five or more anarchists identified from Police seizures of revolutionary material at PNC headquarters in May 1963, Plan X-13. Those people remained at large and active, to citizens' disbelief.

A meeting of the Commonwealth Prime Ministers Conference was planned for July 1964, which Jagan thought would be a good opportunity to raise the troubling constitutional, labour and governance issues. To prepare the ground Jagan repeated his offer to Burnham of a coalition of PPP and PNC with Commonwealth oversight. Burnham's snub was no surprise, except perhaps to Jagan; he had tasted blood and knew he had Jagan on the run. Jagan incredibly turned for help to Washington to whom London had promised "no independence" for BG without US approval. He spoke to the US Consul General Delmar Carlson but Carlson would do nothing without the Governor's approval which really meant referral to London; that Jagan knew was a lost cause. (Incidentally Carlson had denied that the US had any plans to interfere with Guiana's trade in foodstuffs or medicine or similar goods with Cuba).

On June 24, 1964 Jagan wrote British Prime Minister Alec Douglas-Home explaining the rationale of desirable interventions re labour and land tenancy, that had been labelled as terrorist and insupportable by hysterical opponents. He complained defiantly that *"all so-called leaders in the West Indies have betrayed their movement, but we intend to carry this fight to the finish. The people's movement has* been destroyed by force. They tell us that only Communists rule by force, but here is their democracy ruling by force."

As expected Home did little to help; he was engaged in a close election race that I was sure would see a new Prime Minister. Jagan's hopes were raised when the British Labour Party won and assumed office on October 31st with Harold Wilson as Prime Minister and Anthony Greenwood as Colonial Secretary, both "friends" who had encouraged and supported him from their Opposition benches. Indeed Labour official Arthur Bottomley had fulsomely and ironically told him in 1963, *"Cheddi, if we do not (support you) we will be strengthening the hands of the communists!"* But opposition is one reality, governing another. The Labour Party let him down, particularly Greenwood, all the way to Independence.

Jagan had condemned the 1964 BG elections as fraudulent and illegal but in the run-up to them he had made many speeches and many claims, which did not help his position. For example, two days before the crucial elections, on Dec 5, 1964 he said in answer to critics, much suffused with self-praise, *"Let me remind you of these changes which they ask about. Let me take you back to 1943, the year I returned to British Guiana after spending seven years in the United States of America. I found I had returned to a country in which hardly anything had changed for the better. The old wrongs, the terrible injustices–if they can forget them so easily–I knew them all too well. I saw daily the abuses and misery of the people. I felt these and took them as my own and I will never forget them. I am mindful of what great changes have taken place just as I am mindful of the changes that are still absolute necessities for the people of Guiana and I am aware of these things because I look at them with the eyes of the people and not with the prejudiced eyes of the privileged few who have always had things easy and so did not want a change."*

And this: *"There is only one Party which has consistently fought for changes and for independence and it is the People's Progressive Party. I and a handful of others began the long struggle for independence long before there was any chance of holding office or of forming a government. We who fought them, and fight now, have not changed. If we had changed (yes, ask yourself this question), would the old privileged groups go on attacking us as they do? All that has happened is that the old groups now have new allies from among some of those who once claimed to fight for you. Today, there are many who speak of what they will do when in office but when I began my long struggle, the prospect in view was not of holding office but of going to jail. Where were these people then?"*

The assertions were a worrisome distortion of history, as Stanley complained to me later, and distressed many of Jagan's more thoughtful supporters. The strident claims in the two paragraphs expressed Jagan's shameless usurping and distortion of the whole movement to self-determination that had begun much earlier in the century with the enfranchisement of coloureds and the sharing of power with non-whites in the Combined Court and Court of Justice. Through this mechanism Indian voters had improved from 188 out of 4,104 (4.5%) in 1910, to 714/4569 (15.6%) in 1922, and 17,755/59,384 (30%) in 1945 which enabled him to win a seat in 1947. Moreover he had begun to pay *serious* attention to workers' rights in 1945-6, not 1943 as his speech suggested, although he did write articles on universal franchise in 1944 for the obscure *Labour Advocate.*

Constitutional advances towards self-determination achieved by local reformers after WWI had been thwarted by the declaration of Crown Colony status in 1928, a revocation more sweeping and prolonged than the one Jagan had suffered in 1953. If anything, his radical Marxist intervention frustrated reformers, galvanised rightist opposition, and did more to obstruct the progress of the previous decades than any contrivance of the SPA and their allies. The slowdown post-1928 was exacerbated by the Great Depression; nevertheless reformers succeeded in getting the Swettenham Circular revoked in 1934, an act that contributed more to Indian advancement than any subsequent measure, including anything Jagan had done; it finally secured children's education on the estates and punished estate managers as well as errant parents who exploited their children by enrolling them in work gangs.

Managers often defended their role in this exploitation by pointing to the willingness of parents to put their children to work for a few cents each day, which the father often dissipated in rum drinking. Indeed many adults who remained on the estates were the weak, the unthinking and unambitious. My grandfather, Hari, and later my cousin were among the many who had seen and condemned this as *the* sign of despair and want among workers and of the greed and inhumanity of employers who broke agreements and committed unspeakable atrocities.

Groups like the BGEIA had worked to ameliorate conditions for estate and city workers--although with less frenetic energy than Jagan would display--and to advance enfranchisement and self-governance—slowed by two world wars and the economic depression in between, long before he or Burnham had come on the scene, a fact he would consistently ignore in his dismissal of the Association because it had rejected Communism. Indeed by his own admission he did not identify a cause for action until one was suggested to him when probing entry points into Guianese politics and was guided to trade unionism.

As secretary of the BGEIA in 1947 he learned its plans intimately and simply hijacked them, and craftily used the Enmore killings of 1948 to gain attention from an expectant and gullible people, having seized the limelight from the erratic JN Singh. Before that others had worked for reform, such as the Ruhomans, CR Jacob, JB Singh, Indar and many more. King had introduced him physically to East Demerara, an area whose geography and demographics he did not know and I had described to him during our many meetings.

The ignorance and political naiveté of the general population, especially those on sugar estates and remote districts with little or no means of access to news or opinions other than those of local gossip had helped enormously--not to underplay the huge influence of his wife among people to whom white women were almost sacred. He was thus able to present himself to uncritical sugar estate workers as a messiah, claiming originality of thought and uniqueness of purpose, effectively blinding them to his and Janet's purely ideological and selfish agenda.

His familiarity with sugar estates and villages and the role of gossips in a virtually isolated society possessing few media guided his decision to recruit them very early into his fold to spread his message of deliverance, most remaining quite ignorant of the fact that they were becoming an intrinsic tool in promoting the cause of Communism. By the time the more thoughtful or curious had discovered the historical evolution of the independence movement and begun to challenge claims or re-consider previous support and point out the deception, the party had become solidly entrenched, with its own printed propaganda pamphlets. The gossips became irrelevant; those who came to dislike Communism and began to say so became targets of anger and abuse from PPP activists. It remains inconceivable that both Jagan and Burnham[173] would maintain the falsehood that independence was the outcome of *their* efforts, when in fact *their* actions had disrupted the smooth and steady progression of the independence movement and actually *delayed* it by more than a decade.

Despite all Jagan's actions: speeches, letters, personal appearances, Greenwood upheld Sandys' decision re Proportional Representation and fixed Dec 7, 1964 as the date for a general election. Jagan protested again and thought of but could not usefully boycott the elections. When the tally was published his Party had improved its percentage, no doubt by the amount he would have had, had he fielded candidates in Georgetown in 1961; PPP won 45.8% of the votes, PNC 40.5% and UF 12.4%, the last representing a decreased support of over 3%.

Jagan rightly refused to quit. Governor Luyt did not invite him to form a government, as was customary since the PPP had won the most votes. Instead Luyt turned to Burnham despite all the accumulated evidence of Police-baiting, seditious actions and repeated flouting of accepted canons of ethical and due process. Thus was the anarchist rogue rewarded and became head of Government after concluding a surprising coalition with the United Force whose leader D'Aguiar had scathingly condemned Burnham scant days before, but found the offer of the Finance Ministry irresistible.

To Jagan's dismay his protests in the following months and attempts at non-cooperation, far less vehement or effective than those of the PNC in the previous two years, fell on deaf ears in the UK, received no sympathy elsewhere and were generally shrugged off with bland comments that the results had simply confirmed the usefulness of the PR device to rid Guiana of a troublesome regime. PPP assemblymen had never been in the role of Opposition and the only model they had seen in action was the unorthodox and pugnacious Burnhamite one. Their protests were swiftly met with strong responses from the Ministry of Home Affairs and from Burnham's invocation and continued use of Emergency Regulations to squelch opposition. In June 1965 he detained several of Jagan's senior colleagues, including Cedric Nunes, Prakash Persaud, Pandit Ramlall and Joe Jardim, Jagan's advisors in the pre-independence process, thus derailing PPP's attempts to organise an effective opposition. Jagan realised too late that he could not agitate against an opponent who would swiftly use a steamroller to crush a fly! He had been warned repeatedly for 14 years and should not have been surprised.

With the approach of the Independence Conference at the end of October, Jagan stated in July: *"We want more than anyone else the liberation of our country from political colonial domination and imperialist exploitation"* and called for an end to the state of emergency, release of detainees and *correction of imbalances in police and security forces*. The irony of the last demand – which had been raised to a strong point of contention with Greenwood and Burnham--was lost on him. How had he so soon forgotten that as Premier he had vetoed Rai's attempts to do exactly that just three years back, or Janet's remark that Indians had their agricultural jobs so others should get Police and other positions? He felt repeatedly the sting of regret for many things, the latest for not allowing Professor Abraham to announce Burnham's agreements in 1964. So purblind

---

[173] Years later with his dictatorship established Burnham egregiously proclaimed himself "*Father of the Nation*"!

had he made himself that he failed to recognize that his sorry end had stemmed directly from his own political choices and failure to heed years of warnings about Burnham's character and *modus operandi*. To the surprise of many Jagan meekly backed his destroyer as the latter moved to seize the country, having won in a campaign of rebellion and anarchy in open defiance of all forces of law and order, which Jagan during his Premiership had been impotent to mobilise. He ruefully recalled Tulla's warnings that he avoid the limelight of international scrutiny and the unseen powers that would undermine his position by control of forces within his own government.

Jagan declined to attend the Conference, but the Colonial Office concluded plans anyway for independence and despite more ineffectual protests, the day duly arrived as an anti-climax, in mid-1966, ten years later than expected, to a now racially polarised society. Had Jagan paid any attention to the admonitions of those familiar with British high-handedness in India--most recently from an Indian official in London in 1963--he might have been spared his ignominy. Ironically Burnham had chosen May 26th, the second anniversary of the Wismar-Christianburg massacre--a day of mourning for Indians--which the PNC and its black followers would turn into a day of perennial celebration, claiming that it was the date of the Cuffy-Akara-Accabre revolt.

Again Jagan protested in vain, half-heartedly, while welcoming the event and taking another swipe at the US for fraud and for sponsoring a *"neo-colonialist regime to consolidate a Latin American type dictatorship in Guiana"*. He never seemed to appreciate that US self-interest had coincided with his own extremist blundering and Burnham's guile to complete the familiar US ploy of installing a corrupt puppet as governor simply to protect its commercial interests.

Thus it was that Burnham achieved his aim of putting the Indians in their place, by Jagan's dereliction, and cruelly rubbed salt into wounds that Jagan had vowed to avenge back in 1948, when he radically stole the limelight from the volatile JN Singh and launched his personal dreadnought to greatness, and wrecked it! In the next few years Burnham consolidated his power by going along with UF economic and social policies, and revoked several pieces of PPP legislation, even those that the PNP had supported. By devious means he enticed PPP assemblymen to defect and by this means weakened the PPP to the point that he would, with the UF on side, and the rigging of voting machines, oust it from power forever.

The ending for the country and for many was as tragic as it was undeserved, and for most of my family and close friends was a huge slide backwards from the bright visions of rewards for honest enterprise and dedication that had begun to blossom after WWII. But as politics turned far left these tender buds wilted under the combined heat and drought of vain ambition, greed and a political ideology that rejected the notion that individual talent could be left free to innovate and create and promote social upliftment.

In late autumn 1964 I had given a presentation to Commonwealth Scholars and foreign students in London and said, in part:

I have followed Dr Jagan's odyssey from the very beginning. His manic energy was infectious, and I was delighted that QC masters I admired, especially Don Smith and Cameron Tudor, and most of my friends, of all races, thought that his coming to BG politics was "promising as it was stimulating," although in need of cautious nurturing to gain experience and avoid extremism--an inherent risk of Marxism in the colonies--

and the censure of opponents who would find it easier to take down labels than to counter sober argument. In his early years in the PAC, forerunner of the PPP, Jagan had been forthright in promoting his philosophy and vision, and stimulated many novices, like me, to study the merits and suitability to the BG situation of Marxist philosophy, which he had adopted as his political strategy.

After five years of preparation he found his battlefield, the sugar estates, and his cause, estate workers, whom he called "ordinary men"; he focussed on them, bypassing the proprietors, artisans, professionals, officials, managers and businessmen who then dominated the electorate and had given him his first election victory. In the infancy of the PPP, he and his team began a feverish campaign that kindled among workers a hope for better things and promises of instant relief from the drudgery, exploitation and degraded lives they were forced to live. This above all explains the adulation of his public for no one of his calibre had spoken before then so intimately to them, understood them or united them with a vision of emancipation and plenty that finally promised rewards for a century of suffering.

For over a hundred years the estates had remained little more than squalid and cruel fiefdoms of wealthy absentee British landlords--chief among them Booker Bros, Mc Connell and Co.--whose minions ruled the colony. Yet it is almost certain that the current chief officers, Jock Campbell and Anthony Tasker, would support change and improve conditions if they were spared the spectre of a Communist takeover, which they saw looming menacingly over their investments. But it was naïve to believe that the white bosses would give up easily or without guarantees. Indeed the Robertson Commission enquiring into the constitutional suspension of 1953 had rued electoral dominance by "non-light-skin people"; their speculation that Indians wanted an East Indian empire could be construed as fomenting division between Indians and Blacks; Robertson incredibly dismissed the notion of a multiethnic state contrary to conclusions of the Waddington Commission and of the much earlier Snell Commission of 1927. This played directly into Burnham's game and led to the PPP split in '55 replacing "whites vs. others", post WWII, with "blacks and the rest vs. Indians" or "moderates vs. communists" – all of which were merely labels to divide and control rather than show what must be done or reflect the wish of most people for unity or a peaceful planned partition.

By1950, however--after four years of PAC harangues and ample opportunity for objective analyses of BG realities--the weaknesses of his conclusion had become obvious but were obscured by the excitement generated in the strident awakening of political interest that the PAC had achieved among the grass-roots of plantation and labour society, who were about to gain the right to vote and in this respect be the equal of their better-off neighbours in the towns and villages. They were caught up in the magic of the invective that, despite its lack of cunning and depth, did succeed in welding together, in a promising way, working-class Indians and Blacks in a common and worthy national cause. The means to this end was agitation through trade unionism and the political empowerment it underpinned. In the euphoria of the first successes the young militants ignored their own inner circle's imperatives to become more inclusive, to avoid a society divided by wealth or race or religion since all indicators supported the superior strategy of accepting diversity, both social and economic, and working together, all hands, for betterment. But their strategies led instead to divisions that now appear intractable.

Dr Jagan and his comrades divided the population of BG into "exploiters, who were few, and the exploited, the majority", with no room for mobility between the two. This was Jagan's political guiding light. To the former he gave the full venom of his tongue; to the latter he and Burnham made extravagant promises. Both men were heavily influenced by historical practices and intrigues of the US, UK and USSR before and *during WWII, particularly the anti-WWII campaigns of US "isolationists" championed by aviation hero, Charles Lindbergh, the weakness of Neville Chamberlain in appeasing Adolph Hitler and the strength of Josef Stalin in fending off myriad assaults on his dictatorship and his eventual victory over Hitler. In the cause of the Cold War the US had made numerous errors in Latin America, propping up dictators no less ruthless than their Communist enemies. It was said that if American business could have had the same penetration and power in Russia as it had in Latin America and the Caribbean (and elsewhere in the "free" world), America would have stood foremost as protector of Stalin and the Soviets, not their adversary, ideology notwithstanding!*

Tulla Hardeen, my brother-in-law, an entrepreneur and major 'behind-the-scenes' adviser to Jagan pre-1954, followed the developments with mounting concern; he had warned that this sharp polarization would cloud vision, frustrate planning and impede mobilisation of the best minds to the agreed cause of national upliftment. He had urged more thoughtful use of rhetoric and warned that harangue--although useful to energise the target electorate--would be inappropriate for the Party once in government and persisting in it, considering gaps in PPP support base, would limit his chances for success.

To save his people and do the best for them, as he had promised, Jagan had to enlist most of that 15% of influential citizens and the small group within them that controlled the money supply. Tulla had often warned him that Burnham had seen the abyss facing Jagan and was deliberately pushing him towards it, and once there, Burnham would attack his judgement, change tack, jump ship and seize the leadership of the Party. To lead a multiracial party largely supported by Indians would be sweet irony for the man who would work to ruin and subjugate them once again. It was no surprise that the fall of the PPP Government in 1953 would mark the beginning of Burnham's rise to power.

Dr. Jagan's prime success lay in recruiting and uniting the rural Indian majority which made him win three successive fair elections despite all attempts by opponents to displace him. Yet he lost the race for independent prime ministerial honours to a shyster and a dictator, whom he had brought into the PPP against the advice of many advisers, Blacks foremost among them. In his first mandate, he had focussed on ideological issues and disappointed rural supporters by not tackling infrastructure needs at a time when he had goodwill as a new and popular government and might have received CDW funds earmarked for BG but unallocated since 1947.

Fired after six months in office that first time, in 1953, with no achievement other than notoriety, he maintained his focus on Marxist dogma, and faced economic losses as he allied with the USSR in the Cold War. The Robertson Commission had commented upon this aspect of British Guianese politics noting that "the implications of communist influence in the present leadership of the party are not yet fully understood by the ordinary people in British Guiana, and although some of the more discerning may have withdrawn their support, it is the general belief that the P.P.P. could retain all the characteristics which make it incapable of intelligent government and yet still rely on securing a majority if elections were held in the near future on a similar franchise."

It is not difficult to comprehend Jagan's contradictions in his conduct of politics and his self-sacrificial management of government. He was inexperienced and a poor administrator, obdurate and unwilling or slow to grasp the practicalities and intricacies of planning, design and implementation of projects – a "bull in a China shop" rather than a strategist or negotiator. He showed poor judgement in ordering his plans and assigning workable priorities. For example he had a good land use bill which I felt would have passed were it presented by itself in sober language and not burdened with needless baggage. Instead he introduced it in harsh and tactless language e.g., "All so-called leaders in the West Indies have betrayed their movement, but we intend to carry this fight to the finish. The people's movement has been destroyed by force. They tell us that only Communists rule by force, but here is their democracy ruling by force."

Despite his grasp of human psychology he lost the opportunity to befriend or recruit from all sectors of Guianese society and lacked the statesmanship needed to unite all wings of social, economic and political philosophies into a national movement, such as Felix Houphouet-Boigny of Côte d'Ivoire and Lee Quan Yu of Singapore have tried to achieve after abandoning Communism in the late fifties. Nearer to BG fervent socialist Errol Barrow of Barbados has left Communism and formed a moderate Party. Jagan openly promoted a Communist education and ignored the importance of nurturing and preserving a broad base of local talent and expertise. A major error was to reject or ignore BS Rai's early recommendations to correct ethnic imbalance in the Police and Security forces, at least for rural areas, as recommended by the BGEIA, by the PPP's own study groups and by war-time Governor Gordon Lethem, even though it was British policy to use a different race for policing--just as in India they had used sepoys of one tribal group to control Indians of another or rival one. The Police Council, formed in April, 1960, and chaired by Governor Grey, had agreed that there was urgent need for the Police Force to represent as soon as possible a reasonable cross-section of the community. My Afro-Guianese friend Inspector Bacchus had told us on our trip to Wappai that Police top brass supported this once funds were approved. Instead the Jagans schemed to expel Rai just when Rai was making headway with this; today, three years after thwarting Rai's initiatives he pleads with the Colonial Office for more Indian police!

Within the party he favoured his sycophantic protégés above those with superior ability and ideas. Thus doctrinaire Communists such as his wife Janet, Ranji Chandisingh, HJM Hubbard, Brindley Benn, Moses Bhagwan, Rām Karran and others prospered over moderates like lawyers B.S. Rai and Fenton Ramsahoye, educator Cedric Nunes and a host of able persons who were rejected as probable legislators. Yet he favoured unlikely others like Edward Beharry, a small businessmen with big jowls, a smooth tongue and soothing voice, whom Tulla Hardeen had introduced to him. Incredibly and with little experience, Beharry had oiled his way to a ministerial post, which he proceeded to exploit openly for gain. (It was said that Jagan took to him because they shared a taste for bluster and white suits!)

It seemed that Jagan had learned nothing from his 1953 failures perhaps because, as he had often said, he did not see them as his failures but those of recalcitrant opponents and exploiters he was committed to fight--the bourgeoisie. He claimed that he had the full backing of his electorate, yet most of them could not begin a discourse on the virtues of taxation vs. no taxation, or of this ism vs. that ism and certainly would not argue strategy with Jagan since they themselves had been turned on by the militancy of his language and--inured to regard a "good cuss-up" as cathartic--delighted in the excesses of political invective. This response by his flock encouraged Jagan and the PPP hierarchy to maintain their bellicose style so often criticised by sober heads like Tulla and JB Singh. Neither Jagan nor Burnham had shown the guile--or was it desire-- needed to rise above historical hatreds and current hurt to deal with SPA "blood-suckers" and other opposition, seeing only the blood of PPP followers staining those greedy hands. Diplomacy and reconciliation were not in their dictionary.

As feared, the narrow and rigid focus alienated the educated, the urban middle class, the Roman Catholic Church (especially since Janet Jagan's ill-conceived, premature and sudden advocacy of Family Planning in the fifties), the wealthy and influential who effectively ran the country and whom he saw as his polar opposites and natural foes, but whom he could have enlisted--with the generous help and guidance offered by men of means and influence, even as late as last year right here in London–to the cause of national amelioration and development.

In BG as in Trinidad, my friends Winston and Ashley would agree, there was no real opportunity for rational debate since Jagan, Burnham and Eric Williams all condemned dissenters in scathing and insulting language which Burnham had used to browbeat Jagan as well. Marxism trumped reason and debate in public life and gave rise to an equally insane reaction – some said inane –a sweeping ultra-rightist condemnation of socialism that characterised the United Force, and the once-respected Chronicle and Argosy newspapers.

For Jagan this has been a sad time as he genuinely felt he was leading a passive, downtrodden and helpless people out of bondage--a modern Moses; he reminded us at WISU last year that his plan to push transportation, agriculture, power generation and distribution had had prior support of John Adler, a World Bank economist. This Burnham rejected as too pro-Indian! Burnham had by then consolidated his African support base by joining with moderates Carter and Kendall in '57 and moved on to active anti-Indian racism with surprising media support. For Burnham this was merely "testing the waters" to get the measure of opposition and to plan to overcome it: no frontal assault with impotent and effete weaponry, but infiltrative and undermining stratagems to take over from his former colleague and foil whose every word and action had made his task easier. His opposition to partition was apocryphal, a trifling sop to Jagan who had desperately offered him a coalition which Burnham's successful agitation and Jagan's refusal to turn from Communism had rendered pointless.

Jagan surprised and angered many by using his authority to discredit and dismiss Rai, his ablest Minister, and alienated others--middle class Indian professionals, farmers and businessmen who had given him crucial early support, and talented young people who dared to disagree with him or suggest another political strategy. In truculent and intemperate language, especially evident in speeches directed at the USA, he hotly derided all opposition and in doing so sounded more like a petulant child railing at its parents for denial of something trivial or resisting discipline.

By failing to involve non-communists in his dialectic, equating individual enterprise with the worst forms of capitalism and carping about it while seeking its aid, Jagan had degenerated into a rabble-rouser whose sole success was the mobilisation of sugar workers as a uniform and dependable political tool. He never tried to understand what BG needed and could so easily have achieved--orderly and peaceful change, by compromise, as its motto promised--not the mindless, rushed and unnecessary neo-Bolshevik revolution that he, his wife and friends had contrived, which has led directly to damaging constitutional changes, which will end his rule and dash the hopes of Indians.

Having won the initial battles he mismanaged his three terms as head of Government allowing Burnham to win on the eve of independence, despite three years of seditious behaviour beginning with social disruption and unlawful acts in 1961 and sustained by terrorist mobs rampaging through the streets of Georgetown, committing crimes, defying Police, massing at the Legislature and obstructing Government. Failure of the Police to restore order emboldened the mobs and on Feb 16, 1962, they burned down several city blocks containing scores of businesses, more than three-quarters Indian-owned. These acts were blamed on an unpopular Government bill, ineptly or more probably prematurely pursued despite sage counsel to modify, delay or withdraw it.

In 1963, after months of relative calm, opposition-sponsored lawlessness returned, again in response to a Bill. PNC and UF gangs conquered city streets, aided by the CIA and other US agencies, committing acts of robbery, looting, arson, rape and murder, targeting Indians, and generating deep fears amid chaos. They fomented a general strike beginning in April that lasted 80 days which threatened to bring the government down and by its end had left citizens bewildered, jaded and in deep despair; many lost property, numerous were injured, some seriously, and dozens killed. Opposition leaders remained *inflexible as Jagan took the moral high ground claiming the right to govern democratically and civilly, not by the mob.*

To many, removed from the founts of information or partisan propaganda, the events had proceeded with extreme haste, like a riptide that swept away all in its path; they puzzled to explain the vehemence of the decline of a once peaceful society into a state of civil war far worse than the hegemony they had promised to displace. Even ardent partisans had begun to question their allegiance to leaders who had promised so much and had so far failed to deliver even one iota of that promise. The troubled majority, fearful and confused, stood with their leaders, following loyally, like Browning's rats lined up behind the Pied Piper.

That was the situation that I left in July 1963.

It mystifies me that Jagan has remained adamantly opposed to partition and a mixed economy for BG, to moderation and neutrality in world affairs, and collaboration as advocated by his smartest supporters. His former associate, Sidney King, now styled Eusi Kwayana, had quit the PNC in 1961 and had come here last year with Dr Louis Bone to plead for partition. Jagan refused to hear them and had dismissed "visitors" from Suriname as "interfering", despite his own prior militant advocacy in Nickerie; Burnham had followed suit.

But separate development would have allowed each state to pursue its goals unburdened by exigencies of the opponent race. The confidence and progress each achieved could later inspire moves to cooperation, if not national unity and social togetherness. The union of differing elements, even former enemies, to secure desirable goals has occurred repeatedly in world history and even now former mortal enemies in Europe, led by Jean Monnet, the remarkable French internationalist--spurred by a secret cabal of high-ranking Europeans who first met at Bilderberg in 1954--have gone beyond reconciliation to talk of economic and perhaps political association, as a well-placed American friend has told me. In WWII Monnet had negotiated a union between traditional antagonists UK and France to bolster French resistance. The UK or the USA could not have ignored an initiative for partition of BG supported by both sides. That would have prevented the loss of talent, the rise of Burnham and his destructive destabilization of the country which has already cost the Indians so much in morale, in stability, in property and in lives.

Those who know Burnham well fully agree that given charge of an independent Guiana he will appease the US and rapidly consolidate his leadership, by fair means or foul. An indication of future manipulation of the electoral process was given in March '63 in preparation for a by-election in Houston, a semi-rural constituency just south of the capital. Of 298/696 queries re PNC registrants 15 were under age, 204 had left the area and 79 were fictitious! Burnham had at that time told his advisor Singh, "I live for wealth and power; what do I care of these trifles or indeed of history or who says what tomorrow?"

It is said that he consults Trinidad's Eric Williams on the use of voting machines and other easily corruptible voting mechanisms. He will equally swiftly move to subvert and dominate the forces of law and order – already on his side--alienate or marginalise the opposition and establish his dictatorship; he will create a culture of harassment, deep social divisions, economic disruptions, displacement, exile--or worse-- of opponents, aggrandise himself as the ultimate power in the land, Haitian style; or as my friend Winston Hamid so eloquently debated right here recently in proposing that Burnham would adopt "the way of Osagyefo (the redeemer) Kwame Nkrumah" who recently engineered an amendment to Ghana's constitution that passed with an impossible 99% of the vote. It made his Convention People's Party the only legal Party and he forthwith anointed himself President for Life! I remind you too of our Rhodesian friend Henry's *optimistic and generous view--criticised as patrician by some--that Ian Smith can save Blacks in Africa from sure enslavement by their own people if only he can get to stay long enough to accelerate their education for social upliftment, critical judgment and economic independence.*

*I believe with Winston that Burnham, who had in the past few years copied Ghana's United Party's opposition tactics of violence will now switch to Nkrumah's instead and copy his steps to dictatorship, having already used some of the voting tricks. I believe too that when he supported Jagan's withdrawal from the regional UWI in favour of a local university he **must** have had in mind Nkrumah's "Ideological Institute" built in 1961 to train socialist civil servants and promote Pan-Africanism. Jagan's University of Guiana started on a shoestring last winter and does not lack for bright and eager students, who will all do well, but I doubt whether more than a few will ponder the alternative UWI with its established range and quality, so swayed they are by the fervour of Jagan's advocacy of the one and condemnation of the other. This lack of critical thinking will for a long time trap the unwary to merely parrot the latest gem from the leaders' lips, as erudite lackeys. I feared for UG's objectivity under Jagan but that fear is so much greater as Burnham takes over and begins his journey to dictatorship. Thus will he achieve his revenge against Indians and begin the eventual ruination of the country.*

Even as I spoke in London Jessie Burnham was writing an impassioned open letter 5000 miles away to warn about the future under her brother. The tract, titled **Beware my brother Forbes,** said, in part:

"…Mother was a religious woman with strict ideas on morals and proper conduct. She used to speak often about the importance of honesty and the worth of good character. Often, especially as he grew older, I would catch my mother watching Forbes with a worried eye…When he left for studies in England, her fears about the kind of man he was becoming deepened…I have watched this brilliant brother use his brains to scheme, to plot, to put friend against friend, neighbour against neighbour and relative against relative. I have watched him use this one and that one and then quickly discard them when they have served their purpose. I have watched him with his clever wit and charm manipulate people like puppets on a string… today I fear for my country and my people should my brother become PREMIER or PRIME MINISTER.

"It is from this fear, this concern that I speak. 'BEWARE' I say, 'OF MY BROTHER FORBES.' His motto is 'the personal ends of power justify ANY means used to achieve them'. His Bible is The Prince *by Machiavelli. And we the people, should he come to power, will only be pawns in his endless game of self-advancement. Make no mistake about it: the attraction of political life for Forbes is the attainment of the power and the glory… as I look back now, the signs of his selfishness and boastfulness, now so familiar a part of his personality, was evident long before (mother's death)…along with ambition he developed a certain sickness, a sly glibness. He began, even as a boy, to depend more and more on his skill with words to achieve his goals.*

"Today he runs his Party like the way King Henri Christophe once ran Haiti. While terror is no stranger to our country, it has never been used to suppress FREEDOM, THE LIBERTY OF SPEECH, WORSHIP AND THE PRESS. Would these freedoms continue under my brother? It is my concern in this area-personal individual freedom-that causes me to say to my people, to Guiana, 'BEWARE OF MY BROTHER FORBES.' … It is perhaps an indication of his basic indifference to others that my brother has never found occasion to 'help out' or for that matter, to even express his thanks for the sacrifices all of us made to help him get his start. I don't regret assisting him; he is my brother.

"… his love for personal power is so great he will trade anything to achieve it, (and) nothing is safe, no person, no liberty that stands in his way. That is why I say in all

sincerity "BEWARE OF MY BROTHER FORBES. *Behind the jest, that charm, that easy oratory, is a certain dark strain of cruelty which only surfaces when one of his vital interests is threatened. I say BEWARE OF BOTH. I do not want to see my country become a police state where a power-hungry man can sacrifice our liberty for his personal gain. Many men are selfish. Many men are cruel. Many men love power. The world can tolerate such men as individuals, but our beloved country cannot tolerate such men as leaders...*"

My calls from New York to Elizabeth in New Jersey in December 1964 went unanswered. I had written her a letter enclosing the above and drafts of the events and influences in Jagan's career to 1955, leaving my prospective address at Columbia University for replies. None had come by the time I left New York for Jamaica to await a visa. As so often in human affairs fate (*karma*) supervenes; a delay in obtaining the visa (although the Kingston consulate was very helpful and conciliatory) forced me to yield to the pressing necessity to care for a wife and five children and to accept an offer from the University of the West Indies by their mid-June deadline. I apologised to my Columbia "head" who was sympathetic and offered to take me anytime the visa--which he too had pushed for—materialised.

At Easter 1965, I received a re-routed letter from a Lancashire address.

I'm so sorry to have missed you in New York. I took two weeks holiday to be present when I became a grandmother. So quick! But was I not the same? Andrew would be so proud; the boy looks just like his baby picture.

Your London contact returned my letter with a note that you had just sailed for New York en route to BG. Is this wise, with Mr Burnham in charge? The Manchester Guardian had a short story of Dr Jagan's loss. I was sad to read your 'speech' and the story of the men who tried to help show the doctor a sure way. He must be regretting that he did not listen to reason.

At our New Year's staff party my VP--the one I told you about--said things about "that one is now on our side" and later I found out that he meant BG and they were planning secret explorations of that area as soon as a syndicate was formed. That may not amount to much yet as there is greater potential and much expansion in the Middle East. They will however do enough to get an idea of reserves, production costs and so on and secure long-term leases. With land oil so cheap it's not likely that anyone will do much off-shore at this time beyond basic and <u>discreet</u> exploration in shallow water, although some forward planners are looking to the deep seas, especially in the Gulf. So your Burnham could come in for special treatment and nice 'incentives' to keep this secret. I don't think there's a time-table. There probably won't be unless trouble develops in the Middle East. I've overheard talk that many Arabs are upset that they get so little revenue from their oil and only a few princes and sheikhs get that. This will change, perhaps quite dramatically.

Something happened to change my life. My daughter's company is agent for a large American Insurance group that is expanding here and in Europe and had openings in their Public Relations department for someone who can speak French and has corporate experience; she persuaded me to try for it and to stay with her since I had no one in America. I was in two minds about this but after an interview with a very pleasant older woman and her offer of a nice job, working with her, at a fair pay--nothing like what I got in New Jersey-- and opportunity to travel and earn bonuses, since I'm a 'personne d'expérience', I agreed to think about it and flew back home after Christmas. I had difficulty at first but it was easier to think without family pressure, and after finding that

I had worked long enough to get a small pension, and seeing lovely pictures of the child, I decided to return.

So here I am and finally able to read your "book". I like your writing, its intimacy and in some ways prefer it to Mr Naipaul's command and force. Will you finish it soon? How else can I say how I feel; I re-read sections of your draft and relive the storm; I cherish the adventure and feel like I want more, but now here I am, and you are where I used to be. You would say this is my karma, or yours and mine? We are united by our obligations. I had moments of déjà vu reading your interview with Dr Jagan; he sounds just like Andrew did in his élan to fight for socialism, and gave his life for it; even the words the doctor used are the same. I wonder what Andrew would have become had Hitler not taken him so quickly; I'm sure at least that he would be disappointed how the War has failed to make the world a better and kinder place and that he had lost his life to no high purpose.

This job gives me a different insight into how Corporations behave, but chéri, ils sont tous les mêmes, bénéfices surtout. They are so selfish and pushy. Andrew would kill me if he knew that I work for them. Such a socialist he was. I went to France last month for my first international assignment: three days to translate for two American executives and their group, ten of them, at a big meeting to put together insurance for some NATO groups; now I am in the thick of things. I must be careful what I write, since I don't know who might have to open this, if you are not there to receive it...Write me.

Au 'voir and goodbye till we meet again...Élise.

"Cheddi get shack out!" (ejected). Cheddi and Janet Jagan

VIEWS OF THE GENERAL NEGLECT OF STRUCTURES AND SERVICES DURING BURNHAM'S "RULE"

Obstetrics/Gynaecology Block, Georgetown Hospital 1993; note disrepair and decay

Picture taken in 1993:The mob scene of 1963 at the Central Medical Laboratories (centre back) viewed from the rifleman's angle; the gate and fence have been altered and a leanto (L) and guard house (R) added, plus window air conditioner at left (ENT Clinic). The decay is obvious: rusted roofs, broken windows, fungus growth, loose steps, leaks etc!

It didn't take long for Burnham to reduce the physical infrastructure of the Health Services to a shambles of dilapidated, unsanitary buildings that had been slated for replacement since 1947. The broken and neglected sewer line--next page--tells all. It is amazing that his followers who had so raged against Jagan could tolerate scenes like these of people forced to wait in the open for a service which was often not provided. The laboratory which many had praised in times past was reduced to a travesty, a shame for the few who knew better and had any self-respect left.

"Waiting area" for ENT patients (left building; steps face the Laboratories).

Paediatric Clinic: *waiting* area, 1993

Georgetown Hospital; broken sewer line from General Medicine unit emptying into yard

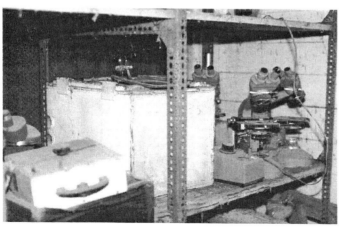

These two 1993. Photos shwo some of the trove of crumbling equipment in the Georgetown Hospital Laboratories,, It is illuminating to note that this decay of an essential service occurred while the US looked on and gave massive support to the dictator who was able to amass a fortune, reported by both Time and Ebony magazines as early as 1974, while bequeathing a gigantic debt to hapless Guyanese.

A row of former fine homes across High St from ours, collapsing from neglect; squatters occupy the yards and rooms.

Guianese Canadian profesionals and buinessfolk visiting Georgetown in 1994 for the celebration of QC's 150th anniversary; picnic on grounds of Canadian embassy.

A drunk off-duty–policeman moonlighting as a taxi-owner veered across 40 feet of new tarmac to collide with me. His 4-seater sedan was laden with 6 large people.They verbally assaulted me for failing to "avoid" them, and desisted from physical assault only when a young Indian fishing in the roadside trench came up with his long machete and pole and stood beside me. He had seen everything. Presently other Indians stopped, one recognising the cop as an illegal taxi operator. A police station a mile from the scene ignored my complaint but after learning who I was reluctantly took a statement but not before another offficer walking into the station unwittingly announced that *"Charlie drunk again and run into a coolie man car!"* The incident took place at 5 pm in full daylight. I was not let go until 8 pm, late for a dinner appointment with old BHS friends, among whom was Kenneth George, then Chief Justice of Guyana! Needless to say my explanation for lateness had a unique context and audience…

$G Before Burnham: Value 42cents US; today .005 cents US; original bright Red

Trashing Indian Industry: Above: Rice Factory *before* and below *during* Burnham's rule

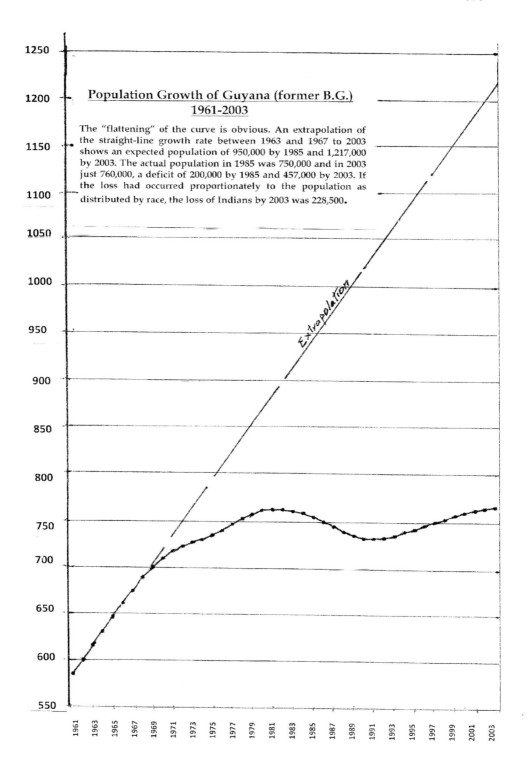

Population Growth of Guyana (former B.G.)
1961-2003

The "flattening" of the curve is obvious. An extrapolation of the straight-line growth rate between 1963 and 1967 to 2003 shows an expected population of 950,000 by 1985 and 1,217,000 by 2003. The actual population in 1985 was 750,000 and in 2003 just 760,000, a deficit of 200,000 by 1985 and 457,000 by 2003. If the loss had occurred proportionately to the population as distributed by race, the loss of Indians by 2003 was 228,500.

Extrapolation

Epilogue

The first casualties of the new hegemony begin to appear overseas, one, a gifted educator and the man who had helped me save my scholarship, landing literally on my doorstep at the UWI where I had started to work after both the UK Commonwealth Office and I had failed in efforts to contact the BG Government. The crudeness and biases shown, even before independence in 1966, presage ill for the future and usher in a cruel and self-aggrandising dictatorship under Burnham engineered and supported by the USA. Eventually both he and Jagan declare themselves Marxist-Leninists. Burnham soon gets rid of the UF and obtains a majority in the first national elections by "massaging" ballot boxes. With total control he emasculates opposition and his repressive policies virtually eliminate small businesses and create a climate of corruption. There is widespread seizure of farmlands and other property and major businesses are nationalized. These measures would increase the exodus of tradesmen, farmers, professionals, civil servants etc., which in time would exceed 300,000 people and trash the country's economy, bringing it under the infamous IMF whose policies would complete the devaluation of its currency from $1G =42 cents US in 1966 to $1G = 0.005 cents US by the turn of the century.

Pervasive despair: Burnham hogs the stage

Even a system based on a democratic constitution may need backing up in the period following independence by emergency measures of a totalitarian kind.   K. Nkrumah, on his dictatorship, Ghana 1964

Finishing a book is like taking a child out in the back and shooting it.   Truman Capote

My younger brother Deo was living with me in Jamaica while completing his degree in Education at the UWI Faculty of Education; I had taken a position in the Faculty of Medicine in 1965 having received no replies from the BG government to the notices that the Commonwealth Office and I had sent separately advising that I had completed my studies and was willing to return despite the tensions. One day he asked me whether I knew Kassim Bacchus[174], who had just joined his Faculty as a lecturer.

I recalled a Kassim Bacchus who when last seen three years earlier was the highly regarded Permanent Secretary in the Ministry of Education in BG and had begun changes in educational foundations for Guianese children which teachers had long desired and to which Kassim had added his research ideas and data, which he had assembled towards a doctoral thesis in the Faculty of Education, University of London.

My first reaction was that this was someone else since those names were not unusual among Muslims. But when I met him he was indeed the Guianese educator, newly recruited by the UWI in 1966, having been "purged" out of office and the newly-independent country by the Prime Minister, Forbes Burnham, who had swiftly begun to clean house hardly had the ink dried on the Independence documents. The moves were overt, disruptive, oppressive and startled many of the senior establishment, who came to realise, only too late that they had backed a viper, or as the Jamaicans would say, "exchanged black dog fo' monkey," or in this case, more aptly, as an Indo-Guianese said, "monkey for a dog!" His "ouster", like mine earlier, was only one of many that would follow as Burnham consolidated his dictatorship.

Kassim was a mild-mannered and patient man of medium height, stocky, with a round face and thick hair; he had a charming and youthful wife with three children, two girls and a boy, a few years older than my own. The children and

---

[174] A gifted academic, a Guianese Indian Muslim, known for tolerance and inclusivity, no relation to Inspector Bacchus, he left the UWI in 1970 for a professorship in Educational Foundations at the University of Alberta, Edmonton, Canada.

our two families became instant friends, and have remained close. On our first social, we made up lost ground on "back home issues", particularly the situation that had led to the incivility he had experienced with Burnham's "victory" in 1964, the harassment, and finally the not-so-veiled threats, when he declined to give way to one of Burnham's Black choices, as by his terms of employment, he could not be fired except for dereliction of duty, while the record clearly showed the opposite. He recalled with regret overlooking and even excusing the many errors that Jagan had made in his Ministry yet he never flinched in his personal regard for or loyalty to the man.

"I thought I knew him;" he mused, "I came quite late into his life and into Guianese affairs, only after returning from California, but in the last few years I worked closely with him and Nunes; I judged him through those meetings and Nunes' eyes. What puzzles me is the dichotomy between what he says and how he acts; his speeches promised accommodation to philosophical differences but his actions focussed to one end only. And on this race thing he remained blind to the fact that a wise government could have united the BG races, economically if not socially, because it's happened in the countryside; people still remember what it was like to be interdependent and friendly, even when hand-to-mouth."

"Well, there's always been racism there, especially in the towns and villages, but people did get along, and quite well," I said. "Sometimes the educated are more intolerant, especially those with prior chips on their shoulders; it's a human thing, I feel, not restricted to a race, unless indoctrinated. At Queen's, and before that at BHS, I was cautious but soon made friends among all races. None showed any of the animosities we've seen in the last fifteen years. Sometimes I found it easier to get along with non-Indians than with Indians. In fact Neville Linton and I became part of the successful Y's Men's Club debating team, and worked together in personnel at the Medical Department after leaving school. Now the major races are fighting and Jagan lost; yet he insists that he is the architect of racial unity and ignores the fact that his support is 95% Indian, whom he always takes for granted, and treats as if he owns them or they owe him."

"I'm a socialist and an Indian, so I'm naturally attracted to his beliefs. But now things have turned so sour," Kassim said dejectedly, "I can't believe he fooled me to believe he was a *wise* man, not a wiseacre; I believed him when he claimed that without him the people of BG would have remained politically naïve, no vote, no nothing; but that was before I learned the truth and the past history of electoral reform; now he's brought Indians to a point they're worse off than they were twenty years ago!"

"Someone, I think it was Churchill, said that '*the inherent vice of capitalism is the unequal sharing of blessings while the inherent virtue of socialism is the equal sharing of misery*'. No socialist state ever really advanced except dictatorially, like USSR, China, Yugoslavia and none of these has so far given the ordinary citizen a better life, only restrictions, harder and less rewarding work, a tough life, terrible shortages of everything even food, and peace only as long as they kept quiet. In London I met several cynical ex-PYO types who'd studied in Moscow; they had no life there, were confined to Lumumba University, to prevent them seeing the conditions of ordinary folk outside. My American friend Elizabeth on the other hand told how people like the Rosenbergs risked or gave their lives believing socialism was better than corporatism. But China might surprise us."

"We wanted a moderate socialism. I have a nephew who studied Physics there, and is now trying to get out of Moscow, but has no exit papers and no good reason yet; he married a Russian girl, which makes it harder. I had denied the harshness because of positive propaganda and published statistics until I heard his stories. Cheddi believed the socialist slogans of the British Labour Party, yet failed to see that Labour succeeded in government only when it behaved moderately and discarded electioneering rhetoric and opposition diatribe. Look how quickly they dumped him." His disillusionment was deeply felt.

"That's exactly what my brother-in-law tried to show him in those critical eight years that could have changed him and saved us. I saw that in the '64 British elections and was so disgusted that I voted for 'Uncle Joe' Grimond, even though the Liberal party was doomed; Labour won the elections and kowtowed to the Americans just as the Conservatives had done! That hit Jagan for six! Poor fool! He should not have been caught like that; so many had warned him, up to the last minute he had offers and advice to salvage his position and the economy and beat Burnham; instead he continued to treat the country as if it was all one big sugar estate and the everybody indentured still. In the end he didn't deserve the time or the sacrifice that so many made who had the *country* at heart, not power for power's sake! I can still hear Tulla detailing to him how capitalism can be made to serve a social good."

"When I was a teen we didn't know much about Georgetown and the racial clubs. People believed him and sided with him against them. But after seeing the evidence for myself I think his big mistake was to dismiss the EIA as racist ideologically when all it did was to assemble an Indian lobby without which he would not have been possible!"

"It is the nature of man to bite the hand that feeds him. Cheddi overlooked and even denied the considerable leg-up the Association had given him even though he failed as its secretary," I said, recalling the trenchant criticisms of Ramroop, Rangela and others of that same Executive.

"I realised very late that he used EIA ideas to form the core of PPP platforms; he did undermine the Association and created divisions instead of working for unity. I believed in him implicitly." He sounded hurt.

"Cheddi behaved anti-Indian," I said, "and used to call people racist who sought equity in public employment, especially in the Police and Volunteer forces, even though he had been their victim; equity was one of the things many saw as key to fairness and justice especially in sugar estates and rural farming districts; incredibly he and Janet both chastised and expelled people, like Rai, for seeking equity. So many people, even senior Black Police officers had shown him how it could be done, long before Burnham took over. And when he finally asked Greenwood for balance it was ten years too late; he's nuts!"

"A bit harsh, but true, and that's more amazing because he knew of the historical abuse of Indians by Black Police; it was a striking feature of colonial BG, and strongly criticised by the BGEIA." Kassim's voice, though soft, conveyed the deep regrets that he was so cruelly denied the opportunity to do good work in a community that he loved; his wife Shami would occasionally shed a tear on recalling the cruelty of their Burnham experience and the "stupidity" of the Jagans that allowed Burnham to win.

"I've never heard him say that it was *Negro* Police that killed Indians at Enmore in 1948, the incident gave him his *cause célèbre*." I recalled years ago asking him why this was so, only to be scolded and lectured on the evils of racism and the temptation to propose it as argument!

"I see now that if he had not messed things up the authorities would have paid more attention to the BGEIA's resolutions on the issues; Lethem began to implement some in the forties, including the franchise issue. The EIA had begun to get results and would have worked with others to secure a more peaceable outcome. Instead we'll get more corruption."

"That's right; Lethem started reforms long before Cheddi." I recalled.

"Instead, he condemned everything, good and bad," Kassim noted. "I believe now that his infernal hurry before Cuba took shape was a Cold War push for the Soviets to get a base. But his bullying style and poor negotiating skills alienated UK, stalled progress and allowed Burnham, who's very very dangerous, to take advantage of oratory and negritude, to take over. Now it's too late for change, especially the Police."

"Cheddi was naïve enough to believe that a Black Police Force would remain as loyal to him as they were to the Governor. I recall how shocked my old schoolmaster, George Forsythe, a fine Black man, was when Jagan in '53 dismissed delegations of Indians, including one he headed, that came to discuss rural policing, and curb the high-handed ways black policemen had of dealing with Indians especially the elderly who spoke Hindi. Forsythe was a strong PPP man and argued for Indian policing of Indian areas."

"Terrible irony," Kassim re-iterated; "he scuttled Rai's equity plan which Police officials had accepted years ago; then, as you say, in '64 he was pleading with Greenwood, supposedly his friend, for more Indian Police! Incredible about-face!"

"That was when Burnham really pumped up his hounds; if people thought that things had been bad in '62 and '63 they had to think again in '64." I observed.

"By then Cheddi had long exhausted US tolerance and was doomed. He had so much going for him, personality, honesty, charisma, majority support, yet lost. No wonder that Blacks felt free to roam and went berserk, killing Indians and tearing Wismar apart.[175]"

"Even more amazing, he acted surprised when all the things about which he had been warned started to happen, and brought the CIA to BG." I said ruefully. "If he'd been patient and acted smart in '53 they'd have left us alone. They took real interest after the suspension and gave BG the scrutiny Jamaica and Trinidad had received several years earlier and sensibly opted for moderate socialism. "

"It puzzles me that neither he nor the Attorney General took legal action against PNC sedition, after Police discovered treasonable material, documents and weapons at PNC HQ in May '63. Yet a year or more later he was blasting the Governor for banning copies of the Police report."

"And to add salt to our wounds," I complained, "he acted with surprise when D'Aguiar said in Trinidad that the only alternative to Jagan was *partition*,

---

[175] Among Burnham's first acts in Opposition was to befriend a few senior Police officers and make them his confidantes. As early as 1951, Tulla had introduced Jagan to Police officers, but Jagan did not follow through, and when later, in August 1961, two Indian officers went to see him at Freedom House, privately and secretly, at great risk, posing as labourers, to warn and advise; he chided them for racism! (See Ch).

.

quoting many prominent, although unpopular Indians who had quit supporting the PPP--Gajraj, Majid, Ghani, Ishmael, Balwant Singh, Unus Hack, Muneshwar and others like us who had to leave or pay the final price. Now I don't care much for most of these chaps but Cheddi dismissed them all as exploiters. He drove them away without examining the position they advocated, without any compromise. That was foolish and fatal."

"That's true. When they were hounding me," Kassim said, voice cracking, almost in tears, "it was PNC people pushing and shoving to get their forces into place. I told Jagan everything; he did object, but by then his word was nothing. That was so sad; how terribly he misjudged Burnham. For my part I was so deep into the challenges of educating children that I did not realise that the US was so irrationally scared of another Cuba in America that it would spend so much in time and people, even Kennedy getting directly into it and plotting to change BG leaders or delay independence. That shocked me; I didn't dream that UK and US would support Burnham since both the Governor and US consul Melby called him dishonest and sly. And of course D'Aguiar's *laissez faire* capitalism was the same as the estates and his claims so fanciful he only boosted the extremists.

"He too was headstrong and should have followed good advice to develop some moderate alternatives. I was not in favour of partition until the Wismar massacre and I saw the refugees and heard their stories personally. Then I heard that a group in London had made him an offer but no details until I came here and heard from someone who knew of the meeting. It was foolish to reject them and leave the constitutional decision to Sandys."

"I hope he realises that Burnham is going along now with a lot of UF-inspired policies, revoking tax bills and levies, and easing restrictions on businesses and foreign ownership, only so far as he needs UF. With independence he takes charge of Police, Security, and the electoral process *He will not lose any election after that's done*. So goodbye D'Aguiar! See what's happening in Africa, and across Mona Passage in Haiti. Brace yourself." I felt an enormous sadness for yet another group of simple trusting people, the salt of the earth, on the brink of deprivation and suffering, under yet another tyrant descended from slaves.

"What about Haiti? Kassim spoke as if from afar.

"You should look into it, now that you've seen Burnham at work and you're next door; visit and see for yourself the similarities; and compare them too with Nkrumah."

"I've read up on Nkrumah and agree with you; I supported UG until the scales fell when I read of Nkrumah's plans for a socialist college to train his civil service. Burnham will abuse UG the same way."

"I wasn't very popular with my friends for opposing UG when I was there; but no one knew of my presentation to Nunes and meetings with his staff; officially they did not happen. Clearly the decision was ideological. Any success it achieves will come purely because of good students seeking an education, not pushing party politics."

"What about Duvalier? I heard a little about his private army and *Voudou* practice; with all the troubles we've had I had no time for them."

"Haiti should become mandatory study for Guianese. It's where Burnham is heading--absolute control and ownership with US help, the real nigger in the woodpile. Their biggest problem is that France made them poor by forcing them to pay reparations after the War of Independence, valuing property lost at *150 million francs in gold*--which, by the way, included the slaves, the biggest slice of that pie--or else face a naval blockade with US and British help. They borrowed from these same nations and were paying up to half their revenue in interest; they finally paid off the loans in 1947. The Haitian National Bank had failed just before WWI; the National City Bank of New York bought it and wanted to collect all customs revenue to repay US business loans, but couldn't. Also other bankers were pressing to get payments of loans they'd made to the Haitian bank.

"For a few years the US had been trying to get Haiti to sign a Convention similar to one signed with the Dominican Republic, but Haiti rejected it as it would give the US powers of occupation. WWII started and Washington used the presence of German businessmen resident in Haiti to send marines to remove half a million dollars from the HNB to New York. Haiti had had troubles with rebels for years and lost several presidents. The US, especially the South, rejected Haiti and recognised it only after the South seceded in 1862.

"At one time the US wanted to annex all of Hispaniola or at least part of Haiti for a naval base. One arrogant asshole in the State Department Alvey Adee, called it *'a public nuisance at our door'*! That was a time when eugenics was all the rage and skull measurements were used to 'prove' that Blacks were inferior to whites. We know today that that's almost all pigshit. Then in 1915, with Haiti's president killed, Woodrow Wilson occupied the country *"to keep order"* and stayed 19 years! FDR who was Secretary of the Navy re-wrote the Constitution deleting the clause that excluded foreigners from owning Haitian property. The place was already open to corruption but then it became fair game for greedy Americans, many from Wall St, who bought up huge acreages in the country.

"The occupation was brutal for Haitians who found themselves working for ignoramuses and looters and with fraud and wrong-doing everywhere by US personnel. The marines took over everything including all sources of funds and in fact enslaved the nation. They did build some roads and other infrastructure but left after saddling Haiti with huge debts and many killed or missing. They failed to educate the people as promised and left Haiti with one of the highest illiteracy rates in the hemisphere. In 1950 Paul Magloire became President and things settled for six years until he too was ousted and Duvalier became President in '57, set up his *Ton Ton M'acoute* who terrorise the people; they believe that *Ton Ton M'acoutes* are zombies raised from the dead by Papa Doc's powerful *Voudou*, and of course he proceeded to loot the treasury and murder his critics, to this day."

"Amazing! I didn't know all that, and I studied in the US for so many years; but I guess LA was more tuned to Mexico. The US knows all this and yet allows Duvalier to steal from poor people?"

"They don't really care; they see it as small price to pay to keep out Communists. Same principle operates for Trujillo in the Dominican Republic. It's worse with Castro making them sweat. Cuba is so close, and USSR tightening up, Berlin Wall and all. It's all Cold War politics."

"How did you come by all this stuff? The *Gleaner* carries these?" he asked, surprised.

"Some, but I followed the changes since '51 on my radio when I was studying languages; I had planned to go there to study creole French, but Medicine ended that. Later I learned some history from a Haitian, M. Dunière[176];

---

[176] He also told me of the historic schism in Haitian society, the obsession with colour and breeding, and their domination of politics. He suggested I read the articles of James Weldon Johnson. I found

I had rented a room from him in '58. He was a mulatto, supposedly one of the privileged but had 'escaped'--his word--years earlier in the early thirties. I'd seen his name first in the ad and when I met him I said it in French; he corrected me saying he was now Dunnery, and Haiti was all *passé*. He wouldn't talk about it or himself, but he condemned the US Military Police, the *Gendarmerie d'Haiti* run by the US Marines, who had built a road by press-ganging people, like slaves, under an old law called *corvée*, and killed many people who resisted, over 3,000 in all. I suspect that was why he fled; he was a teenager when they took over and had to quit high school; he's still angry."

"I can see why you say Guyana is in for bad times. The US backed Burnham for their self-interest, not the interests of the Guianese; it won't take long for him to apply *'the remedy'* and US will give him money which he will steal just like Duvalier, and build his own personal army and bank account. Guyana *might* get a little face-lifting."

"I know Cheddi knows this; years ago Tulla warned him to make good with the Police, if he wished to keep peace; if Guyana were independent in '61, the US would've occupied it."

"And you know, throughout the '63 strike he kept asking the Governor for army patrols and failed to see how that contradicted his demand for independence; how could he manage an independent country without the ability to maintain law and order? It's imbecile and I saw that too late."

"I saw it coming and warned Kass," Shami interjected, "but he said it was far-fetched. You men are often slow to pick up on things. Women are so much closer to the ground."

"I know; that's what gets them into trouble." I teased.

"Naughty you!" she scolded gently.

A little merriment lightened the atmosphere. In the pause Kassim recalled a scene he had witnessed during one with Cheddi's speeches; a woman near Janet whispered, "He looks so handsome tonight."

"And every night," Janet replied reflexly; "He *is* the handsomest man in the world!"

"Handsomest?" Shami asked. "Handsome fool! See where he got us."

"I wonder what Asgar would say if he had heard this conversation." Kassim smiled.

"Who's Asgar?" I asked.

"Asgar Ali, a relative; first batch UG economics graduate; he's coming here to do a Master's; he's PYO, staunch Jaganite and vocal; you'll be amused by what he has to say."[177]

In the 1968 elections Burnham secured an absolute majority, with overt vote-rigging and substitution of ballots plus abuse of proxy and compilations of bogus overseas votes--both of which I witnessed. He severed liaisons with D'Aguiar, a process he had begun earlier and covertly after attaining

---

one much later while in London (*The Nation*, 111, 28 August 1920). The real tragedy was the denial of the validity of the Haitian revolt which was morally justified and really not different from the French or American ones. In fact it was even more justified.

[177] Asgar, confirmed Jaganite, completed his Master's and worked for many years with the Jamaican Central Bank before leaving in 1992 to rejoin Jagan as Guyana's Minister of Finance; he was soon displaced by his deputy, Bharrat Jagdeo, a Moscow-educated Marxist, and split from the PPP under a cloud; he formed his own Party which was trashed in later elections. Jagdeo became President in 1999. Asgar has drifted into obscurity.

independence. In the thirty-one months to that election D'Aguiar had been allowed several measures including severing ties with Cuba. The Americans had been pleased enough with this to make some monetary advances to Burnham, the first $6 million for sea defence repairs and to widen the main road for six miles from Georgetown east to Plaisance.

When the grant was spent with only half the work done, the US sent an auditor to verify accounts. The night before his arrival a fire destroyed the records of the project. Curiously only those specific cabinets were lost, while all others nearby were almost unscathed. The Burnham hegemony had begun with a mysterious blaze, with $3 million unaccounted for, a clear warning of things to come. Many persons were crudely expelled, as Kassim was, from senior positions including the Judiciary. D'Aguiar was end-played and dropped out of sight. Incredibly the US maintained its support.

The PPP declared itself as Marxist-Leninist in 1969 and four years later Burnham did the same for the PNC and soon after declared the *"paramountcy"* of the PNC in Government. He had meanwhile declared Guyana a republic and had become its Executive President by constitutional amendment, secured by flagrant vote-rigging. Dissenters were ignored, but when they persisted, some e.g. socialist University professor Joshua Ramsammy was shot and seriously wounded in 1973, not twenty yards from where I had paused that day on my way towards a crowd of protesters of which he was a part. Later, in 1980, Marxist historian Walter Rodney was murdered as he accepted a booby-trapped radio which promptly exploded in his lap as he sat in his brother's car.

Between these two episodes many Government critics were killed, maimed or simply "disappeared", many into the files of Amnesty International and other agencies. It is significant that during Burnham's reign the main opposition came from the Liberator Party (Ganraj Kumar, J K Richmond) and from the Working People's Alliance, a political movement begun by academics including Walter Rodney, Rupert Roopnarine, Omawale, Joshua Ramsammy, Clive Thomas and others at the University. The PPP became, to all appearances, a passive political partner, its voice hardly heard; Jagan was even accused of collusion with Burnham. Certainly he remained a mere dupe who watched helplessly as Burnham revealed the full extent of his villainy and methodically raped the country, just as his sister, Jessie, in 1964, and Jagan's friend, Tulla, had warned as early as 1952.

Punitive anti-business legislation and taxation, supported by the PPP, compulsory military service, anti-Indian job discrimination, seizure of private property-- including cattle ranches, coconut estates, rice farms and mills--and arbitrary "taxation" of businessmen led to massive uprooting and migrations to North America, Europe, the West Indies and elsewhere that depleted the population by more than one-third[178]. The Government became autarchic and took over retail distribution of food under an organisation founded by Minister of Agriculture and National Development Dr Ptolemy Reid, Burnham's right

---

[178] Figures from 1969-76 show that over 6000 *known* migrants left annually, distributed in 1976 as follows: 43% going to the USA, 31% to Canada, 10% to Britain, 9% to the Caribbean islands and the rest elsewhere. Economic and social pressures increased the exodus to over 14,000 annually between 1976 and 1981. Thereafter the annual drain amounted to up to 30,000 annually, mainly Indian businessmen, professionals and skilled workers.

hand, named *The Knowledge Sharing Institute,* a mystifying appellation if ever there was one, and headed by Burnham's wife, Viola, and patterned, no doubt on Duvalier's scheme to profit from every activity in Haiti. The immediate result was the decimation of all start-ups and small businesses--activities generally carried out by Indians,

Burnham proclamation of the paramountcy of the PNC made the Party the effective Government and the main employment agency for public services at all levels. The health and education services suffered major losses from underfunding and staff losses so that by the 1980s the signs of collapse were everywhere. Some infrastructure was improved, roads and sea defence mainly, while a stupid decision was made to scrap the railway, instantly regretted by Dr Reid in Parliament. Capricious decisions were frequent and fattened party hacks. Through all of this the faces of the Civil Service, commercial houses and many cadres of teachers darkened, became wards of the PNC, followed orders to the letter, and gave stoic and serf-like service of pitiable quality and quantity. Police and other Services ignored human rights. Complainants were ignored or 'disciplined'. The sugar and bauxite enterprises were nationalised and placed in the hands of the inexperienced and soon began to languish. Jamaicans were imported, given land for farming and promptly grew *ganja* (marijuana).

As it had done with Duvalier and the other "anti-Communist', or more aptly pro-US dictators world-wide, the USA blithely ignored the repercussions of these crimes on people and the economies of small poor countries, as long as the dictator maintained his pro-US stance and left its businesses to their own devices. Instead of making friends and becoming the vaunted "good neighbour", the US created resentment and hate among nations emerging form colonial bondage only to fall into a US corporate cauldron. Rather than learn from its abhorrent and bullying behaviour the US remains today rooted in narcissism and a bloated sense of superiority which embarrasses thoughtful and humane members of its citizenry.

In his march to absolute control of the new nation Burnham had taken steps to neutralise Indian opposition to his *"Cooperative Republic"* and enhance his personal Executive Presidential powers by disseminating photos of Indira Gandhi sitting next to him, claiming that he had copied the Indian constitution and that Mrs. Gandhi had endorsed his plans. Mrs. Gandhi had done no such thing, and even if she had, was this a case of one despot supporting another? Burnham had taken to India a few Indians, opportunistic tokens he had attracted to his fiefdom with lucrative rewards, men considered traitors by their fellow Indians and who had used the gifts of learning, reason and expression to serve "the enemy" against the interests and welfare of their Indian brethren, reminiscent of the Indian *Princes Council* and others who had become *coconuts* of the British Raj.

They gave, not for any high-minded cause above race, but purely to facilitate a nefarious dictator's seizure of the minds and assets of a naïve and captive people. Sridath Ramphal and Vincent Teekah were foremost among Burnham's legal advisers. The former would go on to greater opulence and higher office as Burnham's ally while the latter would come to an ignominious end in 1979, shot by an unknown assailant, some allege on order from the dictator himself. Burnham exceeded Indira in both authoritarianism and corruption, becoming, by the end of 1974, one of the richest black men in the world according to the USA's *Ebony* and *Time* magazines!

Health services declined to a level inconceivable in 1950, in facilities, personnel, range and quality and remain a major problem today. I lament the ruined hopes of my many friends who saw so much scope for developing a first-rate service, and although we thought that health services had declined much by 1960 and could go nowhere but up, we saw the impossible happen: the painful disintegration of a proud and aspiring service, which dedicated native sons and daughters at every level of organisation had nurtured. It became a miserable pariah among medical services in the Caribbean which in a spectacular show of poetic justice finally took the life of Forbes Burnham, the architect of its degradation, in 1985, aged 62, some say by "planned misadventure".

I reflected sadly on how, in 1962, in the hope that Jagan would honour the memory of his benefactor Tulla and move to a kinder and more rewarding political stage, Stan and I had planned a comprehensive clinic at DeHoop on land my mother would donate, a few minutes' walk to road or rail. We would involve the community in its operations, and do the many things we saw possible to help an industrious people starving for good and stable medical care, at low cost since neither of us craved wealth from practice. The Luck-Ragbeer Clinic would become a model of community health care applicable to the whole country and to all nations, not just the undeveloped. Such was our grand aim, and everyone who saw our plans supported them[179]. But that did not happen, and could not happen. We broke up as I've· shown and I was not allowed back except on compassionate grounds or for professional work when needed to contribute from afar.

Stan remained in the new Guyana, left the government service and began an inner city practice that was a model of holistic care. His relapses however became troublesome and the political violence took a heavy toll on his wife's endurance. They parted in friendship and she left with the children and eventually settled in Canada, where so many Guyanese from all walks of life would regroup after escaping the intolerable oppression of the Burnham dictatorship. In time after nearly two decades of an exemplary practice Stan succumbed to organ damage, the adverse effect of medications that had controlled his condition.

I had visited him several times during that period as my work took me often to Trinidad and Barbados allowing me a day or two to slip over to Georgetown. On these visits he would introduce me to patients and I would invariably hear uninhibited and effusive appraisals of his work from an adoring clientele; they were largely "inner city" folk but several of the more astute professional and business class — including members of my family-- sought him out and stuck by him to the end, their only complaint being that illness sometimes made him cancel office hours. Years later when I became involved in standards and competence assessment I would think of him, the quality of his practice and the impeccable notes he kept, in copybook handwriting, all carefully catalogued.

Gordon and Honnet completed their surgical specialty training: both remained in Guyana, the former serving for a time as head of the Mackenzie

---

[179] As Dean of the Medical Faculty, UWI, in the early 70's I became a Council member of the Pan-American Federation of Associations and Schools of Medicine and participated in several developments including a major effort in Community Medicine with 10 locations one of which was in Jamaica, of which I was director. It incorporated the ideas that Stan and I had hoped to implement and was well received by my Latin American colleagues and copied in other locations.

(Linden) Hospital, the latter at St Joseph's Hospital, where he became Medical Director. Jan Evertz went to the USA, completed training in dermatology and for many years was the only dermatologist in Wyoming. He eventually married and returned to "sunny Curaçao". Hublall started a practice on the Texas Gulf Coast where he remained until retirement. Chet stayed in Guyana and carried on a highly respected general practice on the Corentyne coast. Bedessie who was interning with Jan and not much involved in our discussions migrated to Kitchener, along with business members of his extended family. Dr Brahmam stayed in Guyana and became Head of Medical Services for the Sugar Producers Association.

Walter left with his family and settled in Toronto, and established a practice as a paediatric cardiologist but could not break the 1960s colour bar past a fellowship at the Sick Children's Hospital where his white associates routinely came to him for problem-solutions! This I saw firsthand. After a short contract as paediatrician at the Georgetown hospital in the early 70s, he returned to Canada and established a private practice in his specialty in Brampton, a small town northwest of Toronto which has since exploded in population and popularity. Harold Hamilton left for his homeland Trinidad soon after the Burnham take-over. One by one the Indian doctors left for parts unknown. Naresh Jain eventually went to the United States.

Many of the technologists left, some to study medicine, others to continue their careers, in the USA, UK, Canada or the West Indies. Gool Khan left to take up a managerial position at the UWI Pathology Department. Several senior technologists retired early. The difficulties of communication and the pervasive social dangers limited efforts to locate others beyond rumours that most had left the country.

A great source of worry to us was the lack of news of Chetram Singh, the hospital administrator I had first met in 1950 when I was a civil servant and came to know, although not well, as a bright and keen administrative cadet at the Georgetown Hospital. He was a great talent with a retinue of female admirers and had qualified as a Hospital administrator and placed in charge of the New Amsterdam Hospital which he promptly proceeded to revitalise. Kassim did not have news. In the seventies I discovered him in Toronto where so many Guianese had settled; he was working with the Ontario Ministry of Health on systems reform. Later he moved to the office of CEO, St Joseph's Hospital, London, Ontario, from which he retired and began work as a consultant to various hospitals and as an advisor to the Jagan Government from 1992 on various projects aimed to mend a dysfunctional and derelict Ministry of Health.

The poignant transformation of a peaceful and unpretentious society and the inculcation of a bellicose culture within it that tore communities apart--with total loss of confidence that one's fellow man would behave civilly--remains for me one of the most destructive elements of Jagan-Burnham politics, plunging it deep into the stifling Cold War, a hand-maiden to the corruption and greed of a dictator pacified by US financial incentives. People like Stanley, Kassim and others in this tale are just a few of the numerous early victims of the dictator whose varied talents and integrity would have contributed faithfully to building a viable and prosperous nation. Jagan and Burnham were a paradox, a rare combination that acting antagonistically achieved the same sorry end each would have achieved had the other not existed. They took the country at its birth into an abyss of sorrow, aggression, racial hatreds--despite Jagan's preferences-- family disruption, suppression of talent and dissent, and ultimately exile, escaping the spreading blight of corruption while those who could not escape sank into depression or worse, drug dealing, smuggling and other criminal behaviour, from which the country still struggles, almost hopelessly, to emerge.

Many who fled Guyana have ironically but bitterly thanked Burnham for forcing them into the wider world of greater opportunity and prosperity, and might have readily accepted the separation had they left their homeland voluntarily or found greater tolerance and knowledge among their hosts. But national ties and youthful ambitions to transform a familiar society and improve it linger nostalgically in many ageing hearts and minds. The yearning to achieve in one's own childhood environment is never really assuaged by contributions to, and fame in a biased foreign land. But this too will fade as the older generation gives way to the new whose feelings and emotions will be for *their* native land and not that of their parents. To them this story will be a blip in history notable only for the memories and longing of their parents and the question that they would ask from time to time, "What if Dr Jagan had…?"

I have no doubt that despite exile old Jagan hands everywhere will reject the viewpoints given, so mesmerising was his personality, and so conditioned are they to a particularly persuasive presentation of their country's history to consider alternatives especially as many of the characters and the closed-door incidents described would be unknown to them. The events described are incontrovertible, except perhaps for a few details. I hope that this account will bring some balance to the extremes of adulation heaped on Jagan and on Burnham by their respective followers.

If Jagan were a victim, as some claim, he was entirely self-made, helped by his indomitable wife and comrade and her resolve to spread the Communist doctrine. She will no doubt rank high among twentieth century female rebels globally, despite the small size of her sphere of operation.

Just as a pathologist can identify a cancer by studying a small sample — a biopsy--of its component cells aspirated with a needle or excised (histology), or even from a few shed cells (cytology) so can we analyse the world scene by examining one of its representative components. This is such an attempt. The Cold War fomented grievous divisions among major nations and allowed pettiness and greed to savage lesser ones and keep them in line. It raged for over forty years and when it was "over" both combatants had taken their peoples so far back into a shadowy past of poverty and terror that Rousseau, the 18th century author of three great revolutions, could once more step in and articulate his *Contrat Social* and be instantly relevant and topical.

American interests dominated the small emerging country and exaggerated its ability to threaten the integrity of the United States, even if it were established as a communist state. Their own foreign policy was poor and too often based on shallow research, with evidence gained from paid informers who were more likely to relate what he/she believed the recipient would like to hear or what suited the recipient's purposes.

America has long forgotten the principles on which it was founded--the "rights of man"-- and instead trumpets, extols and even exports a model that allows aggressive mercantilists to pursue excesses of greed, hoarding, deceit and exploitation, reducing gullible masses to personal chattel or even slaves, as viciously as when Americans were free to buy and sell slaves and whip them in public, or when their British forebears roamed and savaged the East to seize its resources.

The treatment of people generally has changed only in method, not in purpose. It is logical but sad that the Communist philosophy has within it the seeds of its own destruction, as the USSR has found out, and that unbridled capitalism, an equally tyrannical way of national economic organisation, has unhappily worsened since World War II. This *laissez faire* capitalism, or corporatism, ironically egged on by a Russian émigré, Ayn Rand, now threatens to give the world to fewer and fewer powers — mostly private — with no respect for morality, ethics, the spirit of 'live and let live' or the rights of man. By controlling all means of production and trade they wish to enslave the world. This monopoly of control was the aim of Communism too and hotly condemned by merchants and the governments they control. These two forces kept the Cold War going for over 40 years to the aggrandisement of many on both sides. The difference between them lay mainly in the ownership of the assets seized.

If we wish fairness in upholding the rights of all people surely the middle path must be the way to take us there, *the golden mean,* where all can reap the fruits they have sown and be allowed to keep and share as they wish, as Tulla--a key personality in this story--so fervently believed and tried to inculcate in Dr Jagan, and which my sister, Tulla's wife, exemplified in her altruism that positively influenced the careers and lives of so many of her kin. The constraints and weaknesses are more in the mind of man rather than in the heart and hand. Why do we need so much that we must continue to wrest even the nothing that our poorest citizens possess?

END

Appendix: Composition of the 1961 BG Legislature

The members of the **Council of Ministers** and the **Legislative Assembly** are:

The Council of Ministers:

Dr the Honourable Cheddi Jagan, Premier and Chair of Council
Hon Brindley Benn, Minister of Natural Resources
Hon Ram Karran, Minister of Works and Hydraulics
Hon Balram Singh Rai, Minister of Home Affairs
Hon Ranji Chandisingh, Minister of Labour, Health and Housing
Senator, the Hon Jocelyn Hubbard, Minister of Trade and Industry,
Dr the Hon Charles Jacob Jnr, Minister of Finance
Senator the Hon Cedric Nunes, Minister of Education and Social
Development Dr the Hon Fenton Ramsahoye, Attorney General
Hon Gladstone Wilson, Minister of Communications

The Legislative Assembly:

Speaker – The Honourable Rahman Gajraj
The Members of the Council of Minister listed above except the two
Senators
Other Members:
PPP: Messrs George Bowman and Lawrence Mann (Parliamentary
Secretaries); Messrs Mohammed Safee, Moses Bhagwan, Victor Downer,
Harry Lall, George Robertson, John Caldeira, Maccie Hamid, Derek Jagan
and Mohamed Shakoor.
Minority Groups:
PNC: Messrs LFS Burnham, John Carter, WOR Kendall, Eugene Correia,
Neville Bissember, Stanley Hugh, Robert Jordan, HMS Wharton, William
Blair, John Joaquin and Claude Merriman.
UF: Peter D' Aguiar, Randolph Cheeks, Stephen Campbell and Edward
Melville.

The Members of the **Senate**:
President: His Honour Senator Ashton Chase
Members: Senator the Hon HJM Hubbard
Senator the Hon CV Nunes
Senator Claude Christian
Senator Moneer Khan
Senator Pandit CS Persaud
Senator Mrs Christina Ramjattan
Senator Herbert Thomas
Senator Miss Ann Jardim
Senator Antony G Tasker, OBE
Senator CV Too Chung, Deputy President